TYPES OF DRAMA

Plays and Essays

Fifth Edition

SYLVAN BARNET
Tufts University

MORTON BERMAN
Boston University

WILLIAM BURTO
University of Lowell

SCOTT, FORESMAN AND COMPANY
Glenview, Illinois   Boston   London

Library of Congress Cataloging-in-Publication Data

Types of drama.

   1. Drama—Collections.   2. Drama—History and
criticism.   I. Barnet, Sylvan.   II. Berman, Morton.
III. Burto, William.
PN6112.T96   1988   808.82   88-4694
ISBN 0-673-39876-5

3 4 5 6 7 8 9 10—KPF—94 93 92 91 90

PRINTED IN THE UNITED STATES OF AMERICA

Text credits:

Pages 635–647. *Out of Our Fathers' House* by Eve Merriam,
Paula Wagner, and Jack Hofsiss. Reprinted by permission of
International Creative Management, Inc. Copyright © 1975 by
Paula Wagner, Jack Hofsiss, and Eve Merriam.

Pages 70 and 648. Material from "Under Ben Bulben" by W. B.
Yeats. Reprinted with permission of Macmillan Publishing
Company A. P. Watt Ltd. on behalf of Michael B. Yeats and
Macmillan London Ltd. from *Collected Poems* by W. B. Yeats.
Copyright 1940 by Georgie Yeats, renewed 1968 by Bertha
Georgie Yeats, Michael Butler Yeats and Anne Yeats.

PREFACE

In this edition of *Types of Drama* we have added eight plays: Sophocles's *Antigone*, O'Neill's *The Emperor Jones*, García Lorca's *The House of Bernarda Alba*, Williams's *The Glass Menagerie*, Albee's *The Sandbox*, Luce's *Slam the Door Softly*, Merriam, Wagner, and Hofsiss's *Out of Our Fathers' House*, and Wilson's 1987 Pulitzer Prize winner, *Fences*.

We have also added (while retaining Peter Arnott's "The Script and the Stage") two essays on the play in the theater, and we have amplified our section called "Writing About Drama" so that it now discusses not only writing reviews and analyses but also writing an original scene.

The *plays*, apart from the first five, are arranged chronologically. We begin with *A Doll's House*, to introduce students to "The Language of Drama," and then follow it with Clare Boothe Luce's modern one-act reinterpretation of Ibsen. Next, following an introductory essay called "The Nature of Drama," we print one tragedy (*Oedipus*), one comedy (*The Importance of Being Earnest*), and one tragicomedy (*The Sandbox*), thus giving students an idea of the major types of drama. The remaining twenty plays, from *Antigone* and *Lysistrata* to *'night, Mother* and *Fences*, are given in chronological order. (Instructors who prefer to group the plays by genres can, of course, easily do so.) The plays cover a range of years and of types, but in no case were they chosen only to represent a period or a type. All were chosen because of their inherent value. Those not written in English are represented in what we believe are the best modern translations.

The *commentaries* on the plays are relatively short. They are not attempts to explicate the plays but contain, we think, some useful and relevant points that will also be helpful with other plays. Thus, the commentary on *A Midsummer Night's Dream* includes a discussion of two traditions of comedy, "critical" comedy and "romantic" comedy, material that is also relevant to other plays in the book, including *The Misanthrope* and *Arms and the Man*. Similarly, the commentary on *The Glass Menagerie* goes beyond the play by discussing presentational theater, a topic relevant to almost all drama before Ibsen. But even those commentaries that are sharply focused on a given play do not seek to utter the last word. On the contrary, they seek to provide material that will stimulate discussion in class or that may be the topic of a writing assignment. The *topics for discussion* that follow each commentary are similarly designed.

iii

The anthologized *essays* fall into two groups: one group (the authors range from Aristotle to Susanne Langer) consists of relatively theoretical writings on the nature of tragedy, comedy, and tragicomedy; the second group, emphasizing drama as theater rather than as literature, contains essays by directors. Because these discussions are fairly general, almost any essay may be read in conjunction with almost any play.

The *glossary* is a dictionary of two hundred basic critical and historical terms. Though some of the definitions are brief, many are fairly long. Students and instructors have told us that the glossary can actually be read with interest and that the definitions, far from being perfunctory, are genuinely helpful.

The *illustrations* show the plays in performance; further, we have included illustrations of Greek and Elizabethan theaters in an effort to assist students in imagining the plays on unfamiliar stages.

Having briefly described the book, we want (before we turn to the pleasant job of acknowledging our debts) to offer a comment on the theater in the second half of the twentieth century. The 1950s saw the growth of the theater of the absurd; the mid-1960s, in the United States, saw the birth of a very different sort of drama, an affirmative drama that can be called the theater of commitment. Opposition to the war in Vietnam was one great source of commitment; a second source was the civil rights movement, which stimulated black dramatists to affirm black power. Inspired especially by the black power movement, other movements soon developed: gay theater, women's theater, Chicano theater, Asian-American theater, and Native American theater. The products of these movements are highly diverse, and it is too early to say that they constitute a substantial body of enduring works; many of the plays were frankly designed as a means of consciousness-raising. Still, one notices a new eloquence, not an attempt (necessarily doomed) to revive Shakespeare's poetry, but a prose more eloquent or more confident than, say, the language of Albee's characters. In *Types of Drama* this new confidence in language is seen most clearly in *Out of Our Fathers' House*, by Merriam, Wagner, and Hofsiss, in which six women talk lucidly and compellingly. It seems clear that today's dramatists have a new faith in human beings, a faith not simply that people will endure but that they can talk meaningfully. Beckett's characters showed their strength in persistently waiting for Godot; the new theater's characters show their strength in asserting themselves, not as tragic heroes demanding that life make sense, and certainly not as comic figures making an amusing spectacle of themselves, but as men and women on the way to attaining the dignity that is rightfully theirs.

Acknowledgments

We have been fortunate in getting permission to print important modern plays and distinguished translations of older plays; we are grateful to the authors, translators, and publishers who have cooperated. We are also grateful to the many teachers who have given advice that helped us prepare this new edition: Jacob H. Adler, Purdue University; Terry Browne, State University of New York, Geneseo; Leslie Phillips Butterworth, Holyoke Community College; Kenneth Campbell, Virginia Commonwealth University; Charles L. Darn, University of Pittsburgh at Johnstown; Cheryl Faraone, State University of New York, Geneseo; John C. Freeman, El Paso Community college; Catherine Gannon, California State University at San Bernardino; Russell Goldfarb, Western Michigan University; John Gronbeck-Tedesco, University of Kansas; Jo Ann Holonbeck, College of Saint Catherine; Richard L. Homan, Rider College; Grace McLaughlin, Portland Community College; John B. Pieters, University of Florida; George Ray, Washington and Lee University; Gail Salo, George Mason University; David K. Sauer, Spring Hill College; Myron Simon, University of California at Irvine; Keith Slocum, Montclair State College; Lucille Stelling, Normandale Community College; Edna M. Troiano, Charles County Community College; Robert L. Vales, Gannon University; and Bruce E. Woodruff, Baker University.

We also gladly acknowledge our debts to Jeanne Newlin of the Harvard Theatre Collection, and to Arthur Friedman, Oscar Brockett, Harry Ritchie, and Marcia Stubbs. Our thanks also go to Bradford C. Gray, Deirdre McDonald, Carolyn Woznick, and Virginia Shine of Scott, Foresman/Little, Brown, and Ron Newcomer of R. David Newcomer Associates, who never let us get away with anything.

CONTENTS

ESSAYS 735

WRITING ABOUT DRAMA 773

Why Write? Analysis. Finding a Topic. From Topic to Thesis.
A Sample Analysis. Writing a Review. A Sample Review. Writing
a Comparison. Communicating Judgments. Asking Questions to Get
Answers. Organizing an Essay. Summary: How to Write an Effective
Essay. Basic Manuscript Form. Quotation and Quotation Marks.
A Note on Footnotes. A Note on Internal Citations.

WRITING DRAMA 797

Writing a Scene. Construction in Drama. The One-Act Play.
Last Words.

A GLOSSARY OF DRAMATIC TERMS 805

THE LANGUAGE OF DRAMA

Although a play usually tells a story, "the medium of drama," as Ezra Pound observed, "is not words, but persons moving about on a stage using words." Take Ibsen's *A Doll's House* as an example. The gist of the story is this: Nora, without her husband knowing it, forged a document so that she and her husband could spend a year in Italy; this trip to a warm climate was necessary to preserve her husband's life. When Torvald, the husband, learns the truth and is in danger of being exposed as the husband of a forger, instead of either taking the blame or at least standing by Nora, to Nora's amazement he savagely turns on her. When the forged document is returned, so that it can be destroyed rather than made public, he exclaims, "I'm saved," at which point Nora asks, "And I?" Torvald forgives Nora, but Nora now understands that Torvald has never loved her but has only played with her, treating her like a doll and keeping her from making something of her life. Finding that she no longer loves him and that therefore she cannot continue to live with him, at the end of the play she leaves the house for no specified destination. The last thing we hear is the sound of the door closing behind her.

This is moderately interesting, and it has some roots in fact. Ibsen actually knew a woman who had forged a check to pay for a trip that her husband's health required. When the husband learned the truth, he turned on her and had her committed to an asylum, though later, for the sake of their children, he allowed her to return to their home. Ibsen, of course, added a good deal and changed the ending; but even if he had not made these changes, a play about this family would—if it were any good—be very different from an account in *Time* or *People*, because, as Pound says, a play is made not out of words but out of "persons moving about on a stage using words."

Let's begin with the stage and its setting. When the curtain goes up on a   SETTING
performance of *A Doll's House*, the audience sees "a pleasant living room, tastefully but not expensively furnished." Additional details, such as "etchings on the walls," and "a small bookcase with deluxe editions," tell us much about the kind of people who live here. We shall learn more about these people when we see the clothes that they wear and hear the words that they speak, but even now—from seeing their living room—we know that they are people who hold the conventional middle-class values. The "deluxe editions" in the bookcase, for example, are more for show than for reading.

In some plays there are several sets—sometimes in sharp contrast—but in *A Doll's House* there is only one set, and perhaps we come to feel that this omnipresent room is a sort of prison that stifles its inhabitants or, as the title of the play implies, that this room keeps its inhabitants at a distance from the realities of life. At the end of the play, Nora escapes from this box and enters the real world. We might look, too, at the ways in which some of the furniture and the properties work in the play. Very early, when Torvald begins to lecture Nora about incurring debts, she "walks over toward the stove." It is scarcely too subtle to conclude that she is seeking a place of warmth or security when confronted by Torvald's chilling words. We may not *consciously* come to this conclusion, but

A Doll's House: setting as a revelation of values. (Photograph: University of Minnesota Theatre.)

that doesn't matter. Indeed, later in this act, Torvald, sitting near the stove, says quite naturally, "Ah, it's nice and warm in here."

Or consider the use Ibsen makes of the Christmas tree. In Act I, when Nora's world is still relatively undisturbed, the tree, adorned with candles and flowers, is in the center of the stage. By the end of this act Nora is terrified, and when the curtain goes up for the second act, we see the tree thrust into a corner, "stripped, shabby-looking, with burnt-down candles." Again, we may not consciously conclude that Ibsen, through the tree, is telling us something about Nora, but surely the tree—at first gay, then forlorn—somehow has an impact on us.

LIGHTING   Speaking of candles, or of lighting, in the second act a stage direction tells us, as Nora's terror grows, "Darkness begins to fall during the following scene." Later in the scene, when Dr. Rank confesses he loves Nora and thereby adds to her confusion, Nora seeks to regain her composure by ordering the maid to bring in a lamp—a natural desire, given her sense that she is threatened sexually, but also a symbol of illumination, for now the secret is out in the open. Finally, in the last act, when Nora forcefully explains to Torvald that she now sees things clearly, they are sitting on opposite sides of a table with a lighted lamp on it.

The setting of even a realistic play, then, including the furniture and the lighting, is a means by which a playwright communicates. Another realistic play, *The Cherry Orchard*, juxtaposes the orchard (the dying aristocratic way of life) with telephone poles and a town (the new industrial way of life). In *Death of a Salesman*, Willy Loman's "fragile-seeming home" is surrounded by "a solid vault of apartment houses," Miller thereby conveying the vulnerability of the individual.

A bare stage, too (much used in contemporary drama; for example, in the plays of Beckett), by virtue of its barrenness says something about the human being's isolation or alienation. Although one frequently hears that the Elizabethan stage was bare and that Shakespeare's plays are most effective on a bare stage, in fact the Elizabethan stage was an elaborate piece of architecture, suggestive of a completely ordered universe, and when appropriate the stage was decorated with banners. But it could be bleak when bleakness was required. At the end of the second act of *King Lear*, Gloucester tells us what we are to imagine: "Alack, the night comes on, and the high winds / Do sorely ruffle. For many miles about / There's scarce a bush." Again, this locale says something about the impoverished people who move in it.

In returning to *A Doll's House*, and to Ezra Pound's comment on the nature of drama, let us continue for a moment to talk about the ways in which drama even without dialogue says something. Costumes tell us a good deal, on the stage as in life. They do not necessarily tell the truth about their wearers, but they tell us what the wearers want us to believe. If, on the street, we see a man who is wearing workman's clothes, we conclude that he may be a workman—or that for some reason (say, political or sexual) he wants us to think that he is a workman; in any case, the clothes make a statement, conscious or not. COSTUME

In the first act, Nora wears ordinary clothing, but in the middle of the second act she puts on "a long, many-colored shawl" when she frantically rehearses her tarantella. The shawl, of course, is supposed to be appropriate to the Italian dance, but surely its multitude of colors also helps to express Nora's conflicting emotions, her near hysteria, expressed too in the fact that "her hair comes loose and falls down over her shoulders," but "She doesn't notice." The shawl and her disheveled hair, then, *speak* to us as clearly as the dialogue does.

In the middle of the third act, after the party and just before the showdown, Nora appears in her "Italian costume," and Helmer wears "evening dress" under an open black cloak. She is dressed for a masquerade (her whole life has been a masquerade, it turns out), and Torvald's formal suit and black cloak help to express the stiffness and the blight that have forced her to present a false front throughout their years of marriage. A little later, after Nora sees that she has never really known her husband for the selfish creature he is, she leaves the stage, and when she returns she is "in an everyday dress." The pretense is over.

She is no longer Torvald's "doll." When she finally leaves the stage—leaving the house—she "Wraps her shawl around her." This is not the "many-colored shawl" she used in rehearsing the dance, but the "big, black shawl" she wears when she returns from the dance. The blackness of this shawl helps to express the death of her old way of life; Nora is now aware that life is not child's play.

Ibsen did not, of course, invent the use of costumes as dramatic language; it goes back to the beginnings of drama, and one has only to think of Hamlet's "inky cloak," or of Lear tearing off his clothing, or of the fresh clothing in which Lear is garbed after his madness in order to see how eloquently costumes can speak. To this can be added the matter of disguises—for example, Edgar's disguise in *King Lear*—which are removed near the end of plays, when the truth is finally revealed and the characters can be fully themselves. In short, the removal of disguises *says* something.

GESTURES

Gestures, too, are a part of the language of drama. Helmer "playfully pulls [Nora's] ear," showing his affection; Nora claps her hands; Mrs. Linde (an old friend of Nora's) "tries to read but seems unable to concentrate," and so forth. All such gestures clearly and naturally convey states of mind. One of the most delightful and revealing gestures in the play occurs when, in the third act, Helmer demonstrates to Mrs. Linde the ugliness of knitting ("Look here: arms pressed close to the sides") and the elegance of embroidering (". . . with your right [hand] you move the needle—like this—in an easy, elongated arc"). None of his absurd remarks throughout the play is quite so revealing of his absurdity as is this silly demonstration.

Some gestures, or stage directions that imply gestures, are a bit more complex. For example, when Nora "walks cautiously over to the door to the study and listens," this direction conveys Nora's fear that her husband may detect her foibles—or even her crime. We read this stage direction almost at the start of the play, when we do not yet know who is who or what is what, but we do know, from this gesture alone, that Nora is not at ease even in her own home. And when Mrs. Linde sees her former lover, Krogstad, she "starts, looks, turns away toward the window," a natural enough reaction but one that indicates her desire to escape from this confining box-set. Similarly, when Nora "wildly" dances during her rehearsal in the second act, the action of course indicates the terrible agitation in her mind. One other, quieter example: in Act III, when the dying Dr. Rank for the last time visits Nora in order to gain comfort, she lights his cigar, and a moment later Rank replies—these are his last words—"And thanks for the light." Thus we not only hear words about a cigar, but we *see* an act of friendship, a flash of light in this oppressive household.

SOUND
EFFECTS

Like the setting, the costumes, and the gestures, the sound effects in a play are important. Footsteps on stairs, or the swish and slight thud of a letter dropping into a mailbox on the door, can have an electrifying effect. In *A Doll's House* the music of the tarantella communicates Nora's frenzy, but the most famous sound effect is reserved for the very end of the play, when Nora walks out on Helmer: "From downstairs comes the sound of a heavy door slamming shut."

A *Doll's House:* a symbolic gesture. (Photograph: Harvard Theatre Collection.)

Nothing could better "say" anything about Nora's decision to choose a new life.

Simply to widen the canvas, we can add an example from Shakespeare: the sound of the storm in *King Lear* is a reflection of Lear's disordered kingdom, disordered family, and disordered mind. Similarly, the "scream" of the subway in LeRoi Jones's *Dutchman*, the sound of the axes cutting down the trees in *The Cherry Orchard*, and the flute ("telling of grass and trees and the horizon") in *Death of a Salesman* are not merely realism.

But, of course, dialogue is the most persistent sound in a play. A good playwright gives us not a transcript of our chaotic fragmentary sentences but language that continually reveals character and that furthers plot. (As one critic

DIALOGUE

has said, "Dialogue is what the characters *do* to each other.") Look at the first few lines that Nora and her husband exchange:

HELMER (*in his study*): Is that my little lark twittering out there?
NORA (*opening some of the packages*): That's right.
HELMER: My squirrel bustling about?
NORA: Yes.
HELMER: When did squirrel come home?

Helmer's "Is that my little lark twittering out there?" and his "My squirrel bustling about?" are affectionate but horribly condescending; and Nora's brief responses, "That's right" and "Yes," indicate—though probably even she does not know it—her aversion to such oppressive affection. If we contrast her perfunctory words here with her long speeches to Helmer at the end of the play, when she has seen the light, we realize how fully the lark-squirrel has turned into an articulate human being.

PLOT AND CHARACTER

The point need not be labored; there is scarcely a line in the play that does not reveal the speaker's character and at the same time add a twist to the plot. We can briefly examine one episode. When Nora and Helmer, in the first act, discuss Krogstad's forgery, we are getting not only *exposition* (a setting forth of information that the audience must know), and preparation for later events (Helmer will discharge Krogstad from the bank); we are also getting a revelation of Helmer's character (the lecture on dishonesty). But, even more important, we are getting a development in Nora's character, for, unknown to Helmer, Nora sees a resemblance between herself and Krogstad, and Nora is coming to the realization that her supposedly loving husband may judge her (if he learns the truth) as harshly as he judged Krogstad.

THEME

What does the play add up too? What is the underlying theme or meaning of the play? Some critics, arguing that the concept of theme is meaningless, hold that any play gives us only an extremely detailed history of some imaginary people. But surely this view is desperate. Ibsen himself began work on *A Doll's House* by jotting down some "Notes for a Modern Tragedy":

There are two kinds of moral laws, two kinds of conscience, one for men and one, quite different, for women. They don't understand each other; but in practical life, woman is judged by masculine law, as though she weren't a woman but a man.

The wife in the play ends by having no idea what is right and what is wrong; natural feelings on the one hand and belief in authority on the other lead her to utter distraction.

Of course, Ibsen probably began by thinking about the real woman who forged a check to pay for the trip to save her sick husband, but the passage just quoted is the earliest writing relevant to the play. As Ibsen worked on the play, he (not surprisingly) produced characters and a plot that have a life of their own; but even if they depart from his preliminary note, these characters and this plot add up to something. (A *plot* is what happens; a *theme* is what the happenings add up to.) Some readers see in *A Doll's House* a play about a woman's place in a man's world, or a play about women's rights, but Ibsen himself (years after writing the play) said he had a larger theme: "I am not even sure what women's rights really are. To me it has been a question of human rights." Certainly the play deals, as Ibsen implies, with the enslavement of one person by another. At last Torvald dimly seems to recognize that Nora is a human being, not a doll; and Nora perceives that such a recognition could lead to "a true marriage." To the reply that themes such as "marriage must be based on mutual respect" and "self-knowledge is acquired only painfully" are mere truisms, we can counter: Yes, but the truisms are presented in such a way that they take on life and become a part of us, whereas mere truisms are something of which we say, "I've heard it said, and I guess it's so." And surely we are in no danger of equating the play with the theme that we sense underlies it. We never believe that our statement of the theme is really the equivalent of the play itself. The play, we recognize, presents the theme with such detail that our statement of the theme is only a wedge that helps us to enter the play so we may more fully (in Henry James's word) "appropriate" it.

IN BRIEF: HOW TO READ A PLAY

A play is written to be seen and to be heard. We go to *see* a play in a theater (*theater* is derived from a Greek word meaning "to watch"), but in the theater we *hear* it because we become an audience (*audience* is derived from a Latin word meaning "to hear"). In reading a play, we must engage in the difficult job of trying to see and to hear—to see the characters, costumed and moving within a specified setting, and to hear what they say (not only their words but their tone, their joy or hypocrisy or tentativeness or aggression, or whatever). As Harley Granville Barker—a playwright, director, and critic—said, the reader of a play

> must, so to speak, perform the whole play in his imagination; as he reads, each effect must come home to him; the succession and contrast of scenes, the harmony and clash of the music of the dialogue, the action implied, the mere physical opposition of characters, or the silent figure standing aloof—for that can also be eloquent.

When we are in the theater, of course, especially if the actors are competent, the text comes alive without much effort on our part. But when we read a play, we must try to imagine the lines as they might be acted on the stage. That is, remembering that the dialogue takes place in a setting, is spoken in a particular tone of voice, and is accompanied by gestures, we must use both the mind's eye and the mind's ear. Modern playwrights often help us by providing fairly full stage directions. Here, for example, is a passage from Shaw's *Arms and the Man:*

> RAINA (*dreamily*): . . . I wanted to be alone. The stars are so beautiful! What is the matter?
> CATHERINE: Such news! There has been a battle.
> RAINA (*her eyes dilating*): Ah! (*She comes eagerly to* CATHERINE.)

Earlier writers, however—for instance Shakespeare, who assumed that a play was something to see rather than to read—give us very few explicit stage directions, though if we read the dialogue attentively we will perceive that a character is kneeling, or brandishing a sword, or looking down his nose at his hearer. But even the passage from Shaw requires us to use our imagination, for (at least in the context) we must perceive that in her dreaminess and in her ecstasy Raina is putting on an act, posing. Shaw here, like every playwright, is, in the words of Paul Valéry, "a creator who makes others create." The reader-audience must cooperate with the writer. The famous definition of drama as "Three boards, two actors, and a passion" is a bit too concise, for though it includes the state, the performers, and the subject matter, it omits the audience, the responsive reader or spectator who, so to speak, must re-create the play.

If you develop the following principles into habits, you will get far more out of a play than if you simply read it as though it is a novel in dialogue.

1.   Pay attention to the list of characters (the *dramatis personae*, literally "the masks" of the play) and carefully read the descriptions if the playwright has provided them, but don't worry at the start if you can't get the characters clearly in mind. As you read the play you will encounter the characters in action, and thus you will get to know them fully.

2.   Keep in mind the kind of theater for which the play was written. The Greek theater of Sophocles and Aristophanes, the Elizabethan theater of Shakespeare, and the proscenium theater of Ibsen, Chekhov, and their successors are discussed in the Glossary. To take the first of these examples: The Greek theater, open to the heavens, and with a structure representing a palace or temple behind the actors, is itself a kind of image of a society governed by the laws of the state and the laws of the gods. Moreover, the chorus enters the playing space by marching down the side aisles, past the audience, thus helping to unite the world of the audience and of the players. On the other hand, the audience watching a play by Ibsen on a proscenium stage is sitting in its own darkened area, sharply separated from the players in their boxlike setting.

3.   If the playwright describes a set, try to envision it clearly. For those plays whose sets are not illustrated in this book, you may find it useful to make a simple sketch, indicating the exits and any substantial pieces of furniture that are specified. Try to imagine the atmosphere (comfortable, foreboding, oppressive, or whatever) that the set evokes. Equally important, as you read imagine where the action takes place and, drawing on stage directions, imagine where the characters stand in relation to each other as they bounce words off one another.

4.   Don't underestimate the importance of sound effects and of gestures, whether they are stated explicitly in stage directions or are implied in the dialogue.

5.   As you read the dialogue, try to imagine what the speaker is up to. Are the words spoken sincerely? Is the speaker perhaps self-deceived? The speaker is trying to create an impression on his or her listener, but what impression is conveyed to you?

6.   Pay attention, at least during a second reading, to silences, including pauses within speeches or between speeches, or to characters who, though onstage, do not speak at a particular point. Is the silence of such a character a sign of reticence, a sign of moral failure, a sign of ignorance, or what?

A DOLL'S HOUSE

Henrik Ibsen

Translated by Otto Reinert

Henrik Ibsen (1828–1906) was born in Skien, Norway, of wealthy parents who soon after his birth lost their money. Ibsen worked as a pharmacist's apprentice, but at the age of twenty-two he had written his first play, a promising melodrama entitled *Cataline*. He engaged in theater work in Norway, and then in Denmark and Germany. By 1865 his plays had won him a state pension that enabled him to settle in Rome. After writing romantic, historic, and poetic plays, he turned to realistic drama with *The League of Youth* (1869). Among the major realistic "problem plays" are *A Doll's House* (1879), *Ghosts* (1881), and *An Enemy of the People* (1882). In *The Wild Duck* (1884) he moved toward a more symbolic tragic comedy, and his last plays, written in the nineties, are highly symbolic. *Hedda Gabler* (1890) looks backward to the plays of the eighties rather than forward to the plays of the nineties.

CHARACTERS

TORVALD HELMER, *a lawyer*
NORA, *his wife*
DR. RANK
MRS. LINDE
KROGSTAD

THE HELMERS' THREE SMALL CHILDREN
The children's NURSE, *Anne-Marie*
A HOUSEMAID
A PORTER

The Scene: The Helmers' living room

Sam Waterston as Helmer and Liv Ullmann as Nora in the 1975 production directed by Tormod Skagestad. (Photograph: Joseph Abeles Studio.)

ACT I

A pleasant living room, tastefully but not expensively furnished. A door on the rear wall, right, leads to the front hall; another door, left, to HELMER's *study. Between the two doors a piano. A third door in the middle of the left wall; further front a window. Near the window a round table with easy chairs and a small couch. Toward the rear of the right wall a fourth door; further front a tile stove with a rocking chair and a couple of armchairs in front of it. Between the stove and the side door a small table. Copperplate etchings on the walls. A whatnot with porcelain figurines and other small objects. A small bookcase with deluxe editions. A rug on the floor; fire in the stove. Winter day.*

The doorbell rings, then the sound of the front door opening. NORA, *dressed for outdoors, enters, humming cheerfully. She carries several packages, which she puts down on the table, right. She leaves the door to the front hall open; there a* PORTER *is seen holding a Christmas tree and a basket. He gives them to the* MAID, *who has let them in.*

NORA: Be sure to hide the Christmas tree, Helene. The children mustn't see it till after we've trimmed it tonight. (*Opens her purse; to the* PORTER.) How much?

PORTER: Fifty øre.

NORA: Here's a crown. No, keep the change. (*The* PORTER *thanks her, leaves.* NORA *closes the door. She keeps laughing quietly to herself as she takes off her coat, etc. She takes a bag of macaroons from her pocket and eats a couple. She walks cautiously over to the door to the study and listens.*) Yes, he's home. (*Resumes her humming, walks over to the table, right.*)

HELMER (*in his study*): Is that my little lark twittering out there?

NORA (*opening some of the packages*): That's right.

HELMER: My squirrel bustling about?

NORA: Yes.

HELMER: When did squirrel come home?

NORA: Just now. (*Puts the bag of macaroons back in her pocket, wipes her mouth.*) Come out here, Torvald. I want to show you what I've bought.

A Doll's House by Henrik Ibsen, translated by Otto Reinert. Copyright © 1977 by Otto Reinert. Reprinted by permission of Scott, Foresman and Company.

HELMER: I'm busy right now! (*After a little while he opens the door and looks in, pen in hand.*) Bought, eh? All that? So little wastrel has been throwing money around again?

NORA: Oh, but Torvald, this Christmas we can be a little extravagant, can't we? It's the first Christmas we haven't had to watch every penny.

HELMER: I don't know about that. We certainly don't have money to throw away.

NORA: Yes, Torvald, we do. A little, anyway. Just a tiny little bit? Now that you're going to get that big salary and all and make lots and lots of money.

HELMER: Starting at New Year's, yes. But payday isn't till the end of the quarter.

NORA: That doesn't matter. We can always borrow.

HELMER: Nora! (*Goes over to her and playfully pulls her ear.*) There you go being irresponsible again. Suppose I borrowed a thousand crowns today and you spent it all for Christmas and on New Year's Eve a tile from the roof laid me out cold?

NORA (*putting her hand over his mouth*): I won't have you say such horrid things.

HELMER: But suppose it happened. Then what?

NORA: If it did, I wouldn't care whether we owed money or not.

HELMER: But what about the people I had borrowed from?

NORA: Who cares about them! They are strangers!

HELMER: Nora, Nora, you *are* a woman. No, really! You know how I feel about that. No debts! A home in debt isn't a free home, and if it isn't free it isn't beautiful. We've managed nicely so far, you and I, and that's the way we'll go on. It won't be for much longer.

NORA (*walks over toward the stove*): All right, Torvald. Whatever you say.

HELMER (*follows her*): Come, come, my little songbird mustn't droop her wings. What's this? Can't have a pouty squirrel in the house, you know. (*Takes out his wallet.*) Nora, what do you think I have here?

NORA (*turns around quickly*): Money!

HELMER: Here. (*Gives her some bills.*) Don't you think I know Christmas is expensive?

NORA (*counting*): Ten—twenty—thirty—forty. Thank you, thank you, Torvald. This helps a lot.

HELMER: I certainly hope so.

Both characters are playful very playful

NORA: It does, it does! But I want to show you what I got. It was cheap, too. Look. New clothes for Ivar. And a sword. And a horse and a trumpet for Bob. And a doll and a little bed for Emmy. It isn't any good, but it wouldn't last, anyway. And here's some dress material and scarves for the maids. I feel bad about old Anne-Marie, though. She really should be getting much more. *nervous feelings — he is...*

HELMER: And what's in here?

NORA (*cries*): Not till tonight!

HELMER: I see. But now what does my little spendthrift have in mind for herself?

NORA: Oh, nothing. I really don't care.

HELMER: Of course you do. Tell me what you'd like. Within reason.

NORA: Oh, I don't know. Really, I don't. The only thing—

HELMER: Well? *— use costume*

NORA (*fiddling with his buttons, without looking at him*): If you really want to give me something, you might—you could—

HELMER: All right, let's have it.

NORA (*quickly*): Some money, Torvald. Just as much as you think you can spare. Then I'll buy myself something one of these days.

HELMER: No, really, Nora—

NORA: Oh yes, please, Torvald. Please? I'll wrap the money in pretty gold paper and hang it on the tree. Won't that be nice?

HELMER: What's the name for little birds that are always spending money?

NORA: Wastrels, I know. But please let's do it my way, Torvald. Then I'll have time to decide what I need most. Now that's sensible, isn't it?

HELMER (*smiling*): Oh, very sensible. That is, if you really bought yourself something you could use. But it all disappears in the household expenses or you buy things you don't need. And then you come back to me for more.

NORA: Oh, but Torvald—

HELMER: That's the truth, dear little Nora, and you know it. (*Puts his arm around her.*) My wastrel is a little sweetheart, but she *does* go through an awful lot of money awfully fast. You've no idea how expensive it is for a man to keep a wastrel.

NORA: That's not fair, Torvald. I really save all I can.

HELMER (*laughs*): Oh, I believe that. All you can. Meaning, exactly nothing!

NORA (*hums, smiles mysteriously*): You don't know all the things we songbirds and squirrels need money for, Torvald.

HELMER: You know, you're funny. Just like *Nora*

your father. You're always looking for ways to get money, but as soon as you do, it runs through your fingers and you can never say what you spent it for. Well, I guess I'll just have to take you the way you are. It's in your blood. Yes, that sort of thing is hereditary, Nora.

NORA: In that case, I wish I had inherited many of Daddy's qualities.

HELMER: And I don't want you any different from just what you are—my own sweet little songbird. Hey!—I think I just noticed something. Aren't you looking—what's the word?—a little—sly—?

NORA: I am?

HELMER: You definitely are. Look at me.

NORA (*looks at him*): Well?

HELMER (*wagging a finger*): Little sweet tooth hasn't by any chance been on a rampage today, has she?

NORA: Of course not. Whatever makes you think that?

HELMER: A little detour by the pastryshop maybe?

NORA: No, I assure you, Torvald—

HELMER: Nibbled a little jam?

NORA: Certainly not!

HELMER: Munched a macaroon or two?

NORA: No, really, Torvald, honestly—

HELMER: All right. Of course I was only joking.

NORA (*walks toward the table, right*): You know I wouldn't do anything to displease you.

HELMER: I know. And I have your promise. (*Over to her.*) All right, keep your little Christmas secrets to yourself, Nora darling. They'll all come out tonight, I suppose, when we light the tree.

NORA: Did you remember to invite Rank?

HELMER: No, but there's no need to. He knows he'll have dinner with us. Anyway, I'll see him later this morning. I'll ask him then. I did order some good wine. Oh Nora, you've no idea how much I'm looking forward to tonight!

NORA: Me too! And the children, Torvald! They'll have such a good time!

HELMER: You know, it *is* nice to have a good, safe job and a comfortable income. Feels good just thinking about it. Don't you agree?

NORA: Oh, it's wonderful!

HELMER: Remember last Christmas? For three whole weeks you shut yourself up every evening till long after midnight, making ornaments for the Christmas tree and I don't know what else. Some big surprise for all of us, anyway. I'll be damned if I've ever been so bored in my whole life!

Helmer refers always to Nora as an animal

NORA: I wasn't bored at all.

HELMER (*smiling*): But you've got to admit you didn't have much to show for it in the end.

NORA: Oh, don't tease me again about that! Could I help it that the cat got in and tore up everything?

HELMER: Of course you couldn't, my poor little Nora. You just wanted to please the rest of us, and that's the important thing. But I *am* glad the hard times are behind us. Aren't you?

NORA: Oh yes. I think it's just wonderful.

HELMER: This year I won't be bored and lonely. And you won't have to strain your dear eyes and your delicate little hands—

NORA (*claps her hands*): No I won't, will I, Torvald? Oh, how wonderful, how lovely, to hear you say that! (*Puts her arm under his.*) Let me tell you how I think we should arrange things, Torvald. Soon as Christmas is over—(*The doorbell rings.*) Someone's at the door. (*Straightens things up a bit.*) A caller, I suppose. Bother!

HELMER: Remember, I'm not home.

MAID (*in the door to the front hall*): Ma'am, there's a lady here—

NORA: All right. Ask her to come in.

MAID (*to* HELMER): And the Doctor just arrived.

HELMER: Is he in the study?

MAID: Yes, sir.

(HELMER *exits into his study. The* MAID *shows* MRS. LINDE *in and closes the door behind her as she leaves.* MRS. LINDE *is in travel dress.*)

MRS. LINDE (*timid and a little hesitant*): Good morning, Nora.

NORA (*uncertainly*): Good morning.

MRS. LINDE: I don't believe you know who I am.

NORA: No—I'm not sure—Though I know I should—Of course! Kristine! It's you!

MRS. LINDE: Yes, it's me.

NORA: And I didn't even recognize you! I had no idea! (*In a lower voice.*) You've changed, Kristine.

MRS. LINDE: I'm sure I have. It's been nine or ten long years.

NORA: Has it really been that long? Yes, you're right. I've been so happy these last eight years. And now you're here. Such a long trip in the middle of winter. How brave!

MRS. LINDE: I got in on the steamer this morning.

NORA: To have some fun over the holidays, of course. That's lovely. For we *are* going to have fun. But take off your coat! You aren't cold, are you? (*Helps her.*) There, now! Let's sit down here by the fire and just relax and talk. No, you sit

there. I want the rocking chair. (*Takes her hands.*) And now you've got your old face back. It was just for a minute, right at first—Though you are a little more pale, Kristine. And maybe a little thinner.

MRS. LINDE: And much, much older, Nora.

NORA: Maybe a little older. Just a teeny-weeny bit, not much. (*Interrupts herself, serious.*) Oh, but how thoughtless of me, chatting away like this! Sweet, good Kristine, can you forgive me?

MRS. LINDE: Forgive you what, Nora?

NORA (*in a low voice*): You poor dear, you lost your husband, didn't you?

MRS. LINDE: Three years ago, yes.

NORA: I know. I saw it in the paper. Oh please believe me, Kristine. I really meant to write you, but I never got around to it. Something was always coming up.

MRS. LINDE: Of course, Nora. I understand.

NORA: No, that wasn't very nice of me. You poor thing, all you must have been through. And he didn't leave you much, either, did he?

MRS. LINDE: No.

NORA: And no children?

MRS. LINDE: No.

NORA: Nothing at all, in other words?

MRS. LINDE: Not so much as a sense of loss—a grief to live on—

NORA (*incredulous*): But Kristine, how can that be?

MRS. LINDE (*with a sad smile, strokes* NORA'*s hair*): That's the way it sometimes is, Nora.

NORA: All alone. How awful for you. I have three darling children. You can't see them right now, though, they're out with their nurse. But now you must tell me everything—

MRS. LINDE: No, no; I'd rather listen to you.

NORA: No, you begin. Today I won't be selfish. Today I'll think only of you. Except there's one thing I've just got to tell you first. Something marvelous that's happened to us just these last few days. You haven't heard, have you?

MRS. LINDE: No, tell me.

NORA: Just think. My husband's been made manager of the Mutual Bank.

MRS. LINDE: Your husband—! Oh, I'm so glad!

NORA: Yes, isn't that great? You see, private law practice is so uncertain, especially when you won't have anything to do with cases that aren't—you know—quite nice. And of course Torvald won't do that, and I quite agree with him. Oh, you've no idea how delighted we are! He takes over at New Year's, and he'll be getting a big salary and all sorts of extras. From now on we'll be able to live in quite a different way—exactly as we like. Oh,

Kristine! I feel so carefree and happy! It's lovely to have lots and lots of money and not have to worry about a thing! Don't you agree?

MRS. LINDE: It would be nice to have enough, at any rate.

NORA: No, I don't mean just enough. I mean lots and lots!

MRS. LINDE (*smiles*): Nora, Nora, when are you going to be sensible? In school you spent a great deal of money.

NORA (*quietly laughing*): Yes, and Torvald says I still do. (*Raises her finger at* MRS. LINDE.) But "Nora, Nora" isn't so crazy as you all think. Believe me, we've had nothing to be extravagant with. We've both had to work.

MRS. LINDE: You too?

NORA: Yes. Oh, it's been little things mostly— sewing, crocheting, embroidery—that sort of thing. (*Casually.*) And other things too. You know, of course, that Torvald left government service when we got married? There was no chance of promotion in his department, and of course he had to make more money than he had been making. So for the first few years he worked altogether too hard. He took jobs on the side and worked day and night. It turned out to be too much for him. He became seriously ill. The doctors told him he needed to go south.

MRS. LINDE: That's right; you spent a year in Italy, didn't you?

NORA: Yes, we did. But you won't believe how hard it was to get away. Ivar had just been born. But of course we had to go. Oh, it was a wonderful trip. And it saved Torvald's life. But it took a lot of money, Kristine.

MRS. LINDE: I'm sure it did.

NORA: Twelve hundred dollars of the old money.[1] Four thousand eight hundred crowns. That's a lot.

MRS. LINDE: Yes. So it's lucky you have it when something like that happens.

NORA: Well, actually we got the money from Daddy.

MRS. LINDE: I see. That was about the time your father died, I believe.

NORA: Yes, just about then. And I couldn't even go and take care of him. I was expecting little Ivar any day. And I had poor Torvald to look after,

desperately sick and all. My dear, good Daddy! I never saw him again, Kristine. That's the saddest thing that's happened to me since I got married.

MRS. LINDE: I know you were very fond of him. But then you went to Italy?

NORA: Yes, for now we had the money, and the doctors urged us to go. So we left about a month later.

MRS. LINDE: And when you came back your husband was well again?

NORA: Healthy as a horse!

MRS. LINDE: But—the doctor?

NORA: What do you mean?

MRS. LINDE: I thought the maid said it was the doctor, that gentleman who came the same time I did.

NORA: Oh, that's Doctor Rank. He doesn't come as a doctor. He's our closest friend. He looks in at least once every day. No, Torvald hasn't been sick once since then. And the children are strong and healthy, too, and so am I. (*Jumps up and claps her hands.*) Oh god, Kristine! Isn't it wonderful to be alive and happy! Isn't it just lovely!—But now I'm being mean again, talking only about myself and my things. (*Sits down on a footstool close to* MRS. LINDE *and puts her arms on her lap.*) Please, don't be angry with me! Tell me, is it really true that you didn't care for your husband? Then why did you marry him?

MRS. LINDE: Mother was still alive, but she was bedridden and helpless. And I had my two younger brothers to look after. I didn't think I had the right to turn him down.

NORA: No, I suppose. So he had money then?

MRS. LINDE: He was quite well off, I think. But it was an uncertain business, Nora. When he died, the whole thing collapsed and there was nothing left.

NORA: And then—?

MRS. LINDE: Well, I had to manage as best I could. With a little store and a little school and anything else I could think of. The last three years have been one long work day for me, Nora, without any rest. But now it's over. My poor mother doesn't need me anymore. She passed away. And the boys are on their own too. They've both got jobs and support themselves.

NORA: What a relief for you—

MRS. LINDE: No, not relief. Just a great emptiness. Nobody to live for any more. (*Gets up, restlessly.*) That's why I couldn't stand it any longer in that little hole. It's got to be easier to find something to keep me busy and occupy my thoughts here in town. With a little luck I should

---

[1] In 1875 Norway joined the international monetary union based on the gold standard. The monetary unit changed from the old silver specie dollar (*Daler*) to the crown (*Krone*), redeemable in gold. As Nora's remark implies, there were four crowns to a dollar.

be able to find a good, steady job—something in an office—

NORA: Oh but Kristine, that's exhausting work, and you look worn out already. It would be much better if you went to a resort.

MRS. LINDE (*Walks over to the window*): I don't have a Daddy who can give me the money, Nora.

NORA (*getting up*): Oh, don't be angry with me.

MRS. LINDE (*over to her*): Dear Nora, don't *you* be angry with *me*. That's the worst thing about my kind of situation: you become so bitter. You've nobody to work for, and yet you have to look out for yourself, somehow. You got to keep on living, and so you become selfish. Do you know—when you told me about your husband's new position I was delighted not so much for your sake as for my own.

NORA: Why was that? Oh, I see. You think maybe Torvald can give you a job?

MRS. LINDE: That's what I had in mind.

NORA: And he will too, Kristine. Just leave it to me. I'll be ever so subtle about it. I'll think of something nice to tell him, something he'll like. I so much want to help you.

MRS. LINDE: That's very good of you, Nora— making an effort like that for me. Especially since you've known so little trouble and hardship in your own life.

NORA: I—have known so little—?

MRS. LINDE (*smiling*): Oh well, some sewing or whatever it was. You're still a child, Nora.

NORA (*with a toss of her head, walks away*): You shouldn't sound so superior.

MRS. LINDE: I shouldn't?

NORA: You're just like all the others. None of you think I'm good for anything really serious.

MRS. LINDE: Well, now—

NORA: That I've never been through anything difficult.

MRS. LINDE: But Nora! You just told me all your troubles!

NORA: That's nothing! (*Lowers her voice.*) I haven't told you about *it*.

MRS. LINDE: It? What's that? What do you mean?

NORA: You patronize me, Kristine, and that's not fair. You're proud that you worked so long and so hard for your mother.

MRS. LINDE: I don't think I patronize anyone. But it *is* true that I'm both proud and happy that I could make mother's last years comparatively easy.

NORA: And you're proud of all you did for your brothers.

MRS. LINDE: I think I have the right to be.

NORA: And so do I. But now I want to tell you something, Kristine. I have something to be proud and happy about too.

MRS. LINDE: I don't doubt that for a moment. But what exactly do you mean?

NORA: Not so loud! Torvald mustn't hear—not for anything in the world. Nobody must know about this, Kristine. Nobody but you.

MRS. LINDE: But what is it?

NORA: Come here. (*Pulls her down on the couch beside her.*) You see, I *do* have something to be proud and happy about. I've saved Torvald's life.

MRS. LINDE: Saved—? How do you mean— "saved"?

NORA: I told you about our trip to Italy. Torvald would have died if he hadn't gone.

MRS. LINDE: I understand that. And so your father gave you the money you needed.

NORA (*smiles*): Yes, that's what Torvald and all the others think. But—

MRS. LINDE: But what?

NORA: Daddy didn't give us a penny. *I* raised that money.

MRS. LINDE: *You* did? That whole big amount?

NORA: Twelve hundred dollars. Four thousand eight hundred crowns. *Now* what do you say?

MRS. LINDE: But Nora, how could you? Did you win the state lottery?

NORA (*contemptuously*): State lottery! (*Snorts.*) What would be so great about that?

MRS. LINDE: Where did it come from then?

NORA (*humming and smiling, enjoying her secret*): Hmmm. Tra-la-la-la-la!

MRS. LINDE: You certainly couldn't have borrowed it.

NORA: Oh? And why not?

MRS. LINDE: A wife can't borrow money without her husband's consent.

NORA (*with a toss of her head*): Oh, I don't know—take a wife with a little bit of a head for business—a wife who knows how to manage things—

MRS. LINDE: But Nora, I don't understand at all—

NORA: You don't have to. I didn't say I borrowed the money, did I? I could have gotten it some other way. (*Leans back.*) An admirer may have given it to me. When you're as tolerably goodlooking as I am—

MRS. LINDE: Oh, you're crazy.

NORA: I think you're dying from curiosity, Kristine.

MRS. LINDE: I'm beginning to think you've done something very foolish, Nora.

NORA (*sits up*): Is it foolish to save your husband's life?

MRS. LINDE: I say it's foolish to act behind his back.

NORA: But don't you see: he couldn't be told! You're missing the whole point, Kristine. We couldn't even let him know how seriously ill he was. The doctors came to *me* and told me his life was in danger, that nothing could save him but a stay in the south. Don't you think I tried to work on him? I told him how lovely it would be if I could go abroad like other young wives. I cried and I begged. I said he'd better remember what condition I was in, that he had to be nice to me and do what I wanted. I even hinted he could borrow the money. But that almost made him angry with me. He told me I was being irresponsible and that it was his duty as my husband not to give in to my whims and moods—I think that's what he called it. All right, I said to myself, you've got to be saved somehow, and so I found a way—

MRS. LINDE: And your husband never learned from your father that the money didn't come from him?

NORA: Never. Daddy died that same week. I thought of telling him all about it and asking him not to say anything. But since he was so sick—It turned out I didn't have to—

MRS. LINDE: And you've never told your husband?

NORA: Of course not! Good heavens, how could I? He, with his strict principles! Besides, you know how men are. Torvald would find it embarrassing and humiliating to learn that he owed me anything. It would upset our whole relationship. Our happy, beautiful home would no longer be what it is.

MRS. LINDE: Aren't you ever going to tell him?

NORA (*reflectively, half smiling*): Yes—one day, maybe. Many, many years from now, when I'm no longer young and pretty. Don't laugh! I mean when Torvald no longer feels about me the way he does now, when he no longer thinks it's fun when I dance for him and put on costumes and recite for him. Then it will be good to have something in reserve—(*Interrupts herself.*) Oh, I'm just being silly! That day will never come.—Well, now, Kristine, what do you say about my great secret? Don't you think I'm good for something too?—By the way, you wouldn't believe all the worry I've had because of it. It's been very hard to meet my obligations on schedule. You see, in business there's something called quarterly interest and something called installments on the principal,

and those things are terribly hard to come up with. I've had to save a little here and a little there, whenever I could. I couldn't use much of the housekeeping money, for Torvald has to eat well. And I couldn't use what I got for clothes for the children. They have to look nice, and I didn't think it would be right to spend less than I got— the sweet little things!

MRS. LINDE: Poor Nora! So you had to take it from your own allowance?

NORA: Yes, of course. After all, it was my affair. Every time Torvald gave me money for a new dress or what have you, I never used more than half of it. I always bought the cheapest, simplest things for myself. Thank god, everything looks good on me, so Torvald never noticed. But it was hard many times, Kristine, for it's fun to have pretty clothes. Don't you think?

MRS. LINDE: Certainly.

NORA: Anyway, I had other ways of making money too. Last winter I was lucky enough to get some copying work. So I locked the door and sat up writing every night till quite late. God! I often got so tired—! But it was great fun, too, working and making money. It was almost like being a man.

MRS. LINDE: But how much have you been able to pay off this way?

NORA: I couldn't tell you exactly. You see, it's very difficult to keep track of that kind of business. All I know is I have been paying off as much as I've been able to scrape together. Many times I just didn't know what to do. (*Smiles.*) Then I used to imagine a rich old gentleman had fallen in love with me—

MRS. LINDE: What! What old gentleman?

NORA: Phooey! And now he was dead and they were reading his will, and there it said in big letters, "All my money is to be paid in cash immediately to the charming Mrs. Nora Helmer."

MRS. LINDE: But dearest Nora—who *was* this old gentleman?

NORA: For heaven's sake, Kristine, don't you see! There *was* no old gentleman. He was just somebody I made up when I couldn't think of any way to raise the money. But never mind him. The old bore can be anyone he likes to for all I care. I have no use for him or his last will, for now I don't have a single worry in the world. (*Jumps up.*) Dear god, what a lovely thought that is! To be able to play and have fun with the children, to have everything nice and pretty in the house, just the way Torvald likes it! Not a care! And soon spring will be here, and the air will be blue and high.

Maybe we can travel again. Maybe I'll see the ocean again! Oh, yes, yes!—it's wonderful to be alive and happy!

(*The doorbell rings.*)

MRS. LINDE (*getting up*): There's the doorbell. Maybe I better be going.

NORA: No, please stay. I'm sure it's just someone for Torvald—

MAID (*in the hall door*): Excuse me, ma'am. There's a gentleman here who'd like to see Mr. Helmer.

NORA: You mean the Bank Manager.

MAID: Sorry, ma'am; the Bank Manager. But I didn't know—since the Doctor is with him—

NORA: Who is the gentleman?

KROGSTAD (*appearing in the door*): It's just me, Mrs. Helmer.

(MRS. LINDE *starts, looks, turns away toward the window.*)

NORA (*takes a step toward him, tense, in a low voice*): You? What do you want? What do you want with my husband?

KROGSTAD: Bank business—in a way. I have a small job in the Mutual, and I understand your husband is going to be our new manager—

NORA: So it's just—?

KROGSTAD: Just routine business, ma'am. Nothing else.

NORA: All right. In that case, why don't you go through the door to the office. (*Dismisses him casually as she closes the door. Walks over to the stove and tends the fire.*)

MRS LINDE: Nora—who was that man?

NORA: His name's Krogstad. He's a lawyer.

MRS. LINDE: So it *was* him.

NORA: Do you know him?

MRS. LINDE: I used to—many years ago. For a while he worked as a clerk in our part of the country.

NORA: Right. He did.

MRS. LINDE: He has changed a great deal.

NORA: I believe he had a very unhappy marriage.

MRS. LINDE: And now he's a widower, isn't he?

NORA: With many children. There now; it's burning nicely again. (*Closes the stove and moves the rocking chair a little to the side.*)

MRS. LINDE: They say he's into all sorts of business.

NORA: Really? Maybe so. I wouldn't know. But let's not talk about business. It's such a bore.

RANK (*appears in the door to* HELMER's *study*): No, I don't want to be in the way. I'd rather talk to your wife a bit. (*Closes the door and notices* MRS. LINDE.) Oh, I beg your pardon. I believe I'm in the way here too.

NORA: No, not at all. (*Introduces them.*) Doctor Rank. Mrs. Linde.

RANK: Aha. A name often heard in this house. I believe I passed you on the stairs coming up.

MRS. LINDE: Yes. I'm afraid I climb stairs very slowly. They aren't good for me.

RANK: I see. A slight case of inner decay, perhaps?

MRS. LINDE: Overwork, rather.

RANK: Oh, is that all? And now you've come to town to relax at all the parties?

MRS. LINDE: I have come to look for a job.

RANK: A proven cure for overwork, I take it?

MRS. LINDE: One has to live, Doctor.

RANK: Yes, that seems to be the general opinion.

NORA: Come on, Doctor Rank—you want to live just as much as the rest of us.

RANK: Of course I do. Miserable as I am, I prefer to go on being tortured as long as possible. All my patients feel the same way. And that's true of the moral invalids too. Helmer is talking with a specimen right this minute.

MRS. LINDE (*in a low voice*): Ah!

NORA: What do you mean?

RANK: Oh, this lawyer, Krogstad. You don't know him. The roots of his character are decayed. But even he began by saying something about having *to live*—as if it were a matter of the highest importance.

NORA: Oh? What did he want with Torvald?

RANK: I don't really know. All I heard was something about the bank.

NORA: I didn't know that Krog—that this Krogstad had anything to do with the Mutual Bank.

RANK: Yes, he seems to have some kind of job there. (*To* MRS. LINDE) I don't know if you are familiar in your part of the country with the kind of person who is always running around trying to sniff out cases of moral decrepitude and as soon as he finds one puts the individual under observation in some excellent position or other. All the healthy ones are left out in the cold.

MRS. LINDE: I should think it's the sick who need looking after the most.

RANK (*shrugs his shoulders*): There we are. That's the attitude that turns society into a hospital.

(NORA, *absorbed in her own thoughts suddenly starts giggling and clapping her hands.*)

RANK: What's so funny about that? Do you even know what society is?

NORA: What do I care about your stupid society! I laughed at something entirely different—something terribly amusing. Tell me, Doctor Rank—all the employees in the Mutual Bank, from now on they'll all be dependent on Torvald, right?

RANK: Is that what you find so enormously amusing?

NORA (*smiles and hums*): That's my business, that's my business! (*Walks around.*) Yes, I do think it's fun that we—that Torvald is going to have so much influence on so many people's lives. (*Brings out the bag of macaroons.*) Have a macaroon, Doctor Rank.

RANK: Well, well—macaroons. I thought they were banned around here.

NORA: Yes, but these were some that Kristine gave me.

MRS. LINDE: What! I?

NORA: That's all right. Don't look so scared. You couldn't know that Torvald won't let me have macaroons. He's afraid they'll ruin my teeth. But who cares! Just once in a while—! Right, Doctor Rank? Have one! (*Puts a macaroon into his mouth.*) You too, Kristine. And one for me. A very small one. Or at most two. (*Walks around again.*) Yes, I really feel very, very happy. Now there's just one thing I'm dying to do.

RANK: Oh? And what's that?

NORA: Something I want to say so Torvald could hear.

RANK: And why can't you?

NORA: I don't dare to, for it's not nice.

MRS. LINDE: Not nice?

RANK: In that case, I guess you'd better not. But surely to the two of us—? What is it you'd like to say to Helmer?

NORA: I want to say, "goddammit!"

RANK: Are you out of your mind!

MRS. LINDE: For heaven's sake, Nora!

RANK: Say it. Here he comes.

NORA (*hiding the macaroons*): Shhh!

(HELMER *enters from his study, carrying his hat and overcoat.*)

NORA (*going to him*): Well, dear, did you get rid of him?

HELMER: Yes, he just left.

NORA: Torvald, I want you to meet Kristine. She's just come to town.

HELMER: Kristine—? I'm sorry; I don't think—

NORA: Mrs. Linde, Torvald dear. Mrs. Kristine Linde.

HELMER: Oh, yes. A childhood friend of my wife's, I suppose.

MRS. LINDE: Yes, we've known each other for a long time.

NORA: Just think; she has come all this way just to see you.

HELMER: I'm not sure I understand—

MRS. LINDE: Well, not really—

NORA: You see, Kristine is an absolutely fantastic secretary, and she would so much like to work for a competent executive and learn more than she knows already—

HELMER: Very sensible, I'm sure, Mrs. Linde.

NORA: So when she heard about your appointment—they got a wire about it—she came here as fast as she could. How about it, Torvald? Couldn't you do something for Kristine? For my sake? Please?

HELMER: Quite possibly. I take it you're a widow, Mrs. Linde?

MRS. LINDE: Yes.

HELMER: And you've had office experience?

MRS. LINDE: Some—yes.

HELMER: In that case I think it's quite likely that I'll be able to find you a position.

NORA (*claps her hands*): I knew it! I knew it!

HELMER: You've arrived at a most opportune time, Mrs. Linde.

MRS. LINDE: Oh, how can I ever thank you—

HELMER: Not at all, not at all. (*Puts his coat on.*) But today you'll have to excuse me—

RANK: Wait a minute; I'll come with you. (*Gets his fur coat from the front hall, warms it by the stove.*)

NORA: Don't be long, Torvald.

HELMER: An hour or so, no more.

NORA: Are you leaving, too, Kristine?

MRS. LINDE (*putting on her things*): Yes, I better go and find a place to stay.

HELMER: Good. Then we'll be going the same way.

NORA (*helping her*): I'm sorry this place is so small, but I don't think we very well could—

MRS. LINDE: Of course! Don't be silly, Nora. Goodbye, and thank you for everything.

NORA: Goodbye. We'll see you soon. You'll be back this evening, of course. And you too, Doctor Rank; right? If you feel well enough? Of course you will. Just wrap yourself up.

(*General small talk as all exit into the hall. Children's voices are heard on the stairs.*)

NORA: There they are! There they are! (*She runs and opens the door.* THE NURSE ANNE-MARIE *enters with the children.*) Come in! Come in! (*Bends over and kisses them.*) Oh, you sweet, sweet darlings! Look at them, Kristine! Aren't they beautiful?

RANK: No standing around in the draft!

HELMER: Come along, Mrs. Linde. This place isn't fit for anyone but mothers right now.

(DOCTOR RANK, HELMER, *and* MRS. LINDE *go down the stairs. The* NURSE *enters the living room with the* CHILDREN. NORA *follows, closing the door behind her.*)

NORA: My, how nice you all look! Such red cheeks! Like apples and roses. (*The children all talk at the same time.*) You've had so much fun? I bet you have. Oh, isn't that nice! You pulled both Emmy and Bob on your sleigh? Both at the same time? That's very good, Ivar. Oh, let me hold her for a minute, Anne-Marie. My sweet little doll baby! (*Takes the smallest of the children from the* NURSE *and dances with her.*) Yes, yes, of course; Mama'll dance with you too, Bob. What? You threw snowballs? Oh, I wish I'd been there! No, no; *I* want to take their clothes off, Anne-Marie. Please let me; I think it's so much fun. You go on in. You look frozen. There's hot coffee on the stove.

(*The* NURSE *exits into the room to the left.* NORA *takes the children's wraps off and throws them all around. They all keep telling her things at the same time.*)

NORA: Oh, really? A big dog ran after you? But it didn't bite you? Of course not. Dogs don't bite sweet little doll babies. Don't peek at the packages, Ivar! What's in them? Wouldn't you like to know! No, no; that's something terrible! Play? You want to play? What do you want to play? Okay, let's play hide-and-seek. Bob hides first. You want *me* to? All right. I'll go first.

(*Laughing and shouting,* NORA *and the children play in the living room and in the adjacent room, right. Finally,* NORA *hides herself under the table; the children rush in, look for her, can't find her. They hear her low giggle, run to the table, lift the rug that covers it, see her. General hilarity. She crawls out, pretends to scare them. New delight. In the meantime there has been a knock on the door between the living room and the front hall, but nobody has noticed. Now the door is opened halfway;* KROGSTAD *appears. He waits a little. The playing goes on.*)

KROGSTAD: Pardon me, Mrs. Helmer—

NORA (*with a muted cry turns around, jumps up*): Ah! What do you want?

KROGSTAD: I'm sorry. The front door was open. Somebody must have forgotten to close it—

NORA (*standing up*): My husband isn't here, Mr. Krogstad.

KROGSTAD: I know.

NORA: So what do you want?

KROGSTAD: I'd like a word with you.

NORA: With—! (*To the children in a low voice.*) Go in to Anne-Marie. What? No, the strange man won't do anything bad to mama. When he's gone we'll play some more. (*She takes the children into the room to the left and closes the door.*)

NORA (*tense, troubled*): You want to speak with me?

KROGSTAD: Yes I do.

NORA: Today—? It isn't the first of the month yet.

KROGSTAD: No, it's Christmas Eve. It's up to you what kind of holiday you'll have.

NORA: What do you want? I can't possibly—

KROGSTAD: Let's not talk about that just yet. There's something else. You do have a few minutes, don't you?

NORA: Yes. Yes, of course. That is—

KROGSTAD: Good. I was sitting in Olsen's restaurant when I saw your husband go by.

NORA: Yes—?

KROGSTAD: —with a lady.

NORA: What of it?

KROGSTAD: May I be so free as to ask: wasn't that lady Mrs. Linde?

NORA: Yes.

KROGSTAD: Just arrived in town?

NORA: Yes, today.

KROGSTAD: She's a good friend of yours, I understand?

NORA: Yes, she is. But I fail to see—

KROGSTAD: I used to know her myself.

NORA: I know that.

KROGSTAD: So you know that. I thought as much. In that case, let me ask you a simple question. Is Mrs. Linde going to be employed in the bank?

NORA: What makes you think you have the right to cross examine me like this, Mr. Krogstad—you, one of my husband's employees? But since you ask, I'll tell you. Yes, Mrs. Linde is going to be working in the bank. And it was I who recommended her, Mr. Krogstad. Now you know.

KROGSTAD: So I was right.

NORA (*walks up and down*): After all, one does have a little influence, you know. Just because you're a woman, it doesn't mean that—Really, Mr. Krogstad, people in a subordinate position should be careful not to offend someone who—oh well—

KROGSTAD: —has influence?

NORA: Exactly.

KROGSTAD (*changing his tone*): Mrs. Helmer, I must ask you to be good enough to use your influence on my behalf.

NORA: Oh? What do you mean?

KROGSTAD: I want you to make sure that I am going to keep my subordinate position in the bank.

NORA: I don't understand. Who is going to take your position away from you?

KROGSTAD: There's no point in playing ignorant with me, Mrs. Helmer. I can very well appreciate that your friend would find it unpleasant to run into me. So now I know who I can thank for my dismissal.

NORA: But I assure you—

KROGSTAD: Never mind. I just want to say you still have time. I advise you to use your influence to prevent it.

NORA: But Mr. Krogstad, I don't have any influence—none at all.

KROGSTAD: No? I thought you just said—

NORA: Of course I didn't mean it that way. I! Whatever makes you think that I have any influence of that kind on my husband?

KROGSTAD: I went to law school with your husband. I have no reason to think that the Bank Manager is less susceptible than other husbands.

NORA: If you're going to insult my husband, I'll have to ask you to leave.

KROGSTAD: You're brave, Mrs. Helmer.

NORA: I'm not afraid of you any more. After New Year's I'll be out of this thing with you.

KROGSTAD (*more controlled*): Listen, Mrs. Helmer. If necessary, I'll fight as for my life to keep my little job in the bank.

NORA: So it seems.

KROGSTAD: It isn't just the money; that's really the smallest part of it. There is something else— Well, I guess I might as well tell you. It's like this. I'm sure you know, like everybody else, that some years ago I committed—an impropriety.

NORA: I believe I've heard it mentioned.

KROGSTAD: The case never came to trial, but from that moment all doors were closed to me. So I took up the kind of business you know about. I had to do something, and I think I can say about

myself that I have not been among the worst. But now I want to get out of all that. My sons are growing up. For their sake I must get back as much of my good name as I can. This job in the bank was like the first rung on the ladder. And now your husband wants to kick me down and leave me back in the mud again.

NORA: But I swear to you, Mr. Krogstad; it's not at all in my power to help you.

KROGSTAD: That's because you don't want to. But I have the means to force you.

NORA: You don't mean you're going to tell my husband I owe you money?

KROGSTAD: And if I did?

NORA: That would be a mean thing to do. (*Almost crying.*) That secret, which is my joy and my pride—for him to learn about it in such a coarse and ugly way—to learn it from *you*—! It would be terribly unpleasant for me.

KROGSTAD: Just unpleasant?

NORA (*heatedly*): But go ahead! Do it! It will be worse for you than for me. When my husband realizes what a bad person you are, you're certainly going to lose your job.

KROGSTAD: I asked you if it was just domestic unpleasantness you were afraid of?

NORA: When my husband finds out, of course he'll pay off the loan, and then we won't have anything more to do with you.

KROGSTAD (*stepping closer*): Listen, Mrs. Helmer—either you have a very bad memory, or you don't know much about business. I think I had better straighten you out on a few things.

NORA: What do you mean?

KROGSTAD: When your husband was ill, you came to me to borrow twelve hundred dollars.

NORA: I knew nobody else.

KROGSTAD: I promised to get you the money—

NORA: And you did.

KROGSTAD: —I promised to get you the money on certain conditions. At the time you were so anxious about your husband's health and so set on getting him away that I doubt very much that you paid much attention to the details of our transaction. That's why I remind you of them now. Anyway, I promised to get you the money if you would sign an I.O.U., which I drafted.

NORA: And which I signed.

KROGSTAD: Good. But below your signature I added a few lines, making your father security for the loan. Your father was supposed to put his signature to those lines.

NORA: Supposed to—? He did.

KROGSTAD: I had left the date blank. That is, your father was to date his own signature. You recall that, don't you, Mrs. Helmer?

NORA: I guess so—

KROGSTAD: I gave the note to you. You were to mail it to your father. Am I correct?

NORA: Yes.

KROGSTAD: And of course you did so right away, for no more than five or six days later you brought the paper back to me, signed by your father. Then I paid you the money.

NORA: Well? And haven't I been keeping up with the payments?

KROGSTAD: Fairly well, yes. But to get back to what we were talking about—those were difficult days for you, weren't they, Mrs. Helmer?

NORA: Yes, they were.

KROGSTAD: Your father was quite ill, I believe.

NORA: He was dying.

KROGSTAD: And died shortly afterwards?

NORA: That's right.

KROGSTAD: Tell me, Mrs. Helmer; do you happen to remember the date of your father's death? I mean the exact day of the month?

NORA: Daddy died on September 29.

KROGSTAD: Quite correct. I have ascertained that fact. That's why there is something peculiar about this (*takes out a piece of paper*), which I can't account for.

NORA: Peculiar? How? I don't understand—

KROGSTAD: It seems very peculiar, Mrs. Helmer, that your father signed this promissory note three days after his death.

NORA: How so? I don't see what—

KROGSTAD: Your father died on September 29. Now look. He has dated his signature October 2. Isn't that odd?

(NORA *remains silent*)

KROGSTAD: Can you explain it?

(NORA *still silent*)

KROGSTAD: I also find it striking that the date and the month and the year are not in your father's handwriting but in a hand I think I recognize. Well, that might be explained. Your father may have forgotten to date his signature and somebody else may have done it here, guessing at the date before he had learned of your father's death. That's all right. It's only the signature itself that matters. And that is genuine, isn't it, Mrs. Helmer? Your father *did* put his name to this note?

NORA (*after a brief silence tosses her head back and looks defiantly at him*): No, he didn't. I wrote Daddy's name.

KROGSTAD: Mrs. Helmer—do you realize what a dangerous admission you just made?

NORA: Why? You'll get your money soon.

KROGSTAD: Let me ask you something. Why didn't you mail this note to your father?

NORA: Because it was impossible. Daddy was sick—you know that. If I had asked him for his signature I would have had to tell him what the money was for. But I couldn't tell him, as sick as he was, that my husband's life was in danger. That was impossible. Surely you can see that.

KROGSTAD: Then it would have been better for you if you had given up your trip abroad.

NORA: No, that was impossible! That trip was to save my husband's life. I couldn't give it up.

KROGSTAD: But didn't you realize that what you did amounted to fraud against me?

NORA: I couldn't let that make any difference. I didn't care about you at all. I hated the way you made all those difficulties for me, even though you knew the danger my husband was in. I thought you were cold and unfeeling.

KROGSTAD: Mrs. Helmer, obviously you have no clear idea of what you have done. Let me tell you that what I did that time was no more and no worse. And it ruined my name and reputation.

NORA: You! Are you trying to tell me that you did something brave once in order to save your wife's life?

KROGSTAD: The law doesn't ask about motives.

NORA: Then it's a bad law.

KROGSTAD: Bad or not—if I produce this note in court you'll be judged according to the law.

NORA: I refuse to believe you. A daughter shouldn't have the right to spare her dying old father worry and anxiety? A wife shouldn't have the right to save her husband's life? I don't know the laws very well, but I'm sure that somewhere they make allowance for cases like that. And you, a lawyer, don't know that? I think you must be a bad lawyer, Mr. Krogstad.

KROGSTAD: That may be. But business—the kind of business you and I have with one another—don't you think I know something about that? Very well. Do what you like. But let me tell you this: if I'm going to be kicked out again, you'll keep me company. (*He bows and exits through the front hall.*)

NORA (*pauses thoughtfully; then, with a defiant toss of her head*): Oh, nonsense! Trying to scare me like that! I'm not all that silly. (*Starts picking up the children's clothes; soon stops.*) But—? No! That's impossible! I did it for love!

THE CHILDREN (*in the door to the left*): Mama, the strange man just left. We saw him.

NORA: Yes, yes; I know. But don't tell anybody about the strange man. Do you hear? Not even Daddy.

THE CHILDREN: We won't. But now you'll play with us again, won't you, mama?

NORA: No, not right now.

THE CHILDREN: Oh, but mama—you promised.

NORA: I know, but I can't just now. Go to your own room. I've so much to do. Be nice now, my little darlings. Do as I say. (*She nudges them gently into the other room and closes the door. She sits down on the couch, picks up a piece of embroidery, makes a few stitches, then stops.*) No! (*Throws the embroidery down, goes to the hall door and calls out:*) Helene! Bring the Christmas tree in here, please! (*Goes to the table, left, opens the drawer, halts.*) No—that's impossible!

MAID (*with the Christmas tree*): Where do you want it, ma'am?

NORA: There. The middle of the floor.

MAID: You want anything else?

NORA: No, thanks. I have everything I need. (*The* MAID *goes out.* NORA *starts trimming the tree.*) I want candles—and flowers—That awful man! Oh, nonsense! There's nothing wrong. This will be a lovely tree. I'll do everything you want me to, Torvald. I'll sing for you—dance for you—

(HELMER, *a bundle of papers under his arm, enters from outside.*)

NORA: Ah—you're back already?

HELMER: Yes, Has anybody been here?

NORA: Here? No.

HELMER: That's funny. I saw Krogstad leaving just now.

NORA: Oh? Oh yes, that's right. Krogstad was here for just a moment.

HELMER: I can tell from your face that he came to ask you to put in a word for him.

NORA: Yes.

HELMER: And it was supposed to be your own idea, wasn't it? You were not to tell me he'd been here. He asked you that too, didn't he?

NORA: Yes, Torvald, but—

HELMER: Nora, Nora, how could you! Talking to a man like that and making him promises! And lying to me about it afterwards—!

NORA: Lying—?

HELMER: Didn't you say nobody had been here? (*Shakes his finger at her.*) My little songbird must never do that again. Songbirds are supposed to have clean beaks to chirp with—no false notes. (*Puts his arm around her waist.*) Isn't that so? Of course it is. (*Lets her go.*) And that's enough about that. (*Sits down in front of the fireplace.*) Ah, it's nice and warm in here. (*Begins to leaf through his papers.*)

NORA (*busy with the tree. After a brief pause*): Torvald.

HELMER: Yes.

NORA: I'm looking forward so much to the Stenborgs' costume party day after tomorrow.

HELMER: And I can't wait to find out what you're going to surprise me with.

NORA: Oh, that silly idea!

HELMER: Oh?

NORA: I can't think of anything. It all seems so foolish and pointless.

HELMER: Ah, my little Nora admits that?

NORA (*behind his chair, her arms on the back of the chair*): Are you very busy, Torvald?

HELMER: Well—

NORA: What are all those papers?

HELMER: Bank business.

NORA: Already?

HELMER: I've asked the board to give me the authority to make certain changes in organization and personnel. That's what I'll be doing over the holidays. I want it all settled before New Year's.

NORA: So that's why this poor Krogstad—

HELMER: Hm.

NORA (*leisurely playing with the hair on his neck*): If you weren't so busy, Torvald, I'd ask you for a great, big favor.

HELMER: Let's hear it, anyway.

NORA: I don't know anyone with better taste than you, and I want so much to look nice at the party. Couldn't you sort of take charge of me, Torvald, and decide what I'll wear—help me with my costume?

HELMER: Aha! Little Lady Obstinate is looking for someone to rescue her?

NORA: Yes, Torvald. I won't get anywhere without your help.

HELMER: All right, I'll think about it. We'll come up with something.

NORA: Oh, you *are* nice! (*Goes back to the Christmas tree. A pause.*) Those red flowers look so pretty.—Tell me, was it really all that bad what this Krogstad fellow did?

HELMER: He forged signatures. Do you have any idea what that means?

NORA: Couldn't it have been because he felt he had to?

HELMER: Yes, or like so many others he may simply have been thoughtless. I'm not so heartless as to condemn a man absolutely because of a single imprudent act.

NORA: Of course not, Torvald!

HELMER: People like him can redeem themselves morally by openly confessing their crime and taking their punishment.

NORA: Punishment—?

HELMER: But that was not the way Krogstad chose. He got out of it with tricks and evasions. That's what has corrupted him.

NORA: So you think that if—?

HELMER: Can't you imagine how a guilty person like that has to lie and fake and dissemble wherever he goes—putting on a mask before everybody he's close to, even his own wife and children? It's this thing with the children that's the worst part of it, Nora.

NORA: Why is that?

HELMER: Because when a man lives inside such a circle of stinking lies he brings infection into his own home and contaminates his whole family. With every breath of air his children inhale the germs of something ugly.

NORA (moving closer behind him): Are you so sure of that?

HELMER: Of course I am. I have seen enough examples of that in my work. Nearly all young criminals have had mothers who lied.

NORA: Why mothers—particularly?

HELMER: Most often mothers. But of course fathers tend to have the same influence. Every lawyer knows that. And yet, for years this Krogstad has been poisoning his own children in an atmosphere of lies and deceit. That's why I call him a lost soul morally. (Reaches out for her hands.) And that's why my sweet little Nora must promise me never to take his side again. Let's shake on that.— What? What's this? Give me your hand! There! Now that's settled. I assure you, I would find it impossible to work in the same room with that man. I feel litterally sick when I'm around people like that.

NORA (withdraws her hand and goes to the other side of the Christmas tree): It's so hot in here. And I have so much to do.

HELMER (gets up and collects his papers): Yes, and I really should try to get some of this reading done before dinner. I must think about your costume too. And maybe just possibly I'll have something to wrap in gilt paper and hang on the Christmas tree. (Puts his hand on her head.) Oh my adorable little songbird! (Enters his study and closes the door.)

NORA (after a pause, in a low voice): It's all a lot of nonsense. It's not that way at all. It's impossible. It has to be impossible.

NURSE (in the door, left): The little ones are asking ever so nicely if they can't come in and be with their mama.

NORA: No, no, no! Don't let them in here! You stay with them, Anne-Marie.

NURSE: If you say so, ma'am. (Closes the door.)

NORA (pale with terror): Corrupt my little children—! Poison my home—? (Brief pause; she lifts her head.) That's not true. Never. Never in a million years.

ACT II

The same room. The Christmas tree is in the corner by the piano, stripped, shabby-looking, with burnt-down candles. NORA's *outdoor clothes are on the couch.* NORA *is alone. She walks around restlessly. She stops by the couch and picks up her coat.*

NORA (drops the coat again): There's somebody now! (Goes to the door, listens.) No. Nobody. Of course not—not on Christmas. And not tomorrow either.[1]—But perhaps—(Opens the door and looks.) No, nothing in the mailbox. All empty. (Comes forward.) How silly I am! Of course he isn't serious. Nothing like that could happen. After all, I have three small children.

(The NURSE *enters from the room, left, carrying a big carton.*)

NURSE: Well, at last I found it—the box with your costume.

NORA: Thanks. Just put it on the table.

NURSE (does so): But it's all a big mess, I'm afraid.

NORA: Oh, I wish I could tear the whole thing to little pieces!

NURSE: Heavens! It's not as bad as all that. It can

[1] In Norway both December 25 and 26 are legal holidays.

be fixed all right. All it takes is a little patience.

NORA: I'll go over and get Mrs. Linde to help me.

NURSE: Going out again? In this awful weather? You'll catch a cold.

NORA: That might not be such a bad thing. How are the children?

NURSE: The poor little dears are playing with their presents, but—

NORA: Do they keep asking for me?

NURSE: Well, you know, they're used to being with their mama.

NORA: I know. But Anne-Marie, from now on I can't be with them as much as before.

NURSE: Oh well. Little children get used to everything.

NORA: You think so? Do you think they'll forget their mama if I were gone altogether?

NURSE: Goodness me—gone altogether?

NORA: Listen, Anne-Marie; something I've often wondered about. How could you bring yourself to leave your child with strangers?

NURSE: But I had to, if I were to nurse you.

NORA: Yes, but how could you *want* to?

NURSE: When I could get such a nice place? When something like that happens to a poor young girl, she'd better be grateful for whatever she gets. For *he* didn't do a thing for me—the louse!

NORA: But your daughter has forgotten all about you, hasn't she?

NURSE: Oh no! Not at all! She wrote to me both when she was confirmed and when she got married.

NORA (*putting her arms around her neck*): You dear old thing—you were a good mother to me when I was little.

NURSE: Poor little Nora had no one else, you know.

NORA: And if my little ones didn't, I know you'd—oh, I'm being silly! (*Opens the carton.*) Go in to them, please. I really should—. Tomorrow you'll see how pretty I'll be.

NURSE: I know. There won't be anybody at that party half as pretty as you, ma'am. (*Goes out, left.*)

NORA (*begins to take clothes out of the carton. In a moment she throws it all down.*) If only I dared to go out. If only I knew nobody would come—that nothing would happen while I was gone.—How silly! Nobody'll come. Just don't think about it. Brush the muff. Beautiful gloves. Beautiful gloves. Forget it. Forget it. One, two, three, four, five six—(*Cries out.*) There they are! (*Moves toward the door, stops irresolutely.*)

(MRS. LINDE *enters from the hall. She has already taken off her coat.*)

NORA: Oh, it's you, Kristine. There's no one else out there, is there? I'm so glad you're here.

MRS. LINDE: They told me you'd asked for me.

NORA: I just happened to walk by. I need your help with something—badly. Let's sit here on the couch. Look, Torvald and I are going to a costume party tomorrow night—at Consul Stenborg's upstairs—and Torvald wants me to go as a Neapolitan fisher girl and dance the Tarantella. I learned it when we were on Capri, don't you know.

MRS. LINDE: Well, well! So you'll be putting on a whole show?

NORA: Yes. Torvald thinks I should. Look here's the costume. Torvald had it made for me while we were there. But it's so torn and everything. I just don't know—

MRS. LINDE: Oh that can be fixed. It's not that much. The trimmings have come loose in a few places. Do you have needle and thread? Ah, here we are. All set.

NORA: I really appreciate it, Kristine.

MRS. LINDE (*sewing*): So you'll be in disguise tomorrow night, eh? You know—I may come by for just a moment, just to look at you.—Oh dear, I haven't even thanked you for the nice evening last night.

NORA (*gets up, moves around*): Oh I don't know. I don't think last night was as nice as it usually is.—You should have come to town a little earlier, Kristine.—Yes, Torvald knows how to make it nice and pretty around here.

MRS. LINDE: You too, I should think. After all, you're your father's daughter. By the way, is Dr. Rank always as depressed as he was last night?

NORA: No, last night was unusual. He's a very sick man, you know—very sick. Poor Rank, his spine is rotting away or something. Tuberculosis, I think. You see, his father was a nasty old man with mistresses and all that sort of thing. Rank has been sickly ever since he was a little boy.

MRS. LINDE (*dropping her sewing to her lap*): But dearest Nora, where have you learned about things like that?

NORA (*still walking about*): Oh, you know—with three children you sometimes get to talk with—other wives. Some of them know quite a bit about medicine. So you pick up a few things.

MRS. LINDE (*resumes her sewing. After a brief pause*): Does Dr. Rank come here every day?

NORA: Every single day. He's Torvald's oldest and best friend, after all. And my friend too, for that matter. He's part of the family, almost.

MRS. LINDE: But tell me, is he quite sincere? I mean, isn't he the kind of man who likes to say nice things to people?

NORA: No, not at all. Rather the opposite, in fact. What makes you say that?

MRS. LINDE: When you introduced us yesterday, he told me he'd often heard my name mentioned in this house. But later on it was quite obvious that your husband really had no idea who I was. So how could Dr. Rank—?

NORA: You're right, Kristine, but I can explain that. You see, Torvald loves me so very much that he wants me all to himself. That's what he says. When we were first married he got jealous, almost, when I as much as mentioned anybody from back home that I was fond of. So of course I soon stopped doing that. But with Dr. Rank I often talk about home. You see, he likes to listen to me.

MRS. LINDE: Look here, Nora. In many ways you're still a child. After all, I'm quite a bit older than you and have had more experience. I want to give you a piece of advice. I think you should get out of this thing with Dr. Rank.

NORA: Get out of what thing?

MRS. LINDE: Several things in fact, if you want my opinion. Yesterday you said something about a rich admirer who was going to give you money—

NORA: One who doesn't exist, unfortunately. What of it?

MRS. LINDE: Does Dr. Rank have money?

NORA: Yes he does.

MRS. LINDE: And no dependents?

NORA: No. But—?

MRS. LINDE: And he comes here every day?

NORA: Yes, I told you that already.

MRS. LINDE: But how can that sensitive man be so tactless?

NORA: I haven't the slightest idea what you're talking aobut.

MRS. LINDE: Don't play games with me, Nora. Don't you think I know who you borrowed the twelve hundred dollars from?

NORA: Are you out of your mind! The very idea—! A friend of both of us who sees us every day— What a dreadfully uncomfortable position that would be!

MRS. LINDE: So it really isn't Dr. Rank?

NORA: Most certainly not! I would never have dreamed of asking him—not for a moment. Anyway, he didn't have any money then. He inherited it afterwards.

MRS. LINDE: Well, I still think that may have been lucky for you, Nora dear.

NORA: The idea! It would never have occurred to me to ask Dr. Rank—. Though I'm sure that if I *did* ask him—

MRS. LINDE: But of course you won't.

NORA: Of course not. I can't imagine that would ever be necessary. But I am quite sure that if I told Dr. Rank—

MRS. LINDE: Behind your husband's back?

NORA: I must get out of—this other thing. That's also behind his back. I *must* get out of it.

MRS. LINDE: That's what I told you yesterday. But—

NORA (*walking up and down*): A man manages these things so much better than a woman—

MRS. LINDE: One's husband, yes.

NORA: Silly, silly! (*Stops.*) When you've paid off all you owe, you get your I.O.U. back; right?

MRS. LINDE: Yes, of course.

NORA: And you can tear it into a hundred thousand little pieces and burn it—that dirty, filthy paper!

MRS. LINDE (*looks hard at her, puts down her sewing, rises slowly*): Nora—you're hiding something from me.

NORA: Can you tell?

MRS. LINDE: Something's happened to you, Nora, since yesterday morning. What is it?

NORA (*going to her*): Kristine! (*Listens.*) Shhh. Torvald just came back. Listen. Why don't you go in to the children for a while. Torvald can't stand having sewing around. Get Anne-Marie to help you.

MRS. LINDE (*gathers some of the sewing things together*): All right, but I'm not leaving here till you and I have talked.

(*She goes out left, just as* HELMER *enters from the front hall.*)

NORA (*towards him*): I have been waiting and waiting for you, Torvald.

HELMER: Was that the dressmaker?

NORA: No, it was Kristine. She's helping me with my costume. Oh Torvald, just wait till you see how nice I'll look!

HELMER: I told you. Pretty good idea I had, wasn't it?

NORA: Lovely! Marvelous! And wasn't it nice of me to go along with it?

HELMER (*his hand under her chin*): Nice? To do what your husband tells you? All right, you little rascal; I know you didn't mean it that way. But

don't let me interrupt you. I suppose you want to
try it on.

NORA: And you'll be working?

HELMER: Yes. (*Shows her a pile of papers.*) Look.
I've been down to the bank. (*Is about to enter his
study.*)

NORA: Torvald.

HELMER (*halts*): Yes?

NORA: What if your little squirrel asked you ever
so nicely—

HELMER: For what?

NORA: Would you do it?

HELMER: Depends on what it is.

NORA: Squirrel would run around and do all
sorts of fun tricks if you'd be nice and agreeable.

HELMER: All right. What is it?

NORA: Lark would chirp and twitter in all the
rooms, up and down—

HELMER: So what? Lark does that anyway.

NORA: I'll be your elfmaid and dance for you in
the moonlight, Torvald.

HELMER: Nora, don't tell me it's the same thing
you mentioned this morning?

NORA (*closer to him*): Yes, Torvald. I beg you!

HELMER: You really have the nerve to bring that
up again?

NORA: Yes. You've just got to do as I say. You
must let Krogstad keep his job.

HELMER: My dear Nora. It's his job I intend to
give to Mrs. Linde.

NORA: I know. And that's ever so nice of you.
But can't you just fire someone else?

HELMER: This is incredible! You just don't give
up, do you? Because *you* make some foolish
promise, *I* am supposed to—!

NORA: That's not the reason, Torvald. It's for
your own sake. That man writes for the worst
newspapers. You've said so yourself. There's no
telling what he may do to you. I'm scared to death
of him.

HELMER: Ah, I understand. You're afraid because of what happened before.

NORA: What do you mean?

HELMER: You're thinking of your father, of
course.

NORA: Yes. Yes, you're right. Remember the
awful things they wrote about Daddy in the newspapers? I really think they might have forced him
to resign if the ministry hadn't sent you to look into
the charges and if you hadn't been so helpful and
understanding.

HELMER: My dear little Nora, there is a world of
difference between your father and me. Your
father's official conduct was not above reproach.

Mine is, and I intend it to stay that way as long as I
hold my position.

NORA: Oh, but you don't know what vicious
people like him may think of. Oh, Torvald! Now
all of us could be so happy together here in our
own home, peaceful and carefree. Such a good
life, Torvald, for you and me and the children!
That's why I implore you—

HELMER: And it's exactly because you plead for
him that you make it impossible for me to keep
him. It's already common knowledge in the banks
that I intend to let Krogstad go. If it gets out that
the new manager has changed his mind because of
his wife—

NORA: Yes? What then?

HELMER: No, of course, that wouldn't matter at
all as long as little Mrs. Pighead here got her way!
Do you want me to make myself look ridiculous
before my whole staff—make people think I can
be pushed around by just anybody—by outsiders?
Believe me, I'd soon find out what the consequences would be! Besides, there's another thing
that makes it absolutely impossible for Krogstad to
stay on in the bank now that I'm in charge.

NORA: What's that?

HELMER: I suppose in a pinch I could overlook
his moral shortcomings—

NORA: Yes, you could; couldn't you, Torvald?

HELMER: And I understand he's quite a good
worker, too. But we've known each other for a long
time. It's one of those imprudent relationships you
get into when you're young that embarrass you for
the rest of your life. I guess I might as well be frank
with you: he and I are on a first name basis. And
that tactless fellow never hides the fact even when
other people are around. Rather, he seems to think
it entitles him to be familiar with me. Every
chance he gets he comes out with his damn
"Torvald, Torvald." I'm telling you, I find it most
awkward. He would make my position in the bank
intolerable.

NORA: You don't really mean any of this,
Torvald.

HELMER: Oh? I don't? And why not?

NORA: No, for it's all so petty.

HELMER: What! Petty? You think I'm being
petty!

NORA: No, I *don't* think you are petty, Torvald
dear. That's exactly why I—

HELMER: Never mind. You think my reasons
are petty, so it follows that I must be petty too.
Petty! Indeed! By god, I'll put an end to this right
now! (*Opens the door to the front hall and calls
out.*) Helene!

NORA: What are you doing?

HELMER (*searching among his papers*): Making a decision. (*The* MAID *enters.*) Here. Take this letter. Go out with it right away. Find somebody to deliver it. But quick. The address is on the envelope. Wait. Here's money.

MAID: Very good, sir. (*She takes the letter and goes out.*)

HELMER (*collecting his papers*): There now, little Mrs. Obstinate!

NORA (*breathless*): Torvald—what was that letter?

HELMER: Krogstad's dismissal.

NORA: Call it back, Torvald! There's still time! Oh, Torvald, please—call it back! For my sake, for your own sake, for the sake of the children! Listen to me, Torvald! Do it! You don't know what you're doing to all of us!

HELMER: Too late.

NORA: Yes. Too late.

HELMER: Dear Nora, I forgive you this fear you're in, although it really is an insult to me. Yes, it is! It's an insult to think that I am scared of a shabby scrivener's revenge. But I forgive you, for it's such a beautiful proof how much you love me. (*Takes her in his arms.*) And that's the way it should be, my sweet darling. Whatever happens, you'll see that when things get really rough I have both strength and courage. You'll find out that I am man enough to shoulder the whole burden.

NORA (*terrified*): What do you mean by that?

HELMER: All of it, I tell you—

NORA (*composed*): You'll never have to do that.

HELMER: Good. Then we'll share the burden, Nora—like husband and wife, the way it ought to be. (*Caresses her.*) Now are you satisfied? There, there, there. Not that look in your eyes—like a frightened little dove. It's all your own foolish imagination.—Why don't you practice the Tarantella—and your tambourine, too. I'll be in the inner office. When I close both doors I won't hear a thing. You may make as much noise as you like. (*Turning in the doorway.*) And when Rank comes, why don't you tell him where to find me. (*He nods to her, enters his study carrying his papers, and closes the door.*)

NORA (*transfixed by terror, whispers*): He would do it. He'll do it. He'll do it in spite of the whole world.—No, this mustn't happen. Anything rather than that! There must be a way—! (*The doorbell rings.*) Doctor Rank! Anything rather than that! Anything—anything at all!

(*She passes her hand over her face, pulls herself together, and opens the door to the hall.* DR. RANK *is out there, hanging up his coat. Darkness begins to fall during the following scene.*)

NORA: Hello there, Dr. Rank. I recognized your ringing. Don't go in to Torvald yet. I think he's busy.

RANK: And you?

NORA (*as he enters and she closes the door behind him*): You know I always have time for you.

RANK: Thanks. I'll make use of that as long as I can.

NORA: What do you mean by that? "As long as you can"?

RANK: Does that frighten you?

NORA: Well, it's a funny expression. As if something was going to happen.

RANK: Something is going to happen that I've long been expecting. But I admit I hadn't thought it would come quite so soon.

NORA (*seizes his arm*): What is it you've found out? Dr. Rank—tell me!

RANK (*sits down by the stove*): I'm going downhill fast. There's nothing to be done about that.

NORA (*with audible relief*): So it's *you*—

RANK: Who else? No point in lying to myself. I'm in worse shape than any of my other patients, Mrs. Helmer. These last few days I've been conducting an audit on my inner condition. Bankrupt. Chances are that within a month I'll be rotting up in the cemetery.

NORA: Shame on you! Talking that horrid way!

RANK: The thing itself is horrid—damn horrid. The worst of it, though, is all that other horror that comes first. There is only one more test I need to make. After that I'll have a pretty good idea when I'll start coming apart. There is something I want to say to you. Helmer's refined nature can't stand anything hideous. I don't want him in my sick room.

NORA: Oh but Dr. Rank—

RANK: I don't want him there. Under no circumstance. I'll close my door to him. As soon as I have full certainty that the worst is about to begin I'll give you my card with a black cross on it. Then you'll know the last, horrible destruction has started.

NORA: Today you're really quite impossible. And I had hoped you'd be in a particularly good mood.

RANK: With death on my hands? Paying for someone else's sins? Is there justice in that? And yet there isn't a single family that isn't ruled by that

Coat used in [illegible] + Exit

same law of ruthless retribution, in one way or another.

NORA (*puts her hands over her ears*): Poppycock! Be fun! Be fun!

RANK: Well, yes. You may just as well laugh at the whole thing. My poor, innocent spine is suffering for my father's frolics when he was a young lieutenant.

NORA (*over by the table, left*): Right. He was addicted to asparagus and goose liver paté, wasn't he?

RANK: And truffles.

NORA: Of course. Truffles. And oysters too, I think.

RANK: And oysters. Obviously.

NORA: And all the port and champagne that go with it. It's really too bad that goodies like that ruin your backbone.

RANK: Particularly an unfortunate backbone that never enjoyed any of it.

NORA: Ah yes, that's the saddest part of it all.

RANK (*looks searchingly at her*): Hm—

NORA (*after a brief pause*): Why did you smile just then?

RANK: I didn't. It was you who laughed.

NORA: No, it was you who smiled, Dr. Rank!

RANK (*gets up*): I see you're more of a mischief-maker than I thought.

NORA: I feel like mischief today.

RANK: So it seems.

NORA (*with both her hands on his shoulders*): Dear, dear Dr. Rank, don't you go and die and leave Torvald and me.

RANK: Oh, you won't miss me for very long. Those who go away are soon forgotten.

NORA (*with an anxious look*): Do you believe that?

RANK: You'll make new friends, and then—

NORA: Who'll make new friends?

RANK: Both you and Helmer, once I'm gone. You yourself seem to have made a good start already. What was this Mrs. Linde doing here last night?

NORA: Aha—Don't tell me you're jealous of poor Kristine?

RANK: Yes I am. She'll be my successor in this house. As soon as I have made my excuses, that woman is likely to—

NORA: Shh—not so loud. She's in there.

RANK: Today too? There you are!

NORA: She's mending my costume. My god, you really *are* unreasonable. (*Sits down on the couch.*) Now be nice, Dr. Rank. Tomorrow you'll see how beautifully I'll dance, and then you are to

pretend I'm dancing just for you—and for Torvald too, of course. (*Takes several items out of the carton.*) Sit down, Dr. Rank; I want to show you something.

RANK (*sitting down*): What?

NORA: Look.

RANK: Silk stockings.

NORA: Flesh-colored. Aren't they lovely? Now it's getting dark in here, but tomorrow—No, no. You only get to see the foot. Oh well, you might as well see all of it.

RANK: Hm.

NORA: Why do you look so critical? Don't you think they'll fit?

RANK: That's something I can't possibly have a reasoned opinion about.

NORA (*looks at him for a moment*): Shame on you. (*Slaps his ear lightly with the stocking.*) That's what you get. (*Puts the things back in the carton.*)

RANK: And what other treasures are you going to show me?

NORA: Nothing at all, because you're naughty. (*She hums a little and rummages in the carton.*)

RANK (*after a brief silence*): When I sit here like this, talking confidently with you, I can't imagine—I can't possibly imagine what would have become of me if I hadn't had you and Helmer.

NORA (*smiles*): Well, yes—I do believe you like being with us.

RANK (*in a lower voice, lost in thought*) And then to have to go away from it all—

NORA: Nonsense. You're not going anywhere.

RANK (*as before*): —and not leave behind as much as a poor little token of gratitude, hardly a brief memory of someone missed, nothing but a vacant place that anyone can fill.

NORA: And what if I were to ask you—? No—

RANK: Ask me what?

NORA: For a great proof of your friendship—

RANK: Yes, yes—?

NORA: No, I mean—for an enormous favor—

RANK: Would you really for once make me as happy as all that?

NORA: But you don't even know what it is.

RANK: Well, then; tell me.

NORA: Oh, but I can't, Dr. Rank. It's altogether too much to ask—It's advice and help and a favor—

RANK: So much the better. I can't even begin to guess what it is you have in mind. So for heaven's sake tell me! Don't you trust me?

NORA: Yes, I trust you more than anybody I know. You are my best and most faithful friend. I know that. So I will tell you. All right, Dr. Rank.

There is something you can help me prevent. You know how much Torvald loves me—beyond all words. Never for a moment would he hesitate to give his life for me.

RANK (*leaning over her*): Nora—do you really think he's the only one—?

NORA (*with a slight start*): Who—?

RANK: —who'd gladly give his life for you.

NORA (*heavily*): I see.

RANK: I have sworn an oath to myself to tell you before I go. I'll never find a better occasion.—All right, Nora; now you know. And now you also know that you can confide in me, more than in anyone else.

NORA (*gets up. In a calm, steady voice*): Let me get by.

RANK (*makes room for her but remains seated*): Nora—

NORA (*in the door to the front hall*): Helene, bring the lamp in here, please. (*Walks over to the stove.*) Oh, dear Dr. Rank. That really wasn't very nice of you.

RANK (*gets up*): That I have loved you as much as anybody—was that not nice?

NORA: No, not that. But that you told me. There was no need for that.

RANK: What do you mean? Have you known—?

(*The* MAID *enters with the lamp, puts it on the table, and goes out.*)

RANK: Nora—Mrs. Helmer—I'm asking you: did you know?

NORA: Oh, how can I tell you what I knew and didn't know! I really can't say—But that you could be so awkward, Dr. Rank! Just when everything was so comfortable.

RANK: Well, anyway, now you know that I'm at your service with my life and soul. And now you must speak.

NORA (*looks at him*): After what just happened?

RANK: I beg you—let me know what it is.

NORA: There is nothing I can tell you now.

RANK: Yes, yes. You mustn't punish me this way. Please let me do for you whatever anyone *can* do.

NORA: Now there is nothing you can do. Besides, I don't think I really need any help, anyway. It's probably just my imagination. Of course that's all it is. I'm sure of it! (*Sits down in the rocking chair, looks at him, smiles.*) Well, well, well, Dr. Rank! What a fine gentleman you turned out to be! Aren't you ashamed of yourself, now that we have light?

RANK: No, not really. But perhaps I ought to leave—and not come back?

NORA: Don't be silly; of course not! You'll come here exactly as you have been doing. You know perfectly well that Torvald can't do without you.

RANK: Yes, but what about you?

NORA: Oh, I always think it's perfectly delightful when you come.

RANK: That's the very thing that misled me. You are a riddle to me. It has often seemed to me that you'd just as soon be with me as with Helmer.

NORA: Well, you see, there are people you love, and then there are other people you'd almost rather be with.

RANK: Yes, there is something in that.

NORA: When I lived home with Daddy, of course I loved him most. But I always thought it was so much fun to sneak off down to the maids' rooms, for they never gave me good advice and they always talked about such fun things.

RANK: Aha! So it's *their* place I have taken.

NORA (*jumps up and goes over to him*): Oh dear, kind Dr. Rank, you know very well I didn't mean it that way. Can't you see that with Torvald it is the way it used to be with Daddy?

(*The* MAID *enters from the front hall.*)

MAID: Ma'am! (*Whispers to her and gives her a caller's card.*)

NORA (*glances at the card*): Ah! (*Puts it in her pocket.*)

RANK: Anything wrong?

NORA: No, no; not at all. It's nothing—just my new costume—

RANK: But your costume is lying right there!

NORA: Oh yes, that one. But this is another one. I ordered it. Torvald mustn't know—

RANK: Aha. So that's the great secret.

NORA: That's it. Why don't you go in to him, please. He's in the inner office. And keep him there for a while—

RANK: Don't worry. He won't get away. (*Enters* HELMER's *study.*)

NORA (*to the* MAID): You say he's waiting in the kitchen?

MAID: Yes. He came up the back stairs.

NORA: But didn't you tell him there was somebody with me?

MAID: Yes, but he wouldn't listen.

NORA: He won't leave?

MAID: No, not till he's had a word with you, ma'am.

NORA: All right. But try not to make any noise. And, Helene—don't tell anyone he's here. It's supposed to be a surprise for my husband.

MAID: I understand, ma'am—(*She leaves.*)

NORA: The terrible is happening. It's happening,

after all. No, no, no. It can't happen. It won't happen. (*She bolts the study door.*)

(*The* MAID *opens the front hall door for* KROGSTAD *and closes the door behind him. He wears a fur coat for traveling, boots, and a fur hat.*)

NORA (*toward him*): Keep your voice down. My husband's home.

KROGSTAD: That's all right.

NORA: What do you want?

KROGSTAD: To find out something.

NORA: Then hurry. What?

KROGSTAD: I expect you know I've been fired.

NORA: I couldn't prevent it, Mr. Krogstad. I fought for you as long and as hard as I could, but it didn't do any good.

KROGSTAD: Your husband doesn't love you any more than that? He knows what I can do to you, and yet he runs the risk—

NORA: Surely you didn't think I'd tell him?

KROGSTAD: No, I really didn't. It wouldn't be like Torvald Helmer to show that that kind of guts—

NORA: Mr. Krogstad, I insist that you show respect for my husband.

KROGSTAD: By all means. All due respect. But since you're so anxious to keep this a secret, may I assume that you are a little better informed than yesterday about exactly what you have done?

NORA: Better than *you* could ever teach me.

KROGSTAD: Of course. Such a bad lawyer as I am—

NORA: What do you want of me?

KROGSTAD: I just wanted to see how you were, Mrs. Helmer. I've been thinking about you all day. You see, even a bill collector, a pen pusher, a—anyway, someone like me—even he has a little of what they call a heart.

NORA: Then show it. Think of my little children.

KROGSTAD: Have you and your husband thought of mine? Never mind. All I want to tell you is that you don't need to take this business too seriously. I have no intention of bringing charges right away.

NORA: Oh no, you wouldn't; would you? I knew you wouldn't.

KROGSTAD: The whole thing can be settled quite amicably. Nobody else needs to know anything. It will be between the three of us.

NORA: My husband must never find out about this.

KROGSTAD: How are you going to prevent it? Maybe you can pay me the balance on the loan?

NORA: No, not right now.

KROGSTAD: Or do you have some way of raising the money in the next few days?

NORA: None I intend to make use of.

KROGSTAD: It wouldn't do you any good, anyway. Even if you had the cash in your hand right this minute, I wouldn't give you your note back. It wouldn't make any difference *how* much money you offered me.

NORA: Then you'll have to tell me what you plan to use the note *for*.

KROGSTAD: Just keep it; that's all. Have it on hand, so to speak. I won't say a word to anybody else. So if you've been thinking about doing something desperate—

NORA: I have!

KROGSTAD: —like leaving house and home—

NORA: I have!

KROGSTAD: —or even something worse—

NORA: How did you know?

KROGSTAD: —then: don't.

NORA: How did you know I was thinking of *that?*

KROGSTAD: Most of us do, right at first. I did, too, but when it came down to it I didn't have the courage—

NORA (*tonelessly*): Nor do I.

KROGSTAD (*relieved*): See what I mean? I thought so. You don't either.

NORA: I don't. I don't.

KROGSTAD: Besides, it would be very silly of you. Once that first domestic blow-up is behind you—. Here in my pocket is a letter for your husband.

NORA: Telling him everything?

KROGSTAD: As delicately as possible.

NORA (*quickly*): He mustn't get that letter. Tear it up. I'll get you the money somehow.

KROGSTAD: Excuse me, Mrs. Helmer. I thought I just told you—

NORA: I'm not talking about the money I owe you. Just let me know how much money you want from my husband, and I'll get it for you.

KROGSTAD: I want no money from your husband.

NORA: Then, what *do* you want?

KROGSTAD: I'll tell you, Mrs. Helmer. I want to rehabilitate myself, I want to get up in the world; and your husband is going to help me. For a year and a half I haven't done anything disreputable. All that time I have been struggling with the most miserable circumstances. I was content to work my way up step by step. Now I've been kicked out, and I'm no longer satisfied just getting my old job back. I want more than that; I want to get to the top. I'm quite serious. I want the bank to take me back but in a higher position. I want your husband to create a new job for me—

NORA: He'll never do that!

KROGSTAD: He will. I know him. He won't dare not to. And once I'm back inside and he and I are working together, you'll see! Within a year I'll be the manager's right hand. It will be Nils Krogstad and not Torvald Helmer who'll be running the Mutual Bank!

NORA: You'll never see that happen!

KROGSTAD: Are you thinking of—?

NORA: Now I *do* have the courage.

KROGSTAD: You can't scare me. A fine, spoiled lady like you—

NORA: You'll see, you'll see!

KROGSTAD: Under the ice, perhaps? Down in that cold, black water? Then spring comes, and you float up again—hideous, ugly, unrecognizable, hair all gone—

NORA: You don't frighten me.

KROGSTAD: Nor you me. One doesn't do that sort of thing, Mrs. Helmer. Besides, what good would it do? He'd still be in my power.

NORA: Afterwards? When I'm no longer—?

KROGSTAD: Aren't you forgetting that your reputation would be in my hands?

(NORA *stares at him, speechless.*)

KROGSTAD: All right; now I've told you what to expect. So don't do anything foolish. When Helmer gets my letter I expect to hear from him. And don't you forget that it's your husband himself who forces me to use such means again. That I'll never forgive him. Good-bye, Mrs. Helmer. (*Goes out through the hall.*)

NORA (*at the door, opens it a little, listens*): He's going. And no letter. Of course not! That would be impossible! (*Opens the door more.*) What's he doing? He's still there. Doesn't go down. Having second thoughts—? Will he—?

(*The sound of a letter dropping into the mailbox. Then* KROGSTAD's *steps are heard going down the stairs, gradually dying away.*)

NORA (*with a muted cry runs forward to the table by the couch. Brief pause*): In the mailbox. (*Tiptoes back to the door to the front hall.*) There it is. Torvald, Torvald—now we're lost!

MRS. LINDE (*enters from the left, carrying* NORA's *Capri costume*): There now. I think it's all fixed. Why don't we try it on you—

NORA (*in a low, hoarse voice*): Kristine, come here.

MRS. LINDE: What's wrong with you? You look quite beside yourself.

NORA: Come over here. Do you see that letter? There, look—through the glass in the mailbox.

MRS. LINDE: Yes, yes; I see it.

NORA: That letter is from Krogstad.

MRS. LINDE: Nora—it was Krogstad who lent you the money!

NORA: Yes, and now Torvald will find out about it.

MRS. LINDE: Oh believe me, Nora. That's the best thing for both of you.

NORA: There's more to it than you know. I forged a signature—

MRS. LINDE: Oh my god—!

NORA: I just want to tell you this, Kristine, that you must be my witness.

MRS. LINDE: Witness? How? Witness to what?

NORA: If I lose my mind—and that could very well happen—

MRS. LINDE: Nora!

NORA: —or if something were to happen to me—something that made it impossible for me to be here—

MRS. LINDE: Nora, Nora! You're not yourself!

NORA: —and if someone were to take all the blame, assume the whole responsibility—Do you understand—?

MRS. LINDE: Yes, yes; but how can you think—!

NORA: —then you are to witness that that's not so, Kristine. I am not beside myself. I am perfectly rational, and what I'm telling you is that nobody else has known about this. I've done it all by myself, the whole thing. Just remember that.

MRS. LINDE: I will. But I don't understand any of it.

NORA: Oh, how could you! For it's the wonderful that's about to happen.

MRS. LINDE: The wonderful?

NORA: Yes, the wonderful. But it's so terrible, Kristine. It mustn't happen for anything in the whole world!

MRS. LINDE: I'm going over to talk to Krogstad right now.

NORA: No, don't. Don't go to him. He'll do something bad to you.

MRS. LINDE: There was a time when he would have done anything for me.

NORA: He!

MRS. LINDE: Where does he live?

NORA: Oh, I don't know—Yes, wait a minute (*reaches into her pocket*)—here's his card.—But the letter, the letter—!

HELMER (*in his study, knocks on the door*): Nora!

NORA (*cries out in fear*): Oh, what is it? What do you want?

HELMER: That's all right. Nothing to be so

stnl.

scared about. We're not coming in. For one thing, we can't. You've bolted the door, you know. Are you trying on your costume?

NORA: Yes—yes, I am. I'm going to be so pretty, Torvald.

MRS. LINDE (*looking at the card*): He lives just around the corner.

NORA: I know, but it's no use. Nothing can save us now. The letter is in the mailbox.

MRS. LINDE: And your husband has the key?

NORA: Yes. He always keeps it with him.

MRS. LINDE: Krogstad must ask for his letter back, unread. He's got to think up some pretext or other—

NORA: But this is just the time of day when Torvald—

MRS. LINDE: Delay him. Go in to him. I'll be back as soon as I can. (*She hurries out through the hall door.*)

NORA (*walks over to* HELMER's *door, opens it, and peeks in*): Torvald!

HELMER (*still offstage*): Well, well! So now one's allowed in one's own living room again. Come on, Rank. Now we'll see—(*In the doorway.*) But what's this?

NORA: What, Torvald, dear?

HELMER: Rank prepared me for a splendid metamorphosis.

RANK (*in the doorway*): That's how I understood it. Evidently I was mistaken.

NORA: Nobody gets to admire me in my costume before tomorrow.

HELMER: But, dearest Nora—you look all done in. Have you been practicing too hard?

NORA: No. I haven't practiced at all.

HELMER: But you'll have to, you know.

NORA: I know it, Torvald. I simply must. But I can't do a thing unless you help me. I have forgotten everything.

HELMER: Oh it will all come back. We'll work on it.

NORA: Oh yes, please, Torvald. You just have to help me. Promise? I am so nervous. That big party—. You mustn't do anything else tonight. Not a bit of business. Don't even touch a pen. Will you promise, Torvald?

HELMER: I promise. Tonight I'll be entirely at your service—you helpless little thing.—Just a moment, though. First I want to—(*Goes to the door to the front hall.*)

NORA: What are you doing out there?

HELMER: Just looking to see if there's any mail.

NORA: No, no! Don't, Torvald!

HELMER: Why not?

NORA: Torvald, I beg you. There is no mail.

HELMER: Let me just look, anyway. (*Is about to go out.*)

(NORA *by the piano, plays the first bars of the Tarantella dance.*)

HELMER (*halts at the door*): Aha!

NORA: I won't be able to dance tomorrow if I don't get to practice with you.

HELMER (*goes to her*): Are you really all that scared, Nora dear?

NORA: Yes, so terribly scared. Let's try it right now. There's still time before we eat. Oh please, sit down and play for me, Torvald. Teach me, coach me, the way you always do.

HELMER: Of course I will, my darling, if that's what you want. (*Sits down at the piano.*)

NORA (*takes the tambourine out of the carton, as well as a long, many-colored shawl. She quickly drapes the shawl around herself. She leaps into the middle of the floor and cries*): Play for me! I want to dance!

(HELMER *plays and* NORA *dances.* DR. RANK *stands by the piano behind* HELMER *and watches.*)

HELMER (*playing*): Slow down, slow down!

NORA: Can't!

HELMER: Not so violent, Nora!

NORA: It has to be this way.

HELMER (*stops playing*): No, no. This won't do at all.

NORA (*laughing, swinging her tambourine*): What did I tell you?

RANK: Why don't you let me play.

HELMER (*getting up*): Good idea. Then I can direct her better.

(RANK *sits down at the piano and starts playing.* NORA *dances more and more wildly.* HELMER *stands by the stove, repeatedly correcting her. She doesn't seem to hear. Her hair comes loose and falls down over her shoulders. She doesn't notice but keeps on dancing.* MRS. LINDE *enters.*)

MRS. LINDE (*stops by the door, dumbfounded*): Ah—!

NORA (*dancing*): We're having such fun, Kristine!

HELMER: My dearest Nora, you're dancing as if it were a matter of life and death!

NORA: It is! It is!

HELMER: Rank, stop. This is sheer madness. Stop it, I say!

(RANK *stops playing;* NORA *suddenly stops dancing.*)

HELMER (*goes over to her*): If I hadn't seen it I wouldn't have believed it. You've forgotten every single thing I ever taught you.

NORA (*tosses away the tambourine*): See? I told you.

HELMER: Well! You certainly need coaching.

NORA: Didn't I tell you I did? Now you've seen for yourself. I'll need your help till the very minute we're leaving for the party. Will you promise, Torvald?

HELMER: You can count on it.

NORA: You're not to think of anything except me—not tonight and not tomorrow. You're not to read any letters—not to look in the mailbox—

HELMER: Ah, I see. You're still afraid of that man.

NORA: Yes—yes, that too.

HELMER: Nora, I can tell from looking at you. There's a letter from him out there.

NORA: I don't know. I think so. But you're not to read it now. I don't want anything ugly to come between us before it's all over.

RANK (*to* HELMER *in a low voice*): Better not argue with her.

HELMER (*throws his arm around her*): The child shall have her way. But tomorrow night, when you've done your dance—

NORA: Then you'll be free.

MAID (*in the door, right*): Dinner can be served any time, ma'am.

NORA: We want champagne, Helene.

MAID: Very good, ma'am. (*Goes out.*)

HELMER: Aha! Having a party, eh?

NORA: Champagne from now till sunrise! (*Calls out.*) And some macaroons, Helene. Lots!—just this once.

HELMER (*taking her hands*): There, there—I don't like this wild—frenzy—Be my own sweet little lark again, the way you always are.

NORA: Oh, I will. But you go on in. You too, Dr. Rank. Kristine, please help me put up my hair.

RANK (*in a low voice to* HELMER *as they go out*): You don't think she is—you know—expecting—?

HELMER: Oh no. Nothing like that. It's just this childish fear I was telling you about. (*They go out, right.*)

NORA: Well?

MRS. LINDE: Left town.

NORA: I saw it in your face.

MRS. LINDE: He'll be back tomorrow night. I left him a note.

NORA: You shouldn't have. I don't want you to try to stop anything. You see, it's a kind of ecstasy, too, this waiting for the wonderful.

MRS. LINDE: But what is it you're waiting *for*?

NORA: You wouldn't understand. Why don't you go in to the others. I'll be there in a minute.

(MRS. LINDE *enters the dining room, right.*)

NORA (*stands still for a little while, as if collecting herself. She looks at her watch*): Five o'clock. Seven hours till midnight. Twenty-four more hours till next midnight. Then the Tarantella is over. Twenty-four plus seven—thirty-one more hours to live.

HELMER (*in the door, right*): What's happening to my little lark?

NORA (*to him, with open arms*): Here's your lark!

ACT III

The same room. The table by the couch and the chairs around it have been moved to the middle of the floor. A lighted lamp is on the table. The door to the front hall is open. Dance music is heard from upstairs. MRS. LINDE *is seated by the table, idly leafing through the pages of a book. She tries to read but seems unable to concentrate. Once or twice she turns her head in the direction of the door, anxiously listening.*

MRS. LINDE (*looks at her watch*): Not yet. It's almost too late. If only he hasn't—(*Listens again.*) Ah! There he is. (*She goes to the hall and opens the front door carefully. Quiet footsteps on the stairs. She whispers.*) Come in. There's nobody here.

KROGSTAD (*in the door*): I found your note when I got home. What's this all about?

MRS. LINDE: I've got to talk to you.

KROGSTAD: Oh? And it has to be here?

MRS. LINDE: It couldn't be at my place. My room doesn't have a separate entrance. Come in. We're all alone. The maid is asleep and the Helmers are at a party upstairs.

KROGSTAD (*entering*): Really? The Helmers are dancing tonight, are they?

MRS. LINDE: And why not?

KROGSTAD: You're right. Why not, indeed.

MRS. LINDE: All right, Krogstad. Let's talk, you and I.

KROGSTAD: I didn't know we had anything to talk about.

MRS. LINDE: We have much to talk about.

KROGSTAD: I didn't think so.

MRS. LINDE: No, because you've never really understood me.

KROGSTAD: What was there to understand?

What happened was perfectly commonplace. A heartless woman jilts a man when she gets a more attractive offer.

MRS. LINDE: Do you think I'm all that heartless? And do you think it was easy for me to break with you?

KROGSTAD: No?

MRS. LINDE: You really thought it was?

KROGSTAD: If it wasn't, why did you write the way you did that time?

MRS. LINDE: What else could I do? If I had to make a break, I also had the duty to destroy whatever feelings you had for me.

KROGSTAD (clenching his hands): So that's the way it was. And you did—that—just for money!

MRS. LINDE: Don't forget I had a helpless mother and two small brothers. We couldn't wait for you, Krogstad. You know yourself how uncertain your prospects were then.

KROGSTAD: All right. But you still didn't have the right to throw me over for somebody else.

MRS. LINDE: I don't know. I have asked myself that question many times. Did I have that right?

KROGSTAD (in a lower voice): When I lost you I lost my footing. Look at me now. A shipwrecked man on a raft.

MRS. LINDE: Rescue may be near.

KROGSTAD: It was near. Then you came.

MRS. LINDE: I didn't know that, Krogstad. Only today did I find out it's your job I'm taking over in the bank.

KROGSTAD: I believe you when you say so. But now that you do know, aren't you going to step aside?

MRS. LINDE: No, for it wouldn't do you any good.

KROGSTAD: Whether it would or not—I would do it.

MRS. LINDE: I have learned common sense. Life and hard necessity have taught me that.

KROGSTAD: And life has taught me not to believe in pretty speeches.

MRS. LINDE: Then life has taught you a very sensible thing. But you do believe in actions, don't you?

KROGSTAD: How do you mean?

MRS. LINDE: You referred to yourself just now as a shipwrecked man.

KROGSTAD: It seems to me I had every reason to do so.

MRS. LINDE: And I am a shipwrecked woman. No one to grieve for, no one to care for.

KROGSTAD: You made your choice.

MRS. LINDE: I had no other choice that time.

KROGSTAD: Let's say you didn't. What then?

MRS. LINDE: Krogstad, how would it be if we two shipwrecked people got together?

KROGSTAD: What's this!

MRS. LINDE: Two on one wreck are better off than each on his own.

KROGSTAD: Kristine!

MRS. LINDE: Why do you think I came to town?

KROGSTAD: Surely not because of me?

MRS. LINDE: If I'm going to live at all I must work. All my life, for as long as I can remember, I have worked. That's been my one and only pleasure. But now that I'm all alone in the world I feel only this terrible emptiness and desolation. There is no joy in working just for yourself. Krogstad—give me someone and something to work for.

KROGSTAD: I don't believe in this. I think you're just another hysterical female being noble and sacrificing yourself.

MRS. LINDE: Did you ever know me to be hysterical?

KROGSTAD: You really could do this? Listen—do you know about my past? All of it?

MRS. LINDE: Yes.

KROGSTAD: Do you also know what people think of me around here?

MRS. LINDE: A little while ago you sounded as if you thought that together with me you might have become a different person.

KROGSTAD: I'm sure of it.

MRS. LINDE: Couldn't that still be?

KROGSTAD: Kristine—do you know what you are doing? Yes, I see you do. And you really think you have the courage—?

MRS. LINDE: I need someone to be a mother to, and your children need a mother. You and I need one another. Nils, I believe in you—in the real you. Together with you I dare to do anything.

KROGSTAD (seizes her hands): Thanks, thanks, Kristine—now I know I'll raise myself in the eyes of others.—Ah, but I forget—!

MRS. LINDE (listening): Shh!—There's the Tarantella. You must go; hurry!

KROGSTAD: Why? What is it?

MRS. LINDE: Do you hear what they're playing up there? When that dance is over they'll be down.

KROGSTAD: All right. I'm leaving. The whole thing is pointless, anyway. Of course you don't know what I'm doing to the Helmers.

MRS. LINDE: Yes, Krogstad; I do know.

KROGSTAD: Still, you're brave enough—?

MRS. LINDE: I very well understand to what extremes despair can drive a man like you.

KROGSTAD: If only it could be undone!

MRS. LINDE: It could, for your letter is still out there in the mailbox.

KROGSTAD: Are you sure?

MRS. LINDE: Quite sure. But—

KROGSTAD (*looks searchingly at her*): Maybe I'm beginning to understand. You want to save your friend at any cost. Be honest with me. That's it, isn't it?

MRS. LINDE: Krogstad, you may sell yourself for somebody else's sake, but you don't do it twice.

KROGSTAD: I'll ask for my letter back.

MRS. LINDE: No, no.

KROGSTAD: Yes, of course. I'll wait here till Helmer comes down. Then I'll ask him for my letter. I'll tell him it's just about my dismissal— that he shouldn't read it.

MRS. LINDE: No, Krogstad. You are not to do that.

KROGSTAD: But tell me—wasn't that the real reason you wanted to meet me here?

MRS. LINDE: At first it was, because I was so frightened. But that was yesterday. Since then I have seen the most incredible things going on in this house. Helmer must learn the whole truth. This miserable secret must come out in the open; those two must come to a full understanding. They simply can't continue with all this concealment and evasion.

KROGSTAD: All right; if you want to take that chance. But there is one thing I *can* do, and I'll do it right now.

MRS. LINDE (*listening*): But hurry! Go! The dance is over. We aren't safe another minute.

KROGSTAD: I'll be waiting for you downstairs.

MRS. LINDE: Yes, do. You must see me home.

KROGSTAD: I've never been so happy in my whole life. (*He leaves through the front door. The door between the living room and the front hall remains open.*)

MRS. LINDE (*straightens up the room a little and gets her things ready*): What a change! Oh yes!— what a change! People to work for—to live for—a home to bring happiness to. I can't wait to get to work—! If only they'd come soon—(*Listens.*) Ah, there they are. Get my coat on—(*Puts on her coat and hat.*)

(HELMER's and NORA's voices are heard outside. A key is turned in the lock, and HELMER almost forces NORA into the hall. She is dressed in her Italian costume, with a big, black shawl over her shoulders. He is in evening dress under an open, black domino.)

NORA (*in the door, still resisting*): No, no, no! I don't want to! I want to go back upstairs. I don't want to leave so early.

HELMER: But dearest Nora—

NORA: Oh please, Torvald—please! I'm asking you as nicely as I can—just another hour!

HELMER: Not another minute, sweet. You know we agreed. There now. Get inside. You'll catch a cold out here. (*She still resists, but he guides her gently into the room.*)

MRS. LINDE: Good evening.

NORA: Kristine!

HELMER: Ah, Mrs. Linde. Still here?

MRS. LINDE: I know. I really should apologize, but I so much wanted to see Nora in her costume.

NORA: You've been waiting up for me?

MRS. LINDE: Yes, unfortunately I didn't get here in time. You were already upstairs, but I just didn't feel like leaving till I had seen you.

HELMER (*removing NORA's shawl*): Yes, do take a good look at her, Mrs. Linde. I think I may say she's worth looking at. Isn't she lovely?

MRS. LINDE: She certainly is—

HELMER: Isn't she a miracle of loveliness, though? That was the general opinion at the party, too. But dreadfully obstinate—that she is, the sweet little thing. What can we do about that? Will you believe it—I practically had to use force to get her away.

NORA: Oh Torvald, you're going to be sorry you didn't give me even half an hour more.

HELMER: See what I mean, Mrs. Linde? She dances the Tarantella—she is a tremendous success—quite deservedly so, though perhaps her performance was a little too natural—I mean, more than could be reconciled with the rules of art. But all right! The point is: she's a success, a tremendous success. So should I let her stay after that? Spoil the effect? Of course not. So I take my lovely little Capri girl—I might say, my capricious little Capri girl—under my arm—a quick turn around the room—a graceful bow in all directions, and—as they say in the novels—the beautiful apparition is gone. A finale should always be done for effect, Mrs. Linde, but there doesn't seem to be any way of getting that into Nora's head. Poooh—! It's hot in here. (*Throws his cape down on a chair and opens the door to his study.*) Why, it's dark! Oh yes—of course. Excuse me—(*Goes inside and lights a couple of candles.*)

NORA (*in a hurried, breathless whisper*): Well?

MRS. LINDE (*in a low voice*): I have talked to him.

NORA: And—?

MRS. LINDE: Nora—you've got to tell your husband everything.

NORA (*no expression in her voice*): I knew it.

MRS. LINDE: You have nothing to fear from Krogstad. But you must speak.

NORA: I'll say nothing.

MRS. LINDE: Then the letter will.

NORA: Thank you, Kristine. Now I know what I have to do. Shh!

HELMER (*returning*): Well, Mrs. Linde, have you looked your fill?

MRS. LINDE: Yes. And now I'll say goodnight.

HELMER: So soon? Is that your knitting?

MRS. LINDE (*takes it*): Yes, thank you. I almost forgot.

HELMER: So you knit, do you?

MRS. LINDE: Oh yes.

HELMER: You know—you ought to take up embroidery instead.

MRS. LINDE: Oh? Why?

HELMER: Because it's so much more beautiful. Look. You hold the embroidery so—in your left hand. Then with your right you move the needle—like this—in an easy, elongated arc—you see?

MRS. LINDE: Maybe you're right—

HELMER: Knitting, on the other hand, can never be anything but ugly. Look here: arms pressed close to the sides—the needles going up and down—there's something Chinese about it somehow—. That really was an excellent champagne they served us tonight.

MRS. LINDE: Well; goodnight, Nora. And don't be obstinate any more.

HELMER: Well said, Mrs. Linde!

MRS. LINDE: Goodnight, sir.

HELMER (*sees her to the front door*): Goodnight, goodnight. I hope you'll get home all right? I'd be very glad to—but of course you don't have far to walk, do you? Goodnight, goodnight. (*She leaves. He closes the door behind her and returns to the living room.*) There! At last we got rid of her. She really is an incredible bore, that woman.

NORA: Aren't you very tired, Torvald?

HELMER: No, not in the least.

NORA: Not sleepy either?

HELMER: Not at all. Quite the opposite. I feel enormously—animated. How about you. Yes, you do look tired and sleepy.

NORA: Yes, I am very tired. Soon I'll be asleep.

HELMER: What did I tell you? I was right, wasn't I? Good thing I didn't let you stay any longer.

NORA: Everything you do is right.

HELMER (*kissing her forehead*): Now my little lark is talking like a human being. But did you notice what splendid spirits Rank was in tonight?

NORA: Was he? I didn't notice. I didn't get to talk with him.

HELMER: Nor did I—hardly. But I haven't seen him in such a good mood for a long time. (*Looks at her, comes closer to her.*) Ah! It does feel good to be back in our own home again, to be quite alone with you—Oh, how lovely you are!—my exciting young woman!

NORA: Don't look at me like that, Torvald!

HELMER: Am I not to look at my most precious possession? All that loveliness that is mine, nobody's but mine, all of it mine!

NORA (*walks to the other side of the table*): I won't have you talk to me like that tonight.

HELMER (*follows her*): The Tarantella is still in your blood. I can tell. That only makes you all the more alluring. Listen! The guests are beginning to leave. (*Softly.*) Nora—darling—soon the whole house will be quiet.

NORA: I hope so.

HELMER: Yes, don't you, my darling? Do you know—when I'm at a party with you, like tonight—do you know why I hardly ever talk to you, why I keep away from you, only look at you once in a while—a few stolen glances—do you know why I do that? It's because I pretend that you are my secret love, my young, secret bride-to-be, and nobody has the slightest suspicion that there is anything between us.

NORA: Yes, I know. All your thoughts are with me.

HELMER: Then when we're leaving and I lay your shawl around your delicate young shoulders—around that wonderful curve of your neck—then I imagine you're my young bride, that we're coming away from the wedding, that I am taking you to my home for the first time—that I am alone with you for the first time—quite alone with you, you young, trembling beauty! I have desired you all evening—all my longing has only been for you. When you were dancing the Tarantella, chasing, inviting—my blood was on fire; I couldn't stand it any longer—that's why I brought you down so early—

NORA: Leave me now, Torvald. Please! I don't want all this.

HELMER: What do you mean? You're only playing your little teasing bird game with me; aren't you Nora? Don't want to? I'm your husband, aren't I?

(*There is a knock on the front door.*)

NORA (*with a start*): Did you hear that—?

HELMER (*on his way to the hall*): Who is it?

RANK (*outside*): It's me. May I come in for a moment?

HELMER (*in a low voice, annoyed*): Oh, what

does he want now? (*Aloud.*) Just a minute. (*Opens the door.*) Well! How good of you not to pass by our door.

RANK: I thought I heard your voice, so I felt like saying hello. (*Looks around.*) Ah yes—this dear, familiar room. What a cozy, comfortable place you have here, you two.

HELMER: Looked to me as if you were quite comfortable upstairs too.

RANK: I certainly was. And why not? Why not enjoy all you can in this world? As much as you can and for as long as you can, anyway. Excellent wine.

HELMER: The champagne, particularly.

RANK: You noticed that too? Incredible how much I managed to put away.

NORA: Torvald drank a lot of champagne tonight, too.

RANK: Did he?

NORA: Yes, he did, and then he's always so much fun afterwards.

RANK: Well, why not have some fun in the evening after a well spent day?

HELMER: Well spent? I'm afraid I can't claim that.

RANK (*slapping him lightly on the shoulder*): But you see, I can!

NORA: Dr. Rank, I believe you have been conducting a sicentific test today.

RANK: Exactly.

HELMER: What do you know—little Nora talking about scientific experiments!

NORA: May I congratulate you on the result?

RANK: You may indeed.

NORA: It was a good one?

RANK: The best possible for both doctor and patient—certainty.

NORA (*a quick query*): Certainty?

RANK: Absolute certainty. So why shouldn't I have myself an enjoyable evening afterwards?

NORA: I quite agree with you, Dr. Rank. You should.

HELMER: And so do I. If only you don't pay for it tomorrow.

RANK: Oh well—you get nothing for nothing in this world.

NORA: Dr. Rank—you are fond of costume parties, aren't you?

RANK: Yes, particularly when there is a reasonable number of amusing disguises.

NORA: Listen—what are the two of us going to be the next time?

HELMER: You frivolous little thing! Already thinking about the next party!

RANK: You and I? That's easy. You'll be Fortune's Child.

HELMER: Yes, but what is a fitting costume for that?

RANK: Let your wife appear just the way she always is.

HELMER: Beautiful. Very good indeed. But how about yourself? Don't you know what you'll go as?

RANK: Yes, my friend. I know precisely what I'll be.

HELMER: Yes?

RANK: At the next masquerade I'll be invisible.

HELMER: That's a funny idea.

RANK: There's a certain big, black hat—you've heard about the hat that makes you invisible, haven't you? You put that on, and nobody can see you.

HELMER (*suppressing a smile*): I guess that's right.

RANK: But I'm forgetting what I came for. Helmer, give me a cigar—one of your dark Havanas.

HELMER: With the greatest pleasure. (*Offers him his case.*)

RANK (*takes one and cuts off the tip*): Thanks.

NORA (*striking a match*): Let me give you a light.

RANK: Thanks. (*She holds the match; he lights his cigar.*) And now good-bye!

HELMER: Good-bye, good-bye, my friend.

NORA: Sleep well, Dr. Rank.

RANK: I thank you.

NORA: Wish me the same.

RANK: You? Well, if you really want me to—. Sleep well. And thanks for the light. (*He nods to both of them and goes out.*)

HELMER (*in a low voice*): He had had quite a bit to drink.

NORA (*absently*): Maybe so.

(HELMER *takes out his keys and goes out into the hall.*)

NORA: Torvald—what are you doing out there?

HELMER: Got to empty the mailbox. It is quite full. There wouldn't be room for the newspapers in the morning—

NORA: Are you going to work tonight?

HELMER: You know very well I won't.—Say! What's this? Somebody's been at the lock.

NORA: The lock—?

HELMER: Sure. Why, I wonder. I hate to think that any of the maids—. Here's a broken hairpin. It's one of yours, Nora.

NORA (*quickly*): Then it must be one of the children.

HELMER: You better make damn sure they stop

that. Hm, hm.—There! I got it open, finally. (*Gathers up the mail, calls out to the kitchen:*) Helene?—Oh Helene—turn out the light here in the hall, will you? (*He comes back into the living room and closes the door.*) Look how it's been piling up. (*Shows her the bundle of letters. Starts leafing through it.*) What's this?

NORA (*by the window*): The letter! Oh no, no, Torvald!

HELMER: Two calling cards—from Rank.

NORA: From Dr. Rank?

HELMER (*looking at them*): "Doctor of Medicine Rank!" They were on top. He must have put them there when he left just now.

NORA: Anything written on them?

HELMER: A black cross above the name. Look. What a macabre idea. Like announcing his own death.

NORA: That's what it is.

HELMER: Hm? You know about this? Has he said anything to you?

NORA: That card means he's saying good-bye to us. He'll lock himself up to die.

HELMER: My poor friend. I knew of course he wouldn't be with me very long. But so soon—. And this hiding himself away like a wounded animal—

NORA: When it has to be, it's better it happens without words. Don't you think so, Torvald?

HELMER (*walking up and down*): He'd grown so close to us. I find it hard to think of him as gone. With his suffering and loneliness he was like a clouded background for our happy sunshine. Well, it may be better this way. For him, at any rate. (*Stops.*) And perhaps for us, too, Nora. For now we have nobody but each other. (*Embraces her.*) Oh you—my beloved wife! I feel I just can't hold you close enough. Do you know, Nora— many times I have wished some great danger threatened you, so I could risk my life and blood and everything—everything, for your sake.

NORA (*frees herself and says in a strong and firm voice*): I think you should go and read your letters now, Torvald.

HELMER: No, no—not tonight. I want to be with you, my darling.

NORA: With the thought of your dying friend—?

HELMER: You are right. This has shaken both of us. Something not beautiful has come between us. Thoughts of death and dissolution. We must try to get over it—out of it. Till then—we'll each go to our own room.

NORA (*her arms around his neck*): Torvald— good night! Good night!

HELMER (*kisses her forehead*): Goodnight, my little songbird. Sleep well, Nora. Now I'll read my letters. (*He goes into his room, carrying the mail. Closes the door.*)

NORA (*her eyes desperate, her hands groping, finds* HELMER's *domino and throws it around her; she whispers, quickly, brokenly, hoarsely*): Never see him again. Never. Never. Never. (*Puts her shawl over her head.*) And never see the children again, either. Never; never.—The black, icy water—fathomless—this—! If only it was all over.— Now he has it. Now he's reading it. No, no; not yet. Torvald—good-bye—you—the children—

(*She is about to hurry through the hall, when* HELMER *flings open the door to his room and stands there with an open letter in his hand.*)

HELMER: Nora!

NORA (*cries out*): Ah—!

HELMER: What is it? You know what's in this letter?

NORA: Yes, I do! Let me go! Let me out!

HELMER (*holds her back*): Where do you think you're going?

NORA (*trying to tear herself loose from him*): I won't let you save me, Torvald!

HELMER (*tumbles back*): True! Is it true what he writes? Oh my god! No, no—this can't possibly be true.

NORA: It is true. I have loved you more than anything else in the whole world.

HELMER: Oh, don't give me any silly excuses.

NORA (*taking a step towards him*): Torvald—!

HELMER: You wretch! What have you done!

NORA: Let me go. You are not to sacrifice yourself for me. You are not to take the blame.

HELMER: No more playacting. (*Locks the door to the front hall.*) You'll stay here and answer me. Do you understand what you have done? Answer me! Do you understand?

NORA (*gazes steadily at him with an increasingly frozen expression*): Yes. Now I'm beginning to understand.

HELMER (*walking up and down*): What a dreadful awakening. All these years—all these eight years—she, my pride and my joy—a hypocrite, a liar—oh worse! worse!—a criminal! Oh, the bottomless ugliness in all this! Damn! Damn! Damn!

(NORA *silent, keeps gazing at him.*)

HELMER (*stops in front of her*): I ought to have guessed that something like this would happen. I should have expected it. All your father's loose principles—Silence! You have inherited every one of your father's loose principles. No religion, no morals, no sense of duty—. Now I am being punished for my leniency with him. I did it for your sake, and this is how you pay me back.

NORA: Yes. This is how.

HELMER: You have ruined all my happiness. My whole future—you've thrown it away. Oh, it's terrible to think about. I am at the mercy of an unscrupulous man. He can do with me whatever he likes, demand anything of me, command me and dispose of me just as he pleases—I dare not say a word! To go down so miserably, to be destroyed—all because of an irresponsible woman!

NORA: When I am gone from the world, you'll be free.

HELMER: No noble gestures, please. Your father was always full of such phrases too. What good would it do me if you were gone from the world, as you put it? Not the slightest bit of good at all. He could still make the whole thing public, and if he did I wouldn't be surprised if people thought I'd put you up to it. They might even think it was my idea—that it was I who urged you to do it! And for all this I have you to thank—you, whom I've borne on my hands through all the years of our marriage. *Now* do you understand what you've done to me?

NORA (*with cold calm*): Yes.

HELMER: I just can't get it into my head that this is happening; it's all so incredible. But we have to come to terms with it somehow. Take your shawl off. Take it off, I say! I have to satisfy him one way or another. The whole affair must be kept quiet at whatever cost.—And as far as you and I are concerned, nothing must seem to have changed. I'm talking about appearances, of course. You'll go on living here; that goes without saying. But I won't let you bring up the children; I dare not trust you with them.—Oh! Having to say this to one I have loved so much, and whom I still—! But all that has to be past. It's not a question of happiness any more but of hanging on to what can be salvaged—pieces, appearances—(*The doorbell rings.* HELMER *jumps.*) Has he—! Hide, Nora! Say you're sick.

(NORA *doesn't move.* HELMER *opens the door to the hall.*)

MAID (*half dressed, out in the hall*): A letter for your wife, sir.

HELMER: Give it to me. (*Takes the letter and closes the door.*) Yes, it's from him. But I won't let you have it. I'll read it myself.

NORA: Yes—you read it.

HELMER (*by the lamp*): I hardly dare. Perhaps we're lost, both you and I. No; I've got to know. (*Tears the letter open, glances through it, looks at an enclosure, a cry of joy.*) Nora!

(NORA *looks at him with a question in her eyes.*)

HELMER: Nora!—No, I must read it again.—Yes, yes; it is so! I'm saved! Nora, I'm saved!

NORA: And I?

HELMER: You too, of course; we're both saved, both you and I. Look! He's returning your note. He writes that he's sorry, he regrets, a happy turn in his life—oh, it doesn't matter what he writes. We're saved, Nora! Nobody can do anything to you now. Oh Nora, Nora—. No, I want to get rid of this disgusting thing first. Let me see— (*Looks at the signature.*) No, I don't want to see it. I don't want it to be more than a bad dream, the whole thing. (*Tears up the note and both letters, throws the pieces in the stove, and watches them burn.*) There! Now it's gone.—He wrote that ever since Christmas Eve—. Good god, Nora, these must have been three terrible days for you.

NORA: I have fought a hard fight these last three days.

HELMER: And been in agony and seen no other way out than—. No, we won't think of all that ugliness. We'll just rejoice and tell ourselves it's over, it's all over! Oh, listen to me, Nora. You don't seem to understand. It's over. What *is* it? Why do you look like that—that frozen expression on your face? Oh my poor little Nora, don't you think I know what it is? You can't make yourself believe that I have forgiven you. But I have, Nora; I swear to you, I have forgiven you for everything. Of course I know that what you did was for love of me.

NORA: That is true.

HELMER: You have loved me the way a wife ought to love her husband. You just didn't have the wisdom to judge the means. But do you think I love you any less because you don't know how to act on your own? Of course not. Just lean on me. I'll advise you; I'll guide you. I wouldn't be a man if I didn't find you twice as attractive because of your womanly helplessness. You mustn't pay any attention to the hard words I said to you right at first. It was just that first shock when I thought everything was collapsing all around me. I have forgiven you, Nora. I swear to you—I really have forgiven you.

NORA: I thank you for your forgiveness. (*She goes out through the door, right.*)

HELMER: No, stay—(*Looks into the room she entered.*) What are you doing in there?

NORA (*within*): Getting out of my costume.

HELMER (*by the open door*): Good, good. Try to calm down and compose yourself, my poor little frightened songbird. Rest safely; I have broad wings to cover you with. (*Walks around near the door.*) What a nice and cozy home we have, Nora. Here's shelter for you. Here I'll keep you safe like a hunted dove I have rescued from the hawk's talons. Believe me: I'll know how to quiet your beating heart. It will happen by and by, Nora; you'll see. Why, tomorrow you'll look at all this in quite a different light. And soon everything will be just the way it was before. I won't need to keep reassuring you that I have forgiven you; you'll feel it yourself. Did you really think I could have abandoned you, or even reproached you? Oh, you don't know a real man's heart, Nora. There is something unspeakably sweet and satisfactory for a man to know deep in himself that he has forgiven his wife—forgiven her in all the fullness of his honest heart. You see, that way she becomes his very own all over again—in a double sense, you might say. He has, so to speak, given her a second birth; it is as if she had become his wife and his child, both. From now on that's what you'll be to me, you lost and helpless creature. Don't worry about a thing, Nora. Only be frank with me, and I'll be your will and your conscience.—What's this? You're not in bed? You've changed your dress—!

NORA (*in an everyday dress*): Yes, Torvald. I have changed my dress.

HELMER: But why—now—this late—?

NORA: I'm not going to sleep tonight.

HELMER: But my dear Nora—

NORA (*looks at her watch*): It isn't all that late. Sit down here with me, Torvald. You and I have much to talk about. (*Sits down at the table.*)

HELMER: Nora—what is this all about? That rigid face—

NORA: Sit down. This will take a while. I have much to say to you.

HELMER (*sits down, facing her across the table*): You worry me, Nora. I don't understand you.

NORA: No, that's just it. You don't understand me. And I have never understood you—not till tonight. No, don't interrupt me. Just listen to what I have to say.—This is a settling of accounts, Torvald.

HELMER: What do you mean by that?

NORA (*after a brief silence*): Doesn't one thing strike you, now that we are sitting together like this?

HELMER: What would that be?

NORA: We have been married for eight years. Doesn't it occur to you that this is the first time that you and I, husband and wife, are having a serious talk?

HELMER: Well—serious—. What do you mean by that?

NORA: For eight whole years—longer, in fact—ever since we first met, we have never talked seriously to each other about a single serious thing.

HELMER: You mean I should forever have been telling you about worries you couldn't have helped me with anyway?

NORA: I am not talking about worries. I'm saying we have never tried seriously to get to the bottom of anything together.

HELMER: But dearest Nora, I hardly think that would have been something *you*—

NORA: That's the whole point. You have never understood me. Great wrong has been done to me, Torvald. First by Daddy and then by you.

HELMER: What! by us two? We who have loved you more than anyone else?

NORA (*shakes her head*): You never loved me—neither Daddy nor you. You only thought it was fun to be in love with me.

HELMER: But, Nora—what an expression to use!

NORA: That's the way it has been, Torvald. When I was home with Daddy, he told me all his opinions, and so they became my opinions too. If I disagreed with him I kept it to myself, for he wouldn't have liked that. He called me his little doll baby, and he played with me the way I played with my dolls. Then I came to your house—

HELMER: What a way to talk about our marriage!

NORA (*imperturbably*): I mean that I passed from Daddy's hands into yours. You arranged everything according to your taste, and so I came to share it—or I pretended to; I'm not sure which. I think it was a little of both, now one and now the other. When I look back on it now, it seems to me I've been living here like a pauper—just a hand-to-mouth kind of existence. I have earned my keep by doing tricks for you, Torvald. But that's the way you wanted it. You have great sins against me to answer for, Daddy and you. It's your fault that nothing has become of me.

HELMER: Nora, you're being both unreasonable and ungrateful. Haven't you been happy here?

NORA: No, never. I thought I was, but I wasn't.

HELMER: Not—not happy!

NORA: No; just having fun. And you have always been very good to me. But our home has never been more than a playroom. I have been your doll wife here, just the way I used to be Daddy's doll child. And the children have been my dolls. I thought it was fun when you played with me, just as they thought it was fun when I played with them. That's been our marriage, Torvald.

HELMER: There is something in what you are saying—exaggerated and hysterical though it is. But from now on things will be different. Playtime is over; it's time for growing up.

NORA: Whose growing up—mine or the children's?

HELMER: Both yours and the children's, Nora darling.

NORA: Oh Torvald, you're not the man to bring me up to be the right kind of wife for you.

HELMER: How can you say that?

NORA: And I—? What qualifications do I have for bringing up the children?

HELMER: Nora!

NORA: You said so yourself a minute ago—that you didn't dare to trust me with them.

HELMER: In the first flush of anger, yes. Surely, you're not going to count that.

NORA: But you were quite right. I am *not* qualified. Something else has to come first. Somehow I have to grow up myself. And you are not the man to help me do that. That's a job I have to do by myself. And that's why I'm leaving you.

HELMER (*jumps up*): What did you say!

NORA: I have to be by myself if I am to find out about myself and about all those other things too. So I can't stay here any longer.

HELMER: Nora, Nora!

NORA: I'm leaving now. I'm sure Kristine will put me up for tonight.

HELMER: You're out of your mind! I won't let you! I forbid you!

NORA: You can't forbid me anything any more; it won't do any good. I'm taking my own things with me. I won't accept anything from you, either now or later.

HELMER: But this is madness!

NORA: Tomorrow I'm going home—I mean back to my old home town. It will be easier for me to find some kind of job there.

HELMER: Oh, you blinded, inexperienced creature—!

NORA: I must see to it that I get experience, Torvald.

HELMER: Leaving your home, your husband, your children! Not a thought of what people will say!

NORA: I can't worry about that. All I know is that I have to leave.

HELMER: Oh, this is shocking! Betraying your most sacred duties like this!

NORA: And what do you consider my most sacred duties?

HELMER: Do I need to tell you that? They are your duties to your husband and your children.

NORA: I have other duties equally sacred.

HELMER: You do not. What duties would they be?

NORA: My duties to myself.

HELMER: You are a wife and a mother before you are anything else.

NORA: I don't believe that anymore. I believe I am first of all a human being, just as much as you—or at any rate I must try to become one. Oh, I know very well that most people agree with you, Torvald, and that it says something like that in all the books. But what people say and what the books say is no longer enough for me. I have to think about these things myself and see if I can't find the answers.

HELMER: You mean to tell me you don't know what your proper place in your own home is? Don't you have a reliable guide in such matters? Don't you have religion?

NORA: Oh but Torvald—I don't really know what religion is.

HELMER: What's this?

NORA: All I know is what the Reverend Hansen told me when he prepared me for confirmation. He said that religion was *this* and it was *that*. When I get by myself, away from here, I'll have to look into that, too. I have to decide if what the Reverend Hansen said was right, or anyway if it is right for *me*.

HELMER: Oh, this is unheard of in a young woman! If religion can't guide you, let me appeal to your conscience. For surely you have moral feelings? Or—answer me—maybe you don't?

NORA: Well, you see, Torvald, I don't really know what to say. I just don't know. I am confused about these things. All I know is that my ideas are quite different from yours. I have just found out that the laws are different from what I thought they were, but in no way can I get it into my head that those laws are right. A woman shouldn't have the right to spare her dying old father or save her husband's life! I just can't believe that.

HELMER: You speak like a child. You don't understand the society you live in.

NORA: No, I don't. But I want to find out about it. I have to make up my mind who is right, society or I.

HELMER: You are sick, Nora; you have a fever. I really don't think you are in your right mind.

NORA: I have never felt so clearheaded and sure of myself as I do tonight.

HELMER: And clearheaded and sure of yourself you're leaving your husband and your children?

Birds are kept in cages

NORA: Yes.

HELMER: Then there is only one possible explanation.

NORA: What?

HELMER: You don't love me anymore.

NORA: No; that's just it.

HELMER: Nora! How can you say that!

NORA: I am sorry, Torvald, for you have always been so good to me. But I can't help it. I don't love you anymore.

HELMER (*with forced composure*): And this too is a clear and sure conviction?

NORA: Completely clear and sure. That's why I don't want to stay here anymore.

HELMER: And are you ready to explain to me how I came to forfeit your love?

NORA: Certainly, I am. It was tonight, when the wonderful didn't happen. That was when I realized you were not the man I thought you were.

HELMER: You have to explain. I don't understand.

NORA: I have waited patiently for eight years, for I wasn't such a fool that I thought the wonderful is something that happens any old day. Then this— thing—came crashing in on me, and then there wasn't a doubt in my mind that now—now comes the wonderful. When Krogstad's letter was in that mailbox, never for a moment did it even occur to me that you would submit to his conditions. I was so absolutely certain that you would say to him: make the whole thing public—tell everybody. And when that had happened—

HELMER: Yes, then what? When I had surrendered my own wife to shame and disgrace—!

NORA: When that had happened, I was absolutely certain that you would stand up and take the blame and say, "I am the guilty one."

HELMER: Nora!

NORA: You mean I never would have accepted such a sacrifice from you? Of course not. But what would my protests have counted against yours? *That* was the wonderful I was waiting for in hope and terror. And to prevent that I was going to kill myself.

HELMER: I'd gladly work nights and days for you, Nora—endure sorrow and want for your sake. But nobody sacrifices his *honor* for his love.

NORA: A hundred thousand women have done so.

HELMER: Oh, you think and talk like a silly child.

NORA: All right. But you don't think and talk like the man I can live with. When you had gotten over your fright—not because of what threatened

me but because of the risk to *you*—and the whole danger was past, then you acted as if nothing at all had happened. Once again I was your little songbird, your doll, just as before, only now you had to handle her even more carefully, because she was so frail and weak. (*Rises.*) Torvald—that moment I realized that I had been living here for eight years with a stranger and had borne him three children—Oh, I can't stand thinking about it! I feel like tearing myself to pieces!

HELMER (*heavily*): I see it, I see it. An abyss has opened up between us.—Oh but Nora—surely it can be filled?

NORA: The way I am now I am no wife for you.

HELMER: I have it in me to change.

NORA: Perhaps—if your doll is taken from you.

HELMER: To part—to part from you! No, no, Nora! I can't grasp that thought!

NORA (*goes out, right*): All the more reason why it has to be. (*She returns with her street clothes and a small bag, which she sets down on the chair by the table.*)

HELMER: Nora, Nora! Not now! Wait till tomorrow.

NORA (*putting on her coat*): I can't spend the night in a stranger's rooms.

HELMER: But couldn't we live here together like brother and sister—?

NORA (*tying on her hat*): You know very well that wouldn't last long—. (*Wraps her shawl around her.*) Good-bye, Torvald. I don't want to see the children. I know I leave them in better hands than mine. The way I am now I can't be anything to them.

HELMER: But someday, Nora—someday—?

NORA: How can I tell? I have no idea what's going to become of me.

HELMER: But you're still my wife, both as you are now and as you will be.

NORA: Listen, Torvald—when a wife leaves her husband's house, the way I am doing now, I have heard he has no further legal responsibilities for her. At any rate, I now release you from all responsibility. You are not to feel yourself obliged to me for anything, and I have no obligations to you. There has to be full freedom on both sides. Here is your ring back. Now give me mine.

HELMER: Even this?

NORA: Even this.

HELMER: Here it is.

NORA: There. So now it's over. I'm putting the keys here. The maids know everything about the house—better than I. Tomorrow, after I'm gone, Kristine will come over and pack my things from home. I want them sent after me.

HELMER: Over! It's all over! Nora, will you never think of me?

NORA: I'm sure I'll often think of you and the children and this house.

HELMER: May I write to you, Nora?

NORA: No—never. I won't have that.

HELMER: But send you things—? You must let me—

NORA: Nothing, nothing—

HELMER: —help you, when you need help—

NORA: I told you, no; I won't have it. I'll accept nothing from strangers.

HELMER: Nora—can I never again be more to you than a stranger?

NORA (*picks up her bag*): Oh Torvald—then the most wonderful of all would have to happen—

HELMER: Tell me what that would be—!

NORA: For that to happen, both you and I would have to change so that—Oh Torvald, I no longer believe in the wonderful.

HELMER: But I *will* believe. Tell me! Change, so that—?

NORA: So that our living together would become a true marriage. Good-bye. (*She goes out through the hall.*)

HELMER (*sinks down on a chair near the door and covers his face with his hands*): Nora! Nora! (*Looks around him and gets up.*) All empty. She's gone. (*With sudden hope.*) The most wonderful—?!

(*From downstairs comes the sound of a heavy door slamming shut.*)

TOPICS FOR DISCUSSION

1. Near the beginning of the play, how does Mrs. Linde's presence help to define Nora's character? In your opinion, what does Nora's response to Krogstad's entrance tell us about Nora?

2. What do you think Dr. Rank contributes to the play? If he were eliminated, what would be lost? In your answer, consider these two topics among others: (a) his inheritance from his father (how is it relevant to Nora's inheritance from her father?); (b) his love for Nora (what does this tell us about her?).

3. Ibsen very reluctantly acceded to a request for an alternate ending for a German production. In the new ending Helmer forces Nora to look at their sleeping children and reminds her that "tomorrow, when they wake up and call for their mother, they will be—motherless." Nora "struggles with herself" and concludes by saying, "Oh, this is a sin against myself, but I cannot leave them." In view of the fact that the last act several times seems to be moving toward a "happy ending" (e.g., Krogstad promises to recall his letter), do you think this alternate ending is so bad? Why, or why not?

4. Can it be argued that although at the end Nora goes out to achieve self-realization, her abandonment of her children—especially to Torvald's loathsome conventional morality—is a crime? (By the way, exactly why does Nora leave the children? She seems to imply, in some passages, that because she forged a signature she is unfit to bring them up. But do you agree with her?)

5. Michael Meyer, in his splendid biography *Henrik Ibsen*, says that the play is not so much about women's rights as about "the need of every individual to find out the kind of person he or she really is, and to strive to become that person." Did this thought occur to you while reading the play? If not, can you now offer evidence to support this interpretation?

6. In *The Quintessence of Ibsenism* Bernard Shaw says that Ibsen, reacting against a common theatrical preference for strange situations, "saw that . . . the more familiar the situation, the more interesting the play. Shakespeare had put ourselves on the stage but not our situations. Our uncles seldom murder our fathers and . . . marry our

mothers. . . . Ibsen . . . gives us not only ourselves, but ourselves in our own situations. The things that happen to his stage figures are things that happen to us. One consequence is that his plays are much more important to us than Shakespeare's. Another is that they are capable both of hurting us cruelly and of filling us with excited hopes of escape from idealistic tyrannies, and with visions of intenser life in the future." How much of this do you believe?

SLAM THE DOOR SOFTLY

Clare Boothe Luce

Clare Boothe Luce (1903–1987) achieved distinction in two fields, playwrighting and politics. After working on two magazines, *Vogue* and *Vanity Fair* (she was managing editor of *Vanity Fair* from 1933 to 1934), she married Henry Luce, the founder of *Fortune* and *Time*, and began a career as a playwright. Her first play, *Abide with Me* (1935), was unsuccessful, but she soon achieved critical acclaim and financial success with *The Women* (1936), *Kiss the Boys Good-bye* (1938)—both of which are social satires—and a comedy-mystery, *Margin for Error* (1939). She then embarked on a second career, serving two terms in Congress as a representative from Connecticut (1943–1947) and later serving as ambassador to Italy (1953–1956). Ill health compelled her to resign the ambassadorship, but in 1959 she was well enough to be appointed ambassador to Brazil—although because of a controversy she resigned the post in the same year, without having served.

The scene is the Thaw Walds' cheerfully furnished middle-class living room in New York's suburbia. There are a front door and hall, a door to the kitchen area, and a staircase to the bedroom floor. Two easy chairs and two low hassocks with toys on them, grouped around a television, indicate a family of four. Drinks are on a bar cart at one end of a comfortable sofa, and an end table at the other. There are slightly more than the average number of bookshelves. The lamps are on, but as we don't hear the children, we know it is the Parents' Hour.

As the curtain rises, THAW WALD, *a good-looking fellow, about 35, is sitting in one of the easy chairs, smoking and watching TV. His back is to the sofa and staircase, so he does not see his wife coming down the stairs.* NORA WALD *is a rather pretty woman of about 32. She is carrying a suitcase, handbag, and an armful of books.*

Thaw switches channels, and lands in the middle of a panel show. During the TV dialogue that follows Nora somewhat furtively deposits her suitcase in the hall, takes her coat out of the hall closet, and comes back to the sofa carrying coat, purse, and books. She lays her coat on the sofa, and the books on the end table. The books are full of little paper slips—bookmarkers. All of the above actions are unobserved by Thaw. We cannot see the TV screen, but we hear the voices of four women, all talking excitedly at once.)

Slam the Door Softly production at Manhattanville College directed by Tracy Allen. (Photo courtesy of Tracy Allen.)

THAW (*to the screen and the world in general*): God, these Liberation gals! Still at it.

MALE MODERATOR'S VOICE (*full of paternal patience wearing a bit thin*): Ladies! Lay-deez! Can't we switch now from the question of the sex-typing of jobs to what the Women's Liberation Movement thinks about—

OLDER WOMAN'S VOICE: May I finish! In the Soviet Union 83% of the dentists, 75% of the doctors and 37% of the lawyers are women. In Poland and Denmark—

MODERATOR: I think you have already amply made your point, Mrs. Epstein—anything men can do, women can do better!

YOUNG WOMAN'S VOICE (*angrily*): That was *not* her point—and you know it! What she said was, there are very few professional jobs men are doing that women couldn't do, if only—

THAW: Well, for God's sake then, shaddup, and go do 'em—

BLACK WOMAN'S VOICE: What she's been saying, what we've all been saying, and you men just don't want to hear us, is—things are the same for women as they are for us black people. We try to get up, you just sit down on us, like a big elephant sits down on a bunch of poor little mice.

MODERATOR: Well, sometimes moderators have to play the elephant, and sit down on one subject in order to develop another. As I was about to say, ladies, there *is one thing* a woman can do, no man can do—(*in his best holy-night-all-is-bright voice*) give birth to a *child*.

YOUNG WOMAN'S VOICE: So what else is new?

THAW: One gets you ten, she's a Lesbo—

MODERATOR (*forcefully*): And *that* brings us to marriage! Now, if *I* may be permitted to get in just *one* statistic, edgewise: two-thirds of all adult American females are married women. And now! (*At last he's got them where he wants them.*) What *is* the Women's Lib view of Woman's No. 1 job—Occupation Housewife?

THAW: Ha! That's the one none of 'em can handle—

YOUNG WOMAN'S VOICE (*loud and clear*): Marriage, as an institution, is as thoroughly corrupt as prostitution. It is, in fact, legalized and romanticized prostitution. A woman who marries is selling her sexual services and domestic services for permanent bed and board—

BLACK WOMAN'S VOICE: There's no human being a man can buy anymore—except a woman—

THAW (*snapping off the TV*): Crrr-ap! Boy, what a bunch of battle-axes! (*He goes back to studying his TV listings.*)

NORA (*raising her voice*): Thaw! I'd like to say something about what they just said about marriage—

THAW (*in a warning voice*): Uh-uh, Nora! We both agreed months ago, you'd lay off the feminist bit, if I'd lay off watching Saturday football—

NORA: And do something with the children . . . But Thaw, there's something maybe, I ought to try to tell you myself—

(*Thaw is not listening. Nora makes a "what's the use" gesture, then opens her purse, takes out three envelopes, carefully inserts two of them under the covers of the top two books.*)

THAW: Like to hear Senators Smithers, Smethers and Smothers on "How Fast Can We Get Out of Vietnam?"

NORA (*cool mockery*): That bunch of pot-bellied, bald-headed old goats! Not one of them could get a woman—well, yes, maybe for two dollars.

THAW: You don't look at Senators, Nora. You listen to them.

NORA (*nodding*): Women are only to look at. Men are to listen to. Got it.

(*Thaw snaps off the TV. He is now neither looking at her nor listening to her, as he methodically turns pages of the magazine he has picked up.*)

THAW: Finished reading to the kids?

NORA: I haven't been reading to the children. I've been reading to myself—and talking to myself—for a long time now.

THAW: That's good. (*She passes him, carrying the third envelope, and goes into kitchen.*)

THAW (*Unenthusiastically*): Want some help with the dishes?

NORA'S VOICE: I'm not doing the dishes.

THAW (*enthusiastically*): Say, Nora, this is quite an ad we've got in *Life* for Stove Mountain Life Insurance.

NORA'S VOICE: Yes, I saw it. Great. (*She comes back and goes to sofa.*)

THAW: It's the kind of ad that grabs you. This sad-faced, nice-looking woman of 50, sitting on a bench with a lot of discouraged old biddies, in an employment agency. Great caption—(*reading*)

NORA and THAW (*together*): "Could this happen to *your* wife?"

NORA: I'll let you know the answer very shortly. (*A pause.*) You really don't hear me anymore, do you? (*He really doesn't. She buttons herself into her coat, pulls on her gloves.*) Well, there are enough groceries for a week. All the telephone numbers you'll need and menus for the children are in the envelope on the spindle. A girl will come in to take care of them after school—until your mother gets here.

THAW: Uh-huh . . .

NORA (*looks around sadly*): Well, good-bye dear little doll house. Good-bye dear husband. You've had the best ten years of my life.

(*She goes to the staircase, blows two deep kisses upstairs, just as Thaw glances up briefly at her, but returns automatically to his magazine. Nora picks up suitcase, opens the door, goes out, closing it quietly.*)

THAW (*like a man suddenly snapping out of a hypnotic trance*): Nora? Nora? NOR-RA! (*He is out of the door in two seconds.*)

THAW'S and NORA'S VOICES: Nora, where're you going?—I'll miss my train—I don't understand—it's all in my letter—let me go!—You come back—

(*They return. He is pulling her by the arm. He yanks the suitcase away from her, drops it in the hall.*)

NORA: Ouch! You're hurting me!

THAW: Now what is this all about? (*He shoves her into the room, then stands between her and door.*) Why the hell . . . What're you sneaking out of the house . . . What's that suitcase for?

NORA: I wasn't sneaking. I told you. But you weren't listening.

THAW: I was listening . . . it just didn't register. You said you were reading to yourself. Then you started yakking about the kids and the groceries and the doll house mother sent . . . (*flabbergasted.*) Good-bye?! What the hell do you mean, *good-bye*?!

NORA: Just that. I'm leaving you. (*Pointing to books.*) My letter will explain everything—

THAW: Have you blown your mind?

NORA: Thaw, I've got to scoot, or I'll miss the eight-o-nine.

THAW: You'll miss it. (*He backs her to the sofa, pushes her onto it, goes and slams the door and strides back.*) Now, my girl, explain all this.

NORA: That's easy. Muscle. The heavier musculature of the male is a secondary sexual charac-

teristic. Although that's not certain. It could be just the result of selective breeding. In primitive times, of course, the heavier musculature of the male was necessary to protect the pregnant female and the immobile young—

THAW (*his anger evaporates*): Nora, are you sick?

NORA: But what's just happened now shows that nothing has changed—I mean, fundamentally changed—in centuries, in the relations between the sexes. *You* still Tarzan, *me* still Jane.

THAW (*sits on sofa beside her, feels her head*): I've noticed you've been . . . well . . . acting funny lately . . .

NORA: Funny?

THAW: Like there was something on your mind. . . . Tell me, what's wrong, sweetheart? Where does it hurt?

NORA: It hurts (*taps head*) here. Isn't that where thinking hurts *you*? No. You're used to it. I was, too, when I was at Wellesley. But I sort of stopped when I left. It's really hard to think of anything else when you're having babies.

THAW: Nora, isn't it about time for your period?

NORA: But if God had wanted us to think just with our wombs, why did He give us a brain? No matter what men say, Thaw, the female brain is not a vestigial organ, like a vermiform appendix.

THAW: Nora . . .

NORA: Thaw, I can just about make my train. I'll leave the car and keys in the usual place at the station. Now, I have a very important appointment in the morning. (*She starts to rise.*)

THAW: Appointment? (*Grabs her shoulders.*) Nora, look at me! You weren't sneaking out of the house to . . . get an abortion?

NORA: When a man can't explain a woman's actions, the first thing he thinks about is the condition of her uterus. Thaw, if you were leaving me and I didn't know why, would I ask, first thing, if you were having prostate trouble?

THAW: Don't try to throw me off the track, sweetie! Now, if you want another baby . . .

NORA: Thaw, don't you remember, we both agreed about the overpopulation problem—

THAW: To hell with the overpopulation problem. Let Nixon solve that. Nora, I can swing another baby—

NORA: Maybe you can. I can't. For me there are no more splendid, new truths to be learned from scanning the contents of babies' diapers. Thaw, I *am* pregnant. But not in a feminine way. In the way only men are supposed to get pregnant.

THAW: Men, pregnant?

NORA (*nodding*): With ideas. Pregnancies there (*taps his head*) are masculine. And a very superior form of labor. Pregnancies here (*taps her tummy*) are feminine—a very inferior form of labor. That's an example of male linguistic chauvinism. Mary Ellmann is *great* on that. You'll enjoy her *Thinking about Women* . . .

THAW (*going to telephone near bookshelf*): I'm getting the doctor. (*Nora makes a dash for the door, he drops the phone.*) Oh, no you don't!

(*He reaches for her as she passes, misses. Grabs her ponytail and hauls her back by it, and shoves her into the easy chair.*)

NORA: Brother, Millett sure had you taped.

THAW: Milly *who*? (*A new thought comes to him.*) Has one of your goddam-gossipy female friends been trying to break up our marriage? (*He suddenly checks his conscience. It is* not *altogether pure.*) What did she tell you? That she saw me having lunch, uh, dinner, with some girl?

NORA (*nodding to herself*): Right on the button!

THAW: Now, Nora, I can explain about that girl—

NORA: You don't have to. Let's face it. Monogamy is not natural to the male—

THAW: You know I'm not in love with anybody but you—

NORA: It's not natural to the female, either. Making women think it is is man's most successful form of brainwashing—

THAW: Nora, I swear, that girl means nothing to me—

NORA: And you probably mean nothing to her. So whose skin is off whose nose?

THAW (*relieved, but puzzled*): Well, uh, I'm glad you feel that way about—uh—things.

NORA: Oh, it's not the way I *feel*. It's the way things really are. What with the general collapse of the mores, and now the Pill, women are becoming as promiscuous as men. It figures. We're educated from birth to think of ourselves just as man-traps. Of course, in my mother's day, good women thought of themselves as private man-traps. Only bad women were public man-traps. Now we've all gone public. (*Looks at watch.*) I'll have to take the eight-forty.

(*She gets out of her coat, lays it, ready to slip into, on back of sofa.*)

THAW (*a gathering suspicion*): Nora, are you trying to tell me . . . that *you*—

NORA: Of course, a lot of it, today, is the fault of the advertising industry. Making women think they're failures in life if they don't make like sex-pots around the clock. We're even supposed to wear false eyelashes when we're vacuuming. Betty Friedan's great on that. She says many lonely suburban housewives, unable to identify their real problem, think more sex is the answer. So they sleep with the milkman, or the delivery boy. If I felt like sleeping with anybody like that, I'd pick the plumber. When you need *him*, boy you *need* him!

THAW (*the unpleasant thought he has been wrestling with has now jelled*): Nora . . . are you . . . trying to tell me you are leaving me—for someone else?

NORA: Why, Thaw Wald! How could you even *think* such a thing? (*To herself.*) Now, how naïve can I be? What else do men think about, in connection with women, *but sex*? He is saying to himself, she's not having her period, she's not pregnant, she's not jealous; it's *got* to be another man.

THAW: Stop muttering to yourself, and answer my question.

NORA: I forgot what it was. Oh, yes. *No.*

THAW: No what?

NORA: No, I'm not in love with anybody else. I was a virgin when I married you. And intacta. And that wasn't par for the course—even at Wellesley. And I've never slept with anybody else, partly because I never wanted to. And partly because, I suppose, of our family's Presbyterian hangup. So, now that all the vital statistics are out of the way, I'll just drive around until—

(*Begins to slip her arms into coat. He grabs coat, throws it on easy chair.*)

THAW: You're not leaving until you tell me *why.*

NORA: But it's all in my letter. (*Points.*) The fat one sticking out of Simone de Beauvoir's *Second Sex*—

THAW: If you have a bill of particulars against me, I want it—straight. From you.

NORA: Oh, darling, I have no bill of particulars. By all the standards of our present-day society, you are a very good husband. And, mark me, you'll be president of Stove Mountain Life Insurance Company before you're 50. The point is, what will I be when I'm 50—

THAW: You'll be my wife, if I have anything to say. Okay. So you're not leaving me because I'm a bad husband, or because my financial future is dim.

NORA: No. Oh, Thaw, you just wouldn't understand.

THAW (*patiently*): I might, if you would try, for just one minute, to talk logically—

NORA: Thaw, women aren't trained to talk logically. Men don't like women who talk logically. They find them unfeminine—aggressive—

THAW: Dammit, Nora, will you talk sense . . .

NORA: But Boy! does a man get sore when a woman won't talk logically when *he* wants her to, and (*snaps fingers*) like that! And *that* isn't illogical? What women men are! Now, if you will step aside—

THAW (*grabbing her and shaking her*): You're going to tell me why you're walking out on me, if I have to *sock* you!

NORA: Thaw, eyeball to eyeball, *I am leaving you*—and not for a man. For reasons of my own I just don't think you *can* understand. And if you mean to stop me, you'll have to beat me to a pulp. But I'm black and blue already.

THAW: (*seizes her tenderly in his arms, kisses her*): Nora, sweetheart! You know I couldn't really hurt you. (*Kisses, kisses.*) Ba-aaby, what do you say we call it a night? (*Scoops her up in his arms.*) You can tell me *all* about it in bed . . .

NORA: The classical male one-two. Sock 'em and screw 'em.

THAW (*dumping her on sofa*): Well, it's been known to work on a lot of occasions. Something tells me this isn't one of them. (*Pours a drink.*)

NORA: I guess I need one, too. (*He mixes them.*) Thaw?

THAW: Yes.

NORA: I couldn't help being a *little* pleased when you made like a caveman. It shows you really do value my sexual services.

THAW: Jee-zus!

NORA: Well, it can't be my domestic services— you don't realize, yet, what they're worth. (*Drinks.*) Thaw, you do have a problem with me. But you can't solve it with force. And *I* do have a problem. But I can't solve it with sex.

THAW: Could you, would you, *try* to tell me what my-you-our problem is?

NORA: Friedan's *Feminine Mystique* is very good on The Problem. I've marked all the relevant passages. And I've personalized them in my letter—

(*He goes to book. Yanks out letter, starts to tear it up. Nora groans. He changes his mind, and stuffs it in his pocket.*)

THAW: Look, Nora, there's one thing I've always said about you. For a woman, you're pretty damn honest. Don't you think you owe it to me to level and give me a chance to defend myself?

NORA: The trouble is, *you* would have to listen to *me*. And that's hard for you. I *understand why*. Not listening to women is a habit that's been passed on from father to son for generations. You could almost say, tuning out on women is another secondary sexual male characteristic.

THAW: So our problem is that *I* don't listen?

NORA: Thaw, you always go on talking, no matter how hard I'm interrupting.

THAW: Okay. You have the floor.

NORA: Well, let's begin where this started tonight. When you oppressed me, and treated me as an inferior—

THAW: I oppressed . . . (*Hesitates.*) Lay on, MacDuff.

NORA: You honestly don't think that yanking me around by my hair and threatening to sock me are not the oppressive gestures of a superior male toward an inferior female?

THAW: For Chrissake, Nora, a man isn't going to let the woman he loves leave him, if he can stop her!

NORA: Exactly. Domination of the insubordinate female is an almost instinctive male reflex. *In extremis*, Thaw, it is *rape*. Now, would I like it if you should say you were going to leave me? No. But could I drag you back—

THAW: You'd just have to crook your little finger.

NORA: Flattery will get you nowhere this evening. So, where was I?

THAW: I am a born rapist.

NORA: Wasn't that what you had in mind when you tried to adjourn this to our bedroom? But that's just your primitive side. There's your civilized side, too. You are a patriarchal *pater familias*.

THAW: What am I now?

NORA: Thaw, you do realize we all live in a patriarchy, where men govern women by playing sexual politics?

THAW: Look, you're not still sore because I talked you into voting for Nixon? (*She gives him a withering look.*) Okay. So we all live in a patriarchy . . .

NORA: Our little family, the Walds, are just one nuclear patriarchal unit among the millions in our patriarchal male-dominated civilization, which is worldwide. It's all in that book—

THAW: Look Nora, I promise I'll read the damn book—but . . .

NORA: So who's interrupting? Well, Thaw, all

history shows that the hand that cradles the *rock* has ruled the world, *not* the hand that rocks the cradle! Do you know what brutal things men have done to women? Bought and sold them like cattle. Bound their feet at birth to deform them—so they couldn't run away—like in China. Made widows throw themselves on the funeral pyres of their husbands, like in India. Cut off their clitorises, so they could be bred but not enjoy sex. Thaw, did you know that the clitoris is the only sexual organ, in either sex, solely designed by nature for sexual pleasure?

THAW: That fascinating fact, up to now, has escaped me.

NORA: Yes, it's a pity. Well . . . men who committed adultery were almost never punished. But women were always brutally punished. Why, in many countries unfaithful wives were *stoned* to death—

THAW: This is America, 1970, Nora. And here, when wives are unfaithful, *husbands* get stoned. (*Drinks.*) Mind if *I* do?

NORA: By your guest. Oh, there's no doubt that relations between the sexes have been greatly ameliorated . . .

THAW: Now, about *our* relations, Nora. You're not holding it against *me* that men, the dirty bastards, have done a lot of foul things to women in the past?

NORA (*indignant*): What do you mean, in the *past*?

THAW (*determined to be patient*): Past, present, future—what has what other men have done to other women got to do with us?

NORA: Quite a lot. We *are* a male and a female—

THAW: That's the supposition I've always gone on. But Nora, we are a *particular* male and a *particular* female: Thaw Wald and his wife, Nora—

NORA: Yes. That's why it's so shattering when you find out you are such a typical husband and—

THAW (*a new effort to take command*): Nora, how many men do you know who are still in love with their wives after ten years?

NORA: Not many. And, Thaw, listen, maybe the reason is—

THAW: So you agree that's not typical? Okay. Now, do I ever grumble about paying the bills? So that's not typical. I liked my mother-in-law, even when she was alive. And God knows that's not typical. And don't I do every damn thing I can to keep *my* mother off your back? And that's not

typical. I'm even thoughtful about the little things. You said so yourself, remember, when I bought you that black see-through nightgown for Mother's Day. That I went out and chose myself. And which *you* never wear.

NORA: I had to return it. It was too small. And do you know what the saleswoman said? She said, "Men who buy their wives things in this department are in love with them. But why do they all seem to think they are married to midgets?" That's it, Thaw, that's *it!* Men "think little"—like "thinking thin"—even about women they love. They don't think at all about women they don't love or want to sleep with. Now, I can't help it if you think of me as a midget. But don't you see, I've got to stop thinking of myself as one. Thaw, *listen* . . .

THAW: Why the devil should *you* think of yourself as a midget? *I* think you're a great woman. A *real* woman! Why, you're the dearest, sweetest, most understanding little wife—most of the time—a man ever had. And the most intelligent and wonderful little mother! Dammit, those kids are the smartest, best-behaved, most self-reliant little kids . . .

NORA: Oh, I've been pretty good at Occupation Housewife, if I do say so myself. But Thaw, *listen.* Can't you even imagine that there might be something *more* a woman needs and wants—

THAW: My God, Nora, what more can a woman want than a nice home, fine children and a husband who adores her?

NORA: (*discouraged*): You sound like old Dr. Freud, in person.

THAW: I sound like Freud? I wish I were. Then I'd know why you're so uptight.

NORA: Oh, no you wouldn't. Know what Freud wrote in his diary, when he was 77? "What do women want? My God, what do they want?" Fifty years this giant brain spends analyzing women. And he still can't find out what they want. So this makes him the world's greatest expert on feminine psychology? (*She starts to look at her watch.*) To think I bought him, in college.

THAW: You've got plenty of time. You were saying about Freud—(*He lights a cigarette, hands it to her, determined to stick with it to the end.*)

NORA: History is full of ironies! Freud was the foremost exponent of the theory of the natural inferiority of women. You know, "Anatomy is destiny"?

THAW: I was in the School of Business, remember?

NORA: Well, old Freud died in 1939. He didn't

live to see what happened when Hitler adopted his theory that "anatomy is destiny." Six million of his own people went to the gas chambers. One reason, Hitler said, that the Jews were *naturally* inferior was because they were effeminate people, with a slave mentality. He said they were full of those vices which men always identify with women—when they're feeling hostile: You know, sneakiness and deception, scheming and wheedling, whining and pushiness, oh, and materialism, sensuousness and sexuality. Thaw, what's *your* favorite feminine vice?

THAW: At this moment, feminine monologues.

NORA: I didn't think you'd have the nerve to say sneakiness. I saw you sneak a look at your watch, and egg me on to talk about Freud, hoping I'll miss my train. I won't.

THAW: So nothing I've said—what little I've had a chance to say . . . (*she shakes her head*)—you still intend to divorce me?

NORA: Oh, I never said I was divorcing you. I'm deserting you. So you can divorce me.

THAW: You do realize, Nora, that if a wife deserts her husband he doesn't have to pay her alimony?

NORA: I don't want alimony. But I do want severance pay. (*Points to books.*) There's my bill, rendered for ten years of domestic services—the thing sticking in *Woman's Place*, by Cynthia Fuchs Epstein. I figured it at the going agency rates for a full-time cook, cleaning woman, handyman, laundress, seamstress, and part-time gardener and chauffeur, I've worked an average ten-hour day. So I've charged for overtime. Of course, you've paid my rent, taxes, clothing, medical expenses, and food. So I've deducted those. Even though as a housewife, I've had no fringe benefits. Just the same, the bill . . . well, I'm afraid you're going to be staggered. I was. It comes to over $53,000. I'd like to be paid in ten installments.

THAW (*he is staggered*): Mathematics isn't really your bag, Nora.

NORA: I did it on that little calculating machine you gave me at Christmas. If you think it's not really fair, I'll be glad to negotiate. And, please notice, I haven't charged anything for sleeping with you!

THAW: Wow! (*He is really punch drunk.*)

NORA: I'm not a prostitute. And *this* is what I wanted to say about the Lib girls. They're right about women who marry *just* for money. But they're wrong about women who marry for love. It's love makes all the difference—

THAW (*dispirited*): Well, *vive la différence.*

NORA: And, of course, I haven't charged anything for being a nurse. I've adored taking care of the children, especially when they were babies. I'm going to miss them—*awfully*.

THAW: (*on his feet, with outrage*): You're deserting the children, too? My God, Nora, what kind of woman *are* you? You're going to leave those poor little kids alone in this house—

NORA: You're here. And I told you, your mother is coming. I wired her that her son needed her. She'll be happy again—and be needed again—for the first time in years—

THAW (*this is a real blow*): My *mother*! Oh, migod, you *can't*, Nora. You know how she—swarms over me! She thinks I'm still 12 years old . . . (*His head is now in his hands.*) You know she drives me out of my cotton-picking mind.

NORA: Yes. But you never said so before.

THAW: I love my mother. She's been a good mother, and wife. But Nora, she's a *very* limited woman! Yak, yak—food, shopping, the kids . . .

NORA: Thaw, the children love this house, and I don't want to take them out of school. And I can't give them another home. Women, you know, can't borrow money to buy a house. Besides, legally this house and everything in it, except mother's few things, are yours. All the worldly goods with which thou didst me endow seem to be in that suitcase.

THAW: Nora, you know damn well that all my life insurance is in your name. If I died tomorrow—and I may blow my brains out tonight—everything would go to you and the kids.

NORA: Widowhood is one of the few fringe benefits of marriage. But, today, all the money I have is what I've saved in the past year out of my clothes allowance—$260.33. But I hope you will give me my severance pay—

THAW: And if I don't—you know legally I don't have to—how do you propose to support yourself?

NORA: Well, if I can't get a job right away—sell my engagement ring. That's why they say diamonds are a gal's best friend. What else do jobless women *have* they can turn into ready cash—except their bodies?

THAW: What kind of job do you figure on getting?

NORA: Well, I do have a master's in English. So I'm going to try for a spot in *Time* Research. That's the intellectual harem kept by the Time Inc. editors. The starting pay is good.

THAW: How do you know that?

NORA: From your own research assistant, Molly Peapack. We're both Wellesley, you know. She's a friend of the chief researcher at *Time*, Marylois Vega. Also, Molly says, computer programming is a field that may open to women—

THAW (*indignant*): You told Peapack you were leaving me? Before you even told *me*? How do you like *that* for treating a mate like an inferior!

NORA: Thaw, I've told you at least three times a week for the last year that with the kids both in school, I'd like to get a job. You always laughed at me. You said I was too old to be a Playboy Bunny, and that the only job an inexperienced woman my age could get would be as a saleswoman—

THAW: Okay. Where are you going to live? That 200 won't go far—

NORA: Peapack's offered to let me stay with her until I find something.

THAW: I'm going to have a word with Miss Molly Peapack tomorrow. She's been too damned aggressive lately, anyway—

NORA: She's going to have a word with you, too. She's leaving.

THAW: Peapack is leaving? Leaving *me*?

NORA: When you got her from Prudential, you promised her, remember, you'd recommend her for promotion to office manager. So, last week you took on a man. A new man. Now she's got a job offer where she's sure she's got a 40-60 chance for advancement to management. (*Pause.*) So you've lost your home wife and your office wife.

THAW: Jesus! And *this* is a male-dominated world?

NORA: Well, I've got five minutes—

THAW: You've still not told me *why*.

NORA: Oh, Thaw darling! You poor—*man*. I have told you why: I'm leaving because I want a job. I want to do some share, however small, of the world's work, and be paid for it. Isn't the work you do in the world—and the salary you get—what makes you respect yourself, and other men respect you? Women have begun to want to respect themselves a little, too—

THAW: You mean, the real reason you are leaving is that you want a *paying* job?

NORA: Yes.

THAW: God, Nora, why didn't you say that in the beginning. All right, go get a job, if it's that important to you. But that doesn't mean you have to leave me and the kids.

NORA: I'm afraid it does. Otherwise, I'd have to do two jobs. Out there. And here.

THAW: Look, Nora, I heard some of the Lib gals say there are millions of working wives and mothers who are doing two jobs. Housework can't be all that rough—

NORA: Scrubbing floors, walls. Cleaning pots, pans, windows, ovens. Messes—dog messes, toilet messes, children's messes. Garbage. Laundry. Shopping for pounds of stuff. Loading them into the car, out of the car—(A pause.) Not all of it hard. But all of it routine. All of it *boring*.

THAW: Listen, Nora, what say, you work, I work. And we split the housework? How's that for a deal?

NORA: It's a deal you are not quite free to make, Thaw. You sometimes *can't* get home until very late. And you have to travel a lot, you know. Oh, it might work for a little while. But not for long. After ten years, you still won't empty an ashtray, or pick up after yourself in the bathroom. No. I don't have the physical or moral strength to swing two jobs. So I've got to choose the one, before it's too late, that's most important to me—oh, not for me just now, but for when *I'm* 50—

THAW: When you're 50, Nora, if you don't leave me, you'll be the wife of the president of Stove Mountain Life Insurance Company. Sharing my wealth, sharing whatever status I have in the community. And with servants of your own. Now you listen to *me*, Nora. It's a man's world, out there. It's a man's world where there are a lot of women working. I see them every day. What are most of them really doing? Marking time, and looking, always looking, for a man who will offer them a woman's world . . . the world you have here. Marriage is still the best deal that the world has to offer women. And most women know it. It's always been like that. And it's going to be like that for a long, long time.

NORA: Just now I feel that the best deal I, Nora Wald, can hope to get out of life is to learn to esteem myself as a person . . . to stop feeling that every day a little bit more of my mind—and heart—is being washed down the drain with the soapsuds . . . Thaw—listen. If I don't stop shrinking, I'll end up secretly hating you, and trying to cut you—and *your* son—down to my size. The way your poor, dear mother does you and your father. And you'll become like your father, the typical henpecked husband. Thinking of his old wife as the Ball and Chain. You know he has a mistress? (*Thaw knows.*) A smart gal who owns her own shop . . . who doesn't bore him.

THAW: Well, Nora . . . (*Pours drinks.*) One for the road?

NORA: Right. For the road.

THAW: Nora . . . I'll wait. But I don't know how long—

NORA: I've thought of that, too . . . that you might remarry . . . that girl, maybe, who means nothing—

THAW: Goddammit, a man needs a woman of his own—

NORA (*nodding*): I know. A sleep-in, sleep-with body servant of his very own. Well, that's your problem. Just now, I have to wrestle with mine. (*Goes to door, picks up suitcase.*) I'm not bursting with self-confidence, Thaw. I do love you. And I also need . . . a man. So I'm not slamming the door. I'm closing it . . . very . . . softly.

(*Exits. Curtain falls.*)

COMMENTARY

Drama comes from the Greek verb *dran*, meaning "to do" or "to act." The doings in drama often are obvious: characters fall in (and out of) love, they forge letters, they slam doors, and sometimes they even kill each other. But, as we mentioned in our discussion of A *Doll's House*, dialogue is also a sort of doing or action; "Dialogue is what the characters *do* to each other." They act with words as well as with gestures.

In *The Quintessence of Ibsenism* Bernard Shaw argued that the mid-nineteenth-century play before Ibsen usually consisted of "an exposition in the first act, a situation in the second, and unravelling in the third." Ibsen, he said, changed all that with A *Doll's House*:

> Now you have exposition, situation, and discussion; and the discussion is the test of the playwright. . . . Now the serious playwright recognizes in the discussion not only the main test of his highest powers, but also the real center of his play's interest.

"His or her," he should have said, in this analysis of the play with a thesis. (For information about this sort of play, see *pièce à thèse* in the glossary.) Elsewhere Shaw replied to the criticism that his plays are all talk by admitting the truth of the charge: "My plays are all talk, just as Raphael's pictures are all paint, Michaelangelo's statues all marble, Beethoven's symphonies all noise." Shaw is having his fun, but he is also being serious in his assertion that drama can deal not only with action of the obvious sort but also with ideas worth arguing about. The writer of a play of ideas will, of course, make some use of settings, costumes, and gestures to communicate meaning, but the chief interest is in the examination of an idea, or, to use Shaw's word, the center of interest is the "discussion."

Clare Boothe Luce's play is in this tradition. To some degree every writer must see himself or herself as part of a tradition. When Sophocles wrote *Oedipus the King* he presumably said to himself, "The Oedipus story has often been told, by Homer and by the playwrights who are my contemporaries, but this is the way I see it." Furthermore, he must also have said to himself, "Our writers of tragedies do such-and-such; in this play I want to deepen, or enlarge, what tragic drama can do, and I want to deepen or enlarge our sense of the tragic."

Similarly, when Shakespeare wrote *Hamlet* he was working in (and adding to) the tradition of the Elizabethan revenge play, a form already popular; indeed, at least one play on Hamlet had already appeared on the stage. And in his *King Lear* he is similarly indebted to an older play, the anonymous *King Leir*, which ends happily. Shakespeare must have thought, "No, no, no! The story ought to go thus . . ."

Clare Boothe Luce's play is inspired by Ibsen's *A Doll's House* (the title alludes to the end of Ibsen's play). Presumably Luce did not feel that Ibsen got the story wrong, only that in 1970—ninety-one years after Ibsen wrote his play—the story could usefully be set forth a little differently. She follows the main line of Ibsen's plot but uses American characters and customs of the late twentieth century. She also employs her distinctive tone, which is unlike Ibsen's. Part of the fun of reading her play is to imagine Ibsen in the background while at the same time recognizing both what is new in the work and what is essentially Ibsenite. To take a single, simple example, at the end of the play Nora carefully explains that she is not slamming the door, just closing it carefully.

TOPICS FOR DISCUSSION

1. Based on the little that we hear of the television program at the start of the play, characterize the moderator of the program.
2. What dramatic purposes are served by including the bit about the television program?
3. Very early in the dialogue Thaw warns Nora: "Uh-uh, Nora! We both agreed months ago, you'd lay off the feminist bit if I'd lay off watching Saturday football." What does this tell us about Thaw? And about Nora? Do you think they made a fair bargain? (Notice also the first line that Nora speaks after Thaw's line.)
4. What are the implications of the ad by Stove Mountain Life Insurance? Why does Thaw think it is "quite an ad"? What do you think of it?
5. Trace the course of Thaw's methods in his attempts to keep Nora from leaving.
6. How much do you think Thaw has learned by the end of the play?
7. In some ways the play—though certainly serious—is a comedy. What, if anything, do you find funny in it?
8. If you have read Ibsen's *A Doll's House*, compare the treatment of sex in the two plays.

THE NATURE OF DRAMA

1. Tragedy and Comedy

Whimsical assertions that all of us are Platonists or Aristotelians, or liberals or conservatives ("Nature wisely does contrive / That every boy and every gal / That's born into the world alive / Is either a little Liberal / Or else a little Conservative"), reveal a tendency to divide things into two. Two is about right: Peace and war, man and woman, day and night, life and death. There may be middle cases; there is the cold war, and Edmund Burke suggested that no one can point to the precise moment that divides day from night—but Burke also suggested that everyone can make the useful distinction between day and night. The distinction between comedy and tragedy may not always be easy to make, but until the twentieth century it was usually clear enough. *Hamlet,* which in Horatio's words is concerned with "woe or wonder," is a tragedy; *A Midsummer Night's Dream*, which in Puck's words is concerned with things that pleasingly "befall preposterously," is a comedy. The best plays of our century, however, are another thing, and discussion of these plays—somewhat desperately called tragicomedy—will be postponed until later in this chapter.

What befalls—preposterous or not—is the *action of the play*. The gestures on the stage are, of course, "actions," but they are not the action of the play in the sense of Aristotle's use of *praxis* or "action" in *The Poetics*, a fragmentary treatise of the fourth century B.C. that remains the starting point for most discussions of drama. For Aristotle, drama is the imitation (i.e., representation, re-presentation, re-creation) by impersonators, of an action. In tragedy the action is serious and important, something that matters, done by people who count (e.g., King Oedipus's discovery that he has killed his father and married his mother); in comedy (for Aristotle), the action is done by unimportant laughable people who make mistakes that do not cause us pain. Commonly the tragic action is a man's perception of a great mistake he has made; he suffers intensely and perhaps dies, having exhausted all the possibilities of his life. (Female tragic heroes are rare.) The comic action often is the exposure of folly and the renewal rather than the exhaustion of human nature. Crabby parents, for example, find that they cannot keep young lovers apart, and so they join in the marriage festivities. Byron jocosely put the matter thus:

> All tragedies are finished by a death,
> All comedies are ended by a marriage.

All tragedies and all comedies do not in fact end thus, but the idea is right; tragedy has the solemnity, seriousness, and finality we often associate with death,[1] and comedy has the joy and fertility and suggestion of a new life we often associate with marriage.

(margin note: IMITATION OF AN ACTION)

---

[1] Shakespeare's tragedies all end with the death of the tragic hero, but a good many Greek tragedies do not. In *Oedipus the King* the hero remains alive, but he is blind and banished and seems to have exhausted the possibilities of his life. Some other Greek tragedies have what can

This concept of *an action* (i.e., an underlying motif, not merely gestures) in tragedy and in comedy makes clear that comedy is not a mere matter of jokes or funny bits of business. It also makes clear what the Greek comic playwright Menander meant when he told a friend that he had composed a play, and now had only to write the dialogue: he had worked out the happenings that would embody the action, and there remained only the slighter task of providing the spirited words. The same idea is implicit in Ibsen's comment that the drafts of his plays differed "very much from each other in characterization, not in action." The action or happening dramatized in a tragedy or a comedy may be conceived of as a single course or train of events manifested on the stage by a diversity of activities. Think of such expressions as "the closing of the frontier," or "the revival of learning"; each might be said to denote an action, though such action is seen only in its innumerable manifestations.

HAPPENINGS
AND
HAPPENINGS

Tragic playwrights take some happening, from history (for example, the assassination of Julius Caesar), or from fiction (Shakespeare derived Othello from an Italian short story), or from their own imagination, and they make or shape or arrange episodes that clarify the action. They make (in common terminology) a *plot* that embodies the action or spiritual content. Even when playwrights draw on history, they make their own plot because they select and rearrange the available historical facts. A reenactment of everything that Julius Caesar did during his last days or hours would not be a play with an action, for drama is not so much concerned with what in fact *happened* as with some sort of typical and coherent or unified thing that *happens*, a significant action. Sometimes, of course, history provides substantial material for drama, but even Shakespeare's *Julius Caesar* takes frequent liberties with the facts as Shakespeare knew them, and Shakespeare's source, the biographer Plutarch, doubtless had already assimilated the facts to a literary form. At most we can say that history provided Shakespeare with a man whose life lent itself well to an established literary form. Not every life does lend itself thus. We are told that Aeschylus, the earliest tragic playwright who has left us any complete plays, was killed when an eagle mistook his bald head for a rock and dropped a turtle on it to break the shell. Aeschylus's death was a great loss, but it did not have the unified significant action required of tragedy. By chance an eagle that had captured a turtle was near to Aeschylus, and Aeschylus by chance (or rather by his chemistry) was bald. There is no relation between these two circumstances; Aeschylus's death (allegedly) happened this way, and we can account for it, but

UNITY

the event has no intelligible unity. (A sentence from Vladimir Nabokov's *Pale Fire* comes to mind: If one is contemplating suicide, "jumping from a high bridge is not recommended even if you cannot swim, for wind and water abound

---

reasonably be called a happy ending; i.e., some sort of joyful reconciliation. For example, in Sophocles's *Philoctetes*, the weapon which has been taken from the sick Philoctetes is returned to him, and Heracles, a messenger from Zeus, announces that Philoctetes will be healed. But these tragedies with happy endings, like those with unhappy endings, deal with "important" people, and they are about "serious" things. If there is finally joy, it is a solemn joy.

in weird contingencies, and tragedy ought not to culminate in a record dive or a policeman's promotion.")

In tragedy things cohere. The hero normally does some deed and suffers as a consequence. Actions have consequences in the moral world no less than in the materialistic world of the laboratory. The tragic playwright's solemn presentation of "the remorseless working of things," Alfred North Whitehead pointed out (in his *Science and the Modern World*, 1925), is "the vision possessed by science," and it cannot be accidental that the two great periods of tragic drama, fifth-century B.C. Athens and England around 1600, were periods of scientific inquiry.

This emphasis on causality means that the episodes are related, connected, and not merely contiguous. Generally the formula is to show the tragic hero moving toward committing some deed that will cause great unintended suffering, committing it, and then, by seeing the consequences, learning the true nature of his deed. The plot, that is, involves a credible character whose doings are related to his nature. For Aristotle, in the best sort of tragedy the tragic hero is an important person, almost preeminently virtuous, who makes some sort of great mistake that entails great suffering. Calamity does not descend upon him from above, does not happen *to* him, nor does he consciously will a destructive act; he merely makes a great mistake. The mistake is Aristotle's *hamartia*, sometimes translated as "error," sometimes as "flaw." Probably Aristotle did not mean by hamartia a trait, such as rashness or ambition, which the translation "flaw" implies, but simply meant an action based on a mental error, a sort of false step. Oedipus, erroneously thinking that Polybus and Meropê are his parents, flees from them when he hears that he will kill his father and sleep with his mother. His action is commendable, but it happens to be a great mistake because it brings him to his real parents. Nevertheless, despite the scholarly elucidations of Aristotle, we can sometimes feel that the erring action proceeds from a particular kind of character, that a person with different traits would not have acted in the same way. The Oedipus that we see in the play, for example, is a self-assured quick-tempered man—almost a rash man, we might say—who might well have neglected to check the facts before he fled from Corinth. There are at least times, even when reading *Oedipus the King*, when one feels with George Meredith (1828–1909) that

> in tragic life, God wot,
> No villain need be! Passions spin the plot:
> We are betrayed by what is false within.

From this it is only a short step to identifying hamartia with a flaw, and the flaw most often attributed to the tragic hero is *hybris*, a word that for the Greeks meant something like "bullying," "abuse of power," but in dramatic criticism usually is translated as "overweening pride." The tragic hero forgets that (in Montaigne's words) "on the loftiest throne in the world we are still sitting only on our own rear," and he believes his actions are infallible. King Lear, for example, banishes his daughter Cordelia with "Better thou / Hadst not been born than not

THE
TRAGIC
HERO

HAMARTIA

HYBRIS

t' have pleased me better." Macbeth, told that he will be king of Scotland, chooses to make the prophecy come true by murdering his guest, King Duncan; Brutus decides that Rome can be saved from tyranny only by killing Caesar, and he deludes himself into thinking he is not murdering Caesar but sacrificing Caesar for the welfare of Rome.

PERIPETEIA   We have talked of hamartia and hybris in tragedy; two more Greek words, *peripeteia* and *anagnorisis*, also common in discussions of tragedy, ought to be mentioned. A peripeteia (sometimes anglicized to *peripety* or translated as "reversal") occurs when the action takes a course not intended by the doer. Aristotle gives two examples: (1) the Messenger comes to cheer up Oedipus by freeing him from fears but the message heightens Oedipus' fears; (2) Danaus (in a lost play) prosecutes a man but is himself killed.

A few other examples may be useful: Oedipus fled from Corinth to avoid contact with his parents, but his flight brought him to them; Macbeth kills Duncan to gain the crown but his deed brings him fearful nights instead of joyful days; Lear, seeking a peaceful old age, puts himself in the hands of two daughters who maltreat him, and banishes the one daughter who later will comfort him. The Bible—especially the Old Testament—is filled with such peripeties or ironic actions. For example, the Philistines brought Samson before them to entertain them, and he performed his most spectacular feat by destroying his audience. But the archetypal tragic story is that of Adam and Eve: aiming to be like gods, they lost their immortality and the earthly paradise, and brought death to themselves.

ANAGNORISIS   The other Greek word, *anagnorisis*, translated as "recognition" or "discovery" or "disclosure," seems to have meant for Aristotle a clearing up of some misunderstanding, such as the proper identification of someone or the revelation of some previously unknown fact. But later critics have given it a richer meaning and used it to describe the hero's perception of his true nature or his true plight. In the narrow sense, it is an anagnorisis or "recognition" when King Lear learns that Regan and Goneril are ungrateful and cruel. In the wider sense, the anagnorisis is in his speech in Act III, Scene IV, when he confesses his former ignorance and his neglect of his realm:

> Poor naked wretches, wheresoe'er you are,
> That bide the pelting of this pitiless storm,
> How shall your houseless heads and unfed sides,
> Your looped and windowed raggedness, defend you
> From seasons such as these? O, I have ta'en
> Too little care of this! Take physic, pomp;
> Expose thyself to feel what wretches feel,
> That thou mayst shake the superflux to them,
> And show the heavens more just.

Similarly Hamlet's "There is special providence in the fall of a sparrow," and Othello's "one that loved not wisely, but too well," may be called recognition scenes. Here is Macbeth's recognition that his purpose has been frustrated, that his deed has been ironic:

> My way of life
> Is fall'n into the sear, the yellow leaf,
> And that which should accompany old age,
> As honor, love, obedience, troops of friends,
> I must not look to have.

"Troops of friends" abound in comedy. Where tragedy is primarily the dramatization of the single life that ripens and then can only rot, that reaches its fullest and then is destroyed, comedy is primarily the dramatization of the renewing of the self and of social relationships. The tragic hero is isolated from society, partly by his different nature, and partly by his tragic act; comedy suggests that selfhood is found not in assertion of individuality, but in joining in the fun, in becoming part of the flow of common humanity. Where tragedy suggests an incompatibility between the energy or surge of the individual life and the laws of life or the norms of society, comedy suggests that norms are valid and necessary. Tragic heroes do what they feel compelled to do; they assert themselves, and are intensely aware that they are special persons and not members of the crowd. But that their mistake always reveals that they are hybristic is not at all certain. The Greek tragic hero is commonly set against a chorus of ordinary mortals who caution him, wring their hands, and lament his boldness, but these ordinary mortals are always aware that if they are law-abiding people, they are also less fully human beings than the hero. That they obey society's laws is not due to superior virtue, to the triumph of reason over will, to self-discipline; rather, their obedience is due to a lower vision, or to timidity, and indeed sometimes to a fear of what resides in their own breasts.

THE SOCIAL WORLD OF COMEDY

TRAGIC ISOLATION

Tragic heroes are, of course, in one way inferior to those about them; their mistakes cost them great suffering, and they are thus immobilized as the others are not. But their greatness remains indisputable; the anguish that at times paralyzes Hamlet also makes him greater than, say, Horatio and Laertes. In fact, tragic heroes are circumscribed, certainly after the deed, when they are necessarily subject to the consequences (Brutus kills Caesar and finds that he brings to Rome a turmoil that makes him flee from Rome and that ultimately makes him take his own life); even before doing the tragic deed, the heroes are circumscribed because their action proceeds from something, either from their personality or from their circumstances. Still, their action seems to them to be freely theirs, and indeed we feel that it is an action that lesser persons could not perform. This perception is almost a way of arguing that a tragic hero may err not so much from weakness as from strength. Why can Iago so easily deceive Othello? Not because Othello is an unthinking savage, or an unsophisticated foreigner, but because (as Iago admits) Othello is of a "loving noble nature," and, again,

TRAGIC VIRTUE

> The Moor is of *a free and open nature*
> *That thinks men honest* that but seem to be so;

> And will as tenderly be led by th' nose
> As asses are.

Why can Claudius see to it that Laertes murders Hamlet during a fencing match? Not because Hamlet is a poor fencer, or a coward, but because Hamlet

> *Most generous, and free from all contriving,*
> Will not peruse the foils.

TRAGIC JOY

This is not to say that tragic heroes are faultless, or that they are quite happy with themselves and with their action; but they do experience a kind of exultation even in their perception that disaster is upon them. If they grieve over their deeds, we sense a glory in their grief, for they find, like Captain Ahab, that in their topmost grief lies their topmost greatness. At last they see everything and know that nothing more can be experienced. They have lived their lives to the limits. Othello put it thus:

> Here is my journey's end, here is my butt,
> And very seamark of my utmost sail.

(In a comedy Shakespeare tells us that "journeys end in lovers meeting," that is, the end is a new beginning.)

In "Under Ben Bulben" William Butler Yeats (1865–1939) suggests the sense of completeness that the tragic hero experiences when, under the influence of a great passion, he exhausts his nature and seems to be not a man among men but a partner (rather than a subject) of fate:

> Know that when all words are said
> And a man is fighting mad,
> Something drops from eyes long blind,
> He completes his partial mind,
> For an instant stands at ease,
> Laughs aloud, his heart at peace.
> Even the wisest man grows tense
> With some sort of violence
> Before he can accomplish fate,
> Know his work or choose his mate.

Elsewhere Yeats put his distinction between the tragic hero and the world the hero is up against thus: "Some Frenchman[2] has said that farce is the struggle against a ridiculous object, comedy against a movable object, tragedy against an immovable; and because the will, or energy, is greatest in tragedy, tragedy is the more noble; but I add that 'will or energy is eternal delight,' and when its limit is reached it may become a pure, aimless joy, though the man, the shade, still mourns his lost object."

What of the contexts and times when we find passionate self-assertion

---

[2] Yeats is rather freely summarizing Ferdinand Brunetière's *La Loi du théâtre*. A translation of Brunetière's treatise is available in *European Theories of the Drama*, ed. Barrett H. Clark.

funny? Much depends on what is being asserted, and on what or who the COMIC
antagonist is. King Lear against his tigerish daughters is a tragic figure, but a ASSERTION
pedant against a dull schoolboy may be a comic one. The lament of the tragic
hero is proportionate to the event, but the effort extended by the comic figure is
absurdly disproportionate. Furthermore, as Henri Bergson (1859–1941) pointed
out, the comic figure usually is a sort of mechanism, repeating his actions and
catch phrases with clocklike regularity in contexts where they are inappropriate.
He quotes Latin on every occasion, or he never travels without his pills, or she
always wants to know how much something costs, or he is forever spying on his
wife. Bergson, who suggested that the comic is "the mechanical encrusted on
the living," illustrated his point by telling of the customs officers who bravely
rescue the crew of a sinking vessel, and then ask, the moment the shore is
reached, "Have you anything to declare?" The mechanical question, inappropriate in the situation, reveals that the officers value trivial regulations as
much as they do life itself. In *The Circus* Charlie Chaplin is dusting things off;
he comes upon the magician's bowl of goldfish, takes the fish out and wipes
them, and then returns them to the bowl.

The comic world seems to be presided over by a genial, tolerant deity who COMIC JOY
enjoys the variety that crosses the stage. The sketchbooks of the Japanese artist
Hokusai (1760–1849) wonderfully reveal this comic delight in humanity. There
are pages of fat men, pages of thin men (no less engagingly drawn), pages of men
making funny faces, and there is a delightful drawing of a man holding a
magnifying glass in front of his face so that his nose seems enormous. Comic
playwrights give us something of this range of types and grotesques, and they give
us also variety in language (e.g., puns, inverted clichés, malapropisms) and
variety in episodes (much hiding behind screens, dressing in disguise). The
characters, then, who insist on being themselves, who mechanically hold to a
formula of language or of behavior, are laughably out of place in the world of
varied people who live and let live. What comedy does not tolerate is COMIC
intolerance; it regularly suggests that the intolerant—for example, the pedant ISOLATION
and the ascetic—are fools and probably hypocrites. Here is the self-righteous
Alceste, in Molière's *The Misanthrope*:

> Some men I hate for being rogues: the others,
> I hate because they treat the rogues like brothers,
> And, lacking a virtuous scorn for what is vile,
> Receive the villain with a complaisant smile.
> Notice how tolerant people choose to be
> Toward that bold rascal who's at law with me.

Philinte genially replies,

> Let's have an end of rantings and of railings,
> And show some leniency toward human failings.
> This world requires a pliant rectitude;
> Too stern a virtue makes one stiff and rude.

Here is the puritanical Malvolio in *Twelfth Night*, trying to quiet down some tipsy but genial revelers:

> My masters, are you mad? Or what are you? Have you no wit, manners nor honesty, but to gabble like tinkers at this time of night? Do ye make an alehouse of my lady's house? . . . Is there not respect of place, persons, nor time in you?

He is aptly answered: "Art any more than a steward? Dost thou think, because thou art virtuous, there shall be no more cakes and ale?" This suspicion of a "virtue" that is opposed to cakes and ale runs through the history of comedy.

In Shakespeare's *Love's Labor Lost*, the young noblemen who vow to devote themselves to study, and to forgo the company of women, are laughed at until they accept their bodies and admit interest in those of the ladies. The celebration of the human body, or at least the good-natured acceptance of it which is present in comedy, is well-put by the General in Anouilh's *The Waltz of the Toreadors*:

> You're in the ocean, splashing about, doing your damndest not to drown, in spite of whirlpools and cross currents. The main thing is to do the regulation breast-stroke and if you're not a clod, never to let the life-buoy ["the ideal"] out of sight. No one expects any more than that out of you. Now if you relieve yourself in the water now and then, that's your affair. The sea is big, and if the top half of your body still looks as though it's doing the breaststroke, nobody will say a word.

DETACH-
MENT AND
ENGAGE-
MENT

One way of distinguishing between comedy and tragedy is summarized in Horace Walpole's aphorism "This world is a comedy to those that think, a tragedy to those that feel." Life seen thoughtfully, with considerable detachment, viewed from above, as it were, is an amusing pageant, and the comic writer gives us something of this view. With Puck we look at the antics in the forest, smile tolerantly, and say with a godlike perspective, "Lord, what fools these mortals be!" But in tragedy we are to a greater degree engaged; the tragic dramatist manages to make us in large measure identify ourselves with the hero, feel his plight as if it were our own, and value his feelings as he values them.[3] Yeats noticed this when he said that "character is continuously present in comedy alone," and that "tragedy must always be a drowning and breaking of the dykes that separate man from man. . . . It is upon these dykes comedy keeps house." And Yeats again: "Nor when the tragic reverie is at its height do we say, 'How well that man is realised, I should know him were I to meet him in the street,' for it is always ourselves that we see upon the [tragic] stage."

One consequence of this distinction between tragedy and comedy, between looking-at and feeling-with, is that the comic plot is usually more intricate than

---

[3] Bergson's theory that a human being—an organism—is comical when it behaves mechanically requires, as Bergson said, a modification: feelings must be suppressed. A crippled man is not comic despite his mechanical limp, because we feel for him. Comedy requires, Bergson said, an "anesthesia of the heart."

the tragic plot, and less plausible. The comic plot continues to trip up its characters, bringing them into numerous situations that allow them to display their folly over and again. The complex comic plot is often arbitrary, full of the workings of Fortune or Chance, and we delight at each new unexpected or unlikely happening. In tragedy, Fate (sometimes in the form that "character is destiny") or Necessity rules, there is the consistency and inevitability, the "remorseless working of things," that has already been mentioned. If Macbeth were struck dead by a falling roof tile while he dozed in the palace after a good meal, instead of dying on Macduff's sword, or if Brutus were to die by slipping in his bath, instead of dying on the very sword with which he killed Caesar, we would have arbitrary happenings that violate the spirit of everything that precedes. But the unexpected letters and the long-lost relatives that often turn up at the close of a comedy are thoroughly in the spirit of the comic vision, which devalues not only rigidly consistent character but rigidity of every sort, even of plot. Tragedy usually follows a straight course, comedy a delightfully twisted one.

TRAGIC FATE AND COMIC FORTUNE IN PLOTS

    The rigid behavior of some of comedy's laughably serious characters (e.g., misers, jealous husbands, stern fathers) is paralleled in the rigid circumstances that often are sketched at the beginning of a comedy. In *A Midsummer Night's Dream* the Athenian law requires that a young woman marry the man of her father's choice, or be put to death, or live chastely in a nunnery. Gilbert and Sullivan, to draw on familiar material, afford plenty of examples of comedy's fondness for a cantankerous beginning: *The Mikado* opens with a chorus of Japanese noblemen whose code of etiquette makes them appear to be "worked by strings"; they live in a town where a law ordered that "all who flirted, leered or winked / Should forthwith be beheaded." (Comedy often begins with a society dominated by some harsh law.) Although this law has been suspended, another harsh decree is in effect: the pretty Yum-Yum is betrothed to her old guardian, Ko-Ko. We learn, too, that her appropriate wooer, Nanki-Poo, is a prince who has had to disguise himself as a humble wandering minstrel to escape his father's decree that he marry Katisha, an old and ugly lady of the court.

COMIC BEGINNINGS AND ENDINGS

    After various doings in a comedy, a new—presumably natural, prosperous, fertile, and free—society is formed, usually centered around lovers who are going to be married. Yum-Yum and Nanki-Poo finally contrive to get married, evading Katisha and Ko-Ko, who make the best of things by marrying each other. The whole business is satisfactorily explained to the Mikado, who affably accepts, and ruffled tempers are soothed:

> The threatened cloud has passed away,
> And brightly shines the dawning day;
> What though the night may come too soon,
> We've years and years of afternoon!
>
>   Then let the throng
>   Our joy advance,
> With laughing song
>   And merry dance,

> With joyous shout and ringing cheer,
> Inaugurate our new career!

The first four lines are sung by the young lovers, the remaining six are sung by "All," the new, or renewed, society, free from unnatural law. *H.M.S. Pinafore* begins with lovers who cannot marry because of disparity in rank, but ends with appropriate shifts in rank so that there can be "three loving pairs on the same day united."

In comedy there is often not only an improbable turn in events but an improbable (but agreeable) change in character—or at least in rank; troublesome persons become enlightened, find their own better nature, and join in the fun, commonly a marriage-feast. Finding one's own nature is common in tragedy, too, but there self-knowledge is co-terminous with death or some death-like condition, such as blindness. *Oedipus the King* ends with a note of finality, even though Oedipus is alive at the end; the fact that twenty-five years later Sophocles decided to write a play showing Oedipus's apotheosis does not allow us to see the earlier play as less than complete. The chorus in *Oedipus the King* has the last word:

SELF-
KNOWL-
EDGE

> This man was Oedipus.
> That mighty King, who knew the riddle's mystery,
> Whom all the city envied, Fortune's favorite.
> Behold, in the event, the storm of his calamities,
> And, being mortal, think on that last day of death,
> Which all must see, and speak of no man's happiness
> Till, without sorrow, he hath passed the goal of life.

Or consider the irreparable loss at the end of Shakespeare's tragedies: "This was the noblest Roman of them all"; "We that are young / Shall never see so much, nor live so long"; "The rest is silence." But comedy ends with a new beginning, a newly formed society, usually a wedding party; the tragic figure commonly awakens to the fact that he has made a big mistake and his life is over, but the comic figure commonly awakens to his better nature. He usually sheds his aberration and is restored to himself and to a renewed society. Alceste's refusal to change, at the end of *The Misanthrope*, helps to push that comedy toward the borderline between comedy and tragedy. Oedipus learns that his parents were not those whom he had supposed, and he learns that even the mighty Oedipus can be humbled. Othello comes to see himself as a man "that loved not wisely but too well," and, having reached his journey's end, he executes justice upon himself by killing himself. That is, at the end of the play he finds himself, but this finding of the self separates him forever from those around him, whereas the comic figure who finds himself usually does so by putting aside in some measure his individuality and by submitting himself to a partner or to the group.

Comedy and tragedy offer different visions and represent different psychological states. And they are equally useful. The tragic vision may have more prestige, but it is no small thing to make people laugh, to call attention amusingly to the follies and joys of life, and to help develop the sense of humor—and humility—that may be indispensable to survival in a world continually threatened by aggressive ideals that demand uncritical acceptance. Infants smile easily, and children laugh often, but growing up is often attended by a frightening seriousness. True, hostile laughter, the scarcely veiled aggressiveness that manifests itself in derision, remains an adult possession, but the laughter evoked by the best comedy is good-natured while it is critical, and it is in part directed at ourselves. We look at bumbling humanity and we recall Puck's words, "Lord, what fools these mortals be." This is not to say that the comic vision is cynical; rather, it attributes to folly what less generous visions attribute to ill will or to hopeless corruption, and when it laughs it forgives. Analyses of laughter are sometimes funny but more often they are tedious; still, they at least pay the comic spirit the compliment of recognizing it as worthy of our best efforts.

2. Tragicomedy

The word *tragicomedy* is much newer than the words *tragedy* and *comedy*; it first appeared about 186 B.C., when Plautus spoke of *tragicocomoedia* in his *Amphitryon*, a Roman comedy in which gods assume mortal shapes in order to dupe a husband and seduce his wife. Mercury, in a joking prologue to the play, explains the author's dilemma:

> I'll make it a mixture, a tragicomedy. It wouldn't be right for me to make it all
> a comedy since kings and gods appear. Well, then, since there's a slave part
> too, I'll do as I said and make it a tragicomedy.

But the play is a traditional comedy, unalloyed with the solemnity, terror, and pity of tragedy. It shows laughable activities that finally turn out all right. It should be mentioned again, however, that although tragedy and comedy were clearly separated in the ancient world, not all ancient tragedies ended with death, or even ended unhappily. Aeschylus's trilogy, *The Oresteia*, ends with reconciliation and solemn joy (but it has been bought at the price of great suffering), and Sophocles's *Philoctetes* and Euripides's *Iphigeneia at Taurus* end with catastrophes averted. They were tragic for the Greeks because momentous issues were treated seriously, though we might say that the plots have a comic structure because they end happily. In the Renaissance there was much fussing over the meanings of tragedy, comedy, and tragicomedy, but most theoreticians inclined to the view that tragedy dealt with noble figures engaged in serious actions, was written in a lofty style, and ended unhappily; comedy dealt with humbler figures engaged in trivial actions, was written in relatively common diction, and ended happily. Tragicomedy, whether defined as some mixture (e.g., high people in trivial actions) or as a play in which, to quote Sir Philip Sidney, the writer "thrust in the clown by head and shoulders to play a part in majestical matters," was for the most part scorned by academic critics as a

TRAGI-
COMEDY
BEFORE
1900

mongrel. It was merely additive, bits of comedy added to a tragedy. At best the advocates for tragicomedy could argue that a play without the terror of tragedy and the absurdity of comedy can cover a good deal of life and can please a good many tastes. But this sort of play, unlike modern tragicomedy, is not so much a union of tragedy and comedy as an exclusion of both, lacking, for example, the awe we associate with tragedy and the fun we associate with comedy.

In the twentieth century the word and the form have become thoroughly respectable; indeed, it is now evident that most of the best plays of our century are best described not as tragedies or as comedies but as tragicomedies—distinctive fusions (not mere aggregations) of tragedy and comedy. For a start we can take William Hazlitt's statement that "man is the only animal that laughs and weeps; for he is the only animal that is struck with the difference between what things are, and what they ought to be." Another way of putting it is to say that human beings have an ideal of conduct, but circumstances and human limitations prevent them from fulfilling this ideal. This pursuit of the ideal thus can seem noble, or foolish, or a mixture of the two.

Most of the best playwrights of the twentieth century have adopted the more complicated mixed view. Comedy had customarily invoked a considerable degree of detachment; in Bergson's (1900) formula, already quoted, comedy requires an anesthesia of the spectators' hearts as they watch folly on the stage. Tragedy, on the other hand, has customarily invoked a considerable degree of involvement or sympathy; in Walpole's formula, also already quoted, "The world is a comedy to those that think, a tragedy to those that feel." But tragicomedy shows us comic characters for whom we feel deep sympathy. Pirandello, in his essay *Umorismo* (1908), gives an interesting example of the

**DETACH-
MENT AND
ENGAGE-
MENT
AGAIN**

phenomenon. Suppose, he says, we see an elderly woman with dyed hair and much too much makeup. We find her funny; but if we realize that she is trying to hold the attention of her husband, our sympathy is aroused. Our sense of her absurdity is not toally dissipated, but we feel for her and so our laughter is combined with pity.

**THEATER
OF THE
ABSURD**

In the third quarter of the twentieth century the theater that was most vital was not the Broadway musical, the earnest problem-play, or the well-made drawing-room comedy (although these continued to be written) but a fairly unified body of drama called the absurd, whose major writers are Beckett, Genet, Ionesco, Pinter, and Albee. Their theme is human anguish, but their techniques are those of comedy: improbable situations and unheroic characters who say funny things. These writers differ, of course, and differ from play to play, but they are all preoccupied with the loneliness of people in a world without the certainties afforded by God or by optimistic rationalism. This loneliness is heightened by a sense of impotence derived partly from an awareness of our inability to communicate in a society that has made language meaningless, and partly from an awareness of the precariousness of our existence in an atomic age. Behind this vision are some two hundred years of thinking that have conspired to make it difficult to think of any man as a hero who confronts a mysterious cosmic order. Man, Ionesco says in *Notes and Counter Notes*, is "cut off from his religious and metaphysical roots." One of the milestones in the journey toward contemporary nihilism is the bourgeois drama of the middle of the eighteenth century, which sought to show the dignity of the common people but which, negatively put, undermined the concept of a tragic *hero*. Instead of showing a heroic yet universal figure, it showed ordinary people in relation to their society, thus paving the way for Arthur Miller's Willy Loman, who apparently would have been okay, as we all would be, if our economic system allowed for early retirement. Miller's play makes no claim for Willy's grandeur or for the glory of life; it claims only that he is an ordinary man at the end of his rope in a deficient society and that he is entitled to a fair deal.

Other landmarks on the road to our awareness of our littleness are, like bourgeois drama, developments in thinking that were believed by their builders to be landmarks on the road to our progressive conquest of fear. Among these we can name Darwin's *The Origin of Species* (1859), which, in the popular phrase, seemed to record progress "up from apes," but which, more closely read, reduced human beings to the product of "accidental variations" and left God out of the picture, substituting for a cosmic order a barbaric struggle for existence. (In the second edition, 1860, Darwin spoke of life as "breathed by the creator," but the creator was not Darwin's concern and he later abandoned all religious beliefs. Probably he retained his belief that the process of "natural selection works solely by and for the good of each being," but by 1889 his disciple Huxley saw it differently. Huxley said he knew of no study "so unutterably saddening as that of the evolution of humanity.") Karl Marx, studying the evolution of societies at about the same time, was attributing our sense of alienation to economic forces, thereby implying that we have no identity we can properly call our own. Moreover, Marxist thinking, like Darwinian thinking, suggested that human beings could not do anything of really great importance, nor could they be blamed for their misfortunes. At the end of the nineteenth century, and in the early twentieth century, Freud, also seeking to free us from tyranny, turned to the forces within our mind. Ironically, the effort to chart our unconscious drives and anarchic impulses in order to help us to know ourselves induced a profound distrust of the self: we can scarcely be confident of our behavior, for we know that apparently heroic behavior has unconscious unheroic motives rooted in the experiences of infancy. Tragic heroes are people with complexes, and religious codes are only wishful thinking.

The result of such developments in thought seems to be that a "tragic sense" in the twentieth century commonly means a despairing or deeply uncertain view, something very different from what it meant in Greece and in Elizabethan England. This uncertainty is not merely about the cosmos but even about character or identity. In 1888, in the Preface to *Miss Julie*, August Strindberg called attention to the new sense of the instability of character:

> I have made the people in my play fairly "characterless." The middle-class conception of a fixed character was transferred to the stage, where the middle class has always ruled. A character there came to mean an actor who was always one and the same, always drunk, always comic or always melancholy,

DIMINUTION OF HUMAN BEINGS

DISSOLUTION OF CHARACTER AND PLOT

and who needed to be characterized only by some physical defect such as a club foot, a wooden leg, or a red nose, or by the repetition of some such phrase such as, "That's capital," or "Barkis is willin'." . . . Since the persons in my play are modern characters, living in a transitional era more hurried and hysterical than the previous one at least, I have depicted them as more unstable, as torn and divided, a mixture of the old and the new.

In 1902, in his preface to A Dream Play, he is more explicit: "Anything may happen, anything seems possible and probable. . . . The characters split, double, multiply, vanish, solidify, blur, clarify." Strindberg's view of the fluidity of character—the characterlessness of character, one might say—has continued and is apparent in O'Neill's *The Emperor Jones*, in almost all of Pirandello's work, in the underground film, and in much of the Theater of the Absurd. Ionesco, in *Fragments of a Journal*, says, "I often find it quite impossible to hold an opinion about a fact, a thing or a person. Since it's all a matter of interpretation, one has to choose a particular interpretation." In *Notes and Counter Notes* Ionesco said, "chance formed us," and that we would be different if we had different experiences; characteristically a few years later he said that he was no longer sure that he believed in chance.

Along with the sense of characterlessness, or at least of the mystery of character, there developed in the drama (and in the underground film and the novel) a sense of plotlessness, or fundamental untruthfulness of the traditional plot that moved by cause and effect. "Plots," Ionesco has said in *Conversations*, "are never interesting," and again he has said that a play should be able to stop at any point; it ends only because "the audience has to go home to bed. . . . It's true for real life. Why should it be different for art?" Ionesco has treated his own plots very casually, allowing directors to make "all the cuts needed" and suggesting that endings other than those he wrote are possibilities. After all, in a meaningless world one can hardly take a dramatic plot seriously. In Ionesco's *Victims of Duty* a character defends a new kind of irrational, anti-Aristotelian drama: "The theater of my dreams would be irrationalist. . . . The contemporary theater doesn't reflect the cultural tone of our period, it's not in harmony with the general drift of the other manifestations of the modern spirit. . . . We'll get rid of the principle of identity and unity of character. . . . Personality doesn't exist." A policeman-psychologist (a materialist who demands law and order) offers an old-fashioned view: "I don't believe in the absurd, everything hangs together, everything can be comprehended . . . thanks to the achievements of human thought and science," but he is murdered by the anti-Aristotelian.

Thus, Beckett's *Waiting for Godot* ends—as the first act ended—without anything ending:

> VLADIMIR: Well? Shall we go?
> ESTRAGON: Yes, let's go.
>
> *They do not move.*
> *Curtain.*

To bring an action to a completion, as drama traditionally did, is to imply an orderly world of cause and effect, of beginnings and endings, but for the dramatists of the absurd, there is no such pattern. At best it is *Hamlet* as Tom Stoppard's Rosencrantz and Guildenstern see it: they are supposed to do a job they don't understand, and instead of a pattern or "order" they encounter only "Incidents! Incidents! Dear God, is it too much to expect a little sustained action?" Well, yes; it is too much to expect.

There can be no tragedy, because, as Ionesco explains in *Notes*, tragedy admits the existence of fate or destiny, which is to say it admits the existence of objective (however incomprehensible) laws ruling the universe, whereas the new comic perception of incongruity is that existence itself is absurd because there is no objective law. The new comic vision is far darker than the old tragic vision; it has nothing in it of what Yeats called "tragic joy." But what is our reaction to this joyless comedy? Let Ionesco, whose plays sometimes include meaningless babble, have the last word:

> The fact of being astonishes us, in a world that now seems all illusion and pretense, in which all human behavior tells of absurdity and all history of absolute futility; all reality and all language appear to lose their articulation, to disintegrate and collapse, so what possible reaction is there left, when everything has ceased to matter, but laugh at it all.[4]

3. A Note on the Origins of Greek Drama and on the Structure of Greek Tragedy

Although the ancient Greeks were fairly confident that they knew the origin and history of drama, modern scholars are less certain. The Greeks—notably Aristotle (384–322 B.C.)—said that both tragedy and comedy originated in improvisations; tragedy, according to Aristotle, originated in improvisations in choral poems honoring Dionysus (the god of fertility and wine), and comedy originated in improvisations in phallic songs. Around the middle of the sixth century B.C. a man named Thespis stepped out of the chorus and, singing in a different meter, became an impersonator who sang not *about* a god but *in the role of* a god. Thespis thus was the first actor, and by taking on an identity apart from the chorus, he and his successors made possible dialogue between a character and the chorus. Later the playwright Aeschylus (525–456 B.C.) added a second actor, thus increasing the dramatic (as opposed to the lyric and narrative) element, and still later Sophocles (c. 496–406 B.C.) added the third. The number of actors became fixed at three, so in ancient Greek drama there are never more than three speaking parts onstage at one time. However, since the actors could double in roles, there may be eight or even ten speaking parts in a play.

THE TRAGEDY OF COMEDY

THE ORIGINS

---

[4] *Notes and Counter Notes: Writings on the Theatre* (New York: Grove Press, 1964), p. 163.

Greek Theatre of Epidaurus on the Peloponnesus east of Nauplia. (Photograph: Frederick Ayer, Photo Researchers, Inc.)

Unfortunately, there is little evidence to support the assertion that Greek tragedy originated in festivals honoring Dionysus. The chief evidence for the theory, aside from Aristotle's assertion (made some three centuries after the supposed fact), is that tragic plays from 534 B.C. were indeed performed at a festival called the Dionysia, honoring Dionysus. But, surprisingly, Dionysus figures importantly in only one Greek tragedy, which is puzzling if Greek tragedy really did originate in songs honoring him. The old view dies hard, however, and one still usually reads that tragedy originated in choral songs sung at fertility festivals honoring Dionysus, and that at some decisive moment Thespis impersonated him or some other god, and tragic drama was born.

A sort of corollary goes thus: Since Dionysus was god of the vine, the original songs were performed during revels in honor of the rebirth of the vine, which was seen as the rebirth of the year, the renewal of life after the death of the year in winter. The celebration of the renewal of the "year spirit" involved dramatizing the death of this divine power, and that's what Greek tragedy supposedly shows, though the "divine power" or "year spirit" came to be put into the forms of Greek heroes rather than of the god Dionysus. This is all pretty imaginative; skeptics have asked not only why Dionysus virtually disappears from the plays but also why these plays, supposedly rooted in festivals honoring the renewal of the year, end with death and lamentation rather than with renewal and joy. To the second objection, the answer is sometimes made that the plays do indeed include a suggestion of renewal; the hero comes to perceive his or her fate, and in recognizing it, and in magnificently singing about it, shows a sort of spiritual rebirth. Confronted with this answer, skeptics remain (justifiably) skeptical.

One other alleged connection with ritual should be mentioned. We know that Greek actors wore masks when they performed. Advocates of the ritual origin of Greek drama argue that the masks derived from masks that priests wore for two reasons: to impersonate the gods, and to disguise themselves lest the gods be displeased with them. Skeptics reply that the masks, with their bold, stylized features, were necessary in order to identify the characters to the audience in the vast theaters, since a Greek theater held some 15,000 people. That is, even a spectator at a great distance from the stage would immediately be able to know, upon seeing a character enter with a stereotyped mask, that this was a tragic king, or a young woman, or a messenger, or whatever. It is also argued that the mouths of the masks were designed to serve as megaphones, though in fact the acoustics in Greek theaters are so remarkably good that megaphones seem unnecessary.

A tragedy commonly begins with a *prologue*, during which the exposition is given. Next comes the chorus's *ode* of entrance, sung while the chorus marches into the theater, through the side aisles and onto the orchestra. The ensuing *scene* is followed by a choral song. Usually there are four or five scenes, alternating with odes. Each of these choral odes has a *strophe* (lines presumably sung while the chorus dances in one direction) and an *antistrophe* (lines presumably sung while the chorus retraces its steps). Sometimes a third part, an

THE STRUCTURE OF GREEK TRAGEDY

epode, concludes an ode. (In addition to odes that are *stasima,* there can be odes within episodes; the fourth episode of *Antigonê* contains an ode complete with *epode.*) After the last part of the last ode comes the epilogue or final scene.

The actors (all male) seem to have chanted much of the play. Perhaps the total result of combining speech with music and dancing was a sort of music-drama roughly akin to opera with some spoken dialogue, such as Mozart's *Magic Flute.*

For a brief additional remark about Dionysus, see the entry on him in the Glossary; for information about the Greek theater, see the illustration on page 80, and the entry on *Greek theater* in the Glossary. These entries include suggestions for further reading.

OEDIPUS THE KING

Sophocles

Translated into English verse by H. D. F. Kitto

> Sophocles (c. 496–406 B.C.), the son of a wealthy Athenian, is one of the three Greek tragic writers whose work survives. (The other two are Aeschylus and Euripides.) Of Sophocles's more than 120 plays, we have 7. The exact dates of most of Sophocles's plays are unknown. *Antigone* probably was written about 441 B.C.; *Oedipus the King*, which deals with earlier material concerning the House of Oedipus, was written later, about 430 B.C. Some twenty-five years later, when he was almost ninety, Sophocles wrote *Oedipus at Colonus*, dramatizing Oedipus's last deeds.

DRAMATIS PERSONAE

OEDIPUS, *King of Thebes*
PRIEST OF ZEUS
CREON, *brother of Iocasta*
TEIRESIAS, *a Seer*
IOCASTA, *Queen of Thebes*
A CORINTHIAN SHEPHERD
A THEBAN SHEPHERD
A MESSENGER
CHORUS *of Theban citizens*
PRIESTS, ATTENDANTS, *etc.*

Scene: Thebes, before the royal palace.

Greek National Theatre Company production at the Epidaurus Festival of Ancient Greek Drama with Alexis Minotis as Oedipus. (Photo by Dimitrios Harissiadis.)

OEDIPUS:

My children, latest brood of ancient Cadmus,
What purpose brings you here, a multitude
Bearing the boughs that mark the suppliant?
Why is our air so full of frankincense,
5 So full of hymns and prayers and lamentations?
This, children, was no matter to entrust
To others: therefore I myself am come
Whose fame is known to all—I, Oedipus.
—You, Sir, are pointed out by length of years
10 To be the spokesman: tell me, what is in
Your hearts? What fear? What sorrow? Count on all
That I can do, for I am not so hard
As not to pity such a supplication.

PRIEST:

Great King of Thebes, and sovereign Oedipus,
15 Look on us, who now stand before the altars—
Some young, still weak of wing; some bowed with age—
The priests, as I, of Zeus; and these, the best
Of our young men; and in the market-place,
And by Athena's temples and the shrine
20 Of fiery divination, there is kneeling,
Each with his suppliant branch, the rest of Thebes.
The city, as you see yourself, is now
Storm-tossed, and can no longer raise its head
Above the waves and angry surge of death.
25 The fruitful blossoms of the land are barren,
The herds upon our pastures, and our wives
In childbirth, barren. Last, and worst of all,
The withering god of fever swoops on us
To empty Cadmus' city and enrich
30 Dark Hades with our groans and lamentations.
No god we count you, that we bring our prayers,
I and these children, to your palace-door,
But wise above all other men to read
Life's riddles, and the hidden ways of Heaven;
35 For it was you who came and set us free
From the blood-tribute that the cruel Sphinx
Had laid upon our city; without our aid
Or our instruction, but, as we believe,
With god as ally, you gave us back our life.
40 So now, most dear, most mighty Oedipus,
We all entreat you on our bended knees,
Come to our rescue, whether from the gods
Or from some man you can find means to save.

For I have noted, *that* man's counsel is
Of best effect, who has been tried in action.   45
Come, noble Oedipus! Come, save our city.
Be well advised; for that past service given
This city calls you Savior; of your kingship
Let not the record be that first we rose
From ruin, then to ruin fell again.   50
No, save our city, let it stand secure.
You brought us gladness and deliverance
Before; now do no less. You rule this land;
Better to rule it full of living men
Than rule a desert; citadel or ship   55
Without its company of men is nothing.

OEDIPUS:

My children, what you long for, that I know
Indeed, and pity you. I know how cruelly
You suffer; yet, though sick, not one of you
Suffers a sickness half as great as mine.   60
Yours is a single pain; each man of you
Feels but his own. My heart is heavy with
The city's pain, my own, and yours together.
You come to me not as to one asleep
And needing to be wakened; many a tear   65
I have been shedding, every path of thought
Have I been pacing; and what remedy,
What single hope my anxious thought has found
That I have tried. Creon, Menoeceus' son,
My own wife's brother, I have sent to Delphi   70
To ask in Phoebus' house what act of mine,
What word of mine, may bring deliverance.
Now, as I count the days, it troubles me
What he is doing; his absence is prolonged
Beyond the proper time. But when he comes   75
Then write me down a villain, if I do
Not each particular that the god discloses.

PRIEST:

You give us hope.—And here is more, for they
Are signaling that Creon has returned.

OEDIPUS:

O Lord Apollo, even as Creon smiles,   80
Smile now on us, and let it be deliverance!

PRIEST:

The news is good; or he would not be wearing
That ample wreath of richly berried laurel.

OEDIPUS:

We soon shall know; my voice will reach so far:
Creon my lord, my kinsman, what response   85
Do you bring with you from the god of Delphi?

[*Enter* CREON.]

CREON:

Good news! Our sufferings, if they are guided right,
Can even yet turn to a happy issue.

OEDIPUS:
This only leaves my fear and confidence
90 In equal balance: what did Phoebus say?
CREON:
Is it your wish to hear it now, in public,
Or in the palace? I am at your service.
OEDIPUS:
Let them all hear! Their sufferings distress
Me more than if my own life were at stake.
CREON:
95 Then I will tell you what Apollo said—
And it was very clear. There is pollution
Here in our midst, long-standing. This must we
Expel, nor let it grow past remedy.
OEDIPUS:
What has defiled us? and how are we to purge it?
CREON:
100 By banishing or killing one who murdered,
And so called down this pestilence upon us.
OEDIPUS:
Who is the man whose death the god denounces?
CREON:
Before the city passed into your care,
My lord, we had a king called Laius.
OEDIPUS:
105 So I have often heard.—I never saw him.
CREON:
His death, Apollo clearly charges us,
We must avenge upon his murderers.
OEDIPUS:
Where are they now? And where shall we disclose
The unseen traces of that ancient crime?
CREON:
110 The god said, Here.—A man who hunts with care
May often find what other men will miss.
OEDIPUS:
Where was he murdered? In the palace here?
Or in the country? Or was he abroad?
CREON:
He made a journey to consult the god,
115 He said—and never came back home again.
OEDIPUS:
But was there no report? no fellow traveler
Whose knowledge might have helped you in your
        search?
CREON:
All died, except one terror-stricken man,
And he could tell us nothing—next to nothing.
OEDIPUS:
And what was that? One thing might lead to
120   much,
If only we could find one ray of light.

CREON:
He said they met with brigands—not with one,
But a whole company; they killed Laius.
OEDIPUS:
A brigand would not *dare*—unless perhaps
Conspirators in Thebes had bribed the man.   125
CREON:
There *was* conjecture; but disaster came
And we were leaderless, without our king.
OEDIPUS:
Disaster? With a king cut down like that
You did not seek the cause? Where was the hin-
        drance?
CREON:
The Sphinx. *Her* riddle pressed us harder still;   130
For Laius—out of sight was out of mind.
OEDIPUS:
I will begin again; *I'll* find the truth.
The dead man's cause has found a true defender
In Phoebus, and in you. And I will join you
In seeking vengeance on behalf of Thebes   135
And Phoebus too; indeed, I must: if I
Remove this taint, it is not for a stranger,
But for myself: the man who murdered him
Might make the same attempt on me; and so,
Avenging him, I shall protect myself.—   140
    Now you, my sons, without delay, arise,
Take up your suppliant branches.—Someone, go
And call the people here, for I will do
What can be done; and either, by the grace
Of God we shall be saved—or we shall fall.   145
PRIEST:
My children, we will go: the King has promised
All that we came to ask.—O Phoebus, thou
Hast given us an answer: give us too
Protection! grant remission of the plague!
                    [*Exeunt* CREON, PRIESTS, *etc.*
                        OEDIPUS *remains.*]

[*Enter the* CHORUS *representing the citizens of
Thebes.*]

Strophe 1

CHORUS:
Sweet is the voice of the god, that
[*mainly dactyls:* ♩]¹   sounds in the   150
Golden shrine of Delphi.

¹ Taking a hint from the French translators for the
Budé series I have here and there added to the lyrical
portions a quasi-musical indication of tempo or mood,
on no authority except that of common sense. These

What message has it sent to Thebes? My trembling
Heart is torn with anguish.
Thou god of Healing, Phoebus Apollo,
155 How do I fear! What hast thou in mind
To bring upon us now? what is to be fulfilled
From days of old?
Tell me this, O Voice divine,
Thou child of golden Hope.

Antistrophe 1

First on the Daughter of Zeus I call for
160 Help, divine Athene;
And Artemis, whose throne is all the earth, whose
Shrine is in our city;
Apollo too, who shoots from afar:
Trinity of Powers, come to our defense!
165 If ever in the past, when ruin threatened us,
You stayed its course
And turned aside the flood of Death,
O then, protect us now!

Strophe 2

[*agitated*: ⅜] Past counting are the woes we suffer;
170 Affliction bears on all the city, and
Nowhere is any defense against destruction.
The holy soil can bring no increase,
Our women suffer and cry in childbirth
But do not bring forth living children.
175 The souls of those who perish, one by one,
Unceasingly, swift as raging fire,
Rise and take their flight to the dark realms of the
dead.

Antistrophe 2

Past counting, those of us who perish:
They lie upon the ground, unpitied,
180 Unburied, infecting the air with deadly pollution.

---

may at least serve to remind the reader, if he needs
reminding, that the lyrics were not recited; they were a
fusion of intense poetry, music, and dancing. Of the
music we know nothing; of the dance we can at least
infer that its range extended from grave processional
movements to the expression of great excitement,
whether of joy or despair. [Kitto.] **dactyls**: lines consisting of feet composed of two short syllables followed by
one long syllable

Young wives, and gray-haired mothers with them,
From every quarter approach the altars
And cry aloud in supplication.
The prayer for healing, the loud wail of lament,
Together are heard in dissonance: 185
O thou golden Daughter of Zeus, grant thy aid!

Strophe 3

[*mainly iambic*: ⅜][2] The fierce god of War has laid
aside
His spear; but yet his terrible cry
Rings in our ears; he spreads death and
destruction.
Ye gods, drive him back to his distant home!   190
For what the light of day has spared,
That the darkness of night destroys.
Zeus our father! All power is thine:
The lightning-flash is thine: hurl upon him
Thy thunderbolt, and quell this god of War!   195

Antistrophe 3

We pray, Lord Apollo: draw thy bow
In our defense. Thy quiver is full of
Arrows unerring: shoot! slay the destroyer!
And thou, radiant Artemis, lend thy aid!
Thou whose hair is bound in gold,   200
Bacchus, lord of the sacred dance,
Theban Bacchus! Come, show thyself!
Display thy blazing torch; drive from our midst
The savage god, abhorred by other gods!
OEDIPUS:
Would you have answer to these prayers? Then
hear   205
My words; give heed; your help may bring
Deliverance, and the end of all our troubles.
Here do I stand before you all, a stranger
Both to the deed and to the story.—What
Could I have done alone, without a clue?   210
But I was yet a foreigner; it was later
That I became a Theban among Thebans.
So now do I proclaim to all the city:
If any Theban knows by what man's hand
He perished, Laius, son of Labdacus,   215
Him I command to tell me all he can;
And if he is afraid, let him annul
Himself the charge he fears; no punishment
Shall fall on him, save only to depart

---

[2] **iambic**: referring to a metrical foot consisting of one
short syllable followed by one long syllable

220 Unharmed from Thebes. Further, if any knows
The slayer to be a stranger from abroad,
Let him speak out; I will reward him, and
Besides, he will have all my gratitude.
But if you still keep silent, if any man
225 Fearing for self or friend shall disobey me,
This will I do—and listen to my words:
Whoever he may be, I do forbid
All in this realm, of which I am the King
And high authority, to shelter in their houses
230 Or speak to him, or let him be their partner
In prayers or sacrifices to the gods, or give
Him lustral water; I command you all
To drive him from your doors; for he it is
That brings this plague upon us, as the god
235 Of Delphi has but now declared to me.—
So stern an ally do I make myself
Both of the god and of our murdered king.—
And for the man that slew him, whether he
Slew him alone, or with a band of helpers,
240 I lay this curse upon him, that the wretch
In wretchedness and misery may live.
And more: if with my knowledge he be found
To share my hearth and home, then upon me
Descend that doom that I invoke on him.
245 This charge I lay upon you, to observe
All my commands: to aid myself, the god,
And this our land, so spurned of Heaven, so
    ravaged.
For such a taint we should not leave unpurged—
The death of such a man, and he your king—
250 Even if Heaven had not commanded us,
But we should search it out. Now, since 'tis I
That wear the crown that he had worn before me,
And have his Queen to wife, and common
    children
Were born to us, but that his own did perish,
255 And sudden death has carried him away—
Because of this, I will defend his cause
As if it were my father's; nothing I
Will leave undone to find the man who killed
The son of Labdacus, and offspring of
260 Polydorus, Cadmus, and of old Agenor.
On those that disobey, this is my curse:
May never field of theirs give increase, nor
Their wives have children; may our present
    plagues,
And worse, be ever theirs, for their destruction.
265 But for the others, all with whom my words
Find favour, this I pray: Justice and all
The gods be ever at your side to help you.
    CHORUS-LEADER:
Your curse constrains me; therefore will I speak.
I did not kill him, neither can I tell

Who did. It is for Phoebus, since he laid   270
The task upon us, to declare the man.
    OEDIPUS:
True; but to force the gods against their will—
    That is a thing beyond all human power.
    CHORUS-LEADER:
All I could say is but a second best.
    OEDIPUS:
Though it were third best, do not hold it back.   275
    CHORUS-LEADER:
I know of none that reads Apollo's mind
So surely as the lord Teiresias;
Consulting him you best might learn the truth.
    OEDIPUS:
Not even this have I neglected: Creon
Advised me, and already I sent   280
Two messengers.—Strange he has not come.
    CHORUS-LEADER:
There's nothing else but old and idle gossip.
    OEDIPUS:
And what was that? I clutch at any straw.
    CHORUS-LEADER:
They said that he was killed by travelers.
    OEDIPUS:
So I have heard; but no one knows a witness.   285
    CHORUS-LEADER:
But if he is not proof against *all* fear
He'll not keep silent when he hears your curse.
    OEDIPUS:
And will they fear a curse, who dared to kill?
    CHORUS-LEADER:
Here is the one to find him, for at last
They bring the prophet here. He is inspired.   290
The only man whose heart is filled with truth.

[*Enter* TEIRESIAS, *led by a boy.*]

    OEDIPUS:
Teiresias, by your art you read the signs
And secrets of the earth and of the sky;
Therefore you know, although you cannot see,
The plague that is besetting us; from this   295
No other man but you, my lord, can save us.
Phoebus has said—you may have heard already—
In answer to our question, that this plague
Will never cease unless we can discover
What men they were who murdered Laius,   300
And punish them with death or banishment.
Therefore give freely all that you have learned
From birds or other form of divination;
Save us; save me, the city, and yourself,
From the pollution that his bloodshed causes.   305
No finer task, than to give all one has
In helping others; we are in your hands.

TEIRESIAS:
Ah! what a burden knowledge is, when knowledge
Can be of no avail! I knew this well,
310 And yet forgot, or I should not have come.
OEDIPUS:
Why, what is this? Why are you so despondent?
TEIRESIAS:
Let me go home! It will be best for you,
And best for me, if you will let me go.
OEDIPUS:
But to withhold your knowledge! This is wrong,
315 Disloyal to the city of your birth.
TEIRESIAS:
I know that what you say will lead you on
To ruin; therefore, lest the same befall me too . . .
OEDIPUS:
No, by the gods! Say all you know, for we
Go down upon our knees, your suppliants.
TEIRESIAS:
320 Because *you* do *not* know! I never shall
Reveal my burden—I will not say *yours*.
OEDIPUS:
You know, and will not tell us? Do you wish
To ruin Thebes and to destroy us all?
TEIRESIAS:
My pain, and yours, will not be caused by me.
325 Why these vain questions?—for I will not speak.
OEDIPUS:
You villain!—for you would provoke a stone
To anger: you'll not speak, but show yourself
So hard of heart and so inflexible?
TEIRESIAS:
You heap the blame on me; but what is yours
330 You do not know—therefore *I* am the villain!
OEDIPUS:
And who would not be angry, finding that
You treat our people with such cold disdain?
TEIRESIAS:
The truth will come to light, without *my* help.
OEDIPUS:
If it is bound to come, you ought to speak it.
TEIRESIAS:
335 I'll say no more, and you, if so you choose,
May rage and bluster on without restraint.
OEDIPUS:
Restraint? Then I'll show none! I'll tell you all
That I can see in you: I do believe
This crime was planned and carried out by you,
340 All but the killing; and were you not blind
I'd say your hand alone had done that murder.
TEIRESIAS:
So? Then I tell you this: submit yourself
To that decree that you have made; from now
Address no word to these men or to me:
345 *You* are the man whose crimes pollute our city.

OEDIPUS:
What, does your impudence extend thus far?
And do you hope that it will go scot-free?
TEIRESIAS:
It will. I have a champion—the truth.
OEDIPUS:
Who taught you that? For it was not your art.
TEIRESIAS:
No; you! You made me speak, against my will.   350
OEDIPUS:
Speak what? Say it again, and say it clearly.
TEIRESIAS:
Was I not clear? Or are you tempting me?
OEDIPUS:
Not clear enough for me. Say it again.
TEIRESIAS:
You are yourself the murderer you seek.
OEDIPUS:
You'll not affront me twice and go unpunished!   355
TEIRESIAS:
Then shall I give you still more cause for rage?
OEDIPUS:
Say what you will; you'll say it to no purpose.
TEIRESIAS:
I know, *you* do not know, the hideous life
Of shame you lead with those most near to you.
OEDIPUS:
You'll pay most dearly for this insolence!   360
TEIRESIAS:
No, not if Truth is strong, and can prevail.
OEDIPUS:
It is—except in you; for you are blind
In eyes and ears and brains and everything.
TEIRESIAS:
You'll not forget these insults that you throw
At me, when all men throw the same at you.   365
OEDIPUS:
You live in darkness; you can do no harm
To me or any man who has his eyes.
TEIRESIAS:
No; *I* am not to bring you down, because
Apollo is enough; he'll see to it.
OEDIPUS:
Creon, or you? Which of you made this plot?   370
TEIRESIAS:
Creon's no enemy of yours; you are your own.
OEDIPUS:
O Wealth! O Royalty! whose commanding art
Outstrips all other arts in life's contentions!
How great a store of envy lies upon you,
If for this scepter, that the city gave   375
Freely to me, unasked—if now my friend,
The trusty Creon, burns to drive me hence
And steal it from me! So he has suborned
This crafty schemer here, this mountebank,

380 Whose purse alone has eyes, whose art is blind.—
Come, prophet, show your title! When the Sphinx
Chanted her music here, why did not *you*
Speak out and save the city? Yet such a question
Was one for augury, not for mother wit.
385 You were no prophet then; your birds, your voice
From Heaven, were dumb. But I, who came by
chance,
I, knowing nothing, put the Sphinx to flight,
Thanks to my wit—no thanks to divination!
And now you try to drive me out; you hope
390 When Creon's king to bask in Creon's favor.
You'll expiate the curse? Ay, and repent it,
Both you and your accomplice. But that you
Seem old, I'd teach you what you gain by treason!
  CHORUS-LEADER:
My lord, he spoke in anger; so I think,
395 Did you. What help in angry speeches? Come,
This is the task, how we can best discharge
The duty that the god has laid on us.
  TEIRESIAS:
King though you are, I claim the privilege
Of equal answer. No, I have the right;
400 I am no slave of yours—I serve Apollo,
And therefore am not listed *Creon's* man.
Listen—since you have taunted me with
blindness!
You have your sight, and yet you cannot see
Where, nor with whom, you live, nor in what
horror.
405 Your parents—do you know them? or that you
Are enemy to your kin, alive or dead?
And that a father's and a mother's curse
Shall join to drive you headlong out of Thebes
And change the light that now you see to darkness?
410 Your cries of agony, where will they reach?
Where on Cithaeron will they not re-echo?
Where you have learned what meant the mar-
riage-song
Which bore you to an evil haven here
After so fair a voyage? And you are blind
415 To other horrors, which shall make you one
With your own children. Therefore, heap your
scorn
On Creon and on me, for no man living
Will meet a doom more terrible than yours.
  OEDIPUS:
What? Am I to suffer words like this from him?
420 Ruin, damnation seize you! Off at once
Out of our sight! Go! Get you whence you came!
  TEIRESIAS:
Had you not called me, I should not be here.
  OEDIPUS:
And had I known that you would talk such folly,
I'd not have called you to a house of mine.

  TEIRESIAS:
To you I seem a fool, but to your parents, 425
To those who did beget you, I was wise.
  OEDIPUS:
Stop! Who were they? Who *were* my parents? Tell
me!
  TEIRESIAS:
This day will show your birth and your
destruction.
  OEDIPUS:
You are too fond of dark obscurities.
  TEIRESIAS:
But do you not excel in reading riddles? 430
  OEDIPUS:
I scorn your taunts; my skill has brought me glory.
  TEIRESIAS:
And this success brought you to ruin too.
  OEDIPUS:
I am content, if so I saved this city.
  TEIRESIAS:
Then I will leave you. Come, boy, take my hand.
  OEDIPUS:
Yes, let him take it. You are nothing but 435
Vexation here. Begone, and give me peace!
  TEIRESIAS:
When I have had my say. No frown of yours
Shall frighten *me*; you cannot injure me.
Here is my message: that man whom you seek
With threats and proclamations for the death 440
Of Laius, he is living here; he's thought
To be a foreigner, but shall be found
Theban by birth—and little joy will this
Bring *him*; when, with his eyesight turned to
blindness,
His wealth to beggary, on foreign soil 445
With staff in hand he'll tap his way along,
His children with him; and he will be known
Himself to be their father and their brother,
The husband of the mother who gave him birth,
Supplanter of his father, and his slayer. 450
—There! Go, and think on this; and if you find
That I'm deceived, say then—and not before—
That I am ignorant in divination.
  [*Exeunt severally* TEIRESIAS *and* OEDIPUS.]

Strophe 1

  CHORUS:
The voice of god rang out in the holy cavern,
Denouncing one who has killed a King—the
crime of crimes. 455
  Who is the man? Let him begone in
  Headlong flight, swift as a horse!

[*anapests*]³ For the terrible god, like a warrior armed,
Stands ready to strike with a lightning-flash:
460   The Furies who punish crime, and never fail,
Are hot in their pursuit.

Antistrophe 1

The snow is white on the cliffs of high Parnassus.
It has flashed a message: Let every Theban join the hunt!
Lurking in caves among the mountains,
465   Deep in the woods—where is the man?
[*anapests*]³ In wearisome flight, unresting, alone,
An outlaw, he shuns Apollo's shrine;
    But ever the living menace of the god
    Hovers around his head.

Strophe 2

470   [*choriambics*]⁴ Strange, disturbing, what the wise
Prophet has said. What can he mean?
Neither can I believe, nor can I disbelieve;
I do not know what to say.
I look here, and there; nothing can I find—
475   No strife, either now or in the past,
Between the kings of Thebes and Corinth.
A hand unknown struck down the King;
Though I would learn who it was dealt the blow,
That *he* is guilty whom all revere—
480   How can I believe this with no proof?

Antistrophe 2

Zeus, Apollo—they have knowledge;
They understand the ways of life.
Prophets are men, like me; that they can understand
More than is revealed to me—
485   Of that, I can find nowhere certain proof,
Though one man is wise, another foolish.
Until the charge is manifest
I will not credit his accusers.

³ **anapests**: metrical feet consisting of two short syllables followed by one long syllable
⁴ **choriambics**: metrical feet consisting of a trochee (a long syllable followed by a short syllable) and an iamb (a short syllable followed by a long syllable)

I saw myself how the Sphinx challenged him:
He proved his wisdom; he saved our city;   490
Therefore how can I now condemn him?

[*Enter* CREON]

CREON:
They tell me, Sirs, that Oedipus the King
Has made against me such an accusation
That I will not endure. For if he thinks
That in this present trouble I have done   495
Or said a single thing to do him harm,
Then let me die, and not drag out my days
With such a name as that. For it is not
One injury this accusation does me;
It touches my whole life, if you, my friends,   500
And all the city are to call me traitor.
CHORUS-LEADER:
The accusation may perhaps have come
From heat of temper, not from sober judgment.
CREON:
What was it made him think contrivances
Of mine suborned the seer to tell his lies?   505
CHORUS-LEADER:
Those were his words; I do not know his reasons.
CREON:
Was he in earnest, master of himself,
When he attacked me with this accusation?
CHORUS-LEADER:
I do not closely scan what kings are doing.—
But here he comes in person from the palace.   510

[*Enter* OEDIPUS.]

OEDIPUS:
What, *you*? You dare come here? How can you find
The impudence to show yourself before
My house, when you are clearly proven
To have sought my life and tried to steal my crown?
Why, do you think me then a coward, or   515
A fool, that you should try to lay this plot?
Or that I should not see what you were scheming,
And so fall unresisting, blindly, to you?
But you were mad, so to attempt the throne,
Poor and unaided; this is not encompassed   520
Without the strong support of friends and money!
CREON:
This you must do: now you have had your say
Hear my reply; then yourself shall judge.
OEDIPUS:
A ready tongue! But I am bad at listening—
To you. For I have found how much you hate me.   525
CREON:
One thing: first listen to what I have to say.

OEDIPUS:
One thing: do not pretend you're not a villain.
CREON:
If you believe it is a thing worth having,
Insensate stubbornness, then you are wrong.
OEDIPUS:
530 If you believe that one can harm a kinsman
Without retaliation, you are wrong.
CREON:
With this I have no quarrel; but explain
What injury you say that I have done you.
OEDIPUS:
Did you advise, or did you not, that I
Should send a man for that most reverend
535   prophet?
CREON:
I did, and I am still of that advice.
OEDIPUS:
How long a time is it since Laius . . .
CREON:
Since Laius did *what*? How can I say?
OEDIPUS:
Was seen no more, but met a violent death?
CREON:
540 It would be many years now past and gone.
OEDIPUS:
And had this prophet learned his art already?
CREON:
Yes, his repute was great—as it is now.
OEDIPUS:
Did he make any mention then of me?
CREON:
He never spoke of you within my hearing.
OEDIPUS:
545 Touching the murder: did you make no search?
CREON:
No search? Of course we did; but we found
   nothing.
OEDIPUS:
And why did this wide prophet not speak *then*?
CREON:
Who knows? Where I know nothing I say nothing.
OEDIPUS:
This much you know—and you'll do well to
   answer:
CREON:
550 What is it? If I know, I'll tell you freely.
OEDIPUS:
That if he had not joined with you, he'd not
Have said that I was Laius' murderer.
CREON:
If he said this, I did not know.—But I
May rightly question you, as you have me.

OEDIPUS:
Ask what you will. You'll never prove *I* killed him.   555
CREON:
Why then: are you not married to my sister?
OEDIPUS:
I am indeed; it cannot be denied.
CREON:
You share with her the sovereignty of Thebes?
OEDIPUS:
She need but ask, and anything is hers.
CREON:
And am I not myself conjoined with you?   560
OEDIPUS:
You are; not rebel therefore, but a traitor!
CREON:
Not so, if you will reason with yourself,
As I with you. This first: would any man,
To gain no increase of authority,
Choose kingship, with its fears and sleepless
   nights?   565
Not I. What I desire, what every man
Desires, if he has wisdom, is to take
The substance, not the show, of royalty.
For now, through you, I have both power and
   ease,
But were I king, I'd be oppressed with cares.   570
Not so: while I have ample sovereignty
And rule in peace, why should I want the crown?
I am not yet so mad as to give up
All that which brings me honor and advantage.
Now, every man greets me, and I greet him;   575
Those who have need of you make much of me,
Since I can make or mar them. Why should I
Surrender this to load myself with that?
A man of sense was never yet a traitor;
I have no taste for that, nor could I force   580
Myself to aid another's treachery.
   But you can test me: go to Delphi; ask
If I reported rightly what was said.
And further: if you find that I had dealings
With that diviner, you may take and kill me   585
Not with your single vote, but yours and mine,
But not on bare suspicion, unsupported.
How wrong it is, to use a random judgment
And think the false man true, the true man false!
To spurn a loyal friend, that is no better   590
Than to destroy the life to which we cling.
This you will learn in time, for Time alone
Reveals the upright man; a single day
Suffices to unmask the treacherous.
CHORUS-LEADER:
My lord, he speaks with caution, to avoid   595
Grave error. Hasty judgment is not sure.

OEDIPUS:
But when an enemy is quick to plot
And strike, I must be quick in answer too.
If I am slow, and wait, then I shall find
600   That he has gained his end, and I am lost.
CREON:
What do you wish? To drive me into exile?
OEDIPUS:
No, more than exile: I will have your life.[5]
CREON:
<When will it cease, this monstrous rage of
    yours?>
OEDIPUS:
When your example shows what comes of envy.
CREON:
605   Must you be stubborn? Cannot you believe me?
OEDIPUS:
<You speak to me as if I were a fool!>
CREON:
Because I know you're wrong.
OEDIPUS: Right, for myself!
CREON:
It is not right for me!
OEDIPUS: But you're a traitor.
CREON:
What if your charge is false?
OEDIPUS: I have to govern.
CREON:
Not govern badly!
610   OEDIPUS: Listen to him, Thebes!
CREON:
You're not the city! I am Theban too.
CHORUS-LEADER:
My lords, no more! Here comes the Queen, and
    not

---

[5] The next two verses, as they stand in the mss., are
impossible. Editors are agreed on this, though no single
remedy has found general acceptance. The mss. attribute v. 604 [Oedipus' next speech] to Creon, and v. 605
[Creon's next speech] to Oedipus. I can make no real
sense of this: the only φθόνος, "envy," that is in question
is the envy of his royal power that Oedipus is attributing
to Creon; and the words ὑπείξων, "yield," "not to be
stubborn," and πιστεύσων, "believe," must surely be
used by Creon of Oedipus, not by Oedipus of Creon.
Since a translator who hopes to be acted must give the
actors something to say, preferably good sense, and
cannot fob them off with a row of dots, I have recon-
structed the passage by guesswork, putting my guesses
within brackets. I have assumed that two verses were lost,
one after v. 603 and one after v. 605, and that the wrong
attribution of vv. 604 and 605 followed almost inevitably. [Kitto.]

Too soon, to join you. With her help, you must
Compose the bitter strife that now divides you.

[*Enter* IOCASTA.]

IOCASTA:
You frantic men! What has aroused this wild   615
Dispute? Have you no shame, when such a plague
Afflicts us, to indulge in private quarrels?
Creon, go home, I pray. You, Oedipus,
Come in; do not make much of what is nothing.
CREON:
My sister: Oedipus, your husband here,   620
Has thought it right to punish me with one
Of two most awful dooms: exile, or death.
OEDIPUS:
I have: I have convicted him, Iocasta,
Of plotting secretly against my life.
CREON:
If I am guilty in a single point   625
Of such a crime, then may I die accursed.
IOCASTA:
O, by the gods, believe him, Oedipus!
Respect the oath that he has sworn, and have
Regard for me, and for these citizens.

[*In what follows, the parts given to the chorus are
sung, the rest, presumably, spoken. The rhythm
of the music and dance is either dochmiac,*[6] *five-
time, or a combination of three- and five-time.*]

Strophe

CHORUS:
My lord, I pray, give consent.   630
Yield to us; ponder well.
OEDIPUS:
What is it you would have me yield?
CHORUS:
Respect a man ripe in years,
Bound by this mighty oath he has sworn.
OEDIPUS:
Your wish is clear?
CHORUS: It is.
OEDIPUS: Then tell it me.   635
CHORUS:
Not to repel, and drive out of our midst a friend,
    Scorning a solemn curse, for uncertain cause.

---

[6] **dochmiac**: usually, but not necessarily, a metrical
foot consisting of three long and two short syllables

OEDIPUS:
I tell you this: your prayer will mean for me
My banishment from Thebes, or else my death.
CHORUS:
640 No, no! by the Sun, the chief of gods,
      Ruin and desolation and all evil come upon me
If I harbor thoughts such as these!
No; our land racked with plague breaks my heart.
    Do not now deal a new wound on Thebes to
      crown the old!
OEDIPUS:
645 Then let him be, though I must die twice over,
Or be dishonored, spurned and driven out.
It's your entreaty, and not his, that moves
My pity; he shall have my lasting hatred.
CREON:
You yield ungenerously; but when your wrath
650 Has cooled, how it will prick you! Natures such
As yours give most vexation to themselves.
OEDIPUS:
O, let me be! Get from my sight.
CREON: I go,
Misjudged by you—but these will judge me better
    [*indicating* CHORUS].
                                    [*Exit* CREON.]

Antistrophe

CHORUS:
My lady, why now delay?
655 Let the King go in with you.
IOCASTA:
When you have told me what has passed.
CHORUS:
Suspicion came.—Random words, undeserved,
Will provoke men to wrath.
IOCASTA:
It was from both?
CHORUS: It was.
IOCASTA: And what was said?
CHORUS:
It is enough for me, more than enough, when I
660 Think of our ills, that this should rest where it lies.
OEDIPUS:
You and your wise advice, blunting my wrath,
Frustrated me—and it has come to this!
CHORUS:
This, O my King, I said, and say again:
665 I should be mad, distraught,
      I should be a fool, and worse,
      If I sought to drive you away.
      Thebes was near sinking; you brought her safe

Through the storm. Now again we pray that you
    may save us.
IOCASTA:
In Heaven's name, my lord, I too must know   670
What was the reason for this blazing anger.
OEDIPUS:
There's none to whom I more defer; and so.
I'll tell you: Creon and his vile plot against me.
IOCASTA:
What has he done, that you are so incensed?
OEDIPUS:
He says that I am Laius' murderer.   675
IOCASTA:
From his own knowledge? Or has someone told
    him?
OEDIPUS:
No; that suspicion should not fall upon
Himself, he used a tool—a crafty prophet.
IOCASTA:
Why, have no fear of *that*. Listen to me,
And you will learn that the prophetic art   680
Touches our human fortunes not at all.
I soon can give you proof.—An oracle
Once came to Laius—from the god himself
I do not say, but from his ministers:
His fate it was, that should he have a son   685
By me, that son would take his father's life.
But he was killed—or so they said—by strangers,
By brigands, at a place where three ways meet.
As for the child, it was not three days old
When Laius fastened both its feet together   690
And had it cast over a precipice.
Therefore Apollo failed; for neither did
His son kill Laius, nor did Laius meet
The awful end he feared, killed by his son.
    So much for what prophetic voices uttered. 695
Have no regard for them. The god will bring
To light himself whatever thing he chooses.
OEDIPUS:
Iocasta, terror seizes me, and shakes
My very soul, at one thing you have said.
IOCASTA:
Why so? What have I said to frighten you?   700
OEDIPUS:
I think I heard you say that Laius
Was murdered at a place where three ways meet?
IOCASTA:
So it was said—indeed, they say it still.
OEDIPUS:
Where is the place where this encounter
    happened?
IOCASTA:
They call the country Phokis, and a road   705
From Delphi joins a road from Daulia.

OEDIPUS:
Since that was done, how many years have passed?
IOCASTA:
It was proclaimed in Thebes a little time
Before the city offered you the crown.
OEDIPUS:
710 O Zeus, what fate hast thou ordained for me?
IOCASTA:
What is the fear that so oppresses you?
OEDIPUS:
One moment yet: tell me of Laius.
What age was he? and what was his appearance?
IOCASTA:
A tall man, and his hair was touched with white;
715 In figure he was not unlike yourself.
OEDIPUS:
O God! Did I, then, in my ignorance,
Proclaim that awful curse against myself?
IOCASTA:
What are you saying? How you frighten me!
OEDIPUS:
I greatly fear that prophet was not blind.
720 But yet one question; that will show me more.
IOCASTA:
For all my fear, I'll tell you what I can.
OEDIPUS:
Was he alone, or did he have with him
A royal bodyguard of men-at-arms?
IOCASTA:
The company in all were five; the King
725 Rode in a carriage, and there was a Herald.
OEDIPUS:
Ah God! How clear the picture is! . . . But who,
Iocasta, brought report of this to Thebes?
IOCASTA:
A slave, the only man that was not killed.
OEDIPUS:
And is he round about the palace now?
IOCASTA:
730 No, he is not. When he returned, and saw
You ruling in the place of the dead King,
He begged me, on his bended knees, to send him
Into the hills as shepherd, out of sight,
As far as could be from the city here.
735 I sent him, for he was a loyal slave;
He well deserved this favor—and much more.
OEDIPUS:
Could he be brought back here—at once—to see
  me?
IOCASTA:
He could; but why do you desire his coming?
OEDIPUS:
I fear I have already said, Iocasta,
740 More than enough; and therefore I will see him.

IOCASTA:
Then he shall come. But, as your wife, I ask you,
What is the terror that possesses you?
OEDIPUS:
And you shall know it, since my fears have grown
So great; for who is more to me than you,
That I should speak to *him* at such a moment?   745
  My father, then, was Polybus of Corinth;
My mother, Merope. My station there
Was high as any man's—until a thing
Befell me that was strange indeed, though not
Deserving of the thought I gave to it.   750
A man said at a banquet—he was full
Of wine—that I was not my father's son.
It angered me; but I restrained myself
That day. The next I went and questioned both
My parents. They were much incensed with him   755
Who had let fall the insult. So, from them,
I had assurance. Yet the slander spread
And always chafed me. Therefore secretly,
My mother and my father unaware,
I went to Delphi. Phoebus would return   760
No answer to my question, but declared
A thing most horrible: he foretold that I
Should mate with my own mother, and beget
A brood that men would shudder to behold,
And that I was to be the murderer   765
Of my own father.
                    Therefore, back to Corinth
I never went—the stars alone have told me
Where Corinth lies—that I might never see
Cruel fulfillment of that oracle.
So journeying, I came to that same spot   770
Where, as you say, this King was killed. And now,
This is the truth, Iocasta: when I reached
The place where three ways meet, I met a herald,
And in a carriage drawn by colts was such
A man as you describe. By violence   775
The herald and the older man attempted
To push me off the road, I, in my rage,
Struck at the driver, who was hustling me.
The old man, when he saw me level with him,
Taking a double-goad, aimed at my head   780
A murderous blow. He paid for that, full measure.
Swiftly I hit him with my staff; he rolled
Out of his carriage, flat upon his back.
I killed them all.—But if, between this stranger
And Laius there was any bond of kinship,   785
Who could be in more desperate plight than I?
Who more accursèd in the eyes of Heaven?
For neither citizen nor stranger may
Receive me in his house, nor speak to me,
But he must bar the door. And it was none   790
But I invoked this curse on my own head!

And I pollute the bed of him I slew
With my own hands! Say, am I vile? Am I
Not all impure? Seeing I must be exiled,
795 And even in my exile must not go
And see my parents, nor set foot upon
My native land; or, if I do, I must
Marry my mother, and kill Polybus
My father, who engendered me and reared me.
800 If one should say it was a cruel god
Brought this upon me, would he not speak right?
   No, no, you holy powers above! Let me
Not see that day! but rather let me pass
Beyond the sight of men, before I see
805 The stain of such pollution come upon me!
   CHORUS-LEADER:
My lord, this frightens me. But you must hope,
Until we hear the tale from him that saw it.
   OEDIPUS:
That is the only hope that's left to me;
We must await the coming of the shepherd.
   IOCASTA:
810 What do you hope from him, when he is here?
   OEDIPUS:
I'll tell you: if his story shall be found
The same as yours, then I am free of guilt.
   IOCASTA:
But what have I said of especial note?
   OEDIPUS:
You said that he reported it was brigands
815 Who killed the King. If he still speaks of "men,"
It was not I; a single man, and "men,"
Are not the same. But if he says it was
A traveler journeying alone, why then,
The burden of the guilt must fall on me.
   IOCASTA:
820 But that is what he said, I do assure you!
He cannot take it back again! Not I
Alone, but the whole city heard him say it!
But even if he should revoke the tale
He told before, not even so, my lord,
825 Will he establish that the King was slain
According to the prophecy. For that was clear:
His son, and mine, should slay him.—He, poor
   thing,
Was killed himself, and never killed his father.
Therefore, so far as divination goes,
830 Or prophecy, I'll take no notice of it.
   OEDIPUS:
And that is wise.—But send a man to bring
The shepherd; I would not have that neglected.
   IOCASTA:
I'll send at once.—But come with me; for I
Would not do anything that could displease you.
                [Exeunt OEDIPUS and IOCASTA.]

Strophe 1

   CHORUS:
I pray that I may pass my life   835
[in a steady rhythm] In reverent holiness of word
   and deed.
For there are laws enthroned above;
Heaven created them,
Olympus was their father.
And mortal men had no part in their birth;   840
Nor ever shall their power pass from sight
In dull forgetfulness;
A god moves in them; he grows not old.

Antistrophe 1

Pride makes the tyrant—pride of wealth
And power, too great for wisdom and restraint;   845
For Pride will climb the topmost height;
Then is the man cast down
To uttermost destruction.
There he finds no escape, no resource.
But high contention for the city's good   850
May the gods preserve.
For me—may the gods be my defense!

Strophe 2

If there is one who walks in pride
Of word or deed, and has no fear of Justice,
No reverence for holy shrines—   855
May utter ruin fall on him!
So may his ill-starred pride be given its reward.
Those who seek dishonorable advantage
And lay violent hands on holy things
And do not shun impiety—   860
Who among these will secure himself from the
   wrath of God?
If deeds like these are honored,
Why should I join in the sacred dance?

Antistrophe 2

No longer shall Apollo's shrine,
The holy center of the Earth, receive my worship; 865
No, nor his seat at Abae, nor
The temple of Olympian Zeus,
If what the god foretold does not come to pass.
Mighty Zeus—if so I should address Thee—
O great Ruler of all things, look on this!   870

Now are thy oracles falling into contempt, and
   men
Deny Apollo's power.
Worship of the gods is passing away.

[*Enter* IOCASTA, *attended by a girl carrying a*
wreath and incense.]

IOCASTA:
My lords of Thebes, I have bethought myself
To approach the altars of the gods, and lay
875 These wreaths on them, and burn this
   frankincense.
For every kind of terror has laid hold
On Oedipus; his judgment is distracted.
He will not read the future by the past
880 But yields himself to any who speaks fear.
Since then no words of mine suffice to calm him
I turn to Thee Apollo—Thou art nearest—
Thy suppliant, with these votive offerings.
Grant us deliverance and peace, for now
885 Fear is on all, when we see Oedipus,
The helmsman of the ship, so terrified.

[*A reverent silence, while* IOCASTA *lays the*
wreath at the altar and sets fire to the incense.
The wreath will remain and the incense smoke
during the rest of the play.]
[*Enter a* SHEPHERD *from Corinth.*]

CORINTHIAN:
Might I inquire of you where I may find
The royal palace of King Oedipus?
Or, better, where himself is to be found?

CHORUS-LEADER:
890 There is the palace; himself, Sir, is within,
But here his wife and mother of his children.

CORINTHIAN:
Ever may happiness attend on her,
And hers, the wedded wife of such a man.

IOCASTA:
May you enjoy the same; your gentle words
895 Deserve no less.—Now, Sir, declare your purpose;
With what request, what message have you come?

CORINTHIAN:
With good news for your husband and his house.

IOCASTA:
What news is this? And who has sent you here?

CORINTHIAN:
I come from Corinth, and the news I bring
900 Will give you joy, though joy be crossed with grief.

IOCASTA:
What is this, with its two-fold influence?

CORINTHIAN:
The common talk in Corinth is that they
Will call on Oedipus to be their king.

IOCASTA:
What? Does old Polybus no longer reign?

CORINTHIAN:
Not now, for Death has laid him in his grave.   905

IOCASTA:
Go quickly to your master, girl; give him
The news.—You oracles, where are you now?
This is the man whom Oedipus so long
Has shunned, fearing to kill him; now he's dead,
And killed by Fortune, not by Oedipus.   910

[*Enter* OEDIPUS, *very nervous.*]

OEDIPUS:
My dear Iocasta, tell me, my dear wife,
Why have you sent to fetch me from the palace?

IOCASTA:
Listen to *him*, and as you hear, reflect
What has become of all those oracles.

OEDIPUS:
Who is this man?—What has he to tell me?   915

IOCASTA:
He is from Corinth, and he brings you news
About your father. Polybus is dead.

OEDIPUS:
What say you, sir? Tell me the news yourself.

CORINTHIAN:
If you would have me first report on this,
I tell you; death has carried him away.   920

OEDIPUS:
By treachery? Or did sickness come to him?

CORINTHIAN:
A small mischance will lay an old man low.

OEDIPUS:
Poor Polybus! He died, then, of a sickness?

CORINTHIAN:
That, and the measure of his many years.

OEDIPUS:
Ah me! Why then, Iocasta, should a man   925
Regard the Pythian house of oracles,
Or screaming birds, on whose authority
I was to slay my father? But he is dead;
The earth has covered him; and here am I,
My sword undrawn—unless perchance *my* loss   930
Has killed him; so might I be called his slayer.
But for those oracles about my father,
Those he has taken with him to the grave
Wherein he lies, and they are come to nothing.

IOCASTA:
Did I not say long since it would be so?   935

OEDIPUS:
You did; but I was led astray by fear.

IOCASTA:
So none of this deserves another thought.

OEDIPUS:
Yet how can I not fear my mother's bed?
IOCASTA:
Why should we fear, seeing that man is ruled
By chance, and there is room for no clear fore-
940   thought?
No; live at random, live as best one can.
So do not fear this marriage with your mother;
Many a man has suffered this before—
But only in his dreams. Whoever thinks
945 The least of this, he lives most comfortably.
OEDIPUS:
Your every word I do accept, if she
That bore me did not live; but as she does—
Despite your wisdom, how can I but tremble?
IOCASTA:
Yet there is comfort in your father's death.
OEDIPUS:
950 Great comfort, but still fear of her who lives.
CORINTHIAN:
And who is this who makes you so afraid?
OEDIPUS:
Merope, my man, the wife of Polybus.
CORINTHIAN:
And what in *her* gives cause of fear in *you*?
OEDIPUS:
There was an awful warning from the gods.
CORINTHIAN:
955 Can it be told, or must it be kept secret?
OEDIPUS:
No secret. Once Apollo said that I
Was doomed to lie with my own mother, and
Defile my own hands with my father's blood.
Wherefore has Corinth been, these many years,
960 My home no more. My fortunes have been fair.—
But it is good to see a parent's face.
CORINTHIAN:
It was for fear of *this* you fled the city?
OEDIPUS:
This, and the shedding of my father's blood.
CORINTHIAN:
Why then, my lord, since I am come in
    friendship,
965 I'll rid you here and now of that misgiving.
OEDIPUS:
Be sure, your recompense would be in keeping.
CORINTHIAN:
It was the chief cause of my coming here
That your return might bring me some advantage.
OEDIPUS:
Back to my parents I will never go.
CORINTHIAN:
970 My son, it is clear, you know not what you do . . .

OEDIPUS:
Not know? What is this? Tell me what you mean.
CORINTHIAN:
If for this reason you avoid your home.
OEDIPUS:
Fearing Apollo's oracle may come true.
CORINTHIAN:
And you incur pollution from your parents?
OEDIPUS:
That is the thought that makes me live in terror. 975
CORINTHIAN:
I tell you then, this fear of yours is idle.
OEDIPUS:
How? Am I not their child, and they my parents?
CORINTHIAN:
Because there's none of Polybus in you.
OEDIPUS:
How can you say so? Was he not my father?
CORINTHIAN:
I am your father just as much as he!   980
OEDIPUS:
A stranger equal to the father? How?
CORINTHIAN:
Neither did he beget you, nor did I.
OEDIPUS:
Then for what reason did he call me son?
CORINTHIAN:
He had you as a gift—from my own hands.
OEDIPUS:
And showed such love to me? Me, not his own? 985
CORINTHIAN:
Yes, his own childlessness so worked on him.
OEDIPUS:
You, when you gave me: had you bought, or
    found me?
CORINTHIAN:
I found you in the woods upon Cithaeron.
OEDIPUS:
Why were you traveling in that neighborhood?
CORINTHIAN:
I tended flocks of sheep upon the mountain. 990
OEDIPUS:
You were a shepherd, then, wandering for hire?
CORINTHIAN:
I was, my son; but that day, your preserver.
OEDIPUS:
How so? What ailed me when you took me up?
CORINTHIAN:
For that, your ankles might give evidence.
OEDIPUS:
Alas! why speak of this, my life-long trouble? 995
CORINTHIAN:
I loosed the fetters clamped upon your feet.

OEDIPUS:
A pretty gift to carry from the cradle!
CORINTHIAN:
It was for this they named you Oedipus.
OEDIPUS:
Who did, my father or my mother? Tell me.
CORINTHIAN:
1000   I cannot; he knows more, from whom I had you.
OEDIPUS:
It was another, not yourself, that found me?
CORINTHIAN:
Yes, you were given me by another shepherd.
OEDIPUS:
Who? Do you know him? Can you name the
        man?
CORINTHIAN:
They said that he belonged to Laius.
OEDIPUS:
1005   What—him who once was ruler here in Thebes?
CORINTHIAN:
Yes, he it was for whom this man was shepherd.
OEDIPUS:
And is he still alive, that I can see him?
CORINTHIAN [turning to the CHORUS]:
You that are native here would know that best.
OEDIPUS:
Has any man of you now present here
Acquaintance with this shepherd, him he speaks
1010   of?
Has any seen him, here, or in the fields?
Speak; on this moment hangs discovery.
CHORUS-LEADER:
It is, I think, the man that you have sent for,
The slave now in the country. But who should
        know
1015   The truth of this more than Iocasta here?
OEDIPUS:
The man he speaks of: do you think, Iocasta,
He is the one I have already summoned?
IOCASTA:
What matters who he is? Pay no regard.—
The tale is idle; it is best forgotten.
OEDIPUS:
1020   It cannot be that I should have this clue
And then not find the secret of my birth.
IOCASTA:
In God's name stop, if you have any thought
For your own life! My ruin is enough.
OEDIPUS:
Be not dismayed; nothing can prove you base.
1025   Not though I find my mother thrice a slave.
IOCASTA:
O, I beseech you, do not! Seek no more!

OEDIPUS:
You cannot move me. I *will* know the truth.
IOCASTA:
I know that what I say is for the best.
OEDIPUS:
This "best" of yours! I have no patience with it.
IOCASTA:
O may you never learn what man you are!   1030
OEDIPUS:
Go, someone, bring the herdsman here to me,
And leave her to enjoy her pride of birth.
IOCASTA:
O man of doom! For by no other name
Can I address you now or evermore.
                        [*Exit* IOCASTA.]
CHORUS-LEADER:
The Queen has fled, my lord, as if before   1035
Some driving storm of grief. I fear that from
Her silence may break forth some great disaster.
OEDIPUS:
Break forth what will! My birth, however humble,
I am resolved to find. But she, perhaps,   1040
Is proud, as women will be; is ashamed
Of my low birth. But I do rate myself
The child of Fortune, giver of all good,
And I shall not be put to shame, for I
Am born of Her; the Years who are my kinsmen
Distinguished my estate, now high, now low;   1045
So born, I could not make me someone else
And not do all to find my parentage.

Strophe

CHORUS:
If I have power of prophecy,
[*animated rhythm*] If I have judgment wise and
        sure, Cithaeron
(I swear by Olympus),   1050
Thou shalt be honored when the moon
Next is full, as mother and foster-nurse
And birthplace of Oedipus, with festival and
        dancing,
For thou hast given great blessings to our King.
To Thee, Apollo, now we raise our cry: 1055
O grant our prayer find favor in thy sight!

Antistrophe

Who is thy mother, O my son?
Is she an ageless nymph among the mountains,
That bore thee to Pan?

1060 Or did Apollo father thee?
For dear to him are the pastures in the hills.
Or Hermes, who ruleth from the summit of
    Kyllene?
Or Dionysus on the mountain-tops,
Did he receive thee from thy mother's arms,
1065 A nymph who follows him on Helicon?
    OEDIPUS:
If I, who never yet have met the man,
May risk conjecture, I think I see the herdsman
Whom we have long been seeking. In his age
He well accords; and more, I recognize
1070 Those who are with him as of my own household.
But as for knowing, you will have advantage
Of me, if you have seen the man before.
    CHORUS-LEADER:
'Tis he, for certain—one of Laius's men,
One of the shepherds whom he trusted most.

[*Enter the* THEBAN SHEPHERD.]

    OEDIPUS:
You first I ask, you who have come from Corinth:
1075 Is that the man you mean?
    CORINTHIAN: That very man.
    OEDIPUS:
Come here, my man; look at me; answer me
My questions. Were you ever Laius's man?
    THEBAN:
I was; his slave—born in the house, not bought.
    OEDIPUS:
1080 What was your charge, or what your way of life?
    THEBAN:
Tending the sheep, the most part of my life.
    OEDIPUS:
And to what regions did you most resort?
    THEBAN:
Now it was Cithaeron, now the country round.
    OEDIPUS:
And was this man of your acquaintance there?
    THEBAN:
In what employment? Which is the man you
1085   mean?
    OEDIPUS:
Him yonder. Had you any dealings with him?
    THEBAN:
Not such that I can quickly call to mind.
    CORINTHIAN:
No wonder, Sir, but though he has forgotten
I can remind him. I am very sure,
1090 He knows the time when, round about Cithaeron,
He with a double flock, and I with one,
We spent together three whole summer seasons,

From spring until the rising of Arcturus.
Then, with the coming on of winter, I
Drove my flocks home, he his, to Laius's folds. 1095
Is this the truth? or am I telling lies?
    THEBAN:
It is true, although it happened long ago.
    CORINTHIAN:
Then tell me: do you recollect a baby
You gave me once to bring up for my own?
    THEBAN:
Why this? Why are you asking me this question? 1100
    CORINTHIAN:
My friend, *here* is the man who was that baby!
    THEBAN:
O, devil take you! Cannot you keep silent?
    OEDIPUS:
Here, Sir! This man needs no reproof from you.
Your tongue needs chastisement much more than
    his.
    THEBAN:
O best of masters, how am I offending?   1105
    OEDIPUS:
Not telling of the child of whom he speaks.
    THEBAN:
He? He knows nothing. He is wasting time.
    OEDIPUS [*threatening*]:
If you'll not speak from pleasure, speak from pain.
    THEBAN:
No, no, I pray! Not torture an old man!
    OEDIPUS:
Here, someone quickly! Twist this fellow's arms! 1110
    THEBAN:
Why, wretched man? What would you know
    besides?
    OEDIPUS:
That child: you have it him, the one he speaks of?
    THEBAN:
I did. Ah God, would I have died instead!
    OEDIPUS:
And die you shall, unless you speak the truth.
    THEBAN:
And if I do, then death is still more certain.   1115
    OEDIPUS:
This man, I think, is trying to delay me.
    THEBAN:
Not I! I said I gave the child—just now.
    OEDIPUS:
And got it—where? Your own? or someone else's?
    THEBAN:
No, not my own. Someone had given it me.
    OEDIPUS:
Who? Which of these our citizens? From what
    house?   1120

THEBAN:
No, I implore you, master! Do not ask!
OEDIPUS:
You die if I must question you again.
THEBAN:
Then, 'twas a child of one in Laius' house.
OEDIPUS:
You mean a slave? Or someone of his kin?
THEBAN:
1125   God! I am on the verge of saying it.
OEDIPUS:
And I of hearing it, but hear I must.
THEBAN:
His own, or so they said. But she within
Could tell you best—your wife—the truth of it.
OEDIPUS:
What, did she give you it?
THEBAN: She did, my lord.
OEDIPUS:
With what intention?
1130   THEBAN: That I should destroy it.
OEDIPUS:
Her own?—How could she?
THEBAN: Frightened by oracles.
OEDIPUS:
What oracles?
THEBAN: That it would kill its parents.
OEDIPUS:
Why did you let it go to this man here?
THEBAN:
I pitied it, my lord. I thought to send
1135   The child abroad, whence this man came. And he
Saved it, for utter doom. For if you are
The man he says, then you were born for ruin.
OEDIPUS:
Ah God! Ah God! This is the truth, at last!
O Sun, let me behold thee this once more,
1140   I who am proved accursed in my conception,
And in my marriage, and in him I slew.
                    [*Exeunt severally* OEDIPUS,
                      CORINTHIAN, THEBAN.]

Strophe 1

CHORUS:
Alas! you generations of men!
[*glyconics*][7] Even while you live you are next to
    nothing!

Has any man won for himself
More than the shadow of happiness,   1145
A shadow that swiftly fades away?
Oedipus, now as I look on you,
See your ruin, how can I say that
Mortal man can be happy?

Antistrophe 1

For who won greater prosperity?   1150
Sovereignty and wealth beyond all desiring?
The crooked-clawed, riddling Sphinx,
Maiden and bird, you overcame;
You stood like a tower of strength to Thebes.
So you received our crown, received the   1155
Highest honors that we could give—
King in our mighty city.

Strophe 2

Who more wretched, more afflicted now,
With cruel misery, with fell disaster,
Your life in dust and ashes?   1160
    O noble Oedipus!
    How could it be? to come again
A bridegroom of her who gave you birth!
How could such a monstrous thing
Endure so long, unknown?   1165

ANTISTROPHE 2

Time sees all, and Time, in your despite,
Disclosed and punished your unnatural mar-
    riage—
A child, and then a husband.
    O son of Laius,
    Would I had never looked on you!   1170
I mourn you as one who mourns the dead.
First you gave me back my life,
And now, that life is death.

    [*Enter, from the palace, a* MESSENGER.]

MESSENGER:
My Lords, most honored citizens of Thebes,
What deeds am I to tell of, you to see!   1175
What heavy grief to bear, if still remains

---

[7] **glyconics**.: metrical feet consisting of a spondee (two long syllables), a dactyl (two short syllables followed by one long syllable), and an amphimacer, or cretic (one long syllable followed by one short syllable followed by one long syllable)

Your native loyalty to our line of kings.
For not the Ister, no, or Phasis's flood.
Could purify this house, such things it hides,
1180 Such others will it soon display to all,
Evils self-sought. Of all our sufferings
Those hurt the most that we ourselves inflict.
CHORUS-LEADER:
Sorrow enough—too much—in what was known
Already. What new sorrow do you bring?
MESSENGER:
1185 Quickest for me to say and you to hear:
It is the Queen, Iocasta—she is dead.
CHORUS-LEADER:
Iocasta, dead? But how? What was the cause?
MESSENGER:
By her own hand. Of what has passed, the worst
Cannot be yours: that was, to see it.
1190 But you shall hear, so far as memory serves,
The cruel story.—In her agony
She ran across the courtyard, snatching at
Her hair with both her hands. She made her way
Straight to her chamber; she barred fast the doors
1195 And called on Laius, these long years dead,
Remembering their by-gone procreation.
"Through this did you meet death yourself, and
        leave
To me, the mother, child-bearing accursed
To my own child." She cried aloud upon
1200 The bed where she had borne a double brood,
Husband from husband, children from a child.
And thereupon she died, I know not how;
For, groaning, Oedipus burst in, and we,
For watching him, saw not *her* agony
1205 And how it ended. He, raging through the palace,
Came up to each man calling for a sword,
Calling for her whom he had called his wife,
Asking where was she who had borne them all,
Himself and his own children. So he raved.
1210 And then some deity showed him the way,
For it was none of us that stood around;
He cried aloud, as if to someone who
Was leading him; he leapt upon the doors,
Burst from their sockets the yielding bars, and fell
1215 Into the room; and there, hanged by the neck,
We saw his wife, held in a swinging cord.
He, when he saw it, groaned in misery
And loosed her body from the rope. When now
She lay upon the ground, awful to see
1220 Was that which followed: from her dress he tore
The golden brooches that she had been wearing,
Raised them, and with their points struck his own
        eyes,
Crying aloud that they should never see
What he had suffered and what he had done,

But in the dark henceforth they should behold   1225
Those whom they ought not; nor should recognize
Those whom he longed to see. To such refrain
He smote his eyeballs with the pins, not once,
Nor twice; and as he smote them, blood ran down
His face, not dripping slowly, but there fell   1230
Showers of black rain and blood-red hail together.
    Not on his head alone, but on them both,
Husband and wife, this common storm has
        broken.
Their ancient happiness of early days
Was happiness indeed; but now, today,   1235
Death, ruin, lamentation, shame—of all
The ills there are, not one is wanting here.
CHORUS-LEADER:
Now is there intermission in his agony?
MESSENGER:
He shouts for someone to unbar the gates,
And to display to Thebes the parricide,   1240
His mother's—no, I cannot speak the words;
For, by the doom he uttered, he will cast
Himself beyond our borders, not remain
To be a curse at home. But he needs strength,
And one to guide him; for these wounds are greater   1245
Than he can bear—as you shall see; for look!
They draw the bolts. A sight you will behold
To move the pity even of any enemy.

[*The doors open,* OEDIPUS *slowly advances.*]

CHORUS:
O horrible, dreadful sight. More dreadful far

[*These verses sung or chanted in a slow march-
time.*]

Than any I have yet seen. What cruel frenzy   1250
Came over you? What spirit with superhuman
        leap
Came to assist your grim destiny?
Ah, most unhappy man!
But no! I cannot bear even to look at you,
Though there is much that I would ask and see and
        hear.   1255
But I shudder at the very sight of you.
OEDIPUS [*sings in the dochmiac rhythm*]:
Alas! alas! and woe for my misery!
Where are my steps taking me?
My random voice is lost in the air.
O God! how hast thou crushed me!   1260
CHORUS-LEADER [*spoken*]:
Too terribly for us to hear or see.
OEDIPUS [*sings*]:
O cloud of darkness abominable,
My enemy unspeakable,
In cruel onset insuperable.

1265 Alas! alas! Assailed at once by pain
Of pin-points and of memory of crimes.
CHORUS-LEADER:
In such tormenting pains you well may cry
A double grief and feel a double woe.
OEDIPUS [sings]:
Ah, my friend!
1270 Still at my side? Still steadfast?
Still you can endure me?
Still care for me, a blind man?
[Speaks.] For it is you, my friend; I know 'tis you;
Though all is darkness, yet I know your voice.
CHORUS-LEADER:
1275 O, to destroy your sight! How could you bring
Yourself to do it? What god incited you?
OEDIPUS [sings]:
It was Apollo, friends, Apollo.
He decreed that I should suffer what I suffer;
But the hand that struck, alas! was my own,
1280 And not another's.
For why should I have sight,
When sight of nothing could give me pleasure?
CHORUS:
It was even as you say.
OEDIPUS:
What have I left, my friends, to see,
1285 To cherish, whom to speak with, or
To listen to, with joy?
Lead me away at once, far from Thebes;
Lead me away, my friends!
I have destroyed; I am accursed, and, what is
more,
1290 Hateful to Heaven, as no other.
CHORUS-LEADER [speaks]:
Unhappy your intention, and unhappy
Your fate. O would that I had never known you!
OEDIPUS [sings]:
Curses on him, whoever he was,
Who took the savage fetters from my feet,
1295 Snatched me from death, and saved me.
No thanks I owe him,
For had I died that day
Less ruin had I brought on me and mine.
CHORUS:
That wish is my wish too.
OEDIPUS:
1300 I had not then come and slain my father.
Nor then would men have called me
Husband of her that bore me.
Now am I God's enemy, child of the guilty,
And she that bore me has borne too my children;
1305 And if there is evil surpassing evil,
That has come to Oedipus.

CHORUS-LEADER:
How can I say that you have counseled well?
Far better to be dead than to be blind.
OEDIPUS:
That what is done was not done for the best
Seek not to teach me: counsel me no more. 1310
I know not how I could have gone to Hades
And with these eyes have looked upon my father
Or on my mother; such things have I done
To them, death is no worthy punishment.
Or could I look for pleasure in the sight 1315
Of my own children, born as they were born?
Never! No pleasure there, for eyes of mine,
Nor in this city, nor its battlements
Nor sacred images. From these—ah, miser-
able!—
I, the most nobly born of any Theban 1320
Am banned forever by my own decree
That the defiler should be driven forth,
The man accursed of Heaven and Laius's house.
Was I to find such taint in me, and then
With level eyes to look *them* in the face? 1325
Nay more: if for my ears I could have built
Some dam to stay the flood of sound, that I
Might lose both sight and hearing, and seal up
My wretched body—that I would have done.
How good to dwell beyond the reach of pain! 1330
Cithaeron! Why did you accept me? Why
Did you not take and kill me? Never then
Should I have come to dwell among the Thebans.
O Polybus! Corinth! and that ancient home
I thought my father's—what a thing you nurtured! 1335
How fair, how foul beneath! For I am found
Foul in myself and in my parentage.
O you three ways, that in a hidden glen
Do meet: you narrow branching roads within
The forest—you, through my own hands, did
drink 1340
My father's blood, that was my own.—Ah! do you
Remember what you saw me do? And what
I did again in Thebes? You marriages!
You did beget me: then, having begotten,
Bore the same crop again, and brought to light 1345
Commingled blood of fathers, brothers, sons,
Brides, mothers, wives; all that there can be
Among the human kind most horrible!
But that which it is foul to do, it is
Not fair to speak of. Quick as you can, I beg, 1350
Banish me, hide me, slay me! Throw me forth
Into the sea, where I may sink from view.
I pray you, deign to touch one so afflicted,
And do not fear: there is no man alive
Can bear this load of evil but myself. 1355

CHORUS-LEADER:

To listen to your prayers, Creon is here,
For act or guidance opportune; for he,
In your defection, is our champion.

[*Enter* CREON.]

OEDIPUS:

Alas! alas! How can I speak to him?
1360 What word of credit find? In all my commerce
With him aforetime I am proven false.

CREON:

No exultation, Oedipus, and no reproach
Of injuries inflicted brings me here;
But if the face of men moves not your shame,
1365 Then reverence show to that all-nurturing fire.
The holy Sun, that he be not polluted
By such accursèd sight, which neither Earth
Nor rain from Heaven nor sunlight can endure.
    Take him within, and quickly: it is right
1370 His kinsmen only should behold and hear
Evils that chiefly on his kinsmen fall.

OEDIPUS:

In Heaven's name—since you cheat my
    expectation,
So noble towards my baseness—grant me this:
It is for you I ask it, not myself.

CREON:

1375 What is this supplication that you make?

OEDIPUS:

Drive me at once beyond your bounds, where I
Shall be alone, and no one speak to me.

CREON:

I would have done it; but I first desired
To ask the God what he would have me do.

OEDIPUS:

1380 No, his command was given in full, to slay
Me, the polluter and the parricide.

CREON:

Those were his words; but in our present need
It would be wise to ask what we should do.

OEDIPUS:

You will inquire for such a wretch as I?

CREON:

1385 I will: for now *you* may believe the god.

OEDIPUS:

Yes; and on you I lay this charge and duty:
Give burial, as you will, to her who lies
Within—for she is yours, and this is proper:
And, while I live, let not my father's city
1390 Endure to have me as a citizen.
My home must be the mountains—on Cithaeron,
Which, while they lived, my parents chose to be

My tomb: they wished to slay me; now they shall.
For this I know: sickness can never kill me,
Nor any other evil; I was not saved   1395
That day from death, except for some strange
    doom,
My fate must take the course it will.—Now, for
    my sons,
Be not concerned for them: they can, being men,
Fend for themselves, wherever they may be:
But my unhappy daughters, my two girls,   1400
Whose chairs were always set beside my own
At table—they who shared in every dish
That was prepared for me—oh Creon! these
Do I commend to you. And grant me this:
To take them in my arms, and weep for them.   1405
My lord! most noble Creon! could I now
But hold them in my arms, then I should think
I had them as I had when I could see them.
Ah! what is this?
Ah Heaven! do I not hear my dear ones, sobbing? 1410
Has Creon, in his pity, sent to me
My darling children? Has he? Is it true?

CREON:

It is; they have been always your delight;
So, knowing this, I had them brought to you.

OEDIPUS:

Then Heaven reward you, and for this kind service 1415
Protect you better than it protected me!
    Where are you, children? Where? O come to
    me!
Come, let me clasp you with a brother's arms,
These hands, which helped your father's eyes,
    once bright,
To look upon you as they see you now—   1420
Your father who, not seeing, nor inquiring,
Gave you for mother her who bore himself.
See you I cannot; but I weep for you,
For the unhappiness that must be yours,
And for the bitter life that you must lead.   1425
What gathering of the citizens, what festivals,
Will you have part in? Your high celebrations
Will be to go back home, and sit in tears.
And when the time for marriage comes, what man
Will stake upon the ruin and the shame   1430
That *I* am to my parents and to you?
Nothing is wanting there: your father slew
His father, married her who gave him birth,
And then, from that same source whence he
    himself
Had sprung, got you.—With these things they will
    taunt you;   1435
And who will take you then in marriage?—
    Nobody;

But you must waste, unwedded and unfruitful.
  Ah, Creon! Since they have no parent now
But you—for both of us who gave them life
1440 Have perished—suffer them not to be cast out
Homeless and beggars; for they are your kin.
Have pity on them, for they are so young,
So desolate, except for you alone.
Say "Yes," good Creon! Let your hand confirm it.
1445 And now, my children, for my exhortation
You are too young; but you can pray that I
May live henceforward—where I should; and you
More happily than the father who begot you.
  CREON:
Now make an end of tears, and go within.
  OEDIPUS:
1450 Then I must go—against my will.
  CREON:
There is a time for everything.
  OEDIPUS:
You know what I would have you do?
  CREON:
If you will tell me, I shall know.
  OEDIPUS:
Send me away, away from Thebes.
  CREON:
1455 The God, not I, must grant you this.
  OEDIPUS:
The gods hate no man more than me!
  CREON:
Then what you ask they soon will give.
  OEDIPUS:
You promise this?

  CREON: Ah no! When I
Am ignorant, I do not speak.
  OEDIPUS:
Then lead me in; I say no more.   1460
  CREON:
Release the children then, and come.
  OEDIPUS:
What? Take these children from me? No!
  CREON:
Seek not to have your way in all things:
Where you had your way before,
Your mastery broke before the end.   1465

[*There was no doubt a short concluding utterance from the* CHORUS. *What stands in the mss. appears to be spurious.*][8]

[8] Few other scholars share Professor Kitto's suspicion that the concluding lines in the manuscript are spurious. The passage is translated thus by J. T. Sheppard:
  CHORUS:
Look, ye who dwell in Thebes. This man was
  Oedipus.
That mighty King, who knew the riddle's mystery,
Whom all the city envied, Fortune's favorite.
Behold, in the event, the storm of his calamities,
And, being mortal, think on that last day of death,
Which all must see, and speak of no man's
  happiness
Till, without sorrow, he hath passed the goal of life.
                        [Eds.]

COMMENTARY

    Classroom discussions of *Oedipus the King*, like discussions in books, are usually devoted to the problem of fate versus free will. Students (who ought to be filled with youthful confidence in the freedom of the will) generally argue that Oedipus is fated; instructors (who ought to be old enough to know that the inexplicable and unwilled often comes about) generally argue that Oedipus is free and of his own accord performed the actions that fulfilled the prophecy. Prophecy or prediction or foreknowledge, instructors patiently explain, is not the same as foreordination. The physician who says that the newborn babe will never develop mentally beyond the age of six is predicting, not ordaining or willing. So, the argument usually runs, the oracle who predicted that Oedipus would kill his father and marry his mother was not *causing* Oedipus to do these things but was simply, in his deep knowledge, announcing what a man like

Oedipus would do. But that may be too sophisticated a reading, and a reading that derives from the much later European view of human beings as creatures who can shape their destiny. It is hard for us—especially if the tragedy we know best is Shakespeare's—to recognize the possibility of another sort of tragic drama that does not relate the individual's suffering to his or her own actions but that postulates some sort of Necessity that works within an individual.

Whatever the merits of these views, the spectators or readers undeniably already know, when they set out to see or read the play, that Oedipus must end wretchedly. The story is known to all, fixed in Sophocles's text, and Oedipus cannot extricate himself from it. Something along these lines was suggested in the middle of the fourth century B.C. when a Greek comic dramatist complained that the comic writer's task was harder than the tragic writer's: "Tragedy has the best of it since the stories are known beforehand to the spectators even before anyone speaks; so the poet only has to remind them. For if I merely say the name Oedipus, they all know the rest—his father Laius, mother Iocasta, daughters, who his sons are, what will happen to him, what he did."

In fact, it should be mentioned, the tragic writer's task was not quite so easy. First of all, we have Aristotle's statement that "even the known legends are known to only a few," and, second, we have evidence that the tragic writer could vary the details. In Homer's *Iliad* we read that Oedipus continued to rule even after his dreadful history was known, but Sophocles exiles him. And a fragment of Euripides indicates that his Oedipus was blinded by Laius's followers, whereas Sophocles's Oedipus blinds himself. These are details, but they are rather important ones. Probably the ancient Greeks knew the legends in a rough sort of way, as most of us know the Bible or some nuggets of Roman history. Robert Frost and Archibald MacLeish have both drawn from the Book of Job, but their works are enormously different. Writers who uses Job can scarcely omit Job's great suffering, and they can assume that their audience will know that Job had a wife and some comforters, but they are free to go on from there.

Still, the main outline of Oedipus's life must have been fixed, and for us even the details are forever fixed in Sophocles's version. (We know that the Greeks wrote a dozen plays about Oedipus's discovery of his terrible actions, but only Sophocles's survives.) This means that as we read or watch it, each speech has for us a meaning somewhat different from the meaning it has for the speaker and the audience on the stage. Oedipus says he will hunt out the polluted man; we know, as he and the Thebans do not, that *he* is the hunted as well as the hunter. Oedipus says the killer of King Laius may well try to strike at him; we know that Oedipus will find himself out and will strike out his own eyes. A messenger from Corinth tries to allay Oedipus's fears, but he sets them going. What we are talking about, of course, is tragic irony, or Sophoclean irony, in which words and deeds have a larger meaning for the spectator than for the dramatis personae. And surely it is in part because Sophocles so persistently uses this device of giving speeches a second, awesome significance that we feel the plot is a masterpiece of construction in which Oedipus is caught. If ever a man had confidence in his will, it was Oedipus, but if ever a man moved toward a predicted point, it was Oedipus. He had solved the riddle of the sphinx (by himself, without the aid of birds, he somewhat hybristically boasts), but he did not yet know himself. That knowledge was to come later, when he commendably pursued the quest for Laius's slayer and inevitably found himself. The thing is as inevitable as the history described in the sphinx's riddle, which in J. T. Sheppard's version goes thus:

> A thing there is whose voice is one;
> Whose feet are four and two and three.
> So mutable a thing is none
> That moves in earth or sky or sea.
> When on most feet this thing doth go,
> Its strength is weakest and its pace most slow.

This is the history of humanity, willy-nilly. In Sophocles's time people grew from crawling infancy, through erect adulthood, to bent old age supported by a stick, and so they do in our time, as the child's rhyme still claims:

> Walks on four feet,
> On two feet, on three,
> The more feet it walks on,
> The weaker it be.

There was scarcely an infant weaker than the maimed Oedipus; there was scarcely a man stronger than King Oedipus at his height; and there was scarcely a man more in need of a staff than the blind exile. However free each of his actions—and we can only feel that the figure whom we see on the stage is acting freely when he abuses Teiresias and Creon—Oedipus was by fate a human being, and thus the largest pattern of his life could be predicted easily enough.

TOPICS FOR DISCUSSION

1. On the basis of the lines 1–149, characterize Oedipus. What additional traits are revealed in lines 205–491?
2. In your opinion, how fair is it to say that Oedipus is morally guilty? Does he argue that he is morally innocent because he did not intend to do immoral deeds? Can it be said that he is guilty of *hybris* but that *hybris* (see page 67) has nothing to do with his fall?
3. Oedipus says that he blinds himself in order not to look upon people he should not. What further reasons can be given? Why does he not (like Iocasta) commit suicide?
4. How fair is it to say that the play shows the contemptibleness of human efforts to act intelligently?
5. How fair is it to say that in *Oedipus* the gods are evil?
6. Are the choral odes lyrical interludes that serve to separate the scenes, or do they advance the dramatic action?
7. Matthew Arnold said that Sophocles saw life steadily and saw it whole. But in this play is Sophocles facing the facts of life, or, on the contrary, is he avoiding life as it usually is and presenting a series of unnatural and outrageous coincidences?

8. Can you describe your emotions at the end of the play? Do they include pity for Oedipus? Pity for all human beings, including yourself? Fear that you might be punished for some unintended transgression? Awe, engendered by a perception of the interrelatedness of things? Relief that the story is only a story? Exhilaration?

THE IMPORTANCE OF BEING EARNEST

A Trivial Comedy for Serious People

Oscar Wilde

Oscar Wilde (1854–1900) was born in Dublin. He distinguished himself as a student at Trinity College, Dublin, and at Oxford, and then turned to a career of writing, lecturing, and in other ways making himself a public figure in England: his posture as an aesthete (he was alleged to have walked down Piccadilly with a flower in his hand) was caricatured by Gilbert and Sullivan in *Patience*. But it became no laughing matter when in 1895 he was arrested and convicted of homosexuality. After serving two years at hard labor, he was released from jail. He then went to France, where he lived under an assumed name until he died. His Irish birth did not ally him to the Irish Renaissance at the end of the nineteenth century; when W. B. Yeats was writing plays on Irish legends, Wilde was writing drawing-room comedies.

CHARACTERS

JOHN WORTHING, J. P.
ALGERNON MONCRIEFF
REV. CANON CHASUBLE, D.D.
MERRIMAN, *butler*
LANE, *manservant*
LADY BRACKNELL
HON.[1] GWENDOLEN FAIRFAX
CECILY CARDEW
MISS PRISM, *governess*

---

[1] **Hon.:** The prefix *Hon.* (Honorable) indicates that she is the daughter of a viscount or a baron.

A scene from the 1947 Theatre Guild production, directed by John Geilgud, with Geilgud as John Worthing, J. P., Pamela Browne as Gwendolen, Margaret Rutherford as Lady Bracknell, and Robert Fleming as Algernon. (Photograph courtesy of the New York Public Library Vandamm Collection.)

ACT I

Morning room in ALGERNON's *flat in Half-Moon Street. The room is luxuriously and artistically furnished. The sound of a piano is heard in the adjoining room.* LANE *is arranging afternoon tea on the table, and after the music has ceased,* ALGERNON *enters.*

ALGERNON: Did you hear what I was playing, Lane?

LANE: I didn't think it polite to listen, sir.

ALGERNON: I'm sorry for that, for your sake. I don't play accurately—anyone can play accurately—but I play with wonderful expression. As far as the piano is concerned, sentiment is my forte. I keep science for Life.

LANE: Yes, sir.

ALGERNON: And, speaking of the science of Life, have you got the cucumber sandwiches cut for Lady Bracknell?

LANE: Yes, sir. (*Hands them on a salver.*)

ALGERNON (*inspects them, takes two, and sits down on the sofa*): Oh! . . . by the way, Lane, I see from your book that on Thursday night, when Lord Shoreman and Mr. Worthing were dining with me, eight bottles of champagne are entered as having been consumed.

LANE: Yes, sir; eight bottles and a pint.

ALGERNON: Why is it that at a bachelor's establishment the servants invariably drink the champagne? I ask merely for information.

LANE: I attribute it to the superior quality of the wine, sir. I have often observed that in married households the champagne is rarely of a first-rate brand.

ALGERNON: Good heavens! Is marriage so demoralizing as that?

LANE: I believe it *is* a very pleasant state, sir. I have had very little experience of it myself up to the present. I have only been married once. That was in consequence of a misunderstanding between myself and a young person.

ALGERNON (*languidly*): I don't know that I am much interested in your family life, Lane.

LANE: No, sir; it is not a very interesting subject. I never think of it myself.

ALGERNON: Very natural, I am sure. That will do, Lane, thank you.

LANE: Thank you, sir.

LANE *goes out.*

ALGERNON: Lane's views on marriage seem somewhat lax. Really, if the lower orders don't set us a good example, what on earth is the use of them? They seem, as a class, to have absolutely no sense of moral responsibility.

Enter LANE.

LANE: Mr. Ernest Worthing.

Enter JACK. LANE *goes out.*

ALGERNON: How are you, my dear Ernest? What brings you up to town?

JACK: Oh, pleasure, pleasure! What else should bring one anywhere? Eating as usual, I see, Algy!

ALGERNON (*stiffly*): I believe it is customary in good society to take some slight refreshment at five o'clock. Where have you been since last Thursday?

JACK (*sitting down on the sofa*): In the country.

ALGERNON: What on earth do you do there?

JACK (*pulling off his gloves*): When one is in town one amuses oneself. When one is in the country one amuses other people. It is excessively boring.

ALGERNON: And who are the people you amuse?

JACK (*airily*): Oh, neighbors, neighbors.

ALGERNON: Got nice neighbors in your part of Shropshire?

JACK: Perfectly horrid! Never speak to one of them.

ALGERNON: How immensely you must amuse them! (*Goes over and takes sandwich.*) By the way, Shropshire is your country, is it not?

JACK: Eh? Shropshire? Yes, of course. Hallo! Why all these cups? Why cucumber sandwiches? Why such reckless extravagance in one so young? Who is coming to tea?

ALGERNON: Oh! merely Aunt Augusta and Gwendolen.

JACK: How perfectly delightful!

ALGERNON: Yes, that is all very well; but I am afraid Aunt Augusta won't quite approve of your being here.

JACK: May I ask why?

ALGERNON: My dear fellow, the way you flirt with Gwendolen is perfectly disgraceful. It is almost as bad as the way Gwendolen flirts with you.

JACK: I am in love with Gwendolen. I have come up to town expressly to propose to her.

ALGERNON: I thought you had come up for pleasure? . . . I call that business.

JACK: How utterly unromantic you are!

ALGERNON: I really don't see anything romantic in proposing. It is very romantic to be in love. But there is nothing romantic about a definite proposal. Why, one may be accepted. One usually is, I believe. Then the excitement is all over. The very essence of romance is uncertainty. If ever I get married, I'll certainly try to forget the fact.

JACK: I have no doubt about that, dear Algy. The Divorce Court was specially invented for people whose memories are so curiously constituted.

ALGERNON: Oh! there is no use speculating on that subject. Divorces are made in Heaven—(JACK *puts out his hand to take a sandwich.* ALGERNON *at once interferes.*) Please don't touch the cucumber sandwiches. They are ordered especially for Aunt Augusta. (*Takes one and eats it.*)

JACK: Well, you have been eating them all the time.

ALGERNON: That is quite a different matter. She is my aunt. (*Takes plate from below.*) Have some bread and butter. The bread and butter is for Gwendolen. Gwendolen is devoted to bread and butter.

JACK (*advancing to table and helping himself*): And very good bread and butter it is too.

ALGERNON: Well, my dear fellow, you need not eat as if you were going to eat it all. You behave as if you were married to her already. You are not married to her already, and I don't think you ever will be.

JACK: Why on earth do you say that?

ALGERNON: Well, in the first place, girls never marry the men they flirt with. Girls don't think it right.

JACK: Oh, that is nonsense!

ALGERNON: It isn't. It is a great truth. It accounts for the extraordinary number of bachelors that one sees all over the place. In the second place, I don't give my consent.

JACK: Your consent!

ALGERNON: My dear fellow, Gwendolen is my first cousin. And before I allow you to marry her, you will have to clear up the whole question of Cecily. (*Rings bell.*)

JACK: Cecily! What on earth do you mean? What do you mean, Algy, by Cecily! I don't know anyone of the name of Cecily.

Enter LANE.

ALGERNON: Bring me that cigarette case Mr. Worthing left in the smoking room the last time he dined here.

LANE: Yes, sir.

LANE *goes out.*

JACK: Do you mean to say you have had my cigarette case all this time? I wish to goodness you had let me know. I have been writing frantic letters to Scotland Yard[2] about it. I was very nearly offering a large reward.

ALGERNON: Well, I wish you would offer one. I happen to be more than usually hard up.

JACK: There is no good offering a large reward now that the thing is found.

Enter LANE *with the cigarette case on a salver.* ALGERNON *takes it at once.* LANE *goes out.*

ALGERNON: I think that is rather mean of you, Ernest, I must say. (*Opens case and examines it.*) However, it makes no matter, for, now that I look at the inscription inside, I find that the thing isn't yours after all.

JACK: Of course it's mine. (*Moving to him.*) You have seen me with it a hundred times, and you have no right whatsoever to read what is written inside. It is a very ungentlemanly thing to read a private cigarette case.

ALGERNON: Oh! It is absurd to have a hard and fast rule about what one should read and what one shouldn't. More than half of modern culture depends on what one shouldn't read.

JACK: I am quite aware of the fact, and I don't propose to discuss modern culture. It isn't the sort of thing one should talk of in private. I simply want my cigarette case back.

ALGERNON: Yes; but this isn't your cigarette case. This cigarette case is a present from someone of the name of Cecily, and you said you didn't know anyone of that name.

JACK: Well, if you want to know, Cecily happens to be my aunt.

ALGERNON: Your aunt!

JACK: Yes. Charming old lady she is, too. Lives at Tunbridge Wells.[3] Just give it back to me, Algy.

ALGERNON (*retreating to back of sofa*): But why does she call herself little Cecily if she is your aunt and lives at Tunbridge Wells? (*Reading.*) "From little Cecily with her fondest love."

JACK (*moving to sofa and kneeling upon it*): My dear fellow, what on earth is there in that? Some aunts are tall, some aunts are not tall. That is a matter that surely an aunt may be allowed to decide for herself. You seem to think that every aunt should be exactly like your aunt! That is absurd. For Heaven's sake give me back my cigarette case. (*Follows* ALGERNON *round the room.*)

---

[2] **Scotland Yard:** Headquarters of the London Police
[3] **Tunbridge Wells:** A fashionable town south of London in Kent

ALGERNON: Yes. But why does your aunt call you her uncle? "From little Cecily, with her fondest love to her dear Uncle Jack." There is no objection, I admit, to an aunt being a small aunt, but why an aunt, no matter what her size may be, should call her own nephew her uncle, I can't quite make out. Besides, your name isn't Jack at all, it is Ernest.

JACK: It isn't Ernest; it's Jack.

ALGERNON: You have always told me it was Ernest. I have introduced you to everyone as Ernest. You answer to the name of Ernest. You look as if your name was Ernest. You are the most earnest-looking person I ever saw in my life. It is perfectly absurd your saying that your name isn't Ernest. It's on your cards. Here is one of them (*taking it from case*). "Mr. Ernest Worthing, B.4, The Albany."[4] I'll keep this as a proof that your name is Ernest if ever you attempt to deny it to me, or to Gwendolen, or to any one else. (*Puts the card in his pocket.*)

JACK: Well, my name is Ernest in town and Jack in the country, and the cigarette case was given to me in the country.

ALGERNON: Yes, but that does not account for the fact that your small Aunt Cecily, who lives at Tunbridge Wells, calls you her dear uncle. Come, old boy, you had much better have the thing out at once.

JACK: My dear Algy, you talk exactly as if you were a dentist. It is very vulgar to talk like a dentist when one isn't a dentist. It produces a false impression.

ALGERNON: Well, that is exactly what dentists always do. Now, go on! Tell me the whole thing. I may mention that I have always suspected you of being a confirmed and secret Bunburyist; and I am quite sure of it now.

JACK: Bunburyist? What on earth do you mean by a Bunburyist?

ALGERNON: I'll reveal to you the meaning of that incomparable expression as soon as you are kind enough to inform me why you are Ernest in town and Jack in the country.

JACK: Well, produce my cigarette case first.

ALGERNON: Here it is. (*Hands cigarette case.*) Now produce your explanation, and pray make it improbable. (*Sits on sofa.*)

JACK: My dear fellow, there is nothing improbable about my explanation at all. In fact it's perfectly ordinary. Old Mr. Thomas Cardew, who adopted me when I was a little boy, made me in his will guardian to his granddaughter, Miss Cecily Cardew. Cecily, who addresses me as her uncle from motives of respect that you could not possibly appreciate, lives at my place in the country under the charge of her admirable governess, Miss Prism.

ALGERNON: Where is that place in the country, by the way?

JACK: That is nothing to you, dear boy. You are not going to be invited. . . . I may tell you candidly that the place is not in Shropshire.

ALGERNON: I suspected that, my dear fellow! I have Bunburyed all over Shropshire on two separate occasions. Now, go on. Why are you Ernest in town and Jack in the country?

JACK: My dear Algy, I don't know whether you will be able to understand my real motives. You are hardly serious enough. When one is placed in the position of guardian, one has to adopt a very high moral tone on all subjects. It's one's duty to do so. And as a high moral tone can hardly be said to conduce very much to either one's health or one's happiness, in order to get up to town I have always pretended to have a younger brother of the name of Ernest, who lives in the Albany, and gets into the most dreadful scrapes. That, my dear Algy, is the whole truth pure and simple.

ALGERNON: The truth is rarely pure and never simple. Modern life would be very tedious if it were either, and modern literature a complete impossibility!

JACK: That wouldn't be at all a bad thing.

ALGERNON: Literary criticism is not your forte, my dear fellow. Don't try it. You should leave that to people who haven't been at a University. They do it so well in the daily papers. What you really are is a Bunburyist. I was quite right in saying you were a Bunburyist. You are one of the most advanced Bunburyists I know.

JACK: What on earth do you mean?

ALGERNON: You have invented a very useful younger brother called Ernest, in order that you may be able to come up to town as often as you like. I have invented an invaluable permanent invalid called Bunbury, in order that I may be able to go down into the country whenever I choose. Bunbury is perfectly invaluable. If it wasn't for Bunbury's extraordinary bad health, for instance, I wouldn't be able to dine with you at Willis's[5]

---

[4] **The Albany:** Fashionable apartments in Piccadilly near the center of London

[5] **Willis's:** Popular restaurant

tonight, for I have been really engaged to[6] Aunt Augusta for more than a week.

JACK: I haven't asked you to dine with me anywhere tonight.

ALGERNON: I know. You are absurdly careless about sending out invitations. It is very foolish of you. Nothing annoys people so much as not receiving invitations.

JACK: You had much better dine with your Aunt Augusta.

ALGERNON: I haven't the smallest intention of doing anything of the kind. To begin with, I dined there on Monday, and once a week is quite enough to dine with one's own relations. In the second place, whenever I do dine there I am always treated as a member of the family, and sent down with[7] either no woman at all, or two. In the third place, I know perfectly well whom she will place me next to, tonight. She will place me next Mary Farquhar, who always flirts with her own husband across the dinner table. That is not very pleasant. Indeed, it is not even decent . . . and that sort of thing is enormously on the increase. The amount of women in London who flirt with their own husbands is perfectly scandalous. It looks so bad. It is simply washing one's clean linen in public. Besides, now that I know you to be a confirmed Bunburyist I naturally want to talk to you about Bunburying. I want to tell you the rules.

JACK: I'm not a Bunburyist at all. If Gwendolen accepts me, I am going to kill my brother, indeed I think I'll kill him in any case. Cecily is a little too much interested in him. It is rather a bore. So I am going to get rid of Ernest. And I strongly advise you to do the same with Mr. . . . with your invalid friend who has the absurd name.

ALGERNON: Nothing will induce me to part with Bunbury, and if you ever get married, which seems to be extremely problematic, you will be very glad to know Bunbury. A man who marries without knowing Bunbury has a very tedious time of it.

JACK: That is nonsense. If I marry a charming girl like Gwendolen, and she is the only girl I ever saw in my life that I would marry, I certainly won't want to know Bunbury.

ALGERNON: Then your wife will. You don't seem to realize, that in married life three is company and two is none.

JACK (*sententiously*): That, my dear young

friend, is the theory that the corrupt French Drama has been propounding for the last fifty years.

ALGERNON: Yes; and that the happy English home has proved in half the time.

JACK: For heaven's sake, don't try to be cynical. It's perfectly easy to be cynical.

ALGERNON: My dear fellow, it isn't easy to be anything nowadays. There's such a lot of beastly competition about. (*The sound of an electric bell is heard.*) Ah! that must be Aunt Augusta. Only relatives, or creditors, ever ring in that Wagnerian manner.[8] Now, if I get her out of the way for ten minutes, so that you can have an opportunity for proposing to Gwendolen, may I dine with you tonight at Willis's?

JACK: I suppose so, if you want to.

ALGERNON: Yes, but you must be serious about it. I hate people who are not serious about meals. It is so shallow of them.

Enter LANE.

LANE: Lady Bracknell and Miss Fairfax.

ALGERNON *goes forward to meet them. Enter* LADY BRACKNELL *and* GWENDOLEN.

LADY BRACKNELL: Good afternoon, dear Algernon, I hope you are behaving very well.

ALGERNON: I'm feeling very well, Aunt Augusta.

LADY BRACKNELL: That's not quite the same thing. In fact the two things rarely go together. (*Sees* JACK *and bows to him with icy coldness.*)

ALGERNON (*to* GWENDOLEN): Dear me, you are smart![9]

GWENDOLEN: I am always smart! Am I not, Mr. Worthing?

JACK: You're quite perfect, Miss Fairfax.

GWENDOLEN: Oh! I hope I am not that. It would leave no room for developments, and I intend to develop in many directions. (GWENDOLEN *and* JACK *sit down together in the corner.*)

LADY BRACKNELL: I'm sorry if we are a little late, Algernon, but I was obliged to call on dear Lady Harbury. I hadn't been there since her poor husband's death. I never saw a woman so altered; she looks quite twenty years younger. And now I'll have a cup of tea and one of those nice cucumber sandwiches you promised me.

---

[6] **engaged to:** i.e., promised to attend her dinner party
[7] **sent down with:** i.e., ordered to escort

[8] **Wagnerian manner:** Loudly
[9] **smart:** Elegantly dressed

ALGERNON: Certainly, Aunt Augusta. (*Goes over to tea table.*)

LADY BRACKNELL: Won't you come and sit here, Gwendolen?

GWENDOLEN: Thanks, mamma, I'm quite comfortable where I am.

ALGERNON (*picking up empty plate in horror*): Good heavens! Lane! Why are there no cucumber sandwiches? I ordered them specially.

LANE (*gravely*): There were no cucumbers in the market this morning, sir. I went down twice.

ALGERNON: No cucumbers!

LANE: No, sir. Not even for ready money.

ALGERNON: That will do, Lane, thank you.

LANE: Thank you, sir. (*Goes out.*)

ALGERNON: I am greatly distressed, Aunt Augusta, about there being no cucumbers, not even for ready money.

LADY BRACKNELL: It really makes no matter, Algernon. I had some crumpets[10] with Lady Harbury, who seems to me to be living entirely for pleasure now.

ALGERNON: I hear her hair has turned quite gold from grief.

LADY BRACKNELL: It certainly has changed its color. From what cause I, of course, cannot say. (*ALGERNON crosses and hands tea.*) Thank you. I've quite a treat for you tonight, Algernon. I am going to send you down with Mary Farquhar. She is such a nice woman, and so attentive to her husband. It's delightful to watch them.

ALGERNON: I am afraid, Aunt Augusta, I shall have to give up the pleasure of dining with you tonight after all.

LADY BRACKNELL (*frowning*): I hope not, Algernon. It would put my table completely out. Your uncle would have to dine upstairs. Fortunately he is accustomed to that.

ALGERNON: It is a great bore, and, I need hardly say, a terrible disappointment to me, but the fact is I have just had a telegram to say that my poor friend Bunbury is very ill again. (*Exchanges glances with* JACK). They seem to think I should be with him.

LADY BRACKNELL: It is very strange. This Mr. Bunbury seems to suffer from curiously bad health.

ALGERNON: Yes; poor Bunbury is a dreadful invalid.

LADY BRACKNELL: Well, I must say, Algernon, that I think it is high time that Mr. Bunbury made up his mind whether he was going to live or to die. This shilly-shallying with the question is absurd. Nor do I in any way approve of the modern sympathy with invalids. I consider it morbid. Illness of any kind is hardly a thing to be encouraged in others. Health is the primary duty of life. I am always telling that to your poor uncle, but he never seems to take much notice . . . as far as any improvement in his ailments goes. I should be much obliged if you would ask Mr. Bunbury, from me, to be kind enough not to have a relapse on Saturday, for I rely on you to arrange my music for me. It is my last reception, and one wants something that will encourage conversation, particularly at the end of the season[11] when everyone has practically said whatever they had to say, which, in most cases, was probably not much.

ALGERNON: I'll speak to Bunbury, Aunt Augusta, if he is still conscious, and I think I can promise you he'll be all right by Saturday. Of course the music is a great difficulty. You see, if one plays good music, people don't listen, and if one plays bad music, people don't talk. But I'll run over the program I've drawn out, if you will kindly come into the next room for a moment.

LADY BRACKNELL: Thank you, Algernon. It is very thoughtful of you. (*Rising, and following* ALGERNON.) I'm sure the program will be delightful, after a few expurgations. French songs I cannot possibly allow. People always seem to think that they are improper, and either look shocked, which is vulgar, or laugh, which is worse. But German sounds a thoroughly respectable language, and, indeed I believe is so. Gwendolen, you will accompany me.

GWENDOLEN: Certainly, mamma.

LADY BRACKNELL *and* ALGERNON *go into the music room;* GWENDOLEN *remains behind.*

JACK: Charming day it has been, Miss Fairfax.

GWENDOLEN: Pray don't talk to me about the weather, Mr. Worthing. Whenever people talk to me about the weather, I always feel quite certain that they mean something else. And that makes me so nervous.

JACK: I do mean something else.

GWENDOLEN: I thought so. In fact, I am never wrong.

JACK: And I would like to be allowed to take

---

[10] **crumpets:** Lightly toasted bread (similar to English muffins)

[11] **season:** The social season

advantage of Lady Bracknell's temporary absence . . .

GWENDOLEN: I would certainly advise you to do so. Mamma has a way of coming back suddenly into a room that I have often had to speak to her about.

JACK (*nervously*): Miss Fairfax, ever since I met you I have admired you more than any girl . . . I have ever met since . . . I met you.

GWENDOLEN: Yes, I am quite aware of the fact. And I often wish that in public, at any rate, you had been more demonstrative. For me you have always had an irresistible fascination. Even before I met you I was far from indifferent to you. (JACK *looks at her in amazement.*) We live, as I hope you know, Mr. Worthing, in an age of ideals. The fact is constantly mentioned in the more expensive monthly magazines, and has reached the provincial pulpits, I am told; and my ideal has always been to love someone of the name of Ernest. There is something in that name that inspires absolute confidence. The moment Algernon first mentioned to me that he had a friend called Ernest, I knew I was destined to love you.

JACK: You really love me, Gwendolen?

GWENDOLEN: Passionately!

JACK: Darling! You don't know how happy you've made me.

GWENDOLEN: My own Ernest!

JACK: But you don't really mean to say that you couldn't love me if my name wasn't Ernest?

GWENDOLEN: But your name is Ernest.

JACK: Yes, I know it is. But supposing it was something else? Do you mean to say you couldn't love me then?

GWENDOLEN (*glibly*): Ah! that is clearly a metaphysical speculation, and like most metaphysical speculations has very little reference at all to the actual facts of real life, as we know them.

JACK: Personally, darling, to speak quite candidly, I don't much care about the name of Ernest . . . I don't think the name suits me at all.

GWENDOLEN: It suits you perfectly. It is a divine name. It has a music of its own. It produces vibrations.

JACK: Well, really, Gwendolen, I must say that I think there are lots of other much nicer names. I think Jack, for instance, a charming name.

GWENDOLEN: Jack? . . . No, there is very little music in the name Jack, if any at all, indeed. It does not thrill. It produces absolutely no vibrations. . . . I have known several Jacks, and they all, without exception, were more than usually plain. Besides, Jack is a notorious domesticity for John!

And I pity any woman who is married to a man called John. She would probably never be allowed to know the entrancing pleasure of a single moment's solitude. The only really safe name is Ernest.

JACK: Gwendolen, I must get christened at once—I mean we must get married at once. There is no time to be lost.

GWENDOLEN: Married, Mr. Worthing?

JACK (*astounded*): Well . . . surely. You know that I love you, and you led me to believe, Miss Fairfax, that you were not absolutely indifferent to me.

GWENDOLEN: I adore you. But you haven't proposed to me yet. Nothing has been said at all about marriage. The subject has not even been touched on.

JACK: Well . . . may I propose to you now?

GWENDOLEN: I think it would be an admirable opportunity. And to spare you any possible disappointment, Mr. Worthing, I think it only fair to tell you quite frankly beforehand that I am fully determined to accept you.

JACK: Gwendolen!

GWENDOLEN: Yes, Mr. Worthing, what have you got to say to me?

JACK: You know what I have got to say to you.

GWENDOLEN: Yes, but you don't say it.

JACK: Gwendolen, will you marry me? (*Goes on his knees.*)

GWENDOLEN: Of course I will, darling. How long you have been about it! I am afraid you have had very little experience in how to propose.

JACK: My own one, I have never loved anyone in the world but you.

GWENDOLEN: Yes, but men often propose for practice. I know my brother Gerald does. All my girl friends tell me so. What wonderfully blue eyes you have, Ernest! They are quite, quite blue. I hope you will always look at me just like that, especially when there are other people present.

Enter LADY BRACKNELL.

LADY BRACKNELL: Mr. Worthing! Rise sir, from this semi-recumbent posture. It is most indecorous.

GWENDOLEN: Mamma! (*He tries to rise; she restrains him.*) I must beg you to retire. This is no place for you. Besides, Mr. Worthing has not quite finished yet.

LADY BRACKNELL: Finished what, may I ask?

GWENDOLEN: I am engaged to Mr. Worthing, Mamma. (*They rise together.*)

LADY BRACKNELL: Pardon me, you are not

engaged to anyone. When you do become engaged to someone, I, or your father, should his health permit him, will inform you of the fact. An engagement should come on a young girl as a surprise, pleasant or unpleasant, as the case may be. It is hardly a matter that she could be allowed to arrange for herself. . . . And now I have a few questions to put to you, Mr. Worthing. While I am making these inquiries, you, Gwendolen, will wait for me below in the carriage.

GWENDOLEN (*reproachfully*): Mamma!

LADY BRACKNELL: In the carriage, Gwendolen! (GWENDOLEN *goes to the door. She and* JACK *blow kisses to each other behind* LADY BRACKNELL's *back.* LADY BRACKNELL *looks vaguely about as if she could not understand what the noise was. Finally turns round.*) Gwendolen, the carriage!

GWENDOLEN: Yes, Mamma. (*Goes out, looking back at* JACK.)

LADY BRACKNELL (*sitting down*): You can take a seat, Mr. Worthing. (*Looks in her pocket for notebook and pencil.*)

JACK: Thank you, Lady Bracknell, I prefer standing.

LADY BRACKNELL (*pencil and notebook in hand*): I feel bound to tell you that you are not down on my list of eligible young men, although I have the same list as the dear Duchess of Bolton has. We work together, in fact. However, I am quite ready to enter your name, should your answers be what a really affectionate mother requires. Do you smoke?

JACK: Well, yes, I must admit I smoke.

LADY BRACKNELL: I am glad to hear it. A man should always have an occupation of some kind. There are far too many idle men in London as it is. How old are you?

JACK: Twenty-nine.

LADY BRACKNELL: A very good age to be married at. I have always been of opinion that a man who desires to get married should know either everything or nothing. Which do you know?

JACK (*after some hesitation*): I know nothing, Lady Bracknell.

LADY BRACKNELL: I am pleased to hear it. I do not approve of anything that tampers with natural ignorance. Ignorance is like a delicate exotic fruit; touch it and the bloom is gone. The whole theory of modern education is radically unsound. Fortunately in England, at any rate, education produces no effect whatsoever. If it did, it would prove a serious danger to the upper classes, and probably lead to acts of violence in Grosvenor Square. What is your income?

JACK: Between seven and eight thousand a year.

LADY BRACKNELL (*makes a note in her book*): In land, or in investments?

JACK: In investments, chiefly.

LADY BRACKNELL: That is satisfactory. What between the duties expected of one during one's lifetime, and the duties[12] exacted from one after one's death, land has ceased to be either a profit or a pleasure. It gives one position, and prevents one from keeping it up. That's all that can be said about land.

JACK: I have a country house with some land, of course, attached to it, about fifteen hundred acres, I believe; but I don't depend on that for my real income. In fact, as far as I can make out, the poachers are the only people who make anything out of it.

LADY BRACKNELL: A country house! How many bedrooms? Well, that point can be cleared up afterwards. You have a town house, I hope? A girl with a simple, unspoiled nature, like Gwendolen, could hardly be expected to reside in the country.

JACK: Well, I own a house in Belgrave Square, but it is let by the year to Lady Bloxham. Of course, I can get it back whenever I like, at six months' notice.

LADY BRACKNELL: Lady Bloxham? I don't know her.

JACK: Oh, she goes about very little. She is a lady considerably advanced in years.

LADY BRACKNELL: Ah, nowadays that is no guarantee of respectability of character. What number in Belgrave Square?

JACK: 149.

LADY BRACKNELL (*shaking her head*): The unfashionable side. I thought there was something. However, that could easily be altered.

JACK: Do you mean the fashion, or the side?

LADY BRACKNELL (*sternly*): Both, if necessary, I presume. What are your politics?

JACK: Well, I am afraid I really have none. I am a Liberal Unionist.

LADY BRACKNELL: Oh, they count as Tories. They dine with us. Or come in the evening, at any rate. Now to minor matters. Are your parents living?

JACK: I have lost both my parents.

LADY BRACKNELL: To lose one parent, Mr. Worthing, may be regarded as a misfortune; to lose both looks like carelessness. Who was your father? He was evidently a man of some wealth. Was he

---

[12] **duties:** Inheritance taxes

born in what the Radical papers call the purple of commerce, or did he rise from the ranks of the aristocracy?

JACK: I am afraid I really don't know. The fact is, Lady Bracknell, I said I had lost my parents. It would be nearer the truth to say that my parents seem to have lost me . . . I don't actually know who I am by birth. I was . . . well, I was found.

LADY BRACKNELL: Found!

JACK: The late Mr. Thomas Cardew, an old gentleman of a very charitable and kindly disposition, found me, and gave me the name of Worthing, because he happened to have a first-class ticket for Worthing in his pocket at the time. Worthing is a place in Sussex. It is a seaside resort.

LADY BRACKNELL: Where did the charitable gentleman who had a first-class ticket for this seaside resort find you?

JACK (*gravely*): In a handbag.

LADY BRACKNELL: A handbag?

JACK (*very seriously*): Yes, Lady Bracknell. I was in a handbag—a somewhat large, black leather handbag, with handles to it—an ordinary handbag in fact.

LADY BRACKNELL: In what locality did this Mr. James, or Thomas, Cardew come across this ordinary handbag?

JACK: In the cloakroom at Victoria Station. It was given to him in mistake for his own.

LADY BRACKNELL: The cloakroom at Victoria Station?

JACK: Yes. The Brighton line.

LADY BRACKNELL: The line is immaterial. Mr. Worthing, I confess I feel somewhat bewildered by what you have just told me. To be born, or at any rate bred, in a handbag, whether it had handles or not, seems to me to display a contempt for the ordinary decencies of family life that reminds one of the worst excesses of the French Revolution. And I presume you know what that unfortunate movement led to? As for the particular locality in which the handbag was found, a cloakroom at a railway station might serve to conceal a social indiscretion—had probably, indeed, been used for that purpose before now—but it could hardly be regarded as an assured basis for a recognized position in good society.

JACK: May I ask you then what you would advise me to do? I need hardly say I would do anything in the world to ensure Gwendolen's happiness.

LADY BRACKNELL: I would strongly advise you, Mr. Worthing, to try and acquire some relations as soon as possible, and to make a definite effort to produce at any rate one parent, of either sex, before the season is quite over.

JACK: Well, I don't see how I could possibly manage to do that. I can produce the handbag at any moment. It is in my dressing room at home. I really think that should satisfy you, Lady Bracknell.

LADY BRACKNELL: Me, sir! What has it to do with me? You can hardly imagine that I and Lord Bracknell would dream of allowing our only daughter—a girl brought up with the utmost care—to marry into a cloakroom, and form an alliance with a parcel. Good morning, Mr. Worthing!

(LADY BRACKNELL *sweeps out in majestic indignation.*)

JACK: Good morning! (ALGERNON, *from the other room, strikes up the Wedding March.* JACK *looks perfectly furious, and goes to the door.*) For goodness' sake don't play that ghastly tune, Algy! How idiotic you are!

The music stops and ALGERNON *enters cheerily.*

ALGERNON: Didn't it go off all right, old boy? You don't mean to say Gwendolen refused you? I know it is a way she has. She is always refusing people. I think it is most ill-natured of her.

JACK: Oh, Gwendolen is as right as a trivet.[13] As far as she is concerned, we are engaged. Her mother is perfectly unbearable. Never met such a Gorgon[14] . . . I don't really know what a Gorgon is like, but I am quite sure that Lady Bracknell is one. In any case, she is a monster, without being a myth, which is rather unfair. . . . I beg your pardon, Algy, I suppose I shouldn't talk about your own aunt in that way before you.

ALGERNON: My dear boy, I love hearing my relations abused. It is the only thing that makes me put up with them at all. Relations are simply a tedious pack of people, who haven't got the remotest knowledge of how to live, nor the smallest instinct about when to die.

JACK: Oh, that is nonsense!

ALGERNON: It isn't!

JACK: Well, I won't argue about the matter. You always want to argue about things.

---

[13] **trivet:** Proverbial expression meaning reliable (like a trivet used to support a kettle over a fire)
[14] **Gorgon:** Mythical female figure with writhing snakes for hair; her face turned anyone who looked at her into stone

ALGERNON: That is exactly what things were originally made for.

JACK: Upon my word, if I thought that, I'd shoot myself. . . . (*A pause.*) You don't think there is any chance of Gwendolen becoming like her mother in about a hundred and fifty years, do you, Algy?

ALGERNON: All women become like their mothers. That is their tragedy. No man does. That's his.

JACK: Is that clever?

ALGERNON: It is perfectly phrased! and quite as true as any observation in civilized life should be.

JACK: I am sick to death of cleverness. Everybody is clever nowadays. You can't go anywhere without meeting clever people. The thing has become an absolute public nuisance. I wish to goodness we had a few fools left.

ALGERNON: We have.

JACK: I should extremely like to meet them. What do they talk about?

ALGERNON: The fools? Oh! about the clever people, of course.

JACK: What fools.

ALGERNON: By the way, did you tell Gwendolen the truth about your being Ernest in town, and Jack in the country?

JACK (*in a very patronizing manner*): My dear fellow, the truth isn't quite the sort of thing one tells to a nice, sweet, refined girl. What extraordinary ideas you have about the way to behave to a woman!

ALGERNON: The only way to behave to a woman is to make love[15] to her, if she is pretty, and to someone else, if she is plain.

JACK: Oh, that is nonsense.

ALGERNON: What about your brother? What about the profligate Ernest?

JACK: Oh, before the end of the week I shall have got rid of him. I'll say he died in Paris of apoplexy. Lots of people die of apoplexy, quite suddenly, don't they?

ALGERNON: Yes, but it's hereditary, my dear fellow. It's a sort of thing that runs in families. You had much better say a severe chill.

JACK: You are sure a severe chill isn't hereditary, or anything of that kind?

ALGERNON: Of course it isn't!

JACK: Very well, then. My poor brother Ernest is carried off suddenly, in Paris, by a severe chill. That gets rid of him.

ALGERNON: But I thought you said that . . . Miss Cardew was a little too much interested in your poor brother Ernest? Won't she feel his loss a good deal?

JACK: Oh, that is all right. Cecily is not a silly romantic girl, I am glad to say. She has got a capital appetite, goes long walks, and pays no attention at all to her lessons.

ALGERNON: I would rather like to see Cecily.

JACK: I will take very good care you never do. She is excessively pretty, and she is only eighteen.

ALGERNON: Have you told Gwendolen yet that you have an excessively pretty ward who is only just eighteen?

JACK: Oh! one doesn't blurt these things out to people. Cecily and Gwendolen are perfectly certain to be extremely great friends. I'll bet you anything you like that half an hour after they have met, they will be calling each other sister.

ALGERNON: Women only do that when they have called each other a lot of other things first. Now, my dear boy, if we want to get a good table at Willis's, we really must go and dress. Do you know it is nearly seven?

JACK (*irritably*): Oh! it always is nearly seven.

ALGERNON: Well, I'm hungry.

JACK: I never knew you when you weren't. . . .

ALGERNON: What shall we do after dinner? Go to a theater?

JACK: Oh no! I loathe listening.

ALGERNON: Well, let us go to the Club?

JACK: Oh, no! I hate talking.

ALGERNON: Well, we might trot round to the Empire[16] at ten?

JACK: Oh, no! I can't bear looking at things. It is so silly.

ALGERNON: Well, what shall we do?

JACK: Nothing!

ALGERNON: It is awfully hard work doing nothing. However, I don't mind hard work where there is no definite object of any kind.

Enter LANE.

LANE: Miss Fairfax.

Enter GWENDOLEN, LANE *goes out.*

ALGERNON: Gwendolen, upon my word!

GWENDOLEN: Algy, kindly turn your back. I have something very particular to say to Mr. Worthing.

ALGERNON: Really, Gwendolen, I don't think I can allow this at all.

---

[15] **make love:** To pay court to her, to woo

[16] **Empire:** A music hall or variety theater

GWENDOLEN: Algy, you always adopt a strictly immoral attitude towards life. You are not quite old enough to do that. (ALGERNON *retires to the fireplace.*)

JACK: My own darling!

GWENDOLEN: Ernest, we may never be married. From the expression on mamma's face I fear we never shall. Few parents nowadays pay any regard to what their children say to them. The old-fashioned respect for the young is fast dying out. Whatever influence I ever had over mamma, I lost at the age of three. But although she may prevent us from becoming man and wife, and I may marry someone else, and marry often, nothing that she can possibly do can alter my eternal devotion to you.

JACK: Dear Gwendolen!

GWENDOLEN: The story of your romantic origin, as related to me by mamma, with unpleasing comments, has naturally stirred the deeper fibers of my nature. Your Christian name has an irresistible fascination. The simplicity of your character makes you exquisitely incomprehensible to me. Your town address at the Albany I have. What is your address in the country?

JACK: The Manor House, Woolton, Hertfordshire.

ALGERNON, *who has been carefully listening, smiles to himself, and writes the address on his shirt-cuff. Then picks up the* Railway Guide.

GWENDOLEN: There is a good postal service, I suppose? It may be necessary to do something desperate. That of course will require serious consideration. I will communicate with you daily.

JACK: My own one!

GWENDOLEN: How long do you remain in town?

JACK: Till Monday.

GWENDOLEN: Good! Algy, you may turn round now.

ALGERNON: Thanks, I've turned round already.

GWENDOLEN: You may also ring the bell.

JACK: You will let me see you to your carriage, my own darling?

GWENDOLEN: Certainly.

JACK (*to* LANE, *who now enters*): I will see Miss Fairfax out.

LANE: Yes, sir. (JACK *and* GWENDOLEN *go off.*)

LANE *presents several letters on a salver to* ALGERNON. *It is to be surmised that they are bills, as* ALGERNON, *after looking at the envelopes, tears them up.*

ALGERNON: A glass of sherry, Lane.

LANE: Yes, sir.

ALGERNON: Tomorrow, Lane, I'm going Bunburying.

LANE: Yes, sir.

ALGERNON: I shall probably not be back till Monday. You can put up my dress clothes, my smoking jacket, and all the Bunbury suits . . .

LANE: Yes, sir. (*Handing sherry.*)

ALGERNON: I hope tomorrow will be a fine day, Lane.

LANE: It never is, sir.

ALGERNON: Lane, you're a perfect pessimist.

LANE: I do my best to give satisfaction, sir.

Enter JACK. LANE *goes off.*

JACK: There's a sensible, intellectual girl! the only girl I ever cared for in my life. (ALGERNON *is laughing immoderately.*) What on earth are you so amused at?

ALGERNON: Oh, I'm a little anxious about poor Bunbury, that is all.

JACK: If you don't take care, your friend Bunbury will get you into a serious scrape some day.

ALGERNON: I love scrapes. They are the only things that are never serious.

JACK: Oh, that's nonsense, Algy. You never talk anything but nonsense.

ALGERNON: Nobody ever does.

JACK *looks indignantly at him, and leaves the room.* ALGERNON *lights a cigarette, reads his shirt-cuff, and smiles.*

ACT DROP[17]

ACT II

Garden at the Manor House. A flight of gray stone steps leads up to the house. The garden, an old-fashioned one, full of roses. Time of year, July. Basket chairs, and a table covered with books, are set under a large yew tree.

MISS PRISM *discovered seated at the table.* CECILY *is at the back, watering flowers.*

MISS PRISM (*calling*): Cecily, Cecily! Surely such a utilitarian occupation as the watering of flowers is rather Moulton's duty than yours? Especially at a moment when intellectual pleasures

---

[17] **act drop**: A curtain lowered in a theater during intermission

await you. Your German grammar is on the table. Pray open it at page fifteen. We will repeat yesterday's lesson.

CECILY (*coming over very slowly*): But I don't like German. It isn't at all a becoming language. I know perfectly well that I look quite plain after my German lesson.

MISS PRISM: Child, you know how anxious your guardian is that you should improve yourself in every way. He laid particular stress on your German, as he was leaving for town yesterday. Indeed, he always lays stress on your German when he is leaving for town.

CECILY: Dear Uncle Jack is so very serious! Sometimes he is so serious that I think he cannot be quite well.

MISS PRISM (*drawing herself up*): Your guardian enjoys the best of health, and his gravity of demeanor is especially to be commended in one so comparatively young as he is. I know no one who has a higher sense of duty and responsibility.

CECILY: I suppose that is why he often looks a little bored when we three are together.

MISS PRISM: Cecily! I am surprised at you. Mr. Worthing has many troubles in his life. Idle merriment and triviality would be out of place in his conversation. You must remember his constant anxiety about that unfortunate young man his brother.

CECILY: I wish Uncle Jack would allow that unfortunate young man, his brother, to come down here sometimes. We might have a good influence over him, Miss Prism. I am sure you certainly would. You know German, and geology, and things of that kind influence a man very much. (CECILY *begins to write in her diary*.)

MISS PRISM (*shaking her head*): I do not think that even I could produce any effect on a character that according to his own brother's admission is irretrievably weak and vacillating. Indeed I am not sure that I would desire to reclaim him. I am not in favor of this modern mania for turning bad people into good people at a moment's notice. As a man sows so let him reap.[1] You must put away your diary, Cecily. I really don't see why you should keep a diary at all.

CECILY: I keep a diary in order to enter the wonderful secrets of my life. If I didn't write them down, I should probably forget all about them.

MISS PRISM: Memory, my dear Cecily, is the diary that we all carry about with us.

CECILY: Yes, but it usually chronicles the things that have never happened, and couldn't possibly have happened. I believe that Memory is responsible for nearly all the three-volume novels that Mudie[2] sends us.

MISS PRISM: Do not speak slightingly of the three-volume novel, Cecily. I wrote one myself in earlier days.

CECILY: Did you really, Miss Prism? How wonderfully clever you are! I hope it did not end happily? I don't like novels that end happily. They depress me so much.

MISS PRISM: The good ended happily, and the bad unhappily. That is what Fiction means.

CECILY: I suppose so. But it seems very unfair. And was your novel ever published?

MISS PRISM: Alas! no. The manuscript unfortunately was abandoned. (CECILY *starts*.) I used the word in the sense of lost or mislaid. To your work, child, these speculations are profitless.

CECILY (*smiling*): But I see dear Dr. Chasuble coming up through the garden.

MISS PRISM (*rising and advancing*): Dr. Chasuble! This is indeed a pleasure.

Enter CANON CHASUBLE.

CHASUBLE: And how are we this morning? Miss Prism, you are, I trust, well?

CECILY: Miss Prism has just been complaining of a slight headache. I think it would do her so much good to have a short stroll with you in the Park, Dr. Chasuble.

MISS PRISM: Cecily, I have not mentioned anything about a headache.

CECILY: No, dear Miss Prism, I know that, but I felt instinctively that you had a headache. Indeed I was thinking about that, and not about my German lesson, when the Rector came in.

CHASUBLE: I hope, Cecily, you are not inattentive.

CECILY: Oh, I am afraid I am.

CHASUBLE: That is strange. Were I fortunate enough to be Miss Prism's pupil, I would hang upon her lips. (MISS PRISM *glares*.) I spoke metaphorically.—My metaphor was drawn from bees. Ahem! Mr. Worthing, I suppose, has not returned from town yet?

MISS PRISM: We do not expect him till Monday afternoon.

CHASUBLE: Ah yes, he usually likes to spend his Sunday in London. He is not one of those whose

---

[1] . . . **reap:** Galatians vi.7

[2] **Mudie:** A lending library

sole aim is enjoyment, as, by all accounts, that unfortunate young man his brother seems to be. But I must not disturb Egeria[3] and her pupil any longer.

MISS PRISM: Egeria? My name is Laetitia, Doctor.

CHASUBLE (*bowing*): A classical allusion merely, drawn from the Pagan authors. I shall see you both no doubt at Evensong?[4]

MISS PRISM: I think, dear Doctor, I will have a stroll with you. I find I have a headache after all, and a walk might do it good.

CHASUBLE: With pleasure, Miss Prism, with pleasure. We might go as far as the schools and back.

MISS PRISM: That would be delightful. Cecily, you will read your Political Economy in my absence. The chapter on the Fall of the Rupee you may omit. It is somewhat too sensational. Even these metallic problems have their melodramatic side. (*Goes down the garden with* DR. CHASUBLE.)

CECILY (*picks up books and throws them back on table*): Horrid Political Economy! Horrid Geography! Horrid, horrid German!

Enter MERRIMAN *with a card on a salver.*

MERRIMAN: Mr. Ernest Worthing has just driven over from the station. He has brought his luggage with him.

CECILY (*takes the card and reads it*): "Mr. Ernest Worthing, B.4, The Albany, W." Uncle Jack's brother! Did you tell him Mr. Worthing was in town?

MERRIMAN: Yes, Miss. He seemed very much disappointed. I mentioned that you and Miss Prism were in the garden. He said he was anxious to speak to you privately for a moment.

CECILY: Ask Mr. Ernest Worthing to come here. I suppose you had better talk to the housekeeper about a room for him.

MERRIMAN: Yes, Miss. (MERRIMAN *goes off.*)

CECILY: I have never met any really wicked person before. I feel rather frightened. I am so afraid he will look just like everyone else.

Enter ALGERNON, *very gay and debonair.*

He does!

ALGERNON (*raising his hat*): You are my little cousin Cecily, I'm sure.

CECILY: You are under some strange mistake. I am not little. In fact, I believe I am more than usually tall for my age. (ALGERNON *is rather taken aback.*) But I am your cousin Cecily. You, I see from your card, are Uncle Jack's brother, my cousin Ernest, my wicked cousin Ernest.

ALGERNON: Oh! I am not really wicked at all, Cousin Cecily. You mustn't think that I am wicked.

CECILY: If you are not, then you have certainly been deceiving us all in a very inexcusable manner. I hope you have not been leading a double life, pretending to be wicked and being really good all the time. That would be hypocrisy.

ALGERNON (*looks at her in amazement*): Oh! Of course I have been rather reckless.

CECILY: I am glad to hear it.

ALGERNON: In fact, now you mention the subject, I have been very bad in my own small way.

CECILY: I don't think you should be so proud of that, though I am sure it must have been very pleasant.

ALGERNON: It is much pleasanter being here with you.

CECILY: I can't understand how you are here at all. Uncle Jack won't be back till Monday afternoon.

ALGERNON: That is a great disappointment. I am obliged to go up by the first train on Monday morning. I have a business appointment that I am anxious . . . to miss!

CECILY: Couldn't you miss it anywhere but in London?

ALGERNON: No: the appointment is in London.

CECILY: Well, I know, of course, how important it is not to keep a business engagement, if one wants to retain any sense of the beauty of life, but still I think you had better wait till Uncle Jack arrives. I know he wants to speak to you about your emigrating.

ALGERNON: About my what?

CECILY: Your emigrating. He has gone up to buy your outfit.

ALGERNON: I certainly wouldn't let Jack buy my outfit. He has no taste in neckties at all.

CECILY: I don't think you will require neckties. Uncle Jack is sending you to Australia.

ALGERNON: Australia! I'd sooner die.

CECILY: Well, he said at dinner on Wednesday night, that you would have to choose between this world, the next world, and Australia.

ALGERNON: Oh, well! The accounts I have received of Australia and the next world are not

---

[3] **Egeria:** Mythical Roman female advisor of statesmen
[4] **Evensong:** Evening church service

particularly encouraging. This world is good enough for me, Cousin Cecily.

CECILY: Yes, but are you good enough for it?

ALGERNON: I'm afraid I'm not that. That is why I want you to reform me. You might make that your mission, if you don't mind, Cousin Cecily.

CECILY: I'm afraid I've no time, this afternoon.

ALGERNON: Well, would you mind my reforming myself this afternoon?

CECILY: It is rather Quixotic of you. But I think you should try.

ALGERNON: I will. I feel better already.

CECILY: You are looking a little worse.

ALGERNON: That is because I am hungry.

CECILY: How thoughtless of me. I should have remembered that when one is going to lead an entirely new life, one requires regular and wholesome meals. Won't you come in?

ALGERNON: Thank you. Might I have a buttonhole first?[5] I never have any appetite unless I have a buttonhole first.

CECILY: A Maréchal Niel?[6] (*Picks up scissors.*)

ALGERNON: No, I'd sooner have a pink rose.

CECILY: Why? (*Cuts a flower.*)

ALGERNON: Because you are like a pink rose, Cousin Cecily.

CECILY: I don't think it can be right for you to talk to me like that. Miss Prism never says such things to me.

ALGERNON: Then Miss Prism is a shortsighted old lady. (CECILY *puts the rose in his buttonhole.*) You are the prettiest girl I ever saw.

CECILY: Miss Prism says that all good looks are a snare.

ALGERNON: They are a snare that every sensible man would like to be caught in.

CECILY: Oh, I don't think I would care to catch a sensible man. I shouldn't know what to talk to him about.

They pass into the house. MISS PRISM *and* DR. CHASUBLE *return.*

MISS PRISM: You are too much alone, dear Dr. Chasuble. You should get married. A misanthrope I can understand—a womanthrope, never!

CHASUBLE (*with a scholar's shudder*): Believe me, I do not deserve so neologistic a phrase. The precept as well as the practice of the Primitive Church was distinctly against matrimony.

MISS PRISM (*sententiously*): That is obviously the reason why the Primitive Church has not lasted up to the present day. And you do not seem to realize, dear Doctor, that by persistently remaining single, a man converts himself into a permanent public temptation. Men should be more careful; this very celibacy leads weaker vessels astray.

CHASUBLE: But is a man not equally attractive when married?

MISS PRISM: No married man is ever attractive except to his wife.

CHASUBLE: And often, I've been told, not even to her.

MISS PRISM: That depends on the intellectual sympathies of the woman. Maturity can always be depended on. Ripeness can be trusted. Young women are green. (DR. CHASUBLE *starts.*) I spoke horticulturally. My metaphor was drawn from fruits. But where is Cecily?

CHASUBLE: Perhaps she followed us to the schools.

Enter JACK *slowly from the back of the garden. He is dressed in the deepest mourning, with crepe hatband and black gloves.*

MISS PRISM: Mr. Worthing!

CHASUBLE: Mr. Worthing?

MISS PRISM: This is indeed a surprise. We did not look for you till Monday afternoon.

JACK (*shakes* MISS PRISM's *hand in a tragic manner*): I have returned sooner than I expected. Dr. Chasuble, I hope you are well?

CHASUBLE: Dear Mr. Worthing, I trust this garb of woe does not betoken some terrible calamity?

JACK: My brother.

MISS PRISM: More shameful debts and extravagance?

CHASUBLE: Still leading his life of pleasure?

JACK (*shaking his head*): Dead!

CHASUBLE: Your brother Ernest dead?

JACK: Quite dead.

MISS PRISM: What a lesson for him! I trust he will profit by it.

CHASUBLE: Mr. Worthing, I offer you my sincere condolence. You have at least the consolation of knowing that you were always the most generous and forgiving of brothers.

JACK: Poor Ernest! He had many faults, but it is a sad, sad blow.

CHASUBLE: Very sad indeed. Were you with him at the end?

JACK: No. He died abroad; in Paris, in fact. I had a telegram last night from the manager of the Grand Hotel.

---

[5] **buttonhole:** A flower for the buttonhole of a man's jacket

[6] **Maréchal Niel:** A variety of rose

CHASUBLE: Was the cause of death mentioned?

JACK: A severe chill, it seems.

MISS PRISM: As a man sows, so shall he reap.

CHASUBLE (*raising his hand*): Charity, dear Miss Prism, charity! None of us are perfect. I myself am peculiarly susceptible to draughts. Will the interment take place here?

JACK: No. He seems to have expressed a desire to be buried in Paris.

CHASUBLE: In Paris! (*Shakes his head.*) I fear that hardly points to any very serious state of mind at the last. You would no doubt wish me to make some slight allusion to this tragic domestic affliction next Sunday. (JACK *presses his hand convulsively.*) My sermon on the meaning of the manna in the wilderness can be adapted to almost any occasion, joyful, or, as in the present case, distressing. (*All sigh.*) I have preached it at harvest celebrations, christening, confirmations, on days of humiliation and festal days. The last time I delivered it was in the Cathedral, as a charity sermon on behalf of the Society for the Prevention of Discontent among the Upper Orders. The Bishop, who was present, was much struck by some of the analogies I drew.

JACK: Ah! that reminds me, you mentioned christenings I think, Dr. Chasuble? I suppose you know how to christen all right? (DR. CHASUBLE *looks astounded.*) I mean, of course, you are continually christening, aren't you?

MISS PRISM: It is, I regret to say, one of the Rector's most constant duties in this parish. I have often spoken to the poorer classes on the subject. But they don't seem to know what thrift is.

CHASUBLE: But is there any particular infant in whom you are interested, Mr. Worthing? Your brother was, I believe, unmarried, was he not?

JACK: Oh yes.

MISS PRISM (*bitterly*): People who live entirely for pleasure usually are.

JACK: But it is not for any child, dear Doctor. I am very fond of children. No! the fact is, I would like to be christened myself, this afternoon, if you have nothing better to do.

CHASUBLE: But surely, Mr. Worthing, you have been christened already?

JACK: I don't remember anything about it.

CHASUBLE: But have you any grave doubts on the subject?

JACK: I certainly intend to have. Of course I don't know if the thing would bother you in any way, or if you think I am a little too old now.

CHASUBLE: Not at all. The sprinkling, and, indeed, the immersion of adults is a perfectly canonical practice.

JACK: Immersion!

CHASUBLE: You need have no apprehensions. Sprinkling is all that is necessary, or indeed I think advisable. Our weather is so changeable. At what hour would you wish the ceremony performed?

JACK: Oh, I might trot round about five if that would suit you.

CHASUBLE: Perfectly, perfectly! In fact I have two similar ceremonies to perform at that time. A case of twins that occurred recently in one of the outlying cottages on your own estate. Poor Jenkins the carter, a most hard-working man.

JACK: Oh! I don't see much fun in being christened along with other babies. It would be childish. Would half-past five do?

CHASUBLE: Admirably! Admirably! (*Takes out watch.*) And now, dear Mr. Worthing, I will not intrude any longer into a house of sorrow. I would merely beg you not to be too much bowed down by grief. What seems to us bitter trials are often blessings in disguise.

MISS PRISM: This seems to me a blessing of an extremely obvious kind.

Enter CECILY *from the house.*

CECILY: Uncle Jack! Oh, I am pleased to see you back. But what horrid clothes you have got on. Do go and change them.

MISS PRISM: Cecily!

CHASUBLE: My child! My child! (CECILY *goes towards* JACK; *he kisses her brow in a melancholy manner.*)

CECILY: What is the matter, Uncle Jack? Do look happy! You look as if you had toothache, and I have got such a surprise for you. Who do you think is in the dining room? Your brother!

JACK: Who?

CECILY: Your brother Ernest. He arrived about half an hour ago.

JACK: What nonsense! I haven't got a brother.

CECILY: Oh, don't say that. However badly he may have behaved to you in the past he is still your brother. You couldn't be so heartless as to disown him. I'll tell him to come out. And you will shake hands with him, won't you, Uncle Jack? (*Runs back into the house.*)

CHASUBLE: These are very joyful tidings.

MISS PRISM: After we had all been resigned to his loss, his sudden return seems to me peculiarly distressing.

JACK: My brother is in the dining room? I don't

know what it all means. I think it is perfectly absurd.

Enter ALGERNON *and* CECILY *hand in hand. They come slowly up to* JACK.

JACK: Good heavens! (*Motions* ALGERNON *away*.)

ALGERNON: Brother John, I have come down from town to tell you that I am very sorry for all the trouble I have given you, and that I intend to lead a better life in the future. (JACK *glares at him and does not take his hand.*)

CECILY: Uncle Jack, you are not going to refuse your own brother's hand?

JACK: Nothing will induce me to take his hand. I think his coming down here disgraceful. He knows perfectly well why.

CECILY: Uncle Jack, do be nice. There is some good in everyone. Ernest has just been telling me about his poor invalid friend Mr. Bunbury whom he goes to visit so often. And surely there must be much good in one who is kind to an invalid, and leaves the pleasures of London to sit by a bed of pain.

JACK: Oh! he has been talking about Bunbury, has he?

CECILY: Yes, he has told me all about poor Mr. Bunbury, and his terrible state of health.

JACK: Bunbury! Well, I won't have him talk to you about Bunbury or about anything else. It is enough to drive one perfectly frantic.

ALGERNON: Of course I admit that the faults were all on my side. But I must say that I think that Brother John's coldness to me is peculiarly painful. I expected a more enthusiastic welcome, especially considering it is the first time I have come here.

CECILY: Uncle Jack, if you don't shake hands with Ernest I will never forgive you.

JACK: Never forgive me?

CECILY: Never, never, never!

JACK: Well, this is the last time I shall ever do it. (*Shakes hands with* ALGERNON *and glares.*)

CHASUBLE: It's pleasant, is it not, to see so perfect a reconciliation? I think we might leave the two brothers together.

MISS PRISM: Cecily, you will come with us.

CECILY: Certainly, Miss Prism. My little task of reconciliation is over.

CHASUBLE: You have done a beautiful action today, dear child.

MISS PRISM: We must not be premature in our judgments.

CECILY: I feel very happy. (*They all go off except* JACK *and* ALGERNON.)

JACK: You young scoundrel, Algy, you must get out of this place as soon as possible. I don't allow any Bunburying here.

Enter MERRIMAN.

MERRIMAN: I have put Mr. Ernest's things in the room next to yours, sir. I suppose that is all right?

JACK: What?

MERRIMAN: Mr. Ernest's luggage, sir. I have unpacked it and put it in the room next to your own.

JACK: His luggage?

MERRIMAN: Yes, sir. Three portmanteaus,[7] a dressing case, two hatboxes, and a large luncheon basket.

ALGERNON: I am afraid I can't stay more than a week this time.

JACK: Merriman, order the dogcart[8] at once. Mr. Ernest has been suddenly called back to town.

MERRIMAN: Yes, sir. (*Goes back into the house.*)

ALGERNON: What a fearful liar you are, Jack. I have not been called back to town at all.

JACK: Yes, you have.

ALGERNON: I haven't heard anyone call me.

JACK: Your duty as a gentleman calls you back.

ALGERNON: My duty as a gentleman has never interfered with my pleasures in the smallest degree.

JACK: I can quite understand that.

ALGERNON: Well, Cecily is a darling.

JACK: You are not to talk of Miss Cardew like that. I don't like it.

ALGERNON: Well, I don't like your clothes. You look perfectly ridiculous in them. Why on earth don't you go up and change? It is perfectly childish to be in deep mourning for a man who is actually staying for a whole week with you in your house as a guest. I call it grotesque.

JACK: You are certainly not staying with me for a whole week as a guest or anything else. You have got to leave . . . by the four-five train.

ALGERNON: I certainly won't leave you so long as you are in mourning. It would be most unfriendly. If I were in mourning you would stay with me, I suppose. I should think it very unkind if you didn't.

---

[7] **portmanteaus:** Large suitcases
[8] **dogcart:** A vehicle drawn by a horse and accommodating two persons

JACK: Well, will you go if I change my clothes?

ALGERNON: Yes, if you are not too long. I never saw anybody take so long to dress, and with such little result.

JACK: Well, at any rate, that is better than being always overdressed as you are.

ALGERNON: If I am occasionally a little overdressed, I make up for it by being always immensely overeducated.

JACK: Your vanity is ridiculous, your conduct an outrage, and your presence in my garden utterly absurd. However, you have got to catch the four-five, and I hope you will have a pleasant journey back to town. This Bunburying, as you call it, has not been a great success for you. (*Goes into the house.*)

ALGERNON: I think it has been a great success. I'm in love with Cecily, and that is everything.

Enter CECILY *at the back of the garden. She picks up the can and begins to water the flowers.*

But I must see her before I go, and make arrangements for another Bunbury. Ah, there she is.

CECILY: Oh, I merely came back to water the roses. I thought you were with Uncle Jack.

ALGERNON: He's gone to order the dogcart for me.

CECILY: Oh, is he going to take you for a nice drive?

ALGERNON: He's going to send me away.

CECILY: Then have we got to part?

ALGERNON: I am afraid so. It's a very painful parting.

CECILY: It is always painful to part from people whom one has known for a very brief space of time. The absence of old friends one can endure with equanimity. But even a momentary separation from anyone to whom one has just been introduced is almost unbearable.

ALGERNON: Thank you.

Enter MERRIMAN.

MERRIMAN: The dogcart is at the door, sir.

(ALGERNON *looks appealing at* CECILY.)

CECILY: It can wait, Merriman . . . for . . . five minutes.

MERRIMAN: Yes, miss.

Exit MERRIMAN.

ALGERNON: I hope, Cecily, I shall not offend you if I state quite frankly and openly that you seem to me to be in every way the visible personification of absolute perfection.

CECILY: I think your frankness does you great credit, Ernest. If you will allow me, I will copy your remarks into my diary. (*Goes over to table and begins writing in diary.*)

ALGERNON: Do you really keep a diary? I'd give anything to look at it. May I?

CECILY: Oh no. (*Puts her hand over it.*) You see, it is simply a very young girl's record of her own thoughts and impressions, and consequently meant for publication. When it appears in volume form I hope you will order a copy. But pray, Ernest, don't stop. I delight in taking down from dictation. I have reached "absolute perfection." You can go on. I am quite ready for more.

ALGERNON (*somewhat taken aback*): Ahem! Ahem!

CECILY: Oh, don't cough, Ernest. When one is dictating one should speak fluently and not cough. Besides, I don't know how to spell a cough. (*Writes as* ALGERNON *speaks.*)

ALGERNON (*speaking very rapidly*): Cecily, ever since I first looked upon your wonderful and incomparable beauty, I have dared to love you wildly, passionately, devotedly, hopelessly.

CECILY: I don't think that you should tell me that you love me wildly, passionately, devotedly, hopelessly. Hopelessly doesn't seem to make much sense, does it?

ALGERNON: Cecily.

Enter MERRIMAN.

MERRIMAN: The dogcart is waiting, sir.

ALGERNON: Tell it to come round next week, at the same hour.

MERRIMAN (*looks at* CECILY, *who makes no sign*): Yes, sir.

MERRIMAN *retires.*

CECILY: Uncle Jack would be very much annoyed if he knew you were staying on till next week, at the same hour.

ALGERNON: Oh, I don't care about Jack. I don't care for anybody in the whole world but you. I love you, Cecily. You will marry me, won't you?

CECILY: You silly boy! Of course. Why, we have been engaged for the last three months.

ALGERNON: For the last three months?

CECILY: Yes, it will be exactly three months on Thursday.

ALGERNON: But how did we become engaged?

CECILY: Well, ever since dear Uncle Jack first confessed to us that he had a younger brother who was very wicked and bad, you of course have formed the chief topic of conversation between myself and Miss Prism. And of course a man who is much talked about is always very attractive. One feels there must be something in him, after all. I daresay it was foolish of me, but I fell in love with you, Ernest.

ALGERNON: Darling. And when was the engagement actually settled?

CECILY: On the 14th of February last. Worn out by your entire ignorance of my existence, I determined to end the matter one way or the other, and after a long struggle with myself I accepted you under this dear old tree here. The next day I bought this little ring in your name, and this is the little bangle with the true lovers' knot I promised you always to wear.

ALGERNON: Did I give you this? It's very pretty, isn't it?

CECILY: Yes, you've wonderfully good taste, Ernest. It's the excuse I've always given for your leading such a bad life. And this is the box in which I keep all your dear letters. (*Kneels at table, opens box, and produces letters tied up with blue ribbon.*)

ALGERNON: My letters! But, my own sweet Cecily, I have never written you any letters.

CECILY: You need hardly remind me of that, Ernest. I remember only too well that I was forced to write your letters for you. I wrote always three times a week, and sometimes oftener.

ALGERNON: Oh, do let me read them, Cecily?

CECILY: Oh, I couldn't possibly. They would make you far too conceited. (*Replaces box.*) The three you wrote me after I had broken off the engagement are so beautiful, and so badly spelled, that even now I can hardly read them without crying a little.

ALGERNON: But was our engagement ever broken off?

CECILY: Of course it was. On the 22nd of last March. You can see the entry if you like. (*Shows diary.*) "Today I broke off my engagement with Ernest. I feel it is better to do so. The weather still continues charming."

ALGERNON: But why on earth did you break it off? What had I done? I had done nothing at all. Cecily, I am very much hurt indeed to hear you broke it off. Particularly when the weather was so charming.

CECILY: It would hardly have been a really serious engagement if it hadn't been broken off at least once. But I forgave you before the week was out.

ALGERNON (*crossing to her, and kneeling*): What a perfect angel you are, Cecily.

CECILY: You dear romantic boy. (*He kisses her, she puts her fingers through his hair.*) I hope your hair curls naturally, does it?

ALGERNON: Yes, darling, with a little help from others.

CECILY: I am so glad.

ALGERNON: You'll never break off our engagement again. Cecily?

CECILY: I don't think I could break it off now that I have actually met you. Besides, of course, there is the question of your name.

ALGERNON: Yes, of course. (*Nervously.*)

CECILY: You must not laugh at me, darling, but it had always been a girlish dream of mine to love someone whose name was Ernest. (ALGERNON *rises*, CECILY *also.*) There is something in that name that seems to inspire absolute confidence. I pity any poor married woman whose husband is not called Ernest.

ALGERNON: But, my dear child, do you mean to say you could not love me if I had some other name?

CECILY: But what name?

ALGERNON: Oh, any name you like—Algernon—for instance. . . .

CECILY: But I don't like the name of Algernon.

ALGERNON: Well, my own dear, sweet, loving little darling, I really can't see why you should object to the name of Algernon. It is not at all a bad name. In fact, it is rather an aristocratic name. Half of the chaps who get into the Bankruptcy Court are called Algernon. But seriously, Cecily . . . (*moving to her*) if my name was Algy, couldn't you love me?

CECILY (*rising*): I might respect you, Ernest, I might admire your character, but I fear that I should not be able to give you my undivided attention.

ALGERNON: Ahem! Cecily! (*Picking up hat.*) Your Rector here is, I suppose, thoroughly experienced in the practice of all the rites and ceremonials of the Church?

CECILY: Oh, yes. Dr. Chasuble is a most learned man. He has never written a single book, so you can imagine how much he knows.

ALGERNON: I must see him at once on a most important christening—I mean on most important business.

CECILY: Oh!

ALGERNON: I shan't be away more than half an hour.

CECILY: Considering that we have been engaged since February the 14th, and that I only met you today for the first time, I think it is rather hard that you should leave me for so long a period as half an hour. Couldn't you make it twenty minutes?

ALGERNON: I'll be back in no time. (*Kisses her and rushes down the garden.*)

CECILY: What an impetuous boy he is! I like his hair so much. I must enter his proposal in my diary.

Enter MERRIMAN.

MERRIMAN: A Miss Fairfax just called to see Mr. Worthing. On very important business, Miss Fairfax states.

CECILY: Isn't Mr. Worthing in his library?

MERRIMAN: Mr. Worthing went over in the direction of the Rectory some time ago.

CECILY: Pray ask the lady to come out here; Mr. Worthing is sure to be back soon. And you can bring tea.

MERRIMAN: Yes, Miss. (*Goes out.*)

CECILY: Miss Fairfax! I suppose one of the many good elderly women who are associated with Uncle Jack in some of his philanthropic work in London. I don't quite like women who are interested in philanthropic work. I think it is so forward of them.

Enter MERRIMAN.

MERRIMAN: Miss Fairfax.

Enter GWENDOLEN. *Exit* MERRIMAN.

CECILY (*advancing to meet her*): Pray let me introduce myself to you. My name is Cecily Cardew.

GWENDOLEN: Cecily Cardew? (*Moving to her and shaking hands.*) What a very sweet name! Something tells me that we are going to be great friends. I like you already more than I can say. My first impressions of people are never wrong.

CECILY: How nice of you to like me so much after we have known each other such a comparatively short time. Pray sit down.

GWENDOLEN (*still standing up*): I may call you Cecily, may I not?

CECILY: With pleasure!

GWENDOLEN: And you will always call me Gwendolen, won't you?

CECILY: If you wish.

GWENDOLEN: Then that is all quite settled, is it not?

CECILY: I hope so. (*A pause. They both sit down together.*)

GWENDOLEN: Perhaps this might be a favorable opportunity for my mentioning who I am. My father is Lord Bracknell. You have never heard of papa, I suppose?

CECILY: I don't think so.

GWENDOLEN: Outside the family circle, papa, I am glad to say, is entirely unknown. I think that is quite as it should be. The home seems to me to be the proper sphere for the man. And certainly once a man begins to neglect his domestic duties he becomes painfully effeminate, does he not? And I don't like that. It makes men so very attractive. Cecily, mamma, whose views on education are remarkably strict, has brought me up to be extremely shortsighted; it is part of her system; so do you mind my looking at you through my glasses?

CECILY: Oh! not at all, Gwendolen. I am very fond of being looked at.

GWENDOLEN (*after examining* CECILY *carefully through a lorgnette*): You are here on a short visit, I suppose.

CECILY: Oh no! I live here.

GWENDOLEN (*severely*): Really? Your mother, no doubt, or some female relative of advanced years, resides here also?

CECILY: Oh no! I have no mother, nor, in fact, any relations.

GWENDOLEN: Indeed?

CECILY: My dear guardian, with the assistance of Miss Prism, has the arduous task of looking after me.

GWENDOLEN: Your guardian?

CECILY: Yes, I am Mr. Worthing's ward.

GWENDOLEN: Oh! It is strange he never mentioned to me that he had a ward. How secretive of him! He grows more interesting hourly. I am not sure, however, that the news inspires me with feelings of unmixed delight. (*Rising and going to her.*) I am very fond of you, Cecily; I have liked you ever since I met you! But I am bound to state that now that I know that you are Mr. Worthing's ward, I cannot help expressing a wish you were— well, just a little older than you seem to be—and not quite so very alluring in appearance. In fact, if I may speak candidly—

CECILY: Pray do! I think that whenever one has anything unpleasant to say, one should always be quite candid.

GWENDOLEN: Well, to speak with perfect candor, Cecily, I wish that you were fully forty-two, and more than usually plain for your age. Ernest has a strong upright nature. He is the very soul of truth and honor. Disloyalty would be as impossible to him as deception. But even men of the noblest possible moral character are extremely susceptible to the influence of the physical charms of others. Modern, no less than Ancient History, supplies us with many most painful examples of what I refer to. If it were not so, indeed, History would be quite unreadable.

CECILY: I bet your pardon, Gwendolen, did you say Ernest?

GWENDOLEN: Yes.

CECILY: Oh, but it is not Ernest Worthing who is my guardian. It is his brother—his elder brother.

GWENDOLEN (*sitting down again*): Ernest never mentioned to me that he had a brother.

CECILY: I am sorry to say they have not been on good terms for a long time.

GWENDOLEN: Ah! that accounts for it. And now that I think of it I have never heard any man mention his brother. The subject seems distasteful to most men. Cecily, you have lifted a load from my mind. I was growing almost anxious. It would have been terrible if any cloud had come across a friendship like ours, would it not? Of course you are quite, quite sure that it is not Mr. Ernest Worthing who is your guardian?

CECILY: Quite sure. (*A pause.*) In fact, I am going to be his.

GWENDOLEN (*inquiringly*): I beg your pardon?

CECILY (*rather shy and confidingly*): Dearest Gwendolen, there is no reason why I should make a secret of it to you. Our little country newspaper is sure to chronicle the fact next week. Mr. Ernest Worthing and I are engaged to be married.

GWENDOLEN (*quite politely, rising*): My darling Cecily, I think there must be some slight error. Mr. Ernest Worthing is engaged to me. The announcement will appear in the *Morning Post* on Saturday at the latest.

CECILY (*very politely, rising*): I am afraid you must be under some misconception. Ernest proposed to me exactly ten minutes ago. (*Shows diary.*)

GWENDOLEN (*examines diary through her lorgnette carefully*): It is very curious, for he asked me to be his wife yesterday afternoon at 5:30. If you would care to verify the incident, pray do so. (*Produces diary of her own.*) I never travel without my diary. One should always have something sensational to read in the train. I am so sorry, dear Cecily, if it is any disappointment to you, but I am afraid I have the prior claim.

CECILY: It would distress me more than I can tell you, dear Gwendolen, if it caused you any mental or physical anguish, but I feel bound to point out

that since Ernest proposed to you he clearly has changed his mind.

GWENDOLEN (*meditatively*): If the poor fellow has been entrapped into any foolish promise I shall consider it my duty to rescue him at once, and with a firm hand.

CECILY (*thoughtfully and sadly*): Whatever unfortunate entanglement my dear boy may have got into, I will never reproach him with it after we are married.

GWENDOLEN: Do you allude to me, Miss Cardew, as an entanglement? You are presumptuous. On an occasion of this kind it becomes more than a moral duty to speak one's mind. It becomes a pleasure.

CECILY: Do you suggest, Miss Fairfax, that I entrapped Ernest into an engagement? How dare you? This is no time for wearing the shallow mask of manners. When I see a spade I call it a spade.

GWENDOLEN (*satirically*): I am glad to say that I have never seen a spade. It is obvious that our social spheres have been widely different.

Enter MERRIMAN, *followed by the footman. He carries a salver, tablecloth, and plate stand.* CECILY *is about to retort. The presence of the servants exercises a restraining influence, under which both girls chafe.*

MERRIMAN: Shall I lay tea here as usual, Miss?

CECILY (*sternly, in a calm voice*): Yes, as usual. (MERRIMAN *begins to clear table and lay cloth. A long pause.* CECILY *and* GWENDOLEN *glare at each other.*)

GWENDOLEN: Are there many interesting walks in the vicinity, Miss Cardew?

CECILY: Oh! yes! a great many. From the top of one of the hills quite close one can see five counties.

GWENDOLEN: Five counties! I don't think I should like that; I hate crowds.

CECILY (*sweetly*): I suppose that is why you live in town? (GWENDOLEN *bites her lip, and beats her foot nervously with her parasol.*)

GWENDOLEN (*looking round*): Quite a well-kept garden this is, Miss Cardew.

CECILY: So glad you like it, Miss Fairfax.

GWENDOLEN: I had no idea there were any flowers in the country.

CECILY: Oh, flowers are as common here, Miss Fairfax, as people are in London.

GWENDOLEN: Personally I cannot understand how anybody manages to exist in the country, if anybody who is anybody does. The country always bores me to death.

CECILY: Ah! This is what the newspapers call agricultural depression, is it not? I believe the aristocracy are suffering very much from it just at present. It is almost an epidemic amongst them, I have been told. May I offer you some tea, Miss Fairfax?

GWENDOLEN (*with elaborate politeness*): Thank you. (*Aside.*) Detestable girl! But I require tea!

CECILY (*sweetly*): Sugar?

GWENDOLEN (*superciliously*): No, thank you. Sugar is not fashionable any more. (CECILY *looks angrily at her, takes up the tongs and puts four lumps of sugar into the cup.*)

CECILY (*severely*): Cake or bread and butter?

GWENDOLEN (*in a bored manner*): Bread and butter, please. Cake is rarely seen at the best houses nowadays.

CECILY (*cuts a very large slice of cake and puts it on the tray*): Hand that to Miss Fairfax.

MERRIMAN *does so, and goes out with footman.* GWENDOLEN *drinks the tea and makes a grimace. Puts down cup at once, reaches out her hand to the bread and butter, looks at it, and finds it is cake. Rises in indignation.*

GWENDOLEN: You have filled my tea with lumps of sugar, and though I asked most distinctly for bread and butter, you have given me cake. I am known for the gentleness of my disposition, and the extraordinary sweetness of my nature, but I warn you, Miss Cardew, you may go too far.

CECILY (*rising*): To save my poor, innocent, trusting boy from the machinations of any other girl there are no lengths to which I would not go.

GWENDOLEN: From the moment I saw you I distrusted you. I felt that you were false and deceitful. I am never deceived in such matters. My first impressions of people are invariably right.

CECILY: It seems to me, Miss Fairfax, that I am trespassing on your valuable time. No doubt you have many other calls of a similar character to make in the neighborhood.

Enter JACK.

GWENDOLEN (*catches sight of him*): Ernest! My own Ernest!

JACK: Gwendolen! Darling! (*Offers to kiss her.*)

GWENDOLEN (*drawing back*): A moment! May I ask if you are engaged to be married to this young lady? (*Points to* CECILY).

JACK (*laughing*): To dear little Cecily! Of course not! What could have put such an idea into your pretty little head?

GWENDOLEN: Thank you. You may! (*Offers her cheek.*)

CECILY (*very sweetly*): I knew there must be some misunderstanding, Miss Fairfax. The gentleman whose arm is at present round your waist is my dear guardian, Mr. John Worthing.

GWENDOLEN: I beg your pardon?

CECILY: This is Uncle Jack.

GWENDOLEN (*receding*): Jack! Oh!

Enter ALGERNON.

CECILY: Here is Ernest.

ALGERNON (*goes straight over to* CECILY *without noticing anyone else*): My own love! (*Offers to kiss her.*)

CECILY (*drawing back*): A moment, Ernest! May I ask you—are you engaged to be married to this young lady?

ALGERNON (*looking round*): To what young lady? Good heavens! Gwendolen!

CECILY: Yes, to good heavens, Gwendolen, I mean to Gwendolen.

ALGERNON (*laughing*): Of course not. What could have put such an idea into your pretty little head?

CECILY: Thank you. (*Presenting her cheek to be kissed.*) You may. (ALGERNON *kisses her.*)

GWENDOLEN: I felt there was some slight error, Miss Cardew. The gentleman who is now embracing you is my cousin, Mr. Algernon Moncrieff.

CECILY (*breaking away from* ALGERNON): Algernon Moncrieff! Oh! (*The two girls move towards each other and put their arms around each other's waists as if for protection.*)

CECILY: Are you called Algernon?

ALGERNON: I cannot deny it.

CECILY: Oh!

GWENDOLEN: Is your name really John?

JACK (*standing rather proudly*): I could deny it if I liked. I could deny anything if I liked. But my name certainly is John. It has been John for years.

CECILY (*to* GWENDOLEN): A gross deception has been practiced on both of us.

GWENDOLEN: My poor wounded Cecily!

CECILY: My sweet wronged Gwendolen!

GWENDOLEN (*slowly and seriously*): You will call me sister, will you not? (*They embrace.* JACK *and* ALGERNON *groan and walk up and down.*)

CECILY (*rather brightly*): There is just one question I would like to be allowed to ask my guardian.

GWENDOLEN: An admirable idea! Mr. Worthing, there is just one question I would like to be permitted to put to you. Where is your brother

Ernest? We are both engaged to be married to your brother Ernest, so it is a matter of some importance to us to know where your brother Ernest is at present.

JACK (*slowly and hesitatingly*): Gwendolen—Cecily—it is very painful for me to be forced to speak the truth. It is the first time in my life that I have ever been reduced to such a painful position, and I am really quite inexperienced in doing anything of the kind. However, I will tell you quite frankly that I have no brother Ernest. I have no brother at all. I never had a brother in my life, and I certainly have not the smallest intention of ever having one in the future.

CECILY (*surprised*): No brother at all?

JACK (*cheerily*): None!

GWENDOLEN (*severely*): Had you never a brother of any kind?

JACK (*pleasantly*): Never. Not even of any kind.

GWENDOLEN: I am afraid it is quite clear, Cecily, that neither of us is engaged to be married to anyone.

CECILY: It is not a very pleasant position for a young girl suddenly to find herself in. Is it?

GWENDOLEN: Let us go into the house. They will hardly venture to come after us there.

CECILY: No, men are so cowardly, aren't they?

They retire into the house with scornful looks.

JACK: This ghastly state of things is what you call Bunburying, I suppose?

ALGERNON: Yes, and a perfectly wonderful Bunbury it is. The most wonderful Bunbury I have ever had in my life.

JACK: Well, you've no right whatsoever to Bunbury here.

ALGERNON: That is absurd. One has a right to Bunbury anywhere one chooses. Every serious Bunburyist knows that.

JACK: Serious Bunburyist? Good heavens!

ALGERNON: Well, one must be serious about something, if one wants to have any amusement in life. I happen to be serious about Bunburying. What on earth you are serious about I haven't got the remotest idea. About everything, I should fancy. You have such an absolutely trivial nature.

JACK: Well, the only small satisfaction I have in the whole of this wretched business is that your friend Bunbury is quite exploded. You won't be able to run down to the country quite so often as you used to do, dear Algy. And a very good thing too.

ALGERNON: Your brother is a little off color, isn't he, dear Jack? You won't be able to disappear to London quite so frequently as your wicked custom was. And not a bad thing either.

JACK: As for your conduct towards Miss Cardew, I must say that your taking in a sweet, simple, innocent girl like that is quite inexcusable. To say nothing of the fact that she is my ward.

ALGERNON: I can see no possible defense at all for your deceiving a brilliant, clever, thoroughly experienced young lady like Miss Fairfax. To say nothing of the fact that she is my cousin.

JACK: I wanted to be engaged to Gwendolen, that is all. I love her.

ALGERNON: Well, I simply wanted to be engaged to Cecily. I adore her.

JACK: There is certainly no chance of your marrying Miss Cardew.

ALGERNON: I don't think there is much likelihood, Jack, of you and Miss Fairfax being united.

JACK: Well, that is no business of yours.

ALGERNON: If it was my business, I wouldn't talk about it. (*Begins to eat muffins.*) It is very vulgar to talk about one's business. Only people like stockbrokers do that, and then merely at dinner parties.

JACK: How you can sit there, calmly eating muffins when we are in this horrible trouble, I can't make out. You seem to me to be perfectly heartless.

ALGERNON: Well, I can't eat muffins in an agitated manner. The butter would probably get on my cuffs. One should always eat muffins quite calmly. It is the only way to eat them.

JACK: I say it's perfectly heartless your eating muffins at all, under the circumstances.

ALGERNON: When I am in trouble, eating is the only thing that consoles me. Indeed, when I am in really great trouble, as anyone who knows me intimately will tell you, I refuse everything except food and drink. At the present moment I am eating muffins because I am unhappy. Besides, I am particularly fond of muffins. (*Rising.*)

JACK (*rising*): Well, there is no reason why you should eat them all in that greedy way. (*Takes muffins from* ALGERNON.)

ALGERNON (*offering teacake*): I wish you would have teacake instead. I don't like teacake.

JACK: Good heavens! I suppose a man may eat his own muffins in his own garden.

ALGERNON: But you have just said it was perfectly heartless to eat muffins.

JACK: I said it was perfectly heartless of you, under the circumstances. That is a very different thing.

ALGERNON: That may be. But the muffins are the same. (*He seizes the muffin dish from* JACK.)

JACK: Algy, I wish to goodness you would go.

ALGERNON: You can't possibly ask me to go without having some dinner. It's absurd. I never go without my dinner. No one ever does, except vegetarians and people like that. Besides I have just made arrangements with Dr. Chasuble to be christened at a quarter to six under the name of Ernest.

JACK: My dear fellow, the sooner you give up that nonsense the better. I made arrangements this morning with Dr. Chasuble to be christened myself at 5:30, and I naturally will take the name of Ernest. Gwendolen would wish it. We can't both be christened Ernest. It's absurd. Besides, I have a perfect right to be christened if I like. There is no evidence at all that I have ever been christened by anybody. I should think it extremely probable I never was, and so does Dr. Chasuble. It is entirely different in your case. You have been christened already.

ALGERNON: Yes, but I have not been christened for years.

JACK: Yes, but you have been christened. That is the important thing.

ALGERNON: Quite so. So I know my constitution can stand it. If you are not quite sure about your ever having been christened, I must say I think it rather dangerous your venturing on it now. It might make you very unwell. You can hardly have forgotten that someone very closely connected with you was very nearly carried off this week in Paris by a severe chill.

JACK: Yes, but you said yourself that a severe chill was not hereditary.

ALGERNON: It usen't to be, I know—but I daresay it is now. Science is always making wonderful improvements in things.

JACK (*picking up the muffin dish*): Oh, that is nonsense; you are always talking nonsense.

ALGERNON: Jack, you are at the muffins again! I wish you wouldn't. There are only two left. (*Takes them.*) I told you I was particularly fond of muffins.

JACK: But I hate teacake.

ALGERNON: Why on earth then do you allow teacake to be served up for your guests? What ideas you have of hospitality!

JACK: Algernon! I have already told you to go. I don't want you here. Why don't you go!

ALGERNON: I haven't quite finished my tea yet! and there is one muffin left. (JACK *groans, and sinks into a chair.* ALGERNON *still continues eating.*)

ACT III

Morning room at the Manor House. GWEN-DOLEN *and* CECILY *are at the window, looking out into the garden.*

GWENDOLEN: The fact that they did not follow us at once into the house, as anyone else would have done, seems to me to show that they have some sense of shame left.

CECILY: They have been eating muffins. That looks like repentance.

GWENDOLEN (*after a pause*): They don't seem to notice us at all. Couldn't you cough?

CECILY: But I haven't got a cough.

GWENDOLEN: They're looking at us. What effrontery!

CECILY: They're approaching. That's very forward of them.

GWENDOLEN: Let us preserve a dignified silence.

CECILY: Certainly. It's the only thing to do now.

Enter JACK *followed by* ALGERNON. *They whistle some dreadful popular air from a British opera.*

GWENDOLEN: This dignified silence seems to produce an unpleasant effect.

CECILY: A most distasteful one.

GWENDOLEN: But we will not be the first to speak.

CECILY: Certainly not.

GWENDOLEN: Mr. Worthing, I have something very particular to ask you. Much depends on your reply.

CECILY: Gwendolen, your common sense is invaluable. Mr. Moncrieff, kindly answer me the following question. Why did you pretend to be my guardian's brother?

ALGERNON: In order that I might have an opportunity of meeting you.

CECILY (*to* GWENDOLEN): That certainly seems a satisfactory explanation, does it not?

GWENDOLEN: Yes, dear, if you can believe him.

CECILY: I don't. But that does not affect the wonderful beauty of his answer.

GWENDOLEN: True. In matters of grave importance, style, not sincerity, is the vital thing. Mr. Worthing, what explanation can you offer to me for pretending to have a brother? Was it in order that you might have an opportunity of coming up to town to see me as often as possible?

JACK: Can you doubt it, Miss Fairfax?

GWENDOLEN: I have the gravest doubts upon the subject. But I intend to crush them. This is not the moment for German skepticism. (*Moving to* CECILY.) Their explanations appear to be quite satisfactory, especially Mr. Worthing's. That seems to me to have the stamp of truth upon it.

CECILY: I am more than content with what Mr. Moncrieff said. His voice alone inspires one with absolute credulity.

GWENDOLEN: Then you think we should forgive them?

CECILY: Yes. I mean no.

GWENDOLEN: True! I had forgotten. There are principles at stake that one cannot surrender. Which of us should tell them? The task is not a pleasant one.

CECILY: Could we not both speak at the same time?

GWENDOLEN: An excellent idea! I nearly always speak at the same time as other people. Will you take the time from me?

CECILY: Certainly. (GWENDOLEN *beats time with uplifted finger.*)

GWENDOLEN *and* CECILY (*speaking together*): Your Christian names are still an insuperable barrier. That is all!

JACK *and* ALGERNON (*speaking together*): Our Christian names! Is that all? But we are going to be christened this afternoon.

GWENDOLEN (*to* JACK): For my sake you are prepared to do this terrible thing?

JACK: I am.

CECILY (*to* ALGERNON): To please me you are ready to face this fearful ordeal?

ALGERNON: I am!

GWENDOLEN: How absurd to talk of the equality of the sexes! Where questions of self-sacrifice are concerned, men are infinitely beyond us.

JACK: We are. (*Clasps hands with* ALGERNON.)

CECILY: They have moments of physical courage of which we women know absolutely nothing.

GWENDOLEN (*to* JACK): Darling!

ALGERNON (*to* CECILY): Darling! (*They fall into each other's arms.*)

Enter MERRIMAN. *When he enters he coughs loudly, seeing the situation.*

MERRIMAN: Ahem! Ahem! Lady Bracknell.

JACK: Good heavens!

Enter LADY BRACKNELL. *The couples separate in alarm.*

Exit MERRIMAN.

LADY BRACKNELL: Gwendolen! What does this mean?

GWENDOLEN: Merely that I am engaged to be married to Mr. Worthing, Mamma.

LADY BRACKNELL: Come here. Sit down. Sit down immediately. Hesitation of any kind is a sign of mental decay in the young, of physical weakness in the old. (*Turns to* JACK.) Apprised, sir, of my daughter's sudden flight by her trusty maid, whose confidence I purchased by means of a small coin, I followed her at once by a luggage train. Her unhappy father is, I am glad to say, under the impression that she is attending a more than usually lengthy lecture by the University Extension Scheme on the Influence of a permanent income on Thought. I do not propose to undeceive him. Indeed I have never undeceived him on any question. I would consider it wrong. But of course, you will clearly understand that all communication between yourself and my daughter must cease immediately from this moment. On this point, as indeed on all points, I am firm.

JACK: I am engaged to be married to Gwendolen, Lady Bracknell!

LADY BRACKNELL: You are nothing of the kind, sir. And now as regards Algernon! . . . Algernon!

ALGERNON: Yes, Aunt Augusta.

LADY BRACKNELL: May I ask if it is in this house that your invalid friend Mr. Bunbury resides?

ALGERNON (*stammering*): Oh! No! Bunbury doesn't live here. Bunbury is somewhere else at present. In fact, Bunbury is dead.

LADY BRACKNELL: Dead! When did Mr. Bunbury die? His death must have been extremely sudden.

ALGERNON (*airily*): Oh! I killed Bunbury this afternoon. I mean poor Bunbury died this afternoon.

LADY BRACKNELL: What did he die of?

ALGERNON: Bunbury? Oh, he was quite exploded.

LADY BRACKNELL: Exploded! Was he the victim of a revolutionary outrage? I was not aware that Mr. Bunbury was interested in social legislation. If so, he is well punished for his morbidity.

ALGERNON: My dear Aunt Augusta, I mean he was found out! The doctors found out that Bunbury could not live, that is what I mean—so Bunbury died.

LADY BRACKNELL: He seems to have had great confidence in the opinion of his physicians. I am glad, however, that he made up his mind at the last to some definite course of action, and acted upon proper medical advice. And now that we have finally got rid of this Mr. Bunbury, may I ask, Mr. Worthing, who is that young person whose hand my nephew Algernon is now holding in what seems to me a pecularily unnecessary manner?

JACK: That lady is Miss Cecily Cardew, my ward. (LADY BRACKNELL *bows coldly to* CECILY.)

ALGERNON: I am engaged to be married to Cecily, Aunt Augusta.

LADY BRACKNELL: I beg your pardon?

CECILY: Mr. Moncrieff and I are engaged to be married, Lady Bracknell.

LADY BRACKNELL (*with a shiver, crossing to the sofa and sitting down*): I do not know whether there is anything peculiarly exciting in the air of this particular part of Hertfordshire, but the number of engagements that go on seems to be considerably above the proper average that statistics have laid down for our guidance. I think some preliminary inquiry on my part would not be out of place. Mr. Worthing, is Miss Cardew at all connected with any of the larger railway stations in London? I merely desire information. Until yesterday I had no idea that there were any families or persons whose origin was a Terminus.[1] (JACK *looks perfectly furious, but restrains himself*.)

JACK (*in a cold, clear voice*): Miss Cardew is the granddaughter of the late Mr. Thomas Cardew of 149 Belgrave Square, S.W.; Gervase Park, Dorking, Surrey; and the Sporran, Fifeshire, N.B.[2]

LADY BRACKNELL: That sounds not unsatisfactory. Three addresses always inspire confidence, even in tradesmen. But what proof have I of their authenticity?

JACK: I have carefully preserved the Court Guides of the period. They are open to your inspection, Lady Bracknell.

LADY BRACKNELL (*grimly*): I have known strange errors in that publication.

JACK: Miss Cardew's family solicitors are Messrs. Markby, Markby, and Markby.

LADY BRACKNELL: Markby, Markby, and Markby? A firm of the very highest position in their profession. Indeed I am told that one of the Mr. Markbys is occasionally to be seen at dinner parties. So far I am satisfied.

JACK (*very irritably*): How extremely kind of you, Lady Bracknell! I have also in my possession, you will be pleased to hear, certificates of Miss Cardew's birth, baptism, whooping cough, registration, vaccination, confirmation, and the measles; both the German and the English variety.

LADY BRACKNELL: Ah! A life crowded with incident, I see; though perhaps somewhat too exciting for a young girl. I am not myself in favour of premature experiences. (*Rises, looks at her watch.*) Gwendolen! the time approaches for our departure. We have not a moment to lose. As a matter of form, Mr. Worthing, I had better ask you if Miss Cardew has any little fortune?

JACK: Oh! about a hundred and thirty thousand pounds in the Funds.[3] That is all. Good-bye, Lady Bracknell. So pleased to have seen you.

LADY BRACKNELL (*sitting down again*): A moment, Mr. Worthing. A hundred and thirty thousand pounds! And in the Funds! Miss Cardew seems to me a most attractive young lady, now that I look at her. Few girls of the present day have any really solid qualities, any of the qualities that last, and improve with time. We live, I regret to say, in an age of surfaces. (*To* CECILY.) Come over here, dear. (CECILY *goes across*.) Pretty child! your dress is sadly simple, and your hair seems almost as Nature might have left it. But we can soon alter all that. A thoroughly experienced French maid produces a really marvelous result in a very brief space of time. I remember recommending one to young Lady Lancing, and after three months her own husband did not know her.

JACK: And after six months nobody knew her.

LADY BRACKNELL (*glares at* JACK *for a few moments. Then bends, with a practiced smile, to* CECILY): Kindly turn round, sweet child. (CECILY *turns completely round*.) No, the side view is what I want. (CECILY *presents her profile*.) Yes, quite as I expected. There are distinct social possibilities in your profile. The two weak points in our age are its want of principle and its want of profile. The chin a little higher, dear. Style largely depends on the way the chin is worn. They are worn very high, just at present. Algernon!

ALGERNON: Yes, Aunt Augusta!

LADY BRACKNELL: There are distinct social possibilities in Miss Cardew's profile.

ALGERNON: Cecily is the sweetest, dearest, prettiest girl in the whole world. And I don't care twopence about social possibilities.

LADY BRACKNELL: Never speak disrespectfully of Society, Algernon. Only people who can't get into it do that. (*To* CECILY.) Dear child, of course you know that Algernon has nothing but his debts to depend upon. But I do not approve of mercenary marriages. When I married Lord Bracknell I had no fortune of any kind. But I never dreamed for a

---

[1] **Terminus:** Railway station
[2] **N.B.:** North Britain, i.e., Scotland

[3] **Funds:** Interest-bearing government bonds

moment of allowing that to stand in my way. Well, I suppose I must give my consent.

ALGERNON: Thank you, Aunt Augusta.

LADY BRACKNELL: Cecily, you may kiss me!

CECILY (*kisses her*): Thank you, Lady Bracknell.

LADY BRACKNELL: You may also address me as Aunt Augusta for the future.

CECILY: Thank you, Aunt Augusta.

LADY BRACKNELL: The marriage, I think, had better take place quite soon.

ALGERNON: Thank you, Aunt Augusta.

CECILY: Thank you, Aunt Augusta.

LADY BRACKNELL: To speak frankly, I am not in favor of long engagements. They give people the opportunity of finding out each other's character before marriage, which I think is never advisable.

JACK: I beg your pardon for interrupting you, Lady Bracknell, but this engagement is quite out of the question. I am Miss Cardew's guardian, and she cannot marry without my consent until she comes of age. That consent I absolutely decline to give.

LADY BRACKNELL: Upon what grounds, may I ask? Algernon is an extremely, I may almost say an ostentatiously, eligible young man. He has nothing, but he looks everything. What more can one desire?

JACK: It pains me very much to have to speak frankly to you, Lady Bracknell, about your nephew, but the fact is that I do not approve at all of his moral character. I suspect him of being untruthful. (ALGERNON *and* CECILY *look at him in indignant amazement.*)

LADY BRACKNELL: Untruthful! My nephew Algernon? Impossible! He is an Oxonian.[4]

JACK: I fear there can be no possible doubt about the matter. This afternoon during my temporary absence in London on an important question of romance, he obtained admission to my house by means of the false pretense of being my brother. Under an assumed name he drank, I've just been informed by my butler, an entire pint bottle of my Perrier-Jouet, Brut, '89; wine I was specially reserving for myself. Continuing his disgraceful deception, he succeeded in the course of the afternoon in alienating the affections of my only ward. He subsequently stayed to tea, and devoured every single muffin. And what makes his conduct all the more heartless is, that he was perfectly well aware from the first that I have no brother, that I never had a brother, and that I don't intend to have

a brother, not even of any kind. I distinctly told him so myself yesterday afternoon.

LADY BRACKNELL: Ahem! Mr. Worthing, after careful consideration I have decided entirely to overlook my nephew's conduct to you.

JACK: That is very generous of you, Lady Bracknell. My own decision, however, is unalterable. I decline to give my consent.

LADY BRACKNELL (*to* CECILY): Come here, sweet child. (CECILY *goes over.*) How old are you, dear?

CECILY: Well, I am really only eighteen, but I always admit to twenty when I go to evening parties.

LADY BRACKNELL: You are perfectly right in making some slight alteration. Indeed, no woman should ever be quite accurate about her age. It looks so calculating. . . . (*In a meditative manner.*) Eighteen, but admitting to twenty at evening parties. Well, it will not be very long before you are of age and free from the restraints of tutelage. So I don't think your guardian's consent is, after all, a matter of any importance.

JACK: Pray excuse me, Lady Bracknell, for interrupting you again, but it is only fair to tell you that according to the terms of her grandfather's will Miss Cardew does not come legally of age till she is thirty-five.

LADY BRACKNELL: That does not seem to me to be a grave objection. Thirty-five is a very attractive age. London society is full of women of the very highest birth who have, of their own free choice, remained thirty-five for years. Lady Dumbleton is an instance in point. To my own knowledge she has been thirty-five ever since she arrived at the age of forty, which was many years ago now. I see no reason why our dear Cecily should not be even still more attractive at the age you mention than she is at present. There will be a large accumulation of property.

CECILY: Algy, could you wait for me till I was thirty-five?

ALGERNON: Of course I could, Cecily. You know I could.

CECILY: Yes, I felt it instinctively, but I couldn't wait all that time. I hate waiting even five minutes for anybody. It always makes me rather cross. I am not punctual myself, I know, but I do like punctuality in others, and waiting, even to be married, is quite out of the question.

ALGERNON: Then what is to be done, Cecily?

CECILY: I don't know, Mr. Moncrieff.

LADY BRACKNELL: My dear Mr. Worthing, as Miss Cardew states positively that she cannot wait

---

[4] **Oxonian:** A graduate of Oxford

till she is thirty-five—a remark which I am bound to say seems to me to show a somewhat impatient nature—I would beg of you to reconsider your decision.

JACK: But my dear Lady Bracknell, the matter is entirely in your own hands. The moment you consent to my marriage with Gwendolen, I will most gladly allow your nephew to form an alliance with my ward.

LADY BRACKNELL (*rising and drawing herself up*): You must be quite aware that what you propose is out of the question.

JACK: Then a passionate celibacy is all that any of us can look forward to.

LADY BRACKNELL: That is not the destiny I propose for Gwendolen. Algernon, of course, can choose for himself. (*Pulls out her watch.*) Come, dear (GWENDOLEN *rises*), we have already missed five, if not six, trains. To miss any more might expose us to comment on the platform.

Enter DR. CHASUBLE.

CHASUBLE: Everything is quite ready for the christenings.

LADY BRACKNELL: The christenings, sir! Is not that somewhat premature?

CHASUBLE (*looking rather puzzled, and pointing to* JACK *and* ALGERNON): Both these gentlemen have expressed a desire for immediate baptism.

LADY BRACKNELL: At their age? The idea is grotesque and irreligious! Algernon, I forbid you to be baptized. I will not hear of such excesses. Lord Bracknell would be highly displeased if he learned that that was the way in which you wasted your time and money.

CHASUBLE: Am I to understand then that there are to be no christenings at all this afternoon?

JACK: I don't think that, as things are now, it would be of much practical value to either of us, Dr. Chasuble.

CHASUBLE: I am grieved to hear such sentiments from you, Mr. Worthing. They savor of the heretical views of the Anabaptists, views that I have completely refuted in four of my unpublished sermons. However, as your present mood seems to be one peculiarly secular, I will return to the church at once. Indeed, I have just been informed by the pew-opener that for the last hour and a half Miss Prism has been waiting for me in the vestry.

LADY BRACKNELL (*starting*): Miss Prism! Did I hear you mention a Miss Prism?

CHASUBLE: Yes, Lady Bracknell. I am on my way to join her.

LADY BRACKNELL: Pray allow me to detain you for a moment. This matter may prove to be one of vital importance to Lord Bracknell and myself. Is this Miss Prism a female of repellent aspect, remotely connected with education?

CHASUBLE (*somewhat indignantly*): She is the most cultivated of ladies, and the very picture of respectability.

LADY BRACKNELL: It is obviously the same person. May I ask what position she holds in your household?

CHASUBLE (*severely*): I am a celibate, madam.

JACK (*interposing*): Miss Prism, Lady Bracknell, has been for the last three years Miss Cardew's esteemed governess and valued companion.

LADY BRACKNELL: In spite of what I hear of her, I must see her at once. Let her be sent for.

CHASUBLE (*looking off*): She approaches; she is nigh.

Enter MISS PRISM *hurriedly.*

MISS PRISM: I was told you expected me in the vestry, dear Canon. I have been waiting for you there for an hour and three-quarters. (*Catches sight of* LADY BRACKNELL, *who has fixed her with a stony glare.* MISS PRISM *grows pale and quails. She looks anxiously round as if desirous to escape.*)

LADY BRACKNELL (*in a severe, judicial voice*): Prism! (MISS PRISM *bows her head in shame.*) Come here, Prism! (MISS PRISM *approaches in a humble manner.*) Prism! Where is that baby? (*General consternation. The* CANON *starts back in horror.* ALGERNON *and* JACK *pretend to be anxious to shield* CECILY *and* GWENDOLEN *from hearing the details of a terrible public scandal.*) Twenty-eight years ago, Prism, you left Lord Bracknell's house, Number 104, Upper Grosvenor Square, in charge of a perambulator that contained a baby of the male sex. You never returned. A few weeks later, through the elaborate investigations of the Metropolitan police, the perambulator was discovered at midnight standing by itself in a remote corner of Bayswater. It contained the manuscript of a three-volume novel of more than usually revolting sentimentality. (MISS PRISM *starts in involuntary indignation.*) But the baby was not there. (*Everyone looks at* MISS PRISM.) Prism! Where is that baby? (*A pause.*)

MISS PRISM: Lady Bracknell, I admit with shame that I do not know. I only wish I did. The plain facts of the case are these. On the morning of the day you mention, a day that is forever branded on my memory, I prepared as usual to take the baby out in its perambulator. I had also with me a somewhat old, but capacious handbag in which I had intended to place the manuscript of a work of fiction that I had written during my few unoccupied hours. In a moment of mental abstraction, for which I can never forgive myself, I deposited the manuscript in the bassinette and placed the baby in the handbag.

JACK (*who has been listening attentively*): But where did you deposit the handbag?

MISS PRISM: Do not ask me, Mr. Worthing.

JACK: Miss Prism, this is a matter of no small importance to me. I insist on knowing where you deposited the handbag that contained that infant.

MISS PRISM: I left it in the cloakroom of one of the larger railway stations in London.

JACK: What railway station?

MISS PRISM (*quite crushed*): Victoria. The Brighton line. (*Sinks into a chair.*)

JACK: I must retire to my room for a moment. Gwendolen, wait here for me.

GWENDOLEN: If you are not too long, I will wait here for you all my life. (*Exit* JACK *in great excitement.*)

CHASUBLE: What do you think this means, Lady Bracknell?

LADY BRACKNELL: I dare not even suspect, Dr. Chasuble. I need hardly tell you that in families of high position strange coincidences are not supposed to occur. They are hardly considered the thing.

Noises heard overhead as if someone was throwing trunks about. Every one looks up.

CECILY: Uncle Jack seems strangely agitated.

CHASUBLE: Your guardian has a very emotional nature.

LADY BRACKNELL: This noise is extremely unpleasant. It sounds as if he was having an argument. I dislike arguments of any kind. They are always vulgar, and often convincing.

CHASUBLE (*looking up*): It has stopped now. (*The noise is redoubled.*)

LADY BRACKNELL: I wish he would arrive at some conclusion.

GWENDOLEN: This suspense is terrible. I hope it will last.

ENTER JACK *with a handbag of black leather in his hand.*

JACK (*rushing over to* MISS PRISM): Is this the handbag, Miss Prism? Examine it carefully before you speak. The happiness of more than one life depends on your answer.

MISS PRISM (*calmly*): It seems to be mine. Yes, here is the injury it received through the upsetting of a Gower Street omnibus in younger and happier days. Here is the stain on the lining caused by the explosion of a temperance beverage, an incident that occurred at Leamington. And here, on the lock, are my initials. I had forgotten that in an extravagant mood I had had them placed there. The bag is undoubtedly mine. I am delighted to have it so unexpectedly restored to me. It has been a great inconvenience being without it all these years.

JACK (*in a pathetic voice*): Miss Prism, more is restored to you than this handbag. I was the baby you placed in it.

MISS PRISM (*amazed*): You?

JACK (*embracing her*): Yes . . . mother!

MISS PRISM (*recoiling in indignant astonishment*): Mr. Worthing. I am unmarried!

JACK: Unmarried! I do not deny that is a serious blow. But after all, who has the right to cast a stone against one who has suffered? Cannot repentance wipe out an act of folly? Why should there be one law for men, and another for women? Mother, I forgive you. (*Tries to embrace her again.*)

MISS PRISM (*still more indignant*): Mr. Worthing, there is some error. (*Pointing to* LADY BRACKNELL.) There is the lady who can tell you who you really are.

JACK (*after a pause*): Lady Bracknell, I hate to seem inquisitive, but would you kindly inform me who I am?

LADY BRACKNELL: I am afraid that the news I have to give you will not altogether please you. You are the son of my poor sister, Mrs. Moncrieff, and consequently Algernon's elder brother.

JACK: Algy's elder brother! Then I have a brother after all. I knew I had a brother! I always said I had a brother! Cecily—how could you have ever doubted that I had a brother? (*Seizes hold of* ALGERNON.) Dr. Chasuble, my unfortunate brother. Miss Prism, my unfortunate brother. Gwendolen, my unfortunate brother. Algy, you young scoundrel, you will have to treat me with more respect in the future. You have never behaved to me like a brother in all your life.

ALGERNON: Well, not till today, old boy, I admit. I did my best, however, though I was out of practice.

(*Shakes hands.*)

GWENDOLEN (*to* JACK): My own! But what own are you? What is your Christian name, now that you have become someone else?

JACK: Good heavens! . . . I had quite forgotten

that point. Your decision on the subject of my name is irrevocable, I suppose?

GWENDOLEN: I never change, except in my affections.

CECILY: What a noble nature you have, Gwendolen!

JACK: Then the question had better be cleared up at once. Aunt Augusta, a moment. At the time when Miss Prism left me in the handbag, had I been christened already?

LADY BRACKNELL: Every luxury that money could buy, including christening, had been lavished on you by your fond and doting parents.

JACK: Then I was christened! That is settled. Now, what name was I given? Let me know the worst.

LADY BRACKNELL: Being the eldest son you were naturally christened after your father.

JACK (*irritably*): Yes, but what was my father's Christian name?

LADY BRACKNELL (*meditatively*): I cannot at the present moment recall what the General's Christian name was. But I have no doubt he had one. He was eccentric, I admit. But only in later years. And that was the result of the Indian climate, and marriage, and indigestion, and other things of that kind.

JACK: Algy! Can't you recollect what our father's Christian name was?

ALGERNON: My dear boy, we were never even on speaking terms. He died before I was a year old.

JACK: His name would appear in the Army Lists of the period, I suppose, Aunt Augusta?

LADY BRACKNELL: The General was essentially a man of peace, except in his domestic life. But I have no doubt his name would appear in any military directory.

JACK: The Army Lists of the last forty years are here. These delightful records should have been my constant study. (*Rushes to bookcase and tears the books out.*) M. Generals . . . Mallam, Maxbohm, Magley—what ghastly names they have—Markby, Migsby, Mobbs, Moncrieff! Lieutenant 1840, Captain, Lieutenant-Colonel, Colonel, General 1869, Christian names, Ernest John. (*Puts book very quietly down and speaks quite calmly.*) I always told you, Gwendolen, my name was Ernest, didn't I? Well, it is Ernest after all. I mean it naturally is Ernest.

LADY BRACKNELL: Yes, I remember now that the General was called Ernest. I knew I had some particular reason for disliking the name.

GWENDOLEN: Ernest! My own Ernest! I felt from the first that you could have no other name!

JACK: Gwendolen, it is a terrible thing for a man to find out suddenly that all his life he has been speaking nothing but the truth. Can you forgive me?

GWENDOLEN: I can. For I feel that you are sure to change.

JACK: My own one!

CHASUBLE (*to* MISS PRISM): Laetitia! (*Embraces her.*)

MISS PRISM (*enthusiastically*): Frederick! At last!

ALGERNON: Cecily! (*Embraces her.*) At last!

JACK: Gwendolen! (*Embraces her.*) At last!

LADY BRACKNELL: My nephew, you seem to be displaying signs of triviality.

JACK: On the contrary, Aunt Augusta, I've now realized for the first time in my life the vital Importance of Being Earnest.

TABLEAU

COMMENTARY

The gist of the plot of *The Importance of Being Earnest* is the gist of the plot of many comedies: a young man and a young woman wish to marry, but an apparently insurmountable obstacle interposes. The obstacle, however, is surmounted, and so at the end we get a happy, united society. Wilde doubles the lovers, giving us two young men and two young women, but this is scarcely an innovation, for we get two pairs of lovers in several of Shakespeare's comedies, including *A Midsummer Night's Dream*, which, after what has been called an obstacle race to the altar, similarly concludes with all of the lovers happily paired.

Our entry on *farce* in the Glossary suggests that farce is "a sort of comedy based not on clever language or subtleties of character, but on broadly humorous situations," such as a man mistakenly entering the ladies' locker room. Generally the emphasis in farce is on surprise and on swift physical action, with much frantic hiding under beds, desperate putting on of absurd disguises, and so forth. But it is widely (though not universally) agreed that *The Importance of Being Earnest* is a farce, an utterly improbable play with virtually no connection with life as we know or feel it. Those who hold this view, however, see this play as unique, the one farce that depends on language rather than physical action. Writing in 1902, at a revival staged seven years after the original production of *The Importance of Being Earnest*, Max Beerbohm said:

> In scheme, of course, it is a hackneyed farce—the story of a young man coming up to London "on the spree," and of another young man going down conversely to the country, and of the complications that ensue. . . . [But] the fun depends mainly on what the characters say, rather than on what they do. They speak a kind of beautiful nonsense—the language of high comedy, twisted into fantasy. Throughout the dialogue is the horse-play of a distinguished intellect and a distinguished imagination—a horse-play among words and ideas, conducted with poetic dignity.

A few critics, however, have insisted that under the glittering but apparently trivial surface (Wilde said this play was "written by a butterfly for butterflies") there are serious topics, and that Wilde is indeed saying serious things— disguised as nonsense—about society. He is, in this view, joking in earnest; that is, he is writing satirically, and only pretending to be playful. (On *satire*, see the Glossary entry.) Among the topics that critics have singled out are marriage, money, education, sincerity (the importance—or unimportance—of being earnest), class relationships, and death. In effect, the question comes down to this: When we hear, for instance, Lady Bracknell commenting on the absurd circumstances of Jack's infancy, do our minds turn to a criticism of the snobbish speaker, or do they (delighting in the absurd speech) relish the lines themselves and take pleasure in the speaker? Here is the passage in question:

> To be born, or at any rate, bred in a handbag, whether it had handles or not, seems to me to display a contempt for the ordinary decencies of family life that reminds one of the worst excesses of the French Revolution. And I presume you know what that unfortunate movement led to?

Readers are invited to try thinking about the play both ways—as a work of art divorced from reality, and as a work of art that repeatedly if indirectly comments on life—and to come to their own conclusions about the truth of the two views we have set forth. Possibly they will conclude, with Algernon, that "The truth is rarely pure, and never simple."

TOPICS FOR DISCUSSION

1. Speaking of this play, Wilde said in an interview: "It has as its philosophy . . . that we should treat all the trivial things of life seriously, and all the serious things of life with

sincere and studied triviality." Was he kidding? To what extent does the play dramatize such a view?

2. Can it be argued that the play presents a fanciful world utterly remote from the real world, and that attempts to see it as in any way related to our world do it an injustice? If this is the case, what value does the play have?

3. Describe some of Wilde's chief devices of verbal humor. Once such device, for instance, is to turn a proverb inside out, as with the proverbial "Marriages are made in heaven." What other examples of this device do you find? And what other kinds of humor?

4. What are Lady Bracknell's values? What is your response to her—not to her values, but to her? Why?

5. Take one part of one act—Lady Bracknell's examination of Jack in Act I would be a good choice—and indicate what stage business you would use if you were directing the play. A simple example: When Lady Bracknell finishes questioning Jack about his finances and his social standing, she might close her notebook and invitingly pat the seat beside her as she says, "Now to minor matters. Are your parents living?" A little later, when Jack confesses that he cannot identify his parents, she might tear the page out of her notebook.

THE SANDBOX

Edward Albee

Edward Albee (b. 1928) in infancy was adopted by the multimillionaires who owned the chain of Albee theaters. Though surrounded by material comfort, he was an unhappy child who disliked his adopted parents. The only member of his family with whom he seems to have had an affectionate relationship was his grandmother. His work at school and in college was poor, but he wrote a good deal even as an adolescent; when in 1960 he achieved sudden fame with *Zoo Story* (written in 1958), he had already written plays for more than a decade. Among his other plays are *The Death of Bessie Smith* (1960), *The Sandbox* (1960), *The American Dream* (1961), *Who's Afraid of Virginia Woolf* (1962), A *Delicate Balance* (1966), and *The Man Who Had Three Arms* (1983).

PLAYERS

THE YOUNG MAN, 25, *a good-looking, well-built boy in a bathing suit*
MOMMY, 55, *a well-dressed, imposing woman*
DADDY, 60, *a small man; gray, thin*

GRANDMA, 86, *a tiny, wizened woman with bright eyes*
THE MUSICIAN, *no particular age, but young would be nice*

Note: When, in the course of the play, MOMMY *and* DADDY *call each other by these names, there should be no suggestion of regionalism. These names are of empty affection and point up the presenility and vacuity of their characters.*

The Scene: A bare stage, with only the following: Near the footlights, far stage-right, two simple chairs set side by side, facing the audience; near the footlights, far stage-left, a chair facing stage-right with a music stand before it; farther back, and stage-center, slightly elevated and raked, a large child's sandbox with a toy pail and shovel; the background is the sky, which alters from brightest day to deepest night.

At the beginning, it is brightest day; the YOUNG MAN *is alone on stage to the rear of the sandbox, and to one side. He is doing calisthenics; he does calisthenics until quite at the very end of the play. These calisthenics, employing the arms only, should suggest the beating and fluttering of wings. The* YOUNG MAN *is, after all, the Angel of Death.*

The Sandbox production by CSU Summer Arts '87, Cal Poly, San Luis Obispo.

MOMMY *and* DADDY *enter from stage-left,* MOMMY *first.*

MOMMY (*motioning to* DADDY): Well, here we are; this is the beach.

DADDY (*whining*): I'm cold.

MOMMY (*dismissing him with a little laugh*): Don't be silly; it's as warm as toast. Look at that nice young man over there; *he* doesn't think it's cold. (*Waves to the* YOUNG MAN) Hello.

YOUNG MAN (*with an endearing smile*): Hi!

MOMMY (*looking about*): This will do perfectly . . . don't you think so, Daddy? There's sand there . . . and the water beyond. What do you think, Daddy?

DADDY (*vaguely*): Whatever you say, Mommy.

MOMMY (*with the same little laugh*): Well, of course . . . whatever I say. Then, it's settled, is it?

DADDY (*shrugs*): She's *your* mother, not mine.

MOMMY: *I* know she's my mother. What do you take me for? (*A pause*) All right, now; let's get on with it. (*She shouts into the wings, stage-left*) You! Out there! You can come in now.

The MUSICIAN *enters, seats himself in the chair, stage-left, places music on the music stand, is ready to play.* MOMMY *nods approvingly.*

MOMMY: Very nice; very nice. Are you ready, Daddy? Let's go get Grandma.

DADDY: Whatever you say, Mommy.

MOMMY (*leading the way out, stage-left*): Of course, whatever I say. (*To the* MUSICIAN) You can begin now.

The MUSICIAN *begins playing;* MOMMY *and* DADDY *re-enter, carrying* GRANDMA. *She is borne in by their hands under her armpits; she is quite rigid; her legs are drawn up; her feet do not touch the ground; the expression on her ancient face is that of puzzlement and fear.*

DADDY: Where do we put her?

MOMMY (*the same little laugh*): Wherever I say, of course. Let me see . . . well . . . all right, over there . . . in the sandbox. (*Pause*) Well, what are you waiting for, Daddy? . . . The sandbox!

Together they carry GRANDMA *over to the sandbox and more or less dump her in.*

GRANDMA (*righting herself to a sitting position, her voice a cross between a baby's laugh and cry*): Ahhhhhh! Graaaa!

DADDY (*dusting himself*): What do we do now?

MOMMY (*to the* MUSICIAN): You can stop now. (*The* MUSICIAN *stops. Back to* DADDY) What do you mean, what do we do now? We go over there and sit down, of course. (*To the* YOUNG MAN) Hello there.

YOUNG MAN (*again smiling*): Hi!

MOMMY *and* DADDY *move to the chairs, stage-right, and sit down. A pause.*

GRANDMA (*same as before*): Ahhhhhh! Ah-haaa-aaa! Graaaaaa!

DADDY Do you think . . . do you think she's . . . comfortable?

MOMMY (*impatiently*): How would I know?

DADDY (*pause*): What do we do now?

MOMMY (*as if remembering*): We . . . wait. We . . . sit here . . . and we wait . . . that's what we do.

DADDY (*after a pause*): Shall we talk to each other?

MOMMY (*with that little laugh; picking something off her dress*): Well, *you* can talk, if you want to . . . if you can think of anything to say . . . if you can think of anything *new*.

DADDY (*thinks*): No . . . I suppose not.

MOMMY (*with a triumphant laugh*): Of course not!

GRANDMA (*banging the toy shovel against the pail*): Haaaaaa! Ah-haaaaaa!

MOMMY (*out over the audience*): Be quiet, Grandma . . . just be quiet, and wait.

GRANDMA *throws a shovelful of sand at* MOMMY.

MOMMY (*still out over the audience*): She's throwing sand at me! You stop that, Grandma; you stop throwing sand at Mommy! (*To* DADDY) She's throwing sand at me.

DADDY *looks around at* GRANDMA, *who screams at him.*

GRANDMA: GRAAAAAA!

MOMMY: Don't look at her. Just . . . sit here . . . be very still . . . and wait. (*To the* MUSICIAN) You . . . uh . . . you go ahead and do whatever it is you do.

The MUSICIAN *plays.* MOMMY *and* DADDY *are fixed, staring out beyond the audience.* GRANDMA *looks at them, looks at the* MUSICIAN, *looks at the sandbox, throws down the shovel.*

GRANDMA: Ah-haaaaaa! Graaaaaa! (*Looks for reaction; gets none. Now . . . directly to the audience*) Honestly! What a way to treat an old woman! Drag her out of the house . . . stick her in a car . . . bring her out here from the city . . . dump her in a pile of sand . . . and leave her here to set. I'm eighty-six years old! I was married when I was seventeen. To a farmer. He died when I was thirty. (*To the* MUSICIAN) Will you stop that, please? (*The* MUSICIAN *stops playing*) I'm a feeble old woman . . . how do you expect anybody to hear me over that peep! peep! peep! (*To herself*) There's no respect around here. (*To the* YOUNG MAN) There's no respect around here!

YOUNG MAN (*same smile*): Hi!

GRANDMA (*after a pause, a mild double-take, continues, to the audience*): My husband died when I was thirty (*indicates* MOMMY), and I had to raise that big cow over there all by my lonesome. You can imagine what *that was like*. Lordy! (*To the* YOUNG MAN) Where'd they get *you*?

YOUNG MAN: Oh . . . I've been around for a while.

GRANDMA: I'll bet you have! Heh, heh, heh. Will you look at you!

YOUNG MAN (*flexing his muscles*): Isn't that something? (*Continues his calisthenics*)

GRANDMA: Boy, oh boy; I'll say. Pretty good.

YOUNG MAN (*sweetly*): I'll say.

GRANDMA: Where ya from?

YOUNG MAN: Southern California.

GRANDMA (*nodding*): Figgers; figgers. What's your name, honey?

YOUNG MAN: I don't know . . .

GRANDMA (*to the audience*): Bright, too!

YOUNG MAN: I mean . . . I mean, they haven't given me one yet . . . the studio . . .

GRANDMA (*giving him the once-over*): You don't say . . . you don't say. Well . . . uh, I've got to talk some more . . . don't you go 'way.

YOUNG MAN: Oh, no.

GRANDMA (*turning her attention back to the audience*): Fine; fine. (*Then, once more, back to the* YOUNG MAN) You're . . . you're an actor, hunh?

YOUNG MAN (*beaming*): Yes. I am.

GRANDMA (*to the audience again; shrugs*): I'm smart that way. *Anyhow*, I had to raise . . . *that* over there all by my lonesome; and what's next to her there . . . that's what she married. Rich? I tell you . . . money, money, money. They took me off the *farm* . . . which was real decent of them . . . and they moved me into the big townhouse with *them* . . . fixed a nice place for me under the stove . . . gave me an army blanket . . . and my own dish . . . my very own dish! So, what have I got to complain about? Nothing, of course. I'm not complaining. (*She looks up at the sky, shouts to*

someone off stage) Shouldn't it be getting dark now, dear?

The lights dim; night comes on. The MUSICIAN *begins to play; it becomes deepest night. There are spots on all the players, including the* YOUNG MAN, *who is, of course, continuing his calisthenics.*

DADDY (*stirring*): It's nighttime.

MOMMY: Shhhh. Be still . . . wait.

DADDY (*whining*): It's so hot.

MOMMY: Shhhhhh. Be still . . . wait.

GRANDMA (*to herself*): That's better. Night. (*To the* MUSICIAN) Honey, do you play all through this part? (*The* MUSICIAN *nods*.) Well, keep it nice and soft; that's a good boy. (*The* MUSICIAN *nods again; plays softly*.) That's nice.

There is an off-stage rumble.

DADDY (*starting*): What was that?

MOMMY (*beginning to weep*): It was nothing.

DADDY: It was . . . it was . . . thunder . . . or a wave breaking . . . or something.

MOMMY (*whispering, through her tears*): It was an off-stage rumble . . . and you know what *that* means . . .

DADDY: I forget . . .

MOMMY (*barely able to talk*): It means the time has come for poor Grandma . . . and I can't bear it!

DADDY (*vacantly*): I . . . suppose you've got to be brave.

GRANDMA (*mocking*): That's right, kid; be brave. You'll bear up; you'll get over it.

Another off-stage rumble . . . louder.

MOMMY: Ohhhhhhhhhh . . . poor Grandma . . . poor Grandma . . .

GRANDMA (*to* MOMMY): I'm fine! I'm all right! It hasn't happened yet!

A violent off-stage rumble. All the lights go out, save the spot on the YOUNG MAN; *the* MUSICIAN *stops playing.*

MOMMY: Ohhhhhhhh . . . Ohhhhhhhhh . . .

Silence.

GRANDMA: Don't put the lights up yet . . . I'm not ready; I'm not quite ready. (*Silence*) All right, dear . . . I'm about done.

The lights come up again, to brightest day; the MUSICIAN *begins to play.* GRANDMA *is discovered, still in the sandbox, lying on her side, propped up on an elbow, half covered, busily shoveling sand over herself.*

GRANDMA (*muttering*): I don't know how I'm supposed to do anything with this goddam toy shovel . . .

DADDY: Mommy! It's daylight!

MOMMY (*brightly*): So it is! Well! Our long night is over. We must put away our tears, take off our mourning . . . and face the future. It's our duty.

GRANDMA (*still shoveling; mimicking*): . . . take off our mourning . . . face the future . . . Lordy!

MOMMY *and* DADDY *rise, stretch.* MOMMY *waves to the* YOUNG MAN.

YOUNG MAN (*with that smile*): Hi!

GRANDMA *plays dead.* (!) MOMMY *and* DADDY *go over to look at her; she is a little more than half buried in the sand; the toy shovel is in her hands, which are crossed on her breast.*

MOMMY (*before the sandbox; shaking her head*): Lovely! It's . . . it's hard to be sad . . . she looks . . . so happy. (*With pride and conviction*) It pays to do things well. (*To the* MUSICIAN) All right, you can stop now, if you want to. I mean, stay around for a swim, or something, it's all right with us. (*She sighs heavily.*) Well, Daddy . . . off we go.

DADDY: Brave Mommy!

MOMMY: Brave Daddy!

They exit, stage-left.

GRANDMA (*after they leave; lying quite still*): It pays to do things well . . . Boy, oh boy! (*She tries to sit up*) . . . well, kids . . . (*but she finds she can't*) . . . I . . . I can't get up. I . . . I can't move . . .

The YOUNG MAN *stops his calisthenics, nods to the* MUSICIAN, *walks over to* GRANDMA, *kneels down by the sandbox.*

GRANDMA: I . . . can't move . . .

YOUNG MAN: Shhhhh . . . be very still . . .

GRANDMA: I . . . I can't move . . .

YOUNG MAN: Uh . . . ma'am; I . . . I have a line here.

GRANDMA: Oh, I'm sorry, sweetie; you go right ahead.

YOUNG MAN: I am . . . uh . . .

GRANDMA: Take your time, dear.

YOUNG MAN (*prepares; delivers the line like a real amateur*): I am the Angel of Death. I am . . . uh . . . I am come for you.

GRANDMA: What . . . wha . . . (*then, with resignation*) . . . ohhhh . . . ohhhh, I see.

The YOUNG MAN *bends over, kisses* GRANDMA *gently on the forehead.*

GRANDMA (*her eyes closed, her hands folded on her breast again, the shovel between her hands, a sweet smile on her face*): Well . . . that was very nice, dear . . .

YOUNG MAN (*still kneeling*): Shhhhh . . . be still . . .

GRANDMA: What I meant was . . . you did that very well, dear . . .

YOUNG MAN (*blushing*): . . . oh . . .

GRANDMA: No; I mean it. You've got that . . . you've got a quality.

YOUNG MAN (*with his endearing smile*): Oh . . . thank you; thank you very much . . . ma'am.

GRANDMA (*slowly; softly—as the* YOUNG MAN *puts his hands on top of* GRANDMA's): You're . . . you're welcome . . . dear.

Tableau. The MUSICIAN *continues to play as the curtain slowly comes down.*

COMMENTARY

In our discussion of tragicomedy (p. 76), and in the Glossary, we talk about the movement called the theater of the absurd—the theater of such writers as Beckett, Ionesco, Pinter, and Albee—but here we can briefly list the characteristics usually found in the works of these playwrights. We do not mean, of course, that all of these qualities are found in all of their works. In fact, we urge you, after reading this list, to think about the ways in which Albee's *The Sandbox* does *not* quite fit the list. (One of life's great truths is, in Bishop Butler's words, "Every thing is what it is, and not another thing.")

In the theater of the absurd:

1. The plays are "theatrical" rather than realistic, often setting forth obviously impossible situations with obviously unreal characters.

2. The plays are serious but often (or at least intermittently) comic, especially satiric.

3. The basic themes are (a) human loneliness in a world without God, (b) the inability to communicate, (c) the dehumanization and impotence of individuals in a bourgeois society, and (d) the meaninglessness of life.

4. Characters behave illogically, speak in clichés, rarely if ever communicate with each other, and seem to have no clearly defined coherent character.

5. The plays are relatively plotless (nothing much seems to happen).

In thinking about (and in rereading) *The Sandbox*, you may find that it does indeed embody some of these characteristics, but of course it may embody other qualities, too, and some of the points listed may not be relevant. In fact, the most useful function of this list may be that it will stimulate you to think about ways in which the play departs from it.

TOPICS FOR DISCUSSION

1. In a sentence, characterize Mommy, and in another sentence characterize Daddy. By the way, why doesn't Albee give them names?

2. Of the four characters in the play, which do you find the most sympathetic? Exactly why? Set forth your answer, with supporting evidence, in a paragraph, or perhaps in two paragraphs—the first devoted to the three less sympathetic characters, and the second devoted to the most sympathetic character.

3. Why, in your opinion, does Albee insist in the first stage direction that the scene be "a bare stage"? Do you think a naturalistic setting would in some way diminish the play? Explain.

4. What do you make of the sandbox? Is it an image of the grave, with suggestions that life is meaningless and sterile? Or is it an image only of the sterility of life in the United States in the second half of the twentieth century? Does the fact that Grandma was married to a farmer suggest an alternative way of life? Explain.

5. In a longer play, *The American Dream*, Albee uses the same four characters that he uses in *The Sandbox*. Of *The American Dream* he wrote:

> The play . . . is a condemnation of complacency, cruelty, emasculation and vacuity; it is a stand against the fiction that everything in this slipping land of ours is peachy-keen.

To what extent does this statement help you to understand (and to enjoy) *The Sandbox*?

6. In *The New York Times Magazine* (February 25, 1962), Albee protested against the view that his plays, and others of the so-called theater of the absurd, are depressing. He includes a quotation from Martin Esslin's book *The Theatre of the Absurd*:

> Ultimately . . . the Theatre of the Absurd does not reflect despair or a return to dark irrational forces but expresses modern man's endeavor to come to terms with the world in which he lives. It attempts to make him face up to the human condition as it really is, to free him from illusions that are bound to cause constant maladjustment and disappointment. . . . For the dignity of man lies in his reality in all its senselessness; to accept it freely, without fear, without illusions—and to laugh at it.

In what what ways do you find this statement helpful? In what ways do you find it not helpful? Explain.

7. In an interview in 1979 Albee said:

> I like to think people are forced to rethink some things as a result of the experience of seeing some of my plays, that they are not left exactly the way they came in.

Has reading *The Sandbox* forced you to rethink anything? If so, what?

ADDITIONAL PLAYS

ANTIGONE

Sophocles

Translated into English verse by H. D. F. Kitto

Sophocles (c. 495–406 B.C.), the son of a wealthy Athenian, is one of the three Greek tragic writers whose work survives. (The other two are Aeschylus and Euripides.) Of Sophocles's more than 120 plays, we have 7. The exact dates of most of his plays are unknown. *Antigone* was written about 441 B.C.; *Oedipus the King,* which deals with earlier material concerning the house of Oedipus, was written later, probably about 430 B.C.

DRAMATIS PERSONAE

ANTIGONE, *daughter of Oedipus and Iocasta*
ISMENE, *her sister*
CREON, *King of Thebes, brother of Iocasta*
HAEMON, *his son*
A GUARD
TEIRESIAS, *a Seer*
MESSENGER *or messengers*[1]
EURYDICE, *wife of Creon*
CHORUS *of Theban nobles*

Scene: Thebes, before the royal palace

> *Antigone and Ismene are the last members of a royal line that stretched back, through Oedipus and Laius, to Cadmus, who had founded the city by sowing the Dragon's teeth from which sprang its warrior-race.*

[1] There is not the slightest indication in the text whether the messenger who brings the news of Eurydice's death is a man or a woman. Presumably Sophocles used the same man who had brought the news from the cavern, but it is a matter of complete indifference. [Kitto.]

1984 production of *Antigone* at Cottesloe with Jane Lapotaire as Antigone. Directed by John Burgess and Peter Gill. (Photo by Donald Cooper © Photostage.)

[*Enter, from the palace,* ANTIGONE *and* ISMENE.]

ANTIGONE:

Ismene, my own sister, dear Ismene,
How many miseries our father caused!
And is there one of them that does not fall
On us while yet we live? Unhappiness,
5 Calamity, disgrace, dishonor—which
Of these have you and I not known? And now
Again: there is the order which they say
Brave Creon has proclaimed to all the city.
You understand? or do you not yet know
10 What outrage threatens one of those we love?

ISMENE:

Of them, Antigone, I have not heard
Good news or bad—nothing, since we two sisters
Were robbed of our two brothers on one day
When each destroyed the other. During the night
15 The enemy has fled: so much I know,
But nothing more, either for grief or joy.

ANTIGONE:

I knew it; therefore I have brought you here,
Outside the doors, to tell you secretly.

ISMENE:

What is it? Some dark shadow is upon you.

ANTIGONE:

20 Our brothers' burial.—Creon has ordained
Honor for one, dishonor for the other.
Eteocles, they say, has been entombed
With every solemn rite and ceremony
To do him honor in the world below;
25 But as for Polyneices, Creon has ordered
That none shall bury him or mourn for him;
He must be left to lie unwept, unburied,
For hungry birds of prey to swoop and feast
On his poor body. So he has decreed,
30 Our noble Creon, to all the citizens:
To you, to me. To me! And he is coming
To make it public here, that no one may
Be left in ignorance; nor does he hold it
Of little moment: he who disobeys
35 In any detail shall be put to death
By public stoning in the streets of Thebes.
So it is now for you to show if you
Are worthy, or unworthy, of your birth.

ISMENE:

O my poor sister! If it has come to this
40 What can I do, either to help or hinder?

ANTIGONE:

Will you join hands with me and share my task?

ISMENE:

What dangerous enterprise have you in mind?

ANTIGONE:

Will you join me in taking up the body?

ISMENE:

What? Would you bury him, against the law?

ANTIGONE:

No one shall say *I* failed him! I will bury   45
My brother—and yours too, if you will not.

ISMENE:

You reckless girl! When Creon has forbidden?

ANTIGONE:

He has no right to keep me from my own!

ISMENE:

Think of our father, dear Antigone,
And how we saw him die, hated and scorned,   50
When his own hands had blinded his own eyes
Because of sins which he himself disclosed;
And how his mother-wife, two names in one,
Knotted a rope, and so destroyed herself.
And, last of all, upon a single day   55
Our brothers fought each other to the death
And shed upon the ground the blood that joined
    them.
Now you and I are left, alone; and think:
If we defy the King's prerogative
And break the law, our death will be more
    shameful   60
Even than theirs. Remember too that we
Are women, not made to fight with men. Since
    they
Who rule us now are stronger far than we,
In this and worse than this we must obey them.
Therefore, beseeching pardon from the dead,   65
Since what I do is done on hard compulsion,
I yield to those who have authority;
For useless meddling has no sense at all.

ANTIGONE:

I will not urge you. Even if you should wish
To give your help I would not take it now.   70
Your choice is made. But I shall bury him.
And if I have to die for this pure crime,
I am content, for I shall rest beside him;
His love will answer mine. I have to please
The dead far longer than I need to please   75
The living; with them, I have to dwell for ever.
But you, if so you choose, you may dishonor
The sacred laws that Heaven holds in honor.

ISMENE:

I do them no dishonor, but to act
Against the city's will I am too weak.   80

ANTIGONE:

Make that your pretext! I will go and heap
The earth upon the brother whom I love.

ISMENE:

You reckless girl! I tremble for your life.

ANTIGONE:
Look to yourself and do not fear for me.
ISMENE:
85   At least let no one hear of it, but keep
Your purpose secret, and so too will I.
ANTIGONE:
Go and denounce me! I shall hate you more
If you keep silent and do not proclaim it.
ISMENE:
Your heart is hot upon a wintry work!
ANTIGONE:
90   I know I please whom most I ought to please.
ISMENE:
But can you do it? It is impossible!
ANTIGONE:
When I can do no more, then I will stop.
ISMENE:
But why attempt a hopeless task at all?
ANTIGONE:
O stop, or I shall hate you! He will hate
95   You too, forever, justly. Let me be,
Me and my folly! I will face the danger
That so dismays you, for it cannot be
So dreadful as to die a coward's death.
ISMENE:
Then go and do it, if you must. It is
Blind folly—but those who love you love you
100   dearly.

[*Exeunt severally.*]

FIRST ODE

Strophe 1

CHORUS:
Welcome, light of the Sun, the fairest
[*glyconics*][2] Sun that ever has dawned upon
Thebes, the city of seven gates!
At last thou art arisen, great
105   Orb of shining day, pouring
Light across the gleaming water of Dirkê.
Thou hast turned into headlong flight,
Galloping faster and faster, the foe who
Bearing a snow-white shield in full
110   Panoply came from Argos.

[*anapests*][3] He had come to destroy us, in
Polyneices's

---

[2] **glyconics:** metrical feet consisting of a spondee (two
long syllables), a dactyl (two short syllables followed by
one long syllable), and an amphimacer or cretic (one
long syllable followed by one short syllable followed by
one long syllable)
[3] **anapests:** metrical feet consisting of two short syllables followed by one long syllable

Fierce quarrel. *He* brought them against our land;
And like some eagle screaming his rage
From the sky he descended upon us,
With his armour about him, shining like snow,   115
   With spear upon spear,
And with plumes that swayed on their helmets.

Antistrophe 1

[*glyconics*] Close he hovered above our houses,
Circling around our seven gates, with
Spears that thirsted to drink our blood.   120
He's gone! gone before ever his jaws
Snapped on our flesh, before he sated
Himself with our blood, before his blazing fire-
   brand
Seized with its fire our city's towers.
Terrible clangor of arms repelled him,   125
Driving him back, for hard it is to
Strive with the sons of a Dragon.

[*anapests*] For the arrogant boast of an impious
   man
Zeus hateth exceedingly. So, when he saw
This army advancing in swollen flood   130
In the pride of its gilded equipment,
He struck them down from the rampart's edge
   With a fiery bolt
In the midst of their shout of "Triumph!"

Strophe 2

[*more strongly marked rhythm*] Heavily down to
   the earth did he fall, and lie there,   135
He who with torch in his hand and possessed with
   frenzy
   Breathed forth bitterest hate
   Like some fierce tempestuous wind.
   So it fared then with him;
And of the rest, each met his own terrible doom, 140
Given by the great War-god, our deliverer.

[*anapests*] Seven foemen appointed to our seven
   gates
Each fell to a Theban, and Argive arms
Shall grace our Theban temple of Zeus:
Save two, those two of unnatural hate,   145
Two sons of one mother, two sons of one King;
They strove for the crown, and shared with the
   sword
Their estate, each slain by his brother.

Antistrophe 2

Yet do we see in our midst, and acclaim with
   gladness,
150 Victory, glorious Victory, smiling, welcome.
   Now, since danger is past,
    Thoughts of war shall pass from our minds.
    Come! let all thank the gods,
Dancing before temple and shrine all through the
   night,
155 Following Thee, Theban Dionysus.
   CHORUS-LEADER:
But here comes Creon, the new king of Thebes,
In these new fortunes that the gods have given us.
What purpose is he furthering, that he
Has called this gathering of his Counsellors?

[*Enter* CREON, *attended.*]

   CREON:
160 My lords: for what concerns the state, the gods
Who tossed it on the angry surge of strife
Have righted it again; and therefore you
By royal edict I have summoned here,
Chosen from all our number. I know well
165 How you revered the thrones of Laius;
And then, when Oedipus maintained our state,
And when he perished, round his sons you rallied,
Still firm and steadfast in your loyalty.
Since they have fallen by a double doom
170 Upon a single day, two brothers each
Killing the other with polluted sword,
I now possess the throne and royal power
By right of nearest kinship with the dead.
   There is no art that teaches us to know
175 The temper, mind or spirit of any man
Until he has been proved by government
And lawgiving. A man who rules a state
And will not ever steer the wisest course,
But is afraid, and says not what he thinks,
180 That man is worthless; and if any holds
A friend of more account than his own city,
I scorn him; for if I should see destruction
Threatening the safety of my citizens,
185 I would not hold my peace, nor would I count
That man my friend who was my country's foe,
Zeus be my witness. For be sure of this:
It is the city that protects us all;
She bears us through the storm; only when she
Rides safe and sound can we make loyal friends.
190   This I believe, and thus will I maintain
Our city's greatness.—Now, conformably,
Of Oedipus's two sons I have proclaimed
This edict: he who in his country's cause
Fought gloriously and so laid down his life,
195 Shall be entombed and graced with every rite

That men can pay to those who die with honor;
But for his brother, him called Polyneices,
Who came from exile to lay waste his land,
To burn the temples of his native gods,
To drink his kindred blood, and to enslave   200
The rest, I have proclaimed to Thebes that none
Shall give him funeral honors or lament him,
But leave him there unburied, to be devoured
By dogs and birds, mangled most hideously.
Such is my will; never shall I allow   205
The villain to win more honor than the upright;
But any who show love to this our city
In life and death alike shall win my praise.
   CHORUS-LEADER:
Such is your will, my lord; so you requite
Our city's champion and our city's foe.   210
You, being so sovereign, make what laws you will
Both for the dead and those of us who live.
   CREON:
See then that you defend the law now made.
   CHORUS-LEADER:
No, lay that burden on some younger men.
   CREON:
I have appointed guards to watch the body.   215
   CHORUS-LEADER:
What further charge, then, do you lay on us?
   CREON:
Not to connive at those that disobey me.
   CHORUS-LEADER:
None are so foolish as to long for death.
   CREON:
Death is indeed the price, but love of gain
Has often lured a man to his destruction.   220

[*Enter a* GUARD.]

   GUARD:
My lord: I cannot say that I am come
All out of breath with running. More than once
I stopped and thought and turned round in my
   path
And started to go back. My mind had much
To say to me. One time it said "You fool!   225
Why do you go to certain punishment?"
Another time "What? Standing still, you wretch?
You'll smart for it, if Creon comes to hear
From someone else." And so I went along
Debating with myself, not swift nor sure.   230
This way, a short road soon becomes a long one.
At last this was the verdict: I must come
And tell you. It may be worse than nothing; still,
I'll tell you. I can suffer nothing more
Than what is in my fate. There is my comfort!   235
   CREON:
And what is this that makes you so despondent?

GUARD:
First for myself: I did not see it done,
I do not know who did it. Plainly then,
I cannot rightly come to any harm.
CREON:
240 You are a cautious fellow, building up
This barricade. You bring unpleasant news?
GUARD:
I do, and peril makes a man pause long.
CREON:
O, won't you tell your story and be gone?
GUARD:
Then, here it is. The body: someone has
245 Just buried it, and gone away. He sprinkled
Dry dust on it, with all the sacred rites.
CREON:
What? Buried it? What man has so defied me?
GUARD:
How can I tell? There was no mark of pickaxe,
No sign of digging; the earth was hard and dry
250 And undisturbed; no wagon had been there;
He who had done it left no trace at all.
So, when the first day-watchman showed it to us,
We were appalled. We could not see the body;
It was not buried but was thinly covered
255 With dust, as if by someone who had sought
To avoid a curse. Although we looked, we saw
No sign that any dog or bird had come
And torn the body. Angry accusations
Flew up between us; each man blamed another,
260 And in the end it would have come to blows,
For there was none to stop it. Each single man
Seemed guilty, yet proclaimed his ignorance
And could not be convicted. We were all
Ready to take hot iron in our hands,
265 To walk through fire, to swear by all the gods
We had not done it, nor had secret knowledge
Of any man who did it or contrived it.
We could not find a clue. Then one man spoke:
It made us hang our heads in terror, yet
270 No one could answer him, nor could we see
Much profit for ourselves if we should do it.
He said "We must report this thing to Creon;
We dare not hide it"; and his word prevailed.
I am the unlucky man who drew the prize
275 When we cast lots, and therefore I am come
Unwilling and, for certain, most unwelcome:
Nobody loves the bringer of bad news.
CHORUS-LEADER:
My lord, the thought has risen in my mind:
Do we not see in this the hand of God?
CREON:
280 Silence! or you will anger me. You are
An old man: must you be a fool as well?
Intolerable, that you suppose the gods

Should have a single thought for this dead
  body.
What? should they honor him with burial
As one who served them well, when he had come   285
To burn their pillared temples, to destroy
Their treasuries, to devastate their land
And overturn its laws? Or have you noticed
The gods prefer the vile? No, from the first
There was a muttering against my edict,   290
Wagging of heads in secret, restiveness
And discontent with my authority.
I know that some of these perverted others
And bribed them to this act. Of all vile things
Current on earth, none is so vile as money.   295
For money opens wide the city-gates
To ravishers, it drives the citizens
To exile, it perverts the honest mind
To shamefulness, it teaches men to practice
All forms of wickedness and impiety.   300
These criminals who sold themselves for money
Have bought with it their certain punishment;
For, as I reverence the throne of Zeus,
I tell you plainly, and confirm it with
My oath: unless you find, and bring before me,   305
The very author of this burial-rite
Mere death shall not suffice; you shall be hanged
Alive, until you have disclosed the crime,
That for the future you may ply your trade
More cleverly, and learn not every pocket   310
Is safely to be picked. Ill-gotten gains
More often lead to ruin than to safety.
GUARD:
May I reply? Or must I turn and go?
CREON:
Now, as before, your very voice offends me.
GUARD:
Is it your ears that feel it, or your mind?   315
CREON:
Why must you probe the seat of our displeasure?
GUARD:
The rebel hurts your mind; I but your ears.
CREON:
No more of this! You are a babbling fool!
GUARD:
If so, I cannot be the one who did it.
CREON:
Yes, but you did—selling your life for money!   320
GUARD:
It's bad, to judge at random, and judge wrong!
CREON:
You judge my judgment as you will—but bring
The man who did it, or you shall proclaim
What punishment is earned by crooked dealings.
GUARD:
God grant he may be found! But whether he   325

Be found or not—for this must lie with chance—
You will not see me coming *here* again.
Alive beyond my hope and expectation,
I thank the gods who have delivered me.

[*Exeunt severally* CREON *and* GUARD.]

SECOND ODE

Strophe 1

CHORUS:
330 Wonders are many, yet of all
[*glyconics*] Things is Man the most wonderful.
He can sail on the stormy sea
Though the tempest rage, and the loud
Waves roar around, as he makes his
335 Path amid the towering surge.

[*dactyls*]⁴ Earth inexhaustible, ageless, he wearies, as
Backwards and forwards, from season to season, his
Ox-team drives along the ploughshare.

Antistrophe 1

340 He can entrap the cheerful birds,
Setting a snare, and all the wild
Beasts of the earth he has learned to catch, and
Fish that teem in the deap sea, with
Nets knotted of stout cords; of
345 Such inventiveness is man.
Through his inventions he becomes lord
Even of the beasts of the mountain: the long-haired
Horse he subdues to the yoke on his neck, and the
Hill-bred bull, of strength untiring.

Strophe 2

350 And speech he has learned, and thought
So swift, and the temper of mind
To dwell within cities, and not to lie bare
Amid the keen, biting frosts
Or cower beneath pelting rain;
355 Full of resource against all that comes to him

⁴ **dactyls**: metrical feet consisting of two short syllables followed by one long syllable

Is Man. Against Death alone
He is left with no defense.
But painful sickness he can cure
By his own skill.

Antistrophe 2

Surpassing belief, the device and   360
Cunning that Man has attained,
And it bringeth him now to evil, now to good.
If he observe Law, and tread
The righteous path God ordained,
Honored is he; dishonored, the man whose
reckless heart   365
Shall make him join hands with sin:
May I not think like him,
Nor may such an impious man
Dwell in my house.

[*Enter* GUARD, *with* ANTIGONE.]

CHORUS-LEADER:
What evil spirit is abroad? I know   370
Her well: Antigone. But how can I
Believe it? Why, O you unlucky daughter
Of an unlucky father, what is this?
Can it be you, so mad and so defiant,
So disobedient to a King's decree?   375
GUARD:
Here is the one who did the deed, this girl;
We caught her burying him.—But where is
Creon?
CHORUS-LEADER:
He comes, just as you need him, from the palace.

[*Enter* CREON, *attended.*]

CREON:
How? What occasion makes my coming timely?
GUARD:
Sir, against nothing should a man take oath,   380
For second thoughts belie him. Under your threats
That lashed me like a hailstorm, I'd have said
I would not quickly have come here again;
But joy that comes beyond our dearest hope
Surpasses all in magnitude. So I   385
Return, though I had sworn I never would,
Bringing this girl detected in the act
Of honoring the body. This time no lot
Was cast; the windfall is my very own.
And so, my lord, do as you please: take her   390
Yourself, examine her, cross-question her.
I claim the right of free and final quittance.
CREON:
Why do you bring this girl? Where was she taken?

GUARD:
In burying the body. That is all.
CREON:
395 You know what you are saying? Do you mean it?
GUARD:
I saw her giving burial to the corpse
You had forbidden. Is that plain and clear?
CREON:
How did you see and take her so red-handed?
GUARD:
It was like this. When we had reached the place,
400 Those dreadful threats of yours upon our heads,
We swept aside each grain of dust that hid
The clammy body, leaving it quite bare,
And sat down on a hill, to the windward side
That so we might avoid the smell of it.
405 We kept sharp look-out; each man roundly cursed
His neighbor, if he should neglect his duty.
So the time passed, until the blazing sun
Reached his mid-course and burned us with his
heat.
Then, suddenly, a whirlwind came from heaven
410 And raised a storm of dust, which blotted out
The earth and sky; the air was filled with sand
And leaves ripped from the trees. We closed our
eyes
And bore this visitation as we could.
At last it ended; then we saw the girl.
415 She raised a bitter cry, as will a bird
Returning to its nest and finding it
Despoiled, a cradle empty of its young.
So, when she saw the body bare, she raised
A cry of anguish mixed with imprecations
420 Laid upon those who did it; then at once
Brought handfuls of dry dust, and raised aloft
A shapely vase of bronze, and three times poured
The funeral libation for the dead.
We rushed upon her swiftly, seized our prey,
425 And charged her both with this offense and that.
She faced us calmly; she did not disown
The double crime. How glad I was!—and yet
How sorry too; it is a painful thing
To bring a friend to ruin. Still, for me,
430 My own escape comes before everything.
CREON:
You there, who keep your eyes fixed on the
ground,
Do you admit this, or do you deny it?
ANTIGONE:
No, I do not deny it. I admit it.
CREON [to GUARD]:
Then you may go; go where you like. You have
435 Been fully cleared of that grave accusation.
[Exit GUARD.]

You: tell me briefly—I want no long speech:
Did you not know that this had been forbidden?
ANTIGONE:
Of course I knew. There was a proclamation.
CREON:
And so you dared to disobey the law?
ANTIGONE:
It was not Zeus who published this decree, 440
Nor have the Powers who rule among the dead
Imposed such laws as this upon mankind;
Nor could I think that a decree of yours—
A man—could override the laws of Heaven
Unwritten and unchanging. Not of today 445
Or yesterday is their authority;
They are eternal; no man saw their birth.
Was I to stand before the gods' tribunal
For disobeying *them*, because I feared
A man? I knew that I should have to die, 450
Even without your edict; if I die
Before my time, why then, I count it gain;
To one who lives as I do, ringed about
With countless miseries, why, death is welcome.
For me to meet this doom is little grief; 455
But when my mother's son lay dead, had I
Neglected him and left him there unburied,
That would have caused me grief; this causes
none.
And if you think it folly, then perhaps
I am accused of folly by the fool. 460
CHORUS-LEADER:
The daughter shows her father's temper—fierce,
Defiant; she will not yield to any storm.
CREON:
But it is those that are most obstinate
Suffer the greatest fall; the hardest iron,
Most fiercely tempered in the fire, that is 465
Most often snapped and splintered. I have seen
The wildest horses tamed, and only by
The tiny bit. There is no room for pride
In one who is a slave! This girl already
Had fully learned the art of insolence 470
When she transgressed the laws that I established;
And now to that she adds a second outrage—
To boast of what she did, and laugh at us.
Now she would be the man, not I, if she
Defeated me and did not pay for it. 475
But though she be my niece, or closer still
Than all our family, she shall not escape
The direst penalty; no, nor shall her sister:
I judge her guilty too; she played her part
In burying the body. Summon her. 480
Just now I saw her raving and distracted
Within the palace. So it often is:
Those who plan crime in secret are betrayed

Despite themselves; they show it in their faces.
485 But this is worst of all: to be convicted
And then to glorify the crime as virtue.

[*Exeunt some* GUARDS.]

ANTIGONE:
Would you do more than simply take and kill me?
CREON:
I will have nothing more, and nothing less.
ANTIGONE:
Then why delay? To me no word of yours
490 Is pleasing—God forbid it should be so!—
And everything in me displeases you.
Yet what could I have done to win renown
More glorious than giving burial
To my own brother? These men too would say it,
495 Except that terror cows them into silence.
A king has many a privilege: the greatest,
That he can say and do all that he will.
CREON:
You are the only one in Thebes to think it!
ANTIGONE:
These think as I do—but they dare not speak.
CREON:
500 Have you no shame, not to conform with others?
ANTIGONE:
To reverence a brother is no shame.
CREON:
Was he no brother, he who died for Thebes?
ANTIGONE:
One mother and one father gave them birth.
CREON:
Honoring the traitor, you dishonor *him*.
ANTIGONE:
505 He will not bear this testimony, in death.
CREON:
Yes! if the traitor fare the same as he.
ANTIGONE:
It was a brother, not a slave who died!
CREON:
He died attacking Thebes; the other saved us.
ANTIGONE:
Even so, the god of Death demands these rites.
CREON:
510 The good demand more honor than the wicked.
ANTIGONE:
Who knows? In death they may be reconciled.
CREON:
Death does not make an enemy a friend!
ANTIGONE:
Even so, I give both love, not share their hatred.
CREON:
Down then to Hell! Love there, if love you must.
515 While I am living, no woman shall have rule.

[*Enter* GUARDS, *with* ISMENE.]

CHORUS-LEADER:
See where Ismene leaves the palace-gate,
In tears shed for her sister. On her brow
A cloud of grief has blotted out her sun,
And breaks in rain upon her comeliness.
CREON:
You, lurking like a serpent in my house,   520
Drinking my life-blood unawares; nor did
I know that I was cherishing two fiends,
Subverters of my throne: come, tell me this:
Do you confess you shared this burial,
Or will you swear you had no knowledge of it?   525
ISMENE:
I did it too, if she allows my claim;
I share the burden of this heavy charge.
ANTIGONE:
No! Justice will not suffer that; for you
Refused, and I gave you no part in it.
ISMENE:
But in your stormy voyage I am glad   530
To share the danger, traveling at your side.
ANTIGONE:
Whose was the deed the god of Death knows well;
I love not those who love in words alone.
ISMENE:
My sister, do not scorn me, nor refuse
That I may die with you, honoring the dead.   535
ANTIGONE:
You shall not die with me, nor claim as yours
What you rejected. My death will be enough.
ISMENE:
What life is left to me if I lose you?
ANTIGONE:
Ask Creon! It was Creon that you cared for.
ISMENE:
O why taunt me, when it does not help you?   540
ANTIGONE:
If I do taunt you, it is to my pain.
ISMENE:
Can I not help you, even at this late hour?
ANTIGONE:
Save your own life. I grudge not your escape.
ISMENE:
Alas! Can I not join you in your fate?
ANTIGONE:
You cannot: you chose life, and I chose death.   545
ISMENE:
But not without the warning that I gave you!
ANTIGONE:
Some thought *you* wise; the dead commended me.
ISMENE:
But my offense has been as great as yours.

ANTIGONE:
Be comforted; you live, but I have given
550 My life already, in service of the dead.
CREON:
Of these two girls, one has been driven frantic,
The other has been frantic since her birth.
ISMENE:
Not so, my lord; but when disaster comes
The reason that one has cannot stand firm.
CREON:
555 Yours did not, when you chose to partner crime!
ISMENE:
But what is life to me, without my sister?
CREON:
Say not "my sister": sister you have none.
ISMENE:
But she is Haemon's bride—and can you kill her?
CREON:
Is she the only woman he can bed with?
ISMENE:
560 The only one so joined in love with him.
CREON:
I hate a son to have an evil wife.
ANTIGONE:
O my dear Haemon! How your father wrongs you!
CREON:
I hear too much of you and of your marriage.
ISMENE:
He is your son; how can you take her from him?
CREON:
565 It is not I, but Death, that stops this wedding.
CHORUS-LEADER:
It is determined, then, that she must die?
CREON:
For you, and me, determined. [*To the* GUARDS.]
    Take them in
At once; no more delay. Henceforward let
Them stay at home, like women, not roam
    abroad.
570 Even the bold, you know, will seek escape
When they see death at last standing beside them.
        [*Exeunt* ANTIGONE *and* ISMENE *into the
        palace, guarded.* CREON *remains.*]

THIRD ODE

Strophe 1

CHORUS:
Thrice happy are they who have never known
    disaster!

Once a house is shaken of Heaven, disaster
Never leaves it, from generation to generation.
  'Tis even as the swelling sea,   575
  When the roaring wind from Thrace
Drives blustering over the water and makes it
    black:
  It bears up from below
  A thick, dark cloud of mud,
And groaning cliffs repel the smack of wind and
    angry breakers.   580

Antistrophe 1

I see, in the house of our kings, how ancient
    sorrows
Rise again; disaster is linked with disaster.
Woe again must each generation inherit. Some
    god
  Besets them, nor will give release.
  On the last of royal blood   585
There gleamed a shimmering light in the house of
    Oedipus.
  But Death comes once again
  With blood-stained axe, and hews
The sapling down; and Frenzy lends her aid, and
    vengeful Madness.

Strophe 2

  Thy power, Zeus, is almighty! No   590
  Mortal insolence can oppose Thee!
Sleep, which conquers all else, cannot overcome
    Thee,
  Nor can the never-wearied
  Years, but throughout
  Time Thou art strong and ageless,   595
    In thy own Olympus
  Ruling in radiant splendor.
  For today, and in all past time,
  And through all time to come,
  This is the law: that in Man's   600
Life every success brings with it some disaster.

Antistrophe 2

  Hope springs high, and to many a man
  Hope brings comfort and consolation;
Yet she is to some nothing but fond illusion:
  Swiftly they come to ruin,   605
  As when a man
  Treads unawares on hot fire.

For it was a wise man
First made that ancient saying:
610   To the man whom God will ruin
One day shall evil seem
Good, in his twisted judgment
He comes in a short time to fell disaster.
CHORUS-LEADER:
See, here comes Haemon, last-born of your
children,
615   Grieving, it may be, for Antigone.
CREON:
Soon we shall know, better than seers can tell us.

[*Enter* HAEMON.]

My son:
You have not come in rage against your father
Because your bride must die? Or are you still
620   My loyal son, whatever I may do?
HAEMON:
Father, I am your son; may your wise judgment
Rule me, and may I always follow it.
No marriage shall be thought a greater prize
For me to win than your good government.
CREON:
625   So may you ever be resolved, my son,
In all things to be guided by your father.
It is for this men pray that they may have
Obedient children, that they may requite
Their father's enemy with enmity
630   And honor whom their father loves to honor.
One who begets unprofitable children
Makes trouble for himself, and gives his foes
Nothing but laughter. Therefore do not let
Your pleasure in a woman overcome
635   Your judgment, knowing this, that if you have
An evil wife to share your house, you'll find
Cold comfort in your bed. What other wound
Can cut so deep as treachery at home?
So, think this girl your enemy; spit on her,
640   And let her find her husband down in Hell!
She is the only one that I have found
In all the city disobedient.
I will not make myself a liar. I
Have caught her; I will kill her. Let her sing
645   Her hymns to Sacred Kinship! If I breed
Rebellion in the house, then it is certain
There'll be no lack of rebels out of doors.
No man can rule a city uprightly
Who is not just in ruling his own household.
650   Never will I approve of one who breaks
And violates the law, or would dictate
To those who rule. Lawful authority
Must be obeyed in all things, great or small,

Just and unjust alike; and such a man
Would win my confidence both in command   655
And as a subject; standing at my side
In the storm of battle he would hold his ground,
Not leave me unprotected. But there is
No greater curse than disobedience.
This brings destruction on a city, this   660
Drives men from hearth and home, this brings
about
A sudden panic in the battle-front.
Where all goes well, obedience is the cause.
So we must vindicate the law; we must not be
Defeated by a woman. Better far   665
Be overthrown, if need be, by a man
Than to be called the victim of a woman.
CHORUS-LEADER:
Unless the years have stolen away our wits,
All you say is said most prudently.
HAEMON:
Father, it is the gods who give us wisdom;   670
No gift of theirs more precious. I cannot say
That you are wrong, nor would I ever learn
That impudence, although perhaps another
Might fairly say it. But it falls to me,
Being your son, to note what others say,   675
Or do, or censure in you, for your glance
Intimidates the common citizen;
He will not say, before your face, what might
Displease you; I can listen freely, now
The city mourns this girl. "No other woman,"   680
So they are saying, "so undeservedly
Has been condemned for such a glorious deed.
When her own brother had been slain in battle
She would not let his body lie unburied
To be devoured by dogs or birds of prey.   685
Is not this worthy of a crown of gold?"—
Such is the muttering that spreads everywhere.
    Father, no greater treasure can I have
Than your prosperity; no son can find
A greater prize than his own father's fame,   690
No father than his son's. Therefore let not
This single thought possess you: only what
You say is right, and nothing else. The man
Who thinks that he alone is wise, that he
Is best in speech or counsel, such a man   695
Brought to the proof is found but emptiness.
There's no disgrace, even if one is wise,
In learning more, and knowing when to yield.
See how the trees that grow beside a torrent
Preserve their branches, if they bend; the others, 700
Those that resist, are torn out, root and branch.
So to the captain of a ship; let him
Refuse to shorten sail, despite the storm—

He'll end his voyage bottom uppermost.
705 No, let your anger cool, and be persuaded.
If one who is still young can speak with sense,
Then I would say that he does best who has
Most understanding; second best, the man
Who profits from the wisdom of another.
    CHORUS-LEADER:
710 My lord, he has not spoken foolishly;
You each can learn some wisdom from the other.
    CREON:
What? men of our age go to school again
And take a lesson from a very boy?
    HAEMON:
If it is worth the taking. I am young,
715 But think what should be done, not of my age.
    CREON:
What should be done! To honor disobedience!
    HAEMON:
I would not have you honor criminals.
    CREON:
And is this girl then not a criminal?
    HAEMON:
The city with a single voice denies it.
    CREON:
720 Must I give orders then by their permission?
    HAEMON:
If youth is folly, this is childishness.
    CREON:
Am I to rule for them, not for myself?
    HAEMON:
That is not government, but tyranny.
    CREON:
The king is lord and master of his city.
    HAEMON:
725 Then you had better rule a desert island!
    CREON:
This man, it seems, is the ally of the woman.
    HAEMON:
If you're the woman, yes! I fight for you.
    CREON:
Villain! Do you oppose your father's will?
    HAEMON:
Only because you are opposing Justice.
    CREON:
730 When I regard my own prerogative?
    HAEMON:
Opposing God's, you disregard your own.
    CREON:
Scoundrel, so to surrender to a woman!
    HAEMON:
But not to anything that brings me shame.
    CREON:
Your every word is in defense of her.

    HAEMON:
And me, and you—and of the gods below.   735
    CREON:
You shall not marry her this side the grave!
    HAEMON:
So, she must die—and will not die alone.
    CREON:
What? Threaten me? Are you so insolent?
    HAEMON:
It is no threat, if I reply to folly.
    CREON:
The fool would teach me sense! You'll pay for it.   740
    HAEMON:
I'd call you mad, if you were not my father.
    CREON:
I'll hear no chatter from a woman's plaything.
    HAEMON:
Would you have all the talk, and hear no answer?
    CREON:
So?
I swear to God, you shall not bandy words   745
With me and not repent it! Bring her out,
That loathsome creature! I will have her killed
At once, before her bridegroom's very eyes.
    HAEMON:
How can you think it? I will not see that,
Nor shall you ever see my face again.   750
Those friends of yours who can must tolerate
Your raging madness; I will not endure it.
                [*Exit* HAEMON.]

    CHORUS-LEADER:
How angrily he went, my lord! The young,
When they are greatly hurt, grow desperate.
    CREON:
Then let his pride and folly do their worst!   755
He shall not save these women from their doom.
    CHORUS-LEADER:
Is it your purpose then to kill them both?
    CREON:
Not her who had no part in it.—I thank you.
    CHORUS-LEADER:
And for the other: how is she to die?
    CREON:
I'll find a cave in some deserted spot,   760
And there I will imprison her alive
With so much food—no more—as will avert
Pollution and a curse upon the city.
There let her pray to Death, the only god
Whom she reveres, to rescue her from death,   765
Or learn at last, though it be late, that it
Is wanton folly to respect the dead.

    [CREON *remains on the stage.*]

FOURTH ODE

Strophe

CHORUS:
Invincible, implacable Love, O
Love, that makes havoc of all wealth;
770 That peacefully keeps his night-watch
On tender cheek of a maiden:
The Sea is no barrier, nor
Mountainous waste to Love's flight; for
No one can escape Love's domination,
775 Man, no, nor immortal god. Love's
Prey is possessed by madness.

Antistrophe

By Love, the mind even of the just
Is bent awry; he becomes unjust.
So here: it is Love that stirred up
780 This quarrel of son with father.
The kindling light of Love in the soft
Eye of a bride conquers, for
Love sits on his throne, one of the great Powers;
Nought else can prevail against
785 Invincible Aphrodite.

[*Enter* ANTIGONE, *under guard. From this point
up to the end of the fifth ode everything is sung,
except the two speeches in blank verse.*]

CHORUS:
I too, when I see this sight, cannot stay
[*anapests*] Within bounds; I cannot keep back my
    tears
Which rise like a flood. For behold, they bring
Antigone here, on the journey that all
790 Must make, to the silence of Hades.

COMMOS

Strophe 1

ANTIGONE:
Behold me, O lords of my native city!
[*glyconics*] Now do I make my last journey;
    Now do I see the last
Sun that ever I shall behold.
795 Never another! Death, that lulls
All to sleep, takes me while I live

Down to the grim shore of Acheron.
    No wedding day can be
Mine, no hymn will be raised to honor
Marriage of mine; for I   800
Go to espouse the bridegroom, Death.
CHORUS:
Yet a glorious death, and rich in fame
[*anapests*] Is yours; you go to the silent tomb
Not smitten with wasting sickness, nor
Repaying a debt to the sharp-edged sword;   805
But alone among mortals you go to the home
Of the dead while yet you are living.

Antistrophe 1

ANTIGONE:
They tell of how cruelly she did perish,
[*glyconics*] Niobe, Queen in Thebes;
For, as ivy grows on a tree,   810
Strangling it, so she slowly turned to
Stone on a Phrygian mountain-top.
Now the rain-storms wear her away—
    So does the story run—and
Snow clings to her always: 815
Tears fall from her weeping eyes for
Ever and ever. Like to hers, the
Cruel death that now awaits me.
CHORUS:
But she was a goddess, and born of the gods;
[*anapests*] We are but mortals, of mortals born. 820
For a mortal to share in the doom of a god,
That brings her renown while yet she lives,
And a glory that long will outlive her.

Strophe 2

ANTIGONE:
Alas, they laugh! O by the gods of Thebes, my
[*more passionate rhythm*]   native city,
    Mock me, if you must, when I am gone, not
        to my face!   825
O Thebes my city, O you lordly men of Thebes!
O water of Dirkê's stream! Holy soil where our
        chariots run!
You, you do I call upon; you, you shall testify
How all unwept of friends, by what harsh decree,
They send me to the cavern that shall be my
        everlasting grave.   830
Ah, cruel doom! to be banished from earth, nor
        welcomed
Among the dead, set apart, for ever!

CHORUS:
Too bold, too reckless, you affronted
[*more spirited*] Justice. Now that awful power
835 Takes terrible vengeance, O my child.
For some old sin you make atonement.

Antistrophe 2

ANTIGONE:
My father's sin! There is the source of all my
anguish.
Harsh fate that befell my father! Harsh fate that has
held
Fast in its grip the whole renowned race of
Labdacus!
840 O the blind madness of my father's and my
mother's marriage!
O cursed union of a son with his own mother!
From such as those I draw my own unhappy life;
And now I go to dwell with them, unwedded and
accursed.
O brother, through an evil marriage you were
slain; and I
845 Live—but your dead hand destroys me.
CHORUS:
Such loyalty is a holy thing.
Yet none that holds authority
Can brook disobedience, O my child.
Your self-willed pride has been your ruin.

Epode

ANTIGONE:
850 Unwept, unwedded and unbefriended,
Alone, pitilessly used,
Now they drag me to death.
Never again, O thou Sun in the heavens,
May I look on thy holy radiance!
855 Such is my fate, and no one laments it;
No friend is here to mourn me.
CREON:
Enough of this! If tears and lamentations
Could stave off death they would go on forever.
Take her away at once, and wall her up
860 Inside a cavern, as I have commanded,
And leave her there, alone, in solitude.
Her home shall be her tomb; there she may live
Or die, as she may choose: my hands are clean;
But she shall live no more among the living.
ANTIGONE:
865 O grave, my bridal-chamber, everlasting
Prison within a rock: now I must go

To join my own, those many who have died
And whom Persephone has welcomed home;
And now to me, the last of all, so young,
Death comes, so cruelly. And yet I go 870
In the sure hope that you will welcome me,
Father, and you, my mother; you, my brother.
For when you died it was my hands that washed
And dressed you, laid you in your graves, and
poured
The last libations. Now, because to you, 875
Polyneices, I have given burial,
To me they give a recompense like this!
Yet what I did, the wise will all approve.
For had I lost a son, or lost a husband,
Never would I have ventured such an act 880
Against the city's will. And wherefore so?
My husband dead, I might have found another;
Another son from him, if I had lost
A son. But since my mother and my father
Have both gone to the grave, there can be none 885
Henceforth that I can ever call my brother.
It was for this I paid you such an honor,
Dear Polyneices, and in Creon's eyes
Thus wantonly and gravely have offended.
So with rude hands he drags me to my death. 890
No chanted wedding-hymn, no bridal-joy,
No tender care of children can be mine;
But like an outcast, and without a friend,
They take me to the cavernous home of death.
What ordinance of the gods have I transgressed? 895
Why should I look to Heaven any more
For help, or seek an ally among men?
If this is what the gods approve, why then,
When I am dead I shall discern my fault;
If theirs the sin, may they endure a doom 900
No worse than mine, so wantonly inflicted!
CHORUS:
Still from the same quarter the same
wild winds
[*anapests*] Blow fiercely, and shake her stubborn
soul.
CREON:
And therefore, for this, these men shall
have cause,
[*anapests*] Bitter cause, to lament their tardiness. 905
CHORUS:
I fear these words bring us closer yet
To the verge of death.
CREON:
I have nothing to say, no comfort to give:
The sentence is passed, and the end is here.
ANTIGONE:
O city of Thebes where my fathers dwelt, 910
O gods of our race,

Now at last their hands are upon me!
You princes of Thebes, O look upon me,
The last that remain of a line of kings!
915 How savagely impious men use me,
For keeping a law that is holy.
[*Exit* ANTIGONE, *under guard.* CREON *remains.*]

FIFTH ODE

Strophe 1

CHORUS:
There was one in days of old who was imprisoned
[*slow three-time*] In a chamber like a grave, within
a tower:
Fair Danaë, who in darkness was held, and never
saw the pure daylight.
920 Yet she too, O my child, was of an ancient line,
Entrusted with divine seed that had come in
shower of gold.
Mysterious, overmastering, is the power of Fate.
[*faster three-time*] From this, nor wealth nor force
of arms
Nor strong encircling city-walls
925 Nor storm-tossed ship can give deliverance.

Antistrophe 1

Close bondage was ordained by Dionysus
For one who in a frenzy had denied
His godhead: in a cavern Lycurgus, for his sin, was
imprisoned.
In such wise did his madness bear a bitter fruit,
Which withered in a dungeon. So he learned it
930 was a god
He had ventured in his blindness to revile and
taunt.
The sacred dances he had tried
To quell, and end the Bacchic rite,
Offending all the tuneful Muses.

Strophe 2

[*fairly fast, becoming faster; three- and four-time
mixed*] There is a town by the rocks where a
935 sea meets another sea,
Two black rocks by the Bosphorus, near the Thracian coast,

Salmŷdessus; and there a wife had been spurned,
Held close in bitter constraint. [5]
Then upon both her children
A blinding wound fell from her cruel rival: 940
With shuttle in hand she smote the open eyes with
sharp
And blood-stained point, and brought to Phineus'
Two sons a darkness that cried for vengeance.

Antistrophe 2

In bitter grief and despair they bewailed their
unhappy lot,
Children born to a mother whose marriage proved
accursed. 945
Yet she came of a race of ancient kings,
Her sire the offspring of gods.
Reared in a distant country,
Among her fierce, northern father's tempests,
She went, a Boread, swift as horses, over the lofty 950
Mountains. Yet not even she was
Safe against the long-lived Fates, my daughter.

[*Enter* TEIRESIAS, *led by a boy.*]

TEIRESIAS:
My lords, I share my journey with this boy
Whose eyes must see for both; for so the blind
Must move abroad, with one to guide their steps. 955
CREON:
Why, what is this? Why are *you* here, Teiresias?
TEIRESIAS:
I will explain; you will do well to listen.
CREON:
Have I not always followed your good counsel?
TEIRESIAS:
You have; therefore we have been guided well.
CREON:
I have had much experience of your wisdom. 960
TEIRESIAS:
Then think: once more you tread the razor's edge.
CREON:
You make me tremble! What is it you mean?
TEIRESIAS:
What divination has revealed to me,
That I will tell you. To my ancient seat

[5] These two verses are a paraphrase rather than a
translation. It seemed better to give the audience something which it could follow rather than the mythological
reference in the Greek, which it certainly would not.
[Kitto.]

965 Of augury I went, where all the birds
Foregather. There I sat, and heard a clamor
Strange and unusual—birds screaming in rage.
I knew that they were tearing at each other
With murderous claws: the beating of their wings
970 Meant nothing less than that; and I was frightened.
I made a blazing fire upon the altar
And offered sacrifice: it would not burn;
The melting fat oozed out upon the embers
And smoked and bubbled; high into the air
975 The bladder spurted gall, and from the bones
The fatty meat slid off and left them bare.
Such omens, baffling, indistinct, I learned
From him who guides me, as I am guide to others.
Sickness has come upon us, and the cause
980 Is you: our altars and our sacred hearths
Are all polluted by the dogs and birds
That have been gorging on the fallen body
Of Polyneices. Therefore heaven will not
Accept from us our prayers, no fire will burn
985 Our offerings, nor will birds give out clear sounds,
For they are glutted with the blood of men.
Be warned, my son. No man alive is free
From error, but the wise and prudent man
When he has fallen into evil courses
990 Does not persist, but tries to find amendment.
It is the stubborn man who is the fool.
Yield to the dead, forbear to strike the fallen;
To slay the slain, is that a deed of valor?
Your good is what I seek; and that instruction
995 Is best that comes from wisdom, and brings profit.

CREON:
Sir, all of you, like bowmen at a target,
Let fly your shafts at me. Now they have turned
Even diviners on me! By that tribe
I am bought and sold and stowed away on board.
1000 Go, make your profits, drive your trade
In Lydian silver or in Indian gold,
But him you shall not bury in a tomb,
No, not though Zeus' own eagles eat the corpse
And bear the carrion to their master's throne:
1005 Not even so, for fear of that defilement,
Will I permit his burial—for well I know
That mortal man can not defile the gods.
But, old Teiresias, even the cleverest men
Fall shamefully when for a little money
1010 They use fair words to mask their villainy.

TEIRESIAS:
Does any man reflect, does any know . . .

CREON:
Know *what*? Why do you preach at me like this?

TEIRESIAS:
How much the greatest blessing is good counsel?

CREON:
As much, I think, as folly is his plague.

TEIRESIAS:
Yet with this plague you are yourself infected. 1015

CREON:
I will not bandy words with any prophet.

TEIRESIAS:
And yet you say my prophecies are dishonest!

CREON:
Prophets have always been too fond of gold.

TEIRESIAS:
And tyrants, of the shameful use of power.

CREON:
You know it is your King of whom you speak? 1020

TEIRESIAS:
King of the land I saved from mortal danger.

CREON:
A clever prophet—but an evil one.

TEIRESIAS:
You'll rouse me to awaken my dark secret.

CREON:
Awaken it, but do not speak for money.

TEIRESIAS:
And do you think that I am come to *that*? 1025

CREON:
You shall not buy and sell *my* policy.

TEIRESIAS:
Then I will tell you this: you will not live
Through many circuits of the racing sun
Before you give a child of your own body
To make amends for murder, death for death; 1030
Because you have thrust down within the earth
One who should walk upon it, and have lodged
A living soul dishonorably in a tomb;
And impiously have kept upon the earth
Unburied and unblest one who belongs 1035
Neither to you nor to the upper gods
But to the gods below, who are despoiled
By you. Therefore the gods arouse against you
Their sure avengers; they lie in your path
Even now to trap you and to make you pay 1040
Their price.—Now think: do I say *this* for money?
Not many hours will pass before your house
Rings loud with lamentation, men and women.
Hatred for you is moving in those cities
Whose mangled sons had funeral-rites from dogs 1045
Or from some bird of prey, whose wings have
carried
The taint of dead men's flesh to their own homes,
Polluting hearth and altar.
These are the arrows that I launch at you,
Because you anger me. I shall not miss 1050
My aim, and you shall not escape their smart.

Boy, lead me home again, that he may vent
His rage upon some younger man, and learn
To moderate his violent tongue, and find
1055   More understanding than he has today.
                                    [*Exit* TEIRESIAS.]

CHORUS-LEADER:
And so, my lord, he leaves us, with a threat
Of doom. I have lived long, but I am sure
Of this: no single prophecy that he
Has made to Thebes has gone without fulfillment.
CREON:
1060   I know it too, and I am terrified.
To yield is very hard, but to resist
And meet disaster, that is harder still.
CHORUS-LEADER:
Creon, this is no time for wrong decision.
CREON:
What shall I do? Advise me; I will listen.
CHORUS-LEADER:
1065   Release Antigone from her rock-hewn dungeon,
And lay the unburied body in a tomb.
CREON:
Is this your counsel? You would have me yield?
CHORUS-LEADER:
I would, and quickly. The destroying hand
Of Heaven is quick to punish human error.
CREON:
1070   How hard it is! And yet one cannot fight
Against Necessity.—I will give way.
CHORUS-LEADER:
Go then and do it; leave it not to others.
CREON:
Just as I am I go.—You men-at-arms,
You here, and those within: away at once
1075   Up to the hill, and take your implements.
Now that my resolution is reversed
I who imprisoned her will set her free.—
    I fear it may be wiser to observe
Throughout one's life the laws that are established.
                                    [*Exit* CREON.]

SIXTH ODE

Strophe 1

CHORUS:
1080   Thou Spirit whose names are many, Dionysus,
    Born to Zeus the loud-thunderer,
    Joy of thy Theban mother-nymph,
    Lover of famous Italy:
    King art thou in the crowded shrine

Where Demeter has her abode, O   1085
Bacchus! Here is thy mother's home,
Here is thine, by the smooth Is-
mênus's flood, here where the savage
Dragon's teeth had offspring.

Antistrophe 1

Thou art seen by the nymphs amid the smoky
        torchlight,   1090
    Where, upon Parnassus' height,
    They hold revels to honor Thee
    Close to the spring of Castaly.
    Thou art come from the ivy-clad
    Slopes of Asian hills, and vineyards   1095
    Hanging thick with clustering grapes.
    Mystic voices chant: "O
    Bacchus! O Bacchus!" in
    The roads and ways of Thebê.

Strophe 2

    Here is thy chosen home,   1100
    In Thebes above all lands,
    With thy mother, bride of Zeus.
    Wherefore, since a pollution holds
    All our people fast in its grip,
O come with swift healing across the wall of high
        Parnassus,   1105
    Or over the rough Eurîpus.

Antistrophe 2

    Stars that move, breathing flame,
    Honor Thee as they dance;
    Voices cry to Thee in the night.
    Son begotten of Zeus, appear!   1110
    Come, Lord, with thy company,
Thy own nymphs, who with wild, nightlong
        dances praise Thee,
    Bountiful Dionysus!

            [*Enter a* MESSENGER.]

MESSENGER:
You noblemen of Thebes, how insecure
Is human fortune! Chance will overthrow   1115
The great, and raise the lowly; nothing's firm,
Either for confidence or for despair;
No one can prophesy what lies in store.
An hour ago, how much I envied Creon!

1120 He had saved Thebes, we had accorded him
The sovereign power; he ruled our land
Supported by a noble prince, his son.
Now all is lost, and he who forfeits joy
Forfeits his life; he is a breathing corpse.
1125 Heap treasures in your palace, if you will,
And wear the pomp of royalty; but if
You have no happiness, I would not give
A straw for all of it, compared with joy.
    CHORUS-LEADER:
What is this weight of heavy news you bring?
    MESSENGER:
1130 Death!—and the blood-guilt rests upon the living.
    CHORUS-LEADER:
Death? Who is dead? And who has killed him?
   Tell me.
    MESSENGER:
Haemon is dead, and by no stranger's hand.
    CHORUS-LEADER:
But by his father's? Or was it his own?
    MESSENGER:
His own—inflamed with anger at his father.
    CHORUS-LEADER:
1135 Yours was no idle prophecy, Teiresias!
    MESSENGER:
That is my news. What next, remains with you.
    CHORUS-LEADER:
But look! There is his wife, Eurydice;
She is coming from the palace. Has she heard
About her son, or is she here by chance?

[*Enter* EURYDICE.]

    EURYDICE:
1140 You citizens of Thebes, I overheard
When I was standing at the gates, for I
Had come to make an offering at the shrine
Of Pallas, and my hand was on the bar
That holds the gate, to draw it; then there fell
1145 Upon my ears a voice that spoke of death.
My terror took away my strength; I fell
Into my servants' arms and swooned away.
But tell it me once more; I can endure
To listen; I am no stranger to bad news.
    MESSENGER:
1150 Dear lady, I was there, and I will tell
The truth; I will not keep it back from you.
Why should I gloze it over? You would hear
From someone else, and I should seem a liar.
The truth is always best.
                I went with Creon
1155 Up to the hill where Polyneices' body
Still lay, unpitied, torn by animals.
We gave it holy washing, and we prayed

To Hecate and Pluto that they would
Restrain their anger and be merciful.
And then we cut some branches, and we burned 1160
What little had been left, and built a mound
Over his ashes of his native soil.
Then, to the cavern, to the home of death,
The bridal-chamber with its bed of stone.
One of us heard a cry of lamentation 1165
From that unhallowed place; he went to Creon
And told him. On the wind, as he came near,
Cries of despair were borne. He groaned aloud
In anguish: "O, and are my fears come true?
Of all the journeys I have made, am I 1170
To find this one the most calamitous?
It is my son's voice greets me. Hurry, men;
Run to the place, and when you reach the tomb
Creep in between the gaping stones and see
If it be Haemon there, or if the gods 1175
Are cheating me." Upon this desperate order
We ran and looked. Within the furthest chamber
We saw her hanging, dead; strips from her dress
Had served her for a rope. Haemon we saw
Embracing her dead body and lamenting 1180
His loss, his father's deed, and her destruction.
When Creon saw him he cried out in anguish,
Went in, and called to him: "My son! my son!
O why? What have you done? What brought you
   here?
What is this madness? O come out, my son, 1185
Come, I implore you!" Haemon glared at him
With anger in his eyes, spat in his face,
Said nothing, drew his double-hilted sword,
But missed his aim as Creon leapt aside.
Then in remorse he leaned upon the blade 1190
And drove it half its length into his body.
While yet the life was in him he embraced
The girl with failing arms, and breathing hard
Poured out his life-blood on to her white face.
So side by side they lie, and both are dead. 1195
Not in this world but in the world below
He wins his bride, and shows to all mankind
That folly is the worst of human evils.
                [*Exit* EURYDICE.]
    CHORUS-LEADER:
What can we think of this? The Queen is gone
Without one word of good or evil omen. 1200
    MESSENGER:
What can it mean? But yet we may sustain
The hope that she would not display her grief
In public, but will rouse the sad lament
For Haemon's death among her serving-women
Inside the palace. She has true discretion, 1205
And she would never do what is unseemly.

CHORUS-LEADER:
I cannot say, but wild lament would be
Less ominous than this unnatural silence.

MESSENGER:
It *is* unnatural; there may be danger.
1210 I'll follow her; it may be she is hiding
Some secret purpose in her passionate heart.

[*Exit* MESSENGER, *into the palace.*]

CHORUS:
          Look, Creon draws near, and the bur-
          den he bears
[*anapests*] Gives witness to his misdeeds; the cause
          Lies only in his blind error.

[*Enter* CREON *and the* GUARDS, *with the body of*
HAEMON.]⁶

Strophe 1

CREON:
1215 Alas!
The wrongs I have done by ill-counselling!
     Cruel and fraught with death.
     You behold, men of Thebes,
The slayer, the slain; a father, a son.
1220 My own stubborn ways have borne bitter fruit.
My son! Dead, my son! So soon torn from me,
     So young, so young!
The fault only mine, not yours, O my son.
CHORUS-LEADER:
Too late, too late you see the path of wisdom.
CREON:
1225 Alas!
A bitter lesson I have learned! The god
Coming with all his weight has borne down on
     me,
     And smitten me with all his cruelty;
My joy overturned, trampled beneath his feet.
1230 What suffering besets the whole race of men!

[*Enter* MESSENGER, *from the palace.*]

MESSENGER:
My master, when you came you brought a burden
Of sorrow with you; now, within your house,
A second store of misery confronts you.
CREON:
Another sorrow come to crown my sorrow?

⁶ From this point up to the final utterance of the
chorus the dialogue is in strictly strophic form. Creon's
lines, except those rendered in blank verse, are sung;
they are in the strongly marked dochmiac rhythm.
[Kitto.]

MESSENGER:
The Queen, true mother of her son, is dead;   1235
In grief she drove a blade into her heart.

Antistrophe 1

CREON:
Alas!
Thou grim hand of death, greedy and unappeased,
     Why so implacable?
     Voice of doom, you who bring   1240
Such dire news of grief, O, can it be true?
What have you said, my son? O, you have slain
     the slain!
Tell me, can it be true? Is death crowning death?
     My wife! my wife!
My son dead, and now my wife taken too!   1245

[EURYDICE's *body is discovered.*]

CHORUS-LEADER:
But raise your eyes: there is her lifeless body.
CREON:
Alas!
Here is a sorrow that redoubles sorrow.
Where will it end? What else can Fate hold in
     store?
While yet I clasp my dead son in my arms   1250
Before me there lies another struck by death.
Alas cruel doom! the mother's and the son's.
MESSENGER:
She took a sharp-edged knife, stood by the altar,
And made lament for Megareus who was killed
Of old, and next for Haemon. Then at last,   1255
Invoking evil upon you, the slayer
Of both her sons, she closed her eyes in death.

Strophe 2

CREON:
A curse, a thing of terror! O, is there none
Who unsheathe a sword to end all my woes
With one deadly thrust? My grief crushes me.   1260
MESSENGER:
She cursed you for the guilt of Haemon's death
And of the other son who died before.
CREON:
What did she do? How did she end her life?
MESSENGER:
She heard my bitter story; then she put
A dagger to her heart and drove it home.   1265
CREON:
The guilt falls on me alone; none but I

Have slain her; no other shares in the sin.
'Twas I dealt the blow. This is the truth, my
    friends.
Away, take me away, far from the sight of men!
1270 My life now is death. Lead me away from here.
  CHORUS-LEADER:
That would be well, if anything is well.
Briefest is best when such disaster comes.

Antistrophe 2

CREON:
O come, best of all the days I can see,
The last day of all, the day that brings death.
1275 O come quickly! Come, thou night with no dawn!
  CHORUS-LEADER:
That's for the future; here and now are duties
That fall on those to whom they are allotted.

CREON:
I prayed for death; I wish for nothing else.
  CHORUS-LEADER:
Then pray no more; from suffering that has been
Decreed no man will ever find escape. 1280
  CREON:
Lead me away, a rash, a misguided man,
Whose blindness has killed a wife and a son.
O where can I look? What strength can I find?
On me has fallen a doom greater than I can bear.
  [*Exeunt* CREON *and* GUARDS *into the palace.*]

CHORUS:
Of happiness, far the greatest part 1285
[*anapests*] Is wisdom, and reverence towards the
  gods.
Proud words of the arrogant man, in the end,
Meet punishment, great as his pride was great,
Till at last he is schooled in wisdom.

COMMENTARY

In 1849 Matthew Arnold published a splendid poem in which he said that Sophocles "saw life steadily, and saw it whole." But Arnold, no indiscriminate admirer of Sophocles's work, a few years later granted that the interests of the ancient writers were sometimes so remote from ours that "we can no longer sympathize. An action like the action of the *Antigone* of Sophocles, which turns upon the conflict between the heroine's duty to her brother's corpse and that to the laws of her country, is no longer one in which it is possible that we should feel a deep interest."

One might indeed think that a play that makes a fuss about ancient Greek burial rites could be of only remote interest to later readers, and yet Sophocles's *Antigone* has seemed highly relevant to later ages. Modern writers have sometimes shown this interest by rewriting the play, finding in the old story a new meaning. For instance, during World War II, when France was occupied by the Nazis, Jean Anouilh produced his own version of *Antigone* in which it was evident that Antigone stood for the French resistance and that Creon, efficient and ruthless, stood for the Nazis. But Sophocles's play itself—not merely the gist of his plot as reinterpreted by later playwrights—continues to hold our interest, too—although a few words about the plot may be helpful to begin our discussion.

Behind the story of Antigone is the story of her father, Oedipus (as told in Sophocles's *Oedipus the King*; see pp. 85–106), who unknowingly killed his own father and slept with his own mother. The curse on the house of Oedipus outlived him and descended to his children: His sons Polyneices and Eteocles quarreled and killed each other, and his daughter Antigone was put to death when she sought to confer on Polyneices the burial rites she felt were his due.

More precisely, after the fall of Oedipus his two sons inherited the rule of Thebes. They were to rule jointly, but they quarreled and Eteocles banished his brother Polyneices. Polyneices returned to Thebes, armed with allies, and in the ensuing conflict both brothers were killed. Creon, their maternal uncle (and Antigone's), thereupon set about ruling the city. One of his first acts was to order that Eteocles be given a state funeral but that Polyneices, who had come in arms against his own city and had thereby (in Creon's opinion) assaulted the gods of the city, be denied burial. For the Greeks, the denial of funeral rites—a fate reserved for the worst criminals—meant that the soul of the corpse could not enter the next world and be honored. Antigone defied her uncle's edict, gave the corpse a symbolic burial, was caught, and was sent to death. Creon ultimately relented, but his change of mind came too late: Antigone was dead, and so were Creon's wife and son.

This brief summary has done little to suggest that Matthew Arnold may have been mistaken when he said that a modern audience could not be much interested in *Antigone*. And yet even a single reading of the play will let a reader see that it is not simply about ancient rites. Nor is it about the workings of fate, for although the household curse is several times mentioned in the play, the tragic outcome does not seem to be arbitrarily imposed on the characters. But what, then, is the play about?

The German philosopher Georg Wilhelm Friedrich Hegel, in the early nineteenth century, offered a view that makes a good starting point, although few have accepted it without qualification. For Hegel, the play is not a conflict of right against wrong; rather, it shows "a collision between the two highest moral powers," the rightful demands of the family versus those of the state. "The public law of the state and the instinctive family-love and duty towards a brother are here set in conflict." And elsewhere in Hegel: "Each of these two sides realizes only one of the moral powers . . . , and the meaning of eternal justice is shown in this, that both end in injustice because they are one-sided." Moreover, this conflict between ties of kinship and the claims of society reflects or is rooted in a conflict of divine law (the duty of the ruler to govern so as to preserve order, and of the citizen to obey). For Hegel, then, Sophocles's *Antigone* denies neither the claim of the family nor the claim of the state; what it denies is the absoluteness of either claim.

Few modern readers have agreed with Hegel that Creon and Antigone are equally right and equally wrong. Most readers find Antigone much more sympathetic than Creon. Suppose, then, we briefly make a case for Antigone. We can say, first of all, that she is right and Creon is wrong. (Even Creon's strongest defenders finally cannot say that Creon is right and Antigone is wrong.) She acts bravely, persisting in a course that she knows will bring her to suffering. And she does this not out of any hope of private gain. Moreover, she persists even though she sees that her course of action isolates her from everyone else— from her sister Ismene, and from the chorus of men (Creon's counselors).

What can be said against Antigone? Some readers have found her to be a bit too eager for martyrdom, a bit too headstrong, a bit too aware of her superiority to Ismene. There is, perhaps, also some validity to Hegel's comment that "the gods she reveres are the Gods of the Underworld, the instinctive powers of feeling, love, and blood, not the daylight gods of a free, self-conscious life of nation and people."

And what of Creon? The play itself, of course, refutes his early view that he is right in denying burial to Polyneices. And he is in many ways, even from the start, unattractive. One can note, for instance, his touchy male chauvinism, in such a passage as this:

> Now she would be the man, not I, if she
> Defeated me and did not pay for it. (Lines 474–75)

He soon comes to feel that the city is his personal property, so that his word is law, whether just or not. Can anything be said on his behalf? Perhaps at least this: First, he is new on the throne, and his inexperience apparently makes him suspicious, uneasy, and quick to act. Second, as ruler, he does indeed have the responsibility of maintaining order in a city that has recently undergone a civil war. Third, his refusal to allow Polyneices to be buried is not based on personal hatred of Polyneices; he believes (wrongly, it turns out, but perhaps understandably) that the gods cannot sympathize with a man who has come to burn their shrines. Fourth, perhaps it can be said in his behalf that the last third of the play arouses some sympathy (or at least pity) for him; although he repents, he is nevertheless terribly punished by the deaths of his son and his wife, and he must live with the knowledge that these deaths, as well as Antigone's, are his responsibility.

Much more, of course, can be said—must be said—about both Antigone and Creon; a reader of the play may well feel that not only can more be said but that less can be said, since several of the assertions just made about the two chief figures may strike some readers as scarcely relevant. For instance, one might say, "Yes, Creon is new on the throne, and, yes, he is ruling during a state of emergency, but that's of no importance since he is so clearly in the wrong." One might tentatively test this assertion by looking to see what the chorus has to say. To what degree does it support Creon, and to what degree does it support Antigone? But of course there is a problem here: the chorus is a character in the play, not simply Sophocles's spokesperson. Indeed, it is quite interesting to study this chorus of rather conventional male advisers to Creon. They give Antigone a little sympathy when she is led off to her death, but not until after they hear Teiresias (the seer) do they advise Creon to reverse his order. And, to take only one passage, we can notice that at the end of the first choral ode, celebrating civilization and the city, the chorus utters cautious words to the effect that the laws must be observed, and the "anarchic" person must be shunned. These words seem aimed at the rebel who has defied Creon, but at the end of the play the audience may well apply them not to Antigone but to Creon.

The more one reads the play and thinks about it, the more subtle it becomes. This is not to suggest that one cannot (perhaps) come out and say, for instance, "Antigone is the tragic hero, and Creon is clearly wrong"; but it is to suggest that as soon as one has come out and said such a thing, one realizes that there is more to be said. For instance, to continue with the position just taken, one wants to see and to say exactly why and how Creon is "wrong," and even while listing his faults one finds that he holds one's attention. And of course even those few who find Antigone a headstrong girl (readers of *Oedipus the King* may think she has inherited her father's irritability), a bit too intent on martyrdom, must, on reading the play, admit that she compels our admiration. Scholarly books on ancient Greece rightly tell us that women played a severely limited role in Athenian society. Pericles, the Athenian statesman and general, probably summed up the average man's view when he said, "A woman's glory is not to show more weakness than is natural to her sex, and not to be talked about, for good or for evil, among men." The scholarly books on ancient Athens are probably right, in the main. Luckily, Sophocles didn't read them.

TOPICS FOR DISCUSSION

1. Would you use masks for some (or all) of the characters? If so, would they be masks that fully cover the face, Greek-style, or some sort of half-masks? (A full mask enlarges the face, and conceivably the mouthpiece can amplify the voice, but only an exceptionally large theater might require such help. Perhaps half-masks are enough if the aim is chiefly to distance the actors from the audience and from daily reality, and to force the actors to develop resources other than facial gestures. One director, arguing in favor of half-masks, has said that an actor who wears even a half-mask learns to act not with his eyes but with his neck.)

2. How would you costume the players? Would you dress them as the Greeks might have? Why? One argument sometimes used by those who hold that modern productions of Greek drama should use classical costumes is that Greek drama *ought* to be remote and ritualistic. Evaluate this view. What sort of modern dress might be effective?

3. If you were directing a college production of *Antigone*, how large a chorus would you use? (Sophocles is said to have used a chorus of fifteen.) Would you have the chorus recite (or chant) the odes in unison, or would you assign lines to single speakers?

4. If you have read *Oedipus the King*, compare and contrast the Creon of *Antigone* with the Creon of *Oedipus*.

5. Although Sophocles called his play *Antigone*, many critics say that Creon is the real tragic hero, pointing out that Antigone is absent from the last third of the play. Evaluate this view.

6. In some Greek tragedies, fate plays a great role in bringing about the downfall of the tragic hero. Though there are references to the curse on the House of Oedipus in *Antigone*, do we feel that Antigone goes to her death as a result of the workings of fate? Do we feel that fate is responsible for Creon's fall? Are both Antigone and Creon the creators of their own tragedy?

7. Are the words *hamartia* and *hybris* (page 67) relevant to Antigone? To Creon?

8. Why does Creon, contrary to the Chorus's advice (lines 1065–66), bury the body of Polyneices before he releases Antigone? Does his action show a zeal for piety as short-sighted as his earlier zeal for law? Is his action plausible, in view of the facts that Teiresias has dwelt on the wrong done to Polyneices and that Antigone has ritual food to sustain her? Or are we not to worry about Creon's motive?

9. A *foil* is a character who, by contrast, sets off or helps define another character. To what extent is Ismene a foil to Antigone? Is she entirely without courage?

10. What function does Eurydice serve? How deeply do we feel about her fate?

LYSISTRATA

Aristophanes

English version by Dudley Fitts

Nothing of much interest is known about Aristophanes (c. 450 to c. 385 B.C.). An Athenian, he competed for about forty years in the annual festivals of comic drama to which three playwrights each contributed one play. His first play was produced in 427 B.C., his last extant play in 388 B.C., but he is known to have written two comedies after this date. Of the forty or so plays he wrote, eleven survive. *Lysistrata* was produced in 411 B.C.

PERSONS REPRESENTED

LYSISTRATA [*pronounced* Ly SIS tra ta]
KALONIKE [*pronounced* Ka lo NI kee]
MYRRHINE [*pronounced* MYR rhi nee]
LAMPITO [*pronounced* LAM pee toe]
CHORUS
COMMISSIONER
KINESIAS [*pronounced* ki NEE see as]
SPARTAN HERALD
SPARTAN AMBASSADOR
A SENTRY

Until the exodos, *the* CHORUS *is divided into two hemichori: the first, of Old Men; the second, of Old Women. Each of these had its* KORYPHAIOS *(i.e., leader). In the* exodos, *the hemichori return as Athenians and Spartans.*

The supernumeraries include the BABY SON *of Kinesias:* STRATYLLIS, *a member of the hemichorus of Old Women; various individual speakers, both Spartan and Athenian.*

Scene: Athens. First, a public square; later, beneath the walls of the Akropolis; later, a courtyard within the Akropolis.

Patrick Hines in the Phoenix Theater production of *Lysistrata* in New York, 1959. (Photograph: Joseph Abeles Studio.)

PROLOGUE

[*Athens; a public square; early morning;* LYSISTRATA *alone.*]

LYSISTRATA:
If someone had invited them to a festival—
of Bacchos, say; or to Pan's shrine, or to
    Aphrodite's°[1]
over at Kolias—, you couldn't get through the
    streets,
what with the drums and the dancing. But now,
not a woman in sight!

5   Except—oh, yes!

[*Enter* KALONIKE.]

Here's one of my neighbors, at last. Good
morning, Kalonike.
KALONIKE:
                    Good morning, Lysistrata. Darling,
don't frown so! You'll ruin your face!
LYSISTRATA: Never mind my face.
Kalonike,
the way we women behave! Really, I don't blame

10   the men
for what they say about us.
KALONIKE: No; I imagine they're right.
LYSISTRATA:
For example: I call a meeting
to think out a most important matter—and what
    happens?
The women all stay in bed!
KALONIKE: Oh, they'll be along.

15 It's hard to get away, you know: a husband, a cook,
a child . . . Home life can be *so* demanding!
LYSISTRATA:
What I have in mind is even more demanding.
KALONIKE:
Tell me: what is it?

Lysistrata: An English Version by Dudley Fitts, copyright 1954 by Harcourt Brace Jovanovich, Inc.; renewed 1982 by Cornelia Fitts, Daniel H. Fitts, and Deborah W. Fitts, is reprinted by permission of the publisher. CAUTION: All rights, including professional, amateur, motion picture, recitation, lecturing, public reading, radio reading, radio broadcasting, and television are strictly reserved. Inquiries on all rights should be addressed to Harcourt Brace Jovanovich, Inc., Orlando, Florida 32887.
[1] The degree sign (°) indicates a footnote, which is keyed to the text by the line number. Text references are printed in **boldface** type; the annotation follows in lightface type.
2 **Bacchos, Pan, Aphrodite:** The first two are gods associated with wine; Aphrodite is the goddess of love.

LYSISTRATA: It's big.
KALONIKE: Goodness! *How* big?
LYSISTRATA:
Big enough for all of us.
KALONIKE: But we're not all here!
LYSISTRATA:
We would be, if *that's* what was up!
                                No, Kalonike,   20
this is something I've been turning over for nights,
long sleepless nights.
KALONIKE:
                    It must be getting worn down, then,
if you've spent so much time on it.
LYSISTRATA: Worn down or not,
it comes to this: Only we women can save Greece!
KALONIKE:
Only we women? Poor Greece!
LYSISTRATA: Just the same,   25
it's up to us. First, we must liquidate
the Peloponnesians—
KALONIKE: Fun, fun!
LYSISTRATA: —and then the Boiotians.°
KALONIKE:
Oh! But not those heavenly eels!
LYSISTRATA: You needn't worry.
I'm not talking about eels.—But here's the point:
If we can get the women from those places—   30
all those Boiotians and Pelopennesians—
to join us women here, why, we can save
all Greece!
KALONIKE: But dearest Lysistrata!
How can women do a thing so austere, so
political? We belong at home. Our only armor's   35
our perfumes, our saffron dresses and
our pretty little shoes!
LYSISTRATA: Exactly. Those
transparent dresses, the saffron, the
perfume, those pretty shoes—
KALONIKE: Oh?
LYSISTRATA: Not a single man would lift
his spear—
KALONIKE:
            I'll send my dress to the dyer's tomorrow!   40
LYSISTRATA:
—or grab a shield—
KALONIKE: The sweetest little negligée—
LYSISTRATA:
—or haul out his sword.

27 **Boiotia:** A country north of Attika, noted for the crudity of its inhabitants and the excellence of its seafood.

KALONIKE: I know where I can buy
the dreamiest sandals!
LYSISTRATA:
                        Well, so you see. Now shouldn't
the women have come?
KALONIKE: Come? They should have *flown!*
LYSISTRATA:
Athenians are always late.
45   But imagine!
There's no one here from the South Shore, or
      from Salamis.
KALONIKE:
Things are hard over in Salamis, I swear.
They have to get going at dawn.
LYSISTRATA: And nobody from Acharnai.
I thought they'd be here hours ago.
KALONIKE: Well, you'll get
50   that awful Theagenes woman: she'll be
a sheet or so in the wind.
                        But look!
Someone at last! Can you see who they are?

[*Enter* MYRRHINE *and other women.*]

LYSISTRATA:
They're from Anagyros.
KALONIKE: They certainly are.
You'd know them anywhere, by the scent.
MYRRHINE:
Sorry to be late, Lysistrata.
55   Oh come,
don't scowl so. Say something!
LYSISTRATA: My dear Myrrhine,
what is there to say? After all,
you've been pretty casual about the whole thing.
MYRRHINE: Couldn't find
my girdle in the dark, that's all.
                              But what *is*
"the whole thing"?
60   KALONIKE: No, we've got to wait
for those Boiotians and Peloponnesians.
LYSISTRATA:
That's more like it.—But, look!
Here's Lampito!

[*Enter* LAMPITO *with women from Sparta.*]

LYSISTRATA: Darling Lampito,
how pretty you are today! What a nice color!
Goodness, you look as though you could strangle a
65   bull!
LAMPITO:
Ah think Ah could! It's the work-out
In the gym every day; and, of co'se that dance of
      ahs
where y' kick yo' own tail.

KALONIKE: What an adorable figure!
LAMPITO:
Lawdy, when y' touch me lahk that,
Ah feel lahk a heifer at the altar!
LYSISTRATA: And this young lady?   70
Where is she from?
LAMPITO: Boiotia. Social-Register type.
LYSISTRATA:
Ah. "Boiotia of the fertile plain."
KALONIKE: And if you look,
you'll find the fertile plain has just been mowed.
LYSISTRATA:
And this lady?
LAMPITO: Hagh, wahd, handsome. She comes
      from Korinth.
KALONIKE:
High and wide's the word for it.
LAMPITO: Which one of you   75
called this heah meeting, and why?
LYSISTRATA: I did.
LAMPITO: Well, then, tell us:
What's up?
MYRRHINE:Yes, darling, what *is* on your mind,
      after all?
LYSISTRATA:
I'll tell you.—But first, one little question.
MYRRHINE: Well?
LYSISTRATA:
It's your husbands. Fathers of your children.
      Doesn't it bother you
that they're always off with the Army? I'll stake my
      life,   80
not one of you has a man in the house this minute!
KALONIKE:
Mine's been in Thrace the last five months, keep-
      ing an eye
on that General.
MYRRHINE: Mine's been in Pylos for seven.
LAMPITO: And mahn,
whenever he gets a *dis*charge, he goes raht back
with that li'l ole shield of his, and enlists again!   85
LYSISTRATA:
And not the ghost of a lover to be found!
From the very day the war began—
                              those Milesians!
I could skin them alive!
                    —I've not seen so much, even,
as one of those leather consolation prizes.—
But there! What's important is: If I've found a
      way   90
to end the war, are you with me?
MYRRHINE: I should *say* so!
Even if I have to pawn my best dress and
drink up the proceeds.

KALONIKE: Me, too! Even if they split me
right up the middle, like a flounder.
LAMPITO: Ah'm shorely with you.
95 Ah'd crawl up Taygetos° on mah knees
if that'd bring peace.
LYSISTRATA: All right, then; here it is:
Women! Sisters!
If we really want our men to make peace,
we must be ready to give up—
MYRRHINE: Give up what?
Quick, tell us!
LYSISTRATA:
               But *will* you?
100 MYRRHINE: We will, even if it kills us.
LYSISTRATA:
Then we must give up going to bed with our men.
[*Long silence.*]
Oh? So now you're sorry? Won't look at me?
Doubtful? Pale? All teary-eyed?
               But come: be frank with me.
Will you do it, or not? Well? Will you do it?
MYRRHINE: I couldn't. No.
Let the war go on.
105 KALONIKE: Nor I. Let the war go on.
LYSISTRATA:
You, you little flounder,
ready to be split up the middle?
KALONIKE: Lysistrata, no!
I'd walk through the fire for you—you *know* I
     would!—but don't
ask us to give up *that!* Why, there's nothing like it!
LYSISTRATA:
And you?
BOIOTIAN:
110 No. I must say *I'd* rather walk through fire.
LYSISTRATA:
What an utterly perverted sex we women are!
No wonder poets write tragedies about us.
There's only one thing we can think of.
               But you from Sparta:
If you stand by me, we may win yet! Will you?
It means so much!
115 LAMPITO: Ah sweah, it means *too* much!
By the Two Goddesses, it does! Asking a girl
to sleep—Heaven knows how long!—in a great
     big bed
with nobody there but herself! But Ah'll stay with
     you!
Peace comes first!
LYSISTRATA: Spoken like a true Spartan!

95 **Taygetos:** A mountain range.

KALONIKE:
But if—
     oh dear!
               —if we give up what you tell us to,   120
will there *be* any peace?
LYSISTRATA:
               Why, mercy, of course there will!
We'll just sit snug in our very thinnest gowns,
perfumed and powdered from top to bottom, and
     those men
simply won't stand still! And when we say No,
they'll go out of their minds! And there's your
     peace.   125
You can take my word for it.
LAMPITO: Ah seem to remember
that Colonel Menelaos threw his sword away
when he saw Helen's breast all bare.
KALONIKE: But, goodness me!
What if they just get up and leave us?
LYSISTRATA: In that case
we'll have to fall back on ourselves, I suppose.   130
But they won't.
KALONIKE:
               I must say that's not much help. But
what if they drag us into the bedroom?
LYSISTRATA: Hang on to the door.
KALONIKE:
What if they slap us?
LYSISTRATA: If they do, you'd better give in.
But be sulky about it. Do I have to teach you how?
You know there's no fun for men when they have
     to force you.   135
There are millions of ways of getting them to see
     reason.
Don't you worry: a man
doesn't like it unless the girl co-operates.
KALONIKE:
I suppose so. Oh, all right. We'll go along.
LAMPITO:
Ah imagine us Spahtans can arrange a peace. But
     you   140
Athenians! Why, you're just war-mongerers!
LYSISTRATA: Leave that to me.
I know how to make them listen.
LAMPITO: Ah don't see how.
After all, they've got their boats; and there's lots of
     money
piled up in the Akropolis.°

144 **Akropolis:** At the beginning of the war, Perikles
stored emergency funds in the Akropolis, the citadel
sacred to Athene.

LYSISTRATA: The Akropolis? Darling,
we're taking over the Akropolis today!
That's the older women's job. All the rest of us
are going to the Citadel to sacrifice—you under-
      stand me?
And once there, we're in for good!
LAMPITO: Whee! Up the rebels!
Ah can see you're a good strat*eeg*ist.
LYSISTRATA: Well, then, Lampito,
what we have to do now is take a solemn oath.
LAMPITO:
Say it. We'll sweah.
LYSISTRATA: This is it.
—But where's our Inner Guard?
            —Look, Guard: you see this shield?
Put it down here. Now bring me the victim's
      entrails.
KALONIKE:
But the oath?
LYSISTRATA:
            You remember how in Aischylos' *Seven*
they killed a sheep and swore on a shield? Well,
      then?
KALONIKE:
But I don't see how you can swear for peace on a
      shield.
LYSISTRATA:
What else do you suggest?
KALONIKE: Why not a white horse?
We could swear by that.
LYSISTRATA:
            And where will you get a white horse?
KALONIKE:
I never thought of that. *What* can we do?
LYSISTRATA: I have it!
Let's set this big black wine-bowl on the ground
and pour in a gallon or so of Thasian, and swear
not to add one drop of water.
LAMPITO: Ah lahk *that* oath!
LYSISTRATA:
Bring the bowl and the wine-jug.
KALONIKE: Oh, what a simply *huge* one!
LYSISTRATA:
Set it down. Girls, place your hands on the gift-
      offering.
O Goddess of Persuasion! And thou, O Loving-
      cup:
Look upon this our sacrifice, and
be gracious!
KALONIKE:
See the blood spill out. How red and pretty it is!
LAMPITO:
And Ah must say it smells good.

MYRRHINE: Let me swear first!
KALONIKE:
No, by Aphrodite, we'll match for it!
LYSISTRATA:
Lampito: all of you women: come, touch the
      bowl,
and repeat after me—remember, this is an oath—:
I WILL HAVE NOTHING TO DO WITH MY
      HUSBAND OR MY LOVER
KALONIKE:
*I will have nothing to do with my husband or my
      lover*
LYSISTRATA:
THOUGH HE COME TO ME IN PITIABLE
      CONDITION
KALONIKE:
Though he come to me in pitiable condition
(Oh Lysistrata! This is killing me!)
LYSISTRATA:
IN MY HOUSE I WILL BE UNTOUCHABLE
KALONIKE:
In my house I will be untouchable
LYSISTRATA:
IN MY THINNEST SAFFRON SILK
KALONIKE:
In my thinnest saffron silk
LYSISTRATA:
AND MAKE HIM LONG FOR ME.
KALONIKE:
And make him long for me.
LYSISTRATA:
I WILL NOT GIVE MYSELF
KALONIKE:
I will not give myself
LYSISTRATA:
AND IF HE CONSTRAINS ME
KALONIKE:
And if he constrains me
LYSISTRATA:
I WILL BE COLD AS ICE AND NEVER
      MOVE
KALONIKE:
I will be cold as ice and never move
LYSISTRATA:
I WILL NOT LIFT MY SLIPPERS TOWARD
      THE CEILING
KALONIKE:
I will not lift my slippers toward the ceiling
LYSISTRATA:
OR CROUCH ON ALL FOURS LIKE THE
      LIONESS IN THE CARVING
KALONIKE:
Or crouch on all fours like the lioness in the carving

LYSISTRATA:
AND IF I KEEP THIS OATH LET ME DRINK
    FROM THIS BOWL
KALONIKE:
195 *And if I keep this oath let me drink from this bowl*
LYSISTRATA:
IF NOT, LET MY OWN BOWL BE FILLED
    WITH WATER.
KALONIKE:
If not, let my own bowl be filled with water.
LYSISTRATA:
You have all sworn?
    MYRRHINE: We have.
    LYSISTRATA: Then thus
I sacrifice the victim.

    [*Drinks largely.*]

    KALONIKE: Save some for us!
200 Here's to you, darling, and to you, and to you!
                    [*Loud cries off-stage.*]
    LAMPITO:
What's all *that* whoozy-goozy?
    LYSISTRATA: Just what I told you.
The older women have taken the Akropolis.
Now you, Lampito,
rush back to Sparta. We'll take care of things here.
    Leave
these girls here for hostages.
205   The rest of you,
up to the Citadel: and mind you push in the bolts.
    KALONIKE:
But the men? Won't they be after us?
    LYSISTRATA: Just you leave
the men to me. There's not fire enough in the
    world,
or threats either, to make me open these doors
except on my own terms.
210   KALONIKE: I hope not, by Aphrodite!
After all,
we've got a reputation for bitchiness to live up to.
                    [*Exeunt.*]

PARADOS:
CHORAL EPISODE

[*The hillside just under the Akropolis. Enter*
CHORUS OF OLD MEN *with burning torches and*
braziers; much puffing and coughing.]

KORYPHAIOS(man):
Forward march, Drakes, old friend: never you
    mind
that damn big log banging hell down on your back.

STROPHE 1

CHORUS(men):
There's this to be said for longevity:
You see things you thought that you'd never see.
    Look, Strymodoros, who would have thought
        it?   5
    We've caught it—
                    the New Femininity!
The wives of our bosom, our board, our bed—
Now, by the gods, they've gone ahead
And taken the Citadel (Heaven knows why!),
Profanèd the sacred statuar-y,   10
                    And barred the doors,
                    The subversive whores!
KORYPHAIOS(m):
Shake a leg there, Philurgos, man: the Akropolis
    or bust!
Put the kindling around here. We'll build one
    almighty big
bonfire for the whole bunch of bitches, every last
    one;   15
and the first we fry will be old Lykon's woman.

ANTISTROPHE 1

CHORUS(m):
They're not going to give me the old horselaugh!
No, by Demeter, they won't pull this off!
    Think of Kleomenes: even he
    Didn't go free
                    till he brought me his stuff.   20
A good man he was, all stinking and shaggy,
Bare as an eel except for the bag he
Covered his rear with. God, what a mess!
Never a bath in six years, I'd guess.
                    Pure Sparta, man!   25
                    He also ran.
KORYPHAIOS(m):
That was a siege, friends! Seventeen ranks strong
we slept at the Gate. And shall we not do as much
against these women, whom God and Euripides
    hate?
If we don't, I'll turn in my medals from Marathon.   30

STROPHE 2

CHORUS(m):
Onward and upward! A little push,
    And we're there.
Ouch, my shoulders! I could wish
    For a pair
Of good strong oxen. Keep your eye   35
    On the fire there, it mustn't die.
                    Akh! Akh!
The smoke would make a cadaver cough!

ANTISTROPHE 2

Holy Herakles, a hot spark
40   Bit my eye!
Damn this hellfire, damn this work!
    So say I.
Onward and upward just the same.
(Laches, remember the Goddess: for shame!)
45   Akh! Akh!
    The smoke would make a cadaver cough!
KORYPHAIOS(m):
At last (and let us give suitable thanks to God
for his infinite mercies) I have managed to bring
my personal flame to the common goal. It
    breathes, it lives.
50 Now, gentlemen, let us consider. Shall we insert
the torch, say, into the brazier, and thus extract
a kindling brand? And shall we then, do you think,
push on to the gate like valiant sheep? On the
    whole, yes.
But I would have you consider this, too: if they—
55 I refer to the women—should refuse to open,
what then? Do we set the doors afire
and smoke them out? At ease, men. Meditate.
Akh, the smoke! Woof! What we really need
is the loan of a general or two from the Samos
    Command.
60 At least we've got this lumber off our backs.
That's something. And now let's look to our fire.
O Pot, brave Brazier, touch my torch with flame!
Victory, Goddess, I invoke thy name!
Strike down these paradigms of female pride,
65 And we shall hang our trophies up inside.

[*Enter* CHORUS OF OLD WOMEN *on the walls of
the Akropolis, carrying jars of water.*]

KORYPHAIOS(woman):
Smoke, girls, smoke! There's smoke all over the
    place!
Probably fire, too. Hurry, girls! Fire! Fire!

STROPHE 1

CHORUS(women):
    Nikodike, run!
    Or Kalyke's done
70   To a turn, and poor Kritylla's
    Smoked like a ham.
              Damn
    These old men! Are we too late?
    I nearly died down at the place
    Where we fill our jars:
75   Slaves pushing and jostling—
      Such a hustling
    I never saw in all my days.

ANTISTROPHE 1

But here's water at last.
Haste, sisters, haste!
Slosh it on them, slosh it down,   80
The silly old wrecks!
           Sex
Almighty! What they want's
A hot bath? Good. Send one down.
Athena of Athens town,
    Trito-born!° Helm of Gold!   85
    Cripple the old
Firemen! Help us help them drown!

[*The* OLD MEN *capture a woman,* STRATYLLIS.]

STRATYLLIS:
Let me go! Let me go!
KORYPHAIOS(w):   You walking corpses,
have you no shame?
KORYPHAIOS(m):
              I wouldn't have believed it!
An army of women in the Akropolis!   90
KORYPHAIOS(w):
So we scare you, do we? Grandpa, you've seen
only our pickets yet!
KORYPHAIOS(m):   Hey, Phaidrias!
Help me with the necks of these jabbering hens!
KORYPHAIOS(w):
Down with your pots, girls! We'll need both hands
if these antiques attack us.
KORYPHAIOS(m):   Want your face kicked in?   95
KORYPHAIOS(w):
Want your balls chewed off?
KORYPHAIOS(m):   Look out! I've got a stick!
KORYPHAIOS(w):
You lay a half-inch of your stick on Stratyllis,
and you'll never stick again!
KORYPHAIOS(m):
Fall apart!
KORYPHAIOS(w):
        I'll spit up your guts!
KORYPHAIOS(m):   Euripedes!° Master!
How well you knew women!
KORYPHAIOS(w):   Listen to him, Rhodippe,   100
up with the pots!
KORYPHAIOS(m):
        Demolition of God,
what good are your pots?
KORYPHAIOS(w):
        You refugee from the tomb,
what good is your fire?

85 **Trito-born:** Athene, said to be born near Lake
Tritonis, in Libya.
99 **Euripedes:** A tragic dramatist.

KORYPHAIOS(m):
                    Good enough to make a pyre
to barbecue you!

KORYPHAIOS(w):
                    We'll squizzle your kindling!

KORYPHAIOS(m):
You think so?

KORYPHAIOS(w):
                    Yah! Just hang around a while!

105

KORYPHAIOS(m):
Want a touch of my torch?

KORYPHAIOS(w):   It needs a good soaping.

KORYPHAIOS(m):
How about you?

KORYPHAIOS(w):
                    Soap for a senile bridegroom!

KORYPHAIOS(m):
Senile? Hold your trap!

KORYPHAIOS(w):   Just *you* try to hold it!

KORYPHAIOS(m):
The yammer of women!

KORYPHAIOS(w):   Oh is that so?

110 You're not in the jury room now, you know.

KORYPHAIOS(m):
Gentlemen, I beg you, burn off that woman's hair!

KORYPHAIOS(w):
Let it come down!

[*They empty their pots on the men.*]

KORYPHAIOS(m):
What a way to drown!

KORYPHAIOS(w):   Hot, hey?

KORYPHAIOS(m):   Say,
enough!

KORYPHAIOS(w):
            Dandruff

115 needs watering. I'll make you
nice and fresh.

KORYPHAIOS(m):
                    For God's sake, you,
hold off!

SCENE 1

[*Enter a* COMMISSIONER *accompanied by four
constables.*]

COMMISSIONER:
These degenerate women! What a racket of little
      drums,
what a yapping for Adonis on every house-top!
It's like the time in the Assembly when I was
      listening
to a speech—out of order, as usual—by that fool

Demostratos,° all about troops for Sicily,°   5
that kind of nonsense—
                    and there was his wife
trotting around in circles howling
Alas for Adonis!°—
                    and Demostratos insisting
we must draft every last Zakynthian that can
      walk—
and his wife up there on the roof,   10
drunk as an owl, yowling
Oh weep for Adonis!—
                    and that damned ox Demostratos
mooing away through the rumpus. That's what we
      get
for putting up with this wretched woman-business!

KORYPHAIOS(m):
Sir, you haven't heard the half of it. They laughed
      at us!   15
Insulted us! They took pitchers of water
and nearly drowned us! We're still wringing out
      our clothes,
for all the world like unhousebroken brats.

COMMISSIONER:
Serves you right, by Poseidon!
Whose fault is it if these women-folk of ours   20
get out of hand? We coddle them,
we teach them to be wasteful and loose. You'll see
      a husband
go into a jeweler's. "Look," he'll say,
"jeweler," he'll say, "you remember that gold
      choker
you made for my wife? Well, she went to a dance
      last night   25
and broke the clasp. Now, I've got to go to
      Salamis,
and can't be bothered. Run over to my house
      tonight,
will you, and see if you can put it together for her."
Or another one
goes to a cobbler—a good strong workman, too,   30
with an awl that was never meant for child's play.
      "Here,"
he'll tell him, "one of my wife's shoes is pinching
her little toe. Could you come up about noon
and stretch it out for her?"
                    Well, what do you expect?
Look at me, for example, I'm a Public Officer,   35
and it's one of my duties to pay off the sailors.
And where's the money? Up there in the
      Akropolis!

5 **Demostratos:** Athenian orator and jingoist politician; **Sicily:** A reference to the Sicilian Expedition (416
B.C.), in which Athens was decisively defeated.
8 **Adonis:** Fertility god.

And those blasted women slam the door in my
     face!
But what are we waiting for?
                              —Look here, constable,
40   stop sniffing around for a tavern, and get us
some crowbars. We'll force their gates! As a matter
     of fact,
I'll do a little forcing myself.

[*Enter* LYSISTRATA, *above, with* MYRRHINE, KA-
LONIKE, *and the* BOIOTIAN.]

LYSISTRATA: No need of forcing.
Here I am, of my own accord. And all this talk
about locked doors—! We don't need locked
     doors,
45   but just the least bit of common sense.
     COMMISSIONER:
Is that so, ma'am!
                         —Where's my constable?
                              —Constable,
arrest that woman, and tie her hands behind her.
     LYSISTRATA:
If he touches me, I swear by Artemis
there'll be one scamp dropped from the public
     payroll tomorrow!
     COMMISSIONER:
Well, constable? You're not afraid, I suppose?
50   Grab her,
two of you, around the middle!
     KALONIKE: No, by Pandrosos!
Lay a hand on her, and I'll jump on you so hard
your guts will come out the back door!
     COMMISSIONER: That's what *you* think!
Where's the sergeant?—Here, you: tie up that
     trollop first,
the one with the pretty talk!
55   MYRRHINE: By the Moon-Goddess,
just try! They'll have to scoop you up with a spoon!
     COMMISSIONER:
Another one!
                    Officer, seize that woman!
                                        I swear
I'll put an end to this riot!
     BOIOTIAN: By the Taurian,
one inch closer, you'll be one screaming bald-
     head!
     COMMISSIONER:
Lord, what a mess! And my constables seem
60   ineffective.
But—women get the best of us? By God, no!
                              —Skythians!
Close ranks and forward march!
     LYSISTRATA: "Forward," indeed!
By the Two Goddesses, what's the sense in *that*?

They're up against four companies of women
armed from top to bottom.
     COMMISSIONER: Forward, my Skythians!   65
     LYSISTRATA:
Forward, yourselves, dear comrades!
You grainlettucebeanseedmarket girls!
You garlicandonionbreadbakery girls!
Give it to 'em! Knock 'em down! Scratch 'em!
Tell 'em what you think of 'em!

[*General mêlée; the Skythians yield.*]

                              —Ah, that's enough!   70
Sound a retreat: good soldiers don't rob the dead.
     COMMISSIONER:
A nice day *this* has been for the police!
     LYSISTRATA:
Well, there you are.—Did you really think we
     women
would be driven like slaves? Maybe now you'll
     admit
that a woman knows something about spirit.
     COMMISSIONER: Spirit enough,   75
especially spirits in bottles! Dear Lord Apollo!
     KORYPHAIOS[(m)]:
Your Honor, there's no use talking to them.
     Words
mean nothing whatever to wild animals like these.
Think of the sousing they gave us! and the water
was not, I believe, of the purest.   80
     KORYPHAIOS[(w)]:
You shouldn't have come after us. And if you try it
     again,
you'll be one eye short!—Although, as a matter of
     fact,
what I like best is just to stay at home and read,
like a sweet little bride: never hurting a soul, no,
never going out. But if you *must* shake hornets'
     nests,   85
look out for the hornets.

STROPHE

CHORUS[(m)]:
Of all the beasts that God hath wrought
     What monster's worse than woman?
Who shall encompass with his thought
     Their guile unending? No man.   90

They've seized the Heights, the Rock, the Shrine—
     But to what end? I wot not.
Sure there's some clue to their design!
     Have you the key? I thought not.
KORYPHAIOS[(m)]:
We might question them, I suppose. But I warn
     you, sir,   95

don't believe anything you hear! It would be un-
  Athenian
not to get to the bottom of this plot.
  COMMISSIONER: Very well.
My first question is this: Why, so help you God,
did you bar the gates of the Akropolis?
  LYSISTRATA: Why?
100 To keep the money, of course. No money, no war.
  COMMISSIONER:
You think that money's the cause of war?
  LYSISTRATA: I do.
Money brought about that Peisandros° business
and all the other attacks on the State. Well and
  good!
They'll not get another cent here!
  COMMISSIONER: And what will you do?
  LYSISTRATA:
105 What a question! From now on, we intend
to control the Treasury.
  COMMISSIONER: Control the Treasury!
  LYSISTRATA:
Why not? Does that seem strange? After all,
we control our household budgets.
  COMMISSIONER: But that's different!
  LYSISTRATA:
"Different"? What do you mean?
  COMMISSIONER: I mean simply this:
110 it's the Treasury that pays for National Defense.
  LYSISTRATA:
Unnecessary. We propose to abolish war.
  COMMISSIONER:
Good God.—And National Security?
  LYSISTRATA: Leave that to us.
  COMMISSIONER:
You?
  LYSISTRATA:
  Us.
  COMMISSIONER:
      We're done for, then!
  LYSISTRATA: Never mind.
We women will save you in spite of yourselves.
  COMMISSIONER: What nonsense!
  LYSISTRATA:
115 If you like. But you must accept it, like it or not.
  COMMISSIONER:
Why, this is downright subversion!
  LYSISTRATA: Maybe it is.
But we're going to save you, Judge.
  COMMISSIONER: I don't *want* to be saved.
  LYSISTRATA:
Tut. The death-wish. All the more reason.
  COMMISSIONER: But the idea

102 **Peisandros:** A plotter against the Athenian
democracy.

of women bothering themselves about peace and
  war!
  LYSISTRATA:
Will you listen to me?
  COMMISSIONER: Yes. But be brief, or I'll— 120
  LYSISTRATA:
This is no time for stupid threats.
  COMMISSIONER: By the gods,
I can't stand any more!
  AN OLD WOMAN: Can't stand? Well, well.
  COMMISSIONER:
That's enough out of you, you old buzzard!
Now, Lysistrata: tell me what you're thinking.
  LYSISTRATA:
Glad to.
          Ever since this war began   125
We women have been watching you men, agree-
  ing with you,
keeping our thoughts to ourselves. That doesn't
  mean
we were happy: we weren't, for we saw how things
  were going;
but we'd listen to you at dinner
arguing this way and that.
                      —Oh you, and your big 130
Top Secrets!—
            And then we'd grin like little patriots
(though goodness knows we didn't feel like grinning) and ask you:
"Dear, did the Armistice come up in Assembly
  today?"
And you'd say, "None of your business! Pipe
  down!," you'd say.
And so we would.
  AN OLD WOMAN: *I* wouldn't have, by God! 135
  COMMISSIONER:
You'd have taken a beating, then!
                              —Go on.
  LYSISTRATA:
Well, we'd be quiet. But then, you know, all at
  once
you men would think up something worse than
  ever.
Even *I* could see it was fatal. And, "Darling," I'd
  say,
"have you gone completely mad?" And my husband would look at me   140
and say, "Wife, you've got your weaving to attend
  to.
Mind your tongue, if you don't want a slap. 'War's
a man's affair!'"°

143 **War's a man's affair:** Quoted from Homer's *Iliad*,
VI, 492, Hector to his wife Andromache.

COMMISSIONER:
             Good words, and well pronounced.
LYSISTRATA:
You're a fool if you think so.
                                    It was hard enough
145 to put up with all this banquet-hall strategy.
But then we'd hear you out in the public square:
"Nobody left for the draft-quota here in Athens?"
you'd say; and, "No," someone else would say,
     "not a man!"
And so we women decided to rescue Greece.
You might as well listen to us now: you'll have to,
150   later.
COMMISSIONER:
You rescue Greece? Absurd.
LYSISTRATA: You're the absurd one.
COMMISSIONER:
You expect me to take orders from a woman?
                                    I'd die first!
LYSISTRATA:
Heavens, if that's what's bothering you, take my
     veil,
here, and wrap it around your poor head.
KALONIKE: Yes,
155 and you can have my market-basket, too.
Go home, tighten your girdle, do the washing,
     mind
your beans! "War's
a woman's affair!"
KORYPHAIOS(w):
                  Ground pitchers! Close ranks!

ANTISTROPHE

CHORUS(w):
This is a dance that I know well,
160   My knees shall never yield.
Wobble and creak I may, but still
   I'll keep the well-fought field.
Valor and grace march on before,
   Love prods us from behind.
165 Our slogan is EXCELSIOR,
   Our watchword SAVE MANKIND.
KORYPHAIOS(w):
Women,   remember   your   grandmothers!
     Remember
that little old mother of yours, what a stinger she
     was!
On, on, never slacken. There's a strong wind
     astern!
LYSISTRATA:
170 O Eros of delight! O Aphrodite! Kyprian!
If ever desire has drenched our breasts or dreamed
in our thighs, let it work so now on the men of
     Hellas

that they shall tail us through the land, slaves,
     slaves
to Woman, Breaker of Armies!
COMMISSIONER: And if we do?
LYSISTRATA:
Well, for one thing, we shan't have to watch you   175
going to market, a spear in one hand, and heaven
     knows
what in the other.
KALONIKE: Nicely said, by Aphrodite!
LYSISTRATA:
As things stand now, you're neither men nor
     women.
Armor clanking with kitchen pans and pots—
you sound like a pack of Korybantes!   180
COMMISSIONER:
A man must do what a man must do.
LYSISTRATA: So I'm told.
But to see a General, complete with Gorgon-
     shield,
jingling along the dock to buy a couple of herrings!
KALONIKE:
I saw a Captain the other day—lovely fellow he
     was,
nice curly hair—sitting on his horse; and—can
     you believe it?—   185
he'd just bought some soup, and was pouring it
     into his helmet!
And there was a soldier from Thrace
swishing his lance like something out of Euripides,
and the poor fruit-store woman got so scared
that she ran away and let him have his figs free!   190
COMMISSIONER:
All this is beside the point
                              Will you be so kind
as to tell me how you mean to save Greece?
LYSISTRATA.   Of course.
Nothing could be simpler.
COMMISSIONER: I assure you, I'm all ears.
LYSISTRATA:
Do you know anything about weaving?
Say the yarn gets tangled: we thread it   195
this way and that through the skein, up and down,
until it's free. And it's like that with war.
We'll send our envoys
up and down, this way and that, all over Greece,
until it's finished.
COMMISSIONER: Yarn? Thread? Skein?   200
Are you out of your mind? I tell you,
war is a serious business.
LYSISTRATA: So serious
that I'd like to go on talking about weaving.
COMMISSIONER:
All right. Go ahead.
LYSISTRATA: The first thing we have to do

205 is to wash our yarn, get the dirt out of it.
You see? Isn't there too much dirt here in Athens?
You must wash those men away.
　　　　　　　Then our spoiled wool—
that's like your job-hunters, out for a life
of no work and big pay. Back to the basket,
210 citizens or not, allies or not,
or friendly immigrants.
　　　　　　　And your colonies?
Hanks of wool lost in various places. Pull them
together, weave them into one great whole,
and our voters are clothed for ever.
　　　COMMISSIONER:　　　It would take a woman
to reduce state questions to a matter of carding and
215 　　weaving.
　　　LYSISTRATA:
You fool! Who were the mothers whose sons sailed
　　off
to fight for Athens in Sicily?
　　　COMMISSIONER:　　　Enough!
I beg you, do not call back those memories.
　　　LYSISTRATA:　　　And then,
instead of the love that every woman needs,
220 we have only our single beds, where we can dream
of our husbands off with the Army.
　　　　　　　Bad enough for wives!
But what about our girls, getting older every day,
and older, and no kisses?
　　　COMMISSIONER:　　　Men get older, too.
　　　LYSISTRATA:
Not in the same sense.
　　　　　　A soldier's discharged,
225 and he may be bald and toothless, yet he'll find
a pretty young thing to go to bed with.
　　　　　　　But a woman!
Her beauty is gone with the first gray hair.
She can spend her time
consulting the oracles and the fortune-tellers,
230 but they'll never send her a husband.
　　　COMMISSIONER:
Still, if a man can rise to the occasion—
　　　LYSISTRATA:
Rise? Rise, yourself!

[Furiously.]

Go invest in a coffin!
　　　　　　You've money enough.
　　　　　　　I'll bake you
a cake for the Underworld.
　　　　　　And here's your funeral
wreath!

[She pours water upon him.]

MYRRHINE:
　　And here's another!

[More water.]

KALONIKE:
　　　　　　　And here's　　　235
my contribution!

[More water.]

LYSISTRATA:　　What are you waiting for?
All aboard Styx Ferry!
　　　　　　Charon's° calling for you!
It's sailing-time: don't disrupt the schedule!
　　　COMMISSIONER:
The insolence of women! And to me!
No, by God, I'll go back to town and show　　240
the rest of the Commission what might happen to
　　them.
　　　　　　　[Exit COMMISSIONER.]
　　　LYSISTRATA:
Really, I suppose we should have laid out his
　　corpse
on the doorstep, in the usual way.
　　　　　　　But never mind.
We'll give him the rites of the dead tomorrow
　　morning.
　　　　　　[Exit LYSISTRATA with MYRRHINE and
　　　　　　　　　　　　　　KALONIKE.]

PARABIS: CHORAL EPISODE

ODE 1

KORYPHAIOS(m):
Sons of Liberty, awake! The day of glory is at
　　hand.
CHORUS(m):
I smell tyranny afoot, I smell it rising from the
　　land.
I scent a trace of Hippias,° I sniff upon the breeze
A dismal Spartan hogo that suggests King
　　Kleisthenes.°
　　Strip, strip for action, brothers!　　　　　　5
　　Our wives, aunts, sisters, mothers
Have sold us out: the streets are full of godless
　　female rages.

237 **Charon:** God who ferried the souls of the newly
dead across the Styx to Hades.
　　3 **Hippias:** An Athenian tyrant (d. 490 B.C.).
　　4 **Kleisthenes:** An ambisexual Athenian.

Shall we stand by and let our women confiscate
our wages?

EPIRRHEMA 1

KORYPHAIOS(m):

Gentlemen, it's a disgrace to Athens, a disgrace
to all that Athens stands for, if we allow these
10 grandmas
to jabber about spears and shields and making
friends
with the Spartans. What's a Spartan? Give me a
wild wolf
any day. No. They want the Tyranny back, I
suppose.
Are we going to take that? No. Let us look like
15 the innocent serpent, but be the flower under it,
as the poet sings. And just to begin with,
I propose to poke a number of teeth
down the gullet of that harridan over there.

ANTODE 1

KORYPHAIOS(w):

Oh, is that so? When you get home, your own
mammá won't know you!

CHORUS(w):

Who do you think we are, you senile bravos?
20 Well, I'll show you.
I bore the sacred vessels in my eighth year, and at
ten
I was pounding out the barley for Athena Goddess;
then
They made me Little Bear
At the Braunonian Fair;
25 I'd held the Holy Basket by the time I was of age,
The Blessed Dry Figs had adorned my plump
décolletage.

ANTEPIRRHEMA 1

KORYPHAIOS(w):

A "disgrace to Athens," am I, just at the moment
I'm giving Athens the best advice she ever had?
Don't I pay taxes to the State? Yes, I pay them
30 in baby boys. And what do you contribute,
you impotent horrors? Nothing but waste: all
our Treasury,° dating back to the Persian Wars,

32 **Treasury:** Money originally contributed by Athens
and her allies, intended to finance an extension of the
sea-war against Persia. Since the failure of the Sicilian
Expedition, the contributions of the allies had fallen off;
and the fund itself was now being raided by Athenian
politicans.

gone! rifled! And not a penny out of your pockets!
Well, then? Can you cough up an answer to that?
Look out for your own gullet, or you'll get a crack   35
from this old brogan that'll make your teeth see
stars!

ODE 2

CHORUS(m):

    Oh insolence!
    Am I unmanned?
    Incontinence!
    Shall my scarred hand   40
    Strike never a blow
    To curb this flow-
    ing female curse?

    Leipsydrion!°
    Shall I betray   45
    The laurels won
    On that great day?
    Come, shake a leg,
    Shed old age, beg
    The years reverse!   50

EPIRRHEMA 2

KORYPHAIOS(m):

Give them an inch, and we're done for! We'll have
them
launching boats next and planning naval strategy,
sailing down on us like so many Artemisias.
Or maybe they have ideas about the cavalry.
That's fair enough, women are certainly good   55
in the saddle. Just look at Mikon's paintings,
All those Amazons wrestling with all those men!
On the whole, a straitjacket's their best uniform.

ANTODE 2

CHORUS(w):

    Tangle with me,
    And you'll get cramps.   60
    Ferocity
    's no use now, Gramps!
    By the Two,
    I'll get through
    To you wrecks yet!   65

    I'll scramble your eggs,
    I'll burn your beans,
    With my two legs.
    You'll see such scenes
    As never yet   70

44 **Leipsydrion:** A place where patriots had gallantly
fought.

Your two eyes met.
A curse? You bet!

ANTEPIRRHEMA 2

KORYPHAIOS^(w):
If Lampito stands by me, and that delicious
    Theban girl,
Ismenia—what good are *you*? You and your seven
75 Resolutions! Resolutions? Rationing Boiotian eels
and making our girls go with them at Hekate's
    Feast!
That was statesmanship! And we'll have to put up
    with it
and all the rest of your decrepit legislation
until some patriot—God give him strength!—
80 grabs you by the neck and kicks you off the Rock.

SCENE II

[*Re-enter* LYSISTRATA *and her lieutenants.*]

KORYPHAIOS^(w) [*Tragic tone*]:
Great Queen, fair Architect of our emprise,
Why lookst thou on us with foreboding eyes?
    LYSISTRATA:
The behavior of these idiotic women!
There's something about the female temperament
that I can't bear!
    KORYPHAIOS^(w):
5   What in the world do you mean?
    LYSISTRATA:
Exactly what I say.
    KORYPHAIOS^(w):
                    What dreadful thing has happened?
Come, tell us: we're all your friends.
    LYSISTRATA: It isn't easy
to say it; yet, God knows, we can't hush it up.
    KORYPHAIOS^(w):
Well, then? Out with it!
    LYSISTRATA: To put it bluntly,
we're dying to get laid.
10   KORYPHAIOS^(w):   Almighty God!
    LYSISTRATA:
Why bring God into it?—No, it's just as I say.
I can't manage them any longer: they've gone
    man-crazy,
they're all trying to get out.
                    Why, look:
one of them was sneaking out the back door
15 over there by Pan's cave; another
was sliding down the walls with rope and tackle;
another was climbing aboard a sparrow, ready to
    take off

for the nearest brothel—I dragged *her* back by the
    hair!
They're all finding some reason to leave.
                                Look there!
There goes another one.
                      —Just a minute, you!   20
Where are you off to so fast?
    FIRST WOMAN: I've got to get home.
I've a lot of Milesian wool, and the worms are
    spoiling it.
    LYSISTRATA:
Oh bother you and your worms! Get back inside!
    FIRST WOMAN:
I'll be back right away, I swear I will.
I just want to get it stretched out on my bed.   25
    LYSISTRATA:
You'll do no such thing. You'll stay right here.
    FIRST WOMAN: And my wool?
You want it ruined?
    LYSISTRATA: Yes, for all I care.
    SECOND WOMAN:
Oh dear! My lovely new flax from Amorgos—
I left it at home, all uncarded!
    LYSISTRATA: Another one!
And all she wants is someone to card her flax.   30
Get back in there!
    SECOND WOMAN:
                But I swear by the Moon-Goddess,
the minute I get it done, I'll be back!
    LYSISTRATA: I say No.
If you, why not all the other women as well?
    THIRD WOMAN:
O Lady Eileithyia!° Radiant goddess! Thou
intercessor for women in childbirth! Stay, I pray
    thee,   35
oh stay this parturition. Shall I pollute
a sacred spot?
    LYSISTRATA:
                And what's the matter with *you*?
    THIRD WOMAN:
I'm having a baby—any minute now.
    LYSISTRATA:
But you weren't pregnant yesterday.
    THIRD WOMAN: Well, I am today.
Let me go home for a midwife, Lysistrata: 40
there's not much time.
    LYSISTRATA: I never heard such nonsense.
What's that bulging under your cloak?
    THIRD WOMAN: A little baby boy.
    LYSISTRATA:
It certainly isn't. But it's something hollow,

---

34 **Eileithyia**: Goddess of childbirth.

like a basin or—Why, it's the helmet of Athena!
And you said you were having a baby.

45   THIRD WOMAN: Well, I am! So there!
     LYSISTRATA:
Then why the helmet?
     THIRD WOMAN: I was afraid that my pains
might begin here in the Akropolis; and I wanted
to drop my chick into it, just as the dear doves do.
     LYSISTRATA:
Lies! Evasions!—But at least one thing's clear:
50   you can't leave the place before your purification.
     THIRD WOMAN
But I can't stay here in the Akropolis! Last night I
    dreamed
of the Snake.
     FIRST WOMAN:
 And those horrible owls, the noise they make!
I can't get a bit of sleep; I'm just about dead.
     LYSISTRATA:
You useless girls, that's enough: Let's have no
    more lying.
Of course you want your men. But don't you
55   imagine
that they want you just as much? I'll give you my
    word,
their nights must be pretty hard.
                    Just stick it out!
A little patience, that's all, and our battle's won.
I have heard an Oracle. Should you like to hear it?
     FIRST WOMAN:
An Oracle? Yes, tell us!
60   LYSISTRATA: Here is what it says:
WHEN SWALLOWS SHALL THE HOÖPOE
    SHUN
    AND SPURN HIS HOT DESIRE,
ZEUS WILL PERFECT WHAT THEY'VE
    BEGUN
    AND SET THE LOWER HIGHER.
     FIRST WOMAN:
65   Does that mean we'll be on top?
     LYSISTRATA:
BUT IF THE SWALLOWS SHALL FALL OUT
    AND TAKE THE HOÖPOE'S BAIT,
A CURSE MUST MARK THEIR HOUR OF
    DOUBT,
    INFAMY SEAL THEIR FATE.
     THIRD WOMAN:
I swear, *that* Oracle's all too clear.
70   FIRST WOMAN: Oh the dear gods!
     LYSISTRATA:
Let's not be downhearted, girls. Back to our places!
The god has spoken. How can we possibly fail
    him?
       [*Exit* LYSISTRATA *with the dissident women.*]

CHORAL EPISODE

STROPHE

CHORUS(m):
I know a little story that I learned way back in
    school.
Goes like this:
Once upon a time there was a young man—and
    no fool—
Named Melanion; and his
One aversion was marriage. He loathed the very
    thought.   5
So he ran off to the hills, and in a special grot
Raised a dog, and spent his days
Hunting rabbits. And it says
That he never never never did come home.
It might be called a refuge *from* the womb.   10
All right,
       all right,
             all right!
We're as bright as young Melanion, and we hate
    the very sight
Of you women!
     A MAN:
How about a kiss, old lady?
     A WOMAN:
Here's an onion for your eye!   15
     A MAN:
A kick in the guts, then?
     A WOMAN:
Try, old bristle-tail, just try!
     A MAN:
Yet they say Myronides
On hands and knees
Looked just as shaggy fore and aft as I!   20

ANTISTROPHE

CHORUS(w):
Well, *I* know a little story, and it's just as good as
    yours.
Goes like this:
Once there was a man named Timon—a rough
    diamond, of course,
And that whiskery face of his
Looked like murder in the shrubbery. By God, he
    was a son   25
Of the Furies, let me tell you! And what did he do
    but run
From the world and all its ways,
Cursing mankind! And it says
That his choicest execrations as of then
Were leveled almost wholly at *old* men.   30

All right,
        all right,
                all right!
But there's one thing about Timon: he could
    always stand the sight
Of us women.

A WOMAN:
How about a crack in the jaw, Pop?

A MAN:
35 I can take it, Ma—no fear!

A WOMAN:
How about a kick in the face?

A MAN:
You'd reveal your old caboose?

A WOMAN:
What I'd show,
I'll have you know,
40 Is an instrument you're too far gone to use.

SCENE III

[*Re-enter* LYSISTRATA.]

LYSISTRATA:
Oh, quick, girls, quick! Come here!

A WOMAN: What is it?

LYSISTRATA: A man.
A man simply bulging with love.
                    O Kyprian Queen,°
O Paphian, O Kythereian! Hear us and aid us!

A WOMAN:
Where is this enemy?

LYSISTRATA: Over there, by Demeter's shrine.

A WOMAN:
Damned if he isn't. But who *is* he?

5   MYRRHINE: My husband.
Kinesias.

LYSISTRATA:
            Oh, then, get busy! Tease him! Under-
mine him!
Wreck him! Give him everything—kissing, tick-
ling, nudging,
whatever you generally torture him with—: give
    him everything
except what we swore on the wine we would not
    give.

MYRRHINE:
Trust me.

LYSISTRATA:
            I do. But I'll help you get him started.
10 The rest of you women, stay back.

2 **Kyprian Queen:** Aphrodite, goddess of love.

[*Enter* KINESIAS.]

KINESIAS: Oh God! Oh my God!
I'm stiff from lack of exercise. All I can do to stand
    up.

LYSISTRATA:
Halt! Who are you, approaching our lines?

KINESIAS: Me? I.

LYSISTRATA:
A man?

KINESIAS:
            You have eyes, haven't you?

LYSISTRATA: Go away.

KINESIAS:
Who says so?

LYSISTRATA:
            Officer of the Day.

KINESIAS: Officer, I beg you,   15
by all the gods at once, bring Myrrhine out.

LYSISTRATA:
Myrrhine? And who, my good sir, are you?

KINESIAS:
Kinesias. Last name's Pennison. Her husband.

LYSISTRATA:
Oh, of course. I beg your pardon. We're glad to
    see you.
We've heard so much about you. Dearest Myrrhine   20
is always talking about Kinesias—never nibbles an
    egg
or an apple without saying
"Here's to Kinesias!"

KINESIAS: Do you really mean it?

LYSISTRATA: I do.
When we're discussing men, she always says
"Well, after all, there's nobody like Kinesias!"   25

KINESIAS:
Good God.—Well, then, please send her down
    here.

LYSISTRATA:
And what do *I* get out of it?

KINESIAS: A standing promise.

LYSISTRATA:
I'll take it up with her.

                    [*Exit* LYSISTRATA.]

KINESIAS: But be quick about it!
Lord, what's life without a wife? Can't eat. Can't
    sleep.
Every time I go home, the place is so empty, so   30
insufferably sad. Love's killing me, Oh,
hurry!

[*Enter* MANES, *a slave, with* KINESIAS' *baby;
the voice of* MYRRHINE *is heard off-stage.*]

MYRRHINE:
            But of course I love him! Adore him—

But no,
he hates love. No. I won't go down.

[*Enter* MYRRHINE, *above.*]

KINESIAS: Myrrhine!
Darlingest Myrrhinette! Come down quick!
MYRRHINE:
Certainly not.
35   KINESIAS: Not? But why, Myrrhine?
MYRRHINE:
Why? You don't need me.
KINESIAS:
                        Need you? My God, *look* at me!
MYRRHINE:
So long!

[*Turns to go.*]

KINESIAS:
            Myrrhine, Myrrhine, Myrrhine!
If not for my sake, for our child!

[*Pinches* BABY.]

                            —All right, you: pipe up!
BABY:
Mummie! Mummie! Mummie!
KINESIAS: You hear that?
40   Pitiful, I call it. Six days now
with never a bath; no food; enough to break your
    heart!
MYRRHINE:
My darlingest child! What a father *you* acquired!
KINESIAS:
At least come down for his sake.
MYRRHINE: I suppose I must.
Oh, this mother business!

                                    [*Exit.*]
KINESIAS: How pretty she is! And younger!
The harder she treats me, the more bothered I get.

[MYRRHINE *enters, below.*]

MYRRHINE:
45   Dearest child,
you're as sweet as your father's horrid. Give me a
    kiss.
KINESIAS:
Now don't you see how wrong it was to get
    involved
in this scheming League of women? It's bad
for us both.
MYRRHINE:
            Keep both hands to yourself!
KINESIAS: But our house
going to rack and ruin?
MYRRHINE: *I* don't care.

KINESIAS: And your knitting   50
all torn to pieces by the chickens? Don't you care?
MYRRHINE:
Not at all.
KINESIAS:
            And our debt to Aphrodite?
Oh, *won't* you come back?
MYRRHINE:
                        No.—At least, not until you men
make a treaty and stop this war.
KINESIAS: Why, I suppose
that might be arranged.
MYRRHINE: Oh? Well, I suppose   55
I might come down then. But meanwhile,
I've sworn not to.
KINESIAS:
                Don't worry.—Now let's have fun.
MYRRHINE:
No! Stop it! I said no!
                        —Although, of course,
I *do* love you.
KINESIAS:
                I know you do. Darling Myrrhine:
come, shall we?
MYRRHINE: Are you out of your mind? In
    front of the child?   60
KINESIAS:
Take him home, Manes.
                    [*Exit* MANES *with* BABY.]
                        There. He's gone.
                                        Come on!
There's nothing to stop us now.
MYRRHINE: You devil! But where?
KINESIAS:
In Pan's cave. What could be snugger than that?
MYRRHINE:
But my purification before I go back to the Citadel?
KINESIAS:
Wash in the Klepsydra.°
MYRRHINE: And my oath?
KINESIAS: Leave the oath to me.   65
After all, I'm the man.
MYRRHINE: Well . . . if you say so.
                        I'll go find a bed.
KINESIAS:
Oh, bother a bed! The ground's good enough for
    me.
MYRRHINE:
No. You're a bad man, but you deserve something
    better than dirt.

65 **Klepsydra:** A sacred spring beneath the walls of the
Akropolis. Kinesias' suggestion has overtones of
blasphemy.

[*Exit* MYRRHINE.]

KINESIAS:
What a love she is! And how thoughtful!

[*Re-enter* MYRRHINE.]

MYRRHINE: Here's your bed.
Now let me get my clothes off.
70   But good horrors!
We haven't a mattress.
    KINESIAS: Oh, forget the mattress!
MYRRHINE: No.
Just lying on blankets? Too sordid.
    KINESIAS: Give me a kiss.
MYRRHINE:
Just a second.
                              [*Exit* MYRRHINE.]
    KINESIAS: I swear, I'll explode!

[*Re-enter* MYRRHINE.]

MYRRHINE: Here's your mattress.
I'll just take my dress off.
                        But look—
where's our pillow?
    KINESIAS: I don't *need* a pillow!
75   MYRRHINE: Well, *I* do.
                              [*Exit* MYRRHINE.]

KINESIAS:
I don't suppose even Herakles
would stand for this!

[*Re-enter* MYRRHINE.]

MYRRHINE: There we are. Ups-a-daisy!
    KINESIAS:
So we are. Well, come to bed.
    MYRRHINE: But I wonder:
is everything ready now?
    KINESIAS:
              I can swear to that. Come, darling!
    MYRRHINE:
Just getting out of my girdle.
80   But remember, now.
what you promised about the treaty.
    KINESIAS: Yes, yes, yes!
    MYRRHINE:
But no coverlet!
    KINESIAS: Damn it, I'll be
your coverlet!
    MYRRHINE:
              Be right back.
                          [*Exit* MYRRHINE.]
    KINESIAS: This girl and her coverlets
will be the death of me.

[*Re-enter* MYRRHINE.]

MYRRHINE: Here we are. Up you go!
    KINESIAS:
Up? I've been up for ages.
    MYRRHINE: Some perfume?   85
    KINESIAS:
No, by Apollo!
    MYRRHINE: Yes, by Aphrodite!
I don't care whether you want it or not.
                          [*Exit* MYRRHINE.]
    KINESIAS:
For love's sake, hurry!

[*Re-enter* MYRRHINE.]

MYRRHINE:
Here, in your hand. Rub it right in.
    KINESIAS: Never cared for perfume.
And this is particularly strong. Still, here goes.   90
    MYRRHINE:
What a nitwit I am! I brought the Rhodian bottle.
    KINESIAS:
Forget it.
    MYRRHINE:
              No trouble at all. You just wait here.
                          [*Exit* MYRRHINE.]
    KINESIAS:
God damn the man who invented perfume!

[*Re-enter* MYRRHINE.]

MYRRHINE:
At last! The right bottle!
    KINESIAS: I've got the rightest
bottle of all, and it's right here waiting for you.   95
Darling, forget everything else. Do come to bed.
    MYRRHINE:
Just let me get my shoes off.
                        —And, by the way,
you'll vote for the treaty?
    KINESIAS: I'll think about it.
                    [MYRRHINE *runs away.*]
There! That's done it! The damned woman,
she gets me all bothered, she half kills me,   100
and off she runs! What'll I do? Where
can I get laid?
              —And you, little prodding pal,
who's going to take care of *you*? No, you and I
had better get down to old Foxdog's Nursing
    Clinic.
CHORUS[(m)]:
Alas for the woes of man, alas   105
    Specifically for you.
She's brought you to a pretty pass:
    What are you going to do?
Split, heart! Sag, flesh! Proud spirit, crack!
Myrrhine's got you on your back.   110

KINESIAS:
The agony, the protraction!
KORYPHAIOS(m):   Friend,
  What woman's worth a damn?
They bitch us all, world without end.
KINESIAS:
  Yet they're so damned sweet, man!
KORYPHAIOS(m):
115   Calamitous, that's what I say.
You should have learned that much today.
    CHORUS(m):
O blessed Zeus, roll womankind.
  Up into one great ball;
Blast them aloft on a high wind,
120   And once there, let them fall.
Down, down they'll come, the pretty dears,
And split themselves on our thick spears.
                 [*Exit* KINESIAS.]

SCENE IV

[*Enter a* SPARTAN HERALD.]

HERALD:
Gentlemen, Ah beg you will be so kind
as to direct me to the Central Committee.
Ah have a communication.

[*Re-enter* COMMISSIONER.]

COMMISSIONER: Are you a man,
or a fertility symbol?
    HERALD:
           Ah refuse to answer that question!
Ah'm a certified herald from Spahta, and Ah've
5   come
to talk about an ahmistice.
    COMMISSIONER: Then why
that spear under your cloak?
    HERALD: Ah have no speah!
    COMMISSIONER:
You don't walk naturally, with your tunic
poked out so. You have a tumor, maybe,
or a hernia?
    HERALD: You lost yo' mahnd, man?
10   COMMISSIONER: Well,
something's up, I can see that. And I don't like it.
    HERALD:
Colonel, Ah resent this.
    COMMISSIONER: So I see. But what *is* it?
    HERALD: A staff
with a message from Spahta.
    COMMISSIONER:
           Oh. I know about those staffs.

Well, then, man, speak out: How are things in
  Sparta?
    HERALD:
Hahd, Colonel, hahd! We're at a standstill.   15
Cain't seem to think of anything but women.
    COMMISSIONER:
How curious! Tell me, do you Spartans think
that maybe Pan's to blame?
    HERALD:
Pan? No. Lampito and her little naked friends.
They won't let a man come nigh them.   20
    COMMISSIONER:
How are you handling it?
    HERALD: Losing our mahnds,
if y' want to know, and walking around hunched
  over
lahk men carrying candles in a gale.
The women have swohn they'll have nothing to do
  with us
until we get a treaty.
    COMMISSIONER: Yes. I know.   25
It's a general uprising, sir, in all parts of Greece.
But as for the answer—
               Sir: go back to Sparta
and have them send us your Armistice Commission.
I'll arrange things in Athens.
               And I may say
that my standing is good enough to make them
  listen.   30
    HERALD:
A man after mah own haht! Seh, Ah thank you.
                 [*Exit* HERALD.]

CHORAL EPISODE

STROPHE

CHORUS(m):
Oh these women! Where will you find
A slavering beast that's more unkind?   Where a
  hotter fire?
Give me a panther, any day.
He's not so merciless as they,   5
  And panthers don't conspire.

ANTISTROPHE

CHORUS(w):
We may be hard, you silly old ass,
  But who brought you to this stupid pass?
    You're the ones to blame.
Fighting with us, your oldest friends,
Simply to serve your selfish ends—   10
    Really, you have no shame!

KORYPHAIOS(m):
No, I'm through with women forever.
KORYPHAIOS(w): If you say so.
Still, you might put some clothes on. You look too absurd
standing around naked. Come, get into this cloak.
KORYPHAIOS(m):
Thank you; you're right. I merely took it off
because I was in such a temper.
KORYPHAIOS(w): That's much better
Now you resemble a man again.
Why have you been so horrid?
And look: there's some sort of insect in your eye.
Shall I take it out?
KORYPHAIOS(m):
An insect, is it? So that's
what's been bothering me. Lord, yes: take it out!
KORYPHAIOS(w):
You might be more polite.
—But, heavens!
What an enormous mosquito!
KORYPHAIOS(m): You've saved my life.
That mosquito was drilling an artesian well
in my left eye.
KORYPHAIOS(w):
Let me wipe
those tears away.—And now: one little kiss?
KORYPHAIOS(m):
No, no kisses.
KORYPHAIOS(w):
You're so difficult.
KORYPHAIOS(m):
You impossible women! How you do get around us!
The poet was right: Can't live with you, or without you.
But let's be friends.
And to celebrate, you might join us in an Ode.

STROPHE 1

CHORUS(m and w):
    Let it never be said
    That my tongue is malicious:
    Both by word and by deed
I would set an example that's noble and gracious.
    We've had sorrow and care
    Till we're sick of the tune.
    Is there anyone here
    Who would like a small loan?
        My purse is crammed,
        As you'll soon find;
And you needn't pay me back if the Peace gets signed.

STROPHE 2

    I've invited to lunch
    Some Karystian rips—
    An esurient bunch,
But I've ordered a menu to water their lips.
    I can still make soup
    And slaughter a pig.
    You're all coming, I hope?
    But a bath first, I beg!
        Walk right up
        As though you owned the place,
And you'll get the front door slammed to in your face.

SCENE V

[*Enter* SPARTAN AMBASSADOR, *with entourage.*]

KORYPHAIOS(m):
The Commission has arrived from Sparta.
How oddly
they're walking!
Gentlemen, welcome to Athens!
How is life in Lakonia?
AMBASSADOR: Need we discuss that?
Simply use your eyes.
CHORUS(m): The poor man's right:
What a sight!
AMBASSADOR: Words fail me.
But come, gentlemen, call in your Commissioners,
and let's get down to a Peace.
CHORAGOS(m): The state we're in! Can't bear
a stitch below the waist. It's a kind of pelvic
paralysis.
COMMISSIONER:
Won't somebody call Lysistrata?—
Gentlemen,
we're no better off than you.
AMBASSADOR: So I see.
A SPARTAN:
Seh, do y'all feel a certain strain
early in the morning?
AN ATHENIAN:
I do, sir. It's worse than a strain.
A few more days, and there's nothing for us but Kleisthenes,
that broken blossom.
CHORAGOS(m):
But you'd better get dressed again.
You know these people going around Athens with chisels,

looking for statues of Hermes.°

ATHENIAN: Sir, you are right.

SPARTAN:

He certainly is! Ah'll put mah own clothes back
on.

[*Enter* ATHENIAN COMMISSIONERS.]

COMMISSIONER:

Gentlemen from Sparta, welcome. This is a sorry
business.

SPARTAN [*To one of his own group*]:

Colonel, we got dressed just in time. Ah sweah,
if they'd seen us the way we were, there'd have
been a new wah

between the states.

COMMISSIONER:

Shall we call the meeting to order?

Now, Lakonians,
what's your proposal?

AMBASSADOR:

We propose to consider peace.

COMMISSIONER:

Good. That's on our minds, too.

—Summon Lysistrata.

We'll never get anywhere without her.

AMBASSADOR: Lysistrata?

Summon Lysis-*any*body! Only, summon!

KORYPHAIOS(m):   No need to summon:
here she is, herself.

[*Enter* LYSISTRATA.]

COMMISSIONER: Lysistrata! Lion of women!

This is your hour to be
hard and yielding, outspoken and shy, austere and
gentle. You see here
the best brains of Hellas (confused, I admit,
by your devious charming) met as one man
to turn the future over to you.

LYSISTRATA: That's fair enough,
unless you men take it into your heads
to turn to each other instead of us. But I'd know
soon enough if you did.

—Where is Reconciliation?

Go, some of you: bring her here.

[*Exeunt two women.*]

And now, women,
lead the Spartan delegates to me: not roughly

or insultingly, as our men handle them, but
gently,
politely, as ladies should. Take them by the hand,   40
or by anything else if they won't give you their
hands.

[*The* SPARTANS *are escorted over.*]

There.—The Athenians next, by any convenient
handle.

[*The* ATHENIANS *are escorted.*]

Stand there, please.—Now, all of you, listen to
me.

[*During the following speech the two women re-
enter, carrying an enormous statue of a naked
girl; this is* RECONCILIATION.]

I'm only a woman, I know; but I've a mind,
and, I think, not a bad one: I owe it to my father   45
and to listening to the local politicians.
So much for that.

Now, gentlemen,
since I have you here, I intend to give you a
scolding.
We are all Greeks.
Must I remind you of Thermopylai,° of Olympia,   50
of Delphoi? names deep in all our hearts?
Are they not a common heritage?

Yet you men
go raiding through the country from both sides,
Greek killing Greek, storming down Greek cities—
and all the time the Barbarian across the sea   55
is waiting for his chance!

—That's my first point.

AN ATHENIAN:

Lord! I can hardly contain myself.

LYSISTRATA: As for you Spartans:

Was it so long ago that Perikleides°
came here to beg our help? I can see him still,
his gray face, his sombre gown. And what did he
want?   60
An army from Athens. All Messene
was hot at your heels, and the sea-god splitting
your land.
Well, Kimon and his men,
four thousand strong, marched out and saved all
Sparta.

---

16 **statues of Hermes:** The statues were the Hermai,
stone posts set up in various parts of Athens. Just before
the sailing of the Sicilian Expedition, a group of anonymous vandals mutilated these statues with chisels. This
was considered an unhappy augury.

50 **Thermopylai:** A narrow pass where, in 480 B.C.,
an army of 300 Spartans held out for three days against a
vastly superior Persian force.

58 **Perikleides:** A Spartan ambassador to Athens who
successfully urged Athenians to aid Sparta in putting
down a rebellion.

And what thanks do we get? You come back to
65   murder us.
AN ATHENIAN:
They're aggressors, Lysistrata!
A SPARTAN: Ah admit it.
When Ah look at those laigs, Ah sweah Ah'll
    aggress mahself!
LYSISTRATA:
And you, Athenians: do you think you're blameless?
Remember that bad time when we were helpless,
70   and an army came from Sparta,
and that was the end of the Thessalian menace,
the end of Hippias and his allies.
                    And that was Sparta,
and only Sparta; but for Sparta, we'd be
cringing slaves today, not free Athenians.

[*From this point, the male responses are less to*
LYSISTRATA *than to the statue.*]

A SPARTAN:
A well shaped speech.
75   AN ATHENIAN: Certainly it has its points.
LYSISTRATA:
Why are we fighting each other? With all this
    history
of favors given and taken, what stands in the way
of making peace?
AMBASSADOR: Spahta is ready, ma'am,
so long as we get that place back.
LYSISTRATA: What place, man?
AMBASSADOR:
Ah refer to Pylos.
COMMISSIONER:
                    Not a chance, by God!
80
LYSISTRATA:
Give it to them, friend.
COMMISSIONER:
        But—what shall we have to bargain with?
LYSISTRATA:
Demand something in exchange.
COMMISSIONER: Good idea.—Well, then:
Cockeville first, and the Happy Hills, and the
    country
between the Legs of Megara.
AMBASSADOR: Mah government objects.
LYSISTRATA:
85   Over-ruled. Why fuss about a pair of legs?

[*General assent. The statue is removed.*]

AN ATHENIAN:
I want to get out of these clothes and start my
    plowing.
A SPARTAN:
Ah'll fertilize mahn first, by the Heavenly Twins!

LYSISTRATA:
And so you shall,
once you've made peace. If you are serious,
go, both of you, and talk with your allies.   90
COMMISSIONER:
Too much talk already. No, we'll stand together.
We've only one end in view. All that we want
is our women; and I speak for our allies.
AMBASSADOR:
Mah government concurs.
AN ATHENIAN: So does Karystos.
LYSISTRATA:
Good.—But before you come inside   95
to join your wives at supper, you must perform
the usual lustration. Then we'll open
our baskets for you, and all that we have is yours.
But you must promise upright good behavior
from this day on. Then each man home with his
    woman!   100
AN ATHENIAN:
Let's get it over with.
A SPARTAN: Lead on. Ah follow.
AN ATHENIAN:
Quick as a cat can wink!
                    [*Exeunt all but the* CHORUSES.]

ANTISTROPHE 1

CHORUS(w):
        Embroideries and
        Twinkling ornaments and
        Pretty dresses—I hand   105
Them all over to you, and with never a qualm.
        They'll be nice for your daughters
        On festival days.
        When the girls bring the Goddess
        The ritual prize.   110
                Come in, one and all:
                Take what you will.
I've nothing here so tightly corked that you can't
    make it spill.

ANTISTROPHE 2

        You may search my house
        But you'll not find   115
        The least thing of use,
Unless your two eyes are keener than mine.
        Your numberless brats
        Are half starved? and your slaves?
        Courage, grandpa! I've lots   120
        Of grain left, and big loaves.
                I'll fill your guts,
                I'll go the whole hog;
But if you come too close to me, remember: 'ware
    the dog!
                    [*Exeunt* CHORUSES.]

EXODOS

[A DRUNKEN CITIZEN *enters, approaches the gate, and is halted by a sentry.*]

CITIZEN:
Open. The. Door.
    SENTRY: Now, friend, just shove along!
—So you want to sit down. If it weren't such an
    old joke,
I'd tickle your tail with this torch. Just the sort of
    gag
this audience appreciates.
    CITIZEN: I. Stay. Right. Here.
    SENTRY:
Get away from there, or I'll scalp you! The gentle-
5   men from Sparta
are just coming back from dinner.

[*Exit* CITIZEN; *the general company reenters; the two* CHORUSES *now represent* SPARTANS *and* ATHENIANS.]

    A SPARTAN: Ah must say,
Ah never tasted better grub.
    AN ATHENIAN: And those Lakonians!
They're gentlemen, by the Lord! Just goes to show,
a drink to the wise is sufficient.
    COMMISSIONER: And why not?
10 A sober man's an ass.
Men of Athens, mark my words: the only efficient
Ambassador's a drunk Ambassador. Is that clear?
Look: we go to Sparta,
and when we get there we're dead sober. The
    result?
Everyone cackling at everyone else. They make
15   speeches;
and even if we understand, we get it all wrong
when we file our reports in Athens. But today—!
Everybody's happy. Couldn't tell the difference
between *Drink to Me Only* and
The Star-Spangled Athens.
20   What's a few lies,
washed down in good strong drink?

[*Re-enter the* DRUNKEN CITIZEN.]

    SENTRY: God almighty,
he's back again!
    CITIZEN: I. Resume. My. Place.
    A SPARTAN [*To an* ATHENIAN]:
Ah beg yo', seh,
take yo' instrument in yo' hand and play for us.
25 Ah'm told
yo' understand the in*t*ricacies of the floot?
Ah'd lahk to execute a song and dance

in honor of Athens,
                and, of cohse, of Spahta.
    CITIZEN:
Toot. On. Your. Flute.

[*The following song is a solo—an aria—accompanied by the flute. The* CHORUS OF SPARTANS *begins a slow dance.*]

    A SPARTAN:
O Memory,   30
Let the Muse speak once more
In my young voice. Sing glory.
Sing Artemision's shore,
Where Athens fluttered the Persians. *Alalai*,
Sing glory, that great   35
Victory! Sing also
Our Leonidas and his men,
Those wild boars, sweat and blood
Down in a red drench. Then, then
The barbarians broke, though they had stood   40
Numberless as the sands before!

O Artemis,°
Virgin Goddess, whose darts
Flash in our forests: approve
This pact of peace and join our hearts,   45
From this day on, in love.
Huntress, descend!
    LYSISTRATA:
All that will come in time.
                       But now, Lakonians,
take home your wives. Athenians, take yours.
Each man be kind to his woman; and you, women,   50
be equally kind. Never again, pray God,
shall we lose our way in such madness.
    KORYPHAIOS(Athenian):   And now
let's dance our joy.

[*From this point the dance becomes general.*]

    CHORUS(Athenian):
Dance, you Graces
                Artemis, dance
Dance, Phoibos,° Lord of dancing
                      Dance,   55
In a scurry of Maenads, Lord Dionysos°
               Dance, Zeus Thunderer

42 **Artemis:** Goddess of virginity, of the hunt, and of childbirth.
   55 **Phoibos:** God of the sun.
   56 **Maenads, Lord Dionysos:** The maenads were ecstatic women in the train of Dionysos, god of wine.

Dance, Lady Hera°
Queen of the sky
Dance, dance, all you gods
Dance witness everlasting of our pact
60 *Evohí Evohé*
Dance for the dearest
the Bringer of Peace
Deathless Aphrodite!

COMMISSIONER:
Now let us have another song from Sparta.

CHORUS(Spartan):
From Taygetos, from Taygetos,
65   Lakonian Muse, come down.
Sing to the Lord Apollo
Who rules Amyklai Town.

Sing Athena of the House of Brass!°
Sing Leda's Twins,° that chivalry

Resplendent on the shore   70
Of our Eurotas; sing the girls
That dance along before:

Sparkling in dust their gleaming feet,
Their hair a Bacchant fire,
And Leda's daughter, thyrsos° raised,   75
Leads their triumphant choir.

CHORUSES(S and A):
Evohé!
Evohaí!
Evohé!
We pass
Dancing
dancing
to greet
Athena of the House of Brass.

57 **Hera:** Wife of Zeus.
68 **Athena of the House of Brass:** A temple standing
on the Akropolis of Sparta.
69 **Leda's Twins:** Leda, raped by Zeus, bore quadru-

plets: two daughters, Helen and Klytaimnestra, and two
sons, Kastor and Polydeukes.
75 **thyrsos:** A staff twined with ivy, carried by Dionysos and his followers.

COMMENTARY

Of the hundreds of ancient Greek comedies that were written, only eleven
by Aristophanes and four by Menander (c. 342–299 B.C.) are extant, and three
of Menander's four survive only in long fragments. Aristophanes seems to have
written about forty plays, Menander more than twice as many. Hundreds of
other men wrote comedies in ancient Greece, but they are mere names, or
names attached to brief fragments. This means that when we talk about Greek
comedy we are really talking about a fraction of Aristophanes's work, and an
even smaller fraction of Menander's.

Greek comedy is customarily divided into three kinds: Old Comedy (486
B.C., when comedy was first given official recognition at the festival called the
City Dionysia, to 404 B.C., the end of the Pelopennesian War, when Athens was
humbled and freedom of speech was curtailed); Middle Comedy (404 B.C. to
336 B.C., the accession of Alexander, when Athens was no longer free); and New
Comedy (336 B.C. to c. 250 B.C., the approximate date of the last fragments). Of
Old Comedy, there are Aristophanes's plays; of Middle Comedy, there is *Plutus*,
one of Aristophanes's last plays; of New Comedy, there are Menander's
fragments and his recently discovered *Dyskolos* (*The Disagreeable Man*).

Old Comedy is a curious combination of obscenity, farce, political
allegory, satire, and lyricism. Puns, literary allusions, phallic jokes, political
jibes, and so on periodically give way to joyful song; Aristophanes seems to have
been something of a combination of Joyce, Swift, and Shelley. Other comparisons may be helpful. Perhaps we can say that in their loosely connected episodes

and their rapid shifts from lyricism and fantasy to mockery the plays are something like a Marx Brothers movie (Harpo's musicl episodes juxtaposed with Groucho's irreverent wisecracks and outrageous ogling), though the plays are more explicitly political; and they are something like the rock musical *Hair*, which combined lyricism and politics with sex.

Normally Aristophanes's plays have the following structure:

1. *Prologos:* prologue or exposition. Someone has a bright idea, and sets it forth either in monologue or dialogue. In *Lysistrata*, the prologue consists of lines 1–212, in which Lysistrata persuades the women to refrain from sex with their husbands and thus compel their husbands to give up the war.

2. *Parados:* entrance to the chorus. The twenty-four or so members of the chorus express their opinion of the idea. (The *koryphaios*, or leader of the chorus, perhaps sings some lines by himself.) *Lysistrata* is somewhat unusual in having two half-choruses (*hemichori*), one of Old Men and another of Old Women, each with its own leader. Probably each half-chorus had twelve members.

3. *Epeisodion:* episode or scene. In the first scene of *Lysistrata* the women defeat the Commissioner. (A scene in this position, that is, before the *parabasis*, is sometimes called the *agon*, or debate.)

4. *Parabasis:* usually an elaborate composition in which the leader of the chorus ordinarily sheds his dramatic character and addresses the audience on the poet's behalf, the other actors having briefly retired. The *parabasis* in *Lysistrata* is unusual; it is much shorter than those in Aristophanes's earlier plays, and the chorus does not speak directly for the playwright.

5. *Epeisodia;* episodes or scenes, sometimes briefly separated by choral songs. These episodes have to do with the working out of the original bright idea. In *Lysistrata* the first scene of this group (labeled Scene II because we have already had one scene before the *parabasis*) shows the women seeking to desert the cause, the second shows Myrrhine–loyal to the idea–tormenting her husband Kinesias, the third shows the Spartan herald discomfited by an erection, and the fourth shows the Spartan ambassadors similarly discomfited.

6. *Exodos:* final scene, customarily of reconciliation and rejoicing. There is often talk of a wedding and a feast. In this play a Spartan sings in praise not only of Sparta but also of Athens, and the chorus praises the deities worshipped in both states.

Perhaps all Old Comedy was rather like this, but it should be remembered that even Aristophanes's eleven plays do not all follow the pattern exactly. *Lysistrata*, for example, is unusual in having two hemichori and in having the chorus retain its identity during the parabasis. But *Lysistrata* (the accent is on the second syllable, and the name in effect means "Disbander-of-the-Army") is typical in its political concern, in its fantasy, in its bawdry, and in its revelry. It touches on serious, destructive themes, but it is joyous and extravagant, ending with a newly unified society. These points require some explanation.

First, Aristophanes's political concern. *Lysistrata* is the last of Aristophanes's three plays opposing the Peloponnesian War (the earlier two are *Acharnians* and *Peace*). This drawn-out war (431–404 B.C.), named for a peninsula forming the southern part of Greece, was fought between Athens (with some allies) and a confederacy headed by Sparta. Though enemies at the time of the play, in 478 B.C. Athens and Sparta and other communities had become allied in order to defeat a common enemy, the Persians, but once the Persian threat was destroyed, Athens deprived most of its allies of their autonomy and, in effect, Athens ruled an empire.

Moreover, Athens tried to extend its empire. The war ultimately cost Athens its overseas empire and its leadership on the mainland. In 413 B.C. Athens had suffered an especially disastrous naval defeat; it had made something of a recovery by the time of *Lysistrata* (performed 411 B.C.), but the cost in manpower and money was enormous. Yet Athens persisted in its dream of conquest and of colonizing.

To counter this fantastic idea Aristophanes holds up another fantastic idea: the women will end the war by a sex strike. Actually, this is not one fantastic idea but two, for the idea of a sex strike is no more fantastic (for Athenians of the fifth century B.C.) than the idea of women playing a role—not to speak of a decisive role—in national affairs. Lysistrata, reporting her husband's view, is reporting the view of every Athenian: "War's a man's affair." (He was quoting from Homer's *Iliad*, so the point was beyond dispute.) And so there is something wild in her suggestion that the women can save the Greek cities (her hope goes beyond Athens, to Sparta and the other combatants), and in her comparison of the state to a ball of tangled yarn:

COMMISSIONER:
All this is beside the point.
                                Will you be so kind
as to tell me how you mean to save Greece?
    LYSISTRATA: Of course.
Nothing could be simpler.
    COMMISSIONER: I assure you, I'm all ears.
    LYSISTRATA:
Do you know anything about weaving?
Say the yarn gets tangled: we thread it
this way and that through the skein, up and down,
until it's free. And it's like that with war.
We'll send our envoys
up and down, this way and that, all over Greece,
until it's finished.
    COMMISSIONER: Yarn? Thread? Skein?
Are you out of your mind? I tell you,
war is a serious business.
    LYSISTRATA: So serious
that I'd like to go on talking about weaving.
    COMMISSIONER:
All right. Go ahead.

LYSISTRATA: The first thing we have to do
is to wash our yarn, get the dirt out of it.
You see? Isn't there too much dirt here in Athens?
You must wash those men away.
                         Then our spoiled wool—
that's like your job-hunters, out for a life
of no work and big pay. Back to the basket,
citizens or not, allies or not,
or friendly immigrants.
                         And your colonies?
Hanks of wool lost in various places. Pull them
together, weave them into one great whole,
and our voters are clothed for ever.

To the Commissioner, this is utterly fantastic:

COMMISSIONER: It would take a woman
to reduce state questions to a matter of carding and weaving.

Such is the male view, and so these fantastic women, in order to exert
influence, must resort to another fantastic idea, the sex strike, and here we
encounter Aristophanes's famous bawdry. In fact the play's reputation for
bawdry is grossly exaggerated. Until recently, when pornography was hard to get,
Lysistrata–because it was literature–provided one of the few available texts that
talked of erections and of female delight in sex, and Aubrey Beardsley's
illustrations (1896) doubtless helped to establish the book's reputation as a sexual
stimulus. But it is really pretty tame stuff compared to what is now readily
available, and the play, for all its sexual jokes, is not really about sex but about
peace, harmony, union—union between husbands and wives, between all in
Athens, and between Athens and the other Greeks-speaking communities.

One final point: the whole play, of course, not only is utterly improbable
but also is utterly impossible: The women complain that they are sex-starved
because the men are away at the war, but we soon find that the women will
remedy this situation by withholding sex from the men—who, we thought, were
away at war. How can one withhold sex from men who are supposedly not
present? But Old Comedy never worried about such consistency.

A few words should be said about Middle Comedy and New Comedy.
Middle Comedy is a convenient label to apply to the lost plays that must have
marked the transition from Old Comedy to New Comedy—that is, to the
surviving work of Menander. In New Comedy, written when Athens's political
greatness was gone, and when political invective was impossible, the chorus has
dwindled to musicians and dancers who perform intermittently, characters tend
to be types (the young lover, the crabby old father, etc.), and the plot is regularly
a young man's wooing of a maid. Fortune seems unfair and unpredictable, but
in the end the virtuous are rewarded. The personal satire and obscenity of Old
Comedy are gone, and in their place is a respectably conducted tale showing
how, after humorous difficulties, the young man achieves his goal. The plot
steadily moves toward the happy ending, which is far more integral than the

more or less elusive allegoric (or metaphoric) union at the end of *Lysistrata*. It was New Comedy that influenced Rome (which could scarcely have imitated the political satire of Old Comedy), and through Rome modern Europe. Shakespeare, for example, whose comedies have been described as obstacle races to the altar, was a descendant of Menander though he knew nothing of Menander's work first-hand.

TOPICS FOR DISCUSSION

1. According to *Lysistrata*, what are the causes of war? What do you think are the causes of war?
2. What connection, if any, is there between the sex strike and the seizure of the Akropolis?
3. An antiwar play might be expected to call attention to cruelty, innocent suffering, and death. How much of this do you find in *Lysistrata*?
4. There is much about sex here. How much is there about love?
5. How much horseplay do you find in the *exodos*? Why?
6. Evaluate the view that the real heroine of the play is not Lysistrata but the nude female statue of Reconciliation.

A MIDSUMMER NIGHT'S DREAM

William Shakespeare

Edited by Wolfgang Clemen

William Shakespeare (1564–1616) was born in Stratford, England, of middle-class parents. Nothing of interest is known about his early years, but by 1590 he was acting and writing plays in London. He early worked in all three Elizabethan dramatic genres—tragedy, comedy, and history. *Romeo and Juliet*, for example, was written about 1595, the year of *Richard II*, and in the following year he wrote *A Midsummer Night's Dream*. Other major comedies are *The Merchant of Venice* (1596–1597), *As You Like It* (1599–1600), and *Twelfth Night* (1599–1600). His last major works, *The Winter's Tale* (1610–1611) and *The Tempest* (1611), are usually called "romances"; these plays have happy endings but they seem more meditative and less joyful than the earlier comedies.

[DRAMATIS PERSONAE

THESEUS, *Duke of Athens*
EGEUS, *father to Hermia*
LYSANDER ⎫ *in love with Hermia*
DEMETRIUS ⎭
PHILOSTRATE, *Master of the Revels to Theseus*
PETER QUINCE, *a carpenter;* PROLOGUE *in the play*
SNUG, *a joiner;* LION *in the play*
NICK BOTTOM, *a weaver;* PYRAMUS *in the play*
FRANCIS FLUTE, *a bellows mender;* THISBY *in the play*
TOM SNOUT, *a tinker;* WALL *in the play*
ROBIN STARVELING, *a tailor;* MOONSHINE *in the play*
HYPPOLYTA, *Queen of the Amazons, betrothed to Theseus*
HERMIA, *daughter to Egeus, in love with Lysander*
HELENA, *in love with Demetrius*
OBERON, *King of the Fairies*
TITANIA, *Queen of the Fairies*
PUCK, *or Robin Goodfellow*
PEASEBLOSSOM ⎫
COBWEB ⎪
MOTH ⎬ *fairies*
MUSTARDSEED ⎭
Other FAIRIES *attending their King and Queen*
ATTENDANTS *on Theseus and Hippolyta*

Scene: Athens, and a wood near it.]

Oberon (Alan Howard), Puck (John Kane), Titania (Sara Kestelman), and Nick Bottom (David Waller) in a 1970 Stratford-upon-Avon production of *A Midsummer Night's Dream* directed by Peter Brook. (Photo by David Farrell, Shakespeare Centre Library, Stratford-upon-Avon.)

[ACT I]

[SCENE I. *The palace of* THESEUS.]

Enter THESEUS, HIPPOLYTA, [PHILOSTRATE,] *with others.*

THESEUS:
Now, fair Hippolyta, our nuptial hour
Draws on apace. Four happy days bring in
Another moon; but, O, methinks, how slow
This old moon wanes! She lingers°¹ my desires,
5　Like to a stepdame, or a dowager,
Long withering out a young man's revenue.°
　　HIPPOLYTA:
Four days will quickly steep themselves in night,
Four nights will quickly dream away the time;
And then the moon, like to a silver bow
10　New-bent in heaven, shall behold the night
Of our solemnities.
　　THESEUS:　　　　Go, Philostrate,
Stir up the Athenian youth to merriments,
Awake the pert° and nimble spirit of mirth,
Turn melancholy forth to funerals;
15　The pale companion° is not for our pomp.°
　　　　　　　　　　　[*Exit* PHILOSTRATE.]
Hippolyta, I wooed thee with my sword,°
And won thy love, doing thee injuries;
But I will wed thee in another key,
With pomp, with triumph, and with reveling.

Enter EGEUS *and his daughter* HERMIA, *and*
LYSANDER, *and* DEMETRIUS.

　　EGEUS:
20　Happy be Theseus, our renownèd Duke!
　　THESEUS:
Thanks, good Egeus.° What's the news with thee?

EGEUS:
Full of vexation come I, with complaint
Against my child, my daughter Hermia.
Stand forth, Demetrius. My noble lord,
This man hath my consent to marry her.　　　　　25
Stand forth, Lysander. And, my gracious Duke,
This man hath bewitched the bosom of my child.
Thou, thou, Lysander, thou hast given her
　　rhymes,
And interchanged love tokens with my child.
Thou hast by moonlight at her window sung,　　30
With feigning voice, verses of feigning love,
And stol'n the impression of her fantasy°
With bracelets of thy hair, rings, gauds, conceits,
Knacks,° trifles, nosegays, sweetmeats, messengers
Of strong prevailment in unhardened youth.　　35
With cunning hast thou filched my daughter's
　　heart,
Turned her obedience, which is due to me,
To stubborn harshness. And my gracious Duke,
Be it so she will not here before your Grace
Consent to marry with Demetrius,　　　　　　40
I beg the ancient privilege of Athens:
As she is mine, I may dispose of her,
Which shall be either to this gentleman
Or to her death, according to our law
Immediately° provided in that case.　　　　　45
　　THESEUS:
What say you, Hermia? Be advised, fair maid.
To you your father should be as a god,
One that composed your beauties; yea, and one
To whom you are but as a form in wax
By him imprinted and within his power　　　　50
To leave the figure or disfigure it.
Demetrius is a worthy gentleman.
　　HERMIA:
So is Lysander.
　　THESEUS:　　In himself he is;
But in this kind, wanting your father's voice,°　55
The other must be held the worthier.
　　HERMIA:
I would my father looked but with my eyes.
　　THESEUS:
Rather your eyes must with his judgment look.

From *A Midsummer Night's Dream* by William Shakespeare, edited by Wolfgang Clemen. Copyright © 1963
by Wolfgang Clemen. Reprinted by arrangement with
NAL Penguin Inc., New York, N.Y.

¹ The degree sign (°) indicates a footnote, which is
keyed to the text by line number. Text references are
printed in boldface type; the annotation follows in roman type.
I.i. 4 **lingers** makes to linger, delays　6 **Long withering
out a young man's revenue** diminishing the young
man's money (because she must be supported by
him)　13 **pert** lively　15 **companion** fellow (contemptuous)　15 **pomp** festive procession　16 **I wooed thee
with my sword** (Theseus had captured Hippolyta when
he conquered the Amazons)　21 **Egeus** (pronounced
"E-gé-us")

32 **stol'n the impression of her fantasy** fraudulently impressed your image upon her imagination　33–34 **gauds,
conceits, Knacks** trinkets, cleverly devised tokens, knick-
knacks　45 **Immediately** expressly　55 **But in . . .
father's voice** but in this particular respect, lacking your
father's approval

HERMIA:
I do entreat your Grace to pardon me.
60 I know not by what power I am made bold,
Nor how it may concern my modesty,
In such a presence here to plead my thoughts;
But I beseech your Grace that I may know
The worst that may befall me in this case,
65 If I refuse to wed Demetrius.

THESEUS:
Either to die the death, or to abjure
Forever the society of men.
Therefore, fair Hermia, question your desires;
Know of° your youth, examine well your blood,°
70 Whether, if you yield not to your father's choice,
You can endure the livery of a nun,
For aye to be in shady cloister mewed,°
To live a barren sister all your life,
Chanting faint hymns to the cold fruitless moon.°
75 Thrice-blessèd they that master so their blood,
To undergo such maiden pilgrimage;
But earthlier happy is the rose distilled,°
Than that which, withering on the virgin thorn,
Grows, lives, and dies in single blessedness.

HERMIA:
80 So will I grow, so live, so die, my lord,
Ere I will yield my virgin patent° up
Unto his lordship, whose unwished yoke
My soul consents not to give sovereignty.

THESEUS:
Take time to pause; and, by the next new moon—
85 The sealing day betwixt my love and me,
For everlasting bond of fellowship—
Upon that day either prepare to die
For disobedience to your father's will,
Or else to wed Demetrius, as he would,
90 Or on Diana's altar to protest
For aye austerity and single life.

DEMETRIUS:
Relent, sweet Hermia: and Lysander, yield
Thy crazèd title° to my certain right.

LYSANDER:
You have her father's love, Demetrius;
95 Let me have Hermia's: do you marry him.

EGEUS:
Scornful Lysander! True, he hath my love,
And what is mine my love shall render him.

And she is mine, and all my right of her
I do estate unto° Demetrius.

LYSANDER:
I am, my lord, as well derived as he,   100
As well possessed,° my love is more than his;
My fortunes every way as fairly ranked
(If not with vantage°) as Demetrius';
And, which is more than all these boasts can be,
I am beloved of beauteous Hermia.   105
Why should not I then prosecute my right?
Demetrius, I'll avouch it to his head,°
Made love to Nedar's daughter, Helena,
And won her soul; and she, sweet lady, dotes,
Devoutly dotes, dotes in idolatry,   110
Upon this spotted° and inconstant man.

THESEUS:
I must confess that I have heard so much,
And with Demetrius thought to have spoken
   thereof;
But, being overfull of self-affairs,
My mind did lose it. But, Demetrius, come;   115
And come, Egeus. You shall go with me;
I have some private schooling for you both.
For you, fair Hermia, look you arm yourself
To fit your fancies to your father's will;
Or else the law of Athens yields you up—   120
Which by no means we may extenuate—
To death, or to a vow of single life.
Come, my Hippolyta. What cheer, my love?
Demetrius and Egeus, go along.
I must employ you in some business   125
Against° our nuptial, and confer with you
Of something nearly° that concerns yourselves.

EGEUS:
With duty and desire we follow you
       Exeunt [all but LYSANDER *and* HERMIA].

LYSANDER:
How now, my love! Why is your cheek so pale?
How chance° the roses there do fade so fast?   130

HERMIA:
Belike° for want of rain, which I could well
Beteem° them from the tempest of my eyes.

LYSANDER:
Ay me! For aught that I could ever read,
Could ever hear by tale or history,

69 **Know of** ascertain from 69 **blood** passions 72
mewed cage 74 **moon** i.e., Diana, goddess of chastity 77 **distilled** made into perfumes 81 **patent** privilege 93 **crazèd title** flawed claim

99 **estate unto** settle upon 101 **As well possessed** as rich 103 **If not with vantage** if not better 107 **to his head** in his teeth 111 **spotted** i.e., morally stained 126 **Against** in preparation for 127 **nearly** closely 130 **How chance** how does it come that 131 **Belike** perhaps 132 **Beteem** bring forth

135 The course of true love never did run smooth;
    But, either it was different in blood—
      HERMIA:
    O cross! Too high to be enthralled to low!
      LYSANDER:
    Or else misgraffèd° in respect of years—
      HERMIA:
    O spite! Too old to be engaged to young!
      LYSANDER:
140 Or else it stood upon the choice of friends—
      HERMIA:
    O hell! To choose love by another's eyes!
      LYSANDER:
    Or, if there were a sympathy in choice,
    War, death, or sickness did lay siege to it,
    Making it momentany° as a sound,
145 Swift as a shadow, short as any dream,
    Brief as the lightning in the collied° night,
    That, in a spleen,° unfolds both heaven and earth,
    And ere a man hath power to say "Behold!"
    The jaws of darkness do devour it up:
150 So quick bright things come to confusion.
      HERMIA:
    If then true lovers have been ever crossed,
    It stands as an edict in destiny:
    Then let us teach our trial patience,°
    Because it is a customary cross,
155 As due to love as thoughts and dreams and sighs,
    Wishes and tears, poor Fancy's° followers.
      LYSANDER:
    A good persuasion.° Therefore, hear me, Hermia.
    I have a widow aunt, a dowager
    Of great revenue, and she hath no child.
160 From Athens is her house remote seven leagues,
    And she respects me as her only son.
    There, gentle Hermia, may I marry thee,
    And to that place the sharp Athenian law
    Cannot pursue us. If thou lovest me, then,
165 Steal forth thy father's house tomorrow night;
    And in the wood, a league without the town,
    Where I did meet thee once with Helena,
    To do observance to a morn of May,
    There will I stay for thee.
      HERMIA: My good Lysander!
170 I swear to thee, by Cupid's strongest bow,
    By his best arrow with the golden head,°

By the simplicity of Venus' doves,
By that which knitteth souls and prospers loves,
And by that fire which burned the Carthage
    queen,°
When the false Troyan under sail was seen,   175
By all the vows that ever men have broke,
In number more than ever women spoke,
In that same place thou hast appointed me,
Tomorrow truly will I meet with thee.
  LYSANDER:
Keep promise, love. Look, here comes Helena.   180

  Enter HELENA.

  HERMIA:
God speed fair Helena! Whither away?
  HELENA:
Call you me fair? That fair again unsay.
Demetrius loves your fair.° O happy fair!
Your eyes are lodestars,° and your tongue's sweet
    air°
More tunable than lark to shepherd's ear,   185
When wheat is green, when hawthorn buds
    appear.
Sickness is catching. O, were favor° so,
Yours would I catch, fair Hermia, ere I go;
My ear should catch your voice, my eye your eye,
My tongue should catch your tongue's sweet
    melody.   190
Were the world mine, Demetrius being bated,°
The rest I'd give to be to you translated.°
O, teach me how you look, and with what art
You sway the motion of Demetrius' heart!
  HERMIA:
I frown upon him, yet he loves me still.   195
  HELENA:
O that your frowns would teach my smiles such
    skill!
  HERMIA:
I give him curses, yet he gives me love.
  HELENA:
O that my prayers could such affection move!
  HERMIA:
The more I hate, the more he follows me.
  HELENA:
The more I love, the more he hateth me.   200
  HERMIA:
His folly, Helena, is no fault of mine.

138 **misgraffèd** ill matched, misgrafted 144 **momentany** momentary, passing 146 **collied** blackened 147 **spleen** flash 153 **teach our trial patience** teach ourselves to be patient 156 **Fancy's** Love's 157 **persuasion** principle 171 **arrow with the golden head** (Cupid's gold-headed arrows caused love, the leaden ones dislike)

174 **Carthage queen** Dido (who burned herself on a funeral pyre when the Trojan Aeneas left her) 183 **fair** beauty 184 **lodestars** guiding stars 184 **air** music 187 **favor** looks 191 **bated** excepted 192 **translated** transformed

HELENA:

None, but your beauty: would that fault were
    mine!

HERMIA:

Take comfort. He no more shall see my face;
Lysander and myself will fly this place.

205 Before the time I did Lysander see,
Seemed Athens as a paradise to me.
O, then, what graces in my love do dwell,
That he hath turned a heaven unto a hell!

LYSANDER:

Helen, to you our minds we will unfold.

210 Tomorrow night, when Phoebe° doth behold
Her silver visage in the wat'ry glass,
Decking with liquid pearl the bladed grass,
A time that lovers' flights doth still° conceal,
Through Athens' gates have we devised to steal.

HERMIA:

215 And in the wood, where often you and I
Upon faint primrose beds were wont to lie,
Emptying our bosoms of their counsel sweet,
There my Lysander and myself shall meet,
And thence from Athens turn away our eyes,

220 To seek new friends and stranger companies.°
Farewell, sweet playfellow. Pray thou for us;
And good luck grant thee thy Demetrius!
Keep word, Lysander. We must starve our sight
From lovers' food till tomorrow deep midnight.

LYSANDER:

I will, my Hermia.   *Exit* HERMIA.

225   Helena, adieu.
As you on him, Demetrius dote on you!

                                Exit LYSANDER.

HELENA:

How happy some o'er other some° can be!
Through Athens I am thought as fair as she.
But what of that? Demetrius thinks not so;

230 He will not know what all but he do know.
And as he errs, doting on Hermia's eyes,
So I, admiring of his qualities.
Things base and vile, holding no quantity,°
Love can transpose to form and dignity.

235 Love looks not with the eyes, but with the mind,
And therefore is winged Cupid painted blind.
Nor hath Love's mind of any judgment taste;
Wings, and no eyes, figure° unheedy haste:
And therefore is Love said to be a child,

240 Because in choice he is so oft beguiled.

---

210 **Phoebe** the moon   213 **still** always   220 **stranger companies** the company of strangers   227 **some o'er other some** some in comparison with others   233 **holding no quantity** having no proportion (therefore unattractive)   238 **figure** symbolize

As waggish boys in game themselves forswear,
So the boy Love is perjured everywhere.
For ere Demetrius looked on Hermia's eyne,°
He hailed down oaths that he was only mine;
And when this hail some heat from Hermia felt,   245
So he dissolved, and show'rs of oaths did melt.
I will go tell him of fair Hermia's flight.
Then to the wood will he tomorrow night
Pursue her; and for this intelligence°
If I have thanks, it is a dear expense:°   250
But herein mean I to enrich my pain,
To have his sight thither and back again.

                                Exit.

[SCENE II. QUINCE's *house.*]

Enter QUINCE *the Carpenter, and* SNUG *the
Joiner, and* BOTTOM *the Weaver, and* FLUTE *the
Bellows Mender, and* SNOUT *the Tinker, and*
STARVELING *the Tailor.*°

QUINCE: Is all our company here?

BOTTOM: You were best to call them generally,°
man by man, according to the scrip.

QUINCE: Here is the scroll of every man's name,
which is thought fit, through all Athens, to play in   5
our interlude° before the Duke and the Duchess,
on his wedding day at night.

BOTTOM: First, good Peter Quince, say what the
play treats on; then read the names of the actors;
and so grow to a point.   10

QUINCE: Marry,° our play is, "The most lamentable comedy, and most cruel death of Pyramus
and Thisby."

BOTTOM: A very good piece of work, I assure
you, and a merry. Now, good Peter Quince, call   15
forth your actors by the scroll. Masters, spread
yourselves.

QUINCE: Answer as I call you. Nick Bottom, the
weaver.

BOTTOM: Ready. Name what part I am for, and   20
proceed.

---

243 **eyne** eyes   249 **intelligence** piece of news   250 **dear expense** (1) expense gladly incurred (2) heavy cost (in Demetrius' opinion)   I.ii.s.d. The names of the clowns suggest their trades—*Bottom:* skein on which the yarn is wound; *Quince:* quines, blocks of wood used for building; *Snug:* close-fitting; *Flute:* suggesting fluted bellows (for church organs); *Snout:* spout of a kettle; *Starveling:* an allusion to the proverbial thinness of tailors   2 **generally** (Bottom means "individually")   6 **interlude** dramatic entertainment   11 **Marry** (an interjection, originally an oath, "By the Virgin Mary")

QUINCE: You, Nick Bottom, are set down for Pyramus.

BOTTOM: What is Pyramus? A lover, or a tyrant?

25   QUINCE: A lover that kills himself, most gallant, for love.

BOTTOM: That will ask some tears in the true performing of it: if I do it, let the audience look to their eyes. I will move storms, I will condole° in
30   some measure. To the rest: yet my chief humor° is for a tyrant. I could play Ercles° rarely, or a part to tear a cat in, to make all split.

> The raging rocks
> And shivering shocks
35   > Shall break the locks
> Of prison gates;
> And Phibbus' car°
> Shall shine from afar,
> And make and mar
40   > The foolish Fates.

This was lofty! Now name the rest of the players. This is Ercles' vein, a tyrant's vein. A lover is more condoling.

QUINCE: Francis Flute, the bellows mender.

45   FLUTE: Here, Peter Quince.

QUINCE: Flute, you must take Thisby on you.

FLUTE: What is Thisby? A wand'ring knight?

QUINCE: It is the lady that Pyramus must love.

FLUTE: Nay, faith, let not me play a woman. I
50   have a beard coming.

QUINCE: That's all one.° You shall play it in a mask, and you may speak as small° as you will.

BOTTOM: An° I may hide my face, let me play Thisby too, I'll speak in a monstrous little voice,
55   "Thisne, Thisne!" "Ah Pyramus, my lover dear! Thy Thisby dear, and lady dear!"

QUINCE: No, no; you must play Pyramus: and, Flute, you Thisby.

BOTTOM: Well, proceed.

60   QUINCE: Robin Starveling, the tailor.

STARVELING: Here, Peter Quince.

QUINCE: Robin Starveling, you must play Thisby's mother. Tom Snout, the tinker.

SNOUT: Here, Peter Quince.

65   QUINCE: You, Pyramus' father: myself, Thisby's father: Snug, the joiner; you, the lion's part. And I hope here is a play fitted.

SNUG: Have you the lion's part written? Pray you, if it be, give it me, for I am slow of study.

QUINCE: You may do it extempore, for it is   70
nothing but roaring.

BOTTOM: Let me play the lion too. I will roar that° I will do any man's heart good to hear me. I will roar, that I will make the Duke say, "Let him roar again, let him roar again."   75

QUINCE: An you should do it too terribly, you would fright the Duchess and the ladies, that they would shriek; and that were enough to hang us all.

ALL: That would hang us, every mother's son.

BOTTOM: I grant you, friends, if you should   80
fright the ladies out of their wits, they would have no more discretion but to hang us: but I will aggravate° my voice so that I will roar you as gently as any sucking dove; I will roar you an 'twere° any nightingale.   85

QUINCE: You can play no part but Pyramus; for Pyramus is a sweet-faced man; a proper° man as one shall see in a summer's day; a most lovely, gentlemanlike man: therefore you must needs play Pyramus.   90

BOTTOM: Well, I will undertake it. What beard were I best to play it in?

QUINCE: Why, what you will.

BOTTOM: I will discharge it in either your straw-color beard, your orange-tawny beard, your pur-   95
ple-in-grain° beard, or your French-crown-color° beard, your perfit° yellow.

QUINCE: Some of your French crowns° have no hair at all, and then you will play barefaced.° But, masters, here are your parts; and I am to entreat   100
you, request you, and desire you, to con° them by tomorrow night; and meet me in the palace wood, a mile without the town, by moonlight. There will we rehearse, for if we meet in the city, we shall be dogged with company, and our devices° known. In   105
the meantime I will draw a bill of properties,° such as our play wants. I pray you, fail me not.

BOTTOM: We will meet; and there we may rehearse most obscenely° and courageously. Take pains; be perfit; adieu.   110

QUINCE: At the Duke's Oak we meet.

---

73 **that** so that   83 **aggravate** (Bottom means "moderate")   84 **an 'twere** as if it were   87 **proper** handsome   95–96 **purple-in-grain** dyed with a fast purple   96–97 **French-crown-color** color of French gold coin   97 **perfit** perfect   98 **crowns** (1) gold coins (2) heads bald from the French disease (syphilis)   99 **barefaced** (1) bald (2) brazen   101 **con** study   105 **devices** plans   106 **bill of properties** list of stage furnishings   109 **obscenely** (Bottom means "seemly")

---

29 **condole** lament   30 **humor** disposition   32 **Ercles** Hercules (a part notorious for ranting)   37 **Phibbus' car** (mispronunciation for "Phoebus' car," or chariot, i.e., the sun)   51 **That's all one** it makes no difference   52 **small** softly   53 **An** if

BOTTOM: Enough; hold or cut bowstrings.°

Exeunt.

[ACT II

SCENE I. A *wood near Athens.*]

Enter a FAIRY *at one door, and* ROBIN GOOD-
FELLOW [PUCK] *at another.*

PUCK:
How now, spirit! Whither wander you?

FAIRY:
Over hill, over dale,
Thorough bush, thorough brier,
Over park, over pale,°
5   Thorough flood, thorough fire,
I do wander everywhere,
Swifter than the moon's sphere;°
And I serve the Fairy Queen,
To dew her orbs° upon the green.
10   The cowslips tall her pensioners° be:
In their gold coats spots you see;
Those be rubies, fairy favors,
In this freckles live their savors.°
I must go seek some dewdrops here,
15   And hang a pearl in every cowslip's ear.
Farewell, thou lob° of spirits; I'll be gone.
Our Queen and all her elves come here anon.

PUCK:
The King doth keep his revels here tonight.
Take heed the Queen come not within his sight.
20   For Oberon is passing fell and wrath,°
Because that she as her attendant hath
A lovely boy, stolen from an Indian king;
She never had so sweet a changeling.°
And jealous Oberon would have the child
25   Knight of his train, to trace° the forests wild.
But she perforce withholds the lovèd boy,
Crowns him with flowers, and makes him all her
joy.

And now they never meet in grove or green,
By fountain clear, or spangled starlight sheen,°
But they do square,° that all their elves for fear   30
Creep into acorn cups and hide them there.

FAIRY:
Either I mistake your shape and making quite,
Or else you are that shrewd and knavish sprite
Called Robin Goodfellow. Are not you he
That frights the maidens of the villagery,°   35
Skim milk, and sometimes labor in the quern,°
And bootless° make the breathless housewife
churn,
And sometime make the drink to bear no barm,°
Mislead night wanderers, laughing at their harm?
Those that Hobgoblin call you, and sweet Puck,   40
You do their work, and they shall have good luck.
Are not you he?

PUCK: Thou speakest aright;
I am that merry wanderer of the night.
I jest to Oberon, and make him smile,
When I a fat and bean-fed horse beguile,   45
Neighing in likeness of a filly foal:
And sometime lurk I in a gossip's° bowl,
In very likeness of a roasted crab;°
And when she drinks, against her lips I bob
And on her withered dewlap° pour the ale.   50
The wisest aunt, telling the saddest° tale,
Sometime for three-foot stool mistaketh me;
Then slip I from her bum, down topples she,
And "tailor"° cries, and falls into a cough;
And then the whole quire° hold their hips and
laugh,   55
And waxen° in their mirth, and neeze,° and swear
A merrier hour was never wasted° there.
But, room, fairy! Here comes Oberon.

FAIRY:
And here my mistress. Would that he were gone!

Enter [OBERON,] *the King of Fairies, at one
door, with his train; and* [TITANIA,] *the Queen,
at another, with hers.*

OBERON:
Ill met by moonlight, proud Titania.   60

---

112 **hold or cut bowstrings** i.e., keep your word or give it
up (?)
II.i. 4 **pale** enclosed land, park   7 **moon's sphere** (according to the Ptolemaic system the moon was fixed in a
hollow sphere that surrounded and revolved about the
earth)   9 **orbs** fairy rings, i.e., circles of darker grass
10 **pensioners** bodyguards (referring to Elizabeth I's
bodyguard of fifty splendid young noblemen)   12 **favors**
gifts   13 **savors** perfumes   16 **lob** lubber, clumsy fellow   20 **passing fell and wrath** very fierce and angry
23 **changeling** (usually a child left behind by fairies in
exchange for one stolen, but here applied to the stolen
child)   25 **trace** traverse

29 **starlight sheen** brightly shining starlight   30 **square**
clash, quarrel   35 **villagery** villagers   36 **quern** hand
mill for grinding grain   37 **bootless** in vain   38 **barm**
yeast, froth   47 **gossip's** old woman's   48 **crab** crab
apple   50 **dewlap** fold of skin on the throat   51 **saddest**
most serious   54 **tailor** (suggesting the posture of a tailor
squatting; or a term of abuse: Middle English *taillard*,
"thief")   55 **quire** company, choir   56 **waxen** increase
56 **neeze** sneeze   57 **wasted** passed

TITANIA:
What, jealous Oberon! Fairy, skip hence.
I have forsworn his bed and company.
OBERON:
Tarry, rash wanton;° am not I thy lord?
TITANIA:
Then I must be thy lady: but I know
65   When thou hast stolen away from fairy land
And in the shape of Corin° sat all day,
Playing on pipes of corn,° and versing love
To amorous Phillida. Why art thou here,
Come from the farthest steep of India?
70   But that, forsooth, the bouncing° Amazon,
Your buskined°mistress and your warrior love,
To Theseus must be wedded, and you come
To give their bed joy and prosperity.
OBERON:
How canst thou thus for shame, Titania,
75   Glance at my credit with Hippolyta,
Knowing I know thy love to Theseus?
Didst not thou lead him through the glimmering
      night
From Perigenia, whom he ravishèd?
And make him with fair Aegles break his faith,
80   With Ariadne and Antiopa?°
TITANIA:
These are the forgeries of jealousy:
And never, since the middle summer's spring,°
Met we on hill, in dale, forest, or mead,
By pavèd° fountain or by rushy brook,
85   Or in the beachèd margent° of the sea,
To dance our ringlets to the whistling wind,
But with thy brawls thou hast disturbed our sport.
Therefore the winds, piping to us in vain,
As in revenge, have sucked up from the sea
90   Contagious° fogs; which, falling in the land,
Hath every pelting° river made so proud,
That they have overborne their continents.°
The ox hath therefore stretched his yoke in vain,
The plowman lost his sweat, and the green corn°
95   Hath rotted ere his youth attained a beard;
The fold stands empty in the drownèd field,

And crows are fatted with the murrion flock;°
The nine men's morris° is filled up with mud;
And the quaint mazes° in the wanton green,°
For lack of tread, are undistinguishable.   100
The human mortals want their winter here;
No night is now with hymn or carol blest.
Therefore the moon, the governess of floods,
Pale in her anger, washes all the air,
That rheumatic diseases do abound.   105
And thorough this distemperature° we see
The seasons alter: hoary-headed frosts
Fall in the fresh lap of the crimson rose,
And on old Hiems'° thin and icy crown
An odorous chaplet° of sweet summer buds   110
Is, as in mockery, set. The spring, the summer,
The childing° autumn, angry winter, change
Their wonted liveries;° and the mazèd° world,
By their increase, now knows not which is which.
And this same progeny of evils comes   115
From our debate,° from our dissension;
We are their parents and original.
OBERON:
Do you amend it, then; it lies in you:
Why should Titania cross her Oberon?
I do but beg a little changeling boy,   120
To be my henchman.°
TITANIA: Set your heart at rest.
The fairy land buys not° the child of me.
His mother was a vot'ress° of my order,
And, in the spicèd Indian air, by night,
Full often hath she gossiped by my side,   125
And sat with me on Neptune's yellow sands,
Marking th' embarkèd traders on the flood;
When we have laughed to see the sails conceive
And grow big-bellied with the wanton wind;
Which she, with pretty and with swimming gait   130
Following—her womb then rich with my young
      squire—
Would imitate, and sail upon the land,
To fetch me trifles, and return again,
As from a voyage, rich with merchandise.

---

97 **murrion flock** flock dead of cattle disease (murrain)   98 **nine men's morris** square cut in the turf (for a game in which each player has nine counters or "men")   99 **quaint mazes** intricate meandering paths on the grass (kept fresh by running along them)   99 **wanton green** grass growing without check   106 **distemperature** disturbance in nature   109 **old Hiems'** the winter's   110 **chaplet** wreath   112 **childing** breeding, fruitful   113 **wonted liveries** accustomed apparel   113 **mazèd** bewildered   116 **debate** quarrel   121 **henchman** page   122 **The fairy land buys not** i.e., even your whole domain could not buy   123 **vot'ress** woman who has taken a vow

63 **rash wanton** hasty willful creature   66 **Corin** (like *Phillida*, line 68, a traditional name for a lover in pastoral poetry)   67 **pipes of corn** musical instruments made of grain stalks   70 **bouncing** swaggering   71 **buskined** wearing a hunter's boot (buskin)   78–80 **Perigenia, Aegles, Ariadne, Antiopa** (girls Theseus loved and deserted)   82 **middle summer's spring** beginning of midsummer   84 **pavèd** i.e., with pebbly bottom   85 **margent** margin, shore   90 **contagious** generating pestilence   91 **pelting** petty   92 **continents** containers (i.e., banks)   94 **corn** grain

135 But she, being mortal, of that boy did die;
And for her sake do I rear up her boy,
And for her sake I will not part with him.
    OBERON:
How long within this wood intend you stay?
    TITANIA:
Perchance till after Theseus' wedding day.
140 If you will patiently dance in our round,°
And see our moonlight revels, go with us.
If not, shun me, and I will spare° your haunts.
    OBERON:
Give me that boy, and I will go with thee.
    TITANIA:
Not for thy fairy kingdom. Fairies, away!
145 We shall chide downright, if I longer stay.
         Exeunt [TITANIA *with her train*].
    OBERON:
Well, go thy way. Thou shalt not from this grove
Till I torment thee for this injury.
My gentle Puck, come hither. Thou rememb'rest
Since° once I sat upon a promontory,
150 And heard a mermaid, on a dolphin's back,
Uttering such dulcet and harmonious breath,
That the rude sea grew civil° at her song,
And certain stars shot madly from their spheres,
To hear the sea maid's music.
    PUCK: I remember.
    OBERON:
155 That very time I saw, but thou couldsn't not,
Flying between the cold moon and the earth,
Cupid all armed. A certain aim he took
At a fair vestal° thronèd by the west,
And loosed his love shaft smartly from his bow,
160 As it should° pierce a hundred thousand hearts.
But I might° see young Cupid's fiery shaft
Quenched in the chaste beams of the wat'ry
    moon,
And the imperial vot'ress passèd on,
In maiden meditation, fancy-free.°
165 Yet marked I where the bolt of Cupid fell.
It fell upon a little western flower,
Before milk-white, now purple with love's wound,
And maidens call it love-in-idleness.°
Fetch me that flow'r; the herb I showed thee once:
170 The juice of it on sleeping eyelids laid
Will make or man or woman° madly dote

Upon the next live creature that it sees.
Fetch me this herb, and be thou here again
Ere the leviathan° can swim a league.
    PUCK:
I'll put a girdle round about the earth   175
In forty minutes.   [*Exit.*]
    OBERON: Having once this juice,
I'll watch Titania when she is asleep,
And drop the liquor of it in her eyes.
The next thing then she waking looks upon,
Be it on lion, bear, or wolf, or bull,   180
On meddling monkey, or on busy° ape,
She shall pursue it with the soul of love.
And ere I take this charm from off her sight,
As I can take it with another herb,
I'll make her render up her page to me.   185
But who comes here? I am invisible,
And I will overhear their conference.

    Enter DEMETRIUS, HELENA *following him.*

    DEMETRIUS:
I love thee not, therefore pursue me not.
Where is Lysander and fair Hermia?
The one I'll slay, the other slayeth me.   190
Thou told'st me they were stol'n unto this wood;
And here am I, and wood° within this wood,
Because I cannot meet my Hermia.
Hence, get thee gone, and follow me no more!
    HELENA:
You draw me, you hardhearted adamant;°   195
But yet you draw not iron, for my heart
Is true as steel. Leave you your power to draw,
And I shall have no power to follow you.
    DEMETRIUS:
Do I entice you? Do I speak you fair?°
Or, rather, do I not in plainest truth   200
Tell you, I do not nor I cannot love you?
    HELENA:
And even for that do I love you the more.
I am your spaniel; and, Demetrius,
The more you beat me, I will fawn on you.
Use me but as your spaniel, spurn me, strike me,   205
Neglect me, lose me; only give me leave,
Unworthy as I am, to follow you.
What worser place can I beg in your love—
And yet a place of high respect with me—
Than to be usèd as you use your dog?   210

---

140 round circular dance   **142 spare** keep away from
149 Since when   **152 civil** well behaved   **158 vestal**
virgin (possibly an allusion to Elizabeth, the Virgin
Queen)   **160 As it should** as if it would   **161 might**
could   **164 fancy-free** free from the power of love   **168**
love-in-idleness pansy   **171 or man or woman** either
man or woman

174 leviathan sea monster, whale   **181 busy** meddle-
some   **192 wood** out of my mind (with perhaps an
additional pun on "wooed")   **195 adamant** (1) very hard
gem (2) loadstone, magnet   **199 speak you fair** speak
kindly to you

DEMETRIUS:
Tempt not too much the hatred of my spirit,
For I am sick when I do look on thee.
HELENA:
And I am sick when I look not on you.
DEMETRIUS:
You do impeach° your modesty too much,
215   To leave the city, and commit yourself
Into the hands of one that loves you not,
To trust the opportunity of night
And the ill counsel of a desert° place
With the rich worth of your virginity.
HELENA:
220   Your virtue is my privilege.° For that
It is not night when I do see your face,
Therefore I think I am not in the night;
Nor doth this wood lack worlds of company,
For you in my respect° are all the world.
225   Then how can it be said I am alone
When all the world is here to look on me?
DEMETRIUS:
I'll run from thee and hide me in the brakes,°
And leave thee to the mercy of wild beasts.
HELENA:
The wildest hath not such a heart as you.
230   Run when you will, the story shall be changed:
Apollo flies, and Daphne° holds the chase;
The dove pursues the griffin;° the mild hind°
Makes speed to catch the tiger; bootless speed,
When cowardice pursues, and valor flies.
DEMETRIUS:
235   I will not stay° thy questions. Let me go!
Or, if thou follow me, do not believe
But I shall do thee mischief in the wood.
HELENA:
Ay, in the temple, in the town, the field,
You do me mischief. Fie, Demetrius!
240   Your wrongs do set a scandal on my sex.
We cannot fight for love, as men may do;
We should be wooed, and were not made to woo.
                                   [Exit DEMETRIUS.]
I'll follow thee, and make a heaven of hell,
To die upon° the hand I love so well.
                                          [Exit.]

OBERON:
Fare thee well, nymph: ere he do leave this grove,   245
Thou shalt fly him, and he shall seek thy love.

Enter PUCK.

Hast thou the flower there? Welcome, wanderer.
PUCK:
Ay, there it is.
OBERON: I pray thee, give it me.
I know a bank where the wild thyme blows,
Where oxlips and the nodding violet grows,   250
Quite overcanopied with luscious woodbine,
With sweet musk roses, and with eglantine.
There sleeps Titania sometime of the night,
Lulled in these flowers with dances and delight;
And there the snake throws° her enameled skin,   255
Weed° wide enough to wrap a fairy in.
And with the juice of this I'll streak her eyes,
And make her full of hateful fantasies.
Take thou some of it, and seek through this grove.
A sweet Athenian lady is in love   260
With a disdainful youth. Anoint his eyes;
But do it when the next thing he espies
May be the lady. Thou shalt know the man
By the Athenian garments he hath on.
Effect it with some care that he may prove   265
More fond on her° than she upon her love:
And look thou meet me ere the first cock crow.
PUCK:
Fear not, my lord, your servant shall do so.
                                          Exeunt.

[SCENE II. *Another part of the wood.*]

Enter TITANIA, *Queen of Fairies, with her train.*

TITANIA:
Come, now a roundel° and a fairy song;
Then, for the third part of a minute, hence;
Some to kill cankers in the musk-rose buds,
Some war with reremice° for their leathern wings
To make my small elves coats, and some keep back   5
The clamorous owl, that nightly hoots and
    wonders
At our quaint° spirits. Sing me now asleep.
Then to your offices, and let me rest.

FAIRIES *sing.*

214 **impeach** expose to reproach   218 **desert** deserted,
uninhabited   220 **Your virtue is my privilege** your
inherent power is my warrant   224 **in my respect** in my
opinion   227 **brakes** thickets   231 **Daphne** a nymph
who fled from Apollo (at her prayer she was changed into
a laurel tree)   232 **griffin** fabulous monster with an
eagle's head and a lion's body   232 **hind** doe   235 **stay**
wait for   244 **To die upon** dying by

255 **throws** casts off   256 **Weed** garment   266 **fond on
her** foolishly in love with her
II.ii.1 **roundel** dance in a ring   4 **reremice** bats   7
quaint dainty

1ST FAIRY:
You spotted snakes with double tongue,
10   Thorny hedgehogs, be not seen;
Newts and blindworms,° do no wrong,
   Come not near our Fairy Queen.

CHORUS:
   Philomele,° with melody
   Sing in our sweet lullaby;
15 Lulla, lulla, lullaby, lulla, lulla, lullaby:
     Never harm
     Nor spell nor charm,
   Come our lovely lady nigh;
   So, good night, with lullaby.

1ST FAIRY:
20 Weaving spiders, come not here;
   Hence, you long-legged spinners, hence!
Beetles black, approach not near;
   Worm nor snail, do no offense.

CHORUS:
   Philomele, with melody, &c.

2ND FAIRY:
25 Hence, away! Now all is well.
One aloof stand sentinel.
     [*Exeunt* FAIRIES. TITANIA *sleeps.*]

Enter OBERON [*and squeezes the flower on* TI-
TANIA's *eyelids*].

OBERON:
What thou seest when thou dost wake,
Do it for thy truelove take;
Love and languish for his sake.
30 Be it ounce,° or cat, or bear,
Pard,° or boar with bristled hair,
In thy eye that shall appear
When thou wak'st, it is thy dear.
Wake when some vile thing is near.   [*Exit.*]

Enter LYSANDER *and* HERMIA

LYSANDER:
35 Fair love, you faint with wand'ring in the wood;
And to speak troth,° I have forgot our way.
We'll rest us, Hermia, if you think it good,
And tarry for the comfort of the day.
HERMIA:
Be't so, Lysander. Find you out a bed;
40 For I upon this bank will rest my head.
LYSANDER:
One turf shall serve as pillow for us both,
One heart, one bed, two bosoms, and one troth.

11 **blindworms** small snakes   13 **Philomele** nightingale
30 **ounce** lynx   31 **Pard** leopard   36 **troth** truth

HERMIA:
Nay, good Lysander. For my sake, my dear,
Lie further off yet, do not lie so near.
   LYSANDER:
O, take the sense,° sweet, of my innocence!   45
Love takes the meaning° in love's conference.
I mean, that my heart unto yours is knit,
So that but one heart we can make of it:
Two bosoms interchainèd with an oath;
So then two bosoms and a single troth.°   50
Then by your side no bed-room me deny,
For lying so, Hermia, I do not lie.°
   HERMIA:
Lysander riddles very prettily.
Now much beshrew° my manners and my pride,
If Hermia meant to say Lysander lied.   55
But, gentle friend, for love and courtesy
Lie further off, in human modesty.
Such separation as may well be said
Becomes a virtuous bachelor and a maid,
So far be distant; and, good night, sweet friend.   60
Thy love ne'er alter till they sweet life end!
   LYSANDER:
Amen, amen, to that fair prayer, say I,
And then end life when I end loyalty!
Here is my bed. Sleep give thee all his rest!
   HERMIA:
With half that wish the wisher's eyes be pressed!   65
          [*They sleep.*]

Enter PUCK.

PUCK:
   Through the forest have I gone,
   But Athenian found I none,
   On whose eyes I might approve°
   This flower's force in stirring love.
   Night and silence.—Who is here?   70
   Weeds° of Athens he doth wear:
   This is he, my master said,
   Despisèd the Athenian maid;
   And here the maiden, sleeping sound,
   On the dank and dirty ground.   75
   Pretty soul! She durst not lie
   Near this lack-love, this kill-courtesy.
   Churl,° upon thy eyes I throw
   All the power this charm doth owe.°

45 **take the sense** understand the true meaning   46
Love takes the meaning lovers understand the true
meaning of what they say to each other   50 **troth**
faithful love   52 **lie** be untrue   54 **beshrew** curse (but
commonly, as here, in a light sense)   68 **approve**
try   71 **Weeds** garments   78 **Churl** boorish fellow   79
owe possess

80 When thou wak'st, let love forbid
    Sleep his seat on they eyelid.
    So awake when I am gone,
        For I must now to Oberon.

                                                    Exit.

    Enter DEMETRIUS *and* HELENA, *running.*

    HELENA:
    Stay, though thou kill me, sweet Demetrius.
    DEMETRIUS:
85 I charge thee, hence, and do not haunt me thus.
    HELENA:
    O, wilt thou darkling° leave me? Do not so.
    DEMETRIUS:
    Stay, on thy peril! I alone will go.

                                                    [*Exit.*]

    HELENA:
    O, I am out of breath in this fond° chase!
    The more my prayer, the lesser is my grace.
90 Happy is Hermia, wheresoe'er she lies,
    For she hath blessèd and attractive eyes.
    How came her eyes so bright? Not with salt tears.
    If so, my eyes are oft'ner washed than hers.
    No, no, I am as ugly as a bear,
95 For beasts that meet me run away for fear.
    Therefore no marvel though Demetrius
    Do, as a monster, fly my presence thus.
    What wicked and dissembling glass of mine
    Made me compare with Hermia's sphery eyne?°
100 But who is here? Lysander! On the ground!
    Dead? Or asleep? I see no blood, no wound.
    Lysander, if you live, good sir, awake.
    LYSANDER [*awaking*]:
    And run through fire I will for thy sweet sake.
    Transparent° Helena! Nature shows art,
105 That through thy bosom makes me see thy heart.
    Where is Demetrius? O, how fit a word
    Is that vile name to perish on my sword!
    HELENA:
    Do not say so, Lysander, say not so.
    What though he love your Hermia? Lord, what
        though?
110 Yet Hermia still loves you. Then be content.
    LYSANDER:
    Content with Hermia! No; I do repent
    The tedious minutes I with her have spent.
    Not Hermia but Helena I love:
    Who will not change a raven for a dove?
115 The will° of man is by his reason swayed

And reason says you are the worthier maid.
Things growing are not ripe until their season:
So I, being young, till now ripe not° to reason.
And touching now the point of human skill,°
Reason becomes the marshal to my will,   120
And leads me to your eyes, where I o'erlook
Love's stories, written in love's richest book.
    HELENA:
Wherefore was I to this keen mockery born?
When at your hands did I deserve this scorn?
Is't not enough, is't not enough, young man,   125
That I did never, no, nor never can,
Deserve a sweet look from Demetrius' eye,
But you must flout° my insufficiency?
Good troth,° you do me wrong, good sooth, you
    do,
In such disdainful manner me to woo.   130
But fare you well. Perforce I must confess
I thought you lord of more true gentleness.°
O, that a lady, of one man refused,
Should of another therefore be abused!

                                                Exit.

    LYSANDER:
She sees not Hermia. Hermia, sleep thou there, 135
And never mayst thou come Lysander near!
For as a surfeit of the sweetest things
The deepest loathing to the stomach brings,
Or as the heresies that men do leave
Are hated most of those they did deceive,   140
So thou, my surfeit and my heresy,
Of all be hated, but the most of me!
And, all my powers, address° your love and might
To honor Helen and to be her knight!

                                                Exit.

    HERMIA [*awaking*]:
Help me, Lysander, help me! Do thy best   145
To pluck this crawling serpent from my breast!
Ay me, for pity! What a dream was here!
Lysander, look how I do quake with fear.
Methought a serpent eat° my heart away,
And you sat smiling at his cruel prey.°   150
Lysander! What, removed? Lysander! Lord!
What, out of hearing? Gone? No sound, no word?
Alack, where are you? Speak, an if° you hear;
Speak, of° all loves! I swoon almost with fear.

---

86 **darkling** in the dark 88 **fond** (1) doting (2) foolish 99 **sphery eyne** starry eyes 104 **Transparent**
bright 115 **will** desire

118 **ripe not** have not ripened 119 **touching now** . . .
human skill now reaching the fullness of human reason 128 **flout** jeer at 129 **Good troth** indeed (an
expletive, like "good sooth") 132 **gentleness** noble
character 143 **address** apply 149 **eat** ate (pronounced
"et") 150 **prey** act of preying 153 **an if** if 154 **of** for
the sake of

155 No? Then I well perceive you are not nigh.
Either death or you I'll find immediately.

Exit.

[ACT III

SCENE I. *The wood.* TITANIA *lying asleep.*]

Enter the clowns: [QUINCE, SNUG, BOTTOM,
FLUTE, SNOUT, *and* STARVELING].

BOTTOM: Are we all met?

QUINCE: Pat,° pat; and here's a marvail's° convenient place for our rehearsal. This green plot
shall be our stage, this hawthorn brake° our tiring
5 house,° and we will do it in action as we will do it
before the Duke.

BOTTOM: Peter Quince?

QUINCE: What sayest thou, bully° Bottom?

BOTTOM: There are things in this comedy of
10 Pyramus and Thisby that will never please. First,
Pyramus must draw a sword to kill himself; which
the ladies cannot abide. How answer you that?

SNOUT: By'r lakin,° a parlous° fear.

STARVELING: I believe we must leave the killing
15 out, when all is done.

BOTTOM: Not a whit. I have a device to make all
well. Write me a prologue, and let the prologue
seem to say, we will do no harm with our swords,
and that Pyramus is not killed indeed; and, for the
20 more better assurance, tell them that I Pyramus
am not Pyramus, but Bottom the weaver. This will
put them out of fear.

QUINCE: Well, we will have such a prologue,
and it shall be written in eight and six.°

25 BOTTOM: No, make it two more; let it be written
in eight and eight.

SNOUT: Will not the ladies be afeared of the lion?

STARVELING: I fear it, I promise you.

BOTTOM: Masters, you ought to consider with
30 yourselves. To bring in—God shield us!—a lion
among ladies, is a most dreadful thing. For there is
not a more fearful wild fowl than your lion living;
and we ought to look to't.

SNOUT: Therefore another prologue must tell he
35 is not a lion.

BOTTOM: Nay, you must name his name, and
half his face must be seen through the lion's neck,

and he himself must speak through, saying thus,
or to the same defect—"Ladies"—or, "Fair
ladies—I would wish you"—or, "I would request 40
you"—or, "I would entreat you—not to fear, not
to tremble: my life for yours. If you think I come
hither as a lion, it were pity of my life.° No, I am
no such thing. I am a man as other men are." And
there indeed let him name his name, and tell them 45
plainly, he is Snug the joiner.

QUINCE: Well, it shall be so. But there is two
hard things; that is, to bring the moonlight into a
chamber; for, you know, Pyramus and Thisby
meet by moonlight. 50

SNOUT: Doth the moon shine that night we play
our play?

BOTTOM: A calendar, a calendar! Look in the
almanac; find out moonshine, find out
moonshine. 55

QUINCE: Yes, it doth shine that night.

BOTTOM: Why, then may you leave a casement
of the great chamber window, where we play,
open, and the moon may shine in at the casement.

QUINCE: Ay; or else one must come in with a 60
bush of thorns° and a lantern, and say he comes to
disfigure,° or to present, the person of Moonshine.
Then, there is another thing: we must have a wall
in the great chamber; for Pyramus and Thisby,
says the story, did talk through the chink of a wall. 65

SNOUT: You can never bring in a wall. What say
you, Bottom?

BOTTOM: Some man or other must present
Wall: and let him have some plaster, or some
loam, or some roughcast° about him, to signify 70
Wall; and let him hold his fingers thus, and
through that cranny shall Pyramus and Thisby
whisper.

QUINCE: If that may be, then all is well. Come,
sit down, every mother's son, and rehearse your 75
parts. Pyramus, you begin. When you have spoken your speech, enter into that brake; and so
everyone according to his cue.

Enter Robin [PUCK].

PUCK:
What hempen homespuns° have we swagg'ring
here,

III.i.2. **Pat** exactly, on the dot   2 **marvail's** (Quince
means "marvelous")   4 **brake** thicket   5 **tiring house**
attiring house, dressing room   8 **bully** good fellow   14
By'r lakin by our lady (ladykin = little lady)   14 **parlous**
perilous, terrible   23 **in eight and six** in alternate lines
of eight and six syllables (ballad stanza)

43 **pity of my life** a bad thing for me   61 **bush of thorns**
(legend held that the man in the moon had been placed
there for gathering firewood on Sunday)   62 **disfigure**
(Bottom means "figure," "represent")   70 **roughcast**
lime mixed with gravel to plaster outside walls   79
hempen homespuns coarse fellows (clad in homespun
cloth of hemp)

80 So near the cradle of the Fairy Queen?
    What, a play toward!° I'll be an auditor;
    An actor too perhaps, if I see cause.
        QUINCE: Speak, Pyramus. Thisby, stand forth.
        PYRAMUS [BOTTOM]:
    Thisby, the flowers of odious savors sweet—
85   QUINCE: Odors, odors.
        PYRAMUS:
    —odors savors sweet:
        So hath thy breath, my dearest Thisby dear.
    But hark, a voice! Stay thou but here awhile,
        And by and by° I will to thee appear.
                                                    Exit.

        PUCK:
90 A stranger Pyramus than e'er played here!
                                                    [Exit.]
        THISBY [FLUTE]: Must I speak now?
        QUINCE: Ay, marry, must you. For you must
    understand he goes but to see a noise that he
    heard, and is to come again.
        THISBY:
95 Most radiant Pyramus, most lily-white of hue,
        Of color like the red rose on triumphant brier,
    Most brisky juvenal,° and eke° most lovely Jew,
        As true as truest horse, that yet would never tire,
    I'll meet thee, Pyramus, at Ninny's° tomb.
100   QUINCE: "Ninus' tomb," man. Why, you must
    not speak that yet. That you answer to Pyramus.
    You speak all your part at once, cues and all.
    Pyramus enter. Your cue is past; it is "never tire."
        THISBY:
    O—as true as truest horse, that yet would never
        tire.

        [Re-enter PUCK, and BOTTOM with an ass's
        head.]

        PYRAMUS:
105   If I were fair, Thisby, I were only thine.
        QUINCE: O monstrous! O strange! We are
    haunted. Pray, masters! Fly, masters! Help!
                        [Exeunt all the clowns but BOTTOM.]
        PUCK:
    I'll follow you, I'll lead you about a round,°
        Through bog, through bush, through brake,
            through brier.
110 Sometime a horse I'll be, sometime a hound,
        A hog, a headless bear, sometime a fire;

And neigh, and bark, and grunt, and roar, and
    burn,
Like horse, hound, hog, bear, fire, at every turn.
                                                    Exit.
    BOTTOM: Why do they run away? This is a
knavery of them to make me afeared.   115

    Enter SNOUT.

    SNOUT: O Bottom, thou art changed! What do I
see on thee?
    BOTTOM: What do you see? You see an ass head
of your own, do you?   [Exit SNOUT.]

    Enter QUINCE.

    QUINCE: Bless thee, Bottom! Bless thee! Thou   120
art translated.°   Exit.
    BOTTOM: I see their knavery. This is to make an
ass of me; to fright me, if they could. But I will not
stir from this place, do what they can. I will walk
up and down here, and will sing, that they shall   125
hear I am not afraid.   [Sings.]
    The woosel° cock so black of hue,
        With orange-tawny bill,
    The throstle with his note so true,
        The wren with little quill°—   130
    TITANIA [awakening]:
What angel wakes me from my flow'ry bed?
    BOTTOM [sings]:
    The finch, the sparrow, and the lark,
        The plain-song cuckoo° gray,
    Whose note full many a man doth mark,
        And dares not answer nay—   135
for, indeed, who would set his wit° to so foolish a
bird? Who would give a bird the lie,° though he
cry "cuckoo" never so?°
    TITANIA:
I pray thee, gentle mortal, sing again:
Mine ear is much enamored of thy note;   140
So is mine eye enthrallèd to thy shape;
And thy fair virtue's force perforce doth move me
On the first view to say, to swear, I love thee.
    BOTTOM: Methinks, mistress, you should have
little reason for that. And yet, to say the truth,   145
reason and love keep little company together now-

121 **translated** transformed   127 **woosel** ouzel, black-
bird   130 **quill** (literally, "reed pipe"; here, "piping
voice")   133 **the plain-song cuckoo** the cuckoo, who
sings a simple song   136 **set his wit** use his intelligence
to answer   137 **give a bird the lie** contradict a bird (the
cuckoo's song supposedly tells a man he is a cuckold)
138 **never so** ever so often

81 **toward** in preparation   89 **by and by** shortly   97
juvenal youth   97 **eke** also   99 **Ninny's** (blunder for
"Ninus'"; Ninus was the legendary founder of Nine-
veh)   108 **about a round** roundabout

adays; the more the pity, that some honest neighbors will not make them friends. Nay, I can gleek° upon occasion.

TITANIA:
150 Thou art as wise as thou art beautiful.

BOTTOM: Not so, neither; but if I had wit enough to get out of this wood, I have enough to serve mine own turn.

TITANIA:
Out of this wood do not desire to go.
155 Thou shalt remain here, whether thou wilt or no.
I am a spirit of no common rate.°
The summer still doth tend° upon my state;
And I do love thee. Therefore, go with me.
I'll give thee fairies to attend on thee,
160 And they shall fetch thee jewels from the deep,
And sing, while thou on pressèd flowers dost sleep:
And I will purge thy mortal grossness so,
That thou shalt like an airy spirit go.
Peaseblossom! Cobweb! Moth!° And Mustardseed!

Enter four Fairies [PEASEBLOSSOM, COBWEB, MOTH, *and* MUSTARDSEED].

PEASEBLOSSOM:
Ready.

COBWEB:
    And I.

MOTH: And I.

MUSTARDSEED: And I.
165 ALL: Where shall we go.

TITANIA:
Be kind and courteous to this gentleman;
Hop in his walks, and gambol in his eyes;
Feed him with apricocks and dewberries,°
With purple grapes, green figs, and mulberries;
170 The honey bags steal from the humblebees,°
And for night tapers crop their waxen thighs,
And light them at the fiery glowworm's eyes,
To have my love to bed and to arise;
And pluck the wings from painted butterflies,
175 To fan the moonbeams from his sleeping eyes.
Nod to him, elves, and do him courtesies.

PEASEBLOSSOM:
Hail mortal!

COBWEB: Hail!

MOTH: Hail!

MUSTARDSEED: Hail!

BOTTOM: I cry your worships mercy,° heartily: I beseech your worship's name.

COBWEB:
Cobweb.   180

BOTTOM: I shall desire you of more acquaintance,° good Master Cobweb: if I cut my finger,° I shall make bold with you. Your name, honest gentleman?

PEASEBLOSSOM:
Peaseblossom.   185

BOTTOM: I pray you, commend me to Mistress Squash,° your mother, and to Master Peascod, your father. Good Master Peaseblossom. I shall desire you of more acquaintance too. Your name, I beseech you, sir?   190

MUSTARDSEED:
Mustardseed.

BOTTOM: Good Master Mustardseed, I know your patience well. That same cowardly, giantlike ox-beef hath devoured° many a gentleman of your house. I promise you your kindred hath made my   195 eyes water ere now. I desire you of more acquaintance, good Master Mustardseed.

TITANIA:
Come, wait upon him; lead him to my bower.
The moon methinks looks with a wat'ry eye;
And when she weeps, weeps every little flower,   200
Lamenting some enforcèd° chastity.
Tie up my lover's tongue, bring him silently.
    Exit [TITANIA *with* BOTTOM *and* FAIRIES].

[SCENE II. *Another part of the wood.*]

Enter [OBERON,] *King of Fairies, and Robin Goodfellow* [PUCK].

OBERON:
I wonder if Titania be awaked;
Then, what it was that next came in her eye,
Which she must dote on in extremity.°
Here comes my messenger. How now, mad spirit!
What night-rule° now about this haunted grove?   5

PUCK:
My mistress with a monster is in love.
Near to her close° and consecrated bower,

148 **gleek** make a satirical jest   156 **rate** rank   157 **still doth tend** always waits upon   164 **Moth** (pronounced "mote," and probably a speck rather than an insect is denoted)   168 **apricocks and dewberries** apricots and blackberries   170 **humblebees** bumblebees

178 **I cry your worships mercy** I beg pardon of your honors   181–182 **I shall desire you of more acquaintance** I shall want to be better acquainted with you   182 **if I cut my finger** (cobweb was used for stanching blood)   187 **Squash** unripe pea pod   194 **devoured** (because beef is often eaten with mustard)   201 **enforcèd** violated
III.ii.3 **in extremity** to the extreme   5 **night-rule** happenings during the night   7 **close** private, secret

While she was in her dull and sleeping hour,
A crew of patches,° rude mechanicals,°
10 That work for bread upon Athenian stalls,
Were met together to rehearse a play,
Intended for great Theseus' nuptial day.
The shallowest thickskin of that barren sort,°
Who Pyramus presented in their sport,
15 Forsook his scene, and entered in a brake.
When I did him at this advantage take,
An ass's nole° I fixèd on his head.
Anon° his Thisby must be answerèd,
And forth my mimic comes. When they him spy,
20 As wild geese that the creeping fowler eye,
Or russet-pated choughs, many in sort,°
Rising and cawing at the gun's report,
Sever themselves and madly sweep the sky,
So, at his sight, away his fellows fly;
25 And, at our stamp, here o'er and o'er one falls;
He murder cries, and help from Athens calls.
Their sense thus weak, lost with their fears thus
     strong,
Made senseless things begin to do them wrong;
For briers and thorns at their apparel snatch;
Some sleeves, some hats, from yielders all things
30   catch.
I led them on in this distracted fear,
And left sweet Pyramus translated there:
When in that moment, so it came to pass,
Titania waked, and straightway loved an ass.
     OBERON:
35 This falls out better than I could devise.
But hast thou yet latched° the Athenian's eyes
With the love juice, as I did bid thee do?
     PUCK:
I took him sleeping—that is finished too—
And the Athenian woman by his side;
40 That, when he waked, of force° she must be eyed.

Enter DEMETRIUS *and* HERMIA.

     OBERON:
Stand close:° this is the same Athenian.
     PUCK:
This is the woman, but not this the man.
     DEMETRIUS:
O, why rebuke you him that loves you so?
Lay breath so bitter on your bitter foe.

     HERMIA:
Now I but chide; but I should use thee worse,   45
For thou, I fear, hast given me cause to curse.
If thou hast slain Lysander in his sleep,
Being o'er shoes in blood, plunge in the deep,
And kill me too.
The sun was not so true unto the day   50
As he to me. Would he have stolen away
From sleeping Hermia? I'll believe as soon
This whole° earth may be bored, and that the
     moon
May through the center creep, and so displease
Her brother's° noontide with th' Antipodes.   55
It cannot be but thou hast murd'red him.
So should a murderer look, so dead,° so grim.
     DEMETRIUS:
So should the murdered look; and so should I,
Pierced through the heart with your stern cruelty.
Yet you, the murderer, look as bright, as clear, 60
As yonder Venus in her glimmering sphere.
     HERMIA:
What's this to my Lysander? Where is he?
Ah, good Demetrius, wilt thou give him me?
     DEMETRIUS:
I had rather give his carcass to my hounds.
     HERMIA:
Out, dog! Out, cur! Thou driv'st me past the
     bounds   65
Of maiden's patience. Hast thou slain him, then?
Henceforth be never numb'red among men!
O, once tell true! Tell true, even for my sake!
Durst thou have looked upon him being awake?
And hast thou killed him sleeping? O brave
     touch!°   70
Could not a worm, an adder, do so much?
An adder did it; for with doubler tongue
Than thine, thou serpent, never adder stung.
     DEMETRIUS:
You spend your passion on a misprised mood:°
I am not guilty of Lysander's blood;   75
Nor is he dead, for aught that I can tell.
     HERMIA:
I pray thee, tell me then that he is well.
     DEMETRIUS:
An if I could, what should I get therefore?°
     HERMIA:
A privilege, never to see me more.
And from thy hated presence part I so.   80

---

9 **patches** fools, clowns   9 **rude mechanicals** uneducated workingmen   13 **barren sort** stupid group   17 **nole** "noodle," head   18 **Anon** presently   21 **russet-pated . . . in sort** gray-headed jackdaws, many in a flock   36 **latched** fastened (or possibly "moistened")   40 **of force** by necessity   41 **close** concealed

53 **whole** solid   55 **Her brother's** i.e., the sun's   57 **dead** deadly pale   70 **brave touch** splendid exploit (ironic)   74 **misprised mood** mistaken anger   78 **therefore** in return

See me no more, whether he be dead or no.
Exit.

DEMETRIUS:
There is no following her in this fierce vein.
Here therefore for a while I will remain.
So sorrow's heaviness doth heavier grow

85 For debt that bankrout sleep doth sorrow owe;°
Which now in some slight measure it will pay,
If for his tender° here I make some stay.

Lies down [and sleeps].

OBERON:
What hast thou done? Thou has mistaken quite,
And laid the love juice on some truelove's sight.

90 Of thy misprision° must perforce ensue
Some true love turned, and not a false turned true.

PUCK:
Then fate o'errules, that, one man holding troth,
A million fail, confounding oath on oath.°

OBERON:
About the wood go swifter than the wind,

95 And Helena of Athens look thou find.
All fancy-sick° she is and pale of cheer,°
With sighs of love, that costs the fresh blood dear:
By some illusion see thou bring her here.
I'll charm his eyes against she do appear.°

PUCK:
100 I go, I go; look how I go,
Swifter than arrow from the Tartar's bow.
[Exit.]

OBERON:
Flower of this purple dye,
Hit with Cupid's archery,
Sink in apple of his eye.

105 When his love he doth espy,
Let her shine as gloriously
As the Venus of the sky.
When thou wak'st, if she be by,
Bet of her for remedy.

Enter PUCK.

PUCK:
110 Captain of our fairy band,
Helena is here at hand;
And the youth, mistook by me,
Pleading for a lover's fee.
Shall we their fond pageant° see?

115 Lord, what fools these mortals be!

OBERON:
Stand aside. The noise they make
Will cause Demetrius to awake.

PUCK:
Then will two at once woo one;
That must needs be sport alone;°
And those things do best please me   120
That befall prepost'rously

Enter LYSANDER and HELENA.

LYSANDER:
Why should you think that I should woo in scorn?
Scorn and derision never come in tears:
Look, when I vow, I weep; and vows so born,
In their nativity all truth appears.   125
How can these things in me seem scorn to you,
Bearing the badge of faith,° to prove them true?

HELENA:
You do advance° your cunning more and more.
When truth kills truth, O devilish-holy fray!
These vows are Hermia's: will you give her o'er?   130
Weigh oath with oath, and you will nothing
weigh.
Your vows to her and me, put in two scales,
Will even weigh; and both as light as tales.

LYSANDER:
I had no judgment when to her I swore.

HELENA:
Nor none, in my mind, now you give her o'er.   135

LYSANDER:
Demetrius loves her, and he loves not you.

DEMETRIUS (*awakening*):
O Helen, goddess, nymph, perfect, divine!
To what, my love, shall I compare thine eyne?
Crystal is muddy. O, how ripe in show°
Thy lips, those kissing cherries, tempting grow!   140
That pure congealèd white, high Taurus'° snow,
Fanned with the eastern wind, turns to a crow
When thou hold'st up thy hand: O, let me kiss
This princess of pure white, this seal of bliss!

HELENA:
O spite! O hell! I see you all are bent   145
To set against me for your merriment:
If you were civil° and knew courtesy,
You would not do me thus much injury.
Can you not hate me, as I know you do,
But you must join in souls to mock me too?   150
If you were men, as men you are in show,

---

85 **For debt . . . sorrow owe** because of the debt that
bankrupt sleep owes to sorrow 87 **tender** offer 90
misprision mistake 93 **confounding oath on oath**
breaking oath after oath 96 **fancy-sick** love-sick 96
cheer face 99 **against she do appear** in preparation for
her appearance

114 **fond pageant** foolish exhibition 119 **alone**
unique, supreme 127 **badge of faith** (Lysander means
his tears) 128 **advance** exhibit, display 139 **show** appearance 141 **Taurus'** of the Taurus Mountains (in
Turkey) 147 **civil** civilized

You would not use a gentle° lady so;
To vow, and swear, and superpraise my parts,°
When I am sure you hate me with your hearts.
155 You both are rivals, and love Hermia;
And now both rivals to mock Helena:
A trim° exploit, a many enterprise,
To conjure tears up in a poor maid's eyes
With your derision! None of noble sort
160 Would so offend a virgin, and extort°
A poor soul's patience, all to make you sport.
    LYSANDER:
You are unkind, Demetrius. Be not so;
For you love Hermia; this you know I know.
And here, with all good will, with all my heart,
165 In Hermia's love I yield you up my part;
And yours of Helena to me bequeath,
Whom I do love, and will do till my death.
    HELENA:
Never did mockers waste more idle° breath.
    DEMETRIUS:
Lysander, keep thy Hermia; I will none.
170 If e'er I loved her, all that love is gone.
My heart to her but as guestwise sojourned,
And now to Helen it is home returned,
There to remain.
    LYSANDER: Helen, it is not so.
    DEMETRIUS:
Disparage not the faith thou dost not know,
175 Lest, to thy peril, thou aby it dear.°
Look, where thy love comes; yonder is thy dear.

    Enter HERMIA.

    HERMIA:
Dark night, that from the eye his° function takes,
The ear more quick of apprehension makes;
Wherein it doth impair the seeing sense,
180 It pays the hearing double recompense.
Thou art not by mine eye, Lysander, found;
Mine ear, I thank it, brought me to thy sound.
But why unkindly didst thou leave me so?
    LYSANDER:
Why should he stay, whom love doth press to go?
    HERMIA:
185 What love could press Lysander from my side?
    LYSANDER:
Lysander's love, that would not let him bide,
Fair Helena, who more engilds the night
Than all yon fiery oes° and eyes of light.
Why seek'st thou me? Could not this make thee
    know,

The hate I bare thee made me leave thee so?   190
    HERMIA:
You speak not as you think: it cannot be.
    HELENA:
Lo, she is one of this confederacy!
Now I perceive they have conjoined all three
To fashion this false sport, in spite of me.
Injurious° Hermia! Most ungrateful maid!   195
Have you conspired, have you with these
    contrived
To bait° me with this foul derision?
Is all the counsel that we two have shared,
The sister's vows, the hours that we have spent,
When we have chid the hasty-footed time   200
For parting us—O, is all forgot?
All school days friendship, childhood innocence?
We, Hermia, like two artificial° gods,
Have with our needles created both one flower,
Both on one sampler,° sitting on one cushion,   205
Both warbling of one song, both in one key;
As if our hands, our sides, voices, and minds,
Had been incorporate.° So we grew together,
Like to a double cherry, seeming parted,
But yet an union in partition;   210
Two lovely berries molded on one stem;
So, with two seeming bodies, but one heart;
Two of the first, like coats in heraldry,
Due but to one, and crownèd with one crest.°
And will you rent° our ancient love asunder,   215
To join with men in scorning your poor friend?
It is not friendly, 'tis not maidenly.
Our sex, as well as I, may chide you for it,
Though I alone do feel the injury.
    HERMIA:
I am amazèd at your passionate words.   220
I scorn you not. It seems that you scorn me.
    HELENA:
Have you not set Lysander, as in scorn,
To follow me and praise my eyes and face?
And made your other love, Demetrius
(Who even but now did spurn me with his foot),   225
To call me goddess, nymph, divine and rare,
Precious, celestial? Wherefore speaks he this
To her he hates? And wherefore doth Lysander
Deny your love,° so rich within his soul,
And tender me (forsooth) affection,   230

195 **Injurious** insulting   196–197 **contrived To bait**
plotted to assail   203 **artificial** skilled in art   205 **sampler** work of embroidery   208 **incorporate** one
body   213–214 **Two of . . . one crest** (Helena apparently envisages a shield on which the coat of arms
appears twice but which has a single crest; Helena and
Hermia have two bodies but a single heart)   215 **rent**
rend, tear   229 **your love** his love for you

152 **gentle** well-born   153 **parts** qualities   157 **trim**
splendid (ironical)   160 **extort** wear out by torturing
168 **idle** vain, futile   175 **aby it dear** pay dearly for
it   177 **his** its (the eye's)   188 **oes** orbs

But by your setting on, by your consent?
What though I be not so in grace° as you,
So hung upon with love, so fortunate,
But miserable most, to love unloved?
235 This you should pity rather than despise.
    HERMIA:
I understand not what you mean by this.
    HELENA:
Ay, do! Persever,° counterfeit sad° looks,
Make mouths° upon me when I turn my back;
Wink each at other; hold the sweet jest up.
240 This sport, well carried, shall be chronicled.
If you have any pity, grace, or manners,
You would not make me such an argument.°
But fare ye well. 'Tis partly my own fault,
Which death or absence soon shall remedy.
    LYSANDER:
245 Stay, gentle Helena; hear my excuse:
My love, my life, my soul, fair Helena!
    HELENA:
O excellent!
    HERMIA:
           Sweet, do not scorn her so.
    DEMETRIUS:
If she cannot entreat,° I can compel.
    LYSANDER:
Thou canst compel no more than she entreat.
Thy threats have no more strength than her weak
250   prayers.
Helen, I love thee; by my life, I do!
I swear by that which I will lose for thee,
To prove him false that says I love thee not.
    DEMETRIUS:
I say I love thee more than he can do.
    LYSANDER:
255 If thou say so, withdraw and prove it too.
    DEMETRIUS:
Quick, come!
    HERMIA: Lysander, whereto tends all this?
    LYSANDER:
Away, you Ethiope!°
    DEMETRIUS: No, no; he'll
Seem to break loose; take on as° you would follow,
But yet come not: you are a tame man, go!
    LYSANDER:
Hang off, thou cat, thou burr! Vile thing, let
260   loose,

Or I will shake thee from me like a serpent!
    HERMIA:
Why are you grown so rude! What change is this,
Sweet love?
    LYSANDER:
           Thy love! Out, tawny Tartar, out!
Out, loathèd med'cine! O hated potion, hence!
    HERMIA:
Do you not jest?
    HELENA: Yes, sooth;° and so do you.   265
    LYSANDER:
Demetrius, I will keep my word° with thee.
    DEMETRIUS:
I would I had your bond, for I perceive
A weak bond holds you. I'll not trust your word.
    LYSANDER:
What, should I hurt her, strike her, kill her dead?
Although I hate her, I'll not harm her so.   270
    HERMIA:
What, can you do me greater harm than hate?
Hate me! Wherefore? O me! What news, my love!
Am not I Hermia? Are not you Lysander?
I am as fair now as I was erewhile.°
Since night° you loved me; yet since night you left
    me.   275
Why, then you left me—O, the gods forbid!—
In earnest, shall I say?
    LYSANDER: Ay, by my life!
And never did desire to see thee more.
Therefore be out of hope, of question, of doubt;
Be certain, nothing truer. 'Tis no jest   280
That I do hate thee, and love Helena.
    HERMIA:
O me! You juggler! You canker blossom!°
You thief of love! What, have you come by night
And stol'n my love's heart from him?
    HELENA: Fine, i' faith!
Have you no modesty, no maiden shame,   285
No touch of bashfulness? What, will you tear
Impatient answers from my gentle tongue?
Fie, fie! You counterfeit, you puppet, you!
    HERMIA:
Puppet? Why so? Ay, that way goes the game.
Now I perceive that she hath made compare°   290
Between our statures; she hath urged her height,
And with her personage, her tall personage,
Her height, forsooth, she hath prevailed with him.
And are you grown so high in his esteem,

---

232 **in grace** in favor 237 **persever** persevere (but accented on second syllable) 237 **sad** grave 238 **Make mouths** make mocking faces 242 **argument** subject (of scorn) 248 **entreat** prevail by entreating 257 **Ethiope** blackamoor (brunette) 258 **take on as** make a fuss as if

265 **sooth** truly 266 **my word** my promise to fight with you 274 **erewhile** a little while ago 275 **Since night** since the beginning of this night 282 **canker blossom** dog rose (or possibly worm that cankers the blossom) 290 **compare** comparison

295 Because I am so dwarfish and so low?
How low am I, thou painted maypole? Speak!
How low am I? I am not yet so low
But that my nails can reach unto thine eyes.
    HELENA:
I pray you, though you mock me, gentlemen,
300 Let her not hurt me, I was never curst;°
I have no gift at all in shrewishness;
I am a right maid° for my cowardice.
Let her not strike me. You perhaps may think,
Because she is something lower than myself,
That I can match her.
305   HERMIA: Lower! Hark, again!
    HELENA:
Good Hermia, do not be so bitter with me.
I evermore did love you, Hermia,
Did ever keep your counsels, never wronged you;
Save that, in love unto Demetrius,
310 I told him of your stealth unto this wood.
He followed you; for love I followed him.
But he hath chid me hence, and threatened me
To strike me, spurn me, nay, to kill me too.
And now, so you will let me quiet go,
315 To Athens will I bear my folly back.
And follow you no further. Let me go.
You see how simple and how fond° I am.
    HERMIA:
Why, get you gone. Who is't that hinders you?
    HELENA:
A foolish heart, that I leave here behind.
    HERMIA:
What, with Lysander?
320   HELENA: With Demetrius.
    LYSANDER:
Be not afraid. She shall not harm thee, Helena.
    DEMETRIUS:
No, sir, she shall not, though you take her part.
    HELENA:
O, when she's angry, she is keen and shrewd!°
She was a vixen when she went to school;
325 And though she be but little, she is fierce.
    HERMIA:
"Little" again! Nothing but "low" and "little"!
Why will you suffer her to flout me thus?
Let me come to her.
    LYSANDER: Get you gone, you dwarf;
You minimus,° of hind'ring knotgrass° made;
You bead, you acorn!

    DEMETRIUS: You are too officious   330
In her behalf that scorns your services.
Let her alone. Speak not of Helena;
Take not her part; for, if thou dost intend°
Never so little show of love to her,
Thou shalt aby° it.
    LYSANDER: Now she holds me not.   335
Now follow, if thou dar'st, to try whose right,
Of thine or mine, is most in Helena.
    DEMETRIUS:
Follow! Nay, I'll go with thee, cheek by jowl.
              [*Exeunt* LYSANDER *and* DEMETRIUS.]
    HERMIA:
You, mistress, all this coil is 'long of you:°
Nay, go not back.
    HELENA: I will not trust you, I,   340
Nor longer stay in your curst company.
Your hands than mine are quicker for a fray,
My legs are longer though, to run away.
    HERMIA:
I amazed,° and know not what to say.
              Exeunt [HELEN *and* HERMIA].
    OBERON:
This is thy negligence. Still thou mistak'st,   345
Or else committ'st thy knaveries willfully.
    PUCK:
Believe me, king of shadows, I mistook.
Did you not tell me I should know the man
By the Athenian garments he had on?
And so far blameless proves my enterprise,   350
That I have 'nointed an Athenian's eyes;
And so far am I glad it so did sort,°
As this their jangling I esteem a sport.
    OBERON:
Thou see'st these lovers seek a place to fight.
Hie therefore, Robin, overcast the night.   355
The starry welkin° cover thou anon
With drooping fog, as black as Acheron;°
And lead these testy° rivals so astray,
As° one come not within another's way.
Like to Lysander sometime frame thy tongue,   360
Then stir Demetrius up with bitter wrong;°
And sometime rail thou like Demetrius.
And from each other look thou lead them thus,
Till o'er their brows death-counterfeiting sleep

---

300 **curst** quarrelsome   302 **right maid** true young woman   317 **fond** foolish   323 **keen and shrewd** sharp-tongued and shrewish   329 **minimus** smallest thing   329 **knotgrass** (a weed that allegedly stunted one's growth)

333 **intend** give sign, direct (or possibly "pretend")   335 **aby** pay for   339 **all this coil is 'long of you** all this turmoil is brought about by you   344 **amazed** in confusion   352 **sort** turn out   356 **welkin** sky   357 **Acheron** one of the rivers of the underworld   358 **testy** excited, angry   359 **As** that   361 **wrong** insult

365   With leaden legs and batty° wings doth creep.
Then crush this herb into Lysander's eye,
Whose liquor hath this virtuous° property,
To take from thence all error with his might,
And make his eyeballs roll with wonted sight.
370   When they next wake, all this derision°
Shall seem a dream and fruitless vision,
And back to Athens shall the lovers wend,
With league whose date° till death shall never end.
Whiles I in this affair do thee employ,
375   I'll to my queen and beg her Indian boy;
And then I will her charmèd eye release
From monster's view, and all things shall be
    peace.

PUCK:
My fairy lord, this must be done with haste,
For night's swift dragons cut the clouds full fast,
380   And yonder shines Aurora's harbinger;°
At whose approach, ghosts, wand'ring here and
    there,
Troop home to churchyards: damnèd spirits all,
That in crossways and floods have burial,
Already to their wormy beds are gone.
385   For fear lest day should look their shames upon,
They willfully themselves exile from light,
And must for aye consort with black-browed night.

OBERON:
But we are spirits of another sort.
I with the Morning's love° have oft made sport;
390   And, like a forester, the groves may tread,
Even till the eastern gate, all fiery-red,
Opening on Neptune with fair blessèd beams,
Turns into yellow gold his salt green streams.
But, notwithstanding, haste; make no delay.
395   We may effect this business yet ere day.
                            [*Exit.*]

PUCK:
    Up and down, up and down,
    I will lead them up and down:
    I am feared in field and town:
    Goblin,° lead them up and down.
400   Here comes one.

Enter LYSANDER.

LYSANDER:
Where art thou, proud Demetrius? Speak thou
    now.

PUCK:
Here, villain; drawn° and ready. Where art thou?
LYSANDER:
I will be with thee straight.
PUCK: Follow me, then,
To plainer° ground.
                     [*Exit* LYSANDER.]

Enter DEMETRIUS.

DEMETRIUS: Lysander! Speak again!
Thou runaway, thou coward, art thou fled?   405
Speak! In some bush? Where dost thou hide thy
    head?
PUCK:
Thou coward, art thou bragging to the stars,
Telling the bushes that thou look'st for wars,
And wilt not come? Come, recreant! Come, thou
    child!
I'll whip thee with a rod. He is defiled   410
That draws a sword on thee.
DEMETRIUS: Yea, art thou there?
PUCK:
Follow my voice. We'll try no manhood° here.
                          Exeunt.

[*Enter* LYSANDER.]

LYSANDER:
He goes before me and still dares me on:
When I come where he calls, then he is gone.
The villain is much lighter-heeled than I.   415
I followed fast, but faster he did fly,
That fallen am I in dark uneven way,
And here will rest me. [*Lies down.*] Come, thou
    gentle day!
For if but once thou show me thy gray light,
I'll find Demetrius, and revenge this spite.   420
                          [*Sleeps.*]

[*Enter*] *Robin* [PUCK] *and* DEMETRIUS.

PUCK:
Ho, ho, ho! Coward, why com'st thou not?
DEMETRIUS:
Abide me,° if thou dar'st; for well I wot°
Thou runn'st before me, shifting every place,
And dar'st not stand, nor look me in the face.
Where art thou now?
PUCK: Come hither. I am here.   425

---

365 **batty** batlike   367 **virtuous** potent   370 **derision** i.e., ludicrous delusion   373 **With league whose date** in union whose term   380 **Aurora's harbinger** dawn's herald (i.e., the morning star)   389 **the Morning's love** Aurora (or possibly her lover Cephalus)   399 **Goblin** Hobgoblin (one of Puck's names)

402 **drawn** with drawn sword   404 **plainer** more level   412 **try no manhood** have no test of valor   422 **Abide me** wait for me   422 **wot** know

DEMETRIUS:
Nay, then, thou mock'st me. Thou shalt buy this
    dear,°
If ever I thy face by daylight see.
Now, go thy way. Faintness constraineth me
To measure out my length on this cold bed.
430 By day's approach look to be visited.°
               [*Lies down and sleeps.*]

    Enter HELENA.

HELENA:
O weary night, O long and tedious night,
    Abate° thy hours! Shine comforts from the east,
That I may back to Athens by daylight,
    From these that my poor company detest:
435 And sleep, that sometimes shuts up sorrow's eye,
Steal me awhile from mine own company.
                      Sleep.

    PUCK:
        Yet but three? Come one more.
        Two of both kinds makes up four.
        Here she comes, curst° and sad:
440   Cupid is a knavish lad,
        Thus to make poor females mad.

    [*Enter* HERMIA.]

    HERMIA:
Never so weary, never so in woe;
    Bedabbled with the dew and torn with briers,
I can no further crawl, no further go;
    My legs can keep no pace with my desires.
445 Here will I rest me till the break of day.
Heavens shield Lysander, if they mean a fray!
               [*Lies down and sleeps.*]

    PUCK:
        On the ground
        Sleep sound:
450   I'll apply
        To your eye,
    Gentle lover, remedy.

    [*Squeezing the juice on* LYSANDER's *eye.*]

        When thou wak'st,
        Thou tak'st
455   · True delight
        In the sight
Of thy former lady's eye:
    And the country proverb known,
That every man should take his own,

In your waking shall be shown.   460
    Jack shall have Jill;
    Nought shall go ill;
The man shall have his mare again, and all shall
    be well.

                      [*Exit.*]

[ACT IV

SCENE I. *The wood.* LYSANDER, DEMETRIUS,
    HELENA, *and* HERMIA, *lying asleep.*]

Enter [TITANIA,] *Queen of Fairies, and* [BOT-
TOM *the*] *Clown, and* FAIRIES; *and* [OBERON,]
the King, behind them.

TITANIA:
Come, sit thee down, upon this flow'ry bed,
    While I thy amiable cheeks do coy,°
And stick musk roses in thy sleek smooth head,
    And kiss thy fair large ears, my gentle joy.
BOTTOM: Where's Peaseblossom?   5
    PEASEBLOSSOM:
Ready.
    BOTTOM: Scratch my head, Peaseblossom.
Where's Mounsieur Cobweb?
    COBWEB:
Ready.
    BOTTOM: Mounsieur Cobweb, good moun- 10
sieur, get you your weapons in your hand, and kill
me a red-hipped humblebee on the top of a thistle;
and, good mounsieur, bring me the honey bag.
Do not fret yourself too much in the action,
mounsieur; and, good mounsieur, have a care the 15
honey bag break not; I would be loath to have you
overflown with a honey bag, signior. Where's
Mounsieur Mustardseed?
    MUSTARDSEED:
Ready.
    BOTTOM: Give me your neaf,° Mounsieur Mus- 20
tardseed. Pray you, leave your curtsy,° good
mounsieur.
    MUSTARDSEED:
What's your will?
    BOTTOM: Nothing, good mounsieur, but to help
Cavalery° Cobweb to scratch. I must to the bar- 25
ber's, mounsieur; for methinks I am marvail's°

---

426 **buy this dear** pay dearly for this   430 **look to be
visited** be sure to be sought out   432 **Abate** make
shorter   439 **curst** cross

IV.i.2   **While I . . . do coy** while I caress your lovely
cheeks   20 **neaf** fist, hand   21 **leave your curtsy** i.e.,
stop bowing, leave your hat on (a curtsy was any gesture
of respect)   25 **Cavalery** i.e., Cavalier   26 **marvail's**
(Bottom means "marvelous")

hairy about the face; and I am such a tender ass, if
my hair do but tickle me, I must scratch.

TITANIA:
What, wilt thou hear some music, my sweet love?
30   BOTTOM: I have a reasonable good ear in music.
Let's have the tongs and the bones.°

TITANIA:
Or say, sweet love, what thou desirest to eat.

     BOTTOM: Truly, a peck of provender. I could
munch your good dry oats. Methinks I have a great
35   desire to a bottle° of hay. Good hay, sweet hay,
hath no fellow.°

TITANIA:
I have a venturous fairy that shall seek
The squirrel's hoard, and fetch thee new nuts.

     BOTTOM: I had rather a handful or two of dried
40   peas. But, I pray you, let none of your people stir
me: I have an exposition of° sleep come upon me.

TITANIA:
Sleep thou, and I will wind thee in my arms.
Fairies, be gone, and be all ways° away.
                       [Exeunt FAIRIES.]
So doth the woodbine the sweet honeysuckle
45 Gently entwist; the female ivy° so
Enrings the barky fingers of the elm.
O, how I love thee! How I dote on thee!
                       [They sleep.]

     Enter Robin Goodfellow [PUCK].

OBERON (advancing):
Welcome, Good Robin. See'st thou this sweet
      sight?
Her dotage now I do begin to pity:
50 For, meeting her of late behind the wood,
Seeking sweet favors° for this hateful fool,
I did upbraid her, and fall out with her.
For she his hairy temples then had rounded
With coronet of fresh and fragrant flowers;
55 And that same dew, which sometime° on the buds
Was wont° to swell, like round and orient° pearls,
Stood now within the pretty flouriets'° eyes,
Like tears, that did their own disgrace bewail.
When I had at my pleasure taunted her,
60 And she in mild terms begged my patience,

31 **the tongs and the bones** rustic music, made by tongs
struck with metal and by bone clappers held between the
fingers   35 **bottle** bundle   36 **fellow** equal   41 **exposition of** (Bottom means "disposition for")   43 **all ways** in
every direction   45 **female ivy** (called female because it
clings to the elm and is supported by it)   51 **favors** love
tokens (probably flowers)   55 **sometime** formerly   56
Was wont used to   56 **orient** lustrous   57 **flouriets'**
flowerets'

I then did ask of her her changeling child;
Which straight she gave me, and her fairy sent
To bear him to my bower in fairy land.
And now I have the boy, I will undo
This hateful imperfection of her eyes: 65
And, gentle Puck, take this transformèd scalp
From off the head of this Athenian swain,
That, he awaking when the other° do,
May all to Athens back again repair,
And think no more of this night's accidents,°   70
But as the fierce vexation of a dream.
But first I will release the Fairy Queen.
      Be as thou wast wont to be;
      See as thou wast wont to see.
      Dian's bud o'er Cupid's flower   75
      Hath such force and blessèd power.
Now, my Titania, wake you, my sweet Queen.

TITANIA:
My Oberon, what visions have I seen!
Methought I was enamored of an ass.

OBERON:
There lies your love.

TITANIA: How came these things to pass?   80
O, how mine eyes do loathe his visage now!

OBERON:
Silence awhile. Robin, take off this head.
Titania, music call; and strike more dead
Than common sleep of all these five the sense.

TITANIA:
Music, ho, music! Such as charmeth sleep!   85

PUCK:
Now, when thou wak'st, with thine own fool's eyes
      peep.

OBERON:
Sound, music! [Music.] Come, my Queen, take
      hands with me,
And rock the ground whereon these sleepers be.
      [Dance.]
Now thou and I are new in amity,
And will tomorrow midnight solemnly°   90
Dance in Duke Theseus' house triumphantly,°
And bless it to all fair prosperity.
There shall the pairs of faithful lovers be
Wedded, with Theseus, all in jollity.

PUCK:
      Fairy King, attend, and mark: 95
      I do hear the morning lark.

OBERON:
      Then, my Queen, in silence sad,°

68 **other** others   70 **accidents** happenings   90 **solemnly** ceremoniously   91 **triumphantly** in festive procession   97 **sad** serious, solemn

Trip we after night's shade.
We the globe can compass soon,
100   Swifter than the wand'ring moon.
TITANIA:
Come, my lord; and in our flight,
Tell me how it came this night,
That I sleeping here was found
With these mortals on the ground.

           Exeunt.

Wind horn. Enter THESEUS, *and all his train;*
[HIPPOLYTA, EGEUS].

THESEUS:
105 Go, one of you, find out the forester,
For now our observation° is performed;
And since we have the vaward° of the day,
My love shall hear the music of my hounds.
Uncouple in the western valley; let them go.
110 Dispatch, I say, and find the forester.
         [*Exit an* ATTENDANT.]
We will, fair Queen, up to the mountain's top,
And mark the musical confusion
Of hounds and echo in conjunction.
HIPPOLYTA:
I was with Hercules and Cadmus once,
115 When in a wood of Crete they bayed° the bear
With hounds of Sparta. Never did I hear
Such gallant chiding; for, besides the groves,
The skies, the fountains, every region near
Seemed all one mutual cry. I never heard
120 So musical a discord, such sweet thunder.
THESEUS:
My hounds are bred out of the Spartan kind,
So flewed, so sanded;° and their heads are hung
With ears that sweep away the morning dew;
Crook-kneed, and dew-lapped like Thessalian
  bulls;
125 Slow in pursuit, but matched in mouth like bells,
Each under each.° A cry° more tunable
Was never holloed to, nor cheered with horn,
In Crete, in Sparta, nor in Thessaly.
Judge when you hear. But, soft!° What nymphs
  are these?
EGEUS:
130 My lord, this is my daughter here asleep;
And this, Lysander; this Demetrius is;

This Helena, old Nedar's Helena:
I wonder of their being here together.
THESEUS:
No doubt they rose up early to observe
The rite of May; and, hearing our intent,   135
Came here in grace of our solemnity.°
But speak, Egeus. Is not this the day
That Hermia should give answer of her choice?
EGEUS:
It is, my lord.
THESEUS:
Go, bid the huntsmen wake them with their
  horns.   140

Shout within. They all start up. Wind horns.

Good morrow, friends. Saint Valentine is past:
Begin these wood birds but to couple now?°
LYSANDER:
Pardon, my lord.
THESEUS: I pray you all, stand up.
I know you two are rival enemies.
How comes this gentle concord in the world,   145
That hatred is so far from jealousy,°
To sleep by hate, and fear no enmity?
LYSANDER:
My lord, I shall reply amazedly,°
Half sleep, half waking: but as yet, I swear,
I cannot truly say how I came here.   150
But, as I think—for truly would I speak,
And now I do bethink me, so it is—.
I came with Hermia hither. Our intent
Was to be gone from Athens, where we might,
Without° the peril of the Athenian law—   155
EGEUS:
Enough, enough, my lord; you have enough.
I beg the law, the law, upon his head.
They would have stol'n away; they would,
  Demetrius,
Thereby to have defeated° you and me,
You of your wife and me of my consent,   160
Of my consent that she should be your wife.
DEMETRIUS:
My lord, fair Helen told me of their stealth,°
Of this their purpose hither to this wood,
And I in fury hither followed them,
Fair Helena in fancy° following me.   165

---

106 **observation** observance, i.e., of the rite of May (cf. I.i.167) 107 **vaward** vanguard, i.e., morning 115 **bayed** brought to bay 122 **So flewed, so sanded** i.e., like Spartan hounds, with hanging cheeks and of sandy color 126 **Each under each** of different tone (like the chime of bells) 126 **cry** pack of hounds 129 **soft** stop

136 **in grace of our solemnity** in honor of our festival 142 **Begin these . . . couple now** (it was supposed that birds began to mate on February 14, St. Valentine's Day) 146 **jealousy** suspicion 148 **amazedly** confusedly 155 **Without** outside of 159 **defeated** deprived by fraud 162 **stealth** stealthy flight 165 **in fancy** in love, doting

But, my good lord, I wot not by what power—
But by some power it is—my love to Hermia,
Melted as the snow, seems to me now
As the remembrance of an idle gaud,°
170 Which in my childhood I did dote upon;
And all the faith, the virtue° of my heart,
The object and the pleasure of mine eye,
Is only Helena. To her, my lord,
Was I betrothed ere I saw Hermia:
175 But, like a sickness,° did I loathe this food;
But, as in health, come to my natural taste,
Now I do wish it, love it, long for it,
And will for evermore be true to it.

THESEUS:
Fair lovers, you are fortunately met.
180 Of this discourse we more will hear anon.
Egeus, I will overbear your will,
For in the temple, by and by,° with us
These couples shall eternally be knit;
And, for the morning now is something worn,°
185 Our purposed hunting shall be set aside.
Away with us to Athens! Three and three,
We'll hold a feast in great solemnity.
Come, Hippolyta.

                 [Exeunt THESEUS, HIPPOLYTA, EGEUS,
                                        and train.]

DEMETRIUS:
These things seem small and undistinguishable,
190 Like far-off mountains turnèd into clouds.

HERMIA:
Methinks I see these things with parted eye,°
When everything seems double.

HELENA: So methinks:
And I have found Demetrius like a jewel,
Mine own, and not mine own.

DEMETRIUS: Are you sure
195 That we are awake? It seems to me
That yet we sleep, we dream. Do not you think
The Duke was here, and bid us follow him?

HERMIA:
Yea, and my father.

HELENA: And Hippolyta.

LYSANDER:
And he did bid us follow to the temple.

DEMETRIUS:
200 Why, then, we are awake. Let's follow him,
And by the way let us recount our dreams.
                                        [Exeunt.]

BOTTOM [awaking]: When my cue comes, call
me, and I will answer. My next is, "Most fair
Pyramus." Heigh-ho! Peter Quince? Flute, the
bellows mender? Snout, the tinker? Starveling?   205
God's my life,° stol'n hence, and left me asleep? I
have had a most rare vision. I have had a dream,
past the wit of man to say what dream it was. Man
is but an ass, if he go about° to expound this
dream. Methought I was—there is no man can   210
tell what. Methought I was—and methought I
had—but man is but a patched° fool if he will offer
to say what methought I had. The eye of man hath
not heard, the ear of man hath not seen, man's
hand is not able to taste, his tongue to conceive,   215
nor his heart to report, what my dream was. I will
get Peter Quince to write a ballet° of this dream. It
shall be called "Bottom's Dream," because it hath
no bottom; and I will sing it in the latter end of a
play, before the Duke. Peradventure to make it the   220
more gracious, I shall sing it at her death.°
                                        [Exit.]

[SCENE II. Athens. QUINCE's house.]

Enter QUINCE, FLUTE,° Thisby and the rabble
[SNOUT, STARVELING].

QUINCE: Have you sent to Bottom's house? Is he
come home yet?
STARVELING: He cannot be heard of. Out of
doubt he is transported.°
FLUTE: If he come not, then the play is marred.   5
It goes not forward, doth it?
QUINCE: It is not possible. You have not a man
in all Athens able to discharge° Pyramus but he.
FLUTE: No, he hath simply the best wit of any
handicraft man in Athens.   10
QUINCE: Yea, and the best person too; and he is
a very paramour for a sweet voice.
FLUTE: You must say "paragon." A paramour is,
God bless us, a thing of nought.°

Enter SNUG the Joiner.

SNUG: Masters, the Duke is coming from the   15

206 **God's my life** an oath (possibly from "God bless my life")   209 **go about** endeavor   212 **patched** (referring to the patchwork dress of jesters)   217 **ballet** ballad   221 **her death** i.e., Thisby's death in the play   IV.ii.s.d. **Flute** (Shakespeare seems to have forgotten that Flute and Thisby are the same person)   4 **transported** carried off (by the fairies)   8 **discharge** play   14 **a thing of nought** a wicked thing

169 **idle gaud** worthless trinket   171 **virtue** power   175 **like a sickness** like one who is sick   182 **by and by** shortly   184 **something worn** somewhat spent   191 **with parted eye** i.e., with the eyes out of focus

temple, and there is two or three lords and ladies more married. If our sport had gone forward, we had all been made men.°

FLUTE: O sweet bully Bottom! Thus hath he lost
20 sixpence a day° during his life. He could not have scaped sixpence a day. And the Duke had not given him sixpence a day for playing Pyramus, I'll be hanged. He would have deserved it. Sixpence a day in Pyramus, or nothing.

Enter BOTTOM.

25   BOTTOM: Where are these lads? Where are these hearts?

QUINCE: Bottom! O most courageous° day! O most happy hour!

BOTTOM: Masters, I am to discourse wonders:
30 but ask me not what; for if I tell you, I am not true Athenian. I will tell you everything, right as it fell out.

QUINCE: Let us hear, sweet Bottom.

BOTTOM: Not a word of me.° All that I will tell
35 you is, that the Duke hath dined. Get your apparel together, good strings to your beards, new ribbons to your pumps; meet presently° at the palace; every man look o'er his part; for the short and the long is, our play is preferred.° In any case, let Thisby have
40 clean linen; and let not him that plays the lion pare his nails, for they shall hang out for the lion's claws. And, most dear actors, eat no onions nor garlic, for we are to utter sweet breath,° and I do not doubt but to hear them say it is a sweet
45 comedy. No more words. Away! Go, away!

[*Exeunt.*]

[ACT V

SCENE I. *Athens. The palace of* THESEUS.]

Enter THESEUS, HIPPOLYTA, *and* PHILOSTRATE, [LORDS, *and* ATTENDANTS].

HIPPOLYTA:
'Tis strange, my Theseus, that these lovers speak of.

THESEUS:
More strange than true. I never may believe
These antique° fables, nor these fairy toys.°

Lovers and madmen have such seething brains,
Such shaping fantasies,° that apprehend   5
More than cool reason ever comprehends.
The lunatic, the lover and the poet
Are of imagination all compact.°
One sees more devils than vast hell can hold,
That is the madman. The lover, all as frantic,   10
Sees Helen's beauty in a brow of Egypt.°
The poet's eye, in a fine frenzy rolling,
Doth glance from heaven to earth, from earth to
    heaven;
And as imagination bodies forth
The forms of things unknown, the poet's pen   15
Turns them to shapes, and gives to airy nothing
A local habitation and a name.
Such tricks hath strong imagination,
That, if it would but apprehend some joy,
It comprehends some bringer of that joy;°   20
Or in the night, imagining some fear,°
How easy is a bush supposed a bear!

HIPPOLYTA:
But all the story of the night told over,
And all their minds transfigured so together,
More witnesseth than fancy's images,   25
And grows to something of great constancy;°
But, howsoever, strange and admirable.°

Enter Lovers: LYSANDER, DEMETRIUS, HERMIA
and HELENA.

THESEUS:
Here come the lovers, full of joy and mirth.
Joy, gentle friends! Joy and fresh days of love
Accompany your hearts!

LYSANDER: More than to us   30
Wait in your royal walks, your board, your bed!

THESEUS:
Come now, what masques,° what dances shall we
    have,
To wear away this long age of three hours
Between our aftersupper° and bedtime?
Where is our usual manager of mirth?   35
What revels are in hand? Is there no play,
To ease the anguish of a torturing hour?
Call Philostrate.

PHILOSTRATE: Here, mighty Theseus.

---

18 **made men** men whose fortunes are made   20 **sixpence a day** (a pension)   27 **courageous** brave, splendid   34 **of me** from me   37 **presently** immediately   39 **preferred** put forward, recommended   43 **breath** (1) exhalation (2) words
V.i.3 **antique** (1) ancient (2) grotesque (antic)   3 **fairy toys** trifles about fairies

5 **fantasies** imagination   8 **compact** composed   11 **brow of Egypt** face of a gypsy   20 **It comprehends . . . that joy** it includes an imagined bringer of the joy   21 **fear** object of fear   26 **constancy** consistency (and reality)   27 **admirable** wonderful   32 **masques** courtly entertainments with masked dancers   34 **aftersupper** refreshment served after early supper

THESEUS:
Say, what abridgment° have you for this evening?
40 What masque? What music? How shall we beguile
The lazy time, if not with some delight?
PHILOSTRATE:
There is a brief° how many sports are ripe:°
Make choice of which your Highness will see first.
[Giving a paper.]
THESEUS:
"The battle with the Centaurs, to be sung
45 By an Athenian eunuch to the harp."
We'll none of that. That have I told my love,
In glory of my kinsman Hercules.
"The riot of the tipsy Bacchanals,
Tearing the Thracian singer° in their rage."
50 That is an old device;° and it was played
When I from Thebes came last a conqueror.
"The thrice three Muses mourning for the death
Of Learning, late deceased in beggary."
That is some satire, keen and critical,
55 Not sorting with° a nuptial ceremony.
"A tedious brief scene of young Pyramus
And his love Thisby; very tragical mirth."
Merry and tragical? Tedious and brief?
That is, hot ice and wondrous strange snow.
60 How shall we find the concord of this discord?
PHILOSTRATE:
A play there is, my lord, some ten words long,
Which is as brief as I have known a play;
But by ten words, my lord, it is too long,
Which makes it tedious. For in all the play
65 There is not one word apt, one player fitted.
And tragical, my noble lord, it is,
For Pyramus therein doth kill himself.
Which, when I saw rehearsed, I must confess,
Made mine eyes water; but more merry tears
70 The passion° of loud laughter never shed.
THESEUS:
What are they that do play it?
PHILOSTRATE:
Hard-handed men, that work in Athens here,
Which never labored in their minds till now;
And now have toiled their unbreathed° memories
75 With this same play, against° your nuptial.
THESEUS:
And we will hear it.
PHILOSTRATE: No, my noble lord;

It is not for you. I have heard it over,
And it is nothing, nothing in the world;
Unless you can find sport in their intents,
Extremely stretched and conned with cruel pain, 80
To do you service.
THESEUS: I will hear that play;
For never anything can be amiss,
When simpleness and duty tender it.
Go, bring them in: and take your places, ladies.
[Exit PHILOSTRATE.]
HIPPOLYTA:
I love not to see wretchedness 'oercharged,°   85
And duty in his service perishing.
THESEUS:
Why, gentle sweet, you shall see no such thing.
HIPPOLYTA:
He says they can do nothing in this kind.°
THESEUS:
The kinder we, to give them thanks for nothing.
Our sport shall be to take what they mistake: 90
And what poor duty cannot do, noble respect
Takes it in might,° not merit.
Where I have come, great clerks° have purposèd
To greet me with premeditated welcomes;
Where I have seen them shiver and look pale,   95
Make periods in the midst of sentences,
Throttle their practiced accent in their fears,
And, in conclusion, dumbly have broke off,
Not paying me a welcome. Trust me, sweet,
Out of this silence yet I picked a welcome;   100
And in the modesty of fearful duty
I read as much as from the rattling tongue
Of saucy and audacious eloquence.
Love, therefore, and tongue-tied simplicity
In least speak most, to my capacity.°   105

[Enter PHILOSTRATE.]

PHILOSTRATE:
So please your Grace, the Prologue is addressed.°
THESEUS:
Let him approach.   [Flourish trumpets.]

Enter the PROLOGUE [QUINCE].

PROLOGUE:
If we offend, it is with our good will.
   That you should think, we come not to offend,
But with good will. To show our simple skill,   110

---

39 **abridgment** entertainment (to abridge or shorten the time) 42 **brief** written list 42 **ripe** ready to be presented 49 **Thracian singer** Orpheus 50 **device** show 55 **sorting with** suited to 70 **passion** strong emotion 74 **unbreathed** unexercised 75 **against** in preparation for

85 **wretchedness o'ercharged** lowly people overburdened 88 **in this kind** in this kind of thing (i.e., acting) 92 **Takes it in might** considers the ability and the effort made 93 **clerks** scholars 105 **to my capacity** according to my understanding 106 **addressed** ready

That is the true beginning of our end.°
Consider, then, we come but in despite.
We do not come, as minding to content you,
Our true intent is. All for your delight,
We are not here. That you should here repent
115   you,
The actors are at hand; and, by their show,°
You shall know all, that you are like to know.
THESEUS: This fellow doth not stand upon
points°
120   LYSANDER: He hath rid his prologue like a rough
colt; he knows not the stop.° A good moral, my
lord: it is not enough to speak, but to speak true.
HIPPOLYTA: Indeed he hath played on this prologue like a child on a recorder;° a sound, but not
125   in government.°
THESEUS: His speech was like a tangled chain;
nothing impaired, but all disordered. Who is next?

Enter PYRAMUS *and* THISBY *and* WALL *and*
MOONSHINE *and* LION [*as in dumbshow*].

PROLOGUE:
Gentles, perchance you wonder at this show;
But wonder on, till truth make all things plain.
130   This man is Pyramus, if you would know;
This beauteous lady Thisby is certain.
This man, with lime and roughcast, doth present
Wall, that vile Wall which did these lovers
sunder;
And through Wall's chink, poor souls, they are
content
135   To whisper. At the which let no man wonder.
This man, with lantern, dog, and bush of thorn,
Presenteth Moonshine; for, if you will know,
By moonshine did these lovers think no scorn
To meet at Ninus' tomb, there, there to woo.
140   This grisly beast, which Lion hight° by name,
The trusty Thisby, coming first by night,
Did scare away, or rather did affright;
And, as she fled, her mantle she did fall,°
Which Lion vile with bloody mouth did stain.
145   Anon comes Pyramus, sweet youth and tall.°
And finds his trusty Thisby's mantle slain:
Whereat, with blade, with bloody blameful blade,

He bravely broached° his boiling bloody breast;
And Thisby, tarrying in mulberry shade,
His dagger drew, and died. For all the rest,   150
Let Lion, Moonshine, Wall, and lovers twain
At large° discourse, while here they do remain.
THESEUS: I wonder if the lion be to speak.
DEMETRIUS: No wonder, my lord. One lion
may, when many asses do.   155
        Exit LION, THISBY *and* MOONSHINE.
WALL:
In this same interlude it doth befall
That I, one Snout by name, present a wall;
And such a wall, as I would have you think,
That had in it a crannied hole or chink,
Through which the lovers, Pyramus and Thisby,   160
Did whisper often very secretly.
This loam, this roughcast, and this stone, doth
show
That I am that same wall; the truth is so;
And this the cranny is, right and sinister,°
Through which the fearful lovers are to whisper.   165
THESEUS: Would you desire lime and hair to
speak better?
DEMETRIUS: It is the wittiest partition° that ever
I heard discourse, my lord.
THESEUS: Pyramus draws near the wall. Silence!   170
PYRAMUS:
O grim-looked night! O night with hue so black!
O night, which ever art when day is not!
O night, O night! Alack, alack, alack,
I fear my Thisby's promise is forgot!
And thou, O wall, O sweet, O lovely wall,   175
That stand'st between her father's ground and
mine!
Thou wall, O wall, O sweet and lovely wall,
Show me thy chink, to blink through with mine
eyne!

[*Wall holds up his fingers.*]

Thanks, courteous wall. Jove shield thee well for
this!
But what see I? No Thisby do I see.   180
O wicked wall, through whom I see no bliss!
Cursed be thy stones for thus deceiving me!
THESEUS: The wall, methinks, being sensible,°
should curse again.°

---

111 **end** aim   116 **show** (probably referring to a kind of
pantomime—"dumb show"—that was to follow, in
which the action of the play was acted without words
while the Prologue gave his account)   119 **stand upon
points** (1) care about punctuation (2) worry about nice-
ties   121 **stop** (1) technical term for the checking of a
horse (2) mark of punctuation   124 **recorder** flutelike
instrument   125 **government** control   140 **hight** is
called   143 **fall** let fall   145 **tall** brave

148 **bravely broached** gallantly stabbed   152 **At large** at
length   164 **right and sinister** i.e., running right and
left, horizontal   168 **wittiest partition** most intelligent
wall (with a pun on "partition," a section of a book or of
an oration)   183 **sensible** conscious   184 **again** in
return

PYRAMUS: No, in truth, sir, he should not. "Deceiving me" is Thisby's cue. She is to enter now, and I am to spy her through the wall. You shall see it will fall pat° as I told you. Yonder she comes.

Enter THISBY.

THISBY:
O wall, full often hast thou heard my moans,
    For parting my fair Pyramus and me!
My cherry lips have often kissed thy stones,
    Thy stones with lime and hair knit up in thee.
PYRAMUS:
I see a voice: now will I to the chink,
To spy an I can hear my Thisby's face.
Thisby!
THISBY:
My love thou art, my love I think.
PYRAMUS:
Think what thou wilt, I am thy lover's grace;°
And, like Limander,° am I trusty still.
THISBY:
And I like Helen,° till the Fates me kill.
PYRAMUS:
Not Shafalus to Procrus° was so true.
THISBY:
As Shafalus to Procrus, I to you.
PYRAMUS:
O kiss me through the hole of this vile wall!
THISBY:
I kiss the wall's hole, not your lips at all.
PYRAMUS:
Wilt thou at Ninny's tomb meet me straightway?
THISBY:
'Tide life, 'tide death,° I come without delay.
                    [*Exeunt* PYRAMUS *and* THISBY.]
WALL:
Thus have I, Wall, my part dischargèd so;
And, being done, this wall away doth go.
                                        [*Exit.*]
THESEUS: Now is the moon used° between the two neighbors.
DEMETRIUS: No remedy, my lord, when walls

are so willful to hear without warning.°
HIPPOLYTA: This is the silliest stuff that ever I heard.
THESEUS: The best in this kind° are but shadows; and the worst are no worse, if imagination amend them.
HIPPOLYTA: It must be your imagination then, and not theirs.
THESEUS: If we imagine no worse of them than they of themselves, they may pass for excellent men. Here come two noble beasts in, a man and a lion.

Enter LION *and* MOONSHINE.

LION:
You, ladies, you, whose gentle hearts do fear
The smallest monstrous mouse that creeps on floor,
May now perchance both quake and tremble here,
    When lion rough in wildest rage doth roar.
Then know that I, as Snug the joiner, am
A lion fell,° nor else no lion's dam;
For, if I should as lion come in strife
Into this place, 'twere pity on my life.°
THESEUS: A very gentle° beast, and of a good conscience.
DEMETRIUS: The very best at a beast, my lord, that e'er I saw.
LYSANDER: The lion is a very fox for his valor.
THESEUS: True; and a goose for his discretion.
DEMETRIUS: Not so, my lord; for his valor cannot carry° his discretion, and the fox carries the goose.
THESEUS: His discretion, I am sure, cannot carry his valor; for the goose carries not the fox. It is well. Leave it to his discretion, and let us listen to the moon.
MOONSHINE:
This lanthorn° doth the hornèd moon present—
DEMETRIUS: He should have worn the horns on his head.°
THESEUS: He is no crescent, and his horns are invisible within the circumference.

---

188 **pat** exactly   198 **thy lover's grace** thy gracious lover   199 **Limander** (Bottom means Leander, but blends him with Alexander)   200 **Helen** (Hero, beloved of Leander, is probably meant)   201 **Shafalus to Procrus** (Cephalus and Procris are meant, legendary lovers)   206 **'Tide life, 'tide death** come (betide) life or death   209 **moon used** (the quartos read thus, the Folio reads *morall downe.* Among suggested emendations are "mural down," and "moon to see")

212 **when walls . . . without warning** i.e., when walls are so eager to listen without warning the parents (?)   215 **in this kind** of this sort, i.e., plays (or players?)   229 **lion fell** fierce lion (perhaps with a pun on *fell* = "skin")   231 **pity on my life** an dangerous thing for me   232 **gentle** gentlemanly, courteous   239 **carry** carry away   245 **lanthorn** so spelled, and perhaps pronounced "lant-horn," because lanterns were commonly made of horn)   246–247 **horns on his head** (cuckolds were said to have horns)

MOONSHINE:
250 This lanthorn doth the hornèd moon present;
Myself the man i' th' moon do seem to be.
THESEUS: This is the greatest error of all the rest.
The man should be put into the lanthorn. How is
it else the man i' th' moon?
255 DEMETRIUS: He dares not come there for the
candle; for, you see, it is already in snuff.°
HIPPOLYTA: I am aweary of this moon. Would
he would change!
THESEUS: It appears, by his small light of discre-
260 tion, that he is in the wane; but yet, in courtesy, in
all reason, we must stay the time.
LYSANDER: Proceed, Moon.
MOONSHINE: All that I have to say is to tell you
that the lanthorn is the moon; I, the man i' th'
265 moon; this thorn bush, my thorn bush; and this
dog, my dog.
DEMETRIUS: Why, all these should be in the
lanthorn; for all these are in the moon. But,
silence! Here comes Thisby.

Enter THISBY.

THISBY:
270 This is old Ninny's tomb. Where is my love?
LION: Oh—[*The* LION *roars.* THISBY *runs off.*]
DEMETRIUS: Well roared, Lion.
THESEUS: Well run, Thisby.
HIPPOLYTA: Well shone, Moon. Truly, the
275 moon shines with a good grace.
[*The* LION *shakes* THISBY's *mantle, and exit.*]
THESEUS: Well moused,° Lion.
DEMETRIUS: And then came Pyramus.
LYSANDER: And so the lion vanished.

Enter PYRAMUS.

PYRAMUS:
Sweet Moon, I thank thee for thy sunny beams;
280 I thank thee, Moon, for shining now so bright;
For, by thy gracious, golden, glittering gleams,
I trust to take of truest Thisby sight.
But stay, O spite!°
But mark, poor knight,
285 What dreadful dole° is here!
Eyes, do you see?
How can it be?
O dainty duck! O dear!
Thy mantle good,
290 What, stained with blood!

Approach, ye Furies fell!°
O Fates, come, come,
Cut thread and thrum;°
Quail,° crush, conclude, and quell!°
THESEUS: This passion, and the death of a dear   295
friend, would go near to make a man look sad.
HIPPOLYTA: Beshrew° my heart, but I pity the
man.
PYRAMUS:
O wherefore, Nature, didst thou lions frame?
Since lion vile hath here deflow'red my dear: 300
Which is—no, no—which was the fairest dame
That lived, that loved, that liked, that looked
with cheer.°
Come, tears, confound;
Out, sword, and wound
The pap of Pyramus;   305
Ay, that left pap,
Where heart doth hop.
[*Stabs himself.*]
Thus die I, thus, thus, thus.
Now am I dead,
Now am I fled;   310
My soul is in the sky.
Tongue, lose thy light;
Moon, take thy flight.
[*Exit* MOONSHINE.]
Now die, die, die, die, die.   [*Dies.*]
DEMETRIUS: No die, but an ace,° for him; for he   315
is but one.
LYSANDER: Less than an ace, man; for he is
dead, he is nothing.
THESEUS: With the help of a surgeon he might
yet recover, and yet prove an ass.   320
HIPPOLYTA: How chance° Moonshine is gone
before Thisby comes back and finds her lover?
THESEUS: She will find him by starlight. Here
she comes; and her passion° ends the play.

[*Enter* THISBY.]

HIPPOLYTA: Methinks she should not use a long   325
one for such a Pyramus. I hope she will be brief.
DEMETRIUS: A mote will turn the balance,
which Pyramus, which Thisby, is the better; he for
a man, God warr'nt us; she for a woman, God
bless us!   330

---

291 **fell** fierce 293 **thread and thrum** i.e., everything
(*thrum* = the end of the warp thread) 294 **Quail**
destroy 294 **quell** kill 297 **Beshrew** curse (but a mild
word) 302 **cheer** countenance 315 **No die, but an**
ace not a die (singular of "dice"), but a one-spot on a
die 321 **How chance** how does it come that 324
passion passionate speech

---

256 **in snuff** (1) in need of snuffing (2) resentful 276
moused shaken (like a mouse) 283 **spite** vexation
285 **dole** sorrowful thing

LYSANDER: She hath spied him already with those sweet eyes.

DEMETRIUS: And thus she means,° videlicet:

THISBY:

Asleep, my love?
What, dead, my dove?
O Pyramus, arise!
Speak, speak. Quite dumb?
Dead, dead? A tomb
Must cover thy sweet eyes.
These lily lips,
This cherry nose,
These yellow cowslip cheeks,
Are gone, are gone.
Lovers, make moan.
His eyes were green as leeks.
O Sisters Three,°
Come, come to me,
With hands as pale as milk;
Lay them in gore,
Since you have shore°
With shears his thread of silk.
Tongue, not a word.
Come, trusty sword,
Come, blade, my breast imbrue!°

[Stabs herself.]

And, farewell, friends.
Thus Thisby ends.
Adieu, adieu, adieu. [Dies.]

THESEUS: Moonshine and Lion are left to bury the dead.

DEMETRIUS: Ay, and Wall too.

BOTTOM [starting up]: No, I assure you; the wall is down that parted their fathers. Will it please you to see the epilogue, or to hear a Bergomask dance° between two of our company?

THESEUS: No epilogue, I pray you; for your play needs no excuse. Never excuse, for when the players are all dead, there need none to be blamed. Marry, if he that writ it had played Pyramus and hanged himself in Thisby's garter, it would have been a fine tragedy: and so it is, truly; and very notably discharged. But, come, your Bergomask. Let your epilogue alone.

[A dance.]

The iron tongue of midnight hath told° twelve. Lovers, to bed; 'tis almost fairy time.

I fear we shall outsleep the coming morn, 375
As much as we this night have overwatched.
This palpable-gross° play hath well beguiled
The heavy gait of night. Sweet friends, to bed.
A fortnight hold we this solemnity,
In nightly revels and new jollity. Exeunt. 380

Enter PUCK [with a broom].

PUCK:

Now the hungry lion roars,
And the wolf behowls the moon;
Whilst the heavy plowman snores,
All with weary task fordone.°
Now the wasted° brands do glow, 385
Whilst the screech owl, screeching loud,
Puts the wretch that lies in woe
In remembrance of a shroud.
Now it is the time of night,
That the graves, all gaping wide, 390
Every one lets forth his sprite,
In the churchway paths to glide:
And we fairies, that do run
By the triple Hecate's team,°
From the presence of the sun, 395
Following darkness like a dream,
Now are frolic.° Not a mouse
Shall disturb this hallowed house:
I am sent, with broom, before,
To sweep the dust behind the door.° 400

Enter King and Queen of Fairies with all their train.

OBERON:

Through the house give glimmering light,
By the dead and drowsy fire:
Every elf and fairy sprite
Hop as light as bird from brier;
And this ditty, after me, 405
Sing, and dance it trippingly.

TITANIA:

First, rehearse your song by rote,
To each word a warbling note:
Hand in hand, with fairy grace,
Will we sing, and bless this place. 410

---

333 **means** laments 346 **Sisters Three** the three Fates 350 **shore** shorn 354 **imbrue** stain with blood 363 **Bergomask dance** rustic dance 373 **told** counted, tolled

377 **palpable-gross** obviously grotesque 384 **fordone** worn out 385 **wasted** used up 394 **triple Hecate's team** i.e., because she had three names: Phoebe in Heaven, Diana on Earth, Hecate in Hades. (Like her chariot—drawn by black horses or dragons—the elves were abroad only at night; but III.ii.388–391 says differently) 397 **frolic** frolicsome 400 **behind the door** i.e., from behind the door (Puck traditionally helped with household chores)

[*Song and dance.*]

OBERON:
Now, until the break of day,
Through this house each fairy stray.
To the best bride-bed will we,
Which by us shall blessèd be;
415   And the issue there create°
Ever shall be fortunate.
So shall all the couples three
Ever true in loving be;
And the blots of Nature's hand
420   Shall not in their issue stand.
Never mole, harelip, nor scar.
Nor mark prodigious,° such as are
Despisèd in nativity.
Shall upon their children be.
425 · With this field-dew consecrate,
Every fairy take his gait,°
And each several° chamber bless,
Through this palace, with sweet peace,
And the owner of it blest
430   Ever shall in safety rest.

415 **create** created   422 **mark prodigious** ominous
birthmark   426 **take his gait** proceed   427 **several**
individual

Trip away; make no stay;
Meet me all by break of day.
                        Exeunt [*all but* PUCK].

PUCK:
If we shadows have offended,
Think but this, and all is mended:
That you have but slumb'red here,   435
While these visions did appear.
And this weak and idle° theme,
No more yielding but° a dream,
Gentles, do not reprehend:
If you pardon, we will mend.   440
And, as I am an honest Puck,
If we have unearnèd luck
Now to scape the serpent's tongue,°
We will make amends ere long;
Else the Puck a liar call: 445
So, good night unto you all.
Give me your hands,° if we be friends,
And Robin shall restore amends.°   [*Exit.*]
                   FINIS

437 **idle** foolish   438 **No more yielding but** yielding no
more than   443 **to scape the serpent's tongue** i.e., to
escape hisses from the audience   447 **Give me your
hands** applaud   448 **restore amends** make amends

COMMENTARY

Speaking broadly, there are in the Renaissance two comic traditions, which
may be called "critical comedy" (or "bitter comedy") and "romantic comedy" (or
"sweet comedy"). The former claims, in Hamlet's words, that the "purpose of
playing . . . is to hold, as 'twere, the mirror up to nature; to show virtue her own
feature, scorn her own image, and the very age and body of the time his form
and pressure." Because it aims to hold a mirror up to the audience, its dramatis
personae are usually urban citizens—jealous husbands, foolish merchants, and
the like. These are ultimately punished, at times merely by exposure, at times by
imprisonment or fines or some such thing. The second kind of comedy,
romantic comedy, seeks less to correct than to delight with scenes of pleasant
behavior. It does not hold a mirror to the audience; rather, it leads the audience
into an elegant dream world where charming gentlefolk live in a timeless
existence. Thomas Heywood, a playwright contemporary with Shakespeare,
briefly set forth the characteristics of both traditions in *An Apology for Actors*
(1612). A comedy, he said,

> is pleasantly contrived with merry accidents, and intermixed with apt and
> witty jests. . . . And what then is the subject of this harmless mirth? Either in
> the shape of a clown to show others their slovenly behavior, that they may

reform that simplicity in themselves, which others make their sport, . . . or to refresh such weary spirits as are tired with labors or study, to moderate the cares and heaviness of the mind, that they may return to their trades and faculties with more zeal and earnestness, after some small soft and pleasant retirement.

When we think of A *Midsummer Night's Dream*, we think not of critical comedy that seeks to reform "slovenly behavior" but of romantic comedy that offers "harmless mirth," "sport," and the refreshing of "such weary spirits as are tired with labors or study." Yet even A *Midsummer Night's Dream* has its touches of critical comedy, its elements that, in Heywood's words, "may reform" by holding up a mirror to unsocial behavior. There is some satire—a little satire of the crabby father, Egeus, and rather more of the young lovers and of the well-meaning rustics who bumblingly stage a play in an effort to please their duke (and to win pensions), but mostly the play is pervaded by genial spirits and a humane vision that make it moral without moralizing. The first book on Shakespeare's morality, Elizabeth Griffith's *The Morality of Shakespeare's Dramas* (1775), rather impatiently dismissed A *Midsummer Night's Dream*: "I shall not trouble my readers with the Fable of this piece, as I can see no general moral that can be deducted from the Argument."

For one thing, all of the people—including the fairies—in A *Midsummer Night's Dream* are basically decent creatures. Egeus is at first irascible, but at the end of the play we hear no more of his insistence that his daughter marry the young man of his choice; Theseus had engaged in youthful indiscretions, but that was long ago and in another country, and now he is the very model of a benevolent ruler; the fairy king and queen bicker, but at the end they are reconciled and they bless the bridal beds of the newlyweds. The rustics, though inept actors and sometimes too impressed by their own theatrical abilities, are men of good intentions. And if in the last act the young aristocratic lovers are a little too confident of their superiority to the rustic actors, we nevertheless feel that they are fundamentally decent; after all, their comments on the performance are more or less in tune with our own.

If A *Midsummer Night's Dream*, then, employs satire only sparingly, what does it do, and what is it about? Perhaps we can get somewhere near to an answer by briefly looking at some of the interrelationships of the stories that make up the intricate plot. There is the story of Theseus and Hippolyta, who will be married in four days; the story of the four young lovers; the story of Bottom and his fellow craftsmen, who are rehearsing a play; and the story of the quarreling fairies. All these stories are related, and eventually come together: the lovers marry on the same day as Theseus and Hippolyta; the craftsmen perform their play at the wedding; the fairies come to witness the wedding and bless it.

One of the play's themes, of course, is love, as shown in the contrasts between the stately love of Theseus and Hippolyta, the changeable romantic love of the four young Athenians, the love of Pyramus and Thisby in the play that the craftsmen are rehearsing, the quarrel between the fairy king and queen, and even Titania's infatuation with Bottom. All these stories play against one another, sometimes very subtly, and sometimes explicitly, as when Lysander, having shifted his affection from Hermia to Helena, says, "Reason says you are the worthier maid" (2.2.116), and Bottom in the next scene accepts Titania's love, saying, "Reason and love keep little company together nowadays" (3.1.146–47). The nature of reason is also implicitly discussed in the play, in the numerous references to "fantasy" and "fancy," or imagination. There is scarcely a scene that does not touch on the matter of the power of the imagination. In the opening scene, for example, Egeus says that Lysander has corrupted Hermia's fantasy (1.1.32), and Duke Theseus tells Hermia that she must perceive her suitors as her father perceives them. The most famous of these references is Theseus's speech on "the lunatic, the lover, and the poet" (5.1.7). In addition to setting the time and place, the images help to define the nature of fantasy: there is an emphasis on night and moonlight during the period of confusion, and then references to the "morning lark," "day," and so on, when Theseus (the spokesman for reason) enters the woods and the lovers are properly paired (4.1.105 ff.). The last scene reintroduces night, and the lovers have moved from the dark wood back to the civilized world of Athens, and the night will bring them to bed. The plot of A *Midsummer Night's Dream*, then, juxtaposes speech against speech, image against image, and scene against scene, telling not simply a story but a story that "grows to something of great constancy, . . . strange and admirable."[1]

[1] The last two paragraphs of commentary are from *The Complete Signet Classic Shakespeare*, edited by Sylvan Barnet. Copyright © 1972 by Harcourt Brace Jovanovich. Reprinted by permission.

TOPICS FOR DISCUSSION

1. What impression do you get of Theseus in the first scene?
2. Characterize Bottom in the second scene.
3. Take one scene from A *Midsummer Night's Dream* and compose detailed stage directions for it, indicating exactly how you would stage the scene.
4. The love story is really complete by the end of the fourth act. What does the fifth act contribute to the play?
5. What ironies (see the Glossary) do you find in the play?
6. What do you find funny about A *Midsummer Night's Dream*?

THE TRAGEDY OF KING LEAR

William Shakespeare

Edited by Russell Fraser

William Shakespeare (1564–1616) was born in Stratford, England, of middle-class parents. Nothing of interest is known about his early years, but by 1590 he was acting and writing plays in London. He early worked in all three Elizabethan dramatic genres—tragedy, comedy, and history. *Romeo and Juliet,* for example, was written about 1595, the year of *Richard II,* and in the following year he wrote *A Midsummer Night's Dream. Julius Caesar* (1599) probably preceded *As You Like It* by one year, and *Hamlet* probably followed *As You Like It* by less than a year. Among the plays that followed *King Lear* (1605–1606) were *Macbeth* (1605–1606) and several "romances"—plays that have happy endings but that seem more meditative and closer to tragedy than such comedies as A *Midsummer Night's Dream, As You Like It,* and *Twelfth Night.*

[DRAMATIS PERSONAE

LEAR, *King of Britain*
KING OF FRANCE
DUKE OF BURGUNDY
DUKE OF CORNWALL, *husband to Regan*
DUKE OF ALBANY, *husband to Goneril*
EARL OF KENT
EARL OF GLOUCESTER
EDGAR, *son to Gloucester*
EDMUND, *bastard son to Gloucester*
CURAN, *a courtier*
OSWALD, *steward to Goneril*
OLD MAN, *tenant to Gloucester*

DOCTOR
LEAR'S FOOL
A CAPTAIN *subordinate to Edmund*
GENTLEMEN *attending on Cordelia*
A HERALD
SERVANTS *to Cornwall*
GONERIL ⎫
REGAN ⎬ *daughters to Lear*
CORDELIA ⎭
KNIGHTS *attending on Lear,* OFFICERS,
  MESSENGERS, SOLDIERS, ATTENDANTS

Scene: Britain]

The faithful Earl of Kent (James Blendick), unfairly put in the stocks for defending his master King Lear, warns Lear (Len Cariou) that his daughter is turning against him as the Fool (Nicholas Kepros) observes in the Guthrie Theater Company's 1974 production of Shakespeare's *King Lear.* Directed by Michael Langham. (Photo by the Guthrie Theatre.)

241

ACT I

SCENE I. [*King* LEAR's *palace.*]

Enter KENT, GLOUCESTER, *and* EDMUND.

KENT: I thought the king had more affected°¹ the Duke of Albany° than Cornwall.

GLOUCESTER: It did always seem so to us; but now, in the division of the kingdom, it appears not
5 which of the dukes he values most, for equalities are so weighed that curiosity in neither can make choice of either's moiety.°

KENT: Is not this your son, my lord?

GLOUCESTER: His breeding,° sir, hath been at
10 my charge. I have so often blushed to acknowledge him that now I am brazed° to't.

KENT: I cannot conceive° you.

GLOUCESTER: Sir, this young fellow's mother could; whereupon she grew round-wombed, and
15 had indeed, sir, a son for her cradle ere she had a husband for her bed. Do you smell a fault?

KENT: I cannot wish the fault undone, the issue° of it being so proper.°

GLOUCESTER: But I have a son, sir, by order of
20 law, some year elder than this, who yet is no dearer in my account:° though this knave° came something saucily° to the world before he was sent for, yet was his mother fair, there was good sport at his making, and the whoreson° must be ac-
25 knowledged. Do you know this noble gentleman, Edmund?

EDMUND: No, my lord.

GLOUCESTER: My Lord of Kent. Remember him hereafter as my honorable friend.
30 EDMUND: My services to your lordship.

From *The Tragedy of King Lear* by William Shakespeare, edited by Russell Fraser. Copyright © 1963 by Russell Fraser. Reprinted by arrangement with NAL Penguin Inc., New York, NY.

¹The degree sign (°) indicates a footnote, which is keyed to the text by the line number. Text references are printed in **boldface** type; the annotation follows in lightface type. The notes are Russell Fraser's.

I.i.1 **affected** loved   2 **Albany** Albanacte, whose domain extended "from the river Humber to the point of Caithness" (Holinshed)   5–7 **equalities . . . moiety** shares are so balanced against one another that careful examination by neither can make him wish the other's portion   9 **breeding** upbringing   11 **brazed** made brazen, hardened   12 **conceive** understand (pun follows)   17 **issue** result (child)   18 **proper** handsome   21 **account** estimation   21 **knave** fellow (without disapproval)   22 **saucily** (1) insolently (2) lasciviously   24 **whoreson** fellow (literally, son of a whore)

KENT: I must love you, and sue° to know you better.

EDMUND: Sir, I shall study deserving.

GLOUCESTER: He hath been out° nine years, and away he shall again. The king is coming. 35

Sound a sennet.° Enter one bearing a coronet,° then King LEAR, *then the Dukes of* CORNWALL *and* ALBANY, *next* GONERIL, REGAN, CORDELIA, *and* ATTENDANTS.

LEAR:
Attend the lords of France and Burgundy, Gloucester.

GLOUCESTER:
I shall, my lord.   *Exit,* [*with* EDMUND].

LEAR:
Meantime we shall express our darker purpose.°
Give me the map there. Know that we have divided
In three our kingdom; and 'tis our fast° intent 40
To shake all cares and business from our age,
Conferring them on younger strengths, while we
Unburthened crawl toward death. Our son of Cornwall,
And you our no less loving son of Albany,
We have this hour a constant will to publish° 45
Our daughters' several° dowers, that future strife
May be prevented° now. The princes, France and Burgundy,
Great rivals in your youngest daughter's love,
Long in our court have made their amorous sojourn,
And here are to be answered. Tell me, my daughters 50
(Since now we will divest us both of rule,
Interest° of territory, cares of state),
Which of you shall we say doth love us most,
That we our largest bounty may extend
Where nature doth with merit challenge.° 55
Goneril,
Our eldest-born, speak first.

31 **sue** entreat   34 **out** away, abroad   35 s.d. **sennet** set of notes played on a trumpet, signaling the entrance or departure of a procession; **coronet** small crown, intended for Cordelia   38 **darker purpose** hidden intention   40 **fast** fixed   45 **constant . . . publish** fixed intention to proclaim   46 **several** separate   47 **prevented** forestalled   52 **Interest** legal right   55 **nature . . . challenge** natural affection contends with desert for (or lays claim to) bounty

GONERIL:

Sir, I love you more than word can wield° the
     matter;
Dearer than eyesight, space,° and liberty;
Beyond what can be valued, rich or rare;
No less than life, with grace, health, beauty,
60   honor;
As much as child e'er loved, or father found;
A love that makes breath° poor, and speech
     unable:°
Beyond all manner of so much° I love you.

CORDELIA [aside]:

What shall Cordelia speak? Love, and be silent.

LEAR:

65 Of all these bounds, even from this line to this,
With shadowy forests, and with champains
     riched,°
With plenteous rivers, and wide-skirted meads,°
We make thee lady. To thine and Albany's issues°
Be this perpetual.° What says our second
     daughter,
70 Our dearest Regan, wife of Cornwall? Speak.

REGAN:

I am made of that self mettle° as my sister,
And prize me at her worth.° In my true heart
I find she names my very deed of love;°
Only she comes too short, that° I profess
75 Myself an enemy to all other joys
Which the most precious square of sense
     professes,°
And find I am alone felicitate°
In your dear highness' love.

CORDELIA [aside]:   Then poor Cordelia!
And yet not so, since I am sure my love's
80 More ponderous° than my tongue.

LEAR:

To thee and thine hereditary ever
Remain this ample third of our fair kingdom,
No less in space, validity,° and pleasure
Than that conferred on Goneril. Now, our joy,
85 Although our last and least;° to whose young love

The vines of France and milk° of Burgundy
Strive to be interest;° what can you say to draw
A third more opulent than your sisters? Speak.

CORDELIA:

Nothing, my lord.

LEAR: Nothing?   90

CORDELIA: Nothing.

LEAR:

Nothing will come of nothing. Speak again.

CORDELIA:

Unhappy that I am, I cannot heave
My heart into my mouth. I love your majesty
According to my bond,° no more nor less.   95

LEAR:

How, how, Cordelia? Mend your speech a little,
Lest you may mar your fortunes.

CORDELIA: Good my lord,
You have begot me, bred me, loved me. I
Return those duties back as are right fit,°
Obey you, love you, and most honor you.   100
Why have my sisters husbands, if they say
They love you all? Haply,° when I shall wed,
That lord whose hand must take my plight° shall
     carry
Half my love with him, half my care and duty.
Sure I shall never marry like my sisters,   105
To love my father all.

LEAR:

But goes thy heart with this?

CORDELIA: Ay, my good lord.

LEAR:

So young, and so untender?

CORDELIA:

So young, my lord, and true.

LEAR:

Let it be so, thy truth then be thy dower!   110
For, by the sacred radiance of the sun,
The mysteries of Hecate° and the night,
By all the operation of the orbs°
From whom we do exist and cease to be,
Here I disclaim all my paternal care,   115
Propinquity and property of blood,°
And as a stranger to my heart and me
Hold thee from this for ever. The barbarous
     Scythian,°

---

57 **wield** handle 58 **space** scope 62 **breath** language 62 **unable** impotent 63 **Beyond . . . much**
beyond all these comparisons 66 **champains riched**
enriched plains 67 **wide-skirted meads** extensive grass-
lands 68 **issues** descendants 69 **perpetual** in perpetu-
ity 71 **self mettle** same material or temperament 72
prize . . . worth value me the same (imperative) 73 **my
. . . love** what my love really is (a legalism) 74 **that** in
that 76 **Which . . . professes** which the choicest
estimate of sense avows 77 **felicitate** made happy 80
ponderous weighty 83 **validity** value 85 **least** youngest, smallest

86 **milk** i.e., pastures 87 **interest** closely connected, as
interested parties 95 **bond** filial obligation 99 **Return
. . . fit** i.e., am correspondingly dutiful 102 **Haply**
perhaps 103 **plight** troth plight 112 **mysteries of
Hecate** secret rites of Hecate (goddess of the infernal
world, and of witchcraft) 113 **operation . . . orbs**
astrological influence 116 **Propinquity . . . blood**
relationship and common blood 118 **Scythian** type of
the savage

Or he that makes his generation messes°
120 To gorge his appetite, shall to my bosom
Be as well neighbored, pitied, and relieved,
As thou my sometime° daughter.
    KENT: Good my liege—
    LEAR:
Peace, Kent!
Come not between the dragon° and his wrath.
125 I loved her most, and thought to set my rest°
On her kind nursery.° Hence and avoid my sight!
So be my grave my peace, as here I give
Her father's heart from her! Call France. Who
    stirs?
Call Burgundy. Cornwall and Albany,
130 With my two daughters' dowers digest° the third;
Let pride, which she calls plainness, marry her.°
I do invest you jointly with my power,
Preeminence, and all the large effects
That troop with majesty.° Ourself,° by monthly
    course,
135 With reservation° of an hundred knights,
By you to be sustained, shall our abode
Make with you by due turn. Only we shall retain
The name, and all th' addition° to a king. The
    sway,
Revènue, execution of the rest,
140 Belovèd sons, be yours; which to confirm,
This coronet° part between you.
    KENT: Royal Lear,
Whom I have ever honored as my king,
Loved as my father, as my master followed,
As my great patron thought on in my prayers—
    LEAR:
145 The bow is bent and drawn; make from the shaft.°
    KENT:
Let it fall° rather, though the fork° invade
The region of my heart. Be Kent unmannerly
When Lear is mad. What wouldst thou do, old
    man?
Thinkst thou that duty shall have dread to speak

When power to flattery bows? To plainness
    honor's bound   150
When majesty falls to folly. Reserve thy state,°
And in thy best consideration° check
This hideous rashness. Answer my life my
    judgment,°
Thy youngest daughter does not love thee least,
Nor are those empty-hearted whose low sounds   155
Reverb° no hollowness.°
    LEAR: Kent, on thy life, no more!
    KENT:
My life I never held but as a pawn°
To wage° against thine enemies; nor fear to lose it,
Thy safety being motive.°
    LEAR: Out of my sight!
    KENT:
See better, Lear, and let me still° remain   160
The true blank° of thine eye.
    LEAR:
Now by Apollo—
    KENT: Now by Apollo, king,
Thou swear'st thy gods in vain.
    LEAR: O vassal! Miscreant!°

[Laying his hand on his sword.]

ALBANY, CORNWALL: Dear sir, forbear!
    KENT:
Kill thy physician, and the fee bestow   165
Upon the foul disease. Revoke thy gift,
Or, whilst I can vent clamor° from my throat,
I'll tell thee thou dost evil.
    LEAR: Hear me, recreant!°
On thine allegiance,° hear me!
That thou hast sought to make us break our vows, 170
Which we durst never yet, and with strained° pride
To come betwixt our sentence° and our power,
Which nor our nature nor our place can bear,
Our potency made good,° take thy reward.
Five days we do allot thee for provision°   175

---

119 **makes . . . messes** eats his own offspring   122
sometime former   124 **dragon** (1) heraldic device of
Britain (2) emblem of ferocity   125 **set my rest** (1) stake
my all (a term from the card game of primero) (2) find
my rest   126 **nursery** care, nursing   130 **digest** ab-
sorb   131 **Let . . . her** Let her pride be her dowry and
gain her a husband   133–134 **effects . . . majesty**
accompaniments that go with kingship   134 **Ourself** the
royal "we"   135 **reservation** the action of reserving a
privilege (a legalism)   138 **addition** titles and honors
141 **coronet** the crown that was to have been Cordelia's   145 **make . . . shaft** avoid the arrow   146 **fall**
strike   146 **fork** forked head of the arrow

151 **Reserve thy state** retain your kingly authority   152
best consideration most careful reflection   153 **Answer
. . . judgment** I will stake my life on my opinion   156
Reverb reverberate   156 **hollowness** (1) emptiness (2)
insincerity   157 **pawn** stake in a wager   158 **wage** (1)
wager (2) carry on war   159 **motive** moving cause   160
still always   161 **blank** the white spot in the center of
the target (at which Lear should aim)   163 **vassal!
Miscreant!** base wretch! Misbeliever!   167 **vent clamor**
utter a cry   168 **recreant** traitor   169 **On thine allegiance** to forswear, which is to commit high treason
171 **strained** forced (and so excessive)   172 **sentence**
judgment, decree   174 **Our . . . good** my royal authority being now asserted   175 **for provision** for making
preparation

To shield thee from diseases° of the world,
And on the sixth to turn thy hated back
Upon the kingdom. If, on the tenth day following,
Thy banished trunk° be found in our dominions,
180 The moment is thy death. Away! By Jupiter,
This shall not be revoked.

KENT:
Fare thee well, king. Sith° thus thou wilt appear,
Freedom lives hence, and banishment is here.

[*To* CORDELIA.]

The gods to their dear shelter take thee, maid,
185 That justly think'st, and hast most rightly said.

[*To* REGAN *and* GONERIL.]

And your large speeches may your deeds approve,°
That good effects° may spring from words of love.
Thus, Kent, O princes, bids you all adieu;
He'll shape his old course° in a country new.
Exit.

Flourish.° Enter GLOUCESTER, *with* FRANCE
and BURGUNDY; ATTENDANTS.

GLOUCESTER:
190 Here's France and Burgundy, my noble lord.
LEAR:
My Lord of Burgundy,
We first address toward you, who with this king
Hath rivaled for our daughter. What in the least
Will you require in present° dower with her,
Or cease your quest of love?
195 BURGUNDY: Most royal majesty,
I crave no more than hath your highness offered,
Nor will you tender° less.
LEAR: Right noble Burgundy,
When she was dear° to us, we did hold her so;
But now her price is fallen. Sir, there she stands.
200 If aught within that little seeming substance,°
Or all of it, with our displeasure pieced,°
And nothing more, may fitly like° your grace,
She's there, and she is yours.
BURGUNDY: I know no answer.
LEAR:
Will you, with those infirmities she owes°

Unfriended, new adopted to our hate,   205
Dow'red with our curse, and strangered° with our
    oath,
Take her, or leave her?
BURGUNDY: Pardon me, royal sir.
Election makes not up° on such conditions.
LEAR:
Then leave her, sir; for, by the pow'r that made
    me,
I tell you all her wealth. [*To* FRANCE.] For you,
    great king,   210
I would not from your love make such a stray
To° match you where I hate; therefore beseech°
    you
T' avert your liking a more worthier way°
Than on a wretch whom nature is ashamed
Almost t' acknowledge hers.
FRANCE: This is most strange,   215
That she whom even but now was your best
    object,°
The argument° of your praise, balm of your age,
The best, the dearest, should in this trice of time
Commit a thing so monstrous to dismantle°
So many folds of favor. Sure her offense   220
Must be of such unnatural degree
That monsters it,° or your fore-vouched° affection
Fall into taint;° which to believe of her
Must be a faith that reason without miracle
Should never plant in me.°
CORDELIA: I yet beseech your majesty,   225
If for° I want that glib and oily art
To speak and purpose not,° since what I well
    intend
I'll do't before I speak, that you make known
It is no vicious blot, murder, or foulness,
No unchaste action or dishonored step,   230
That hath deprived me of your grace and favor;
But even for want of that for which I am richer,
A still-soliciting° eye, and such a tongue

176 **diseases** troubles   179 **trunk** body   182 **Sith** since
186 **approve** prove true   187 **effects** results   189 **shape
. . . course** pursue his customary way   189 s.d. **Flourish**
trumpet fanfare   194 **present** immediate   197 **tender**
offer   198 **dear** (1) beloved (2) valued at a high price
200 **little seeming substance** person who is (1) inconsid-
erable (2) outspoken   201 **pieced** added to it   202 **fitly
like** please by its fitness   204 **owes** possesses

206 **strangered** made a stranger   208 **Election . . . up**
no one can choose   211–212 **make . . . To** stray so far
as to   212 **beseech** I beseech   213 **avert . . . way** turn
your affections from her and bestow them on a better
person   216 **your best object** the one you loved most
217 **argument** subject   219 **dismantle** strip off   222
That monsters it as makes it monstrous, unnatural   222
fore-vouched previously sworn   223 **Fall into taint**
must be taken as having been unjustified all along; i.e.,
Cordelia was·unworthy of your love from the first
224–225 **reason . . . me** my reason would have to be
supported by a miracle to make me believe   226 **for**
because   227 **purpose not** not mean to do what I
promise   233 **still-soliciting** always begging

That I am glad I have not, though not to have it
Hath lost° me in your liking.
235   LEAR: Better thou
Hadst not been born than not t' have pleased me
     better.
     FRANCE:
Is it but this? A tardiness in nature°
Which often leaves the history unspoke°
That it intends to do. My Lord of Burgundy,
240   What say you° to the lady? Love's not love
When it is mingled with regards° that stands
Aloof from th' entire point.° Will you have her?
She is herself a dowry.
     BURGUNDY: Royal king,
Give but that portion which yourself proposed,
245   And here I take Cordelia by the hand,
Duchess of Burgundy.
     LEAR:
Nothing. I have sworn. I am firm.
     BURGUNDY:
I am sorry then you have so lost a father
That you must lose a husband.
     CORDELIA: Peace be with Burgundy.
250   Since that respects of fortune° are his love,
I shall not be his wife.
     FRANCE:
Fairest Cordelia, that art most rich being poor,
Most choice forsaken, and most loved despised,
Thee and thy virtues here I seize upon.
255   Be it lawful I take up what's cast away.
Gods, gods! 'Tis strange that from their cold'st
     neglect
My love should kindle to inflamed respect.°
Thy dow'rless daughter, king, thrown to my
     chance,°
Is queen of us, of ours, and our fair France.
260   Not all the dukes of wat'rish° Burgundy
Can buy this unprized precious° maid of me.
Bid them farewell, Cordelia, though unkind.
Thou losest here,° a better where° to find.
     LEAR:
Thou hast her, France; let her be thine, for we
265   Have no such daughter, nor shall ever see

235 **lost** ruined   237 **tardiness in nature** natural reticence   238 **leaves . . . unspoke** does not announce the
action   240 **What say you** i.e., will you have   241 **regards** considerations (the dowry)   241–242 **stands . . .
point** have nothing to do with the essential question
(love)   250 **respects of fortune** mercenary considerations   257 **inflamed respect** more ardent affection   258
chance lot   260 **wat'rish** (1) with many rivers (2) weak,
diluted   261 **unprized precious** unappreciated by
others, and yet precious   263 **here** in this place   263
where other place

That face of hers again. Therefore be gone,
Without our grace, our love, our benison.°
Come, noble Burgundy.
          Flourish. Exeunt [LEAR, BURGUNDY,
               CORNWALL, ALBANY, GLOUCESTER,
                                and ATTENDANTS].
     FRANCE:
Bid farewell to your sisters.
     CORDELIA:
The jewels of our father,° with washed° eyes   270
Cordelia leaves you. I know you what you are,
And, like a sister,° am most loath to call
Your faults as they are named.° Love well our
     father.
To your professèd° bosoms I commit him.
But yet, alas, stood I within his grace,   275
I would prefer° him to a better place.
So farewell to you both.
     REGAN:
Prescribe not us our duty.
     GONERIL: Let your study
Be to content your lord, who hath received you
At Fortune's alms.° You have obedience scanted,° 280
And well are worth the want that you have
     wanted.°
     CORDELIA:
Time shall unfold what plighted° cunning hides,
Who covers faults, at last shame them derides.°
Well may you prosper.
     FRANCE: Come, my fair Cordelia.
          Exit FRANCE *and* CORDELIA.
     GONERIL: Sister, it is not little I have to say of 285
what most nearly appertains to us both. I think our
father will hence tonight.
     REGAN: That's most certain, and with you; next
month with us.
     GONERIL: You see how full of changes his age is. 290
The observation we have made of it hath not been
little. He always loved our sister most, and with
what poor judgment he hath now cast her off
appears too grossly.°

267 **benison** blessing   270 **The jewels . . . father** you
creatures prized by our father; **washed** (1) weeping (2)
clearsighted   272 **like a sister** because I am a sister, i.e.,
loyal, affectionate   273 **as . . . named** by their right and
ugly names   274 **professèd** pretending to love   276
prefer recommend   280 **At Fortune's alms** as a charitable bequest from Fortune (and so, by extension, as one
beggared or cast down by Fortune)   280 **scanted** stinted
281 **worth . . . wanted** deserve to be denied, even as you
have denied   282 **plighted** pleated, enfolded   283
Who . . . derides Those who hide their evil are finally
exposed and shamed ("He that hideth his sins, shall not
prosper")   294 **grossly** obviously

295 REGAN: 'Tis the infirmity of his age; yet he hath ever but slenderly known himself.

GONERIL: The best and soundest of his time° hath been but rash; then must we look from his age to receive not alone the imperfections of long-
300 ingrafted° condition,° but therewithal° the unruly waywardness that infirm and choleric years bring with them.

REGAN: Such unconstant starts° are we like to have from him as this of Kent's banishment.
305 GONERIL: There is further compliment° of leave-taking between France and him. Pray you, let's hit° together; if our father carry authority with such disposition as he bears,° this last surrender° of his will but offend° us.
310 REGAN: We shall further think of it.

GONERIL: We must do something, and i' th' heat.°

Exeunt.

SCENE II. [*The Earl of* GLOUCESTER's *castle.*]

Enter EDMUND [*with a letter*].

EDMUND:
Thou, Nature,° art my goddess; to thy law
My services are bound. Wherefore should I
Stand in the plague of custom,° and permit
The curiosity° of nations to deprive me,
5 For that° I am some twelve or fourteen moonshines°
Lag of° a brother? Why bastard? Wherefore base?
When my dimensions are as well compact,°
My mind as generous,° and my shape as true,
As honest° madam's issue? Why brand they us
10 With base? With baseness? Bastardy? Base? Base?
Who, in the lusty stealth of nature, take
More composition° and fierce° quality
Than doth, within a dull, stale, tired bed,
Go to th' creating a whole tribe of fops°

297 **of his time** period of his life up to now   299–300 **long-ingrafted** implanted for a long time   300 **condition** disposition; **therewithal** with them   303 **unconstant starts** impulsive whims   305 **compliment** formal courtesy   307 **hit** agree   307–308 **carry . . . bears** continues, and in such frame of mind, to wield the sovereign power   308 **last surrender** recent abdication   309 **offend** vex   311–312 **i' th' heat** while the iron is hot   I.II.1 **Nature** Edmund's conception of Nature accords with our description of a bastard as a natural child   3 **Stand . . . custom** respect hateful convention   4 **curiosity** nice distinctions   5 **For that** because; **moonshines** months   6 **Lag of** short of being (in age)   7 **compact** framed   8 **generous** gallant   9 **honest** chaste   12 **composition** completeness   12 **fierce** energetic   14 **fops** fools

Got° 'tween asleep and wake? Well then,   15
Legitimate Edgar, I must have your land.
Our father's love is to the bastard Edmund
As to th' legitimate. Fine word, "legitimate."
Well, my legitimate, if this letter speed,°
And my invention° thrive, Edmund the base   20
Shall top th' legitimate. I grow, I prosper.
Now, gods, stand up for bastards.

Enter GLOUCESTER.

GLOUCESTER:
Kent banished thus? and France in choler parted?
And the king gone tonight? prescribed° his pow'r?
Confined to exhibition?° All this done   25
Upon the gad?° Edmund, how now? What news?
EDMUND:
So please your lordship, none.
GLOUCESTER:
Why so earnestly seek you to put up° that letter?
EDMUND:
I know no news, my lord.   *Decestih*
GLOUCESTER:
What paper were you reading? —   30
EDMUND: Nothing, my lord.
GLOUCESTER: No? What needed then that terri-   *can't want to know reality*
ble dispatch° of it into your pocket? The quality of
nothing hath not such need to hide itself. Let's see.
Come, if it be nothing, I shall not need spectacles.   35
EDMUND: I beseech you, sir, pardon me. It is a
letter from my brother that I have not all o'er-read;
and for so much as I have perused, I find it not fit
for your o'erlooking.°
GLOUCESTER: Give me the letter, sir.   40
EDMUND: I shall offend, either to detain or give
it. The contents, as in part I understand them, are
to blame.°   *— curiosity.*
GLOUCESTER: Let's see, let's see.
EDMUND: I hope, for my brother's justification,   45
he wrote this but as an essay or taste° of my virtue.
GLOUCESTER (*reads*): "This policy and rever-
ence° of age makes the world bitter to the best of
our times;° keeps our fortunes from us till our
oldness cannot relish° them. I begin to find an idle   50

15 **Got** begot   19 **speed** prosper   20 **invention** plan
24 **prescribed** limited   25 **exhibition** an allowance or pension   26 **Upon the gad** on the spur of the moment (as if pricked by a gad or goad)   28 **put up** put away, conceal   33 **terrible dispatch** hasty putting away   39 **o'erlooking** inspection   43 **to blame** blameworthy   46 **essay or taste** test   47–48 **policy and reverence** policy of reverencing (hendiadys)   48–49 **best . . . times** best years of our lives (i.e., our youth)   50 **relish** enjoy

and fond° bondage in the oppression of aged tyranny, who sways, not as it hath power, but as it is suffered.° Come to me, that of this I may speak more. If our father would sleep till I waked him, you should enjoy half his revenue° for ever, and live the beloved of your brother, Edgar."

Hum! Conspiracy? "Sleep till I waked him, you should enjoy half his revenue." My son Edgar! Had he a hand to write this? A heart and brain to breed it in? When came you to this? Who brought it?

EDMUND: It was not brought me, my lord; there's the cunning of it. I found it thrown in at the casement of my closet.°

GLOUCESTER: You know the character° to be your brother's?

EDMUND: If the matter were good, my lord, I durst swear it were his; but in respect of that,° I would fain° think it were not.

GLOUCESTER: It is his.

EDMUND: It is his hand, my lord; but I hope his heart is not in the contents.

GLOUCESTER: Has he never before sounded° you in this business?

EDMUND: Never, my lord. But I have heard him oft maintain it to be fit that, sons at perfect° age, and fathers declined, the father should be as ward to the son, and the son manage his revenue.

GLOUCESTER: O villain, villain! His very opinion in the letter. Abhorred villain, unnatural, detested,° brutish villain; worse than brutish! Go, sirrah,° seek him. I'll apprehend him. Abominable villain! Where is he?

EDMUND: I do not well know, my lord. If it shall please you to suspend your indignation against my brother till you can derive from him better testimony of his intent, you should run a certain course;° where, if you violently proceed against him, mistaking his purpose, it would make a great gap° in your own honor and shake in pieces the heart of his obedience. I dare pawn down° my life for him that he hath writ this to feel° my affection

to your honor, and to no other pretense of danger.°

GLOUCESTER: Think you so?

EDMUND: If your honor judge it meet,° I will 95 place you where you shall hear us confer of this, and by an auricular assurance° have your satisfaction, and that without any further delay than this very evening.

GLOUCESTER: He cannot be such a monster. 100

EDMUND: Nor is not, sure.

GLOUCESTER: To his father, that so tenderly and entirely loves him. Heaven and earth! Edmund, seek him out; wind me into him,° I pray you; frame° the business after your own wisdom. I 105 would unstate myself to be in a due resolution.°

EDMUND: I will seek him, sir, presently;° convey° the business as I shall find means, and acquaint you withal.°

GLOUCESTER: These late° eclipses in the sun 110 and moon portend no good to us. Though the wisdom of nature° can reason° it thus and thus, yet nature finds itself scourged by the sequent effects.° Love cools, friendship falls off,° brothers divide. In cities, mutinies;° in countries, discord; in palaces, 115 treason; and the bond cracked 'twixt son and father. This villain of mine comes under the prediction,° there's son against father; the king falls from bias of nature,° there's father against child. We have seen the best of our time.° Machinations, 120 hollowness,° treachery, and all ruinous disorders follow us disquietly° to our graves. Find out this villain, Edmund; it shall lose thee nothing.° Do it carefully. And the noble and true-hearted Kent banished; his offense, honesty. 'Tis strange. 125

Exit.

EDMUND: This is the excellent foppery° of the world, that when we are sick in fortune, often the

---

50–51 **idle and fond** foolish 52–53 **who . . . suffered** which rules, not from its own strength, but from our allowance 55 **revenue** income 64 **casement . . . closet** window of my room 65 **character** handwriting 68 **in . . . that** in view of what it is 69 **fain** prefer to 73 **sounded** sounded you out 76 **perfect** mature 81 **detested** detestable 82 **sirrah** sir (familiar form of address) 87–88 **run . . . course** proceed safely, know where you are going 90 **gap** breach 91 **pawn down** stake 92 **feel** test

93 **pretense of danger** dangerous purpose 95 **meet** fit 97 **auricular assurance** proof heard with your own ears 104 **wind . . . him** insinuate yourself into his confidence for me 105 **frame** manage 106 **unstate . . . resolution** forfeit my earldom to know the truth 107 **presently** at once 108 **convey** manage 109 **withal** with it 110 **late** recent 112 **wisdom of nature** scientific learning; **reason** explain 112–113 **yet . . . effects** nonetheless our world is punished with subsequent disasters 114 **falls off** revolts 115 **mutinies** riots 117–118 **This . . . prediction** my son's villainous behavior is included in these portents, and bears them out 119 **bias of nature** natural inclination (the metaphor is from the game of bowls) 120 **best . . . time** our best days 121 **hollowness** insincerity 122 **disquietly** unquietly 124 **it . . . nothing** you will not lose by it 126 **foppery** folly

surfeits of our own behavior,° we make guilty of our disasters the sun, the moon, and stars; as if we 130 were villains on° necessity; fools by heavenly compulsion; knaves, thieves, and treachers by spherical predominance;° drunkards, liars, and adulterers by an enforced obedience of planetary influence;° and all that we are evil in, by a divine thrusting on.° An 135 admirable evasion of whoremaster° man, to lay his goatish° disposition on the charge of a star. My father compounded° with my mother under the Dragon's Tail,° and my nativity° was under Ursa Major,° so that it follows I am rough and lech- 140 erous. Fut!° I should have been that° I am, had the maidenliest star in the firmament twinkled on my bastardizing. Edgar—

Enter EDGAR.

and pat he comes, like the catastrophe° of the old comedy. My cue is villainous melancholy, with a 145 sigh like Tom o' Bedlam.°—O, these eclipses do portend these divisions. Fa, sol, la, mi.°

EDGAR: How now, brother Edmund; what serious contemplation are you in?

EDMUND: I am thinking, brother, of a predic- 150 tion I read this other day, what should follow these eclipses.

EDGAR: Do you busy yourself with that?

EDMUND: I promise you, the effects he writes of succeed° unhappily: as of unnaturalness° between 155 the child and the parent, death, dearth, dissolutions of ancient amities,° divisions in state, menaces and maledictions against king and nobles, needless diffidences,° banishment of friends, dis-

sipation of cohorts,° nuptial breaches, and I know not what. 160

EDGAR: How long have you been a sectary astronomical?°

EDMUND: Come, come, when saw you my father last?

EDGAR: Why, the night gone by.

EDMUND: Spake you with him? 165

EDGAR: Ay, two hours together.

EDMUND: Parted you in good terms? Found you no displeasure in him by word nor countenance?°

EDGAR: None at all.

EDMUND: Bethink yourself wherein you may 170 have offended him; at at my entreaty forbear his presence° until some little time hath qualified° the heat of his displeasure, which at this instant so rageth in him that with the mischief of your person it would scarcely allay.° 175

EDGAR: Some villain hath done me wrong.

EDMUND: That's my fear, brother. I pray you have a continent forbearance° till the speed of his rage goes slower; and, as I say, retire with me to my lodging, from whence I will fitly° bring you to hear 180 my lord speak. Pray ye, go; there's my key. If you do stir abroad, go armed.

EDGAR: Armed, brother?

EDMUND: Brother, I advise you to the best. Go armed. I am no honest man if there be any good 185 meaning toward you. I have told you what I have seen and heard; but faintly, nothing like the image and horror° of it. Pray you, away.

EDGAR: Shall I hear from you anon?°

EDMUND: I do serve you in this business. 190

Exit EDGAR.

A credulous father, and a brother noble,
Whose nature is so far from doing harms
That he suspects none; on whose foolish honesty
My practices° ride easy. I see the business.
Let me, if not by birth, have lands by wit. 195
All with me's meet° that I can fashion fit.°

Exit.

127–128 **often . . . behavior** often caused by our own excesses 130 **on** of 131–132 **treachers . . . predominance** traitors because of the ascendancy of a particular star at our birth 132–133 **by . . . influence** because we had to submit to the influence of our star 134 **divine thrusting on** supernatural compulsion 135 **whoremaster** lecherous 136 **goatish** lascivious 137 **compounded** (1) made terms (2) formed (a child) 138 **Dragon's Tail** the constellation Draco 138 **nativity** birthday 138–139 **Ursa Major** the Great Bear 140 **Fut** 'S foot (an impatient oath) 140 **that** what 143 **catastrophe** conclusion 144–145 **My . . . Bedlam** I must be doleful, like a lunatic beggar out of Bethlehem (Bedlam) Hospital, the London madhouse 146 **Fa, sol, la, mi** Edmund's humming of the musical notes is perhaps prompted by his use of the word *division*, which describes a musical variation 154 **succeed** follow 154 **unnaturalness** unkindness 156 **amities** friendships 158 **diffidences** distrusts

158–159 **dissipation of cohorts** falling away of supporters 161–162 **sectary astronomical** believer in astrology 168 **countenance** expression 171–172 **forbear his presence** keep away from him 172 **qualified** lessened 174–175 **with . . . allay** even an injury to you would not appease his anger 178 **have . . . forbearance** be restrained and keep yourself withdrawn 180 **fitly** at a fit time 188 **image and horror** true horrible picture 189 **anon** in a little while 194 **practices** plots 196 **meet** proper 196 **fashion fit** shape to my purpose

SCENE III. [*The Duke of* ALBANY'*s palace.*]

Enter GONERIL, *and* [OSWALD, *her*] steward.

GONERIL: Did my father strike my gentleman for chiding of his Fool?°

OSWALD: Ay, madam.

GONERIL:
By day and night he wrongs me. Every hour
5 He flashes into one gross crime° or other
That sets us all at odds. I'll not endure it.
His knights grow riotous,° and himself upbraids us
On every trifle. When he returns from hunting,
I will not speak with him. Say I am sick.
10 If you come slack of former services,°
You shall do well; the fault of it I'll answer.°

[*Horns within.*]

OSWALD: He's coming, madam; I hear him.

GONERIL:
Put on what weary negligence you please,
You and your fellows. I'd have it come to question.°
15 If he distaste° it, let him to my sister,
Whose mind and mine I know in that are one,
Not to be overruled. Idle° old man,
That still would manage those authorities
That he hath given away. Now, by my life,
20 Old fools are babes again, and must be used
With checks as flatteries, when they are seen abused.°
Remember what I have said.

OSWALD: Well, madam.

GONERIL:
And let his knights have colder looks among you.
What grows of it, no matter; advise your fellows so.
25 I would breed from hence occasions, and I shall,
That I may speak.° I'll write straight° to my sister
To hold my course. Go, prepare for dinner.

Exeunt.

SCENE IV. [*A hall in the same.*]

Enter KENT [*disguised*].

KENT:
If but as well I other accents borrow

That can my speech defuse,° my good intent
May carry through itself to that full issue°
For which I razed my likeness.° Now, banished Kent,
If thou canst serve where thou dost stand condemned,   5
So may it come,° thy master whom thou lov'st
Shall find thee full of labors.

Horns within.° Enter LEAR, [KNIGHTS,] *and* ATTENDANTS.

LEAR: Let me not stay° a jot for dinner; go, get it ready. [*Exit an* ATTENDANT.] How now, what art thou?   10

KENT: A man, sir.

LEAR: What dost thou profess?° What wouldst thou with us?

KENT: I do profess° to be no less than I seem, to serve him truly that will put me in trust, to love   15
him that is honest, to converse with him that is wise and says little, to fear judgment,° to fight when I cannot choose, and to eat no fish.°

LEAR: What art thou?

KENT: A very honest-hearted fellow and as poor   20
as the king.

LEAR: If you be'st as poor for a subject as he's for a king, thou art poor enough. What wouldst thou?

KENT: Service.

LEAR: Who wouldst thou serve?   25

KENT: You.

LEAR: Dost thou know me, fellow?

KENT: No, sir, but you have that in your countenance° which I would fain° call master.

LEAR: What's that?   30

KENT: Authority.

LEAR: What services canst thou do?

KENT: I can keep honest counsel,° ride, run, mar a curious tale in telling it,° and deliver a plain message bluntly. That which ordinary men are fit   35
for, I am qualified in, and the best of me is diligence.

LEAR: How old art thou?

I.III.2 **Fool** court jester   5 **crime** offense   7 **riotous** dissolute   10 **come . . . services** are less serviceable to him than formerly   11 **answer** answer for   14 **come to question** be discussed openly   15 **distaste** dislike   17 **Idle** foolish   21 **With . . . abused** with restraints as well as soothing words when they are misguided   25–26 **breed . . . speak** find in this opportunities for speaking out   26 **straight** at once

I.IV.2 **defuse** disguise   3 **full issue** perfect result   4 **razed my likeness** shaved off, disguised my natural appearance   6 **So . . . come** so may it fall out   7 s.d. **within** offstage   8 **stay** wait   12 **What . . . profess** What do you do?   14 **profess** claim   17 **judgment** by a heavenly or earthly judge   18 **eat no fish** (1) I am no Catholic, but a loyal Protestant (2) I am no weakling (3) I use no prostitutes   28–29 **countenance** bearing   29 **fain** like to   33 **honest counsel** honorable secrets   34 **mar . . . it** i.e., I cannot speak like an affected courtier ("curious" = elaborate, as against plain)

KENT: Not so young, sir, to love a woman for
40 singing, nor so old to dote on her for anything. I
have years on my back forty-eight.

LEAR: Follow me; thou shalt serve me. If I like
thee no worse after dinner, I will not part from
thee yet. Dinner, ho, dinner! Where's my knave?°
45 My Fool? Go you and call my Fool hither.

[*Exit an* ATTENDANT.]

Enter OSWALD.

You, you, sirrah, where's my daughter?
OSWALD: So please you—   *Exit.*
LEAR: What says the fellow there? Call the
clotpoll° back. [*Exit a* KNIGHT.] Where's my Fool?
50 Ho, I think the world's asleep.

[*Reenter* KNIGHT.]

How now? Where's that mongrel?
KNIGHT: He says, my lord, your daughter is not
well.
LEAR: Why came not the slave back to me when
55 I called him?
KNIGHT: Sir, he answered me in the roundest°
manner, he would not.
LEAR: He would not?
KNIGHT: My lord, I know not what the matter is;
60 but to my judgment your highness is not enter-
tained° with that ceremonious affection as you
were wont. There's a great abatement of kindness
appears as well in the general dependants° as in the
duke himself also and your daughter.
65 LEAR: Ha? Say'st thou so?
KNIGHT: I beseech you pardon me, my lord, if I
be mistaken; for my duty cannot be silent when I
think your highness wronged.
LEAR: Thou but rememb'rest° me of mine own
70 conception.° I have perceived a most faint neglect°
of late, which I have rather blamed as mine own
jealous curiosity° than as a very pretense° and
purpose of unkindness. I will look further into't.
But where's my Fool? I have not seen him this two
75 days.
KNIGHT: Since my young lady's going into
France, sir, the Fool hath much pined away.
LEAR: No more of that; I have noted it well. Go

you and tell my daughter I would speak with her.
Go you, call hither my Fool.   80

[*Exit an* ATTENDANT.]

Enter OSWALD.

O, you, sir, you! Come you hither, sir. Who am I,
sir?
OSWALD: My lady's father.
LEAR: "My lady's father"? My lord's knave, you
whoreson dog, you slave, you cur!   85
OSWALD: I am none of these, my lord; I beseech
your pardon.
    pardon.
LEAR: Do you bandy° looks with me, you rascal?

[*Striking him.*]

OSWALD:
I'll not be strucken,° my lord.
KENT: Nor tripped neither, you base football°   90
player.

[*Tripping up his heels.*]

LEAR: I thank thee, fellow. Thou serv'st me, and
I'll love thee.
KENT: Come, sir, arise, away. I'll teach you
differences.° Away, away. If you will measure your   95
lubber's° length again, tarry; but away. Go to°!
Have you wisdom?° So.°

[*Pushes* OSWALD *out.*]

LEAR: Now, my friendly knave, I thank thee.
There's earnest° of thy service. [*Giving* KENT
money.]

Enter FOOL.

FOOL: Let me hire him too. Here's my coxcomb.°   100

[*Offering* KENT *his cap.*]

LEAR: How now, my pretty knave? How dost
thou?
FOOL: Sirrah, you were best° take my coxcomb.
KENT: Why, Fool?
FOOL: Why? For taking one's part that's out of   105
favor. Nay, an° thou canst not smile as the wind

---

44 **knave** boy   49 **clotpoll** clodpoll, blockhead   56
roundest rudest   60–61 **entertained** treated   63 **dependants** servants   69 **rememb'rest** remindest   70
conception idea   70 **faint neglect** i.e., "weary negligence" (I.III.13)   71–72 **mine . . . curiosity** suspicious
concern for my own dignity   72 **very pretense** actual
intention

88 **bandy** exchange insolently (metaphor from tennis)
89 **strucken** struck   90 **football** a low game played by
idle boys, to the scandal of sensible men   95 **differences**
of rank   96 **lubber's** lout's   96 **Go to** expression of
derisive incredulity   97 **Have you wisdom** i.e., Do you
know what's good for you?   97 **So** good   99 **earnest**
money for services rendered   100 **coxcomb** professional
fool's cap, shaped like a coxcomb   103 **you were best**
you had better   106 **an** if

sits,° thou'lt catch cold shortly. There, take my
coxcomb. Why, this fellow has banished° two on's
daughters, and did the third a blessing against his
110 will. If thou follow him, thou must needs wear my
coxcomb.—How now, nuncle?° Would I had two
coxcombs and two daughters.

LEAR: Why, my boy?

FOOL: If I gave them all my living,° I'd keep my
115 coxcombs myself. There's mine; beg another of
thy daughters.

LEAR: Take heed, sirrah—the whip.

FOOL: Truth's a dog must to kennel; he must be
whipped out, when Lady the Brach° may stand by
120 th' fire and stink.

LEAR: A pestilent gall° to me.

FOOL: Sirrah, I'll teach thee a speech.

LEAR: Do.

FOOL: Mark it, nuncle.

125   Have more than thou showest,
             Speak less than thou knowest,
             Lend less than thou owest,°
             Ride more than thou goest,°
             Learn more than thou trowest,°
130   Set less than thou throwest;°
             Leave thy drink and thy whore,
             And keep in-a-door,
             And thou shalt have more
             Than two tens to a score.°

135 KENT: This is nothing, Fool.

FOOL: Then 'tis like the breath of an unfee'd°
lawyer—you gave me nothing for't. Can you make
no use of nothing, nuncle?

LEAR: Why, no, boy. Nothing can be made out
140 of nothing.

FOOL [to KENT]: Prithee tell him, so much the
rent of his land comes to; he will not believe a fool.

LEAR: A bitter° fool.

FOOL: Dost thou know the difference, my boy,
145 between a bitter fool and a sweet one?

LEAR: No, lad; teach me.

FOOL:

             That lord that counseled thee
             To give away thy land,

Come place him here by me,
    Do thou for him stand.   150
The sweet and bitter fool
    Will presently appear;
The one in motley° here,
    The other found out° there.°

LEAR: Dost thou call me fool, boy?   155

FOOL: All thy other titles thou hast given away;
that thou wast born with.

KENT: This is not altogether fool, my lord.

FOOL: No, faith; lords and great men will not let
me.° If I had a monopoly° out, they would have   160
part on't. And ladies too, they will not let me have
all the fool to myself; they'll be snatching. Nuncle,
give me an egg, and I'll give thee two crowns.

LEAR: What two crowns shall they be?

FOOL: Why, after I have cut the egg i' th' middle   165
and eat up the meat, the two crowns of the egg.
When thou clovest thy crown i' th' middle and
gav'st away both parts, thou bor'st thine ass on thy
back o'er the dirt.° Thou hadst little wit in thy bald
crown when thou gav'st thy golden one away. If I   170
speak like myself° in this, let him be whipped° that
first finds it so. [Singing.]

             Fools had ne'er less grace in a year,
                 For wise men are grown foppish,
             And know not how their wits to wear,   175
                 Their manners are so apish.°

LEAR: When were you wont to be so full of
songs, sirrah?

FOOL: I have used° it, nuncle, e'er since thou
mad'st thy daughters thy mothers; for when thou 180
gav'st them the rod, and put'st down thine own
breeches, [Singing.]

             Then they for sudden joy did weep,
                 And I for sorrow sung,

106–107 **smile . . . sits** ingratiate yourself with those in
power   108 **banished** alienated (by making them independent)   111 **nuncle** contraction of "mine uncle"
114 **living** property   119 **Brach** bitch   121 **gall** sore
127 **owest** ownest   128 **goest** walkest   129 **trowest**
knowest   130 **Set . . . throwest** bet less than you play for
(get odds from your opponent)   133–134 **have . . . score**
i.e., come away with more than you had (two tens, or
twenty shillings, make a score, or one pound)   136
unfee'd unpaid for   143 **bitter** satirical

153 **motley** the drab costume of the professional jester
154 **found out** revealed   154 **there** the Fool points at
Lear, as a fool in the grain   159–160 **let me** i.e., let me
have all the folly to myself   160 **monopoly** James I gave
great scandal by granting to his "snatching" courtiers
royal patents to deal exclusively in some commod-
ity   168–169 **bor'st . . . dirt** like the foolish and
unnatural countryman in Aesop's fable   171 **like myself**
like a fool   171 **let . . . whipped** i.e., let the man be
whipped for a fool who thinks my true saying to be
foolish   173–176 **Fools . . . apish** i.e., fools were never
in less favor than now, and the reason is that wise men,
turning foolish, and not knowing how to use their
intelligence, imitate the professional fools and so make
them unnecessary   179 **used** practiced

185   That such a king should play bo-peep°
        And go the fools among.
Prithee, nuncle, keep a schoolmaster that can
teach thy Fool to lie. I would fain learn to lie.
    LEAR: And° you lie, sirrah, we'll have you
190 whipped.
    FOOL: I marvel what kin thou and thy daughters
are. They'll have me whipped for speaking true;
thou'lt have me whipped for lying; and sometimes
I am whipped for holding my peace. I had rather
195 be any kind o' thing than a fool, and yet I would
not be thee, nuncle: thou hast pared thy wit o' both
sides and left nothing i' th' middle. Here comes
one o' the parings.

    Enter GONERIL.

    LEAR: How now, daughter? What makes that
200 frontlet° on? Methinks you are too much of late i'
th' frown.
    FOOL: Thou wast a pretty fellow when thou
hadst no need to care for her frowning. Now
thou art an O without a figure.° I am better than
205 thou art now: I am a fool, thou art nothing. [*To*
GONERIL.] Yes, forsooth, I will hold my tongue.
So your face bids me, though you say nothing,
Mum, mum,
      He that keeps nor crust nor crum,°
210   Weary of all, shall want° some.

    [*Pointing to* LEAR.]

That's a shealed peascod.°
    GONERIL:
Not only, sir, this your all-licensed° Fool,
But other° of your insolent retinue
Do hourly carp and quarrel, breaking forth
215 In rank° and not-to-be-endurèd riots. Sir,
I had thought by making this well known unto you
To have found a safe° redress, but now grow
    fearful,
By what yourself too late° have spoke and done,
That you protect this course, and put it on
220 By your allowance;° which if you should, the fault

Would not 'scape censure, nor the redresses sleep,°
Which, in the tender of° a wholesome weal,°
Might in their working do you that offense,
Which else were shame, that then necessity
Will call discreet proceeding.°   225
    FOOL: For you know, nuncle,
      The hedge-sparrow fed the cuckoo° so long
      That it had it head bit off by it° young.
So out went the candle, and we were left darkling.°
    LEAR: Are you our daughter?   230
    GONERIL:
Come, sir,
I would you would make use of your good wisdom
Whereof I know you are fraught° and put away
These dispositions° which of late transport you
From what you rightly are.   235
    FOOL: May not an ass know when the cart draws
the horse? Whoop, Jug,° I love thee!
    LEAR:
Does any here know me? This is not Lear.
Does Lear walk thus? Speak thus? Where are his
    eyes?
Either his notion° weakens, or his discernings°   240
Are lethargied°—Ha! Waking? 'Tis not so.
Who is it that can tell me who I am?
    FOOL: Lear's shadow.
    LEAR: I would learn that; for, by the marks of
sovereignty,° knowledge, and reason, I should be   245
false° persuaded I had daughters.
    FOOL: Which° they will make an obedient
father.
    LEAR: Your name, fair gentlewoman?
    GONERIL:
This admiration,° sir, is much o' th' savor°   250
Of other your° new pranks. I do beseech you
To understand my purposes aright.
As you are old and reverend, should be wise.
Here do you keep a hundred knights and squires,

221 **redresses sleep** correction fail to follow   222 **tender
of** desire for   222 **weal** state   222–225 **Might . . .
proceeding** as I apply it, the correction might humiliate
you; but the need to take action cancels what would
otherwise be unfilial conduct in me   227 **cuckoo** which
lays its eggs in the nests of other birds   228 **it** its   229
darkling in the dark   233 **fraught** endowed   234 **dispo-
sitions** moods   237 **Jug** Joan (a quotation from a popular song?)   240 **notion** understanding   240 **discernings**
faculties   241 **lethargied** paralyzed   244–245 **marks of
sovereignty** i.e., tokens that Lear is king, and hence
father to his daughters   246 **false** falsely   247 **Which**
whom (Lear)   250 **admiration** (affected) wonderment
250 **is . . . savor** smacks much   251 **other your** others
of your

185 **play bo-peep** (1) act like a child (2) blind himself   189 **And** if   200 **frontlet** frown (literally, ornamental band)   204 **figure** digit, to give value to the
cipher (Lear is a nought)   209 **crum** soft bread inside
the loaf   210 **want** lack   211 **shealed peascod** empty
pea pod   212 **all-licensed** privileged to take any liberties   213 **other** others   215 **rank** gross   217 **safe** sure
218 **too late** lately   219–220 **put . . . allowance** promote it by your approval

255 Men so disordered, so deboshed,° and bold,
That this our court, infected with their manners,
Shows° like a riotous inn. Epicurism° and lust
Makes it more like a tavern or a brothel
Than a graced° palace. The shame itself doth speak
260 For instant remedy. Be then desired°
By her, that else will take the thing she begs,
A little to disquantity your train,°
And the remainders° that shall still depend,°
To be such men as may besort° your age,
Which know themselves, and you.
265   LEAR: Darkness and devils!
Saddle my horses; call my train together.
Degenerate° bastard, I'll not trouble thee:
Yet have I left a daughter.
  GONERIL:
You strike my people, and your disordered rabble
270 Make servants of their betters.

   Enter ALBANY.

  LEAR:
Woe, that too late repents. O, sir, are you come?
Is it your will? Speak, sir. Prepare my horses.
Ingratitude! thou marble-hearted fiend,
More hideous when thou show'st thee in a child
Than the sea-monster.
275   ALBANY: Pray, sir, be patient.
  LEAR:
Detested kite,° thou liest.
My train are men of choice and rarest parts,°
That all particulars of duty know,
And, in the most exact regard,° support
280 The worships° of their name. O most small fault,
How ugly didst thou in Cordelia show!
Which, like an engine,° wrenched my frame of nature
From the fixed place;° drew from my heart all love,
And added to the gall.° O Lear, Lear, Lear!
285 Beat at this gate that let thy folly in

[*Striking his head.*]
And thy dear judgment out. Go, go, my people.
  ALBANY:
My lord, I am guiltless, as I am ignorant
Of what hath moved you.
  LEAR: It may be so, my lord.
Hear, Nature, hear; dear goddess, hear:
Suspend thy purpose if thou didst intend   290
To make this creature fruitful.
Into her womb convey sterility,
Dry up in her the organs of increase,°
And from her derogate° body never spring
A babe to honor her. If she must teem,°   295
Create her child of spleen,° that it may live
And be a thwart disnatured° torment to her.
Let it stamp wrinkles in her brow of youth,
With cadent° tears fret° channels in her cheeks,
Turn all her mother's pains and benefits°   300
To laughter and contempt, that she may feel
How sharper than a serpent's tooth it is
To have a thankless child. Away, away!
                               Exit.

  ALBANY:
Now, gods that we adore, whereof comes this?
  GONERIL:
Never afflict yourself to know the cause,   305
But let his disposition° have that scope
As° dotage gives it.

   Enter LEAR.

  LEAR:
What, fifty of my followers at a clap?°
Within a fortnight?
  ALBANY: What's the matter, sir?
  LEAR:
I'll tell thee. [*To* GONERIL.] Life and death, I am ashamed   310
That thou hast power to shake my manhood° thus!
That these hot tears, which break from me perforce,°
Should make thee worth them. Blasts and fogs upon thee!
Th' untented woundings° of a father's curse
Pierce every sense about thee! Old fond° eyes,   315

---

255 **deboshed** debauched   257 **Shows** appears   257 **Epicurism** riotous living   259 **graced** dignified   260 **desired** requested   262 **disquantity your train** reduce the number of your dependents   263 **remainders** those who remain   263 **depend** attend on you   264 **besort** befit   267 **Degenerate** unnatural   276 **kite** scavenging bird of prey   277 **parts** accomplishments   279 **exact regard** strict attention to detail   280 **worships** honor   282 **engine** destructive contrivance   282–283 **wrenched . . . place** i.e., disorders my natural self   284 **gall** bitterness

293 **increase** childbearing   294 **derogate** degraded   295 **teem** conceive   296 **spleen** ill humor   297 **thwart disnatured** perverse unnatural   299 **cadent** falling   299 **fret** wear   300 **benefits** the mother's beneficent care of her child   306 **disposition** mood   307 **As** that   308 **at a clap** at one stroke   311 **shake my manhood** i.e., with tears   312 **perforce** involuntarily, against my will   314 **untented woundings** wounds too deep to be probed with a tent (a roll of lint)   315 **fond** foolish

Beweep° this cause again, I'll pluck ye out
And cast you, with the waters that you loose,°
To temper° clay. Yea, is it come to this?
Ha! Let it be so. I have another daughter,
320 Who I am sure is kind and comfortable.°
When she shall hear this of thee, with her nails
She'll flay thy wolvish visage. Thou shalt find
That I'll resume the shape° which thou dost think
I have cast off for ever.

Exit [LEAR, *with* KENT
and ATTENDANTS].

GONERIL: Do you mark that?
ALBANY:
325 I cannot be so partial, Goneril,
To the great love I bear you°—
GONERIL:
Pray you, content. What, Oswald, ho!

[*To the* FOOL].

You, sir, more knave than fool, after your master!
FOOL: Nuncle Lear, nuncle Lear, tarry. Take
330 the Fool° with thee.

A fox, when one has caught her,
And such a daughter,
Should sure to the slaughter,
If my cap would buy a halter.°
335 So the Fool follows after.°   *Exit.*

GONERIL:
This man hath had good counsel. A hundred
knights!
'Tis politic° and safe to let him keep
At point° a hundred knights: yes, that on every
dream,
Each buzz,° each fancy, each complaint, dislike,
340 He may enguard° his dotage with their pow'rs
And hold our lives in mercy.° Oswald, I say!
ALBANY:
Well, you may fear too far.
GONERIL: Safer than trust too far.
Let me still take away the harms I fear,
Not fear still to be taken.° I know his heart.
345 What he hath uttered I have writ my sister.

If she sustain him and his hundred knights,
When I showed th' unfitness—

Enter OSWALD.

How now, Oswald?
What, have you writ that letter to my sister?
OSWALD: Ay, madam.
GONERIL:
Take you some company,° and away to horse.   350
Inform her full of my particular° fear,
And thereto add such reasons of your own
As may compact° it more. Get you gone,
And hasten your return. [*Exit* OSWALD.] No, no,
my lord,
This milky gentleness and course° of yours,   355
Though I condemn not,° yet under pardon,
You are much more attasked° for want of wisdom
Than praised for harmful mildness.°
ALBANY:
How far your eyes may pierce I cannot tell;
Striving to better, oft we mar what's well.   360
GONERIL: Nay then—
ALBANY: Well, well, th' event.°   *Exeunt.*

SCENE V. [*Court before the same.*]

Enter LEAR, KENT, *and* FOOL.

LEAR: Go you before to Gloucester with these
letters. Acquaint my daughter no further with
anything you know than comes from her demand
out of the letter.° If your diligence be not speedy, I
shall be there afore you.   5
KENT: I will not sleep, my lord, till I have
delivered your letter.   *Exit.*
FOOL: If a man's brains were in's heels, were't°
not in danger of kibes?°
LEAR: Ay, boy.   10
FOOL: Then I prithee be merry. Thy wit shall
not go slipshod.°
LEAR: Ha, ha, ha.
FOOL: Shalt° see thy other daughter will use

---

316 **Beweep** if you weep over   317 **loose** (1) let loose (2) lose, as of no avail   318 **temper** mix with and soften 320 **comfortable** ready to comfort   323 **shape** i.e., kingly role 325–326 **I cannot . . . you** i.e., even though my love inclines me to you, I must protest   330 **Fool** (1) the Fool himself (2) the epithet or character of "fool" 334–335 **halter, after** pronounced "hauter," "auter"   337 **politic** good policy   338 **At point** armed 339 **buzz** rumor   340 **enguard** protect   341 **in mercy** at his mercy   344 **Not . . . taken** rather than remain fearful of being overtaken by them

350 **company** escort   351 **particular** own   353 **compact** strengthen   355 **milky . . . course** mild and gentle way (hendiadys)   356 **condemn not** condemn it not 357 **attasked** taken to task, blamed   358 **harmful mildness** dangerous indulgence   362 **th' event** i.e., we'll see what happens
I.v.3–4 **than . . . letter** than her reading of the letter brings her to ask   8 **were't** i.e., the brains   9 **kibes** chilblains   11–12 **Thy . . . slipshod** Your brains shall not go in slippers (because you have no brains to be protected from chilblains)   14 **Shalt** thou shalt

15 thee kindly;° for though she's as like this as a crab's°
like an apple, yet I can tell what I can tell.
    LEAR: Why, what canst thou tell, my boy?
    FOOL: She will taste as like this as a crab does to
a crab. Thou canst tell why one's nose stands i' th'
20 middle on's° face?
    LEAR: No.
    FOOL: Why, to keep one's eyes of° either side's
nose, that what a man cannot smell out, he may
spy into.
25 LEAR: I did her wrong.
    FOOL: Canst tell how an oyster makes his shell?
    LEAR: No.
    FOOL: Nor I neither; but I can tell why a snail
has a house.
30 LEAR: Why?
    FOOL: Why, to put's head in; not to give it away
to his daughters, and leave his horns° without a
case.
    LEAR: I will forget my nature.° So kind a father!
35 Be my horses ready?
    FOOL: Thy asses are gone about 'em. The reason
why the seven stars° are no moe° than seven is a
pretty° reason.
    LEAR: Because they are not eight.
40 FOOL: Yes indeed. Thou wouldst make a good
fool.
    LEAR: To take't again perforce!° Monster
ingratitude!
    FOOL: If thou wert my fool, nuncle, I'd have
45 thee beaten for being old before thy time.
    LEAR: How's that?
    FOOL: Thou shouldst not have been old till thou
hadst been wise.
    LEAR:
O, let me not be mad, not mad, sweet heaven!
50 Keep me in temper;° I would not be mad!

    [Enter GENTLEMAN.]

How now, are the horses ready?
    GENTLEMAN: Ready, my lord.
    LEAR: Come, boy.
    FOOL:
She that's a maid now, and laughs at my departure,

Shall not be a maid long, unless things be cut
    shorter.°   55
                                          Exeunt.

ACT II

SCENE I. [The Earl of GLOUCESTER's castle.]

Enter EDMUND and CURAN, severally.°

    EDMUND: Save° thee, Curan.
    CURAN: And you, sir. I have been with your
father, and given him notice that the Duke of
Cornwall and Regan his duchess will be here with
him this night.   5
    EDMUND: How comes that?
    CURAN: Nay, I know not. You have heard of the
news abroad? I mean the whispered ones, for they
are yet but ear-kissing arguments.°
    EDMUND: Not I. Pray you, what are they?   10
    CURAN: Have you heard of no likely° wars
toward,° 'twixt the Dukes of Cornwell and Albany?
    EDMUND: Not a word.
    CURAN: You may do, then, in time. Fare you
well, sir.   Exit.   15
    EDMUND:
The duke be here tonight? The better!° best!
This weaves itself perforce° into my business.
My father hath set guard to take my brother,
And I have one thing of a queasy question°
Which I must act. Briefness° and Fortune, work! 20
Brother, a word; descend. Brother, I say!

    Enter EDGAR.

My father watches. O sir, fly this place.
Intelligence° is given where you are hid.
You have now the good advantage of the night.
Have you not spoken 'gainst the Duke of Cornwall? 25
He's coming hither, now i' th' night, i' th' haste,°
And Regan with him. Have you nothing said

54–55 She . . . shorter The maid who laughs, missing
the tragic implications of this quarrel, will not have sense
enough to preserve her virginity ("things" = penises)
II.i.s.d. severally separately (from different entrances
onstage)   1 Save God save   9 ear-kissing arguments
subjects whispered in the ear   11 likely probable   12
toward impending   16 The better So much the better   17 perforce necessarily   19 of . . . question that
requires delicate handling (to be "queasy" is to be on the
point of vomiting)   20 Briefness speed   23 Intelligence
information   26 i' th' haste in great haste

15 kindly (1) affectionately (2) after her kind or nature   15 crab crab apple   20 on's of his   22 of on   32
horns (1) snail's horns (2) cuckold's horns   34 nature
paternal instincts   37 seven stars the Pleiades   37 moe
more   38 pretty apt   42 To . . . perforce (1) of Goneril, who has forcibly taken away Lear's privileges; or (2)
of Lear, who meditates a forcible resumption of authority   50 in temper sane

Upon his party° 'gainst the Duke of Albany?
Advise yourself°
   EDGAR: I am sure on't,° not a word.
   EDMUND:
30 I hear my father coming. Pardon me:
In cunning° I must draw my sword upon you.
Draw, seem to defend yourself; now quit you°
   well.
Yield! Come before my father! Light ho, here!
Fly, brother. Torches, torches!—So farewell.
                         Exit EDGAR.
35 Some blood drawn on me would beget opinion°

[*Wounds his arm.*]

Of my more fierce endeavor. I have seen drunkards
Do more than this in sport. Father, father!
Stop, stop! No help?

Enter GLOUCESTER, *and* SERVANTS *with torches.*

   GLOUCESTER:
Now, Edmund, where's the villain?
   EDMUND:
40 Here stood he in the dark, his sharp sword out,
Mumbling of wicked charms, conjuring the moon.
To stand auspicious mistress.
   GLOUCESTER: But where is he?
   EDMUND:
Look, sir, I bleed.
   GLOUCESTER: Where is the villain, Edmund?
   EDMUND:
45 Fled this way, sir, when by no means he could—
   GLOUCESTER:
Pursue him, ho! Go after. [*Exeunt some* SER-
   VANTS.] By no means what?
   EDMUND:
Persuade me to the murder of your lordship;
But that I told him the revenging gods
'Gainst parricides did all the thunder bend;°
50 Spoke with how manifold and strong a bond
The child was bound to th' father. Sir, in fine,°
Seeing how loathly opposite° I stood
To his unnatural purpose, in fell° motion°
With his preparèd sword he charges home
55 My unprovided° body, latched° mine arm;
But when he saw my best alarumed° spirits

Bold in the quarrel's right,° roused to th' encounter,
Or whether gasted° by the noise I made,
Full suddenly he fled.
   GLOUCESTER: Let him fly far.
Not in this land shall he remain uncaught;   60
And found—dispatch.° The noble duke my master,
My worthy arch° and patron, comes tonight.
By his authority I will proclaim it,
That he which finds him shall deserve our thanks,
Bringing the murderous coward to the stake.   65
He that conceals him, death.°
   EDMUND:
When I dissuaded him from his intent,
And found him pight° to do it, with curst° speech
I threatened to discover° him. He replied,
"Thou unpossessing° bastard, dost thou think,   70
If I would stand against thee, would the reposal°
Of any trust, virtue, or worth in thee
Make thy words faithed?° No. What I should
   deny—
As this I would, ay, though thou didst produce
My very character°—I'd turn it all   75
To thy suggestion,° plot, and damnèd practice.°
And thou must make a dullard of the world,°
If they not thought° the profits of my death
Were very pregnant° and potential spirits°
To make thee seek it."   80
   GLOUCESTER:
O strange and fastened° villain!
Would he deny his letter, said he? I never got°
   him.

Tucket° within.

Hark, the duke's trumpets. I know not why he
   comes.
All ports° I'll bar; the villain shall not 'scape;
The duke must grant me that. Besides, his picture   85
I will send far and near, that all the kingdom
May have due note of him; and of my land,

---

28 **Upon his party** censuring his enmity 29 **Advise
yourself** Reflect 29 **on't** of it 31 **In cunning** as a
pretense 32 **quit you** acquaint yourself 35 **beget
opinion** create the impression 49 **bend** aim 51 **in
fine** finally 52 **loathly opposite** bitterly opposed 53
fell deadly 53 **motion** thrust (a term from fencing) 55
unprovided unprotected 55 **latched** wounded (lanced)
56 **best alarumed** wholly aroused

57 **Bold . . . right** confident in the rightness of my
cause 58 **gasted** struck aghast 61 **dispatch** i.e., he
will be killed 62 **arch** chief 66 **death** the same ellipti-
cal form that characterizes "dispatch," line 61 68 **pight**
determined; **curst** angry 69 **discover** expose 70 **un-
possessing** beggarly (landless) 71 **reposal** placing 73
faithed believed 75 **character** handwriting 76 **suggestion** instigation 76 **practice** device 77 **make . . .
world** think everyone stupid 78 **not thought** did not
think 79 **pregnant** teeming with incitement 79 **potential spirits** powerful evil spirits 81 **fastened** hardened 82 **got** begot 82 s.d. **Tucket** Cornwall's special
trumpet call 84 **ports** exits, of whatever sort

Loyal and natural° boy, I'll work the means
To make thee capable.°

Enter CORNWALL, REGAN, *and* ATTENDANTS.

CORNWALL:
90 How now, my noble friend! Since I came hither,
Which I can call but now, I have heard strange
        news.
REGAN:
If it be true, all vengeance comes too short
Which can pursue th' offender. How dost, my
        lord?
GLOUCESTER:
O madam, my old heart is cracked, it's cracked.
REGAN:
95 What, did my father's godson seek your life?
He whom my father named, your Edgar?
GLOUCESTER:
O lady, lady, shame would have it hid.
REGAN:
Was he not companion with the riotous knights
That tended upon my father?
GLOUCESTER:
100 I know not, madam. 'Tis too bad, too bad.
EDMUND:
Yes, madam, he was of that consort.°
REGAN:
No marvel then, though he were ill affected.°
'Tis they have put° him on the old man's death,
To have th' expense and waste° of his revenues.
105 I have this present evening from my sister
Been well informed of them, and with such cautions
That, if they come to sojourn at my house,
I'll not be there.
        CORNWALL: Nor I, assure thee, Regan.
Edmund, I hear that you have shown your father
A childlike° office.
110   EDMUND: It was my duty, sir.
GLOUCESTER:
He did bewray his practice,° and received
This hurt you see, striving to apprehend him.
        CORNWALL:
Is he pursued?
        GLOUCESTER:
                Ay, my good lord.
        CORNWALL:
If he be taken, he shall never more

Be feared of doing° harm. Make your own purpose, 115
How in my strength you please.° For you, Edmund,
Whose virtue and obedience° doth this instant
So much commend itself, you shall be ours.
Natures of such deep trust we shall much need;
You we first seize on.
        EDMUND: I shall serve you, sir, 120
Truly, however else.
        GLOUCESTER: For him I thank your grace.
CORNWALL:
You know not why we came to visit you?
        REGAN:
Thus out of season, threading dark-eyed night.
Occasions, noble Gloucester, of some prize,°
Wherein we must have use of your advice.   125
Our father he hath writ, so hath our sister,
Of differences,° which° I best thought it fit
To answer from° our home. The several messengers
From hence attend dispatch.° Our good old friend,
Lay comforts to your bosom,° and bestow   130
Your needful° counsel to our businesses,
Which craves the instant use.°
        GLOUCESTER: I serve you, madam.
Your graces are right welcome.
                        Exeunt. Flourish.

SCENE II. [*Before* GLOUCESTER's *castle.*]

Enter KENT *and* OSWALD, *severally.*

OSWALD: Good dawning° to thee, friend. Art of
this house?°
KENT: Ay.
OSWALD: Where may we set our horses?
KENT: I' th' mire.   5
OSWALD: Prithee, if thou lov'st me, tell me.
KENT: I love thee not.
OSWALD: Why then, I care not for thee.
KENT: If I had thee in Lipsbury Pinfold,° I would
make thee care for me.   10

---

115 **of doing** because he might do   115–116 **Make . . .
please** Use my power freely, in carrying out your plans
for his capture   117 **virtue and obedience** virtuous
obedience   124 **prize** importance   127 **differences**
quarrels   127 **which** referring not to "differences," but
to the letter Lear has written   128 **from** away from
129 **attend dispatch** are waiting to be sent off
130 **Lay . . . bosom** console yourself (about Edgar's
supposed treason)   131 **needful** needed   132 **craves . . .
use** demands immediate transaction
II.II.1 **dawning** dawn is impending, but not yet arrived   1–2 **Art . . . house** Do you live here?   9
Lipsbury Pinfold a pound or pen in which strayed
animals are enclosed ("Lipsbury" may denote a particular place, or may be slang for "between my teeth")

---

88 **natural** (1) kind (filial) (2) illegitimate   89 **capable**
able to inherit   101 **consort** company   102 **ill affected**
disposed to evil   103 **put** set   104 **expense and waste**
squandering   110 **childlike** filial   111 **bewray his practice** disclose his plot

OSWALD: Why dost thou use me thus? I know thee not.

KENT: Fellow, I know thee.

OSWALD: What dost thou know me for?

15 KENT: A knave, a rascal, an eater of broken meats;° a base, proud, shallow, beggarly, three-suited,° hundred-pound,° filthy worsted-stocking° knave; a lily-livered, action-taking,° whoreson, glass-gazing,° superserviceable,° finical° rogue; 20 one-trunk-inheriting° slave; one that wouldst be a bawd in way of good service,° and art nothing but the composition° of a knave, beggar, coward, pander, and the son and heir of a mongrel bitch; one whom I will beat into clamorous whining if 25 thou deniest the least syllable of thy addition.°

OSWALD: Why, what a monstrous fellow art thou, thus to rail on one that is neither known of thee nor knows thee!

KENT: What a brazen-faced varlet art thou to 30 deny thou knowest me! Is it two days since I tripped up thy heels and beat thee before the king? [Drawing his sword.] Draw, you rogue, for though it be night, yet the moon shines. I'll make a sop o' th' moonshine° of you. You whoreson cullionly 35 barbermonger,° draw!

OSWALD: Away, I have nothing to do with thee.

KENT: Draw, you rascal. You come with letters against the king, and take Vanity the puppet's° part against the royalty of her father. Draw, you rogue, 40 or I'll so carbonado° your shanks. Draw, you rascal. Come your ways!°

OSWALD: Help, ho! Murder! Help!

KENT: Strike, you slave! Stand, rogue! Stand, you neat° slave! Strike!

[Beating him.]

OSWALD: Help, ho! Murder, murder!   45

Enter EDMUND, with his rapier drawn, CORN-WALL, REGAN, GLOUCESTER, SERVANTS.

EDMUND: How now? What's the matter? Part!

KENT: With you,° goodman boy,° if you please! Come, I'll flesh° ye, come on, young master.

GLOUCESTER: Weapons? Arms? What's the matter here?   50

CORNWALL: Keep peace, upon your lives. He dies that strikes again. What is the matter?

REGAN: The messengers from our sister and the king.

CORNWALL: What is your difference?° Speak.   55

OSWALD: I am scarce in breath, my lord.

KENT: No marvel, you have so bestirred° your valor. You cowardly rascal, nature disclaims in thee.° A tailor made thee.°

CORNWALL: Thou art a strange fellow. A tailor   60 make a man?

KENT: A tailor, sir. A stonecutter or a painter could not have made him so ill, though they had been but two years o' th' trade.

CORNWALL: Speak yet, how grew your quarrel?   65

OSWALD: This ancient ruffian, sir, whose life I have spared at suit of° his gray beard—

KENT: Thou whoreson zed,° thou unnecessary letter! My lord, if you will give me leave, I will tread this unbolted° villain into mortar and daub   70 the wall of a jakes° with him. Spare my gray beard, you wagtail!°

CORNWALL: Peace, sirrah! You beastly° knave, know you no reverence?

KENT: Yes, sir, but anger hath a privilege.   75

15–16 **broken meats** scraps of food   16–17 **three-suited** the wardrobe permitted to a servant or "knave"   17 **hundred-pound** the extent of Oswald's wealth, and thus a sneer at his aspiring to gentility   17 **worsted-stocking** worn by servants   18 **action-taking** one who refuses a fight and goes to law instead   19 **glass-gazing** conceited   19 **superserviceable** sycophantic, serving without principle   19 **finical** overfastidious   20 **one-trunk-inheriting** possessing only a trunkful of goods   21 **bawd . . . service** pimp, to please his master   22 **composition** compound   25 **addition** titles   33–34 **sop . . . moon-shine** i.e., Oswald will admit the moonlight, and so sop it up, through the open wounds Kent is preparing to give him   34–35 **cullionly barber-monger** base patron of hairdressers (effeminate man)   38 **Vanity the puppet's** Goneril, here identified with one of the personified characters in the morality plays, which were sometimes put on as puppet shows   40 **carbonado** cut across, like a piece of meat before cooking   41 **Come your ways** Get along!

44 **neat** (1) foppish (2) unmixed, as in "neat wine"   47 **With you** i.e., the quarrel is with you; **goodman boy** young man (peasants are "goodmen"; "boy" is a term of contempt)   48 **flesh** introduce to blood (term from hunting)   55 **difference** quarrel   57 **bestirred** exercised   58–59 **nature . . . thee** nature renounces any part in you   59 **A tailor made thee** from the proverb "The tailor makes the man"   67 **at suit of** out of pity for   68 **zed** the letter Z, generally omitted in contemporary dictionaries   70 **unbolted** unsifted, i.e., altogether a villain   71 **jakes** privy   72 **wagtail** a bird that bobs its tail up and down, and thus suggests obsequiousness   74 **beastly** irrational

CORNWALL:
Why art thou angry?
KENT:
That such a slave as this should wear a sword,
Who wears no honesty. Such smiling rogues as
  these,
Like rats, oft bite the holy cords° atwain
Which are too intrince° t' unloose; smooth° every
80   passion
That in the natures of their lords rebel,
Being oil to fire, snow to the colder moods;
Renege,° affirm, and turn their halcyon beaks°
With every gale and vary° of their masters,
85 Knowing naught, like dogs, but following.
A plague upon your epileptic° visage!
Smile you° my speeches, as I were a fool?
Goose, if I had you upon Sarum Plain,°
I'd drive ye cackling home to Camelot.°
CORNWALL:
90 What, art thou mad, old fellow?
GLOUCESTER:
How fell you out? Say that.
KENT:
No contraries° hold more antipathy
Than I and such a knave.
CORNWALL:
Why dost thou call him knave? What is his fault?
KENT:
95 His countenance likes° me not.
CORNWALL:
No more perchance does mine, nor his, nor hers.
KENT:
Sir, 'tis my occupation to be plain:
I have seen better faces in my time
Than stands on any shoulder that I see
Before me at this instant.
100   CORNWALL: This is some fellow
Who, having been praised for bluntness, doth
  affect
A saucy roughness, and constrains the garb

Quite from his nature.° He cannot flatter, he;
An honest mind and plain, he must speak truth.
And° they will take it, so; if not, he's plain.   105
These kind of knaves I know, which in this plainness
Harbor more craft and more corrupter ends
Than twenty silly-ducking observants°
That stretch their duties nicely.°
KENT:
Sir, in good faith, in sincere verity,   110
Under th' allowance° of your great aspect,°
Whose influence,° like the wreath of radiant fire
On flick'ring Phoebus' front°—
CORNWALL: What mean'st by this?
KENT: To go out of my dialect,° which you
discommend so much. I know, sir, I am no   115
flatterer. He° that beguiled you in a plain accent
was a plain knave, which, for my part, I will not
be, though I should win your displeasure to entreat
me to't.°
CORNWALL:
What was th' offense you gave him?   120
OSWALD:
I never gave him any.
It pleased the king his master very late°
To strike at me, upon his misconstruction;°
When he, compact,° and flattering his displeasure,
Tripped me behind; being down, insulted, railed, 125
And put upon him such a deal of man°
That worthied him,° got praises of the king
For him attempting who was self-subdued;°
And, in the fleshment° of this dread exploit,
Drew on me here again.

103–104 **constrains . . . nature** forces the manner of
candid speech to be a cloak, not for candor but for
craft   105 **And** if   108 **silly-ducking observants** ridicu-
lously obsequious attendants   109 **nicely** punctiliously
111 **allowance** approval   111 **aspect** (1) appearance (2)
position of the heavenly bodies   112 **influence** astrological power   113 **Phoebus' front** forehead of the sun
114 **dialect** customary manner of speaking   116 **He**
i.e., the sort of candid-crafty man Cornwall has been
describing   118–119 **though . . . to't** even if I were to
succeed in bringing your graceless person ("displeasure"
personified, and in lieu of the expected form, "your
grace") to beg me to be a plain knave   122 **very late**
recently   123 **misconstruction** misunderstanding   124
compact in league with the king   126 **put . . . man**
pretended such manly behavior   127 **worthied him**
made him seem heroic   128 **For . . . self-subdued** for
attacking a man (Oswald) who offered no resistance
129 **fleshment** the bloodthirstiness excited by his first
success or "fleshing"

---

79 **holy cords** sacred bonds of affection (as between
husbands and wives, parents and children)   80 **intrince**
entangled, intricate   80 **smooth** appease   83 **Renege**
deny   83 **halcyon beaks** the halcyon or kingfisher serves
here as a type of the opportunist because, when hung up
by the tail or neck, it was supposed to turn with the wind,
like a weathervane   84 **gale and vary** varying gale (hendiadys)   86 **epileptic** distorted by grinning   87 **Smile
you** do you smile at   88 **Sarum Plain** Salisbury Plain
89 **Camelot** the residence of King Arthur (presumably a
particular point, now lost, is intended here)   92 **con-
traries** opposites   95 **likes** pleases

130   KENT: None of these rogues and cowards
But Ajax is their fool.°
       CORNWALL: Fetch forth the stocks!
You stubborn° ancient knave, you reverent°
     braggart,
We'll teach you.
       KENT: Sir, I am too old to learn.
Call not your stocks for me, I serve the king,
135 On whose employment I was sent to you.
You shall do small respect, show too bold malice
Against the grace and person° of my master,
Stocking his messenger.
       CORNWALL:
Fetch forth the stocks. As I have life and honor,
140 There shall he sit till noon.
       REGAN:
Till noon? Till night, my lord, and all night too.
       KENT:
Why, madam, if I were your father's dog,
You should not use me so.
       REGAN: Sir, being his knave, I will.
       CORNWALL:
This is a fellow of the selfsame color°
145 Our sister speaks of. Come, bring away° the stocks.

     Stocks brought out.

       GLOUCESTER:
Let me beseech your grace not to do so.
His fault is much, and the good king his master
Will check° him for't. Your purposed° low
     correction
Is such as basest and contemnèd'st° wretches
150 For pilf'rings and most common trespasses
Are punished with.
The king his master needs must take it ill
That he, so slightly valued in° his messenger,
Should have him thus restrained.
       CORNWALL: I'll answer° that.
       REGAN:
155 My sister may receive it much more worse,
To have her gentleman abused, assaulted,
For following her affairs. Put in his legs.

[KENT *is put in the stocks.*]

Come, my good lord, away!

                        [*Exeunt all but*
                  GLOUCESTER *and* KENT.]
       GLOUCESTER:
I am sorry for thee, friend. 'Tis the duke's pleasure,
Whose disposition° all the world well knows   160
Will not be rubbed° nor stopped. I'll entreat for
     thee.
       KENT:
Pray do not, sir. I have watched° and traveled
     hard.
Some time I shall sleep out, the rest I'll whistle.
A good man's fortune may grow out at heels.°
Give° you good morrow.   165
       GLOUCESTER:
The duke's to blame in this. 'Twill be ill taken.°
                                        Exit.
       KENT:
Good king, that must approve° the common saw,°
Thou out of heaven's benediction com'st
To the warm sun.°
Approach, thou beacon to this under globe,°   170
That by thy comfortable° beams I may
Peruse this letter. Nothing almost sees miracles
But misery.° I know 'tis from Cordelia,
Who hath most fortunately been informed
Of my obscurèd° course. And shall find time   175
Form this enormous state, seeking to give
Losses their remedies.° All weary and o'er-watched,
Take vantage,° heavy eyes, not to behold
This shameful lodging. Fortune, good night;
Smile once more, turn thy wheel.°   180

     Sleeps.

130–131 **None . . . fool** i.e., cowardly rogues like
Oswald always impose on fools like Cornwall (who is
likened to Ajax: [1] the braggart Greek-warrior [2] a jakes
or privy   132 **stubborn** rude   132 **reverent** old   137
grace and person i.e., Lear as sovereign and in his
personal character   144 **color** kind   145 **away** out   148
check correct   148 **purposed** intended   149 **contemnèd'st** most despised   153 **slightly valued in** little honored in the person of   154 **answer** answer for

160 **disposition** inclination   161 **rubbed** diverted (metaphor from the game of bowls)   162 **watched** gone
without sleep   164 **A . . . heels** Even a good man may
have bad fortune   165 **Give** God give   166 **taken** received   167 **approve** confirm   167 **saw** proverb   168–
169 **Thou . . . sun** i.e., Lear goes from better to worse,
from heaven's blessing or shelter to lack of shelter   170
beacon . . . globe i.e., the sun, whose rising Kent
anticipates   171 **comfortable** comforting   172–173
Nothing . . . misery i.e., True perception belongs only
to the wretched   175 **obscurèd** disguised   175–177
shall . . . remedies a possible reading: Cordelia, away
from this monstrous state of things, will find occasion to
right the wrongs we suffer   178 **vantage** advantage (of
sleep)   180 **turn thy wheel** i.e., so that Kent, who is at
the bottom, may climb upward

[SCENE III. A *wood*.]

Enter EDGAR.

EDGAR:
I heard myself proclaimed,
And by the happy° hollow of a tree
Escaped the hunt. No port is free, no place
That guard and most unusual vigilance
5　Does not attend my taking.° Whiles I may 'scape,
I will preserve myself; and am bethought°
To take the basest and most poorest shape
That ever penury, in contempt of man,
Brought near to beast;° my face I'll grime with
　　filth,
10　Blanket° my loins, elf° all my hairs in knots,
And with presented° nakedness outface°
The winds and persecutions of the sky.
The country gives me proof° and precedent
Of Bedlam° beggars, who, with roaring voices,
15　Strike° in their numbed and mortified° bare arms
Pins, wooden pricks,° nails, sprigs of rosemary;
And with this horrible object° from low° farms,
Poor pelting° villages, sheepcotes, and mills,
Sometimes with lunatic bans,° sometime with
　　prayers,
20　Enforce their charity. Poor Turlygod, Poor Tom,°
That's something yet: Edgar I nothing am.°
　　　　　　　　　　　　　　　　　　Exit.

[SCENE IV. *Before* GLOUCESTER's *castle*.
KENT *in the stocks*.]

Enter LEAR, FOOL, *and* GENTLEMAN.

LEAR:
'Tis strange that they should so depart from home,
And not send back my messenger.
　　GENTLEMAN:　　　　　　　As I learned,
The night before there was no purpose° in them
Of this remove.°

KENT:　　　　　　Hail to thee, noble master.
　　LEAR: Ha!　　　　　　　　　　　　　　5
Mak'st thou this shame thy pastime?°
　　KENT:　　　　　　　　　No, my lord.
　　FOOL: Ha, ha, he wears cruel° garters. Horses
are tied by the heads, dogs and bears by th' neck,
monkeys by th' loins, and men by th' legs. When a
man's overlusty at legs,° then he wears wooden　10
netherstocks.°
　　LEAR:
What's he that hath so much thy place mistook
To set thee here?
　　KENT:　　　　　It is both he and she,
Your son and daughter.
　　LEAR: No.　　　　　　　　　　　　　15
　　KENT: Yes.
　　LEAR: No, I say.
　　KENT: I say yea.
　　LEAR: No, no, they would not.
　　KENT: Yes, they have.　　　　　　　　20
　　LEAR:
By Jupiter, I swear no!
　　KENT:
By Juno, I swear ay!
　　LEAR:　　　　　　They durst not do't;
They could not, would not do't. 'Tis worse than
　　murder
To do upon respect° such violent outrage.
Resolve° me with all modest° haste which way　25
Thou mightst deserve or they impose this usage,
Coming from us.
　　KENT:　　　　　My lord, when at their home
I did commend° your highness' letters to them,
Ere I was risen from the place that showed
My duty kneeling, came there a reeking post,°　30
Stewed° in his haste, half breathless, panting forth
From Goneril his mistress salutations,
Delivered letters, spite of intermission,°
Which presently° they read; on° whose contents
They summoned up their meiny,° straight took
　　horse,　　　　　　　　　　　　　　　35
Commanded me to follow and attend

II.III.2 **happy** lucky　5 **attend my taking** watch to
capture me　6 **am bethought** have decided　8–9 **penury** . . . **beast** poverty, to show how contemptible man
is, reduced to the level of a beast　10 **Blanket** cover only
with a blanket　10 **elf** tangle (into "elflocks," supposed
to be caused by elves)　11 **presented** the show of　11
outface brave　13 **proof** example　14 **Bedlam** see
I.II.144–145　15 **Strike** stick　15 **mortified** not alive to
pain　16 **pricks** skewers　17 **object** spectacle　17 **low**
humble　18 **pelting** paltry　19 **bans** curses　20 **Poor**
. . . **Tom** Edgar recites the names a Bedlam beggar gives
himself　21 **That's** . . . **am** There's a chance for me in
that I am no longer known for myself
II.IV.3 **purpose** intention　4 **remove** removal

6 **Mak'st** . . . **pastime** Are you doing this to amuse
yourself?　7 **cruel** (1) painful (2) "crewel," a worsted
yarn used in garters　10 **overlusty at legs** (1) a vagabond
(2) sexually promiscuous (?)　11 **netherstocks** stockings
(as opposed to knee breeches, or upperstocks)　24 **upon
respect** (1) on the respect due to the king (2) deliberately　25 **Resolve** inform　25 **modest** becoming　28
commend deliver　30 **reeking post** sweating messenger　31 **stewed** steaming　33 **spite of intermission** in
spite of the interrupting of my business　34 **presently** at
once　34 **on** on the strength of　35 **meiny** retinue

The leisure of their answer, gave me cold looks,
And meeting here the other messenger,
Whose welcome I perceived had poisoned mine,
40 Being the very fellow which of late
Displayed° so saucily against your highness,
Having more man than wit° about me, drew;
He raised° the house, with loud and coward cries.
Your son and daughter found this trespass worth°
45 The shame which here it suffers.

    FOOL: Winter's not gone yet, if the wild geese fly
that way.°

      Fathers that wear rags
        Do make their children blind,°
50   But fathers that bear bags°
        Shall see their children kind.
      Fortune, that arrant whore,
        Ne'er turns the key° to th' poor.

But for all this, thou shalt have as many dolors° for
55 thy daughters as thou canst tell° in a year.

    LEAR:
O, how this mother swells up toward my heart!
Hysterica passio,° down, thou climbing sorrow,
Thy element's° below. Where is this daughter?

    KENT:
With the earl, sir, here within.

    LEAR: Follow me not;
60 Stay here.   *Exit.*

    GENTLEMAN:
Made you no more offense but what you speak of?

    KENT: None.
How chance° the king comes with so small a
number?

65   FOOL: And° thou hadst been set i' th' stocks for
that question, thou'dst well deserved it.

KENT: Why, Fool?

FOOL: We'll set thee to school to an ant, to teach
thee there's no laboring i' th' winter.° All that
follow their noses are led by their eyes but blind 70
men, and there's not a nose among twenty but can
smell him that's stinking.° Let go thy hold when a
great wheel runs down a hill, lest it break thy neck
with following. But the great one that goes upward, let him draw thee after. When a wise man 75
gives thee better counsel, give me mine again. I
would have none but knaves follow it since a fool
gives it.

    That sir, which serves and seeks for gain,
      And follows but for form,°   80
    Will pack,° when it begins to rain,
      And leave thee in the storm.
    But I will tarry; the Fool will stay,
      And let the wise man fly.
    The knave turns Fool that runs away,   85
    The Fool no knave,° perdy.°

KENT: Where learned you this, Fool?

FOOL: Not i' th' stocks, fool.

Enter LEAR *and* GLOUCESTER.

    LEAR:
Deny° to speak with me? They are sick, they are
    weary,
They have traveled all the night? Mere fetches,° 90
The images° of revolt and flying off!°
Fetch me a better answer.

    GLOUCESTER: My dear lord,
You know the fiery quality° of the duke,
How unremovable and fixed he is
In his own course.

    LEAR: Vengeance, plague, death, confusion! 95
Fiery? What quality? Why, Gloucester, Gloucester,
I'd speak with the Duke of Cornwall and his wife.

    GLOUCESTER:
Well, my good lord, I have informed them so.

    LEAR:
Informed them? Dost thou understand me, man?

    GLOUCESTER:
Ay, my good lord.   100

---

41 **Displayed** showed off 42 **more . . . wit** more
manhood than sense 43 **raised** aroused 44 **worth**
deserving 46–47 **Winter's . . . way** More trouble is to
come, since Cornwall and Regan act so ("geese" is used
contemptuously, as in Kent's quarrel with Oswald,
II.II.88–89) 49 **blind** i.e., indifferent 50 **bags** mon-
eybags 53 **turns the key** i.e., opens the door 54
dolors (1) sorrows (2) dollars (English name for Spanish
and German coins) 55 **tell** (1) about (2) count 56–57
mother . . . Hysterica passio hysteria, causing suffoca-
tion or choking 58 **element** proper place 63 **How
chance** how does it happen that 65 **And** if 68–69
We'll . . . winter in the popular fable the ant, unlike the
improvident grasshopper, anticipates the winter when
none can labor by laying up provisions in the summer;
Lear, trusting foolishly to summer days, finds himself
unprovided for, and unable to provide, now that "winter" has come

69–72 **All . . . stinking** i.e., all can smell out the decay
of Lear's fortunes 80 **form** show 81 **pack** be off 85–
86 **The . . . knave** i.e., the faithless man is the true fool,
for wisdom requires fidelity; Lear's Fool, who remains
faithful, is at least no knave 86 **perdy** by God (French
par Dieu) 89 **Deny** refuse 90 **fetches** subterfuges, acts
of tacking (nautical metaphor) 91 **images** exact like-
nesses 91 **flying off** desertion 93 **quality** temperament

LEAR:
The king would speak with Cornwall. The dear father
Would with his daughter speak, commands—tends°—service.
Are they informed of this? My breath and blood!
Fiery? The fiery duke, tell the hot duke that—
105 No, but not yet. May be he is not well.
Infirmity doth still neglect all office
Whereto our health is bound.° We are not ourselves
When nature, being oppressed, commands the mind
To suffer with the body. I'll forbear;
110 And am fallen out° with my more headier will°
To take the indisposed and sickly fit
For the sound man. [*Looking on* KENT.] Death on my state!° Wherefore
Should he sit here? This act persuades me
That this remotion° of the duke and her
115 Is practice° only. Give me my servant forth.°
Go tell the duke and's wife I'd speak with them!
Now, presently!° Bid them come forth and hear me,
Or at their chamber door I'll beat the drum
Till it cry sleep to death.°
GLOUCESTER:
120 I would have all well betwixt you.   *Exit.*
LEAR:
O me, my heart, my rising heart! But down!
    FOOL: Cry to it, nuncle, as the cockney° did to the eels when she put 'em i' th' paste° alive. She knapped° 'em o' th' coxcombs° with a stick and
125 cried, "Down, wantons,° down!" 'Twas her brother that, in pure kindness to his horse, buttered his hay.°

Enter CORNWALL, REGAN, GLOUCESTER, SERVANTS.

102 **tends** attends (i.e., awaits); with, possibly, an ironic second meaning, "tenders," or "offers"   107 **Whereto . . . bound** duties which we are required to perform, when in health   110 **fallen out** angry   110 **headier will** headlong inclination   112 **state** royal condition   114 **remotion** (1) removal (2) remaining aloof   115 **practice** pretense   115 **forth** i.e., out of the stocks   117 **presently** at once   119 **cry . . . death** follow sleep, like a cry or pack of hounds, until it kills it   122 **cockney** Londoner (ignorant city dweller)   123 **paste** pastry pie   124 **knapped** rapped   124 **coxcombs** heads   125 **wantons** i.e., playful things (with a sexual implication)   126–127 **buttered his hay** i.e., the city dweller does from ignorance what the dishonest ostler does from craft: greases the hay the traveler has paid for, so that the horse will not eat

LEAR:
Good morrow to you both.
    CORNWALL: Hail to your grace.

KENT *here set at liberty*.

REGAN:
I am glad to see your highness.
LEAR:
Regan, I think you are. I know what reason   130
I have to think so. If thou shouldst not be glad,
I would divorce me from thy mother's tomb,
Sepulchring an adultress.° [*To* KENT.] O, are you free?
Some other time for that. Beloved Regan,
Thy sister's naught.° O Regan, she hath tied   135
Sharp-toothed unkindness, like a vulture, here.

[*Points to his heart.*]

I can scarce speak to thee. Thou'lt not believe
With how depraved a quality°—O Regan!
REGAN:
I pray you, sir, take patience, I have hope
You less know how to value her desert   140
Than she to scant her duty.°
    LEAR: Say? how is that?
REGAN:
I cannot think my sister in the least
Would fail her obligation. If, sir, perchance
She have restrained the riots of your followers,
'Tis on such ground, and to such wholesome end,   145
As clears her from all blame.
LEAR:
My curses on her!
    REGAN: O, sir, you are old,
Nature in you stands on the very verge
Of his confine.° You should be ruled, and led
By some discretion that discerns your state   150
Better than you yourself.° Therefore I pray you
That to our sister you do make return,
Say you have wronged her.
    LEAR: Ask her forgiveness?
Do you but mark how this becomes the house:°
"Dear daughter, I confess that I am old.   155

132–133 **divorce . . . adultress** i.e., repudiate your dead mother as having conceived you by another man   135 **naught** wicked   138 **quality** nature   139–141 **I have . . . duty** despite the double negative, the passage means, "I believe that you fail to give Goneril her due, rather than that she fails to fulfill her duty"   148–149 **Nature . . . confine** i.e., you are nearing the end of your life   150–151 **some . . . yourself** some discreet person who understands your condition more than you do   154 **becomes the house** suits my royal and paternal position

[*Kneeling.*]

Age is unnecessary. On my knees I beg
That you'll vouchsafe me raiment, bed, and
    food."
REGAN:
Good sir, no more. These are unsightly tricks.
Return you to my sister.
    LEAR [*rising*]:   Never, Regan.
160 She hath abated° me of half my train,
Looked black upon me, struck me with her
    tongue,
Most serpentlike, upon the very heart.
All the stored vengeances of heaven fall
On her ingrateful top!° Strike her young bones,°
You taking° airs, with lameness.
165   CORNWALL: Fie, sir, fie!
    LEAR:
You nimble lightnings, dart your blinding flames
Into her scornful eyes! Infect her beauty,
You fen-sucked° fogs, drawn by the pow'rful sun,
To fall and blister° her pride.
    REGAN: O the blest gods!
170 So will you wish on me when the rash mood is on.
    LEAR:
No, Regan, thou shalt never have my curse.
Thy tender-hefted° nature shall not give
Thee o'er to harshness. Her eyes are fierce, but
    thine
Do comfort, and not burn. 'Tis not in thee
175 To grudge my pleasures, to cut off my train,
To bandy° hasty words, to scant my sizes,°
And, in conclusion, to oppose the bolt°
Against my coming in. Thou better know'st
The offices of nature, bond of childhood,°
180 Effects° of courtesy, dues of gratitude.
Thy half o' th' kingdom hast thou not forgot,
Wherein I thee endowed.
    REGAN: Good sir, to th' purpose°

Tucket within.

    LEAR:
Who put my man i' th' stocks?
    CORNWALL: What trumpet's that?

REGAN:
I know't—my sister's. This approves° her letter,
That she would soon be here.

Enter OSWALD.

                Is your lady come?   185
    LEAR:
This is a slave, whose easy borrowed° pride
Dwells in the fickle grace° of her he follows.
Out, varlet,° from my sight.
    CORNWALL: What means your grace?
    LEAR:
Who stocked my servant? Regan, I have good hope
Thou didst not know on't.

Enter GONERIL.

                Who comes here? O heavens!   190
If you do love old men, if your sweet sway
Allow° obedience, if you yourselves are old,
Make it° your cause. Send down, and take my
    part.

[*To* GONERIL.]

Art not ashamed to look upon this beard?
O Regan, will you take her by the hand?   195
    GONERIL:
Why not by th' hand, sir? How have I offended?
All's not offense that indiscretion finds°
And dotage terms so.
    LEAR: O sides,° you are too tough!
Will you yet hold? How came my man i' th'
    stocks?
    CORNWALL:
I set him there, sir; but his own disorders°   200
Deserved much less advancement.°
    LEAR: You? Did you?
    REGAN:
I pray you, father, being weak, seem so.°
If till the expiration of your month
You will return and sojourn with my sister,
Dismissing half your train, come then to me.   205
I am now from home, and out of that provision
Which shall be needful for your entertainment.°
    LEAR:
Return to her, and fifty men dismissed?

160 **abated** curtailed   164 **top** head   164 **young bones**
the reference may be to unborn children, rather than to
Goneril herself   165 **taking** infecting   168 **fen-sucked**
drawn up from swamps by the sun   169 **fall and blister**
fall upon and raise blisters   172 **tender-hefted** gently
framed   176 **bandy** volley (metaphor from tennis)   176
scant my sizes reduce my allowances   177 **oppose the
bolt** bar the door   179 **offices . . . childhood** natural
duties, a child's duty to its parent   180 **Effects** manifestations   182 **to th' purpose** come to the point

184 **approves** confirms   186 **easy borrowed** (1) facile
and taken from another (2) acquired without anything to
back it up (like money borrowed without security)   187
grace favor   188 **varlet** base fellow   192 **Allow** approve
of   193 **it** my cause   197 **finds** judges   198 **sides**
breast   200 **disorders** misconduct   201 **advancement**
promotion   202 **seem so** act weak   207 **entertainment**
maintenance

No, rather I abjure all roofs, and choose
210 To wage° against the enmity o' th' air,
To be a comrade with the wolf and owl,
Necessity's sharp pinch.° Return with her?
Why, the hot-blooded° France, that dowerless took
Our youngest born, I could as well be brought
215 To knee° his throne, and, squirelike,° pension beg
To keep base life afoot. Return with her?
Persuade me rather to be slave and sumpter°
To this detested groom. [*Pointing at* OSWALD.]
    GONERIL: At your choice, sir.
    LEAR:
I prithee, daughter, do not make me mad.
220 I will not trouble thee, my child; farewell.
We'll no more meet, no more see one another.
But yet thou art my flesh, my blood, my daughter,
Or rather a disease that's in my flesh,
Which I must needs call mine. Thou art a boil,
225 A plague-sore, or embossèd carbuncle°
In my corrupted blood. But I'll not chide thee.
Let shame come when it will, I do not call it.
I do not bid the Thunder-bearer° shoot,
Nor tell tales of thee to high-judging° Jove.
230 Mend when thou canst, be better at thy leisure,
I can be patient, I can stay with Regan,
I and my hundred knights.
    REGAN: Not altogether so.
I looked not for you yet, nor am provided
For your fit welcome. Give ear, sir, to my sister,
235 For those that mingle reason with your passion°
Must be content to think you old, and so—
But she knows what she does.
    LEAR: Is this well spoken?
    REGAN:
I dare avouch° it, sir. What, fifty followers?
Is it not well? What should you need of more?
Yea, or so many, sith that° both charge° and
240   danger
Speak 'gainst so great a number? How in one house
Should many people, under two commands,
Hold° amity? 'Tis hard, almost impossible.

    GONERIL:
Why might not you, my lord, receive attendance
From those that she calls servants, or from mine?   245
    REGAN:
Why not, my lord? If then they chanced to slack°
    ye,
We could control them. If you will come to me
(For now I spy a danger), I entreat you
To bring but five-and-twenty. To no more
Will I give place or notice.°   250
    LEAR:
I gave you all.
    REGAN: And in good time you gave it.
    LEAR:
Made you my guardians, my depositaries,°
But kept a reservation° to be followed
With such a number. What, must I come to you
With five-and-twenty? Regan, said you so?   255
    REGAN:
And speak't again, my lord. No more with me.
    LEAR:
Those wicked creatures yet do look well-favored°
When others are more wicked; not being the worst
Stands in some rank of praise.° [*To* GONERIL.] I'll
    go with thee.
Thy fifty yet doth double five-and-twenty,   260
And thou art twice her love.°
    GONERIL: Hear me, my lord.
What need you five-and-twenty? ten? or five?
To follow° in a house where twice so many
Have a command to tend you?
    REGAN: What need one?
    LEAR:
O reason° not the need! Our basest beggars   265
Are in the poorest thing superfluous.°
Allow not nature more than nature needs,°
Man's life is cheap as beast's. Thou art a lady:
If only to go warm were gorgeous,
Why, nature needs not what thou gorgeous wear'st,   270
Which scarcely keeps thee warm.° But, for true
    need—

---

210 **wage** fight   212 **Necessity's sharp pinch** a summing up of the hard choice he has just announced   213 **hot-blooded** passionate   215 **knee** kneel before; **squirelike** like a retainer   217 **sumpter** pack horse   225 **embossèd carbuncle** swollen boil   228 **Thunder-bearer** Jupiter   229 **high-judging** (1) supreme (2) judging from heaven   235 **mingle . . . passion** i.e, consider your turbulent behavior coolly and reasonably   238 **avouch** swear by   240 **sith that** since   240 **charge** expense   243 **Hold** preserve

246 **slack** neglect   250 **notice** recognition   252 **depositaries** trustees   253 **reservation** condition   257 **well-favored** handsome   258–259 **not . . . praise** i.e., that Goneril is not so bad as Regan is one thing in her favor   261 **her love** i.e., as loving as she   263 **follow** attend on you   265 **reason** scrutinize   266 **Are . . . superfluous** have some trifle not absolutely necessary   267 **needs** i.e., to sustain life   269–271 **If . . . warm** If to satisfy the need for warmth were to be gorgeous, you would not need the clothing you wear, which is worn more for beauty than warmth

You heavens, give me that patience, patience I
    need.
You see me here, you gods, a poor old man,
As full of grief as age, wretched in both.
275 If it be you that stirs these daughters' hearts
Against their father, fool° me not so much
To bear° it tamely; touch me with noble anger,
And let not women's weapons, water drops,
Stain my man's cheeks. No, you unnatural hags!
280 I will have such revenges on you both
That all the world shall—I will do such things—
What they are, yet I know not; but they shall be
The terrors of the earth. You think I'll weep.
No, I'll not weep.

    Storm and tempest.

285 I have full cause of weeping, but this heart
Shall break into a hundred thousand flaws°
Or ere° I'll weep. O Fool, I shall go mad!
                Exeunt LEAR, GLOUCESTER,
                      KENT, *and* FOOL.
  CORNWALL:
Let us withdraw, 'twill be a storm.
  REGAN:
This house is little; the old man and's people
290 Cannot be well bestowed.°
  GONERIL:
'Tis his own blame; hath° put himself from rest°
And must needs taste his folly.
  REGAN:
For his particular,° I'll receive him gladly,
But not one follower.
  GONERIL: So am I purposed.°
295 Where is my Lord of Gloucester?
  CORNWALL:
Followed the old man forth.

    Enter GLOUCESTER.

                He is returned.
  GLOUCESTER:
The king is in high rage.
  CORNWALL: Whither is he going?
  GLOUCESTER:
He calls to horse, but will I know not whither.

  CORNWALL:
'Tis best to give him way, he leads himself.°
  GONERIL:
My lord, entreat him by no means to stay.   300
  GLOUCESTER:
Alack, the night comes on, and the high winds
Do sorely ruffle.° For many miles about
There's scarce a bush.
  REGAN: O, sir, to willful men
The injuries that they themselves procure
Must be their schoolmasters. Shut up your doors. 305
He is attended with a desperate train,
And what they may incense° him to, being apt
To have his ear abused,° wisdom bids fear.
  CORNWALL:
Shut up your doors, my lord; 'tis a wild night.
My Regan counsels well. Come out o' th' storm. 310
                            Exeunt.

ACT III

SCENE I. [*A heath.*]

Storm still.° Enter KENT *and a* GENTLEMAN
severally.

  KENT:
Who's there besides foul weather?
  GENTLEMAN:
One minded like the weather most unquietly.°
  KENT:
I know you. Where's the king?
  GENTLEMAN:
Contending with the fretful elements;
Bids the wind blow the earth into the sea,   5
Or swell the curlèd waters 'bove the main,°
That things might change° or cease; tears his white
    hair,
Which the impetuous blasts, with eyeless° rage,
Catch in their fury, and make nothing of;
Strives in his little world of man° to outscorn 10

---

299 **give . . . himself** let him go; he insists on his own
way 302 **ruffle** rage 307 **incense** incite 307–308
being . . . abused he being inclined to harken to bad
counsel
III.i.s.d. **still** continually 2 **minded . . . unquietly**
disturbed in mind, like the weather 6 **main** land 7
change (1) be destroyed (2) be exchanged (i.e., turned
upside down) (3) change for the better 8 **eyeless** (1)
blind (2) invisible 10 **little . . . man** the microcosm, as
opposed to the universe or macrocosm, which it copies
in little

276 **fool** humiliate 277 **To bear** as to make me bear
286 **flaws** (1) pieces (2) cracks (3) gusts of passion 287
Or ere before 290 **bestowed** lodged 291 **hath** he
hath; **rest** (1) place of residence (2) repose of mind
293 **his particular** himself personally 294 **purposed**
determined

The to-and-fro conflicting wind and rain.
This night, wherein the cub-drawn° bear would
   couch,°
The lion, and the belly-pinchèd° wolf
Keep their fur dry, unbonneted° he runs,
And bids what will take all.°
15   KENT: But who is with him?
    GENTLEMAN:
None but the Fool, who labors to outjest
His heart-struck injuries.
    KENT: Sir, I do know you,
And dare upon the warrant of my note°
Commend a dear thing° to you. There is division,
20 Although as yet the face of it is covered
With mutual cunning, 'twixt Albany and Cornwall;
Who have—as who have not, that° their great stars
Throned° and set high?—servants, who seem no
   less,°
Which are to France the spies and speculations
25 Intelligent° of our state. What hath been seen,
Either in snuffs and packings° of the dukes,
Or the hard rein which both of them hath borne°
Against the old king, or something deeper,
Whereof, perchance, these are but furnishings°—
30 But, true it is, from France there comes a power°
Into this scattered° kingdom, who already,
Wise in our negligence, have secret feet
In some of our best ports, and are at point°
To show their open banner. Now to you:
35 If on my credit you dare build° so far
To° make your speed to Dover, you shall find
Some that will thank you, making° just° report
Of how unnatural and bemadding° sorrow
The king hath cause to plain.°
40 I am a gentleman of blood and breeding,°

And from some knowledge and assurance° offer
This office° to you.
    GENTLEMAN:
I will talk further with you.
    KENT: No, do not.
For confirmation that I am much more
Than my out-wall,° open this purse and take   45
What it contains. If you shall see Cordelia,
As fear not but you shall, show her this ring,
And she will tell you who that fellow° is
That yet you do not know. Fie on this storm!
I will go seek the king.   50
    GENTLEMAN:
Give me your hand. Have you no more to say?
    KENT:
Few words, but, to effect,° more than all yet:
That when we have found the king—in which
   your pain°
That way, I'll this—he that first lights on him,
Holla the other.   Exeunt [severally].   55

SCENE II. [*Another part of the heath.*]

Storm still. Enter LEAR *and* FOOL.

    LEAR:
Blow, winds, and crack your cheeks. Rage, blow!
You cataracts and hurricanes,° spout
Till you have drenched our steeples, drowned the
   cocks.°
You sulph'rous and thought-executing° fires,
Vaunt-couriers° of oak-cleaving thunderbolts,   5
Singe my white head. And thou, all-shaking
   thunder,
Strike flat the thick rotundity° o' th' world,
Crack Nature's molds,° all germains spill° at once,
That makes ingrateful° man.
    FOOL: O nuncle, court holy-water° in a dry   10
house is better than this rain water out o' door.

12 **cub-drawn** sucked dry by her cubs, and so ravenously hungry 12 **couch** take shelter in its lair 13 **belly-pinchèd** starved 14 **unbonneted** hatless 15 **take all** like the reckless gambler, staking all he has left 18 **warrant . . . note** strength of what I have taken note (of you) 19 **Commend . . . thing** entrust important business 22 **that** whom 22–23 **stars Throned** destinies have throned 23 **seem no less** seem to be so 24–25 **speculations Intelligent** giving intelligence 26 **snuffs and packings** quarrels and plots 27 **hard . . . borne** close and cruel control they have exercised 29 **furnishings** excuses 30 **power** army 31 **scattered** disunited 33 **at point** ready 35 **If . . . build** if you can trust me, proceed 36 **To** as to 37 **making** for making 37 **just** accurate 38 **bemadding** maddening 39 **plain** complain of 40 **blood and breeding** noble family

41 **knowledge and assurance** sure and trustworthy information 42 **office** service (i.e., the trip to Dover) 45 **out-wall** superficial appearance 48 **fellow** companion 52 **to effect** in their importance 53 **pain** labor III.II.2 **hurricanoes** waterspouts 3 **cocks** weathercocks 4 **thought-executing** (1) doing execution as quick as thought (2) executing or carrying out the thought of him who hurls the lightning 5 **Vaunt-couriers** heralds, scouts who range before the main body of the army 7 **rotundity** i.e., not only the sphere of the globe, but the roundness of gestation (Delius) 8 **Nature's molds** the molds or forms in which men are made 8 **all germains spill** destroy the basic seeds of life 9 **ingrateful** ungrateful 10 **court holy-water** flattery

Good nuncle, in; ask thy daughters' blessing.
Here's a night pities neither wise men nor fools.

LEAR:
Rumble thy bellyful. Spit, fire. Spout, rain!
15 Nor rain, wind, thunder, fire are my daughters.
I tax° not you, you elements, with unkindness.
I never gave you kingdom, called you children,
You owe me no subscription.° Then let fall
Your horrible pleasure.° Here I stand your slave,
20 A poor, infirm, weak, and despised old man.
But yet I call you servile ministers,°
That will with two pernicious daughters join
Your high-engendered battles° 'gainst a head
So old and white as this. O, ho! 'tis foul.

25 FOOL: He that has a house to put's head in has a
good headpiece.°

       The codpiece° that will house
          Before the head has any,
       The head and he° shall louse:
30   So beggars marry many.°
       The man that makes his toe
          What he his heart should make
       Shall of a corn cry woe,
          And turn his sleep to wake.°

35 For there was never yet fair woman but she made
mouths in a glass.°

Enter KENT.

LEAR:
No, I will be the pattern of all patience,
I will say nothing.

KENT: Who's there?

40 FOOL: Marry,° here's grace and a codpiece;
that's a wise man and a fool.°

16 **tax** accuse   18 **subscription** allegiance, submission   19 **pleasure** will   21 **ministers** agents   23 **high-
engendered battles** armies formed in the heavens   26
headpiece (1) helmet (2) brain   27 **codpiece** penis
(literally, padding worn at the crotch of a man's hose)
29 **he** it   30 **many** i.e., lice   29–30 **The . . . many** The
man who gratifies his sexual appetites before he has a
roof over his head will end up a lousy beggar   31–34
The . . . wake The man who, ignoring the fit order of
things, elevates what is base above what is noble, will
suffer for it as Lear has, in banishing Cordelia and
enriching her sisters   35–36 **made . . . glass** posed
before a mirror (irrelevant nonsense, except that it calls
to mind the general theme of vanity and folly)   40
Marry a mild oath, from "By the Virgin Mary"   40–41
here's . . . fool Kent's question is unanswered: the king
("grace") is here, and the Fool—who customarily wears
an exaggerated codpiece; but which is which is left ambiguous, since Lear has previously been called a codpiece

KENT:
Alas, sir, are you here? Things that love night
Love not such nights as these. The wrathful skies
Gallow° the very wanderers of the dark
And make them keep° their caves. Since I was
man,   45
Such sheets of fire, such bursts of horrid° thunder,
Such groans of roaring wind and rain, I never
Remember to have heard. Man's nature cannot
carry°
Th' affliction nor the fear.

LEAR: Let the great gods
That keep this dreadful pudder° o'er our heads   50
Find out their enemies now.° Tremble, thou
wretch,
That hast within thee undivulgèd crimes
Unwhipped of justice. Hide thee, thou bloody
hand,
Thou perjured,° and thou simular° of virtue
That art incestuous. Caitiff,° to pieces shake,   55
That under covert and convenient seeming°
Has practiced on° man's life. Close° pent-up guilts,
Rive° your concealing continents° and cry
These dreadful summoners grace.° I am a man
More sinned against than sinning.

KENT: Alack, bareheaded?   60
Gracious my lord,° hard by here is a hovel;
Some friendship will it lend you 'gainst the tempest.
Repose you there, while I to this hard house
(More harder than the stones whereof 'tis raised,
Which even but now, demanding after° you,   65
Denied me to come in) return, and force
Their scanted° courtesy.

LEAR: My wits begin to turn.
Come on, my boy. How dost, my boy? Art cold?
I am cold myself. Where is this straw, my fellow?
The art° of our necessities is strange,   70
That can make vile things precious. Come, your
hovel.

44 **Gallow** frighten   45 **keep** remain inside   46 **horrid**
horrible   48 **carry** endure   50 **pudder** turmoil   51
Find . . . now i.e., discover sinners by the terror they
reveal   54 **perjured** perjurer   54 **simular** counter-
feiter   55 **Caitiff** wretch   56 **seeming** hypocrisy   57
practiced on plotted against   57 **Close** hidden   58 **Rive**
split open   58 **continents** containers   58–59 **cry . . .
grace** beg mercy from the vengeful gods (here figured as
officers who summoned a man charged with immorality
before the ecclesiastical court)   61 **Gracious my lord**
my gracious lord   65 **demanding after** asking for   67
scanted stinted   70 **art** magic powers of the alchemists,
who sought to transmute base metals into precious

Poor Fool and knave, I have one part in my heart
That's sorry yet for thee.

FOOL [*Singing.*]

He that has and a little tiny wit,
    With heigh-ho, the wind and the rain,
Must make content with his fortunes fit,°
    Though the rain it raineth every day.

LEAR: True, my good boy. Come, bring us to
this hovel.   *Exit, [with* KENT].
FOOL: This is a brave° night to cool a courtesan.
I'll speak a prophecy ere I go:

When priests are more in word than matter;
When brewers mar their malt with water;
When nobles are their tailors' tutors,
No heretics burned, but wenches' suitors;°
When every case in law is right,
No squire in debt nor no poor knight;
When slanders do not live in tongues;
Nor cutpurses come not to throngs;
When usurers tell their gold i' th' field,°
And bawds and whores do churches build,°
Then shall the realm of Albion°
Come to great confusion.
Then comes the time, who lives to see't,
That going shall be used with feet.°

This prophecy Merlin° shall make, for I live before
his time.   *Exit.*

SCENE III. [GLOUCESTER'*s castle.*]

Enter GLOUCESTER *and* EDMUND.

GLOUCESTER: Alack, alack, Edmund, I like not
this unnatural dealing. When I desired their leave
that I might pity° him, they took from me the use
of mine own house, charged me on pain of

perpetual displeasure neither to speak of him,   5
entreat for him, or any way sustain° him.
EDMUND: Most savage and unnatural.
GLOUCESTER: Go to; say you nothing. There is
division° between the dukes, and a worse° matter
than that. I have received a letter this night—'tis   10
dangerous to be spoken°—I have locked the letter
in my closet.° These injuries the king now bears
will be revenged home;° there is part of a power°
already footed;° we must incline to° the king. I will
look° him and privily° relieve him. Go you and   15
maintain talk with the duke, that my charity be not
of° him perceived. If he ask for me, I am ill and
gone to bed. If I die for it, as no less is threatened
me, the king my old master must be relieved.
There is strange things toward,° Edmund; pray you   20
be careful.   *Exit.*
EDMUND:
This courtesy forbid° thee shall the duke
Instantly know, and of that letter too.
This seems a fair deserving,° and must draw me
That which my father loses—no less than all.   25
The younger rises when the old doth fall.
                                            Exit.

SCENE IV. [*The heath, Before a hovel.*]

Enter LEAR, KENT, *and* FOOL.

KENT:
Here is the place, my lord. Good my lord, enter.
The tyranny of the open night's too rough
For nature to endure.

Storm still.

LEAR: Let me alone.
KENT:
Good my lord, enter here.
LEAR: Wilt break my heart?°
KENT:
I had rather break mine own. Good my lord,
    enter.   5
LEAR:
Thou think'st 'tis much that this contentious storm

76 **Must . . . fit** must be satisfied with a fortune as tiny as
his wit   80 **brave** fine   84–85 **When . . . suitors** the
first four prophecies are fulfilled already, and hence
"confusion" has come to England: the priest does not
suit his action to his words; the brewer adulterates his
beer; the nobleman is subservient to his tailor (i.e., cares
only for fashion); religious heretics escape, and only
those burn (i.e., suffer) who are afflicted with venereal
disease   90 **tell . . . field** count their money in the
open   86–91 **When . . . build** the last six prophecies, as
they are Utopian, are meant ironically; they will never
be fulfilled   92 **Albion** England   95 **going . . . feet**
people will walk on their feet   96 **Merlin** King Arthur's
great magician who, according to Holinshed's *Chronicles,* lived later than Lear
III.III.3 **pity** show pity to

6 **sustain** care for   9 **division** falling out   9 **worse** more
serious (i.e., the French invasion)   11 **spoken** spoken
of   12 **closet** room   13 **home** to the utmost   13 **power**
army   14 **footed** landed   14 **incline to** take the side
of   15 **look** search for   15 **privily** secretly   17 **of** by
20 **toward** impending   22 **courtesy forbid** kindness forbidden (i.e., to Lear)   24 **fair deserving** an action deserving reward
III.IV.4 **break my heart** i.e., by shutting out the storm
which distracts me from thinking

Invades us to the skin: so 'tis to thee;
But where the greater malady is fixed,°
The lesser is scarce felt. Thou'dst shun a bear;
10   But if thy flight lay toward the roaring sea,
Thou'dst meet the bear i' th' mouth.° When the
          mind's free,°
The body's delicate. The tempest in my mind
Doth from my senses take all feeling else,
Save what beats there. Filial ingratitude,
15   Is it not as° this mouth should tear this hand
For lifting food to't? But I will punish home.°
No, I will weep no more. In such a night
To shut me out! Pour on, I will endure.
In such a night as this! O Regan, Goneril,
20   Your old kind father, whose frank° heart gave all—
O, that way madness lies; let me shun that.
No more of that.
          KENT: Good my lord, enter here.
          LEAR:
Prithee go in thyself; seek thine own ease.
This tempest will not give me leave to ponder
25   On things would hurt me more, but I'll go in.

          [*To the* FOOL.]

In, boy; go first. Houseless poverty°—
Nay, get thee in. I'll pray, and then I'll sleep.
                                        Exit [FOOL].
Poor naked wretches, wheresoe'er you are,
That bide° the pelting of this pitiless storm,
30   How shall your houseless heads and unfed sides,
Your looped and windowed° raggedness, defend
          you
From seasons such as these? O, I have ta'en
Too little care of this! Take physic, pomp;°
Expose thyself to feel what wretches feel,
35   That thou mayst shake the superflux° to them,
And show the heavens more just.
          EDGAR [*within*]: Fathom and half, fathom and
half!° Poor Tom!

          Enter FOOL.

          FOOL: Come not in here, nuncle, here's a spirit.
40   Help me, help me!

          KENT:
Give me thy hand. Who's there?
          FOOL: A spirit, a spirit. He says his name's Poor
Tom.
          KENT:
What art thou that dost grumble there i' th' straw?
Come forth.   45

          Enter EDGAR [*disguised as a madman*].

          EDGAR: Away! the foul fiend follows me.
Through the sharp hawthorn blows the cold
wind.° Humh! Go to thy cold bed, and warm
thee.°
          LEAR: Didst thou give all to thy daughters? And   50
art thou come to this?
          EDGAR: Who gives anything to Poor Tom?
Whom the foul fiend hath led through fire and
through flame, through ford and whirlpool, o'er
bog and quagmire; that hath laid knives under his   55
pillow and halters in his pew,° set ratsbane° by his
porridge,° made him proud of heart, to ride on a
bay trotting horse over four-inched bridges,° to
course° his own shadow for° a traitor. Bless thy five
wits,° Tom's a-cold. O, do, de, do, de, do, de.   60
Bless thee from whirlwinds, star-blasting,° and
taking.° Do Poor Tom some charity, whom the
foul fiend vexes. There could I have him now—
and there—and there again—and there.

          Storm still.

          LEAR:
What, have his daughters brought him to this
          pass?°   65
Couldst thou save nothing? Wouldst thou give 'em
          all?
          FOOL: Nay, he reserved a blanket,° else we had
been all shamed.
          LEAR:
Now all the plagues that in the pendulous° air

47–48 **Through . . . wind** a line from the ballad of "The
Friar of Orders Gray"   48–49 **Go . . . thee** a reminiscence of *The Taming of the Shrew*, Induction, line 10,
which itself is an echo of a line in Thomas Kyd's *The
Spanish Tragedy*   55–56 **knives . . . halters . . .
ratsbane** the fiend tempts Poor Tom to suicide   56 **pew**
gallery or balcony outside a window   57 **porridge** broth
57–58 **ride . . . bridges** i.e., risk his life   59 **course**
chase   59 **for** as   60 **five wits** common wit, imagination, fantasy, estimation, memory   61 **star-blasting** the
evil caused by malignant stars   62 **taking** pernicious
influences   65 **pass** wretched condition   67 **blanket**
i.e., to cover his nakedness   69 **pendulous** overhanging

8 **fixed** lodged (in the mind)   11 **i' th' mouth** in the
teeth   11 **free** i.e., from care   15 **as** as if   16 **home** to
the utmost   20 **frank** liberal (magnanimous)   26
houseless poverty the unsheltered poor, abstracted   29
bide endure   31 **looped and windowed** full of holes
33 **Take physic, pomp** Take medicine to cure yourselves, you great men   35 **superflux** superfluity
37–38 **Fathom and half** Edgar, because of the down-
pour, pretends to take soundings

70 Hang fated o'er° men's faults light on thy daughters!
    KENT:
He hath no daughters, sir.
    LEAR:
Death, traitor; nothing could have subdued° nature
To such a lowness but his unkind daughters.
Is it the fashion that discarded fathers
75 Should have thus little mercy on° their flesh?
Judicious punishment—'twas this flesh begot
Those pelican° daughters.
    EDGAR: Pillicock sat on Pillicock Hill.° Alow,
alow, loo, loo!°
80 FOOL: This cold night will turn us all to fools
and madmen.
    EDGAR: Take heed o' th' foul fiend; obey thy
parents; keep thy word's justice;° swear not; commit not° with man's sworn spouse; set not thy sweet
85 heart on proud array. Tom's a-cold.
    LEAR: What hast thou been?
    EDGAR: A servingman, proud in heart and
mind; that curled my hair, wore gloves in my cap;°
served the lust of my mistress' heart, and did the
90 act of darkness with her; swore as many oaths as I
spake words, and broke them in the sweet face of
heaven. One that slept in the contriving of lust,
and waked to do it. Wine loved I deeply, dice
dearly; and in woman out-paramoured the Turk.°
95 False of heart, light of ear,° bloody of hand; hog in
sloth, fox in stealth, wolf in greediness, dog in
madness, lion in prey.° Let not the creaking° of
shoes nor the rustling of silks betray thy poor heart
to woman. Keep thy foot out of brothels, thy hand
100 out of plackets,° thy pen from lenders' books,° and
defy the foul fiend. Still through the hawthorn
blows the cold wind; says suum, mun, nonny.°
Dolphin° my boy, boy, sessa!° let him trot by.

---

70 **fated o'er** destined to punish   72 **subdued** reduced
75 **on** i.e., shown to   77 **pelican** supposed to feed on its
parent's blood   78 **Pillicock . . . Hill** probably quoted
from a nursery rhyme, and suggested by "pelican";
"pillicock" is a term of endearment and the phallus
78–79 **Alow . . . loo** a hunting call, or the refrain of the
song (?)   83 **keep . . . justice** i.e., do not break thy
word   83–84 **commit not** i.e., adultery   88 **gloves . . .
cap** i.e., as a pledge from his mistress   94 **out-paramoured the Turk** had more concubines than the sul-
tan   95 **light of ear** ready to hear flattery and slander
97 **prey** preying   97 **creaking** deliberately cultivated, as
fashionable   100 **plackets** opening in skirts   100 **pen
. . . books** i.e., do not enter your name in the mon-
eylender's account book   102 **suum, mun, nonny** the
noise of the wind   103 **Dolphin** the French dauphin
(identified by the English with the devil; Poor Tom is
presumably quoting from a ballad)   103 **sessa** an interjection: "Go on!"

Storm still.

    LEAR: Thou wert better in a grave than to
answer° with thy uncovered body this extremity° of   105
the skies. Is man no more than this? Consider him
well. Thou ow'st° the worm no silk, the beast no
hide, the sheep no wool, the cat° no perfume. Ha!
here's three on's° are sophisticated.° Thou art the
thing itself; unaccommodated° man is no more but   110
such a poor, bare, forked° animal as thou art. Off,
off, you lendings!° Come, unbutton here.

    [*Tearing off his clothes.*]

    FOOL: Prithee, nuncle, be contented, 'tis a
naughty° night to swim in. Now a little fire in a
wild° field were like an old lecher's heart—a small   115
spark, all the rest on's° body, cold. Look, here
comes a walking fire.

Enter GLOUCESTER *with a torch.*

    EDGAR: This is the foul fiend Flibbertigibbet.°
He begins at curfew,° and walks till the first cock.°
He gives the web and the pin,° squints° the eye,   120
and makes the harelip; mildews the white° wheat,
and hurts the poor creature of earth.

    Swithold footed thrice the old;°
    He met the nightmare,° and her nine fold;°
        Bid her alight°   125
        And her troth plight,°
    And aroint° thee, witch, aroint thee!

    KENT:
How fares your grace?
    LEAR: What's he?
    KENT:
Who's there? What is't you seek?   130
    GLOUCESTER:
What are you there? Your names?
    EDGAR: Poor Tom, that eats the swimming frog,

---

105 **answer** confront, bear the brunt of   105 **extremity**
extreme severity   107 **ow'st** have taken from   108 **cat**
civet cat, whose glands yield perfume   109 **on's of**
us   109 **sophisticated** adulterated, made artificial   110
unaccommodated uncivilized   111 **forked** two-legged
112 **lendings** borrowed garments   114 **naughty** wicked
115 **wild** barren   116 **on's** of his   118 **Flibbertigibbet**
a figure from Elizabethan demonology   119 **curfew** 9
P.M.   119 **first cock** midnight   120 **web . . . pin**
cataract   120 **squints** crosses   121 **white** ripening
123 **Swithold . . . old** Withold (an Anglo-Saxon saint
who subdued demons) walked three times across the
open country   124 **nightmare** demon   124 **fold** offspring   125 **alight** i.e., from the horse she had possessed   126 **her troth plight** pledge her word   127
aroint be gone

the toad, the todpole, the wall-newt and the water;° that in the fury of his heart, when the foul
135 fiend rages, eats cow-dung for sallets,° swallows
the old rat and the ditch-dog,° drinks the green
mantle° of the standing° pool; who is whipped
from tithing° to tithing, and stocked, punished,
and imprisoned; who hath had three suits to his
140 back, six shirts to his body,

　　Horse to ride, and weapon to wear,
　　But mice and rats, and such small deer,°
　　Have been Tom's food for seven long year.°

Beware my follower!° Peace, Smulkin,° peace,
145 thou fiend!
　　GLOUCESTER:
What, hath your grace no better company?
　　EDGAR:
The Prince of Darkness is a gentleman.
Modo° he's called, and Mahu.°
　　GLOUCESTER:
Our flesh and blood, my lord, is grown so vile
150 That it doth hate what gets° it.
　　EDGAR: Poor Tom's a-cold.
　　GLOUCESTER:
Go in with me. My duty cannot suffer°
T' obey in all your daughters' hard commands.
Though their injunction be to bar my doors
155 And let this tyrannous night take hold upon you,
Yet have I ventured to come seek you out
And bring you where both fire and food is ready.
　　LEAR:
First let me talk with this philosopher.
What is the cause of thunder?
　　KENT:
160 Good my lord, take his offer; go into th' house.
　　LEAR:
I'll talk a word with this same learnèd Theban.°
What is your study?°
　　EDGAR:
How to prevent° the fiend, and to kill vermin.
　　LEAR:
Let me ask you one word in private.

　　KENT:
Importune him once more to go, my lord.   165
His wits begin t' unsettle.
　　GLOUCESTER: Canst thou blame him?

Storm still.

His daughters seek his death. Ah, that good Kent,
He said it would be thus, poor banished man!
Thou say'st the king grows mad—I'll tell thee,
　　friend,
I am almost mad myself. I had a son,   170
Now outlawed from my blood;° he sought my life
But lately, very late.° I loved him, friend,
No father his son dearer. True to tell thee,
The grief hath crazed my wits. What a night's this!
I do beseech your grace—
　　LEAR: O, cry you mercy,° sir.   175
Noble philosopher, your company.
　　EDGAR: Tom's a-cold.
　　GLOUCESTER:
In, fellow, there, into th' hovel; keep thee warm.
　　LEAR:
Come, let's in all.
　　KENT: This way, my lord.
　　LEAR: With him!
I will keep still with my philosopher.   180
　　KENT:
Good my lord, soothe° him; let him take the
　　fellow.
　　GLOUCESTER:
Take him you on.°
　　KENT:
Sirrah, come on; go along with us.
　　LEAR:
Come, good Athenian.°
　　GLOUCESTER:
No words, no words! Hush.   185
　　EDGAR:
Child Rowland to the dark tower came;°
His word was still,° "Fie, foh, and fum,
I smell the blood of a British man."°
　　　　　　　　　　　　　　　　　Exeunt.

133–134 **todpole . . . water** tadpole, wall lizard, water
newt   135 **sallets** salads   136 **ditch-dog** dead dog in a
ditch   137 **mantle** scum; **standing** stagnant   138 **tithing** a district comprising ten families   142 **deer** game
142–143 **But . . . year** adapted from a popular romance,
"Bevis of Hampton"   144 **follower** familiar   144–148
Smulkin . . . Modo . . . Mahu Elizabethan devils, from
Samuel Harsnett's *Declaration* of 1603   150 **gets** begets   152 **suffer** permit me   161 **Theban** i.e., Greek
philosopher   162 **study** particular scientific study   163
prevent balk

171 **outlawed . . . blood** disowned and tainted, like a
carbuncle in the corrupted blood   172 **late** recently
175 **cry you mercy** I beg your pardon   181 **soothe**
humor   182 **you on** with you   184 **Athenian** i.e.,
philosopher (like "Theban")   186 **Child . . . came** from
a lost ballad (?); "child" = a candidate for knighthood;
"Rowland" was Charlemagne's nephew, the hero of *The
Song of Roland*   187 **His . . . still** his motto was
always   187–188 **Fie . . . man** a deliberately absurd
linking of the chivalric hero with the nursery tale of Jack
the Giant-Killer

SCENE V. [GLOUCESTER's *castle.*]

Enter CORNWALL *and* EDMUND.

CORNWALL: I will have my revenge ere I depart his house.

EDMUND: How, my lord, I may be censured,° that nature thus gives way to loyalty, something
5 fears° me to think of.

CORNWALL: I now perceive it was not altogether your brother's evil disposition made him seek his death; but a provoking merit, set a-work by a reprovable badness in himself.°
10 EDMUND: How malicious is my fortune that I must repent to be just! This is the letter which he spoke of, which approves° him an intelligent party° to the advantages° of France. O heavens, that his treason were not! or not I the detector!
15 CORNWALL: Go with me to the duchess.

EDMUND: If the matter of this paper be certain, you have mighty business in hand.

CORNWALL: True or false, it hath made thee Earl of Gloucester. Seek out where thy father is,
20 that he may be ready for our apprehension.°

EDMUND [*aside*]: If I find him comforting° the king, it will stuff his suspicion more fully.—I will persever° in my course of loyalty, though the conflict be sore between that and my blood.°
25 CORNWALL: I will lay trust upon° thee, and thou shalt find a dearer father in my love.

Exeunt.

SCENE VI. [A *chamber in a farmhouse adjoining the castle.*]

Enter KENT *and* GLOUCESTER.

GLOUCESTER: Here is better than the open air; take it thankfully. I will piece out the comfort with what addition I can. I will not be long from you.

KENT: All the power of his wits have given way to
5 his impatience.° The gods reward your kindness.

Exit [GLOUCESTER].

Enter LEAR, EDGAR, *and* FOOL.

EDGAR: Frateretto° calls me, and tells me Nero° is an angler in the lake of darkness. Pray, innocent,° and beware the foul fiend.

FOOL: Prithee, nuncle, tell me whether a madman be a gentleman or a yeoman.° 10

LEAR:
A king, a king.

FOOL: No, he's a yeoman that has a gentleman to his son; for he's a mad yeoman that sees his son a gentleman before him.

LEAR:
To have a thousand with red burning spits 15
Come hizzing° in upon 'em—

EDGAR: The foul fiend bites my back.

FOOL: He's mad that trusts in the tameness of a wolf, a horse's health, a boy's love, or a whore's oath. 20

LEAR:
It shall be done; I will arraign° them straight.°

[*To* EDGAR.]

Come, sit thou here, most learned justice.°

[*To the* FOOL.]

Thou, sapient° sir, sit here. Now, you she-foxes—

EDGAR: Look, where he° stands and glares.
Want'st thou eyes at trial, madam?° 25
Come o'er the bourn,° Bessy, to me.

FOOL:
Her boat hath a leak,
And she must not speak
Why she dares not come over to thee.°

EDGAR: The foul fiend haunts Poor Tom in the 30
voice of a nightingale.° Hoppedance° cries in Tom's belly for two white herring.° Croak° not, black angel; I have no food for thee.

III.v.3 **censured** judged   4–5 **something fears** somewhat frightens   8–9 **a provoking . . . himself** a stimulating goodness in Edgar, brought into play by a blamable badness in Gloucester   12 **approves** proves   12 **intelligent party** (1) spy (2) well-informed person   13 **to the advantages** on behalf of   20 **apprehension** arrest   21 **comforting** supporting (a legalism)   23 **persever** persevere   24 **blood** natural feelings   25 **lay trust upon** (1) trust (2) advance
III.vi.5 **impatience** raging

6 **Frateretto** Elizabethan devil, from Harsnett's *Declaration*   6 **Nero** who is mentioned by Harsnett, and whose angling is reported by Chaucer in "The Monk's Tale"   8 **innocent** fool   10 **yeoman** farmer (just below a gentleman in rank; the Fool asks what class of man has most indulged his children, and thus been driven mad)   16 **hizzing** hissing   21 **arraign** bring to trial   21 **straight** straight away   22 **justice** justicer, judge   23 **sapient** wise   24 **he** i.e., a fiend   25 **Want'st . . . madam** (to Goneril) i.e., Do you want eyes to look at you during your trial? The fiend serves that purpose   26 **bourn** brook (Edgar quotes from a popular ballad)   27–29 **Her . . . thee** the Fool parodies the ballad   31 **nightingale** i.e., the Fool's singing   31 **Hoppedance** Hoberdidance (another devil from Harsnett's *Declaration*)   32 **white herring** unsmoked (as against the black and sulfurous devil?)   32 **Croak** rumble (because his belly is empty)

KENT:

How do you, sir? Stand you not so amazed.°
35 Will you lie down and rest upon the cushions?
LEAR:

I'll see their trial first. Bring in their evidence.°

[*To* EDGAR.]

Thou, robèd man of justice, take thy place.

[*To the* FOOL.]

And thou, his yokefellow of equity,°
Bench° by his side. [*To* KENT.] You are o' th'
commission;°
40 Sit you too.
EDGAR: Let us deal justly.

Sleepest or wakest thou, jolly shepherd?
  Thy sheep be in the corn;°
And for one blast of thy minikin° mouth
45   Thy sheep shall take no harm.°

Purr, the cat is gray.°
LEAR: Arraign her first. 'Tis Goneril, I here take
my oath before this honorable assembly, she
kicked the poor king her father.
50 FOOL: Come hither, mistress. Is your name
Goneril?
LEAR: She cannot deny it.
FOOL: Cry you mercy, I took you for a joint
stool.°
LEAR:

55 And here's another, whose warped looks proclaim
What store° her heart is made on. Stop her there!
Arms, arms, sword, fire! Corruption in the place!°
False justicer, why hast thou let her 'scape?
EDGAR: Bless thy five wits!
KENT:

60 O pity! Sir, where is the patience now
That you so oft have boasted to retain?

EDGAR [*aside*]:

My tears begin to take his part so much
They mar my counterfeiting.°
LEAR:

The little dogs and all,
Tray, Blanch, and Sweetheart—see, they bark at
me.   65
EDGAR: Tom will throw his head at them.
Avaunt, you curs.

  Be thy mouth or black or° white,
  Tooth that poisons if it bite;
  Mastiff, greyhound, mongrel grim,   70
  Hound or spaniel, brach° or lym,°
  Or bobtail tike, or trundle-tail°—
  Tom will make him weep and wail;
  For, with throwing° thus my head,
  Dogs leaped the hatch,° and all are fled.   75

Do, de, de, de. Sessa!° Come, march to wakes°
and fairs and market towns. Poor Tom, thy horn°
is dry.
LEAR: Then let them anatomize Regan. See
what breeds about her heart.° Is there any cause in   80
nature that make° these hard hearts? [*To* EDGAR.]
You, sir, I entertain° for one of my hundred;° only
I do not like the fashion of your garments. You will
say they are Persian;° but let them be changed.
KENT:

Now, good my lord, lie here and rest awhile.   85
LEAR:

Make no noise, make no noise; draw the curtains.°
So, so. We'll go to supper i' th' morning.
FOOL: And I'll go to bed at noon.°

Enter GLOUCESTER.

GLOUCESTER:

Come hither, friend. Where is the king my master?

63 **counterfeiting** i.e., feigned madness   68 **or . . . or**
either . . . or   71 **brach** bitch   71 **lym** bloodhound
(from the liam or leash with which he was led)   72
bobtail . . . trundle-tail short-tailed or long-tailed
cur   74 **throwing** jerking (as a hound lifts its head from
the ground, the scent having been lost)   75 **leaped the
hatch** leaped over the lower half of a divided door (i.e.,
left in a hurry)   76 **Sessa** Be off!   76 **wakes** feasts
attending the dedication of a church   77 **horn** horn
bottle which the Bedlam used in begging a drink (Edgar
is suggesting that he is unable to play his role any
longer)   79–80 **Then . . . heart** i.e., If the Bedlam's
horn is dry, let Regan, whose heart has become as hard
as horn, be dissected   81 **make** subjunctive   82 **entertain** engage   82 **hundred** i.e., Lear's hundred knights
84 **Persian** gorgeous (ironically of Edgar's rags)   86
curtains Lear imagines himself in bed   88 **And . . .
noon** the Fool's last words

34 **amazed** astonished   36 **evidence** the evidence of
witnesses against them   38 **yokefellow of equity** partner
in justice   39 **Bench** sit on the bench   39 **commission**
those commissioned as king's justices   43 **corn** wheat
44 **minikin** shrill   42–45 **Sleepest . . . harm** probably
quoted or adapted from an Elizabethan song   46 **gray**
devils were thought to assume the shape of a gray
cat   53–54 **Cry . . . stool** proverbial and deliberately
impudent apology for overlooking a person; a joint stool
was a low stool made by a joiner, perhaps here a stage
property to represent Goneril and, in line 55, Regan;
"joint stool" can also suggest the judicial bench; hence
Goneril may be identified by the Fool, ironically, with
those in power, who judge   56 **store** stuff   57 **Corruption . . . place** bribery in the court

KENT:
90 Here, sir, but trouble him not; his wits are gone.
GLOUCESTER:
Good friend, I prithee take him in thy arms.
I have o'erheard a plot of death upon him.
There is a litter ready; lay him in't
And drive toward Dover, friend, where thou shalt
    meet
95 Both welcome and protection. Take up thy master.
If thou shouldst dally half an hour, his life,
With thine and all that offer to defend him,
Stand in assurèd loss. Take up, take up,
And follow me, that will to some provision°
Give thee quick conduct.°
100   KENT: Oppressèd nature sleeps.
This rest might yet have balmed thy broken sinews,°
Which, if convenience° will not allow,
Stand in hard cure.° [*To the* FOOL.] Come, help to
    bear thy master.
Thou must not stay behind.
    GLOUCESTER: Come, come, away!
                       Exeunt [*all but* EDGAR].
EDGAR:
105 When we our betters see bearing our woes,
We scarcely think our miseries our foes.°
Who alone suffers suffers most i' th' mind,
Leaving free° things and happy shows° behind;
But then the mind much sufferance° doth o'erskip
110 When grief hath mates, and bearing fellowship.°
How light and portable° my pain seems now,
When that which makes me bend makes the king
    bow.
He childed as I fathered. Tom, away.
Mark the high noises,° and thyself bewray°
When false opinion, whose wrong thoughts° defile
115   thee,
In thy just proof repeals and reconciles thee.°
What will hap more° tonight, safe 'scape the king!
Lurk,° lurk.   [*Exit.*]

---

99 **provision** maintenance   100 **conduct** direction   101
balmed . . . **sinews** soothed thy racked nerves   102
convenience fortunate occasion   103 **Stand** . . . **cure**
will be hard to cure   106 **our foes** enemies peculiar to
ourselves   108 **free** carefree   108 **shows** scenes   109
sufferance suffering   110 **bearing fellowship** suffering
has company   111 **portable** able to be supported or
endured   114 **Mark** . . . **noises** observe the rumors of
strife among those in power   114 **bewray** reveal   115
wrong thoughts misconceptions   116 **In** . . . **thee** on
the manifesting of your innocence recalls you from
outlawry and restores amity between you and your
father   117 **What** . . . **more** whatever else happens
118 **Lurk** hide

SCENE VII. [GLOUCESTER'*s castle.*]

Enter CORNWALL, REGAN, GONERIL, EDMUND,
and SERVANTS.

CORNWALL [*to* GONERIL]: Post speedily to my
lord your husband; show him this letter. The army
of France is landed. [*To* SERVANTS.] Seek out the
traitor Gloucester.
                [*Exeunt some of the* SERVANTS.]
REGAN: Hang him instantly.   5
GONERIL: Pluck out his eyes.
CORNWALL: Leave him to my displeasure. Edmund, keep you our sister company. The revenges
we are bound° to take upon your traitorous father
are not fit for your beholding. Advise the duke   10
where you are going, to a most festinate° preparation. We are bound to the like. Our posts° shall be
swift and intelligent° betwixt us. Farewell, dear
sister; farewell, my Lord of Gloucester.°

Enter OSWALD.

How now? Where's the king?   15
OSWALD:
My Lord of Gloucester hath conveyed him hence.
Some five or six and thirty of his knights,
Hot questrists° after him, met him at gate;
Who, with some other of the lords dependants,°
Are gone with him toward Dover, where they
    boast   20
To have well-armèd friends.
    CORNWALL: Get horses for your mistress.
                          [*Exit* OSWALD.]
GONERIL:
Farewell, sweet lord, and sister.
    CORNWALL:
Edmund, farewell.
                 [*Exeunt* GONERIL *and* EDMUND.]
             Go seek the traitor Gloucester,
Pinion him like a thief, bring him before us.
                 [*Exeunt other* SERVANTS.]
Though well we may not pass upon° his life   25
Without the form of justice, yet our power
Shall do a court'sy to° our wrath, which men
May blame, but not control.

Enter GLOUCESTER, *brought in by two or three.*

III.VII.9 **bound** (1) forced (2) purposing to   11 **festinate**
speedy   12 **posts** messengers   13 **intelligent** full of
information   14 **Lord of Gloucester** Edmund, now
elevated to the title   18 **questrists** searchers   19 **lords
dependants** attendant lords (members of Lear's retinue)   25 **pass upon** pass judgment on   27 **do** . . . **to**
indulge

Who's there, the traitor?

REGAN:
Ingrateful fox, 'tis he.

CORNWALL:
30 Bind fast his corky° arms.

GLOUCESTER:
What means your graces? Good my friends, consider
You are my guests. Do me no foul play, friends.

CORNWALL:
Bind him, I say. [SERVANTS *bind him.*]

REGAN: Hard, hard! O filthy traitor.

GLOUCESTER:
Unmerciful lady as you are, I'm none.

CORNWALL:
35 To this chair bind him. Villain, thou shalt find—

[REGAN *plucks his beard.*°]

GLOUCESTER:
By the kind gods, 'tis most ignobly done
To pluck me by the beard.

REGAN:
So white, and such a traitor?

GLOUCESTER: Naughty° lady,
These hairs which thou dost ravish from my chin
40 Will quicken° and accuse thee. I am your host.
With robber's hands my hospitable favors°
You should not ruffle° thus. What will you do?

CORNWALL:
Come, sir, what letters had you late° from France?

REGAN:
Be simple-answered,° for we know the truth.

CORNWALL:
45 And what confederacy have you with the traitors
Late footed in the kingdom?

REGAN:
To whose hands you have sent the lunatic king:
Speak.

GLOUCESTER:
I have a letter guessingly° set down,
50 Which came from one that's of a neutral heart,
And not from one opposed.

CORNWALL: Cunning.

REGAN: And false.

CORNWALL:
Where hast thou sent the king?

GLOUCESTER:
To Dover.

REGAN:
Wherefore to Dover? Wast thou not charged at
peril°—

CORNWALL:
Wherefore to Dover? Let him answer that.   55

GLOUCESTER:
I am tied to th' stake, and I must stand the course.°

REGAN:
Wherefore to Dover?

GLOUCESTER:
Because I would not see thy cruel nails
Pluck out his poor old eyes; nor thy fierce sister
In his anointed° flesh rash° boarish fangs.   60
The sea, with such a storm as his bare head
In hell-black night endured, would have buoyed°
up
And quenched the stellèd° fires.
Yet, poor old heart, he holp° the heavens to rain.
If wolves had at thy gate howled that dearn° time, 65
Thou shouldst have said, "Good porter, turn the
key."°
All cruels else subscribe.° But I shall see
The wingèd° vengeance overtake such children.

CORNWALL:
See't shalt thou never. Fellows, hold the chair.
Upon these eyes of thine I'll set my foot.   70

GLOUCESTER:
He that will think° to live till he be old,
Give me some help.—O cruel! O you gods!

REGAN:
One side will mock° another. Th' other too.

CORNWALL:
If you see vengeance—

FIRST SERVANT: Hold your hand, my lord!
I have served you ever since I was a child;   75
But better service have I never done you
Than now to bid you hold.

REGAN: How now, you dog?

FIRST SERVANT:
If you did wear a beard upon your chin,

---

54 **charged at peril** ordered under penalty   56 **course**
coursing (in which a relay of dogs baits a bull or bear tied
in the pit)   60 **anointed** holy (because king)   60 **rash**
strike with the tusk, like a boar   62 **buoyed** risen   63
stellèd (1) fixed (as opposed to the planets or wandering
stars) (2) starry   64 **holp** helped   65 **dearn** dread   66
turn the key i.e., unlock the gate   67 **All . . . subscribe**
All cruel creatures but man are compassionate   68
wingèd (1) heavenly (2) swift   71 **will think** expects   73
mock make ridiculous (because of the contrasts)

---

30 **corky** sapless (because old)   36 s.d. **plucks his beard**
a deadly insult   38 **Naughty** wicked   40 **quicken** come
to life   41 **hospitable favors** face of your host   42 **ruffle**
tear at violently   43 **late** recently   44 **simple-answered**
straight forward in answering   49 **guessingly** without
certain knowledge

I'd shake it° on this quarrel. What do you mean!°

80   CORNWALL: My villain!°

Draw and fight.

FIRST SERVANT:
Nay, then, come on, and take the chance of anger.

REGAN:
Give me thy sword. A peasant stand up thus?

*She takes a sword and runs at him behind, kills
him.*

FIRST SERVANT:
O, I am slain! my lord, you have one eye left
To see some mischief° on him. O!

CORNWALL:
85   Lest it see more, prevent it. Out, vile jelly.
Where is thy luster now?

GLOUCESTER:
All dark and comfortless. Where's my son Edmund?
Edmund, enkindle all the sparks of nature°
To quit° this horrid act.

REGAN: Out, treacherous villain,
90   Thou call'st on him that hates thee. It was he
That made the overture° of thy treasons to us;
Who is too good to pity thee.

GLOUCESTER:
O my follies! Then Edgar was abused.°
Kind gods, forgive me that, and prosper him.

REGAN:
95   Go thrust him out at gates, and let him smell
His way to Dover.

                    Exit [one], with GLOUCESTER.
                    How is't, my lord? How look you?°

CORNWALL:
I have received a hurt. Follow me, lady.
Turn out that eyeless villain. Throw this slave
Upon the dunghill. Regan, I bleed apace.
100   Untimely comes this hurt. Give me your arm.
                                        Exeunt.

SECOND SERVANT:
I'll never care what wickedness I do,
If this man come to good.

THIRD SERVANT: If she live long,
And in the end meet the old course of death,°
Women will all turn monsters.

SECOND SERVANT:
Let's follow the old earl, and get the Bedlam   105
To lead him where he would. His roguish madness
Allows itself to anything.°

THIRD SERVANT:
Go thou. I'll fetch some flax and whites of eggs
To apply to his bleeding face. Now heaven help
him.

                              [*Exeunt severally.*]

ACT IV

SCENE I. [*The heath.*]

Enter EDGAR.

EDGAR:
Yet better thus, and known to be contemned,°
Than still contemned and flattered. To be worst,
The lowest and most dejected° thing of fortune,
Stands still in esperance,° lives not in fear:
The lamentable change is from the best,   5
The worst returns to laughter.° Welcome then,
Thou unsubstantial air that I embrace!
The wretch that thou hast blown unto the worst
Owes° nothing to thy blasts.

Enter GLOUCESTER, *led by an* OLD MAN.

                              But who comes here?
My father, poorly led?° World, world, O world!   10
But that thy strange mutations make us hate thee,
Life would not yield to age.°

OLD MAN: O, my good lord,
I have been your tenant, and your father's tenant,
These fourscore years.

GLOUCESTER:
Away, get thee away; good friend, be gone: 15
Thy comforts° can do me no good at all;
Thee they may hurt.°

OLD MAN: You cannot see your way.

GLOUCESTER:
I have no way and therefore want° no eyes;
I stumbled when I saw. Full oft 'tis seen,

---

79 **shake it** an insult comparable to Regan's plucking of
Gloucester's beard   79 **What . . . mean** i.e., What
terrible thing are you doing?   80 **villain** serf (with a
suggestion of the modern meaning)   84 **mischief** injury   88 **enkindle . . . nature** fan your natural feeling
into flame   89 **quit** requite   91 **overture** disclosure
93 **abused** wronged   96 **How look you** How are you?
103 **meet . . . death** die the customary death of old age

107 **His . . . anything** his lack of all self-control leaves
him open to any suggestion
IV.I.1 **known . . . contemned** conscious of being
despised   3 **dejected** abased   4 **esperance** hope   6 **returns to laughter** changes for the better   9 **Owes** is in
debt for   10 **poorly led** (1) led like a poor man, with
only one attendant (2) led by a poor man   11–12 **But
. . . age** We should not agree to grow old and hence
die, except for the hateful mutability of life   16 **comforts** ministrations   17 **hurt** injure   18 **want** require

20 Our means secure us, and our mere defects
Prove our commodities.° Oh, dear son Edgar,
The food° of thy abusèd° father's wrath!
Might I but live to see thee in° my touch,
I'd say I had eyes again!
    OLD MAN: How now! Who's there?
    EDGAR [aside]:
25 O gods! Who is't can say, "I am at the worst"?
I am worse than e'er I was.
    OLD MAN: 'Tis poor mad Tom.
    EDGAR [aside]:
And worse I may be yet: the worst is not
So long as we can say, "This is the worst."°
    OLD MAN:
Fellow, where goest?
    GLOUCESTER: Is it a beggar-man?
    OLD MAN:
30 Madman and beggar too.
    GLOUCESTER:
He has some reason,° else he could not beg.
I' th' last night's storm I such a fellow saw,
Which made me think a man a worm. My son
Came then into my mind, and yet my mind
Was then scarce friends with him. I have heard
35   more since.
As flies to wanton° boys, are we to th' gods,
They kill us for their sport.
    EDGAR [aside]:   How should this be°
Bad is the trade that must play fool to sorrow,
Ang'ring° itself and others. Bless thee, master!
    GLOUCESTER:
Is that the naked fellow?
40   OLD MAN: Ay, my lord.
    GLOUCESTER:
Then, prithee, get thee gone: if for my sake
Thou wilt o'ertake us hence a mile or twain
I' th' way toward Dover, do it for ancient° love,
And bring some covering for this naked soul,
Which I'll entreat to lead me.
45   OLD MAN: Alack, sir, he is mad.

    GLOUCESTER:
'Tis the time's plague,° when madmen lead the
    blind.
Do as I bid thee, or rather do thy pleasure;°
Above the rest,° be gone.
    OLD MAN:
I'll bring him the best 'parel° that I have,
Come on 't what will.   Exit.   50
    GLOUCESTER:
Sirrah, naked fellow—
    EDGAR:
Poor Tom's a-cold. [Aside.] I cannot daub it°
    further.
    GLOUCESTER:
Come hither, fellow.
    EDGAR [aside]:
And yet I must.—Bless thy sweet eyes, they bleed.
    GLOUCESTER:
Know'st thou the way to Dover?   55
    EDGAR:
Both stile and gate, horse-way and footpath.
Poor Tom hath been scared out of his good wits.
Bless thee, good man's son, from the foul fiend!
Five fiends have been in Poor Tom at once; of lust,
as Obidicut;° Hobbididence, prince of dumbness;° 60
Mahu, of stealing; Modo, of murder; Flibber-
tigibett, of mopping and mowing;° who since
possesses chambermaids and waiting-women. So,
bless thee, master!
    GLOUCESTER:
Here, take this purse, thou whom the heavens'
    plagues   65
Have humbled to all strokes:° that I am wretched
Makes thee the happier. Heavens, deal so still!
Let the superfluous° and lust-dieted° man,
That slaves° your ordinance,° that will not see
Because he does not feel, feel your pow'r quickly; 70
So distribution should undo excess,°

20–21 **Our . . . commodities** Our resources make us overconfident, while our afflictions make for our advantage 22 **food** i.e., the object on which Gloucester's anger fed 22 **abusèd** deceived 23 **in** i.e., with, by means of 27–28 **the . . . worst** so long as a man continues to suffer (i.e., is still alive), even greater suffering may await him 31 **reason** faculty of reasoning 36 **wanton** (1) playful (2) reckless 37 **How . . . be** i.e., How can this horror be? 39 **Ang'ring** offending 43 **ancient** (1) the love the Old Man feels, by virtue of his long tenancy (2) the love that formerly obtained between master and man

46 **time's plague** characteristic disorder of this time 47 **thy pleasure** as you like it 48 **the rest** all 49 **'parel** apparel 52 **daub it** lay it on (figure from plastering mortar) 60 **Obidicut** Hoberdicut, a devil (like the four that follow, from Harsnett's *Declaration*) 60 **dumbness** muteness (like the crimes and afflictions in the next lines, the result of diabolic possession) 62 **mopping and mowing** grimacing and making faces 66 **humbled . . . strokes** brought so low as to bear anything humbly 68 **superfluous** possessed of superfluities 68 **lust-dieted** whose lust is gratified (like Gloucester's) 69 **slaves** (1) tramples, spurns like a slave (2) tears, rends (Old English *slaefan*) (?) 69 **ordinance** law 71 **So . . . excess** Then the man with too much wealth would distribute it among those with too little

And each man have enough. Dost thou know
    Dover?
EDGAR: Ay, master
GLOUCESTER:
There is a cliff whose high and bending° head
75 Looks fearfully° in the confinèd deep:°
Bring me but to the very brim of it,
And I'll repair the misery thou dost bear
With something rich about me: from that place
I shall no leading need.
   EDGAR: Give me thy arm:
80 Poor Tom shall lead thee.   *Exeunt.*

SCENE II. [*Before the Duke of* ALBANY'*s palace.*]

Enter GONERIL *and* EDMUND.

GONERIL:
Welcome, my lord: I marvel our mild husband
Not met° us on the way.

Enter OSWALD.

             Now, where's your master?
OSWALD:
Madam, within; but never man so changed.
I told him of the army that was landed:
5 He smiled at it. I told him you were coming;
His answer was, "The worse." Of Gloucester's
    treachery,
And of the loyal service of his son
When I informed him, then he called me sot,°
And told me I had turned the wrong side out:
What most he should dislike seems pleasant to
10   him;
What like,° offensive.
   GONERIL [*to* EDMUND]:
Then shall you go no further.
It is the cowish° terror of his spirit,
That dares not undertake:° he'll not feel wrongs,
Which tie him to an answer.° Our wishes on the
15   way
May prove effects.° Back, Edmund, to my brother;
Hasten his musters° and conduct his pow'rs.°

I must change names° at home and give the distaff°
Into my husband's hands. This trusty servant
Shall pass between us: ere long you are like to
    hear,   20
If you dare venture in your own behalf,
A mistress's° command. Wear this; spare speech;

[*Giving a favor.*]

Decline your head.° This kiss, if it durst speak,
Would stretch thy spirits up into the air:
Conceive,° and fare thee well.   25
EDMUND:
Yours in the ranks of death.
   GONERIL: My most dear Gloucester!
                    Exit [EDMUND].
O, the difference of man and man!
To thee a woman's services are due:
My fool usurps my body.°
   OSWALD: Madam, here comes my lord.
                         Exit.

Enter ALBANY.

GONERIL:
I have been worth the whistle.°
   ALBANY: O Goneril!   30
You are not worth the dust which the rude wind
Blows in your face. I fear your disposition:°
That nature which contemns° its origin
Cannot be bordered certain in itself;°
She that herself will sliver and disbranch°   35
From her material sap,° perforce must wither
And come to deadly use.°
   GONERIL:
No more; the text° is foolish.

---

74 **bending** overhanging   75 **fearfully** occasioning fear;
confinèd deep the sea, hemmed in below
IV.II.2 **Not met** did not meet   8 **sot** fool   11 **What like**
what he should like   13 **cowish** cowardly   14 **undertake** venture   15 **tie . . . answer** oblige him to retali-
ate   15–16 **Our . . . effects** Our desires (that you might
be my husband), as we journeyed here, may be fulfilled
17 **musters** collecting of troops   17 **conduct his pow'rs**
lead his army

18 **change names** i.e., exchange the name of "mistress"
for that of "master"   18 **distaff** spinning stick (wifely
symbol)   22 **mistress's** lover's (and also, Albany having
been disposed of, lady's or wife's)   23 **Decline your
head** i.e., that Goneril may kiss him   25 **Conceive**
understand (with a sexual implication, that includes
"stretch thy spirits," line 24; and "death," line 26: "to
die," meaning "to experience sexual intercourse")   29
My . . . body My husband wrongfully enjoys me   30 **I
. . . whistle** i.e., Once you valued me (the proverb is
implied, "It is a poor dog that is not worth the whistling")   32 **disposition** nature   33 **contemns** despises
34 **bordered . . . itself** kept within its normal bounds
35 **sliver and disbranch** cut off   36 **material sap** essential and life-giving sustenance   37 **come . . . use** i.e., be
as a dead branch for the burning   38 **text** i.e., on which
your sermon is based

ALBANY:
Wisdom and goodness to the vile seem vile:
40 Filths savor but themselves.° What have you done?
Tigers, not daughters, what have you performed?
A father, and a gracious agèd man,
Whose reverence even the head-lugged bear°
      would lick,
Most barbarous, most degenerate, have you
      madded.°
45 Could my good brother suffer you to do it?
A man, a prince, by him so benefited!
If that the heavens do not their visible spirits°
Send quickly down to tame these vile offenses,
It will come,
50 Humanity must perforce prey on itself,
Like monsters of the deep.
      GONERIL: Milk-livered° man!
That bear'st a cheek for blows, a head for wrongs;
Who hast not in thy brows an eye discerning
Thine honor from thy suffering;° that not know'st
55 Fools do those villains pity who are punished
Ere they have done their mischief.° Where's thy
      drum?
France spreads his banners in our noiseless° land,
With plumèd helm° thy state begins to threat,°
Whilst thou, a moral° fool, sits still and cries,
"Alack, why does he so?"
60   ALBANY: See thyself, devil!
Proper° deformity seems not in the fiend
So horrid as in woman.
      GONERIL: O vain fool!
      ALBANY:
Thou changèd and self-covered° thing, for shame,

Be-monster not thy feature.° Were't my fitness°
To let these hands obey my blood,°   65
They are apt enough to dislocate and tear
Thy flesh and bones: howe'er° thou art a fiend,
A woman's shape doth shield thee.
      GONERIL:
Marry, your manhood mew°—

Enter a MESSENGER.

ALBANY: What news?   70
MESSENGER:
O, my good lord, the Duke of Cornwall's dead,
Slain by his servant, going to° put out
The other eye of Gloucester.
      ALBANY: Gloucester's eyes!
MESSENGER:
A servant that he bred,° thrilled with remorse,°
Opposed against the act, bending his sword   75
To his great master, who thereat enraged
Flew on him, and amongst them felled° him dead,
But not without that harmful stroke which since
Hath plucked him after.°
      ALBANY: This shows you are above,
You justicers,° that these our nether° crimes   80
So speedily can venge.° But, O poor Gloucester!
Lost he his other eye?
      MESSENGER: Both, both, my lord.
This letter, madam, craves° a speedy answer;
'Tis from your sister.
      GONERIL [*aside*]:   One way I like this well;
But being widow, and my Gloucester with her,   85
May all the building in my fancy pluck
Upon my hateful life.° Another way,°
The news is not so tart.°—I'll read, and answer.
                                                      Exit.
      ALBANY:
Where was his son when they did take his eyes?

---

40 **Filths . . . themselves** the filthy relish only the taste of
filth   43 **head-lugged bear** bear-baited by the dogs, and
hence enraged   44 **madded** made mad   47 **visible
spirits** avenging spirits in material form   51 **Milk-liv-
ered** lily-livered (hence cowardly, the liver being regarded as the seat of courage)   53–54 **discerning . . .
suffering** able to distinguish between insults that ought to
be resented and ordinary pain that is to be borne   55–56
Fools . . . mischief Only fools are sorry for criminals
whose intended criminality is prevented by punishment   57 **noiseless** i.e., the drum, signifying preparation for war, is silent   58 **helm** helmet   58 **thy . . .
threat** France begins to threaten Albany's realm   59
moral moralizing; but also with the implication that
morality and folly are one   61 **Proper** (1) natural (to a
fiend) (2) fair-appearing   63 **changèd and self-covered**
i.e., transformed, by the contorting of her woman's face,
on which appears the fiendish behavior she has allowed
herself (Goneril has disguised nature by wickedness)

64 **Be-monster . . . feature** do not change your appearance into a fiend's   64 **my fitness** appropriate for me
65 **blood** passion   67 **howe'er** but even if   69 **your
manhood mew** (1) coop up or confine (pretended)
manhood (2) molt or shed it, if that is what is supposed to
"shield" me from you   72 **going to** as he was about
to   74 **bred** reared   74 **thrilled with remorse** pierced by
compassion   77 **amongst them felled** others assisting,
they felled   79 **plucked him after** i.e., brought Cornwall to death with his servant   80 **justicers** judges   80
nether committed below (on earth)   81 **venge** avenge
83 **craves** demands   86–87 **May . . . life** These things
(line 85) may send my future hopes, my castles in air,
crashing down upon the hateful (married) life I lead
now   87 **Another way** looked at another way   88 **tart**
sour

MESSENGER:
Come with my lady hither.

90 ALBANY: He is not here.

MESSENGER:
No, my good lord; I met him back° again.

ALBANY:
Knows he the wickedness?

MESSENGER:
Ay, my good lord; 'twas he informed against him,
And quit the house on purpose, that their
    punishment
Might have the freer course.

95 ALBANY: Gloucester, I live
To thank thee for the love thou showed'st the king,
And to revenge thine eyes. Come hither, friend:
Tell me what more thou know'st.   *Exeunt.*

[SCENE III. *The French camp near Dover.*]

Enter KENT *and a* GENTLEMAN.

KENT: Why the King of France is so suddenly
gone back, know you no reason?

GENTLEMAN: Something he left imperfect in
the state,° which since his coming forth is thought
5 of, which imports° to the kingdom so much fear
and danger that his personal return was most
required and necessary.

KENT: Who hath he left behind him general?

GENTLEMAN: The Marshal of France, Monsier
10 La Far.

KENT: Did your letters pierce° the queen to any
demonstration of grief?

GENTLEMAN:
Ay, sir; she took them, read them in my presence,
And now and then an ample tear trilled° down
15 Her delicate cheek: it seemed she was a queen
Over her passion, who most rebel-like
Sought to be king o'er her.

KENT: O, then it moved her.

GENTLEMAN:
Not to a rage: patience and sorrow strove
Who should express her goodliest.° You have seen
20 Sunshine and rain at once: her smiles and tears
Were like a better way:° those happy smilets°
That played on her ripe lip seemed not to know
What guests were in her eyes, which parted thence

As pearls from diamonds dropped. In brief,
Sorrow would be a rarity most belovèd,   25
If all could so become it.°

KENT: Made she no verbal question?

GENTLEMAN:
Faith, once or twice she heaved° the name of
    "father"
Pantingly forth, as if it pressed her heart;
Cried, "Sisters! Sisters! Shame of ladies! Sisters!
Kent! Father! Sisters! What, i' th' storm? i' th'
    night?   30
Let pity not be believed!"° There she shook
The holy water from her heavenly eyes,
And clamor moistened:° then away she started
To deal with grief alone.

KENT: It is the stars,
The stars above us, govern our conditions;°   35
Else one self mate and make could not beget
Such different issues.° You spoke not with her
    since?

GENTLEMAN: No.

KENT:
Was this before the king returned?

GENTLEMAN: No, since.

KENT:
Well, sir, the poor distressèd Lear's i' th' town; 40
Who sometime in his better tune° remembers
What we are come about, and by no means
Will yield to see his daughter.

GENTLEMAN: Why, good sir?

KENT:
A sovereign° shame so elbows° him: his own
    unkindness
That stripped her from his benediction, turned her 45
To foreign casualties,° gave her dear rights
To his dog-hearted daughters: these things sting
His mind so venomously that burning shame
Detains him from Cordelia.

GENTLEMAN: Alack, poor gentleman!

KENT:
Of Albany's and Cornwall's powers you heard not? 50

---

91 **back** going back
IV.III.3–4 **imperfect . . . state** unsettled in his own
kingdom   5 **imports** portends   11 **pierce** impel   14
trilled trickled   19 **Who . . . goodliest** which should
give her the most becoming expression   21 **Were . . .
way** i.e., improved on that spectacle   21 **smilets** little
smiles

25–26 **Sorrow . . . it** sorrow would be a coveted jewel if it
became others as it does her   27 **heaved** expressed with
difficulty   31 **Let . . . believed** Let it not be believed for
pity   33 **clamor moistened** moistened clamor, i.e.,
mixed (and perhaps assuaged) her outcries with tears
35 **govern our conditions** determine what we are   36–
37 **Else . . . issues** otherwise the same husband and wife
could not produce such different children   41 **better
tune** composed, less jangled intervals   44 **sovereign**
overpowering   44 **elbows** jogs his elbow (i.e., reminds
him)   46 **casualties** chances

GENTLEMAN:
'Tis so;° they are afoot.
KENT:
Well, sir, I'll bring you to our master Lear,
And leave you to attend him: some dear cause°
Will in concealment wrap me up awhile;
55 When I am known aright, you shall not grieve
Lending me this acquaintance. I pray you, go
Along with me.   [*Exeunt.*]

[SCENE IV. *The same. A tent.*]

Enter, with drum and colors, CORDELIA, DOC-
TOR, *and* SOLDIERS.

CORDELIA:
Alack, 'tis he: why, he was met even now
As mad as the vexed sea; singing aloud;
Crowned with rank femiter and furrow-weeds,
With hardocks, hemlock, nettles, cuckoo-flow'rs,
5 Darnel,° and all the idle weeds that grow
In our sustaining corn.° A century° send forth;
Search every acre in the high-grown field.
And bring him to our eye. [*Exit an* OFFICER.]
    What can man's wisdom°
In the restoring his bereavèd° sense?
10 He that helps him take all my outward° worth.
DOCTOR:
There is means, madam:
Our foster-nurse° of nature is repose,
The which he lacks: that to provoke° in him,
Are many simples operative,° whose power
Will close the eye of anguish.
15 CORDELIA: All blest secrets,
All you unpublished virtues° of the earth,
Spring with my tears! be aidant and remediate°
In the good man's distress! Seek, seek for him,
Lest his ungoverned rage dissolve the life
That wants the means to lead it.°

51 **'Tis so** i.e., I have heard of them   53 **dear cause**
important reason
IV.IV.3–5 **femiter . . . Darnel:** *femiter* fumitory, whose
leaves and juice are bitter; *furrow-weeds* weeds that grow
in the furrow, or plowed land; *hardocks* hoar or white
docks (?), burdocks, harlocks; *hemlock* a poison; *nettles*
plants that sting and burn; *cuckoo-flow'rs* identified with
a plant employed to remedy diseases of the brain; *Darnel*
tares, noisome weeds   6 **sustaining corn** life-maintain-
ing wheat   6 **century** sentry (?); troop of a hundred
soldiers   8 **What . . . wisdom** what can science accomplish   9 **bereavèd** impaired   10 **outward** material   12
foster-nurse fostering nurse   13 **provoke** induce   14
simples operative efficacious medicinal herbs   16 **unpublished virtues** i.e., secret remedial herbs   17 **reme-
diate** remedial   20 **wants . . . it** i.e., lacks the reason to
control the rage

Enter MESSENGER.

MESSENGER: News, madam;   20
The British pow'rs are marching hitherward.
CORDELIA:
'Tis known before. Our preparation stands
In expectation of them. O dear father,
It is thy business that I go about;
Therefore° great France   25
My mourning and importuned° tears hath pitied.
No blown° ambition doth our arms incite,
But love, dear love, and our aged father's right:
Soon may I hear and see him!   *Exeunt.*

[SCENE V. GLOUCESTER's *castle.*]

Enter REGAN *and* OSWALD.

REGAN:
But are my brother's pow'rs set forth?
OSWALD: Ay, madam.
Himself in person there?
OSWALD: Madam, with much ado:°
Your sister is the better soldier.
REGAN:
Lord Edmund spake not with your lord at home?
OSWALD:
No, madam.   5
REGAN:
What might import° my sister's letter to him?
OSWALD:
I know not, lady.
REGAN:
Faith, he is posted° hence on serious matter.
It was great ignorance,° Gloucester's eyes being
    out,
To let him live. Where he arrives he moves   10
All hearts against us: Edmund, I think, is gone,
In pity of his misery, to dispatch
His nighted° life; moreover, to descry
The strength o' th' enemy.
OSWALD:
I must needs after him, madam, with my letter.   15
REGAN:
Our troops set forth tomorrow: stay with us;
The ways are dangerous.
OSWALD: I may not, madam:
My lady charted my duty° in this business.

25 **Therefore** because of that   26 **importuned** importu-
nate   27 **blown** puffed up
IV.V.2 **ado** bother and persuasion   6 **import** purport,
carry as its message   8 **is posted** has ridden speedily   9
ignorance folly   13 **nighted** (1) darkened, because
blinded (2) benighted   18 **charged my duty** ordered me
as a solemn duty

REGAN:
Why should she write to Edmund? Might not you
20 Transport her purposes° by word? Belike,°
Some things I know not what. I'll love thee much,
Let me unseal the letter.
OSWALD: Madam, I had rather—
REGAN:
I know your lady does not love her husband;
I am sure of that: and at her late° being here
25 She gave strange eliads° and most speaking looks
To noble Edmund. I know you are of her bosom.°
OSWALD: I, madam?
REGAN:
I speak in understanding: y' are; I know't:
Therefore I do advise you, take this note:°
30 My lord is dead; Edmund and I have talked;
And more convenient° is he for my hand
Than for your lady's: you may gather more.°
If you do find him, pray you, give him this;°
And when your mistress hears thus much from
you,
35 I pray, desire her call° her wisdom to her.
So, fare you well.
If you do chance to hear of that blind traitor,
Preferment° falls on him that cuts him off.
OSWALD:
Would I could meet him, madam! I should show
What party I do follow.
40 REGAN: Fare thee well. *Exeunt.*

[SCENE VI. *Fields near Dover.*]

Enter GLOUCESTER *and* EDGAR.

GLOUCESTER:
When shall I come to th' top of that same hill?
EDGAR:
You do climb up it now. Look, how we labor.
GLOUCESTER:
Methinks the ground is even.
EDGAR: Horrible steep.
Hark, do you hear the sea?
GLOUCESTER: No, truly.
EDGAR:
5 Why then your other senses grow imperfect
By your eyes' anguish.°
GLOUCESTER: So may it be indeed.

Methinks thy voice is altered, and thou speak'st
In better phrase and matter than thou didst.
EDGAR:
Y' are much deceived: in nothing am I changed
But in my garments.
GLOUCESTER: Methinks y' are better spoken. 10
EDGAR:
Come on, sir; here's the place: stand still. How
fearful
And dizzy 'tis to cast one's eyes so low!
The crows and choughs° that wing the midway air°
Show scarce so gross° as beetles. Half way down
Hangs one that gathers sampire,° dreadful trade! 15
Methinks he seems no bigger than his head.
The fishermen that walk upon the beach
Appear like mice; and yond tall anchoring° bark
Diminished to her cock;° her cock, a buoy
Almost too small for sight. The murmuring surge 20
That on th' unnumb'red idle pebble° chafes
Cannot be heard so high. I'll look no more,
Lest my brain turn and the deficient sight
Topple° down headlong.
GLOUCESTER: Set me where you stand.
EDGAR:
Give me your hand: you are now within a foot 25
Of th' extreme verge: for all beneath the moon
Would I not leap upright.°
GLOUCESTER: Let go my hand.
Here, friend, 's another purse; in it a jewel
Well worth a poor man's taking. Fairies° and gods
Prosper it with thee! Go thou further off; 30
Bid me farewell, and let me hear thee going.
EDGAR:
Now fare ye well, good sir.
GLOUCESTER: With all my heart.
EDGAR [*aside*]:
Why I do trifle thus with his despair
Is done to cure it.°
GLOUCESTER: O you mighty gods!

He kneels.

This world I do renounce, and in your sights 35

20 **Transport her purposes** convey her intentions 20
Belike probably 24 **late** recently 25 **eliads** amorous
looks 26 **of her bosom** in her confidence 29 **take this
note** take note of this 31 **convenient** fitting 32 **gather
more** surmise more yourself 33 **this** this advice 35
call recall 38 **Preferment** promotion
IV.VI.6 **anguish** pain

13 **choughs** a kind of crow 13 **midway air** i.e., halfway
down the cliff 14 **gross** large 15 **sampire** samphire,
an aromatic herb associated with Dover Cliffs 18 **an-
choring** anchored 19 **cock** cockboat, a small boat
usually towed behind the ship 21 **unnumb'red idle
pebble** innumerable pebbles, moved to and fro by the
waves to no purpose 23–24 **the . . . Topple** my failing
sight topple me 27 **upright** i.e., even up in the air, to
say nothing of forward, over the cliff 29 **Fairies** who are
supposed to guard and multiply hidden treasure 33–34
Why . . . it I play on his despair in order to cure it

Shake patiently my great affliction off:
If I could bear it longer and not fall
To quarrel with° your great opposeless° wills,
My snuff° and loathèd part of nature should
40 Burn itself out. If Edgar live, O bless him!
Now, fellow, fare thee well.

He falls.

EDGAR: Gone, sir, farewell.
And yet I know not how° conceit° may rob
The treasury of life, when life itself
Yields to° the theft. Had he been where he thought,
45 By this had thought been past. Alive or dead?
Ho, you sir! friend! Hear you, sir! speak!
Thus might he pass° indeed: yet he revives.
What are you, sir?

GLOUCESTER: Away, and let me die.

EDGAR:
Hadst thou been aught but gossamer, feathers, air,
50 So many fathom down precipitating,°
Thou'dst shivered like an egg: but thou dost breathe;
Hast heavy substance; bleed'st not; speak'st; art
sound.
Ten masts at each° make not the altitude
Which thou hast perpendicularly fell:
55 Thy life's° a miracle. Speak yet again.

GLOUCESTER:
But have I fall'n, or no?

EDGAR:
From the dread summit of this chalky bourn.°
Look up a-height;° the shrill-gorged° lark so far
Cannot be seen or heard: do but look up.

GLOUCESTER:
60 Alack, I have no eyes.
Is wretchedness deprived that benefit,
To end itself by death? 'Twas yet some comfort,
When misery could beguile° the tyrant's rage
And frustrate his proud will.

EDGAR: Give me your arm
65 Up, so. How is't? Feel you° your legs? You stand.

GLOUCESTER:
Too well, too well.

EDGAR: This is above all strangeness.
Upon the crown o' th' cliff, what thing was that
Which parted from you?

37–38 **fall . . . with** rebel against   38 **opposeless** not to
be, and not capable of being, opposed   39 **snuff** the
guttering (and stinking) wick of a burnt-out candle   42
how but what; **conceit** imagination   44 **Yields to** allows   47 **pass** die   50 **precipitating** falling   53 **at each**
one on top of the other   55 **life's** survival is   57 **bourn**
boundary   58 **a-height** on high   58 **gorged** throated,
voiced   63 **beguile** cheat (i.e., by suicide)   65 **Feel you**
have you any feeling in

GLOUCESTER: A poor unfortunate beggar.

EDGAR:
As I stood here below, methought his eyes
Were two full moons; he had a thousand noses,   70
Horns whelked° and waved like the enridgèd° sea:
It was some fiend; therefore; thou happy father,°
Think that the clearest° gods, who make them
honors
Of men's impossibilities,° have preserved thee.

GLOUCESTER:
I do remember now: henceforth I'll bear   75
Affliction till it do cry out itself,
"Enough, enough," and die. That thing you speak
of,
I took it for a man; often 'twould say,
"The fiend, the fiend"—he led me to that place.

EDGAR:
Bear free° and patient thoughts.

Enter LEAR *[fantastically dressed with wild
flowers].*

                     But who comes here?   80
The safer° sense will ne'er accommodate°
His master thus.

LEAR: No, they cannot touch me for coining;° I
am the king himself.

EDGAR:
O thou side-piercing sight!   85

LEAR: Nature's above art in that respect.° There's
your press-money.° That fellow handles his bow
like a crow-keeper;° draw me a clothier's yard.°
Look, look a mouse! Peace, peace; this piece of
toasted cheese will do't. There's my gauntlet;° I'll   90

71 **whelked** twisted   71 **enridgèd** i.e., furrowed into
waves   72 **happy father** fortunate old man   73 **clearest**
purest   73–74 **who . . . impossibilities** who cause
themselves to be honored and revered by performing
miracles of which men are incapable   80 **free** i.e.,
emancipated from grief and despair, which fetter the
soul   81 **safer** sounder, saner   81 **accommodate** dress,
adorn   83 **touch . . . coining** arrest me for minting
coins (the king's prerogative)   86 **Nature's . . . respect**
i.e., a born king is superior to legal (and hence artificial)
inhibition; there is also a glance here at the popular
Renaissance debate concerning the relative importance
of nature (inspiration) and art (training)   87 **press-
money** paid to conscripted soldiers   88 **crow-keeper** a
farmer scaring away crows   88 **clothier's yard** the standard English arrow was a cloth-yard long; here the
injunction is to draw the arrow back, like a powerful
archer, a full yard to the ear   90 **gauntlet** armored
glove, thrown down as a challenge

prove it on° a giant. Bring up the brown bills.° O,
well flown,° bird! i' th' clout, i' th' clout:° hewgh!°
Give the word.°

EDGAR: Sweet marjoram.°

95   LEAR: Pass.

GLOUCESTER: I know that voice.

LEAR: Ha! Goneril, with a white beard! They
flattered me like a dog,° and told me I had white
hairs in my beard ere the black ones were there.°
100   To say "ay" and "no" to everything that I said!
"Ay" and "no" too was no good divinity.° When
the rain came to wet me once and the wind to
make me chatter; when the thunder would not
peace at my bidding; there I found 'em, there I
105   smelt 'em out. Go to, they are not men o' their
words: they told me I was everything; 'tis a lie, I am
not ague-proof.°

GLOUCESTER:
The trick° of that voice I do well remember:
Is't not the king?

LEAR: Ay, every inch a king.
110   When I do stare, see how the subject quakes.
I pardon that man's life. What was thy cause?°
Adultery?
Thou shalt not die: die for adultery! No:
The wren goes to't, and the small gilded fly
115   Does lecher° in my sight.
Let copulation thrive; for Gloucester's bastard son
Was kinder to his father than my daughters
Got° 'tween the lawful sheets.
To't, luxury,° pell-mell! for I lack soldiers.°
120   Behold yond simp'ring dame,

Whose face between her forks presages snow,°
That minces° virtue and does shake the head
To hear of pleasure's name.°
The fitchew,° nor the soilèd° horse, goes to't
With a more riotous appetite.   125
Down from the waist they are Centaurs,°
Though women all above:
But to the girdle° do the gods inherit,°
Beneath is all the fiend's.
There's hell, there's darkness, there is the sul-   130
phurous pit, burning, scalding, stench, consump-
tion; fie, fie, fie! pah, pah! Give me an ounce of
civet;° good apothecary, sweeten my imagination:
there's money for thee.

GLOUCESTER:
O, let me kiss that hand!   135

LEAR:
Let me wipe it first; it smells of mortality.°

GLOUCESTER:
O ruined piece of nature! This great world
Shall so wear out to nought.° Dost thou know me?

LEAR: I remember thine eyes well enough. Dost
thou squiny° at me? No, do thy worst, blind   140
Cupid;° I'll not love. Read thou this challenge;°
mark but the penning of it.

GLOUCESTER:
Were all thy letters suns, I could not see.

EDGAR:
I would not take° this from report: it is,
And my heart breaks at it.   145

LEAR: Read.

GLOUCESTER:
What, with the case° of eyes?

LEAR: O, ho, are you there with me?° No eyes
in your head, nor no money in your purse? Your
eyes are in a heavy case,° your purse in a light,° yet   150
you see how this world goes.

---

91 **prove it on** maintain my challenge even against
91 **brown bills** halberds varnished to prevent rust (here
the reference is to the soldiers who carry them)   92 **well
flown** falconer's cry; and perhaps a reference to the flight
of the arrow   92 **clout** the target shot at   92 **hewgh**
imitating the whizzing of the arrow (?)   93 **word** pass-
word   94 **Sweet marjoram** herb, used as a remedy for
brain disease   98 **like a dog** as a dog flatters   98–99 **I . . .
there** I was wise before I had even grown a beard   101
no good divinity bad theology, because contrary to the
biblical saying (II Corinthians 1:18), "Our word toward
you was not yea and nay"; see also James 5:12, "But let
your yea be yea, and your nay, nay; lest ye fall into
condemnation"; and Matthew 5:36–37   107 **ague-
proof** secure against fever   108 **trick** intonation   111
cause offense   115 **lecher** copulate   118 **Got** begot
119 **luxury** lechery   119 **for . . . soldiers** i.e., (1) whom
copulation will supply (?) (2) and am therefore powerless (?)

121 **Whose . . . snow** whose cold demeanor seems to
promise chaste behavior ("forks" = legs)   122 **minces**
squeamishly pretends to   123 **pleasure's name** the very
name of sexual pleasure   124 **fitchew** polecat (and slang
for prostitute)   124 **soilèd** put to pasture, and hence
wanton with feeding   126 **Centaurs** lustful creatures,
half man and half horse   128 **girdle** waist   128 **inherit**
possess   133 **civet** perfume   136 **mortality** (1) death (2)
existence   137–138 **This . . . nought** i.e., The universe
(macrocosm) will decay to nothing in the same way as
the little world of man (microcosm)   140 **squiny** squint,
look sideways, like a prostitute   140–141 **blind Cupid**
the sign hung before a brothel   141 **challenge** a reminiscence of lines 90–91   144 **take** believe   147 **case**
empty sockets   148 **are . . . me** is that what you tell
me   150 **heavy case** sad plight (pun on line 147)   150
light i.e., empty

GLOUCESTER:
I see it feelingly.°

LEAR: What, art mad? A man may see how this
world goes with no eyes. Look with thine ears: see
155 how yond justice rails upon yond simple° thief.
Hark, in thine ear: change places, and, handy-
dandy,° which is the justice, which is the thief?
Thou hast seen a farmer's dog bark at a beggar?

GLOUCESTER: Ay, sir.

160 LEAR: And the creature run from the cur? There
thou mightst behold the great image of authority:°
a dog's obeyed in office.°
Thou rascal beadle,° hold thy bloody hand!
Why dost thou lash that whore? Strip thy own
back;
165 Thou hotly lusts to use her in that kind°
For which thou whip'st her. The usurer hangs the
cozener.°
Through tattered clothes small vices do appear;
Robes and furred gowns° hide all. Plate sin with
gold,
And the strong lance of justice hurtless° breaks;
170 Arm it in rags, a pygmy's straw does pierce it.
None does offend, none, I say, none; I'll able° 'em:
Take that° of me, my friend, who have the power
To seal th' accuser's lips. Get thee glass eyes,°
And, like a scurvy politician,° seem
To see the things thou dost not. Now, now, now,
175 now.
Pull off my boots: harder, harder: so.

EDGAR:
O, matter and impertinency° mixed!
Reason in madness!

LEAR:
If thou wilt weep my fortunes, take my eyes.
180 I know thee well enough; thy name is Gloucester:
Thou must be patient; we came crying hither:

Thou know'st, the first time that we smell the air
We wawl and cry. I will preach to thee: mark.

GLOUCESTER:
Alack, alack the day!

LEAR:
When we are born, we cry that we are come   185
To this great stage of fools. This'° a good block.°
It were a delicate° stratagem, to shoe
A troop of horse with felt: I'll put't in proof;°
And when I have stol'n upon these son-in-laws,
Then, kill, kill, kill, kill, kill, kill!   190

Enter a GENTLEMAN, [*with* ATTENDANTS].

GENTLEMAN:
O, here he is: lay hand upon him. Sir,
Your most dear daughter—

LEAR:
No rescue? What, a prisoner? I am even
The natural fool° of fortune. Use me well;
You shall have ransom. Let me have surgeons;   195
I am cut° to th' brains.

GENTLEMAN: You shall have anything.

LEAR:
No seconds?° all myself?
Why, this would make a man a man of salt,°
To use his eyes for garden water-pots,
Ay, and laying autumn's dust.   200

GENTLEMAN:
Good sir—

LEAR:
I will die bravely,° like a smug° bridegroom.°
What!

152 **feelingly** (1) by touch (2) by feeling pain (3) with
emotion   155 **simple** common, of low estate   157
handy-dandy i.e., choose, guess (after the children's
game—"Handy-dandy, prickly prandy"—of choosing
the correct hand)   161 **image of authority** symbol revealing the true meaning of authority   162 **a dog's . . .
office** i.e., whoever has power is obeyed   163 **beadle**
parish constable   165 **kind** i.e., sexual act   166 **The
usurer . . . cozener** i.e., The powerful money-lender, in
his role as judge, puts to death the petty cheat   168
Robes . . . gowns worn by a judge   169 **hurtless** i.e.,
without hurting the sinner   171 **able** vouch for   172
that the immunity just conferred (line 171)   173 **glass
eyes** spectacles   174 **scurvy politician** vile politic man
177 **matter and impertinency** sense and nonsense

186 **This** this is   186 **block** various meanings have been
suggested, for example, the stump of a tree, on which
Lear is supposed to climb; a mounting-block, which
suggests "horse" (line 188); a hat (which Lear or another
must be made to wear), from the block on which a felt
hat is molded, and which would suggest a "felt" (line
188); the proposal here is that "block" be taken to denote
the quintain, whose function is to bear blows, "a mere
lifeless block" (*As You Like It*, I.ii.247), an object shaped
like a man and used for tilting practice; see also *Much
Ado About Nothing*, II.i.231–232, "She misused me
past the endurance of a block!" and, in the same passage,
the associated reference, "I stood like a man at a mark
[target]" (lines 237–238)   187 **delicate** subtle   188
put't in proof test it   194 **natural fool** born sport (with
pun on "natural" = imbecile)   196 **cut** wounded   197
seconds supporters   198 **man of salt** i.e., all (salt)
tears   202 **bravely** (1) smartly attired (2) courageously
202 **smug** spick and span   202 **bridegroom** whose
"brave" sexual feats are picked up in the pun on "die"

I will be jovial: come, come; I am a king;
Masters, know you that?
GENTLEMAN:
205 You are a royal one, and we obey you.
  LEAR: Then there's life in't.° Come, and you get
it, you shall get it by running. Sa, sa, sa, sa.°

            Exit [running; ATTENDANTS *follow*].

  GENTLEMAN:
A sight most pitiful in the meanest wretch,
Past speaking of in a king! Thou hast one daughter
210 Who redeems Nature from the general curse
Which twain have brought her to.°
  EDGAR:
Hail, gentle° sir.
  GENTLEMAN: Sir, speed° you: what's your will?
  EDGAR:
Do you hear aught, sir, of a battle toward?°
  GENTLEMAN:
Most sure and vulgar:° every one hears that,
Which can distinguish sound.
215   EDGAR: But, by your favor,
How near's the other army?
  GENTLEMAN:
Near and on speedy foot; the main descry
Stands on the hourly thought.°
  EDGAR: I thank you, sir: that's all.
  GENTLEMAN:
Though that the queen on special cause is here,
Her army is moved on.
220   EDGAR: I thank you, sir.
                         *Exit [*GENTLEMAN*]*.
  GLOUCESTER:
You ever-gentle gods, take my breath from me;
Let not my worser spirit° tempt me again
To die before you please.
  EDGAR: Well pray you, father.
  GLOUCESTER:
Now, good sir, what are you?
  EDGAR:
225 A most poor man, made tame° to fortune's blows;
Who, by the art of known and feeling sorrows,°

206 **there's life in't** there's still hope   207 **Sa . . . sa**
hunting and rallying cry; also an interjection of defiance   210–211 **general . . . to** (1) universal condemnation which Goneril and Regan have made for (2)
damnation incurred by the original sin of Adam and
Eve   212 **gentle** noble   212 **speed** God speed   213
toward impending   214 **vulgar** common knowledge
217–218 **the main . . . thought** we expect to see the
main body of the army any hour   222 **worser spirit** bad
angel, evil side of my nature   225 **tame** submissive
226 **art . . . sorrows** instruction of sorrows painfully
experienced

Am pregnant° to good pity. Give me your hand,
I'll lead you to some biding.°
  GLOUCESTER: Hearty thanks;
The bounty and the benison° of heaven
To boot, and boot.°

  Enter OSWALD.

  OSWALD:
                A proclaimed prize!° Most happy!°   230
That eyeless head of thine was first framed° flesh
To raise my fortunes. Thou old unhappy traitor,
Briefly thyself remember:° the sword is out
That must destroy thee.
  GLOUCESTER: Now let thy friendly° hand
Put strength enough to't.   [EDGAR *interposes.*]
  OSWALD: Wherefore, bold peasant,   235
Dar'st thou support a published° traitor? Hence!
Lest that th' infection of his fortune take
Like hold on thee. Let go his arm.
  EDGAR:
Chill° not let go, zir, without vurther 'casion.°
  OSWALD:
Let go, slave, or thou diest!   240
  EDGAR: Good gentleman, go your gait,° and let
poor volk° pass. And chud ha' bin zwaggered° out
of my life, 'twould not ha' bin zo long as 'tis by a
vortnight. Nay, come not near th' old man; keep
out, che vor' ye,° or I'se° try whether your costard°   245
or my ballow° be the harder: chill be plain with
you.
  OSWALD: Out, dunghill!
  They fight.
  EDGAR: Chill pick your teeth,° zir: come; no
matter vor your foins.°   250
  [OSWALD *falls.*]
  OSWALD:
Slave, thou hast slain me. Villain, take my purse:

227 **pregnant** disposed   228 **biding** place of refuge
229 **benison** blessing   230 **To . . . boot** also, and in the
highest degree   230 **proclaimed prize** i.e., one with a
price on his head   230 **happy** fortunate (for Oswald)
231 **framed** created   233 **thyself remember** i.e., pray,
think of your sins   234 **friendly** i.e., because it offers the
death Gloucester covets   236 **published** proclaimed
239 **Chill** I will (Edgar speaks in rustic dialect)   239
vurther 'casion further occasion   241 **gait** way   242
volk folk   242 **And . . . zwaggered** if I could have been
swaggered   245 **che vor' ye** I warrant you   245 **I'se** I
shall   245 **costard** head (literally, "apple")   246 **ballow**
cudgel   249 **Chill . . . teeth** I will knock your teeth
out   250 **foins** thrusts

If ever thou wilt thrive, bury my body,
And give the letters which thou find'st about° me
To Edmund Earl of Gloucester; seek him out
255   Upon the English party.° O, untimely death!
Death!   (*He dies.*)
    EDGAR:
I know thee well. A serviceable° villain,
As duteous° to the vices of thy mistress
As badness would desire.
    GLOUCESTER: What, is he dead?
    EDGAR:
260   Sit you down, father; rest you.
Let's see these pockets: the letters that he speaks of
May be my friends. He's dead; I am only sorry
He had no other deathsman.° Let us see:
Leave,° gentle wax;° and, manners, blame us not:
265   To know our enemies' minds, we rip their hearts;
Their papers° is more lawful.

   Reads the letter.

"Let our reciprocal vows be remembered. You
have many opportunities to cut him off: if your will
want not,° time and place will be fruitfully offered.
270   There is nothing done, if he return the conqueror:
then am I the prisoner, and his bed my jail; from
the loathed warmth whereof deliver me, and supply the place for your labor.
   "Your—wife, so I would° say—affectionate servant, and for you her own for venture,°
275   Goneril."
O indistinguished space of woman's will!°
A plot upon her virtuous husband's life;
And the exchange° my brother! Here in the sands
Thee I'll rake up,° the post unsanctified°
280   Of murderous lechers; and in the mature° time,
With this ungracious paper° strike° the sight
Of the death-practiced° duke: for him 'tis well
That of thy death and business I can tell.

253 **about** upon   255 **party** side   257 **serviceable** ready
to be used   258 **duteous** obedient   263 **deathsman**
executioner   264 **Leave** by your leave   264 **wax** with
which the letter is sealed   266 **Their papers** i.e., to rip
their papers   268–69 **if . . . not** if your desire (and lust)
be not lacking   274 **would** would like to   275 **and . . .
venture** i.e., and one who holds you her own for
venturing (Edmund had earlier been promised union by
Goneril, "If you dare venture in your own behalf,"
IV.II.21)   276 **indistinguished . . . will** unlimited range
of woman's lust   278 **exchange** substitute   279 **rake up**
cover up, bury   279 **post unsanctified** unholy messenger   280 **mature** ripe   281 **ungracious paper** wicked
letter   281 **strike** blast   282 **death-practiced** whose
death is plotted

    GLOUCESTER:
The king is mad: how stiff° is my vile sense,°
That I stand up, and have ingenious° feeling   285
Of my huge sorrows! Better I were distract:°
So should my thoughts be severed from my griefs,
And woes by wrong imaginations° lose
The knowledge of themselves.
                    Drum afar off.
    EDGAR: Give me your hand:
Far off, methinks, I hear the beaten drum.   290
Come, father, I'll bestow° you with a friend.
                      Exeunt.

SCENE VII. [*A tent in the French camp.*]

Enter CORDELIA, KENT, DOCTOR, *and*
GENTLEMAN.

    CORDELIA:
O thou good Kent, how shall I live and work,
To match thy goodness? My life will be too short,
And every measure fail me.
    KENT:
To be acknowledged, madam, is o'erpaid.
All my reports go° with the modest truth,   5
Nor more nor clipped,° but so.
    CORDELIA: Be better suited:°
These weeds° are memories° of those worser hours:
I prithee, put them off.
    KENT: Pardon, dear madam:
Yet to be known shortens my made intent:°
My boon I make it,° that you know me not   10
Till time and I think meet.°
    CORDELIA:
Then be't so, my good lord. [*To the* DOCTOR.]
   How does the king?
    DOCTOR:
Madam, sleeps still.
    CORDELIA:
O you kind gods!
Cure this great breach in his abusèd° nature.   15
Th' untuned and jarring senses, O, wind up°
Of this child-changèd° father.
    DOCTOR: So please your majesty

284 **stiff** unbending   284 **vile sense** hateful capacity for
feeling   285 **ingenious** conscious   286 **distract** distracted, mad   288 **wrong imaginations** delusions   291
bestow lodge
IV.VII.5 **go** conform   6 **clipped** curtailed; **suited** attired   7 **weeds** clothes   7 **memories** reminders   9 **Yet
. . . intent** to reveal myself just yet interferes with the
plan I have made   10 **My . . . it** I ask this reward   11
meet fitting   15 **abusèd** disturbed   16 **wind up** tune
17 **child-changèd** changed, deranged (and also, reduced
to a child) by the cruelty of his children

That we may wake the king: he hath slept long.

CORDELIA:

Be governed by your knowledge, and proceed

20 I' th' sway of° your own will. Is he arrayed?

Enter LEAR *in a chair carried by* SERVANTS.

GENTLEMAN:

Ay, madam; in the heaviness of sleep

We put fresh garments on him.

DOCTOR:

Be by good madam, when we do awake him;

I doubt not of his temperance.°

CORDELIA: Very well.

DOCTOR:

25 Please you, draw near. Louder the music there!

CORDELIA:

O my dear father, restoration hang

Thy medicine on my lips, and let this kiss

Repair those violent harms that my two sisters

Have in thy reverence° made.

KENT: Kind and dear princess

CORDELIA:

30 Had you not been their father, these white flakes°

Did challenge° pity of them. Was this a face

To be opposed against the warring winds?

To stand against the deep dread-bolted° thunder?

In the most terrible and nimble stroke

35 Of quick, cross° lightning to watch—poor perdu!°—

With this thin helm?° Mine enemy's dog,

Though he had bit me, should have stood that

    night

Against my fire; and wast thou fain,° poor father,

To hovel thee with swine and rogues° forlorn,

40 In short° and musty straw? Alack, alack!

'Tis wonder that thy life and wits at once

Had not concluded all.° He wakes; speak to him.

DOCTOR:

Madam, do you, 'tis fittest.

CORDELIA:

How does my royal lord? How fares your majesty?

LEAR:

You do me wrong to take me out o' th' grave: 45

Thou art a soul in bliss; but I am bound

Upon a wheel of fire,° that mine own tears

Do scald like molten lead.

CORDELIA: Sir, do you know me?

LEAR:

You are a spirit, I know. Where did you die?

CORDELIA:

Still, still, far wide.°   50

DOCTOR:

He's scarce awake: let him alone awhile.

LEAR:

Where have I been? Where am I? Fair daylight?

I am mightily abused.° I should ev'n die with pity,

To see another thus. I know not what to say.

I will not swear these are my hands: let's see; 55

I feel this pin prick. Would I were assured

Of my condition.

CORDELIA: O, look upon me, sir,

And hold your hand in benediction o'er me.

You must not kneel.

LEAR: Pray, do not mock me:

I am a very foolish fond° old man, 60

Fourscore and upward, not an hour more nor less;

And, to deal plainly,

I fear I am not in my perfect mind.

Methinks I should know you and know this man,

Yet I am doubtful; for I am mainly° ignorant 65

What place this is, and all the skill I have

Remembers not these garments, nor I know not

Where I did lodge last night. Do not laugh at me,

For, as I am a man, I think this lady

To be my child Cordelia.

CORDELIA: And so I am, I am. 70

LEAR:

Be your tears wet? Yes, faith. I pray, weep not.

If you have poison for me, I will drink it.

I know you do not love me; for your sisters

Have, as I do remember, done me wrong.

You have some cause, they have not.

CORDELIA: No cause, no cause. 75

LEAR:

Am I in France?

KENT: In your own kingdom, sir.

LEAR:

Do not abuse° me.

DOCTOR:

Be comforted, good madam: the great rage,°

---

20 **I' . . . of** according to 24 **temperance** sanity 29 **reverence** revered person 30 **flakes** hairs (in long strands) 31 **challenge** claim 33 **deep dread-bolted** deep-voiced and furnished with the dreadful thunderbolt 35 **cross** zigzag 35 **perdu** (1) sentry in a forlorn position (2) lost one 36 **helm** helmet (his scanty hair) 38 **fain** pleased 39 **rogues** vagabonds 40 **short** when straw is freshly cut, it is long, and suitable for bedding, given its flexibility and crispness; as it is used, it becomes musty, shreds into pieces, is "short"; in contemporary Maine usage, "short manure" refers to dung mixed with straw that has been broken up, "long manure" to dung mixed with coarse new straw 42 **concluded all** come to a complete end

47 **wheel of fire** torment associated by the Middle Ages with hell, where Lear thinks he is 50 **wide** i.e., of the mark (of sanity) 53 **abused** deluded 60 **fond** in dotage 65 **mainly** entirely 77 **abuse** deceive 78 **rage** frenzy

You see, is killed in him: and yet it is danger
80 To make him even o'er° the time he has lost.
Desire him to go in; trouble him no more
Till further settling.°

CORDELIA:
Will't please your highness walk?°

LEAR: You must bear with me.
Pray you now, forget and forgive. I am old and
   foolish.

Exeunt. Mane[n]t° KENT
and GENTLEMAN.

85 GENTLEMAN: Holds it true, sir, that the Duke of
Cornwall was so slain?

KENT: Most certain, sir.

GENTLEMAN: Who is conductor of his people?

KENT: As 'tis said, the bastard son of Gloucester.

90 GENTLEMAN: They say Edgar, his banished son,
is with the Earl of Kent in Germany.

KENT: Report is changeable.° 'Tis time to look
about; the powers° of the kingdom approach apace.

GENTLEMAN: The arbitrement° is like to be
95 bloody. Fare you well, sir.   [*Exit.*]

KENT:
My point and period will be throughly wrought,°
Or well or ill, as this day's battle's fought.

Exit.

ACT V

SCENE I. [*The British camp near Dover.*]

Enter, with drum and colors, EDMUND, REGAN,
GENTLEMEN, *and* SOLDIERS.

EDMUND:
Know° of the duke if his last purpose hold,°
Or whether since he is advised° by aught
To change the course: he's full of alteration
And self-reproving: bring his constant pleasure.°
                  [*To a* GENTLEMAN, *who goes out.*]

REGAN:
5 Our sister's man is certainly miscarried.°

EDMUND:
'Tis to be doubted,° madam.

REGAN: Now, sweet lord,
You know the goodness I intend upon you:
Tell me, but truly, but then speak the truth,
Do you not love my sister?

EDMUND: In honored° love.

REGAN:
But have you never found my brother's way   10
To the forfended° place?

EDMUND: That thought abuses° you.

REGAN:
I am doubtful that you have been conjunct
And bosomed with her, as far as we call hers.°

EDMUND:
No, by mine honor, madam.

REGAN:
I shall never endure her: dear my lord,   15
Be not familiar with her.

EDMUND: Fear° me not.—
She and the duke her husband!

Enter, with drum and colors, ALBANY, GONERIL,
[*and*] SOLDIERS.

GONERIL [*aside*]:
I had rather lose the battle than that sister
Should loosen° him and me.

ALBANY:
Our very loving sister, well be-met°   20
Sir, this I heard, the king is come to his daughter,
With others whom the rigor of our state°
Forced to cry out. Where I could not be honest,°
I never yet was valiant: for this business,
It touches us, as° France invades our land,   25
Not bolds the king, with others, whom, I fear,
Most just and heavy causes make oppose.°

EDMUND:
Sir, you speak nobly.

REGAN: Why is this reasoned?°

GONERIL:
Combine together 'gainst the enemy;

---

80 **even o'er** smooth over by filling in; and hence,
"recollect"   82 **settling** calming   83 **walk** perhaps in
the sense of "withdraw"   84 s.d. **Mane[n]t** remain   92
Report is changeable rumors are unreliable   93 **powers**
armies   94 **arbitrement** deciding encounter   96 **My . . .
wrought** the aim and end, the close of my life, will be
completely worked out
V.i.1 **Know** learn   1 **last purpose hold** most recent
intention (to fight) be maintained   2 **advised** induced
4 **constant pleasure** fixed (final) decision   5 **miscarried**
come to grief

6 **doubted** feared   9 **honored** honorable   11 **forfended**
forbidden   11 **abuses** (1) deceives (2) demeans, is unworthy of   12–13 **I . . . hers** I fear that you have united
with her intimately, in the fullest possible way   16 **Fear**
distrust   19 **loosen** separate   20 **be-met** met   22 **rigor
. . . state** tyranny of our government   23 **honest** honorable   25 **touches us, as** concerns me, only in that   26–
27 **Not . . . oppose** and not in that France emboldens
the king and others, who have been led, by real and
serious grievances, to take up arms against us   28 **reasoned** argued

30   For these domestic and particular broils°
     Are not the question° here.
          ALBANY: Let's then determine
     With th' ancient of war° on our proceeding.
          EDMUND:
     I shall attend you presently at your tent.
          REGAN:
     Sister, you'll go with us?°
35   GONERIL: No.
          REGAN:
     'Tis most convenient;° pray you, go with us.
          GONERIL [aside]:
     O, ho, I know the riddle.°—I will go.
                              Exeunt both the ARMIES.

     Enter EDGAR [disguised].

          EDGAR:
     If e'er your grace had speech with man so poor,
     Hear me one word.
          ALBANY [To those going out]:
               I'll overtake you. [To EDGAR.] Speak.
               Exeunt [all but ALBANY and EDGAR].
          EDGAR:
40   Before you fight the battle, ope this letter.
     If you have victory, let the trumpet sound
     For° him that brought it: wretched though I seem,
     I can produce a champion that will prove°
     What is avouchèd° there. If you miscarry,
45   Your business of° the world hath so an end,
     And machination° ceases. Fortune love you.
          ALBANY:
     Stay till I have read the letter.
          EDGAR: I was forbid it.
     When time shall serve, let but the herald cry,
     And I'll appear again.
          ALBANY:
50   Why, fare thee well: I will o'erlook° thy paper.
                              Exit [EDGAR].

     Enter EDMUND.

          EDMUND:
     The enemy's in view: draw up your powers.
     Here is the guess° of their true strength and forces

By diligent discovery;° but your haste
Is now urged on you.
     ALBANY: We will greet° the time.
                              Exit.
     EDMUND:
To both these sisters have I sworn my love;   55
Each jealous° of the other, as the stung
Are of the adder. Which of them shall I take?
Both? One? Or neither? Neither can be enjoyed,
If both remain alive: to take the widow
Exasperates, makes mad her sister Goneril;   60
And hardly° shall I carry out my side,°
Her husband being alive. Now then, we'll use
His countenance° for the battle; which being done,
Let her who would be rid of him devise
His speedy taking off. As for the mercy   65
Which he intends to Lear and to Cordelia,
The battle done, and they within our power,
Shall never see his pardon; for my state
Stands on me to defend, not to debate.°
                              Exit.

SCENE II. [A field between the two camps.]

Alarum° within. Enter, with drum and colors,
LEAR, CORDELIA, and SOLDIERS, over the stage;
and exeunt.
     Enter EDGAR and GLOUCESTER.

     EDGAR:
Here, father,° take the shadow of this tree
For your good host; pray that the right may thrive.
If ever I return to you again,
I'll bring you comfort.
     GLOUCESTER: Grace go with you, sir.
                              Exit [EDGAR].

Alarum and retreat° within. [Re]enter EDGAR.

     EDGAR:
Away, old man; give me thy hand; away!   5
King Lear hath lost, he and his daughter ta'en:°
Give me thy hand; come on.

---

53 **By diligent discovery** obtained by careful recon-
noitering   54 **greet** i.e., meet the demands of   56
jealous suspicious   61 **hardly** with difficulty   61 **carry
. . . side** (1) satisfy my ambition (2) fulfill my bargain
(with Goneril)   63 **countenance** authority   68–69 **for
. . . debate** my position requires me to act, not to reason
about right and wrong
V.II.s.d. **Alarum** a trumpet call to battle   1 **father** i.e.,
venerable old man (Edgar has not yet revealed his
identity)   4 s.d. **retreat** signaled by a trumpet   6 **ta'en**
captured

30 **particular broils** private quarrels   31 **question** issue   32 **th' ancient of war** experienced commanders
34 **us** me (rather than Edmund)   36 **convenient** fitting,
desirable   37 **riddle** real reason (for Regan's curious
request)   41–42 **sound For** summon   43 **prove** i.e., by
trial of combat   44 **avouchèd** maintained   45 **of** in
46 **machination** plotting   50 **o'erlook** read over   52
guess estimate

GLOUCESTER:
No further, sir; a man may rot even here.
EDGAR:
What, in ill thoughts again? Men must endure
10   Their going hence, even as their coming hither:
Ripeness° is all. Come on.
GLOUCESTER: And that's true too.
                                              Exeunt.

SCENE III. [*The British camp near Dover.*]

Enter, in conquest, with drum and colors, ED-
MUND; LEAR *and* CORDELIA, *as prisoners;* SOL-
DIERS, CAPTAIN.

EDMUND:
Some officers take them away: good guard,°
Until their greater pleasures° first be known
That are to censure° them.
CORDELIA: We are not the first
Who with best meaning° have incurred the worst.
5   For thee, oppressèd king, I am cast down;
Myself could else out-frown false Fortune's frown.
Shall we not see these daughters and these sisters?
LEAR:
No, no, no, no! Come, let's away to prison:
We two alone will sing like birds i' th' cage:
10   When thou dost ask me blessing, I'll kneel down
And ask of thee forgiveness: so we'll live,
And pray, and sing, and tell old tales, and laugh
At gilded butterflies,° and hear poor rogues
Talk of court news; and we'll talk with them too,
15   Who loses and who wins, who's in, who's out;
And take upon's the mystery of things,
As if we were God's spies:° and we'll wear out,°
In a walled prison, packs and sects of great ones
That ebb and flow by th' moon.°
EDMUND: Take them away.
LEAR:
20   Upon such sacrifices, my Cordelia,
The gods themselves throw incense.° Have I
    caught thee?

He that parts us shall bring a brand from heaven,
And fire us hence like foxes.° Wipe thine eyes;
The good years° shall devour them,° flesh and
    fell,°
Ere they shall make us weep. We'll see 'em starved
    first.   25
Come. [*Exeunt* LEAR *and* CORDELIA, *guarded.*]
EDMUND:
Come hither, captain; hark.
Take thou this note: go follow them to prison:
One step I have advanced thee; if thou dost
As this instructs thee, thou dost make thy way   30
To noble fortunes: know thou this, that men
Are as the time is:° to be tender-minded
Does not become a sword:° thy great employment
Will not bear question;° either say thou'lt do't,
Or thrive by other means.
CAPTAIN: I'll do't, my lord.   35
EDMUND:
About it; and write happy° when th' hast done.
Mark; I say, instantly, and carry it so°
As I have set it down.
CAPTAIN:
I cannot draw a cart, nor eat dried oats;
If it be man's work, I'll do't.   40
                                    Exit CAPTAIN.

Flourish. Enter ALBANY, GONERIL, REGAN [*another* CAPTAIN, *and*] SOLDIERS.

ALBANY:
Sir, you have showed today your valiant strain,°
And fortune led you well: you have the captives
Who were the opposites of° this day's strife:
I do require them of you, so to use them
As we shall find their merits° and our safety   45
May equally determine.
EDMUND: Sir, I thought it fit
To send the old and miserable king

11 **Ripeness** maturity, as of fruit that is ready to fall
V.iii.1 **good guard** let them be well guarded   2 **their greater pleasures** the will of those in command, the great ones   3 **censure** pass judgment on   4 **meaning** intentions   13 **gilded butterflies** i.e., gorgeously attired courtiers, fluttering after nothing   16–17 **take . . . spies** profess to read the riddle of existence, as if endowed with divine omniscience   17 **wear out** outlast   18–19 **packs . . . moon** intriguing and partisan cliques of those in high station, whose fortunes change every month   20–21 **Upon . . . incense** i.e., the gods approve our renunciation of the world

22–23 **He . . . foxes** No human agency can separate us, but only divine interposition, as of a heavenly torch parting us like foxes that are driven from their place of refuge by fire and smoke   24 **good years** plague and pestilence ("undefined malefic power or agency," *Oxford English Dictionary*)   24 **them** the enemies of Lear and Cordelia   24 **fell** skin   32 **as . . . is** i.e., absolutely determined by the exigencies of the moment   33 **become a sword** befit a soldier   34 **bear question** admit of discussion   36 **write happy** style yourself fortunate   37 **carry it so** manage the affair in exactly that manner (as if Cordelia had taken her own life)   41 **strain** (1) stock (2) character   43 **opposites of** opponents in   45 **merits** deserts

To some retention and appointed guard;°
Whose° age had charms in it, whose title more,
50 To pluck the common bosom on his side,°
And turn our impressed lances in our eyes°
Which do command them. With him I sent the
    queen:
My reason all the same; and they are ready
Tomorrow, or at further space,° t'appear
55 Where you shall hold your session.° At this time
We sweat and bleed: the friend hath lost his friend;
And the best quarrels, in the heat, are cursed
By those that feel their sharpness.°
The question of Cordelia and her father
Requires a fitter place.
60   ALBANY: Sir, by your patience,
I hold you but a subject of° this war,
Not as a brother.
    REGAN: That's as we list to grace° him.
Methinks our pleasure might have been demanded,
Ere you had spoke so far. He led our powers,
65 Bore the commission of my place and person;
The which immediacy may well stand up
And call itself your brother.°
    GONERIL: Not so hot:
In his own grace he doth exalt himself
More than in your addition.°
    REGAN: In my rights,
70 By me invested, he compeers° the best.
    GONERIL:
That were the most,° if he should husband you.°
    REGAN:
Jesters do oft prove prophets.
    GONERIL: Holla, holla!
That eye that told you so looked but a-squint.°
    REGAN:
Lady, I am not well; else I should answer

From a full-flowing stomach.° General,   75
Take thou my soldiers, prisoners, patrimony;°
Dispose of them, of me; the walls is thine:°
Witness the world, that I create thee here
My lord, and master.
    GONERIL: Mean you to enjoy him?
    ALBANY:
The let-alone° lies not in your good will.   80
    EDMUND:
Nor in thine, lord.
    ALBANY: Half-blooded° fellow, yes.
    REGAN [to EDMUND]:
Let the drum strike, and prove my title thine.°
    ALBANY:
Stay yet; hear reason. Edmund, I arrest thee
On capital treason; and in thy attaint°
This gilded serpent [pointing to GONERIL]. For   85
    your claim, fair sister,
I bar it in the interest of my wife;
'Tis she is subcontracted° to this lord,
And I, her husband, contradict your banes.°
If you will marry, make your loves° to me;
My lady is bespoke.°
    GONERIL: An interlude!°   90
    ALBANY:
Thou art armed, Gloucester: let the trumpet sound:
If none appear to prove upon thy person
Thy heinous, manifest, and many treasons,
There is my pledge° [throwing down a glove]: I'll
    make° it on thy heart,
Ere I taste bread, thou art in nothing less   95
Than I have here proclaimed thee.
    REGAN: Sick, O, sick!
    GONERIL [aside]:
If not, I'll ne'er trust medicine.°
    EDMUND [throwing down a glove]:
There's my exchange:° what in the world he is

---

48 **retention . . . guard** confinement under duly appointed guard 49 **Whose** i.e., Lear's 50 **pluck . . . side** win the sympathy of the people to himself 51 **turn . . . eyes** turn our conscripted lancers against us 54 **further space** a later time 55 **session** trial 57–58 **best . . . sharpness** worthiest causes may be judged badly by those who have been affected painfully by them, and whose passion has not yet cooled 61 **subject of** subordinate in 62 **list to grace** wish to honor 65–67 **Bore . . . brother** was authorized, as my deputy, to take command; his present status, as my immediate representative, entitles him to be considered your equal 69 **your addition** honors you have bestowed on him 70 **compeers** equals 71 **most** most complete investing in your rights 71 **husband you** become your husband 73 **a-squint** cross-eyed

75 **From . . . stomach** angrily 76 **patrimony** inheritance 77 **walls is thine** i.e., Regan's person, which Edmund has stormed and won 80 **let-alone** power to prevent 81 **Half-blooded** bastard, and so only half noble 82 **prove . . . thine** prove by combat your entitlement to my rights 84 **in thy attaint** as a sharer in the treason for which you are impeached 87 **subcontracted** pledged by a contract which is called into question by the existence of a previous contract (Goneril's marriage) 88 **contradict your banes** forbid your announced intention to marry (by citing the precontract) 89 **loves** love-suits 90 **bespoke** already pledged 90 **interlude** play 94 **pledge** gage 94 **make** prove 97 **medicine** poison 98 **exchange** technical term, denoting the glove Edmund throws down

That names me traitor, villainlike he lies:°
100 Call by the trumpet:° he that dares approach,
On him, on you—who not?—I will maintain
My truth and honor firmly.
    ALBANY:
A herald, ho!
    EDMUND: A herald, ho, a herald!
    ALBANY:
Trust to thy single virtue;° for thy soldiers,
105 All levied in my name, have in my name
Took their discharge.
    REGAN: My sickness grows upon me.
    ALBANY:
She is not well; convey her to my tent.

                          [*Exit* REGAN, *led.*]

Enter a HERALD.

Come hither, herald. Let the trumpet sound—
And read out this.
110 CAPTAIN: Sound, trumpet!

A trumpet sounds.

HERALD (*reads*): "If any man of quality or de-
gree° within the lists° of the army will maintain
upon Edmund, supposed Earl of Gloucester, that
he is a manifold traitor, let him appear by the third
115 sound of the trumpet: he is bold in his defense."
    EDMUND: Sound!

First trumpet.

HERALD: Again!

Second trumpet.

HERALD: Again!

Third trumpet.
    Trumpet answers within. Enter EDGAR, *at the
third sound, armed, a trumpet before him.*°

    ALBANY:
Ask him his purpose, why he appears
Upon this call o' th' trumpet.
120   HERALD: What are you?
Your name, your quality,° and why you answer
This present summons?
    EDGAR: Know, my name is lost;
By treason's tooth bare-gnawn and canker-bit:°

Yet am I noble as the adversary
I come to cope.°
    ALBANY: Which is that adversary?   125
    EDGAR:
What's he that speaks for Edmund, Earl of
    Gloucester?
    EDMUND:
Himself: what say'st thou to him?
    EDGAR: Draw thy sword,
That if my speech offend a noble heart,
Thy arm do thee justice: here is mine.
Behold it is my privilege,   130
The privilege of mine honors,
My oath, and my profession.° I protest,
Maugre° thy strength, place, youth, and eminence,
Despite thy victor sword and fire-new° fortune,
Thy valor and thy heart,° thou art a traitor,   135
False to thy gods, thy brother, and thy father,
Conspirant° 'gainst this high illustrious prince,
And from th' extremest upward° of thy head
To the descent and dust below thy foot,°
A most toad-spotted traitor.° Say thou "No,"   140
This sword, this arm and my best spirits are bent°
To prove upon thy heart, whereto I speak,°
Thou liest.
    EDMUND:
               In wisdom° I should ask thy name,
But since thy outside looks so fair and warlike,
And that thy tongue some say° of breeding breathes,   145
What safe and nicely° I might well delay°
By rule of knighthood, I disdain and spurn:
Back do I toss these treasons° to thy head;
With the hell-hated° lie o'erwhelm thy heart;
Which for they yet glance by and scarcely bruise,   150
This sword of mine shall give them instant way,

---

99 **villainlike he lies** the lie direct, a challenge to mortal
combat 100 **trumpet** trumpeter 104 **single virtue** unaided valor 111–112 **quality or degree** rank or position 112 **lists** rolls 118 s.d. **trumpet before him**
trumpeter preceding him 121 **quality** rank 123 **canker-bit** eaten by the caterpillar

125 **cope** encounter 130–132 **it . . . profession** my
knighthood entitles me to challenge you, and to have my
challenge accepted 133 **Maugre** despite 134 **fire-new**
fresh from the forge or mint 135 **heart** courage 137
Conspirant conspiring, a conspirator 138 **extremest
upward** the very top 139 **the . . . foot** your lowest part
(sole) and the dust beneath it 140 **toad-spotted traitor**
spotted with treason (and hence venomous, as the toad is
allegedly marked with spots that exude venom) 141
bent directed 142 **whereto I speak** Edgar speaks from
the heart, and speaks to the heart of Edmund 143
wisdom prudence (since he is not obliged to fight with
one of lesser rank) 145 **say** assay (i.e., touch, sign)
146 **safe and nicely** cautiously and punctiliously 146
delay i.e., avoid 148 **treasons** accusations of treason 149 **hell-hated** hated like hell

Where they shall rest for ever.° Trumpets, speak!

Alarums. [They] fight. [EDMUND *falls.*]

ALBANY:
Save° him, save him!
    GONERIL: This is practice,° Gloucester:
By th' law of war thou wast not bound to answer
155 An unknown opposite;° thou art not vanquished,
But cozened and beguiled.
    ALBANY: Shut your mouth, dame,
Or with this paper shall I stop it. Hold, sir;°
Thou° worse than any name, read thine own evil.
No tearing, lady; I perceive you know it.
    GONERIL:
160 Say, if I do, the laws are mine, not thine:
Who can arraign me for't?
    ALBANY: Most monstrous! O!
Know'st thou this paper?
    GONERIL: Ask me not what I know.
                                Exit.

ALBANY:
Go after her; she's desperate; govern° her.
    EDMUND:
What you have charged me with, that have I done;
165 And more, much more; the time will bring it out.
'Tis past, and so am I. But what art thou
That hast this fortune on° me? If thou'rt noble,
I do forgive thee.
    EDGAR: Let's exchange charity.°
I am no less in blood° than thou art, Edmund;
170 If more,° the more th' hast wronged me.
My name is Edgar, and thy father's son.
The gods are just, and of our pleasant° vices
Make instruments to plague us:
The dark and vicious place° where thee he got°
Cost him his eyes.
175   EDMUND: Th' hast spoken right, 'tis true;
The wheel is come full circle; I am here.°

ALBANY:
Methought thy very gait did prophesy°
A royal nobleness: I must embrace thee:
Let sorrow split my heart, if ever I
Did hate thee or thy father!
    EDGAR: Worthy° prince, I know't. 180
    ALBANY:
Where have you hid yourself?
How have you known the miseries of your father?
    EDGAR:
By nursing them, my lord. List a brief tale;
And when 'tis told, O, that my heart would burst!
The bloody proclamation to escape° 185
That followed me so near—O, our lives' sweetness,
That we the pain of death would hourly die
Rather than die at once!°—taught me to shift
Into a madman's rags, t' assume a semblance
That very dogs disdained: and in this habit° 190
Met I my father with his bleeding rings,°
Their precious stones new lost; became his guide,
Led him, begged for him, saved him from despair;
Never—O fault!—revealed myself unto him,
Until some half-hour past, when I was armed, 195
Not sure, though hoping, of this good success,
I asked his blessing, and from first to last
Told him our pilgrimage.° But his flawed° heart—
Alack too weak the conflict to support—
'Twixt two extremes of passion, joy and grief, 200
Burst smilingly.
    EDMUND: This speech of yours hath moved me,
And shall perchance do good: but speak you on;
You look as you had something more to say.
    ALBANY:
If there be more, more woeful, hold it in;
For I am almost ready to dissolve,° 205
Hearing of this.
    EDGAR: This would have seemed a period°
To such as love not sorrow; but another,
To amplify too much, would make much more,
And top extremity.°
Whilst I was big in clamor,° came there in a man, 210

150–152 **Which . . . ever** which accusations of treason, since as yet they do no harm, even though I have hurled them back, I now thrust upon you still more forcibly, with my sword, so that they may remain with you permanently 153 **Save** spare 153 **practice** trickery 155 **opposite** opponent 157 **Hold, sir** to Edmund: "Just a moment!" 158 **Thou** probably Goneril 163 **govern** control 167 **fortune on** victory over 168 **charity** forgiveness and love 169 **blood** lineage 170 **If more** if I am more noble (since legitimate) 172 **of our pleasant** out of our pleasurable 174 **place** i.e., the adulterous bed 174 **got** begot 176 **wheel . . . here** i.e., Fortune's wheel, on which Edmund ascended, has now, in its downward turning, deposited him at the bottom, whence he began

177 **gait did prophesy** carriage did promise 180 **Worthy** honorable 185 **to escape** (my wish) to escape the sentence of death 186–188 **O . . . once** How sweet is life, that we choose to suffer death every hour rather than make an end at once 190 **habit** attire 191 **rings** sockets 198 **our pilgrimage** of our (purgatorial) journey 198 **flawed** cracked 205 **dissolve** i.e., into tears 206 **period** limit 207–209 **but . . . extremity** just one woe more, described too fully, would go beyond the extreme limit 210 **big in clamor** loud in lamentation

Who, having seen me in my worst estate,°
Shunned my abhorred° society; but then, finding
Who 'twas that so endured, with his strong arms
He fastened on my neck, and bellowed out
215 As he'd burst heaven; threw him on my father;
Told the most piteous tale of Lear and him
That ever ear received: which in recounting
His grief grew puissant,° and the strings of life
Began to crack: twice then the trumpets sounded,
And there I left him tranced.°
220   ALBANY: But who was this?
     EDGAR:
Kent, sir, the banished Kent; who in disguise
Followed his enemy° king, and did him service
Improper for a slave.

Enter a GENTLEMAN, *with a bloody knife.*

GENTLEMAN:
Help, help, O, help!
     EDGAR: What kind of help?
     ALBANY: Speak, man.
     EDGAR:
What means this bloody knife?
225   GENTLEMAN: 'Tis hot, it smokes;°
It came even from the heart of—O, she's dead!
     ALBANY:
Who dead? Speak, man.
     GENTLEMAN:
Your lady, sir, your lady: and her sister
By her is poisoned; she confesses it.
     EDMUND:
230 I was contracted° to them both: all three
Now marry° in an instant.
     EDGAR: Here comes Kent.
     ALBANY:
Produce the bodies, be they alive or dead.
                              [*Exit* GENTLEMAN.]
This judgment of the heavens, that makes us
     tremble,
Touches us not with pity.

     Enter KENT.

                              O, is this he?
235 The time will not allow the compliment°
Which very manners° urges.

     KENT: I am come
To bid my king and master aye° good night:
Is he not here?
     ALBANY: Great thing of° us forgot!
Speak, Edmund, where's the king? and where's
     Cordelia?
See'st thou this object,° Kent?   240

     The bodies of Goneril and Regan are brought in.

     KENT:
Alack, why thus?
     EDMUND: Yet° Edmund was beloved:
The one the other poisoned for my sake,
And after slew herself.
     ALBANY:
Even so. Cover their faces.
     EDMUND:
I pant for life:° some good I mean to do,   245
Despite of mine own nature. Quickly send,
Be brief in it, to th' castle; for my writ°
Is on the life of Lear and on Cordelia:
Nay, send in time.
     ALBANY: Run, run, O, run!
     EDGAR:
To who, my lord? Who has the office?° Send   250
Thy token of reprieve.°
     EDMUND:
Well thought on: take my sword,
Give it the captain.
     EDGAR: Haste thee, for thy life.
                              [*Exit* MESSENGER.]
     EDMUND:
He hath commission from thy wife and me
To hang Cordelia in the prison, and   255
To lay the blame upon her own despair,
That she fordid° herself.
     ALBANY:
The gods defend her! Bear him hence awhile.
                              [EDMUND *is borne off.*]

     Enter LEAR, *with* CORDELIA *in his arms,* [GEN-
     TLEMAN, *and others following.*].

     LEAR:
Howl, howl, howl, howl! O, you are men of
     stones:
Had I your tongues and eyes, I'd use them so   260
That heaven's vault should crack. She's gone for
     ever.

---

211 **estate** condition 212 **abhorred** abhorrent 218
puissant overmastering 220 **tranced** insensible 222
enemy hostile 225 **smokes** steams 230 **contracted**
betrothed 231 **marry** i.e., unite in death 235 **compli-**
ment ceremony 236 **very manners** ordinary civility

237 **aye** forever 238 **thing of** matter by 240 **object**
sight (the bodies of Goneril and Regan) 241 **Yet** in
spite of all 245 **pant for life** gasp for breath 247 **writ**
command (ordering the execution) 250 **office** commission 251 **token of reprieve** sign that they are re-
prieved 257 **fordid** destroyed

I know when one is dead and when one lives;
She's dead as earth. Lend me a looking-glass;
If that her breath will moist or stain the stone,°
Why, then she lives.

265   KENT: Is this the promised end?°
EDGAR:
Or image° of that horror?
   ALBANY: Fall and cease.°
   LEAR:
This feather stirs; she lives. If it be so,
It is a chance which does redeem° all sorrows
That ever I have felt.
   KENT: O my good master.
   LEAR:
Prithee, away.

270   EDGAR: 'Tis noble Kent, your friend.
   LEAR:
A plague upon you, murderers, traitors all!
I might have saved her; now she's gone for ever.
Cordelia, Cordelia, stay a little. Ha,
What is't thou say'st? Her voice was ever soft,

275   Gentle and low, an excellent thing in woman.
I killed the slave that was a-hanging thee.
   GENTLEMAN:
'Tis true, my lords, he did.
   LEAR: Did I not, fellow?
I have seen the day, with my good biting falchion°
I would have made them skip: I am old now,

280   And these same crosses° spoil me.° Who are you?
Mine eyes are not o' th' best: I'll tell you straight.°
   KENT:
If Fortune brag of two° she loved and hated,
One of them we behold.
   LEAR:
This is a dull sight.° Are you not Kent?
   KENT: The same,

285   Your servant Kent. Where is your servant Caius?°
   LEAR:
He's a good fellow, I can tell you that;
He'll strike, and quickly too: he's dead and rotten.

KENT:
No, my good lord; I am the very man.
   LEAR:
I'll see that straight.°
   KENT:
That from your first of difference and decay°   290
Have followed your sad steps.
   LEAR: You are welcome hither.
   KENT:
Nor no man else:° all's cheerless, dark and deadly.
Your eldest daughters have fordone° themselves,
And desperately° are dead.
   LEAR: Ay, so I think.
   ALBANY:
He knows not what he says, and vain is it   295
That we present us to him.
   EDGAR: Very bootless.°

Enter a MESSENGER.

MESSENGER:
Edmund is dead, my lord.
   ALBANY: That's but a trifle here.
You lords and noble friends, know our intent.
What comfort to this great decay may come°
Shall be applied. For us, we° will resign,   300
During the life of this old majesty,
To him our absolute power: [*to* EDGAR *and* KENT]
   you, to your rights;
With boot,° and such addition° as your honors
Have more than merited. All friends shall taste
The wages of their virtue, and all foes   305
The cup of their deservings. O, see, see!
   LEAR:
And my poor fool° is hanged: no, no, no life?
Why should a dog, a horse, a rat, have life,
And thou no breath at all? Thou'lt come no more,
Never, never, never, never, never.   310
Pray you, undo this button.° Thank you, sir.
Do you see this? Look on her. Look, her lips.
Look there, look there.

He dies.

264 **stone** i.e., the surface of the crystal looking-glass
265 **promised end** doomsday   266 **image** exact likeness   266 **Fall and cease** i.e., Let the heavens fall, and
all things finish   268 **redeem** make good   278 **falchion**
small curved sword   280 **crosses** troubles   280 **spoil me**
i.e., my prowess as a swordsman   281 **tell you straight**
recognize you straightaway   282 **two** i.e., Lear, and
some hypothetical second, who is also a prime example
of Fortune's inconstancy ("loved and hated")   284 **dull
sight** (1) melancholy spectacle (2) faulty eyesight (Lear's
own, clouded by weeping)   285 **Caius** Kent's name, in
disguise

289 **see that straight** attend to that in a moment   290
your . . . decay beginning of your decline in fortune   292 **Nor . . . else** no, I am not welcome, nor is
anyone else   293 **fordone** destroyed   294 **desperately**
in despair   296 **bootless** fruitless   299 **What . . . come**
whatever aid may present itself to this great ruined
man   300 **us, we** the royal "we"   303 **boot** good measure   303 **addition** additional titles and rights   307 **fool**
Cordelia ("fool" being a term of endearment; but it is
perfectly possible to take the word as referring also to the
Fool)   311 **undo this button** i.e., to ease the suffoca-
tion Lear feels

EDGAR: He faints. My lord, my lord!
KENT:
Break, heart; I prithee, break.
EDGAR: Look up, my lord!
KENT:
315 Vex not his ghost:° O, let him pass! He hates him
That would upon the rack° of this tough world
Stretch him out longer.°
EDGAR: He is gone indeed.
KENT:
The wonder is he hath endured so long:
He but usurped° his life.

ALBANY:
Bear them from hence. Our present business   320
Is general woe. [*To* KENT *and* EDGAR.] Friends of
    my soul, you twain,
Rule in this realm and the gored state sustain.
KENT:
I have a journey, sir, shortly to go;
My master calls me, I must not say no.
EDGAR:
The weight of this sad time we must obey,°   325
Speak what we feel, not what we ought to say.
The oldest hath borne most: we that are young
Shall never see so much, nor live so long.
                    Exeunt, with a dead march.

315 **Vex . . . ghost** do not trouble his departing spirit
316 **rack** instrument of torture, stretching the victim's
joints to dislocation   317 **longer** (1) in time (2) in bodily
length   319 **usurped** possessed beyond the allotted term

325 **obey** submit to

COMMENTARY

The best way to understand Shakespeare's tragic vision is, of course, to see
and read the tragedies very intelligently, but some help may be gained from a
brief consideration of two speeches in *Hamlet*. In the final scene, when
Fortinbras and others enter the stage looking for Claudius, they find to their
amazement the corpses of Claudius, Gertrude, Laertes, and Hamlet. Horatio,
Hamlet's friend, endeavors to bring the visitors up to date:

> What is it you would see?
> If aught of woe or wonder, cease your search.

Fortinbras and his associates are indeed struck with woe and wonder:

> FORTINBRAS: O proud Death,
> What feast is toward in thine eternal cell
> That thou so many princes at a shot
> So bloodily hast struck?
> AMBASSADOR: The sight is dismal.

Horatio seeks to explain: the visitors will hear

> Of carnal, bloody, and unnatural acts,
> Of accidental judgments, casual slaughters,
> Of deaths put on by cunning and forced cause,
> And, in this upshot, purposes mistook
> Fall'n on th'inventors' heads.

The spectators of the play itself have indeed seen "unnatural acts," "deaths put
on by cunning," etc., and presumably these spectators have experienced the
"woe" and "wonder" that the new arrivals will experience as Horatio sets forth
the details.

Let us now look at a second passage from *Hamlet*. The speaker is the despicable Rosencrantz, and there is some flattery of King Claudius in his speech, but the gist of his argument about the death of a king rings true, makes sense:

> The cess of majesty
> Dies not alone, but like a gulf doth draw
> What's near it with it; or it is a massy wheel
> Fixed on the summit of the highest mount,
> To whose huge spokes ten thousand lesser things
> Are mortised and adjoined, which when it falls,
> Each small annexment, petty consequence,
> Attends the boist'rous ruin. Never alone
> Did the King sigh, but with a general groan.

Surely it is understandable that the deaths of, say, Lincoln and Kennedy had a vastly greater effect upon America than the deaths of any number of private citizens. Put crudely, they mattered more.

The speeches together afford some justification of the Elizabethan view that tragedy is concerned with violence done to and by people of high rank. The fall of a person in high position evokes deeper woe and wonder than the snuffing out of a nonentity. The latter may evoke pity, but scarcely awe at the terrifying power of destructiveness or at the weakness that is at the heart of power.

Shakespeare does not merely slap the label of king or prince or general on a character and then assume that greatness has been established. His characters speak great language and perform great deeds. (And, no less important, they have the capacity to suffer greatly.) Lear, in the first scene, gives away—almost seems to create—fertile kingdoms:

> Of all these bounds, even from this line to this,
> With shadowy forests, and with champains riched,
> With plenteous rivers, and wide-skirted meads,
> We make thee lady.

Even in injustice, when he banishes his daughter, Cordelia, for speaking the truth as she sees it, he has a kind of terrible grandeur:

> Let it be so, thy truth then be thy dower!
> For, by the sacred radiance of the sun,
> The mysteries of Hecate and the night,
> By all the operation of the orbs
> From whom we do exist and cease to be,
> Here I disclaim all my paternal care,
> Propinquity and property of blood,
> And as a stranger to my heart and me
> Hold thee from this for ever.

Finally, even in his madness—"a sight most pitiful in the meanest wretch, / Past speaking of in a king"—he has grandeur. To Gloucester's "Is't not the king?" he replies:

> Ay, every inch a king.
> When I do stare, see how the subject quakes.

> I pardon that man's life. What was thy cause?
> Adultery?
> Thou shalt not die: die for adultery! No:
> The wren goes to 't, and the small gilded fly
> Does lecher in my sight.
> Let copulation thrive. . . .

We might contrast Lear's noble voice with Edmund's materialistic comment on the way of the world:

> This is the excellent foppery of the world, that when we are sick in fortune, often the surfeits of our own behavior, we make guilty of our disasters the sun, the moon, and stars; as if we were villains on necessity; fools by heavenly compulsion; knaves, thieves, and treachers by spherical predominance; drunkards, liars, and adulterers by an enforced obedience of planetary influence; and all that we are evil in, by a divine thrusting on. An admirable evasion of whoremaster man, to lay his goatish disposition on the charge of a star. . . . Fut! I should have been that I am, had the maidenliest star in the firmament twinkled on my bastardizing.

Lear seems to be displacing Hamlet as the play that speaks to our time. Hamlet was especially popular with nineteenth-century audiences, who often found in the uncertain prince an image of their own doubts in a world in which belief in a benevolent divine order was collapsing under the influence of scientific materialism and bourgeois aggressiveness. Many audiences in our age find in Lear—where "for many miles about / There's scarce a bush"—a play thoroughly in the spirit of Beckett's Waiting for Godot, where the scenery consists of a single tree. Moreover, Lear denounces the hypocrisy of the power structure and exposes the powerlessness of the disenfranchised: "Robes and furred gowns hide all. Plate sin with gold, / And the strong lance of justice hurtless breaks; / Arm it in rags, a pygmy's straw does pierce it." And what of the gods? There are several comments about their nature, but perhaps the most memorable reference to the gods is not a mere comment but one followed by an action: learning that Cordelia is in danger, Albany cries out, "The gods defend her!" and immediately his words are mocked by Lear's entrance on the stage, with the dead Cordelia in his arms.

But the interpretation of King Lear as a revelation of the emptiness of life fails to consider at least two things. First, there is an affirmation in those passages in which Lear comes, through heart-rending anguish, to see that he was not what he thought he was. Second, this anagnorisis or recognition is several times associated with love or charity, as when (3.4) Lear invites the Fool to enter the hovel first and then confesses his guilt in having cared too little for humanity. And this care for humanity is seen in Cordelia, who comes—though ineffectually in the long run—to the aid of her father. It is seen, too, in the nameless servant who at the end of 3.7 promises to apply medicine to Gloucester's eyeless sockets; it is seen even in the villainous Edmund, who in dying repents and says, "Some good I mean to do, / Despite mine own nature" (5.3), and who thereupon tries, unsuccessfully, to save Cordelia. No one would say that these actions turn King Lear into a happy vision, but it is perverse to ignore them and to refuse to see that in this play love humanizes as surely as egoism dehumanizes. If the play dramatizes human desolation, it also dramatizes the love that, while providing no protection against pain or death, makes a human being's life different from the life of "a dog, a horse, a rat."

TOPICS FOR DISCUSSION

1. On the basis of his remarks in the first 36 lines of the play, how would you characterize Gloucester?
2. Coleridge found in Cordelia's "Nothing" (1.1.89) "some little, faulty admixture of pride or sullenness." Do you think that Cordelia is blameworthy here, or can she be exonerated?
3. Characterize the Lear of the first act. Regan and Goneril offer a characterization in 1.1.290–304. Do you find their description acceptable?
4. Explain in a sentence or two what Edmund means by "Nature" in 1.2.1–22. On the basis of 1.2, characterize Edmund.
5. In 1.4, what evidence is there that Lear is perceiving a "recognition" or *anagnorisis* (see Glossary)? On the other hand, which of his speeches in this scene especially indicate that he still has much to learn?
6. At the end of 2.2, Kent is put in the stocks. In a sentence, characterize him on the basis of the last speech in the scene.
7. If you were directing a production of *King Lear*, how would you suggest Kent perform 2.4.1–27? Exactly what tone would you like him to use?
8. The last two lines of 2.4 (Cornwall's speech) are often deleted in performances. Why? What do you think is gained or lost?
9. Characterize Lear in 3.2 and 3.4.
10. In 4.1.19, what does Gloucester mean when he says, "I stumbled when I saw"?
11. In 5.3 why does Edmund confess and tell of the plan to murder Lear and Cordelia?
12. What motives do Goneril and Regan have for their behavior? What motive does Edmund have for his?
13. How much self-knowledge do you think Lear achieves?
14. What function does the Fool perform?
15. Some critics insist that Lear dies joyfully, but others insist that he dies angrily and blindly. What can be said on behalf of each of these views? Which view strikes you as truer?
16. In what ways is the subplot (Gloucester and his sons) related to the main plot of Lear and his daughters?
17. Gloucester says: "As flies to wanton boys, are we to th' gods, / They kill us for their sport" (4.1.36). Do you think that this is an adequate summary of the theme of *King Lear*?

THE MISANTHROPE

Molière

English version by Richard Wilbur

Jean Baptiste Poquelin (1622–1673), who took the name Molière, was born into a prosperous middle-class family. For a while he studied law and philosophy, but by 1643 he was acting. He became the head of a theatrical company that had initial difficulties but later, thanks largely to Molière's comedies, great successes. In 1662 he married Armande Béjart. The marriage apparently was unhappy, but the capricious and flirtatious Armande proved to be an accomplished actress. Molière continued to act, with great success in comedy, until his death. In one of those improbable things that happen in real life but that are too strange for art, Molière died of a hemorrhage that he suffered while playing the title role in his comedy *The Hypochondriac*. The early plays are highly farcical; among the later and greater plays are *The Highbrow Ladies* (1659), *Tartuffe* (1664), *Don Juan* (1665), *The Misanthrope* (1666), and *The Miser* (1668).

CHARACTERS

ALCESTE, *in love with Célimène*
PHILINTE, *Alceste's friend*
ORONTE, *in love with Célimène*
CÉLIMÈNE, *Alceste's beloved*
ÉLIANTE, *Célimène's cousin*
ARSINOÉ, *a friend of Célimène's*
ACASTE
CLITANDRE } *Marquesses*
BASQUE, *Célimène's servant*
A GUARD *of the Marshalsea*
DUBOIS, *Alceste's valet*

The Scene throughout is in Célimène's house at Paris.

1983 production of *Le Misanthrope*. (Photograph by Martha Swope.)

ACT I

SCENE I. [PHILINTE, ALCESTE.]

PHILINTE:
Now, what's got into you?
ALCESTE (*seated*):   Kindly leave me alone.
PHILINTE:
Come, come, what is it? This lugubrious tone . . .
ALCESTE:
Leave me, I said; you spoil my solitude.
PHILINTE:
Oh, listen to me, now and don't be rude.
ALCESTE:
5   I choose to be rude, Sir, and to be hard of hearing.
PHILINTE:
These ugly moods of yours are not endearing;
Friends though we are, I really must insist . . .
ALCESTE (*abruptly rising*):
Friends? Friends, you say? Well, cross me off your
    list.
I've been your friend till now, as you well know;
10   But after what I saw a moment ago
I tell you flatly that our ways must part.
I wish no place in a dishonest heart.
PHILINTE:
Why, what have I done, Alceste? Is this quite just?
ALCESTE:
My God, you ought to die of self-disgust.
15   I call your conduct inexcusable, Sir,
And every man of honor will concur.
I see you almost hug a man to death,
Exclaim for joy until you're out of breath,
And supplement these loving demonstrations
20   With endless offers, vows, and protestations;
Then when I ask you "Who was that?" I find
That you can barely bring his name to mind!
Once the man's back is turned, you cease to love
    him,
And speak with absolute indifference of him!
25   By God, I say it's base and scandalous
To falsify the heart's affections thus;

If I caught myself behaving in such a way,
I'd hang myself for shame, without delay.
PHILINTE:
It hardly seems a hanging matter to me;
I hope that you will take it graciously   30
If I extend myself a slight reprieve,
And live a little longer, by your leave.
ALCESTE:
How dare you joke about a crime so grave?
PHILINTE:
What crime? How else are people to behave?
ALCESTE:
I'd have them be sincere, and never part   35
With any word that isn't from the heart.
PHILINTE:
When someone greets us with a show of pleasure,
It's but polite to give him equal measure,
Return his love the best that we know how,
And trade him offer for offer, vow for vow.   40
ALCESTE:
No, no, this formula you'd have me follow,
However fashionable, is false and hollow,
And I despise the frenzied operations
Of all these barterers of protestations,
These lavishers of meaningless embraces,   45
These utterers of obliging commonplaces,
Who court and flatter everyone on earth
And praise the fool no less than the man of worth.
Should you rejoice that someone fondles you,
Offers his love and service, swears to be true,   50
And fills your ears with praises of your name,
When to the first damned fop he'll say the same?
No, no: no self-respecting heart would dream
Of prizing so promiscuous an esteem;
However high the praise, there's nothing worse   55
Than sharing honors with the universe.
Esteem is founded on comparison:
To honor all men is to honor none.
Since you embrace this indiscriminate vice,
Your friendship comes at far too cheap a price: 60
I spurn the easy tribute of a heart
Which will not set the worthy man apart:
I choose, Sir, to be chosen; and in fine,
The friend of mankind is no friend of mine.
PHILINTE:
But in polite society, custom decrees   65
That we show certain outward courtesies. . . .
ALCESTE:
Ah, no! we should condemn with all our force
Such false and artificial intercourse.

Let men behave like men; let them display
70 Their inmost hearts in everything they say;
Let the heart speak, and let our sentiments
Not mask themselves in silly compliments.

PHILINTE:
In certain cases it would be uncouth
And most absurd to speak the naked truth;
75 With all respect for your exalted notions,
It's often best to veil one's true emotions.
Wouldn't the social fabric come undone
If we were wholly frank with everyone?
Suppose you met with someone you couldn't bear;
80 Would you inform him of it then and there?

ALCESTE:
Yes.

PHILINTE:
        Then you'd tell old Emilie it's pathetic
The way she daubs her features with cosmetic
And plays the gay coquette at sixty-four?

ALCESTE:
I would.

PHILINTE:
            And you'd call Dorilas a bore,
85 And tell him every ear at court is lame
From hearing him brag about his noble name?

ALCESTE:
Precisely.

PHILINTE:
        Ah, your joking.

ALCESTE: Au contraire:
In this regard there's none I'd choose to spare.
All are corrupt; there's nothing to be seen
90 In court or town but aggravates my spleen.
I fall into deep gloom and melancholy
When I survey the scene of human folly,
Finding on every hand base flattery,
Injustice, fraud, self-interest, treachery. . . .
95 Ah, it's too much; mankind has grown so base,
I mean to break with the whole human race.

PHILINTE:
This philosophic rage is a bit extreme;
You've no idea how comical you seem;
Indeed, we're like those brothers in the play
Called *School for Husbands*, one of whom was
100   prey . . .

ALCESTE:
Enough, now! None of your stupid similes.

PHILINTE:
Then let's have no more tirades, if you please.
The world won't change, whatever you say or do;
And since plain speaking means so much to you,
105 I'll tell you plainly that by being frank

You've earned the reputation of a crank,
And that you're thought ridiculous when you rage
And rant against the manners of the age.

ALCESTE:
So much the better; just what I wish to hear.
No news could be more grateful to my ear.   110
All men are so detestable in my eyes,
I should be sorry if they thought me wise.

PHILINTE:
Your hatred's very sweeping, is it not?

ALCESTE:
Quite right: I hate the whole degraded lot.

PHILINTE:
Must all poor human creatures be embraced,   115
Without distinction, by your vast distaste?
Even in these bad times, there are surely a few . . .

ALCESTE:
No, I include all men in one dim view:
Some men I hate for being rogues: the others
I hate because they treat the rogues like brothers, 120
And, lacking a virtuous scorn for what is vile,
Receive the villain with a complaisant smile.
Notice how tolerant people choose to be
Toward that bold rascal who's at law with me.
His social polish can't conceal his nature;   125
One sees at once that he's a treacherous creature;
No one could possibly be taken in
By those soft speeches and that sugary grin.
The whole world knows the shady means by which
The low-brow's grown so powerful and rich,   130
And risen to a rank so bright and high
That virtue can but blush, and merit sigh.
Whenever his name comes up in conversation,
None will defend his wretched reputation;
Call him knave, liar, scoundrel, and all the rest,   135
Each head will nod, and no one will protest.
And yet his smirk is seen in every house,
He's greeted everywhere with smiles and bows,
And when there's any honor that can be got
By pulling strings, he'll get it, like as not.   140
My God! It chills my heart to see the ways
Men come to terms with evil nowadays;
Sometimes, I swear, I'm moved to flee and find
Some desert land unfouled by humankind.

PHILINTE:
Come, let's forget the follies of the times   145
And pardon mankind for its petty crimes;
Let's have an end of rantings and of railings,
And show some leniency toward human failings.
This world requires a pliant rectitude;
Too stern a virtue makes one stiff and rude;   150
Good sense views all extremes with detestation,

And bids us to be noble in moderation.
The rigid virtues of the ancient days
Are not for us; they jar with all our ways
155   And ask of us too lofty a perfection.
Wise men accept their times without objection,
And there's no greater folly, if you ask me,
Than trying to reform society.
Like you, I see each day a hundred and one
160   Unhandsome deeds that might be better done,
But still, for all the faults that meet my view,
I'm never known to storm and rave like you.
I take men as they are, or let them be,
And teach my soul to bear their frailty;
165   And whether in court or town, whatever the scene,
My phlegm's as philosophic as your spleen.

ALCESTE:
This phlegm which you so eloquently commend,
Does nothing ever rile it up, my friend?
Suppose some man you trust should treacherously
170   Conspire to rob you of your property,
And do his best to wreck your reputation?
Wouldn't you feel a certain indignation?

PHILINTE:
Why, no. These faults of which you so complain
Are part of human nature, I maintain,
175   And it's no more a matter for disgust
That men are knavish, selfish and unjust,
Than that the vulture dines upon the dead,
And wolves are furious, and apes ill-bred.

ALCESTE:
Shall I see myself betrayed, robbed, torn to bits,
180   And not . . . Oh, let's be still and rest our wits.
Enough of reasoning, now. I've had my fill.

PHILINTE:
Indeed, you would do well, Sir, to be still.
Rage less at your opponent, and give some thought
To how you'll win this lawsuit that he's brought.

ALCESTE:
185   I assure you I'll do nothing of the sort.

PHILINTE:
Then who will plead your case before the court?

ALCESTE:
Reason and right and justice will plead for me.

PHILINTE:
Oh, Lord. What judges do you plan to see?

ALCESTE:
Why, none. The justice of my cause is clear.

PHILINTE:
190   Of course, man; but there's politics to fear . . .

ALCESTE:
No, I refuse to lift a hand. That's flat.

I'm either right, or wrong.
    PHILINTE: Don't count on that.
ALCESTE:
No, I'll do nothing.
    PHILINTE: Your enemy's influence
Is great, you know . . .
    ALCESTE: That makes no difference.
PHILINTE:
It will; you'll see.
    ALCESTE: Must honor bow to guile?   195
If so, I shall be proud to lose the trial.
    PHILINTE:
O, really . . .
    ALCESTE: I'll discover by this case
Whether or not men are sufficiently base
And impudent and villainous and perverse
To do me wrong before the universe.   200
    PHILINTE:
What a man!
    ALCESTE:
                Oh, I could wish, whatever the cost,
Just for the beauty of it, that my trial were lost.
    PHILINTE:
If people heard you talking so, Alceste,
They'd split their sides. Your name would be a
    jest.
    ALCESTE:
So much the worse for jesters.
    PHILINTE: May I enquire   205
Whether this rectitude you so admire,
And these hard virtues you're enamored of
Are qualities of the lady whom you love?
It much surprises me that you, who seem
To view mankind with furious disesteem,   210
Have yet found something to enchant your eyes
Amidst a species which you so despise.
And what is more amazing, I'm afraid,
Is the most curious choice your heart has made.
The honest Éliante is fond of you,   215
Arsinoé, the prude, admires you too;
And yet your spirit's been perversely led
To choose the flighty Célimène instead,
Whose brittle malice and coquettish ways
So typify the manners of our days.   220
How is it that the traits you most abhor
Are bearable in this lady you adore?
Are you so blind with love that you can't find
    them?
Or do you contrive, in her case, not to mind them?
    ALCESTE:
My love for that young widow's not the kind   225

That can't perceive defects; no, I'm not blind.
I see her faults, despite my ardent love,
And all I see I fervently reprove.
And yet I'm weak; for all her falsity,
230 That woman knows the art of pleasing me,
And though I never cease complaining of her,
I swear I cannot manage not to love her.
Her charm outweighs her faults; I can but aim
To cleanse her spirit in my love's pure flame.

    PHILINTE:
235 That's no small task; I wish you all success.
You think then that she loves you?

    ALCESTE: Heavens, yes!
I wouldn't love her did she not love me.

    PHILINTE:
Well, if her taste for you is plain to see,
Why do these rivals cause you such despair?

    ALCESTE:
240 True love, Sir, is possessive, and cannot bear
To share with all the world. I'm here today
To tell her she must send that mob away.

    PHILINTE:
If I were you, and had your choice to make,
Éliante, her cousin, would be the one I'd take;
245 That honest heart, which cares for you alone,
Would harmonize far better with your own.

    ALCESTE:
True, true: each day my reason tells me so;
But reason doesn't rule in love, you know.

    PHILINTE:
I fear some bitter sorrow is in store;
This love . . .

SCENE II.[ORONTE, ALCESTE, PHILINTE.]

ORONTE (to ALCESTE):
                The servants told me at the door
That Éliante and Célimène were out,
But when I heard, dear Sir, that you were about,
I came to say, without exaggeration,
5 That I hold you in the vastest admiration,
And that it's always been my dearest desire
To be the friend of one I so admire.
I hope to see my love of merit requited,
And you and I in friendship's bond united.
10 I'm sure you won't refuse—if I may be frank—
A friend of my devotedness—and rank.

(During this speech of ORONTE's ALCESTE is
abstracted, and seems unaware that he is being

spoken to. He only breaks off his reverie when
ORONTE says:)

It was for you, if you please, that my words were
    intended.

    ALCESTE:
For me, Sir?

    ORONTE:
             Yes, for you. You're not offended?

    ALCESTE:
By no means. But this much surprises me . . .
The honor comes most unexpectedly . . .   15

    ORONTE:
My high regard should not astonish you;
The whole world feels the same. It is your due.

    ALCESTE:
Sir . . .

    ORONTE:
        Why, in all the State there isn't one
Can match your merits; they shine, Sir, like the
    sun.

    ALCESTE:
Sir . . .

    ORONTE:
        You are higher in my estimation   20
Than all that's most illustrious in the nation.

    ALCESTE:
Sir . . .

    ORONTE:
        If I lie, may heaven strike me dead!
To show you that I mean what I have said,
Permit me, Sir, to embrace you most sincerely,
And swear that I will prize our friendship dearly. 25
Give me your hand. And now, Sir, if you choose,
We'll make our vows.

    ALCESTE: Sir . . .

    ORONTE: What! You refuse?

    ALCESTE:
Sir, it's a very great honor you extend:
But friendship is a sacred thing, my friend;
It would be profanation to bestow   30
The name of friend on one you hardly know.
All parts are better played when well-rehearsed;
Let's put off friendship, and get acquainted first.
We may discover it would be unwise
To try to make our natures harmonize.   35

    ORONTE:
By heaven! You're sagacious to the core;
This speech has made me admire you even more.
Let time, then, bring us closer day by day;
Meanwhile, I shall be yours in every way.

40 If, for example, there should be anything
You wish at court, I'll mention it to the King.
I have his ear, of course; it's quite well known
That I am much in favor with the throne.
In short, I am your servant. And now, dear friend,
45 Since you have such fine judgment, I intend
To please you, if I can, with a small sonnet
I wrote not long ago. Please comment on it,
And tell me whether I ought to publish it.

ALCESTE:
You must excuse me, Sir; I'm hardly fit
To judge such matters.
ORONTE: Why not?
50 ALCESTE: I am, I fear,
Inclined to be unfashionably sincere.

ORONTE:
Just what I ask; I'd take no satisfaction
In anything but your sincere reaction.
I beg you not to dream of being kind.

ALCESTE:
55 Since you desire it, Sir, I'll speak my mind.

ORONTE:
Sonnet. It's a sonnet . . . Hope . . . The poem's
addressed
To a lady who wakened hopes within my breast.
Hope . . . this is not the pompous sort of thing,
Just modest little verses, with a tender ring.

ALCESTE:
Well, we shall see.
60 ORONTE: Hope . . . I'm anxious to hear
Whether the style seems properly smooth and
clear,
And whether the choice of words is good or bad.

ALCESTE:
We'll see, we'll see.
ORONTE: Perhaps I ought to add
That it took me only a quarter-hour to write it.

ALCESTE:
65 The time's irrelevant, Sir: kindly recite it.

ORONTE (reading):
Hope comforts us awhile, 'tis true,
Lulling our cares with careless laughter,
And yet such joy is full of rue,
My Phillis, if nothing follows after.

PHILINTE:
70 I'm charmed by this already; the style's delightful.

ALCESTE (sotto voce, to PHILINTE):
How can you say that? Why, the thing is frightful.

ORONTE:
Your fair face smiled on me awhile,
But was it kindness so to enchant me?

'Twould have been fairer not to smile,
If hope was all you meant to grant me.   75

PHILINTE:
What a clever thought! How handsomely you
phrase it!

ALCESTE (sotto voce, to PHILINTE):
You know the thing is trash. How dare you praise
it?

ORONTE:
If it's to be my passion's fate.
Thus everlastingly to wait,
Then death will come to set me free: 80
For death is fairer than the fair;
Phyllis, to hope is to despair
When one must hope eternally.

PHILINTE:
The close is exquisite—full of feeling and grace.

ALCESTE (sotto voce, aside):
Oh, blast the close; you'd better close your face   85
Before you send your lying soul to hell.

PHILINTE:
I can't remember a poem I've liked so well.

ALCESTE (sotto voce, aside):
Good Lord!

ORONTE (to PHILINTE):
            I fear you're flattering me a bit.

PHILINTE:
Oh, no!

ALCESTE (sotto voce, aside):
            What else d'you call it, you hypocrite?

ORONTE (to ALCESTE):
But you, Sir, keep your promise now: don't shrink   90
From telling me sincerely what you think.

ALCESTE:
Sir, these are delicate matters; we all desire
To be told that we've the true poetic fire.
But once, to one whose name I shall not mention,
I said, regarding some verse of his invention,   95
That gentlemen should rigorously control
That itch to write which often afflicts the soul;
That one should curb the heady inclination
To publicize one's little avocation;
And that in showing off one's works of art   100
One often plays a very clownish part.

ORONTE:
Are you suggesting in a devious way
That I ought not . . .

ALCESTE: Oh, that I do not say.
Further, I told him that no fault is worse
Than that of writing frigid, lifeless verse,   105
And that the merest whisper of such a shame
Suffices to destroy a man's good name.

ORONTE:

D'you mean to say my sonnet's dull and trite?

ALCESTE:

I don't say that. But I went on to cite
110 Numerous cases of once-respected men
Who came to grief by taking up the pen.

ORONTE:

And am I like them? Do I write so poorly?

ALCESTE:

I don't say that. But I told this person, "Surely
You're under no necessity to compose;
115 Why you should wish to publish, heaven knows.
There's no excuse for printing tedious rot
Unless one writes for bread, as you do not.
Resist temptation, then, I beg of you;
Conceal your pastimes from the public view;
120 And don't give up, on any provocation,
Your present high and courtly reputation,
To purchase at a greedy printer's shop
The name of silly author and scribbling fop."
These were the points I tried to make him see.

ORONTE:

125 I sense that they are also aimed at me;
But now—about my sonnet—I'd like to be told . . .

ALCESTE:

Frankly, that sonnet should be pigeonholed.
You've chosen the worst models to imitate.
The style's unnatural. Let me illustrate:
130 For example, *Your fair face smiled on me awhile,*
Followed by, *'Twould have been fairer not to smile!*
Or this: *such joy is full of rue;*
Or this: *For death is fairer than the fair;*
Or, *Phyllis, to hope is to despair*
135 *When one must hope eternally!*
This artificial style, that's all the fashion,
Has neither taste, nor honesty, nor passion;
It's nothing but a sort of wordy play,
And nature never spoke in such a way.
140 What, in this shallow age, is not debased?
Our fathers, though less refined, had better taste;
I'd barter all that men admire today
For one old love song I shall try to say:
    If the King had given me for my own
145 *Paris, his citadel,*
    And I for that must leave alone
    Her whom I love so well,
    I'd say then to the Crown,
    Take back your glittering town;
150 *My darling is more fair, I swear,*
    My darling is more fair.
The rhyme's not rich, the style is rough and old,
But don't you see that it's the purest gold

Beside the tinsel nonsense now preferred,
And that there's passion in its every word?   155
    If the King had given me for my own
    Paris, his citadel,
    And I for that must leave alone
    Her whom I love so well,
    I'd say then to the Crown,   160
    Take back your glittering town;
    My darling is more fair, I swear,
    My darling is more fair.
There speaks a loving heart. (*To* PHILINTE.) You're
    laughing, eh?
Laugh on, my precious wit. Whatever you say,   165
I hold that song's worth all the bibelots
That people hail today with ah's and oh's.

ORONTE:

And I maintain my sonnet's very good.

ALCESTE:

It's not at all surprising that you should.
You have your reasons; permit me to have mine   170
For thinking that you cannot write a line.

ORONTE:

Others have praised my sonnet to the skies.

ALCESTE:

I lack their art of telling pleasant lies.

ORONTE:

You seem to think you've got no end of wit.

ALCESTE:

To praise your verse, I'd need still more of it.   175

ORONTE:

I'm not in need of your approval, Sir.

ALCESTE:

That's good; you couldn't have it if you were.

ORONTE:

Come now, I'll lend you the subject of my sonnet;
I'd like to see you try to improve upon it.

ALCESTE:

I might, by chance, write something just as shoddy;   180
But then I wouldn't show it to everybody.

ORONTE:

You're most opinionated and conceited.

ALCESTE:

Go find your flatterers, and be better treated.

ORONTE:

Look here, my little fellow, pray watch your tone.

ALCESTE:

My great big fellow, you'd better watch your own.   185

PHILINTE (*stepping between them*):

Oh, please, please, gentlemen! This will never do.

ORONTE:

The fault is mine, and I leave the field to you.
I am your servant, Sir, in every way.

ALCESTE:
And I, Sir, am your most abject valet.

SCENE III. [PHILINTE, ALCESTE.]

PHILINTE:
Well, as you see, sincerity in excess
Can get you into a very pretty mess;
Oronte was hungry for appreciation . . .
   ALCESTE:
Don't speak to me.
     PHILINTE: What?
     ALCESTE: No more conversation.
     PHILINTE:
Really, now . . .
     ALCESTE: Leave me alone.
     PHILINTE: If I . . .
5   ALCESTE: Out of my sight!
     PHILINTE:
But what . . .
     ALCESTE: I won't listen.
     PHILINTE: But . . .
     ALCESTE: Silence!
     PHILINTE: Now, is it polite . . .
     ALCESTE:
By heaven, I've had enough. Don't follow me.
     PHILINTE:
Ah, you're just joking. I'll keep you company.

ACT II

SCENE I. [ALCESTE, CÉLIMÈNE.]

ALCESTE:
Shall I speak plainly, Madam? I confess
Your conduct gives me infinite distress,
And my resentment's grown too hot to smother.
Soon, I foresee, we'll break with one another.
5 If I said otherwise, I should deceive you;
Sooner or later, I shall be forced to leave you,
And if I swore that we shall never part,
I should misread the omens of my heart.
     CÉLIMÈNE:
You kindly saw me home, it would appear,
10 So as to pour invectives in my ear.
     ALCESTE:
I've no desire to quarrel. But I deplore
Your inability to shut the door
On all these suitors who beset you so.
There's what annoys me, if you care to know.
     CÉLIMÈNE:
15 Is it my fault that all these men pursue me?
Am I to blame if they're attracted to me?

And when they gently beg an audience,
Ought I to take a stick and drive them hence?
     ALCESTE:
Madam, there's no necessity for a stick;
A less responsive heart would do the trick.   20
Of your attractiveness I don't complain;
But those your charms attract, you then detain
By a most melting and receptive manner,
And so enlist their hearts beneath your banner.
It's the agreeable hopes which you excite   25
That keep these lovers round you day and night;
Were they less liberally smiled upon,
That sighing troop would very soon be gone.
But tell me, Madam, why is it that lately
This man Clitandre interests you so greatly?   30
Because of what high merits do you deem
Him worthy of the honor of your esteem?
Is it that your admiring glances linger
On the splendidly long nail of his little finger?
Or do you share the general deep respect   35
For the blond wig he chooses to affect?
Are you in love with his embroidered hose?
Do you adore his ribbons and his bows?
Or is it that this paragon bewitches
Your tasteful eye with his vast German breeches?   40
Perhaps his giggle, or his falsetto voice,
Makes him the latest gallant of your choice?
     CÉLIMÈNE:
You're much mistaken to resent him so.
Why I put up with him you surely know:
My lawsuit's very shortly to be tried,   45
And I must have his influence on my side.
     ALCESTE:
Then lose your lawsuit, Madam, or let it drop;
Don't torture me by humoring such a fop.
     CÉLIMÈNE:
You're jealous of the whole world, Sir.
     ALCESTE: That's true,
Since the whole world is well-received by you.   50
     CÉLIMÈNE:
That my good nature is so unconfined
Should serve to pacify your jealous mind;
Were I to smile on one, and scorn the rest,
Then you might have some cause to be distressed.
     ALCESTE:
Well, if I mustn't be jealous, tell me, then,   55
Just how I'm better treated than other men.
     CÉLIMÈNE:
You know you have my love. Will that not do?
     ALCESTE:
What proof have I that what you say is true?
     CÉLIMÈNE:
I would expect, Sir, that my having said it

60 Might give the statement a sufficient credit.
ALCESTE:
But how can I be sure that you don't tell
The selfsame thing to other men as well?
CÉLIMÈNE:
What a gallant speech! How flattering to me!
What a sweet creature you make me out to be!
65 Well then, to save you from the pangs of doubt,
All that I've said I hereby cancel out;
Now, none but yourself shall make a monkey of
    you:
Are you content?
ALCESTE:
              Why, why am I doomed to love you?
I swear that I shall bless the blissful hour
70 When this poor heart's no longer in your power!
I make no secret of it: I've done my best
To exorcise this passion from my breast;
But thus far all in vain; it will not go;
It's for my sins that I must love you so.
CÉLIMÈNE:
75 Your love for me is matchless, Sir; that's clear.
ALCESTE:
Indeed, in all the world it has no peer;
Words can't describe the nature of my passion,
And no man ever loved in such a fashion.
CÉLIMÈNE:
Yes, it's a brand-new fashion, I agree:
80 You show your love by castigating me,
And all your speeches are enraged and rude.
I've never been so furiously wooed.
ALCESTE:
Yet you could calm that fury, if you chose.
Come, shall we bring our quarrels to a close?
85 Let's speak with open hearts, then, and begin . . .

SCENE II. [CÉLIMÈNE, ALCESTE, BASQUE.]

CÉLIMÈNE:
What is it?
BASQUE: Acaste is here.
CÉLIMÈNE:
                    Well, send him in.

SCENE III. [CÉLIMÈNE, ALCESTE.]

ALCESTE:
What! Shall we never be alone at all?
You're always ready to receive a call,
And you can't bear, for ten ticks of the clock,
Not to keep open house for all who knock.
CÉLIMÈNE:
5 I couldn't refuse him: he'd be most put out.
ALCESTE:
Surely that's not worth worrying about.

CÉLIMÈNE:
Acaste would never forgive me if he guessed
That I consider him a dreadful pest.
ALCESTE:
If he's a pest, why bother with him then?
CÉLIMÈNE:
Heavens! One can't antagonize such men;   10
Why, they're the chartered gossips of the court,
And have a say in things of every sort.
One must receive them, and be full of charm;
They're no great help, but they can do you harm,
And though your influence be ever so great,   15
They're hardly the best people to alienate.
ALCESTE:
I see, dear lady, that you could make a case
For putting up with the whole human race;
These friendships that you calculate so nicely . . .

SCENE IV. [ALCESTE, CÉLIMÈNE, BASQUE.]

BASQUE:
Madam, Clitandre is here as well.
ALCESTE: Precisely.
CÉLIMÈNE:
Where are you going?
ALCESTE: Elsewhere.
CÉLIMÈNE: Stay.
ALCESTE: No, no.
CÉLIMÈNE:
Stay, Sir.
ALCESTE:
        I can't.
CÉLIMÈNE: I wish it.
ALCESTE: No, I must go.
I beg you, Madam, not to press the matter;
You know I have no taste for idle chatter.   5
CÉLIMÈNE:
Stay. I command you.
ALCESTE: No, I cannot stay.
CÉLIMÈNE:
Very well; you have my leave to go away.

SCENE V. [ÉLIANTE, PHILINTE, ACASTE,
CLITANDRE, ALCESTE, CÉLIMÈNE, BASQUE.]

ÉLIANTE (to CÉLIMÈNE):
The Marquesses have kindly come to call.
Were they announced?
CÉLIMÈNE:
                    Yes. Basque, bring chairs for all.

(BASQUE provides the chairs, and exits.)

(To ALCESTE.) You haven't gone?
ALCESTE: No; and I shan't depart
Till you decide who's foremost in your heart.

CÉLIMÈNE:
O, hush.

ALCESTE:

5   It's time to choose; take them, or me.

CÉLIMÈNE:
You're mad.

ALCESTE:
            I'm not, as you shall shortly see.

CÉLIMÈNE:
Oh?

ALCESTE:
    You'll decide.

CÉLIMÈNE: You're joking now, dear friend.

ALCESTE:
No, no; you'll choose; my patience is at an end.

CLITANDRE:
Madam, I come from court, where poor Cleónte

10 Behaved like a perfect fool, as is his wont.
Has he no friend to counsel him, I wonder,
And teach him less unerringly to blunder?

CÉLIMÈNE:
It's true, the man's a most accomplished dunce;
His gauche behavior charms the eye at once;

15 And every time one sees him, on my word,
His manner's grown a trifle more absurd.

ACASTE:
Speaking of dunces, I've just now conversed
With old Damon, who's one of the very worst;
I stood a lifetime in the broiling sun

20 Before his dreary monologue was done.

CÉLIMÈNE:
Oh, he's a wondrous talker, and has the power
To tell you nothing hour after hour:
If, by mistake, he ever came to the point,
The shock would put his jawbone out of joint.

ÉLIANTE (to PHILINTE):

25 The conversation takes its usual turn,
And all our dear friends' ears will shortly burn.

CLITANDRE:
Timante's a character, Madam.

CÉLIMÈNE: Isn't he, though?
A man of mystery from top to toe,
Who moves about in a romantic mist

30 On secret missions which do not exist.
His talk is full of eyebrows and grimaces;
How tired one gets of his momentous faces;
He's always whispering something confidential
Which turns out to be quite inconsequential;

35 Nothing's too slight for him to mystify;
He even whispers when he says "good-bye."

ACASTE:
Tell us about Géralde.

CÉLIMÈNE: That tiresome ass.
He mixes only with the titled class,

And fawns on dukes and princes, and is bored
With anyone who's not as least a lord.   40
The man's obsessed with rank, and his discourses
Are all of hounds and carriages and horses;
He uses Christian names with all the great,
And the word Milord, with him, is out of date.

CLITANDRE:
He's very taken with Bélise, I hear.   45

CÉLIMÈNE:
She is the dreariest company, poor dear.
Whenever she comes to call, I grope about
To find some topic which will draw her out,
But, owing to her dry and faint replies,
The conversation wilts, and droops, and dies.   50
In vain one hopes to animate her face
By mentioning the ultimate commonplace;
But sun or shower, even hail or frost
Are matters she can instantly exhaust.
Meanwhile her visit, painful though it is,   55
Drags on and on through mute eternities,
And though you ask the time, and yawn, and
    yawn,
She sits there like a stone and won't be gone.

ACASTE:
Now for Adraste.

CÉLIMÈNE: Oh, that conceited elf
Has a gigantic passion for himself;   60
He rails against the court, and cannot bear it
That none will recognize his hidden merit;
All honors given to others give offense
To his imaginary excellence.

CLITANDRE:
What about young Cléon? His house, they say,   65
Is full of the best society, night and day.

CÉLIMÈNE:
His cook has made him popular, not he:
It's Cléon's table that people come to see.

ÉLIANTE:
He gives a splendid dinner, you must admit.

CÉLIMÈNE:
But must he serve himself along with it?   70
For my taste, he's a most insipid dish
Whose presence sours the wine and spoils the fish.

PHILINTE:
Damis, his uncle, is admired no end.
What's your opinion, Madam?

CÉLIMÈNE: Why, he's my friend.

PHILINTE:
He seems a decent fellow, and rather clever.   75

CÉLIMÈNE:
He works too hard at cleverness, however.
I hate to see him sweat and struggle so
To fill his conversation with bons mots.
Since he's decided to become a wit

80   His taste's so pure that nothing pleases it;
    He scolds at all the latest books and plays,
    Thinking that wit must never stoop to praise,
    That finding fault's a sign of intellect,
    That all appreciation is abject,
85   And that by damning everything in sight
    One shows oneself in a distinguished light.
    He's scornful even of our conversations:
    Their trivial nature sorely tries his patience;
    He folds his arms, and stands above the battle,
90   And listens sadly to our childish prattle.

ACASTE:
Wonderful, Madam! You've hit him off precisely.

CLITANDRE:
No one can sketch a character so nicely.

ALCESTE:
How bravely, Sirs, you cut and thrust at all
These absent fools, till one by one they fall:
95   But let one come in sight, and you'll at once
Embrace the man you lately called a dunce,
Telling him in a tone sincere and fervent
How proud you are to be his humble servant.

CLITANDRE:
Why pick on us? *Madame's* been speaking, Sir.
100   And you should quarrel, if you must, with her.

ALCESTE:
No, no, by God, the fault is yours, because
You lead her on with laughter and applause,
And make her think that she's the more delightful
The more her talk is scandalous and spiteful.
105   Oh, she would stoop to malice far, far less
If no such claque approved her cleverness.
It's flatterers like you whose foolish praise
Nourishes all the vices of these days.

PHILINTE:
But why protest when someone ridicules
Those you'd condemn, yourself, as knaves or
110   fools?

CÉLIMÈNE:
Why, Sir? Because he loves to make a fuss.
You don't expect him to agree with us,
When there's an opportunity to express
His heaven-sent spirits of contrariness?
115   What other people think, he can't abide;
Whatever they say, he's on the other side;
He lives in deadly terror of agreeing;
'Twould make him seem an ordinary being.
Indeed, he's so in love with contradiction,
120   He'll turn against his most profound conviction
And with a furious eloquence deplore it,
If only someone else is speaking for it.

ALCESTE:
Go on, dear lady, mock me as you please;
You have your audience in ecstasies.

PHILINTE:
But what she says is true: you have a way   125
Of bridling at whatever people say;
Whether they praise or blame, your angry spirit
Is equally unsatisfied to hear it.

ALCESTE:
Men, Sir, are always wrong, and that's the reason
That righteous anger's never out of season;   130
All that I hear in all their conversation
Is flattering praise or reckless condemnation.

CÉLIMÈNE:
But . . .

ALCESTE:
         No, no, Madam, I am forced to state
That you have pleasures which I deprecate,
And that these others, here, are much to blame   135
For nourishing the faults which are your shame.

CLITANDRE:
I shan't defend myself, Sir; but I vow
I'd thought this lady faultless until now.

ACASTE:
I see her charms and graces, which are many;
But as for faults, I've never noticed any.   140

ALCESTE:
I see them, Sir; and rather than ignore them,
I strenuously criticize her for them.
The more one loves, the more one should object
To every blemish, every least defect.
Were I this lady, I would soon get rid   145
Of lovers who approved of all I did,
And by their slack indulgence and applause
Endorsed my follies and excused my flaws.

CÉLIMÈNE:
If all hearts beat according to your measure,
The dawn of love would be the end of pleasure;   150
And love would find its perfect consummation
In ecstasies of rage and reprobation.

ÉLIANTE:
Love, as a rule, affects men otherwise,
And lovers rarely love to criticize.
They see their lady as a charming blur,   155
And find all things commendable in her.
If she has any blemish, fault, or shame,
They will redeem it by a pleasing name.
The pale-faced lady's lily-white, perforce;
The swarthy one's a sweet brunette, of course;   160
The spindly lady has a slender grace;
The fat one has a most majestic pace;
The plain one, with her dress in disarray,
They classify as *beauté négligée*;
The hulking one's a goddess in their eyes,   165
The dwarf, a concentrate of Paradise;
The haughty lady has a noble mind;
The mean one's witty, and the dull one's kind;

The chatterbox has liveliness and verve,
170 The mute one has a virtuous reserve.
So lovers manage, in their passion's cause,
To love their ladies even for their flaws.
   ALCESTE:
But I still say . . .
   CÉLIMÈNE: I think it would be nice
To stroll around the gallery once or twice.
What! You're not going, Sirs?
175 CILANDRE *and* ACASTE: No, Madam, no.
   ALCESTE:
You seem to be in terror lest they go.
Do what you will, Sirs; leave, or linger on,
But I shan't go till after you are gone.
   ACASTE:
I'm free to linger, unless I should perceive
180 *Madame* is tired, and wishes me to leave.
   CLITANDRE:
And as for me, I needn't go today
Until the hour of the King's *coucher*.
   CÉLIMÈNE (*to* ALCESTE):
You're joking, surely?
   ALCESTE: Not in the least; we'll see
Whether you'd rather part with them, or me.

SCENE VI. [ALCESTE, CÉLIMÈNE, ÉLIANTE,
   ACASTE, PHILINTE, CLITANDRE, BASQUE.]

   BASQUE (*to* ALCESTE):
Sir, there's a fellow here who bids me state
That he must see you, and that it can't wait.
   ALCESTE:
Tell him that I have no such pressing affairs.
   BASQUE:
It's a long tailcoat that this fellow wears,
With gold all over.
   CÉLIMÈNE (*to* ALCESTE):
5   You'd best go down and see.
Or—have him enter.

SCENE VII. [ALCESTE, CÉLIMÈNE, ÉLIANTE,
   ACASTE, PHILINTE, CLITANDRE, GUARD.]

   ALCESTE (*confronting the* GUARD):
        Well, what do you want with me?
Come in, Sir.
   GUARD: I've a word, Sir, for your ear.
   ALCESTE:
Speak it aloud, Sir; I shall strive to hear.
   GUARD:
The Marshals have instructed me to say
5 You must report to them without delay.
   ALCESTE:
Who? Me, Sir?

   GUARD: Yes, Sir; you.
   ALCESTE: But what do they want?
   PHILINTE (*to* ALCESTE):
To scotch your silly quarrel with Oronte.
   CÉLIMÈNE (*to* PHILINTE):
What quarrel?
   PHILINTE: Oronte and he have fallen out
Over some verse he spoke his mind about;
The Marshals wish to arbitrate the matter.   10
   ALCESTE:
Never shall I equivocate or flatter!
   PHILINTE:
You'd best obey their summons; come, let's go.
   ALCESTE:
How can they mend our quarrel, I'd like to know?
Am I to make a cowardly retraction,
And praise those jingles to his satisfaction?   15
I'll not recant; I've judged that sonnet rightly,
It's bad.
   PHILINTE:
        But you might say so more politely. . . .
   ALCESTE:
I'll not back down; his verses make me sick.
   PHILINTE:
If only you could be more politic!
But come, let's go.
   ALCESTE: I'll go, but I won't unsay   20
A single word.
   PHILINTE: Well, let's be on our way.
   ALCESTE:
Till I am ordered by my lord the King
To praise that poem, I shall say the thing
Is scandalous, by God, and that the poet
Ought to be hanged for having the nerve to show
    it.   25

(*To* CLITANDRE *and* ACASTE, *who are laughing.*)

By heaven, Sirs, I really didn't know
That I was being humorous.
   CÉLIMÈNE: Go, Sir, go;
Settle your business.
   ALCESTE: I shall, and when I'm through,
I shall return to settle things with you.

ACT III

SCENE I. [CLINTANDRE, ACASTE.]

   CLITANDRE:
Dear Marquess, how contented you appear;
All things delight you, nothing mars your cheer.
Can you, in perfect honesty, declare
That you've a right to be so debonair?

ACASTE:

5   By Jove, when I survey myself, I find
No cause whatever for distress of mind.
I'm young and rich; I can in modesty
Lay claim to an exalted pedigree;
And owing to my name and my condition
10 I shall not want for honors and position.
Then as to courage, that most precious trait,
I seem to have it, as was proved of late
Upon the field of honor, where my bearing,
They say, was very cool and rather daring.
15 I've wit, of course; and taste in such perfection
That I can judge without the least reflection,
And at the theater, which is my delight,
Can make or break a play on opening night,
And lead the crowd in hisses or bravos,
20 And generally be known as one who knows.
I'm clever, handsome, gracefully polite;
My waist is small, my teeth are strong and white;
As for my dress, the world's astonished eyes
Assure me that I bear away the prize.
25 I find myself in favor everywhere,
Honored by men, and worshiped by the fair;
And since these things are so, it seems to me
I'm justified in my complacency.

CLITANDRE:

Well, if so many ladies hold you dear,
30 Why do you press a hopeless courtship here?

ACASTE:

Hopeless, you say? I'm not the sort of fool
That likes his ladies difficult and cool.
Men who are awkward, shy, and peasantish
May pine for heartless beauties, if they wish,
35 Grovel before them, bear their cruelties,
Woo them with tears and sighs and bended knees,
And hope by dogged faithfulness to gain
What their poor merits never could obtain.
For men like me, however, it makes no sense
40 To love on trust, and foot the whole expense.
Whatever any lady's merits be,
I think, thank God, that I'm as choice as she;
That if my heart is kind enough to burn
For her, she owes me something in return;
45 And that in any proper love affair
The partners must invest an equal share.

CLITANDRE:

You think, then, that our hostess favors you?

ACASTE:

I've reason to believe that that is true.

CLITANDRE:

How did you come to such a mad conclusion?
50 You're blind, dear fellow. This is sheer delusion.

ACASTE:

All right, then: I'm deluded and I'm blind.

CLITANDRE:

Whatever put the notion in your mind?

ACASTE:

Delusion.

CLITANDRE:

What persuades you that you're right?

ACASTE:

I'm blind.

CLITANDRE:

But have you any proofs to cite?

ACASTE:

I tell you I'm deluded.

CLITANDRE: Have you, then,   55
Received some secret pledge from Célimène?

ACASTE:

Oh, no: she scorns me.

CLITANDRE: Tell me the truth, I beg.

ACASTE:

She just can't bear me.

CLITANDRE: Ah, don't pull my leg.
Tell me what hope she's given you, I pray.

ACASTE:

I'm hopeless, and it's you who win the day.   60
She hates me thoroughly, and I'm so vexed
I mean to hang myself on Tuesday next.

CLITANDRE:

Dear Marquess, let us have an armistice
And make a treaty. What do you say to this?
If ever one of us can plainly prove   65
That Célimène encourages his love,
The other must abandon hope, and yield,
And leave him in possession of the field.

ACASTE:

Now there's a bargain that appeals to me;
With all my heart, dear Marquess, I agree.   70
But hush.

SCENE II. [CÉLIMÈNE, ACASTE, CLITANDRE.]

CÉLIMÈNE:

Still here?

CLITANDRE: 'Twas love that stayed our feet.

CÉLIMÈNE:

I think I heard a carriage in the street.
Whose is it? D'you know?

SCENE III. [CÉLIMÈNE, ACASTE,
CLITANDRE, BASQUE.]

BASQUE: Arsinoé is here,
Madame.

CÉLIMÈNE:

Arsinoé, you say? Oh, dear.

BASQUE:

Éliante is entertaining her below.

CÉLIMÈNE:
What brings the creature here, I'd like to know?
ACASTE:
5   They say she's dreadfully prudish, but in fact
I think her piety . . .
CÉLIMÈNE: It's all an act.
At heart she's worldly, and her poor success
In snaring men explains her prudishness.
It breaks her heart to see the beaux and gallants
10 Engrossed by other women's charms and talents,
And so she's always in a jealous rage
Against the faulty standards of the age.
She lets the world believe that she's a prude
To justify her loveless solitude,
15 And strives to put a brand of moral shame
On all the graces that she cannot claim.
But still she'd love a lover; and Alceste
Appears to be the one she'd love the best.
His visits here are poison to her pride;
20 She seems to think I've lured him from her side;
And everywhere, at court or in the town,
The spiteful, envious woman runs me down.
In short, she's just as stupid as can be,
Vicious and arrogant in the last degree,
25 And . . .

SCENE IV. [ARSINOÉ, CÉLIMÈNE,
CLITANDRE, ACASTE.]

CÉLIMÈNE:
        Ah! What happy chance has brought
you here?
I've thought about you ever so much, my dear.
ARSINOÉ:
I've come to tell you something you should know.
CÉLIMÈNE:
How good of you to think of doing so!

(CLITANDRE and ACASTE go out, laughing.)

SCENE V. [ARSINOÉ, CÉLIMÈNE.]

ARSINOÉ:
It's just as well those gentlemen didn't tarry.
CÉLIMÈNE:
Shall we sit down?
ARSINOÉ: That won't be necessary.
Madam, the flame of friendship ought to burn
Brightest in matters of the most concern,
5   And as there's nothing which concerns us more
Than honor, I have hastened to your door
To bring you, as your friend, some information
About the status of your reputation.
I visited, last night, some virtuous folk,
10 And, quite by chance, it was of you they spoke;
There was, I fear, no tendency to praise

Your light behavior and your dashing ways.
The quantity of gentlemen you see
And your by now notorious coquetry
Were both so vehemently criticized   15
By everyone, that I was much surprised.
Of course, I needn't tell you where I stood;
I came to your defense as best I could,
Assured them you were harmless, and declared
Your soul was absolutely unimpaired.   20
But there are some things, you must realize,
One can't excuse, however hard one tries,
And I was forced at last into conceding
That your behavior, Madam, is misleading,
That it makes a bad impression, giving rise   25
To ugly gossip and obscene surmise,
And that if you were more *overtly* good,
You wouldn't be so much misunderstood.
Not that I think you've been unchaste—no! no!
The saints preserve me from a thought so low!   30
But mere good conscience never did suffice:
One must avoid the outward show of vice.
Madam, you're too intelligent, I'm sure,
To think my motives anything but pure
In offering you this counsel—which I do   35
Out of a zealous interest in you.
CÉLIMÈNE:
Madam, I haven't taken you amiss;
I'm very much obliged to you for this;
And I'll at once discharge the obligation
By telling you about *your* reputation.   40
You've been so friendly as to let me know
What certain people say of me, and so
I mean to follow your benign example
By offering you a somewhat similar sample.
The other day, I went to an affair   45
And found some most distinguished people there
Discussing piety, both false and true.
The conversation soon came round to you.
Alas! Your prudery and bustling zeal
Appeared to have a very slight appeal.   50
Your affectation of a grave demeanor,
Your endless talk of virtue and of honor,
The aptitude of your suspicious mind
For finding sin where there is none to find,
Your towering self-esteem, that pitying face   55
With which you contemplate the human race,
Your sermonizings and your sharp aspersions
On people's pure and innocent diversions—
All these were mentioned, Madam, and, in fact,
Were roundly and concertedly attacked.   60
"What good," they said, "are all these outward
    shows,
When everything belies her pious pose?
She prays incessantly; but then, they say,

She beats her maids and cheats them of their pay;
65 She shows her zeal in every holy place,
But still she's vain enough to paint her face;
She holds that naked statues are immoral,
But with a naked *man* she'd have no quarrel."
Of course, I said to everybody there
70 That they were being viciously unfair;
But still they were disposed to criticize you,
And all agreed that someone should advise you
To leave the morals of the world alone,
And worry rather more about your own.
75 They felt that one's self-knowledge should be great
Before one thinks of setting others straight;
That one should learn the art of living well
Before one threatens other men with hell,
And that the Church is best equipped, no doubt,
80 To guide our souls and root our vices out.
Madam, you're too intelligent, I'm sure,
To think my motives anything but pure
In offering you this counsel—which I do
Out of a zealous interest in you.
    ARSINOÉ:
85 I dared not hope for gratitude, but I
Did not expect so acid a reply;
I judge, since you've been so extremely tart,
That my good counsel pierced you to the heart.
    CÉLIMÈNE:
Far from it, Madam. Indeed, it seems to me
90 We ought to trade advice more frequently.
One's vision of oneself is so defective
That it would be an excellent corrective.
If you are willing, Madam, let's arrange
Shortly to have another frank exchange
95 In which we'll tell each other, *entre nous,*
What you've heard tell of me, and I of you.
    ARSINOÉ:
Oh, people never censure you, my dear;
It's me they criticize. Or so I hear.
    CÉLIMÈNE:
Madam, I think we either blame or praise
100 According to our taste and length of days.
There is a time of life for coquetry,
And there's a season, too, for prudery.
When all one's charms are gone, it is, I'm sure,
Good strategy to be devout and pure:
105 It makes one seem a little less forsaken.
Some day, perhaps, I'll take the road you've taken:
Time brings all things. But I have time aplenty,
And see no cause to be a prude at twenty.
    ARSINOÉ:
You give your age in such a gloating tone
110 That one would think I was an ancient crone;
We're not so far apart, in sober truth,
That you can mock me with a boast of youth!

Madam, you baffle me. I wish I knew
What moves you to provoke me as you do.
    CÉLIMÈNE:
For my part, Madam, I should like to know   115
Why you abuse me everywhere you go.
Is it my fault, dear lady, that your hand
Is not, alas, in very great demand?
If men admire me, if they pay me court
And daily make me offers of the sort   120
You'd dearly love to have them make to you,
How can I help it? What would you have me do?
If what you want is lovers, please feel free
To take as many as you can from me.
    ARSINOÉ:
Oh, come. D'you think the world is losing sleep   125
Over the flock of lovers which you keep,
Or that we find it difficult to guess
What price you pay for their devotedness?
Surely you don't expect us to suppose
Mere merit could attract so many beaux?   130
It's not your virtue that they're dazzled by;
Nor is it virtuous love for which they sigh.
You're fooling no one, Madam; the world's not
        blind;
There's many a lady heaven has designed
To call men's noblest, tenderest feelings out,   135
Who has no lovers dogging her about;
From which it's plain that lovers nowadays
Must be acquired in bold and shameless ways,
And only pay one court for such reward
As modesty and virtue can't afford.   140
Then don't be quite so puffed up, if you please,
About your tawdry little victories;
Try, if you can, to be a shade less vain,
And treat the world with somewhat less disdain.
If one were envious of your amours,   145
One soon could have a following like yours;
Lovers are no great trouble to collect
If one prefers them to one's self-respect.
    CÉLIMÈNE:
Collect them then, my dear; I'd love to see
You demonstrate that charming theory;   150
Who knows, you might . . .
    ARSINOÉ: Now, Madam, that will do;
It's time to end this trying interview.
My coach is late in coming to your door,
Or I'd have taken leave of you before.
    CÉLIMÈNE:
Oh, please don't feel that you must rush away;   155
I'd be delighted, Madam, if you'd stay.
However, lest my conversation bore you,
Let me provide some better company for you;
This gentleman, who comes most apropos,
Will please you more than I could do, I know.   160

SCENE VI. [ALCESTE, CÉLIMÈNE, ARSINOÉ.]

CÉLIMÈNE:
Alceste, I have a little note to write
Which simply must go out before tonight;
Please entertain *Madame*; I'm sure that she
Will overlook my incivility.

SCENE VII. [ALCESTE, ARSINOÉ.]

ARSINOÉ:
Well, Sir, our hostess graciously contrives
For us to chat until my coach arrives;
And I shall be forever in her debt
For granting me this little tête-à-tête.
5 We women very rightly give our hearts
To men of noble character and parts,
And your especial merits, dear Alceste,
Have roused the deepest sympathy in my breast.
Oh, how I wish they had sufficient sense
10 At court, to recognize your excellence!
They wrong you greatly, Sir. How it must hurt you
Never to be rewarded for your virtue!

ALCESTE:
Why, Madam, what cause have I to feel aggrieved?
What great and brilliant thing have I achieved?
15 What service have I rendered to the King
That I should look to him for anything?

ARSINOÉ:
Not everyone who's honored by the State
Has done great services. A man must wait
Till time and fortune offer him the chance.
20 Your merit, Sir, is obvious at a glance,
And . . .

ALCESTE:
          Ah, forget my merit; I am not neglected.
The court, I think, can hardly be expected
To mine men's souls for merit, and unearth
Our hidden virtues and our secret worth.

ARSINOÉ:
25 *Some* virtues, though are far too bright to hide;
Yours are acknowledged, Sir, on every side.
Indeed, I've heard you warmly praised of late
By persons of considerable weight.

ALCESTE:
This fawning age has praise for everyone,
30 And all distinctions, Madam, are undone.
All things have equal honor nowadays,
And no one should be gratified by praise.
To be admired, one only need exist,
And every lackey's on the honors list.

ARSINOÉ:
35 I only wish, Sir, that you had your eye
On some position at court, however high;
You'd only have to hint at such a notion

For me to set the proper wheels in motion;
I've certain friendships I'd be glad to use
To get you any office you might choose.   40

ALCESTE:
Madam, I fear that any such ambition
Is wholly foreign to my disposition.
The soul God gave me isn't of the sort
That prospers in the weather of a court.
It's all too obvious that I don't possess   45
The virtues necessary for success.
My one great talent is for speaking plain;
I've never learned to flatter or to feign;
And anyone so stupidly sincere
Had best not seek a courtier's career.   50
Outside the court, I know, one must dispense
With honors, privilege, and influence;
But still one gains the right, forgoing these,
Not to be tortured by the wish to please.
One needn't live in dread of snubs and slights,   55
Nor praise the verse that every idiot writes,
Nor humor silly Marquesses, nor bestow
Politic sighs on Madam So-and-So.

ARSINOÉ:
Forget the court, then; let the matter rest.
But I've another cause to be distressed   60
About your present situation, Sir.
It's to your love affair that I refer.
She whom you love, and who pretends to love
    you,
Is, I regret to say, unworthy of you.

ALCESTE:
Why, Madam? Can you seriously intend   65
To make so grave a charge against your friend?

ARSINOÉ:
Alas, I must. I've stood aside too long
And let that lady do you grievous wrong;
But now my debt to conscience shall be paid:
I tell you that your love has been betrayed.   70

ALCESTE:
I thank you, Madam; you're extremely kind.
Such words are soothing to a lover's mind.

ARSINOÉ:
Yes, though she *is* my friend, I say again
You're very much too good for Célimène.
She's wantonly misled you from the start.   75

ALCESTE:
You may be right; who knows another's heart?
But ask yourself if it's the part of charity
To shake my soul with doubts of her sincerity.

ARSINOÉ:
Well, if you'd rather be a dupe than doubt her,
That's your affair. I'll say no more about her.   80

ALCESTE:
Madam, you know that doubt and vague suspicion

Are painful to a man in my position;
It's most unkind to worry me this way
Unless you've some real proof of what you say.
    ARSINOÉ:
85 Sir, say no more: all doubts shall be removed,
And all that I've been saying shall be proved.
You've only to escort me home, and there
We'll look into the heart of this affair.
I've ocular evidence which will persuade you
90 Beyond a doubt, that Célimène's betrayed you.
Then, if you're saddened by that revelation,
Perhaps I can provide some consolation.

ACT IV

SCENE I. [ÉLIANTE, PHILINTE.]

    PHILINTE:
Madam, he acted like a stubborn child;
I thought they never would be reconciled;
In vain we reasoned, threatened, and appealed;
He stood his ground and simply would not yield.
5   The Marshals, I feel sure, have never heard
An argument so splendidly absurd.
"No, gentlemen," said he, "I'll not retract.
His verse is bad: extremely bad, in fact.
Surely it does the man no harm to know it.
10 Does it disgrace him, not to be a poet?
A gentleman may be respected still,
Whether he writes a sonnet well or ill.
That I dislike his verse should not offend him;
In all that touches honor, I commend him;
15 He's noble, brave, and virtuous—but I fear
He can't in truth be called a sonneteer.
I'll gladly praise his wardrobe; I'll endorse
His dancing, or the way he sits a horse;
But, gentlemen, I cannot praise his rhyme.
20 In fact, it ought to be a capital crime
For anyone so sadly unendowed
To write a sonnet, and read the thing aloud."
At length he fell into a gentler mood
And, striking a concessive attitude,
25 He paid Oronte the following courtesies:
"Sir, I regret that I'm so hard to please,
And I'm profoundly sorry that your lyric
Failed to provoke me to a panegyric."
After these curious words, the two embraced,
30 And then the hearing was adjourned—in haste.
    ÉLIANTE:
His conduct has been very singular lately;
Still, I confess that I respect him greatly.
The honesty in which he takes such pride
Has—to my mind—it's noble, heroic side.

In this false age, such candor seems outrageous;   35
But I could wish that it were more contagious.
    PHILINTE:
What most intrigues me in our friend Alceste
Is the grand passion that rages in his breast.
The sullen humors he's compounded of
Should not, I think, dispose his heart to love;   40
But since they do, it puzzles me still more
That he should choose your cousin to adore.
    ÉLIANTE:
It does, indeed, belie the theory
That love is born of gentle sympathy,
And that the tender passion must be based   45
On sweet accords of temper and of taste.
    PHILINTE:
Does she return his love, do you suppose?
    ÉLIANTE:
Ah, that's a difficult question, Sir. Who knows?
How can we judge the truth of her devotion?
Her heart's a stranger to its own emotion.   50
Sometimes it thinks it loves, when no love's there;
At other times it loves quite unaware.
    PHILINTE:
I rather think Alceste is in for more
Distress and sorrow than he's bargained for;
Were he of my mind, Madam, his affection   55
Would turn in quite a different direction,
And we would see him more responsive to
The kind regard which he receives from you.
    ÉLIANTE:
Sir, I believe in frankness, and I'm inclined,
In matters of the heart, to speak my mind.   60
I don't oppose his love for her; indeed,
I hope with all my heart that he'll succeed,
And were it in my power, I'd rejoice
In giving him the lady of his choice.
But if, as happens frequently enough   65
In love affairs, he meets with a rebuff—
If Célimène should grant some rival's suit—
I'd gladly play the role of substitute;
Nor would his tender speeches please me less
Because they'd once been made without success.   70
    PHILINTE:
Well, Madam, as for me, I don't oppose
Your hopes in this affair; and heaven knows
That in my conversations with the man
I plead your cause as often as I can.
But if those two should marry, and so remove   75
All chance that he will offer you his love,
Then I'll declare my own, and hope to see
Your gracious favor pass from him to me.
In short, should you be cheated of Alceste,
I'd be most happy to be second best.   80

ÉLIANTE:
Philinte, you're teasing.

PHILINTE:　　　　　Ah, Madam, never fear;
No words of mine were ever so sincere,
And I shall live in fretful expectation
Till I can make a fuller declaration.

SCENE II. [ALCESTE, ÉLIANTE, PHILINTE.]

ALCESTE:
Avenge me, Madam! I must have satisfaction,
Or this great wrong will drive me to distraction!

ÉLIANTE:
Why, what's the matter? What's upset you so?

ALCESTE:
Madam, I've had a mortal, mortal blow.
5　If Chaos repossessed the universe,
I swear I'd not be shaken any worse.
I'm ruined . . . I can say no more . . . My soul . . .

ÉLIANTE:
Do try, Sir, to regain your self-control.

ALCESTE:
Just heaven! Why were so much beauty and grace
10　Bestowed on one so vicious and so base?

ÉLIANTE:
Once more, Sir, tell us. . . .

ALCESTE:　　　　My world has gone to wrack;
I'm—I'm betrayed; she's stabbed me in the back:
Yes, Célimène (who would have thought it of
　　her?)
Is false to me, and has another lover.

ÉLIANTE:
15　Are you quite certain? Can you prove these things?

PHILINTE:
Lovers are prey to wild imaginings
And jealous fancies. No doubt there's some mis-
　　take . . .

ALCESTE:
Mind your own business, Sir, for heaven's sake.
(To ÉLIANTE.) Madam, I have the proof that you
　　demand
20　Here in my pocket, penned by her own hand.
Yes, all the shameful evidence one could want
Lies in this letter written to Oronte—
Oronte! whom I felt sure she couldn't love,
And hardly bothered to be jealous of.

PHILINTE:
25　Still, in a letter, appearances may deceive;
This may not be so bad as you believe.

ALCESTE:
Once more I beg you, Sir, to let me be;
Tend to your own affairs; leave mine to me.

ÉLIANTE:
Compose yourself; this anguish that you feel . . .

ALCESTE:
Is something, Madam, you alone can heal.　30
My outraged heart, beside itself with grief,
Appeals to you for comfort and relief.
Avenge me on your cousin, whose unjust
And faithless nature has deceived my trust;
Avenge a crime your pure soul must detest.　35

ÉLIANTE:
But how, Sir?

ALCESTE:　　Madam, this heart within my breast
Is yours; pray take it; redeem my heart from her,
And so avenge me on my torturer.
Let her be punished by the fond emotion,
The ardent love, the bottomless devotion,　40
The faithful worship which this heart of mine
Will offer up to yours as to a shrine.

ÉLIANTE:
You have my sympathy, Sir, in all you suffer;
Nor do I scorn the noble heart you offer;
But I suspect you'll soon be mollified,　45
And this desire for vengeance will subside.
When some belovèd hand has done us wrong
We thirst for retribution—but not for long;
However dark the deed that she's committed,
A lovely culprit's very soon acquitted.　50
Nothing's so stormy as an injured lover,
And yet no storm so quickly passes over.

ALCESTE:
No, Madam, no—this is no lovers' spat;
I'll not forgive her; it's gone too far for that;
My mind's made up; I'll kill myself before　55
I waste my hopes upon her any more.
Ah, here she is. My wrath intensifies.
I shall confront her with her tricks and lies,
And crush her utterly, and bring you then
A heart no longer slave to Célimène.　60

SCENE III. [CÉLIMÈNE, ALCESTE.]

ALCESTE (aside):
Sweet heaven, help me to control my passion.

CÉLIMÈNE (aside):
Oh, Lord. (To ALCESTE.) Why stand there staring
　　in that fashion?
And what d'you mean by those dramatic sighs,
And that malignant glitter in your eyes?

ALCESTE:
I mean that sins which cause the blood to freeze　5
Look innocent beside your treacheries;
That nothing Hell's or Heaven's wrath could do
Ever produced so bad a thing as you.

CÉLIMÈNE:
Your compliments were always sweet and pretty.

ALCESTE:
Madam, it's not the moment to be witty.　10

No, blush and hang your head; you've ample
   reason,
Since I've the fullest evidence of your treason.
Ah, this is what my sad heart prophesied;
Now all my anxious fears are verified;
15 My dark suspicion and my gloomy doubt
Divined the truth, and now the truth is out.
For all your trickery, I was not deceived;
It was my bitter stars that I believed.
But don't imagine that you'll go scot-free;
20 You shan't misuse me with impunity.
I know that love's irrational and blind;
I know the heart's not subject to the mind,
And can't be reasoned into beating faster;
I know each soul is free to choose its master;
25 Therefore had you but spoken from the heart,
Rejecting my attention from the start,
I'd have no grievance, or at any rate
I could complain of nothing but my fate.
Ah, but so falsely to encourage me—
30 That was a treason and a treachery
For which you cannot suffer too severely,
And you shall pay for that behavior dearly.
Yes, now I have no pity, not a shred;
My temper's out of hand; I've lost my head;
35 Shocked by the knowledge of your double dealings,
My reason can't restrain my savage feelings;
A righteous wrath deprives me of my senses,
And I won't answer for the consequences.

CÉLIMÈNE:
What does this outburst mean? Will you please
   explain?
40 Have you, by any chance, gone quite insane?

ALCESTE:
Yes, yes, I went insane the day I fell
A victim to your black and fatal spell,
Thinking to meet with some sincerity
Among the treacherous charms that beckoned me.

CÉLIMÈNE:
45 Pooh. Of what treachery can you complain?

ALCESTE:
How sly you are, how cleverly you feign!
But you'll not victimize me any more.
Look: here's a document you've seen before.
This evidence, which I acquired today,
50 Leaves you, I think, without a thing to say.

CÉLIMÈNE:
Is this what sent you into such a fit?

ALCESTE:
You should be blushing at the sight of it.

CÉLIMÈNE:
Ought I to blush? I truly don't see why.

ALCESTE:
Ah, now you're being bold as well as sly;

Since there's no signature, perhaps you'll claim . . . 55

CÉLIMÈNE:
I wrote it, whether or not it bears my name.

ALCESTE:
And you can view with equanimity
This proof of your disloyalty to me!

CÉLIMÈNE:
Oh, don't be so outrageous and extreme.

ALCESTE:
You take this matter lightly, it would seem. 60
Was it no wrong to me, no shame to you,
That you should send Oronte this billet-doux?

CÉLIMÈNE:
Oronte! Who said it was for him?

ALCESTE: Why, those
Who brought me this example of your prose.
But what's the difference? If you wrote the letter 65
To someone else, it pleases me no better.
My grievance and your guilt remain the same.

CÉLIMÈNE:
But need you rage, and need I blush for shame,
If this was written to a *woman* friend?

ALCESTE:
Ah! Most ingenious. I'm impressed no end; 70
And after that incredible evasion
Your guilt is clear. I need no more persuasion.
How dare you try so clumsy a deception?
D'you think I'm wholly wanting in perception?
Come, come, let's see how brazenly you'll try 75
To bolster up so palpable a lie:
Kindly construe this ardent closing section
As nothing more than sisterly affection!
Here, let me read it. Tell me, if you dare to,
That this is for a woman . . .

CÉLIMÈNE: I don't care to. 80
What right have you to badger and berate me,
And so highhandedly interrogate me?

ALCESTE:
Now, don't be angry; all I ask of you
Is that you justify a phrase or two . . .

CÉLIMÈNE:
No, I shall not. I utterly refuse, 85
And you may take those phrases as you choose.

ALCESTE:
Just show me how this letter could be meant
For a woman's eyes, and I shall be content.

CÉLIMÈNE:
No, no, it's for Oronte; you're perfectly right.
I welcome his attentions with delight, 90
I prize his character and his intellect,
And everything is just as you suspect.
Come, do your worst now; give your rage free rein;
But kindly cease to bicker and complain.

ALCESTE (*aside*):

95 Good God! Could anything be more inhuman?
Was ever a heart so mangled by a woman?
When I complain of how she has betrayed me,
She bridles, and commences to upbraid me!
She tries my tortured patience to the limit;
100 She won't deny her guilt; she glories in it!
And yet my heart's too faint and cowardly
To break these chains of passion, and be free,
To scorn her as it should, and rise above
This unrewarded, mad, and bitter love.
(*To* CÉLIMÈNE.) Ah, traitress, in how confident a
105   fashion
You take advantage of my helpless passion,
And use my weakness for your faithless charms
To make me once again throw down my arms!
But do at least deny this black transgression;
110 Take back that mocking and perverse confession;
Defend this letter and your innocence,
And I, poor fool, will aid in your defense.
Pretend, pretend, that you are just and true,
And I shall make myself believe in you.

CÉLIMÈNE:

115 Oh, stop it. Don't be such a jealous dunce,
Or I shall leave off loving you at once.
Just why should I *pretend*? What could impel me
To stoop so low as that? And kindly tell me
Why, if I loved another, I shouldn't merely
120 Inform you of it, simply and sincerely!
I've told you where you stand, and that admission
Should altogether clear me of suspicion;
After so generous a guarantee,
What right have you to harbor doubts of me?
125 Since women are (from natural reticence)
Reluctant to declare their sentiments,
And since the honor of our sex requires
That we conceal our amorous desires,
Ought any man for whom such laws are broken
130 To question what the oracle has spoken?
Should he not rather feel an obligation
To trust that most obliging declaration?
Enough, now. Your suspicions quite disgust me;
Why should I love a man who doesn't trust me?
135 I cannot understand why I continue,
Fool that I am, to take an interest in you.
I ought to choose a man less prone to doubt,
And give you something to be vexed about.

ALCESTE:

Ah, what a poor enchanted fool I am;
140 These gentle words, no doubt, were all a sham,
But destiny requires me to entrust
My happiness to you, and so I must.
I'll love you to the bitter end, and see

How false and treacherous you dare to be.

CÉLIMÈNE:

No, you don't really love me as you ought.   145

ALCESTE:

I love you more than can be said or thought;
Indeed, I wish you were in such distress
That I might show my deep devotedness.
Yes, I could wish that you were wretchedly poor,
Unloved, uncherished, utterly obscure;   150
That fate had set you down upon the earth
Without possessions, rank, or gentle birth;
Then, by the offer of my heart, I might
Repair the great injustice of your plight;
I'd raise you from the dust, and proudly prove   155
The purity and vastness of my love.

CÉLIMÈNE:

This is a strange benevolence indeed!
God grant that I may never be in need. . . .
Ah, here's Monsier Dubois, in quaint disguise.

SCENE IV. [CÉLIMÈNE, ALCESTE, DUBOIS.]

ALCESTE:

Well, why this costume? Why those frightened
    eyes?
What ails you?

DUBOIS:

        Well, Sir, things are most mysterious.

ALCESTE:

What do you mean?

DUBOIS:

        I fear they're very serious.

ALCESTE:

What?

DUBOIS:

    Shall I speak more loudly?

ALCESTE:

            Yes; speak out.

DUBOIS:

Isn't there someone here, Sir?

ALCESTE:

            Speak, you lout!   5
Stop wasting time.

DUBOIS:

    Sir, we must slip away.

ALCESTE:

How's that?

DUBOIS: We must decamp without delay.

ALCESTE:

Explain yourself.

DUBOIS:

    I tell you we must fly.

ALCESTE:

What for?

DUBOIS:

    We mustn't pause to say good-by.

ALCESTE:

Now what d'you mean by all of this, you clown?   10

DUBOIS:
I mean, Sir, that we've got to leave this town.
ALCESTE:
I'll tear you limb from limb and joint from joint
If you don't come more quickly to the point.
DUBOIS:
Well, Sir, today a man in a black suit,
15 Who wore a black and ugly scowl to boot,
Left us a document scrawled in such a hand
As even Satan couldn't understand.
It bears upon your lawsuit, I don't doubt;
But all hell's devils couldn't make it out.
ALCESTE:
20 Well, well, go on. What then? I fail to see
How this event obliges us to flee.
DUBOIS:
Well, Sir, an hour later, hardly more,
A gentleman who's often called before
Came looking for you in an anxious way.
25 Not finding you, he asked me to convey
(Knowing I could be trusted with the same)
The following message . . . Now, what *was* his
     name?
ALCESTE:
Forget his name, you idiot. What did he say?
DUBOIS:
Well, it was one of your friends, Sir, anyway.
30 He warned you to begone, and he suggested
That if you stay, you may well be arrested.
ALCESTE:
What? Nothing more specific? Think, man, think!
DUBOIS:
No, Sir. He had me bring him pen and ink,
And dashed you off a letter which, I'm sure,
35 Will render things distinctly less obscure.
ALCESTE:
Well—let me have it!
CÉLIMÈNE: What *is* this all about?
ALCESTE:
God knows; but I have hopes of finding out.
How long am I to wait, you blitherer?
DUBOIS (*after a protracted search for the letter*):
I must have left it on your table, Sir.
ALCESTE:
I ought to . . .
CÉLIMÈNE:
40   No, no, keep yourself-control;
Go find out what's behind this rigmarole.
ALCESTE:
It seems that fate, no matter what I do,
Has sworn that I may not converse with you;
But, Madam, pray permit your faithful lover
45 To try once more before the day is over.

ACT V

SCENE I. [ALCESTE, PHILINTE.]

ALCESTE:
No, it's too much. My mind's made up, I tell you.
PHILINTE:
Why should this blow, however hard, compel
     you . . .
ALCESTE:
No, no, don't waste your breath in argument;
Nothing you say will alter my intent;
This age is vile, and I've made up my mind   5
To have no further commerce with mankind.
Did not truth, honor, decency, and the laws
Oppose my enemy and approve my cause?
My claims were justified in all men's sight;
I put my trust in equity and right;   10
Yet, to my horror and the world's disgrace,
Justice is mocked, and I have lost my case!
A scoundrel whose dishonesty is notorious
Emerges from another lie victorious!
Honor and right condone his brazen fraud,   15
While rectitude and decency applaud!
Before his smirking face, the truth stands charmed,
And virtue conquered, and the law disarmed!
His crime is sanctioned by a court decree!
And not content with what he's done to me,   20
The dog now seeks to ruin me by stating
That I composed a book now circulating,
A book so wholly criminal and vicious
That even to speak its title is seditious!
Meanwhile Oronte, my rival, lends his credit   25
To the same libelous tale, and helps to spread it!
Oronte! a man of honor and of rank,
With whom I've been entirely fair and frank;
Who sought me out and forced me, willy-nilly,
To judge some verse I found extremely silly;   30
And who, because I properly refused
To flatter him, or see the truth abused,
Abets my enemy in a rotten slander!
There's the reward of honesty and candor!
The man will hate me to the end of time   35
For failing to commend his wretched rhyme!
And not this man alone, but all humanity
Do what they do from interest and vanity;
They prate of honor, truth, and righteousness,
But lie, betray, and swindle nonetheless.   40
Come then: man's villainy is too much to bear;
Let's leave this jungle and this jackal's lair.
Yes! treacherous and savage race of men,
You shall not look upon my face again.

PHILINTE:

45 Oh, don't rush into exile prematurely;
Things aren't as dreadful as you make them,
   surely.
It's rather obvious, since you're still at large,
That people don't believe your enemy's charge.
Indeed, his tale's so patently untrue
50 That it may do more harm to him than you.

   ALCESTE:

Nothing could do that scoundrel any harm:
His frank corruption is his greatest charm,
And, far from hurting him, a further shame
Would only serve to magnify his name.

   PHILINTE:

55 In any case, his bald prevarication
Has done no injury to your reputation,
And you may feel secure in that regard.
As for your lawsuit, it should not be hard
To have the case reopened, and contest
This judgment . . .

60   ALCESTE: No, no, let the verdict rest.
Whatever cruel penalty it may bring,
I wouldn't have it changed for anything.
It shows the times' injustice with such clarity
That I shall pass it down to our posterity
65 As a great proof and signal demonstration
Of the black wickedness of this generation.
It may cost twenty thousand francs; but I
Shall pay their twenty thousand, and gain thereby
The right to storm and rage at human evil,
70 And send the race of mankind to the devil.

   PHILINTE:

Listen to me . . .

   ALCESTE:

       Why? What can you possibly say?
Don't argue, Sir; your labor's thrown away.
Do you propose to offer lame excuses
For men's behavior and the times' abuses?

   PHILINTE:

75 No, all you say I'll readily concede:
This is a low, conniving age indeed;
Nothing but trickery prospers nowadays,
And people ought to mend their shabby ways.
Yes, man's a beastly creature; but must we then
80 Abandon the society of men?
Here in the world, each human frailty
Provides occasion for philosophy,
And that is virtue's noblest exercise;
If honesty shone forth from all men's eyes,
85 If every heart were frank and kind and just.
What could our virtues do but gather dust
(Since their employment is to help us bear
The villainies of men without despair)?
A heart well-armed with virtue can endure . . .

   ALCESTE:

Sir, you're a matchless reasoner, to be sure;   90
Your words are fine and full of cogency;
But don't waste time and eloquence on me.
My reason bids me go, for my own good.
My tongue won't lie and flatter as it should;
God knows what frankness it might next commit,   95
And what I'd suffer on account of it.
Pray let me wait for Célimène's return
In peace and quiet. I shall shortly learn,
By her response to what I have in view,
Whether her love for me is feigned or true.   100

   PHILINTE:

Till then, let's visit Éliante upstairs.

   ALCESTE:

No, I am too weighed down with somber cares.
Go to her, do; and leave me with my gloom
Here in the darkened corner of this room.

   PHILINTE:

Why, that's no sort of company, my friend;   105
I'll see if Éliante will not descend.

SCENE II. [CÉLIMÈNE, ORONTE, ALCESTE.]

   ORONTE:

Yes, Madam, if you wish me to remain
Your true and ardent lover, you must deign
To give me some more positive assurance.
All this suspense is quite beyond endurance.
If your heart shares the sweet desires of mine,   5
Show me as much by some convincing sign;
And here's the sign I urgently suggest:
That you no longer tolerate Alceste,
But sacrifice him to my love, and sever
All your relations with the man forever.   10

   CÉLIMÈNE:

Why do you suddenly dislike him so?
You praised him to the skies not long ago.

   ORONTE:

Madam, that's not the point. I'm here to find
Which way your tender feelings are inclined.
Choose, if you please, between Alceste and me,   15
And I shall stay or go accordingly.

   ALCESTE (emerging from the corner):

Yes, Madam, choose; this gentleman's demand
Is wholly just, and I support his stand.
I too am true and ardent; I too am here
To ask you that you make your feelings clear.   20
No more delays, now; no equivocation;
The time has come to make your declaration.

   ORONTE:

Sir, I've no wish in any way to be
An obstacle to your felicity.

ALCESTE:

25 Sir, I've no wish to share her heart with you;
    That may sound jealous, but at least it's true.
    ORONTE:
    If, weighing us, she leans in your direction . . .
    ALCESTE:
    If she regards you with the least affection . . .
    ORONTE:
    I swear I'll yield her to you there and then.
    ALCESTE:
30 I swear I'll never see her face again.
    ORONTE:
    Now, Madam, tell us what we've come to hear.
    ALCESTE:
    Madam, speak openly and have no fear.
    ORONTE:
    Just say which one is to remain your lover.
    ALCESTE:
    Just name one name, and it will all be over.
    ORONTE:
35 What! Is it possible that you're undecided?
    ALCESTE:
    What! Can your feelings possibly be divided?
    CÉLIMÈNE:
    Enough: this inquisition's gone too far:
    How utterly unreasonable you are!
    Not that I couldn't make the choice with ease;
40 My heart has no conflicting sympathies;
    I know full well which one of you I favor,
    And you'd not see me hesitate or waver.
    But how can you expect me to reveal
    So cruelly and bluntly what I feel?
45 I think it altogether too unpleasant
    To choose between two men when both are present;
    One's heart has means more subtle and more kind
    Of letting its affections be divined,
    Nor need one be uncharitably plain
50 To let a lover know he loves in vain.
    ORONTE:
    No, no, speak plainly; I for one can stand it.
    I beg you to be frank.
    ALCESTE: And I demand it.
    The simple truth is what I wish to know,
    And there's no need for softening the blow.
55 You've made an art of pleasing everyone,
    But now your days of coquetry are done:
    You have no choice now, Madam, but to choose,
    For I'll know what to think if you refuse;
    I'll take your silence for a clear admission
60 That I'm entitled to my worst suspicion.
    ORONTE:
    I thank you for this ultimatum, Sir,
    And I may say I heartily concur.

CÉLIMÈNE:
Really, this foolishness is very wearing:
Must you be so unjust and overbearing?
Haven't I told you why I must demur?   65
Ah, here's Éliante; I'll put the case to her.

SCENE III. [ÉLIANTE, PHILINTE, CÉLIMÈNE,
            ORONTE, ALCESTE.]

CÉLIMÈNE:
Cousin, I'm being persecuted here
By these two persons, who, it would appear,
Will not be satisfied till I confess
Which one I love the more, and which the less,
And tell the latter to his face that he   5
Is henceforth banished from my company.
Tell me, has ever such a thing been done?
ÉLIANTE:
You'd best not turn to me; I'm not the one
To back you in a matter of this kind:
I'm all for those who frankly speak their mind. 10
ORONTE:
Madam, you'll search in vain for a defender.
ALCESTE:
You're beaten, Madam, and may as well surrender.
ORONTE:
Speak, speak, you must; and end this awful strain.
ALCESTE:
Or don't, and your position will be plain.
ORONTE:
A single word will close this painful scene.   15
ALCESTE:
But if you're silent, I'll know what you mean.

SCENE IV. [ARSINOÉ, CÉLIMÈNE,
        ÉLIANTE, ALCESTE, PHILINTE, ACASTE,
            CLITANDRE, ORONTE.]

ACASTE (to CÉLIMÈNE):
Madam, with all due deference, we two
Have come to pick a little bone with you.
CLITANDRE (to ORONTE and ALCESTE):
I'm glad you're present, Sirs, as you'll soon learn,
Our business here is also your concern.
ARSINOÉ (to CÉLIMÈNE:):
Madam, I visit you so soon gain   5
Only because of these two gentlemen,
Who came to me indignant and aggrieved
About a crime too base to be believed.
Knowing your virtue, having such confidence in
    it,
I couldn't think you guilty for a minute,   10
In spite of all their telling evidence;
And, rising above our little difference,
I've hastened here in friendship's name to see

You clear yourself of this great calumny.
ACASTE:

15 Yes, Madam, let us see with what composure
You'll manage to respond to this disclosure.
You lately sent Clitandre this tender note.
CLITANDRE:
And this one, for Acaste, you also wrote.
ACASTE (*to* ORONTE *and* ALCESTE):
You'll recognize this writing, Sirs, I think;
20 The lady is so free with pen and ink
That you must know it all too well, I fear.
But listen: this is something you should hear.

"How absurd you are to condemn my light-
heartedness in society, and to accuse me of being
25 happiest in the company of others. Nothing could
be more unjust; and if you do not come to me
instantly and beg pardon for saying such a thing, I
shall never forgive you as long as I live. Our big
bumbling friend the Viscount . . ."

30 What a shame that he's not here.

"Our big bumbling friend the Viscount, whose
name stands first in your complaint, is hardly a
man to my taste; and ever since the day I watched
him spend three-quarters of an hour spitting into a
35 well, so as to make circles in the water, I have been
unable to think highly of him. As for the little
Marquess . . ."

In all modesty, gentlemen, that is I.

"As for the little Marquess, who sat squeezing
40 my hand for such a long while yesterday, I find
him in all respects the most trifling creature alive;
and the only things of value about him are his cape
and his sword. As for the man with the green
ribbons . . ."

45 (*To* ALCESTE.) It's your turn now, Sir.

"As for the man with the green ribbons, he
amuses me now and then with his bluntness and
his bearish ill-humor; but there are many times
indeed when I think him the greatest bore in the
50 world. And as for the sonneteer . . ."

(*To* ORONTE.) Here's your helping.

"And as for the sonneteer, who has taken it into
his head to be witty, and insists on being an author
in the teeth of opinion, I simply cannot be both-
55 ered to listen to him, and his prose wearies me
quite as much as his poetry. Be assured that I am
not always so well-entertained as you suppose; that
I long for your company, more than I dare to say,

at all these entertainments to which people drag
me; and that the presence of those one loves is the   60
true and perfect seasoning to all one's pleasures."

CLITANDRE: And now for me.

"Clitandre, whom you mention, and who so
pesters me with his saccharine speeches, is the last
man on earth for whom I could feel any affection.   65
He is quite mad to suppose that I love him, and so
are you, to doubt that you are loved. Do come to
your senses; exchange your suppositions for his;
and visit me as often as possible, to help me bear
the annoyance of his unwelcome attentions."   70

It's sweet character that these letters show,
And what to call it, Madam, you well know.
Enough. We're off to make the world acquainted
With this sublime self-portrait that you've painted.
ACASTE:
Madam, I'll make no farewell oration;   75
No, you're not worthy of my indignation.
Far choicer hearts than yours, as you'll discover,
Would like this little Marquess for a lover.

SCENE V. [CÉLIMÈNE, ÉLIANTE, ASRINOÉ,
ALCESTE, ORONTE, PHILINTE.]

ORONTE:
So! After all those loving letters you wrote,
You turn on me like this, and cut my throat!
And your dissembling, faithless heart, I find,
Has pledged itself by turns to all mankind!
How blind I've been! But now I clearly see;   5
I thank you, Madam, for enlightening me.
My heart is mine once more, and I'm content;
The loss of it shall be your punishment.
(*To* ALCESTE.) Sir, she is yours; I'll seek no more to
stand
Between your wishes and this lady's hand.   10

SCENE VI. [CÉLIMÈNE, ÉLIANTE, ARSINOÉ,
ALCESTE, PHILINTE.]

ARSINOÉ (*to* CÉLIMÈNE):
Madam, I'm forced to speak. I'm far too stirred
To keep my counsel, after what I've heard.
I'm shocked and staggered by our want of morals.
It's not my way to mix in others' quarrels;
But really, when this fine and noble spirit,   5
This man of honor and surpassing merit,
Laid down the offering of his heart before you,
How *could* you . . .
ALCESTE:
Madam, permit me, I implore you,

To represent myself in this debate.
10 Dont' bother, please, to be my advocate.
My heart, in any case, could not afford
To give your services their due reward;
And if I chose, for consolation's sake,
Some other lady, 'twould not be you I'd take.

ARSINOÉ:
What makes you think you could, Sir? And how
15   dare you
Imply that I've been trying to ensnare you?
If you can for a moment entertain
Such flattering fancies, you're extremely vain.
I'm not so interested as you suppose
20 In Célimène's discarded gigolos.
Get rid of that absurd illusion, do.
Women like me are not for such as you.
Stay with this creature, to whom you're so attached;
I've never seen two people better matched.

SCENE VII. [CÉLIMÈNE, ÉLIANTE, ALCESTE, PHILINTE.]

ALCESTE (*to* CÉLIMÈNE):
Well, I've been still throughout this exposé,
Till everyone but me has said his say.
Come, have I shown sufficient self-restraint?
And may I now . . .

CÉLIMÈNE: Yes, make your just complaint.
5 Reproach me freely, call me what you will;
You've every right to say I've used you ill.
I've wronged you, I confess it; and in my shame
I'll make no effort to escape the blame.
The anger of those others I could despise;
10 My guilt toward you I sadly recognize.
Your wrath is wholly justified, I fear;
I know how culpable I must appear,
I know all things bespeak my treachery,
And that, in short, you've grounds for hating me.
Do so; I give you leave.

ALCESTE: Ah, traitress—how,
15 How should I cease to love you, even now?
Though mind and will were passionately bent
On hating you, my heart would not consent.
(*To* ÉLIANTE *and* PHILINTE.) Be witness to my
     madness, both of you;
20 See what infatuation drives one to;
But wait; my folly's only just begun,
And I shall prove to you before I'm done
How strange the human heart is, and how far
From rational we sorry creatures are.
(*To* CÉLIMÈNE:.) Woman, I'm willing to forget
25   your shame,
And clothe your treacheries in a sweeter name;

I'll call them youthful errors, instead of crimes,
And lay the blame on these corrupting times.
My one condition is that you agree
To share my chosen fate, and fly with me   30
To that wild, trackless, solitary place
In which I shall forget the human race.
Only by such a course can you atone
For those atrocious letters; by that alone
Can you remove my present horror of you,   35
And make it possible for me to love you.

CÉLIMÈNE:
What! I renounce the world at my young age,
And die of boredom in some hermitage?

ALCESTE:
Ah, if you really loved me as you ought,
You wouldn't give the world a moment's thought;   40
Must you have me, and all the world beside?

CÉLIMÈNE:
Alas, at twenty one is terrified
Of solitude. I fear I lack the force
And depth of soul to take so stern a course.
But if my hand in marriage will content you,   45
Why, there's a plan which I might well consent to,
And . . .

ALCESTE:
       No, I detest you now. I could excuse
Everything else, but since you thus refuse
To love me wholly, as a wife should do,
And see the world in me, as I in you,   50
Go! I reject your hand, and disenthrall
My heart from your enchantments, once for all.

SCENE VIII. [ÉLIANTE, ALCESTE, PHILINTE.]

ALCESTE (*to* ÉLIANTE):
Madam, your virtuous beauty has no peer;
Of all this world you only are sincere;
I've long esteemed you highly as you know;
Permit me ever to esteem you so,
And if I do not now request your hand,   5
Forgive me, Madam, and try to understand.
I feel unworthy of it; I sense that fate
Does not intend me for the married state,
That I should do you wrong by offering you
My shattered heart's unhappy residue,   10
And that in short . . .

ÉLIANTE: Your argument's well taken:
Nor need you fear that I shall feel forsaken.
Were I to offer him this hand of mine,
Your friend, Philinte, I think, would not decline.

PHILINTE:
Ah, Madam, that's my heart's most cherished
     goal,   15

For which I'd gladly give my life and soul.
   ALCESTE (*to* ÉLIANTE *and* PHILINTE):
May you be true to all you now profess,
And so deserve unending happiness.
Meanwhile, betrayed and wronged in everything,
20 I'll flee this bitter world where vice is king,
And seek some spot unpeopled and apart
Where I'll be free to have an honest heart.
   PHILINTE:
Come, Madam, let's do everything we can
To change the mind of this unhappy man.

COMMENTARY

The introduction to this book makes the rather obvious point that in both tragedy and comedy we have characters who are motivated by some ideal and that (for example) the tragic hero who hunts out the polluted man in Thebes or who kills his wife because he thinks she is unfaithful is neither more nor less impassioned than the comic lover who writes sonnets to his mistress's eyebrow. Whether the passion is noble or comic depends not on its depth, or its persistence, but on its context, and especially on its object.

The passion for honesty that drives Molière's misanthrope, Alceste, is said by the equable Éliante to have "its noble, heroic side," and her view has found wide acceptance among audiences and readers. Alceste is sometimes seen as a tragic figure caught in a comic world, and the play is sometimes said to be a sort of tragic comedy. Alceste demands honesty, and he fulminates against flattery and other forms of insincerity that apparently compose the entire life of the other figures. Surrounded by trimmers and gossips and worse, he alone (if we except the gentle Éliante) seems to hold to a noble ideal. The only other ideal given much prominence is Philinte's, a code of such easy tolerance that it is at times almost indistinguishable from mere passive acceptance of everything.

What case can be made that Alceste is comic, not tragic? A few points suggest themselves. First, this champion of honesty is in love (or thinks he is) with a coquette. What can be more comic than the apostle of plain-dealing being himself in the power of the irrational, especially when this power deposits him at the feet of Célimène, a woman who employs all the devices that in others infuriate him? Second, his demand for honesty is indiscriminate; he is as offended at trivial courtesies as at the law's injustice. Philinte "ought to die of self-disgust" for his "crime" of effusively greeting a casual acquaintance whose name he cannot even recall. So disproportionate is Alceste's passion that when he pops onstage in IV.II, saying to Éliante, "Avenge me, Madam," he is funny, though the words in themselves are scarcely amusing.

Alceste's remark about joking provides a thread that may be followed usefully. He cannot take a joke. Whenever he is laughed at, he becomes indignant, but indignation (when motivated by a desire to protect the self from criticism) itself evokes further laughter because of the gap between the indignant man's presentation of himself and his real worth. Comedy does not allow people to strike attitudes. The man who protests that his argument *is* valid, dammit, or that he *has* a sense of humor, or that his opponent is a fool, is likely to evoke laughter by his monolithic insistence on his merit. When Philinte laughs at the old poem Alceste quotes, Alceste resorts to bitter irony, and when told that his frankness has made him ridiculous, he irritably replies:

> So much the better; just what I wish to hear.
> No news could be more grateful to my ear.
> All men are so detestable in my eyes.
> I should be sorry if they thought me otherwise.

When his persistent refusal to praise a trivial poem moves two auditors to laughter, he again employs frigid irony, and concludes the scene ominously:

> By heavens, Sirs, I really didn't know
> That I was being humorous.
>   CÉLIMÈNE: Go, Sir; go;
> Settle your business.
>   ALCESTE: I shall, and when I'm through,
> I shall return to settle things with you.

Alceste, unable to laugh at the folly of others, cannot, of course, tolerate laughter at himself. When Philinte puts into practice the frankness Alceste stormily advocates, Alceste's response is the indignation we have been commenting on. A sense of humor (as distinct from derisive laughter) involves the ability to laugh at what one values, and among the things one values is the self. Children can laugh at surprises and at the distress of other children, but they cannot laugh at themselves because they cannot see themselves in perspective, at a distance, as it were. Mature people can laugh at (for example) mimicry of themselves, but the child or the immature adult will, like Alceste, sulk or fly into a rage.

In *The Misanthrope* it is entirely possible that Molière is in some degree mimicking himself. In 1662 Molière at forty married Armande Béjart, a woman less than half his age. The marriage seems to have been unhappy, apparently because his wife enjoyed attracting the attentions of other men. Some critics, pressing this point, assume that if the play is autobiographical, Alceste must be expressing Molière's point of view, and therefore he cannot be a comic figure. If anything, the autobiographic origin shows only that Molière had (which no one has doubted) a sense of humor. He could laugh at himself. Alceste's courtship of Célimène may in some degree represent Molière's unhappy marriage to a flirtatious and unappreciative woman, but the point is that Molière apparently could stand back and laugh at his own exasperation, which Alceste cannot do. (Molière subtitled the play "The Atrabilious Man in Love"; one cannot hear Alceste speaking thus of himself.) Alceste can only, rather childishly, try to maintain his way, and demand that his special merit be noted and rewarded:

> However high the praise, there's nothing worse
> Than sharing honors with the universe.
> Esteem is founded on comparison:
> To honor all men is to honor none.
> Since you embrace this indiscriminate vice,
> Your friendship comes at far too cheap a price;

> I spurn the easy tribute of a heart
> Which will not set the worthy man apart:
> I choose, Sir, to be chosen; and in fine,
> The friend of mankind is no friend of mine.

Once or twice, when he confesses that his love for Célimène is irrational, he seems to have some perspective, but mostly the scenes of Alceste as lover serve to reveal again and again his consuming egotism. His love is so great, he tells Célimène, that he wishes she were in some peril so that he could prove his love by saving her. Célimène aptly replies that Alceste's is "a strange benevolence indeed."

The argument thus far has tried to make the point that Alceste is funny—funny because (among other things) his anger is indiscriminate and disproportionate, because he is a sort of philosopher and yet is in love, and because his *idée fixe*, frankness, when turned against him, exasperates him. But when we return to Éliante's reference to his "noble, heroic side," and we recall his passion for honesty and his passionate desire to be himself, and when we see the hollowness all about him, the comic figure begins to take on a tragic aspect; and when at the end he departs from the stage unrepentant and bitter, banishing himself from society, we feel that the usual comic plot too has taken on a tragic aspect. But this is hardly to say that Alceste is tragic and *The Misanthrope* a tragedy. One cannot, for example, imagine Alceste committing suicide. He is not a Romeo or an Othello.

TOPICS FOR DISCUSSION

1. Does Alceste want to win or lose his lawsuit? Why?
2. Alceste bases his claims on reason. Do you think his own tone is always reasonable? Is his love of Célimène reasonable?
3. Jean-Jacques Rousseau said (in 1758) that Alceste is a man "who detests the morals of his age . . . , who, precisely because he loves mankind, despises in them the wrong they inflict upon one another." In somewhat the same vein, Jean-Louis Barrault, who has often performed the role of Alceste, says that Alceste "loved people too well. That was why he couldn't stand them as they were." How much evidence do you find of this love?
4. Evaluate Francois Mauriac's comment:

   In a world where a decent man . . . has so many reasons if not for protest, at least for examining his own conscience, Alceste only attacks the most harmless practices, those "lies" which do not take anyone in but which are necessary if social life is to go on at all. . . . In a world where injustice is rife, where crime is everywhere, he is up in arms against trivialities. He feels no horror for what is really horrible—beginning with himself. All his attacks are directed to things outside himself; he only compares himself with other people in order to demonstrate his own superiority.

5. Like King Lear, Alceste is greatly distressed at the discrepancy between reality and appearance, between what is said and what is believed or felt. But why—at least to some degree—does Alceste's distress strike you as funny?

6. Alceste scarcely appears in the third act. Is there any decline of interest? If not, why not? Is it reasonable to argue that Molière has not lost sight of the issues, that (for example) Acaste in III.I gives us something of Alceste and that Arsinoé in III.V gives us a sample of the outspokenness Alceste desires? Do you find Arsinoé's sincerity engaging?

7. What is the difference between Éliante's view of Alceste and Philinte's view? What do you think are the strengths and weaknesses of Philinte's speech on "philosophy" and "virtue" in V.I.80–89?

8. Philinte's marriage to Éliante is in accord with the usual ending of comedy, but what is the dramatic relevance of Molière's emphasis on the unromantic aspects of the marriage?

9. If we grant that Alceste's sincerity is at least in part rooted in self-love, does it follow that an audience sees no validity in his indictment of society?

ARMS AND THE MAN

A Pleasant Play

Bernard Shaw

Bernard Shaw (1856–1950) was born in Dublin of Anglo-Irish stock. His father drank too much, and his mother—something of an Ibsenite "new woman"—went to London to make her way as singer and voice teacher. Shaw worked in a Dublin real estate office for a while (he did not attend a college or university), and then followed his mother to London, where he wrote critical reviews and five novels (1879–1883) before turning playwright. His first play, begun with William Archer (playwright and translator of Ibsen), was abandoned in 1885, and then entirely revised by Shaw into *Widowers' Houses* (1892). He had already shown, in a critical study entitled *The Quintessence of Ibsenism* (1891), that he regarded the stage as a pulpit and soap box; before the nineteenth century was over, he wrote nine more plays, in order (he said) to espouse socialism effectively. *Arms and the Man* (1894) is among his early comic masterpieces, but at least a dozen of his plays have established themselves in the repertoire, including one tragedy, *Saint Joan*.

Shaw's idiosyncratic use (or nonuse) of the apostrophe is preserved in our text, as is his use of extra space between the letters of a word to indicate emphasis.

Raina retrieves the photograph she left for Captain Bluntschli in the pocket of her father's coat in a scene from the 1980 Guthrie Theater production directed by Michael Langham. (Photograph by Bruce Goldstein courtesy of the Guthrie Theater, Minneapolis, Minnesota.)

ACT I

Night: A lady's bedchamber in Bulgaria, in a small town near the Dragoman Pass, late in November in the year 1885. Through an open window with a little balcony a peak of the Balkans, wonderfully white and beautiful in the starlit snow, seems quite close at hand, though it is really miles away. The interior of the room is not like anything to be seen in the west of Europe. It is half rich Bulgarian, half cheap Viennese. Above the head of the bed, which stands against a little wall cutting off the left hand corner of the room, is a painted wooden shrine, blue and gold, with an ivory image of Christ, and a light hanging before it in a pierced metal ball suspended by three chains. The principal seat, placed towards the other side of the room and opposite the window, is a Turkish ottoman. The counterpane and hangings of the bed, the window curtains, the little carpet, and all the ornamental textile fabrics in the room are oriental and gorgeous; the paper on the walls is occidental and paltry. The washstand, against the wall on the side nearest the ottoman and window, consists of an enamelled iron basin with a pail beneath it in a painted metal frame, and a single towel on the rail at the side. The dressing table, between the bed and the window, is a common pine table, covered with a cloth of many colors, with an expensive toilet mirror on it. The door is on the side nearest the bed; and there is a chest of drawers between. This chest of drawers is also covered by a variegated native cloth; and on it there is a pile of paper backed novels, a box of chocolate creams, and a miniature easel with a large photograph of an extremely handsome officer, whose lofty bearing and magnetic glance can be felt even from the portrait. The room is lighted by a candle on the chest of drawers, and another on the dressing table with a box of matches beside it.

The window is hinged doorwise and stands wide open. Outside, a pair of wooden shutters, opening outwards, also stand open. On the balcony a young lady, intensely conscious of the romantic beauty of the night, and of the fact that her own youth and beauty are part of it, is gazing at the snowy Balkans. She is in her nightgown, well covered by a long mantle of furs, worth, on a moderate estimate, about three times the furniture of the room.

Her reverie is interrupted by her mother, CATHERINE PETKOFF, *a woman over forty, imperiously energetic, with magnificent black hair and eyes, who might be a very splendid specimen of the wife of a mountain farmer, but is determined to be a Viennese lady, and to that end wears a fashionable tea gown on all occasions.*

CATHERINE (*entering hastily, full of good news*): Raina! (*She pronounces it Rah-eena, with the stress on the ee.*) Raina! (*She goes to the bed, expecting to find* RAINA *there.*) Why, where—? (RAINA *looks into the room.*) Heavens, child! are you out in the night air instead of in your bed? You'll catch your death. Louka told me you were asleep.

RAINA (*dreamily*): I sent her away. I wanted to be alone. The stars are so beautiful! What is the matter?

CATHERINE: Such news! There has been a battle.

RAINA (*her eyes dilating*): Ah! (*She comes eagerly to* CATHERINE.)

CATHERINE: A great battle at Slivnitza! A victory! And it was won by Sergius.

RAINA (*with a cry of delight*): Ah! (*They embrace rapturously.*) Oh, mother! (*Then, with sudden anxiety*) is father safe?

CATHERINE: Of course! he sends me the news. Sergius is the hero of the hour, the idol of the regiment.

RAINA: Tell me, tell me. How was it? (*Ecstatically.*) Oh, mother! mother! mother! (*She pulls her mother down on the ottoman; and they kiss one another frantically.*)

CATHERINE (*with surging enthusiasm*): You cant guess how splendid it is. A cavalry charge! think of that! He defied our Russian commanders—acted without orders—led a charge on his own responsibility—headed it himself—was the first man to sweep through their guns. Cant you see it, Raina: our gallant splendid Bulgarians with their swords and eyes flashing, thundering down like an avalanche and scattering the wretched Serbs and their dandified Austrian officers like chaff. And you! you kept Sergius waiting a year before you would be betrothed to him. Oh, if you have a drop of Bulgarian blood in your veins, you will worship him when he comes back.

RAINA: What will he care for my poor little worship after the acclamations of a whole army of heroes? But no matter: I am so happy! so proud! (*She rises and walks about excitedly.*) It proves that all our ideas were real after all.

CATHERINE (*indignantly*): Our ideas real! What do you mean?

RAINA: Our ideas of what Sergius would do. Our patriotism. Our heroic ideals. I sometimes used to doubt whether they were anything but dreams. Oh, what faithless little creatures girls are! When I buckled on Sergius's sword he looked so noble: it was treason to think of disillusion or humiliation or failure. And yet—and yet—(*She sits down again suddenly.*) Promise me you'll never tell him.

CATHERINE: Dont ask me for promises until I know what I'm promising.

RAINA: Well, it came into my head just as he was holding me in his arms and looking into my eyes, that perhaps we only had our heroic ideas because we are so fond of reading Byron and Pushkin, and because we were so delighted with the opera that season at Bucharest. Real life is so seldom like that! Indeed never, as far as I knew it then. (*Remorsefully.*) Only think, mother: I doubted him: I wondered whether all his heroic qualities and his soldiership might not prove mere imagination when he went into a real battle. I had an uneasy fear that he might cut a poor figure there beside all those clever officers from the Tsar's court.

CATHERINE: A poor figure! Shame on you! The Serbs have Austrian officers who are just as clever as the Russians; but we have beaten them in every battle for all that.

RAINA (*laughing and snuggling against her mother*): Yes: I was only a prosaic little coward. Oh, to think that it was all true! that Sergius is just as splendid and noble as he looks! that the world is really a glorious world for women who can see its glory and men who can act its romance! What happiness! what unspeakable fulfillment!

They are interrupted by the entry of LOUKA, *a handsome proud girl in a pretty Bulgarian peasant's dress with double apron, so defiant that her servility to* RAINA *is almost insolent. She is afraid of* CATHERINE, *but even with her goes as far as she dares.*

LOUKA: If you please, madam, all the windows are to be closed and the shutters made fast. They say there may be shooting in the streets. (RAINA *and* CATHERINE *rise together, alarmed.*) The Serbs are being chased right back through the pass; and they say they may run into the town. Our cavalry will be after them; and our people will be ready for them, you may be sure, now theyre running away. (*She goes out on the balcony, and pulls the outside shutters to; then steps back into the room.*)

CATHERINE (*businesslike, housekeeping instincts aroused*): I must see that everything is made safe downstairs.

RAINA: I wish our people were not so cruel. What glory is there in killing wretched fugitives?

CATHERINE: Cruel! Do you suppose they would hesitate to kill you—or worse?

RAINA (*to* LOUKA): Leave the shutters so that I can just close them if I hear any noise.

CATHERINE (*authoritatively, turning on her way to the door*): Oh no, dear: you must keep them fastened. You would be sure to drop off to sleep and leave them open. Make them fast, Louka.

LOUKA: Yes, madam. (*She fastens them.*)

RAINA: Dont be anxious about me. The moment I hear a shot, I shall blow out the candles and roll myself up in bed with my ears well covered.

CATHERINE: Quite the wisest thing you can do, my love. Good night.

RAINA: Goodnight. (*Her emotion comes back for a moment.*) Wish me joy. (*They kiss.*) This is the happiest night of my life—if only there are no fugitives.

CATHERINE: Go to bed, dear; and dont think of them. (*She goes out.*)

LOUKA (*secretly to* RAINA): If you would like the shutters open, just give them a push like this (*she pushes them: they open: she pulls them to again*). One of them ought to be bolted at the bottom; but the bolt's gone.

RAINA (*with dignity, reproving her*): Thanks, Louka; but we must do what we are told. (LOUKA *makes a grimace.*) Good night.

LOUKA (*carelessly*): Good night. (*She goes out, swaggering.*)

RAINA, *left alone, takes off her fur cloak and throws it on the ottoman. Then she goes to the chest of drawers, and adores the portrait there with feelings that are beyond all expression. She does not kiss it or press it to her breast, or shew it any mark of bodily affection; but she takes it in her hands and elevates it, like a priestess.*

RAINA (*looking up at the picture*): Oh, I shall never be unworthy of you any more, my soul's hero: never, never, never. (*She replaces it reverently. Then she selects a novel from the little pile of books. She turns over the leaves dreamily; finds her page; turns the book inside out at it; and, with a happy sigh, gets into bed and prepares to read herself to sleep. But before abandoning herself to fiction, she raises her eyes once more, thinking of the blessed reality, and murmurs*) My hero! my hero!

A distant shot breaks the quiet of the night. She starts, listening; and two more shots, much nearer, follow, startling her so that she scrambles out of bed, and hastily blows out the candle on the chest of drawers. Then, putting her fingers in her ears, she runs to the dressing table, blows out the light there, and hurries back to bed in the dark, nothing being visible but the glimmer of the light in the pierced ball before the image, and the starlight seen through the slits at the top of the shutters. The firing breaks out again: there is a startling fusillade quite close at hand. Whilst it is still echoing, the shutters disappear, pulled open from without; and for an instant the rectangle of snowy starlight flashes out with the figure of a man silhouetted in black upon it. The shutters close immediately; and the room is dark again. But the silence is now broken by the sound of panting. Then there is a scratch; and the flame of a match is seen in the middle of the room.

RAINA (*crouching on the bed*): Who's there? (*The match is out instantly.*) Who's there? Who is that?

A MAN'S VOICE (*in the darkness, subduedly, but threateningly*): Sh—Sh! Dont call out; or youll be shot. Be good; and no harm will happen to you. (*She is heard leaving her bed, and making for the door.*) Take care: it's no use trying to run away.

RAINA: But who—

THE VOICE (*warning*): Remember: if you raise your voice my revolver will go off. (*Commandingly*) Strike a light and let me see you. Do you hear? (*Another moment of silence and darkness as she retreats to the chest of drawers. Then she lights a candle; and the mystery is at an end. He is a man of about 35, in a deplorable plight, bespattered with mud and blood and snow, his belt and the strap of his revolver case keeping together the torn ruins of the blue tunic of a Serbian artillery officer. All that the candlelight and his unwashed unkempt condition make it possible to discern is that he is of middling stature and undistinguished appearance, with strong neck and shoulders, roundish obstinate looking head covered with short crisp bronze curls, clear quick eyes and good brows and mouth, hopelessly prosaic nose like that of a strong minded baby, trim soldierlike carriage and energetic manner, and with all his wits about him in spite of his desperate predicament: even with a sense of the*

humor of it, without, however, the least intention of trifling with it or throwing away a chance. Reckoning up what he can guess about RAINA: *her age, her social position, her character, and the extent to which she is frightened, he continues, more politely but still most determinedly.*) Excuse my disturbing you; but you recognize my uniform? Serb! If I'm caught I shall be killed. (*Menacingly*) Do you understand that?

RAINA: Yes.

THE MAN: Well I dont intend to get killed if I can help it. (*Still more formidably*) Do you understand that? (*He locks the door quickly but quietly.*)

RAINA (*disdainfully*): I suppose not. (*She draws herself up superbly, and looks him straight in the face, adding, with cutting emphasis*) S o m e soldiers, I know, are afraid to die.

THE MAN (*with grim goodhumor*): All of them, dear lady, all of them, believe me. It is our duty to live as long as we can. Now, if you raise an alarm—

RAINA (*cutting him short*): You will shoot me. How do you know that I am afraid to die?

THE MAN (*cunningly*): Ah; but suppose I dont shoot you, what will happen then? A lot of your cavalry will burst into this pretty room of yours and slaughter me here like a pig; for I'll fight like a demon: they shant get m e into the street to amuse themselves with: I know what they are. Are you prepared to receive that sort of company in your present undress? (RAINA, *suddenly conscious of her nightgown, instinctively shrinks and gathers it more closely about her neck. He watches her and adds pitilessly*) Hardly presentable, eh? (*She turns to the ottoman. He raises his pistol instantly, and cries*) Stop! (*She stops.*) Where are you going?

RAINA (*With dignified patience*): Only to get my cloak.

THE MAN (*passing swiftly to the ottoman and snatching the cloak*): A good idea! I'll keep the cloak; and youll take care that nobody comes in and sees you without it. This is a better weapon than the revolver: eh? (*He throws the pistol down on the ottoman.*)

RAINA (*revolted*): It is not the weapon of a gentleman!

THE MAN: It's good enough for a man with only you to stand between him and death. (*As they look at one another for a moment,* RAINA *hardly able to believe that even a Serbian officer can be so cynically and selfishly unchivalrous, they are startled by a sharp fusillade in the street. The chill of imminent death hushes the man's voice as he adds*)

Do you hear? If you are going to bring those blackguards in on me you shall receive them as you are.

Clamor and disturbance. The pursuers in the street batter at the house door, shouting Open the door! Open the door! Wake up, will you! *A man servant's voice calls to them angrily from within* This is Major Petkoff's house: you cant come in here; *but a renewal of the clamor, and a torrent of blows on the door, end with his letting a chain down with a clank, followed by a rush of heavy footsteps and a din of trimphant yells, dominated at last by the voice of* CATHERINE, *indignantly addressing an officer with* What does this mean, sir? Do you know where you are? *The noise subsides suddenly.*

LOUKA (*outside, knocking at the bedroom door*): My lady! my lady! get up quick and open the door. If you dont they will break it down.

The fugitive throws up his head with the gesture of a man who sees that it is all over with him, and drops the manner he has been assuming to intimidate RAINA.

THE MAN (*sincerely and kindly*): No use, dear: I'm done for. (*Flinging the cloak to her.*) Quick! wrap yourself up: theyre coming.
RAINA: Oh, thank you. (*She wraps herself up with intense relief.*)
THE MAN (*between his teeth*): Dont mention it.
RAINA (*anxiously*): What will you do?
THE MAN (*grimly*): The first man in will find out. Keep out of the way; and dont look. It wont last long; but it will not be nice. (*He draws his sabre and faces the door, waiting.*)
RAINA (*impulsively*): I'll help you. I'll save you.
THE MAN: You cant.
RAINA: I can. I'll hide you. (*She drags him towards the window.*) Here! behind the curtains.
THE MAN (*yielding to her*): Theres just half a chance, if you keep your head.
RAINA (*drawing the curtain before him*): S-sh! (*She makes for the ottoman.*)
THE MAN (*putting out his head*): Remember—
RAINA (*running back to him*): Yes?
THE MAN: —nine soldiers out of ten are born fools.
RAINA: Oh! (*She draws the curtain angrily before him.*)
THE MAN (*looking out at the other side*): If they find me, I promise you a fight: a devil of a fight.

She stamps at him. He disappears hastily. She

takes off her cloak, and throws it across the foot of the bed. Then, with a sleepy, disturbed air, she opens the door. LOUKA *enters excitedly.*

LOUKA: One of those beasts of Serbs has been seen climbing up the waterpipe to your balcony. Our men want to search for him; and they are so wild and drunk and furious. (*She makes for the other side of the room to get as far from the door as possible.*) My lady says you are to dress at once and to—(*She sees the revolver lying on the ottoman, and stops, petrified.*)
RAINA (*as if annoyed at being disturbed*): They shall not search here. Why have they been let in?
CATHERINE (*coming in hastily*): Raina, darling, are you safe? Have you seen anyone or heard anything?
RAINA: I heard the shooting. Surely the soldiers will not dare come in here?
CATHERINE: I have found a Russian officer, thank Heaven: he knows Sergius. (*Speaking through the door to someone outside.*) Sir: will you come in now. My daughter will receive you.

A young Russian officer, in Bulgarian uniform, enters, sword in hand.

OFFICER (*with soft feline politeness and stiff military carriage*) Good evening, gracious lady. I am sorry to intrude; but there is a Serb hiding on the balcony. Will you and the gracious lady your mother please to withdraw whilst we search?
RAINA (*petulantly*): Nonsense, sir: you can see that there is no one on the balcony. (*She throws the shutters wide open and stands with her back to the curtain where the man is hidden, pointing to the moonlit balcony. A couple of shots are fired right under the window; and a bullet shatters the glass opposite* RAINA, *who winks and gasps, but stands her ground; whilst* CATHERINE *screams, and the officer, with a cry of* Take care! *rushes to the balcony.*)
THE OFFICER (*on the balcony, shouting savagely down to the street*): Cease firing there, you fools: do you hear? Cease firing, damn you! (*He glares down for a moment; then turns to* RAINA, *trying to resume his polite manner.*) Could anyone have got in without your knowledge? Were you asleep?
RAINA: No: I have not been to bed.
THE OFFICER (*impatiently, coming back into the room*): Your neighbors have their heads so full of runaway Serbs that they see them everywhere. (*Politely*) Gracious lady: a thousand pardons. Goodnight. (*Military bow, which* RAINA *returns*

coldly. Another to CATHERINE, *who follows him out.*)

RAINA *closes the shutters. She turns and sees* LOUKA, *who has been watching the scene curiously.*

RAINA: Dont leave my mother, Louka, until the soldiers go away.

LOUKA *glances at* RAINA, *at the ottoman, at the curtain; then purses her lips secretively, laughs insolently, and goes out.* RAINA, *highly offended by this demonstration, follows her to the door, and shuts it behind her with a slam, locking it violently. The man immediately steps out from behind the curtain, sheathing his sabre. Then, dismissing the danger from his mind in a businesslike way, he comes affably to* RAINA.

THE MAN: A narrow shave; but a miss is as good as a mile. Dear young lady: your servant to the death. I wish for your sake I had joined the Bulgarian army instead of the other one. I am not a native Serb.

RAINA (*haughtily*): No: you are one of the Austrians who set the Serbs on to rob us of our national liberty, and who officer their army for them. We hate them!

THE MAN: Austrian! not I. Dont hate me, dear young lady. I am a Swiss, fighting merely as a professional soldier. I joined the Serbs because they came first on the road from Switzerland. Be generous: youve beaten us hollow.

RAINA: Have I not been generous?

THE MAN: Noble! Heroic! But I'm not saved yet. This particular rush will soon pass through; but the pursuit will go on all night by fits and starts. I must take my chance to get off in a quiet interval. (*Pleasantly*) You dont mind my waiting just a minute or two, do you?

RAINA (*putting on her most genteel society manner*): Oh, not at all. Wont you sit down?

THE MAN: Thanks. (*He sits on the foot of the bed.*)

RAINA *walks with studied elegance to the ottoman and sits down. Unfortunately she sits on the pistol, and jumps up with a shriek. The man, all nerves, shies like a frightened horse to the other side of the room.*

THE MAN (*irritably*): Dont frighten me like that. What is it?

RAINA: Your revolver! It was staring that officer in the face all the time. What an escape!

THE MAN (*vexed at being unnecessarily terrified*): Oh, is that all?

RAINA (*staring at him rather superciliously as she conceives a poorer and poorer opinion of him, and feels proportionately more and more at her ease*): I am sorry I frightened you. (*She takes up the pistol and hands it to him.*) Pray take it to protect yourself against me.

THE MAN (*grinning wearily at the sarcasm as he takes the pistol*): No use, dear young lady: there's nothing in it. It's not loaded. (*He makes a grimace at it, and drops it disparingly into his revolver case.*)

RAINA: Load it by all means.

THE MAN: Ive no ammunition. What use are cartridges in battle? I always carry chocolate instead; and I finished the last cake of that hours ago.

RAINA (*outraged in her most cherished ideals of manhood*): Chocolate! Do you stuff your pockets with sweets—like a schoolboy—even in the field?

THE MAN (*grinning*): Yes: isnt it contemptible? (*Hungrily*) I wish I had some now.

RAINA: Allow me. (*She sails away scornfully to the chest of drawers, and returns with the box of confectionery in her hand.*) I am sorry I have eaten them all except these. (*She offers him the box.*)

THE MAN (*ravenously*): Youre an angel! (*He gobbles the contents.*) Creams! Delicious! (*He looks anxiously to see whether there are any more. There are none: he can only scrape the box with his fingers and suck them. When that nourishment is exhausted he accepts the inevitable with pathetic goodhumor, and says, with grateful emotion*) Bless you, dear lady! You can always tell an old soldier by the inside of his holsters and cartridge boxes. The young ones carry pistols and cartridges: the old ones, grub. Thank you. (*He hands back the box. She snatches it contemptuously from him and throws it away. He shies again, as if she had meant to strike him.*) Ugh! Dont do things so suddenly, gracious lady. It's mean to revenge yourself because I frightened you just now.

RAINA (*loftily*): Frighten me! Do you know, sir, that though I am only a woman, I think I am at heart as brave as you.

THE MAN: I should think so. You havent been under fire for three days as I have. I can stand two days without shewing it much; but no man can stand three days: I'm as nervous as a mouse. (*He sits down on the ottoman, and takes his head in his hands.*) Would you like to see me cry?

RAINA (*alarmed*): No.

THE MAN: If you would, all you have to do is to scold me just as if I were a little boy and you my nurse. If I were in camp now, they'd play all sorts of tricks on me.

RAINA (*a little moved*): I'm sorry. I wont scold you. (*Touched by the sympathy in her tone, he raises his head and looks gratefully at her: she immediately draws back and says stiffly*) You must excuse me: o u r soldiers are not like that. (*She moves away from the ottoman.*)

THE MAN: Oh yes they are. There are only two sorts of soldiers: old ones and young ones. Ive served fourteen years: half of your fellows never smelt powder before. Why, how is it that youve just beaten us? Sheer ignorance of the art of war, nothing else. (*Indignantly*) I never saw anything so unprofessional.

RAINA (*ironically*): Oh! was it unprofessional to beat you?

THE MAN: Well, come! is it professional to throw a regiment of cavalry on a battery of machine guns, with the dead certainty that if the guns go off not a horse or man will ever get within fifty yards of the fire? I couldnt believe my eyes when I saw it.

RAINA (*eagerly turning to him, as all her enthusiasm and her dreams of glory rush back on her*): Did you see the great cavalry charge? Oh, tell me about it. Describe it to me.

THE MAN: You never saw a cavalry charge, did you?

RAINA: How could I?

THE MAN: Ah, perhaps not. No: of course not! Well, it's a funny sight: It's like slinging a handful of peas against a window pane: first one comes; then two or three close behind him; and then all the rest in a lump.

RAINA (*her eyes dilating as she raises her clasped hands ecstatically*): Yes, first One! the bravest of the brave!

THE MAN (*prosaically*): Hm! you should see the poor devil pulling at his horse.

RAINA: Why should he pull at his horse!

THE MAN (*impatient of so stupid a question*): It's running away with him, of course: do you suppose the fellow wants to get there before the others and be killed? Then they all come. You can tell the young ones by their wildness and their slashing. The old ones come bunched up under the number one guard: they know that theyre mere projectiles, and that it's no use trying to fight. The wounds are mostly broken knees, from the horses cannoning together.

RAINA: Ugh! But I dont believe the first man is a coward. I know he is a hero!

THE MAN (*goodhumoredly*): Thats what youd have said if youd seen the first man in the charge today.

RAINA (*breathless, forgiving him everything*): Ah, I knew it! Tell me. Tell me about him.

THE MAN: He did it like an operatic tenor. A regular handsome fellow, with flashing eyes and lovely moustache, shouting his war-cry and charging like Don Quixote at the windmills. We did laugh.

RAINA: You dared to laugh!

THE MAN: Yes; but when the sergeant ran up as white as a sheet, and told us theyd sent us the wrong ammunition, and that we couldnt fire a round for the next ten minutes, we laughed at the other side of our mouths. I never felt so sick in my life; though Ive been in one or two very tight places. And I hadnt even a revolver cartridge: only chocolate. We'd no bayonets: nothing. Of course, they just cut us to bits. And there was Don Quixote flourishing like a drum major, thinking he'd done the cleverest thing ever known, whereas he ought to be courtmartialled for it. Of all the fools ever let loose on a field of battle, that man must be the very maddest. He and his regiment simply committed suicide; only the pistol missed fire: thats all.

RAINA (*deeply wounded, but steadfastly loyal to her ideals*): Indeed! Would you know him again if you saw him?

THE MAN: Shall I ever forget him!

She again goes to the chest of drawers. He watches her with a vague hope that she may have something more for him to eat. She takes the portrait from its stand and brings it to him.

RAINA: That is a photograph of the gentleman— the patriot and hero—to whom I am betrothed.

THE MAN (*recognizing it with a shock*): I'm really very sorry. (*Looking at her*) Was it fair to lead me on? (*He looks at the portrait again*) Yes: thats Don Quixote; not a doubt of it. (*He stifles a laugh.*)

RAINA (*quickly*): Why do you laugh?

THE MAN (*apologetic, but still greatly tickled*): I didnt laugh, I assure you. At least I didnt mean to. But when I think of him charging the windmills and imagining he was doing the finest thing—(*He chokes with suppressed laughter.*)

RAINA (*sternly*): Give me back the portrait, sir.

THE MAN (*with sincere remorse*): Of course. Certainly. I'm really very sorry. (*He hands her the picture. She deliberately kisses it and looks him straight in the face before returning to the chest of drawers to replace it. He follows her, apologizing.*) Perhaps I'm quite wrong, you know: no doubt I am. Most likely he had got wind of the cartridge business somehow, and knew it was a safe job.

RAINA: That is to say, he was a pretender and a coward! You did not dare say that before.

THE MAN (*With a comic gesture of despair*): It's no use, dear lady: I cant make you see it from the professional point of view. (*As he turns away to get back to the ottoman, a couple of distant shots threaten renewed trouble.*

RAINA (*sternly, as she sees him listening to the shots*): So much the better for you!

THE MAN (*turning*): How?

RAINA: You are my enemy; and you are at my mercy. What would I do if I were a professional soldier?

THE MAN: Ah, true, dear young lady: youre always right. I know how good youve been to me: to my last hour I shall remember those three chocolate creams. It was unsoldierly; but it was angelic.

RAINA (*coldly*): Thank you. And now I will do a soldierly thing. You cannot stay here after what you have just said about my future husband; but I will go out on the balcony and see whether it is safe for you to climb down into the street. (*She turns to the window.*)

THE MAN (*changing countenance*): Down that waterpipe! Stop! Wait! I cant! I darent! The very thought of it makes me giddy. I came up it fast enough with death behind me. But to face it now in cold blood—! (*He sinks on the ottoman.*) It's no use; I give up: I'm beaten. Give the alarm. (*He drops his head on his hands in the deepest dejection.*)

RAINA: (*disarmed by pity*): Come: dont be disheartened. (*She stoops over him almost maternally: he shakes his head.*) Oh, you are a very poor soldier: a chocolate cream soldier! Come, cheer up! it takes less courage to climb down than to face capture: remember that.

THE MAN (*dreamily, lulled by her voice*): No: capture only means death; and death is sleep: oh, sleep, sleep, sleep, undisturbed sleep! Climbing down the pipe means doing something—exerting myself—thinking! Death ten times over first.

RAINA (*softly and wonderingly, catching the rhythm of his weariness*): Are you as sleepy as that?

THE MAN: Ive not had two hours undisturbed sleep since I joined. I havnt closed my eyes for forty-eight hours.

RAINA (*at her wit's end*): But what am I to do with you?

THE MAN (*staggering up, roused by her desperation*): Of course. I must do something. (*He shakes himself; pulls himself together; and speaks with rallied vigor and courage.*) You see, sleep or no sleep, hunger or no hunger, tired or not tired, you can always do a thing when you know it must be done. Well, that pipe must be got down: (*he hits himself on the chest*) do you hear that, you chocolate cream soldier? (*He turns to the window.*)

RAINA (*anxiously*): But if you fall?

THE MAN: I shall sleep as if the stones were a feather bed. Good-bye. (*He makes boldly for the window; and his hand is on the shutter when there is a terrible burst of firing in the street beneath.*)

RAINA (*rushing to him*): Stop! (*She seizes him recklessly, and pulls him quite round.*) Theyll kill you.

THE MAN (*coolly, but attentively*): Never mind: this sort of thing is all in my day's work. I'm bound to take my chance. (*Decisively*) Now do what I tell you. Put out the candle; so that they shant see the light when I open the shutters. And keep away from the window, whatever you do. If they see me theyre sure to have a shot at me.

RAINA (*clinging to him*): Theyre sure to see you: it's bright moonlight. I'll save you. Oh, how can you be so indifferent! You want me to save you, dont you?

THE MAN: I really dont want to be troublesome. (*She shakes him in her impatience.*) I am not indifferent, dear young lady, I assure you. But how is it to be done?

RAINA: Come away from the window. (*She takes him firmly back to the middle of the room. The moment she releases him he turns mechanically towards the window again. She seizes him and turns him back, exclaiming*) Please! (*He becomes motionless, like a hypnotized rabbit, his fatigue gaining fast on him. She releases him, and addresses him patronizingly.*) Now listen. You must trust to our hospitality. You do not yet know in whose house you are. I am a Petkoff.

THE MAN: A pet what?

RAINA (*rather indignantly*): I mean that I belong to the family of the Petkoffs, the richest and best known in our country.

THE MAN: Oh yes, of course. I beg your pardon. The Petkoffs, to be sure. How stupid of me!

RAINA: You know you never heard of them until this moment. How can you stoop to pretend!

THE MAN: Forgive me: I'm too tired to think; and the change of subject was too much for me. Dont scold me.

RAINA: I forgot. It might make you cry. (*He nods, quite seriously. She pouts and then resumes her patronizing tone.*) I must tell you that my father holds the highest command of any Bulgarian in our army. He is (*proudly*) a Major.

THE MAN (*pretending to be deeply impressed*): A Major! Bless me! Think of that!

RAINA: You shewed great ignorance in thinking that it was necessary to climb up to the balcony because ours is the only private house that has two rows of windows. There is a flight of stairs inside to get up and down by.

THE MAN: Stairs! How grand! You live in great luxury indeed, dear young lady.

RAINA: Do you know what a library is?

THE MAN: A library? A roomful of books?

RAINA: Yes. We have one, the only one in Bulgaria.

THE MAN: Actually a real library! I should like to see that.

RAINA (*affectedly*): I tell you these things to shew you that you are not in the house of ignorant country folk who would kill you the moment they saw your Serbian uniform, but among civilized people. We go to Bucharest every year for the opera season; and I have spent a whole month in Vienna.

THE MAN: I saw that, dear young lady. I saw at once that you knew the world.

RAINA: Have you ever seen the opera of Ernani?

THE MAN: Is that the one with the devil in it in red velvet, and a soldier's chorus?

RAINA (*contemptuously*): No!

THE MAN (*stifling a heavy sigh of weariness*): Then I dont know it.

RAINA: I thought you might have remembered the great scene where Ernani, flying from his foes just as you are tonight, takes refuge in the castle of his bitterest enemy, an old Castilian noble. The noble refuses to give him up. His guest is sacred to him.

THE MAN (*quickly, waking up a little*): Have your people got that notion?

RAINA (*with dignity*): My mother and I can understand that notion, as you call it. And if instead of threatening me with your pistol as you did you had simply thrown yourself as a fugitive on our hospitality, you would have been as safe as in your father's house.

THE MAN: Quite sure?

RAINA (*turning her back on him in disgust*): Oh, it is useless to try to make y o u understand.

THE MAN: Dont be angry: you see how awkward it would be for me if there was any mistake. My father is a very hospitable man: he keeps six hotels; but I couldnt trust him as far as that. What about your father?

RAINA: He is away at Slivnitza fighting for his country. I answer for your safety. There is my hand in pledge of it. Will that reassure you? (*She offers him her hand.*)

THE MAN (*looking dubiously at his own hand*): Better not touch my hand, dear young lady. I must have a wash first.

RAINA (*touched*): That is very nice of you. I see that you are a gentleman.

THE MAN (*puzzled*): Eh?

RAINA: You must not think I am surprised. Bulgarians of really good standing—people in o u r position—wash their hands nearly every day. So you see I can appreciate your delicacy. You may take my hand. (*She offers it again.*)

THE MAN (*kissing it with his hands behind his back*): Thanks, gracious young lady: I feel safe at last. And now would you mind breaking the news to your mother? I had better not stay here secretly longer than is necessary.

RAINA: If you will be so good as to keep perfectly still whilst I am away.

THE MAN: Certainly. (*He sits down on the ottoman.*)

RAINA *goes to the bed and wraps herself in the fur cloak. His eyes close. She goes to the door. Turning for a last look at him, she sees that he is dropping off to sleep.*

RAINA (*at the door*): You are not going asleep, are you? (*He murmurs inarticulately: she runs to him and shakes him.*) Do you hear? Wake up: you are falling asleep.

THE MAN: Eh? Falling aslee—? Oh no: not the least in the world: I was only thinking. It's all right: I'm wide awake.

RAINA (*severely*): Will you please stand up while I am away. (*He rises reluctantly.*) All the time, mind.

THE MAN (*standing unsteadily*): Certainly. Certainly: you may depend on me.

RAINA *looks doubtfully at him. He smiles weakly. She goes reluctantly, turning again at the door, and almost catching him in the act of yawning. She goes out.*

THE MAN (*drowsily*): Sleep, sleep, sleep, sleep, slee— (*The words trail off into a murmur. He wakes again with a shock on the point of falling.*) Where am I? Thats what I want to know: where am I? Must keep awake. Nothing keeps me awake except danger: remember that: (*intently*) danger, danger, danger, dan— (*trailing off again: another shock.*) Wheres danger? Mus' find it. (*He starts off vaguely round the room in search of it.*) What am I looking for? Sleep—danger—dont know. (*He stumbles against the bed.*) Ah yes: now I know. I'm to go to bed, but not to sleep. Be sure not to sleep, because of danger. Not to lie down either, only sit down. (*He sits on the bed. A blissful expression comes into his face.*) Ah! (*With a happy sigh he sinks back at full length; lifts his boots into the bed with a final effort; and falls fast asleep instantly.*)

CATHERINE *comes in, followed by* RAINA.

RAINA (*looking at the ottoman*): He's gone! I left him here.

CATHERINE: Here! Then he must have climbed down from the—

RAINA (*seeing him*): Oh! (*She points.*)

CATHERINE (*scandalized*): Well! (*She strides to the bed,* RAINA *following until she is opposite her on the other side.*) He's fast asleep. The brute!

RAINA (*anxiously*): Sh!

CATHERINE (*shaking him*): Sir! (*Shaking him again, harder*) Sir!! (*Vehemently, shaking very hard*) Sir!!!

RAINA (*catching her arm*): Dont, mamma; the poor darling is worn out. Let him sleep.

CATHERINE (*letting him go, and turning amazed to* RAINA): The poor darling! Raina!!! (*She looks sternly at her daughter.*)

The man sleeps profoundly.

ACT II

The sixth of March, 1886. In the garden of MAJOR PETKOFF's *house. It is a fine spring morning: the garden looks fresh and pretty. Beyond the paling the tops of a couple of minarets can be seen, shewing that there is a valley there, with the little town in it. A few miles further the Balkan mountains rise and shut in the landscape. Looking towards them from within the garden, the side of the house is seen on the left, with a garden door reached by a little flight of steps. On the right the stable yard, with its gateway, encroaches on the garden. There are fruit bushes along the paling and house, covered with washing spread out to dry. A path runs by the house, and rises by two steps at the corner, where it turns out of sight. In the middle, a small table, with two bent wood chairs at it, is laid for breakfast with Turkish coffee pot, cups, rolls, etc.; but the cups have been used and the bread broken. There is a wooden garden seat against the wall on the right.*

LOUKA, *smoking a cigaret, is standing between the table and the house, turning her back* *with angry disdain on a man servant who is lecturing her. He is a middle-aged man of cool temperament and low but clear and keen intelligence, with the complacency of the servant who values himself on his rank in servitude, and the imperturbability of the accurate calculator who has no illusions. He wears a white Bulgarian costume: jacket with embroidered border, sash, wide knickerbockers, and decorated gaiters. His head is shaved up to the crown, giving him a high Japanese forehead. His name is* NICOLA.

NICOLA: Be warned in time, Louka: mend your manners. I know the mistress. She is so grand that she never dreams that any servant could dare be disrespectful to her; but if she once suspects that you are defying her, out you go.

LOUKA: I do defy her. I will defy her. What do I care for her?

NICOLA: If you quarrel with the family, I never can marry you. It's the same as if you quarrelled with me!

LOUKA: You take her part against me, do you?

NICOLA (*sedately*): I shall always be dependent on the good will of the family. When I leave their service and start a shop in Sofia, their custom will be half my capital: their bad word would ruin me.

LOUKA: You have no spirit. I should like to catch them saying a word against me!

NICOLA (*pityingly*): I should have expected more sense from you, Louka. But youre young: youre young!

LOUKA: Yes; and you like me the better for it, dont you? But I know some family secrets they wouldnt care to have told, young as I am. Let them quarrel with me if they dare!

NICOLA (*with compassionate superiority*): Do you know what they would do if they heard you talk like that?

LOUKA: What could they do?

NICOLA: Discharge you for untruthfulness. Who would believe any stories you told after that? Who would give you another situation? Who in this house would dare be seen speaking to you ever again? How long would your father be left on his little farm? (*She impatiently throws away the end of her cigaret, and stamps on it.*) Child: you dont know the power such high people have over the like of you and me when we try to rise out of our poverty against them. (*He goes close to her and lowers his voice.*) Look at me, ten years in their service. Do you think I know no secrets? I know things about the mistress that she wouldnt have the master know for a thousand levas. I know things about him that she wouldnt let him hear the last of for six months if I blabbed them to her. I know things about Raina that would break off her match with Sergius if—

LOUKA (*turning on him quickly*): How do you know? I never told you!

NICOLA (*opening his eyes cunningly*): So thats your little secret, is it? I thought it might be something like that. Well, you take my advice and be respectful; and make the mistress feel that no matter what you know or dont know, she can depend on you to hold your tongue and serve the family faithfully. Thats what they like; and thats how youll make most out of them.

LOUKA (*with searching scorn*): You have the soul of a servant, Nicola.

NICOLA (*complacently*): Yes: thats the secret of success in service.

A loud knocking with a whip handle on a wooden door is heard from the stable yard.

MALE VOICE OUTSIDE: Hollo! Hollo there! Nicola!

LOUKA: Master! back from the war!

NICOLA (*quickly*): My word for it, Louka, the war's over. Off with you and get some fresh coffee. (*He runs out into the stable yard.*)

LOUKA (*as she collects the coffee pot and cups on the tray, and carries it into the house*): Youll never put the soul of a servant into me.

MAJOR PETKOFF *comes from the stable yard, followed by* NICOLA. *He is a cheerful, excitable, insignificant, unpolished man of about 50, naturally unambitious except as to his income and his importance in local society, but just now greatly pleased with the military rank which the war has thrust on him as a man of consequence in his town. The fever of plucky patriotism which the Serbian attack roused in all the Bulgarians has pulled him through the war; but he is obviously glad to be home again.*

PETKOFF (*pointing to the table with his whip*): Breakfast out here, eh?

NICOLA: Yes, sir. The mistress and Miss Raina have just gone in.

PETKOFF (*sitting down and taking a roll*): Go in and say Ive come; and get me some fresh coffee.

NICOLA: It's coming sir. (*He goes to the house door.* LOUKA, *with fresh coffee, a clean cup, and a brandy bottle on her tray, meets him.*) Have you told the mistress?

LOUKA: Yes: she's coming.

NICOLA *goes into the house.* LOUKA *brings the coffee to the table.*

PETKOFF: Well: The Serbs havnt run away with you, have they?

LOUKA: No, sir.

PETKOFF: Thats right. Have you brought me some cognac?

LOUKA (*putting the bottle on the table*): Here, sir.

PETKOFF: That's right. (*He pours some into his coffee.*)

CATHERINE, *who, having at this early hour made only a very perfunctory toilet, wears a Bulgarian apron over a once brilliant but now half worn-out dressing gown, and a colored handkerchief tied over her thick black hair, comes from the house with Turkish slippers on her bare feet, looking astonishingly handsome and stately under all the circumstances.* LOUKA *goes into the house.*

CATHERINE: My dear Paul: what a surprise for us! (*She stoops over the back of his chair to kiss him.*) Have they brought you fresh coffee?

PETKOFF: Yes: Louka's been looking after me. The war's over. The treaty was signed three days ago at Bucharest; and the decree for our army to demobilize was issued yesterday.

CATHERINE (*springing erect, with flashing eyes*): Paul: have you let the Austrians force you to make peace?

PETKOFF (*submissively*): My dear: they didnt consult me. What could I do? (*She sits down and turns away from him.*) But of course we saw to it that the treaty was an honorable one. It declares peace—

CATHERINE (*outraged*): Peace!

PETKOFF (*appeasing her*):—but not friendly relations: remember that. They wanted to put that in; but I insisted on its being struck out. What more could I do?

CATHERINE: You could have annexed Serbia and made Prince Alexander Emperor of the Balkans. Thats what I would have done.

PETKOFF: I dont doubt it in the least, my dear. But I should have had to subdue the whole Austrian Empire first; and that would have kept me too long away from you. I missed you greatly.

CATHERINE (*relenting*): Ah! (*She stretches her hand affectionately across the table to squeeze his.*)

PETKOFF: And how have you been, my dear?

CATHERINE: Oh, my usual sore throats, thats all.

PETKOFF (*with conviction*): That comes from washing your neck every day. Ive often told you so.

CATHERINE: Nonsense, Paul!

PETKOFF (*over his coffee and cigaret*): I dont believe in going too far with these modern customs. All this washing cant be good for the health: it's not natural. There was an Englishman at Philippopolis who used to wet himself all over with cold water every morning when he got up. Disgusting! It all comes from the English: their climate makes them so dirty that they have to be perpetually washing themselves. Look at my father! he never had a bath in his life; and he lived to be ninety-eight, the healthiest man in Bulgaria. I dont mind a good wash once a week to keep up my position; but once a day is carrying the thing to a ridiculous extreme.

CATHERINE: You are a barbarian at heart still, Paul. I hope you behaved yourself before all those Russian officers.

PETKOFF: I did my best. I took care to let them know that we have a library.

CATHERINE: Ah; but you didnt tell them that we have an electric bell in it? I have had one put up.

PETKOFF: Whats an electric bell?

CATHERINE: You touch a button; something tinkles in the kitchen; and then Nicola comes up.

PETKOFF: Why not shout for him?

CATHERINE: Civilized people never shout for their servants. Ive learnt that while you were away.

PETKOFF: Well, I'll tell you something Ive learnt too. Civilized people dont hang out their washing to dry where visitors can see it; so youd better have all that (*indicating the clothes on the bushes*) put somewhere else.

CATHERINE: Oh, thats absurd, Paul: I dont believe really refined people notice such things.

SERGIUS (*knocking at the stable gates*): Gate, Nicola!

PETKOFF: Theres Sergius. (*Shouting*) Hollo, Nicola!

CATHERINE: Oh, dont shout, Paul: it really isnt nice.

PETKOFF: Bosh! (*He shouts louder than before.*) Nicola!

NICOLA (*appearing at the house door*): Yes, sir.

PETKOFF: Are you deaf? Dont you hear Major Saranoff knocking? Bring him round this way. (*He pronounces the name with the stress on the second syllable: Sarahnoff.*)

NICOLA: Yes, Major. (*He goes into the stable yard.*)

PETKOFF: You must talk to him, my dear, until Raina takes him off our hands. He bores my life out about our not promoting him. Over m y head, if you please.

CATHERINE: He certainly ought to be promoted when he marries Raina. Besides, the country should insist on having at least one native general.

PETKOFF: Yes; so that he could throw away whole brigades instead of regiments. It's no use, my dear: he hasnt the slightest chance of promotion until we're quite sure that the peace will be a lasting one.

NICOLA (*at the gate, announcing*): Major Sergius Saranoff! (*He goes into the house and returns presently with a third chair, which he places at the table. He then withdraws.*)

MAJOR SERGIUS SARANOFF, *the original of the portrait in* RAINA's *room, is a tall romantically handsome man, with the physical hardihood, the high spirit, and the susceptible imagination of an untamed mountaineer chieftain. But his remarkable personal distinction is of a characteristically civilized type. The ridges of his eyebrows, curving with an interrogative twist round the projections at the outer corners; his jealously observant eye; his nose, thin, keen, and apprehensive in spite of the pugnacious high bridge and large nostril; his assertive chin would not be out of place in a Parisian salon, shewing that the clever imaginative barbarian has an acute critical faculty which has been thrown into intense activity by the arrival of western civilization in the Balkans. The result is precisely what the advent of nineteenth-century thought first produced in England: to wit, Byronism. By his brooding on the perpetual failure, not only of others, but of himself, to live up to his ideals; by his consequent cynical scorn for humanity; by his jejune credulity as to the absolute validity of his concepts and the unworthiness of the world in disregarding them; by his wincings and mockeries under the sting of the petty disillusions which every hour spent among men brings to his sensitive observation, he has acquired the half tragic, half ironic air, the mysterious moodiness, the suggestion of a strange and terrible history that has left nothing but undying remorse, by which Childe Harold fascinated the grandmothers of his English contemporaries. It is clear that here or nowhere is* RAINA's *ideal hero.* CATHERINE *is hardly less enthusiastic about him than her daughter, and much less reserved in shewing her enthusiasm. As he enters from the stble gate, she rises effusively to greet him.* PETKOFF *is distinctly less disposed to make a fuss about him.*

PETKOFF: Here already, Sergius! Glad to see you.

CATHERINE: My dear Sergius! (*She holds out both her hands.*)

SERGIUS (*kissing them with scrupulous gallantry*): My dear mother, if I may call you so.

PETKOFF (*drily*): Mother-in-law, Sergius: mother-in-law! Sit down; and have some coffee.

SERGIUS: Thank you: none for me. (*He gets away from the table with a certain distaste for* PETKOFF's *enjoyment of it, and posts himself with conscious dignity against the rail of the steps leading to the house.*)

CATHERINE: You look superb. The campaign has improved you, Sergius. Everybody here is mad about you. We were all wild with enthusiasm about that magnificent cavalry charge.

SERGIUS (*with grave irony*): Madam: it was the cradle and the grave of my military reputation.

CATHERINE: How so?

SERGIUS: I won the battle the wrong way when our worthy Russian generals were losing it the right way. In short, I upset their plans, and wounded their self-esteem. Two Cossack colonels had their regiments routed on the most correct principles of scientific warfare. Two major-generals got killed strictly according to military etiquette. The two colonels are now major-generals; and I am still a simple major.

CATHERINE: You shall not remain so, Sergius. The women are on your side; and they will see that justice is done you.

SERGIUS: It is too late. I have only waited for the peace to send in my resignation.

PETKOFF (*dropping his cup in his amazement*): Your resignation!

CATHERINE: Oh, you must withdraw it!

SERGIUS (*with resolute measured emphasis, folding his arms*): I never withdraw.

PETKOFF (*vexed*): Now who could have supposed you were going to do such a thing?

SERGIUS (*with fire*): Everyone that knew me. But enough of myself and my affairs. How is Raina; and where is Raina?

RAINA (*suddenly coming round the corner of the house and standing at the top of the steps in the path*: Raina is here.

She makes a charming picture as they turn to look at her. She wears an underdress of pale green silk, draped with an overdress of thin ecru canvas embroidered with gold. She is crowned with a dainty eastern cap of gold tinsel. SERGIUS *goes impulsively to meet her. Posing regally, she presents her hand: he drops chivalrously on one knee and kisses it.*

PETKOFF (*aside to* CATHERINE, *beaming with parental pride*): Pretty, isnt it? She always appears at the right moment.

CATHERINE (*impatiently*): Yes; she listens for it. It is an abominable habit.

SERGIUS *leads* RAINA *forward with splendid gallantry. When they arrive at the table, she turns to him with a bend of the head: he bows; and thus they separate, he coming to his place and she going behind her father's chair.*

RAINA (*stooping and kissing her father*): Dear father! Welcome home!

PETKOFF (*patting her cheek*): My little pet girl. (*He kisses her. She goes to the chair left by* NICOLA *for* SERGIUS, *and sits down.*)

CATHERINE: And so youre no longer a soldier, Sergius.

SERGIUS: I am no longer a soldier. Soldiering, my dear madam, is the coward's art of attacking mercilessly when you are strong, and keeping out of harm's way when you are weak. That is the whole secret of successful fighting. Get your enemy at a disadvantage; and never, on any account, fight him on equal terms.

PETKOFF: They wouldnt let us make a fair stand-up fight of it. However, I suppose soldiering has to be a trade like any other trade.

SERGIUS: Precisely. But I have no ambition to shine as a tradesman; so I have taken the advice of that bagman of a captain that settled the exchange of prisoners with us at Pirot, and given it up.

PETKOFF: What! that Swiss fellow? Sergius: I've often thought of that exchange since. He over-reached us about those horses.

SERGIUS: Of course he over-reached us. His father was a hotel and livery stable keeper; and he owed his first step to his knowledge of horse-dealing. (*With mock enthusiasm*) Ah, he was a soldier: every inch a soldier! If only I had bought the horses for my regiment instead of foolishly leading it into danger, I should have been a field-marshal now!

CATHERINE: A Swiss? What was he doing in the Serbian army?

PETKOFF: A volunteer, of course: keen on picking up his profession. (*Chuckling*) We shouldnt have been able to begin fighting if these foreigners hadnt shewn us how to do it: we knew nothing about it; and neither did the Serbs. Egad, there'd have been no war without them!

RAINA: Are there many Swiss officers in the Serbian Army?

PETKOFF: No. All Austrians, just as our officers

were all Russians. This was the only Swiss I came across. I'll never trust a Swiss again. He humbugged us into giving him fifty ablebodied men for two hundred worn out chargers. They werent even eatable!

SERGIUS: We were two children in the hands of that consummate soldier, Major: simply two innocent little children.

RAINA: What was he like?

CATHERINE: Oh, Raina, what a silly question!

SERGIUS: He was like a commercial traveller in uniform. Bourgeois to his boots!

PETKOFF (*grinning*): Sergius: tell Catherine that queer story his friend told us about how he escaped after Slivnitza. You remember. About his being hid by two women.

SERGIUS (*with bitter irony*): Oh yes: quite a romance! He was serving in the very battery I so unprofessionally charged. Being a thorough soldier, he ran away like the rest of them, with our cavalry at his heels. To escape their sabres he climbed a waterpipe and made his way into the bedroom of a young Bulgarian lady. The young lady was enchanted by his persuasive commercial traveller's manners. She very modestly entertained him for an hour or so, and then called in her mother lest her conduct should appear unmaidenly. The old lady was equally fascinated; and the fugitive was sent on his way in the morning, disguised in an old coat belonging to the master of the house, who was away at the war.

RAINA (*rising with marked stateliness*): Your life in the camp has made you coarse, Sergius. I did not think you would have repeated such a story before me. (*She turns away coldly.*)

CATHERINE (*also rising*): She is right, Sergius. If such women exist, we should be spared the knowledge of them.

PETKOFF: Pooh! nonsense! what does it matter?

SERGIUS (*ashamed*): No, Petkoff: I was wrong. (*To* RAINA *with earnest humility*) I beg your pardon. I have behaved abominably. Forgive me, Raina. (*She bows reservedly.*) And you too, madam. (CATHERINE *bows graciously and sits down. He proceeds solemnly, again addressing* RAINA.) The glimpses I have had of the seamy side of life during the last few months have made me cynical; but I should not have brought my cynicism here: least of all into your presence, Raina. I—(*Here, turning to the others, he is evidently going to begin a long speech when the* MAJOR *interrupts him.*)

PETKOFF: Stuff and nonsense, Sergius! Thats quite enough fuss about nothing: a soldier's daughter should be able to stand up without flinching to

a little strong conversation. (*He rises.*) Come: it's time for us to get to business. We have to make up our minds how those three regiments are to get back to Philippopolis: theres no forage for them on the Sofia route. (*He goes towards the house.*) Come along. (SERGIUS *is about to follow him when* CATHERINE *rises and intervenes.*)

CATHERINE: Oh, Paul, cant you spare Sergius for a few moments? Raina has hardly seen him yet. Perhaps I can help you to settle about the regiments.

SERGIUS (*protesting*): My dear madam, impossible: you—

CATHERINE (*stopping him playfully*): You stay here, my dear Sergius: theres no hurry. I have a word or two to say to Paul. (SERGIUS *instantly bows and steps back.*) Now, dear (*taking* PETKOFF's *arm*): come and see the electric bell.

PETKOFF: Oh, very well, very well.

They go into the house together affectionately. SERGIUS, *left alone with* RAINA, *looks anxiously at her, fearing that she is still offended. She smiles, and stretches out her arms to him.*

SERGIUS (*hastening to her*): Am I forgiven?

RAINA (*placing her hands on his shoulders as she looks up at him with admiration and worship*): My hero! My king!

SERGIUS: My queen! (*He kisses her on the forehead.*)

RAINA: How I have envied you, Sergius! You have been out in the world, on the field of battle, able to prove yourself there worthy of any woman in the world; whilst I have had to sit at home inactive—dreaming—useless—doing nothing that could give me the right to call myself worthy of any man.

SERGIUS: Dearest: all my deeds have been yours. You inspired me. I have gone through the war like a knight in a tournament with his lady looking down at him!

RAINA: And you have never been absent from my thoughts for a moment. (*Very solemnly*) Sergius: I think we two have found the higher love. When I think of you, I feel that I could never do a base deed, or think an ignoble thought.

SERGIUS: My lady and my saint! (*He clasps her reverently.*)

RAINA (*returning his embrace*): My lord and my—

SERGIUS: Sh—sh! Let me be the worshipper, dear. You little know how unworthy even the best man is of a girl's pure passion!

RAINA: I trust you. I love you. You will never

disappoint me, Sergius. (LOUKA *is heard singing within the house. They quickly release each other.*) I cant pretend to talk indifferently before her: my heart is too full. (LOUKA *comes from the house with her tray. She goes to the table, and begins to clear it, with her back turned to them.*) I will get my hat; and then we can go out until lunch time. Wouldnt you like that?

SERGIUS: Be quick. If you are away five minutes, it will seem five hours. (RAINA *runs to the top of the steps, and turns there to exchange looks with him and wave him a kiss with both hands. He looks after her with emotion for a moment; then turns slowly away, his face radiant with the loftiest exaltation. The movement shifts his field of vision, into the corner of which there now comes the tail of* LOUKA's *double apron. His attention is arrested at once. He takes a stealthy look at her, and begins to twirl his moustache mischievously, with his left hand akimbo on his hip. Finally, striking the ground with his heels in something of a cavalry swagger, he strolls over to the other side of the table, opposite her, and says*): Louka: do you know what the higher love is?

LOUKA (*astonished*): No, sir.

SERGIUS: Very fatiguing thing to keep up for any length of time, Louka. One feels the need of some relief after it.

LOUKA (*innocently*): Perhaps you would like some coffee, sir? (*She stretches her hand across the table for the coffee pot.*)

SERGIUS (*taking her hand*): Thank you, Louka.

LOUKA (*pretending to pull*): Oh, sir, you know I didn't mean that. I'm surprised at you!

SERGIUS (*coming clear of the table and drawing her with him*): I am surprised at myself, Louka. What would Sergius, the hero of Slivnitza, say if he saw me now? What would Sergius, the apostle of the higher love, say if he saw me now? What would the half dozen Sergiuses who keep popping in and out of this handsome figure of mine say if they caught us here? (*Letting go her hand and slipping his arm dexterously round her waist*) Do you consider my figure handsome, Louka?

LOUKA: Let me go, sir. I shall be disgraced. (*She struggles: he holds her inexorably.*) Oh, will you let go?

SERGIUS (*looking straight into her eyes*): No.

LOUKA: Then stand back where we cant be seen. Have you no common sense?

SERGIUS: Ah! thats reasonable. (*He takes her into the stable yard gateway, where they are hidden from the house.*)

LOUKA (*plaintively*): I may have been seen from the windows: Miss Raina is sure to be spying about after you.

SERGIUS (*stung: letting her go*): Take care, Louka. I may be worthless enough to betray the higher love; but do not you insult it.

LOUKA (*demurely*): Not for the world, sir, I'm sure. May I go on with my work, please, now?

SERGIUS (*again putting his arm around her*): You are a provoking little witch, Louka. If you were in love with me, would you spy out of windows on me?

LOUKA: Well, you see, sir, since you say you are half a dozen different gentlemen all at once, I should have a great deal to look after.

SERGIUS (*charmed*): Witty as well as pretty. (*He tries to kiss her*)

LOUKA (*avoiding him*): No: I dont want your kisses. Gentlefolk are all alike: you making love to me behind Miss Raina's back; and she doing the same behind yours.

SERGIUS (*recoiling a step*): Louka!

LOUKA: It shews how little you really care.

SERGIUS (*dropping his familiarity, and speaking with freezing politeness*): If our conversation is to continue, Louka, you will please remember that a gentleman does not discuss the conduct of the lady he is engaged to with her maid.

LOUKA: It's so hard to know what a gentleman considers right. I thought from your trying to kiss me that you had given up being so particular.

SERGIUS (*turning from her and striking his forehead as he comes back into the garden from the gateway*): Devil! devil!

LOUKA: Ha! ha! I expect one of the six of you is very like me, sir; though I am only Miss Raina's maid. (*She goes back to her work at the table, taking no further notice of him.*)

SERGIUS (*speaking to himself*): Which of the six is the real man? thats the question that torments me. One of them is a hero, another a buffoon, another a humbug, another perhaps a bit of a blackguard. (*He pauses, and looks furtively at* LOUKA *as he adds, with a deep bitterness.*) And one, at least, is a coward: jealous, like all cowards. (*He goes to the table.*) Louka.

LOUKA: Yes?

SERGIUS: Who is my rival?

LOUKA: You shall never get that out of me, for love or money.

SERGIUS: Why?

LOUKA: Never mind why. Besides, you would tell that I told you; and I should lose my place.

SERGIUS (*holding out his right hand in affirmation*): No! on the honor of a—(*He checks himself;*

*and his hand drops, nerveless, as he concludes sardonically)—*of a man capable of behaving as I have been behaving for the last five minutes. Who is he?

LOUKA: I dont know. I never saw him. I only heard his voice through the door of her room.

SERGIUS: Damnation! How dare you?

LOUKA (*retreating*): Oh, I mean no harm: youve no right to take up my words like that. The mistress knows all about it. And I tell you that if that gentleman ever comes here again, Miss Raina will marry him, whether he likes it or not. I know the difference between the sort of manner you and she put on before one another and the real manner.

SERGIUS *shivers as if she had stabbed him. Then, setting his face like iron, he strides grimly to her, and grips her above the elbows with both hands.*

SERGIUS: Now listen you to me.

LOUKA (*wincing*): Not so tight: youre hurting me.

SERGIUS: That doesnt matter. You have stained my honor by making me a party to your eavesdropping. And you have betrayed your mistress.

LOUKA (*writhing*): Please—

SERGIUS: That shews that you are an abominable little clod of common clay, with the soul of a servant. (*He lets her go as if she were an unclean thing, and turns away, dusting his hands of her, to the bench by the wall, where he sits down with averted head, meditating gloomily.*)

LOUKA (*whimpering angrily with her hands up her sleeves, feeling her bruised arms*): You know how to hurt with your tongue as well as with your hands. But I dont care, now Ive found out that whatever clay I'm made of, youre made of the same. As for her, she's a liar; and her fine airs are a cheat; and I'm worth six of her. (*She shakes the pain off hardily; tosses her head; and sets to work to put the things on the tray.*)

He looks doubtfully at her. She finishes packing the tray, and laps the cloth over the edges, so as to carry all out together. As she stoops to lift it, he rises.

SERGIUS: Louka! (*She stops and looks defiantly at him.*) A gentleman has no right to hurt a woman under any circumstances. (*With profound humility, uncovering his head.*) I beg your pardon.

LOUKA: That sort of apology may satisfy a lady. Of what use is it to a servant?

SERGIUS (*rudely crossed in his chivalry, throws it off with a bitter laugh, and says slightingly*): Oh!

you wish to be paid for the hurt? (*He puts on his shako, and takes some money from his pocket.*)

LOUKA (*her eyes filling with tears in spite of herself*): No: I want my hurt made well.

SERGIUS (*sobered by her tone*): How?

She rolls up her left sleeve; clasps her arm with the thumb and fingers of her right hand; and looks down at the bruise. Then she raises her head and looks straight at him. Finally, with a superb gesture, she presents her arm to be kissed. Amazed, he looks at her; at the arm; at her again; hesitates; and then, with shuddering intensity, exclaims Never! *and gets away as far as possible from her.*

Her arm drops. Without a word, and with unaffected dignity, she takes her tray, and is approaching the house when RAINA *returns, wearing a hat and jacket in the height of the Vienna fashion of the previous year, 1885.* LOUKA *makes way proudly for her, and then goes into the house.*

RAINA: I'm ready. Whats the matter? (*Gaily*) Have you been flirting with Louka?

SERGIUS (*hastily*): No, no. How can you think such a thing?

RAINA (*ashamed of herself*): Forgive me, dear: it was only a jest. I am so happy today.

He goes quickly to her, and kisses her hand remorsefully. CATHERINE *comes out and calls to them from the top of the steps.*

CATHERINE (*coming down to them*): I am sorry to disturb you, children; but Paul is distracted over those three regiments. He doesnt know how to send them to Philippopolis; and he objects to every suggestion of mine. You must go and help him, Sergius. He is in the library.

RAINA (*disappointed*): But we are just going out for a walk.

SERGIUS: I shall not be long. Wait for me just five minutes. (*He runs up the steps to the door.*)

RAINA (*following him to the foot of the steps and looking up at him with timid coquetry*): I shall go round and wait in full view of the library windows. Be sure you draw father's attention to me. If you are a moment longer than five minutes, I shall go in and fetch you, regiments or no regiments.

SERGIUS (*laughing*): Very well. (*He goes in.*)

RAINA *watches him until he is out of her sight. Then, with a perceptible relaxation of manner, she begins to pace up and down the garden in a brown study.*

CATHERINE: Imagine their meeting that Swiss and hearing the whole story! The very first thing your father asked for was the old coat we sent him off in. A nice mess you have got us into!

RAINA (*gazing thoughtfully at the gravel as she walks*): The little beast!

CATHERINE: Little beast! What little beast?

RAINA: To go and tell! Oh, if I had him here, I'd cram him with chocolate creams til he couldnt ever speak again!

CATHERINE: Dont talk such stuff. Tell me the truth Raina. How long was he in your room before you came to me?

RAINA (*whisking round and recommencing her march in the opposite direction*): Oh, I forget.

CATHERINE: You cannot forget! Did he really climb up after the soldiers were gone; or was he there when that officer searched the room?

RAINA: No. Yes: I think he must have been there then.

CATHERINE: You think! Oh, Raina! Raina! Will anything ever make you straightforward? If Sergius finds out, it will be all over between you.

RAINA (*with cool impertinence*): Oh, I know Sergius is your pet. I sometimes wish you could marry him instead of me. You would just suit him. You would pet him, and spoil him, and mother him to perfection.

CATHERINE (*opening her eyes very widely indeed*): Well, upon my word!

RAINA (*capriciously: half to herself*): I always feel a longing to do or say something dreadful to him— to shock his propriety—to scandalize the five senses out of him. (*To* CATHERINE, *perversely*) I dont care whether he finds out about the chocolate cream soldier or not. I half hope he may. (*She again turns and strolls flippantly away up the path to the corner of the house.*)

CATHERINE: And what should I be able to say to your father, pray?

RAINA (*over her shoulder, from the top of the two steps*): Oh, poor father! As if he could help himself! (*She turns the corner and passes out of sight.*)

CATHERINE (*looking after her, her fingers itching*): Oh, if you were only ten years younger! (LOUKA *comes from the house with a salver, which she carries hanging down by her side.*) Well?

LOUKA: Theres a gentleman just called, madam. A Serbian officer.

CATHERINE (*flaming*): A Serb! And how dare he—(*checking herself bitterly*) Oh, I forgot. We are at peace now. I suppose we shall have them calling every day to pay their compliments. Well: if he is

an officer why dont you tell your master? He is in the library with Major Saranoff. Why do you come to me?

LOUKA: But he asks for you, madam. And I dont think he knows who you are: he said the lady of the house. He gave me this little ticket for you. (*She takes a card out of her bosom; puts it on the salver; and offers it to* CATHERINE.)

CATHERINE (*reading*): "Captain Bluntschli"? Thats a German name.

LOUKA: Swiss, madam, I think.

CATHERINE (*with a bound that makes* LOUKA *jump back*): Swiss! What is he like?

LOUKA (*timidly*): He has a big carpet bag, madam.

CATHERINE: Oh Heavens! he's come to return the coat. Send him away: say we're not at home: ask him to leave his address and I'll write to him. Oh stop: that will never do. Wait! (*She throws herself into a chair to think it out.* LOUKA *waits.*) The master and Major Saranoff are busy in the library, arnt they?

LOUKA: Yes, madam.

CATHERINE (*decisively*): Bring the gentleman out here at once. (*Peremptorily.*) And be very polite to him. Dont delay. Here (*impatiently snatching the salver from her*): leave that here; and go straight back to him.

LOUKA: Yes, madam (*going*).

CATHERINE: Louka!

LOUKA (*stopping*): Yes, madam.

CATHERINE: Is the library door shut?

LOUKA: I think so, madam.

CATHERINE: If not, shut it as you pass through.

LOUKA: Yes, madam (*going*).

CATHERINE: Stop (LOUKA *stops*). He will have to go that way (*indicating the gate of the stable yard*) Tell Nicola to bring his bag here after him. Dont forget.

LOUKA (*surprised*): His bag?

CATHERINE: Yes: here: as soon as possible. (*Vehemently.*) Be quick! (LOUKA *runs into the house.* CATHERINE *snatches her apron off and throws it behind a bush. She then takes up the salver and uses it as a mirror, with the result that the handkerchief tied round her head follows the apron. A touch to her hair and shake to her dressing gown make her presentable.*) Oh, how? how? how can a man be such a fool! Such a moment to select! (LOUKA *appears at the door of the house, announcing* CAPTAIN BLUNTSCHLI. *She stands aside at the top of the steps to let him pass before she goes in again. He is the man of the midnight adventure in* RAINA's *room, clean, well brushed, smartly uni-*

formed, and out of trouble, but still unmistakably the same man. The moment LOUKA's back is turned, CATHERINE swoops on him with impetuous, urgent, coaxing appeal.) Captain Bluntschi: I am very glad to see you; but you must leave this house at once. (He raises his eyebrows.) My husband has just returned with my future son-in-law; and they know nothing. If they did, the consequences would be terrible. You are a foreigner: you do not feel our national animosities as we do. We still hate the Serbs: the effect of the peace on my husband has been to make him feel like a lion baulked of his prey. If he discovers our secret, he will never forgive me; and my daughter's life will hardly be safe. Will you, like the chivalrous gentleman and soldier you are, leave at once before he finds you here?

BLUNTSCHLI (disappointed, but philosophical): At once, gracious lady. I only came to thank you and return the coat you lent me. If you will allow me to take it out of my bag and leave it with your servant as I pass out, I need detain you no further. (He turns to go into the house.)

CATHERINE (catching him by the sleeve): Oh, you must not think of going back that way. (Coaxing him across to the stable gates.) This is the shortest way out. Many thanks. So glad to have been of service to you. Good-bye.

BLUNTSCHLI: But my bag?

CATHERINE: It shall be sent on. You will leave me your address.

BLUNTSCHLI: True. Allow me. (He takes out his card-case, and stops to write his address, keeping CATHERINE in an agony of impatience. As he hands her the card, PETKOFF, hatless, rushes from the house in a fluster of hospitality, followed by SERGIUS.)

PETKOFF (as he hurries down the steps): My dear Captain Bluntschli—

CATHERINE: Oh Heavens! (She sinks on the seat against the wall.)

PETKOFF (too preoccupied to notice her as he shakes BLUNTSCHLI's hand heartily): Those stupid people of mine thought I was out here, instead of in the—haw!—library (he cannot mention the library without betraying how proud he is of it). I saw you through the window. I was wondering why you didnt come in. Saranoff is with me: you remember him, dont you?

SERGIUS (saluting humorously, and then offering his hand with great charm of manner): Welcome, our friend the enemy!

PETKOFF: No longer the enemy, happily.

(Rather anxiously) I hope youve called as a friend, and not about horses or prisoners.

CATHERINE: Oh, quite as a friend, Paul. I was just asking Captain Bluntschli to stay to lunch; but he declares he must go at once.

SERGIUS (sardonically): Impossible, Bluntschli. We want you here badly. We have to send on three cavalry regiments to Philippopolis; and we dont in the least know how to do it.

BLUNTSCHLI (suddenly attentive and business-like): Philippopolis? The forage is the trouble, I suppose.

PETKOFF (eagerly): Yes: thats it. (To SERGIUS.) He sees the whole thing at once.

BLUNTSCHLI: I think I can shew you how to manage that.

SERGIUS: Invaluable man! Come along! (Towering over BLUNTSCHLI, he puts his hand on his shoulder and takes him to the steps, PETKOFF following.)

RAINA comes from the house as BLUNTSCHLI puts his foot on the first step.

RAINA: Oh! The chocolate cream soldier!

BLUNTSCHLI stands rigid. SERGIUS, amazed, looks at RAINA, then at PETKOFF, who looks back at him and then at his wife.

CATHERINE (with commanding presence of mind): My dear Raina, dont you see that we have a guest here? Captain Bluntschli: one of our new Serbian friends.

RAINA bows: BLUNTSCHLI bows.

RAINA: How silly of me! (She comes down into the centre of the group, between BLUNTSCHLI and PETKOFF.) I made a beautiful ornament this morning for the ice pudding; and that stupid Nicola has just put down a pile of plates on it and spoilt it. (To BLUNTSCHLI, winningly) I hope you didnt think that you were the chocolate cream soldier, Captain Bluntschli.

BLUNTSCHLI (laughing): I assure you I did. (Stealing a whimsical glance at her) Your explanation was a relief.

PETKOFF (suspiciously, to RAINA): And since when, pray, have you taken to cooking?

CATHERINE: Oh, whilst you were away. It is her latest fancy.

PETKOFF (testily): And has Nicola taken to drinking? He used to be careful enough. First he shews Captain Bluntschli out here when he knew quite well I was in the library; and then he goes downstairs and breaks Raina's chocolate soldier. He must—(NICOLA appears at the top of the steps with the bag. He descends; places it respectfully *before* BLUNTSCHLI; *and waits for further orders. General amazement.* NICOLA, *unconscious of the effect he is producing, looks perfectly satisfied with himself. When* PETKOFF *recovers his power of speech, he breaks out at him with*) Are you mad, Nicola?

NICOLA (*taken aback*): Sir?

PETKOFF: What have you brought that for?

NICOLA: My lady's orders, major. Louka told me that—

CATHERINE (*interrupting him*): My orders! Why should I order you to bring Captain Bluntschli's luggage out here? What are you thinking of, Nicola?

NICOLA (*after a moment's bewilderment, picking up the bag as he addresses* BLUNTSCHLI *with the very perfection of servile discretion*): I beg your pardon, captain, I am sure. (To CATHERINE.) My fault, madam: I hope you shall overlook it. (*He bows, and is going to the steps with the bag, when* PETKOFF *addresses him angrily.*)

PETKOFF: Youd better go and slam that bag, too, down on Miss Raina's ice pudding! (*This is too much for* NICOLA. *The bag drops from his hand almost on his master's toes, eliciting a roar of*) Begone, you butter-fingered donkey.

NICOLA (*snatching up the bag, and escaping into the house*): Yes, Major.

CATHERINE: Oh, never mind, Paul: dont be angry.

PETKOFF (*blustering*): Scoundrel! He's got out of hand while I was away. I'll teach him. Infernal blackguard! The sack next Saturday! I'll clear out the whole establishment—

(*He is stifled by the caresses of his wife and daughter, who hang round his neck, petting him.*)

CATHERINE } [*together*] { Now, now, now it
RAINA   { Wow, wow, wow:

{ mustnt be angry. He meant
{ not on your first day at home.
{ no harm. Be good to please
{ I'll make another ice pudding.
{ me, dear. Sh-sh-sh-sh!
{ Tch-ch-ch!

PETKOFF (*yielding*): Oh well, never mind. Come, Bluntschli: lets have no more nonsense about going away. You know very well youre not going back to Switzerland yet. Until you do go back youll stay with us.

RAINA: Oh, do, Captain Bluntschli.

PETKOFF (*to* CATHERINE): Now, Catherine: it's of you he's afraid. Press him: and he'll stay.

CATHERINE: Of course I shall be only too delighted if (*appealingly*) Captain Bluntschli really wishes to stay. He knows my wishes.

BLUNTSCHLI (*in his driest military manner*): I am at madam's orders.

SERGIUS (*cordially*): That settles it!

PETKOFF (*heartily*): Of course!

RAINA: You see you must stay.

BLUNTSCHLI (*smiling*): Well, if I must, I must. *Gesture of despair from* CATHERINE.

ACT III

In the library after lunch. It is not much of a library. Its literary equipment consists of a single fixed shelf stocked with old paper covered novels, broken backed, coffee stained, torn and thumbed; and a couple of little hanging shelves with a few gift books on them: the rest of the wall space being occupied by trophies of war and the chase. But it is a most comfortable sitting room. A row of three large windows shews a mountain panorama, just now seen in one of its friendliest aspects in the mellowing afternoon light. In the corner next the right hand window a square earthenware stove, a perfect tower of glistening pottery, rises nearly to the ceiling and guarantees plenty of warmth. The ottoman is like that in RAINA's *room, and similarly placed; and the window seats are luxurious with decorated cushions. There is one object, however, hopelessly out of keeping with its surroundings. This is a small kitchen table, much the worse for wear, fitted as a writing table with an old canister full of pens, an eggcup filled with ink, and a deplorable scrap of heavily used pink blotting paper.*

At the side of this table, which stands to the left of anyone facing the window, BLUNTSCHLI *is hard at work with a couple of maps before him, writing orders. At the head of it sits* SERGIUS, *who is supposed to be also at work, but is actually gnawing the feather of a pen, and contemplating* BLUNTSCHLI's *quick, sure, businesslike progress with a mixture of envious irritation at his own incapacity and awestruck wonder at an ability which seems to him almost miraculous, though its prosaic character forbids him to esteem it. The* MAJOR *is comfortably established on the ottoman, with a newspaper in his hand and the tube of his hookah within easy reach.*

CATHERINE *sits at the stove, with her back to them, embroidering.* RAINA, *reclining on the divan, is gazing in a daydream out at the Balkan landscape, with a neglected novel in her lap.*

The door is on the same side as the stove, farther from the window. The button of the electric bell is at the opposite side, behind BLUNTSCHLI.

PETKOFF (*looking up from his paper to watch how they are getting on at the table*): Are you sure I cant help in any way, Bluntschli?

BLUNTSCHLI (*without interrupting his writing or looking up*): Quite sure, thank you. Saranoff and I will manage it.

SERGIUS (*grimly*): Yes: we'll manage it. He finds out what to do; draws up the orders; and I sign em. Division of labor! (BLUNTSCHLI *passes him a paper.*) Another one? Thank you. (*He plants the paper squarely before him; sets his chair carefully parallel to it; and signs with his cheek on his elbow and his protruded tongue following the movements of his pen.*) This hand is more accustomed to the sword than to the pen.

PETKOFF: It's very good of you, Bluntschli: it is indeed, to let yourself be put upon in this way. Now are you quite sure I can do nothing?

CATHERINE (*in a low warning tone*): You can stop interrupting, Paul.

PETKOFF (*starting and looking round at her*): Eh? Oh! Quite right. (*He takes his newspaper up again, but presently lets it drop.*) Ah, you havnt been campaigning, Catherine: you dont know how pleasant it is for us to sit here, after a good lunch, with nothing to do but enjoy ourselves. Theres only one thing I want to make me thoroughly comfortable.

CATHERINE: What is that?

PETKOFF: My old coat. I'm not at home in this one: I feel as if I were on parade.

CATHERINE: My dear Paul, how absurd you are about that old coat! It must be hanging in the blue closet where you left it.

PETKOFF: My dear Catherine, I tell you Ive looked there. Am I to believe my own eyes or not? (CATHERINE *rises and crosses the room to press the button of the electric bell.*) What are you shewing off that bell for? (*She looks at him majestically, and silently resumes her chair and her needlework.*) My dear: if you think the obstinacy of your sex can make a coat out of two old dressing gowns of Raina's, your waterproof, and my mackintosh, youre mistaken. Thats exactly what the blue closet contains at present.

NICOLA *presents himself.*

CATHERINE: Nicola: go to the blue closet and bring your master's old coat here: the braided one he wears in the house.

NICOLA: Yes, madam. (*He goes out.*)

PETKOFF: Catherine.

CATHERINE: Yes, Paul.

PETKOFF: I bet you any piece of jewellery you like to order from Sofia against a week's housekeeping money that the coat isnt there.

CATHERINE: Done, Paul!

PETKOFF (*excited by the prospect of a gamble*): Come: heres an opportunity for some sport. Wholl bet on it? Bluntschli: I'll give you six to one.

BLUNTSCHLI (*imperturbably*): It would be robbing you, Major. Madam is sure to be right. (*Without looking up, he passes another batch of papers to* SERGIUS.)

SERGIUS (*also excited*): Bravo, Switzerland! Major: I bet my best charger against an Arab mare for Raina that Nicola finds the coat in the blue closet.

PETKOFF (*eagerly*): Your best char—

CATHERINE (*hastily interrupting him*): Dont be foolish, Paul. An Arabian mare will cost you 50,000 levas.

RAINA (*suddenly coming out of her picturesque revery*): Really, mother, if you are going to take the jewellery, I dont see why you should grudge me my Arab.

NICOLA *comes back with the coat, and brings it to* PETKOFF, *who can hardly believe his eyes.*

CATHERINE: Where was it, Nicola?

NICOLA: Hanging in the blue closet, madam.

PETKOFF: Well, I am d—

CATHERING (*stopping him*): Paul!

PETKOFF: I could have sworn it wasnt there. Age is beginning to tell on me. I'm getting hallucinations. (*To* NICOLA.) Here: help me to change. Excuse me, Bluntschli. (*He begins changing coats,* NICOLA *acting as valet.*) Remember: I didnt take that bet of yours, Sergius. Youd better give Raina that Arab steed yourself, since youve roused her expectations. Eh, Raina? (*He looks round at her; but she is again rapt in the landscape. With a little gush of parental affection and pride, he points her out to them, and says*) She's dreaming, as usual.

SERGIUS: Assuredly she shall not be the loser.

PETKOFF: So much the better for her. I shant come off so cheaply, I expect. (*The change is now complete.* NICOLA *goes out with the discarded coat.*) Ah, now I feel at home at last. (*He sits down and takes his newspaper with a grunt of relief.*)

BLUNTSCHLI (*to* SERGIUS, *handing a paper*): Thats the last order.

PETKOFF (*jumping up*): What! Finished?

BLUNTSCHLI: Finished.

PETKOFF (*with childlike envy*): Havnt you anything for me to sign?

BLUNTSCHLI: Not necessary. His signature will do.

PETKOFF (*inflating his chest and thumping it.*): Ah well, I think weve done a thundering good day's work. Can I do anything more?

BLUNTSCHLI: You had better both see the fellows that are to take these. (SERGIUS *rises.*) Pack them off at once; and shew them that Ive marked on the orders the time they should hand them in by. Tell them that if they stop to drink or tell stories—if theyre five minutes late, theyll have the skin off their backs.

SERGIUS (*stiffening indignantly*): I'll say so. (*He strides to the door.*) And if one of them is man enough to spit in my face for insulting him, I'll buy his discharge and give him a pension. (*He goes out.*)

BLUNTSCHLI (*confidentially*): Just see that he talks to them properly, Major, will you?

PETKOFF (*officiously*): Quite right, Bluntschli, quite right. I'll see to it. (*He goes to the door importantly, but hesitates on the threshold.*) By the bye, Catherine, you may as well come too. Theyll be far more frightened of you than of me.

CATHERINE (*putting down her embroidery*): I daresay I had better. You would only splutter at them. (*She goes out,* PETKOFF *holding the door for her and following her.*)

BLUNTSCHLI: What an army! They make cannons out of cherry trees; and the officers send for their wives to keep discipline! (*He begins to fold and docket the papers.*)

RAINA, *who has risen from the divan, marches slowly down the room with her hands clasped behind her, and looks mischievously at him.*

RAINA: You look ever so much nicer than when we last met. (*He looks up, surprised.*) What have you done to yourself?

BLUNTSCHLI: Washed; brushed; good night's sleep and breakfast. Thats all.

RAINA: Did you get back safely that morning?

BLUNTSCHLI: Quite, thanks.

RAINA: Were they angry with you for running away from Sergius's charge?

BLUNTSCHLI (*grinning*): No: they were glad; because theyd all just run away themselves.

RAINA (*going to the table, and leaning over it towards him*): It must have made a lovely story for them: all that about me and my room.

BLUNTSCHLI: Capital story. But I only told it to one of them: a particular friend.

RAINA: On whose discretion you could absolutely rely?

BLUNTSCHLI: Absolutely.

RAINA: Hm! He told it all to my father and Sergius the day you exchanged the prisoners. (*She turns away and strolls carelessly across to the other side of the room.*)

BLUNTSCHLI (*deeply concerned, and half incredulous*): No! You dont mean that, do you?

RAINA (*turning, with sudden earnestness*): I do indeed. But they dont know that it was in this house you took refuge. If Sergius knew, he would challenge you and kill you in a duel.

BLUNTSCHLI: Bless me! then dont tell him.

RAINA: Please be serious, Captain Bluntschli. Can you not realize what it is to me to deceive him? I want to be quite perfect with Sergius: no meanness, no smallness, no deceit. My relation to him is the one really beautiful and noble part of my life. I hope you can understand that.

BLUNTSCHLI (*sceptically*): You mean that you wouldnt like him to find out that the story about the ice pudding was a—a—a— You know.

RAINA (*wincing*): Ah, dont talk of it in that flippant way. I lied: I know it. But I did it to save your life. He would have killed you. That was the second time I ever uttered a falsehood. (BLUNTSCHLI *rises quickly and looks doubtfully and somewhat severely at her.*) Do you remember the first time?

BLUNTSCHLI: I! No. Was I present?

RAINA: Yes; and I told the officer who was searching for you that you were not present.

BLUNTSCHLI: True. I should have remembered it.

RAINA (*greatly encouraged*): Ah, it is natural that you should forget it first. It cost you nothing: it cost me a lie! A lie!

She sits down on the ottoman, looking straight before her with her hands clasped around her knee. BLUNTSCHLI, *quite touched, goes to the ottoman with a particularly reassuring and considerate air, and sits down beside her.*

BLUNTSCHLI: My dear young lady, dont let this worry you. Remember: I'm a soldier. Now what are the two things that happen to a soldier so often that he comes to think nothing of them? One is hearing people tell lies (RAINA *recoils*): the other is getting his life saved in all sorts of ways by all sorts of people.

RAINA (*rising in indignant protest*): And so he becomes a creature incapable of faith and of gratitude.

BLUNTSCHLI (*making a wry face*): Do you like gratitude? I dont. If pity is akin to love, gratitude is akin to the other thing.

RAINA: Gratitude! (*Turning on him*) If you are incapable of gratitude you are incapable of any noble sentiment. Even animals are grateful. Oh, I see now exactly what you think of me! You were not surprised to hear me lie. To you it was something I probably did every day! every hour!! That is how men think of women. (*She paces the room tragically.*)

BLUNTSCHLI (*dubiously*): Theres reason in everything. You said youd told only two lies in your whole life. Dear young lady: isnt that rather a short allowance? I'm quite a straightforward man myself; but it wouldnt last me a whole morning.

RAINA (*staring haughtily at him*): Do you know, sir, that you are insulting me?

BLUNTSCHLI: I cant help it. When you strike that noble attitude and speak in that thrilling voice, I admire you; but I find it impossible to believe a single word you say.

RAINA (*superbly*): Captain Bluntschli!

BLUNTSCHLI (*unmoved*): Yes?

RAINA (*standing over him, as if she could not believe her senses*): Do you mean what you said just now? Do you k n o w what you said just now?

BLUNTSCHLI: I do.

RAINA (*gasping*): I! I!!! (*She points to herself incredulously, meaning "I, Raina Petkoff tell lies!" He meets her gaze unflinchingly. She suddenly sits down beside him, and adds, with a complete change of manner from the heroic to a babyish familiarity*) How did you find me out?

BLUNTSCHLI (*promptly*): Instinct, dear young lady. Instinct, and experience of the world.

RAINA (*wonderingly*): Do you know, you are the first man I ever met who did not take me seriously?

BLUNTSCHLI: You mean, dont you, that I am the first man that has ever taken you quite seriously?

RAINA: Yes: I suppose I do mean that. (*Cosily, quite at her ease with him*) How strange it is to be talked to in such a way! You know, Ive always gone on like that.

BLUNTSCHLI: You mean the—?

RAINA: I mean the noble attitude and the thrilling voice. (*They laugh together.*) I did it when I was a tiny child to my nurse. She believed in it. I do it

before my parents. They believe in it. I do it before Sergius. He believes in it.

BLUNTSCHLI: Yes: he's a little in that line himself, isnt he?

RAINA (*startled*): Oh! Do you think so?

BLUNTSCHLI: You know him better than I do.

RAINA: I wonder—I wonder is he? If I thought that—! (*Discouraged*) Ah, well; what does it matter? I suppose, now youve found me out, you despise me.

BLUNTSCHLI (*warmly, rising*): No, my dear young lady, no, no, no a thousand times. It's part of your youth: part of your charm. I'm like all the rest of them: the nurse, your parents, Sergius: I'm your infatuated admirer.

RAINA (*pleased*): Really?

BLUNTSCHLI (*slapping his breast smartly with his hand, German fashion*): Hand aufs Herz! Really and truly.

RAINA (*very happy*): But what did you think of me for giving you my portrait?

BLUNTSCHLI (*astonished*): Your portrait! You never gave me your portrait.

RAINA (*quickly*): Do you mean to say you never got it?

BLUNTSCHLI: No. (*He sits down beside her, with renewed interest, and says, with some complacency*) When did you send it to me?

RAINA (*indignantly*): I did not send it to you. (*She turns her head away, and adds, reluctantly*) It was in the pocket of that coat.

BLUNTSCHLI (*pursing his lips and rounding his eyes*) Oh-o-oh! I never found it. It must be there still.

RAINA (*springing up*): There still! for my father to find the first time he puts his hand in his pocket! Oh, how could you be so stupid?

BLUNTSCHLI (*rising also*): It doesn't matter: I suppose it's only a photograph: how can he tell who it was intended for? Tell him he put it there himself.

RAINA (*bitterly*): Yes: that is so clever! isnt it? (*Distractedly*) Oh! what shall I do?

BLUNTSCHLI: Ah, I see. You wrote something on it. That was rash.

RAINA (*vexed almost to tears*): Oh, to have done such a thing for y o u, who care no more—except to laugh at me—oh! Are you sure nobody has touched it?

BLUNTSCHLI: Well, I cant be quite sure. You see, I couldnt carry it about with me all the time: one cant take much luggage on active service.

RAINA: What did you do with it?

BLUNTSCHLI: When I got through to Pirot I had to put it in safe keeping somehow. I thought of the railway cloak room; but thats the surest place to get looted in modern warfare. So I pawned it.

RAINA: Pawned it!!!

BLUNTSCHLI: I know it doesnt sound nice; but it was much the safest plan. I redeemed it the day before yesterday. Heaven only knows whether the pawnbroker cleared out the pockets or not.

RAINA (*furious: throwing the words right into his face*): You have a low shopkeeping mind. You think of things that would never come into a gentleman's head.

BLUNTSCHLI: (*phlegmatically*): Thats the Swiss national character, dear lady. (*He returns to the table.*)

RAINA: Oh, I wish I had never met you. (*She flounces away, and sits at the window fuming.*)

LOUKA *comes in with a heap of letters and telegrams on her salver, and crosses, with her bold free gait, to the table. Her left sleeve is looped up to the shoulder with a brooch, shewing her naked arm, with a broad gilt bracelet covering the bruise.*

LOUKA (*to* BLUNTSCHLI): For you. (*She empties the salver with a fling on to the table.*) The messenger is waiting. (*She is determined not to be civil to an enemy, even if she must bring him his letters.*)

BLUNTSCHLI (*to* RAINA): Will you excuse me: the last postal delivery that reached me was three weeks ago. These are the subsequent accumulations. Four telegrams: a week old. (*He opens one.*) Oho! Bad news!

RAINA (*rising and advancing a little remorsefully*): Bad news?

BLUNTSCHLI: My father's dead. (*He looks at the telegram with his lips pursed, musing on the unexpected changes in his arrangements.* LOUKA *crosses herself hastily.*)

RAINA: Oh, how very sad!

BLUNTSCHLI: Yes: I shall have to start for home in an hour. He has left a lot of big hotels behind him to be looked after. (*He takes up a fat letter in a long blue envelope.*) Here's a whacking letter from the family solicitor. (*He pulls out the enclosures and glances over them.*) Great Heavens! Seventy! Two hundred! (*In a crescendo of dismay.*) Four hundred! Four thousand!! Nine thousand six hundred!!! What on earth am I to do with them all?

RAINA (*timidly*): Nine thousand hotels?

BLUNTSCHLI: Hotels! nonsense. If you only knew! Oh, it's too ridiculous! Excuse me: I must give my fellow orders about starting. (*He leaves the room hastily, with the documents in his hand.*)

LOUKA (*knowing instinctively that she cannot annoy* RAINA *by disparaging* BLUNTSCHLI): He has not much heart that Swiss. He has not a word of grief for his poor father.

RAINA (*bitterly*): Grief! A man who has been doing nothing but killing people for years! What does he care? What does any soldier care? (*She goes to the door, restraining her tears with difficulty.*)

LOUKA: Major Saranoff has been fighting too; and he has plenty of heart left. (RAINA, *at the door, draws herself up haughtily and goes out.*) Aha! I thought you wouldnt get much feeling out of your soldier. (*She is following* RAINA *when* NICOLA *enters with an armful of logs for the stove.*)

NICOLA (*grinning amorously at her*): Ive been trying all the afternoon to get a minute alone with you, my girl. (*His countenance changes as he notices her arm.*) Why, what fashion is that of wearing your sleeve, child?

LOUKA (*proudly*): My own fashion.

NICOLA: Indeed! If the mistress catches you, she'll talk to you. (*He puts the logs down, and seats himself comfortably on the ottoman.*)

LOUKA: Is that any reason why y o u should take it on yourself to talk to me?

NICOLA: Come! dont be so contrary with me. Ive some good news for you. (*She sits down beside him. He takes out some paper money.* LOUKA, *with an eager gleam in her eyes, tries to snatch it; but he shifts it quickly to his left hand, out of her reach.*) See! a twenty leva bill! Sergius gave me that, out of pure swagger. A fool and his money are soon parted. Theres ten levas more. The Swiss gave me that for backing up the mistress's and Raina's lies about him. He's no fool, he isnt. You should have heard old Catherine downstairs as polite as you please to me, telling me not to mind the Major being a little impatient; for they knew what a good servant I was—after making a fool and a liar of me before them all! The twenty will go to our savings; and you shall have the ten to spend if youll only talk to me so as to remind me I'm a human being. I get tired of being a servant occasionally.

LOUKA: Yes: sell your manhood for 30 levas, and buy me for 10! (*Rising scornfully*) Keep your money. You were born to be a servant. I was not. When you set up your shop you will only be everybody's servant instead of somebody's servant. (*She goes moodily to the table and seats herself regally in* SERGIUS's *chair.*)

NICOLA (*picking up his logs, and going to the stove*): Ah, wait til you see. We shall have our evenings to ourselves; and I shall be master in my own house, I promise you. (*He throws the logs down and kneels at the stove.*)

LOUKA: You shall never be master in mine.

NICOLA (*turning, still on his knees, and squatting down rather forlornly on his calves, daunted by her implacable disdain*): You have a great ambition in you, Louka. Remember: if any luck comes to you, it was I that made a woman of you.

LOUKA: You!

NICOLA (*scrambling up and going to her*): Yes, me. Who was it made you give up wearing a couple of pounds of false black hair on your head and reddening your lips and cheeks like any other Bulgarian girl! I did. Who taught you to trim your nails, and keep your hands clean, and be dainty about yourself, like a fine Russian lady! Me: do you hear that? me! (*She tosses her head defiantly; and he turns away, adding more cooly*) Ive often thought that if Raina were out of the way, and you just a little less of a fool and Sergius just a little more of one, you might come to be one of my grandest customers, instead of only being my wife and costing me money.

LOUKA: I believe you would rather be my servant than my husband. You would make more out of me. Oh, I know that soul of yours.

NICOLA (*going closer to her for greater emphasis*): Never you mind my soul; but just listen to my advice. If you want to be a lady, your present behaviour to me wont do at all, unless when we're alone. It's too sharp and impudent; and impudence is a sort of familiarity: it shews affection for me. And dont you try being high and mighty with me, either. Youre like all country girls: you think it's genteel to treat a servant the way I treat a stableboy. Thats only your ignorance; and dont you forget it. And dont be so ready to defy everybody. Act as if you expected to have your own way, not as if you expected to be ordered about. The way to get on as a lady is the same as the way to get on as a servant: youve got to know your place: thats the secret of it. And you may depend on me to know my place if you get promoted. Think over it, my girl. I'll stand by you: one servant should always stand by another.

LOUKA (*rising impatiently*): Oh, I must behave in my own way. You take all the courage out of me with your cold-blooded wisdom. Go and put those logs in the fire: thats the sort of thing you understand.

Before NICOLA *can retort,* SERGIUS *comes in. He checks himself a moment on seeing* LOUKA; *then goes to the stove.*

SERGIUS (*to* NICOLA): I am not in the way of your work, I hope.

NICOLA (*in a smooth, elderly manner*): Oh no, sir: thank you kindly. I was only speaking to this foolish girl about her habit of running up here to the library whenever she gets a chance, to look at the books. Thats the worst of her education, sir: it gives her habits above her station. (*To* LOUKA) Make that table tidy, Louka, for the Major. (*He goes out sedately.*)

LOUKA, *without looking at* SERGIUS, *pretends to arrange the papers on the table. He crosses slowly to her, and studies the arrangement of her sleeve reflectively.*

SERGIUS: Let me see: is there a mark there? (*He turns up the bracelet and sees the bruise made by his grasp. She stands motionless, not looking at him: fascinated, but on her guard.*) Ffff! Does it hurt?

LOUKA: Yes.

SERGIUS: Shall I cure it?

LOUKA (*instantly withdrawing herself proudly, but still not looking at him*): No. You cannot cure it now.

SERGIUS (*masterfully*): Quite sure? (*He makes a movement as if to take her in his arms.*)

LOUKA: Dont trifle with me, please. An officer should not trifle with a servant.

SERGIUS (*indicating the bruise with a merciless stroke of his forefinger*): That was no trifle, Louka.

LOUKA (*flinching; then looking at him for the first time*): Are you sorry?

SERGIUS (*with measured emphasis, folding his arms*): I am n e v e r sorry.

LOUKA (*wistfully*): I wish I could believe a man could be as unlike a woman as that. I wonder are you really a brave man?

SERGIUS (*unaffectedly, relaxing his attitude*): Yes: I am a brave man. My heart jumped like a woman's at the first shot; but in the charge I found that I was brave. Yes: that at least is real about me.

LOUKA: Did you find in the charge that the men whose fathers are poor like mine were any less brave than the men who are rich like you?

SERGIUS (*with bitter levity*): Not a bit. They all slashed and cursed and yelled like heroes. Psha! the courage to rage and kill is cheap. I have an English bull terrier who has as much of that sort of courage as the whole Bulgarian nation, and the whole Russian nation at its back. But he lets my groom thrash him, all the same. Thats your soldier all over! No, Louka: your poor men can cut throats; but they are afraid of their officers; they put up with insults and blows; they stand by and see one another punished like children: aye, and help to do it when they are ordered. And the officers!!! Well (*with a short harsh laugh*) I am an officer. Oh, (*fervently*) give me the man who will defy to the death any power on earth or in heaven that sets itself up against his own will and conscience: he alone is the brave man.

LOUKA: How easy it is to talk! Men never seem to me to grow up: they all have schoolboy's ideas. You dont know what true courage is.

SERGIUS (*ironically*): Indeed! I am willing to be instructed. (*He sits on the ottoman, sprawling magnificently.*)

LOUKA: Look at me! How much am I allowed to have my own will? I have to get your room ready for you: to sweep and dust, to fetch and carry. How could that degrade me if it did not degrade you to have it done for you? But (*with subdued passion*) if I were Empress of Russia, above everyone in the world, then!! Ah then, though according to you I could shew no courage at all, you should see, you should see.

SERGIUS: What would you do, most noble Empress?

LOUKA: I would marry the man I loved, which no other queen in Europe has the courage to do. If I loved you, though you would be as far beneath me as I am beneath you, I would dare to be the equal of my inferior. Would you dare as much if you loved me? No: if you felt the beginnings of love for me you would not let it grow. You would not dare: you would marry a rich man's daughter because you would be afraid of what other people would say of you.

SERGIUS (*bounding up*): You lie: it is not so, by all the stars! If I loved you, and I were the Czar himself, I would set you on the throne by my side. You know that I love another woman, a woman as high above you as heaven is above earth. And you are jealous of her.

LOUKA: I have no reason to be. She will never marry you now. The man I told you of has come back. She will marry the Swiss.

SERGIUS (*recoiling*): The Swiss!

LOUKA: A man worth ten of you. Then you can come to me; and I will refuse you. You are not good enough for me. (*She turns to the door.*)

SERGIUS (*springing after her and catching her fiercely in his arms*): I will kill the Swiss; and afterwards I will do as I please with you.

LOUKA (*in his arms, passive and steadfast*): The Swiss will kill you, perhaps. He has beaten you in love. He may beat you in war.

SERGIUS (*tormentedly*): Do you think I believe that she—s h e ! whose worst thoughts are higher than your best ones, is capable of trifling with another man behind my back?

LOUKA: Do you think s h e would believe the Swiss if he told her now that I am in your arms?

SERGIUS (*releasing her in despair*): Damnation! Oh, damnation! Mockery! mockery everywhere! everything I think is mocked by everything I do. (*He strikes himself frantically on the breast.*) Coward! liar! fool! Shall I kill myself like a man, or live and pretend to laugh at myself? (*She again turns to go.*) Louka! (*She stops near the door.*) Remember: you belong to me.

LOUKA (*turning*): What does that mean? An insult?

SERGIUS (*commandingly*): It means that you love me, and that I have had you here in my arms, and will perhaps have you there again. Whether that is an insult I neither know nor care: take it as you please. But (*vehemently*) I will not be a coward and a trifler. If I choose to love you, I dare marry you, in spite of all Bulgaria. If these hands ever touch you again, they shall touch my affianced bride.

LOUKA: We shall see whether you dare keep your word. And take care. I will not wait long.

SERGIUS (*again folding his arms and standing motionless in the middle of the room*): Yes: we shall see. And you shall wait my pleasure.

BLUNTSCHLI, *much preoccupied, with his papers still in his hand, enters, leaving the door open for* LOUKA *to go out. He goes across to the table, glancing at her as he passes.* SERGIUS, *without altering his resolute attitude, watches him steadily.* LOUKA *goes out, leaving the door open.*

BLUNTSCHLI (*absently, sitting at the table as before, and putting down his papers*): Thats a remarkable looking young woman.

SERGIUS (*gravely, without moving*): Captain Bluntschli.

BLUNTSCHLI: Eh?

SERGIUS: You have deceived me. You are my rival. I brook no rivals. At six o'clock I shall be in the drilling-ground on the Klissoura road, alone, on horseback, with my sabre. Do you understand?

BLUNTSCHLI (*staring, but sitting quite at his ease*): Oh, thank you: thats a cavalry man's proposal. I'm in the artillery; and I have the choice of weapons. If I go, I shall take a machine gun. And there shall be no mistake about the cartridges this time.

SERGIUS (*flushing, but with deadly coldness*): Take care, sir. It is not our custom in Bulgaria to allow invitations of that kind to be trifled with.

BLUNTSCHLI (*warmly*): Pooh! dont talk to me about Bulgaria. You dont know what fighting is. But have it your own way. Bring your sabre along. I'll meet you.

SERGIUS (*fiercely delighted to find his opponent a man of spirit*): Well said, Switzer. Shall I lend you my best horse?

BLUNTSCHLI: No: damn your horse! thank you all the same, my dear fellow. (RAINA *comes in, and hears the next sentence.*) I shall fight you on foot. Horseback's too dangerous: I dont want to kill you if I can help it.

RAINA (*hurrying forward anxiously*): I have heard what Captain Bluntschli said, Sergius. You are going to fight. Why? (SERGIUS *turns away in silence, and goes to the stove, where he stands watching her as she continues, to* BLUNTSCHLI.) What about?

BLUNTSCHLI: I dont know: he hasnt told me. Better not interfere, dear young lady. No harm will be done: Ive often acted as sword instructor. He wont be able to touch me; and I'll not hurt him. It will save explanations. In the morning I shall be off home; and youll never see me or hear of me again. You and he will then make it up and live happily ever after.

RAINA (*turning away deeply hurt, almost with a sob in her voice*): I never said I wanted to see you again.

SERGIUS (*striding forward*): Ha! That is a confession.

RAINA (*haughtily*): What do you mean?

SERGIUS: You love that man!

RAINA (*scandalized*): Sergius!

SERGIUS: You allow him to make love to you behind my back, just as you treat me as your affianced husband behind his. Bluntschli: you knew our relations; and you deceived me. It is for that I call you to account, not for having received favors I never enjoyed.

BLUNTSCHLI (*jumping up indignantly*): Stuff! Rubbish! I have received no favors. Why, the young lady doesnt even know whether I'm married or not.

RAINA (*forgetting herself*): Oh! (*Collapsing on the ottoman.*) Are you?

SERGIUS: You see the young lady's concern, Captain Bluntschli. Denial is useless. You have enjoyed the privilege of being received in her own room, late at night—

BLUNTSCHLI (*interrupting him pepperily*): Yes, you blockhead! she received me with a pistol at her head. Your cavalry were at my heels. I'd have blown out her brains if she'd uttered a cry.

SERGIUS (*taken aback*): Bluntschli! Raina: is this true?

RAINA (*rising in wrathful majesty*): Oh, how dare you, how dare you?

BLUNTSCHLI: Apologize, man: apologize. (*He resumes his seat at the table.*)

SERGIUS (*with the old measured emphasis, folding his arms*): I never apologize!

RAINA (*passionately*): This is the doing of that friend of yours, Captain Bluntschli. It is he who is spreading this horrible story about me. (*She walks about excitedly.*)

BLUNTSCHLI: No: he's dead. Burnt alive.

RAINA (*stopping, shocked*): Burnt alive!

BLUNTSCHLI: Shot in the hip in a woodyard. Couldnt drag himself out. Your fellows' shells set the timber on fire and burnt him, with half a dozen other poor devils in the same predicament.

RAINA: How horrible!

SERGIUS: And how ridiculous! Oh, war! war! the dream of patriots and heroes! A fraud, Bluntschli. A hollow sham, like love.

RAINA (*outraged*): Like love! You say that before me!

BLUNTSCHLI: Come, Saranoff: that matter is explained.

SERGIUS: A hollow sham, I say. Would you have come back here if nothing had passed between you except at the muzzle of your pistol? Raina is mistaken about your friend who was burnt. He was not my informant.

RAINA: Who then? (*Suddenly guessing the truth*) Ah, Louka! my maid! my servant! You were with her this morning all that time after—after—Oh, what sort of god is this I have been worshipping! (*He meets her gaze with sardonic enjoyment of her disenchantment. Angered all the more, she goes closer to him, and says, in a lower, intenser tone.*) Do you know that I looked out of the window as I went upstairs to have another sight of my hero; and I saw something I did not understand then. I know now that you were making love to her.

SERGIUS (*with grim humor*): You saw that?

RAINA: Only too well. (*She turns away, and throws herself on the divan under the centre window, quite overcome.*)

SERGIUS (*cynically*): Raina: our romance is shattered. Life's a farce.

BLUNTSCHLI (*to* RAINA, *whimsically*): You see: he's found himself out now.

SERGIUS (*going to him*): Bluntschli: I have allowed you to call me blockhead. You may now call me a coward as well. I refuse to fight you. Do you know why?

BLUNTSCHLI: No; but it doesn't matter. I didnt ask the reason when you cried on; and I dont ask the reason now that you cry off. I'm a professional soldier! I fight when I have to, and am very glad to get out of it when I havnt to. Youre only an amateur: you think fighting's an amusement.

SERGIUS (*sitting down at the table, nose to nose with him*): You shall hear the reason all the same, my professional. The reason is that it takes two men—real men—men of heart, blood and honor—to make a genuine combat. I could no more fight with you than I could make love to an ugly woman. Youve no magnetism: youre not a man: youre a machine.

BLUNTSCHLI: (*apologetically*): Quite true, quite true. I always was that sort of chap. I'm very sorry.

SERGIUS: Psha!

BLUNTSCHLI: But now that youve found that life isnt a farce, but something quite sensible and serious, what further obstacle is there to your happiness?

RAINA (*rising*): You are very solicitous about my happiness and his. Do you forget his new love—Louka? It is not you that he must fight now, but his rival, Nicola.

SERGIUS: Rival!! (*bounding half across the room.*)

RAINA: Dont you know that theyre engaged?

SERGIUS: Nicola! Are fresh abysses opening? Nicola!

RAINA (*sarcastically*): A shocking sacrifice, isn't it? Such beauty! such intellect! such modesty! wasted on a middle-aged servant man. Really, Sergius, you cannot stand by and allow such a thing. It would be unworthy of your chivalry.

SERGIUS (*losing all self-control*): Viper! Viper! (*He rushes to and fro, raging.*)

BLUNTSCHLI: Look here, Saranoff: youre getting the worst of this.

RAINA (*getting angrier*): Do you realize what he has done, Captain Bluntschli? He has set this girl

as a spy on us; and her reward is that he makes love to her.

SERGIUS: False! Monstrous!

RAINA: Monstrous. (*Confronting him*) Do you deny that she told you about Captain Bluntschli being in my room?

SERGIUS: No; but—

RAINA (*interrupting*): Do you deny that you were making love to her when she told you?

SERGIUS: No; but I tell you—

RAINA (*cutting him short contemptuously*): It is unnecessary to tell us anything more. That is quite enough for us. (*She turns away from him and sweeps majestically back to the window.*)

BLUNTSCHLI (*quietly, as* SERGIUS, *in an agony of mortification, sinks on the ottoman, clutching his averted head between his fists*): I told you you were getting the worst of it, Saranoff.

SERGIUS: Tiger cat!

RAINA (*running excitedly to* BLUNTSCHLI): You hear this man calling me names, Captain Bluntschli?

BLUNTSCHLI: What else can he do, dear lady? He must defend himself somehow. Come (*very persuasively*): dont quarrel. What good does it do?

RAINA, *with a gasp, sits down on the ottoman, and after a vain effort to look vexedly at* BLUNTSCHLI, *falls a victim to her sense of humor, and actually leans back babyishly against the writhing shoulder of* SERGIUS.

SERGIUS: Engaged to Nicola! Ha! ha! Ah well, Bluntschli, you are right to take this huge imposture of a world coolly.

RAINA (*quaintly to* BLUNTSCHLI, *with an intuitive guess at his state of mind*): I daresay you think us a couple of grown-up babies, dont you?

SERGIUS (*grinning savagely*): He does: he does. Swiss civilization nursetending Bulgarian barbarism, eh?

BLUNTSCHLI (*blushing*): Not at all, I assure you. I'm only very glad to get you two quieted. There! there! let's be pleasant and talk it over in a friendly way. Where is this other young lady?

RAINA: Listening at the door, probably.

SERGIUS (*shivering as if a bullet had struck him, and speaking with quiet but deep indignation*): I will prove that that, at least, is a calumny. (*He goes with dignity to the door and opens it. A yell of fury bursts from him as he looks out. He darts into the passage, and returns dragging in* LOUKA, *whom he flings violently against the table, exclaiming*) Judge her, Bluntschli. Y o u , the cool impartial man: judge the eavesdropper.

LOUKA *stands her ground, proud and silent.*

BLUNTSCHLI (*shaking his head*): I mustnt judge her. I once listened myself outside a tent when there was a mutiny brewing. It's all a question of the degree of provocation. My life was at stake.

LOUKA: My love was at stake. I am not ashamed.

RAINA (*contemptuously*): Your love! Your curiosity, you mean.

LOUKA (*facing her and retorting her contempt with interest*): My love, stronger than anything y o u can feel, even for your chocolate cream soldier.

SERGIUS (*with quick suspicion to* LOUKA): What does that mean?

LOUKA (*fiercely*): It means—

SERGIUS (*interrupting her slightingly*): Oh, I remember: the ice pudding. A paltry taunt, girl!

MAJOR PETKOFF *enters, in his shirtsleeves.*

PETKOFF: Excuse my shirtsleeves, gentlemen. Raina: somebody has been wearing that coat of mine: I'll swear it. Somebody with a differently shaped back. It's all burst open at the sleeve. Your mother is mending it. I wish she'd make haste: I shall catch cold. (*He looks more attentively at them.*) Is anything the matter?

RAINA: No. (*She sits down at the stove, with a tranquil air.*)

SERGIUS: Oh no. (*He sits down at the end of the table, as at first.*)

BLUNTSCHLI (*who is already seated*): Nothing. Nothing.

PETKOFF (*sitting down on the ottoman in his old place*): Thats all right. (*He notices* LOUKA.) Anything the matter, Louka?

LOUKA: No, sir.

PETKOFF (*genially*): Thats all right. (*He sneezes.*) Go and ask your mistress for my coat, like a good girl, will you?

NICOLA *enters with the coat.* LOUKA *makes a pretence of having business in the room by taking the little table with the hookah away to the wall near the windows.*

RAINA (*rising quickly as she sees the coat on* NICOLA's *arm*): Here it is, papa. Give it to me, Nicola; and do you put some more wood on the fire. (*She takes the coat, and brings it to the* MAJOR, *who stands up to put it on.* NICOLA *attends to the fire.*)

PETKOFF (*to* RAINA, *teasing her affectionately*): Aha! Going to be very good to poor old papa just for one day after his return from the wars, eh?

RAINA (*with solemn reproach*): Ah, how can you say that to me, father?

PETKOFF: Well, well, only a joke, little one. Come: give me a kiss. (*She kisses him.*) Now give me the coat.

RAINA: No: I am going to put it on for you. Turn your back. (*He turns his back and feels behind him with his arms for the sleeves. She dexterously takes the photograph from the pocket and throws it on the table before* BLUNTSCHLI, *who covers it with a sheet of paper under the very nose of* SERGIUS, *who looks on amazed, with his suspicions roused in the highest degree. She then helps* PETKOFF *on with his coat.*) There, dear! Now are you comfortable?

PETKOFF: Quite, little love. Thanks. (*He sits down; and* RAINA *returns to her seat near the stove.*) Oh, by the bye, Ive found something funny. Whats the meaning of this? (*He puts his hand into the picked pocket.*) Eh? Hallo! (*He tries the other pocket.*) Well, I could have sworn—! (*Much puzzled, he tries the breast pocket.*) I wonder—(*trying the original pocket.*) Where can it—? (*He rises, exclaiming.*) Your mother's taken it!

RAINA (*very red*): Taken what?

PETKOFF: Your photograph, with the inscription: "Raina, to her Chocolate Cream Soldier: a Souvenir." Now you know theres something more in this than meets the eye; and I'm going to find it out. (*Shouting*) Nicola!

NICOLA (*coming to him*): Sir!

PETKOFF: Did you spoil any pastry of Miss Raina's this morning?

NICOLA: You heard Miss Raina say that I did, sir.

PETKOFF: I know that, you idiot. Was it true?

NICOLA: I am sure Miss Raina is incapable of saying anything that is not true, sir.

PETKOFF: Are you? Then I'm not. (*Turning to the others.*) Come: do you think I dont see it all? (*He goes to* SERGIUS, *and slaps him on the shoulder.*) Sergius: youre the chocolate cream soldier, arnt you?

SERGIUS (*starting up*): I! A chocolate cream soldier! Certainly not.

PETKOFF: Not! (*He looks at them. They are all very serious and very conscious.*) Do you mean to tell me that Raina sends things like that to other men?

SERGIUS (*enigmatically*): The world is not such an innocent place as we used to think, Petkoff.

BLUNTSCHLI (*rising*): It's all right, Major. I'm

the chocolate cream soldier. (PETKOFF and SER-
GIUS are equally astonished.) The gracious young
lady saved my life by giving me chocolate creams
when I was starving: shall I ever forget their
flavour! My late friend Stolz told you the story at
Pirot. I was the fugitive.

PETKOFF: You! (He gasps.) Sergius: do you
remember how those two women went on this
morning when we mentioned it? (SERGIUS smiles
cynically. PETKOFF confronts RAINA severely.)
Youre a nice young woman, arnt you?

RAINA (bitterly): Major Saranoff has changed his
mind. And when I wrote that on the photograph, I
did not know that Captain Bluntschli was married.

BLUNTSCHLI (startled into vehement protest):
I'm not married.

RAINA (with deep reproach): You said you were.

BLUNTSCHLI: I did not. I positively did not. I
never was married in my life.

PETKOFF (exasperated): Raina: will you kindly
inform me, if I am not asking too much, which of
these gentlemen you are engaged to?

RAINA: To neither of them. This young lady
(introducing LOUKA, who faces them all proudly) is
the object of Major Saranoff's affections at present.

PETKOFF: Louka! Are you mad, Sergius? Why,
this girl's engaged to Nicola.

NICOLA: I beg your pardon, sir. There is a
mistake. Louka is not engaged to me.

PETKOFF: Not engaged to you, you scoundrel!
Why, you had twenty-five levas from me on the
day of your betrothal; and she had that gilt bracelet
from Miss Raina.

NICOLA (with cool unction): We gave it out so,
sir. But it was only to give Louka protection. She
had a soul above her station; and I have been no
more than her confidential servant. I intend, as
you know, sir, to set up a shop later on in Sofia;
and I look forward to her custom and recommen-
dation should she marry into the nobility. (He goes
out with impressive discretion, leaving them all
staring after him.)

PETKOFF (breaking the silence): Well, I am—
hm!

SERGIUS: This is either the finest heroism or the
most crawling baseness. Which is it, Bluntschli?

BLUNTSCHLI: Never mind whether it's heroism
or baseness. Nicola's the ablest man Ive met in
Bulgaria. I'll make him manager of a hotel if he
can speak French and German.

LOUKA (suddenly breaking out at SERGIUS): I
have been insulted by everyone here. You set
them the example. You owe me an apology.

SERGIUS, like a repeating clock of which the
spring has been touched, immediately begins to
fold his arms.

BLUNTSCHLI (before he can speak): It's no use.
He never apologizes.

LOUKA: Not to you, his equal and his enemy. To
me, his poor servant, he will not refuse to apologize.

SERGIUS (approvingly): You are right. (He bends
his knee in his grandest manner.) Forgive me.

LOUKA: I forgive you. (She timidly gives him her
hand, which he kisses.) That touch makes me your
affianced wife.

SERGIUS (springing up): Ah! I forgot that.

LOUKA (coldly): You can withdraw if you like.

SERGIUS: Withdraw! Never! You belong to me.
(He puts his arm about her.)

CATHERINE comes in and finds LOUKA in SER-
GIUS's arms, with all the rest gazing at them in
bewildered astonishment.

CATHERINE: What does this mean?

SERGIUS releases LOUKA.

PETKOFF: Well, my dear, it appears that Sergius
is going to marry Louka instead of Raina. (She is
about to break out indignantly at him: he stops her
by exclaiming testily.) Dont blame me: I ve nothing to do with it. (He retreats to the stove.)

CATHERINE: Marry Louka! Sergius: you are
bound by your word to us!

SERGIUS (folding his arms): Nothing binds me.

BLUNTSCHLI (much pleased by this piece of common sense): Saranoff: your hand. My congratulations. These heroics of yours have their practical
side after all. (To LOUKA.) Gracious young lady:
the best wishes of a good Republican! (He kisses her
hand, to RAINA's great disgust, and returns to his
seat.)

CATHERINE: Louka: you have been telling
stories.

LOUKA: I have done Raina no harm.

CATHERINE (haughtily): Raina!

RAINA, equally indignant, almost snorts at the
liberty.

LOUKA: I have a right to call her Raina: she calls
me Louka. I told Major Saranoff she would never
marry him if the Swiss gentleman came back.

BUNTSCHLI (rising, much surprised): Hallo!

LOUKA (turning to RAINA): I thought you were
fonder of him than of Sergius. You know best
whether I was right.

BLUNTSCHLI: What nonsense! I assure you, my dear Major, my dear Madame, the gracious young lady simply saved my life, nothing else. She never cared two straws for me. Why, bless my heart and soul, look at the young lady and look at me. She, rich, young, beautiful, with her imagination full of fairy princes and noble natures and cavalry charges and goodness knows what! And I, a commonplace Swiss soldier who hardly knows what a decent life is after fifteen years of barracks and battles: a vagabond, a man who has spoiled all his chances in life through an incurably romantic disposition, a man—

SERGIUS (*starting as if a needle had pricked him and interrupting* BLUNTSCHLI *in incredulous amazement*): Excuse me, Bluntschli: what did you say had spoiled your chances in life?

BLUNTSCHLI (*promptly*): An incurably romantic disposition. I ran away from home twice when I was a boy. I went into the army instead of into my father's business. I climbed the balcony of this house when a man of sense would have dived into the nearest cellar. I came sneaking back here to have another look at the young lady when any other man of my age would have sent the coat back—

PETKOFF: My coat!

BLUNTSCHLI: —yes: thats the coat I mean—would have sent it back and gone quietly home. Do you suppose I am the sort of fellow a young girl falls in love with? Why, look at our ages! I'm thirty-four: I dont suppose the young lady is much over seventeen. (*This estimate produces a marked sensation, all the rest turning and staring at one another. He proceeds innocently.*) All that adventure which was life or death to me, was only a schoolgirl's game to her—chocolate creams and hide and seek. Heres the proof! (*He takes the photograph from the table.*) Now, I ask you, would a woman who took the affair seriously have sent me this and written on it "Raina, to her Chocolate Cream Soldier: a Souvenir"? (*He exhibits the photograph triumphantly, as if it settled the matter beyond all possibility of refutation.*)

PETKOFF: Thats what I was looking for. How the deuce did it get there? (*He comes from the stove to look at it, and sits down on the ottoman.*)

BLUNTSCHLI (*to* RAINA, *complacently*): I have put everything right, I hope, gracious young lady.

RAINA (*going to the table to face him*): I quite agree with your account of yourself. You are a romantic idiot. (BLUNTSCHLI *is unspeakably taken aback.*) Next time, I hope you will know the difference between a schoolgirl of seventeen and a woman of twenty-three.

BLUNTSCHLI (*stupefied*): Twenty-three!

RAINA *snaps the photograph contemptuously from his hand; tears it up; throws the pieces in his face; and sweeps back to her former place.*

SERGIUS (*with grim enjoyment of his rival's discomfiture*): Bluntschli: my one last belief is gone. Your sagacity is a fraud, like everything else. You have less sense than even I!

BLUNTSCHLI (*overwhelmed*): Twenty-three! Twenty-three!! (*he considers.*) Hm! (*Swiftly making up his mind and coming to his host.*) In that case, Major Petkoff, I beg to propose formally to become a suitor for your daughter's hand, in place of Major Saranoff retired.

RAINA: You dare!

BLUNTSCHLI: If you were twenty-three when you said those things to me this afternoon, I shall take them seriously.

CATHERINE (*loftily polite*): I doubt, sir, whether you quite realize either my daughter's position or that of Major Sergius Saranoff, whose place you propose to take. The Petkoffs and the Saranoffs are known as the richest and most important families in the country. Our position is almost historical: we can go back for twenty years.

PETKOFF: Oh, never mind that, Catherine. (*To* BLUNTSCHLI.) We should be most happy, Bluntschli, if it were only a question of your position; but hang it, you know, Raina is accustomed to a very comfortable establishment. Sergius keeps twenty horses.

BLUNTSCHLI: But who wants twenty horses? We're not going to keep a circus.

CATHERINE (*severely*): My daughter, sir, is accustomed to a first-rate stable.

RAINA: Hush, mother: youre making me ridiculous.

BLUNTSCHLI: Oh well, if it comes to a question of an establishment, here goes! (*He darts impetuously to the table; seizes the papers in the blue envelope; and turns to* SERGIUS.) How many horses did you say?

SERGIUS: Twenty, noble Switzer.

BLUNTSCHLI: I have two hundred horses. (*They are amazed.*) How many carriages?

SERGIUS: Three.

BLUNTSCHLI: I have seventy. Twenty-four of them will hold twelve inside, besides two on the box, without counting the driver and conductor. How many tablecloths have you?

SERGIUS: How the deuce do I know?

BLUNTSCHLI: Have you four thousand?

SERGIUS: No.

BLUNTSCHLI: I have. I have nine thousand six hundred pairs of sheets and blankets, with two thousand four hundred eider-down quilts. I have ten thousand knives and forks, and the same quantity of dessert spoons. I have three hundred servants. I have six palatial establishments, besides two livery stables, a tea gardens, and a private house. I have four medals for distinguished services; I have the rank of an officer and the standing of a gentleman; and I have three native languages. Shew me any man in Bulgaria that can offer as much!

PETKOFF (*with childish awe*): Are you Emperor of Switzerland?

BLUNTSCHLI: My rank is the highest known in Switzerland: I am a free citizen.

CATHERINE: Then, Captain Bluntschli, since you are my daughter's choice—

RAINA (*mutinously*): He's not.

CATHERINE (*ignoring her*):—I shall not stand in the way of her happiness. (PETKOFF *is about to speak.*) That is Major Petkoff's feeling also.

PETKOFF: Oh, I shall be only too glad. Two hundred horses! Whew!

SERGIUS: What says the lady?

RAINA (*pretending to sulk*): The lady says that he can keep his tablecloths and his omnibuses. I am not here to be sold to the highest bidder. (*She turns her back on him.*)

BLUNTSCHLI: I wont take that answer. I appealed to you as a fugitive, a beggar, and a starving man. You accepted me. You gave me your hand to kiss, your bed to sleep in, and your roof to shelter me.

RAINA: I did not give them to the Emperor of Switzerland.

BLUNTSCHLI: Thats just what I say. (*He catches her by the shoulders and turns her face-to-face with him.*) Now tell us whom you did give them to.

RAINA (*succumbing with a shy smile*): To my chocolate cream soldier.

BLUNTSCHLI (*with a boyish laugh of delight*): Thatll do. Thank you. (*He looks at his watch and suddenly becomes businesslike.*) Time's up, Major. Youve managed those regiments so well that youre sure to be asked to get rid of some of the infantry of the Timok division. Send them home by way of Lom Palanka. Saranoff: dont get married until I come back: I shall be here punctually at five in the evening on Tuesday fortnight. Gracious ladies (*his heels click*) good evening. (*He makes them a military bow, and goes.*)

SERGIUS: What a man! Is he a man!

TOPICS FOR DISCUSSION

1. What is Shaw getting at in his description (page 336) of the furniture in Petkoff's house?

2. Raina ends as a realist, but at the outset she is not merely the opposite, a self-deceived romanticist. Do you think the characterization—and the play—would be better if her transformation were from wholehearted romanticist to realist? Aristotle's terms *peripeteia* (reversal) and *anagnorisis* (recognition) are commonly used in discussions of tragedy (see page 68), but they can also be useful in discussions of comedy. What reversals and recognitions do you find in *Arms and the Man*? When Sergius is disenchanted, he claims (page 360) that war is "a hollow sham, like love." Is this recognition the point toward which the play has been moving? Explain.

3. Nicola is not essential to the plot. What, then, does he contribute to the play?

4. Sir Max Beerbohm says in a critique of *Arms and the Man* that we first cudgel our brains over the meaning of Sergius's marriage to Louka and finally must conclude that it has no meaning. Sergius marries her, Sir Max says, merely because Bluntschli will marry Raina, and the symmetry of the plot demands that Sergius marry someone and Louka is the only available unmarried woman. Do you think this marriage is a dramatic weakness? Explain.

5. Shaw once said: "It is the business of a writer of comedy to wound the susceptibilities

of his audience. The classic definition of his function is 'the chastening of morals by ridicule.'" Does *Arms and the Man* wound your susceptibilities? If so, to any purpose? Is the play a serious examination of the nature of soldiers and of war? Or does the clowning, especially in the third act, pretty much obliterate any intellectual content? Explain.

6. Sergius says to Bluntschli: "Youre not a man: youre a machine." W. B. Yeats, Shaw's countryman and contemporary, said something similar: "I listened to *Arms and the Man* with admiration and hatred. It seemed to me inorganic, logical straightness and not the crooked road of life, yet I stood aghast before its energy. . . . Presently I had a nightmare that I was haunted by a sewing machine, that clicked and shone, but the incredible thing was that the machine smiled, smiled perpetually." Have Sergius and Yeats a point? A related matter: On page 71 we quoted Bergson's view that figures who respond mechanically are often the objects of laughter because they are absurdly inadequate in their responses to the complexities of life. Does Bluntschli provide an example of Bergson's "mechanical encrusted on the living"? Or, on the contrary, does he embody a mental flexibility that lets him cut through the encrustations of society? And can it be argued that the romantic Sergius is Bergson's mechanical man?

7. One of the chief theories of laughter is neatly stated in Thomas Hobbes's *Leviathan* (1651):

> *Sudden Glory*, is the passion which maketh those *Grimaces* called Laughter; and is caused either by some sudden act of their own, that pleaseth them; or by the apprehension of some deformed thing in another, in comparison whereof they suddenly applaud themselves.

If *Arms and the Man* evokes laughter, is the laughter of Hobbes's sort? Does Hobbes's theory cover any or all laughable occurrences you can think of?

THE CHERRY ORCHARD

Anton Chekhov

Translated by Laurence Senelick

Anton Chekhov (1860–1904) received his medical degree from the University of Moscow in 1884, but he had already published some stories. His belief that his medical training assisted him in writing about people caused some people to find him cold, but on the whole the evidence suggests that he was a genial, energetic young man with considerable faith in reason and (as befitted a doctor) in science, and with very little faith in religion and in heroics. His major plays are *The Seagull* (1896), *Uncle Vanya* (1899), *Three Sisters* (1901), and, finally, *The Cherry Orchard* (1903), written during his last illness.

THE CAST[1]

RANEVSKAYA, LYUBOV ANDREEVNA, *a landowner* (Lyoo-BAWFF Ahn-DRAY-eff-nah Rahn-YEHFF-skei-ah)

ANYA, *her daughter, age 17* (AHN-yah)

VARYA, *her adopted daughter, age 24* (VAHR-yah)

GAEV, LEONID ANDREEVICH, *Ranevskaya's brother* (Lyaw-NEED Ahn-DRAY-eech GEI-ehff)

LOPAKHIN, YERMOLAI ALEKSEICH, *a businessman* (Yehr-mah-LEI Ah-lihk-SAY-eech Lah-PAH-kheen)

TROFIMOV, PYOTR SERGEEVICH, *a student* (PYAW-tr Trah-FEE-mawff Ser-GAY-veech)

SIMEONOV-PISHCHIK, BORIS BORISOVICH, *a landowner* (Seem-YAWN-awff PEESH-cheek)

CHARLOTTA IVANOVA, *a governess* (Sharh-LAW-tah Ee-VAHN-awff-nah)

YEPIKHODOV, SEMYON PANTELEEVICH, *a bookkeeper* (Sim-YAHN Pahn-til-YAY-eech Ippy-KHAW-dawff)

DUNYASHA, *a parlor-maid* (Doon-YAH-shah)

FIRS NIKOLAEVICH, *a footman, an old fellow of 87* (FEERRSS Nee-kaw-LEI-yeh-veech)

YASHA, *a young manservant* (YAH-shah)

A TRAMP

THE STATIONMASTER

A POSTAL CLERK

GUESTS, SERVANTS

The action takes place on MADAM RANEVSKAYA's *estate.*

---

[1] **Cast.** Unlike earlier dramatists like Gogol or Ostrovsky, Chekhov seldom resorts to word play in naming the characters in his full-length pieces, but to a Russian ear, certain associations can be made. *Lyubov* means "love" (perhaps Amy is the English equivalent), and a kind of indiscriminate love is indeed the soul of Ranevskaya's character. *Gaev* suggests *gaer*, buffoon, while *Lopakhin* may be derived from either *lopata*, a shovel, or *lopat'*, to shovel food down one's gullet—both words of the earth, earthy. *Simeonov-Pishchik* is a Dickensian combination of a noble boyar name and a silly one reminiscent of *pishchat'*, to chirp. A similar English appellation might be Montmorency-Tweet. [All notes are by the translator.]

Leigh Lawson (left), Judy Parfitt (center), and Caroline Langrisile (right) in a recent production of *The Cherry Orchard*. (Photograph by Donald Cooper © Photostage.)

ACT I

*ill known as the Nursery. One
'nto* ANYA's *bedroom. Dawn,
_ʒe up. It is already May, the
_ɩ are in blossom, but it is chilly in the
ʋrchard, there is a frost. The windows in the room
are shut.*

(*Enter* DUNYASHA *carrying a candle, and* LO-
PAKHIN *holding a book.*)

LOPAKHIN: Train's in, thank God. What's the
time?

DUNYASHA: Almost two. (*Blows out the candle.*)
Daylight already.

LOPAKHIN: But just how late was the train? Must
have been two hours at least. (*Yawns and stretches.*)
I'm a fine one, made quite a fool of myself! Drove
over here on purpose, so as to meet them at the
station, and fell asleep just like that . . . dozed off
in a chair. Annoying . . . but you should have
woken me up.

DUNYASHA: I thought you'd gone. (*Listening.*)
Listen, it sounds like they're coming.

LOPAKHIN (*listening*): No . . . the luggage has to
be brought in, and what-have-you. . . . (*Pause.*)
Lyubov Andreevna's been living abroad five years
now. I wonder what she's like these days. . . . She's
a good sort of person. An easygoing, unpretentious
person. I remember, when I was a lad of about
fifteen, my late father—at that time he kept a shop
here in the village—punched me in the face with
his fist, blood was pouring from my nose. . . .
We'd come into the yard for some reason or other,
and he was tipsy. Lyubov Andreevna, I remember
as if it were yesterday, she was still a young lady, so
slender, led me to the washbasin, right here in this
very room, the nursery. "Don't cry," says she,
"peasant boy, it'll heal in time for your wedding . . ."
(*Pause.*) Peasant boy. . . . My father, it's true, was
a peasant, and here am I in a white waistcoat and
tan shoes. Like a pig rooting in a pastry shop. . . .
Now here am I, rich, plenty of money, but if you
think it over and consider, once a peasant, always a
peasant. . . . (*Leafs through the book.*) I was
reading this book and couldn't make head or tail of
it. Reading and dozed off.

(*Pause.*)

DUNYASHA: The dogs didn't sleep all night, they
sense the mistress coming home.

LOPAKHIN: What's got into you, Dunyasha,
you're such a . . .

DUNYASHA: My hands are trembling. I'm going
to swoon.

LOPAKHIN: You're much too delicate, Dunyasha. Dressing up like a lady, fixing your hair like
one too. Mustn't do that. Mustn't forget who you
are.

(YEPIKHODOV *enters with a bouquet; he is wearing a jacket and brightly polished boots, which
squeak noisily. On entering, he drops the bouquet.*)

YEPIKHODOV (*picks up the bouquet*): Here, the
gardener sent them, he says to stick 'em in the
dining room. (*He hands* DUNYASHA *the bouquet.*)

LOPAKHIN: And bring me some beer.

DUNYASHA: Very good. (*She exits.*)

YEPIKHODOV: Three degrees of frost this morning, but the cherries are all in bloom. I can't
condone our climate. (*He sighs.*) I can't. I mean, it
doesn't seem to make an effort. Look, Yermolai
Alekseich, allow me to append, I bought myself
some boots the day before yesterday, and they, I
make bold to assert, squeak so much, it's quite out
of the question. What should I grease them with?

LOPAKHIN: Leave me alone. You're a pest.

YEPIKHODOV: Every day something unlucky
happens to me. But I don't complain, I'm used to
it. I even smile.

(DUNYASHA *enters and gives* LOPAKHIN *some
beer.*)

YEPIKHODOV: I'm on my way. (*Bumps into a
chair which falls over.*) There. . . . (*As if triumphant*) You see, pardon the expression, what a
circumstance, incidentally. . . . It's simply, you
might say conspicuous! (*He exits.*)

DUNYASHA: Just let me tell you, Yermolai Alekseich, Yepikhodov proposed to me.

LOPAKHIN: Ah!

DUNYASHA: I don't know what to do. . . . He's a
quiet sort, but sometimes he starts talking away,
and you can't understand a thing. It's nice and it's
sensitive, only you can't understand it. I kind of
like him. He's madly in love with me. He's an
unlucky sort of fellow, something happens every
day. So we've nicknamed him: twenty-two troubles. . . .

LOPAKHIN (*hearkening*): Listen, I think they're coming. . . .

DUNYASHA: Coming! What's the matter with me . . . I'm all over chills.

LOPAKHIN: They are coming. Let's go meet them. Will she recognize me? We haven't set eyes on one another for five years.

DUNYASHA (*in a flurry*): I'll faint this minute. . . . Ach, I'll faint!

(*We hear the sounds of two carriages drawing up to the house.* LOPAKHIN *and* DUNYASHA *exeunt quickly. The Stage is empty. Noises begin in the adjoining rooms.* FIRS, *leaning on a stick, hurries across the stage; he has just been to meet* LYUBOV ANDREEVNA: *he is wearing an old suit of livery and a top hat; he mutters something to himself, but no words can be made out. The off-stage noises keep growing louder. A voice: "Let's go through here."* LYUBOV ANDREEVNA, ANYA, *and* CHARLOTTA IVANOVNA *with a lapdog on a leash, the three dressed in travelling clothes,* VARYA *in an overcoat and kerchief,* GAEV, SIMEONOV-PISHCHIK, LOPAKHIN, DUNYASHA *with a bundle and a parasol, servants carrying suitcases—all pass through the room.*)

ANYA: Let's go through here. Mama, do you remember what room this was?

LYUBOV ANDREEVNA (*joyously, through tears*): The nursery!

VARYA: It's cold, my hands are numb. (*To* LYUBOV ANDREEVNA) Your rooms, the white and the violet, are still the same as ever, Mama dear.

LYUBOV ANDREEVNA: The nursery, my darling, beautiful room. . . . I slept here when I was a little girl. . . . (*She weeps.*) And now I'm like a little girl. . . . (*She kisses her brother and* VARYA *and then her brother again.*) And Varya is just the same as before, looks like a nun. And I recognized Dunyasha. . . . (*Kisses* DUNYASHA.)

GAEV: The train was two hours late. What's going on? What kind of organization is that?

CHARLOTTA (*to* PISHCHIK): My dog, he even eats nuts.

PISHCHIK (*astounded*): Can you imagine!

(*They all go out, except for* ANYA *and* DUNYASHA.)

DUNYASHA: We've been waiting and waiting. (*Helps to remove* ANYA's *overcoat and hat.*)

ANYA: I couldn't sleep the four nights on the train . . . now I'm so frozen.

DUNYASHA: You left during Lent, then there was snow, frost, and now? My darling! (*She laughs and kisses her.*) We kept waiting for you, my sweet, my precious . . . I'll tell you now, I can't keep it back another minute. . . .

ANYA (*weary*): Now what . . .

DUNYASHA: Yepikhodov the bookkeeper proposed to me right after Easter.

ANYA: You've got a one-track mind. . . . (*Setting her hair to rights.*) I've lost all my hair-pins. . . . (*She is very tired, practically staggering.*)

DUNYASHA: I just don't know what to think. He loves me, loves me so much!

ANYA (*peering through the door to her room, tenderly*): My room, my windows, as if I'd never gone away. I'm home! Tomorrow morning I'll get up, I'll run through the orchard. . . . Oh, if only I could get some sleep! I couldn't sleep the whole way. I was worried to death.

DUNYASHA: Day before yesterday, Pyotr Sergeich arrived.

ANYA (*joyfully*): Petya!

DUNYASHA: Sleeping in the bathhouse, practically lives there. "I'm afraid," says he, "of being a bother." (*Looking at her pocket watch*) Somebody ought to wake him up, but Varvara Mikhailovna gave the order not to. "You mustn't wake him up," she says.

(ENTER VARYA, *with a key-ring on her belt.*)

VARYA: Dunyasha, coffee immediately. . . . Mama dear is asking for coffee.

DUNYASHA: Right this minute. (*She exits.*)

VARYA: Well, thank God, you've come back. You're home again. (*Caressing her.*) My darling's come back! My beauty's come back!

ANYA: I've had so much to put up with.

VARYA: I can imagine!

ANYA: I left during Holy Week, it was so cold then. Charlotta kept on talking the whole way, performing card tricks. Why you stuck me with Charlotta. . . .

VARYA: You couldn't have travelled by yourself, precious. Seventeen years old!

ANYA: We got to Paris, it was cold there too, snowing. I speak awful French. Mama was living on a fifth floor walkup, she had all sorts of French visitors, ladies, some old Catholic priest with a little book, so smoky and tawdry. And all of a sudden I started pitying Mama, pitying her so, I took her head between my hands and couldn't let go. Then Mama kept hugging me, crying. . . .

VARYA (*through tears*): Don't talk about it, don't talk about it. . . .

ANYA: The villa near Menton she'd already sold, she had nothing left, nothing. And I hadn't a kopek left either, we barely got this far. And Mama doesn't understand! We sit down to dine at a station, and she orders the most expensive meal and gives each waiter a ruble tip. Charlotta's the same way. And Yasha insists on his share too, it's simply horrible. Of course Mama has her own valet Yasha, we brought him back. . . .

VARYA: I saw the loafer. . . .

ANYA: Well, how is everything? Have we paid off the interest?

VARYA: What with?

ANYA: Oh dear, oh dear. . . .

VARYA: In August the estate's to be auctioned off. . . .

ANYA: Oh dear. . . .

LOPAKHIN (*sticking his head in the door and bleating*): Me-e-eh. . . . (*Exits.*)

VARYA (*through tears*): I'd like to smack him one. . . . (*Shakes her fist.*)

ANYA (*embraces* VARYA, *quietly*): Varya, has he proposed? (VARYA *shakes her head.*) He *does* love you. . . . Why don't you talk it over, what are you waiting for?

VARYA: I don't think anything will come of it for us. He's got so much work, no time for me . . . and pays me no attention. May he go with God, it's hard for me even to get to see him . . . Everybody talks about our wedding, everybody's congratulating us, but as a matter of fact, there's nothing to it, it's all like a dream. . . . (*In a different tone*) You've got a new brooch like a bumble-bee.

ANYA (*sadly*): Mama bought it. (*Goes to her room, speaks merrily, like a child.*) And in Paris I went up in a balloon!

VARYA: My darling's come back! My beauty's come back!

(DUNYASHA *has returned with a coffee-pot and is making coffee.*)

VARYA (*stands near the door*): I go about the whole day, darling, with my household chores and dream and dream. If only there were a rich man for you to marry, I'd be at peace too, I'd go to a hermitage, then to Kiev . . . to Moscow, and so I'd keep on going to holy places . . . I'd go on and on. Glorious! . . .

ANYA: Birds are singing in the orchard. What's the time now?

VARYA: Must be three. Time for you to be asleep, dearest. (*Going into* ANYA's *room.*) Glorious!

(YASHA *enters with a lap rug, and a travelling bag.*)

YASHA (*crosses the stage; affectedly*): May I pass through here?

DUNYASHA: A body'd hardly recognize you, Yasha. How you've changed abroad.

YASHA: Mm. . . . Who are you?

DUNYASHA: When you left here, I was so high. . . . (*Measures from the floor.*) Dunyasha, Fyodor Kozoedov's daughter. You don't remember!

YASHA: Mm . . . some tomato! (*Glances around, embraces her; she shrieks and drops a saucer.* YASHA *hurriedly exits.*)

VARYA (*in the doorway, crossly*): Now what was that?

DUNYASHA (*through tears*): I broke a saucer. . . .

VARYA: That's good luck.

ANYA (*entering from her room*): We ought to warn Mama that Petya's here. . . .

VARYA: I gave orders not to wake him.

ANYA (*pensively*): Six years ago, a month after father died, brother Grisha drowned in the river, a sweet little boy, seven years old. Mama couldn't stand it, she went away, went away without looking back. . . . (*Shivers.*) How I understand her, if she only knew! (*Pause.*) And Petya Trofimov was Grisha's tutor, he might remind . . .

(*Enter* FIRS *in a jacket and white vest.*)

FIRS (*goes to the coffee pot; preoccupied*): The mistress will take her coffee in here. . . . (*Putting on white gloves*) Coffee ready? (*Sternly to* DUNYASHA) You! Where's the cream?

DUNYASHA: Ach, my God. . . . (*Exits hurriedly.*)

FIRS (*fussing with the coffee-pot*): Ech, you're half-baked. . . . (*Mumbles to himself*) Come home from Paris. . . . And the master went to Paris once upon a time . . . by coach. . . . (*Laughs.*)

VARYA: Firs, what are you on about?

FIRS: What's wanted? (*Joyfully*) My mistress has come home! I've been waiting! Now I can die. . . . (*Weeps with joy.*)

(*Enter* LYUBOV ANDREEVNA, GAEV, *and* SIMEONOV-PISHCHIK, *the last in a peasant coat of excellent cloth and wide trousers.* GAEV, *on entering, moves his arms and torso as if he were playing billiards.*)

LYUBOV ANDREEVNA: How does it go? Let me remember. . . . Yellow to the corner! Doublet to the center!

GAEV: Red to the corner! Once upon a time, sister, we used to sleep together in this very room, and now I'm already fifty-one years old, strange as it seems. . . .

LOPAKHIN: Yes, time flies.

GAEV: How's that?

LOPAKHIN: Time, I say, flies.

GAEV: It smells of cheap perfume in here.

ANYA: I'm going to bed. Good night, Mama. (*Kisses her mother.*)

LYUBOV ANDREEVNA: My precious little princess. (*Kisses her hands.*) Are you glad you're home? I can't pull myself together.

ANYA: Good night, Uncle.

GAEV (*kisses her face, hands*): God bless you. How like your mother you are! (*To his sister*) Lyuba, you were just the same at her age.

(ANYA *gives her hand to* LOPAKHIN *and* PISHCHIK, *exits, and shuts the door behind her.*)

LYUBOV ANDREEVNA: She's very tired.

PISHCHIK: Must be a long trip.

VARYA (*to* LOPAKHIN *and* PISHCHIK): Well, gentlemen? Three o'clock, by this time you've worn out your welcome.

LYUBOV ANDREEVNA (*laughing*): You never change, Varya. (*Draws* VARYA *to her and kisses her.*) First I'll have some coffee, then everybody will go. (FIRS *puts a cushion under her feet.*) Thank you, dear. I've grown accustomed to coffee. I drink it night and day. Thank you, old dear. (*Kisses* FIRS.)

VARYA: I'll see if all the luggage was brought in. . . . (*Exits.*)

LYUBOV ANDREEVNA; Can I really be sitting here? (*Laughs.*) I feel like jumping up and down and swinging my arms. (*Hides her face in her hands.*) But suppose I'm dreaming! God knows, I love my country, love it tenderly. I couldn't look at it from the carriage, couldn't stop crying. (*Through tears*) However, I must drink some coffee. Thank you, Firs, thank you, my old dear. I'm so glad you're still alive.

FIRS: Day before yesterday.

GAEV: He doesn't hear well.

LOPAKHIN: I've got to leave for Kharkov around five. What a nuisance! I wanted to have a look at you, to talk. . . . You're still as lovely as ever.

PISHCHIK (*breathing hard*): Even gotten prettier. . . . Dressed in Parisian fashions. . . . "Lost my cart with all four wheels. Lost my heart head over heels."

LOPAKHIN: Your brother, Leonid Andreich here, says that I'm a boor, a money-grubbing peasant, but it doesn't make the least bit of difference to me. Let him talk. The only thing I want is for you to believe in me as you once did, for your wonderful, heart-breaking eyes to look at me as they once did. Merciful God! My father was your grandfather's serf and your father's, but you, you personally, did so much for me once that I forgot it

all and love you like my own kin—more than my own kin.

LYUBOV ANDREEVNA: I can't sit still. I just can't. . . . (*Leaps up and walks about in great excitement.*) I won't survive the joy. . . . Laugh at me, I'm silly. . . . My dear bookcase! (*Kisses the bookcase.*) My little table.

GAEV: While you were away, Nanny died.

LYUBOV ANDREEVNA (*sits and drinks coffee*): Yes, may she rest in peace. They wrote me.

GAEV: And Anastasy died. Cross-eyed Petrusha left me and now he's working in town for the police. (*Takes a box from his pocket and eats caramels out of it.*)

PISHCHIK: My dear daughter Dashenka . . . says to say hello. . . .

LOPAKHIN: I'd like to tell you something very enjoyable, cheery. (*Looking at his watch.*) I have to go now, never time for a chat . . . well, here it is in two or three words. As you already know, the cherry orchard will be sold to pay your debts, the auction is set for August 22nd but don't you fret, dear lady, don't lose any sleep, there's a way out. . . . Here's my plan. Please pay attention! Your estate lies only thirteen miles from town, the railroad runs alongside it, and if the cherry orchard were divided into building lots and then leased out for summer cottages, you'd be making at the very least twenty-five thousand a year.

GAEV: Excuse me, what poppycock!

LYUBOV ANDREEVNA: I don't quite understand you, Yermolai Alekseich.

LOPAKHIN: You'll get out of the tenants about twenty-five rubles a year per two-and-a-half acres at the very least, and if you advertise now, I'll willingly bet anything that by fall there won't be a single unoccupied plot, it'll all be grabbed up. In a word, congratulations, you're saved. Wonderful location, deep river. Only, of course, we'll have to put it to rights, fix it up . . . for example, say, pull down all the old sheds, and this house, which is absolutely worthless, chop down the old cherry orchard.

LYUBOV ANDREEVNA: Chop it down? My dear, forgive me, but you don't understand anything. If there's one thing of interest in the entire district, even outstanding, it's none other than our cherry orchard.

LOPAKHIN: The only outstanding thing about this orchard is that it's enormous. The cherries grow once in two years, and there's no way of getting rid of them, nobody buys them.

GAEV: This orchard is cited in the Encyclopedia.

LOPAKHIN (*glancing at his watch*): If we don't

think up something and come to some decision, then on the twenty-second of August the cherry orchard and the whole estate will be sold at auction. Make up your mind! There's no other way out, I promise you. Absolutely none!

FIRS: In the old days, some forty–fifty years back—cherries were dried, preserved, pickled, made into jam, and sometimes . . .

GAEV: Be quiet, Firs.

FIRS: And sometimes whole cartloads of dried cherries were sent to Moscow and Kharkov. Then there was money! And in those days the dried cherries were soft, juicy, sweet, tasty. . . . They knew a recipe then. . . .

LYUBOV ANDREEVNA: And where's that recipe today?

FIRS: Forgotten. Nobody remembers.

PISHCHIK (to LYUBOV): What's going on in Paris? How was it? You ate frogs?

LYUBOV ANDREEVNA: I ate crocodiles.

PISHCHIK: Can you imagine . . .

LOPAKHIN: Up till now there were only gentry and peasants in the country, but now the summer tourists have sprung up. Every town, even the smallest, is surrounded these days by summer cottages. And I'll bet that during the next twenty-odd years the summer tourist will multiply fantastically. Now he only drinks tea on his veranda, but it might just happen that on his puny two-and-a-half acres, he goes in for farming and then your cherry orchard will become happy, rich, lush. . . .

GAEV (getting indignant): What poppycock!

(Enter VARYA and YASHA.)

VARYA: Mama dear, here are two telegrams for you. (Selects a key; with a jangle opens the old bookcase.) Here they are.

LYUBOV ANDREEVNA: This is from Paris. (Tears up the telegrams, without reading them.) I'm through with Paris.

GAEV: Lyuba, do you know how old that bookcase is? A week ago I pulled out the bottom drawer, and I looked, and there were numbers burnt into it. This bookcase was built exactly one hundred years ago. How do you like that? Maybe we ought to celebrate its anniversary. An inanimate object, but all the same, any way you look at it, a case to hold books.

PISHCHIK (astounded): A hundred years . . . Can you imagine! . . .

GAEV: Yes. . . . This thing. . . . (Clasping the bookcase) Dear, venerable bookcase! I salute your existence, which for over a century has been dedicated to the enlightened idealism of virtue and justice. Your mute appeal to constructive endeavor has not faltered in the course of a century, upholding (through tears) in generations of our line, courage, faith in a better future and nurturing within us ideals of decency and social consciousness.

(Pause.)

LOPAKHIN: Yes. . . .

LYUBOV ANDREEVNA: You're still the same, Lyonya.

GAEV (somewhat embarrassed): Carom to the right corner! Red to the center!

LOPAKHIN (glancing at his watch): Well, my time's up.

YASHA (handing medicine to LYUBOV): Maybe you'll take your pills now. . . .

PISHCHIK: Shouldn't take medicine, dearest lady. . . . It does no good, or harm. . . . Give that here . . . most respected lady.(He takes the pills, shakes them into his palm, blows on them, pops them into his mouth and drinks some beer.) There!

LYUBOV ANDREEVNA (alarmed): You've gone crazy!

PISHCHIK: I took all the pills.

LOPAKHIN: What a glutton!

(They all laugh.)

FIRS: The gentleman stayed with us during Holy Week, ate half-a-bucket of cucumbers. . . . (Mumbles.)

LYUBOV ANDREEVNA: What is he on about?

VARYA: For three years now he's been mumbling like that. We're used to it.

YASHA: Senility.

(CHARLOTTA IVANOVNA crosses the stage in a white dress. She is very slender, tightly laced, with a pair of pincenez on a cord at her belt.)

LOPAKHIN: Excuse me, Charlotta Ivanovna, I haven't yet had time to say hello to you. (Tries to kiss her hand.)

CHARLOTTA (pulling her hand away): If I let you kiss a hand, then next you'd be after a elbow, then a shoulder. . . .

LOPAKHIN: My unlucky day. (Everybody laughs.) Charlotta Ivanovna, show us a trick!

LYUBOV ANDREEVNA: Charlotta, show us a trick!

CHARLOTTA: No reason. I want to go to bed. (Exits.)

LOPAKHIN: We'll see each other again in three weeks. (Kisses LYUBOV ANDREEVNA's hand.) Meanwhile good-bye. It's time. (To GAEV) Be seeing you. (*Exchanges kisses with* PISHCHIK) Be seeing you. (*Gives his hand to* VARYA, *then to* FIRS *and* YASHA) I don't want to go. (*To* LYUBOV ANDREEVNA) If you think over this business of the cottages and decide, then let me know, I'll arrange a loan of fifty thousand or so. Give it some serious thought.

VARYA (*angrily*): Well, go once and for all!

LOPAKHIN: I'm going, I'm going. . . . (*He leaves.*)

GAEV: Boor. However, I apologize. . . . Varya's going to marry him, that's Varya's little fiancé!

VARYA: Don't say anything uncalled for, Uncle dear.

LYUBOV ANDREEVNA: Anyway, Varya, I shall be delighted. He's a good man.

PISHCHIK: A man, you've got to tell the truth . . . most worthy. . . . And my Dashenka . . . also says that . . . says all sorts of things. (*Snores but immediately wakes up.*) But by the way, most respected lady, will you lend me . . . two hundred forty rubles . . . tomorrow I've got to pay the interest on the mortgage. . . .

VARYA (*alarmed*): We haven't got any, we haven't got any!

LYUBOV ANDREEVNA: As a matter of fact, I haven't a thing.

PISHCHIK: It'll turn up. (*Laughs.*) I never lose hope. There, I think, all is lost, I'm ruined, lo and behold!—the railroad runs across my land and . . . pays me for it. And then, watch, something else will happen, if not today, tomorrow . . . Dashenka will win two hundred thousand . . . she's got a lottery ticket.

LYUBOV ANDREEVNA: The coffee's finished, now we can go to bed.

FIRS (*brushes* GAEV's *clothes, scolding*): You didn't put on them trousers again. What am I going to do with you!

VARYA (*quietly*): Anya's asleep. (*Quietly opens a window.*) The sun's up already, it's not so cold. Look, Mama dear: what wonderful trees! My God, the air! The starlings are singing.

GAEV (*opens another window*): The orchard's all white. You haven't forgotten, Lyuba? There's that long pathway leading straight on, straight on, like a stretched ribbon, it glistens on moonlit nights. You remember? You haven't forgotten?

LYUBOV ANDREEVNA (*looks through the window at the orchard*): O my childhood, my innocence! I slept in this nursery, gazed out at the orchard, happiness awoke with me every morning, and it was just the same then, nothing has changed. (*Laughs with joy.*) All, all white! O my orchard!

After the dark, drizzly autumn and the cold winter, you're young again, full of happiness, the heavenly angels haven't forsaken you. . . . If only I could lift this heavy stone from off my chest and shoulders, if only I could forget my past!

GAEV: Yes, and the orchard will be sold for debts, strange as it seems.

LYUBOV ANDREEVNA: Look, our poor Mama is walking through the orchard . . . in a white dress! (*Laughs with joy.*) There she is.

GAEV: Where?

VARYA: God be with you, Mama dear.

LYUBOV ANDREEVNA: There's nobody there, it just seemed so to me. At the right, by the turning to the summerhouse, a white sapling is bent over, looking like a woman. . . . (*Enter* TROFIMOV *in a shabby student's uniform and eyeglasses.*) What a marvelous orchard! White bunches of blossoms, blue sky . . .

TROFIMOV: Lyubov Andreevna! (*She stares round at him.*) I'll only pay my respects and then leave at once. (*Kisses her hand fervently.*) They told me to wait till morning, but I didn't have the patience. . . .

(LYUBOV ANDREEVNA *stares in bewilderment.*)

VARYA (*through tears*): This is Petya Trofimov.

TROFIMOV: Petya Trofimov, one-time tutor to your Grisha. . . . Can I have changed so much?

(LYUBOV ANDREEVNA *embraces him and weeps quietly.*)

GAEV (*embarrassed*): Come, come, Lyuba.

VARYA (*weeps*): Didn't I tell you, Petya, to wait till tomorrow.

LYUBOV ANDREEVNA: My Grisha . . . my little boy . . . Grisha . . . son. . . .

VARYA: There's no help for it, Mama dear. God's will be done.

TROFIMOV (*gently, through tears*): All right, all right. . . .

LYUBOV ANDREEVNA (*quietly weeping*): A little boy lost, drowned. . . . What for? What for, my friend? (*More quietly*) Anya's asleep in there, and I'm shouting . . . making noise. . . . Well now, Petya? Why have you become so homely? Why have you aged so?

TROFIMOV: On the train an old peasant woman called me "the mangy gent."

LYUBOV ANDREEVNA: You were just a boy in those days, a dear little student, but now your hair is thinning, eyeglasses. Are you really still a student? (*Goes to the door.*)

TROFIMOV: I suppose I'll be a perpetual student.

LYUBOV ANDREEVNA (*kisses her brother, then* VARYA): Well, let's go to bed. . . . You've aged too, Leonid.

PISHCHIK (*follows her*): That means it's time for bed. . . . Och, my gout. I'll stay over with you. . . . And if you would, Lyubov Andreevna, my soul, tomorrow morning early . . . two hundred forty rubles. . . .

GAEV: He never gives up.

PISHCHIK: Two hundred forty rubles . . . to pay the interest on the mortgage.

LYUBOV ANDREEVNA: I haven't any money, dovie.

PISHCHIK: We'll pay it back, dear lady. . . . A trifling sum. . . .

LYUBOV ANDREEVNA: Well, all right, Leonid will let you have it. . . . You give it to him, Leonid.

GAEV: I'll give it to him all right, hold out your pockets.

LYUBOV ANDREEVNA: What can we do, give it to him. . . . He needs it. . . . He'll pay it back.

(LYUBOV ANDREEVNA, TROFIMOV, PISHCHIK, *and* FIRS *exeunt.* GAEV, VARYA *and* YASHA *remain.*)

GAEV: My sister still hasn't outgrown the habit of squandering money. (*To* YASHA.) Out of the way, my good man, you smell like a chicken-coop.

YASHA (*with a sneer*): But you're just the same as you always were, Leonid Andreich.

GAEV: How's that? (*To* VARYA) What did he say?

VARYA (*to* YASHA): Your mother's come from the village, ever since yesterday she's been sitting in the servant's hall, wanting to see you. . . .

YASHA: To hell with her!

VARYA: Ach, disgraceful!

YASHA: That's all I need. She might have come tomorrow. (*Exits.*)

VARYA: Mama dear is just as she was before, she hasn't changed a bit. If it were in her power, she'd give away everything.

GAEV: Yes. . . . (*Pause.*) If a large number of cures is suggested for a particular disease, that means the disease is incurable. I think, wrack my brains, I've come up with all sorts of solutions, all sorts, and that means, actually, none. It would be nice to inherit a fortune from somebody, nice if we married off our Anya to a very rich man, nice to go off to Yaroslavl and try our luck with our auntie the Countess. Auntie's really very, very wealthy.

VARYA (*weeps*): If only God would help us.

GAEV: Stop snivelling. Auntie's very wealthy, but she isn't fond of us. In the first place, Sister married a courtroom lawyer, not a nobleman. . . . (ANYA *appears in the doorway.*) Married a commoner and behaved herself, well, you can't say very virtuously. She's a good, kind, splendid person, I love her very much, but, no matter how much you consider the extenuating circumstances, even so, it must be admitted she's depraved. You can feel it in her slightest movement.

VARYA (*whispering*): Anya's standing in the doorway.

GAEV: How's that? (*Pause.*) Extraordinary, something's got in my right eye. . . . My sight's beginning to fail. And Thursday, when I was at the County Court . . .

(ANYA *enters.*)

VARYA: Why aren't you asleep, Anya?

ANYA: I can't fall asleep. I can't.

GAEV: My little tadpole. (*Kisses* ANYA's *face, hands.*) My little girl. . . . (*Through tears*) You're not my niece, you're my angel, you're everything to me. Believe me, believe . . .

ANYA: I believe you, Uncle. Everybody loves you, respects you . . . but, dear Uncle, you must keep still, simply keep still. What were you saying just now about my Mama, your own sister? Why did you say that?

GAEV: Yes, yes. . . . (*Hides his face in his hands.*) In fact, it was terrible! My God! God, save me! And today I made a speech to the bookcase . . . like a fool! And as soon as I'd finished, I realized what a fool I'd been.

VARYA: True, Uncle dear, you ought to keep still. Just keep still. That's all.

ANYA: If you keep still, you'll be more at peace with yourself.

GAEV: I'll keep still. (*Kisses* ANYA's *and* VARYA's *hands.*) I'll keep still. Only this is business. Thursday I was at the County Court, well, some friends gathered around, started a conversation about this and that, six of one, half a dozen of the other, and it turns out it's possible to borrow money on an I.O.U. to pay the interest to the bank.

VARYA: If only God would help us!

GAEV: I'll go there on Tuesday and have another talk. (*To* VARYA) Stop snivelling. (*To* ANYA) Your Mama will talk to Lopakhin, he won't refuse her, of course. . . . And you, when you're rested up, will go to Yaroslav to your grandmother the Countess. That way we'll have action in three directions—and our business is in the bag! We'll pay off the interest. I'm positive. . . . (*Pops a caramel into his mouth.*) Word of honor. I'll swear by whatever you like, the estate won't be sold!

(*Excited*) I swear by my happiness! Here's my hand on it, call me a trashy, dishonorable man if I permit that auction! I swear with all my heart!

ANYA (*a more peaceful mood comes over her, she is happy*): You're so good, Uncle, so clever! (*Embraces her uncle.*) Now I feel calm! I'm calm! I'm happy!

(*Enter* FIRS.)

FIRS (*scolding*): Leonid Andreich, have you no fear of God? When are you going to bed?

GAEV: Right now, right now. Go along, Firs. I'll even undress myself, how about that. Well, children, beddy-bye. . . . Details tomorrow, but for now go to bed. (*Kisses* ANYA *and* VARYA.) I'm a man of the 'eighties.[1] . . . People don't put much stock in that period, but all the same I can say I've suffered considerably for my convictions in my time. It's not for nothing I'm loved by the peasant. You've got to know the peasant! You've got to know with what . . .

ANYA: You're at it again, Uncle!

VARYA: You must keep still, Uncle dear.

FIRS (*angrily*): Leonid Andreich!

GAEV: Coming, coming. . . . Go to bed. Two cushion carom to the center! I pocket the white . . . (*Exits followed by* FIRS, *hobbling.*)

ANYA: Now I'm calm. I don't want to go to Yaroslavl. I don't like Grandmama, but just the same, I'm calm. Thanks to Uncle. (*Sits down.*)

VARYA: I must get some sleep. I'm off. Oh, there was some unpleasantness while you were away. As you probably know, only the old servants live in the old quarters; Yefimushka, Polya, Yevstignei, oh, and Karp. They started letting certain tramps spend the night with them—I held my peace. Only then, I hear they're spreading the rumor that I gave orders to feed them nothing but peas. Out of stinginess, you see. . . . And this was all Yevstignei's doing. . . . Fine, thinks I. If that's how things are, thinks I, then just you wait. I send for Yevstignei. . . . (*Yawns.*) Up he trots. . . . What's wrong with

---

[1] **A man of the 'eighties:** The 1880s, when Russia was ruled by the reactionary Alexander III, was a period of intensive political repression. Revolutionary movements were forcibly suppressed, as were the more liberal journals, and social activism virtually ceased. The intelligentsia took refuge in the passive resistance of Tolstoyanism and a tame dabbling in "art for art's sake" (which explains Gaev's chatter about the decadents, mentioned in Act II). The feeling of social and political impotence led to the torpid aimlessness that is a common theme in Chekhov's works.

you, I say, Yevstignei . . . you're such a nincompoop. . . . (*Glancing at* ANYA.) Anechka! (*Pause.*) Fallen asleep! . . . (*Takes* ANYA *by the arm.*) Let's go to bed. . . . Let's go!. . . . (*Leads her.*) My darling has fallen asleep! Let's go. . . .

(*They exeunt. Far beyond the orchard a shepherd is playing his pipes.* TROFIMOV *crosses the stage and, seeing* ANYA *and* VARYA, *stops short.*)

VARYA: Ssh. . . . She's asleep . . . asleep. . . . Let's go, dearest.

ANYA (*softly, half-asleep*): I'm so tired . . . all the bells. . . . Uncle . . . dear . . . and mama and uncle . . .

VARYA: Let's go, dearest, let's go. . . . (*Exits into* ANYA's *room.*)

TROFIMOV (*moved*): My sunshine! My springtime!

ACT II

A field. An old, long-abandoned shrine leaning to one side. Beside it a well, large stones which were once, obviously, tombstones, and an old bench. At one side, towering poplars cast their shadows; here the cherry orchard begins. Further off are telegraph poles, and way in the distance, dimly sketched on the horizon, is a large town, which can be seen only in the best and clearest weather. A road to GAEV's *estate can be seen. Soon the sun will set.* CHARLOTTA, YASHA, *and* DUNYASHA *are sitting on the bench.* YEPIKHODOV *stands nearby and strums a guitar; everyone sits rapt in thought.* CHARLOTTA *is wearing an old peaked cap; she has taken a rifle off her shoulder and is adjusting a buckle on the strap.*

CHARLOTTA (*pensively*): I haven't got a proper passport. I don't know how old I am, and I always have the impression I'm still a young thing. When I was a little girl, my father and Mama used to go from fairground to fairground, giving performances, rather good ones. And I would jump the *salto mortale*[1] and do all sorts of different stunts. And when Papa and Mama died, a German lady took me to her house and started teaching me. Fine, I grew up, then turned into a governess. But where I'm from and who I am—I don't know. . . . Who my parents were, maybe they weren't married . . . I don't know. (*Pulls a cucumber from her pocket and eats it.*) I don't know anything. (*Pause.*)

---

[1] **Salto mortale:** Death-defying leap.

I would so like to talk, but there's no one to talk with. . . . No one.

YEPIKHODOV (*strums his guitar and sings*): "What care I for the noisy world, what are friends and foes to me. . . ." How pleasant to play the mandolin!

DUNYASHA: That's a guitar, not a mandolin. (*Looks in a hand-mirror and powders her nose.*)

YEPIKHODOV: To a lovesick lunatic, this is a mandolin. . . . (*Sings quietly*) "Were but my heart aflame with the spark of requited love. . . ."

(YASHA *joins in.*)

CHARLOTTA: These people are rotten singers. . . . Fooey! A pack of hyenas.

DUNYASHA (*to* YASHA): Anyway, how lucky you were to live abroad.

YASHA: Yes, of course. I can't disagree with you there. (*Yawns, then lights a cigar.*)

YEPIKHODOV: Stands to reason. Abroad everything has long since attained its complete maturation point.

YASHA: Goes without saying.

YEPIKHODOV: I'm a cultured fellow, I read all kinds of remarkable books, but somehow I can't figure out my own inclinations, what I personally want, to live or to shoot myself, strictly speaking, but nevertheless I always carry a revolver on my person. Here it is. . . . (*Displays a revolver.*)

CHARLOTTA: I'm done. Now I'll go. (*Slips the gun over her shoulder.*) Yepikhodov, you're a very clever fellow and a very frightening one; the women ought to love you madly. Brr! (*Exiting*) These clever people are all so stupid there's no one for me to talk to. . . . No one. . . . All alone, alone, I've got no one and . . . who I am, why I am, I don't know. (*Exits.*)

YEPIKHODOV: Strictly speaking, not flying off on tangents, I must declare concerning myself, by the way, that Fate treats me ruthlessly, as a storm does a rowboat. If, suppose, I'm wrong about this, then why when I woke up this morning, to give but a single example, I look and there on my chest is a terrifically huge spider. . . . This big. (*Uses both hands to show.*) Or then again, I'll take some beer, so as to drink it, and there, lo and behold, is something in the highest degree improper, such as a cockroach. . . . (*Pause.*) Have you read Buckle?[2]

(*Pause.*) I should like to trouble you with a couple of words, Avdotya Fyodorovna.

DUNYASHA: Go ahead.

YEPIKHODOV: I'm desirous of seeing you in private. . . . (*Sighs.*)

DUNYASHA: (*embarrassed*): All right . . . only first bring me my shawl . . . It's next to the cupboard . . . it's getting damp.

YEPIKHODOV: All right, ma'am . . . I'll fetch it, ma'am. . . . Now I know what I must do with my revolver. . . . (*Takes the guitar and exits playing it.*)

YASHA: Twenty-two troubles! Pretty stupid, take it from me. (*Yawns.*)

DUNYASHA: God forbid he should shoot himself. (*Pause.*) I've gotten jittery, always worrying. When I was still a little girl, they took me to the master's house, now I'm out of touch with the simple life, and my hands are white, as white as can be, like a young lady's. I've gotten sensitive, so delicate, ladylike, afraid of everything. . . . Awfully so. And, Yasha, if you deceive me, then I don't know what'll happen to my nerves.

YASHA (*kisses her*): Some tomato! Of course, every girl ought to know just how far to go, and if there's one thing I hate, it's a girl who misbehaves herself.

DUNYASHA: I love you ever so much, you're educated, you can discuss anything.

(*Pause.*)

YASHA (*yawns*): Yes'm. . . . The way I look at it, it's like this: if a girl loves somebody, that means she's immoral. (*Pause.*) Nice smoking a cigar in the fresh air. . . . (*Listening*) Someone's coming this way. . . . The gentry. . . . (DUNYASHA *impulsively embraces him.*) Go home, as if you'd been to the river for a swim, take this road or you'll run into them and they'll think I've been going out with you. I couldn't stand that.

DUNYASHA (*coughs quietly*): I've got a headache from your cigar. . . . (*Exits.*)

---

[2] **Buckle**: Henry Thomas Buckle—pronounced Bucklee—(1821–1862), whose *History of Civilization in England* (1857, 1861) posited that scepticism was the handmaiden of progress and that credulity (for which, read religion) retarded civilization's advance. He enjoyed immense popularity among progressive Russians in the 1860s, but by the end of the century seemed outmoded. Chekhov himself had read Buckle when a youth and quoted him approvingly in his early correspondence; as the years wore on, however, he began to take issue with many of Buckle's contentions. In *The Cherry Orchard*, he uses the reference to indicate that Yepikhodov's attempts at self-education are jejune and far behind the times.

(YASHA *remains sitting beside the shrine. Enter* LYUBOV ANDREEVNA, GAEV, *and* LOPAKHIN.)

LOPAKHIN: You've got to decide once and for all—time won't stand still. It's really quite a dead issue. Do you agree to rent land for cottages or not? Answer in one word: yes or no? Just one word!

LYUBOV ANDREEVNA: Who's been smoking those revolting cigars here? . . . (*Sits.*)

GAEV: Now that the railroad's in operation, it's become convenient. (*Sits.*) You ride to town and have lunch . . . yellow to the center! I ought to stop off at home, play one game. . . .

LYUBOV ANDREEVNA: You'll have time.

LOPAKHIN: Just one word! (*Pleading.*) Give me an answer!

GAEV (*yawning*): How's that?

LYUBOV ANDREEVNA (*looking into her purse*): Yesterday I had lots of money, but today there's very little. My poor Varya for economy's sake feeds everybody milk soup, in the kitchen the old people get nothing but peas, and somehow I'm spending recklessly. . . . (*Drops the purse, scattering gold coins.*) Oh dear, spilled all over the place. . . . (*Annoyed.*)

YASHA: Allow me, I'll pick them up at once. (*Gathers the money.*)

LYUBOV ANDREEVNA: That's sweet of you, Yasha. And why did I go into town for lunch. . . . That shabby restaurant of yours with its music, the tablecloths smelt of soap. . . . Why drink so much, Lyonya? Why eat so much? Why talk so much? Today in the restaurant you started in talking a lot again and all off the subject. About the 'seventies, about the decadents. And who to? Talking to waiters about the decadents!

LOPAKHIN: Yes.

GAEV (*waves his hands*): I'm incorrigible, it's obvious. . . . (*Irritably, to* YASHA) What's the matter, forever whirling around in front of us. . . .

YASHA (*laughing*): I can't hear your voice without laughing.

GAEV (*to his sister*): Either he goes, or I do. . . .

LYUBOV ANDREEVNA: Go away, Yasha, run along.

YASHA (*handing the purse to* LYUBOV ANDREEVNA): I'll go right now. (*Barely restraining his laughter.*) This very minute. . . . (*Exits.*)

LOPAKHIN: Rich old Deriganov intends to purchase your estate. They say he's coming to the auction.

LYUBOV ANDREEVNA: Where did you hear that?

LOPAKHIN: They were discussing it in town.

GAEV: Our aunt in Yaroslavl promised to send something, but when and how much she'll send I don't know. . . .

LOPAKHIN: How much is she sending? A hundred thousand? Two hundred?

LYUBOV ANDREEVNA: Well . . . ten or fifteen thousand—and we're grateful for that much.

LOPAKHIN: Excuse me, but such frivolous people as you, my friends, such unbusinesslike, peculiar people I never encountered before. Somebody tells you in plain Russian your estate is going to be sold, but you simply refuse to understand.

LYUBOV ANDREEVNA: But what are we going to do? Inform us, what?

LOPAKHIN: I inform you every day. Every day I tell you one and the same thing. Both the cherry orchard and the land have got to be leased as lots for cottages, do it right now, immediately—the auction is staring you in the face! Will you understand! Decide once and for all that there'll be cottages, they'll lend you as much money as you want, and then you'll be saved.

LYUBOV ANDREEVNA: Summer cottages and summer tourists—it's so vulgar, excuse me.

GAEV: I agree with you wholeheartedly.

LOPAKHIN: I'll either burst into tears or scream or fall down in a faint. It's too much for me! You're wearing me out! (*To* GAEV) You old woman!

GAEV: How's that?

LOPAKHIN: Old woman! (*Starts to exit.*)

LYUBOV ANDREEVNA (*frightened*): No, don't go, stay, dovie. Please! Maybe we'll think of something.

LOPAKHIN: What's there to think about?

LYUBOV ANDREEVNA: Don't go, please. With you here somehow it's jollier. . . . (*Pause.*) I keep anticipating something, as if the house were about to collapse on top of us.

GAEV (*in deep meditation*): Off the cushion to the corner . . . double to the center. . . .

LYUBOV ANDREEVNA: We've sinned so very much. . . .

LOPAKHIN: What kind of sins have you got. . . .

GAEV (*pops a caramel into his mouth*): They say I've eaten up my whole estate in caramels. . . . (*Laughs.*)

LYUBOV ANDREEVNA: Oh, my sins. . . . I've always thrown money around recklessly, like a maniac, and married a man who produced nothing but debts. My husband died of champagne—he drank frightfully—and then, to my misfortune, I fell in love with another man, had an affair, and just at that time—this was my first punishment, dropped right on my head—the river over there . . . my little boy drowned, and I went abroad, went for good, so as never to return, never see that river again . . . I shut my eyes, ran away, beside myself, and *he* came after me . . . cruelly, brutally. I bought a villa near Menton, because *he* fell ill there, and for three years I didn't know what it was to rest day or night: the invalid exhausted me, my heart shrivelled up. But the next year, when the villa was sold for debts, I went to Paris, and there he robbed me, ran off and had an affair with another woman, I tried to poison myself . . . so silly, so shameful . . . and suddenly I had a longing for Russia, for my country, my little girl. . . . (*Wipes away her tears.*) Lord, Lord, be merciful, forgive me my sins! Don't punish me anymore! (*Takes a telegram out of her pocket.*) I received this today from Paris. . . . He begs my forgiveness, implores me to come back. . . . (*Tears up telegram.*) Sounds like music somewhere. (*Listens.*)

GAEV: That's our famous Jewish orchestra. You remember, four fiddles, a flute and a double bass.

LYUBOV ANDREEVNA: Does it still exist? We ought to hire them sometime and throw a party.

LOPAKHIN (*listening*): I don't hear it. . . . (*Sings softly*) "And for cash the Prussians will Frenchify the Russians." (*Laughs.*) What a play I saw at the theatre yesterday, very funny.

LYUBOV ANDREEVNA: And most likely there was nothing funny about it. It's not for you to look at plays, you should look at yourselves more. You all lead such gray lives, you talk such utter nonsense.

LOPAKHIN: That's true. I've got to admit, our life is idiotic. . . . (*Pause.*) My daddy was a peasant, an ignoramus, he didn't understand anything, didn't teach me but kept getting drunk and beating me with a stick. When you come down to it, I'm the same kind of idiot and ignoramus. I never studied anything, my handwriting is terrible, I write, I'm ashamed to show it to people, like a pig.

LYUBOV ANDREEVNA: You ought to get married, my friend.

LOPAHKIN: Yes . . . that's true.

LYUBOV ANDREEVNA: You should marry our Varya; she's a good girl.

LOPAKHIN: Yes.

LYUBOV ANDREEVNA: I adopted her from the common folk, she works the livelong day, but the main thing is she loves you. Yes and you've cared for her for a long time.

LOPAKHIN: Why not? I'm not against it. . . . She's a good girl.

(*Pause.*)

GAEV: They've offered me a position at the bank. Six thousand a year. . . . Did you hear?

LYUBOV ANDREEVNA: You indeed! Stay where you are. . . .

(FIRS *enters; he is carrying an overcoat.*)

FIRS (*to* GAEV): Please, sir, put it on, it's damp here.

GAEV (*putting on the overcoat*): You're a pest, my man.

FIRS: Never you mind. . . . You went out this morning, didn't tell me. (*Inspects him.*)

LYUBOV ANDREEVNA: How old you're getting, Firs!

FIRS: What's wanted?

LOPAKHIN: The mistress says, you're getting very old!

FIRS: I've lived a long time. They were planning my wedding, long before your daddy was even born. . . . (*Laughs.*) And when the serfs was freed,[3] I was already head valet. Those days I didn't hanker to be freed, I stayed by the masters. . . . (*Pause.*) And I remember, everybody was glad, but what they was glad about, they didn't know themselves.

LOPAKHIN: It used to be nice all right. For instance, you got flogged.

FIRS (*not having heard*): I'll say. The peasants stood by the masters, the masters stood by the peasants, but now everything is topsy-turvy, can't figure out nothing.

GAEV: Keep quiet, Firs. Tomorrow I have to go to town. They promised to introduce me to some general, who might make us a loan on an I.O.U.

LOPAKHIN: Nothing'll come of it. And you won't pay the interest, you can be sure.

LYUBOV ANDREEVNA: He's raving. There are no such generals.

(*Enter* TROFIMOV, ANYA, *and* VARYA.)

GAEV: And here comes our crowd.

ANYA: Mama's sitting down.

LYUBOV ANDREEVNA (*tenderly*): Come, come. . . . My darlings. . . . (*kissing* ANYA *and* VARYA.) If

---

[3] **When the serfs was freed:** The serfs were emancipated by Alexander II in 1861, two years before Lincoln followed suit. Under the terms of the Emancipation Act, peasants were allotted land but had to pay back the government in annual installments, the sum used to indemnify former landowners. House serfs, on the other hand, were allotted no land. Both these conditions caused tremendous hardship and were responsible for great unrest among the newly manumitted. So there is more than a grain of truth in Firs's jeremiad.

only you both knew how much I love you. Sit beside me, that's right.

(*Everyone sits down.*)

LOPAKHIN: Our perpetual student is always stepping out with the ladies.

TROFIMOV: None of your business.

LOPAKHIN: Soon he'll be fifty and he'll still be a student.

TROFIMOV: Stop your idiotic jokes.

LOPAKHIN: What are you getting angry about, you crank?

TROFIMOV: Stop pestering me.

LOPAKHIN (*laughs*): May I ask, what's your opinion of me?

TROFIMOV: Here's my opinion, Yermolai Alekseich. You're a rich man, soon you'll be a millionaire. And in the same way a wild beast that devours everything that crosses its path is necessary to the conversion of matter, *you're* necessary.

(*Everyone laughs.*)

VARYA: Petya, tell us about the planets instead.

LYUBOV ANDREEVNA: No, let's go with yesterday's conversation.

TROFIMOV: What was that about?

GAEV: About human pride.

TROFIMOV: Yesterday we talked for quite a while, but we didn't get anywhere. In a proud man, according to you, there's something mystical. It may be your viewpoint's the right one, but if we reason it out simply, without frills, what pride can there be, is there any sense to it, if Man is poorly constructed physiologically, if the vast majority is crude, unthinking, profoundly wretched? We ought to stop admiring ourselves. We should just work.

GAEV: You'll die nonetheless.

TROFIMOV: Who knows? What does that mean—you'll die? Maybe Man has a hundred senses and with death only five, the ones known to us, perish, but the remaining ninety-five live on.

LYUBOV ANDREEVNA: Aren't you clever, Petya. . . .

LOPAKHIN (*ironically*): Awfully!

TROFIMOV: Mankind moves forward, perfecting its powers. Everything that's unattainable for us now will some day come within our grasp and our understanding, only we've got to work to help the Truth seekers with all our might. Here in Russia very few people do any work at the moment. The vast majority of educated people, as I know them, are searching for nothing, do nothing, and so far aren't capable of work. They call themselves intellectuals, but they refer to their servants by pet names, treat the peasants like animals, are poorly informed, read nothing serious, do absolutely nothing, just talk about science, barely understand art. They're all intense, they all have glum faces, and all they talk about is major concerns, they philosophize, but meanwhile anybody can see that the working class is abominably fed, sleeps without pillows, thirty or forty to a single room, everywhere bedbugs, foul odors, dampness, moral filth. . . . And obviously all our nice chitchat serves only to shut our own eyes and other people's. Show me, where are the day-care centers we do so much talking about so often, where are the reading rooms? People only write about them in novels, in fact there aren't any. There's only dirt, vulgarity, Asiatic bestiality. . . . I distrust and don't care for very intense faces, I distrust intense conversations. It's better to keep still!

LOPAKHIN: Take me, I get up before five every morning, I work from dawn to dusk, well, I always have money on hand, my own and other people's, and I notice what the people around me are like. You only have to start in business to find out how few honest, decent people there are. Sometimes, when I can't sleep, I think: "Lord, you gave us vast forests, boundless fields, the widest horizons, and living here, we ourselves ought to be regular giants."

LYUBOV ANDREEVNA: What do you need giants for? . . . They're only useful in fairy tales, anywhere else they're scary.

(*Far upstage* YEPIKHODOV *crosses and plays his guitar.*)

LYUBOV ANDREEVNA (*dreamily*): There goes Yepikhodov. . . .

ANYA (*dreamily*): There goes Yepikhodov. . . .

GAEV: The sun is setting ladies and gentlemen.

TROFIMOV: Yes.

GAEV (*quietly, as if declaiming*): Oh, Nature, wondrous creature, aglow with eternal radiance, beautiful yet impassive, you, whom we call Mother, merging within yourself Life and Death, you vitalize and you destroy. . . .

VARYA (*pleading*): Uncle dear!

ANYA: Uncle, you're at it again!

TROFIMOV: You'd better bank the yellow to the center doublet.

GAEV: I'll keep still, keep still.

(*Everyone sits down, absorbed in thought. The*

only sound is FIRS *softly muttering. Suddenly a distant sound is heard, as if from the sky, the sound of a snapped string, dying away, mournfully.*)

LYUBOV ANDREEVNA: What's that?

LOPAKHIN: I don't know. Somewhere far off in a mineshaft a bucket dropped. But somewhere very far off.

GAEV: Or perhaps it was some kind of bird . . . such as a heron.

TROFIMOV: Or an owl . . .

LYUBOV ANDREEVNA (*shivers*): Unpleasant anyway.

(*Pause.*)

FIRS: Before the disaster it was the same: the screech-owl hooted and the samovar hummed non-stop.

GAEV: Before what disaster?

FIRS: Before the serfs were freed.

(*Pause.*)

LYUBOV ANDREEVNA: Come everyone, let's go home. Evening's coming on. (*To* ANYA) You've got tears in your eyes. . . . What is it, my little girl? (*Kisses her.*)

ANYA: Nothing special, Mama. Never mind.

TROFIMOV: Someone's coming.

(*A* TRAMP *appears, in a shabby white peaked cap, and an overcoat; he's tipsy.*)

TRAMP: Allow me to inquire, can I reach the station straight on from here?

GAEV: You can. Follow that road.

TRAMP: I'm extremely obliged to you. (*Coughs.*) Splendid weather. . . . (*Declaiming*) "Brother mine, suffering brother . . . come to Volga, whose laments . . ." (*To* VARYA) Mademoiselle, bestow some thirty kopeks on a famished fellow Russian. . . .

(VARYA *is alarmed, screams.*)

LOPAKHIN (*angrily*): That'll be enough of that!

LYUBOV ANDREEVNA (*flustered*): Take this . . . here you are. . . . (*Looks in her purse.*) No silver. . . . Never mind, here's a gold piece for you. . . .

TRAMP: Extremely obliged to you! (*Exits.*)

(*Laughter.*)

VARYA (*frightened*): I'm going. . . . I'm going. . . . Ach, Mama dear, there's nothing in the house for people to eat, and you gave him a gold-piece.

LYUBOV ANDREEVNA: What can you do with a silly like me! I'll let you have everything I've got

when we get home. Yermolai Alekseich, lend me some more!

LOPAKHIN: Gladly.

LYUBOV ANDREEVNA: Come along, ladies and gentlemen, it's time. And look, Varya, we've made quite a match for you, congratulations.

VARYA (*through tears*): You mustn't joke about this, Mama.

LOPAKHIN: Oldphelia, get thee to a nunnery.[4] . . .

GAEV: My hands are trembling: it's been a long time since I played billiards.

LOPAKHIN: Oldphelia, oh nymph, in thy horizons be all my sins remembered!

LYUBOV ANDREEVNA: Come along, ladies and gentlemen. Almost time for supper.

VARYA: He scared me. My heart's pounding so.

LOPAKHIN: I remind you, ladies and gentlemen, on the twenty-second of August the estate will be auctioned off. Think about that! . . . Think! . . .

(*Exeunt everyone except* TROFIMOV *and* ANYA.)

ANYA (*laughing*): Thank the tramp, he scared off Varya, now we're alone.

TROFIMOV: Varya's afraid we'll suddenly fall in love with one another, so she hangs around us all day long. Her narrow mind can't comprehend that we're above love. Avoiding the petty and specious that keeps us from being free and happy, that's the goal and meaning of our life. Forward! We march irresistibly toward the shining star, glowing there in the distance! Forward! No dropping behind, friends!

ANYA (*stretching up her arms*): You speak so well! (*Pause.*) It's wonderful here today.

TROFIMOV: Yes, superb weather.

ANYA: What you have done to me, Petya, why have I stopped loving the cherry orchard as I did? I loved it so tenderly, there seemed to me no finer place on earth than our orchard.

TROFIMOV: All Russia is our orchard. The world is wide and beautiful and there are many wonderful places in it. (*Pause.*) Just think, Anya: your grandfather, great-grandfather and all your ancestors were slave-owners, owners of living souls, and from every cherry in the orchard, every leaf, every tree trunk there must be human beings watching you, you must hear voices. . . . To own living souls—it's really corrupted all of you, those who lived before and those living now, so that your

---

4 Oldphelia: Lopakhin is apparently an avid theatre-goer and misquotes from one of the many bad Russian translations of Shakespeare. The reference is to Hamlet's admonition to Ophelia.

mother, you, your uncle, no longer notice that you're living in debt, at other peoples' expense, at the expense of those people whom you wouldn't even let beyond your front hall. . . . We're at least two hundred years behind the times, we've still got absolutely nothing, no definite attitude to the past, we just philosophize, complain we're depressed or drink vodka. Yet it's so clear that before we start living in the present, we must first atone for our past, finish with it, and we can atone for it only through suffering, only through extraordinary, incessant labor. Understand that, Anya.

ANYA: The house we live in hasn't been our house for a long time, and I'll go away, I give you my word.

TROFIMOV: If you have the housekeeper's keys, throw them down the well and go away. Be free as the wind.

ANYA (*enraptured*): You speak so well!

TROFIMOV: Believe me, Anya, believe! I'm not yet thirty, I'm young. I'm still a student, but I've already undergone so much! When winter comes, I'm starved, sick, worried, poor as a beggar, and—where haven't I been chased by Fate, where haven't I been! And yet, always, every moment of the day and night, my soul has been full of inexplicable presentiments. I foresee happiness, Anya, I can see it already. . . .

ANYA (*dreamily*): The moon's on the rise.

(*We can hear* YEPIKHODOV *playing the same gloomy tune as before on his guitar. The moon comes up. Somewhere near the poplars* VARYA *is looking for* ANYA *and calling:* "Anya! Where are you?")

TROFIMOV: Yes, the moon's on the rise. (*Pause.*) Here's happiness, here it comes, drawing closer and closer, I can already hear its footsteps. And if we don't see it, can't recognize it, what's wrong with that? Others will see it!

VARYA'S VOICE: Anya! Where are you?

TROFIMOV: That Varya again! (*Angrily*) Appalling!

ANYA: So what? Let's go down to the river. It's nice there.

TROFIMOV: Let's go. (*They exit.*)

VARYA'S VOICE: Anya! Anya!

ACT III

The drawing room, separated from the ballroom by an arch. A chandelier is alight. We can hear, as if in the hallway, a Jewish orchestra, the same mentioned in Act II. *Evening. Grand-rond is being played in the ballroom.* SIMEONOV-PISHCHIK'S *voice:* "Promenade à une paire!" *Enter the drawing room: in the first couple* PISHCHIK *and* CHARLOTTA IVANOVNA, *in the second* TROFIMOV *and* LYUBOV ANDREEVNA, *in the third* ANYA *and the* POSTAL CLERK, *in the fourth* VARYA *and the* STATIONMASTER, *etc.* VARYA *is weeping quietly and while dancing, wipes away the tears. In the last couple* DUNYASHA. *They go through the drawing-room.* PISHCHIK *calls out:* "Grand-rond balancez!" *and* "Les cavaliers à genoux et remerciez vos dames!" FIRS *in a tail-coat crosses the room with seltzer bottle on a tray.* PISHCHIK *and* TROFIMOV *enter the room.*

PISHCHIK: I've got high blood pressure, I've already had two strokes, it's tough dancing, but as the saying goes, when you run with the pack, bark or don't bark, but keep on wagging your tail. Actually I've got the constitution of a horse. My late father, what a cut-up, rest in peace, used to talk of our ancestry as if our venerable line, the Simeonov-Pishchiks, were descended from the very horse Caligula made a Senator. . . . (*Sits down.*) But here's my problem: no money! A hungry dog believes only in meat. . . . (*Snores and immediately wakes up.*) Just like me. . . . I can't think of anything but money. . . .

TROFIMOV: As a matter of fact, there *is* something horsey about your build.

PISHCHIK: So what . . . a horse is a fine beast . . . you could sell a horse. . . .

(*We hear billiards played in the next room.* VARYA *appears under the arch in the ballroom.*)

TROFIMOV (*teasing*): Madam Lopakhin! Madam Lopakhin!

VARYA (*angrily*): Mangy gent!

TROFIMOV: Yes, I'm a mangy gent and proud of it!

VARYA (*brooding bitterly*): Here we've hired musicians and what are we going to pay them with? (*Exits.*)

TROFIMOV (*to* PISHCHIK): If the energy you've wasted in the course of a lifetime tracking down money to pay off interest had gone into something else, then you probably could have turned the world upside-down.

PISHCHIK: Nietzche[1] . . . a philosopher . . . the

---

[1] **Nietzche:** Friedrich Wilhelm Nietzsche (1884–1900), whose philosophy encourages a new "master" morality for Supermen and instigates revolt against the conventional constraints of Western civilization.

greatest, most famous . . . a man of immense intellect, says in his works it's justifiable to counterfeit money.

TROFIMOV: So you've read Nietzsche?

PISHCHIK: Well . . . Dashenka told me. But now I'm in such straits that if it came to counterfeiting money . . . Day after tomorrow three hundred rubles to pay . . . I've already borrowed a hundred and thirty. . . . (*Feeling his pockets, alarmed.*) The money's gone! I've lost the money! (*Through tears*) Where's the money? (*Gleefully*) Here it is, in the lining. . . . I was really sweating for a minute.

(*Enter* LYUBOV ANDREEVNA *and* CHARLOTTA IVANOVNA.)

LYUBOV ANDREEVNA (*humming a lively dance*): Why is Lyonya taking so long? What's he doing in town? (*To* DUNYASHA) Dunyasha, offer the musicians some tea. . . .

TROFIMOV: The auction didn't come off, in all likelihood.

LYUBOV ANDREEVNA: And the musicians arrived at the wrong time and we started the ball at the wrong time. . . . Well, never mind. . . . (*Sits down and hums softly.*)

CHARLOTTA (*hands* PISHCHIK *a deck of cards*): Here's a deck of cards for you, think of one particular card.

PISHCHIK: I've got one.

CHARLOTTA: Now shuffle the deck. Very good. Hand it over. O my dear Mister Pishchik. Ein, zwei, drei! Now look at it, it's in your breast pocket. . . .

PISHCHIK (*pulling a card from his breast pocket*): Eight of spades, absolutely right! (*Astounded*) Can you imagine!

CHARLOTTA (*holds deck of cards on her palm, to* TROFIMOV): Tell me quick, which card's on top.

TROFIMOV: What? Well, the queen of spades.

CHARLOTTA: Right! (*To* PISHCHIK) Well? Which card's on top?

PISHCHIK: The ace of hearts.

CHARLOTTA: Right! (*Claps her hand over her palm, the deck of cards disappears.*) Isn't it lovely weather today! (*She is answered by a mysterious feminine voice, as if from beneath the floor: "Oh yes, marvellous weather, Madam."*) You're so nice, my ideal. . . .

VOICE: Madam, I been liking you ferry much.

STATIONMASTER (*applauding*): Lady ventriloquist, bravo!

PISHCHIK (*astounded*): Can you imagine! Bewitching Charlotta Ivanovna. . . . I'm simply in love with you. . . .

CHARLOTTA: In love? (*Shrugging*) What do you know about love? Guter Mensch, aber schlechter Musikant.[2]

TROFIMOV (*claps* PISHCHIK *on the shoulder*): Good old horse. . . .

CHARLOTTA: Please pay attention, one more trick. (*Takes a rug from a chair.*) Here is a very nice rug. I'd like to sell it . . . (*Shakes it out.*) What am I offered?

PISHCHIK (*astounded*): Can you imagine!

CHARLOTTA: Ein, zwei, drei! (*Quickly lifts the lowered rug.*)

(*Behind the rug stands* ANYA, *who curtsies, runs to her mother, embraces her, and runs back to the ballroom amid the general delight.*)

LYUBOV ANDREEVNA (*applauding*): Bravo, bravo!

CHARLOTTA: One more! Ein, zwei, drei! (*Raises the rug.*)

(*Behind the rug stands* VARYA, *who bows.*)

PISHCHIK (*astounded*): Can you imagine!

CHARLOTTA: The end! (*Throws the rug at* PISHCHIK, *curtsies, and runs into the ballroom.*)

PISHCHIK (*scurrying after her*): You little rascal! . . . How do you like that! How do you like that! (*Exits.*)

LYUBOV ANDREEVNA: And Leonid still isn't back. I don't understand what he can be doing in town all this time! Everything must be over there, either the estate is sold or the auction didn't take place, but why keep us in suspense so long?

VARYA (*trying to solace her*): Uncle dear bought it, I'm sure of it.

TROFIMOV (*sarcastically*): Sure.

VARYA: Granny sent him power of attorney, so he could buy it in her name and transfer the debt. She did it for Anya. And I'm sure, God willing, that Uncle dear bought it.

LYUBOV ANDREEVNA: Granny in Yaroslavl sent fifty thousand to buy the estate in her name—she doesn't trust us—but that money won't even manage to pay off the interest. (*Hides her face in her hands.*) Today my fate will be decided, my fate. . . .

TROFIMOV (*teases* VARYA): Madam Lopakhin!

VARYA (*angrily*): Perpetual student! Twice already you've been expelled from the university.

LYUBOV ANDREEVNA: Why are you getting angry, Varya? He teases you about Lopakhin, what of

---

[2] **Guter Mensch, aber schlecter Musikant:** A good man, but a poor musician.

it? You want to—then marry Lopakhin, he's a good man, an interesting person. You don't want to—don't get married; nobody's forcing you, sweetheart. . . .

VARYA: I regard this as a serious matter, Mama dear, I've got to speak frankly. He's a good man, I like him.

LYUBOV ANDREEVNA: Then marry him. I don't understand what you're waiting for!

VARYA: Mama dear, I can't propose to him myself. It's been two years now they've talked about him, everyone's talking, but he either keeps still or makes jokes. I understand. He's getting rich, involved in business, no time for me. If only I'd had some money, even a little, just a hundred rubles, I'd have dropped everything and gone far away. I'd have gone to a convent.

TROFIMOV: Glorious!

VARYA (to TROFIMOV): A student ought to act intelligent! (In a soft voice, tearfully) How homely you've become, Petya. How old you've grown! (To LYUBOV ANDREEVNA, no longer weeping) Only I can't do without work, Mama dear. I have to do something every minute.

(Enter YASHA.)

YASHA (barely restraining his laughter): Yepikhodov broke a billiard cue!

(He exits.)

VARYA: What's Yepikhodov doing here? Who allowed him to play billiards? I don't understand these people. (She exits.)

LYUBOV ANDREEVNA: Don't tease her, Petya, can't you see she's sad enough without that?

TROFIMOV: She's just too officious, poking her nose in other people's business. All summer long she couldn't leave us alone, me or Anya. She was afraid a romance might spring up between us. What concern is it of hers? And anyway, I didn't show any signs of it, I'm so removed from banality. We're above love!

LYUBOV ANDREEVNA: Well then, I must be beneath love. (Extremely upset) Why isn't Leonid back? If only I knew whether the estate were sold or not. Calamity seems so incredible to me that I don't even know what to think, I'm at a loss. . . . I could scream right this minute. . . . I could do something absurd. Save me, Petya. Say something, tell me. . . .

TROFIMOV: Whether the estate's sold today or not—what's the difference? It's been over and done with for a long time now, no turning back, the bridges are burnt. Calm down, dear lady. You mustn't deceive yourself, for once in your life you've got to look the truth straight in the eye.

LYUBOV ANDREEVNA: What truth? You can see where truth is and where falsehood is, but I seem to have lost my sight. I can't see anything. You boldly settle all the important questions, but tell me, dovie, isn't that because you're young, because you haven't had time to suffer through any of your problems? You boldly look forward, but isn't that because you don't see and don't expect anything awful, because life is still concealed from your young eyes? You're more courageous and more sincere and more profound than we are, but stop and think, be indulgent if only in your fingertips, spare me. Why, I was born here, here lived my father and my mother, my grandfather, I love this house, without the cherry orchard, I couldn't make sense of my life, and if it really has to be sold, then sell me along with the orchard. . . . (Embraces TROFIMOV, kisses him on the forehead.) Why, my son was drowned here. . . . (Weeps.) Show me some pity, dear, kind man.

TROFIMOV: You know I sympathize wholeheartedly.

LYUBOV ANDREEVNA: But you should say so differently, differently. . . . (Takes out a handkerchief, a telegram falls to the floor.) My heart is so heavy today, you can't imagine. Here it's too noisy for me, my soul shudders at every sound, I shudder all over, but I can't go off by myself, it would terrify me to be alone in silence. Don't blame me, Petya . . . I love you like my own flesh-and-blood. I'd gladly have given you Anya's hand, believe me, only, dovie, you've got to study, got to finish your course. You don't do anything, Fate simply hustles you from place to place, it's so odd. . . . Isn't that right? Isn't it? And something's got to be done about your beard, to make it grow somehow. . . . (Laughs.) You look funny!

TROFIMOV (picks up telegram): I've no desire to be a fashion-plate.

LYUBOV ANDREEVNA: This telegram's from Paris. Every day I get one. Yesterday too and today. That wild man has fallen ill again, something's wrong with him again. . . . He begs my forgiveness, implores me to come back, and actually I feel I ought to go to Paris, stay with him for a while. You look so stern, Petya, but what's to be done, dovie, what am I to do, he's ill, he's lonely, unhappy, and who's there to look after him, who'll keep him out of mischief, who'll give him his medicine at the right time? And what's there to hide or keep mum about, I love him, it's obvious. I love him, I love him. . . . It's a millstone around my neck, it's dragging me to the depths, but I love that stone and I can't live without it. (*Presses* TROFIMOV's *hand.*) Don't think harshly of me, Petya, don't say anything, don't talk. . . .

TROFIMOV (*through tears*): Forgive my frankness, for God's sake: but he robbed you blind!

LYUBOV ANDREEVNA: No, no, no, don't talk that way. . . . (*Puts her hands over her ears.*)

TROFIMOV: Why, he's a scoundrel, you're the only one who doesn't realize it! He's an insignificant scoundrel, a nonentity. . . .

LYUBOV ANDREEVNA (*getting angry, but restraining herself*): You're twenty-six or twenty-seven, but you're still a sophomoric schoolboy!

TROFIMOV: So what!

LYUBOV ANDREEVNA: You should act like a man, at your age you should understand people in love. And you should be in love yourself . . . you should fall in love! (*Angrily*) Yes, yes! And there's no purity in you, you're simply "puritanical," a ridiculous crank, a freak. . . .

TROFIMOV (*horrified*): What is she saying!

LYUBOV ANDREEVNA: "I am above love!" You're not above love, but simply, as our Firs here says, you're half-baked. At your age not to have a mistress! . . .

TROFIMOV (*horrified*): This is horrible! What is she saying! (*Rushes to the ballroom clutching his head.*) This is horrible . . . I can't stand it, I'm going. . . . (*Exits, but immediately returns.*) All is over between us! (*Exits into the hall.*)

LYUBOV ANDREEVNA (*shouting after him*): Petya, wait! You funny man, I was joking! Petya!

(*We hear in the hallway, someone running up the stairs and suddenly falling back down with a crash. ANYA and VARYA shriek, but immediately laughter is heard.*)

LYUBOV ANDREEVNA: What's going on in there?

(ANYA *runs in.*)

ANYA (*laughing*): Petya fell down the stairs! (*Runs out.*)

LYUBOV ANDREEVNA: What a character that Petya is! . . .

(*The* STATIONMASTER *stops in the center of the ballroom and recites Aleksei Tolstoi's "The Fallen Woman." The guests listen, but barely has he recited a few lines, when the strains of a waltz reach them from the hallway, and the recitation breaks off. Everyone dances. Enter from the hall,* TROFIMOV, ANYA, VARYA, *and* LYUBOV ANDREEVNA.)

LYUBOV ANDREEVNA: Well, Petya . . . well, my pure-in-heart . . . I apologize . . . let's go dance. . . . (*Dances with* TROFIMOV.)

(ANYA *and* VARYA *dance.*)

(FIRS *enters, leaves his stick by the side-door.* YASHA *also enters the drawing room, watching the dancers.*)

YASHA: How're you doing, Gramps?

FIRS: I'm none too well. In the old days we had generals, barons, admirals dancing at our parties, but now we send for the postal clerk and the stationmaster, yes and they don't come a-running. Somehow I've gotten weak. The late master, the grandfather, doctored everybody with sealing wax for every ailment. I've took sealing wax every day now for twenty-odd years, and maybe more; maybe that's why I'm still alive.

YASHA: You bore me stiff, Gramps. (*Yawns.*) How about dropping dead.

FIRS: Ech, you're . . . half-baked! (*Mutters.*)

(TROFIMOV *and* LYUBOV ANDREEVNA *dance in the ballroom, then in the drawing-room.*)

LYUBOV ANDREEVNA: Merci, I'm going to sit down a bit. . . . (*Sits down.*) I'm tired.

(*Enter* ANYA.)

ANYA (*agitated*): Just now in the kitchen some man was saying that the cherry orchard has already been sold.

LYUBOV ANDREEVNA: Sold to whom?

ANYA: He didn't say. He left. (*Dances with* TROFIMOV.)

(*They both exeunt into the ballroom.*)

YASHA: It was some old coot babbling away there. A stranger.

FIRS: And Leonid Andreich still isn't back, still not returned. He's got on a light topcoat, for between seasons, see if he don't catch cold. Ech, these striplings!

LYUBOV ANDREEVNA: I'll die this instant. Yasha, go and find out whom it's been sold to.

YASHA: He went away a long time ago, that old man. (*Laughs.*)

LYUBOV ANDREEVNA (*somewhat annoyed*): Well, what are you laughing about? What's made you so happy?

YASHA: Yepikhodov's awfully funny. Empty-headed fellow. Twenty-two troubles.

LYUBOV ANDREEVNA: Firs, if the estate is sold, then where will you go?

FIRS: Wherever you order, there I'll go.

LYUBOV ANDREEVNA: Why do you look like that? Aren't you well? You know you ought to go to bed. . . .

FIRS: Yes—(*With a grin*) I go to bed, and with me gone, who'll serve, who'll take care of things? I'm the only one in the whole house.

YASHA (*to* LYUBOV ANDREEVNA): Lyubov Andreevna! Let me ask you a favor, be so kind! If you go off to Paris again, take me with you, please. For me to stay around here is absolutely out of the question. (*Glances around, lowers his voice*) Why bring it up, you see for yourself, an uncivilized country, immoral people, besides it's boring, in the kitchen they feed us disgusting stuff and there's that Firs going around, muttering all sorts of uncalled-for remarks. Take me with you, be so kind!

(*Enter* PISHCHIK.)

PISHCHIK: Allow me to request . . . a little waltz, loveliest of ladies. . . . (LYUBOV ANDREEVNA *goes with him.*) Enchanting lady, I'll borrow that hundred and eighty rubles off you just the same . . . I'll borrow . . . (*Dances*) a hundred and eighty rubles. . . .

(*They pass into the ballroom.*)

YASHA (*singing softly*): "Wilt thou learn my soul's unrest . . ."

(*In the ballroom a figure in a gray top-hat and checked trousers waves its arms and jumps up and down; shouts of "Bravo, Charlotta Ivanovna!"*)

DUNYASHA (*stops to powder her nose*): The young mistress orders me to dance—lots of gentlemen and few ladies—but dancing makes my head swim, my heart pound. Firs Nikolaevich, just now the clerk from the post-office told me something that took my breath away.

(*The music subsides.*)

FIRS: Well, what did he tell you?

DUNYASHA: You, he says, are like a flower.

YASHA (*yawns*): Ignorance. . . . (*Exits.*)

DUNYASHA: Like a flower. . . . I'm such a sensitive girl, I'm frightfully fond of compliments.

FIRS: You'll get your head turned.

(*Enter* YEPIKHODOV.)

YEPIKHODOV: Avdotya Fyodorovna, you refuse to see me . . . as if I were some sort of bug. (*Sighs.*) Ech, life!

DUNYASHA: What can I do for you?

YEPIKHODOV: No doubt you may be right. (*Sighs.*) But, of course, if it's considered from a standpoint, then you, I venture to express myself thus, pardon my outspokenness, positively drove me into a state of mind. I know my fate, every day something unlucky happens to me, and I've grown accustomed to that long ago, so that I look upon my destiny with a smile. You gave me your word, and although I . . .

DUNYASHA: Please, we'll talk later on, but now leave me alone. I'm dreaming now. (*Plays with her fan.*)

YEPIKHODOV: I suffer misfortune every day, and I, I venture to express myself thus, merely smile, even laugh.

(*Enter* VARYA *from the ballroom.*)

VARYA: Haven't you gone yet, Semyon? What a really disrespectful person you are. (*To* DUNYASHA.) Clear out of here, Dunyasha. (*To* YEPIKHODOV.) First you play billards and break the cue, and now you're strolling around the drawing-room like a guest.

YEPIKHODOV: To make demands on me, allow me to inform you, you can't.

VARYA: I'm not making demands on you, I'm just telling you. The only thing you know is walking from place to place, instead of attending to business. We keep a bookkeeper but nobody knows what for.

YEPIKHODOV (*offended*): Whether I work or whether I walk or whether I eat or whether I play billiards may only be discussed by people of understanding, my elders.

VARYA: You dare to talk to me that way? (*Flying into a rage*) You dare? You mean I don't understand anything? Get out of here! This minute!

YEPIKHODOV (*alarmed*): I request you to express yourself in a tactful fashion.

VARYA (*beside herself*): This very minute, out of here! Out! (*He goes to the door, she follows him.*) Twenty-two troubles! Don't draw another breath here! Don't let me set eyes on you! (YEPIKHODOV *exits, behind the door his voice:*)

YEPIKHODOV'S VOICE: I'm going to complain about you.

VARYA: So, you're coming back? (*Seizes the stick, left near the door by* FIRS.) Come on . . . come on . . . come on, I'll show you. . . . Well, are you coming? Are you coming? So take this. . . . (*Swings the stick.*)

(*At the same moment,* LOPAKHIN *enters.*)

LOPAKHIN: My humble thanks.

VARYA (*angrily and sarcastically*): My fault!

LOPAKHIN: Don't mention it. Thank you kindly for the pleasant surprise.

VARYA: It's not worth thanks. (*Starts out, then looks back and asks gently.*) I didn't hurt you?

LOPAKHIN: No, it's nothing. Raised an enormous bump though.

(*Voices in the ballroom: "Lopakhin's arrived! Yermolai Alekseich!"*)

PISHCHIK: Sights to be seen, sounds to be heard. . . . (*He and* LOPAKHIN *kiss.*) You smell a little of cognac, my dear boy, my bucko. But we were making merry here too.

(*Enter* LYUBOV ANDREEVNA.)

LYUBOV ANDREEVNA: Is that you, Yermolai Alekseich? Why so long? Where's Leonid?

LOPAKHIN: Leonid Andreich returned with me, he's on his way. . . .

LYUBOV ANDREEVNA (*agitated*): Well, what? Was there an auction? Tell me!

LOPAKHIN (*embarrassed, afraid to display his joy*): The auction was over by four o'clock. . . . We missed the train, had to wait till half-past nine. (*Sighs heavily.*) Oof! My head's in a bit of a whirl. . . .

(*Enter* GAEV; *his right hand is holding packages, his left is wiping away tears.*)

LYUBOV ANDREEVNA: Lyonya, what? Well, Lyonya? (*Impatiently, tearfully*) Hurry up, for God's sake. . . .

GAEV (*not answering her, only waves his hand, to* FIRS, *weeping*): Here, take this. . . . There's anchovies, Kerch herring. . . . I didn't eat a thing all day. . . . What I've been through!

(*The door to the billiard room opens. We hear the sounds of the balls and* YASHA's *voice: "Seven and Eighteen!"* GAEV's *expression shifts, he stops crying.*)

GAEV: I'm awfully tired. Firs, help me change. (*Exits through the ballroom, followed by* FIRS.)

PISHCHIK: What happened at the auction? Tell us!

LYUBOV ANDREEVNA: Is the cherry orchard sold?

LOPAKHIN: Sold.

LYUBOV ANDREEVNA: Who bought it?

LOPAKHIN: I bought it.

(*Pause.* LYUBOV ANDREEVNA *is overcome; she*

would fall, were she not standing beside an armchair and a table. VARYA *takes the keys from her belt, throws them on the floor in the middle of the drawing-room and exits.*)

LOPAKHIN: I bought it! Wait, ladies and gentlemen, please for a minute, my head's in a muddle, I can't talk. . . . (*Laughs.*) We showed up at the auction, Deriganov was there already. Leonid Andreich only had fifty thousand, and Deriganov right off bid thirty over and above the mortgage. I get the picture, I pitched into him, bid forty. He forty-five. I fifty-five. I mean, he kept adding by fives, I by tens. . . . Well, it ended. Over and above the mortgage I bid ninety thousand, it was knocked down to me. Now the cherry orchard's mine. Mine! (*Chuckling.*) My God, Lord, the cherry orchard's mine! Tell me I'm drunk, out of my mind, that I'm imagining it all. . . . (*Stamps his feet.*) Don't laugh at me! If only my father and grandfather could rise up from their graves and see all that's happened, how their Yermolai, beaten, half-literate Yermolai, who used to run around barefoot in the wintertime; how this same Yermolai bought the estate, the most beautiful thing in the world. I bought the estate where grandfather and father were slaves, where they weren't even allowed in the kitchen. I'm asleep, this is only one of my dreams, it only looks this way. . . . This is a figment of your imagination, hidden by the shadows of ignorance. . . . (*Picks up the keys, smiles gently.*) She threw down the keys, she wants to show that she's no longer mistress here. . . . (*Jingles the keys.*) Well, it's all the same. (*We hear the orchestra tuning up.*) Hey, musicians, play, I want to hear you! Come on, everybody, see how Yermolai Lopakhin will swing an axe in the cherry orchard, how the trees'll come tumbling to the ground!! We'll build cottages, and our grandchildren and greatgrandchildren will see a new life here. . . . Music, play! (*The music plays,* LYUBOV ANDREEVNA *has sunk into a chair, crying bitterly.*) (*Reproachfully*) Why, oh, why didn't you listen to me? My poor, dear lady, you can't undo it now. (*Tearfully*) Oh, if only this were all over quickly, if somehow our clumsy, unhappy life could be changed quickly.

PISHCHIK (*takes him by the arm; in an undertone*): She's crying. Let's go into the ballroom, leave her alone. . . . Let's go. . . . (*Drags him by the arm and leads him into the ballroom.*)

LOPAKHIN: So what? Music, play louder! Let everything be the way I want it! (*Ironically*) Here comes the new landlord, the owner of the cherry orchard! (*He accidentally bumps into a small table and almost knocks over the candelabrum.*) I can pay for everything! (*Exits with* PISHCHIK.)

(*No one is left in the ballroom or drawingroom except* LYUBOV ANDREEVNA, *who is sitting, all bunched up, weeping bitterly. The music is playing, softly.* ANYA *and* TROFIMOV *hurry in.* ANYA *goes up to her mother and kneels before her.* TROFIMOV *remains at the entrance to the ballroom.*)

ANYA: Mama! . . . Mama, you're crying? Dear, kind, good Mama, my own, my beautiful, I love you . . . I bless you. The cherry orchard's sold, there isn't any more, that's true, true, true, but don't cry, Mama, you've got your life ahead of you, you've got your good, pure heart . . . Come with me, come, dearest, away from here, come! . . . We'll plant a new orchard, more splendid than this one, you'll see it, you'll understand, and joy, peaceful, profound joy will sink into your heart, like the sun at nightfall, and you'll smile, Mama! Come, dearest! Come! . . .

ACT IV

First Act set. Neither curtains on the windows, nor pictures on the walls, a few sticks of furniture remain, piled up in a corner, as if for sale. A feeling of emptiness. Near the door to the outside and at the back of the stage are piled suitcases, travelling bags, etc. At the left the door is open, and through it we can hear the voices of VARYA *and* ANYA. LOPAKHIN *stands waiting.* YASHA *is holding a tray of champagne glasses. In the hallway,* YEPIKHODOV *is tying up a carton. Off- stage, at the back, a hum. It's the peasants come to say good-bye.* GAEV's *voice: "Thank you, friends, thank you."*

YASHA: The common folk have come to say good-bye. I'm of the opinion, Yermolai Alekseich, they're decent enough people, but they aren't too bright.

(*The hum subsides. Enter through the hall* LYUBOV ANDREEVNA *and* GAEV. *She isn't cry- ing, but is pale, her face twitches, she can't talk.*)

GAEV: You gave them your purse, Lyuba. You mustn't! You mustn't!

LYUBOV ANDREEVNA: I couldn't help it! I couldn't help it!

(*Both exit.*)

LOPAKHIN (*through the door, after them*): Please, I humbly beseech you! A little drink at parting. It didn't occur to me to bring any from town, and at the station I only found one bottle. Please! (*Pause.*) How about it, ladies and gentlemen? Don't you want any? (*Walks away from the door.*) Had I known, I wouldn't have bought it. Well, I won't drink any either. (YASHA *carefully sets the tray on a chair.*) You drink up, Yasha, anyway.

YASHA: To those departing! And happy days to the stay-at-homes! (*Drinks.*) This champagne isn't the genuine article, you can take it from me.

LOPAKHIN: Eight rubles a bottle. (*Pause.*) It's cold as hell in here.

YASHA: They didn't stoke up today, it doesn't matter, we're leaving. (*Laughs.*)

LOPAKHIN: What's that for?

YASHA: Sheer satisfaction.

LOPAKHIN: Outside it's October, but sunny and mild, like summer. Good building weather. (*Glances at his watch, at the door.*) Ladies and gentlemen, remember, until the train leaves, there's forty-seven minutes in all! Which means, in twenty minutes we start for the station. Get a move on.

(*Enter from outdoors* TROFIMOV *in an overcoat.*)

TROFIMOV: Seems to me it's time to go now. The horses are at the door. Where the hell are my galoshes? Disappeared. (*Through the door*) Anya, my galoshes aren't here! I can't find them!

LOPAKHIN: And I have to be in Kharkov. I'll accompany you on the same train. I'm staying all winter in Kharkov. I've been hanging around here with you, I'm worn out doing nothing. I can't be without work, I don't even know what to do with my hands. They dangle something strange, like somebody else's.

TROFIMOV: We'll be going soon, and you can return to your productive labor.

LOPAKHIN: Do have a little drink.

TROFIMOV: None for me.

LOPAKHIN: Looks like off to Moscow now?

TROFIMOV: Yes, I'll see them as far as town, but tomorrow off to Moscow.

LOPAKHIN: Yes. . . . Hey, the professors are holding off on lectures, I'll bet they're waiting for your arrival!

TROFIMOV: None of your business.

LOPAKHIN: How many years have you been studying at the University?

TROFIMOV: Think up something fresher. That's old and stale. (*Looks for his galoshes.*) By the way, we probably won't see each other again, so let me give you a piece of advice as a farewell: don't wave your arms! Break yourself of that habit—arm-waving. And also cottage-building, figuring that eventually tourists will turn into private house-holders, figuring in that way is just the same as arm-waving. . . . When you come down to it, I'm fond of you anyhow. You've got delicate, gentle fingers, like an artist, you've got a delicate, gentle soul. . . .

LOPAKHIN (*embraces him*): Good-bye, dear boy. Thanks for everything. If you need it, borrow some money from me for the road.

TROFIMOV: What for? No need.

LOPAKHIN: But you've got none!

TROFIMOV: I do. Thank you. I received some for a translation. Here it is, in my pocket. (*Anxiously*) But my galoshes are gone!

VARYA (*from the next room*): Take your nasty things! (*She flings a pair of rubber galoshes on stage.*)

TROFIMOV: What are you upset about, Varya? Hm. . . . But these aren't *my* galoshes!

LOPAKHIN: Last spring I planted twenty-seven hundred acres of poppies, and now I've cleared forty thousand net. And when my poppies bloomed, it was like a picture! Here's what I'm driving at, I cleared forty thousand, which means I offer you a loan because I'm able to. Why turn up your nose? I'm a peasant . . . plain and simple.

TROFIMOV: Your father was a peasant, mine, a druggist, but from that absolutely nothing follows. (LOPAKHIN *pulls out his wallet.*) Don't bother, don't bother. . . . Even if you gave me two hundred thousand, I wouldn't take it. I'm a free man. And everything that's valued so highly and fondly by all of you, rich men and beggars, hasn't the slightest sway over me, it's like fluff floating in the air. I can manage without you, I can pass you by. I'm strong and proud. Humanity is moving toward the most exalted truth, the most exalted happiness possible on earth, and I'm in the front ranks!

LOPAKHIN: Will you get there?

TROFIMOV: I'll get there. (*Pause.*) I'll get there, or I'll show others the way to get there.

(*We hear in the distance an axe striking a tree.*)

LOPAKHIN: Well, good-bye, my boy. Time to go. We turn up our noses at each other, but life keeps slipping by. When I work a long time non-stop, then my thoughts are sharper, and even I seem to know why I exist. But, brother, how many people there are in Russia who have no reason to exist. Well, what's the difference, that's not what

makes the world go round. Leonid Andreich, they say, took a position, he'll be in the bank, six thousand a year. . . . Only he won't keep at it, too lazy. . . .

ANYA (*in the doorway*): Mama begs you: until she's gone, not to chop down the orchard.

TROFIMOV: I mean really, haven't you got any tact. . . . (*Exits through the hall.*)

LOPAKHIN: Right away, right away. . . . These people, honestly! (*Exits after him.*)

ANYA: Did they take Firs to the hospital?

YASHA: I told them to this morning. They took him, I should think.

ANYA (*to* YEPIKHODOV, *who is crossing through the ballroom*): Semyon Panteleich, please find out whether Firs was taken to the hospital.

YASHA (*offended*): I told Yegor this morning. Why ask ten times?

YEPIKHODOV: Superannuated Firs, in my con-clusive opinion, is past all repairing, he should be gathered to his fathers. And I can only envy him. (*Sets a suitcase on top of a cardboard hatbox and crushes it.*) Well, look at that, naturally. I should have known. (*Exits.*)

YASHA (*mocking*): Twenty-two troubles. . . .

YEPIKHODOV: Well, it could have happened to anybody.

VARYA (*from behind door*): Have they sent Firs to the hospital?

ANYA: They have.

VARYA: Then why didn't they take the letter to the doctor?

ANYA: We'll have to send someone after them. . . . (*Exits.*)

VARYA (*from the adjoining room*): Where's Yasha? Tell him his mother's arrived, wants to say good-bye to him.

YASHA (*waves his hand*): They simply try my patience.

(DUNYASHA *in the meantime has been fussing with the luggage; now that* YASHA *is alone, she comes up to him.*)

DUNYASHA: If only you'd take one little look at me, Yasha. You're going away . . . you're leaving me behind. . . . (*Weeps and throws herself around his neck.*)

YASHA: What's to cry about? (*Drinks cham-pagne.*) In six days I'll be in Paris again. Tomorrow we'll board an express train and dash away, just try and spot us. Somehow I can't believe it. Vive la France! . . . It doesn't suit me, here, I can't live . . . nothing going on. I've seen enough ignorance—fed up. (*Drinks champagne.*) What's there to cry about? Behave respectably, then you won't have to cry.

DUNYASHA (*powdering her nose, looks in a hand-mirror*): Drop me a line from Paris. I really loved you, Yasha, loved you so! I'm a soft-hearted creature, Yasha!

YASHA: Someone's coming in here. (*Fusses around with the luggage, humming softly.*)

(*Enter* LYUBOV ANDREEVNA, GAEV, ANYA, *and* CHARLOTTA IVANOVNA.)

GAEV: We should be off. Not much time left. (*Looking at* YASHA) Who's that smelling of herring?

LYUBOV ANDREEVNA: In about ten minutes we ought to be getting into the carriages . . . (*Casting a glance around the room.*) Good-bye, dear old house, old grandfather. Winter will pass, spring will come again, but you won't be here anymore, they'll tear you down. How much these walls have seen! (*Kissing her daughter ardently.*) My precious, you're radiant, your eyes are sparkling like two diamonds. Are you glad? Very?

ANYA: Very! A new life is beginning, Mama!

GAEV: As a matter of fact, everything's fine now. Until the sale of the cherry orchard, we were all upset, distressed, but then, when the dilemma was settled, finally, irrevocably, everyone calmed down, even became cheerful. . . . I'm a bank employee, now; I'm a financier . . . yellow to the center, and you, Lyuba, anyway, you're looking better, that's for sure.

LYUBOV ANDREEVNA: Yes. My nerves are better, that's true. (*They help her on with her hat and coat.*) I'm sleeping well. Carry my things out, Yasha. It's time. (*To* ANYA) My little girl, we'll see each other soon. . . . I'm off to Paris, I'll live there on that money your granny in Yaroslavl sent us to buy the estate—hurray for Granny!—but that money won't last long.

ANYA: Mama, you'll come back soon . . . won't you? I'll study, pass the examination at the high school, and then I'll work to help you. Mama, we'll be together and read all sorts of books . . . won't we? (*Kisses her mother's hand.*) We'll read in the autumn evenings, we'll read lots of books, and before us a new, wonderful world will open up. . . . (*Dreaming*) Mama, come back. . . .

LYUBOV ANDREEVNA: I'll come back, my treasure. (*Embraces her daughter.*)

(*Enter* LOPAKHIN. CHARLOTTA *is quietly singing a song.*)

GAEV: Charlotta's happy! She's singing!

CHARLOTTA (*picks up a bundle that looks like a swaddled baby*): Rock-a-bye, baby, on-the-tree-top. (*We hear a baby crying: "Waa! Waa!"*) Hush, my sweet, my dear little boy. ("*Waa! Waa!*") I'm so sorry for you! (*Tossing back the bundle.*) Will you please find me a position! I can't keep on this way.

LOPAKHIN: We'll find one, Charlotta Ivanovna, don't worry.

GAEV: Everyone's dropping us, Varya's leaving . . . we've suddenly become superfluous.

CHARLOTTA: There's no place to live in town. Have to go away. . . . (*Hums.*) It doesn't matter.

(*Enter* PISHCHIK.)

LOPAKHIN: The freak of nature! . . .

PISHCHIK (*out of breath*): Oy, let me catch my breath.. . . I'm winded . . . my most honored. . . . Give me some water. . . .

GAEV: After money, I suppose? Your humble servant, I'll keep out of temptation's way. . . . (*Exits.*)

PISHCHIK (*out of breath*): I haven't been to see you for a long time . . . loveliest of ladies. . . . (*To* LOPAKHIN) You here . . . glad to see you . . . a man of the widest intellect . . . take . . . go on. . . . (*Hands money to* LOPAKHIN.) Four hundred rubles. . . . I still owe you eight hundred and forty. . . .

LOPAKHIN (*bewildered, shrugs*): It's like a dream. . . .Where did you get this?

PISHCHIK: Wait. . . . Hot. . . . Most amazing thing happened. Some Englishmen stopped by my place and found some kind of white clay on the land. . . . (*To* LYUBOV ANDREEVNA) And four hundred for you . . . beautiful lady, divine. . . . (*Hands her money.*) The rest later. (*Drinks water.*) Just now some young man on the train was relating that a certain . . . great philosopher recommends jumping off roofs . . . "Jump!"—he says, and in that lies the whole problem. (*Astounded.*) Can you imagine! Water! . . .

LOPAKHIN: Who were these Englishmen?

PISHCHIK: I leased them the lot with the clay for twenty-four years. . . . But now, excuse me, no time. . . . Have to run along . . . I'm going to Znoikov's . . . Kardamonov's . . . I owe everybody. . . . (*Drinks.*) I wish you health. . . . On Thursday I'll drop by. . . .

LYUBOV ANDREEVNA: We're just about to move to town, and tomorrow I'll be abroad.

PISHCHIK: What? (*Agitated*) Why to town? Goodness, look at the furniture . . . the suitcases . . . well, never mind. . . . (*Through tears*) Never mind. Persons of the highest intelligence . . . those Englishmen. . . . Never mind. . . . Be happy. . . .

God will aid you. . . . Never mind. . . . Everything in this world comes to an end. . . . (*Kisses* LYUBOV ANDREEVNA's *hand.*) And should rumor reach you that my end has come, just remember this very thing—a horse, and say: "There was on earth thus-and-such . . . Simeonov-Pishchik . . . rest in peace." . . . Incredible weather . . . yes. . . . (*Exits, overcome with emotion, but immediately reappears in the doorway and says*) Dashenka says to say hello! (*Exits.*)

LYUBOV ANDREEVNA: Now we can go. I'm leaving with two things on my mind. First—that Firs is ill. (*Glancing at her watch.*) There's still five minutes. . . .

ANYA: Mama, they've already sent Firs to the hospital. Yasha sent him this morning.

LYUBOV ANDREEVNA: My second anxiety is Varya. She's used to early rising and working, and now without work, she's like a fish out of water. She's got thin, she's got pale, she cries, poor thing. . . . (*Pause.*) You know this perfectly well, Yermolai Alekseich: I had dreamt . . . of marrying her to you, yes and it certainly looked as if you were ready to get married. (*Whispers to* ANYA, *who nods to* CHARLOTTA, *and both leave.*) She loves you, you're fond of her, I don't know, I just don't know why you seem to avoid each other. I don't understand.

LOPAKHIN: Personally I don't understand either, I admit. It's all sort of strange. . . . If there's still time, then I'm ready right now. . . . Let's settle it right away—and there's an end to it, but if it weren't for you I feel I wouldn't propose.

LYUBOV ANDREEVNA: That's excellent. All it takes is one little minute. I'll call her right now. . . .

LOPAKHIN: And there's champagne for the occasion. (*Looks in the glasses.*) Empty, somebody drank it already. (YASHA *coughs.*) I should say, lapped it up. . . .

LYUBOV ANDREEVNA (*lively*): Fine! We'll leave . . . Yasha, allez! I'll call her. . . . (*In the doorway*) Varya, drop everything, come here. Come on! (*Exits with* YASHA.)

LOPAKHIN (*glancing at his watch*): Yes. . . . (*Pause. Behind the door a stifled laugh, whispering, finally* VARYA *enters.*)

VARYA (*scrutinizes the luggage for a long time*): That's odd, I just can't find it. . . .

LOPAKHIN: What are you looking for?

VARYA: I packed it myself and can't remember. (*Pause.*)

LOPAKHIN: Where are you off to now. Varvara Mikhailovna?

VARYA: Me? To the Ragulins'. . . . I've agreed to take charge of their household . . . as a housekeeper, or something.

LOPAKHIN: That's in Yashnevo? On to seventy miles from here. (*Pause.*) So ends life in this house. . . .

VARYA (*examining the luggage*): Where in the world is it. . . . Or maybe I packed it in the trunk. . . . Yes, life in this house is ended . . . there won't be any more.

LOPAKHIN: And I'll be riding to Kharkov soon . . . by the same train. Lots of business. But I'm leaving Yepikhodov on the grounds . . . I hired him.

VARYA: That so!

LOPAKHIN: Last year by this time it was snowing already, if you remember, but now it's mild, sunny. Except that it's cold. . . . About three degrees of frost.

VARYA: I haven't noticed. (*Pause.*) And besides our thermometer is broken. . . .

(*Pause. Voice from the yard through the door:* "Yermolai Alekseich!")

LOPAKHIN (*as if expecting this call for a long time*): Right away! (*Rushes out.*)

(VARYA, *sitting on the floor, laying her head on a pile of dresses, quietly sobs. The door opens,* LYUBOV ANDREEVNA *enters cautiously.*)

LYUBOV ANDREEVNA: Well? (*Pause.*) We've got to go.

VARYA (*has stopped crying, wipes her eyes*): Yes, it's time, Mama dear. I'll get to the Ragulins today, if only I don't miss the train. . . .

LYUBOV ANDREEVNA (*in the doorway*): Anya, put your things on!

(*Enter* ANYA, *then* GAEV, CHARLOTTA IVANOVNA. GAEV *has on a heavy overcoat with a hood. The servants and coachman foregather.* YEPIKHODOV *fusses around with the luggage.*)

LYUBOV ANDREEVNA: Now we can be on our way.

ANYA (*joyously*): On our way!

GAEV: My friends, beloved friends! Leaving this house forever, can I be silent, can I restrain myself from expressing at parting those feelings which now fill my whole being . . .

ANYA (*entreating*): Uncle!

VARYA: Uncle dear, you mustn't!

GAEV (*depressed*): Bank the yellow to the center. . . . I'll keep still. . . .

(*Enter* TROFIMOV, *then* LOPAKHIN.)

TROFIMOV: Well, ladies and gentlemen, time to go!

LOPAKHIN: Yepikhodov, my overcoat!

LYUBOV ANDREEVNA: I'll sit just one more minute. It's as if I'd never before seen what the walls are like in this house, what the ceilings are like, and now I gaze at them greedily, with such tender love. . . .

GAEV: I remember when I was six, on Trinity Sunday I sat in this window and watched my father driving to church. . . .

LYUBOV ANDREEVNA: Is all the luggage loaded?

LOPAKHIN: Everything, I think. (*Putting on his overcoat, to* YEPIKHODOV) You there, Yepikhodov, see that everything's in order.

YEPIKHODOV (*talks in a hoarse voice*): Don't worry, Yermolai Alekseich!

LOPAKHIN: What's the matter with your voice?

YEPIKHODOV: I just drank some water, swallowed something.

YASHA (*comtemptuously*): Ignorance. . . .

LYUBOV ANDREEVNA: We're leaving—and not a soul will be left here. . . .

LOPAKHIN: Until next spring.

VARYA (*pulls a parasol out of a bundle, looking as if she were about to hit somebody.* LOPAKHIN *pretends to be scared*): What are you . . . what are you doing . . . it never crossed my mind. . . .

TROFIMOV: Ladies and gentlemen, let's get into the carriages. . . . It's high time! The train'll be here any minute!

VARYA: Petya, here they are, your galoshes, next to the suitcase. (*Tearfully*) And yours are so muddy, so old. . . .

TROFIMOV (*putting on his galoshes*): Let's go, ladies and gentlemen! . . .

GAEV (*overcome with emotion, afraid he'll cry*): The train. . . the station. . . . Followshot to the center, white doublet to the corner. . . .

LYUBOV ANDREEVNA: Let's go!

LOPAKHIN: Everybody here? Nobody there? (*Locking the side door on the left.*) Things stored here, have to lock up. Let's go! . . .

ANYA: Good-bye, house! Good-bye, old life!

TROFIMOV: Hello, new life! (*Exits with* ANYA.)

(VARYA *casts a glance around the room and exits unhurriedly. Exeunt* YASHA *and* CHARLOTTA *with a lapdog.*)

LOPAKHIN: Which means, till spring. Come along, ladies and gentlemen. . . . Till we meet again! . . . (*Exits.*)

(LYUBOV ANDREEVNA *and* GAEV *are left alone. As if they had been waiting for this, they throw themselves around one another's neck and sob with restraint, quietly, afraid of someone hearing them.*)

GAEV (*in despair*): Sister dear, sister dear. . . .

LYUBOV ANDREEVNA: Oh, my darling, my sweet, beautiful orchard! . . . My life, my youth, my happiness, good-bye! . . . Good-bye! . . .

(ANYA'S *voice, gaily, appealing:* "Mama!" TROFIMOV'S *voice, gaily, excited:* "Yoo-hoo!")

LYUBOV ANDREEVNA: One last look at the walls, the windows. . . . Our poor mother loved to walk about in this room. . . .

GAEV: Sister dear, sister dear! . . .

ANYA'S VOICE: Mama! . . .

TROFIMOV'S VOICE: Yoo-hoo! . . .

LYUBOV ANDREEVNA: We're coming!

(*They exeunt. The stage is empty. We hear the doors being locked with a key, then the carriages driving off. It grows quiet. In the silence there is the dull thud of the axe against a tree, sounding forlorn and doleful. We hear footsteps. From the door at right* FIRS *appears. He's dressed as always, in a jacket and white vest, slippers on his feet. He is ill.*)

FIRS (*crosses to the door, tries the knob*): Locked. They've gone. . . . (*Sits on the sofa.*) Forgot about me. . . . Never mind. . . . I'll sit here a bit. . . . And I guess Leonid Andreich didn't put on his fur-coat, went out in his topcoat. . . . (*Sighs, anxiously.*) I didn't see to it. . . . Young striplings! (*Mutters something that cannot be understood.*) This life's gone by like I hadn't lived. (*Lies down.*) I'll lie down a bit. . . . Ain't no strength in you, nothing left, nothing. . . . Ech, you're . . . half-baked! . . . (*Lies immobile.*)

(*We hear the distant sound, as if from the sky, the sound of a snapped string, dying away mournfully. Silence ensues, and all we hear far away in the orchard is the thud of an axe on a tree.*)

COMMENTARY

At the end of *The Cherry Orchard*, the old servant Firs, forgotten by the family he has long served, wanders onto the stage, locked within the house that is no longer theirs. Is he comic, in his mutterings, in his old-maidish frettings about Leonid Andreevich's inadequate coat, and in his implicit realization that although he is concerned about the aristocrats the aristocrats are unconcerned about him? Or is he tragic, dying in isolation? Or neither? The comedy is scarcely uproarious; if there is humor in his realization that his life has been trivial, this humor is surely tinged with melancholy. And the "tragic" reading is also ambiguous: first, the text does not say that he dies; second, if it can be assumed that he dies, the death of an ill eighty-seven-year-old man can scarcely seem untimely; and third, Firs does not seem particularly concerned about dying.

If this play ends with a death, then, it is not the sort of death that Byron had in mind when he said, "All tragedies are finished by a death, / All comedies are ended by a marriage." We are in the dramatic world that Shaw spoke of when he said that "the curtain no longer comes down on a hero slain or married: it comes down when the audience has seen enough of the life presented to it, . . . and must either leave the theatre or miss its last train."

Chekhov insisted that *The Cherry Orchard* was a comedy, but what sort of comedy? In the latter part of the last act there is almost a proposal of marriage, but, typically, it never gets made. For two years everyone has joked about the anticipated marriage between Lopakhin and Varya, but when these two are thrust together they are overcome by embarrassment, and the interview is dissipated in small talk. Not that (of course) a comedy must end with a marriage; marriage is only the conventional way of indicating a happy union, or reunion, that symbolizes the triumph of life. But in this play we *begin* with a reunion—the family is reunited in the ancestral home—and we end with a separation, the inhabitants scattering when the home is sold.

Another way of getting at *The Cherry Orchard* is to notice that in this play, although there are innumerable references to Time between the first speech, when Lopakhin says "Train's in, thank God! What's the time?" and the last act, where there is much talk about catching the outbound train, Time does not function as it usually functions either in tragedy or in comedy. In tragedy we usually feel: if there had only been more time. . . . For example, in *Romeo and Juliet* Friar Laurence writes a letter to Romeo, explaining that Juliet will take a potion that will put her in a temporary, deathlike trance, but the letter is delayed, Romeo mistakenly hears that Juliet is dead, and he kills himself. A few moments after his suicide Juliet revives. Had Friar Laurence's message arrived on schedule, or had Romeo not been so quick to commit suicide, no great harm would have been done. In *King Lear*, Edmund repents that he has ordered a soldier to kill Cordelia, and a messenger hurries out to change the order, but he is too late.

If in tragedy we usually feel the pressure of time, in comedy there is usually a sense of leisure. Things are difficult now, but in the course of time they will work themselves out. Sooner or later people will realize that the strange goings-on are due to the existence of identical twins; sooner or later the stubborn parents will realize that they cannot forever stand in the way of young lovers; sooner or later the money will turn up and all will be well. In the world of comedy, one is always safe in relying on time. In *The Cherry Orchard*, Lopakhin insists, correctly enough, that the family must act *now* if it is to save the orchard: "You've got to decide once and for all—time won't stand still." There is ample time to act on Lopakhin's suggestion that the orchard be leased for summer houses, and the play covers a period from May to October; but the plan is not acted on because to the aristocrats any sort of selling is unthinkable, and although one Pishchik is in the course of time miraculously redeemed from financial ruin by some Englishmen who discover and buy "some kind of white clay" on *his* land, time brings Mme. Ranevskaya and her brother Gaev no such good fortune. So far as the main happenings in the play are concerned, time neither presses nor preserves; it only passes.

During the passage of time in this play, the orchard is lost (tragic?) and the characters reveal themselves to be funny (comic?). The loss of the orchard is itself a happening of an uncertain kind. It stands, partly, for the end of an old way of life. But if that way once included intelligent and gracious aristocrats, it also included slavery, and in any case it now is embodied in the irresponsible heirs we see on the stage—Mme. Ranevskaya and her brother Gaev, along with their deaf and near-senile servant Firs. For Gaev the orchard is important chiefly because it lends prestige, since it is mentioned in the encyclopedia. Mme. Ranevskaya sees more to it. For her it is "all white" and it is "young again, full of happiness"; we are momentarily touched by her vision, but there is yet another way of seeing the orchard: for Trofimov, a student who envisions a new society as an orchard for all people, the ancestral cherry orchard is haunted by the serfs of the bad old days. Moreover, although the orchard is much talked about, it seems to have decayed to a trivial ornament. Long ago its crop was regularly harvested, pickled, and sold, thus providing food and income, but now "nobody remembers" the pickling formula and nobody buys the crop. There seems to be some truth to Lopakhin's assertion that "the only remarkable thing about this cherry orchard is that it's very big," and although one must point out that this remark is made by a despised merchant, Lopakhin is neither a fool nor the "money grubber" that Gaev thinks he is. Lopakhin delights in nature put to use. He "cleared forty thousand net" from poppies, "And when my poppies bloomed, it was like a picture!" His enthusiasm for the flowers is undercut for us only a little, if at all, by the fact that they were of use to him and to others.

Lopakhin's serious concern, whether for his poppies or for the future of the cherry orchard, contrasts interestingly with Mme. Ranevskaya's and with Gaev's sporadic passion for the orchard. Mme. Ranevskaya says, "Without the cherry orchard, I couldn't make sense of my life," and she doubtless means what she says; but that her words have not much relation to reality is indicated by her meaningless addition, "If it really has to be sold, then sell me along with the orchard." After the orchard has been sold, Gaev confesses, "everything's fine now. Until the sale of the cherry orchard, we were all upset, distressed, but then, when the dilemma was settled, finally, irrevocably, everyone calmed down, even became cheerful . . . I'm a bank employee. . . . Lyuba, anyway, you're looking better, that's for sure." His sister agrees: "Yes. My nerves are better, that's true. . . . I'm sleeping well. Carry my things out, Yasha. It's time." She returns to her lover in Paris, Gaev goes off to a job in the bank, and though we can imagine that the orchard will continue to be an occasional topic of conversation, we cannot imagine that the loss has in any way changed them. The play ends, but things will go on in the same way; neither a tragic nor a comic action has been completed.

The characters no less than the action are tragicomic. Their longings would touch the heart if only these people did not so quickly digress or engage in little actions that call their depth into doubt. Charlotta laments that she had no proper passport and that her deceased parents may not have been married: "Where I came from and who I am I don't know." And then, having touched on the mighty subject of one's identity, the subject that is the stuff of tragedy in which heroes endure the worst in order to know who they are, she begins to eat a cucumber, and somehow that simple and entirely necessary act diminishes her dignity—though it does not totally dissipate our glimpse of her alienation. In the same scene, when Yepikhodov confesses that although he reads "all kinds of remarkable books" he "cannot discover [his] own inclinations," we hear another echo of the tragic hero's quest for self-knowledge, but we also hear an echo from the world of comedy, say of the pedant who guides his life by a textbook. Yepikhodov, perhaps like a tragic hero, is particularly concerned with whether to live or to shoot himself; but this racking doubt is diminished by his prompt explanation that since he may someday decide on suicide, he always carries a revolver, which he proceeds to show to his listeners. Almost all of the characters bare their souls, but their slightly addled minds and their hungry bodies expose them to a gentle satirical treatment so that they evoke a curious amused pathos. One can, for example, sympathize with Mme. Ranevskaya's despair—but one cannot forget that she is scatterbrained and that domestic duties and local pieties occupy her mind only occasionally and that her disreputable lover in Paris means as much as the orchard she thinks she cannot live without. And when Gaev says, "Word of honor I'll swear, by whatever you like, that the estate won't be sold," we know that he has very little honor and even less ability to focus on the problem (mostly he takes refuge in thoughts about billiards, and somehow his habit of eating candy does not enhance his status in our eyes) and that the estate will be sold.

Finally, something must be said about the ambiguous treatment of the future. We know, from his correspondence, that Chekhov looked forward to a new and happier society. Russia, like much of the rest of Europe, was ceasing to be an agrarian society, but if the death throes were evident, one could not be so confident about the birth pangs. Something of the presence of two worlds is hinted at in the stage direction at the beginning of the second act, where we see the estate with its orchard, and also "Further off are telegraph poles, and way in the distance, dimly sketched on the horizon, is a large town." The telegraph poles and the town silently represent the new industrial society, but Trofimov the student speaks at length of the glorious possibilities of the future, and his speeches were sufficiently close to the bone for the censor to delete two passages sharply critical of the present. But we cannot take Trofimov's speeches quite at face value. He is a student, but he is almost thirty and still has not received his degree. His speeches in Act II are moving, especially those on the need to work rather than to talk if the future is to be better than the past, but we cannot quite rid ourselves of the suspicion that Trofimov talks rather than works. Certainly he is contemptuous of the merchant Lopakhin, who delights in work. And, worse, Trofimov frets too much about his overshoes, thinks he is "above love," and is so confounded by Mme. Ranevskaya's remark, "At your age, not to have a mistress!" that he falls down a flight of stairs. None of these personal failings invalidates his noble view of the future; certainly none of them turns this view into a comic pipedream, and yet all of these things, along with a certain nostalgia that we feel for the past, do suffuse even his noblest statements about the future with a delicate irony that puts them, along with the much praised but totally neglected cherry orchard, firmly in the tragicomic world. One understands why Chekhov called the play a comedy, and one understands why Stanislavsky (who directed the first production and played the part of Gaev) told Chekhov, "It is definitely not a comedy . . . but a tragedy." Perhaps neither of the men fully wanted to see the resonant ambiguities in the play.

TOPICS FOR DISCUSSION

1. What do you make of the fact that the opening stage directions specify that the setting for the first act is a room that "is still known as the Nursery"?
2. What do the costumes communicate? (Consider, for example, the brief description of Lopakhin's costume on p. 370.)
3. Characterize Lyubov Andreevna.
4. Can some of the characters clearly be called comic? Do some of these characters help to make Lyubov Andreevna less comic?
5. How might the theme of the play be stated?
6. How seriously do you take Gaev's thoughts?
7. In your opinion, why is Firs in the play?
8. What do you make of the sound of the breaking string at the end of the play?
9. Chekhov said that he wrote "a comedy, in places even a farce." But the director, Stanislavsky, replied, "This is not a comedy or a farce; . . . it is a tragedy." What can be said for each of these views? Try to specify speeches or scenes that can be used to support these judgments. For instance, when Trofimov falls downstairs, is the episode farcical?

TRIFLES

Susan Glaspell

Susan Glaspell (1882–1948) was born in Davenport, Iowa, and educated at Drake University in Des Moines. In 1913 she married George Cram Cook, and with Cook and other writers, actors, and artists in 1915 founded the Provincetown Players, a group that remained vital until 1929. Among the important writers associated with the Provincetown Players were Eugene O'Neill, Sherwood Anderson, E. E. Cummings, and Edna Ferber. Glaspell wrote *Trifles* (1916), as well as other short plays, for the Provincetown Players, but she also wrote stories, novels, and a biography of her husband. In 1931 she won the Pulitzer Prize for *Alison's House*, a play about the family of a deceased poet who in some ways resembles Emily Dickinson.

SCENE: *The kitchen in the now abandoned farmhouse of* JOHN WRIGHT, *a gloomy kitchen, and left without having been put in order—the walls covered with a faded wallpaper. Down right is a door leading to the parlor. On the right wall above this door is a built-in kitchen cupboard with shelves in the upper portion and drawers below. In the rear wall at right, up two steps is a door opening onto stairs leading to the second floor. In the rear wall at left is a door to the shed and from there to the outside. Between these two doors is an old-fashioned black iron stove. Running along the left wall from the shed door is an old iron sink and sink shelf, in which is set a hand pump. Downstage of the sink is an uncurtained window. Near the window is an old wooden rocker. Center stage is an unpainted wooden kitchen table with straight chairs on either side. There is a small chair down right. Unwashed pans under the sink, a loaf of bread outside the breadbox, a dish towel on the table—other signs of incompleted work. At the rear the shed door opens and the* SHERIFF *comes in followed by the* COUNTY ATTORNEY *and* HALE. *The* SHERIFF *and* HALE *are men in middle life, the* COUNTY ATTORNEY *is a young man; all are much bundled up and go at once to the stove. They are followed by the two women—the* SHERIFF's *wife,* MRS. PETERS, *first; she is a slight wiry woman, a thin nervous face.* MRS. HALE *is larger and would ordinarily be called more comfortable looking, but she is disturbed now and looks fearfully about as she enters. The women have come in slowly, and stand close together near the door.*

COUNTY ATTORNEY (*at stove rubbing his hands*): This feels good. Come up to the fire, ladies.

MRS. PETERS (*after taking a step forward*): I'm not—cold.

SHERIFF (*unbuttoning his overcoat and stepping away from the stove to right of table as if to mark the beginning of official business*): Now, Mr. Hale, before we move things about, you explain to Mr. Henderson just what you saw when you came here yesterday morning.

COUNTY ATTORNEY (*crossing down to left of the table*): By the way, has anything been moved? Are things just as you left them yesterday?

SHERIFF (*looking about*): It's just the same. When it dropped below zero last night I thought I'd better send Frank out this morning to make a fire for us—(*sits right of center table*) no use getting pneumonia with a big case on, but I told him not to touch anything except the stove—and you know Frank.

COUNTY ATTORNEY: Somebody should have been left here yesterday.

SHERIFF: Oh—yesterday. When I had to send Frank to Morris Center for that man who went crazy—I want you to know I had my hands full yesterday. I knew you could get back from Omaha by today and as long as I went over everything here myself—

COUNTY ATTORNEY: Well, Mr. Hale, tell just what happened when you came here yesterday morning.

HALE (*crossing down to above table*): Harry and I had started to town with a load of potatoes. We came along the road from my place and as I got here I said, "I'm going to see if I can't get John Wright to go in with me on a party telephone." I spoke to Wright about it once before and he put me off, saying folks talked too much anyway, and all he asked was peace and quiet—I guess you know about how much he talked himself; but I thought maybe if I went to the house and talked about it before his wife, though I said to Harry that I didn't know as what his wife wanted made much difference to John—

COUNTY ATTORNEY: Let's talk about that later, Mr. Hale. I do want to talk about that, but tell now just what happened when you got to the house.

HALE: I didn't hear or see anything; I knocked at the door, and still it was all quiet inside. I knew they must be up, it was past eight o'clock. So I knocked again, and I thought I heard somebody say, "Come in." I wasn't sure, I'm not sure yet, but I opened the door—this door (*indicating the door by which the two women are still standing*) and there in that rocker—(*pointing to it*) sat Mrs. Wright. (*They all look at the rocker down left.*)

COUNTY ATTORNEY: What—what was she doing?

HALE: She was rockin' back and forth. She had her apron in her hand and was kind of—pleating it.

COUNTY ATTORNEY: And how did she—look?

HALE: Well, she looked queer.

COUNTY ATTORNEY: How do you mean—queer?

HALE: Well, as if she didn't know what she was going to do next. And kind of done up.

COUNTY ATTORNEY (*takes out notebook and pencil and sits left of center table*): How did she seem to feel about your coming?

HALE: Why, I don't think she minded—one way or other. She didn't pay much attention. I said, "How do, Mrs. Wright, it's cold, ain't it?" And she said, "Is it?"—and went on kind of pleating at her apron. Well, I was surprised; she didn't ask me to come up to the stove, or to set down, but just sat there, not even looking at me, so I said, "I want to see John." And then she—laughed. I guess you would call it a laugh. I thought of Harry and the team outside, so I said a little sharp: "Can't I see John?" "No," she says, kind o' dull like. "Ain't he home?" says I. "Yes," says she, "he's home." "Then why can't I see him?" I asked her, out of patience. "'Cause he's dead," says she. "*Dead?*" says I. She just nodded her head, not getting a bit excited, but rockin' back and forth. "Why—where is he?" says I, not knowing what to say. She just pointed upstairs—like that. (*Himself pointing to the room above.*) I started for the stairs, with the idea of going up there. I walked from there to here—then I says, "Why, what did he die of?" "He died of a rope round his neck," says she, and just went on pleatin' at her apron. Well, I went out and called Harry. I thought I might—need help. We went upstairs and there he was lyin'—

COUNTY ATTORNEY: I think I'd rather have you go into that upstairs, where you can point it all out. Just go on now with the rest of the story.

HALE: Well, my first thought was to get that rope off. It looked . . . (*stops, his face twitches*) . . . but Harry, he went up to him, and he said, "No, he's dead all right, and we'd better not touch anything." So we went back downstairs. She was still sitting that same way. "Has anybody been notified?" I asked. "No," says she, unconcerned. "Who did this, Mrs. Wright?" said Harry. He said it business-like—and she stopped pleatin' of her apron. "I don't know," she says. "You don't *know?*" says Harry. "No," says she. "Weren't you sleepin' in the bed with him?" says Harry. "Yes," says she, "but I was on the inside." "Somebody slipped a rope round his neck and strangled him and you didn't wake up?" says Harry. "I didn't wake up," she said after him. We musta looked as if we didn't see how that could be, for after a minute she said, "I sleep sound." Harry was going to ask her more questions but I said maybe we ought to let her tell her story first to the coroner, or the sheriff, so Harry went fast as he could to Rivers' place, where there's a telephone.

COUNTY ATTORNEY: And what did Mrs. Wright do when she knew that you had gone for the coroner?

HALE: She moved from the rocker to that chair over there (*pointing to a small chair in the down right corner*) and just sat there with her hands held together and looking down. I got a feeling that I ought to make some conversation, so I said I had come in to see if John wanted to put in a telephone, and at that she started to laugh, and then she stopped and looked at me—scared. (*The* COUNTY ATTORNEY, *who has had his notebook out, makes a note.*) I dunno, maybe it wasn't scared. I wouldn't like to say it was. Soon Harry got back, and then Dr. Lloyd came, and you, Mr. Peters, and so I guess that's all I know that you don't.

COUNTY ATTORNEY (*rising and looking around*): I guess we'll go upstairs first—and then out to the barn and around there. (*To the* SHERIFF) You're convinced that there was nothing important here—nothing that would point to any motive?

SHERIFF: Nothing here but kitchen things. (*The* COUNTY ATTORNEY, *after again looking around the kitchen, opens the door of a cupboard closet in right wall. He brings a small chair from right—gets up on it and looks on a shelf. Pulls his hand away, sticky.*)

COUNTY ATTORNEY: Here's a nice mess. (*The women draw nearer up center.*)

MRS. PETERS (*to the other woman*): Oh, her fruit; it did freeze. (*To the* LAWYER) She worried about that when it turned so cold. She said the fire'd go out and her jars would break.

SHERIFF (*rises*): Well, can you beat the women!

Held for murder and worryin' about her preserves.

COUNTY ATTORNEY (*getting down from chair*): I guess before we're through she may have something more serious than preserves to worry about. (*Crosses down right center.*)

HALE: Well, women are used to worrying over trifles. (*The two women move a little closer together.*)

COUNTY ATTORNEY (*with the gallantry of a young politician*): And yet, for all their worries, what would we do without the ladies? (*The women do not unbend. He goes below the center table to the sink, takes a dipperful of water from the pail and pouring it into a basin, washes his hands. While he is doing this the* SHERIFF *and* HALE *cross to cupboard, which they inspect. The* COUNTY ATTORNEY *starts to wipe his hands on the roller towel, turns it for a cleaner place.*) Dirty towels! (*Kicks his foot against the pans under the sink.*) Not much of a housekeeper, would you say, ladies?

MRS. HALE (*stiffly*): There's a great deal of work to be done on a farm.

COUNTY ATTORNEY: To be sure. And yet (*with a little bow to her*) I know there are some Dickson County farmhouses which do not have such roller towels. (*He gives it a pull to expose its full length again.*)

MRS. HALE: Those towels get dirty awful quick. Men's hands aren't always as clean as they might be.

COUNTY ATTORNEY: Ah, loyal to your sex, I see. But you and Mrs. Wright were neighbors. I suppose you were friends, too.

MRS. HALE (*shaking her head*): I've not seen much of her of late years. I've not been in this house—it's more than a year.

COUNTY ATTORNEY (*crossing to women up center*): And why was that? You didn't like her?

MRS. HALE: I liked her all well enough. Farmers' wives have their hands full, Mr. Henderson. And then—

COUNTY ATTORNEY: Yes——?

MRS. HALE (*looking about*): It never seemed a very cheerful place.

COUNTY ATTORNEY: No—it's not cheerful. I shouldn't say she had the homemaking instinct.

MRS. HALE: Well I don't know as Wright had, either.

COUNTY ATTORNEY: You mean that they didn't get on very well?

MRS. HALE: No, I don't mean anything. But I don't think a place'd be any cheerfuller for John Wright's being in it.

COUNTY ATTORNEY: I'd like to talk more of that a little later. I want to get the lay of things upstairs now. (*He goes past the women to up right where steps lead to a stair door.*)

SHERIFF: I suppose anything Mrs. Peters does'll be all right. She was to take in some clothes for her, you know, and a few little things. We left in such a hurry yesterday.

COUNTY ATTORNEY: Yes, but I would like to see what you take, Mrs. Peters, and keep an eye out for anything that might be of use to us.

MRS. PETERS: Yes, Mr. Henderson. (*The men leave by up right door to stairs. The women listen to the men's steps on the stairs, then look about the kitchen.*)

MRS. HALE (*crossing left to sink*): I'd hate to have men coming into my kitchen, snooping around and criticizing. (*She arranges the pans under sink which the* LAWYER *had shoved out of place.*)

MRS. PETERS: Of course it's no more than their duty. (*Crosses to cupboard up right.*)

MRS. HALE: Duty's all right, but I guess that deputy sheriff that came out to make the fire might have got a little of this on. (*Gives the roller towel a pull.*) Wish I'd thought of that sooner. Seems mean to talk about her for not having things slicked up when she had to come away in such a hurry. (*Crosses right to* MRS. PETERS *at cupboard.*)

MRS. PETERS (*who has been looking through cupboard, lifts one end of a towel that covers a pan*): She had bread set. (*Stands still.*)

MRS. HALE (*eyes fixed on a loaf of bread beside the breadbox, which is on a low shelf of the cupboard*): She was going to put this in there. (*Picks up loaf, then abruptly drops it. In a manner of returning to familiar things*) It's a shame about her fruit. I wonder if it's all gone. (*Gets up on the chair and looks.*) I think there's some here that's all right, Mrs. Peters. Yes—here; (*holding it toward the window*) this is cherries, too. (*Looking again.*) I declare I believe that's the only one. (*Gets down, jar in her hand. Goes to the sink and wipes it off on the outside.*) She'll feel awful bad after all her hard work in the hot weather. I remember the afternoon I put up my cherries last summer. (*She puts the jar on the big kitchen table, center of the room. With a sigh, is about to sit down in the rocking chair. Before she is seated realizes what chair it is; with a slow look at it, steps back. The chair which she has touched rocks back and forth.* MRS. PETERS *moves to center table and they both watch the chair rock for a moment or two.*)

MRS. PETERS (*shaking off the mood which the empty rocking chair has evoked. Now in a businesslike manner she speaks*): Well, I must get those things from the front room closet. (*She goes to the door at the right, but, after looking into the other room, steps back.*) You coming with me, Mrs. Hale? You could help me carry them. (*They go in the other room; reappear,* MRS. PETERS *carrying a dress, petticoat and skirt,* MRS. HALE *following with a pair of shoes.*) My, it's cold in there. (*She puts the clothes on the big table, and hurries to the stove.*)

MRS. HALE (*right of center table examining the skirt*): Wright was close. I think maybe that's why she kept so much to herself. She didn't even belong to the Ladies' Aid. I suppose she felt she couldn't do her part, and then you don't enjoy things when you feel shabby. I heard she used to wear pretty clothes and be lively, when she was Minnie Foster, one of the town girls singing in the choir. But that—oh, that was thirty years ago. This all you was to take in?

MRS. PETERS: She said she wanted an apron. Funny thing to want, for there isn't much to get you dirty in jail, goodness knows. But I suppose just to make her feel more natural. (*Crosses to cupboard.*) She said they was in the top drawer in this cupboard. Yes, here. And then her little shawl that always hung behind the door. (*Opens stair door and looks.*) Yes, here it is. (*Quickly shuts door leading upstairs.*)

MRS. HALE (*abruptly moving toward her*): Mrs. Peters?

MRS. PETERS: Yes, Mrs. Hale? (*At up right door.*)

MRS. HALE: Do you think she did it?

MRS. PETERS (*in a frightened voice*): Oh, I don't know.

MRS. HALE: Well, I don't think she did. Asking for an apron and her little shawl. Worrying about her fruit.

MRS. PETERS (*starts to speak, glances up, where footsteps are heard in the room above. In a low voice*): Mr. Peters says it looks bad for her. Mr. Henderson is awful sarcastic in a speech and he'll make fun of her sayin' she didn't wake up.

MRS. HALE: Well, I guess John Wright didn't wake when they was slipping that rope under his neck.

MRS. PETERS (*crossing slowly to table and placing shawl and apron on table with other clothing*): No, it's strange. It must have been done awful crafty and still. They say it was such a—funny way to kill a man, rigging it all up like that.

MRS. HALE (*crossing to left of* MRS. PETERS *at table*): That's just what Mr. Hale said. There was a gun in the house. He says that's what he can't understand.

MRS. PETERS: Mr. Henderson said coming out that what was needed for the case was a motive; something to show anger, or—sudden feeling.

MRS. HALE (*who is standing by the table*): Well, I don't see any signs of anger around here. (*She puts her hand on the dish towel which lies on the table, stands looking down at table, one-half of which is clean, the other half messy.*) It's wiped to here. (*Makes a move as if to finish work, then turns and looks at loaf of bread outside the breadbox. Drops towel. In that voice of coming back to familiar things*) Wonder how they are finding things upstairs. (*Crossing below table to down right.*) I hope she had it a little more red-up up there. You know, it seems kind of *sneaking.* Locking her up in town and then coming out here and trying to get her own house to turn against her!

MRS. PETERS: But, Mrs. Hale, the law is the law.

MRS. HALE: I s'pose 'tis. (*Unbuttoning her coat*) Better loosen up your things, Mrs. Peters. You won't feel them when you go out. (MRS. PETERS *takes off her fur tippet, goes to hang it on chair back left of table, stands looking at the work basket on floor near down left window.*)

MRS. PETERS: She was piecing a quilt. (*She brings the large sewing basket to the center table and they look at the bright pieces,* MRS. HALE *above the table and* MRS. PETERS *left of it.*)

MRS. HALE: It's a log cabin pattern. Pretty, isn't it? I wonder if she was goin' to quilt it or just knot it? (*Footsteps have been heard coming down the stairs. The* SHERIFF *enters followed by* HALE *and the* COUNTY ATTORNEY.

SHERIFF: They wonder if she was going to quilt it or just knot it! (*The men laugh, the women look abashed.*)

COUNTY ATTORNEY (*rubbing his hands over the stove*): Frank's fire didn't do much up there, did it? Well, let's go out to the barn and get that cleared up. (*The men go outside by up left door.*)

MRS. HALE (*resentfully*): I don't know as there's anything so strange, our takin' up our time with little things while we're waiting for them to get the evidence. (*She sits in chair right of table smoothing out a block with decision.*) I don't see as it's anything to laugh about.

MRS. PETERS (*apologetically*): Of course they've got awful important things on their minds. (*Pulls up a chair and joins* MRS. HALE *at the left of the table.*)

MRS. HALE (*examining another block*): Mrs. Peters, look at this one. Here, this is the one she was working on, and look at the sewing! All the rest of it has been so nice and even. And look at this! It's all over the place! Why, it looks as if she didn't know what she was about! (*After she has said this they look at each other, then start to glance back at the door. After an instant* MRS. HALE *has pulled at a knot and ripped the sewing.*)

MRS. PETERS: Oh, what are you doing, Mrs. Hale?

MRS. HALE (*mildly*): Just pulling out a stitch or two that's not sewed very good. (*Threading a needle.*) Bad sewing always made me fidgety.

MRS. PETERS (*with a glance at door, nervously*): I don't think we ought to touch things.

MRS. HALE: I'll just finish up this end. (*Suddenly stopping and leaning forward*) Mrs. Peters?

MRS. PETERS: Yes, Mrs. Hale?

MRS. HALE: What do you suppose she was so nervous about?

MRS. PETERS: Oh—I don't know. I don't know as she was nervous. I sometimes sew awful queer when I'm just tired. (MRS. HALE *starts to say something, looks at* MRS. PETERS, *then goes on sewing.*) Well, I must get these things wrapped up. They may be through sooner than we think. (*Putting apron and other things together.*) I wonder where I can find a piece of paper, and string. (*Rises.*)

MRS. HALE: In that cupboard, maybe.

MRS. PETERS (*crosses right looking in cupboard*): Why, here's a bird-cage. (*Holds it up.*) Did she have a bird, Mrs. Hale?

MRS. HALE: Why, I don't know whether she did or not—I've not been here for so long. There was a man around last year selling canaries cheap, but I don't know as she took one; maybe she did. She used to sing real pretty herself.

MRS. PETERS (*glancing around*): Seems funny to think of a bird here. But she must have had one, or why would she have a cage? I wonder what happened to it?

MRS. HALE: I s'pose maybe the cat got it.

MRS. PETERS: No, she didn't have a cat. She's got that feeling some people have about cats—being afraid of them. My cat got in her room and she was real upset and asked me to take it out.

MRS. HALE: My sister Bessie was like that. Queer, ain't it?

MRS. PETERS (*examining the cage*): Why, look at this door. It's broke. One hinge is pulled apart. (*Takes a step down to* MRS. HALE's *right.*)

MRS. HALE (*looking too*): Looks as if someone must have been rough with it.

MRS. PETERS: Why, yes. (*She brings the cage forward and puts it on the table.*)

MRS. HALE (*glancing toward up left door*): I wish if they're going to find any evidence they'd be about it. I don't like this place.

MRS. PETERS: But I'm awful glad you came with me, Mrs. Hale. It would be lonesome for me setting here alone.

MRS. HALE: It would, wouldn't it? (*Dropping her sewing*) But I tell you what I do wish, Mrs. Peters. I wish I had come over sometimes when *she* was here. I—(*looking around the room*)—wish I had.

MRS. PETERS: But of course you were awful busy, Mrs. Hale—your house and your children.

MRS. HALE (*rises and crosses left*): I could've come. I stayed away because it weren't cheerful—and that's why I ought to have come. I—(*looking out left window*)—I've never liked this place. Maybe because it's down in a hollow and you don't see the road. I dunno what it is, but it's a lonesome place and always was. I wish I had come over to see Minnie Foster sometimes. I can see now—— (*Shakes her head.*)

MRS. PETERS (*left of table and above it*): Well, you mustn't reproach yourself, Mrs. Hale. Somehow we just don't see how it is with other folks until—something turns up.

MRS. HALE: Not having children makes less work—but it makes a quiet house, and Wright out to work all day, and no company when he did come in. (*Turning from window*) Did you know John Wright, Mrs. Peters?

MRS. PETERS: Not to know him; I've seen him in town. They say he was a good man.

MRS. HALE: Yes—good; he didn't drink, and kept his word as well as most, I guess, and paid his debts. But he was a hard man, Mrs. Peters. Just to pass the time of day with him——(*Shivers.*) Like a raw wind that gets to the bone. (*Pauses, her eye falling on the cage.*) I should think she woulda wanted a bird. But what do you suppose went with it?

MRS. PETERS: I don't know, unless it got sick and died. (*She reaches over and swings the broken door, swings it again, both women watch it.*)

MRS. HALE: You weren't raised round here, were you? (MRS. PETERS *shakes her head.*) You didn't know—her?

MRS. PETERS: Not till they brought her yesterday.

MRS. HALE: She—come to think of it, she was kind of like a bird herself—real sweet and pretty, but kind of timid and—fluttery. How—she—did—change. (*Silence; then as if struck by a happy thought and relieved to get back to everyday things. Crosses right above* MRS. PETERS *to cupboard, replaces small chair used to stand on to its original place down right.*) Tell you what, Mrs. Peters, why don't you take the quilt in with you? It might take up her mind.

MRS. PETERS: Why, I think that's a real nice idea, Mrs. Hale. There couldn't possibly be any objection to it, could there? Now, just what would I take? I wonder if her patches are in here—and her things. (*They look in the sewing basket.*)

MRS. HALE (*crosses to right of table*): Here's some red. I expect this has got sewing things in it. (*Brings out a fancy box.*) What a pretty box. Looks like something somebody would give you. Maybe her scissors are in here. (*Opens box. Suddenly puts her hand to her nose.*) Why——(MRS. PETERS *bends nearer, then turns her face away.*) There's something wrapped up in this piece of silk.

MRS. PETERS: Why, this isn't her scissors.

MRS. HALE (*lifting the silk*): Oh, Mrs. Peters—it's——(MRS. PETERS *bends closer.*)

MRS. PETERS: It's the bird.

MRS. HALE: But, Mrs. Peters—look at it! Its neck! Look at its neck! It's all—other side *to*.

MRS. PETERS: Somebody—wrung—its—neck. (*Their eyes meet. A look of growing comprehension, of horror. Steps are heard outside.* MRS. HALE *slips box under quilt pieces, and sinks into her chair. Enter* SHERIFF *and* COUNTY ATTORNEY. MRS. PETERS *steps down left and stands looking out of window.*)

COUNTY ATTORNEY (*as one turning from serious things to little pleasantries*): Well, ladies, have you decided whether she was going to quilt it or knot it? (*Crosses to center above table.*)

MRS. PETERS: We think she was going to—knot it. (SHERIFF *crosses to right of stove, lifts stove lid and glances at fire, then stands warming hands at stove.*)

COUNTY ATTORNEY: Well, that's interesting, I'm sure. (*Seeing the bird-cage.*) Has the bird flown?

MRS. HALE (*putting more quilt pieces over the box*): We think the—cat got it.

COUNTY ATTORNEY (*preoccupied*): Is there a cat? (MRS. HALE *glances in a quick covert way at* MRS. PETERS.)

MRS. PETERS (*turning from window takes a step in*): Well, not *now*. They're superstitious, you know. They leave.

COUNTY ATTORNEY (*to* SHERIFF PETERS, *continuing an interrupted conversation*): No sign at all of anyone having come from the outside. Their own rope. Now let's go up again and go over it piece by piece. (*They start upstairs.*) It would have to have been someone who knew just the——

(MRS. PETERS *sits down left of table. The two women sit there not looking at one another, but as if peering into something and at the same time holding back. When they talk now it is in the manner of feeling their way over strange ground, as if afraid of what they are saying, but as if they cannot help saying it.*)

MRS. HALE (*hesitatively and in hushed voice*): She liked the bird. She was going to bury it in that pretty box.

MRS. PETERS (*in a whisper*): When I was a girl— my kitten—there was a boy took a hatchet, and before my eyes—and before I could get there—— (*Covers her face an instant.*) If they hadn't held me back I would have—(*catches herself, looks upstairs where steps are heard, falters weakly*)—hurt him.

MRS. HALE (*with a slow look around her*): I wonder how it would seem never to have had any children around. (*Pause.*) No, Wright wouldn't like the bird—a thing that sang. She used to sing. He killed that, too.

MRS. PETERS (*moving uneasily*): We don't know who killed the bird.

MRS. HALE: I knew John Wright.

MRS. PETERS: It was an awful thing done in this house that night, Mrs. Hale. Killing a man while he slept, slipping a rope around his neck that choked the life out of him.

MRS. HALE: His neck. Choked the life out of him. (*Her hand goes out and rests on the birdcage.*)

MRS. PETERS (*with rising voice*): We don't know who killed him. We don't *know*.

MRS. HALE (*her own feeling not interrupted*): If there'd been years and years of nothing, then a bird to sing to you, it would be awful—still, after the bird was still.

MRS. PETERS (*something within her speaking*): I know what stillness is. When we homesteaded in Dakota, and my first baby died—after he was two years old, and me with no other then—

MRS. HALE (*moving*): How soon do you suppose they'll be through looking for the evidence?

MRS. PETERS: I know what stillness is. (*Pulling herself back.*) The law has got to punish crime, Mrs. Hale.

MRS. HALE (*not as if answering that*): I wish you'd seen Minnie Foster when she wore a white dress with blue ribbons and stood up there in the choir and sang. (*A look around the room.*) Oh, I *wish* I'd come over here once in a while! That was a crime! That was a crime! Who's going to punish that?

MRS. PETERS (*looking upstairs*): We mustn't— take on.

MRS. HALE: I might have known she needed help! I know how things can be—for women. I tell you, it's queer, Mrs. Peters. We live close together and we live far apart. We all go through the same things—it's all just a different kind of the same thing. (*Brushes her eyes, noticing the jar of fruit, reaches out for it.*) If I was you I wouldn't tell her her fruit was gone. Tell her it *ain't*. Tell her it's all right. Take this in to prove it to her. She—she may never know whether it was broke or not.

MRS. PETERS (*takes the jar, looks about for something to wrap it in; takes petticoat from the clothes brought from the other room, very nervously begins winding this around the jar. In a false voice*): My, it's a good thing the men couldn't hear us. Wouldn't they just laugh! Getting all stirred up over a little thing like a—dead canary. As if that could have anything to do with—with—wouldn't they *laugh*! (*The men are heard coming downstairs.*)

MRS. HALE (*under her breath*): Maybe they would—maybe they wouldn't.

COUNTY ATTORNEY: No, Peters, it's all perfectly clear except a reason for doing it. But you know juries when it comes to women. If there was some definite thing. (*Crosses slowly to above table.* SHERIFF *crosses down right.* MRS. HALE *and* MRS. PETERS *remain seated at either side of table.*) Something to show—something to make a story about—a thing that would connect up with this strange way of doing it——(*The women's eyes meet for an instant. Enter* HALE *from outer door.*)

HALE (*remaining up left by door*): Well, I've got the team around. Pretty cold out there.

COUNTY ATTORNEY: I'm going to stay awhile by myself. (*To the* SHERIFF) You can send Frank out for me, can't you? I want to go over everything. I'm not satisfied that we can't do better.

SHERIFF: Do you want to see what Mrs. Peters is going to take in? (*The* LAWYER *picks up the apron, laughs.*)

COUNTY ATTORNEY: Oh, I guess they're not very dangerous things the ladies have picked out. (*Moves a few things about, disturbing the quilt pieces which cover the box. Steps back.*) No, Mrs. Peters doesn't need supervising. For that matter a sheriff's wife is married to the law. Ever think of it that way, Mrs. Peters?

MRS. PETERS: Not—just that way.

SHERIFF (*chuckling*): Married to the law. (*Moves to down right door to the other room.*) I just want you to come in here a minute, George. We ought to take a look at these windows.

COUNTY ATTORNEY (*scoffingly*): Oh, windows!

SHERIFF: We'll be right out, Mr. Hale. (HALE *goes outside. The* SHERIFF *follows the* COUNTY ATTORNEY *into the other room. Then* MRS. HALE *rises, hands tight together, looking intensely at* MRS. PETERS, *whose eyes make a slow turn, finally meeting* MRS. HALE's. *A moment* MRS. HALE *holds her, then her own eyes point the way to where the box is concealed. Suddenly* MRS. PETERS *throws back quilt pieces and tries to put the box in the bag she is carrying. It is too big. She opens box, starts to take bird out, cannot touch it, goes to pieces, stands there helpless. Sound of a knob turning in the other room.* MRS. HALE *snatches the box and puts it in the pocket of her big coat. Enter* COUNTY ATTORNEY *and* SHERIFF, *who remains down right.*)

COUNTY ATTORNEY (*crosses to up left door facetiously*): Well, Henry, at least we found out that she was not going to quilt it. She was going to—what is it you call it, ladies?

MRS HALE (*standing center below table facing front, her hand against her pocket*): We call it—knot it, Mr. Henderson.

CURTAIN

COMMENTARY

Trifles is a remarkable play, not only because it was written by a woman at a time when women did not often write for the stage but also because it anticipates some of the views of the women's movement. In our Commentary to *Out of Our Fathers' House* (page 647), where we briefly discuss the history of women who wrote for the theater, we point out that until fairly recently plays by women did not customarily present a feminist point of view. In fact, *Trifles* is the only significant early example we can think of.

Trifles deals with a murder, but the spectator or reader soon perceives that it is not a conventional murder mystery. "Who dunnit?" is something we learn fairly early. There is considerably more suspense at the very end of the play—will the women be able to conceal the dead bird before the men return to the room?—but chiefly the interest in the play is in Mrs. Hale's and Mrs. Peters's growing awareness of what has happened and of their consequent growing solidarity, with each other and with Mrs. Wright. A year after Glaspell wrote this play, she rewrote it as a short story, titled "Jury of Her Peers." The title implies the chief *action* (in the Aristotelian sense) underlying the play: the women come to a decision about Mrs. Wright and act on it.

The short story is extremely close to the play (much of it, after the first page, uses dialogue identical with that of the play), but it begins in Martha Hale's house, rather than in the Wright house. You may be interested in reading the beginning of the story, since the story writer here is conveying information in a way that the dramatist cannot. When you reread the play, notice the ways in which some of this information gets conveyed.

> When Martha Hale opened the storm-door and got a cut of the north wind, she ran back for her big woolen scarf. As she hurriedly wound that round her head her eye made a scandalized sweep of her kitchen. It was no ordinary thing that called her away—it was probably farther from ordinary than anything that had ever happened in Dickson County. But what her eye took in was that her kitchen was in no shape for leaving: her bread all ready for mixing, half the flour sifted and half unsifted.

She hated to see things half done; but she had been at that when the team from town stopped to get Mr. Hale, and then the sheriff came running in to say his wife wished Mrs. Hale would come too—adding, with a grin, that he guessed she was getting scarey and wanted another woman along. So she had dropped everything right where it was.

"Martha!" now came her husband's impatient voice. "Don't keep folks waiting out here in the cold."

TOPICS FOR DISCUSSION

1. In a sentence or two describe the setting, indicating both what it "says" and the atmosphere it evokes.
2. Even before the first word of dialogue is spoken, what does the play tell us (in the entrance of the characers) about the distinction between the men and the women?
3. How would you characterize Mr. Henderson, the county attorney?
4. In what way or ways are Mrs. Peters and Mrs. Hale different from each other?
5. Several times the men "laugh" or "chuckle." In their contexts, what do these expressions of amusement convey?
6. On page 405, *"the women's eyes meet for an instant."* What does this bit of action "say"? What are we to understand by the exchange of glances?
7. On page 405, when Mrs. Peters tells of the boy who killed her cat, she says, "If they hadn't held me back, I would have—(*catches herself, looks upstairs where steps are heard, falters weakly*)—hurt him." What do you think she was about to say before she faltered? Why does Glaspell include this speech about Mrs. Peters's girlhood?
8. On page 403, Mrs. Hale, looking at a quilt, wonders whether Mrs. Wright "was going to quilt it or just knot it." The men are amused by the women's concern with this topic, and the last line of the play returns to this issue. What is the point?
9. What sort of person do you think Minnie Foster was before she married?
10. In what way or ways is the play ironic? (Consult the entry on *irony* in the Glossary.)
11. Can it reasonably be argued that this play is immoral? Explain.

THE EMPEROR JONES

Eugene O'Neill

Eugene O'Neill (1888–1953), the son of an actor, was born in a hotel room near Broadway and spent his early years traveling with his parents throughout the United States. He entered Princeton University in 1906 but left before the end of the first year. In 1909 he traveled to Honduras looking for gold, contracted malaria, and returned to the United States in 1910. After touring briefly with his father's company, he shipped to Buenos Aires, jumped ship there, did odd jobs, shipped to South Africa, and returned to the United States in 1911. The following year he learned that he had tuberculosis. In a sanatorium he began seriously reading plays, and in 1916 he joined the Provincetown Players, who put on some of his one-act plays. *The Emperor Jones* (1920), produced by the Provincetown Players in New York, was his first major play. In time he was awarded four Pulitzer Prizes (one, posthumous, was for *A Long Day's Journey into Night*, written in 1940, but not produced until 1955), and a Nobel Prize. In 1933 *The Emperor Jones* was made into a film starring Paul Robeson. The film, 72 minutes long, devotes the first 30 minutes to showing Jones's life in the United States, and the next 15 minutes to Jones's arrival on the island and his career there. Only the last 27 minutes are devoted to the happenings in O'Neill's play.

CHARACTERS

BRUTUS JONES, *Emperor*
HENRY SMITHERS, *A Cockney Trader*
AN OLD NATIVE WOMAN
LEM, *A Native Chief*
SOLDIERS, *Adherents of Lem*
THE LITTLE FORMLESS FEARS
JEFF

THE NEGRO CONVICTS
THE PRISON GUARD
THE PLANTERS
THE AUCTIONEER
THE SLAVES
THE CONGO WITCH-DOCTOR
THE CROCODILE GOD

The action of the play takes place on an island in the West Indies as yet not self-determined by white Marines. The form of native government is, for the time being, an empire.

Paul Chevalier as Smithers and Habib Benglia as Jones in a 1949 production of *The Emperor Jones* in Paris. (Photograph: Bernand.)

SCENE I

Scene—The audience chamber in the palace of the Emperor—a spacious, high-ceilinged room with bare, white-washed walls. The floor is of white tiles. In the rear, to the left of center, a wide archway giving out on a portico with white pillars. The palace is evidently situated on high ground, for beyond the portico nothing can be seen but a vista of distant hills, their summits crowned with thick groves of palm trees. In the right wall, center, a smaller arched doorway leading to the living quarters of the palace. The room is bare of furniture with the exception of one huge chair made of uncut wood which stands at center, its back to rear. This is very apparently the Emperor's throne. It is painted a dazzling, eye-smiting scarlet. There is a brilliant orange cushion on the seat and another smaller one is placed on the floor to serve as a footstool. Strips of matting, dyed scarlet, lead from the foot of the throne to the two entrances.

It is late afternoon but the sunlight still blazes yellowly beyond the portico and there is an oppressive burden of exhausting heat in the air.

As the curtain rises, a native Negro woman sneaks in cautiously from the entrance on the right. She is very old, dressed in cheap calico, bare-footed, a red bandana handkerchief covering all but a few stray wisps of white hair. A bundle bound in colored cloth is carried over her shoulder on the end of a stick. She hesitates beside the doorway, peering back as if in extreme dread of being discovered. Then she begins to glide noiselessly, a step at a time, toward the doorway in the rear. At this moment, SMITHERS *appears beneath the portico.*

SMITHERS *is a tall, stoop-shouldered man about forty. His bald head, perched on a long neck with an enormous Adam's apple, looks like an egg. The tropics have tanned his naturally pasty face with its small, sharp features to a sickly yellow, and native rum has painted his pointed nose to a startling red. His little, washy-blue eyes are red-rimmed and dart about him like a ferret's. His expression is one of unscrupulous meanness, cowardly and dangerous. He is dressed in a worn riding suit of dirty white drill, puttees, spurs, and wears a white cork helmet. A cartridge belt with an automatic revolver is around his waist. He carries a riding whip in his hand. He sees the woman and stops to watch her suspiciously. Then, making up his mind, he steps quickly on tiptoe into the room. The woman, looking back over her shoulder continually, does not see him until it is too late. When she does,* SMITHERS *springs forward and grabs her firmly by the shoulder. She struggles to get away, fiercely but silently.*

SMITHERS (*tightening his grasp—roughly*): Easy! None o' that, me birdie. You can't wriggle out now. I got me 'ooks on yer.

WOMAN (*seeing the uselessness of struggling, gives way to frantic terror, and sinks to the ground, embracing his knees supplicatingly*): No tell him! No tell him, Mister!

SMITHERS (*with great curiosity*): Tell 'im? (*Then scornfully*) Oh, you mean 'is bloomin' Majesty. What's the gaime, any 'ow? What are you sneakin' away for? Been stealin' a bit, I s'pose. (*He taps her bundle with his riding whip significantly.*)

WOMAN (*shaking her head vehemently*): No, me no steal.

SMITHERS: Bloody liar! But tell me what's up. There's somethin' funny goin' on. I smelled it in the air first thing I got up this mornin'. You blacks are up to some devilment. This palace of 'is is like a bleedin' tomb. Where's all the 'ands?

(*The woman keeps sullenly silent.* SMITHERS *raises his whip threateningly.*)

Ow, yer won't, won't yer? I'll show yer what's what.

WOMAN (*coweringly*): I tell, Mister. You no hit. They go—all go. (*She makes a sweeping gesture toward the hills in the distance.*)

SMITHERS: Run away—to the 'ills?

WOMAN: Yes, Mister. Him Emperor—Great

Father. (*She touches her forehead to the floor with a quick mechanical jerk.*) Him sleep after eat. Then they go—all go. Me old woman. Me left only. Now me go too.

SMITHERS (*his astonishment giving way to an immense, mean satisfaction*): Ow! So that's the ticket! Well, I know bloody well wot's in the air—when they runs orf to the 'ills. The tom-tom 'll be thumping out there bloomin' soon. (*With extreme vindictiveness.*) And I'm bloody glad of it, for one! Serve 'im right! Puttin' on airs, the stinkin' nigger! 'Is Majesty! Gawd blimey! I only 'opes I'm there when they takes 'im out to shoot 'im. (*Suddenly.*) 'E's still 'ere all right, ain't 'e?

WOMAN: Yes. Him sleep.

SMITHERS: 'E's bound to find out soon as 'e wakes up. 'E's cunnin' enough to know when 'is time's come.

(*He goes to the doorway on right and whistles shrilly with his fingers in his mouth. The old woman springs to her feet and runs out of the doorway, rear.* SMITHERS *goes after her, reaching for his revolver.*)

Stop or I'll shoot! (*Then stopping—indifferently.*) Pop orf then, if yer like, yer black cow. (*He stands in the doorway, looking after her.*)

(JONES *enters from the right. He is a tall, powerfully built, full-blooded Negro of middle age. His features are typically negroid, yet there is something decidedly distinctive about his face—an underlying strength of will, a hardy, self-reliant confidence in himself that inspires respect. His eyes are alive with a keen, cunning intelligence. In manner he is shrewd, suspicious, evasive. He wears a light blue uniform coat, sprayed with brass buttons, heavy gold chevrons on his shoulders, gold braid on the collar, cuffs, etc. His pants are bright red with a light blue stripe down the side. Patent-leather laced boots with spurs, and a belt with a long-barreled, pearl-handled revolver in a holster complete his make up. Yet there is something not altogether ridiculous about his grandeur. He has a way of carrying it off.*)

JONES (*not seeing anyone—greatly irritated and blinking sleepily—shouts*): Who dare whistle dat way in my palace? Who dare wake up de Emperor? I'll git de hide fravled off some o' you niggers sho'!

SMITHERS (*showing himself—in a manner half-afraid and half-defiant*): It was me whistled to yer. (*As* JONES *frowns angrily*) I got news for yer.

JONES (*putting on his suavest manner, which fails to cover up his contempt for the white man*): Oh, it's you, Mister Smithers. (*He sits down on his throne with easy dignity.*) What news you got to tell me?

SMITHERS (*coming close to enjoy his discomfiture*): Don't yer notice nothin' funny today?

JONES (*coldly*): Funny? No. I ain't perceived nothin' of de kind!

SMITHERS: Then yer ain't so foxy as I thought yer was. Where's all your court? (*Sarcastically*) The Generals and the Cabinet Ministers and all?

JONES (*imperturbably*): Where dey mostly runs de minute I closes my eyes—drinkin' rum and talkin' big down in de town. (*Sarcastically*) How come you don't know dat? Ain't you sousin' with 'em most every day?

SMITHERS (*stung but pretending indifference—with a wink*): That's part of the day's work. I got ter—ain't I—in my business?

JONES (*contemptuously*): Yo' business!

SMITHERS (*imprudently enraged*): Gawd blimey, you was glad enough for me ter take yer in on it when you landed here first. You didn' 'ave no 'igh and mighty airs in them days!

JONES (*his hand going to his revolver like a flash—menacingly*): Talk polite, white man! Talk polite, you heah me! I'm boss heah now, is you fergettin'? (*The Cockney seems about to challenge this last statement with the facts but something in the other's eyes holds and cows him.*)

SMITHERS (*in a cowardly whine*): No 'arm meant, old top.

JONES (*condescendingly*): I accepts yo' apology. (*Lets his hand fall from his revolver.*) No use'n you rakin' up ole times. What I was den is one thing. What I is now's another. You didn't let me in on yo' crooked work out o' no kind feelin's dat time. I done de dirty work fo' you—and most o' de brain work, too, fo' dat matter—and I was wu'th money to you, dat's de reason.

SMITHERS: Well, blimey, I give yer a start, didn't I—when no one else would. I wasn't afraid to 'ire yer like the rest was—'count of the story about your breakin' jail back in the States.

JONES: No, you didn't have no s'cuse to look down on me fo' dat. You been in jail you'self more'n once.

SMITHERS (*furiously*): It's a lie! (*Then trying to pass it off by an attempt at scorn*) Garn! Who told yer that fairy tale?

JONES: Dey's some tings I ain't got to be tole. I kin see 'em in folk's eyes. (*Then after a pause—meditatively*) Yes, you sho' give me a start. And it didn't take long from dat time to git dese fool, woods' niggers right where I wanted dem. (*With pride*) From stowaway to Emperor in two years! Dat's goin' some!

SMITHERS (*with curiosity*): And I bet you got yer pile o'money 'id safe some place.

JONES (*with satisfaction*): I sho' has! And it's in a foreign bank where no pusson don't ever git it out but me no matter what come. You didn't s'pose I was holdin' down dis Emperor job for de glory in it, did you? Sho'! De fuss and glory part of it, dat's only to turn de heads o' de low-flung, bush niggers dat's here. Dey wants de big circus show for deir money. I gives it to 'em an' I gits de money. (*With a grin*) De long green, dat's me every time! (*Then rebukingly*) But you ain't got no kick agin me, Smithers. I'se paid you back all you done for me many times. Ain't I pertected you and winked at all de crooked tradin' you been doin' right out in de broad day? Sho' I has—and me makin' laws to stop it at de same time! (*He chuckles.*)

SMITHERS (*grinning*): But, meanin' no 'arm, you been grabbin' right and left yourself, ain't yer? Look at the taxes you've put on 'em! Blimey! You've squeezed 'em dry!

JONES (*chuckling*): No, dey ain't *all* dry yet. I'se still heah, ain't I?

SMITHERS (*smiling at his secret thought*): They're dry right now, you'll find out. (*Changing the subject abruptly*) And as for me breakin' laws, you've broke 'em all yerself just as fast as yer made 'em.

JONES: Ain't I de Emperor? De laws don't go for him. (*Judicially*) You heah what I tells you, Smithers. Dere's little stealin' like you does, and dere's big stealin' like I does. For de little stealin' dey gits you in jail soon or late. For de big stealin' dey makes you Emperor and puts you in de Hall o' Fame when you croaks. (*Reminiscently*) If dey's one thing I learns in ten years on de Pullman ca's listenin' to de white quality talk, it's dat same fact. And when I gits a chance to use it I winds up Emperor in two years.

SMITHERS (*unable to repress the genuine admiration of the small fry for the large*): Yes, yer turned the bleedin' trick, all right. Blimey, I never seen a bloke 'as 'ad the bloomin' luck you 'as.

JONES (*severely*): Luck? What you mean—luck?

SMITHERS: I suppose you'll say as that swank about the silver bullet ain't luck—and that was what first got the fool blacks on yer side the time of the revolution, wasn't it?

JONES (*with a laugh*): Oh, dat silver bullet! Sho' was luck! But I makes dat luck, you heah? I loads de dice! Yessuh! When dat murderin' nigger ole Lem hired to kill me takes aim ten feet away and his gun misses fire and I shoots him dead, what you heah me say?

SMITHERS: You said yer'd got a charm so's no lead bullet'd kill yer. You was so strong only a silver bullet could kill yer, you told 'em. Blimey, wasn't that swank for yer—and plain, fat-'eaded luck?

JONES (*proudly*): I got brains and I uses 'em quick. Dat ain't luck.

SMITHERS: Yer know they wasn't 'ardly liable to get no silver bullets. And it was luck 'e didn't 'it you that time.

JONES (*laughing*): And dere all dem fool, bush niggers was kneelin' down and bumpin' deir heads on de ground like I was a miracle out o' de Bible. Oh Lawd, from dat time on I has dem all eatin' out of my hand. I cracks de whip and dey jumps through.

SMITHERS (*with a sniff*): Yankee bluff done it.

JONES: Ain't a man's talkin' big what makes him big—long as he makes folks believe it? Sho', I talks large when I ain't got nothin' to back it up, but I ain't talkin' wild just de same. I knows I kin fool 'em—I *knows* it—and dat's backin' enough fo' my game. And ain't I got to learn deir lingo and teach some of dem English befo' I kin talk to 'em? Ain't dat wuk? You ain't never learned ary word er it, Smithers, in de ten years you been heah, dough yo' knows it's money in yo' pocket tradin' wid 'em if you does. But you'se too shiftless to take de trouble.

SMITHERS (*flushing*): Never mind about me. What's this I've 'eard about yer really 'avin' a silver bullet moulded for yourself?

JONES: It's playin' out my bluff. I has de silver bullet moulded and I tells 'em when de time comes I kills myself wid it. I tells 'em dat's 'cause I'm de on'y man in de world big enuff to git me. No use'n deir tryin'. And dey falls down and bumps deir heads. (*He laughs.*) I does dat so's I kin take a walk in peace widout no jealous nigger gunnin' at me from behind de trees.

SMITHERS (*astonished*): Then you 'ad it made— 'onest?

JONES: Sho' did. Heah she be. (*He takes out his revolver, breaks it, and takes the silver bullet out of one chamber.*) Five lead an' dis silver baby at de last. Don't she shine pretty? (*He holds it in his hand, looking at it admiringly, as if strangely fascinated.*)

SMITHERS: Let me see. (*Reaches out his hand for it.*)

JONES (*harshly*): Keep y' hands whar dey b'long, white man. (*He replaces it in the chamber and puts the revolver back on his hip.*)

SMITHERS (*snarling*): Gawd blimey! Think I'm a bleedin' thief, you would.

JONES: No, 'tain't dat. I knows you'se scared to steal from me. On'y I ain't 'lowin' nary body to touch dis baby. She's my rabbit's foot.

SMITHERS (*sneering*): A bloomin' charm, wot? (*Venomously*) Well, you'll need all the bloody charms you 'as before long, s' 'elp me!

JONES (*judiciously*): Oh, I'se good for six months yit 'fore dey gits sick o' my game. Den, when I sees trouble comin', I makes my get away.

SMITHERS: Ho! You got it all planned, ain't yer?

JONES: I ain't no fool. I knows dis Emperor's time is sho't. Dat why I make hay when de sun shine. Was you thinkin' I'se aimin' to hold down dis job for life? No, suh! What good is gittin' money if you stays back in dis raggedy country? I wants action when I spends. And when I sees dese niggers gittin' up deir nerve to tu'n me out, and I'se got all de money in sight, I resigns on de spot and beats it quick.

SMOTHERS: Where to?

JONES: None o' yo' business.

SMITHERS: Not back to the bloody States, I'll lay my oath.

JONES (*suspiciously*): Why don't I? (*Then with an easy laugh*) You mean 'count of dat story 'bout me breakin' from jail back dere? Dat's all talk.

SMITHERS (*skeptically*): Ho, yes!

JONES (*sharply*): You ain't 'sinuatin' I'se a liar, is you?

SMITHERS (*hastily*): No, Gawd strike me! I was only thinkin' o' the bloody lies you told the blacks 'ere about killin' white men in the States.

JONES (*angered*): How come dey're lies?

SMITHERS: You'd 'ave been in jail if you 'ad, wouldn't yer then? (*With venom*) And from what I've 'eard, it ain't 'ealthy for a black to kill a white man in the States. They burns 'em in oil, don't they?

JONES (*with cool deadliness*): You mean lynchin' 'd scare me? Well, I tells you, Smithers, maybe I does kill one white man back dere. Maybe I does. And maybe I kills another right heah 'fore long if he don't look out.

SMITHERS (*trying to force a laugh*): I was on'y spoofin' yer. Can't yer take a joke? And you was just sayin' you'd never been in jail.

JONES (*in the same tone—slightly boastful*): Maybe I goes to jail dere for gettin' in an argument wid razors ovah a crap game. Maybe I gits twenty years when dat colored man die. Maybe I gits in 'nother argument wid de prison guard was overseer ovah us when we're wukin' de roads. Maybe he hits me wid a whip and I splits his head wid a shovel and runs away and files de chain off my leg and gits away safe. Maybe I does all dat an' maybe I don't. It's a story I tells you so's you knows I'se de kind of man dat if you evah repeats one word of it, I ends yo' stealin' on dis yearth mighty damn quick!

SMITHERS (*terrified*): Think I'd peach on yer? Not me! Ain't I always been yer friend?

JONES (*suddenly relaxing*): Sho' you has—and you better be.

SMITHERS (*recovering his composure—and with it his malice*): And just to show yer I'm yer friend, I'll tell yer that bit o' news I was goin' to.

JONES: Go ahead! Shoot de piece. Must be bad news from de happy way you look.

SMITHERS (*warningly*): Maybe it's gettin' time for you to resign—with that bloomin' silver bullet, wot? (*He finishes with a mocking grin.*)

JONES (*puzzled*): What's dat you say? Talk plain.

SMITHERS: Ain't notice any of the guards or servants about the place today, I 'aven't.

JONES (*carelessly*): Dey're all out in de garden sleepin' under de trees. When I sleeps, dey sneaks a sleep, too, and I pretends I never suspicions it. All I got to do is to ring de bell and dey come flyin', makin' a bluff dey was wukin' all de time.

SMITHERS (*in the same mocking tone*): Ring the bell now an' you'll bloody well see what I means.

JONES (*startled to alertness, but preserving the same careless tone*): Sho' I rings. (*He reaches below the throne and pulls out a big, common dinner bell which is painted the same vivid scarlet as the throne. He rings this vigorously—then stops to listen. Then he goes to both doors, rings again, and looks out.*)

SMITHERS (*watching him with malicious satisfaction, after a pause—mockingly*): The bloody ship is sinkin' an' the bleedin' rats 'as slung their 'ooks.

JONES (*in a sudden fit of anger flings the bell clattering into a corner*): Low-flung, woods' niggers! (*Then catching* SMITHERS' *eye on him, he controls himself and suddenly bursts into a low chuckling laugh.*) Reckon I overplays my hand dis once! A man can't take de pot on a bob-tailed flush all de time. Was I sayin' I'd sit in six months mo'? Well, I's changed my mind den. I cashes in and resigns de job of Emperor right dis minute.

SMITHERS (*with real admiration*): Blimey, but you're a cool bird, and no mistake.

JONES: No use'n fussin'. When I knows de

game's up I kisses it good-bye widout no long waits. Dey've all run off to de hills, ain't dey?

SMITHERS: Yes—every bleedin' man jack of 'em.

JONES: Den de revolution is at de post. And de Emperor better git his feet smokin' up de trail. (*He starts for the door in rear.*)

SMITHERS: Goin' out to look for your 'orse? Yer won't find any. They steals the 'orses first thing. Mine was gone when I went for 'im this mornin'. That's wot first give me a suspicion of wot was up.

JONES (*alarmed for a second, scratches his head, then philosophically*): Well, den I hoofs it. Feet, do yo' duty! (*He pulls out a gold watch and looks at it.*) Three-thuty. Sundown's at six-thuty or dereabouts. (*Puts his watch back—with cool confidence.*) I got plenty o' time to make it easy.

SMITHERS: Don't be so bloomin' sure of it. They'll be after you 'ot and 'eavy. Ole Lem is at the bottom o' this business an' 'e 'ates you like 'ell. 'E'd rather do for you than eat 'is dinner, 'e would!

JONES (*scornfully*): Dat fool no-count nigger! Does you think I'se scared o' him? I stands him on his thick head more'n once befo' dis, and I does it again if he come in my way . . . (*Fiercely*) And dis time I leave him a dead nigger fo' sho'!

SMITHERS: You'll 'ave to cut through the big forest—an' these blacks 'ere can sniff and follow a trail in the dark like 'ounds. You'd 'ave to 'ustle to get through that forest in twelve hours even if you knew all the bloomin' trails like a native.

JONES (*with indignant scorn*): Look-a-heah, white man! Does you think I'se a natural bo'n fool? Give me credit fo' havin' some sense, fo' Lawd's sake! Don't you s'pose I'se looked ahead and made sho' of all de chances? I'se gone out in dat big forest, pretendin' to hunt, so many times dat I knows it high an' low like a book. I could go through on dem trails wid my eyes shut. (*With great contempt*) Think dese ign'rent bush niggers dat ain't got brains enuff to know deir own names even can catch Brutus Jones? Huh, I s'pects not! Not on yo' life! Why, man, de white men went after me wid bloodhounds where I come from an' I jes' laughs at 'em. It's a shame to fool dese black trash around heah, dey're so easy. You watch me, man! I'll make dem look sick, I will. I'll be 'cross de plain to de edge of de forest by time dark comes. Once in de woods in de night, dey got a swell chance o' findin' dis baby! Dawn tomorrow I'll be out at de oder side and on de coast whar dat French gunboat is stayin'. She picks me up, take me to Martinique when she go dar, and dere I is

safe wid a mighty big bankroll in my jeans. It's easy as rollin' off a log.

SMITHERS (*maliciously*): But s'posin' somethin' 'appens wrong an' they do nab yer?

JONES (*decisively*): Dey don't—dat's de answer.

SMITHERS: But, just for argyment's sake— what'd you do?

JONES (*frowning*): I's got five lead bullets in dis gun good enuff fo' common bush niggers—and after dat I got de silver bullet left to cheat 'em out o' gittin' me.

SMITHERS (*jeeringly*): Ho, I was forgettin' that silver bullet. You'll bump yourself orf in style, won't yer? Blimey!

JONES (*gloomily*): You kin bet yo' whole roll on one thing, white man. Dis baby plays out his string to de end and when he quits, he quits wid a bang de way he ought. Silver bullet ain't none too good for him when he go, dat's a fac'! (*Then shaking off his nervousness—with a confident laugh*) So'! What is I talkin' about? Ain't come to dat yit and I never will—not wid trash niggers like dese yer. (*Boastfully*) Silver bullet bring me luck anyway. I kin outguess, outrun, outfight, an' outplay de whole lot o' dem all ovah de board any time o' de day er night! You watch me!

(*From the distant hills comes the faint, steady thump of a tom-tom, low and vibrating. It starts at a rate exactly corresponding to normal pulse beat—72 to the minute—and continues at a gradually accelerating rate from this point uninterruptedly to the very end of the play.*

JONES starts at the sound. A strange look of apprehension creeps into his face for a moment as he listens. Then he asks, with an attempt to regain his most casual manner.)

What's dat drum beatin' fo'?

SMITHERS (*with a mean grin*): For you. That means the bleedin' ceremony 'as started. I've 'eard it before and I knows.

JONES: Cer'mony? What cer'mony?

SMITHERS: The blacks is 'oldin' a bloody meetin', 'avin' a war dance, gettin' their courage worked up b'fore they starts after you.

JONES: Let dem! Dey'll sho' need it!

SMITHERS: And they're there 'oldin' their 'eathen religious service—makin' no end of devil spells and charms to 'elp 'em against your silver bullet. (*He guffaws loudly.*) Blimey, but they're balmy as 'ell!

JONES (*a tiny bit awed and shaken in spite of*

himself): Huh! Takes more'n dat to scare dis chicken!

SMITHERS (*scenting the other's feeling—maliciously*): Ternight when it's pitch black in the forest, they'll 'ave their pet devils and ghosts 'oundin' after you. You'll find yer bloody 'air'll be standin' on end before termorrow mornin'. (*Seriously*) It's a bleedin' queer place, that stinkin' forest, even in daylight. Yer don't know what might 'appen in there, it's that rotten still. Always sends the cold shivers down my back minute I gets in it.

JONES (*with a contemptuous sniff*): I ain't no chicken-liver like you is. Trees an' me, we'se friends, and dar's a full moon comin' bring me light. And let dem po' niggers make all de fool spells dey'se a min' to. Does yo' s'pect I'se silly enuff to b'lieve in ghosts an' ha'nts an' all dat ole woman's talk? G'long, white man! You ain't talkin' to me. (*With a chuckle*) Doesn't you know dey's got to do wid a man was member in good standin' o' de Baptist Church? Sho' I was dat when I was porter on de Pullmans, befo' I gits into my little trouble. Let dem try deir heathen tricks. De Baptist Church done pertect me and land dem all in hell. (*Then with more confident satisfaction*) And I'se got little silver bullet o' my own, don't forgit.

SMITHERS: Ho! You 'aven't give much 'eed to your Baptist Church since you been down 'ere. I've 'eard myself you 'ad turned yer coat an' was takin' up with their blarsted witch-doctors, or whatever the 'ell yer calls the swine.

JONES (*vehemently*): I pretends to! Sho' I pretends! Dat's part o' my game from de fust. If I finds out dem niggers believes dat black is white, den I yells it out louder 'n deir loudest. It don't git me nothin' to do missionary work for de Baptist Church. I'se after de coin, an' I lays my Jesus on de shelf for de time bein'. (*Stops abruptly to look at his watch—alertly.*) But I ain't got de time to waste no more fool talk wid you. I'se gwine away from heah dis secon'. (*He reaches in under the throne and pulls out an expensive Panama hat with a bright multi-colored band and sets it jauntily on his head.*) So long, white man! (*With a grin.*) See you in jail sometime, maybe!

SMITHERS: Not me, you won't. Well, I wouldn't be in yer bloody boots for no bloomin' money, but 'ere's wishin' yer luck just the same.

JONES (*contemptuously*): Yo're de frightenedest man evah I see! I tells you I'se safe's 'f I was in New York City. It takes dem niggers from now to dark to git up de nerve to start somethin'. By dat time, I'se got a head start dey never kotch up wid.

SMITHERS (*maliciously*): Give my regards to any ghosts yer meets up with.

JONES (*grinning*): If dat ghost got money, I'll tell him never ha'nt you less'n he wants to lose it.

SMITHERS (*flattered*): Garn! (*Then curiously*) Ain't yer takin' no luggage with yer?

JONES: I travels light when I wants to move fast. And I got tinned grub buried on de edge o' de forest. (*Boastfully*) Now say dat I don't look ahead an' use my brains! (*With a wide, liberal gesture*) I will all dat's left in de palace to you—and you better grab all you kin sneak away wid befo' dey gits here.

SMITHERS (*gratefully*): Righto—and thanks ter yer. (*As* JONES *walks toward the door in rear—cautioningly*) Say! Look 'ere, you ain't goin 'out that way, are yer?

JONES: Does you think I'd slink out de back door like a common nigger? I'se Emperor yit, ain't I? And de Emperor Jones leaves de way he comes, and dat black trash don't dare stop him—not yit, leastways. (*He stops for a moment in the doorway, listening to the far-off but insistent beat of the tom-tom.*) Listen to dat roll-call, will you? Must be mighty big drum carry dat far. (*Then with a laugh*) Well, if dey ain't no whole brass band to see me off, I sho' got de drum part of it. So long, white man. (*He puts his hands in his pockets and with studied carelessness, whistling a tune, he saunters out of the doorway and off to the left.*)

SMITHERS (*looks after him with a puzzled admiration*): 'E's got 'is bloomin' nerve with 'im, s'elp me! (*Then angrily*) Ho—the bleedin' nigger— puttin' on 'is bloody airs! I 'opes they nabs 'im an' gives 'im what's what! (*Then putting business before the pleasure of this thought, looking around him with cupidity*) A bloke ought to find a 'ole lot in this palace that'd go for a bit of cash. Let's take a look, 'Arry, me lad. (*He starts for the doorway on right as*

THE CURTAIN FALLS

SCENE II

Scene—Nightfall. The end of the plain where the Great Forest begins. The foreground is sandy, level ground dotted by a few stones and clumps of stunted bushes covering close against the earth to escape the buffeting of the trade wind. In the rear the forest is a wall of darkness dividing the world. Only when the eye becomes accustomed to the gloom can the outlines of separate trunks of the nearest trees be made out, enormous pillars of deeper blackness. A somber monotone of wind lost in the leaves moans in the air. Yet this sound serves but to intensify the impression of the forest's relentless immobility, to form a background throwing into relief its brooding, implacable silence.

JONES enters from the left, walking rapidly. He stops as he nears the edge of the forest, looks around him quickly, peering into the dark as if searching for some familiar landmark. Then, apparently, satisfied that he is where he ought to be, he throws himself on the ground, dog-tired.

Well, heah I is. In de nick o' time, too! Little mo' an' it'd be blacker'n de ace of spades heahabouts. (*He pulls a bandana handkerchief from his hip pocket and mops off his perspiring face.*) Sho'! Gimme air! I'se tuckered out sho' 'nuff. Dat soft Emperor job ain't no trainin' fo' a long hike ovah dat plain in de brilin' sun. (*Then with a chuckle*) Cheah up, nigger, de worst is yet to come. (*He lifts his head and stares at the forest. His chuckle peters out abruptly. In a tone of awe*) My goodness, look at dem woods, will you? Dat no-count Smithers said dey'd be black an' he sho' called de turn. (*Turning away from them quickly and looking down at his feet, he snatches at a chance to change the subject—solicitously*) Feet, you is holdin' up yo' end fine an' I sutinly hopes you ain't blisterin' none. It's time you git a rest. (*He takes off his shoes, his eyes studiously avoiding the forest. He feels of the soles of his feet gingerly.*) You is still in de pink—on'y a little mite feverish. Cool yo'selfs. Remember you done got a long journey yit befo' you. (*He sits in a weary attitude, listening to the rhythmic beating of the tom-tom. He grumbles in a loud tone to cover up a growing uneasiness.*) Bush niggers! Wonder dey wouldn' get sick o' beatin' dat drum. Sound louder, seem like. I wonder if dey's startin' after me? (*He scrambles to his feet, looking back across the plain.*) Couldn't see dem now, nohow, if dey was hundred feet away. (*Then shaking himself like a wet dog to get rid of these depressing thoughts.*) Sho', dey's miles an' miles behind. What you gittin' fidgety about? (*But he sits down and begins to lace up his shoes in great haste, all the time muttering reassuringly.*) You know what? Yo' belly is empty, dat's what's de matter wid you. Come time to eat! Wid nothin' but wind on yo' stumach, o' course you feels jiggedy. Well, we eats right heah an' now soon's I gits dese pesky

shoes laced up! (*He finishes lacing up his shoes.*) Dere! Now le's see. (*Gets on his hands and knees and searches the ground around him with his eyes.*) White stone, white stone, where is you? (*He sees the first white stone and crawls to it—with satisfaction.*) Heah you is! I knowed dis was de right place. Box of grub, come to me. (*He turns over the stone and feels in under it—in a tone of dismay*) Ain't heah! Gorry, is I in de right place or isn't I? Dere's 'nother stone. Guess dat's it. (*He scrambles to the next stone and turns it over.*) Ain't heah, neither! Grub, whar is you? Ain't heah. Gorry, has I got to go hungry into dem woods—all de night? (*While he is talking he scrambles from one stone to another, turning them over in frantic haste. Finally, he jumps to his feet excitedly.*) Is I lost de place? Must have! But how dat happen when I was followin' de trail across de plain in broad daylight? (*Almost plaintively*) I'se hungry, I is! I gotta git my feed. Whar's my strength gonna come from if I doesn't? Gorry, I gotta find dat grub high an' low somehow! Why it come dark so quick like dat? Can't see nothin'. (*He scratches a match on his trousers and peers about him. The rate of the beat of the far-off tom-tom increases perceptibly as he does so. He mutters in a bewildered voice.*) How come all dese white stones come heah when I only remembers one? (*Suddenly, with a frightened gasp, he flings the match on the ground and stamps on it.*) Nigger, is you gone crazy mad? Is you lightin' matches to show dem whar you is? Fo' Lawd's sake, use yo' haid. Gorry, I'se got to be careful! (*He stares at the plain behind him apprehensively, his hand on his revolver.*) But how come all dese white stones? And whar's dat tin box o' grub I had all wrapped up in oil cloth?

(*While his back is turned,* THE LITTLE FORMLESS FEARS *creep out from the deeper blackness of the forest. They are black, shapeless, only their glittering little eyes can be seen. If they have any describable form at all it is that of a grubworm about the size of a creeping child. They move noiselessly, but with deliberate, painful effort, striving to raise themselves on end, failing and sinking prone again.* JONES *turns about to face the forest. He stares up at the tops of the trees, seeking vainly to discover his whereabouts by their conformation.*)

Can't tell nothin' from dem trees! Gorry, nothin' 'round heah look like I evah seed it befo'. I'se done lost de place sho' 'nuff! (*With mournful foreboding.*) It's mighty queer! It's mighty queer! (*With sudden forced defiance—in an angry tone*) Woods, is you tryin' to put somethin' ovah on me?

(*From the formless creatures on the ground in front of him comes a tiny gale of low mocking laughter like a rustling of leaves. They squirm upward toward him in twisted attitudes.* JONES *looks down, leaps backward with a yell of terror, yanking out his revolver as he does so.*)

(*In a quavering voice*) What's dat? Who's dar? What is you? Git away from me befo' I shoots you up! You don't? . . .

(*He fires. There is a flash, a loud report, then silence broken only by the far-off, quickened throb of the tom-tom. The formless creatures have scurried back into the forest.* JONES *remains fixed in his position, listening intently. The sound of the shot, the reassuring feel of the revolver in his hand, have somewhat restored his shaken nerve. He addresses himself with renewed confidence.*)

Dey're gone. Dat shot fix 'em. Dey was only little animals—little wild pigs, I reckon. Dey've maybe rooted out yo' grub an' eat it. Sho', you fool nigger, what you think dey is—ha'nts? (*Excitedly*) Gorry, you give de game away when you fire dat shot. Dem niggers heah dat fo' su'tin! Time you beat it in de woods widout no long waits. (*He starts for the forest—hesitates before the plunge—then urging himself in with manful resolution*) Git in, nigger! What you skeered at? Ain't nothin' dere but de trees! Git in! (*He plunges boldly into the forest.*)

SCENE III

Scene—Nine o'clock. In the forest. The moon has just risen. Its beams, drifting through the canopy of leaves, make a barely perceptible, suffused, eerie glow. A dense low wall of underbrush and creepers is in the nearer foreground, fencing in a small triangular clearing. Beyond this is the massed blackness of the forest like an encompassing barrier. A path is dimly discerned leading down to the clearing from left, rear, and winding away from it again toward the right. As the scene opens nothing can be distinctly made out. Except for the beating of the tom-tom, which is a trifle louder and quicker than in the previous scene, there is silence, broken every few seconds by a queer, clicking sound. Then gradually the figure of the Negro, JEFF, *can be dis-*

cerned crouching on his haunches at the rear of the triangle. He is middle-aged, thin, brown in color, is dressed in a Pullman porter's uniform, cap, etc. He is throwing a pair of dice on the ground before him, picking them up, shaking them, casting them out with the regular, rigid, mechanical movements of an automaton. The heavy, plodding footsteps of someone approaching along the trail from the left are heard and JONES' *voice, pitched in a slightly higher key and strained in a cheering effort to overcome its own tremors.*

De moon's rizen. Does you heah dat, nigger? You gits more light from dis out. No mo' buttin' yo' fool head agin' de trunks an' scratchin' de hide off yo' legs in de bushes. Now you sees whar yo'se gwine. So cheer up! From now on you has a snap. (*He steps just to the rear of the triangular clearing and mops off his face on his sleeve. He has lost his Panama hat. His face is scratched, his brilliant uniform shows several large rents.*) What time's it gittin' to be, I wonder? I dassent light no match to find out. Phoo'. It's wa'm an' dat's a fac'! (*Wearily*) How long I been makin' tracks in dese woods? Must be hours an' hours. Seems like fo'evah! Yit can't be, when de moon's jes' riz. Dis am a long night fo' yo', yo' Majesty! (*With a mournful chuckle*) Majesty! Der ain't much majesty 'bout dis baby now. (*With attempted cheerfulness*) Never min'. It's all part o' de game. Dis night come to an end like everything else. And when you gits dar safe and has dat bankroll in yo' hands you laughs at all dis. (*He starts to whistle but checks himself abruptly.*) What yo' whistlin' for, you po' dope! Want all de worl' to heah you? (*He stops talking to listen.*) Heah dat ole drum! Sho' gits nearer from de sound. Dey're packin' it along wid 'em. Time fo' me to move. (*He takes a step forward, then stops—worriedly*) What's dat odder queer clickety sound I heah? Dere it is! Sound close! Sound like—sound like—Fo' God sake, sound like some nigger was shootin' crap! (*Frightenedly*) I better beat it quick when I gits dem notions. (*He walks quickly into the clear space—then stands transfixed as he sees* JEFF—*in a terrified gasp*) Who dar? Who dat? Is dat you, Jeff? (*Starting toward the other, forgetful for a moment of his surroundings and really believing it is a living man that he sees—in a tone of happy relief*) Jeff! I'se sho' mighty glad to see you! Dey tol' me you done died from dat razor cut I gives you. (*Stopping suddenly, bewilderedly*) But how you come to be heah, nigger? (*He stares fascinatedly at the other who continues his mechanical play with the dice.* JONES' *eyes begin to roll wildly. He stutters*) Ain't you gwine—look up—can't you speak to me? Is you— is you—a ha'nt? (*He jerks out his revolver in a frenzy of terrified rage.*) Nigger, I kills you dead once. Has I got to kill you again? You take it den. (*He fires. When the smoke clears away* JEFF *has disappeared.* JONES *stands trembling—then with a certain reassurance*) He's gone, anyway. Ha'nt or no ha'nt, dat shot fix him. (*The beat of the far-off tom-tom is perceptibly louder and more rapid.* JONES *becomes conscious of it—with a start, looking back over his shoulder*) Dey's gittin' near! Dey's comin' fast! And heah I is shootin' shots to let 'em know jes' whar I is. Oh, Gorry, I'se got to run. (*Forgetting the path he plunges wildly into the underbrush in the rear and disappears in the shadow.*)

SCENE IV

Scene—Eleven o'clock. In the forest. A wide dirt road runs diagonally from right, front, to left, rear. Rising sheer on both sides the forest walls it in. The moon is now up. Under its light the road glimmers ghastly and unreal. It is as if the forest had stood aside momentarily to let the road pass through and accomplish its veiled purpose. This done, the forest will fold in upon itself again and the road will be no more. JONES *stumbles in from the forest on the right. His uniform is ragged and torn. He looks about him with numbed surprise when he sees the road, his eyes blinking in the bright moonlight. He flops down exhaustedly and pants heavily for a while. Then with sudden anger.*

I'm meltin' wid heat! Runnin' an' runnin' an' runnin'! Damn dis heah coat! Like a straitjacket! (*He tears off his coat and flings it away from him, revealing himself stripped to the waist.*) Dere! Dat's better! Now I kin breathe! (*Looking down at his feet, the spurs catch his eye.*) And to hell wid dese high-fangled spurs. Dey're what's been a-trippin' me up an' breakin' my neck. (*He unstraps them and flings them away disgustedly.*) Dere! I gits rid o' dem frippety Emperor trappin's an' I travels lighter. Lawd! I'se tired! (*After a pause, listening to the insistent beat of the tom-tom in the distance.*) I must 'a put some distance between myself an' dem—runnin' like dat—and yet—dat damn drum sound jes' de same—nearer, even. Well, I guess I a'most holds my lead anyhow. Dey won't

never catch up. (*With a sigh*) If on'y my fool legs stands up. Oh, I'se sorry I evah went in for dis. Dat Emperor job is sho' hard to shake. (*He looks around him suspiciously.*) How'd dis road evah git heah? Good level road, too. I never remembers seein' it befo'. (*Shaking his head apprehensively*) Dese woods is sho' full o' de queerest things at night. (*With a sudden terror*) Lawd God, don't let me see no more o' dem ha'nts! Dey gits my goat! (*Then trying to talk himself into confidence*) Ha'nts! You fool nigger, dey ain't no such things! Don't de Baptist parson tell you dat many time? Is you civilized, or is you like dese ign'rent black niggers heah? Sho'! Dat was all in yo' own head. Wasn't nothin' dere. Wasn't no Jeff! Know what? You jus' get seein' dem things 'cause yo' belly's empty and you's sick wid hunger inside. Hunger 'fects yo' head and yo' eyes. Any fool know dat. (*Then pleading fervently*) But bless God, I don't come across no more o' dem, whatever dey is! (*Then cautiously*) Rest! Don't talk! Rest! You needs it. Den you gits on yo' way again. (*Looking at the moon*) Night's half gone a'most. Yo hits de coast in de mawning! Den you'se all safe.

(*From the right forward a small gang of Negroes enter. They are dressed in striped convict suits, their heads are shaven, one leg drags limpingly, shackled to a heavy ball and chain. Some carry picks, the others shovels. They are followed by a white man dressed in the uniform of a prison guard. A Winchester rifle is slung across his shoulders and he carries a heavy whip. At a signal from the* GUARD *they stop on the road opposite where* JONES *is sitting.* JONES, *who has been staring up at the sky, unmindful of their noiseless approach, suddenly looks down and sees them. His eyes pop out, he tries to get to his feet and fly, but sinks back, too numbed by fright to move. His voice catches in a choking prayer.*)

Lawd Jesus!

(*The* PRISON GUARD *cracks his whip—noiselessly—and at that signal all the convicts start to work on the road. They swing their picks, they shovel, but not a sound comes from their labor. Their movements, like those of* JEFF *in the preceding scene, are those of automatons—rigid, slow, and mechanical. The* PRISON GUARD *points sternly at* JONES *with his whip, motions him to take his place among the other shovelers.* JONES *gets to his feet in a hypnotized stupor. He mumbles subserviently.*)

Yes, suh! Yes, suh! I'se comin'.

(*As he shuffles, dragging one foot, over to his place, he curses under his breath with rage and hatred.*)

God damn yo' soul, I gits even wid you yit, sometime.

(*As if there were a shovel in his hands he goes through weary, mechanical gestures of digging up dirt, and throwing it to the roadside. Suddenly the* GUARD *approaches him angrily, threateningly. He raises his whip and lashes* JONES *viciously across the shoulders with it.* JONES *winces with pain and cowers abjectly. The* GUARD *turns his back on him and walks away contemptuously. Instantly* JONES *straightens up. With arms upraised as if his shovel were a club in his hands he springs murderously at the unsuspecting* GUARD. *In the act of crashing down his shovel on the white man's skull,* JONES *suddenly becomes aware that his hands are empty. He cries despairingly.*)

Whar's my shovel? Gimme my shovel till I splits his damn head! (*Appealing to his fellow convicts*) Gimme a shovel, one o' you, fo' God's sake!

(*They stand fixed in motionless attitudes, their eyes on the ground. The* GUARD *seems to wait expectantly, his back turned to the attacker.* JONES *bellows with baffled, terrified rage, tugging frantically at his revolver.*)

I kills you, you white debil, if it's de last thing I evah does! Ghost or debil, I kill you again!

(*He frees the revolver and fires point blank at the* GUARD's *back. Instantly the walls of the forest close in from both sides, the road and the figures of the convict gang are blotted out in an enshrouding darkness. The only sounds are a crashing in the underbrush as* JONES *leaps away in mad flight and the throbbing of the tom-tom, still far distant, but increased in volume of sound and rapidity of beat.*)

SCENE V

Scene—One o'clock. A large circular clearing, enclosed by the serried ranks of gigantic trunks of tall trees whose tops are lost to view. In the center is a big dead stump worn by time into a curious resemblance to an auction block. The moon floods the clearing with a clear light. JONES *forces his way in through the forest on the left. He looks wildly about the clearing with hunted, fearful glances: His pants are in tatters, his shoes cut and misshapen, flapping about his feet. He slinks cautiously to the stump in the center and sits down in a tense position, ready for instant flight. Then he holds his head in his hands and rocks back and forth, moaning to himself miserably.*

Oh Lawd, Lawd! Oh Lawd, Lawd! (*Suddenly he throws himself on his knees and raises his clasped hands to the sky—in a voice of agonized pleading*) Lawd Jesus, heah my prayer! I'se a po' sinner, a po' sinner! I knows I done wrong, I knows it! When I cotches Jeff cheatin' wid loaded dice my anger overcomes me and I kills him dead! Lawd, I done wrong! When dat guard hits me wid de whip, my anger overcomes me, and I kills him dead. Lawd, I done wrong! And down heah whar dese fool bush niggers raises me up to the seat o' de mighty, I steals all I could grab. Lawd, I done wrong! I knows it! I'se sorry! Forgive me, Lawd! Forgive dis po' sinner! (*Then beseeching terrifiedly*) And keep dem away, Lawd! Keep dem away from me! And stop dat drum soundin' in my ears! Dat begin to sound ha'nted, too. (*He gets to his feet, evidently slightly reassured by his prayer—with attempted confidence*) De Lawd'll preserve me from dem ha'nts after dis. (*Sits down on the stump again.*) I ain't skeered o' real men. Let dem come. But dem odders . . . (*He shudders—then looks down at his feet, working his toes inside the shoes—with a groan.*) Oh, my po' feet! Dem shoes ain't no use no more 'ceptin' to hurt. I'se better off widout dem. (*He unlaces them and pulls them off—holds the wrecks of the shoes in his hands and regards them mournfully.*) You was real, A-one patin' leather, too. Look at you now. Emperor, you'se gittin' mighty low!

(*He sits dejectedly and remains with bowed shoulders, staring down at the shoes in his hands as if reluctant to throw them away. While his attention is thus occupied, a crowd of figures silently enter the clearing from all sides. All are dressed in Southern costumes of the period of the fifties of the last century. There are middle-aged men who are evidently well-to-do planters. There is one spruce, authoritative individual—the* AUCTIONEER. *There is a crowd of curious spectators, chiefly young belles and dandies who have come to the slave-market for diversion. All exchange courtly greetings in dumb show and chat silently together. There is something stiff, rigid, unreal, marionettish about their movements. They group themselves about the stump. Finally a batch of slaves are led in from the left by an attendant—three men of different ages, two women, one with a baby in her arms, nursing. They are placed to the left of the stump, beside* JONES.

The white planters look them over appraisingly as if they were cattle, and exchange judgments on each. The dandies point with their fingers and make witty remarks. The belles titter bewitchingly. All this in silence save for the ominous throb of the tom-tom. The AUCTIONEER *holds up his hand, taking his place at the stump. The group strain forward attentively. He touches* JONES *on the shoulder peremptorily, motioning for him to stand on the stump—the auction block.*

JONES looks up, sees the figures on all sides, looks wildly for some opening to escape, sees none, screams and leaps madly to the top of the stump to get as far away from them as possible. He stands there, cowering, paralyzed with horror. The AUCTIONEER *begins his silent spiel. He points to* JONES, *appeals to the planters to see for themselves. Here is a good field hand, sound in mind and limb as they can see. Very strong still in spite of his being middle-aged. Look at that back. Look at those shoulders. Look at the muscles in his arms and his sturdy legs. Capable of any amount of hard labor. Moreover, of a good disposition, intelligent and tractable. Will any gentleman start the bidding? The* PLANTERS *raise their fingers, make their bids. They are apparently all eager to possess* JONES. *The bidding is lively, the crowd interested. While this has been going on,* JONES *has been seized by the courage of desperation. He dares to look down and around him. Over his face abject terror gives way to mystification, to gradual realization.*)

(*Stutteringly*) What you all doin', white folks? What's all dis? What you all lookin' at me fo'? What you doin' wid me, anyhow? (*Suddenly convulsed with raging hatred and fear*) Is dis a auction? Is you sellin' me like dey uster befo' de war? (*Jerking out his revolver just as the* AUCTIONEER *knocks him down to one of the planters—glaring from him to the purchaser*) And you sells me? And you buys me? I shows you I'se a free nigger, damn yo' souls!

(*He fires at the* AUCTIONEER *and at the* PLANTER *with such rapidity that the two shots are almost simultaneous. As if this were a signal the walls of the forest fold in. Only blackness remains and silence broken by* JONES *as he rushes off, crying*

with fear—and by the quickened, ever louder beat of the tom-tom.)

SCENE VI

Scene—Three o'clock. A cleared space in the forest. The limbs of the trees meet over it forming a low ceiling about five feet from the ground. The interlocked ropes of creepers reaching upward to entwine the tree trunks give an arched appearance to the sides. The space thus enclosed is like the dark, noisome hold of some ancient vessel. The moonlight is almost completely shut out and only a vague, wan light filters through. There is the noise of someone approaching from the left, stumbling and crawling through the undergrowth. JONES' *voice is heard between chattering moans.*

Oh, Lawd, what I gwine do now? Ain't got no bullet left on'y de silver one. If mo' o' dem ha'nts come after me, how I gwine skeer dem away? Oh, Lawd, on'y de silver one left—an' I gotta save dat fo' luck. If I shoots dat one I'm a goner sho'! Lawd, it's black heah! Whar's de moon? Oh, Lawd, don't dis night evah come to an end? (*By the sounds, he is feeling his way cautiously forward.*) Dere! Dis feels like a clear space. I gotta lie down an' rest. I don't care if dem niggers does cotch me. I gotta rest.

(*He is well forward now where his figure can be dimly made out. His pants have been so torn away that what is left of them is no better than a breech cloth. He flings himself full length, face downward on the ground, panting with exhaustion. Gradually it seems to grow lighter in the enclosed space and two rows of seated figures can be seen behind* JONES. *They are sitting in crumpled, despairing attitudes, hunched, facing one another with their backs touching the forest walls as if they were shackled to them. All are Negroes, naked save for loin cloths. At first they are silent and motionless. Then they begin to sway slowly forward toward each other and back again in unison, as if they were laxly letting themselves follow the long roll of a ship at sea. At the same time, a low, melancholy murmur rises among them, increasing gradually by rhythmic degrees which seem to be directed and controlled by the throb of the tom-tom in the distance, to a long, tremulous wail of despair that reaches a certain pitch, unbearably acute, then falls by slow gradations of tone into silence and is taken up again.* JONES *starts, looks up, sees the figures, and throws himself down again to shut out the sight. A shudder of terror shakes his whole body as the wail rises up about him again. But the next time, his voice, as if under some uncanny compulsion, starts with the others. As their chorus lifts he rises to a sitting posture similar to the others, swaying back and forth. His voice reaches the highest pitch of sorrow, of desolation. The light fades out, the other voices cease, and only darkness is left.* JONES *can be heard scrambling to his feet and running off, his voice sinking down the scale and receding as he moves farther and farther away in the forest. The tom-tom beats louder, quicker, with a more insistent, triumphant pulsation.*)

SCENE VII

Scene—Five o'clock. The foot of a gigantic tree by the edge of a great river. A rough structure of boulders, like an altar, is by the tree. The raised river bank is in the nearer background. Beyond this the surface of the river spreads out, brilliant and unruffled in the moonlight, blotted out and merged into a veil of bluish mist in the distance. JONES' *voice is heard from the left rising and falling in the long, despairing wail of the chained slaves, to the rhythmic beat of the tom-tom. As his voice sinks into silence, he enters the open space. The expression of his face is fixed and stony, his eyes have an obsessed glare, he moves with a strange deliberation like a sleepwalker or one in a trance. He looks around at the tree, the rough stone altar, the moonlit surface of the river beyond, and passes his hand over his head with a vague gesture of puzzled bewilderment. Then, as if in obedience to some obscure impulse, he sinks into a kneeling, devotional posture before the altar. Then he seems to come to himself partly, to have an uncertain realization of what he is doing, for he straightens up and stares about him horrifiedly—in an incoherent mumble.*

What—what is I doin'? What is—dis place? Seems like—seems like I know dat tree—an' dem stones—an' de river. I remember—seems like I been heah befo'. (*Tremblingly*) Oh, Gorry, I'se skeered in dis place! I'se skeered! Oh, Lawd, pertect dis sinner!

(*Crawling away from the altar, he cowers close to the ground, his face hidden, his shoulders heaving with sobs of hysterical fright. From behind the trunk of the tree, as if he had sprung out of it, the figure of the* CONGO WITCH-DOCTOR *appears. He is wizened and old, naked except for the fur of some small animal tied about his waist, its bushy tail hanging down in front. His body is stained all over a bright red. Antelope horns are on each side of his head, branching upward. In one hand he carries a bone rattle, in the other a charm stick with a bunch of white cockatoo feathers tied to the end. A great number of glass beads and bone ornaments are about his neck, ears, wrists, and ankles. He struts noiselessly with a queer prancing step to a position in the clear ground between* JONES *and the altar. Then with a preliminary, summoning stamp of his foot on the earth, he begins to dance and to chant. As if in response to his summons the beating of the tom-tom grows to a fierce, exultant boom whose throbs seem to fill the air with vibrating rhythm.* JONES *looks up, starts to spring to his feet, reaches a half-kneeling, half-squatting position and remains rigidly fixed there, paralyzed with awed fascination by this new apparition. The* WITCH-DOCTOR *sways, stamping with his foot, his bone rattle clicking the time. His voice rises and falls in a weird, monotonous croon, without articulate word divisions. Gradually his dance becomes clearly one of a narrative in pantomime, his croon is an incantation, a charm to allay the fierceness of some implacable deity demanding sacrifice. He flees, he is pursued by devils, he hides, he flees again. Ever wilder and wilder becomes his flight, nearer and nearer draws the pursuing evil, more and more the spirit of terror gains possession of him. His croon, rising to intensity, is punctuated by shrill cries.* JONES *has become completely hypnotized. His voice joins in the incantation, in the cries, he beats time with his hands and sways his body to and fro from the waist. The whole spirit and meaning of the dance has entered into him, has become his spirit. Finally the theme of the pantomime halts on a howl of despair, and is taken up again in a note of savage hope. There is a salvation. The forces of evil demand sacrifice. They must be appeased. The* WITCH-DOCTOR *points with his wand to the sacred tree, to the river beyond, to the altar, and finally to* JONES *with a ferocious command.* JONES *seems to sense the meaning of this. It is he who must offer himself for sacrifice. He beats his forehead abjectly to the ground, moaning hysterically.*)

Mercy, Oh Lawd! Mercy! Mercy on dis po' sinner.

(*The* WITCH-DOCTOR *springs to the river bank. He stretches out his arms and calls to some god within its depths. Then he starts backward slowly, his arms remaining out. A huge head of a crocodile appears over the bank and its eyes, glittering greenly, fasten upon* JONES. *He stares into them fascinatedly. The* WITCH-DOCTOR *prances up to him, touches him with his wand, motions with hideous command toward the waiting monster.* JONES *squirms on his belly nearer and nearer, moaning continually.*)

Mercy, Lawd! Mercy!

(*The crocodile heaves more of his enormous bulk onto the land.* JONES *squirms toward him. The* WITCH-DOCTOR'S *voice shrills out in furious exultation, the tom-tom beats madly.* JONES *cries out in a fierce, exhausted spasm of anguished pleading.*)

Lawd, save me! Lawd Jesus, heah my prayer!

(*Immediately, in answer to his prayer, comes the thought of the one bullet left him. He snatches at his hip, shouting defiantly.*)

De silver bullet! You don't git me yit!

(*He fires at the green eyes in front of him. The head of the crocodile sinks back behind the river bank, the* WITCH-DOCTOR *springs behind the sacred tree and disappears.* JONES *lies with his face to the ground, his arms outstretched, whimpering with fear as the throb of the tom-tom fills the silence about him with a somber pulsation, a baffled but revengeful power.*)

SCENE VIII

Scene—Dawn. Same as Scene II, the dividing line of forest and plain. The nearest tree trunks are dimly revealed but the forest behind them is still a mass of glooming shadows. The tom-tom seems on the very spot, so loud and continuously vibrating are its beats. LEM *enters from the left, followed by a small squad of his soldiers, and by the Cockney trader,* SMITHERS. LEM *is a heavyset, ape-faced old savage of the extreme African type, dressed only in a loin cloth. A revolver and cartridge belt are about his waist. His soldiers are in different degrees of rag-concealed nakedness. All wear broad palm-leaf hats. Each one carries a rifle.* SMITHERS *is the same as in Scene I. One of the soldiers, evidently a tracker, is peering about keenly on the ground. He grunts and*

points to the spot where JONES *entered the forest.* LEM *and* SMITHERS *come to look.*

SMITHERS (*after a glance, turns away in disgust*): That's where 'e went in right enough. Much good it'll do yer. 'E's miles orf by this an' safe to the Coast, damn 'is 'ide! I tole yer yer'd lose 'im, didn't I?—wastin' the 'ole bloomin' night beatin' yer bloody drum and castin' yer silly spells! Gawd blimey, wot a pack!

LEM (*gutturally*): We cotch him. You see. (*He makes a motion to his soldiers who squat down on their haunches in a semicircle.*)

SMITHERS (*exasperatedly*): Well, ain't yer goin' in an' 'unt 'im in the woods? What the 'ell's the good of waitin'?

LEM (*imperturbably—squatting down himself*): We cotch him.

SMITHERS (*turning away from him contemptuously*): Aw! Garn! 'E's a better man than the lot o' you put together. I 'ates the sight o' 'im but I'll say that for 'im.

(*A sound of snapping twigs comes from the forest. The soldiers jump to their feet, cocking their rifles alertly.* LEM *remains sitting with an imperturbable expression, but listening intently. The sound from the woods is repeated.* LEM *makes a quick signal with his hand. His followers creep quickly but noiselessly into the forest, scattering so that each enters at a different spot.*)

SMITHERS (*in the silence that follows—in a contemptuous whisper*): You ain't thinkin' that would be 'im, I 'ope?

LEM (*calmly*): We cotch him.

SMITHERS: Blarsted fat 'eads! (*Then after a second's thought—wonderingly*) Still an' all, it might 'appen. If 'e lost 'is bloody way in these stinkin' woods 'e'd likely turn in a circle without 'is knowin' it. They all does.

LEM (*peremptorily*): Sssh!

(*The reports of several rifles sound from the forest, followed a second later by savage, exultant yells. The beating of the tom-tom abruptly ceases.* LEM *looks up at the white man with a grin of satisfaction.*)

We cotch him. Him dead.

SMITHERS (*with a snarl*): 'Ow d'yer know it's 'im an' 'ow d'yer know 'e's dead?

LEM: My mens dey got 'um silver bullets. Dey kill him shore.

SMITHERS (*astonished*): They got silver bullets?

LEM: Lead bullet no kill him. He got um strong

charm. I cook um money, make um silver bullet, make um strong charm, too.

SMITHERS (*light breaking upon him*): So that's wot you was up to all night, wot? You was scared to put after 'im til you'd moulded silver bullets, eh?

LEM (*simply stating a fact*): Yes. Him got strong charm. Lead no good.

SMITHERS (*slapping his thigh and guffawing*): Haw-haw! If yer don't beat all 'ell! (*Then recovering himself—scornfully*) I'll bet yer it ain't 'im they shot at all, yer bleedin' looney!

LEM (*calmly*): Dey come bring him now.

(*The soldiers come out of the forest, carrying* JONES' *limp body. There is a little reddish-purple hole under his left breast. He is dead. They carry him to* LEM, *who examines his body with great satisfaction.* SMITHERS *leans over his shoulder— in a tone of frightened awe.*)

Well, they did for yer right enough, Jonsey, me lad! Dead as a 'erring! (*Mockingly*) Where's yer 'igh an' mighty airs now, yer bloomin' Majesty? (*Then with a grin*) Silver bullets! Gawd blimey, but yer died in the 'eighth o' style, any'ow!

(LEM *makes a motion to the soldiers to carry the body out left.* SMITHERS *speaks to him sneeringly.*)

SMITHERS: And I s'pose you think it's yer bleedin' charms and yer silly beatin' the drum that made 'im run in a circle when 'e'd lost 'imself, don't yer?

(*But* LEM *makes no reply, does not seem to hear the question, walks out left after his men.* SMITH-ERS *looks after him with contemptuous scorn.*)

Stupid as 'ogs, the lot of 'em! Blarsted niggers!

CURTAIN FALLS

COMMENTARY

The gist of the story of *The Emperor Jones* is simply this: Jones, a black fugitive from a chain gang, has turned up on an island in the West Indies and established himself as Emperor. By his own admission he has tyrannized over his subjects, and he was able to get away with it because they believed that he could be killed only by a silver bullet. (This is the *antecedent action*; we learn it during the play, but it reports what happened before the play begins.) At the beginning of the play, hearing that a rebellion is in progress Jones confidently sets out to leave the island; he becomes increasingly terrified, and at the end of the play he is shot with a silver bullet.

This is moderately interesting, and not totally different from some historical episodes: President Guillaume Sam of Haiti boasted he would kill himself with a silver bullet, but he was hacked to pieces by his oppressed subjects in 1915, only five years before O'Neill wrote *The Emperor Jones*; and a century earlier, Henri Christophe, a slave who had become the merciless ruler of part of Haiti, shot himself when confronted with an insurrection. O'Neill knew these bits of history and used them to shape *The Emperor Jones*, but even if he had not changed some facts, a play about Sam or Christophe inevitably would—if it were any good— be very different from an encyclopedia entry on them because, in Ezra Pound's words, a play is made not out of words but out of "persons moving about on a stage using words."

Let's begin with the stage and its setting. When the curtain goes up on a performance of *The Emperor Jones*, the audience sees "the audience chamber in the palace of the Emperor." It is furnished solely with "one huge chair . . . painted a dazzling eye-smiting scarlet," a cushion that serves as a footstool, and two scarlet mats that go "from the foot of the throne to the two entrances." This stage, at least in the context of what follows, "says" a lot. It conveys Jones's dominance, for he alone can sit in the room, and it conveys something of his bloody career, for if the scarlet throne on which Jones sits at first suggests royalty, it also in retrospect suggests the blood that surrounds his career. Whether or not O'Neill was conscious of the fact when he was writing the play, the huge scarlet chair, which at the start is boldly emblematic of Jones both as Emperor and as murderer, makes a notable contrast to the "little reddish-purple hole under his left breast" when his corpse is brought onstage at the end of the play. The imperial murderer has diminished to this.

The play uses only two other sets, and these are almost one: the edge of the Great Forest, and within the Great Forest. The Forest, again, in the context of the action, says something. O'Neill tells us, in his first description of it, that it gives an impression of "relentless immobility" and of "brooding, implacable silence." Fleeing through the forest Jones becomes terrified, and we see that the dark forest is, in part at least, the jungle of the human mind, the world of inarticulate, elemental passions that seethe beneath the fragile surface of reason. (*The Emperor Jones* belongs, at least roughly, to the movement called expressionism, in which scenery is commonly used not to give an image of the external world but of a character's state of mind—see the Glossary.) The darkness of the jungle, a strong contrast to the brightly illuminated throne room where Jones was the confident master, provides us with an example of the way in which a dramatist uses lighting—or, rather, darkness—symbolically.

Among the stock dramatic types of the black man available to O'Neill in 1920, the chief were the Tom (faithful black retainer), the Buffoon (clownish lazy servant), the Bull (villain who wants to rape white women), and the Tragic Mulatto (hovering between two races.) Almost all depictions of blacks on the American stage of the time fell into these classifications. O'Neill, in a remarkable step forward in the history of American drama, and therefore in the history of American thought, used none of these stereotypes. (In *The Emperor Jones* the lazy man is not the black, who has diligently learned the language of the islanders and who for two years worked hard and efficiently at his job of robbing his subjects; the lazy man is the white man, Smithers, who in ten years has not bothered to learn the language.) Today, some seventy years after O'Neill wrote the play, inevitably we are disturbed by some racist implications in the play, especially the implication that a black more quickly than a white reverts to the condition of the "primitive" human being. But O'Neill was far ahead of most whites of his time in presenting a black whose face showed "an underlying strength of will, a hardy, self-reliant confidence," and whose eyes showed "a keen, cunning intelligence." If these words put us in mind of any type, it is, paradoxically, the rugged white individualist who was so worshipped in the nineteenth and early twentieth centuries. O'Neill gives us not a stereotyped black man (and none of the stereotypes was flattering), but a fresh conception, a black who has the virtues and faults of white society, of America as it was and is, and perhaps of mankind. (The very name "Jones" suggests Everyman—though "Brutus" adds to it both a sense of high Roman dignity, and a sense of grotesque incongruity, as well as a hint of the "brute" that is beneath the clothes of every person, white or black.) Jones is quite explicit about his code: his aim is to get rich in the great white man's way, by hard work and by cunning immorality on a grand scale.

> You heah what I tells you, Smithers. Dere's little stealin' like you does, and dere's big stealin' like I does. For de little stealin' dey gits you in jail soon or late. For de big stealin' dey makes you Emperor and puts you in de Hall o' Fame when you croaks. (*Reminiscently*) If dey's one thing I learns in ten years on de Pullman ca's listenin' to de white quality talk, it's dat same fact. And when I gits a chance to use it I winds up Emperor in two years.

Smithers is no less unscrupulous or cruel than Jones is, but he simply does not have Jones's courage, perseverance, intelligence, and vision. In short, O'Neill gives us a fresh, fully realized picture of believable human beings and we should not be deceived by the funny spelling into thinking that Jones is the conventional black man of the stage up to O'Neill's time.

TOPICS FOR DISCUSSION

1. Smithers is essentially a coward. Why, then, does he talk impudently and even angrily to Jones at the start of the play?
2. How does O'Neill use Jones's costume, at the start and then later in the play, to say something about Jones (and about all of us)?
3. Discuss the organization of the six scenes in the jungle. (O'Neill gives us, first, the "little formless fears," then the memory of the murder of Jeff, the memory of the murder of the prison guard, the slave auction, the slave ship, and the African ceremony.) How are the last three of these fundamentally different from the first three? Dramatically speaking, could the last three be given before the first three? Explain.
4. Jones runs in a circle. Smithers sees in this only a simple fact, but can one say that the symmetry is meaningful? Do you think it is appropriate, for instance, to see in it a return to our inarticulate and mysterious origin? Explain.
5. If you don't recall the time scheme of the play, look again to see at what time of day the play begins and at what time it ends. What do you make out of this structure?
6. *The Emperor Jones* has eight scenes, a large number for a short play. What is the effect of so large a number? After all, the six central, expressionistic scenes between the realistic opening and closing scenes could, with a little rewriting, have been one long scene, but O'Neill chose to put the material into six scenes. Why? Hint: expressionistic drama (see Glossary) often uses lots of scenes—but why?
7. How relevant to the play do you find the concepts of *hybris* and *hamartia* (see page 67 and Glossary)? Explain.
8. The play was enthusiastically received in 1920. Heywood Broun, however, writing in *The New York Tribune*, offered one objection in an otherwise ecstatic review: "We cannot understand just why [O'Neill] has allowed the Emperor to die to the sound of off-stage shots. It is our idea that he should come crawling to the very spot where he meets his death and that the natives should be molding silver bullets there and waiting without so much as stretching out a finger for him." What do you think of Broun's suggestion?

THE HOUSE OF BERNARDA ALBA

Federico García Lorca

Translated by James Graham-Lujan and Richard L. O'Connell

Federico García Lorca (1898–1936) was born in Spain, near Granada, the son of a landowner and an ex-school teacher. He attended the University of Granada, dropped out, lived for a while in a world of writers and artists, but later returned to the university and in 1923 received a law degree. He had by that date already published a book of essays and a book of poetry and had seen the production of one of his plays in Madrid. After graduating, he continued to write, paint (he was close to Salvador Dali), compose music (some with Manuel de Falla), and edit a magazine. In 1929–1930 he lived in the United States, but then he returned to Spain, where he became the director of a traveling theatrical company. Meanwhile, he kept writing plays. Although he had not been active in politics, in 1936, in the first weeks of the Spanish Civil War, he was arrested and murdered by Franco's agents.

García Lorca wrote farces and surrealistic and symbolist works, but his most enduring plays are three relatively bare tragedies: *Blood Wedding* (1933), *Yerma* (1934), and (written shortly before his death) *The House of Bernarda Alba* (1936).

CHARACTERS

A MAID (FIRST SERVANT), *age 50*
LA PONCIA, *a maid, age 60*
MARIA JOSEFA, *Bernarda's mother, age 80*
A BEGGAR WOMAN
HER CHILD
WOMEN IN MOURNING
BERNARDA, *age 60*
FIRST WOMAN
FIRST GIRL
SECOND WOMAN

THIRD WOMAN
SECOND GIRL
ANGUSTIAS, *Bernarda's daughter, age 39*
FOURTH WOMAN
AMELIA, *Bernarda's daughter, age 27*
ADELA, *Bernarda's daughter, age 20*
MARTIRIO, *Bernarda's daughter, age 24*
MAGDALENA, *Bernarda's daughter, age 30*
PRUDENCIA, *age 50*

The writer states that these Three Acts are intended as a photographic document.

Miriam Colon, as Bernarda, in a 1987 Guthrie Theater production directed by Les Waters with sets by Annie Smart, costumes by Martin Pakledinaz, and lighting by James F. Ingalls. (Photo by Greg Helgeson.)

ACT I

A very white room in Bernarda Alba's house. The walls are white. There are arched doorways with jute curtains tied back with tassels and ruffles. Wicker chairs. On the walls, pictures of unlikely landscapes full of nymphs or legendary kings. It is summer. A great brooding silence fills the stage. It is empty when the curtain rises. Bells can be heard tolling outside.

FIRST SERVANT (*entering*): The tolling of those bells hits me right between the eyes.

PONCIA (*she enters, eating bread and sausage*): More than two hours of mumbo jumbo. Priests are here from all the towns. The church looks beautiful. At the first responsory for the dead, Magdalena fainted.

FIRST SERVANT: She's the one who's left most alone.

PONCIA: She's the only one who loved her father. Ay! Thank God we're alone for a little. I came over to eat.

FIRST SERVANT: If Bernarda sees you . . . !

PONCIA: She's not eating today so she'd just as soon we'd all die of hunger! Domineering old tyrant! But she'll be fooled! I opened the sausage crock.

FIRST SERVANT (*with an anxious sadness*): Couldn't you give me some for my little girl, Poncia?

PONCIA: Go ahead! And take a fistful of peas too. She won't know the difference today.

VOICE (*within*): Bernarda!

PONCIA: There's the grandmother! Isn't she locked up tight?

FIRST SERVANT: Two turns of the key.

PONCIA: You'd better put the cross-bar up too. She's got the fingers of a lock-picker!

VOICE (*within*): Bernarda!

PONCIA (*shouting*): She's coming! (*To the* SERVANT) Clean everything up good. If Bernarda doesn't find things shining, she'll pull out the few hairs I have left.

SERVANT: What a woman!

PONCIA: Tyrant over everyone around her. She's perfectly capable of sitting on your heart and watching you die for a whole year without turning off that cold little smile she wears on her wicked face. Scrub, scrub those dishes!

SERVANT: I've got blood on my hands from so much polishing of everything.

PONCIA: She's the cleanest, she's the decentest, she's the highest everything! A good rest her poor husband's earned!

(The bells stop.)

SERVANT: Did all the relatives come?

PONCIA: Just hers. His people hate her. They came to see him dead and make the sign of the cross over him; that's all.

SERVANT: Are there enough chairs?

PONCIA: More than enough. Let them sit on the floor. When Bernarda's father died people stopped coming under this roof. She doesn't want them to see her in her "domain." Curse her!

SERVANT: She's been good to you.

PONCIA: Thirty years washing her sheets. Thirty years eating her leftovers. Nights of watching when she had a cough. Whole days peeking through a crack in the shutters to spy on the neighbors and carry her the tale. Life without secrets one from the other. But in spite of that—curse her! May the "pain of the piercing nail" strike her in the eyes.

SERVANT: Poncia!

PONCIA: But I'm a good watchdog! I bark when I'm told and bite beggars' heels when she sics me on 'em. My sons work in her fields—both of them already married, but one of these days I'll have enough.

SERVANT: And then . . . ?

PONCIA: Then I'll lock myself up in a room with her and spit in her face—a whole year. "Bernarda, here's for this, that and the other!" Till I leave her—just like a lizard the boys have squashed. For that's what she is—she and her whole family! Not that I envy her her life. Five girls are left her, five ugly daughters—not counting Angustias the eldest, by her first husband, who has money—the rest of them, plenty of eyelets to embroider, plenty of linen petticoats, but bread and grapes when it comes to inheritance.

SERVANT: Well, I'd like to have what they've got!

PONCIA: All we have is our hands and a hole in God's earth.

SERVANT: And that's the only earth they'll ever leave to us—to us who have nothing!

PONCIA (at the cupboard): This glass has some specks.

SERVANT: Neither soap nor rag will take them off.

(The bells toll.)

PONCIA: The last prayer! I'm going over and listen. I certainly like the way our priest sings. In the Pater Noster his voice went up, and up—like a pitcher filling with water little by little. Of course, at the end his voice cracked, but it's glorious to hear it. No, there never was anybody like the old Sacristan—Tronchapinos. At my mother's Mass, may she rest in peace, he sang. The walls shook—and when he said "Amen," it was as if a wolf had come into the church. (Imitating him) A-a-a-a-men! (She starts coughing.)

SERVANT: Watch out—you'll strain your windpipe!

PONCIA: I'd rather strain something else! (Goes out laughing.)

(The SERVANT scrubs. The bells toll.)

SERVANT (imitating the bells): Dong, dong, dong. Dong, dong, dong. May God forgive him!

BEGGAR WOMAN (at the door, with a little girl): Blesséd be God!

SERVANT: Dong, dong, dong. I hope he waits many years for us! Dong, dong, dong.

BEGGAR (loudly, a little annoyed): Blesséd be God!

SERVANT (annoyed): Forever and ever!

BEGGAR: I came for the scraps.

(The bells stop tolling.)

SERVANT: You can go right out the way you came in. Today's scraps are for me.

BEGGAR: But you have somebody to take care of you—and my little girl and I are all alone!

SERVANT: Dogs are alone too, and they live.

BEGGAR: They always give them to me.

SERVANT: Get out of here! Who let you in anyway? You've already tracked up the place.

(The BEGGAR WOMAN and LITTLE GIRL leave. The Servant goes on scrubbing.)

Floors finished with oil, cupboards, pedestals, iron beds—but us servants, we can suffer in silence—and live in mud huts with a plate and a spoon. I hope someday not a one will be left to tell it.

(The bells sound again.)

Yes, yes—ring away. Let them put you in a coffin with gold inlay and brocade to carry it on—you're no less dead than I'll be, so take what's coming to you, Antonio María Benavides—stiff in your broadcloth suit and your high boots—take what's coming to you! You'll never again lift my skirts behind the corral door!

(From the rear door, two by two, WOMEN IN MOURNING with large shawls and black skirts and fans, begin to enter. They come in slowly until the stage is full.)

SERVANT (breaking into a wail): Oh, Antonio María Benavides, now you'll never see these walls, nor break bread in this house again! I'm the one who loved you most of all your servants. (Pulling her hair) Must I live on after you've gone? Must I go on living?

(The two hundred women finish coming in, and BERNARDA and her five daughters enter. BERNARDA leans on a cane.)

BERNARDA (to the SERVANT): Silence!

SERVANT (weeping): Bernarda!

BERNARDA: Less shrieking and more work. You should have had all this cleaner for the wake. Get out. This isn't your place.

(The SERVANT goes off crying.)

The poor are like animals—they seem to be made of different stuff.

FIRST WOMAN: The poor feel their sorrows too.

BERNARDA: But they forget them in front of a plateful of peas.

FIRST GIRL (timidly): Eating is necessary for living.

BERNARDA: At your age one doesn't talk in front of older people.

WOMAN: Be quiet, child.

BERNARDA: I've never taken lessons from anyone. Sit down.

(They sit down. Pause.)

(Loudly) Magdalena, don't cry. If you want to cry, get under your bed. Do you hear me?

SECOND WOMAN (to BERNARDA): Have you started to work the fields?

BERNARDA: Yesterday.

THIRD WOMAN: The sun comes down like lead.

FIRST WOMAN: I haven't known heat like this for years.

(*Pause. They all fan themselves.*)

BERNARDA: Is the lemonade ready?

PONCIA: Yes, Bernarda.

(*She brings in a large tray full of little white jars which she distributes.*)

BERNARDA: Give the men some.

PONCIA: They're already drinking in the patio.

BERNARDA: Let them get out the way they came in. I don't want them walking through here.

A GIRL (*to* AUGUSTIAS): Pepe el Romano was with the men during the service.

AUGUSTIAS: There he was.

BERNARDA: His mother was there. She saw his mother. Neither she nor I saw Pepe . . .

GIRL: I thought . . .

BERNARDA The one who *was* there was Darajalí, the widower. Very close to your Aunt. We all of us saw him.

SECOND WOMAN (*aside, in a low voice*): Wicked, worse than wicked woman!

THIRD WOMAN: A tongue like a knife!

BERNARDA: Women in church shouldn't look at any man but the priest—and him only because he wears skirts. To turn your head is to be looking for the warmth of corduroy.

FIRST WOMAN: Sanctimonious old snake!

PONCIA (*between her teeth*): Itching for a man's warmth.

BERNARDA (*beating with her cane on the floor*): Blesséd be God!

ALL (*crossing themselves*): Forever blesséd and praised.

BERNARDA: Rest in peace with holy company at your head.

ALL: Rest in peace!

BERNARDA: With the Angel Saint Michael, and his sword of justice.

ALL: Rest in peace!

BERNARDA: With the key that opens, and the hand that locks.

ALL: Rest in peace!

BERNARDA: With the most blesséd, and the little lights of the field.

ALL: Rest in peace!

BERNARDA: With our holy charity, and all souls on land and sea.

ALL: Rest in peace!

BERNARDA: Grant rest to your servant, Antonio María Benavides, and give him the crown of your blesséd glory.

ALL: Amen.

BERNARDA (*she rises and chants*): Requiem aeternam donat eis domine.[1]

ALL (*standing and chanting in the Gregorian*) (*They cross themselves.*)

fashion): Et lux perpetua luceat eis.[2]

FIRST WOMAN: May you have health to pray for his soul.

(*They start filing out.*)

THIRD WOMAN: You won't lack loaves of hot bread.

SECOND WOMAN: Nor a roof for your daughters.

(*They are all filing in front of* BERNARDA *and going out.*)

(AUGUSTIAS *leaves by the door to the patio.*)

FOURTH WOMAN: May you go on enjoying your wedding wheat.

PONCIA (*she enters, carrying a money bag*): From the men—this bag of money for Masses.

BERNARDA: Thank them—and let them have a glass of brandy.

GIRL (*to* MAGDALENA): Magdalena . . .

BERNARDA (*to* MAGDALENA, *who is starting to cry*): Sh-h-h-h! (*She beats with her cane on the floor.*)

(*All the women have gone out.*)

BERNARDA (*to the women who have just left*). Go back to your houses and criticize everything you've seen! I hope it'll be many years before you pass under the archway of my door again.

PONCIA: You've nothing to complain about. The whole town came.

BERNARDA: Yes, to fill my house with the sweat from their wraps and the poison of their tongues.

AMELIA: Mother, don't talk like that.

BERNARDA: What other way is there to talk about this curséd village with no river—this village full of wells where you drink water always fearful it's been poisoned?

PONCIA: Look what they've done to the floor!

BERNARDA: As though a herd of goats had passed through.

(PONCIA *cleans the floor.*)

[1] **Requiem . . . domine:** "Eternal rest give to them, O Lord"; opening prayer from Catholic Mass for the Dead.

[2] **Et . . . eis:** "And let perpetual light shine upon them"; response to the prayer, above.

Adela, give me a fan.

ADELA: Take this one.

(*She gives her a round fan with green and red flowers.*)

BERNARDA (*throwing the fan on the floor*): Is that the fan to give to a widow? Give me a black one and learn to respect your father's memory.

MARTIRIO: Take mine.

BERNARDA: And you?

MARTIRIO: I'm not hot.

BERNARDA: Well, look for another, because you'll need it. For the eight years of mourning, not a breath of air will get in this house from the street. We'll act as if we'd sealed up doors and windows with bricks. That's what happened in my father's house—and in my grandfather's house. Meantime, you can all start embroidering your hope-chest linens. I have twenty bolts of linen in the chest from which to cut sheets and coverlets. Magdalena can embroider them.

MAGDALENA: It's all the same to me.

ADELA (*sourly*): If you don't want to embroider them—they can go without. That way yours will look better.

MAGDALENA: Neither mine nor yours. I know I'm not going to marry. I'd rather carry sacks to the mill. Anything except sit here day after day in this dark room.

BERNARDA: That's what a woman is for.

MAGDALENA: Cursed be all women.

BERNARDA: In this house you'll do what I order. You can't run with the story to your father any more. Needle and thread for women. Whiplash and mules for men. That's the way it has to be for people who have certain obligations.

(ADELA *goes out.*)

VOICE: Bernarda! Let me out!

BERNARDA (*calling*): Let her out now!

(*The* FIRST SERVANT *enters.*)

FIRST SERVANT: I had a hard time holding her. In spite of her eighty years, your mother's strong as an oak.

BERNARDA: It runs in the family. My grandfather was the same way.

SERVANT: Several times during the wake I had to cover her mouth with an empty sack because she wanted to shout out to you to give her dishwater to drink at least, and some dogmeat, which is what she says you feed her.

MARTIRIO: She's mean!

BERNARDA (*to* SERVANT): Let her get some fresh air in the patio.

SERVANT: She took her rings and the amethyst earrings out of the box, put them on, and told me she wants to get married.

(*The daughters laugh.*)

BERNARDA: Go with her and be careful she doesn't get near the well.

SERVANT: You don't need to be afraid she'll jump in.

BERNARDA: It's not that—but the neighbors can see her there from their windows.

(*The* SERVANT *leaves.*)

MARTIRIO: We'll go change our clothes.

BERNARDA: Yes, but don't take the 'kerchiefs from your heads.

(ADELA *enters.*)

And Augustias?

ADELA (*meaningfully*): I saw her looking out through the cracks of the back door. The men had just gone.

BERNARDA: And you, what were *you* doing at the door?

ADELA: I went there to see if the hens had laid.

BERNARDA: But the men had already gone!

ADELA (*meaningfully*): A group of them were still standing outside.

BERNARDA (*furiously*): Angustias! Angustias!

ANGUSTIAS (*entering*): Did you want something?

BERNARDA: For what—and at whom—were you looking?

ANGUSTIAS: Nobody.

BERNARDA: Is it decent for a woman of your class to be running after a man the day of her father's funeral? Answer me! Whom were you looking at? (*Pause.*)

ANGUSTIAS: I . . .

BERNARDA: Yes, you!

ANGUSTIAS: Nobody.

BERNARDA: Soft! Honeytongue! (*She strikes her.*)

PONCIA (*running to her*): Bernarda, calm down! (*She holds her.*)

(ANGUSTIAS *weeps.*)

BERNARDA: Get out of here, all of you!

(*They all go out.*)

PONCIA: She did it not realizing what she was doing—although it's bad, of course. It really disgusted me to see her sneak along to the patio. Then she stood at the window listening to the men's talk which, as usual, was not the sort one should listen to.

BERNARDA: That's what they come to funerals for. (*With curiosity*) What were they talking about?

PONCIA: They were taking about Paca la Roseta. Last night they tied her husband up in a stall, stuck her on a horse behind the saddle, and carried her away to the depths of the olive grove.

BERNARDA: And what did she do?

PONCIA: She? She was just as happy—they say her breasts were exposed and Maximiliano held on to her as if he were playing a guitar. Terrible!

BERNARDA: And what happened?

PONCIA: What had to happen. They came back almost at daybreak. Paca la Roseta with her hair loose and a wreath of flowers on her head.

BERNARDA: She's the only bad woman we have in the village.

PONCIA: Because she's not from here. She's from far away. And those who went with her are the sons of outsiders too. The men from here aren't up to a thing like that.

BERNARDA: No, but they like to see it, and talk about it, and suck their fingers over it.

PONCIA: They were saying a lot more things.

BERNARDA (*looking from side to side with a certain fear*): What things?

PONCIA: I'm ashamed to talk about them.

BERNARDA: And my daughter heard them?

PONCIA: Of course!

BERNARDA: That one takes after her Aunts: white and mealy-mouthed and casting sheep's eyes at any little barber's compliment. Oh, what one has to go through and put up with so people will be decent and not too wild!

PONCIA: It's just that your daughters are of an age when they ought to have husbands. Mighty little trouble they give you. Angustias must be much more than thirty now.

BERNARDA: Exactly thirty-nine.

PONCIA: Imagine. And she's never had a beau . . .

BERNARDA (*furiously*): None of them has ever had a beau and they've never needed one! They get along very well.

PONCIA: I didn't mean to offend you.

BERNARDA: For a hundred miles around there's no one good enough to come near them. The men in this town are not of their class. Do you want me to turn them over to the first shepherd?

PONCIA: You should have moved to another town.

BERNARDA: That's it. To sell them!

PONCIA: No, Bernarda, to change. . . . Of course, any place else, they'd be the poor ones.

BERNARDA: Hold your tormenting tongue!

PONCIA: One can't even talk to you. Do we, or do we not share secrets?

BERNARDA: We do not. You're a servant and I pay you. Nothing more.

PONCIA: But . . .

FIRST SERVANT (*entering*): Don Arturo's here. He's come to see about dividing the inheritance.

BERNARDA: Let's go. (*To the* SERVANT) You start whitewashing the patio. (*To* LA PONCIA) And you start putting all the dead man's clothes away in the chest.

PONCIA: We could give away some of the things.

BERNARDA: Nothing—not a button even! Not even the cloth we covered his face with.

(*She goes out slowly, leaning on her cane. At the door she turns to look at the two servants. They go out. She leaves.*)

(AMELIA *and* MARTIRIO *enter.*)

AMELIA: Did you take the medicine?

MARTIRIO: For all the good it'll do me.

AMELIA: But you took it?

MARTIRIO: I do things without any faith, but like clockwork.

AMELIA: Since the new doctor came you look livelier.

MARTIRIO: I feel the same.

AMELIA: Did you notice? Adelaida wasn't at the funeral.

MARTIRIO: I know. Her sweetheart doesn't let her go out even to the front doorstep. Before, she was gay. Now, not even powder on her face.

AMELIA: These days a girl doesn't know whether to have a beau or not.

MARTIRIO: It's all the same.

AMELIA: The whole trouble is all these wagging tongues that won't let us live. Adelaida has probably had a bad time.

MARTIRIO: She's afraid of our mother. Mother is the only one who knows the story of Adelaida's father and where he got his lands. Every time she comes here, Mother twists the knife in the wound. Her father killed his first wife's husband in Cuba so he could marry her himself. Then he left her here and went off with another woman who already had one daughter, and then he took up with this other girl, Adelaida's mother, and married her after his second wife died insane.

AMELIA: But why isn't a man like that put in jail?

MARTIRIO: Because men help each other cover up things like that and no one's able to tell on them.

AMELIA: But Adelaida's not to blame for any of that.

MARTIRIO: No. But history repeats itself. I can see that everything is a terrible repetition. And she'll have the same fate as her mother and grand-mother—both of them wife to the man who fathered her.

AMELIA: What an awful thing!

MARTIRIO: It's better never to look at a man. I've been afraid of them since I was a little girl. I'd see them in the yard, yoking the oxen and lifting grain sacks, shouting and stamping, and I was always afraid to grow up for fear one of them would suddenly take me in his arms. God has made me weak and ugly and has definitely put such things away from me.

AMELIA: Don't say that! Enrique Humanas was after you and he liked you.

MARTIRIO: That was just people's ideas! One time I stood in my nightgown at the window until daybreak because he let me know through his shepherd's little girl that he was going to come, and he didn't. It was all just talk. Then he married someone else who had more money than I.

AMELIA: And ugly as the devil.

MARTIRIO: What do men care about ugliness? All they care about is lands, yokes of oxen, and a submissive bitch who'll feed them.

AMELIA: Ay!

(MAGDALENA enters.)

MAGDALENA: What are you doing?

MARTIRIO: Just here.

AMELIA: And you?

MAGDALENA: I've been going through all the rooms. Just to walk a little, and look at Grand-mother's needlepoint pictures—the little woolen dog, and the black man wrestling with the lion—which we liked so much when we were children. Those were happier times. A wedding lasted ten days and evil tongues weren't in style. Today people are more refined. Brides wear white veils, just as in the cities, and we drink bottled wines, but we rot inside because of what people might say.

MARTIRIO: Lord knows what went on then!

AMELIA (to MAGDALENA): One of your shoelaces has come untied.

MAGDALENA: What of it?

AMELIA: You'll step on it and fall.

MAGDALENA: One less!

MARTIRIO: And Adela?

MAGDALENA: Ah! She put on the green dress she made to wear for her birthday, went out to the yard, and began shouting: "Chickens! Chickens, look at me!" I had to laugh.

AMELIA: If Mother had only seen her!

MAGDALENA: Poor little thing! She's the young-est one of us and still has her illusions. I'd give something to see her happy.

(Pause. ANGUSTIAS crosses the stage, carrying some towels.)

ANGUSTIAS: What time is it?

MAGDALENA: It must be twelve.

ANGUSTIAS: So late?

AMELIA: It's about to strike.

(ANGUSTIAS goes out.)

MAGDALENA (meaningfully): Do you know what? (Pointing after ANGUSTIAS.)

AMELIA: No.

MAGDALENA: Come on!

MARTIRIO: I don't know what you're talking about!

MAGDALENA: Both of you know it better than I do, always with your heads together, like two little sheep, but not letting anybody else in on it. I mean about Pepe el Romano!

MARTIRIO: Ah!

MAGDALENA (mocking her): Ah! The whole town's talking about it. Pepe el Romano is coming to marry Angustias. Last night he was walking around the house and I think he's going to send a declaration soon.

MARTIRIO: I'm glad. He's a good man.

AMELIA: Me too. Angustias is well off.

MAGDALENA: Neither one of you is glad.

MARTIRIO: Magdalena! What do you mean?

MAGDALENA: If he were coming because of Angustias' looks, for Angustias as a woman, I'd be glad too, but he's coming for her money. Even though Angustias is our sister, we're her family here and we know she's old and sickly, and always has been the least attractive one of us! Because if she looked like a dressed-up stick at twenty, what can she look like now, now that she's forty?

MARTIRIO: Don't talk like that. Luck comes to the one who least expects it.

AMELIA: But Magdalena's right after all! Angustias has all her father's money; she's the only rich one in the house and that's why, now that Father's dead and the money will be divided, they're coming for her.

MAGDALENA: Pepe el Romano is twenty-five years old and the best-looking man around here. The natural thing would be for him to be after you, Amelia, or our Adela, who's twenty—not looking for the least likely one in this house, a woman who, like her father, talks through her nose.

MARTIRIO: Maybe he likes that!

MAGDALENA: I've never been able to bear your hypocrisy.

MARTIRIO: Heavens!

(ADELA *enters*)

MAGDALENA: Did the chickens see you?

ADELA: What did you want me to do?

AMELIA: If Mother sees you, she'll drag you by your hair!

ADELA: I had a lot of illusions about this dress. I'd planned to put it on the day we were going to eat watermelons at the well. There wouldn't have been another like it.

MARTIRIO: It's a lovely dress.

ADELA: And one that looks very good on me. It's the best thing Magdalena's ever cut.

MAGDALENA: And the chickens, what did they say to you?

ADELA: They presented me with a few fleas that riddled my legs. (*They laugh.*)

MARTIRIO: What you can do is dye it black.

MAGDALENA: The best thing you can do is give it to Angustias for her wedding with Pepe el Romano.

ADELA (*with hidden emotion*): But Pepe el Romano . . .

AMELIA: Haven't you heard about it?

ADELA: No.

MAGDALENA: Well, now you know!

ADELA: But it can't be!

MAGDALENA: Money can do anything.

ADELA: Is that why she went out after the funeral and stood looking through the door? (*Pause.*) And that man would . . .

MAGDALENA: Would do anything. (*Pause.*)

MARTIRIO: What are you thinking, Adela?

ADELA: I'm thinking that this mourning has caught me at the worst moment of my life for me to bear it.

MAGDALENA: You'll get used to it.

ADELA (*bursting out, crying with rage*): I will not get used to it! I can't be locked up. I don't want my skin to look like yours. I don't want my skin's whiteness lost in these rooms. Tomorrow I'm going to put on my green dress and go walking in the streets. I want to go out!

(*The* FIRST SERVANT *enters.*)

MAGDALENA (*in a tone of authority*): Adela!

SERVANT: The poor thing! How she misses her father. . . . (*She goes out.*)

MARTIRIO: Hush!

AMELIA: What happens to one will happen to all of us. [ADELA *grows calm.*]

MAGDALENA: The servant almost heard you.

SERVANT (*entering*): Pepe el Romano is coming along at the end of the street.

(AMELIA, MARTIRIO, *and* MAGDALENA *run hurriedly.*)

MAGDALENA: Let's go see him! (*They leave rapidly.*)

SERVANT (*to* ADELA): Aren't you going?

ADELA: It's nothing to me.

SERVANT: Since he has to turn the corner, you'll see him better from the window of your room.

(*The* SERVANT *goes out.* ADELA *is left on the stage, standing doubtfully; after a moment, she also leaves rapidly, going toward her room.* BERNARDA *and* LA PONCIA *come in.*)

BERNARDA: Damned portions and shares!

PONCIA: What a lot of money is left to Angustias!

BERNARDA: Yes.

PONCIA: And for the others, considerably less.

BERNARDA: You've told me that three times now, when you know I don't want it mentioned! Considerably less; a lot less! Don't remind me any more.

(ANGUSTIAS *comes in, her face heavily made up.*)

Angustias!

ANGUSTIAS: Mother.

BERNARDA: Have you dared to powder your face? Have you dared to wash your face on the day of your father's death?

ANGUSTIAS: He wasn't my father. Mine died a long time ago. Have you forgotten that already?

BERNARDA: You owe more to this man, father of your sisters, than to your own. Thanks to him, your fortune is intact.

ANGUSTIAS: We'll have to see about that first!

BERNARDA: Even out of decency! Out of respect!

ANGUSTIAS: Let me go out, mother!

BERNARDA: Let you go out? After I've taken that powder off your face, I will. Spineless! Painted hussy! Just like your aunts!

(*She removes the powder violently with her handkerchief.*)

Now get out!

PONCIA: Bernarda, don't be so hateful!

BERNARDA: Even though my mother is crazy, I still have my five senses and I know what I'm doing.

(*They all enter.*)

MAGDALENA: What's going on here?

BERNARDA: Nothing's "going on here"!

MAGDALENA (*to* ANGUSTIAS): If you're fighting over the inheritance, you're the richest one and can hang on to it all.

ANGUSTIAS: Keep your tongue in your pocketbook!

BERNARDA (*beating on the floor*): Don't fool yourselves into thinking you'll sway me. Until I go out of this house feet first I'll give the orders for myself and for you!

(*Voices are heard and* MARÍA JOSEFA, *Bernarda's mother, enters. She is very old and has decked out her head and breast with flowers.*)

MARIA JOSEFA: Bernarda, where is my mantilla? Nothing, nothing of what I own will be for any of you. Not my rings nor my black moiré dress. Because not a one of you is going to marry—not a one. Bernarda, give me my necklace of pearls.

BERNARDA (*to the* SERVANT): Why did you let her get in here?

SERVANT (*trembling*): She got away from me!

MARIA JOSEFA: I ran away because I want to marry—I want to get married to a beautiful manly man from the shore of the sea. Because here the men run from women.

BERNARDA: Hush, hush, Mother!

MARIA JOSEFA: No, no—I won't hush. I don't want to see these single women, longing for marriage, turning their hearts to dust; and I want to go to my home town. Bernarda, I want a man to get married to and be happy with!

BERNARDA: Lock her up!

MARIA JOSEFA: Let me go out, Bernarda!

(*The* SERVANT *seizes* MARÍA JOSEFA.)

BERNARDA: Help her, all of you!

(*They all grab the old woman.*)

MARIA JOSEFA: I want to get away from here! Bernarda! To get married by the shore of the sea— by the shore of the sea!

ACT II

A *white room in Bernarda's house. The doors on the left lead to the bedrooms. Bernarda's daughters are seated on low chairs, sewing.* MAGDA-LENA *is embroidering.* LA PONCIA *is with them.*

ANGUSTIAS: I've cut the third sheet.

MARTIRIO: That one goes to Amelia.

MAGDALENA: Angustias, shall I put Pepe's initials here too?

ANGUSTIAS (*dryly*): No.

MAGDALENA (*calling to* ADELA *offstage*): Adela, aren't you coming?

AMELIA: She's probably stretched out on the bed.

PONCIA: Something's wrong with that one. I find her restless, trembling, frightened—as if a lizard were between her breasts.

MARTIRIO: There's nothing, more or less, wrong with her than there is with all of us.

MAGDALENA: All of us except Angustias.

ANGUSTIAS: I feel fine, and anybody who doesn't like it can pop.

MAGDALENA: We all have to admit the nicest things about you are your figure and your tact.

ANGUSTIAS: Fortunately, I'll soon be out of this hell.

MAGDALENA: Maybe you won't get out!

MARTIRIO: Stop this talk!

ANGUSTIAS: Besides, a good dowry is better than dark eyes in one's face!

MAGDALENA: All you say just goes in one ear and out the other.

AMELIA (*to* LA PONCIA): Open the patio door and see if we can get a bit of a breeze.

(LA PONCIA *opens the door.*)

MARTIRIO: Last night I couldn't sleep because of the heat.

AMELIA: Neither could I.

MAGDALENA: I got up for a bit of air. There was a black storm cloud and a few drops even fell.

PONCIA: It was one in the morning and the earth seemed to give off fire. I got up too. Angustias was still at the window with Pepe.

MAGDALENA (*with irony*): That late? What time did he leave?

ANGUSTIAS: Why do you ask, if you saw him?

AMELIA: He must have left about one-thirty.

ANGUSTIAS: Yes. How did you know?

AMELIA: I heard him cough and heard his mare's hoofbeats.

PONCIA: But I heard him leave around four.

ANGUSTIAS: It must have been someone else!

PONCIA: No, I'm sure of it!

AMELIA: That's what it seemed to me, too.

MAGDALENA: That's very strange! (*Pause.*)

PONCIA: Listen, Angustias, what did he say to you the first time he came by your window?

ANGUSTIAS: Nothing. What should he say? Just talked.

MARTIRIO: It's certainly strange that two people who never knew each other should suddenly meet at a window and be engaged.

ANGUSTIAS: Well, I didn't mind.

AMELIA: I'd have felt very strange about it.

ANGUSTIAS: No, because when a man comes to a window he knows, from all the busybodies who come and go and fetch and carry, that he's going to be told "yes."

MARTIRIO: All right, but he'd have to ask you.

ANGUSTIAS: Of course!

AMELIA (*inquisitively*): And how did he ask you?

ANGUSTIAS: Why, no way:—"You know I'm after you. I need a good, well brought up woman, and that's you—if it's agreeable."

AMELIA: These things embarrass me!

ANGUSTIAS: They embarrass me too, but one has to go through it!

PONCIA: And did he say anything more?

ANGUSTIAS: Yes, he did all the talking.

MARTIRIO: And you?

ANGUSTIAS: I couldn't have said a word. My heart was almost coming out of my mouth. It was the first time I'd ever been alone at night with a man.

MAGDALENA: And such a handsome man.

ANGUSTIAS: He's not bad looking!

PONCIA: Those things happen among people who have an idea how to do things, who talk and say and move their hand. The first time my husband, Evaristo the Short-tailed, came to my window . . . Ha! Ha! Ha!

AMELIA: What happened?

PONCIA: It was very dark. I saw him coming along and as he went by he said, "Good evening." "Good evening," I said. Then we were both silent for more than half an hour. The sweat poured down my body. Then Evaristo got nearer and nearer as if he wanted to squeeze in through the bars and said in a very low voice—"Come here and let me feel you!"

(*They all laugh.* AMELIA *gets up, runs and looks through the door.*)

AMELIA: Ay, I thought mother was coming!

MAGDALENA: What she'd have done to us!

(*They go on laughing.*)

AMELIA: Sh-h-h! She'll hear us.

PONCIA: Then he acted very decently. Instead of getting some other idea, he went to raising birds, until he died. You aren't married but it's good for you to know, anyway, that two weeks after the wedding a man gives up the bed for the table, then the table for the tavern, and the woman who doesn't like it can just rot, weeping in a corner.

AMELIA: You liked it.

PONCIA: I learned how to handle him!

MARTIRIO: Is it true that you sometimes hit him?

PONCIA: Yes, and once I almost poked out one of his eyes!

MAGDALENA: All women ought to be like that!

PONCIA: I'm one of your mother's school. One time I don't know what he said to me, and then I killed all his birds—with the pestle!

(*They laugh.*)

MAGDALENA: Adela, child! Don't miss this.

AMELIA: Adela! (*Pause.*)

MAGDALENA: I'll go see! (*She goes out.*)

PONCIA: That child is sick!

MARTIRIO: Of course. She hardly sleeps!

PONCIA: What *does* she do, then?

MARTIRIO: How do I know what she does?

PONCIA: You probably know better than we do, since you sleep with just a wall between you.

ANGUSTIAS: Envy gnaws on people.

AMELIA: Don't exaggerate.

ANGUSTIAS: I can tell it in her eyes. She's getting the look of a crazy woman.

MARTIRIO: Don't talk about crazy women. This is one place you're not allowed to say that word.

(MAGDALENA *and* ADELA *enter.*)

MAGDALENA: Didn't you say she was asleep?

ADELA: My body aches.

MARTIRIO (*with a hidden meaning*): Didn't you sleep well last night?

ADELA: Yes.

MARTIRIO: Then?

ADELA (*loudly*): Leave me alone. Awake or asleep, it's no affair of yours. I'll do whatever I want to with my body.

MARTIRIO: I was just concerned about you!

ADELA: Concerned?—curious! Weren't you sewing? Well, continue! I wish I were invisible so I could pass through a room without being asked where I was going!

SERVANT (*entering*): Bernarda is calling you. The man with the laces is here.

(*All but* ADELA *and* LA PONCIA *go out, and as* MARTIRIO *leaves, she looks fixedly at* ADELA.)

ADELA: Don't look at me like that! If you want, I'll give you my eyes, for they're younger, and my back to improve that hump you have, but look the other way when I go by.

PONCIA: Adela, she's your sister, and the one who most loves you besides!

ADELA: She follows me everywhere. Sometimes she looks in my room to see if I'm sleeping. She won't let me breathe, and always, "Too bad about that face!" "Too bad about that body! It's going to waste!" But I won't let that happen. My body will be for whomever I choose.

PONCIA (*insinuatingly, in a low voice*): For Pepe el Romano, no?

ADELA (*frightened*): What do you mean?

PONCIA: What I said, Adela!

ADELA: Shut up!

PONCIA (*loudly*): Don't you think I've noticed?

ADELA: Lower your voice!

PONCIA: Then forget what you're thinking about!

ADELA: What do you know?

PONCIA: We old ones can see through walls. Where do you go when you get up at night?

ADELA: I wish you were blind!

PONCIA: But my head and hands are full of eyes, where something like this is concerned. I couldn't possibly guess your intentions. Why did you sit almost naked at your window, and with the light on and the window open, when Pepe passed by the second night he came to talk with your sister?

ADELA: That's not true!

PONCIA: Don't be a child! Leave your sister alone. And if you like Pepe el Romano, keep it to yourself.

(ADELA *weeps.*)

Besides, who says you can't marry him? Your sister Angustias is sickly. She'll die with her first child. Narrow waisted, old—and out of my experience I can tell you she'll die. Then Pepe will do what all widowers do in these parts: he'll marry the youngest and most beautiful, and that's you. Live on that hope, forget him, anything; but don't go against God's law.

ADELA: Hush!

PONCIA: I won't hush!

ADELA: Mind your own business. Snooper, traitor!

PONCIA: I'm going to stick to you like a shadow!

ADELA: Instead of cleaning the house and then going to bed and praying for the dead, you root around like an old sow about goings on between men and women—so you can drool over them.

PONCIA: I keep watch; so people won't spit when they pass our door.

ADELA: What a tremendous affection you've suddenly conceived for my sister.

PONCIA: I don't have any affection for any of you. I want to live in a decent house. I don't want to be dirtied in my old age!

ADELA: Save your advice. It's already too late. For I'd leap not over you, just a servant, but over my mother to put out this fire I feel in my legs and

my mouth. What can you possibly say about me? That I lock myself in my room and will not open the door? That I don't sleep? I'm smarter than you! See if you can catch the hare with your hands.

PONCIA: Don't defy me, Adela, don't defy me! Because I can shout, light lamps, and make bells ring.

ADELA: Bring four thousand yellow flares and set them about the walls of the yard. No one can stop what has to happen.

PONCIA: You like him that much?

ADELA: That much! Looking in his eyes I seem to drink his blood in slowly.

PONCIA: I won't listen to you.

ADELA: Well, you'll have to! I've been afraid of you. But now I'm stronger than you!

(ANGUSTIAS *enters.*)

ANGUSTIAS: Always arguing!

PONCIA: Certainly. She insists that in all this heat I have to go bring her I don't know what from the store.

ANGUSTIAS: Did you buy me the bottle of perfume?

PONCIA: The most expensive one. And the face powder. I put them on the table in your room.

(ANGUSTIAS *goes out.*)

ADELA: And be quiet!

PONCIA: We'll see!

(MARTIRIO *and* AMELIA *enter.*)

MARTIRIO (*to* ADELA): Did you see the laces?

AMELIA: Angustias', for her wedding sheets, are beautiful.

ADELA (*to* MARTIRIO, *who is carrying some lace*): And these?

MARTIRIO: They're for me. For a nightgown.

ADELA (*with sarcasm*): One needs a sense of humor around here!

MARTIRIO (*meaningfully*): But only for me to look at. I don't have to exhibit myself before anybody.

PONCIA: No one ever sees us in our nightgowns.

MARTIRIO (*meaningfully, looking at* ADELA): Sometimes they don't! But I love nice underwear. If I were rich, I'd have it made of Holland Cloth. It's one of the few tastes I've left.

PONCIA: These laces are beautiful for babies' caps and christening gowns. I could never afford them for my own. Now let's see if Angustias will use them for hers. Once she starts having children, they'll keep her running night and day.

MAGDALENA: I don't intend to sew a stitch on them.

AMELIA: And much less bring up some stranger's children. Look how our neighbors across the road are—making sacrifices for four brats.

PONCIA: They're better off than you. There at least they laugh and you can hear them fight.

MARTIRIO: Well, you go work for them, then.

PONCIA: No, fate has sent me to this nunnery!

(*Tiny bells are heard distantly as though through several thicknesses of wall.*)

MAGDALENA: It's the men going back to work.

PONCIA: It was three o'clock a minute ago.

MARTIRIO: With this sun!

ADELA (*sitting down*): Ay! If only we could go out in the fields too!

MAGDALENA (*sitting down*): Each class does what it has to!

MARTIRIO (*sitting down*): That's it!

AMELIA (*sitting down*): Ay!

PONCIA: There's no happiness like that in the fields right at this time of year. Yesterday morning the reapers arrived. Forty or fifty handsome young men.

MAGDALENA: Where are they from this year?

PONCIA: From far, far away. They came from the mountains! Happy! Like weathered trees! Shouting and throwing stones! Last night a woman who dresses in sequins and dances, with an accordion, arrived, and fifteen of them made a deal with her to take her to the olive grove. I saw them from far away. The one who talked with her was a boy with green eyes—tight knit as a sheaf of wheat.

AMELIA: Really?

ADELA: Are you sure?

PONCIA: Years ago another one of those women came here, and I myself gave my eldest son some money so he could go. Men need things like that.

ADELA: Everything's forgiven *them*.

AMELIA: To be born a woman's the worst possible punishment.

MAGDALENA: Even our eyes aren't our own.

(*A distant song is heard, coming nearer.*)

PONCIA: There they are. They have a beautiful song.

AMELIA: They're going out to reap now.

CHORUS:
  The reapers have set out
  Looking for ripe wheat;
  They'll carry off the hearts
  Of any girls they meet.

(*Tambourines and carrañacas*[1] *are heard. Pause. They all listen in the silence cut by the sun.*)

AMELIA: And they don't mind the sun!

MARTIRIO: They reap through flames.

ADELA: How I'd like to be a reaper so I could come and go as I pleased. Then we could forget what's eating at us all.

MARTIRIO: What do you have to forget?

ADELA: Each one of us has something.

MARTIRIO (*intensely*): Each one!

PONCIA: Quiet! Quiet!

CHORUS (*very distantly*):
  Throw wide your doors and windows,
  You girls who live in the town.
  The reaper asks you for roses
  With which to deck his crown.

PONCIA: What a song!

MARTIRIO (*with nostalgia*):
  Throw wide your doors and windows,
  You girls who live in the town.

ADELA (*passionately*):
  The reaper asks you for roses
  With which to deck his crown.

(*The song grows more distant.*)

PONCIA: Now they're turning the corner.

ADELA: Let's watch them from the window of my room.

PONCIA: Be careful not to open the shutters too much because they're likely to give them a push to see who's looking.

(*The three leave.* MARTIRIO *is left sitting on the low chair with her head between her hands.*)

AMELIA (*drawing near her*): What's wrong with you?

MARTIRIO: The heat makes me feel ill.

AMELIA: And it's no more than that?

MARTIRIO: I was wishing it were November, the rainy days, the frost—anything except this unending summertime.

AMELIA: It'll pass and come again.

MARTIRIO: Naturally. (*Pause.*) What time did you go to sleep last night?

AMELIA: I don't know. I sleep like a log. Why?

MARTIRIO: Nothing. Only I thought I heard someone in the yard.

AMELIA: Yes?

MARTIRIO: Very late.

[1] **carrañacas:** an instrument used in carnival processions.

AMELIA: And weren't you afraid?

MARTIRIO: No. I've heard it other nights.

AMELIA: We'd better watch out! Couldn't it have been the shepherds?

MARTIRIO: The shepherds come at six.

AMELIA: Maybe a young, unbroken mule?

MARTIRIO (*to herself, with double meaning*): That's it! That's it. An unbroken little mule.

AMELIA: We'll have to set a watch.

MARTIRIO: No. No. Don't say anything. It may be I've just imagined it.

AMELIA: Maybe. (*Pause. She starts to go.*)

MARTIRIO: Amelia!

AMELIA (*at the door*): What? (*Pause.*)

MARTIRIO: Nothing. (*Pause.*)

AMELIA: Why did you call me? (*Pause.*)

MARTIRIO: It just came out. I didn't mean to. (*Pause.*)

AMELIA: Lie down for a little.

ANGUSTIAS (*She bursts in furiously, in a manner that makes a great contrast with previous silence.*): Where's that picture of Pepe I had under my pillow? Which one of you has it?

MARTIRIO: No one.

AMELIA: You'd think he was a silver St. Bartholomew.

ANGUSTIAS: Where's the picture?

(PONCIA, MAGDALENA, *and* ADELA *enter.*)

ADELA: What picture?

ANGUSTIAS: One of you has hidden it on me.

MAGDALENA: Do you have the effrontery to say that?

ANGUSTIAS: I had it in my room, and now it isn't there.

MARTIRIO: But couldn't it have jumped out into the yard at midnight? Pepe likes to walk around in the moonlight.

ANGUSTIAS: Don't joke with me! When he comes I'll tell him.

PONCIA: Don't do that! Because it'll turn up. (*Looking at* ADELA.)

ANGUSTIAS: I'd like to know which one of you has it.

ADELA (*looking at* MARTIRIO): Somebody has it! But not me!

MARTIRIO (*with meaning*): Of course not you!

BERNARDA (*entering, with her cane*): What scandal is this in my house in the heat's heavy silence? The neighbors must have their ears glued to the walls.

ANGUSTIAS: They've stolen my sweetheart's picture!

BERNARDA (*fiercely*): Who? Who?

ANGUSTIAS: They have!

BERNARDA: Which one of you? (*Silence.*) Answer me! (*Silence. To* LA PONCIA) Search their rooms! Look in their beds. This comes of not tying you up with shorter leashes. But I'll teach you now! (*To* ANGUSTIAS) Are you sure?

ANGUSTIAS: Yes.

BERNARDA: Did you look everywhere?

ANGUSTIAS: Yes, Mother.

(*They all stand in an embarrassed silence.*)

BERNARDA: At the end of my life—to make me drink the bitterest poison a mother knows. (*To* PONCIA) Did you find it?

PONCIA: Here it is.

BERNARDA: Where did you find it?

PONCIA: It was . . .

BERNARDA: Say it! Don't be afraid.

PONCIA (*wonderingly*): Between the sheets in Martirio's bed.

BERNARDA (*to* MARTIRIO): Is that true?

MARTIRIO: It's true.

BERNARDA (*advancing on her, beating her with her cane*): You'll come to a bad end yet, you hypocrite! Troublemaker!

MARTIRIO (*fiercely*): Don't hit me, Mother!

BERNARDO: All I want to!

MARTIRIO: If I let you! You hear me? Get back!

PONCIA: Don't be disrespectful to your mother!

ANGUSTIAS (*holding* BERNARDA): Let her go, please!

BERNARDA: Not even tears in your eyes.

MARTIRIO: I'm not going to cry just to please you.

BERNARDA: Why did you take the picture?

MARTIRIO: Can't I play a joke on my sister? What else would I want it for?

ADELA (*leaping forward, full of jealousy*): It wasn't a joke! You never liked to play jokes. It was something else bursting in her breast—trying to come out. Admit it openly now.

MARTIRIO: Hush, and don't make me speak; for if I should speak the walls would close together one against the other with shame.

ADELA: An evil tongue never stops inventing lies.

BERNARDA: Adela!

MAGDALENA: You're crazy.

AMELIA: And you stone us all with your evil suspicions.

MARTIRIO: But some others do things more wicked!

ADELA: Until all at once they stand forth stark naked and the river carries them along.

BERNARDA: Spiteful!

ANGUSTIAS: It's not my fault Pepe el Romano chose me!

ADELA: For your money.

ANGUSTIAS: Mother!

BERNARDA: Silence!

MARTIRIO: For your fields and your orchards.

MAGDALENA: That's only fair.

BERNARDA: Silence, I say! I saw the storm coming but I didn't think it'd burst so soon. Oh, what an avalanche of hate you've thrown on my heart! But I'm not old yet—I have five chains for you, and this house my father built, so not even the weeds will know of my desolation. Out of here!

(*They go out. Bernarda sits down desolately.* LA PONCIA *is standing close to the wall.* BERNARDA *recovers herself, and beats on the floor.*)

I'll have to let them feel the weight of my hand! Bernarda, remember your duty!

PONCIA: May I speak?

BERNARDA: Speak. I'm sorry you heard. A stranger is always out of place in a family.

PONCIA: What I've seen, I've seen.

BERNARDA: Angustias must get married right away.

PONCIA: Certainly. We'll have to get her away from here.

BERNARDA: Not her, him!

PONCIA: Of course. He's the one to get away from here. You've thought it all out.

BERNARDA: I'm not thinking. There are things that shouldn't and can't be thought out. I give orders.

PONCIA: And you think he'll be satisfied to go away?

BERNARDA (*rising*): What are you imagining now?

PONCIA: He will, of course, marry Angustias.

BERNARDA: Speak up! I know you well enough to see that your knife's out for me.

PONCIA: I never knew a warning could be called murder.

BERNARDA: Have you some "warning" for me?

PONCIA: I'm not making any accusations, Bernarda. I'm only telling you to open your eyes and you'll see.

BERNARDA: See what?

PONCIA: You've always been smart, Bernarda. You've seen other people's sins a hundred miles away. Many times I've thought you could read

minds. But, your children are your children, and now you're blind.

BERNARDA: Are you talking about Martirio?

PONCIA: Well, yes—about Martirio . . . (*With curiosity*) I wonder why she hid the picture?

BERNARDA (*shielding her daughter*): After all, she says it was a joke. What else could it be?

PONCIA (*scornfully*): Do you believe that?

BERNARDA (*sternly*): I don't merely believe it. It's so!

PONCIA: Enough of this. We're talking about your family. But if we were talking about your neighbor across the way, what would it be?

BERNARDA: Now you're beginning to pull the point of the knife out.

PONCIA (*always cruelly*): No, Bernarda. Something very grave is happening here. I don't want to put the blame on your shoulders, but you've never given your daughters any freedom. Martirio is lovesick, I don't care what you say. Why didn't you let her marry Enrique Humanas? Why, on the very day he was coming to her window did you send him a message not to come?

BERNARDA (*loudly*): I'd do it a thousand times over! My blood won't mingle with the Humanas' while I live! His father was a shepherd.

PONCIA: And you see now what's happening to you with these airs!

BERNARDA: I have them because I can afford to. And you don't have them because you know where you came from!

PONCIA (*with hate*): Don't remind me! I'm old now. I've always been grateful for your protection.

BERNARDA (*emboldened*): You don't seem so!

PONCIA (*with hate, behind softness*): Martirio will forget this.

BERNARDA: And if she doesn't—the worse for her. I don't believe this is that "very grave thing" that's happening here. Nothing's happening here. It's just that you wish it would! And if it should happen one day, you can be sure it won't go beyond these walls.

PONCIA: I'm not so sure of that! There are people in town who can also read hidden thoughts, from afar.

BERNARDA: How you'd like to see me and my daughters on our way to a whorehouse!

PONCIA: No one knows her own destiny!

BERNARDA: I know my destiny! And my daughters! The whorehouse was for a certain woman, already dead . . .

PONCIA (*fiercely*): Bernarda, respect the memory of my mother!

BERNARDA: Then don't plague me with your evil thoughts! (*Pause.*)

PONCIA: I'd better stay out of everything.

BERNARDA: That's what you ought to do. Work and keep your mouth shut. The duty of all who work for a living.

PONCIA: But we can't do that. Don't you think it'd be better for Pepe to marry Martirio or . . . yes! . . . Adela?

BERNARDA: No, I *don't* think so.

PONCIA (*with meaning*): Adela! She's Romano's real sweetheart!

BERNARDA: Things are never the way we want them!

PONCIA: But it's hard work to turn them from their destined course. For Pepe to be with Angustias seems wrong to me—and to other people—and even to the wind. Who knows if they'll get what they want?

BERNARDA: There you go again! Sneaking up on me—giving me bad dreams. But I won't listen to you, because if all you say should come to pass— I'd scratch your face.

PONCIA: Frighten someone else with that.

BERNARDA: Fortunately, my daughters respect me and have never gone against my will!

PONCIA: That's right! But, as soon as they break loose they'll fly to the rooftops!

BERNARDA: And I'll bring them down with stones!

PONCIA: Oh, yes! You were always the bravest one!

BERNARDA: I've always enjoyed a good fight!

PONCIA: But aren't people strange. You should see Angustias's enthusiasm for her lover, at her age! And he seems very smitten too. Yesterday my oldest son told me that when he passed by with the oxen at four-thirty in the morning they were still talking.

BERNARDA: At four-thirty?

ANGUSTIAS (*entering*): That's a lie!

PONCIA: That's what he told me.

BERNARDA (*to* ANGUSTIAS): Speak up!

ANGUSTIAS: For more than a week Pepe has been leaving at one. May God strike me dead if I'm lying.

MARTIRIO (*entering*): I heard him leave at four too.

BERNARDA: But did you see him with your eyes?

MARTIRIO: I didn't want to look out. Don't you talk now through the side window?

ANGUSTIAS: We talk through my bedroom window.

(*Adela appears at the door*)

MARTIRIO: Then . . .

BERNARDA: What's going on here?

PONCIA: If you're not careful, you'll find out! At least Pepe was at *one* of your windows—and at four in the morning too!

BERNARDA: Are you sure of that?

PONCIA: You can't be sure of anything in this life!

ADELA: Mother, don't listen to someone who wants us to lose everything we have.

BERNARDA: I know how to take care of myself! If the townspeople want to come bearing false witness against me, they'll run into a stone wall! Don't any of you talk about this! Sometimes other people try to stir up a wave of filth to drown us.

MARTIRIO: I don't like to lie.

PONCIA: So there must be something.

BERNARDA: There won't be anything. I was born to have my eyes always open. Now I'll watch without closing them 'til I die.

ANGUSTIAS: I have the right to know.

BERNARDA: You don't have any right except to obey. No one's going to fetch and carry for me. (*To* LA PONCIA) And don't meddle in our affairs. No one will take a step without my knowing it.

SERVANT (*entering*): There's a big crowd at the top of the street, and all the neighbors are at their doors!

BERNARDA (*to* PONCIA): Run see what's happening!

(*The Girls are about to run out.*)

Where are you going? I always knew you for window watching women and breakers of your mourning. All of you, to the patio!

(*They go out.* BERNARDA *leaves. Distant shouts are heard.* MARTIRIO *and* ADELA *enter and listen, not daring to step farther than the front door.*)

MARTIRIO: You can be thankful I didn't happen to open my mouth.

ADELA: I would have spoken too.

MARTIRIO: And what were you going to say? Wanting isn't doing!

ADELA: I do what I can and what happens to suit me. You've wanted to, but haven't been able.

MARTIRIO: You won't go on very long.

ADELA: I'll have everything!

MARTIRIO: I'll tear you out of his arms!

ADELA (*pleadingly*): Martirio, let me be!

MARTIRIO: None of us will have him!

ADELA: He wants me for his house!

MARTIRIO: I saw how he embraced you!

ADELA: I didn't want him to. It's as if I were dragged by a rope.

MARTIRIO: I'll see you dead first!

(MAGDALENA *and* ANGUSTIAS *look in. The tumult is increasing. A* SERVANT *enters with* BERNARDA. PONCIA *also enters from another door.*)

PONCIA: Bernarda!

BERNARDA: What's happening?

PONCIA: Librada's daughter, the unmarried one, had a child and no one knows whose it is!

ADELA: A child?

PONCIA: And to hide her shame she killed it and hid it under the rocks, but the dogs, with more heart than most Christians, dug it out and, as though directed by the hand of God, left it at her door. Now they want to kill her. They're dragging her through the streets—and down the paths and across the olive groves the men are coming, shouting so the fields shake.

BARNARDA: Yes, let them all come with olive whips and hoe handles—let them all come and kill her!

ADELA: No, not to kill her!

MARTIRIO: Yes—and let us go out too!

BERNARDA: And let whoever loses her decency pay for it!

(*Outside a woman's shriek and a great clamor is heard.*)

ADELA: Let her escape! Don't you go out!

MARTIRIO (*looking at* ADELA): Let her pay what she owes!

BERNARDA (*at the archway*): Finish her before the guards come! Hot coals in the place where she sinned!

ADELA (*holding her belly*): No! No!

BERNARDA: Kill her! Kill her!

ACT III

Four white walls, lightly washed in blue, of the interior patio of Bernarda Alba's house. The doorways, illumined by the lights inside the rooms, give a tenuous glow to the stage. At the center there is a table with a shaded oil lamp about which BERNARDA *and her daughters are eating.* LA PONCIA *serves them.* PRUDENCIA *sits apart. When the curtain rises, there is a great*

silence interrupted only by the noise of plates and silverware.

PRUDENCIA: I'm going. I've made you a long visit. (*She rises.*)

BERNARDA: But wait, Prudencia. We never see one another.

PRUDENCIA: Have they sounded the last call to rosary?

PONCIA: Not yet.

(*Prudencia sits down again.*)

BERNARDA: And your husband, how's he getting on?

PRUDENCIA: The same.

BERNARDA: We never see him either.

PRUDENCIA: You know how he is. Since he quarrelled with his brothers over the inheritance, he hasn't used the front door. He takes a ladder and climbs over the back wall.

BERNARDA: He's a real man! And your daughter?

PRUDENCIA: He's never forgiven her.

BERNARDA: He's right.

PRUDENCIA: I don't know what he told you. I suffer because of it.

BERNARDA: A daughter who's disobedient stops being a daughter and becomes an enemy.

PRUDENCIA: I let water run. The only consolation I've left is to take refuge in the church, but, since I'm losing my sight, I'll have to stop coming so the children won't make fun of me.

(*A heavy blow is heard against the walls.*)

What's that?

BERNARDA: The stallion. He's locked in the stall and he kicks against the wall of the house. (*Shouting*) Tether him and take him out in the yard! (*In a lower voice*) He must be too hot.

PRUDENCIA: Are you going to put the new mares to him?

BERNARDA: At daybreak.

PRUDENCIA: You've known how to increase your stock.

BERNARDA: By dint of money and struggling.

PONCIA (*interrupting*): And she has the best herd in these parts. It's a shame that prices are low.

BERNARDA: Do you want a little cheese and honey?

PRUDENCIA: I have no appetite.

(*The blow is heard again*)

PONCIA: My God!

PRUDENCIA: It quivered in my chest!

BERNARDA (*rising, furiously*): Do I have to say things twice? Let him out to roll on the straw.

(*Pause. Then, as though speaking to the Stable-man:*) Well then, lock the mares in the corral, but let him run free or he may kick down the walls. (*She returns to the table and sits again.*) Ay, what a life!

PRUDENCIA: You have to fight like a man.

BERNARDA: That's it.

(ADELA *gets up from the table.*)

Where are you going?

ADELA: For a drink of water.

BERNARDA (*raising her voice*): Bring a pitcher of cool water. (*To* ADELA) You can sit down.

(ADELA *sits down.*)

PRUDENCIA: And Angustias, when will she get married?

BERNARDA: They're coming to ask for her within three days.

PRUDENCIA: You must be happy.

ANGUSTIAS: Naturally!

AMELIA (*to* MAGDALENA): You've spilled the salt!

MAGDALENA: You can't possibly have worse luck than you're having.

AMELIA: It always brings bad luck.

BERNARDA: That's enough!

PRUDENCIA (*to* ANGUSTIAS): Has he given you the ring yet?

ANGUSTIAS: Look at it. (*She holds it out.*)

PRUDENCIA: It's beautiful. Three pearls. In my day, pearls signified tears.

ANGUSTIAS: But things have changed now.

ADELA: I don't think so. Things go on meaning the same. Engagement rings should be diamonds.

PONCIA: The most appropriate.

BERNARDA: With pearls or without them, things are as one proposes.

MARTIRIO: Or as God disposes.

PRUDENCIA: I've been told your furniture is beautiful.

BERNARDA: It cost sixteen thousand *reales*.

PONCIA (*interrupting*): The best is the wardrobe with the mirror.

PRUDENCIA: I never saw a piece like that.

BERNARDA: We had chests.

PRUDENCIA: The important thing is that everything be for the best.

ADELA: And that you never know.

BERNARDA: There's no reason why it shouldn't be.

(*Bells are heard very distantly.*)

PRUDENCIA: The last call. (*To* ANGUSTIAS) I'll

be coming back to have you show me your clothes.

ANGUSTIAS: Whenever you like.

PRUDENCIA: Good evening—God bless you!

BERNARDA: Good-bye, Prudencia.

ALL FIVE DAUGHTERS (*at the same time*): God go with you!

(*Pause.* PRUDENCIA *goes out.*)

BERNARDA: Well, we've eaten.

(*They rise.*)

ADELA: I'm going to walk as far as the gate to stretch my legs and get a bit of fresh air.

(MAGDALENA *sits down in a low chair and leans against the wall.*)

AMELIA: I'll go with you.

MARTIRIO: I too.

ADELA (*with contained hate*): I'm not going to get lost!

AMELIA: One needs company at night.

(*They go out.* BERNARDA *sits down.* ANGUSTIAS *is clearing the table.*)

BERNARDA: I've told you once already! I want you to talk to your sister Martirio. What happened about the picture was a joke and you must forget it.

ANGUSTIAS: You know she doesn't like me.

BERNARDA: Each one knows what she thinks inside. I don't pry into anyone's heart, but I want to put up a good front and have family harmony. You understand?

ANGUSTIAS: Yes.

BERNARDA: Then that's settled.

MAGDALENA (*she is almost asleep*): Besides, you'll be gone in no time. (*She falls asleep.*)

ANGUSTIAS: Not soon enough for me.

BERNARDA: What time did you stop talking last night?

ANGUSTIAS: Twelve-thirty.

BERNARDA: What does Pepe talk about?

ANGUSTIAS: I find him absent-minded. He always talks to me as though he were thinking of something else. If I ask him what's the matter, he answers—"We men have our worries."

BERNARDA: You shouldn't ask him. And when you're married, even less. Speak if he speaks, and look at him when he looks at you. That way you'll get along.

ANGUSTIAS: But, Mother, I think he's hiding things from me.

BERNARDA: Don't try to find out. Don't ask him, and above all, never let him see you cry.

ANGUSTIAS: I should be happy, but I'm not.

BERNARDA: It's all the same.

ANGUSTIAS: Many nights I watch Pepe very closely through the window bars and he seems to fade away—as though he were hidden in a cloud of dust like those raised by the flocks.

BERNARDA: That's just because you're not strong.

ANGUSTIAS: I hope so!

BERNARDA: Is he coming tonight?

ANGUSTIAS: No, he went into town with his mother.

BERNARDA: Good, we'll get to bed early. Magdalena!

ANGUSTIAS: She's asleep. (ADELA, MARTIRIO, and AMELIA enter.)

AMELIA: What a dark night!

ADELA: You can't see two steps in front of you.

MARTIRIO: A good night for robbers, for anyone who needs to hide.

ADELA: The stallion was in the middle of the corral. White. Twice as large. Filling all the darkness.

AMELIA: It's true. It was frightening. Like a ghost.

ADELA: The sky has stars as big as fists.

MARTIRIO: This one stared at them till she almost cracked her neck.

ADELA: Don't you like them up there?

MARTIRIO: What goes on over the roof doesn't mean a thing to me. I have my hands full with what happens under it.

ADELA: Well, that's the way it goes with you!

BERNARDA: And it goes the same for you as for her.

ANGUSTIAS: Good night.

ADELA: Are you going to bed now?

ANGUSTIAS: Yes, Pepe isn't coming tonight. (She goes out.)

ADELA: Mother, why, when a star falls or lightning flashes, does one say:

Holy Barbara, blessed on high
May your name be in the sky
With holy water written high?

BERNARDA: The old people know many things we've forgotten.

AMELIA: I close my eyes so I won't see them.

ADELA: Not I. I like to see what's quiet and been quiet for years on end, running with fire.

MARTIRIO: But all that has nothing to do with us.

BERNARDA: And it's better not to think about it.

ADELA: What a beautiful night! I'd like to stay up till very late and enjoy the breeze from the fields.

BERNARDA: But we have to go to bed. Magdalena!

AMELIA: She's just dropped off.

BERNARDA: Magdalena!

MAGDALENA (annoyed): Leave me alone!

BERNARDA: To bed!

MAGDALENA (rising, in a bad humor): You don't give anyone a moment's peace! (She goes off grumbling.)

AMELIA: Good night! (She goes out.)

BERNARDA: You two get along, too.

MARTIRIO: How is it Angustias's sweetheart isn't coming tonight?

BERNARDA: He went on a trip.

MARTIRIO (looking at ADELA): Ah!

ADELA: I'll see you in the morning!

(She goes out. MARTIRIO drinks some water and goes out slowly, looking at the door to the yard. LA PONCIA enters.)

PONCIA: Are you still here?

BERNARDA: Enjoying this quiet and not seeing anywhere the "very grave thing" that's happening here—according to you.

PONCIA: Bernarda, let's not go any further with this.

BERNARDA: In this house there's no question of a yes or a no. My watchfulness can take care of anything.

PONCIA: Nothing's happening outside. That's true, all right. Your daughters act and are as though stuck in a cupboard. But neither you nor anyone else can keep watch inside a person's heart.

BERNARDA: My daughters breathe calmly enough.

PONCIA: That's your business, since you're their mother. I have enough to do just with serving you.

BERNARDA: Yes, you've turned quiet now.

PONCIA: I keep my place—that's all.

BERNARDA: The trouble is you've nothing to talk about. If there were grass in this house, you'd make it your business to put the neighbors' sheep to pasture here.

PONCIA: I hide more than you think.

BERNARDA: Do your sons still see Pepe at four in the morning? Are they still repeating this house's evil litany?

PONCIA: They say nothing.

BERNARDA: Because they can't. Because there's nothing for them to sink their teeth in. And all because my eyes keep constant watch!

PONCIA: Bernarda, I don't want to talk about this because I'm afraid of what you'll do. But don't you feel so safe.

BERNARDA: Very safe!

PONCIA: Who knows, lightning might strike

suddenly. Who knows but what all of a sudden, in a rush of blood, your heart might stop.

BERNARDA: Nothing will happen here. I'm on guard now against all your suspicions.

PONCIA: All the better for you.

BERNARDA: Certainly, all the better!

SERVANT (*entering*): I've just finished with the dishes. Is there anything else, Bernarda?

BERNARDA (*rising*): Nothing. I'm going to get some rest.

PONCIA: What time do you want me to call you?

BERNARDA: No time. Tonight I intend to sleep well. (*She goes out.*)

PONCIA: When you're powerless against the sea, it's easier to turn your back on it and not look at it.

SERVANT: She's so proud! She herself pulls the blindfold over her eyes.

PONCIA: I can do nothing. I tried to head things off, but now they frighten me too much. You feel this silence?—in each room there's a thunderstorm—and the day it breaks, it'll sweep all of us along with it. But I've said what I had to say.

SERVANT: Bernarda thinks nothing can stand against her, yet she doesn't know the strength a man has among women alone.

PONCIA: It's not all the fault of Pepe el Romano. It's true last year he was running after Adela; and she was crazy about him—but she ought to keep her place and not lead him on. A man's a man.

SERVANT: And some there are who believe he didn't have to talk many times with Adela.

PONCIA: That's true. (*In a low voice*) And some other things.

SERVANT: I don't know what's going to happen here.

PONCIA: How I'd like to sail across the sea and leave this house, this battleground, behind!

SERVANT: Bernarda's hurrying the wedding and it's possible nothing will happen.

PONCIA: Things have gone much too far already. Adela is set no matter what comes, and the rest of them watch without rest.

SERVANT: Martirio too . . . ?

PONCIA: That one's the worst. She's a pool of poison. She sees El Romano is not for her, and she'd sink the world if it were in her hand to do so.

SERVANT: How bad they all are!

PONCIA: They're women without men, that's all. And in such matters even blood is forgotten. Sh-h-h-h! (*She listens.*)

SERVANT: What's the matter?

PONCIA (*she rises*): The dogs are barking.

SERVANT: Someone must have passed by the back door.

(ADELA *enters wearing a white petticoat and corselet.*)

PONCIA: Aren't you in bed yet?

ADELA: I want a drink of water. (*She drinks from a glass on the table.*)

PONCIA: I imagined you were asleep.

ADELA: I got thirsty and woke up. Aren't you two going to get some rest?

SERVANT: Soon now.

(ADELA *goes out.*)

PONCIA: Let's go.

SERVANT: We've certainly earned some sleep. Bernarda doesn't let me rest the whole day.

PONCIA: Take the light.

SERVANT: The dogs are going mad.

PONCIA: They're not going to let us sleep.

(*They go out. The stage is left almost dark.* MARÍA JOSEFA *enters with a lamb in her arms.*)

MARIA JOSEFA (*singing*):
Little lamb, child of mine
Let's go to the shore of the sea,
The tiny ant will be at his doorway,
I'll nurse you and give you your bread.
Bernarda, old leopard-face,
And Magdalena, hyena-face,
Little lamb . . .
Rock, rock-a-bye,
Let's go to the palms at Bethlehem's gate.

(*She laughs.*)

Neither you nor I would want to sleep
The door will open by itself
And on the beach we'll go and hide
In a little coral cabin.

Bernarda, old leopard-face,
And Magdalena, hyena-face,
Little lamb . . .
Rock, rock-a-bye,
Let's go to the palms at Bethlehem's gate.

(*She goes off singing.*)

(ADELA *enters. She looks about cautiously and disappears out the door leading to the corral.* MARTIRIO *enters by another door and stands in anguished watchfulness near the center of the stage. She also is in petticoats. She covers herself with a small black scarf.* MARÍA JOSEFA *crosses before her.*)

MARTIRIO: Grandmother, where are you going?

MARIA JOSEFA: You are going to open the door for me? Who are you?

MARTIRIO: How did you get out here?

MARIA JOSEFA: I escaped. You, who are you?

MARTIRIO: Go back to bed.

MARIA JOSEFA: You're Martirio. Now I see you. Martirio, face of a martyr. And when are you going to have a baby? I've had this one.

MARTIRIO: Where did you get that lamb?

MARIA JOSEFA: I know it's a lamb. But can't a lamb be a baby? It's better to have a lamb than not to have anything. Old Bernarda, leopard-face, and Magdalena, hyena-face!

MARTIRIO: Don't shout.

MARIA JOSEFA: It's true. Everything's very dark. Just because I have white hair you think I can't have babies, but I can—babies and babies and babies. This baby will have white hair, and I'd have *this* baby, and another, and this *one* other; and with all of us with snow white hair we'll be like the waves—one, then another, and another. Then we'll all sit down and all of us will have white heads, and we'll be seafoam. Why isn't there any seafoam here? Nothing but mourning shrouds here.

MARTIRIO: Hush, hush.

MARIA JOSEFA: When my neighbor had a baby, I'd carry her some chocolate and later she'd bring me some, and so on—always and always and always. You'll have white hair, but your neighbors won't come. Now I have to go away, but I'm afraid the dogs will bite me. Won't you come with me as far as the fields? I don't like fields. I like houses, but open houses, and the neighbor women asleep in their beds with their littly tiny tots, and the men outside sitting in their chairs. Pepe el Romano is a giant. All of you love him. But he's going to devour you because you're grains of wheat. No, not grains of wheat. Frogs with no tongues!

MARTIRIO (*angrily*): Come, off to bed with you. (*She pushes her.*)

MARIA JOSEFA: Yes, but then you'll open the door for me, won't you?

MARTIRIO: Of course.

MARIA JOSEFA (*weeping*):
Little lamb, child of mine,
Let's go to the shore of the sea,
The tiny ant will be at his doorway,
I'll nurse you and give you your bread.

(MARTIRIO *locks the door through which* MARÍA JOSEFA *came out and goes to the yard door. There she hesitates, but goes two steps farther.*)

MARTIRIO (*in a low voice*): Adela! (*Pause. She advances to the door. Then, calling*) Adela!

(ADELA *enters. Her hair is disarranged.*)

ADELA: And what are you looking for me for?

MARTIRIO: Keep away from him.

ADELA: Who are you to tell me that?

MARTIRIO: That's no place for a decent woman.

ADELA: How you wish *you'd* been there!

MARTIRIO (*shouting*): This is the moment for me to speak. This can't go on.

ADELA: This is just the beginning. I've had strength enough to push myself forward—the spirit and looks you lack. I've seen death under this roof, and gone out to look for what was mine, what belonged to me.

MARTIRIO: That soulless man came for another woman. You pushed yourself in front of him.

ADELA: He came for the money, but his eyes were always on me.

MARTIRIO: I won't allow you to snatch him away. He'll marry Angustias.

ADELA: You know better than I he doesn't love her.

MARTIRIO: I know.

ADELA: You know because you've seen—he loves me, me!

MARTIRIO (*desperately*): Yes.

ADELA (*close before her*): He loves me, *me*! He loves me, *me*!

MARTIRIO: Stick me with a knife if you like, but don't tell me that again.

ADELA: That's why you're trying to fix it so I won't go away with him. It makes no difference to you if he puts his arms around a woman he doesn't love. Nor does it to me. He could be a hundred years with Angustias, but for him to have his arms around me seems terrible to you—because you too love him! You love him!

MARTIRIO (*dramatically*): Yes! Let me say it without hiding my head. Yes! My breast's bitter, bursting like a pomegranate! I love him!

ADELA (*impulsively, hugging her*): Martirio, Martirio, I'm not to blame!

MARTIRIO: Don't put your arms around me! Don't try to smooth it over. My blood's no longer yours, and even though I try to think of you as a sister, I see you as just another woman. (*She pushes her away.*)

ADELA: There's no way out here. Whoever has to drown—let her drown. Pepe is mine. He'll carry me to the rushes along the river bank . . .

MARTIRIO: He won't!

ADELA: I can't stand this horrible house after the taste of his mouth. I'll be what he wants me to be.

Everybody in the village against me, burning me with their fiery fingers; pursued by those who claim they're decent, and I'll wear, before them all, the crown of thorns that belongs to the mistress of a married man.

MARTIRIO: Hush!

ADELA: Yes, yes. (*In a low voice*) Let's go to bed. Let's let him marry Angustias. I dont' care anymore, but I'll go off alone to a little house where he'll come to see me whenever he wants, whenever he feels like it.

MARTIRIO: That'll never happen! Not while I have a drop of blood left in my body.

ADELA: Not just weak you, but a wild horse I could force to his knees with just the strength of my little finger.

MARTIRIO: Don't raise that voice of yours to me. It irritates me. I have a heart full of a force so evil that, without my wanting to be, I'm drowned by it.

ADELA: You show us the way to love our sisters. God must have meant to leave me alone in the midst of darkness, because I can see you as I've never seen you before.

(*A whistle is heard and* ADELA *runs toward the door, but* MARTIRIO *gets in front of her.*)

MARTIRIO: Where are you going?

ADELA: Get away from that door!

MARTIRIO: Get by me if you can!

ADELA: Get away!

(*They struggle.*)

MARTIRIO (*shouts*): Mother! Mother!

ADELA: Let me go!

(BERNARDA *enters. She wears petticoats and a black shawl.*)

BERNARDA: Quiet! Quiet! How poor I am without even a man to help me!

MARTIRIO (*pointing to* ADELA): She was with him. Look at those skirts covered with straw!

BERNARDA (*going furiously toward* ADELA): That's the bed of a bad woman!

ADELA (*facing her*): There'll be an end to prison voices here! (ADELA *snatches away her mother's cane and breaks it in two.*) This is what I do with the tyrant's cane. Not another step. No one but Pepe commands me!

(MAGDALENA *enters.*)

MAGDALENA: Adela!

(LA PONCIA *and* ANGUSTIAS *enter.*)

ADELA: I'm his. (*To* ANGUSTIAS) Know that— and go out in the yard and tell him. He'll be master in this house.

ANGUSTIAS: My God!

BERNARDA: The gun! Where's the gun?

(*She rushes out. Behind her follows* MARTIRIO. AMELIA *enters and looks on frightened, leaning her head against the wall.*)

ADELA: No one can hold me back! (*She tries to go out.*)

ANGUSTIAS (*holding her*): You're not getting out of here with your body's triumph! Thief! Disgrace of this house!

MAGDALENA: Let her go where we'll never see her again!

(*A shot is heard.*)

BERNARDA (*entering*): Just try looking for him now!

MARTIRIO (*entering*): That does away with Pepe el Romano.

ADELA: Pepe! My God! Pepe! (*She runs out.*)

PONCIA: Did you kill him?

MARTIRIO: No. He raced away on his mare!

BERNARDA: It was my fault. A woman can't aim.

MAGDALENA: Then, why did you say . . . ?

MARTIRIO: For her! I'd like to pour a river of blood over her head!

PONCIA: Curse you!

MAGDALENA: Devil!

BERNARDA: Although it's better this way!

(*A thud is heard.*)

Adela! Adela!

PONCIA (*at her door*): Open this door!

BERNARDA: Open! Don't think the walls will hide your shame!

SERVANT (*entering*): All the neighbors are up!

BERNARDA (*in a low voice, but like a roar*): Open! Or I'll knock the door down!

(*Pause. Everything is silent.*)

Adela! (*She walks away from the door.*) A hammer!

(LA PONCIA *throws herself against the door. It opens and she goes in. As she enters, she screams and backs out.*)

What is it?

PONCIA (*she puts her hands to her throat*): May we never die like that!

(*The* SISTERS *fall back. The* SERVANT *crosses herself.* BERNARDA *screams and goes forward.*)

Don't go in!

BERNARDA: No, not I! Pepe, you're running now, alive in the darkness, under the trees, but another day you'll fall. Cut her down! My daughter died a virgin. Take her to another room and dress her as though she were a virgin. No one will say anything about this! She died a virgin. Tell them, so that at dawn, the bells will ring twice.

MARTIRIO: A thousand times happy she, who had him.

BERNARDA: And I want no weeping. Death must be looked at face to face. Silence! (*To one daughter*) Be still, I said! (*To another daughter*) Tears when you're alone! We'll drown ourselves in a sea of mourning. She, the youngest daughter of Bernarda Alba, died a virgin. Did you hear me? Silence, silence, I said. Silence!

COMMENTARY

Federico García Lorca told a friend that *The House of Bernarda Alba* was rooted in his childhood experience:

> There's a small village, not far from Granada, where my parents owned a little property—Valderrubio. In the house adjacent to ours lived "dona Bernarda," a very old widow who exerted inexorable and tyrannical vigilance over her unmarried daughters. Since they were prisoners deprived of all free will, I never spoke with them, but I could see them pass like shadows, always silent and dressed in black. . . . And that is how *The House of Bernarda Alba* was born.

This bit of experience he shaped into a play that he characterized as "a drama about women in the villages of Spain." He said, too, that the play is "intended as a photographic document" (*un documenta fotográfico*), and certainly in its emphasis on black and white—the black costumes and the white walls and linens—it has the starkness of a documentary photograph of the 1930s. The two statements, taken together, rightly indicate that the play is particularly Spanish, but it is Spanish in other ways also. For instance, the emphasis on love and honor connects the play with Spanish plays of the seventeenth century, a period known as the Golden Age (*el siglo de oro*) of Spanish drama. But *The House of Bernarda Alba* is by no means an attempt to imitate the plays of, say, Lope de Vega or other seventeenth-century writers; it is very much of its own age, and a further Spanish meaning can, perhaps, be found if the play—written shortly before Franco and his fascists rose to power—is viewed as a picture of what Spanish political life might soon become: a society so distrustful of passion and individual freedom that it represses all signs of individuality.

A political reading of the play is not impossible, though it does suffer from the fact that the play was written *before* Franco came to power, and so (if one holds it) one must say that García Lorca was warning his countrymen of what *might* happen. Another interpretation, this one highly private, holds that García Lorca, a homosexual, is expressing (in a disguised form) his own frustrated sexuality, a sexuality that in the 1930s had to be concealed from all in authority. But aside from its documentary interest (whether a document of Spanish public life or a document of García Lorca's private life), what does the play offer to a reader or spectator? One answer is suggested by its very title, *The House of Bernarda Alba*, which brings to mind Greek drama, with its concern for the workings of destiny through the generations of a family or "house," as in "the house of Oedipus." That is, the play, going beyond the local, in tragic fashion sees what Alfred North Whitehead called "the remorseless working of things." Bernarda Alba's attempt to stifle all passion and to impose her will on her daughters (as well, of course, as on her mother, her servants, and her neighbors) destroys not only her daughters but her house. "Alba" means "dawn" as well as "whiteness," but the house of Alba is headed toward darkness.

One related point: Despite García Lorca's insistence that the play is a realistic documentary, a picture of Spanish life, it is richly symbolic. The ironic use of white (which can suggest purity and especially virginity but here equally suggests a concern chiefly for appearances, the whitewash of whited sepulchers) is an obvious example, and so, too, are the references to the stallion, the oppressive heat, and the green (the color of nature, or life, or generation) of Adela's dress. On a larger scale there is the contrast, on the one hand, between the migrant, singing men who work in the fields and who fulfill their sexual drive in the olive grove and, on the other hand, the house-bound women who, sexually frustrated, at best express their passion in wry jokes and taunts, but who for the most part engage in recriminations and bickering.

On one occasion when García Lorca read the play aloud to some friends, he proudly said after each scene, "Not a drop of poetry! Reality! Realism!" Even in the narrowest sense of the word *poetry* García Lorca was mistaken in saying that the play contains no poetry, since we hear María Josefa's cradle song and the songs of the harvesters; and if we keep in mind the broader sense of the word, *poetry* as the imaginative use of language to produce a picture of the human heart, we realize how far from true the author's comment is. Why, then, did he say that the play is all "realism" and no "poetry"? One can only guess, but probably he meant that there is nothing false and nothing fancy about the play; it is (though largely an invention, rooted in a scrap of childhood experience) a true picture of life.

TOPICS FOR DISCUSSION

1. The play has three closely related settings. What do they contribute to the play? The first setting calls for walls with "pictures of unlikely landscapes full of nymphs or legendary kings." What do you make of this?
2. Why do you think García Lorca decided to begin the play with no characters onstage?
3. García Lorca does not specify the lighting or the stage directions for the first two acts, though the dialogue in Act II indicates that the shutters are closed. In Act III the lighting grows progressively darker, so that even by the middle of the act "the stage is left almost dark." If you were directing the play, what sort of lighting would you use for Acts I and II? Why?
4. What do you think Bernarda's mother, Maria Josefa, contributes to the play?
5. Though Pepe el Romano is much talked about, and the migrant harvesters are heard

singing, no male is ever seen in the play. Why does García Lorca keep men offstage?

6. Bernarda Alba holds fanatically to a code of honor. Is this honor rooted in something worthy, such as reverence for God, in a high sense of human dignity, or in an awareness of the fragility of the bonds of civilization? If not, what (if anything) *is* her code rooted in? Can it be said that although she imprisons her daughters, she herself is imprisoned by unworthy ideals?

7. In your opinion, why does Bernarda Alba insist that Adela died a virgin? What does her insistence tell us about Bernarda?

8. Given Aristotle's criteria, are either Bernarda or Adela tragic figures? Does either character evoke pity and terror in the reader? Is the idea of "reversal" or *peripeteia* (see page 68) relevant to both, one, or neither? Explain.

THE GLASS MENAGERIE

Nobody, not even the rain, has such small hands.

—e. e. cummings

Tennessee Williams

Tennessee Williams (1914–1983) was born Thomas Lanier Williams in Columbus, Mississippi. During his childhood his family moved to St. Louis, were his father had accepted a job as manager of a shoe company. Williams has written that neither he nor his sister Rose could adjust to the change from the South to the Midwest, but the children had already been deeply troubled. Nevertheless, at the age of sixteen he achieved some distinction as a writer when his prize-winning essay in a nationwide contest was published. After high school he attended the University of Missouri but flunked ROTC and was therefore withdrawn from school by his father. He worked in a shoe factory for a while, then attended Washington University, where he wrote several plays. He finally graduated from the University of Iowa with a major in playwrighting. After graduation he continued to write, supporting himself with odd jobs such as waiting on tables and running elevators. His first commercial success was *The Glass Menagerie* (produced in Chicago in 1944, and in New York in 1945); among his other plays are *A Streetcar Named Desire* (1947), *Cat on a Hot Tin Roof* (1955), and *Suddenly Last Summer* (1958).

LIST OF CHARACTERS

AMANDA WINGFIELD, *the mother. A little woman of great but confused vitality clinging frantically to another time and place. Her characterization must be carefully created, not copied from type. She is not paranoiac, but her life is paranoia. There is much to admire in Amanda, and as much to love and pity as there is to laugh at. Certainly she has endurance and a kind of heroism, and though her foolishness makes her unwittingly cruel at times, there is tenderness in her slight person.*

LAURA WINGFIELD, *her daughter. Amanda, having failed to establish contact with reality, continues to live vitally in her illusions, but Laura's situation is even graver. A childhood illness has left her crippled, one leg slightly shorter than the other, and held in a brace. This defect need not be more than suggested on the stage. Stemming from this, Laura's separation increases till she is like a piece of her own glass collection, too exquisitely fragile to move from the shelf.*

TOM WINGFIELD, *her son. And the narrator of the play. A poet with a job in a warehouse. His nature is not remorseless, but to escape from a trap he has to act without pity.*

JIM O'CONNOR, *the gentleman caller. A nice, ordinary, young man.*

Scene: *An alley in St. Louis.*

Part I: *Preparation for a Gentleman Caller.*
Part II: *The Gentleman Calls.*

Time: *Now and the Past.*

Laurette Taylor as Amanda Wingfield in the 1945 Broadway production of *The Glass Menagerie*. (Photo by the Harvard Theatre Collection.)

SCENE I

The Wingfield apartment is in the rear of the building, one of those vast hive-like conglomerations of cellular living-units that flower as warty growths in overcrowded urban centers of lower middle-class population and are symptomatic of the impulse of this largest and fundamentally enslaved section of American society to avoid fluidity and differentiation and to exist and function as one interfused mass of automatism.

The apartment faces an alley and is entered by a fire-escape, a structure whose name is a touch of accidental poetic truth, for all of these huge buildings are always burning with the slow and implacable fires of human desperation. The fire-escape is included in the set—that is, the landing of it and steps descending from it.

The scene is memory and is therefore non-realistic. Memory takes a lot of poetic license. It omits some details; others are exaggerated, according to the emotional value of the articles it touches, for memory is seated predominantly in the heart. The interior is therefore rather dim and poetic.

At the rise of the curtain, the audience is faced with the dark, grim rear wall of the Wingfeld tenement. This building, which runs parallel to the footlights, is flanked on both sides by dark, narrow alleys which run into murky canyons of tangled clotheslines, garbage cans and the sinister latticework of neighboring fire-escapes. It is up and down these side alleys that exterior entrances and exits are made, during the play. At the end of Tom's opening commentary, the dark tenement wall slowly reveals (by means of a transparency) the interior of the ground floor Wingfield apartment.

Downstage is the living room, which also serves as a sleeping room for Laura, the sofa unfolding to make her bed. Upstage, center, and divided by a wide arch or second proscenium with transparent faded portieres (or second curtain), is the dining room. In an old-fashioned what-not in the living room are seen scores of transparent glass animals. A blown-up photograph of the father hangs on the wall of the living room, facing the audience, to the left of the archway. It is the face of a very handsome young man in a

doughboy's First World War cap. He is gallantly smiling, ineluctably smiling, as if to say, "I will be smiling forever."

The audience hears and sees the opening scene in the dining room through both the transparent fourth wall of the building and the transparent gauze portieres of the dining-room arch. It is during this revealing scene that the fourth wall slowly ascends, out of sight.

This transparent exterior wall is not brought down again until the very end of the play, during Tom's final speech.

The narrator is an undisguised convention of the play. He takes whatever license with dramatic convention as is convenient to his purposes.

TOM *enters dressed as a merchant sailor from alley, stage left, and strolls across the front of the stage to the fire-escape. There he stops and lights a cigarette. He addresses the audience.*

TOM: Yes, I have tricks in my pocket, I have things up my sleeve. But I am the opposite of a stage magician. He gives you illusion that has the appearance of truth. I give you truth in the pleasant disguise of illusion. To begin with, I turn back time. I reverse it to that quaint period, the thirties, when the huge middle class of America was matriculating in a school for the blind. Their eyes had failed them, or they had failed their eyes, and so they were having their fingers pressed forcibly down on the fiery Braille alphabet of a dissolving economy. In Spain there was revolution. Here there was only shouting and confusion. In Spain there was Guernica. Here there were disturbances of labor, sometimes pretty violent, in otherwise peaceful cities such as Chicago, Cleveland, Saint Louis. . . . This is the social background of the play.

(Music.)

The play is memory. Being a memory play, it is dimly lighted, it is sentimental, it is not realistic. In memory everything seems to happen to music. That explains the fiddle in the wings. I am the narrator of the play, and also a character in it. The other characters are my mother, Amanda, my sister, Laura, and a gentleman caller who appears in the final scenes. He is the most realistic character in the play, being an emissary from a world of reality that we were somehow set apart from. But since I have a poet's weakness for symbols, I am using this character also as a symbol; he is the long delayed but always expected something that we live for. There is a fifth character in the play who doesn't appear except in this larger-than-life photograph over the mantel. This is our father who left us a long time ago. He was a telephone man who fell in love with long distances; he gave up his job with the telephone company and skipped the light fantastic out of town. . . . The last we heard of him was a picture post-card from Mazatlan, on the Pacific coast of Mexico, containing a message of two words—"Hello—Good-bye!" and no address. I think the rest of the play will explain itself. . . .

AMANDA's *voice becomes audible through the portieres.*

(Legend on Screen: "Où Sont Les Neiges.")

He divides the portieres and enters the upstage area. AMANDA *and* LAURA *are seated at a dropleaf table. Eating is indicated by gestures without food or utensils.* AMANDA *faces the audience.* TOM *and* LAURA *are seated in profile. The interior has lit up softly and through the scrim we see* AMANDA *and* LAURA *seated at the table in the upstage area.*

AMANDA (*calling*): Tom?

TOM: Yes, Mother.

AMANDA: We can't say grace until you come to the table!

TOM: Coming, Mother. (*He bows slightly and withdraws, reappearing a few moments later in his place at the table.*)

AMANDA (*to her son*): Honey, don't *push* with your *fingers.* If you have to push with something, the thing to push with is a crust of bread. And chew—chew! Animals have sections in their stomachs which enable them to digest food without mastication, but human beings are supposed to chew their food before they swallow it down. Eat food leisurely, son, and really enjoy it. A well-cooked meal has lots of delicate flavors that have to be held in the mouth for appreciation. So chew your food and give your salivary glands a chance to function!

(*Tom deliberately lays his imaginary fork down and pushes his chair back from the table.*)

TOM: I haven't enjoyed one bite of this dinner because of your constant directions on how to eat it. It's you that makes me rush through meals with your hawk-like attention to every bite I take. Sickening—spoils my appetite—all this discussion of animals' secretion—salivary glands—mastication!

AMANDA (*lightly*): Temperament like a Metropolitan star! (*He rises and crosses downstage.*) You're not excused from the table.

TOM: I am getting a cigarette.

AMANDA: You smoke too much.

(LAURA *rises.*)

LAURA: I'll bring in the blanc mange.

(*He remains standing with his cigarette by the portieres during the following.*)

AMANDA (*rising*) No, sister, no, sister—you be the lady this time and I'll be the darky.

LAURA: I'm already up.

AMANDA: Resume your seat, little sister—I want you to stay fresh and pretty—for gentlemen callers!

LAURA: I'm not expecting any gentlemen callers.

AMANDA (*crossing out to kitchenette. Airily*): Sometimes they come when they are least expected! Why, I remember one Sunday afternoon in Blue Mountain—(*Enters kitchenette.*)

TOM: I know what's coming!

LAURA: Yes. But let her tell it.

TOM: Again?

LAURA: She loves to tell it.

(AMANDA *returns with bowl of dessert.*)

AMANDA: One Sunday afternoon in Blue Mountain—your mother received—*seventeen!*—gentlemen callers! Why, sometimes there weren't chairs enough to accommodate them all. We had to send the nigger over to bring in folding chairs from the parish house.

TOM (*remaining at portieres*): How did you entertain those gentlemen callers?

AMANDA: I understood the art of conversation!

TOM: I bet you could talk.

AMANDA: Girls in those days *knew* how to talk, I can tell you.

TOM: Yes?

(Image: Amanda as a Girl on a Porch Greeting Callers.)

AMANDA: They knew how to entertain their gentlemen callers. It wasn't enough for a girl to be possessed of a pretty face and a graceful figure—although I wasn't slighted in either respect. She also needed to have a nimble wit and a tongue to meet all occasions.

TOM: What did you talk about?

AMANDA: Things of importance going on in the world! Never anything coarse or common or vulgar. (*She addresses* TOM *as though he were seated in the vacant chair at the table though he remains by portieres. He plays this scene as though he held the book.*) My callers were gentlemen—all! Among my callers were some of the most prominent young planters of the Mississippi Delta—planters and sons of planters!

(TOM *motions for music and a spot of light on* AMANDA. *Her eyes lift, her face glows, her voice becomes rich and elegiac.*)

(Screen Legend: "Où Sont Les Neiges.")

There was young Champ Laughlin who later became vice-president of the Delta Planters Bank. Hadley Stevenson who was drowned in Moon Lake and left his widow one hundred and fifty thousand in Government bonds. There were the Cutrere brothers, Wesley and Bates. Bates was one of my bright particular beaux! He got in a quarrel with that wild Wainright boy. They shot it out on the floor of Moon Lake Casino. Bates was shot through the stomach. Died in the ambulance on his way to Memphis. His widow was also well provided for, came into eight or ten thousand acres, that's all. She married him on the rebound—never loved her—carried my picture on him the night he died! And there was that boy that every girl in the Delta had set her cap for! That beautiful, brilliant young Fitzhugh boy from Green County!

TOM: What did he leave his widow?

AMANDA: He never married! Gracious, you talk as though all of my old admirers had turned up their toes to the daisies!

TOM: Isn't this the first you mentioned that still survives?

AMANDA: That Fitzhugh boy went North and made a fortune—came to be known as the Wolf of Wall Street! He had the Midas touch, whatever he touched turned to gold! And I could have been Mrs. Duncan J. Fitzhugh, mind you! But—I picked your *father*!

LAURA (*rising*): Mother, let me clear the table.

AMANDA: No dear, you go in front and study your typewriter chart. Or practice your shorthand a little. Stay fresh and pretty!—It's almost time for our gentlemen callers to start arriving. (*She flounces girlishly toward the kitchenette.*) How many do you suppose we're going to entertain this afternoon?

(Tom *throws down the paper and jumps up with a groan.*)

LAURA (*alone in the dining room*): I don't believe we're going to receive any, Mother.

AMAMDA (*reappearing, airily*): What? No one— not one? You must be joking! (LAURA *nervously echoes her laugh. She slips in a fugitive manner*

through the half-open portieres and draws them gently behind her. A shaft of very clear light is thrown on her face against the faded tapestry of the curtains.) **(Music: "The Glass Menagerie" Under Faintly.)** (*Lightly*) Not one gentleman caller? It can't be true! There must be a flood, there must have been a tornado!

LAURA: It isn't a flood, it's not a tornado, Mother. I'm just not popular like you were in Blue Mountain. . . . (TOM *utters another groan.* LAURA *glances at him with a faint, apologetic smile. Her voice catching a little*) Mother's afraid I'm going to be an old maid.

(The Scene Dims Out with "Glass Menagerie" Music.)

SCENE II

"Laura, Haven't You Ever Liked Some Boy"

On the dark stage the screen is lighted with the image of blue roses. Gradually LAURA's *figure becomes apparent and the screen goes out. The music subsides.* LAURA *is seated in the delicate ivory chair at the small clawfoot table. She wears a dress of soft violet material for a kimono—her hair tied back from her forehead with a ribbon. She is washing and polishing her collection of glass.*

AMANDA *appears on the fire-escape steps. At the sound of her ascent,* LAURA *catches her breath, thrusts the bowl of ornaments away and seats herself stiffly before the diagram of the typewriter keyboard as though it held her spellbound. Something has happened to* AMANDA. *It is written in her face as she climbs to the landing: a look that is grim and hopeless and a little absurd.*

She has on one of those cheap or imitation velvety-looking cloth coats with imitation fur collar. Her hat is five or six years old, one of those dreadful cloche hats that were worn in the late twenties, and she is clasping an enormous black patent-leather pocketbook with nickel clasp and initials. This is her full-dress outfit, the one she usually wears to the D.A.R.

Before entering she looks through the door. She purses her lips, opens her eyes wide, rolls them upward and shakes her head. Then she slowly lets herself in the door. Seeing her mother's expression LAURA *touches her lips with a nervous gesture.*

LAURA: Hello, Mother, I was—(*She makes a nervous gesture toward the chart on the wall.* AMANDA *leans against the shut door and stares at* LAURA *with a martyred look.*)

AMANDA: Deception? Deception? (*She slowly removes her hat and gloves, continuing the swift suffering stare. She lets the hat and gloves fall on the floor—a bit of acting.*)

LAURA (*shakily*): How was the D.A.R. meeting? (AMANDA *slowly opens her purse and removes a dainty white handkerchief which she shakes out delicately and delicately touches to her lips and nostrils.*) Didn't you go to the D.A.R. meeting, Mother?

AMANDA (*faintly, almost inaudibly*):—No.—No. (*Then more forcibly*) I did not have the strength—to go to the D.A.R. In fact, I did not have the courage! I wanted to find a hole in the ground and hide myself in it forever! (*She crosses slowly to the wall and removes the diagram of the typewriter keyboard. She holds it in front of her for a second, staring at it sweetly and sorrowfully— then bites her lips and tears it in two pieces.*)

LAURA (*faintly*): Why did you do that, Mother? (AMANDA *repeats the same procedure with the chart of the Gregg Alphabet.*) Why are you—

AMANDA: Why? Why? How old are you, Laura?

LAURA: Mother, you know my age.

AMANDA: I thought that you were an adult; it seems that I was mistaken. (*She crosses slowly to the sofa and sinks down and stares at* LAURA.)

LAURA: Please don't stare at me, Mother.

(AMANDA *closes her eyes and lowers her head. Count ten.*)

AMANDA: What are we going to do, what is going to become of us, what is the future?

(*Count ten.*)

LAURA: Has something happened, Mother? (AMANDA *draws a long breath and takes out the handkerchief again. Dabbing process.*) Mother, has—something happened?

AMANDA: I'll be all right in a minute. I'm just bewildered—(*count five*)—by life. . . .

LAURA: Mother, I wish that you would tell me what's happened.

AMANDA: As you know, I was supposed to be inducted into my office at the D.A.R. this afternoon. **(Image: A Swarm of Typewriters.)** But I stopped off at Rubicam's Business College to speak to your teachers about your having a cold and ask them what progress they thought you were making down there.

LAURA: Oh. . . .

AMANDA: I went to the typing instructor and introduced myself as your mother. She didn't know who you were. Wingfield, she said. We don't have any such student enrolled at the school! I assured her she did, that you had been going to classes since early in January. "I wonder," she said, "if you could be talking about that terribly shy little girl who dropped out of school after only a few days' attendance?" "No," I said, "Laura, my daughter, has been going to school every day for the past six weeks!" "Excuse me," she said. She took the attendance book out and there was your name, unmistakably printed, and all the dates you were absent until they decided that you had dropped out of school. I still said, "No, there must have been some mistake! There must have been some mix-up in the records!" And she said, "No— I remember her perfectly now. Her hand shook so that she couldn't hit the right keys! The first time we gave a speed-test, she broke down completely— was sick at the stomach and almost had to be carried into the wash-room! After that morning she never showed up any more. We phoned the house but never got any answer"—while I was working at Famous and Barr, I suppose, demonstrating those—Oh! I felt so weak I could barely keep on my feet! I had to sit down while they got me a glass of water! Fifty dollars' tuition, all of our plans—my hopes and ambitions for you—just gone up the spout, just gone up the spout like that. (LAURA *draws a long breath and gets awkwardly to her feet. She crosses to the victrola and winds it up.*) What are you doing?

LAURA: Oh! (*She releases the handle and returns to her seat.*)

AMANDA: Laura, where have you been going when you've gone out pretending that you were going to business college?

LAURA: I've just been going out walking.

AMANDA: That's not true.

LAURA: It is. I just went walking.

AMANDA: Walking? Walking? In winter? Deliberately courting pneumonia in that light coat? Where did you walk to, Laura?

LAURA: It was the lesser of two evils, Mother. **(Image: Winter Scene in Park.)** I couldn't go back up. I—threw up—on the floor!

AMANDA: From half past seven till after five thirty every day you mean to tell me you walked around in the park, because you wanted to make me think that you were still going to Rubicam's Business College?

LAURA: It wasn't as bad as it sounds. I went inside places to get warmed up.

AMANDA: Inside where?

LAURA: I went in the art museum and the birdhouses at the Zoo. I visited the penguins every day! Sometimes I did without lunch and went to the movies. Lately I've been spending most of my afternoons in the Jewel-box, that big glass house where they raise the tropical flowers.

AMANDA: You did all this to deceive me, just for the deception? (LAURA *looks down.*) Why?

LAURA: Mother, when you're disappointed, you get that awful suffering look on your face, like the picture of Jesus' mother in the museum!

AMANDA: Hush!

LAURA: I couldn't face it.

(*Pause. A whisper of strings.*)

(Legend: "The Crust of Humility.")

AMANDA (*hopelessly fingering the huge pocketbook*): So what are we going to do the rest of our lives? Stay home and watch the parades go by? Amuse ourselves with the glass menagerie, darling? Eternally play those worn-out phonograph records your father left as a painful reminder of him? We won't have a business career—we've given that up because it gave us nervous indigestion! (*Laughs wearily.*) What is there left but dependency all our lives? I know so well what becomes of unmarried women who aren't prepared to occupy a position. I've seen such pitiful cases in the South—barely tolerated spinsters living upon the grudging patronage of sister's husband or brother's wife!—stuck away in some little mousetrap of a room—encouraged by one in-law to visit another—little birdlike women without any nest—eating the crust of humility all their life! Is that the future that we've mapped out for ourselves? I swear it's the only alternative I can think of! It isn't a very pleasant alternative, is it? Of course—some girls *do marry.* (LAURA *twists her hands nervously.*) Haven't you ever liked some boy?

LAURA: Yes. I liked one once. (*Rises.*) I came across his picture a while ago.

AMANDA (*with some interest*): He gave you his picture?

LAURA: No, it's in the year-book.

AMANDA (*disappointed*): Oh—a high-school boy.

(Screen Image: Jim as a High-School Hero Bearing a Silver Cup.)

LAURA: Yes. His name was Jim. (*Laura lifts the heavy annual from the clawfoot table.*) Here he is in *The Pirates of Penzance.*

AMANDA (*absently*): The what?

LAURA: The operetta the senior class put on. He had a wonderful voice and we sat across the aisle from each other Mondays, Wednesdays and Fridays in the Aud. Here he is with the silver cup for debating! See his grin?

AMANDA (*absently*): He must have had a jolly disposition.

LAURA: He used to call me—Blue Roses.

(Image: Blue Roses.)

AMANDA: Why did he call you such a name as that?

LAURA: When I had that attack of pleurosis—he asked me what was the matter when I came back. I said pleurosis—he thought that I said Blue Roses! So that's what he always called me after that. Whenever he saw me, he'd holler, "Hello, Blue Roses!" I didn't care for the girl that he went out with. Emily Meisenbach. Emily was the best-dressed girl at Soldan. She never struck me, though, as being sincere. . . . It says in the Personal Section—they're engaged. That's—six years ago! They must be married by now.

AMANDA: Girls that aren't cut out for business careers usually wind up married to some nice man. (*Gets up with a spark of revival.*) Sister, that's what you'll do!

(LAURA *utters a startled, doubtful laugh. She reaches quickly for a piece of glass.*)

LAURA: But, Mother—

AMANDA: Yes? (*Crossing to photograph.*)

LAURA (*in a tone of frightened apology*): I'm—crippled!

(Image: Screen.)

AMANDA: Nonsense! Laura, I've told you never, never to use that word. Why, you're not crippled, you just have a little defect—hardly noticeable, even! When people have some slight disadvantage like that, they cultivate other things to make up for it—develop charm—and vivacity—and—*charm!* That's all you have to do! (*She turns again to the photograph.*) One thing your father had *plenty* of—was *charm!*

(*Tom motions to the fiddle in the wings.*)

(The Scene Fades Out with Music.)

SCENE III

(Legend on the Screen: "After the Fiasco—")

TOM *speaks from the fire-escape landing.*

TOM: After the fiasco at Rubicam's Business College, the idea of getting a gentleman caller for Laura began to play a more important part in Mother's calculations. It became an obsession. Like some archetype of the universal unconscious, the image of the gentleman caller haunted our small apartment. . . . **(Image: Young Man at Door with Flowers.)** An evening at home rarely passed without some allusion to this image, this specter, this hope. . . . Even when he wasn't mentioned, his presence hung in Mother's preoccupied look and in my sister's frightened, apologetic manner— hung like a sentence passed upon the Wingfields! Mother was a woman of action as well as words. She began to take logical steps in the planned direction. Late that winter and in the early spring—realizing that extra money would be needed to properly feather the nest and plume the bird—she conducted a vigorous campaign on the telephone, roping in subscribers to one of those magazines for matrons called *The Home-maker's Companion,* the type of journal that features the serialized sublimations of ladies of letters who think in terms of delicate cup-like breasts, slim, tapering waists, rich, creamy thighs, eyes like wood-smoke in autumn, fingers that soothe and caress like strains of music, bodies as powerful as Etruscan sculpture.

(Screen Image: Glamor Magazine Cover.)

(AMANDA *enters with phone on long extension cord. She is spotted in the dim stage.*)

AMANDA: Ida Scott? This is Amanda Wingfield! We *missed* you at the D.A.R. last Monday! I said to myself: She's probably suffering with that sinus condition! How is that sinus condition? Horrors! Heaven have mercy!—You're a Christian martyr, yes, that's what you are, a Christian martyr! Well, I just now happened to notice that your subscription to the *Companion's* about to expire! Yes, it expires with the next issue, honey!—just when that wonderful new serial by Bessie Mae Hopper is getting off to such an exciting start. Oh, honey, it's something that you can't miss! You remember how *Gone With the Wind* took everybody by storm? You simply couldn't go out if you hadn't read it. All everybody *talked* was Scarlett O'Hara.

Well, this is a book that critics already compare to *Gone With the Wind.* It's the *Gone With the Wind* of the post-World War generation!—What?— Burning?—Oh, honey, don't let them burn, go take a look in the oven and I'll hold the wire! Heavens—I think she's hung up!

(Dim Out.)

(Legend on Screen: "You Think I'm in Love with Continental Shoemakers?")

(*Before the stage is lighted, the violent voices of* TOM *and* AMANDA *are heard. They are quarreling behind the portieres. In front of them stands* LAURA *with clenched hands and panicky expression. A clear pool of light on her figure throughout this scene.*)

TOM: What in Christ's name am I—

AMANDA (*shrilly*): Don't you use that—

TOM: Supposed to do!

AMANDA: Expression! Not in my—

TOM: Ohhh!

AMANDA: Presence! Have you gone out of your senses?

TOM: I have, that's true, *driven* out!

AMANDA: What is the matter with you, you— big—big—IDIOT!

TOM: Look—I've got *no thing,* no single thing—

AMANDA: Lower your voice!

TOM: In my life here that I can call my OWN! Everything is—

AMANDA: Stop that shouting!

TOM: Yesterday you confiscated my books! You had the nerve to—

AMANDA: I took that horrible novel back to the library—yes! That hideous book by that insane Mr. Lawrence. (TOM *laughs wildly.*) I cannot control the output of diseased minds or people who cater to them—(TOM *laughs still more wildly.*) BUT I WON'T ALLOW SUCH FILTH BROUGHT INTO MY HOUSE! No, no, no, no, no!

TOM: House, house! Who pays rent on it, who makes a slave of himself to—

AMANDA (*fairly screeching*): Don't you DARE to—

TOM: No, no, I musn't say things! *I've* got to just—

AMANDA: Let me tell you—

TOM: I don't want to hear any more! (*He tears the portieres open. The upstage area is lit with a turgid smoky red glow.*)

AMANDA's *hair is in metal curlers and she wears a very old bathrobe, much too large for her slight figure, a relic of the faithless Mr. Wingfield. An upright typewriter and a wild disarray of manuscripts are on the drop-leaf table. The quarrel was probably precipitated by Amanda's interruption of his creative labor. A chair lying overthrown on the floor. Their gesticulating shadows are cast on the ceiling by the fiery glow.*

AMANDA: You *will* hear more, you—

TOM: No, I won't hear more, I'm going out!

AMANDA: You come right back in—

TOM: Out, out out! Because I'm—

AMANDA: Come back here, Tom Wingfield! I'm not through talking to you!

TOM: Oh, go—

LAURA (*desperately*): Tom!

AMANDA: You're going to listen, and no more insolence from you! I'm at the end of my patience! (*He comes back toward her.*)

TOM: What do you think I'm at? Aren't I supposed to have any patience to reach the end of, Mother? I know, I know. It seems unimportant to you, what I'm *doing*—what I *want* to do—having a little *difference* between them! You don't think that—

AMANDA: I think you've been doing things that you're ashamed of. That's why you act like this. I don't believe that you go every night to the movies. Nobody goes to the movies night after night. Nobody in their right minds goes to the movies as often as you pretend to. People don't go to the movies at nearly midnight, and movies don't let out at two A.M. Come in stumbling. Muttering to yourself like a maniac! You get three hours' sleep and then go to work. Oh, I can picture the way you're doing down there. Moping, doping, because you're in no condition.

TOM (*wildly*): No, I'm in no condition!

AMANDA: What right have you got to jeopardize your job? Jeopardize the security of us all? How do you think we'd manage if you were—

TOM: Listen! You think I'm crazy *about* the warehouse? (*He bends fiercely toward her slight figure.*) You think I'm in love with the Continental Shoemakers? You think I want to spend fifty-five years down there in that—*celotex interior!* with—*fluorescent—tubes!* Look! I'd rather somebody picked up a crowbar and battered out my brains—than go back mornings! I *go!* Every time you come in yelling that God damn "*Rise and Shine!*" "*Rise and Shine!*" I say to myself "How *lucky dead* people are!" But I get up. I *go!* For sixty-five dollars a month I give up all that I dream of doing and being *ever!* And you say self—*self's* all I ever think

of. Why, listen, if self is what I thought of, Mother, I'd be where he is—GONE! (*Pointing to father's picture.*) As far as the system of transportation reaches! (*He starts past her. She grabs his arm.*) Don't grab at me, Mother!

AMANDA: Where are you going?

TOM: I'm going to the *movies!*

AMANDA: I don't believe that lie!

TOM (*crouching toward her, overtowering her tiny figure. She backs away, gasping*): I'm going to opium dens! Yes, opium dens, dens of vice and criminals' hang-outs, Mother. I've joined the Hogan gang, I'm a hired assassin, I carry a tommy-gun in a violin case! I run a string of cat-houses in the Valley! They call me Killer, Killer Wingfield, I'm leading a double-life, a simple, honest warehouse worker by day, by night a dynamic *czar* of the *underworld, Mother.* I go to gambling casinos, I spin away fortunes on the roulette table! I wear a patch over one eye and a false mustache, sometimes I put on green whiskers. On those occasions the call me—*El Diablo!* Oh, I could tell you things to make you sleepless! My enemies plan to dynamite this place. They're going to blow us all sky-high some night! I'll be glad, very happy, and so will you! You'll go up, up on a broomstick, over Blue Mountain with seventeen gentlemen callers! You ugly—babbling old—*witch.* . . . (*He goes through a series of violent, clumsy movements, seizing his overcoat, lunging to the door, pulling it fiercely open. The women watch him, aghast. His arm catches in the sleeve of the coat as he struggles to pull it on. For a moment he is pinioned by the bulky garment. With an outraged groan he tears the coat off again, splitting the shoulders of it, and hurls it across the room. It strikes against the shelf of Laura's glass collection, there is a tinkle of shattering glass. LAURA cries out as if wounded.*)

(Music Legend: "The Glass Menagerie.")

LAURA (*shrilly*): My glass!—menagerie. . . . (*She covers her face and turns away.*)

(*But* AMANDA *is still stunned and stupefied by the "ugly witch" so that she barely notices this occurrence. Now she recovers her speech.*)

AMANDA (*in an awful voice*): I won't speak to you—until you apologize! (*She crosses through portieres and draws them together behind her.* TOM *is left with* LAURA. LAURA *clings weakly to the mantel with her face averted.* TOM *stares at her stupidly for a moment. Then he crosses to shelf. Drops awkwardly to his knees to collect the fallen glass, glancing at* LAURA *as if he would speak but couldn't.*)

("The Glass Menagerie" steals in as the Scene Dims Out.)

SCENE IV

The interior is dark. Faint light in the alley. A deep-voiced bell in a church is tolling the hour by five as the scene commences.

TOM *appears at the top of the alley. After each solemn boom of the bell in the tower, he shakes a little noise-maker or rattle as if to express the tiny spasm of man in contrast to the sustained power and dignity of the Almighty. This and the un-steadiness of his advance make it evident that he has been drinking.*

As he climbs the few steps to the fire-escape landing light steals up inside. LAURA *appears in night-dress, observing* TOM's *empty bed in the front room.*

TOM *fishes in his pockets for the door-key, removing a motley assortment of articles in the search, including a perfect shower of movie-ticket stubs and an empty bottle. At last he finds the key, but just as he is about to insert it, it slips from his fingers. He strikes a match and crouches below the door.*

TOM (*bitterly*): One crack—and it falls through!

(LAURA *opens the door.*)

LAURA: Tom! Tom, what are you doing?
TOM: Looking for a door-key.
LAURA: Where have you been all this time?
TOM: I have been to the movies.
LAURA: All this time at the movies?
TOM: There was a very long program. There was a Garbo picture and a Mickey Mouse and a travelogue and a newsreel and a preview of coming attractions. And there was an organ solo and a collection for the milk-fund—simultaneously—which ended up in a terrible fight between a fat lady and an usher!
LAURA (*innocently*): Did you have to stay through everything?
TOM: Of course! And, oh, I forgot! There was a big stage show! The headliner on this stage show was Malvolio the Magician. He performed won-derful tricks, many of them, such as pouring water back and forth between pitchers. First it turned to wine and then it turned to beer and then it turned to whiskey. I know it was whiskey it finally turned

into because he needed somebody to come up out of the audience to help him, and I came up—both shows! It was Kentucky Straight Bourbon. A very generous fellow, he gave souvenirs. (*He pulls from his back pocket a shimmering rainbow-colored scarf.*) He gave me this. This is his magic scarf. You can have it, Laura. You wave it over a canary cage and you get a bowl of gold-fish. You wave it over the gold-fish bowl and they fly away canaries. . . . But the wonderfulest trick of all was the coffin trick. We nailed him into a coffin and he got out of the coffin without removing one nail. (*He has come inside.*) There is a trick that would come in handy for me—get me out of this 2 by 4 situation! (*Flops onto bed and starts removing shoes.*)
LAURA: Tom—Shhh!
TOM: What you shushing me for?
LAURA: You'll wake up Mother.
TOM: Goody, goody! Pay 'er back for all those "Rise an' Shines." (*Lies down, groaning.*) You know it don't take much intelligence to get your-self into a nailed-up coffin, Laura. But who in hell ever got himself out of one without removing one nail?

(*As if in answer, the father's grinning photograph lights up.*)

(Scene Dims Out.)

Immediately following: The church bell is heard striking six. At the sixth stroke the alarm clock goes off in Amanda's room, and after a few moments we hear her calling: "Rise and Shine! Rise and Shine! Laura, go tell your brother to rise and shine!"

TOM (*sitting up slowly*). I'll rise—but I won't shine.

(*The light increases.*)

AMANDA: Laura, tell your brother his coffee is ready.

(LAURA *slips into front room.*)

LAURA: Tom! it's nearly seven. Don't make Mother nervous. (*He stares at her stupidly. Be-seechingly*) Tom, speak to Mother this morning. Make up with her, apologize, speak to her!
TOM: She won't to me. It's her that started not speaking.
LAURA: If you just say you're sorry she'll start speaking.
TOM: Her not speaking—is that such a tragedy?
LAURA: Please—please!
AMANDA (*calling from kitchenette*): Laura, are

you going to do what I asked you to do, or do I have to get dressed and go out myself?

LAURA: Going, going—soon as I get on my coat! (*She pulls on a shapeless felt hat with nervous, jerky movement, pleadingly glancing at* TOM. *Rushes awkwardly for coat. The coat is one of* AMANDA's, *inaccurately made-over, the sleeves too short for* LAURA.) Butter and what else?

AMANDA (*entering upstage*): Just butter. Tell them to charge it.

LAURA: Mother, they make such faces when I do that.

AMANDA: Sticks and stones may break my bones, but the expression of Mr. Garfinkel's face won't harm me! Tell your brother his coffee is getting cold.

LAURA (*at door*): Do what I asked you, will you, will you, Tom?

(*He looks sullenly away.*)

AMANDA: Laura, go now or just don't go at all!

LAURA (*rushing out*): Going—going! (*A second later she cries out.* TOM *springs up and crosses to the door.* AMANDA *rushes anxiously in.* TOM *opens the door.*)

TOM: Laura?

LAURA: I'm all right. I slipped, but I'm all right.

AMANDA (*peering anxiously after her*): If anyone breaks a leg on those fire-escape steps, the landlord ought to be sued for every cent he possesses! (*She shuts door. Remembers she isn't speaking and returns to other room.*)

(*As* TOM *enters listlessly for his coffee, she turns her back to him and stands rigidly facing the window on the gloomy gray vault of the areaway. Its light on her face with its aged but childish features is cruelly sharp, satirical as a Daumier print.*)

(Music Under: "Ave Maria.")

(TOM *glances sheepishly but sullenly at her averted figure and slumps at the table. The coffee is scalding hot; he sips it and gasps and spits it back in the cup. At his gasp,* AMANDA *catches her breath and half turns. Then catches herself and turns back to window.*)

TOM *blows on his coffee, glancing sidewise at his mother. She clears her throat.* TOM *clears his. He starts to rise. Sinks back down again, scratches his head, clears his throat again.* AMANDA *coughs.* TOM *raises his cup in both hands to blow on it, his eyes staring over the rim of it at his mother for several moments. Then he*

slowly sets the cup down and awkwardly and hesitantly rises from the chair.

TOM (*hoarsely*): Mother. I—I apologize. Mother. (AMANDA *draws a quick, shuddering breath. Her face works grotesquely. She breaks into childlike tears.*) I'm sorry for what I said, for everything that I said, I didn't mean it.

AMANDA (*sobbingly*): My devotion has made me a witch and so I make myself hateful to my children!

TOM: No, you *don't*.

AMANDA: I worry so much, don't sleep, it makes me nervous!

TOM (*gently*): I understand that.

AMANDA: I've had to put up a solitary battle all these years. But you're my right-hand bower! Don't fall down, don't fail!

TOM (*gently*): I try, Mother.

AMANDA (*with great enthusiasm*): Try and you will SUCCEED! (*The notion makes her breathless.*) Why, you—you're just *full* of natural endowments! Both of my children—they're *unusual* children! Don't you think I know it? I'm so—proud! Happy and—feel I've—so much to be thankful for but—Promise me one thing, son!

TOM: What, Mother?

AMANDA: Promise, son, you'll—never be a drunkard!

TOM (*turns to her grinning*): I will never be a drunkard, Mother.

AMANDA: That's what frightened me so, that you'd be drinking! Eat a bowl of Purina!

TOM: Just coffee, Mother.

AMANDA: Shredded wheat biscuit?

TOM: No. No, Mother, just coffee.

AMANDA: You can't put in a day's work on an empty stomach. You've got ten minutes—don't gulp! Drinking too-hot liquids makes cancer of the stomach. . . . Put cream in.

TOM: No, thank you.

AMANDA: To cool it.

TOM: No! No, thank you, I want it black.

AMANDA: I know, but it's not good for you. We have to do all that we can to build ourselves up. In these trying times we live in, all that we have to cling to is—each other. . . . That's why it's so important to—Tom, I—I sent out your sister so I could discuss something with you. If you hadn't spoken I would have spoken to you. (*Sits down.*)

TOM (*gently*): What is it, Mother, that you want to discuss?

AMANDA: Laura!

(TOM *puts his cup down slowly.*)

(Legend on Screen: "Laura.")

(Music: "The Glass Menagerie.")

TOM: —Oh.—Laura . . .

AMANDA (*touching his sleeve*): You know how Laura is. So quiet but—still water runs deep! She notices things and I think she—broods about them. (TOM *looks up.*) A few days ago I came in and she was crying.

TOM: What about?

AMANDA: You.

TOM: Me?

AMANDA: She has an idea that you're not happy here.

TOM: What gave her that idea?

AMANDA: What gives her any idea? However, you do act strangely. I—I'm not criticizing, understand *that!* I know your ambitions do not lie in the warehouse, that like everybody in the whole wide world—you've had to—make sacrifices, but—Tom—Tom—life's not easy, it calls for—Spartan endurance! There's so many things in my heart that I cannot describe to you! I've never told you but I—*loved* your father. . . .

TOM (*gently*): I know that, Mother.

AMANDA: And you—when I see you taking after his ways! Staying out late—and—well, you *had* been drinking the night you were in that—terrifying condition! Laura says that you hate the apartment and that you go out nights to get away from it! Is that true, Tom?

TOM: No. You say there's so much in your heart that you can't describe to me. That's true of me, too. There's so much in my heart that I can't describe to *you!* So let's respect each other's—

AMANDA: But, why—*why,* Tom—are you always so *restless?* Where do you go to, nights?

TOM: I—go to the movies.

AMANDA: Why do you go to the movies so much, Tom?

TOM: I go to the movies because—I like adventure. Adventure is something I don't have much of at work, so I go to the movies.

AMANDA: But, Tom, you go to the movies *entirely too much!*

TOM: I like a lot of adventure.

(AMANDA *looks baffled, then hurt. As the familiar inquisition resumes he becomes hard and impatient again.* AMANDA *slips back into her querulous attitude toward him.*)

(Image on Screen: **Sailing Vessel with Jolly Roger.**)

AMANDA: Most young men find adventure in their careers.

TOM: Then most young men are not employed in a warehouse.

AMANDA: The world is full of young men employed in warehouses and offices and factories.

TOM: Do all of them find adventure in their careers?

AMANDA: They do or they do without it! Not everybody has a craze for adventure.

TOM: Man is by instinct a lover, a hunter, a fighter, and none of those instincts are given much play at the warehouse!

AMANDA: Man is by instinct! Don't quote instinct to me! Instinct is something that people have got away from! It belongs to animals! Christian adults don't want it!

TOM: What do Christian adults want, then, Mother?

AMANDA: Superior things! Things of the mind and the spirit! Only animals have to satisfy instincts! Surely your aims are somewhat higher than theirs! Than monkeys—pigs—

TOM: I reckon they're not.

AMANDA: You're joking. However, that isn't what I wanted to discuss.

TOM (*rising*): I haven't much time.

AMANDA (*pushing his shoulders*): Sit down.

TOM: You want me to punch in red at the warehouse, Mother?

AMANDA: You have five minutes. I want to talk about Laura.

(Legend: "Plans and Provisions.")

TOM: All right! What about Laura?

AMANDA: We have to be making plans and provisions for her. She's older than you, two years, and nothing has happened. She just drifts along doing nothing. It frightens me terribly how she just drifts along.

TOM: I guess she's the type that people call home girls.

AMANDA: There's no such type, and if there is, it's a pity! That is unless the home is hers, with a husband!

TOM: What?

AMANDA: Oh, I can see the handwriting on the wall as plain as I see the nose in front of my face! It's terrifying! More and more you remind me of your father! He was out all hours without explanation—Then *left! Good-bye!* And me with the bag to hold. I saw that letter you got from the Merchant Marine. I know what you're dreaming of. I'm not standing here blindfolded. Very well, then. Then *do* it! But not till there's somebody to take your place.

TOM: What do you mean?

AMANDA: I mean that as soon as Laura has got somebody to take care of her, married, a home of her own, independent—why, then you'll be free to go wherever you please, on land, on sea, whichever way the wind blows! But until that time you've got to look out for your sister. I don't say me because I'm old and don't matter! I say for your sister because she's young and dependent. I put her in business college—a dismal failure! Frightened her so it made her sick to her stomach. I took her over to the Young People's League at the church. Another fiasco. She spoke to nobody, nobody spoke to her. Now all she does is fool with those pieces of glass and play those worn-out records. What kind of a life is that for a girl to lead!

TOM: What can I do about it?

AMANDA: Overcome selfishness! Self, self, self is all that you ever think of! (TOM *springs up and crosses to get his coat. It is ugly and bulky. He pulls on a cap with earmuffs.*) Where is your muffler? Put your wool muffler on! (*He snatches it angrily from the closet and tosses it around his neck and pulls both ends tight.*) Tom! I haven't said what I had in mind to ask you.

TOM: I'm too late to—

AMANDA (*catching his arms—very importunately. Then shyly.*) Down at the warehouse, aren't there some—nice young men?

TOM: No!

AMANDA: There *must* be—*some.*

TOM: Mother—

(*Gesture.*)

AMANDA: Find out one that's clean-living—doesn't drink and—ask him out for sister!

TOM: What?

AMANDA: For *sister!* To *meet!* Get *acquainted!*

TOM (*stamping to door*): Oh, my go-osh!

AMANDA: Will you? (*He opens door. Imploringly*) Will you? (*He starts down.*) Will you? *Will you, dear?*

TOM (*calling back*): YES!

(AMANDA *closes the door hesitantly and with a troubled but faintly hopeful expression.*)

(Screen Image: Glamor Magazine Cover.)

(*Spot* AMANDA *at phone.*)

AMANDA: Ella Cartwright? This is Amanda Wingfield! How are you, honey? How is that kidney condition? (*Count five.*) Horrors! (*Count*

five.) You're a Christian martyr, yes, honey, that's what you are, a Christian martyr! Well, I just happened to notice in my little red book that your subscription to the *Companion* has just run out! I knew that you wouldn't want to miss out on the wonderful serial starting in this new issue. It's by Bessie Mae Hopper, the first thing she's written since *Honeymoon for Three.* Wasn't that a strange and interesting story? Well, this one is even lovelier, I believe. It has a sophisticated society background. It's all about the horsey set on Long Island!

(Fade Out.)

SCENE V

(Legend on Screen: "Annunciation.") *Fade with music.*

It is early dusk of a spring evening. Supper has just been finished in the Wingfield apartment. AMANDA *and* LAURA *in light-colored dresses are removing dishes from the table, in the upstage area, which is shadowy, their movements formalized almost as a dance or ritual, their moving forms as pale and silent as moths.* TOM, *in white shirt and trousers, rises from the table and crosses toward the fire-escape.*

AMANDA (*as he passes her*): Son, will you do me a favor?

TOM: What?

AMANDA: Comb your hair! You look so pretty when your hair is combed! (TOM *slouches on sofa with evening paper. Enormous caption "Franco Triumphs."*) There is only one respect in which I would like you to emulate your father.

TOM: What respect is that?

AMANDA: The care he always took of his appearance. He never allowed himself to look untidy. (*He throws down the paper and crosses to fire-escape.*) Where are you going?

TOM: I'm going out to smoke.

AMANDA: You smoke too much. A pack a day at fifteen cents a pack. How much would that amount to in a month? Thirty times fifteen is how much, Tom? Figure it out and you will be astounded at what you could save. Enough to give you a night-school course in accounting at Washington U! Just think what a wonderful thing that would be for you, son!

(TOM *is unmoved by the thought.*)

TOM: I'd rather smoke. (*He steps out on landing, letting the screen door slam.*)

AMANDA (*sharply*): I know! That's the tragedy of it. . . . (*Alone, she turns to look at her husband's picture.*)

(Dance Music: "All the World Is Waiting for the Sunrise!")

TOM (*to the audience*): Across the alley from us was the Paradise Dance Hall. On evenings in spring the windows and doors were open and the music came outdoors. Sometimes the lights were turned out except for a large glass sphere that hung from the ceiling. It would turn slowly about and filter the dusk with delicate rainbow colors. Then the orchestra played a waltz or a tango, something that had a slow and sensuous rhythm. Couples would come outside, to the relative privacy of the alley. You could see them kissing behind ashpits and telephone poles. This was the compensation for lives that passed like mine, without any change or adventure. Adventure and change were imminent in this year. They were waiting around the corner for all these kids. Suspended in the mist over Berchtesgaden, caught in the folds of Chamberlain's umbrella—In Spain there was Guernica! But here there was only hot swing music and liquor, dance halls, bars, and movies, and sex that hung in the gloom like a chandelier and flooded the world with brief, deceptive rainbows. . . . All the world was waiting for bombardments!

(AMANDA *turns from the picture and comes outside.*)

AMANDA (*sighing*): A fire-escape landing's a poor excuse for a porch. (*She spreads a newspaper on a step and sits down, gracefully and demurely as if she were settling into a swing on a Mississippi veranda.*) What are you looking at?

TOM: The moon.

AMANDA: Is there a moon this evening?

TOM: It's rising over Garfinkel's Delicatessen.

AMANDA: So it is! A little silver slipper of a moon. Have you made a wish on it yet?

TOM: Um-hum.

AMANDA: What did you wish for?

TOM: That's a secret.

AMANDA: A secret, huh? Well, I won't tell mine either. I will be just as mysterious as you.

TOM: I bet I can guess what yours is.

AMANDA: Is my head so transparent?

TOM: You're not a sphinx.

AMANDA: No, I don't have secrets. I'll tell you what I wished for on the moon. Success and happiness for my precious children! I wish for that whenever there's a moon, and when there isn't a moon, I wish for it, too.

TOM: I thought perhaps you wished for a gentleman caller.

AMANDA: Why do you say that?

TOM: Don't you remember asking me to fetch one?

AMANDA: I remember suggesting that it would be nice for your sister if you brought home some nice young man from the warehouse. I think I've made that suggestion more than once.

TOM: Yes, you have made it repeatedly.

AMANDA: Well?

TOM: We are going to have one.

AMANDA: *What?*

TOM: A gentleman caller!

(The Annunciation Is Celebrated with Music.)

(AMANDA *rises.*)

(Image on Screen: Caller with Bouquet.)

AMANDA: You mean you have asked some nice young man to come over?

TOM: Yep. I've asked him to dinner.

AMANDA: You really did?

TOM: I did!

AMANDA: You did, and did he—*accept?*

TOM: He did!

AMANDA: Well, well—well, well! That's—lovely!

TOM: I thought that you would be pleased.

AMANDA: It's definite, then?

TOM: Very definite.

AMANDA: Soon?

TOM: Very soon.

AMANDA: For heaven's sake, stop putting on and tell me some things, will you?

TOM: What things do you want me to tell you?

AMANDA: Naturally I would like to know when he's *coming!*

TOM: He's coming tomorrow.

AMANDA: *Tomorrow?*

TOM: Yep. Tomorrow.

AMANDA: But, Tom!

TOM: Yes, Mother?

AMANDA: Tomorrow gives me no time!

TOM: Time for what?

AMANDA: Preparations! Why didn't you phone me at once, as soon as you asked him, the minute that he accepted? Then, don't you see, I could have been getting ready!

TOM: You don't have to make any fuss.

AMANDA: Oh, Tom, Tom, Tom, of course I

have to make a fuss! I want things nice, not sloppy! Not thrown together. I'll certainly have to do some fast thinking, won't I?

TOM: I don't see why you have to think at all.

AMANDA: You just don't know. We can't have a gentleman caller in a pig-sty! All my wedding silver has to be polished, the monogrammed table linen ought to be laundered! The windows have to be washed and fresh curtains put up. And how about clothes? We have to *wear* something, don't we?

TOM: Mother, this boy is no one to make a fuss over!

AMANDA: Do you realize he's the first young man we've had introduced to your sister? It's terrible, dreadful, disgraceful that poor little sister has never received a single gentleman caller! Tom, come inside! (*She opens the screen door.*)

TOM: What for?

AMANDA: I want to ask you some things.

TOM: If you're going to make such a fuss, I'll call it off, I'll tell him not to come.

AMANDA: You certainly won't do anything of the kind. Nothing offends people worse than broken engagements. It simply means I'll have to work like a Turk! We won't be brilliant, but we'll pass inspection. Come on inside. (TOM *follows, groaning.*) Sit down.

TOM: Any particular place you would like me to sit?

AMANDA: Thank heavens I've got that new sofa! I'm also making payments on a floor lamp I'll have sent out! And put the chintz covers on, they'll brighten things up! Of course I'd hoped to have these walls re-papered. . . . What is the young man's name?

TOM: His name is O'Connor.

AMANDA: That, of course, means fish—tomorrow is Friday! I'll have that salmon loaf—with Durkee's dressing! What does he do? He works at the warehouse?

TOM: Of course! How else would I—

AMANDA: Tom, he—doesn't drink?

TOM: Why do you ask me that?

AMANDA: Your father *did*!

TOM: Don't get started on that!

AMANDA: He *does* drink, then?

TOM: Not that I know of!

AMANDA: Make sure, be certain! The last thing I want for my daughter's a boy who drinks!

TOM: Aren't you being a little premature? Mr. O'Connor has not yet appeared on the scene!

AMANDA: But will tomorrow. To meet your sister, and what do I know about his character? Nothing! Old maids are better off than wives of drunkards!

TOM: Oh, my God!

AMANDA: Be still!

TOM (*leaning forward to whisper*): Lots of fellows meet girls whom they don't marry!

AMANDA: Oh, talk sensibly, Tom—and don't be sarcastic! (*She has gotten a hairbrush.*)

TOM: What are you doing?

AMANDA: I'm brushing that cow-lick down! What is this young man's position at the warehouse?

TOM (*submitting grimly to the brush and the interrogation*): This young man's position is that of a shipping clerk, Mother.

AMANDA: Sounds to me like a fairly responsible job, the sort of a job *you* would be in if you just had more *get-up*. What is his salary? Have you got any idea?

TOM: I would judge it to be approximately eighty-five dollars a month.

AMANDA: Well—not princely, but—

TOM: Twenty more than I make.

AMANDA: Yes, how well I know! But for a family man, eighty-five dollars a month is not much more than you can just get by on. . . .

TOM: Yes, but Mr. O'Connor is not a family man.

AMANDA: He might be, mightn't he? Some time in the future?

TOM: I see. Plans and provisions.

AMANDA: You are the only young man that I know of who ignores the fact that the future becomes the present, the present the past, and the past turns into everlasting regret if you don't plan for it!

TOM: I will think that over and see what I can make of it.

AMANDA: Don't be supercilious with your mother! Tell me some more about this—what do you call him?

TOM: James D. O'Connor. The D. is for Delaney.

AMANDA: Irish on *both* sides! *Gracious!* And doesn't drink?

TOM: Shall I call him up and ask him right this minute?

AMANDA: The only way to find out about those things is to make discreet inquiries at the proper moment. When I was a girl in Blue Mountain and it was suspected that a young man drank, the girl whose attentions he had been receiving, if any girl *was*, would sometimes speak to the minister of his church, or rather her father would if her father was living, and sort of feel him out on the young man's character. That is the way such things are discreetly handled to keep a young woman from making a tragic mistake!

TOM: Then how did you happen to make a tragic mistake?

AMANDA: That innocent look of your father's had everyone fooled! He *smiled*—the world was *enchanted.!* No girl can do worse than put herself at the mercy of a handsome appearance! I hope that Mr. O'Connor is not too good-looking.

TOM: No, he's not too good-looking. He's covered with freckles and hasn't too much of a nose.

AMANDA: He's not right-down homely, though?

TOM: Not right-down homely. Just medium homely, I'd say.

AMANDA: Character's what to look for in a man.

TOM: That's what I've always said, Mother.

AMANDA: You've never said anything of the kind and I suspect you would never give it a thought.

TOM: Don't be suspicious of me.

AMANDA: At least I hope he's the type that's up and coming.

TOM: I think he really goes in for self-improvement.

AMANDA: What reason have you to think so?

TOM: He goes to night school.

AMANDA (*beaming*): Splendid! What does he do, I mean study?

TOM: Radio engineering and public speaking!

AMANDA: Then he has visions of being advanced in the world! Any young man who studies public speaking is aiming to have an executive job some day! And radio engineering? A thing for the future! Both of these facts are very illuminating. Those are the sort of things that a mother should know concerning any young man who comes to call on her daughter. Seriously or—not.

TOM: One little warning. He doesn't know about Laura. I didn't let on that we had dark ulterior motives. I just said, why don't you come have dinner with us? He said okay and that was the whole conversation.

AMANDA: I bet it was! You're eloquent as an oyster. However, he'll know about Laura when he gets here. When he sees how lovely and sweet and pretty she is, he'll thank his lucky stars he was asked to dinner.

TOM: Mother, you mustn't expect too much of Laura.

AMANDA: What do you mean?

TOM: Laura seems all those things to you and me because she's ours and we love her. We don't even notice she's crippled any more.

AMANDA: Don't say crippled! You know that I never allow that word to be used!

TOM: But face facts, Mother. She is and—that's not all—

AMANDA: What do you mean "not all"?

TOM: Laura is very different from other girls.

AMANDA: I think the difference is all to her advantage.

TOM: Not quite all—in the eyes of others—strangers—she's terribly shy and lives in a world of her own and those things make her seem a little peculiar to people outside the house.

AMANDA: Don't say peculiar.

TOM: Face the facts. She is.

(The Dance-Hall Music Changes to a Tango That Has a Minor and Somewhat Ominous Tone.)

AMANDA: In what way is she peculiar—may I ask?

TOM (*gently*): She lives in a world of her own—a world of—little glass ornaments, Mother. . . . (*Gets up.* AMANDA *remains holding brush, looking at him, troubled.*) She plays old phonograph records and—that's about all—(*He glances at himself in the mirror and crosses to door.*)

AMANDA (*sharply*) Where are you going?

TOM: I'm going to the movies. (*Out screen door.*)

AMANDA: Not to the movies, every night to the movies! (*Follows quickly to screen door.*) I don't believe you always go to the movies! (*He is gone.* AMANDA *looks worriedly after him for a moment. Then vitality and optimism return and she turns from the door. Crossing to portieres.*) Laura! Laura! (*LAURA answers from kitchenette.*)

LAURA: Yes, Mother.

AMANDA: Let those dishes go and come in front! (*LAURA appears with dish towel. Gaily*) Laura, come here and make a wish on the moon!

LAURA (*entering*): Moon—moon?

AMANDA: A little silver slipper of a moon. Look over your left shoulder, Laura, and make a wish! (*LAURA looks faintly puzzled as if called out of sleep.* AMANDA *seizes her shoulders and turns her at angle by the door.*) Now! Now, darling, *wish!*

LAURA: What shall I wish for, Mother?

AMANDA (*her voice trembling and her eyes suddenly filling with tears*). Happiness! Good Fortune!

(*The violin rises and the stage dims out.*)

SCENE VI

(Image: High School Hero.)

TOM: And so the following evening I brought Jim home to dinner. I had known Jim slightly in high school. In high school Jim was a hero. He had tremendous Irish good nature and vitality with the scrubbed and polished look of white chinaware. He seemed to move in a continual spotlight. He was a star in basketball, captain of the debating club, president of the senior class and the glee club and he sang the male lead in the annual light operas. He was always running or bounding, never just walking. He seemed always at the point of defeating the law of gravity. He was shooting with such velocity through his adolescence that you would logically expect him to arrive at nothing short of the White House by the time he was thirty. But Jim apparently ran into more interference after his graduation from Soldan. His speed had definitely slowed. Six years after he left high school he was holding a job that wasn't much better than mine.

(Image: Clerk.)

He was the only one at the warehouse with whom I was on friendly terms. I was valuable to him as someone who could remember his former glory, who had seen him win basketball games and the silver cup in debating. He knew of my secret practice of retiring to a cabinet of the washroom to work on poems when business was slack in the warehouse. He called me Shakespeare. And while the other boys in the warehouse regarded me with suspicious hostility, Jim took a humorous attitude toward me. Gradually his attitude affected the others, their hostility wore off and they also began to smile at me as people smile at an oddly fashioned dog who trots across their path at some distance.

I knew that Jim and Laura had known each other at Soldan, and I had heard Laura speak admiringly of his voice. I didn't know if Jim remembered her or not. In high school Laura had been as unobtrusive as Jim had been astonishing. If he did remember Laura, it was not as my sister, for when I asked him to dinner, he grinned and said, "You know, Shakespeare, I never thought of you as having folks!"

He was about to discover that I did. . . .

(Light upstage.)

(Legend on Screen: "The Accent of a Coming Foot.")

(Friday evening. It is about five o'clock of a late spring evening which comes "scattering poems in the sky." A delicate lemony light is in the Wingfield apartment. AMANDA *has worked like a Turk in preparation for the gentleman caller. The results are astonishing. The new floor lamp with its rose-silk shade is in place, a colored paper lantern conceals the broken light fixture in the ceiling, new billowing white curtains are at the windows, chintz covers are on chairs and sofa, a pair of new sofa pillows make their initial appearance.*

Open boxes and tissue paper are scattered on the floor.

LAURA *stands in the middle with lifted arms while* AMANDA *crouches before her, adjusting the hem of the new dress, devout and ritualistic. The dress is colored and designed by memory. The arrangement of* LAURA's *hair is changed; it is softer and more becoming. A fragile, unearthly prettiness has come out in* LAURA: *she is like a piece of translucent glass touched by light, given a momentary radiance, not actual, not lasting.)*

AMANDA (*impatiently*): Why are you trembling?
LAURA: Mother, you've made me so nervous!
AMANDA: How have I made you nervous?
LAURA: By all this fuss! You make it seem so important!
AMANDA: I don't understand you, Laura. You couldn't be satisfied with just sitting home, and yet whenever I try to arrange something for you, you seem to resist it. (*She gets up.*) Now take a look at yourself. No, wait! Wait just a moment—I have an idea!
LAURA: What is it now?

(Amanda produces two powder puffs which she wraps in handkerchiefs and stuffs in LAURA's *bosom.)*

LAURA: Mother, what are you doing?
AMANDA: They call them "Gay Deceivers"!
LAURA: I won't wear them!
AMANDA: You will!
LAURA: Why should I?
AMANDA: Because, to be painfully honest, your chest is flat.
LAURA: You make it seem like we were setting a trap.
AMANDA: All pretty girls are a trap, a pretty trap, and men expect them to be. (**Legend: "A Pretty Trap."**) Now look at yourself, young lady. This is the prettiest you will ever be! I've got to fix myself now! You're going to be surprised by your mother's

appearance! (*She crosses through portieres, humming gaily.*)

(LAURA *moves slowly to the long mirror and stares solemnly at herself. A wind blows the white curtains inward in a slow, graceful motion and with a faint, sorrowful sighing.*)

AMANDA (*off stage*): It isn't dark enough yet. (*She turns slowly before the mirror with a troubled look.*)

(Legend on Screen: "This Is My Sister: Celebrate Her with Strings!" Music.)

AMANDA (*laughing, off*): I'm going to show you something. I'm going to make a spectacular appearance!

LAURA: What is it, Mother?

AMANDA: Possess your soul in patience—you will see! Something I've resurrected from that old trunk! Styles haven't changed so terribly much after all. . . . (*She parts the portieres.*) Now just look at your mother! (*She wears a girlish frock of yellowed voile with a blue silk sash. She carries a bunch of jonquils—the legend of her youth is nearly revived. Feverishly*) This is the dress in which I led the cotillion. Won the cakewalk twice at Sunset Hill, wore one spring to the Governor's ball in Jackson! See how I sashayed around the ballroom, Laura? (*She raises her skirt and does a mincing step around the room.*) I wore it on Sundays for my gentlemen callers! I had it on the day I met your father—I had malaria fever all that spring. The change of climate from East Tennessee to the Delta—weakened resistance—I had a little temperature all the time—not enough to be serious—just enough to make me restless and giddy! Invitations poured in—parties all over the Delta!—"Stay in bed," said Mother, "you have fever!"—but I just wouldn't.—I took quinine but kept on going, going!—Evenings, dances!—Afternoons, long, long rides! Picnics—lovely!—So lovely, that country in May.—All lacy with dogwood, literally flooded with jonquils!—That was the spring I had the craze for jonquils. Jonquils became an absolute obsession. Mother said, "Honey, there's no more room for jonquils." And still I kept bringing in more jonquils. Whenever, wherever I saw them, I'd say, "Stop! Stop! I see jonquils!" I made the young men help me gather the jonquils! It was a joke, Amanda and her jonquils! Finally there were no more vases to hold them, every available space was filled with jonquils. No vases to hold them? All right, I'll hold them myself! And then I—(*She stops in front of the picture.*) (**Music.**) met your father! Malaria fever and jonquils and then—

this—boy. . . . (*She switches on the rose-colored lamp.*) I hope they get here before it starts to rain. (*She crosses upstage and places the jonquils in bowl on table.*) I gave your brother a little extra change so he and Mr. O'Connor could take the service car home.

LAURA (*with altered look*): What did you say his name was?

AMANDA: O'Connor.

LAURA: What is his first name?

AMANDA: I don't remember. Oh, yes, I do. It was—Jim!

(LAURA *sways slightly and catches hold of a chair.*)

(Legend on Screen: "Not Jim!")

LAURA (*faintly*): Not—Jim!

AMANDA: Yes, that was it, it was Jim! I've never known a Jim that wasn't nice!

(Music: Ominous.)

LAURA: Are you sure his name is Jim O'Connor?

AMANDA: Yes. Why?

LAURA: Is he the one that Tom used to know in high school?

AMANDA: He didn't say so. I think he just got to know him at the warehouse.

LAURA: There was a Jim O'Connor we both knew in high school—(*Then, with effort.*) If that is the one that Tom is bringing to dinner—you'll have to excuse me, I won't come to the table.

AMANDA: What sort of nonsense is this?

LAURA: You asked me once if I'd ever liked a boy. Don't you remember I showed you this boy's picture?

AMANDA: You mean the boy you showed me in the year book?

LAURA: Yes, that boy.

AMANDA: Laura, Laura, were you in love with that boy?

LAURA: I don't know, Mother. All I know is I couldn't sit at the table if it was him!

AMANDA: It won't be him! It isn't the least bit likely. But whether it is or not, you will come to the table. You will not be excused.

LAURA: I'll have to be, Mother.

AMANDA: I don't intend to humor your silliness, Laura. I've had too much from you and your brother, both! So just sit down and compose yourself till they come. Tom has forgotten his key so you'll have to let them in, when they arrive.

LAURA (*panicky*): Oh, Mother—*you* answer the door!

AMANDA (*lightly*): I'll be in the kitchen—busy!

LAURA: Oh, Mother, please answer the door, don't make me do it!

AMANDA (*crossing into kitchenette*): I've got to fix the dressing for the salmon. Fuss, fuss—silliness!—over a gentleman caller!

(*Door swings shut.* LAURA *is left alone.*)

(Legend: "Terror!")

(*She utters a low moan and turns off the lamp— sits stiffly on the edge of the sofa, knotting her fingers together.*)

(Legend on Screen: "The Opening of a Door!")

(TOM *and* JIM *appear on the fire-escape steps and climb to landing. Hearing their approach,* LAURA *rises with a panicky gesture. She retreats to the portieres.*
The doorbell. LAURA *catches her breath and touches her throat. Low drums.*)

AMANDA (*calling*): Laura, sweetheart! The door!

(*Laura stares at it without moving.*)

JIM: I think we just beat the rain.

TOM: Uh-huh. (*He rings again, nervously.* JIM *whistles and fishes for a cigarette.*)

AMANDA (*very, very gaily*): Laura, that is your brother and Mr. O'Connor! Will you let them in, darling?

(LAURA *crosses toward kitchenette door.*)

LAURA (*breathlessly*): Mother—you go to the door!

(AMANDA *steps out of the kitchenette and stares furiously at* LAURA. *She points imperiously at the door.*)

LAURA: Please, please!

AMANDA (*in a fierce whisper*): What is the matter with you, you silly thing?

LAURA (*desperately*): Please, you answer it, *please!*

AMANDA: I told you I wasn't going to humor you, Laura. Why have you chosen this moment to lose your mind?

LAURA: Please, please, please, you go!

AMANDA: You'll have to go to the door because I can't!

LAURA (*despairingly*): I can't either!

AMANDA: Why?

LAURA: I'm *sick!*

AMANDA: I'm sick, too—of your nonsense! Why can't you and your brother be normal people?

Fantastic whims and behavior! (TOM *gives a long ring.*) Preposterous goings on! Can you give me one reason—(*Calls out lyrically.*) COMING! JUST ONE SECOND!—why should you be afraid to open a door? Now you answer it, Laura!

LAURA: Oh, oh, oh . . . (*She returns through the portieres. Darts to the victrola and winds it frantically and turns it on.*)

AMANDA: Laura Wingfield, you march right to that door!

LAURA: Yes—yes, Mother!

(*A faraway, scratchy rendition of "Dardanella" softens the air and gives her strength to move through it. She slips to the door and draws it cautiously open.* TOM *enters with the caller,* JIM O'CONNOR.)

TOM: Laura, this is Jim. Jim, this is my sister, Laura.

JIM (*stepping inside*): I didn't know that Shakespeare had a sister!

LAURA (*retreating stiff and trembling from the door*): How—how do you do?

JIM (*heartily extending his hand*): Okay!

(LAURA *touches it hesitantly with hers.*)

JIM: Your hand's *cold*, Laura!

LAURA: Yes, well—I've been playing the victrola. . . .

JIM: Must have been playing classical music on it! You ought to play a little hot swing music to warm you up!

LAURA: Excuse me—I haven't finished playing the victrola. . . .

(*She turns awkwardly and hurries into the frontroom. She pauses a second by the victrola. Then catches her breath and darts through the portieres like a frightened deer.*)

JIM (*grinning*): What was the matter?

TOM: Oh—with Laura? Laura is—terribly shy.

JIM: Shy, huh? It's unusual to meet a shy girl nowadays. I don't believe you ever mentioned you had a sister.

TOM: Well, now you know. I have one. Here is the *Post Dispatch*. You want a piece of it?

JIM: Uh-huh.

TOM: What piece? The comics?

JIM: Sports! (*Glances at it.*) Ole Dizzy Dean is on his bad behavior.

TOM (*disinterest*): Yeah? (*Lights cigarette and crosses back to fire-escape door.*)

JIM: Where are *you* going?

TOM: I'm gong out on the terrace.

JIM (*goes after him*): You know, Shakespeare—I'm going to sell you a bill of goods!

TOM: What goods?

JIM: A course I'm taking.

TOM: Huh?

JIM: In public speaking! You and me, we're not the warehouse type.

TOM: Thanks—that's good news. But what has public speaking got to do with it?

JIM: It fits you for—executive positions!

TOM: Awww.

JIM: I tell you it's done a helluva lot for me.

(Image: Executive at Desk.)

TOM: In what respect?

JIM: In every! Ask yourself what is the difference between you an' me and men in the office down front? Brains?—No!—Ability?—No! Then what? Just one little thing—

TOM: What is that one little thing?

JIM: Primarily it amounts to—social poise! Being able to square up to people and hold your own on any social level!

AMANDA (*off stage*): Tom?

TOM: Yes, Mother?

AMANDA: Is that you and Mr. O'Connor?

TOM: Yes, Mother.

AMANDA: Well, you just make yourselves comfortable in there.

TOM: Yes, Mother.

AMANDA: Ask Mr. O'Connor if he would like to wash his hands.

JIM: Aw—no—no—thank you—I took care of that at the warehouse. Tom—

TOM: Yes?

JIM: Mr. Mendoza was speaking to me about you.

TOM: Favorably?

JIM: What do you think?

TOM: Well—

JIM: You're going to be out of a job if you don't wake up.

TOM: I am waking up—

JIM: You show no signs.

TOM: The signs are interior.

(Image on Screen: The Sailing Vessel with Jolly Roger Again.)

TOM: I'm planning to change. (*He leans over the rail speaking with quiet exhilaration. The incandescent marquees and signs of the first-run movie houses light his face from across the alley. He looks like a voyager.*) I'm right at the point of committing myself to a future that doesn't include the warehouse and Mr. Mendoza or even a night-school course in public speaking.

JIM: What are you gassing about?

TOM: I'm tired of the movies.

JIM: Movies!

TOM: Yes, movies! Look at them—(*A wave toward the marvels of Grand Avenue.*) All of those glamorous people—having adventures—hogging it all, gobbling the whole thing up! You know what happens? People go to the *movies* instead of *moving!* Hollywood characters are supposed to have all the adventures for everybody in America, while everybody in America sits in a dark room and watches them have them! Yes, until there's a war. That's when adventure becomes available to the masses! *Everyone's* dish, not only Gable's! Then the people in the dark room come out of the dark room to have some adventures themselves—Goody, goody—It's our turn now, to go to the South Sea Island—to make a safari—to be exotic, far-off—But I'm not patient. I don't want to wait till then. I'm tired of the *movies* and I am *about* to move!

JIM (*incredulously*): Move?

TOM: Yes.

JIM: When?

TOM: Soon!

JIM: Where? Where?

(Theme Three: Music Seems to Answer the Question, While Tom Thinks It Over. He Searches Among His Pockets.)

TOM: I'm starting to boil inside. I know I seem dreamy, but inside—well, I'm boiling! Whenever I pick up a shoe, I shudder a little thinking how short life is and what I am doing!—Whatever that means. I know it doesn't mean shoes—except as something to wear on a traveler's feet! (*Finds paper.*) Look—

JIM: What?

TOM: I'm a member.

JIM (*reading*): The Union of Merchant Seamen.

TOM: I paid my dues this month, instead of the light bill.

JIM: You will regret it when they turn the lights off.

TOM: I won't be here.

JIM: How about your mother?

TOM: I'm like my father. The bastard son of a bastard! See how he grins? And he's been absent going on sixteen years!

JIM: You're just talking, you drip. How does your mother feel about it?

TOM: Shhh—Here comes Mother! Mother is not acquainted with my plans!

AMANDA (*enters portieres*): Where are you all?

TOM: On the terrace, Mother.

(*They start inside. She advances to them.* TOM *is distinctly shocked at her appearance. Even* JIM *blinks a little. He is making his first contact with girlish Southern vivacity and in spite of the night-school course in public speaking is somewhat thrown off the beam by the unexpected outlay of social charm. Certain responses are attempted by* JIM *but are swept aside by* AMANDA's *gay laughter and chatter.* TOM *is embarrassed but after the first shock* JIM *reacts very warmly. Grins and chuckles, is altogether won over.*)

(Image: Amanda as a Girl.)

AMANDA (*coyly smiling, shaking her girlish ringlets*): Well, well, well, so this is Mr. O'Connor. Introductions entirely unnecessary. I've heard so much about you from my boy. I finally said to him, Tom—good gracious!—why don't you bring this paragon to supper? I'd like to meet this nice young man at the warehouse!—Instead of just hearing him sing your praises so much! I don't know why my son is so stand-offish—that's not Southern behavior! Let's sit down and—I think we could stand a little more air in here! Tom, leave the door open. I felt a nice fresh breeze a moment ago. Where has it gone? Mmm, so warm already! And not quite summer, even. We're going to burn up when summer really gets started. However, we're having—we're having a very light supper. I think light things are better fo' this time of year. The same as light clothes are. Light clothes an' light food are what warm weather calls fo'. You know our blood gets so thick during th' winter—it takes a while fo' us to *adjust* ou'selves!—when the season changes . . . It's come so quick this year. I wasn't prepared. All of a sudden—heavens! Already summer!—I ran to the trunk an' pulled out this light dress—Terribly old! Historical almost! But feels so good—so good an' co-ol, y'know. . . .

TOM: Mother—

AMANDA: Yes, honey?

TOM: How about—supper?

AMANDA: Honey, you go ask Sister if supper is ready! You know that Sister is in full charge of supper! Tell her you hungry boys are waiting for it. (*To* JIM) Have you met Laura?

JIM: She—

AMANDA: Let you in? Oh, good, you've met already! It's rare for a girl as sweet an' pretty as Laura to be domestic! But Laura is, thank heavens, not only pretty but also very domestic. I'm not at all. I never was a bit. I never could make a thing but angel-food cake. Well, in the South, we had so many servants. Gone, gone, gone. All vestiges of gracious living! Gone completely! I wasn't prepared for what the future brought me. All of my gentlemen callers were sons of planters and so of course I assumed that I would be married to one and raise my family on a large piece of land with plenty of servants. But man proposes—and woman accepts the proposal!—To vary that old, old saying a little bit—I married no planter! I married a man who worked for the telephone company!—that gallantly smiling gentleman over there! (*Points to the picture.*) A telephone man who—fell in love with long distance!—Now he travels and I don't even know where!—But what am I going on for about my—tribulations! Tell me yours—I hope you don't have any! Tom?

TOM (*returning*): Yes, Mother?

AMANDA: Is supper nearly ready?

TOM: It looks to me like supper is on the table.

AMANDA: Let me look—(*She rises prettily and looks through portieres.*) Oh, lovely—But where is Sister?

TOM: Laura is not feeling well and she says that she thinks she'd better not come to the table.

AMANDA: What?—Nonsense!—Laura? Oh, Laura!

LAURA (*off stage, faintly*): Yes, Mother.

AMANDA: You really must come to the table. We won't be seated until you come to the table! Come in, Mr. O'Connor. You sit over there and I'll—Laura? Laura Wingfield! You're keeping us waiting, honey! We can't say grace until you come to the table!

(*The back door is pushed weakly open and* LAURA *comes in. She is obviously quite faint, her lips trembling, her eyes wide and staring. She moves unsteadily toward the table.*)

(Legend: "Terror!")

(*Outside a summer storm is coming abruptly. The white curtains billow inward at the windows and there is a sorrowful murmur and deep blue dusk.* LAURA *suddenly stumbles—She catches at a chair with a faint moan.*)

TOM: Laura!

AMANDA: Laura! (*There is a clap of thunder.*) **(Legend: "Ah!")** (*Despairingly*) Why, Laura, you *are* sick, darling! Tom, help your sister into the living room, dear! Sit in the living room, Laura—rest on the sofa. Well! (*To the gentleman caller*) Standing over the hot stove made her ill!—I told her that it was just too warm this evening, but— (TOM *comes back in.* LAURA *is on the sofa.*) Is Laura all right now?

TOM: Yes.

AMANDA: What *is* that? Rain? A nice cool rain has come up! (*She gives the gentleman caller a frightened look.*) I think we may—have grace—now . . . (TOM *looks at her stupidly.*) Tom, honey—you say grace!

TOM: Oh . . . "For these and all thy mercies—" (*The bow their heads,* AMANDA *stealing a nervous glance at* JIM. *In the living room* LAURA, *stretched on the sofa, clenches her hands to her lips, to hold back a shuddering sob.*) God's Holy Name be praised—

(The Scene Dims Out.)

SCENE VII

A Souvenir

Half an hour later. Dinner is just being finished in the upstage area which is concealed by the drawn portieres.

As the curtain rises LAURA *is still huddled upon the sofa, her feet drawn under her, her head resting on a pale blue pillow, her eyes wide and mysteriously watchful. The new floor lamp with its shade of rose-colored silk gives a soft, becoming light to her face, bringing out the fragile, unearthly prettiness which usually escapes attention. There is a steady murmur of rain, but it is slackening and stops soon after the scene begins; the air outside becomes pale and luminous as the moon breaks out.*

A moment after the curtain rises, the lights in both rooms flicker and go out.

JIM: Hey, there, Mr. Light Bulb!

(AMANDA *laughs nervously.*)

(Legend: "Suspension of a Public Service.")

AMANDA: Where was Moses when the lights went out? Ha-ha. Do you know the answer to that one, Mr. O'Connor?

JIM: No, Ma'am, what's the answer?

AMANDA: In the dark! (JIM *laughs appreciatively.*) Everybody sit still. I'll light the candles. Isn't it lucky we have them on the table? Where's a

match? Which of you gentlemen can provide a match?

JIM: Here.

AMANDA: Thank you, sir.

JIM: Not at all, Ma'am!

AMANDA: I guess the fuse has burnt out. Mr. O'Connor, can you tell a burnt-out fuse? I know I can't and Tom is a total loss when it comes to mechanics. (**Sound: Getting Up: Voices Recede a Little to Kitchenette.**) Oh, be careful you don't bump into something. We don't want our gentleman caller to break his neck. Now wouldn't that be a fine howdy-do?

JIM: Ha-ha! Where is the fuse-box?

AMANDA: Right here next to the stove. Can you see anything?

JIM: Just a minute.

AMANDA: Isn't electricity a mysterious thing? Wasn't it Benjamin Franklin who tied a key to a kite? We live in such a mysterious universe, don't we? Some people say that science clears up all the mysteries for us. In my opinion it only creates more! Have you found it yet?

JIM: No, Ma'am. All these fuses look okay to me.

AMANDA: Tom!

TOM: Yes, Mother?

AMANDA: That light bill I gave you several days ago. The one I told you we got the notices about?

TOM: Oh.—Yeah.

(Legend: "Ha!")

AMANDA: You didn't neglect to pay it by any chance?

TOM: Why, I—

AMANDA: Didnt! I might have known it!

JIM: Shakespeare probably wrote a poem on that light bill, Mrs. Wingfield.

AMANDA: I might have known better than to trust him with it! There's such a high price for negligence in this world!

JIM: Maybe the poem will win a ten-dollar prize.

AMANDA: We'll just have to spend the remainder of the evening in the nineteenth century, before Mr. Edison made the Mazda lamp!

JIM: Candlelight is my favorite kind of light.

AMANDA: That shows you're romantic! But that's no excuse for Tom. Well, we got through dinner. Very considerate of them to let us get through dinner before they plunged us into everlasting darkness, wasn't it, Mr. O'Connor?

JIM: Ha-ha!

AMANDA: Tom, as a penalty for your carelessness you can help me with the dishes.

JIM: Let me give you a hand.

AMANDA: Indeed you will not!

JIM: I ought to be good for something.

AMANDA: Good for something? (*Her tone is rhapsodic.*) *You?* Why, Mr. O'Connor, nobody, *nobody's* given me this much entertainment in years—as you have!

JIM: Aw, now, Mrs. Wingfield!

AMANDA: I'm not exaggerating, not one bit! But Sister is all by her lonesome. You go keep her company in the parlor! I'll give you this lovely old candelabrum that used to be on the altar at the church of the Heavenly Rest. It was melted a little out of shape when the church burnt down. Lightning struck it one spring. Gypsy Jones was holding a revival at the time and he intimated that the church was destroyed because the Episcopalians gave card parties.

JIM: Ha-ha.

AMANDA: And how about coaxing Sister to drink a little wine? I think it would be good for her! Can you carry both at once?

JIM: Sure. I'm Superman!

AMANDA: Now, Thomas, get into this apron!

(*The door of kitchenette swings closed on* AMANDA's *gay laughter; the flickering light approaches the portieres.* LAURA *sits up nervously as he enters. Her speech at first is low and breathless from the almost intolerable strain of being alone with a stranger.*)

(Legend: "I Don't Suppose You Remember Me at All!")

(*In her first speeches in this scene, before* JIM's *warmth overcomes her paralyzing shyness,* LAURA's *voice is thin and breathless as though she has run up a steep flight of stairs.* JIM's *attitude is gently humorous. In playing this scene it should be stressed that while the incident is apparently unimportant, it is to* LAURA *the climax of her secret life.*)

JIM: Hello, there, Laura.

LAURA (*faintly*). Hello. (*She clears her throat.*)

JIM: How are you feeling now? Better?

LAURA: Yes. Yes, thank you.

JIM: This is for you. A little dandelion wine. (*He extends it toward her with extravagant gallantry.*)

LAURA: Thank you.

JIM: Drink it—but don't get drunk! (*He laughs heartily.* LAURA *takes the glass uncertainly; laughs shyly.*) Where shall I set the candles?

LAURA: Oh—oh, anywhere . . .

JIM: How about here on the floor? Any objections?

LAURA: No.

JIM: I'll spread a newspaper under to catch the drippings. I like to sit on the floor. Mind if I do?

LAURA: Oh, no.

JIM: Give me a pillow?

LAURA: What?

JIM: A pillow!

LAURA: Oh . . . (*Hands him one quickly.*)

JIM: How about you? Don't you like to sit on the floor?

LAURA: Oh—yes.

JIM: Why don't you, then?

LAURA: I—will.

JIM: Take a pillow! (LAURA *does. Sits on the other side of the candelabrum.* JIM *crosses his legs and smiles engagingly at her.*) I can't hardly see you sitting way over there.

LAURA: I can—see you.

JIM: I know, but that's not fair, I'm in the limelight. (LAURA *moves her pillow closer.*) Good! Now I can see you! Comfortable?

LAURA: Yes.

JIM: So am I. Comfortable as a cow. Will you have some gum?

LAURA: No, thank you.

JIM: I think that I will indulge, with your permission. (*Musingly unwraps it and holds it up.*) Think of the fortune made by the guy that invented the first piece of chewing gum. Amazing, huh? The Wrigley Building is one of the sights of Chicago.—I saw it summer before last when I went up to the Century of Progress. Did you take in the Century of Progress?

LAURA: No, I didn't.

JIM: Well, it was quite a wonderful exposition. What impressed me most was the Hall of Science. Gives you an idea of what the future will be in America, even more wonderful than the present time is! (*Pause. Smiling at her*) Your brother tells me you're shy. Is that right, Laura?

LAURA: I—don't know.

JIM: I judge you to be an old-fashioned type of girl. Well, I think that's a pretty good type to be. Hope you don't think I'm being too personal—do you?

LAURA (*hastily, out of embarrassment*): I believe I *will* take a piece of gum, if you—don't mind. (*Clearing her throat*) Mr. O'Connor, have you—kept up with your singing?

JIM: Singing? Me?

LAURA: Yes. I remember what a beautiful voice you had.

JIM: When did you hear me sing?

(Voice Offstage in the Pause.)

VOICE (*offstage*):
   O blow, ye winds, heigh-ho,
   A-roving I will go!
   I'm off to my love
   With a boxing glove—
   Ten thousand miles away!

JIM: You say you've heard me sing?

LAURA: Oh, yes! Yes, very often . . . I—don't suppose you remember me—at all?

JIM (*smiling doubtfully*): You know I have an idea I've seen you before. I had that idea soon as you opened the door. It seemed almost like I was about to remember your name. But the name that I started to call you—wasn't a name! And so I stopped myself before I said it.

LAURA: Wasn't it—Blue Roses?

JIM (*springs up, grinning*): Blue Roses! My gosh, yes—Blue Roses! That's what I had on my tongue when you opened the door! Isn't it funny what tricks your memory plays! I didn't connect you with the high school somehow or other. But that's where it was; it was high school. I didn't even know you were Shakespeare's sister! Gosh, I'm sorry.

LAURA: I didn't expect you to. You—barely knew me!

JIM: But we did have a speaking acquaintance, huh?

LAURA: Yes, we—spoke to each other.

JIM: When did you recognize me?

LAURA: Oh, right away!

JIM: Soon as I came in the door?

LAURA: When I heard your name I thought it was probably you. I knew that Tom used to know you a little in high school. So when you came in the door—Well, then I was—sure.

JIM: Why didn't you *say* something, then?

LAURA (*breathlessly*): I didn't know what to say, I was—too surprised!

JIM: For goodness' sakes! You know, this sure is funny!

LAURA: Yes! Yes, isn't it, though . . .

JIM: Didn't we have a class in something together?

LAURA: Yes, we did.

JIM: What class was that?

LAURA: It was—singing—Chorus!

JIM: Aw!

LAURA: I sat across the aisle from you in the Aud.

JIM: Aw.

LAURA: Mondays, Wednesdays and Fridays.

JIM: Now I remember—you always came in late.

LAURA: Yes, it was so hard for me, getting upstairs. I had that brace on my leg—it clumped so loud!

JIM: I never heard any clumping.

LAURA: (*wincing at the recollection*): To me it sounded like—thunder!

JIM: Well, well, well. I never even noticed.

LAURA: And everybody was seated before I came in. I had to walk in front of all those people. My seat was in the back row. I had to go clumping all the way up the aisle with everyone watching!

JIM: You shouldn't have been self-conscious.

LAURA: I know, but I was. It was always such a relief when the singing started.

JIM: Aw, yes, I've placed you now! I used to call you Blue Roses. How was it that I got started calling you that?

LAURA: I was out of school a little while with pleurosis. When I came back you asked me what was the matter. I said I had pleurosis—you thought I said Blue Roses. That's what you always called me after that!

JIM: I hope you didn't mind.

LAURA: Oh, no—I liked it. You see, I wasn't acquainted with many—people. . . .

JIM: As I remember you sort of stuck by yourself.

LAURA: I—I—never had much luck at—making friends.

JIM: I don't see why you wouldn't.

LAURA: Well, I—started out badly.

JIM: You mean being—

LAURA: Yes, it sort of—stood between me—

JIM: You shouldn't have let it!

LAURA: I know, but it did, and—

JIM: You were shy with people!

LAURA: I tried not to be but never could—

JIM: Overcome it?

LAURA: No, I—I never could!

JIM: I guess being shy is something you have to work out of kind of gradually.

LAURA (*sorrowfully*): Yes—I guess it—

JIM: Takes time!

LAURA: Yes—

JIM: People are not so dreadful when you know them. That's what you have to remember! And everybody has problems, not just you, but practically everybody has got some problems. You think of yourself as having the only problems, as being the only one who is disappointed. But just look around you and you will see lots of people as disappointed as you are. For instance, I hoped when I was going to high shcool that I would be further along at this time, six years later, than I am now—You remember that wonderful write-up I had in *The Torch*?

LAURA: Yes! (*She rises and crosses to table.*)

JIM: It said I was bound to succeed in anything I went into! (LAURA *returns with the annual.*) Holy Jeez! *The Torch*! (*He accepts it reverently. They smile across it with mutual wonder.* LAURA *crouches beside him and they begin to turn through it.* LAURA's *shyness is dissolving in his warmth.*)

LAURA: Here you are in *Pirates of Penzance*!

JIM (*wistfully*): I sang the baritone lead in that operetta.

LAURA (*rapidly*): So—*beautifully*!

JIM: (*protesting*): Aw—

LAURA: Yes, yes—beautifully—beautifully!

JIM: You heard me?

LAURA: All three times!

JIM: No!

LAURA: Yes!

JIM: All three performances?

LAURA (*looking down*): Yes.

JIM: Why?

LAURA: I—wanted to ask you to—autograph my program.

JIM: Why didn't you ask me to?

LAURA: You were always surrounded by your own friends so much that I never had a chance to.

JIM: You should have just—

LAURA: Well, I—thought you might think I was—

JIM: Thought I might think you was—what?

LAURA: Oh—

JIM (*with reflective relish*): I was beleaguered by females in those days.

LAURA: You were terribly popular!

JIM: Yeah—

LAURA: You had such a—friendly way—

JIM: I was spoiled in high school.

LAURA: Everybody—liked you!

JIM: Including you?

LAURA: I—yes, I—I did, too—(*She gently closes the book in her lap.*)

JIM: Well, well, well!—Give me that program, Laura. (*She hands it to him. He signs it with a flourish.*) There you are—better late than never!

LAURA: Oh, I—what a—surprise!

JIM: My signature isn't worth very much right now. But some day—maybe—it will increase in value! Being disappointed is one thing and being discouraged is something else. I am disappointed but I'm not discouraged. I'm twenty-three years old. How old are you?

LAURA: I'll be twenty-four in June.

JIM: That's not old age!

LAURA: No, but—

JIM: You finished high school?

LAURA (*with difficulty*): I didn't go back.

JIM: You mean you dropped out?

LAURA: I made bad grades in my final examinations. (*She rises and replaces the book and the program. Her voice strained.*) How is—Emily Meisenbach getting along?

JIM: Oh, that kraut-head!

LAURA: Why do you call her that?

JIM: That's what she was.

LAURA: You're not still—going with her?

JIM: I never see her.

LAURA: It said in the Personal Section that you were—engaged!

JIM: I know, but I wasn't impressed by that—propaganda!

LAURA: It wasn't—the truth?

JIM: Only in Emily's optimistic opinion!

LAURA: Oh—

(Legend: "What Have You Done Since High School?")

JIM *lights a cigarette and leans indolently back on his elbows smiling at* LAURA *with a warmth and charm which light her inwardly with altar candles. She remains by the table and turns in her hands a piece of glass to cover her tumult.*

JIM (*after several reflective puffs on a cigarette*): What have you done since high school? (*She seems not to hear him.*) Huh? (LAURA *looks up.*) I said what have you done since high school, Laura?

LAURA: Nothing much.

JIM: You must have been doing something these six long years.

LAURA: Yes.

JIM: Well, then, such as what?

LAURA: I took a business course at business college—

JIM: How did that work out?

LAURA: Well, not very—well—I had to drop out, it gave me—indigestion—

(JIM *laughs gently.*)

JIM: What are you doing now?

LAURA: I don't do anything—much. Oh, please don't think I sit around doing nothing! My glass collection takes up a good deal of my time. Glass is something you have to take good care of.

JIM: What did you say—about glass?

LAURA: Collection I said—I have one—(*She clears her throat and turns away again, acutely shy.*)

JIM (*abruptly*): You know what I judge to be the trouble with you? Inferiority complex! Know what that is? That's what they call it when someone low-rates himself! I understand it because I had it, too. Although my case was not so aggravated as yours seems to be. I had it until I took up public speaking, developed my voice, and learned that I had an aptitude for science. Before that time I never thought of myself as being outstanding in any way whatsoever! Now I've never made a regular study of it, but I have a friend who says I can analyze people better than doctors that make a profession of it. I don't claim that to be necessarily true, but I can sure guess a person's psychology, Laura! (*Takes out his gum.*) Excuse me, Laura. I always take it out when the flavor is gone. I'll use this scrap of paper to wrap it in. I know how it is to get it stuck on a shoe. Yep—that's what I judge to be your principal trouble. A lack of confidence in yourself as a person. You don't have the proper amount of faith in yourself. I'm basing that fact on a number of your remarks and also on certain observations I've made. For instance that clumping you thought was so awful in high school. You say that you even dreaded to walk into class. You see what you did? You dropped out of school, you gave up an education because of a clump, which as far as I know was practically nonexistent! A little physical defect is what you have. Hardly notice-able even! Magnified thousands of times by imag-ination! You know what my strong advice to you is? Think of yourself as *superior* in some way!

LAURA: In what way would I think?

JIM: Why, man alive, Laura! Just look about you a little. What do you see? A world full of common people! All of 'em born and all of 'em going to die! Which of them has one-tenth of your good points! Or mine! Or anyone else's, as far as that goes— Gosh! Everybody excels in some one thing. Some in many! (*Unconsciously glances at himself in the mirror.*) All you've got to do is discover in *what*! Take me, for instance. (*He adjusts his tie at the mirror.*) My interest happens to lie in electro-dynamics. I'm taking a course in radio engineering at night school, Laura, on top of a fairly responsi-ble job at the warehouse. I'm taking that course and studying public speaking.

LAURA: Ohhhh.

JIM: Because I believe in the future of television! (*Turning back to her.*) I wish to be ready to go up right along with it. Therefore I'm planning to get in on the ground floor. In fact, I've already made the right connections and all that remains is for the industry itself to get under way! Full steam—(*His eyes are starry.*) Knowledge—Zzzzzp! Money— Zzzzzzp!—Power! That's the cycle democracy is built on! (*His attitude is convincingly dynamic. LAURA stares at him, even her shyness eclipsed in her absolute wonder. He suddenly grins.*) I guess you think I think a lot of myself!

LAURA: No—o-o-o, I—

JIM: Now how about you? Isn't there something you take more interest in than anything else?

LAURA: Well, I do—as I said—have my—glass collection—

(*A peal of girlish laughter from the kitchen.*)

JIM: I'm not right sure I know what you're talking about. What kind of glass is it?

LAURA: Little articles of it, they're ornaments mostly! Most of them are little animals made out of glass, the tiniest little animals in the world. Mother calls them a glass menagerie! Here's an example of one, if you'd like to see it! This one is one of the oldest. It's nearly thirteen. (*He stretches out his hand.*) (**Music: "The Glass Menagerie."**) Oh, be careful—if you breathe, it breaks!

JIM: I'd better not take it. I'm pretty clumsy with things.

LAURA: Go on, I trust you with him! (*Places it in his palm.*) There now—you're holding him gen-tly! Hold him over the light, he loves the light! You see how the light shines through him?

JIM: It sure does shine!

LAURA: I shouldn't be partial, but he is my favorite one.

JIM: What kind of a thing is this one supposed to be?

LAURA: Haven't you noticed the single horn on his forehead?

JIM: A unicorn, huh?

LAURA: Mmm-hmmm!

JIM: Unicorns, aren't they extinct in the modern world?

LAURA: I know!

JIM: Poor little fellow, he must feel sort of lonesome.

LAURA (*smiling*): Well, if he does he doesn't complain about it. He stays on a shelf with some horses that don't have horns and all of them seem to get along nicely together.

JIM: How do you know?

LAURA (*lightly*): I haven't heard any arguments among them!

JIM (*grinning*): No arguments, huh? Well, that's a pretty good sign! Where shall I set him?

LAURA: Put him on the table. They all like a change of scenery once in a while!

JIM (*stretching*): Well, well, well, well—Look how big my shadow is when I stretch!

LAURA: Oh, oh, yes—it stretches across the ceiling!

JIM (*crossing to door*): I think it's stopped raining. (*Opens fire-escape door.*) Where does the music come from?

LAURA: From the Paradise Dance Hall across the alley.

JIM: How about cutting the rug a little, Miss Wingfield?

LAURA: Oh, I—

JIM: Or is your program filled up? Let me have a look at it. (*Grasps imaginary card.*) Why, every dance is taken! I'll just have to scratch some out. **(Waltz Music: "La Golondrina.")** Ahhh, a waltz! (*He executes some sweeping turns by himself then holds his arms toward* LAURA.)

LAURA (*breathlessly*): I—can't dance!

JIM: There you go, that inferiority stuff!

LAURA: I've never danced in my life!

JIM: Come on, try!

LAURA: Oh, but I'd step on you!

JIM: I'm not made out of glass.

LAURA: How—how—how do we start?

JIM: Just leave it to me. You hold your arms out a little.

LAURA: Like this?

JIM: A little bit higher. Right. Now don't tighten up, that's the main thing about it—relax.

LAURA (*laughing breathlessly*): It's hard not to.

JIM: Okay.

LAURA: I'm afraid you can't budge me.

JIM: What do you bet I can't? (*He swings her into motion.*)

LAURA: Goodness, yes, you can!

JIM: Let yourself go, now, Laura, just let yourself go.

LAURA: I'm—

JIM: Come on!

LAURA: Trying!

JIM: Not so stiff—Easy does it!

LAURA: I know but I'm—

JIM: Loosen th' backbone! There now, that's a lot better.

LAURA: Am I?

JIM: Lots, lots better! (*He moves her about the room in a clumsy waltz.*)

LAURA: Oh, my!

JIM: Ha-ha!

LAURA: Goodness, yes you can!

JIM: Ha-ha-ha! (*They suddenly bump into the table,* JIM *stops.*) What did we hit on?

LAURA: Table.

JIM: Did something fall off it? I think—

LAURA: Yes.

JIM: I hope that it wasn't the little glass horse with the horn!

LAURA: Yes.

JIM: Aw, aw, aw. Is it broken?

LAURA: Now it is just like all the other horses.

JIM: It's lost its—

LAURA: Horn! It doesn't matter. Maybe it's a blessing in disguise.

JIM: You'll never forgive me. I bet that that was your favorite piece of glass.

LAURA: I don't have favorites much. It's no tragedy, Freckles. Glass breaks so easily. No matter how careful you are. The traffic jars the shelves and things fall off them.

JIM: Still I'm awfully sorry that I was the cause.

LAURA (*smiling*): I'll just imagine he had an operation. The horn was removed to make him feel less—freakish! (*They both laugh.*) Now he will feel more at home with the other horses, the ones that don't have horns. . .

JIM: Ha-ha, that's very funny! (*Suddenly serious*) I'm glad to see that you have a sense of humor. You know—you're—well—very different! Surprisingly different from anyone else I know! (*His voice becomes soft and hesitant with a genuine feeling.*) Do you mind me telling you that? (LAURA *is abashed beyond speech.*) You make me feel sort of—I don't know how to put it! I'm usually pretty good at expressing things, but—This is something that I don't know how to say! (LAURA *touches her throat and clears it—turns the broken unicorn in her hands.*) (*Even softer*) Has anyone ever told you that you were pretty? **(Pause: Music.)** (LAURA *looks up slowly, with wonder, and shakes her head.*) Well, you are! In a very different way from anyone else. And all the nicer because of the difference, too. (*His voice becomes low and husky.* LAURA *turns away, nearly faint with the novelty of her emotions.*) I wish that you were my sister. I'd teach you to have some confidence in yourself. The different people are not like other people, but being different is nothing to be ashamed of. Because other people are not such wonderful people. They're one hundred times one thousand. You're one times one! They walk all over the earth. You just stay here. They're common as—weeds, but—you—well, you're—*Blue Roses!*

(Image on Screen: Blue Roses.)

(Music Changes.)

LAURA: But blue is wrong for—roses. . .

JIM: It's right for you—You're—pretty!

LAURA: In what respect am I pretty?

JIM: In all respects—believe me! Your eyes— your hair—are pretty! Your hands are pretty! (*He catches hold of her hand.*) You think I'm making this up because I'm invited to dinner and have to be nice. Oh, I could do that! I could put on an act for you, Laura, and say lots of things without being very sincere. But this time I am. I'm talking to you sincerely. I happened to notice you had this inferiority complex that keeps you from feeling comfortable with people. Somebody needs to build your confidence up and make you proud instead of shy and turning away and—blushing—Somebody ought to—ought to—*kiss* you, Laura! (*His hand slips slowly up her arm to her shoulder.*) (**Music Swells Tumultuously.**) (*He suddenly turns her about and kisses her on the lips. When he releases her* LAURA *sinks on the sofa with a bright, dazed look.* JIM *backs away and fishes in his pocket for a cigarette.*) (**Legend on Screen: "Souvenir."**) Stumble-john! (*He lights the cigarette, avoiding her look. There is a peal of girlish laughter from* AMANDA *in the kitchen.* LAURA *slowly raises and opens her hand. It still contains the little broken glass animal. She looks at it with a tender, bewildered expression.*) Stumble-john! I shouldn't have done that—That was way off the beam. You don't smoke, do you? (*She looks up, smiling, not hearing the question. He sits beside her a little gingerly. She looks at him speechlessly—waiting. He coughs decorously and moves a little farther aside as he considers the situation and senses her feelings, dimly, with perturbation. Gently*) Would you— care for a—mint? (*She doesn't seem to hear him but her look grows brighter even.*) Peppermint— Life Saver? My pocket's a regular drug store— wherever I go . . . (*He pops a mint in his mouth. Then gulps and decides to make a clean breast of it. He speaks slowly and gingerly.*) Laura, you know, if I had a sister like you, I'd do the same thing as Tom. I'd bring out fellows—introduce her to them. The right type of boys of a type to— appreciate her. Only—well—he made a mistake about me. Maybe I've got no call to be saying this. That may not have been the idea in having me over. But what if it was? There's nothing wrong about that. The only trouble is that in my case— I'm not in a situation to—do the right thing. I can't take down your number and say I'll phone. I can't call up next week and—ask for a date. I

thought I had better explain the situation in case you misunderstood it and—hurt your feelings. . . . (*Pause. Slowly, very slowly,* LAURA's *look changes, her eyes returning slowly from his to the ornament in her palm.*)

(AMANDA *utters another gay laugh in the kitchen.*)

LAURA (*faintly*): You—won't—call again?

JIM: No, Laura, I can't. (*He rises from the sofa.*) As I was just explaining, I've—got strings on me, Laura, I've—been going steady! I go out all the time with a girl named Betty. She's a home-girl like you, and Catholic, and Irish, and in a great many ways we—get along fine. I met her last summer on a moonlight boat trip up the river to Alton, on the *Majestic*. Well—right away from the start it was—love! (**Legend: Love!**) (LAURA *sways slightly forward and grips the arm of the sofa. He fails to notice, now enrapt in his own comfortable being.*) Being in love has made a new man of me! (*Leaning stiffly forward, clutching the arm of the sofa,* LAURA *struggles visibly with her storm. But* JIM *is oblivious, she is a long way off.*) The power of love is really pretty tremendous! Love is something that—changes the whole world, Laura! (*The storm abates a little and* LAURA *leans back. He notices her again.*) It happened that Betty's aunt took sick, she got a wire and had to go to Centralia. So Tom—when he asked me to dinner—I naturally just accepted the invitation, not knowing that you—that he—that I—(*He stops awkwardly.*) Huh—I'm a stumble-john! (*He flops back on the sofa. The holy candles in the altar of* LAURA's *face have been snuffed out! There is a look of almost infinite desolation.* JIM *glances at her uneasily.*) I wish that you would—say something. (*She bites her lip which was trembling and then bravely smiles. She opens her hand again on the broken glass ornament. Then she gently takes his hand and raises it level with her own. She carefully places the unicorn in the palm of his hand, then pushes his fingers closed upon it.*) What are you—doing that for? You want me to have him?—Laura? (*She nods.*) What for?

LAURA: A—souvenir . . .

(*She rises unsteadily and crouches beside the victrola to wind it up.*)

(**Legend on Screen: "Things Have a Way of Turning Out So Badly."**)

(**Or Image: "Gentleman Caller Waving Good-Bye!—Gaily."**)

(*At this moment* AMANDA *rushes brightly back in the front room. She bears a pitcher of fruit punch in an old-fashioned cut-glass pitcher and a plate of macaroons. The plate has a gold border and poppies painted on it.*)

AMANDA: Well, well, well! Isn't the air delightful after the shower? I've made you children a little liquid refreshment. (*Turns gaily to the gentleman caller.*) Jim, do you know that song about lemonade?

"Lemonade, lemonade
Made in the shade and stirred with a spade—
Good enough for any old maid!"

JIM (*uneasily*): Ha-ha! No—I never heard it.
AMANDA: Why, Laura! You look so serious!
JIM: We were having a serious conversation.
AMANDA: Good! Now you're better acquainted!
JIM (*uncertainly*): Ha-ha! Yes.
AMANDA: You modern young people are much more serious-minded than my generation. I was so gay as a girl!
JIM: You haven't changed, Mrs. Wingfield.
AMANDA: Tonight I'm rejuvenated! The gaiety of the occasion, Mr. O'Connor! (*She tosses her head with a peal of laughter. Spills lemonade.*) Oooo! I'm baptizing myself!
JIM: Here—let me—
AMANDA (*setting the pitcher down.*): There now. I discovered we had some maraschino cherries. I dumped them in, juice and all!
JIM: You shouldn't have gone to that trouble, Mrs. Wingfield.
AMANDA: Trouble, trouble? Why it was loads of fun! Didn't you hear me cutting up in the kitchen? I bet your ears were burning! I told Tom how outdone with him I was for keeping you to himself so long a time! He should have brought you over much, much sooner! Well, now that you've found your way, I want you to be a very frequent caller! Not just occasional but all the time. Oh, we're going to have a lot of gay times together! I see them coming! Mmm, just breathe that air! So fresh, and the moon's so pretty! I'll skip back out—I know where my place is when young folks are having a—serious conversation!
JIM: Oh, don't go out, Mrs. Wingfield. The fact of the matter is I've got to be going.
AMANDA: Going, now? You're joking! Why, it's only the shank of the evening, Mr. O'Connor!
JIM: Well, you know how it is.
AMANDA: You mean you're a young workingman and have to keep workingmen's hours. We'll

let you off early tonight. But only on the condition that next time you stay later. What's the best night for you? Isn't Saturday night the best night for you workingmen?
JIM: I have a couple of time-clocks to punch, Mrs. Wingfield. One at morning, another one at night!
AMANDA: My, but you *are* ambitious! You work at night, too?
JIM: No, Ma'am, not work but—Betty! (*He crosses deliberately to pick up his hat. The band at the Paradise Dance Hall goes into a tender waltz.*)
AMANDA: Betty? Betty? Who's—Betty! (*There is an ominous cracking sound in the sky.*)
JIM: Oh, just a girl. The girl I go steady with! (*He smiles charmingly. The sky falls.*)

(Legend: "The Sky Falls.")

AMANDA (*a long-drawn exhalation*) Ohhhh . . . Is it a serious romance, Mr. O'Connor?
JIM: We're going to be married the second Sunday in June.
AMANDA: Ohhhh—how nice! Tom didn't mention that you were engaged to be married.
JIM: The cat's not out of the bag at the warehouse yet. You know how they are. They call you Romeo and stuff like that. (*He stops at the oval mirror to put on his hat. He carefully shapes the brim and the crown to give a discreetly dashing effect.*) It's been a wonderful evening, Mrs. Wingfield. I guess this is what they mean by Southern hospitality.
AMANDA: It really wasn't anything at all.
JIM: I hope it don't seem like I'm rushing off. But I promised Betty I'd pick her up at the Wabash depot, an' by the time I get my jalopy down there her train'll be in. Some women are pretty upset if you keep 'em waiting.
AMANDA: Yes, I know—The tyranny of women! (*Extends her hand.*) Goodbye, Mr. O'Connor. I wish you luck—and happiness—and success! All three of them, and so does Laura!—Don't you, Laura?
LAURA: Yes!
JIM (*taking her hand*): Goodbye, Laura. I'm certainly going to treasure that souvenir. And don't you forget the good advice I gave you. (*Raises his voice to a cheery shout.*) So long, Shakespeare! Thanks again, ladies—Good night!

(*He grins and ducks jauntily out. Still bravely grimacing,* AMANDA *closes the door on the gentleman caller. Then she turns back to the room with a puzzled expression. She and* LAURA *don't* _weird._

dare to face each other. LAURA _crouches beside the victrola to wind it._)

AMANDA (_faintly_): Things have a way of turning out so badly. I don't believe that I would play the victrola. Well, well—well—Our gentleman caller was engaged to be married! Tom!

TOM (_from back_): Yes, Mother?

AMANDA: Come in here a minute. I want to tell you something awfully funny.

TOM (_enters with macaroon and a glass of the lemonade_): Has the gentleman caller gotten away already?

AMANDA: The gentleman caller has made an early departure. What a wonderful joke you played on us!

TOM: How do you mean?

AMANDA: You didn't mention that he was engaged to be married.

TOM: Jim? Engaged?

AMANDA: That's what he just informed us.

TOM: I'll be jiggered! I didn't know about that.

AMANDA: That seems very peculiar.

TOM: What's peculiar about it?

AMANDA: Didn't you call him your best friend down at the warehouse?

TOM: He is, but how did I know?

AMANDA: It seems extremely peculiar that you wouldn't know your best friend was going to be married!

TOM: The warehouse is where I work, not where I know things about people!

AMANDA: You don't know things anywhere! You live in a dream; you manufacture illusions! (_He crosses to door._) Where are you going?

TOM: I'm going to the movies.

AMANDA: That's right, now that you've had us make such fools of ourselves. The effort, the preparations, all the expense! The new floor lamp, the rug, the clothes for Laura! All for what? To entertain some other girl's fiancé! Go to the movies, go! Don't think about us, a mother deserted, an unmarried sister who's crippled and has no job! Don't let anything interfere with your selfish pleasure! Just go, go, go—to the movies!

TOM: All right, I will! The more you shout about my selfishness to me the quicker I'll go, and I won't go to the movies!

AMANDA: Go, then! Then go to the moon—you selfish dreamer!

TOM _smashes his glass on the floor. He plunges out on the fire-escape, slamming the door._ LAURA _screams—cut by door._

Dance-hall music up. TOM _goes to the rail and grips it desperately, lifting his face in the chill white moonlight penetrating the narrow abyss of the alley._

(Legend on Screen: And So Good-Bye . . .")

(TOM's _closing speech is timed with the interior pantomime. The interior scene is played as though viewed through sound-proof glass._ AMANDA _appears to be making a comforting speech to_ LAURA _who is huddled upon the sofa. Now that we cannot hear the mother's speech, her silliness is gone and she has dignity and tragic beauty._ LAURA's _dark hair hides her face until at the end of the speech she lifts it to smile at her mother._ AMANDA's _gestures are slow and graceful, almost dancelike, as she comforts the daughter. At the end of her speech she glances a moment at the father's picture—then withdraws through the portieres. At close of_ TOM's _speech,_ LAURA _blows out the candles, ending the play._)

TOM: I didn't go to the moon, I went much further—for time is the longest distance between two places—Not long after that I was fired for writing a poem on the lid of a shoe-box. I left Saint Louis. I descended the steps of this fire-escape for a last time and followed, from then on, in my father's footsteps, attempting to find in motion what was lost in space—I traveled around a great deal. The cities swept about me like dead leaves, leaves that were brightly colored but torn away from the branches. I would have stopped, but I was pursued by something. It always came upon me unawares, taking me altogether by surprise. Perhaps it was a familiar bit of music. Perhaps it was only a piece of transparent glass—Perhaps I am walking along a street at night, in some strange city, before I have found companions. I pass the lighted window of a shop where perfume is sold. The window is filled with pieces of colored glass, tiny transparent bottles in delicate colors, like bits of a shattered rainbow. Then all at once my sister touches my shoulder. I turn around and look into her eyes . . . Oh, Laura, Laura, I tried to leave you behind me, but I am more faithful than I intended to be! I reach for a cigarette, I cross the street, I run into the movies or a bar, I buy a drink, I speak to the nearest stranger—anything that can blow your candles out! (LAURA _bends over the candles._)—for nowadays the world is lit by lightning! Blow out your candles, Laura—and so goodbye . . .

(_She blows the candles out._)

(The Scene Dissolves.)

[PLAYWRIGHT'S] PRODUCTION NOTES

Being a "memory play," *The Glass Menagerie* can be presented with unusual freedom of convention. Because of its considerably delicate or tenuous material, atmospheric touches and subtleties of direction play a particularly important part. Expressionism and all other unconventional techniques in drama have only one valid aim, and that is a closer approach to truth. When a play employs unconventional techniques, it is not, or certainly shouldn't be, trying to escape its responsibility of dealing with reality, or interpreting experience, but is actually or should be attempting to find a closer approach, a more penetrating and vivid expression of things as they are. The straight realistic play with its genuine frigidaire and authentic ice cubes, its characters that speak exactly as its audience speaks, corresponds to the academic landscape and has the same virtue of a photographic likeness. Everyone should know nowadays the unimportance of the photographic in art: that truth, life, or reality is an organic thing which the poetic imagination can represent or suggest, in essence, only through transformation, through changing into other forms than those which were merely present in appearance.

These remarks are not meant as comments only on this particular play. They have to do with a conception of a new, plastic theater which must take the place of the exhausted theater of realistic conventions if the theater is to resume vitality as a part of our culture.

THE SCREEN DEVICE

There is *only one important difference between the original and acting version of the play* and that is the *omission* in the latter of the device which I tentatively included in my *original* script. This device was the use of a screen on which were projected magic-lantern slides bearing images or titles. I do not regret the omission of this device from the . . . Broadway production. The extraordinary power of Miss Taylor's performance made it suitable to have the utmost simplicity in the physical production. But I think it may be interesting to some readers to see how this device was conceived. So I am putting it into the published manuscript. These images and legends, projected from behind, were cast on a section of wall between the front-room and dining-room areas, which should be indistinguishable from the rest when not in use.

The purpose of this will probably be apparent. It is to give accent to certain values in each scene. Each scene contains a particular point (or several) which is structurally the most important. In an episodic play, such as this, the basic structure or narrative line may be obscured from the audience; the effect may seem fragmentary rather than architectural. This may not be the fault of the play so much as a lack of attention in the audience. The legend or image upon the screen will strengthen the effect of what is merely allusion in the writing and allow the primary point to be made more simply and lightly than if the entire responsibility were on the spoken lines. Aside from this structural value, I think the screen will have a definite emotional appeal, less definable but just as important. An imaginative producer or director may invent many other uses for this device than those indicated in the present script. In fact the possibilities of the device seem much larger to me than the instance of this play can possibly utilize.

THE MUSIC

Another extra-literary accent in this play is provided by the use of music. A single recurring tune, "The Glass Menagerie," is used to give emotional emphasis to suitable passages. This tune is like circus music, not when you are on the grounds or in the immediate vicinity of the parade, but when you are at some distance and very likely thinking of something else. It seems under those circumstances to continue almost interminably and it weaves in and out of your preoccupied consciousness; then it is the lightest, most delicate music in the world and perhaps the saddest. It expresses the surface vivacity of life with the underlying strain of immutable and inexpressible sorrow. When you look at a piece of delicately spun glass you think of two things: how beautiful it is and how easily it can be broken. Both of those ideas should be woven into the recurring tune, which dips in and out of the play as if it were carried on a wind that changes. It serves as a thread of connection and allusion between the narrator with his separate point in time and space and the subject of his story. Between each episode it returns as reference to the emotion, nostalgia, which is the first condition of the play. It is primarily Laura's music and therefore comes out most clearly when the play focuses upon her and the lovely fragility of glass which is her image.

THE LIGHTING

The lighting in the play is not realistic. In keeping with the atmosphere of memory, the stage is dim. Shafts of light are focused on selected areas or actors, sometimes in contradistinction to what is the apparent center. For instance, in the quarrel scene between Tom and Amanda, in which Laura has no active part, the clearest pool of light is on her figure. This is also true of the supper scene. The light upon Laura should be distinct from the others, having a peculiar pristine clarity such as light used in early religious portraits of female saints or madonnas. A certain correspondence to light in religious paintings, such as El Greco's, where the figures are radiant in atmosphere that is relatively dusky, could be effectively used throughout the play. (It will also permit a more effective use of the screen.) A free, imaginative use of light can be of enormous value in giving a mobile, plastic quality to plays of a more or less static nature.

COMMENTARY

Broadly speaking, drama has been divided into two sorts, *conventional* (also called presentational, stylized, or symbolic) and, on the other hand, *realistic* (or naturalistic). Conventional drama, such as the ancient Greek plays of Sophocles or the Elizabethan plays of Shakespeare, makes little pretense of offering an accurate transcription of the surface reality. For instance, in real life we all speak prose, but in Sophocles's *Oedipus the King* it is conventional for the characters to speak verse; a man living in a remote region is summoned and appears on stage a few minutes later; moments after blinding himself, Oedipus enters, not writhing in pain but speaking eloquently. Similarly, in Shakespeare's plays, which were staged during the daytime in an unroofed theater, if a character enters carrying a torch the audience understands, by means of this convention, that the scene—acted in full light—is taking place at night. (A *convention* is literally a "coming together"; the audience and the theatrical personnel come together—reach an understanding—and pretend that what is shown onstage is real.)

Most drama before the middle of the nineteenth century was highly conventional, partly because it had to be. The vast size of a Greek theater required the actors to gesticulate broadly and to speak loudly, even if they were supposed to be whispering inconspicuously. Similarly, before the development of advanced techniques of lighting, night scenes necessarily were played in the daylight, or, if played in roofed theaters that used artificial illumination, they were played with only a suggestion of darkness. If a character looked upward and spoke of the moon, the audience agreed to pretend that the moon was visible. But around the middle of the nineteenth century, new techniques of lighting allowed for relatively realistic effects of, say, the breaking of dawn, or the gradual coming of night. Moreover, the temper of the times (largely dominated by a scientific spirit—which, for instance, invented the art of photography) favored an art that seemed close to the surface of life. The announced aim of art, or at least of some artists, was to give "a slice of life."

In fact, of course, even the most realistic play is in some ways conventional.

For two and a half hours the characters do not digress, and they never seem to have to go to the bathroom. The audience looks at "real" furniture displayed in what seems to be a "real" room, but in fact most of the furniture faces the footlights, and the room is missing a wall (see, for instance, the illustration of the set for A *Doll's House* on page 4) so that the audience may see what goes on in it. At the end of the act the curtain drops, and the audience, knowing that there will be an intermission of fifteen minutes, troops out into the lobby. When the audience returns, it understands from the dialogue (and maybe the program note) that the time is now the next day, or the next week. We are scarcely aware of these conventions because, having grown up with them, we have assimilated them, just as we hardly think it is odd that a photograph in a newspaper is black and white, when in real life the images are colored. Similarly, in film and on television—media that are largely realistic—we are not surprised when we get a close-up of a head, even though such a shot is a convention, since in real life we don't suddenly see heads without bodies.

Although the conventions of realism dominated the serious theater in the later nineteenth century, the very end of the century and the first third of the twentieth century saw a vigorous rebellion against them. Just as the realism of the nineteenth century owed much to a new spirit of scientific thinking (especially to studies of the influence of the environment on the individual), so this new movement owed much to a new science, psychology. Some plays now sought to give not the external reality or surface appearance of life but the inner reality, life as *felt* rather than as seen. Thus, instead of the setting closely imitating a room as the scientific eye sees it, the walls might veer crazily, to represent (or symbolize) the way the main character perceives his or her irrational or oppressive world. (For a bit more on this, see the entry on *expressionism* in the Glossary.)

Tennessee Williams's *The Glass Menagerie* is largely in this expressionistic tradition. Its link to psychology—to feeling rather than seeing—is suggested in the first sentence of the Production Notes, where Williams calls it a "memory play." Notice too that in the Production Notes he says that the play "can be presented with unusual freedom of convention." He does not mean that the play is free from conventions; rather, he means that the conventions are not the old established ones but are relatively fresh ones, invented for the moment. Similarly, when he speaks of expressionist plays as being "unconventional," he does not mean that they do not employ conventions. Rather, he means that they are untraditional, relatively novel, employing new conventions. "Expression-ism," he says,

> and all other unconventional techniques in drama have only one valid aim, and that is a closer approach to truth. When a play employs unconventional techniques, it is not, or certainly shouldn't be, trying to escape its respon-sibility of dealing with reality, or interpreting experience, but is actually or should be attempting to find a closer approach, a more penetrating and vivid expression of things as they are.

In fact, when *The Glass Menagerie* was staged in New York, the conspicuously unrealistic convention of projecting words on a screen was not used, but the New York production nevertheless was essentially unrealistic, following, for instance, his comment that "The lighting in the play is not realistic. . . . Shafts of light are focused on selected areas or actors . . . The light upon Laura should be distinct from the others, having a peculiar pristine clarity such as light used in early religious portraits of female saints or madonnas." Jo Mielziner, who did the sets for this play and for many of Williams's other plays, makes a helpful comment in *Designing for the Theatre*:

> If he had written plays in the days before the technical development of translucent and transparent scenery, I believe he would have invented it. . . . My use of translucent and transparent scenic interior walls was not just another trick. It was a true reflection of the contemporary playwright's interest in—and at times obsession with—the exploration of the inner man. Williams was writing not only a memory play but a play of influences that were not confined within the walls of a room.

TOPICS FOR DISCUSSION

1. In what ways, if any, is the setting relevant to the issues raised in the play?
2. What does the victrola offer to Laura? Why is the typewriter a better symbol (for the purposes of the play) than, say, a piano? After all, Laura could have been taking piano lessons.
3. What do you make out of Laura's glass menagerie? Why is it especially significant that the unicorn is Laura's favorite? How do you interpret the loss of the unicorn's horn? What is Laura saying to Jim in the gesture of giving him the unicorn?
4. Laura escapes to her glass menagerie. To what do Tom and Amanda escape? How complete do you think Tom's escape is at the end of the play?
5. Jim is described as "a nice, ordinary young man." To what extent can it be said that he, like the Wingfields, lives in a dream world? Tom says (speaking of the time of the play, 1939) that "The huge middle class was matriculating in a school for the blind." Does the play suggest that Jim, apparently a spokesman for the American dream, is one of the pupils in this school?
6. There is an implication that had Jim not been going steady he might have rescued Laura, but Jim also seems to represent (for example in his lines about money and power) the corrupt outside world that no longer values humanity. Is this a slip on Williams's part, or is it an interesting complexity?
7. What do you make out of the episode, at the end, when Laura blows out the candles? Is she blowing out illusions? Or her own life? Or both? Explain.
8. Some readers have seen great importance in the religious references in the play. To cite only a few examples: Scene V is called (on the screen) "Annunciation"; Amanda is associated with the music "Ave Maria"; Laura's candelabrum, from the altar of the Church of Heavenly Rest, was melted out of shape when the church burned down. Do you think these references add up to anything? If so, to what?
9. On page 481 Williams says, in a stage direction, "Now that we cannot hear the mother's speech, her silliness is gone and she has dignity and tragic beauty." Is

Williams simply dragging in the word "tragic" because of its prestige, or is it legitimate? *Tragedy* is often distinguished from *pathos*: in the tragic, the suffering is experienced by persons who act and are in some measure responsible for their suffering; in the pathetic, the suffering is experienced by the passive and the innocent. For example, in discussing *The Suppliants*, a play by the ancient Greek dramatist Aeschylus, H. D. F. Kitto (in *Greek Tragedy*) says, "The Suppliants are not only pathetic, as the victims of outrage, but also tragic, as the victims of their own misconceptions." Given this distinction, to what extent are Amanda and Laura tragic? Pathetic? You might take into account the following quote from an interview with Williams, reprinted in *Conversations with Tennessee Williams* (ed. Albert J. Devlin): "The mother's valor is the *core* of *The Glass Menagerie*. . . . She's confused, pathetic, even stupid, but everything has *got* to be all right. She fights to make it that way in the only way she knows how."

10. Before writing *The Glass Menagerie*, Williams wrote a short story with the same plot, "Portrait of a Girl in Glass" (later published in his *Collected Stories*). You may want to compare the two works, noticing especially the ways in which Williams has turned a story into a play.

DEATH OF A SALESMAN

Certain private conversations in two acts and a requiem

Arthur Miller

Arthur Miller was born in New York in 1915. In 1938 he graduated from the University of Michigan, where he won several prizes for drama. Six years later he had his first Broadway production, *The Man Who Had All the Luck,* but the play was unlucky and closed after four days. By the time of his first commercial success, *All My Sons* (1947), he had already written eight or nine plays. In 1949 he won a Pulitzer prize with *Death of a Salesman* and achieved an international reputation. Among his other works are an adaptation (1950) of Ibsen's *Enemy of the People* and a play about the Salem witch trials, *The Crucible* (1953), both containing political implications, and *The Misfits* (1961, a screenplay), *After the Fall* (1964), and *Incident at Vichy* (1965).

LIST OF CHARACTERS

WILLY LOMAN

LINDA

BIFF

HAPPY

BERNARD

THE WOMAN

CHARLEY

UNCLE BEN

HOWARD WAGNER

JENNY

STANLEY

MISS FORSYTHE

LETTA

The action takes place in WILLY LOMAN's *house and yard and in various places he visits in the New York and Boston of today.*

Throughout the play, in the stage directions, left and right mean stage left and stage right.

Top: *Lee J. Cobb starred as Willy Loman in the 1949 original Broadway produc-tion of* Death of a Salesman. *(Photograph: Eileen Darby; reproduced courtesy of Hoblitzelle Theatre Arts, John Gassner Collection, Humanities Research Center, The University of Texas at Austin.) Bottom: Dustin Hoffman as Willy Loman and John Malkovich as Biff face each other in this scene from the 1984 production. (Photograph: Inge Morath; reproduced by permission of Magnum Photos, Inc.)*

ACT I

A melody is heard, played upon a flute. It is small and fine, telling of grass and trees and the horizon. The curtain rises.

Before us is the Salesman's house. We are aware of towering, angular shapes behind it, surrounding it on all sides. Only the blue light of the sky falls upon the house and forestage; the surrounding area shows an angry glow of orange. As more light appears, we see a solid vault of apartment houses around the small, fragile-seeming home. An air of the dream clings to the place, a dream rising out of reality. The kitchen at center seems actual enough, for there is a kitchen table with three chairs, and a refrigerator. But no other fixtures are seen. At the back of the kitchen there is a draped entrance, which leads to the living room. To the right of the kitchen, on a level raised two feet, is a bedroom furnished only with a brass bedstead and a straight chair. On a shelf over the bed a silver athletic trophy stands. A window opens onto the apartment house at the side.

Behind the kitchen, on a level raised six and a half feet, is the boy's bedroom, at present barely visible. Two beds are dimly seen, and at the back of the room a dormer window. (This bedroom is above the unseen living-room.) At the left a stairway curves up to it from the kitchen.

The entire setting is wholly or, in some places, partially transparent. The roof-line of the house is one-dimensional; under and over it we see the apartment buildings. Before the house lies an apron, curving beyond the forestage into the orchestra. This forward area serves as the back yard as well as the locale of all WILLY's *imagin-*

ings and of his city scenes. Whenever the action is in the present the actors observe the imaginary wall-lines, entering the house only through its door at the left. But in the scenes of the past these boundaries are broken, and characters enter or leave a room by stepping "through" a wall onto the forestage.*

From the right, WILLY LOMAN, *the Salesman, enters, carrying two large sample cases. The flute plays on. He hears but is not aware of it. He is past sixty years of age, dressed quietly. Even as he crosses the stage to the doorway of the house, his exhaustion is apparent. He unlocks the door, comes into the kitchen, and thankfully lets his burden down, feeling the soreness of his palms. A word-sigh escapes his lips—it might be "Oh, boy, oh, boy." He closes the door, then carries his cases out into the livingroom, through the draped kitchen doorway.*

LINDA, *his wife, has stirred in her bed at the right. She gets out and puts on a robe, listening. Most often jovial, she has developed an iron repression of her exceptions to* WILLY's *behavior—she more than loves him, she admires him, as though his mercurial nature, his temper, his massive dreams and little cruelties, served her only as sharp reminders of the turbulent longings within him, longings which she shares but lacks the temperament to utter and follow to their end.*

LINDA (*hearing* WILLY *outside the bedroom, calls with some trepidation*): Willy!

WILLY: It's all right. I came back.

LINDA: Why? What happened? (*Slight pause.*) Did something happen, Willy?

WILLY: No, nothing happened.

LINDA: You didn't smash the car, did you?

WILLY (*with casual irritation*): I said nothing happened. Didn't you hear me?

LINDA: Don't you feel well?

WILLY: I am tired to the death. (*The flute has faded away. He sits on the bed beside her, a little numb.*) I couldn't make it. I just couldn't make it, Linda.

LINDA (*very carefully, delicately*): Where were you all day? You look terrible.

WILLY: I got as far as a little above Yonkers. I stopped for a cup of coffee. Maybe it was the coffee.

LINDA: What?

WILLY (*after a pause*): I suddenly couldn't drive

any more. The car kept going off onto the shoulder, y'know?

LINDA (*helpfully*): Oh. Maybe it was the steering again. I don't think Angelo knows the Studebaker.

WILLY: No, it's me, it's me. Suddenly I realize I'm goin' sixty miles an hour and I don't remember the last five minutes. I'm—I can't seem to—keep my mind to it.

LINDA: Maybe it's your glasses. You never went for your new glasses.

WILLY: No, I see everything. I came back ten miles an hour. It took me nearly four hours from Yonkers.

LINDA (*resigned*): Well, you'll just have to take a rest, Willy, you can't continue this way.

WILLY: I just got back from Florida.

LINDA: But you didn't rest your mind. Your mind is overactive, and the mind is what counts, dear.

WILLY: I'll start out in the morning. Maybe I'll feel better in the morning. (*She is taking off his shoes.*) These goddam arch supports are killing me.

LINDA: Take an aspirin. Should I get you an aspirin? It'll soothe you.

WILLY (*with wonder*): I was driving along, you understand? And I was fine. I was even observing the scenery. You can imagine, me looking at scenery, on the road every week of my life. But it's so beautiful up there, Linda, the trees are so thick, and the sun is warm. I opened the windshield and just let the warm air bathe over me. And then all of a sudden I'm goin' off the road! I'm tellin' ya, I absolutely forgot I was driving. If I'd've gone the other way over the white line I might've killed somebody. So I went on again—and five minutes later I'm dreamin' again, and I nearly—(*He presses two fingers against his eyes.*) I have such thoughts, I have such strange thoughts.

LINDA: Willy, dear. Talk to them again. There's no reason why you can't work in New York.

WILLY: They don't need me in New York. I'm the New England man. I'm vital in New England.

LINDA: But you're sixty years old. They can't expect you to keep traveling every week.

WILLY: I'll have to send a wire to Portland. I'm supposed to see Brown and Morrison tomorrow morning at ten o'clock to show the line. Goddammit, I could sell them! (*He starts putting on his jacket.*)

LINDA (*taking the jacket from him*): Why don't you go down to the place tomorrow and tell Howard you've simply got to work in New York? You're too accommodating, dear.

WILLY: If old man Wagner was alive I'd a been in charge of New York now! That man was a prince, he was a masterful man. But that boy of his, that Howard, he don't appreciate. When I went north the first time, the Wagner Company didn't know where New England was!

LINDA: Why don't you tell those things to Howard, dear?

WILLY (*encouraged*): I will, I definitely will. Is there any cheese?

LINDA: I'll make you a sandwich.

WILLY: No, go to sleep. I'll take some milk. I'll be up right away. The boys in?

LINDA: They're sleeping. Happy took Biff on a date tonight.

WILLY (*interested*): That so?

LINDA: It was so nice to see them shaving together, one behind the other, in the bathroom. And going out together. You notice? The whole house smells of shaving lotion.

WILLY: Figure it out. Work a lifetime to pay off a house. You finally own it, and there's nobody to live in it.

LINDA: Well, dear, life is a casting off. It's always that way.

WILLY: No, no, some people—some people accomplish something. Did Biff say anything after I went this morning?

LINDA: You shouldn't have criticized him, Willy, especially after he just got off the train. You mustn't lose your temper with him.

WILLY: When the hell did I lose my temper? I simply asked him if he was making any money. Is that a criticism?

LINDA: But, dear, how could he make any money?

WILLY (*worried and angered*): There's such an undercurrent in him. He became a moody man. Did he apologize when I left this morning?

LINDA: He was crestfallen, Willy. You know how he admires you. I think if he finds himself, then you'll both be happier and not fight any more.

WILLY: How can he find himself on a farm? Is that a life? A farmhand? In the beginning, when he was young, I thought, well, a young man, it's good for him to tramp around, take a lot of different jobs. But it's more than ten years now and he has yet to make thirty-five dollars a week!

LINDA: He's finding himself, Willy.

WILLY: Not finding yourself at the age of thirty-four is a disgrace!

LINDA: Shh!

WILLY: The trouble is he's lazy, goddammit!

LINDA: Willy, please!

WILLY: Biff is a lazy bum!

LINDA: They're sleeping. Get something to eat. Go on down.

WILLY: Why did he come home? I would like to know what brought him home.

LINDA: I don't know. I think he's still lost, Willy. I think he's very lost.

WILLY: Biff Loman is lost. In the greatest country in the world a young man with such—personal attractiveness, gets lost. And such a hard worker. There's one thing about Biff—he's not lazy.

LINDA: Never.

WILLY (with pity and resolve): I'll see him in the morning; I'll have a nice talk with him. I'll get him a job selling. He could be big in no time. My God! Remember how they used to follow him around in high school? When he smiled at one of them their faces lit up. When he walked down the street . . . (He loses himself in reminiscences.)

LINDA (trying to bring him out of it): Willy, dear, I got a new kind of American-type cheese today. It's whipped.

WILLY: Why do you get American when I like Swiss?

LINDA: I just thought you'd like a change—

WILLY: I don't want a change! I want Swiss cheese. Why am I always being contradicted?

LINDA (with a covering laugh): I thought it would be a surprise.

WILLY: Why don't you open a window in here, for God's sake?

LINDA (with infinite patience): They're all open, dear.

WILLY: The way they boxed us in here. Bricks and windows, windows and bricks.

LINDA: We should've bought the land next door.

WILLY: The street is lined with cars. There's not a breath of fresh air in the neighborhood. The grass don't grow any more, you can't raise a carrot in the back yard. They should've had a law against apartment houses. Remember those two beautiful elm trees out there? When I and Biff hung the swing between them?

LINDA: Yeah, like being a million miles from the city.

WILLY: They should've arrested the builder for cutting those down. They massacred the neighborhood. (Lost) More and more I think of those days, Linda. This time of year it was lilac and wisteria. And then the peonies would come out, and the daffodils. What fragrance in this room!

LINDA: Well, after all, people had to move somewhere.

WILLY: No, there's more people now.

LINDA: I don't think there's more people. I think—

WILLY: There's more people! That's what's ruining this country! Population is getting out of control. The competition is maddening! Smell the stink from that apartment house! And another one on the other side . . . How can they whip cheese?

(On WILLY's last line, BIFF and HAPPY raise themselves up in their beds, listening.)

LINDA: Go down, try it. And be quiet.

WILLY (turning to LINDA, guiltily): You're not worried about me, are you, sweetheart?

BIFF: What's the matter?

HAPPY: Listen!

LINDA: You've got too much on the ball to worry about.

WILLY: You're my foundation and my support, Linda.

LINDA: Just try to relax, dear. You make mountains out of molehills.

WILLY: I won't fight with him any more. If he wants to go back to Texas, let him go.

LINDA: He'll find his way.

WILLY: Sure. Certain men just don't get started till later in life. Like Thomas Edison, I think. Or B. F. Goodrich. One of them was deaf. (He starts for the bedroom doorway.) I'll put my money on Biff.

LINDA: And Willy—if it's warm Sunday we'll drive in the country. And we'll open the windshield, and take lunch.

WILLY: No, the windshields don't open on the new cars.

LINDA: But you opened it today.

WILLY: Me? I didn't. (He stops.) Now isn't that peculiar! Isn't that a remarkable—(He breaks off in amazement and fright as the flute is heard distantly.)

LINDA: What, darling?

WILLY: That is the most remarkable thing.

LINDA: What, dear?

WILLY: I was thinking of the Chevvy. (Slight pause.) Nineteen twenty-eight . . . when I had that red Chevvy—(Breaks off.) That funny? I coulda sworn I was driving that Chevvy today.

LINDA: Well, that's nothing. Something must've reminded you.

WILLY: Remarkable. Ts. Remember those days? The way Biff used to simonize that car? The dealer refused to believe there was eighty thousand miles on it. (*He shakes his head.*) Heh! (*To* LINDA.) Close your eyes, I'll be right up. (*He walks out of the bedroom.*)

HAPPY (*to* BIFF): Jesus, maybe he smashed up the car again!

LINDA (*calling after* WILLY): Be careful on the stairs, dear! The cheese is on the middle shelf! (*She turns, goes over to the bed, takes his jacket, and goes out of the bedroom.*)

(*Light has risen on the boys' room. Unseen, WILLY is heard talking to himself, "Eighty thousand miles," and a little laugh. BIFF gets out of bed, comes downstage a bit, and stands attentively. BIFF is two years older than his brother HAPPY, well built, but in these days bears a worn air and seems less self-assured. He has succeeded less, and his dreams are stronger and less acceptable than HAPPY's. HAPPY is tall, powerfully made. Sexuality is like a visible color on him, or a scent that many women have discovered. He, like his brother, is lost, but in a different way, for he has never allowed himself to turn his face toward defeat and is thus more confused and hard-skinned, although seemingly more content.*)

HAPPY (*getting out of bed*): He's going to get his license taken away if he keeps that up. I'm getting nervous about him, y'know, Biff?

BIFF: His eyes are going.

HAPPY: No, I've driven with him. He sees all right. He just doesn't keep his mind on it. I drove into the city with him last week. He stops at a green light and then it turns red and he goes. (*He laughs.*)

BIFF: Maybe he's color-blind.

HAPPY: Pop? Why he's got the finest eye for color in the business. You know that.

BIFF (*sitting down on his bed*): I'm going to sleep.

HAPPY: You're not still sour on Dad, are you, Biff?

BIFF: He's all right, I guess.

WILLY (*underneath them, in the living room*): Yes, sir, eighty thousand miles—eighty-two thousand!

BIFF: You smoking?

HAPPY (*holding out a pack of cigarettes*): Want one?

BIFF (*taking a cigarette*): I can never sleep when I smell it.

WILLY: What a simonizing job, heh!

HAPPY (*with deep sentiment*): Funny, Biff, y'know? Us sleeping in here again? The old beds.

(*He pats his bed affectionately.*) All the talk that went across those two beds, huh? Our whole lives.

BIFF: Yeah. Lotta dreams and plans.

HAPPY (*with a deep and masculine laugh*): About five hundred women would like to know what was said in this room.

(*They share a soft laugh.*)

BIFF: Remember that big Betsy something—what the hell was her name—over on Bushwick Avenue?

HAPPY (*combing his hair*): With the collie dog!

BIFF: That's the one. I got you in there, remember?

HAPPY: Yeah, that was my first time—I think. Boy, there was a pig! (*They laugh, almost crudely.*) You taught me everything I know about women. Don't forget that.

BIFF: I bet you forgot how bashful you used to be. Especially with girls.

HAPPY: Oh, I still am, Biff.

BIFF: Oh, go on.

HAPPY: I just control it, that's all. I think I got less bashful and you got more so. What happened, Biff? Where's the old humor, the old confidence? (*He shakes* BIFF's *knee.* BIFF *gets up and moves restlessly about the room.*) What's the matter?

BIFF: Why does Dad mock me all the time?

HAPPY: He's not mocking you, he—

BIFF: Everything I say there's a twist of mockery on his face. I can't get near him.

HAPPY: He just wants you to make good, that's all. I wanted to talk to you about Dad for a long time, Biff. Something's—happening to him. He—talks to himself.

BIFF: I noticed that this morning. But he always mumbled.

HAPPY: But not so noticeable. It got so embarrassing I sent him to Florida. And you know something? Most of the time he's talking to you.

BIFF: What's he say about me?

HAPPY: I can't make it out.

BIFF: What's he say about me?

HAPPY: I think the fact that you're not settled, that you're still kind of up in the air . . .

BIFF: There's one or two other things depressing him, Happy.

HAPPY: What do you mean?

BIFF: Never mind. Just don't lay it all to me.

HAPPY: But I think if you just got started—I mean—is there any future for you out there?

BIFF: I tell ya, Hap, I don't know what the future is. I don't know—what I'm supposed to want.

HAPPY: What do you mean?

BIFF: Well, I spent six or seven years after high school trying to work myself up. Shipping clerk, salesman, business of one kind or another. And it's a measly manner of existence. To get on that subway on the hot mornings in summer. To devote your whole life to keeping stock, or making phone calls, or selling or buying. To suffer fifty weeks of the year for the sake of a two-week vacation, when all you really desire is to be outdoors, with your shirt off. And always to have to get ahead of the next fella. And still—that's how you build a future.

HAPPY: Well, you really enjoy it on a farm? Are you content out there?

BIFF (*with rising agitation*): Hap, I've had twenty or thirty different kinds of jobs since I left home before the war, and it always turns out the same. I just realized it lately. In Nebraska when I herded cattle, and the Dakotas, and Arizona, and now in Texas. It's why I came home now, I guess, because I realized it. This farm I work on, it's spring there now, see? And they've got about fifteen new colts. There's nothing more inspiring or—beautiful than the sight of a mare and a new colt. And it's cool there now, see? Texas is cool now, and it's spring. And whenever spring comes to where I am, I suddenly get the feeling, my God, I'm not gettin' anywhere! What the hell am I doing, playing around with horses, twenty-eight dollars a week! I'm thirty-four years old, I oughta be makin' my future. That's when I come running home. And now, I get here, and I don't know what to do with myself. (*After a pause.*) I've always made a point of not wasting my life, and every time I come back here I know that all I've done is to waste my life.

HAPPY: You're a poet, you know that, Biff? You're a—you're an idealist!

BIFF: No, I'm mixed up very bad. Maybe I oughta get married. Maybe I oughta get stuck into something. Maybe that's my trouble. I'm like a boy. I'm not married, I'm not in business, I just— I'm like a boy. Are you content, Hap? You're a success, aren't you? Are you content?

HAPPY: Hell, no!

BIFF: Why? You're making money, aren't you?

HAPPY (*moving about with energy, expressiveness*): All I can do now is wait for the merchandise manager to die. And suppose I get to be merchandise manager? He's a good friend of mine, and he just built a terrific estate on Long Island. And he lived there about two months and sold it, and now he's building another one. He can't enjoy it once it's finished. And I know that's just what I would

do. I don't know what the hell I'm workin' for. Sometimes I sit in my apartment—all alone. And I think of the rent I'm paying. And it's crazy. But then, it's what I always wanted. My own apartment, a car, and plenty of women. And still, goddammit, I'm lonely.

BIFF (*with enthusiasm*): Listen, why don't you come out West with me?

HAPPY: You and I, heh?

BIFF: Sure, maybe we could buy a ranch. Raise cattle, use our muscles. Men built like we are should be working out in the open.

HAPPY (*avidly*): The Loman Brothers, heh?

BIFF (*with vast affection*): Sure, we'd be known all over the counties!

HAPPY (*enthralled*): That's what I dream about, Biff. Sometimes I want to just rip my clothes off in the middle of the store and outbox that goddam merchandise manager. I mean I can outbox, outrun, and outlift anybody in that store, and I have to take orders from those common, petty sons-of-bitches till I can't stand it any more.

BIFF: I'm tellin' you, kid, if you were with me I'd be happy out there.

HAPPY (*enthused*): See, Biff, everybody around me is so false that I'm constantly lowering my ideals . . .

BIFF: Baby, together we'd stand up for one another, we'd have someone to trust.

HAPPY: If I were around you—

BIFF: Hap, the trouble is we weren't brought up to grub for money. I don't know how to do it.

HAPPY: Neither can I!

BIFF: Then let's go!

HAPPY: The only thing is—what can you make out there?

BIFF: But look at your friend. Builds an estate and then hasn't the peace of mind to live in it.

HAPPY: Yeah, but when he walks into the store the waves part in front of him. That's fifty-two thousand dollars a year coming through the revolving door, and I got more in my pinky finger than he's got in his head.

BIFF: Yeah, but you just said—

HAPPY: I gotta show some of those pompous, self-important executives over there that Hap Loman can make the grade. I want to walk into the store the way he walks in. Then I'll go with you, Biff. We'll be together yet, I swear. But take those two we had tonight. Now weren't they gorgeous creatures?

BIFF: Yeah, yeah, most gorgeous I've had in years.

HAPPY: I get that any time I want, Biff. Whenever I feel disgusted. The only trouble is, it gets like bowling or something. I just keep knockin' them over and it doesn't mean anything. You still run around a lot?

BIFF: Naa. I'd like to find a girl—steady, somebody with substance.

HAPPY: That's what I long for.

BIFF: Go on! You'd never come home.

HAPPY: I would! Somebody with character, with resistance! Like Mom, y'know? You're gonna call me a bastard when I tell you this. That girl Charlotte I was with tonight is engaged to be married in five weeks. (*He tries on his new hat.*)

BIFF: No kiddin'!

HAPPY: Sure, the guy's in line for the vice-presidency of the store. I don't know what gets into me, maybe I just have an overdeveloped sense of competition or something, but I went and ruined her, and furthermore I can't get rid of her. And he's the third executive I've done that to. Isn't that a crummy characteristic? And to top it all, I go to their weddings! (*Indignantly, but laughing*) Like I'm not supposed to take bribes. Manufacturers offer me a hundred-dollar bill now and then to throw an order their way. You know how honest I am, but it's like this girl, see. I hate myself for it. Because I don't want the girl, and, still, I take it and—I love it!

BIFF: Let's go to sleep.

HAPPY: I guess we didn't settle anything, heh?

BIFF: I just got one idea that I think I'm going to try.

HAPPY: What's that?

BIFF: Remember Bill Oliver?

HAPPY: Sure, Oliver is very big now. You want to work for him again?

BIFF: No, but when I quit he said something to me. He put his arm on my shoulder, and he said, "Biff, if you ever need anything, come to me."

HAPPY: I remember that. That sounds good.

BIFF: I think I'll go to see him. If I could get ten thousand or even seven or eight thousand dollars I could buy a beautiful ranch.

HAPPY: I bet he'd back you. 'Cause he thought highly of you, Biff. I mean, they all do. You're well liked, Biff. That's why I say to come back here, and we both have the apartment. And I'm tellin' you, Biff, any babe you want . . .

BIFF: No, with a ranch I could do the work I like and still be something. I just wonder though. I wonder if Oliver still thinks I stole that carton of basketballs.

HAPPY: Oh, he probably forgot that long ago. It's

almost ten years. You're too sensitive. Anyway, he didn't really fire you.

BIFF: Well, I think he was going to. I think that's why I quit. I was never sure whether he knew or not. I know he thought the world of me, though. I was the only one he'd let lock up the place.

WILLY (*below*): You gonna wash the engine, Biff?

HAPPY: Shh!

(BIFF *looks at* HAPPY, *who is gazing down, listening.* WILLY *is mumbling in the parlor.*)

HAPPY: You hear that?

(*They listen.* WILLY *laughs warmly.*)

BIFF (*growing angry*): Doesn't he know Mom can hear that?

WILLY: Don't get your sweater dirty, Biff!

(*A look of pain crosses* BIFF's *face.*)

HAPPY: Isn't that terrible? Don't leave again, will you? You'll find a job here. You gotta stick around. I don't know what to do about him, it's getting embarrassing.

WILLY: What a simonizing job!

BIFF: Mom's hearing that!

WILLY: No kiddin', Biff, you got a date? Wonderful!

HAPPY: Go on to sleep. But talk to him in the morning, will you?

BIFF (*reluctantly getting into bed*): With her in the house. Brother!

HAPPY (*getting into bed*): I wish you'd have a good talk with him.

(*The light on their room begins to fade.*)

BIFF (*to himself in bed*): That selfish, stupid . . .

HAPPY: Sh . . . Sleep, Biff.

(*Their light is out. Well before they have finished speaking,* WILLY's *form is dimly seen below in the darkened kitchen. He opens the refrigerator, searches in there, and takes out a bottle of milk. The apartment houses are fading out, and the entire house and surroundings become covered with leaves. Music insinuates itself as the leaves appear.*)

WILLY: Just wanna be careful with those girls, Biff, that's all. Don't make any promises. No promises of any kind. Because a girl, y'know, they always believe what you tell 'em, and you're very young, Biff, you're too young to be talking seriously to girls.

(*Light rises on the kitchen.* WILLY, *talking, shuts the refrigerator door and comes downstage to the kitchen table. He pours milk into a glass. He is totally immersed in himself, smiling faintly.*)

WILLY: Too young entirely, Biff. You want to watch your schooling first. Then when you're all set, there'll be plenty of girls for a boy like you. (*He smiles broadly at a kitchen chair.*) That so? The girls pay for you? (*He laughs.*) Boy, you must really be makin' a hit.

(WILLY *is gradually addressing—physically—a point offstage, speaking through the wall of the kitchen, and his voice has been rising in volume to that of a normal conversation.*)

WILLY: I been wondering why you polish the car so careful. Ha! Don't leave the hubcaps, boys. Get the chamois to the hubcaps. Happy, use newspaper on the windows, it's the easiest thing. Show him how to do it, Biff! You see, Happy? Pad it up, use it like a pad. That's it, that's it, good work. You're doin' all right, Hap. (*He pauses, then nods in approbation for a few seconds, then looks upward.*) Biff, first thing we gotta do when we get time is clip that big branch over the house. Afraid it's gonna fall in a storm and hit the roof. Tell you what. We get a rope and sling her around, and then we climb up there with a couple of saws and take her down. Soon as you finish the car, boys, I wanna see ya. I got a surprise for you, boys.

BIFF (*offstage*): Whatta ya got, Dad?

WILLY: No, you finish first. Never leave a job till you're finished—remember that. (*Looking toward the "big trees"*) Biff, up in Albany I saw a beautiful hammock. I think I'll buy it next trip, and we'll hang it right between those two elms. Wouldn't that be something? Just swingin' there under those branches. Boy, that would be . . .

(YOUNG BIFF *and* YOUNG HAPPY *appear from the direction* WILLY *was addressing.* HAPPY *carries rags and a pail of water.* BIFF, *wearing a sweater with a block "S," carries a football.*)

BIFF (*pointing in the direction of the car offstage*): How's that, Pop, professional?

WILLY: Terrific. Terrific job, boys. Good work, Biff.

HAPPY: Where's the surprise, Pop?

WILLY: In the back seat of the car.

HAPPY: Boy! (*He runs off.*)

BIFF: What is it, Dad? Tell me, what'd you buy?

WILLY (*laughing, cuffs him*): Never mind, something I want you to have.

BIFF (*turns and starts off*): What is it, Hap?

HAPPY (*offstage*): It's a punching bag!

BIFF: Oh, Pop!

WILLY: It's got Gene Tunney's signature on it!

(HAPPY *runs onstage with a punching bag.*)

BIFF: Gee, how'd you know we wanted a punching bag?

WILLY: Well, it's the finest thing for the timing.

HAPPY (*lies down on his back and pedals with his feet*): I'm losing weight, you notice, Pop?

WILLY (*to* HAPPY): Jumping rope is good too.

BIFF: Did you see the new football I got?

WILLY (*examining the ball*): Where'd you get a new ball?

BIFF: The coach told me to practice my passing.

WILLY: That so? And he gave you the ball, heh?

BIFF: Well, I borrowed it from the locker room. (*He laughs confidentially.*)

WILLY (*laughing with him at the theft*): I want you to return that.

HAPPY: I told you he wouldn't like it!

BIFF (*angrily*): Well, I'm bringing it back!

WILLY (*stopping the incipient argument, to* HAPPY): Sure, he's gotta practice with a regulation ball, doesn't he? (*To* BIFF) Coach'll probably congratulate you on your initiative!

BIFF: Oh, he keeps congratulating my initiative all the time, Pop.

WILLY: That's because he likes you. If somebody else took that ball there'd be an uproar. So what's the report, boys, what's the report?

BIFF: Where'd you go this time, Dad? Gee we were lonesome for you.

WILLY (*pleased, puts an arm around each boy and they come down to the apron*): Lonesome, heh?

BIFF: Missed you every minute.

WILLY: Don't say? Tell you a secret, boys. Don't breathe it to a soul. Someday I'll have my own business, and I'll never have to leave home any more.

HAPPY: Like Uncle Charley, heh?

WILLY: Bigger than Uncle Charley! Because Charley is not—liked. He's liked, but he's not—well liked.

BIFF: Where'd you go this time, Dad?

WILLY: Well, I got on the road, and I went north to Providence. Met the Mayor.

BIFF: The Mayor of Providence!

WILLY: He was sitting in the hotel lobby.

BIFF: What'd he say?

WILLY: He said, "Morning!" And I said, "You got a fine city here, Mayor." And then he had coffee with me. And then I went to Waterbury. Waterbury is a fine city. Big clock city, the famous Waterbury clock. Sold a nice bill there. And then Boston—Boston is the cradle of the Revolution. A fine city. And a couple of other towns in Mass., and on to Portland and Bangor and straight home!

BIFF: Gee, I'd love to go with you sometime, Dad.

WILLY: Soon as summer comes.

HAPPY: Promise?

WILLY: You and Hap and I, and I'll show you all the towns. America is full of beautiful towns and fine, upstanding people. And they know me, boys, they know me up and down New England. The finest people. And when I bring you fellas up, there'll be open sesame for all of us, 'cause one thing, boys: I have friends. I can park my car in any street in New England, and the cops protect it like their own. This summer, heh?

BIFF AND HAPPY (together): Yeah! You bet!

WILLY: We'll take our bathing suits.

HAPPY: We'll carry your bags, Pop!

WILLY: Oh, won't that be something! Me comin' into the Boston stores with you boys carryin' my bags. What a sensation!

(BIFF is prancing around, practicing passing the ball.)

WILLY: You nervous, Biff, about the game?

BIFF: Not if you're gonna be there.

WILLY: What do they say about you in school, now that they made you captain?

HAPPY: There's a crowd of girls behind him every time the classes change.

BIFF (taking WILLY's hand): This Saturday, Pop, this Saturday—just for you, I'm going to break through for a touchdown.

HAPPY: You're supposed to pass.

BIFF: I'm takin' one play for Pop. You watch me, Pop, and when I take off my helmet, that means I'm breakin' out. Then you watch me crash through that line!

WILLY (kisses BIFF): Oh, wait'll I tell this in Boston!

(BERNARD enters in knickers. He is younger than BIFF, earnest and loyal, a worried boy.)

BERNARD: Biff, where are you? You're supposed to study with me today.

WILLY: Hey, looka Bernard. What're you lookin' so anemic about, Bernard?

BERNARD: He's gotta study, Uncle Willy. He's got Regents next week.

HAPPY (tauntingly, spinning BERNARD around): Let's box, Bernard!

BERNARD: Biff! (He gets away from HAPPY.) Listen, Biff, I heard Mr. Birnbaum say that if you don't start studyin' math he's gonna flunk you, and you won't graduate. I heard him!

WILLY: You better study with him, Biff. Go ahead now.

BERNARD: I heard him!

BIFF: Oh, Pop, you didn't see my sneakers! (He holds up a foot for WILLY to look at.)

WILLY: Hey, that's a beautiful job of printing!

BERNARD (wiping his glasses): Just because he printed University of Virginia on his sneakers doesn't mean they've got to graduate him, Uncle Willy!

WILLY (angrily): What're you talking about? With scholarships to three universities they're gonna flunk him?

BERNARD: But I heard Mr. Birnbaum say—

WILLY: Don't be a pest, Bernard! (To his boys) Whan an anemic!

BERNARD: Okay, I'm waiting for you in my house, Biff.

(Bernard goes off. THE LOMANS laugh.)

WILLY: Bernard is not well liked, is he?

BIFF: He's liked, but he's not well liked.

HAPPY: That's right, Pop.

WILLY: That's just what I mean. Bernard can get the best marks in school, y'understand, but when he gets out in the business world, y'understand, you are going to be five times ahead of him. That's why I thank Almighty God you're both built like Adonises. Because the man who makes an appearance in the business world, the man who creates personal interest, is the man who gets ahead. Be liked and you will never want. You take me, for instance. I never have to wait in line to see a buyer. "Willy Loman is here!" That's all they have to know, and I go right through.

BIFF: Did you knock them dead, Pop?

WILLY: Knocked 'em cold in Providence, slaughtered 'em in Boston.

HAPPY (on his back, pedaling again): I'm losing weight, you notice, Pop?

(LINDA enters, as of old, a ribbon in her hair, carrying a basket of washing.)

LINDA (with youthful energy): Hello, dear!

WILLY: Sweetheart!

LINDA: How'd the Chevvy run?

WILLY: Chevrolet, Linda, is the greatest car ever

built. (*To the boys*) Since when do you let your mother carry wash up the stairs?

BIFF: Grab hold there, boy!

HAPPY: Where to, Mom?

LINDA: Hang them up on the line. And you better go down to your friends, Biff. The cellar is full of boys. They don't know what to do with themselves.

BIFF: Ah, when Pop comes home they can wait!

WILLY (*laughs appreciatively*): You better go down and tell them what to do, Biff.

BIFF: I think I'll have them sweep out the furnace room.

WILLY: Good work, Biff.

BIFF (*goes through wall-line of kitchen to doorway at back and calls down*): Fellas! Everybody sweep out the furnace room! I'll be right down!

VOICES: All right! Okay, Biff.

BIFF: George and Sam and Frank, come out back! We're hangin' up the wash! Come on, Hap, on the double! (*He and HAPPY carry out the basket.*)

LINDA: The way they obey him!

WILLY: Well, that's training, the training. I'm tellin' you, I was sellin' thousands and thousands, but I had to come home.

LINDA: Oh, the whole block'll be at that game. Did you sell anything?

WILLY: I did five hundred gross in Providence and seven hundred gross in Boston.

LINDA: No! Wait a minute, I've got a pencil. (*She pulls pencil and paper out of her apron pocket.*) That makes your commission . . . Two hundred—my God! Two hundred and twelve dollars!

WILLY: Well, I didn't figure it yet, but . . .

LINDA: How much did you do?

WILLY: Well, I—I did—abouta hundred and eighty gross in Providence. Well, no—it came to—roughly two hundred gross on the whole trip.

LINDA (*without hesitation*): Two hundred gross. That's . . . (*She figures.*)

WILLY: The trouble was that three of the stores were half closed for inventory in Boston. Otherwise I woulda broke records.

LINDA: Well, it makes seventy dollars and some pennies. That's very good.

WILLY: What do we owe?

LINDA: Well, on the first there's sixteen dollars on the refrigerator—

WILLY: Why sixteen?

LINDA: Well, the fan belt broke, so it was a dollar eighty.

WILLY: But it's brand new.

LINDA: Well, the man said that's the way it is. Till they work themselves in, y'know.

(*They move through the wall-line into the kitchen.*)

WILLY: I hope we didn't get stuck on that machine.

LINDA: They got the biggest ads of any of them!

WILLY: I know, it's a fine machine. What else?

LINDA: Well, there's nine-sixty for the washing machine. And for the vacuum cleaner there's three and a half due on the fifteenth. Then the roof, you got twenty-one dollars remaining.

WILLY: It don't leak, does it?

LINDA: No, they did a wonderful job. Then you owe Frank for the carburetor.

WILLY: I'm not going to pay that man! That goddam Chevrolet, they ought to prohibit the manufacture of that car!

LINDA: Well, you owe him three and a half. And odds and ends, comes to around a hundred and twenty dollars by the fifteenth.

WILLY: A hundred and twenty dollars! My God, if business don't pick up I don't know what I'm gonna do!

LINDA: Well, next week you'll do better.

WILLY: Oh, I'll knock 'em dead next week. I'll go to Hartford. I'm very well liked in Hartford. You know, the trouble is, Linda, people don't seem to take to me.

(*They move onto the forestage.*)

LINDA: Oh, don't be foolish.

WILLY: I know it when I walk in. They seem to laugh at me.

LINDA: Why? Why would they laugh at you? Don't talk that way, Willy.

(*WILLY moves to the edge of the stage.* LINDA *goes into the kitchen and starts to darn stockings.*)

WILLY: I don't know the reason for it, but they just pass me by. I'm not noticed.

LINDA: But you're doing wonderful, dear. You're making seventy to a hundred dollars a week.

WILLY: But I gotta be at it ten, twelve hours a day. Other men—I don't know—they do it easier. I don't know why—I can't stop myself—I talk too much. A man oughta come in with a few words. One thing about Charley. He's a man of few words, and they respect him.

LINDA: You don't talk too much, you're just lively.

WILLY (*smiling*): Well, I figure, what the hell,

life is short, a couple of jokes. (*To himself*) I joke too much! (*The smiles goes.*)

LINDA: Why? You're—

WILLY: I'm fat. I'm very—foolish to look at, Linda. I didn't tell you, but Christmas time I happened to be calling on F. H. Stewarts, and a salesman I know, as I was going in to see the buyer I heard him say something about—walrus. And I—I cracked him right across the face. I won't take that. I simply will not take that. But they do laugh at me. I know that.

LINDA: Darling . . .

WILLY: I gotta overcome it. I know I gotta overcome it. I'm not dressing to advantage, maybe.

LINDA: Willy, darling, you're the handsomest man in the world—

WILLY: Oh, no, Linda.

LINDA: To me you are. (*Slight pause.*) The handsomest.

(*From the darkness is heard the laughter of a woman.* WILLY *doesn't turn to it, but it continues through* LINDA'*s lines.*)

LINDA: And the boys, Willy. Few men are idolized by their children the way you are.

(*Music is heard as behind a scrim, to the left of the house,* THE WOMAN, *dimly seen, is dressing.*)

WILLY (*with great feeling*): You're the best there is, Linda, you're a pal, you know that? On the road—on the road I want to grab you sometimes and just kiss the life outa you.

(*The laughter is loud now, and he moves into a brightening area at the left, where* THE WOMAN *has come from behind the scrim and is standing, putting on her hat, looking into a "mirror" and laughing.*)

WILLY: 'Cause I get so lonely—especially when business is bad and there's nobody to talk to. I get the feeling that I'll never sell anything again, that I won't make a living for you, or a business, a business for the boys. (*He talks through* THE WOMAN'*s subsiding laughter;* THE WOMAN *primps at the "mirror."*) There's so much I want to make for—

THE WOMAN: Me? You didn't make me, Willy. I picked you.

WILLY (*pleased*): You picked me?

THE WOMAN (*who is quite proper-looking,* WILLY'*s age*): I did. I've been sitting at that desk watching all the salesmen go by, day in, day out.

But you've got such a sense of humor, and we do have such a good time together, don't we?

WILLY: Sure, sure. (*He takes her in his arms.*) Why do you have to go now?

THE WOMAN: It's two o'clock . . .

WILLY: No, come on in! (*He pulls her.*)

THE WOMAN: . . . my sisters'll be scandalized. When'll you be back?

WILLY: Oh, two weeks about. Will you come up again?

THE WOMAN: Sure thing. You do make me laugh. It's good for me. (*She squeezes his arm, kisses him.*) And I think you're a wonderful man.

WILLY: You picked me, heh?

THE WOMAN: Sure. Because you're so sweet. And such a kidder.

WILLY: Well, I'll see you next time I'm in Boston.

THE WOMAN: I'll put you right through to the buyers.

WILLY (*slapping her bottom*): Right. Well, bottoms up!

THE WOMAN (*slaps him gently and laughs*): You just kill me, Willy. (*He suddenly grabs her and kisses her roughly.*) You kill me. And thanks for the stockings. I love a lot of stockings. Well, good night.

WILLY: Good night. And keep your pores open!

THE WOMAN: Oh, Willy!

(THE WOMAN *bursts out laughing, and* LINDA'*s laughter blends in.* THE WOMAN *disappears into the dark. Now the area at the kitchen table brightens.* LINDA *is sitting where she was at the kitchen table, but now is mending a pair of her silk stockings.*)

LINDA: You are, Willy. The handsomest man. You've got no reason to feel that—

WILLY (*coming out of* THE WOMAN'*s dimming area and going over to* LINDA): I'll make it all up to you, Linda, I'll—

LINDA: There's nothing to make up, dear. You're doing fine, better than—

WILLY (*noticing her mending*): What's that?

LINDA: Just mending my stockings. They're so expensive—

WILLY (*angrily, taking them from her*): I won't have you mending stockings in this house! Now throw them out!

(LINDA *puts the stockings in her pocket.*)

BERNARD (*entering on the run*): Where is he? If he doesn't study!

WILLY (*moving to the forestage, with great agitation*): You'll give him the answers!

BERNARD: I do, but I can't on a Regents! That's a state exam! They're liable to arrest me!

WILLY: Where is he? I'll whip him, I'll whip him!

LINDA: And he'd better give back that football, Willy, it's not nice.

WILLY: Biff! Where is he? Why is he taking everything?

LINDA: He's too rough with the girls, Willy. All the mothers are afraid of him!

WILLY: I'll whip him!

BERNARD: He's driving the car without a license!

(THE WOMAN's *laugh is heard.*)

WILLY: Shut up!

LINDA: All the mothers—

WILLY: Shut up!

BERNARD (*backing quietly away and out*): Mr. Birnbaum says he's stuck up.

WILLY: Get outa here!

BERNARD: If he doesn't buckle down he'll flunk math! (*He goes off.*)

LINDA: He's right, Willy, you've gotta—

WILLY (*exploding at her*): There's nothing the matter with him! You want him to be a worm like Bernard? He's got spirit, personality . . .

(As *he speaks,* LINDA, *almost in tears, exits into the living room.* WILLY *is alone in the kitchen, wilting and staring. The leaves are gone. It is night again, and the apartment houses look down from behind.*)

WILLY: Loaded with it. Loaded! What is he stealing? He's giving it back, isn't he? Why is he stealing? What did I tell him? I never in my life told him anything but decent things.

(HAPPY *in pajamas has come down the stairs;* WILLY *suddenly becomes aware of* HAPPY's *presence.*)

HAPPY: Let's go now, come on.

WILLY (*sitting down at the kitchen table*): Huh! Why did she have to wax the floors herself? Everytime she waxes the floors she keels over. She knows that!

HAPPY: Shh! Take it easy. What brought you back tonight?

WILLY: I got an awful scare. Nearly hit a kid in Yonkers. God! Why didn't I go to Alaska with my brother Ben that time! Ben! That man was a genius, that man was success incarnate! What a mistake! He begged me to go.

HAPPY: Well, there's no use in—

WILLY: You guys! There was a man started with the clothes on his back and ended up with diamond mines!

HAPPY: Boy, someday I'd like to know how he did it.

WILLY: What's the mystery? The man knew what he wanted and went out and got it! Walked into a jungle, and comes out, the age of twenty-one, and he's rich! The world is an oyster, but you don't crack it open on a mattress!

HAPPY: Pop, I told you I'm gonna retire you for life.

WILLY: You'll retire me for life on seventy goddam dollars a week? And your women and your car and your apartment, and you'll retire me for life! Christ's sake, I couldn't get past Yonkers today! Where are you guys, where are you? The woods are burning! I can't drive a car!

(CHARLEY *has appeared in the doorway. He is a large man, slow of speech, laconic, immovable. In all he says, despite what he says, there is pity, and, now, trepidation. He has a robe over pajamas, slippers on his feet. He enters the kitchen.*)

CHARLEY: Everything all right?

HAPPY: Yeah, Charley, everything's . . .

WILLY: What's the matter?

CHARLEY: I heard some noise. I thought something happened. Can't we do something about the walls? You sneeze in here, and in my house hats blow off.

HAPPY: Let's go to bed, Dad. Come on.

(CHARLEY *signals to* HAPPY *to go.*)

WILLY: You go ahead, I'm not tired at the moment.

HAPPY (*to* WILLY): Take it easy, huh? (*He exits.*)

WILLY: What're you doin' up?

CHARLEY (*sitting down at the kitchen table opposite* WILLY): Couldn't sleep good. I had a heartburn.

WILLY: Well, you don't know how to eat.

CHARLEY: I eat with my mouth.

WILLY: No, you're ignorant. You gotta know about vitamins and things like that.

CHARLEY: Come on, let's shoot. Tire you out a little.

WILLY (*hesitantly*): All right. You got cards?

CHARLEY (*taking a deck from his pocket*): Yeah, I got them. Someplace. What is it with those vitamins?

WILLY (*dealing*): They build up your bones. Chemistry.

CHARLEY: Yeah, but there's no bones in a heartburn.

WILLY: What are you talkin' about? Do you know the first thing about it?

CHARLEY: Don't get insulted.

WILLY: Don't talk about something you don't know anything about.

(*They are playing. Pause.*)

CHARLEY: What're you doin' home?

WILLY: A little trouble with the car.

CHARLEY: Oh. (*Pause.*) I'd like to take a trip to California.

WILLY: Don't say.

CHARLEY: You want a job?

WILLY: I got a job, I told you that. (*After a slight pause*) What the hell are you offering me a job for?

CHARLEY: Don't get insulted.

WILLY: Don't insult me.

CHARLEY: I don't see no sense in it. You don't have to go on this way.

WILLY: I got a good job. (*Slight pause.*) What do you keep comin' in here for?

CHARLEY: You want me to go?

WILLY (*after a pause, withering*): I can't understand it. He's going back to Texas again. What the hell is that?

CHARLEY: Let him go.

WILLY: I got nothin' to give him, Charley, I'm clean, I'm clean.

CHARLEY: He won't starve. None a them starve. Forget about him.

WILLY: Then what have I got to remember?

CHARLEY: You take it too hard. To hell with it. When a deposit bottle is broken you don't get your nickel back.

WILLY: That's easy enough for you to say.

CHARLEY: That ain't easy for me to say.

WILLY: Did you see the ceiling I put up in the living room?

CHARLEY: Yeah, that's a piece of work. To put up a ceiling is a mystery to me. How do you do it?

WILLY: What's the difference?

CHARLEY: Well, talk about it.

WILLY: You gonna put up a ceiling?

CHARLEY: How could I put up a ceiling?

WILLY: Then what the hell are you bothering me for?

CHARLEY: You're insulted again.

WILLY: A man who can't handle tools is not a man. You're disgusting.

CHARLEY: Don't call me disgusting, Willy.

(UNCLE BEN, *carrying a valise and an umbrella, enters the forestage from around the right corner of the house. He is a stolid man, in his sixties, with a mustache and an authoritative air. He is utterly certain of his destiny, and there is an aura of far places about him. He enters exactly as* WILLY *speaks.*)

WILLY: I'm getting awfully tired, Ben.

(BEN's *music is heard.* BEN *looks around at everything.*)

CHARLEY: Good, keep playing; you'll sleep better. Did you call me Ben?

(BEN *looks at his watch.*)

WILLY: That's funny. For a second there you reminded me of my brother Ben.

BEN: I only have a few minutes. (*He strolls, inspecting the place.* WILLY *and* CHARLEY *continue playing.*)

CHARLEY: You never heard from him again, heh? Since that time?

WILLY: Didn't Linda tell you? Couple of weeks ago we got a letter from his wife in Africa. He died.

CHARLEY: That so.

BEN (*chuckling*): So this is Brooklyn, eh?

CHARLEY: Maybe you're in for some of his money.

WILLY: Naa, he had seven sons. There's just one opportunity I had with that man . . .

BEN: I must make a train, William. There are several properties I'm looking at in Alaska.

WILLY: Sure, sure! If I'd gone with him to Alaska that time, everything would've been totally different.

CHARLEY: Go on, you'd froze to death up there.

WILLY: What're you talking about?

BEN: Opportunity is tremendous in Alaska, William. Surprised you're not up there.

WILLY: Sure, tremendous.

CHARLEY: Heh?

WILLY: There was the only man I ever met who knew the answers.

CHARLEY: Who?

BEN: How are you all?

WILLY (*taking a pot, smiling*): Fine, fine.

CHARLEY: Pretty sharp tonight.

BEN: Is Mother living with you?

WILLY: No, she died a long time ago.

CHARLEY: Who?

BEN: That's too bad. Fine specimen of a lady, Mother.

WILLY (*to* CHARLEY): Heh?

BEN: I'd hoped to see the old girl.

CHARLEY: Who died?

BEN: Heard anything from Father, have you?

WILLY (*unnerved*): What do you mean, who died?

CHARLEY (*taking a pot*): What're you talkin' about?

BEN (*looking at his watch*): William, it's half-past eight!

WILLY (*as though to dispel his confusion he angrily stops* CHARLEY'*s hand*): That's my build!

CHARLEY: I put the ace—

WILLY: If you don't know how to play the game I'm not gonna throw my money away on you!

CHARLEY (*rising*): It was my ace, for God's sake!

WILLY: I'm through, I'm through!

BEN: When did Mother die?

WILLY: Long ago. Since the beginning you never knew how to play cards.

CHARLEY (*picks up the cards and goes to the door*): All right! Next time I'll bring a deck with five aces.

WILLY: I don't play that kind of game!

CHARLEY (*turning to him*): You ought to be ashamed of yourself!

WILLY: Yeah?

CHARLEY: Yeah! (*He goes out.*)

WILLY (*slamming the door after him*): Ignoramus!

BEN (*as* WILLY *comes toward him through the wall-line of the kitchen*): So you're William.

WILLY (*shaking* BEN'*s hand*): Ben! I've been waiting for you so long! What's the answer? How did you do it?

BEN: Oh, there's a story in that.

(LINDA *enters the forestage, as of old, carrying the wash basket.*)

LINDA: Is this Ben?

BEN (*gallantly*): How do you do, my dear.

LINDA: Where've you been all these years? Willy's always wondered why you—

WILLY (*pulling* BEN *away from her impatiently*): Where is Dad? Didn't you follow him? How did you get started?

BEN: Well, I don't know how much you remember.

WILLY: Well, I was just a baby, of course, only three or four years old—

BEN: Three years and eleven months.

WILLY: What a memory, Ben!

BEN: I have many enterprises, William, and I have never kept books.

WILLY: I remember I was sitting under the wagon in—was it Nebraska?

BEN: It was South Dakota, and I gave you a bunch of wild flowers.

WILLY: I remember you walking away down some open road.

BEN (*laughing*): I was going to find Father in Alaska.

WILLY: Where is he?

BEN: At that age I had a very faulty view of geography, William. I discovered after a few days that I was heading due south, so instead of Alaska, I ended up in Africa.

LINDA: Africa!

WILLY: The Gold Coast!

BEN: Principally diamond mines.

LINDA: Diamond mines!

BEN: Yes, my dear. But I've only a few minutes—

WILLY: No! Boys! Boys! (YOUNG BIFF *and* HAPPY *appear.*) Listen to this. This is your Uncle Ben, a great man! Tell my boys, Ben!

BEN: Why, boys, when I was seventeen I walked into the jungle, and when I was twenty-one I walked out. (*He laughs.*) And by God I was rich.

WILLY (*to the boys*): You see what I been talking about? The greatest things can happen!

BEN (*glancing at his watch*): I have an appointment in Ketchikan Tuesday week.

WILLY: No, Ben! Please tell about Dad. I want my boys to hear. I want them to know the kind of stock they spring from. All I remember is a man with a big beard, and I was in Mamma's lap, sitting around a fire, and some kind of high music.

BEN: His flute. He played the flute.

WILLY: Sure, the flute, that's right!

(*New music is heard, a high, rollicking tune.*)

BEN: Father was a very great and a very wild-hearted man. We would start in Boston, and he'd toss the whole family into the wagon, and then he'd drive the team right across the country; through Ohio, and Indiana, Michigan, Illinois, and all the Western states. And we'd stop in the towns and sell the flutes that he'd made on the way. Great inventor, Father. With one gadget he made more in a week than a man like you could make in a lifetime.

WILLY: That's just the way I'm bringing them up, Ben—rugged, well liked, all-around.

BEN: Yeah? (*To* BIFF): Hit that, boy—hard as you can. (*He pounds his stomach.*)

BIFF: Oh, no, sir!

BEN (*taking boxing stance*): Come on, get to me! (*He laughs.*)

WILLY: Go to it, Biff! Go ahead, show him!

BIFF: Okay! (*He cocks his fists and starts in.*)

LINDA (*to* WILLY): Why must he fight, dear?

BEN (*sparring with* BIFF): Good boy! Good boy!

WILLY: How's that, Ben, heh?

HAPPY: Give him the left, Biff!

LINDA: Why are you fighting?

BEN: Good boy! (*Suddenly comes in, trips* BIFF, *and stands over him, the point of his umbrella poised over* BIFF'*s eye.*)

LINDA: Look out, Biff!

BIFF: Gee!

BEN (*patting* BIFF'*s knee*): Never fight fair with a stranger, boy. You'll never get out of the jungle that way. (*Taking* LINDA'*s hand and bowing*) It was an honor and a pleasure to meet you, Linda.

LINDA (*withdrawing her hand coldly, frightened*): Have a nice—trip.

BEN (*to* WILLY): And good luck with your—what do you do?

WILLY: Selling.

BEN: Yes. Well . . . (*He raises his hand in farewell to all.*)

WILLY: No, Ben, I don't want you to think . . . (*He takes* BEN'*s arm to show him.*) It's Brooklyn, I know, but we hunt too.

BEN: Really, now.

WILLY: Oh, sure, there's snakes and rabbits and—that's why I moved out here. Why, Biff can fell any one of these trees in no time! Boys! Go right over to where they're building the apartment house and get some sand. We're gonna rebuild the entire front stoop right now! Watch this, Ben!

BIFF: Yes, sir! On the double, Hap!

HAPPY (*as he and* BIFF *run off*): I lost weight, Pop, you notice?

(CHARLEY *enters in knickers, even before the boys are gone.*)

CHARLEY: Listen, if they steal any more from that building the watchman'll put the cops on them!

LINDA (*to* WILLY): Don't let Biff . . .

(BEN *laughs lustily.*)

WILLY: You shoulda seen the lumber they brought home last week. At least a dozen six-by-tens worth all kinds a money.

CHARLEY: Listen, if that watchman—

WILLY: I gave them hell, understand. But I got a couple of fearless characters there.

CHARLEY: Willy, the jails are full of fearless characters.

BEN (*clapping* WILLY *on the back, with a laugh at* CHARLEY): And the stock exchange, friend!

WILLY (*joining in* BEN'*s laughter*): Where are the rest of your pants?

CHARLEY: My wife bought them.

WILLY: Now all you need is a golf club and you can go upstairs and go to sleep. (*To* BEN) Great athlete! Between him and his son Bernard they can't hammer a nail!

BERNARD (*rushing in*): The watchman's chasing Biff!

WILLY (*angrily*): Shut up! He's not stealing anything!

LINDA (*alarmed, hurrying off left*): Where is he? Biff, dear! (*She exits.*)

WILLY (*moving toward the left, away from* BEN): There's nothing wrong. What's the matter with you?

BEN: Nervy boy. Good!

WILLY (*laughing*): Oh, nerves of iron, that Biff!

CHARLEY: Don't know what it is. My New England man comes back and he's bleedin', they murdered him up there.

WILLY: It's contacts, Charley, I got important contacts!

CHARLEY (*sarcastically*): Glad to hear it, Willy. Come in later, we'll shoot a little casino. I'll take some of your Portland money. (*He laughs at* WILLY *and exits.*)

WILLY (*turning to* BEN): Business is bad, it's murderous. But not for me, of course.

BEN: I'll stop by on my way back to Africa.

WILLY (*longingly*): Can't you stay for a few days? You're just what I need, Ben, because I—I have a fine position here, but I—well, Dad left when I was such a baby and I never had a chance to talk to him and I still feel—kind of temporary about myself.

BEN: I'll be late for my train.

(*They are at opposite ends of the stage.*)

WILLY: Ben, my boys—can't we talk? They'd go into the jaws of hell for me, see, but I—

BEN: William, you're being first-rate with your boys. Outstanding, manly chaps!

WILLY (*hanging on to his words*): Oh, Ben, that's good to hear! Because sometimes I'm afraid that I'm not teaching them the right kind of—Ben, how should I teach them?

BEN (*giving great weight to each word, and with a certain vicious audacity*): William, when I walked into the jungle, I was seventeen. When I walked out I was twenty-one. And, by God, I was rich! (*He goes off into darkness around the right corner of the house.*)

WILLY: . . . was rich! That's just the spirit I want to imbue them with! To walk into a jungle! I was right! I was right! I was right!

(BEN *is gone, but* WILLY *is still speaking to him as* LINDA, *in nightgown and robe, enters the kitchen, glances around for* WILLY, *then goes to the door of the house, looks out and sees him. Comes down to his left. He looks at her.*)

LINDA: Willy, dear? Willy?

WILLY: I was right!

LINDA: Did you have some cheese? (*He can't answer.*) It's very late, darling. Come to bed, heh?

WILLY (*looking straight up*): Gotta break your neck to see a star in this yard.

LINDA: You coming in?

WILLY: Whatever happened to that diamond watch fob? Remember? When Ben came from Africa that time? Didn't he give me a watch fob with a diamond in it?

LINDA: You pawned it, dear. Twelve, thirteen years ago. For Biff's radio correspondence course.

WILLY: Gee, that was a beautiful thing. I'll take a walk.

LINDA: But you're in your slippers.

WILLY (*starting to go around the house at the left*): I was right! I was! (*Half to* LINDA, *as he goes, shaking his head*) What a man! There was a man worth talking to. I was right!

LINDA (*calling after* WILLY): But in your slippers, Willy!

(WILLY *is almost gone when* BIFF, *in his pajamas, comes down the stairs and enters the kitchen.*)

BIFF: What is he doing out there?

LINDA: Sh!

BIFF: God Almighty, Mom, how long has he been doing this?

LINDA: Don't, he'll hear you.

BIFF: What the hell is the matter with him?

LINDA: It'll pass by morning.

BIFF: Shouldn't we do anything?

LINDA: Oh, my dear, you should do a lot of things, but there's nothing to do, so go to sleep.

(HAPPY *comes down the stairs and sits on the steps.*)

HAPPY: I never heard him so loud, Mom.

LINDA: Well, come around more often; you'll hear him. (*She sits down at the table and mends the lining of* WILLY'*s jacket.*)

BIFF: Why didn't you ever write me about this, Mom?

LINDA: How could I write to you? For over three months you had no address.

BIFF: I was on the move. But you know I thought of you all the time. You know that, don't you, pal?

LINDA: I know, dear, I know. But he likes to have a letter. Just to know that there's still a possibility for better things.

BIFF: He's not like this all the time, is he?

LINDA: It's when you come home he's always the worst.

BIFF: When I come home?

LINDA: When you write you're coming, he's all smiles, and talks about the future, and—he's just wonderful. And then the closer you seem to come, the more shaky he gets, and then, by the time you get here, he's arguing, and he seems angry at you. I think it's just that maybe he can't bring himself to—to open up to you. Why are you so hateful to each other? Why is that?

BIFF (*evasively*): I'm not hateful, Mom.

LINDA: But you no sooner come in the door than you're fighting!

BIFF: I don't know why. I mean to change. I'm tryin', Mom, you understand?

LINDA: Are you home to stay now?

BIFF: I don't know. I want to look around, see what's doin'.

LINDA: Biff, you can't look around all your life, can you?

BIFF: I just can't take hold, Mom. I can't take hold of some kind of a life.

LINDA: Biff, a man is not a bird, to come and go with the springtime.

BIFF: Your hair . . . (*He touches her hair.*) Your hair got so gray.

LINDA: Oh, it's been gray since you were in high school. I just stopped dyeing it, that's all.

BIFF: Dye it again, will ya? I don't want my pal looking old. (*He smiles.*)

LINDA: You're such a boy! You think you can go away for a year and . . . You've got to get it into your head now that one day you'll knock on this door and there'll be strange people here—

BIFF: What are you talking about? You're not even sixty, Mom.

LINDA: But what about your father?

BIFF (*lamely*): Well, I meant him too.

HAPPY: He admires Pop.

LINDA: Biff, dear, if you don't have any feeling for him, then you can't have any feeling for me.

BIFF: Sure I can, Mom.

LINDA: No. You can't just come to see me, because I love him. (*With a threat, but only a threat, of tears*) He's the dearest man in the world to me, and I won't have anyone making him feel unwanted and low and blue. You've got to make up your mind now, darling, there's no leeway any more. Either he's your father and you pay him that respect, or else you're not to come here. I know he's not easy to get along with—nobody knows that better than me—but . . .

WILLY (*from the left, with a laugh*): Hey, hey, Biffo!

BIFF (*starting to go out after* WILLY): What the hell is the matter with him? (HAPPY *stops him.*)

LINDA: Don't—don't go near him!

BIFF: Stop making excuses for him! He always, always wiped the floor with you. Never had an ounce of respect for you.

HAPPY: He's always had respect for—

BIFF: What the hell do you know about it?

HAPPY (*surlily*): Just don't call him crazy!

BIFF: He's got no character—Charley wouldn't do this. Not in his own house—spewing out that vomit from his mind.

HAPPY: Charley never had to cope with what he's got to.

BIFF: People are worse off then Willy Loman. Believe me, I've seen them!

LINDA: Then make Charley your father, Biff. You can't do that, can you? I don't say he's a great man. Willy Loman never made a lot of money. His name was never in the paper. He's not the finest character that ever lived. But he's a human being, and a terrible thing is happening to him. So attention must be paid. He's not to be allowed to fall into his grave like an old dog. Attention, attention must be finally paid to such a person. You called him crazy—

BIFF: I didn't mean—

LINDA: No, a lot of people think he's lost his—balance. But you don't have to be very smart to know what his trouble is. The man is exhausted.

HAPPY: Sure!

LINDA: A small man can be just as exhausted as a great man. He works for a company thirty-six years this March, opens up unheard-of territories to their trademark, and now in his old age they take his salary away.

HAPPY (*indignantly*): I didn't know that, Mom.

LINDA: You never asked, my dear! Now that you get your spending money someplace else you don't trouble your mind with him.

HAPPY: But I gave you money last—

LINDA: Christmas time, fifty dollars! To fix the hot water it cost ninety-seven fifty! For five weeks he's been on straight commission, like a beginner, an unknown!

BIFF: Those ungrateful bastards!

LINDA: Are they any worse than his sons? When he brought them business, when he was young, they were glad to see him. But now his old friends, the old buyers that loved him so and always found some order to hand him in a pinch—they're all dead, retired. He used to be able to make six, seven calls a day in Boston. Now he takes his valises out of the car and puts them back and takes them out again and he's exhausted. Instead of walking he talks now. He drives seven hundred miles, and when he gets there no one knows him any more, no one welcomes him. And what goes through a man's mind, driving seven hundred miles home without having earned a cent? Why shouldn't he talk to himself? Why? When he has to go to Charley and borrow fifty dollars a week and pretend to me that it's his pay? How long can that go on? How long? You see what I'm sitting here and waiting for? And you tell me he has no character? The man who never worked a day but for your benefit? When does he get the medal for that? Is this his reward—to turn around at the age of sixty-three and find his sons, who he loved better than his life, one a philandering bum—

HAPPY: Mom!

LINDA: That's all you are, my baby! (*To* BIFF.) And you! What happened to the love you had for him? You were such pals! How you used to talk to him on the phone every night! How lonely he was till he could come home to you!

BIFF: All right, Mom. I'll live here in my room, and I'll get a job. I'll keep away from him, that's all.

LINDA: No, Biff. You can't stay here and fight all the time.

BIFF: He threw me out of this house, remember that.

LINDA: Why did he do that? I never knew why.

BIFF: Because I know he's a fake and he doesn't like anybody around who knows!

LINDA: Why a fake? In what way? What do you mean?

BIFF: Just don't lay it all at my feet. It's between me and him—that's all I have to say. I'll chip in from now on. He'll settle for half my paycheck. He'll be all right. I'm going to bed. (*He starts for the stairs.*)

LINDA: He won't be all right.

BIFF (*turning on the stairs, furiously*): I hate this city and I'll stay here. Now what do you want?

LINDA: He's dying, Biff.

(HAPPY *turns quickly to her, shocked.*)

BIFF (*after a pause*): Why is he dying?

LINDA: He's been trying to kill himself.

BIFF (*with great horror*): How?

LINDA: I live from day to day.

BIFF: What're you talking about?

LINDA: Remember I wrote you that he smashed up the car again? In February?

BIFF: Well?

LINDA: The insurance inspector came. He said that they have evidence. That all these accidents in the last year—weren't—weren't—accidents.

HAPPY: How can they tell that? That's a lie.

LINDA: It seems there's a woman . . . (*She takes a breath as—*)

BIFF (*sharply but contained*): What woman?
LINDA (*simultaneously*): . . . and this woman . . .

LINDA: What?

BIFF: Nothing. Go ahead.

LINDA: What did you say?

BIFF: Nothing. I just said what woman?

HAPPY: What about her?

LINDA: Well, it seems she was walking down the road and saw his car. She says that he wasn't driving fast at all, and that he didn't skid. She says he came to that little bridge, and then deliberately smashed into the railing, and it was only the shallowness of the water that saved him.

BIFF: Oh, no, he probably just fell asleep again.

LINDA: I don't think he fell asleep.

BIFF: Why not?

LINDA: Last month . . . (*With great difficulty*) Oh, boys, it's so hard to say a thing like this! He's just a big stupid man to you, but I tell you there's more good in him than in many other people. (*She chokes, wipes her eyes.*) I was looking for a fuse. The lights blew out, and I went down the cellar. And behind the fuse box—it happened to fall out—was a length of rubber pipe—just short.

HAPPY: No kidding?

LINDA: There's a little attachment on the end of it. I knew right away. And sure enough, on the bottom of the water heater there's a new little nipple on the gas pipe.

HAPPILY (*angrily*): That—jerk.

BIFF: Did you have it taken off?

LINDA: I'm—I'm ashamed to. How can I mention it to him? Every day I go down and take away that little rubber pipe. But, when he comes home, I put it back where it was. How can I insult him that way? I don't know what to do. I live from day to day, boys. I tell you, I know every thought in his mind. It sounds so old-fashioned and silly, but I tell you he put his whole life into you and you've turned your backs on him. (*She is bent over in the chair, weeping, her face in her hands.*) Biff, I swear to God! Biff, his life is in your hands!

HAPPY (*to* BIFF): How do you like that damned fool!

BIFF (*kissing her*): All right, pal, all right. It's all settled now. I've been remiss. I know that, Mom. But now I'll stay, and I swear to you, I'll apply myself. (*Kneeling in front of her, in a fever of self-reproach*) It's just—you see, Mom, I don't fit in business. Not that I won't try. I'll try, and I'll make good.

HAPPY: Sure you will. The trouble with you in business was you never tried to please people.

BIFF: I know, I—

HAPPY: Like when you worked for Harrison's. Bob Harrison said you were tops, and then you go and do some damn fool thing like whistling whole songs in the elevator like a comedian.

BIFF (*against* HAPPY): So what? I like to whistle sometimes.

HAPPY: You don't raise a guy to a responsible job who whistles in the elevator!

LINDA: Well, don't argue about it now.

HAPPY: Like when you'd go off and swim in the middle of the day instead of taking the line around.

BIFF (*his resentment rising*): Well, don't you run off? You take off sometimes, don't you? On a nice summer day?

HAPPY: Yeah, but I cover myself!

LINDA: Boys!

HAPPY: If I'm going to take a fade the boss can call any number where I'm supposed to be and they'll swear to him that I just left. I'll tell you something that I hate to say, Biff, but in the business world some of them think you're crazy.

BIFF (*angered*): Screw the business world!

HAPPY: All right, screw it! Great, but cover yourself!

LINDA: Hap, Hap!

BIFF: I don't care what they think! They've laughed at Dad for years, and you know why? Because we don't belong in this nut-house of a city! We should be mixing cement on some open plain, or—or carpenters. A carpenter is allowed to whistle!

(WILLY *walks in from the entrance of the house, at left.*)

WILLY: Even your grandfather was better than a carpenter. (*Pause. They watch him.*) You never grew up. Bernard does not whistle in the elevator, I assure you.

BIFF (*as though to laugh* WILLY *out of it*): Yeah, but you do, Pop.

WILLY: I never in my life whistled in an elevator! And who in the business world thinks I'm crazy?

BIFF: I didn't mean it like that, Pop. Now don't make a whole thing out of it, will ya?

WILLY: Go back to the West! Be a carpenter, a cowboy, enjoy yourself!

LINDA: Willy, he was just saying—

WILLY: I heard what he said!

HAPPY (*trying to quiet* WILLY): Hey, Pop, come on now . . .

WILLY (*continuing over* HAPPY'*s line*) They laugh at me, heh? Go to Filene's, go to the Hub, go to Slattery's, Boston. Call out the name Willy Loman and see what happens! Big shot!

BIFF: All right, Pop.

WILLY: Big!

BIFF: All right!

WILLY: Why do you always insult me?

BIFF: I didn't say a word. (*To* LINDA) Did I say a word?

LINDA: He didn't say anything, Willy.

WILLY (*going to the doorway of the living room*): All right, good night, good night.

LINDA: Willy, dear, he just decided . . .

WILLY (*to* BIFF): If you get tired hanging around tomorrow, paint the ceiling I put up in the living-room.

BUFF: I'm leaving early tomorrow.

HAPPY: He's going to see Bill Oliver, Pop.

WILLY (*interestedly*): Oliver? For what?

BIFF (*with reserve, but trying, trying*): He always said he'd stake me. I'd like to go into business, so maybe I can take him up on it.

LINDA: Isn't that wonderful?

WILLY: Don't interrupt. What's wonderful about it? There's fifty men in the City of New York who'd stake him. (*To* BIFF) Sporting goods?

BIFF: I guess so. I know something about it and—

WILLY: He knows something about it! You know sporting goods better than Spalding, for God's sake! How much is he giving you?

BIFF: I don't know, I didn't even see him yet, but—

WILLY: Then what're you talkin' about?

BIFF (*getting angry*): Well, all I said was I'm gonna see him, that's all!

WILLY (*turning away*): Ah, you're counting your chickens again.

BIFF (*starting left for the stairs*): Oh, Jesus, I'm going to sleep!

WILLY (*calling after him*): Don't curse in this house!

BIFF (*turning*): Since when did you get so clean?

HAPPY (*trying to stop them*): Wait a . . .

WILLY: Don't use that language to me! I won't have it!

HAPPY (*grabbing* BIFF, *shouts*): Wait a minute! I got an idea. I got a feasible idea. Come here, Biff, let's talk this over now, let's talk some sense here. When I was down in Florida last time, I thought of a great idea to sell sporting goods. It just came back to me. You and I, Biff—we have a line, the Loman Line. We train a couple of weeks, and put on a couple of exhibitions, see?

WILLY: That's an idea!

HAPPY: Wait! We form two basketball teams, see? Two water-polo teams. We play each other. It's a million dollars' worth of publicity. Two brothers, see? The Loman Brothers. Displays in the Royal Palms—all the hotels. And banners over the ring and the basketball court: "Loman Brothers." Baby, we could sell sporting goods!

WILLY: That is a one-million-dollar idea!

LINDA: Marvelous!

BIFF: I'm in great shape as far as that's concerned.

HAPPY: And the beauty of it is, Biff, it wouldn't be like a business. We'd be out playin' ball again . . .

BIFF (*enthused*): Yeah, that's . . .

WILLY: Million-dollar . . .

HAPPY: And you wouldn't get fed up with it, Biff. It'd be the family again. There'd be the old honor, and comradeship, and if you wanted to go off for a swim or somethin'—well, you'd do it! Without some smart cooky gettin' up ahead of you!

WILLY: Lick the world! You guys together could absolutely lick the civilized world.

BIFF: I'll see Oliver tomorrow. Hap, if we could work that out . . .

LINDA: Maybe things are beginning to—

WILLY (*wildly enthused, to* LINDA): Stop interrupting! (*To* BIFF) But don't wear sport jacket and slacks when you see Oliver.

BIFF: No, I'll—

WILLY: A business suit, and talk as little as possible, and don't crack any jokes.

BIFF: He did like me. Always liked me.

LINDA: He loved you!

WILLY (*to* LINDA): Will you stop! (*To* BIFF) Walk in very serious. You are not applying for a boy's job. Money is to pass. Be quiet, fine, and serious. Everybody likes a kidder, but nobody lends him money.

HAPPY: I'll try to get some myself, Biff. I'm sure I can.

WILLY: I see great things for you kids, I think your troubles are over. But remember, start big and you'll end big. Ask for fifteen. How much you gonna ask for?

BIFF: Gee, I don't know—

WILLY: And don't say "Gee." "Gee" is a boy's word. A man walking in for fifteen thousand dollars does not say "Gee!"

BIFF: Ten, I think, would be top though.

WILLY: Don't be so modest. You always started too low. Walk in with a big laugh. Don't look worried. Start off with a couple of your good stories to lighten things up. It's not what you say, it's how you say it—because personality always wins the day.

LINDA: Oliver always thought the highest of him—

WILLY: Will you let me talk?

BIFF: Don't yell at her, Pop, will ya?

WILLY (*angrily*): I was talking, wasn't I?

BIFF: I don't like you yelling at her all the time, and I'm tellin' you, that's all.

WILLY: What're you, takin' over this house?

LINDA: Willy—

WILLY (*turning on her*): Don't take his side all the time, goddammit!

BIFF (*furiously*): Stop yelling at her!

WILLY (*suddenly pulling on his cheek, beaten down, guilt ridden*): Give my best to Bill Oliver—he may remember me. (*He exits through the living room doorway.*)

LINDA (*her voice subdued*): What'd you have to start that for? (BIFF *turns away*) You see how sweet he was as soon as you talked hopefully? (*She goes over to* BIFF) Come up and say good night to him. Don't let him go to bed that way.

HAPPY: Come on, Biff, let's buck him up.

LINDA: Please, dear. Just say good night. It takes so little to make him happy. Come. (*She goes through the living room doorway, calling upstairs from within the living room*) Your pajamas are hanging in the bathroom, Willy!

HAPPY (*looking toward where* LINDA *went out*): What a woman! They broke the mold when they made her. You know that, Biff?

BIFF: He's off salary. My god, working on commission!

HAPPY: Well, let's face it: he's no hot-shot selling man. Except that sometimes, you have to admit, he's a sweet personality.

BIFF (*deciding*): Lend me ten bucks, will ya? I want to buy some new ties.

HAPPY: I'll take you to a place I know. Beautiful stuff. Wear one of my striped shirts tomorrow.

BIFF: She got gray. Mom got awful old. Gee, I'm gonna go in to Oliver tomorrow and knock him for a—

HAPPY: Come on up. Tell that to Dad. Let's give him a whirl. Come on.

BIFF (*steamed up*): You know, with ten thousand bucks, boy!

HAPPY (*as they go into the living room*): That's the talk, Biff, that's the first time I've heard the old confidence out of you! (*From within the living room, fading off.*) You're gonna live with me, kid, and any babe you want just say the word . . . (*The last lines are hardly heard. They are mounting the stairs to their parents' bedroom.*)

LINDA (*entering her bedroom and addressing* WILLY, *who is in the bathroom. She is straightening the bed for him*): Can you do anything about the shower? It drips.

WILLY (*from the bathroom*): All of a sudden everything falls to pieces! Goddam plumbing, oughta be sued, those people. I hardly finished putting it in and the thing . . . (*His words rumble off.*)

LINDA: I'm just wondering if Oliver will remember him. You think he might?

WILLY (*coming out of the bathroom in his pajamas*): Remember him? What's the matter with you, you crazy? If he'd've stayed with Oliver he'd be on top by now! Wait'll Oliver gets a look at him. You don't know the average caliber any more. The average young man today—(*he is getting into bed*)—is got a caliber of zero. Greatest thing in the world for him was to bum around.

(BIFF *and* HAPPY *enter the bedroom. Slight pause.*)

WILLY (*stops short, looking at* BIFF): Glad to hear it, boy.

HAPPY: He wanted to say good night to you, sport.

WILLY (*to* BIFF): Yeah. Knock him dead, boy. What'd you want to tell me?

BIFF: Just take it easy, Pop. Good night. (*He turns to go.*)

WILLY (*unable to resist*): And if anything falls off the desk while you're talking to him—like a package or something—don't you pick it up. They have office boys for that.

LINDA: I'll make a big breakfast—

WILLY: Will you let me finish? (*To* BIFF) Tell him you were in the business in the West. Not farm work.

BIFF: All right, Dad.

LINDA: I think everything—

WILLY (*going right through her speech*): And don't undersell yourself. No less than fifteen thousand dollars.

BIFF (*unable to bear him*): Okay. Good night, Mom. (*He starts moving.*)

WILLY: Because you got a greatness in you, Biff, remember that. You got all kinds a greatness . . . (*He lies back, exhausted.* BIFF *walks out.*)

LINDA (*calling after* BIFF): Sleep well, darling!

HAPPY: I'm gonna get married, Mom. I wanted to tell you.

LINDA: Go to sleep, dear.

HAPPY (*going*): I just wanted to tell you.

WILLY: Keep up the good work. (HAPPY *exits.*) God . . . remember that Ebbets Field game? The championship of the city?

LINDA: Just rest. Should I sing to you?

WILLY: Yeah. Sing to me. (LINDA *hums a soft lullaby.*) When that team came out—he was the tallest, remember?

LINDA: Oh, yes. And in gold.

(BIFF *enters the darkened kitchen, takes a cigarette, and leaves the house. He comes downstage into a golden pool of light. He smokes, staring at the night.*)

WILLY: Like a young god. Hercules—something like that. And the sun, the sun all around him. Remember how he waved to me? Right up from the field, with the representatives of three colleges standing by? And the buyers I brought, and the cheers when he came out—Loman, Loman, Loman! God Almighty, he'll be great yet. A star like that, magnificent, can never really fade away!

(*The light on* WILLY *is fading. The gas heater begins to glow through the kitchen wall, near the stairs, a blue flame beneath red coils.*)

LINDA (*timidly*): Willy dear, what has he got against you?

WILLY: I'm so tired. Don't talk any more.

(BIFF *slowly returns to the kitchen. He stops, stares toward the heater.*)

LINDA: Will you ask Howard to let you work in New York?

WILLY: First thing in the morning. Everything'll be all right.

(BIFF *reaches behind the heater and draws out a length of rubber tubing. He is horrified and turns his head toward* WILLY's *room, still dimly lit, from which the strains of* LINDA's *desperate but monotonous humming rise.*)

WILLY (*staring through the window into the moonlight*): Gee, look at the moon moving between the buildings!

(BIFF *wraps the tubing around his hand and quickly goes up the stairs.*)

CURTAIN

ACT II

Music is heard, gay and bright. The curtain rises as the music fades away. WILLY, *in shirt sleeves, is sitting at the kitchen table, sipping coffee, his hat in his lap.* LINDA *is filling his cup when she can.*

WILLY: Wonderful coffee. Meal in itself.

LINDA: Can I make you some eggs?

WILLY: No. Take a breath.

LINDA: You look so rested, dear.

WILLY: I slept like a dead one. First time in months. Imagine, sleeping till ten on a Tuesday morning. Boys left nice and early, heh?

LINDA: They were out of here by eight o'clock.

WILLY: Good work!

LINDA: It was so thrilling to see them leaving together. I can't get over the shaving lotion in this house!

WILLY (*smiling*): Mmm—

LINDA: Biff was very changed this morning. His whole attitude seemed to be hopeful. He couldn't wait to get downtown to see Oliver.

WILLY: He's heading for a change. There's no question, there simply are certain men that take longer to get—solidified. How did he dress?

LINDA: His blue suit. He's so handsome in that suit. He could be a—anything in that suit!

(WILLY *gets up from the table.* LINDA *holds his jacket for him.*)

WILLY: There's no question, no question at all. Gee, on the way home tonight I'd like to buy some seeds.

LINDA (*laughing*): That'd be wonderful. But not enough sun gets back there. Nothing'll grow any more.

WILLY: You wait, kid, before it's all over we're gonna get a little place out in the country, and I'll raise some vegetables, a couple of chickens . . .

LINDA: You'll do it yet, dear.

(WILLY *walks out of his jacket.* LINDA *follows him.*)

WILLY: And they'll get married, and come for a weekend. I'd build a little guest house. 'Cause I got so many fine tools, all I'd need would be a little lumber and some peace of mind.

LINDA (*joyfully*): I sewed the lining . . .

WILLY: I could build two guest houses, so they'd both come. Did he decide how much he's going to ask Oliver for?

LINDA (*getting him into the jacket*): He didn't

mention it, but I imagine ten or fifteen thousand. You going to talk to Howard today?

WILLY: Yeah. I'll put it to him straight and simple. He'll just have to take me off the road.

LINDA: And Willy, don't forget to ask for a little advance, because we've got the insurance premium. It's the grace period now.

WILLY: That's a hundred . . . ?

LINDA: A hundred and eight, sixty-eight. Because we're a little short again.

WILLY: Why are we short?

LINDA: Well, you had the motor job on the car . . .

WILLY: That goddam Studebaker!

LINDA: And you got one more payment on the refrigerator . . .

WILLY: But it just broke again!

LINDA: Well, it's old, dear.

WILLY: I told you we should've bought a well-advertised machine. Charley bought a General Electric and it's twenty years old and it's still good, that son-of-a-bitch.

LINDA: But, Willy—

WILLY: Whoever heard of a Hastings refrigerator? Once in my life I would like to own something outright before it's broken! I'm always in a race with the junkyard! I just finished paying for the car and it's on its last legs. The refrigerator consumes belts like a goddam maniac. They time those things. They time them so when you finally paid for them, they're used up.

LINDA (buttoning up his jacket as he unbuttons it): All told, about two hundred dollars would carry us, dear. But that includes the last payment on the mortgage. After this payment, Willy, the house belongs to us.

WILLY: It's twenty-five years!

LINDA: Biff was nine years old when we bought it.

WILLY: Well, that's a great thing. To weather a twenty-five year mortgage is—

LINDA: It's an accomplishment.

WILLY: All the cement, the lumber, the reconstruction I put in this house! There ain't a crack to be found in it any more.

LINDA: Well, it served its purpose.

WILLY: What purpose? Some stranger'll come along, move in, and that's that. If only Biff would take this house, and raise a family . . . (He starts to go.) Good-bye, I'm late.

LINDA (suddenly remembering): Oh, I forgot! You're supposed to meet them for dinner.

WILLY: Me?

LINDA: At Frank's Chop House on Forty-eighth near Sixth Avenue.

WILLY: Is that so! How about you?

LINDA: No, just the three of you. They're gonna blow you to a big meal!

WILLY: Don't say! Who thought of that?

LINDA: Biff came to me this morning, Willy, and he said, "Tell Dad, we want to blow him to a big meal." Be there six o'clock. You and your two boys are going to have dinner.

WILLY: Gee whiz! That's really somethin'. I'm gonna knock Howard for a loop, kid. I'll get an advance, and I'll come home with a New York job. Goddammit, now I'm gonna do it!

LINDA: Oh, that's the spirit, Willy!

WILLY: I will never get behind a wheel the rest of my life!

LINDA: It's changing, Willy, I can feel it changing!

WILLY: Beyond a question. G'by, I'm late. (He starts to go again.)

LINDA (calling after him as she runs to the kitchen table for a handkerchief): You got your glasses?

WILLY (feels for them, then comes back in): Yeah, yeah, got my glasses.

LINDA (giving him the handkerchief): And a handkerchief.

WILLY: Yeah, handkerchief.

LINDA: And your saccharine?

WILLY: Yeah, my saccharine.

LINDA: Be careful on the subway stairs.

(She kisses him, and a silk stocking is seen hanging from her hand. WILLY notices it.)

WILLY: Will you stop mending stockings? At least while I'm in the house. It gets me nervous. I can't tell you. Please.

(LINDA hides the stocking in her hand as she follows WILLY across the forestage in front of the house.)

LINDA: Remember, Frank's Chop House.

WILLY (passing the apron): Maybe beets would grow out there.

LINDA (laughing): But you tried so many times.

WILLY: Yeah. Well, don't work hard today. (He disappears around the right corner of the house.)

LINDA: Be careful!

(As WILLY vanishes, LINDA waves to him. Suddenly the phone rings. She runs across the stage and into the kitchen and lifts it.)

LINDA: Hello? Oh, Biff! I'm so glad you called, I just . . . Yes, sure, I just told him. Yes, he'll be there for dinner at six o'clock, I didn't forget. Listen, I was just dying to tell you. You know that

little rubber pipe I told you about? That he connected to the gas heater? I finally decided to go
down the cellar this morning and take it away and
destroy it. But it's gone! Imagine? He took it away
himself, it isn't there! (*She listens.*) When? Oh,
then you took it. Oh—nothing, it's just that I'd
hoped he'd taken it away himself. Oh, I'm not
worried, darling, because this morning he left in
such high spirits, it was like the old days! I'm not
afraid any more. Did Mr. Oliver see you? . . .
Well, you wait there then. And make a nice
impression on him, darling. Just don't perspire too
much before you see him. And have a nice time
with Dad. He may have big news too! . . . That's
right, a New York job. And be sweet to him
tonight, dear. Be loving to him. Because he's only
a little boat looking for a harbor. (*She is trembling
with sorrow and joy.*) Oh, that's wonderful, Biff,
you'll save his life. Thanks, darling. Just put your
arm around him when he comes into the restaurant. Give him a smile. That's the boy . . . Good-
bye, dear. . . . You got your comb? . . . That's
fine. Good-bye, Biff dear.

(*In the middle of her speech,* HOWARD WAGNER,
*thirty-six, wheels in a small typewriter table on
which is a wire-recording machine and proceeds
to plug it in. This is on the left forestage. Light
slowly fades on* LINDA *as it rises on* HOWARD.
HOWARD *is intent on threading the machine and
only glances over his shoulder as* WILLY *appears.*)

WILLY: Pst! Pst!

HOWARD: Hello, Willy, come in.

WILLY: Like to have a little talk with you,
Howard.

HOWARD: Sorry to keep you waiting. I'll be with
you in a minute.

WILLY: What's that, Howard?

HOWARD: Didn't you ever see one of these?
Wire recorder.

WILLY: Oh. Can we talk a minute?

HOWARD: Records things. Just got delivery yesterday. Been driving me crazy, the most terrific
machine I ever saw in my life. I was up all night
with it.

WILLY: What do you do with it?

HOWARD: I bought it for dictation, but you can
do anything with it. Listen to this. I had it home
last night. Listen to what I picked up. The first one
is my daughter. Get this. (*He flicks the switch and
"Roll out the Barrel" is heard being whistled.*)
Listen to that kid whistle.

WILLY: That is lifelike, isn't it?

HOWARD: Seven years old. Get that tone.

WILLY: Ts, ts. Like to ask a little favor of you . . .

(*The whistling breaks off, and the voice of* HOW-
ARD'S DAUGHTER *is heard.*)

HIS DAUGHTER: "Now you, Daddy."

HOWARD: She's crazy for me! (*Again the same
song is whistled.*) That's me! Ha! (*He winks.*)

WILLY: You're very good!

(*The whistling breaks off again. The machine
runs silent for a moment.*)

HOWARD: Sh! Get this now, this is my son.

HIS SON: "The capital of Alabama is Montgom-
ery; the capital of Arizona is Phoenix; the capital of
Arkansas is Little Rock; the capital of California is
Sacramento . . ." (*And on, and on.*)

HOWARD (*holding up five fingers*): Five years
old, Willy!

WILLY: He'll make an announcer some day!

HIS SON (*continuing*): "The capital . . ."

HOWARD: Get that—alphabetical order! (*The
machine breaks off suddenly.*) Wait a minute. The
maid kicked the plug out.

WILLY: It certainly is a—

HOWARD: Sh, for God's sake!

HIS SON: "It's nine o'clock, Bulova watch time.
So I have to go to sleep."

WILLY: That really is—

HOWARD: Wait a minute! The next is my wife.

(*They wait.*)

HOWARD'S VOICE: "Go on, say something."
(*Pause.*) "Well, you gonna talk?"

HIS WIFE: "I can't think of anything."

HOWARD'S VOICE: "Well, talk—it's turning."

HIS WIFE (*shyly, beaten*): "Hello." (*Silence.*)
"Oh, Howard, I can't talk into this . . ."

HOWARD (*snapping the machine off*): That was
my wife.

WILLY: That is a wonderful machine. Can we—

HOWARD: I tell you, Willy, I'm gonna take my
camera, and my bandsaw, and all my hobbies, and
out they go. This is the most fascinating relaxation
I ever found.

WILLY: I think I'll get one myself.

HOWARD: Sure, they're only a hundred and a
half. You can't do without it. Supposing you
wanna hear Jack Benny, see? But you can't be at
home at that hour. So you tell the maid to turn the
radio on when Jack Benny comes on, and this
automatically goes on with the radio . . .

WILLY: And when you come home you . . .

HOWARD: You can come home twelve o'clock,
one o'clock, any time you like, and you get
yourself a Coke and sit yourself down, throw the
switch, and there's Jack Benny's program in the
middle of the night!

WILLY: I'm definitely going to get one. Because lots of time I'm on the road, and I think to myself, what I must be missing on the radio!

HOWARD: Don't you have a radio in the car?

WILLY: Well, yeah, but who ever thinks of turning it on?

HOWARD: Say, aren't you supposed to be in Boston?

WILLY: That's what I want to talk to you about, Howard. You got a minute? (*He draws a chair in from the wing.*)

HOWARD: What happened? What're you doing here?

WILLY: Well . . .

HOWARD: You didn't crack up again, did you?

WILLY: Oh, no. No . . .

HOWARD: Geez, you had me worried there for a minute. What's the trouble?

WILLY: Well, tell you the truth, Howard. I've come to the decision that I'd rather not travel any more.

HOWARD: Not travel! Well, what'll you do?

WILLY: Remember, Christmas time, when you had the party here? You said you'd try to think of some spot for me here in town.

HOWARD: With us?

WILLY: Well, sure.

HOWARD: Oh, yeah, yeah. I remember. Well, I couldn't think of anything for you, Willy.

WILLY: I tell ya, Howard. The kids are all grown up, y'know. I don't need much any more. If I could take home—well, sixty-five dollars a week, I could swing it.

HOWARD: Yeah, but Willy, see I—

WILLY: I tell ya why, Howard. Speaking frankly and between the two of us, y'know—I'm just a little tired.

HOWARD: Oh, I could understand that, Willy. But you're a road man, Willy, and we do a road business. We've only got a half-dozen salesmen on the floor here.

WILLY: God knows, Howard, I never asked a favor of any man. But I was with the firm when your father used to carry you in here in his arms.

HOWARD: I know that, Willy, but—

WILLY: Your father came to me the day you were born and asked me what I thought of the name of Howard, may he rest in peace.

HOWARD: I appreciate that, Willy, but there just is no spot here for you. If I had a spot I'd slam you right in, but I just don't have a single solitary spot.

(*He looks for his lighter.* WILLY *has picked it up and gives it to him. Pause.*)

WILLY (*with increasing anger*): Howard, all I need to set my table is fifty dollars a week.

HOWARD: But where am I going to put you, kid?

WILLY: Look, it isn't a question of whether I can sell merchandise, is it?

HOWARD: No, but it's a business, kid, and everybody's gotta pull his own weight.

WILLY (*desperately*): Just let me tell you a story, Howard—

HOWARD: 'Cause you gotta admit, business is business.

WILLY (*angrily*): Business is definitely business, but just listen for a minute. You don't understand this. When I was a boy—eighteen, nineteen—I was already on the road. And there was a question in my mind as to whether selling had a future for me. Because in those days I had a yearning to go to Alaska. See, there were three gold strikes in one month in Alaska, and I felt like going out. Just for the ride, you might say.

HOWARD (*barely interested*): Don't say.

WILLY: Oh, yeah, my father lived many years in Alaska. He was an adventurous man. We've got quite a little streak of self-reliance in our family. I thought I'd go out with my older brother and try to locate him, and maybe settle in the North with the old man. And I was almost decided to go, when I met a salesman in the Parker House. His name was Dave Singleman. And he was eighty-four years old, and he'd drummed merchandise in thirty-one states. And old Dave, he'd go up to his room, y'understand, put on his green velvet slippers—I'll never forget—and pick up his phone and call the buyers, and without ever leaving his room, at the age of eighty-four, he made his living. And when I saw that, I realized that selling was the greatest career a man could want. 'Cause what could be more satisfying than to be able to go, at the age of eighty-four, into twenty or thirty different cities, and pick up a phone, and be remembered and loved and helped by so many different people? Do you know? when he died—and by the way he died the death of a salesman, in his green velvet slippers in the smoker of the New York, New Haven and Hartford, going into Boston—when he died, hundreds of salesmen and buyers were at his funeral. Things were sad on a lotta trains for months after that. (*He stands up.* HOWARD *has not looked at him.*) In those days there was personality in it, Howard. There was respect, and comradeship, and gratitude in it. Today, it's all cut and dried, and there's no chance for bringing friendship to bear—or personality. You see what I mean? They don't know me any more.

HOWARD (*moving away, to the right*): That's just the thing, Willy.

WILLY: If I had forty dollars a week—that's all I'd need. Forty dollars, Howard.

HOWARD: Kid, I can't take blood from a stone, I—

WILLY (*desperation is on him now*): Howard, the year Al Smith was nominated, your father came to me and—

HOWARD (*starting to go off*): I've got to see some people kid.

WILLY (*stopping him*): I'm talking about your father! There were promises made across this desk! You mustn't tell me you've got people to see—I put thirty-four years into this firm, Howard, and now I can't pay my insurance! You can't eat the orange and throw the peel away—a man is not a piece of fruit! (*After a pause*) Now pay attention. Your father—in 1928 I had a big year. I averaged a hundred and seventy dollars a week in commissions.

HOWARD (*impatiently*) Now, Willy, you never averaged—

WILLY (*banging his hand on the desk*): I averaged a hundred and seventy dollars a week in the year of 1928! And your father came to me—or rather, I was in the office here—it was right over this desk—and he put his hand on my shoulder—

HOWARD (*getting up*): You'll have to excuse me, Willy, I gotta see some people. Pull yourself together. (*Going out.*) I'll be back in a little while.

(*On* HOWARD's *exit, the light on his chair grows very bright and strange.*)

WILLY: Pull myself together! What the hell did I say to him? My God, I was yelling at him! How could I! (WILLY *breaks off, staring at the light, which occupies the chair, standing across the desk from it.*) Frank, Frank, don't you remember what you told me that time? How you put your hand on my shoulder, and Frank . . . (*He leans on the desk and as he speaks the dead man's name he accidentally switches on the recorder, and instantly—*)

HOWARD'S SON: ". . . of New York is Albany. The capital of Ohio is Cincinnati, the capital of Rhode Island is . . ." (*The recitation continues.*)

WILLY (*leaping away with fright, shouting*): Ha! Howard! Howard! Howard!

HOWARD (*rushing in*): What happened?

WILLY (*pointing at the machine, which continues nasally, childishly, with the capital cities*): Shut it off! Shut if off!

HOWARD (*pulling the plug out*): Look, Willy . . .

WILLY (*pressing his hands to his eyes*): I gotta get myself some coffee. I'll get some coffee . . .

(WILLY *starts to walk out.* HOWARD *stops him.*)

HOWARD (*rolling up the cord*): Willy, look . . .

WILLY: I'll go to Boston.

HOWARD: Willy, you can't go to Boston for us.

WILLY: Why can't I go?

HOWARD: I don't want you to represent us. I've been meaning to tell you for a long time now.

WILLY: Howard, are you firing me?

HOWARD: I think you need a good long rest, Willy.

WILLY: Howard—

HOWARD: And when you feel better, come back, and we'll see if we can work something out.

WILLY: But I gotta earn money, Howard. I'm in no position to—

HOWARD: Where are your sons? Why don't your sons give you a hand?

WILLY: They're working on a very big deal.

HOWARD: This is no time for false pride, Willy. You go to your sons and you tell them that you're tired. You've got two great boys, haven't you?

WILLY: Oh, no question, no question, but in the meantime . . .

HOWARD: Then that's that, heh?

WILLY: All right, I'll go to Boston tomorrow.

HOWARD: No, no.

WILLY: I can't throw myself on my sons. I'm not a cripple!

HOWARD: Look, kid, I'm busy this morning.

WILLY (*grasping* HOWARD's *arm*): Howard, you've got to let me go to Boston!

HOWARD (*hard, keeping himself under control*): I've got a line of people to see this morning. Sit down, take five minutes, and pull yourself together, and then go home, will ya? I need the office, Willy. (*He starts to go, turns, remembering the recorder, starts to push off the table holding the recorder.*) Oh, yeah. Whenever you can this week, stop by and drop off the samples. You'll feel better, Willy, and then come back and we'll talk. Pull yourself together, kid, there's people outside.

(HOWARD *exits, pushing the table off left.* WILLY *stares into space, exhausted. Now the music is heard—*BEN's *music—first distantly, then closer, closer. As* WILLY *speaks,* BEN *enters from the right. He carries valise and umbrella.*)

WILLY: Oh, Ben, how did you do it? What is the answer? Did you wind up the Alaska deal already?

BEN: Doesn't take much time if you know what you're doing. Just a short business trip. Boarding ship in an hour. Wanted to say good-bye.

WILLY: Ben, I've got to talk to you.

BEN (*glancing at his watch*): Haven't the time, William.

WILLY (*crossing the apron to* BEN): Ben, nothing's working out. I don't know what to do.

BEN: Now, look here, William. I've bought timberland in Alaska and I need a man to look after things for me.

WILLY: God, timberland! Me and my boys in those grand outdoors!

BEN: You've a new continent at your doorstep, William. Get out of these cities, they're full of talk and time payments and courts of law. Screw on your fists and you can fight for a fortune up there.

WILLY: Yes, yes! Linda, Linda!

(LINDA *as of old, with the wash.*)

LINDA: Oh, you're back?

BEN: I haven't much time.

WILLY: No, wait! Linda, he's got a proposition for me in Alaska.

LINDA: But you've got—(*To* BEN) He's got a beautiful job here.

WILLY: But in Alaska, kid, I could—

LINDA: You're doing well enough, Willy!

BEN (*to* LINDA): Enough for what, my dear?

LINDA (*frightened of* BEN *and angry at him*): Don't say those things to him! Enough to be happy right here, right now. (*To* WILLY, *while* BEN *laughs*) Why must everybody conquer the world? You're well liked, and the boys love you, and someday—(*to* BEN)—why, old man Wagner told him just the other day that if he keeps it up he'll be a member of the firm, didn't he, Willy?

WILLY: Sure, sure. I am building something with this firm, Ben, and if a man is building something he must be on the right track, mustn't he?

BEN: What are you building? Lay your hand on it. Where is it?

WILLY (*hesitantly*): That's true, Linda, there's nothing.

LINDA: Why? (*To* BEN) There's a man eighty-four years old—

WILLY: That's right, Ben, that's right. When I look at that man I say, what is there to worry about?

BEN: Bah!

WILLY: It's true, Ben. All he has to do is go into any city, pick up the phone, and he's making his living and you know why?

BEN (*picking up his valise*): I've got to go.

WILLY (*holding* BEN *back*): Look at this boy!

(BIFF, *in his high school sweater, enters carrying suitcase.* HAPPY *carries* BIFF's *shoulder guards, gold helmet, and football pants.*)

WILLY: Without a penny to his name, three great universities are begging for him, and from there the sky's the limit, because it's not what you do, Ben. It's who you know and the smile on your face! It's contacts, Ben, contacts! The whole wealth of Alaska passes over the lunch table at the Commodore Hotel, and that's the wonder, the wonder of this country, that a man can end with diamonds here on the basis of being liked! (*He turns to* BIFF) And that's why when you get out on that field today it's important. Because thousands of people will be rooting for you and loving you. (*To* BEN, *who has again begun to leave*) And Ben! when he walks into a business office his name will sound out like a bell and all the doors will open to him! I've seen it, Ben, I've seen it a thousand times! You can't feel it with your hand like timber, but it's there!

BEN: Good-bye, William.

WILLY: Ben, am I right? Don't you think I'm right? I value your advice.

BEN: There's a new continent at your doorstep, William. You could walk out rich. Rich! (*He is gone.*)

WILLY: We'll do it here, Ben! You hear me? We're gonna do it here!

(YOUNG BERNARD *rushes in. The gay music of the boys is heard.*)

BERNARD: Oh, gee, I was afraid you left already!

WILLY: Why? What time is it?

BERNARD: It's half-past one!

WILLY: Well, come on, everybody! Ebbets Field next stop! Where's the pennants? (*He rushes through the wall-line of the kitchen and out into the living room.*)

LINDA (*to* BIFF): Did you pack fresh underwear?

BIFF (*who has been limbering up*): I want to go!

BERNARD: Biff, I'm carrying your helmet, ain't I?

HAPPY: No, I'm carrying the helmet.

BERNARD: Oh, Biff, you promised me.

HAPPY: I'm carrying the helmet.

BERNARD: How am I going to get in the locker room?

LINDA: Let him carry the shoulder guards. (*She puts her coat and hat on in the kitchen.*)

BERNARD: Can I, Biff? 'Cause I told everybody I'm going to be in the locker room.

HAPPY: In Ebbets Field it's the clubhouse.

BERNARD: I meant the clubhouse. Biff!

HAPPY: Biff!

BIFF (*grandly, after a slight pause*): Let him carry the shoulder guards.

HAPPY (*as he gives* BERNARD *the shoulder guards*): Stay close to us now.

(WILLY *rushes in with the pennants.*)

WILLY (*handing them out*): Everybody wave when Biff comes out on the field. (HAPPY *and* BERNARD *run off.*) You set now, boy?

(*The music has died away.*)

BIFF: Ready to go, Pop. Every muscle is ready.

WILLY (*at the edge of the apron*): You realize what this means?

BIFF: That's right, Pop.

WILLY (*feeling* BIFF's *muscles*): You're comin' home this afternoon captain of the All-Scholastic Championship Team of the City of New York.

BIFF: I got it, Pop. And remember, pal, when I take off my helmet, that touchdown is for you.

WILLY: Let's go! (*He is starting out, with his arm around* BIFF, *when* CHARLEY *enters, as of old, in knickers.*) I got no room for you, Charley.

CHARLEY: Room? For what?

WILLY: In the car.

CHARLEY: You goin' for a ride? I wanted to shoot some casino.

WILLY (*furiously*): Casino! (*Incredulously*) Don't you realize what today is?

LINDA: Oh, he knows, Willy. He's just kidding you.

WILLY: That's nothing to kid about!

CHARLEY: No, Linda, what's goin' on?

LINDA: He's playing in Ebbets Field.

CHARLEY: Baseball in this weather?

WILLY: Don't talk to him. Come on, come on! (*He is pushing them out.*)

CHARLEY: Wait a minute, didn't you hear the news?

WILLY: What?

CHARLEY: Don't you listen to the radio? Ebbets Field just blew up.

WILLY: You go to hell! (CHARLEY *laughs. Pushing them out.*) Come on, come on! We're late.

CHARLEY (*as they go*): Knock a homer, Biff, knock a homer!

WILLY (*the last to leave, turning to* CHARLEY): I don't think that was funny, Charley. This is the greatest day of his life.

CHARLEY: Willy, when are you going to grow up?

WILLY: Yeah, heh? When this game is over, Charley, you'll be laughing out of the other side of your face. They'll be calling him another Red Grange. Twenty-five thousand a year.

CHARLEY (*kidding*): Is that so?

WILLY: Yeah, that's so.

CHARLEY: Well, then, I'm sorry, Willy. But tell me something.

WILLY: What?

CHARLEY: Who is Red Grange?

WILLY: Put up your hands. Goddam you, put up your hands!

(CHARLEY, *chuckling, shakes his head and walks away, around the left corner of the stage.* WILLY *follows him. The music rises to a mocking frenzy.*)

WILLY: Who the hell do you think you are, better than everybody else? You don't know everything, you big, ignorant, stupid . . . Put up your hands!

(*Light rises, on the right side of the forestage, on a small table in the reception room of* CHARLEY's *office. Traffic sounds are heard.* BERNARD, *now mature, sits whistling to himself. A pair of tennis rackets and an overnight bag are on the floor beside him.*)

WILLY (*offstage*): What are you walking away for? Don't walk away! If you're going to say something say it to my face! I know you laugh at me behind my back. You'll laugh out of the other side of your goddam face after this game. Touchdown! Touchdown! Eighty thousand people! Touchdown! Right between the goal posts.

(BERNARD *is a quiet, earnest, but self-assured young man.* WILLY's *voice is coming from right upstage now.* BERNARD *lowers his feet off the table and listens.* JENNY, *his father's secretary, enters.*)

JENNY (*distressed*): Say, Bernard, will you go out in the hall?

BERNARD: What is that noise? Who is it?

JENNY: Mr. Loman. He just got off the elevator.

BERNARD (*getting up*): Who's he arguing with?

JENNY: Nobody. There's nobody with him. I can't deal with him any more, and your father gets all upset everytime he comes. I've got a lot of typing to do, and your father's waiting to sign it. Will you see him?

WILLY (*entering*): Touchdown! Touch—(*He sees* JENNY) Jenny, Jenny, good to see you. How're ya? Workin'? Or still honest?

JENNY: Fine. How've you been feeling?

WILLY: Not much any more, Jenny. Ha, ha! (*He is surprised to see the rackets.*)

BERNARD: Hello, Uncle Willy.

WILLY (*almost shocked*): Bernard! Well, look who's here! (*He comes quickly, guiltily, to* BERNARD *and warmly shakes his hand.*)

BERNARD: How are you? Good to see you.

WILLY: What are you doing here?

BERNARD: Oh, just stopped by to see Pop. Get off my feet till my train leaves. I'm going to Washington in a few minutes.

WILLY: Is he in?

BERNARD: Yes, he's in his office with the accountant. Sit down.

WILLY (*sitting down*): What're you going to do in Washington?

BERNARD: Oh, just a case I've got there, Willy.

WILLY: That so? (*Indicating the rackets*) You going to play tennis there?

BERNARD: I'm staying with a friend who's got a court.

WILLY: Don't say. His own tennis court. Must be fine people, I bet.

BERNARD: They are, very nice. Dad tells me Biff's in town.

WILLY (*with a big smile*): Yeah, Biff's in. Working on a very big deal, Bernard.

BERNARD: What's Biff doing?

WILLY: Well, he's been doing very big things in the West. But he decided to establish himself here. Very big. We're having dinner. Did I hear your wife had a boy?

BERNARD: That's right. Our second.

WILLY: Two boys! What do you know!

BERNARD: What kind of a deal has Biff got?

WILLY: Well, Bill Oliver—very big sporting-goods man—he wants Biff very badly. Called him in from the West. Long distance, carte blanche, special deliveries. Your friends have their own private tennis court?

BERNARD: You still with the old firm, Willy?

WILLY (*after a pause*): I'm—I'm overjoyed to see how you made the grade, Bernard, overjoyed. It's an encouraging thing to see a young man really—really—Looks very good for Biff—very—(*He breaks off, then*) Bernard—(*He is so full of emotion, he breaks off again.*)

BERNARD: What is it, Willy?

WILLY (*small and alone*): What—what's the secret?

BERNARD: What secret?

WILLY: How—how did you? Why didn't he ever catch on?

BERNARD: I wouldn't know that, Willy.

WILLY (*confidentially, desperately*): You were his friend, his boyhood friend. There's something I don't understand about it. His life ended after that Ebbets Field game. From the age of seventeen nothing good ever happened to him.

BERNARD: He never trained himself for anything.

WILLY: But he did, he did. After high school he took so many correspondence courses. Radio mechanics; television; God knows what, and never made the slightest mark.

BERNARD (*taking off his glasses*): Willy, do you want to talk candidly?

WILLY (*rising, faces* BERNARD): I regard you as a very brilliant man, Bernard. I value your advice.

BERNARD: Oh, the hell with the advice, Willy. I couldn't advise you. There's just one thing I've always wanted to ask you. When he was supposed to graduate, and the math teacher flunked him—

WILLY: Oh, that son-of-a-bitch ruined his life.

BERNARD: Yeah, but, Willy, all he had to do was go to summer school and make up that subject.

WILLY: That's right, that's right.

BERNARD: Did you tell him not to go to summer school?

WILLY: Me? I begged him to go. I ordered him to go!

BERNARD: Then why wouldn't he go?

WILLY: Why? Why! Bernard, that question has been trailing me like a ghost for the last fifteen years. He flunked the subject, and laid down and died like a hammer hit him!

BERNARD: Take it easy, kid.

WILLY: Let me talk to you—I got nobody to talk to. Bernard, Bernard, was it my fault? Y'see? It keeps going around in my mind, maybe I did something to him. I got nothing to give him.

BERNARD: Don't take it so hard.

WILLY: Why did he lay down? What is the story there? You were his friend!

BERNARD: Willy, I remember, it was June, and our grades came out. And he'd flunked math.

WILLY: That son-of-a-bitch!

BERNARD: No, it wasn't right then. Biff just got very angry, I remember, and he was ready to enroll in summer school.

WILLY (*surprised*): He was?

BERNARD: He wasn't beaten by it at all. But then, Willy, he disappeared from the block for almost a month. And I got the idea that he'd gone up to New England to see you. Did he have a talk with you then?

(WILLY *stares in silence.*)

BERNARD: Willy?

WILLY (*with a strong edge of resentment in his voice*): Yeah, he came to Boston. What about it?

BERNARD: Well, just that when he came back— I'll never forget this, it always mystifies me. Because I'd thought so well of Biff, even though he'd always taken advantage of me. I loved him, Willy, y'know? And he came back after that month and took his sneakers—remember those sneakers with "University of Virginia" printed on them? He was so proud of those, wore them every day. And he took them down in the cellar, and burned them up in the furnace. We had a fist fight. It lasted at least half an hour. Just the two of us, punching each other down the cellar, and crying right through it. I've often thought of how strange it was that I knew he'd given up his life. What happened in Boston, Willy?

(WILLY *looks at him as at an intruder.*)

BERNARD: I just bring it up because you asked me.

WILLY (*angrily*): Nothing. What do you mean, "What happened?" What's that got to do with anything?

BERNARD: Well, don't get sore.

WILLY: What are you trying to do, blame it on me? If a boy lays down is that my fault?

BERNARD: Now, Willy, don't get—

WILLY: Well, don't—don't talk to me that way! What does that mean, "What happened?"

(CHARLEY *enters. He is in his vest, and he carries a bottle of bourbon.*)

CHARLEY: Hey, you're going to miss that train. (*He waves the bottle.*)

BERNARD: Yeah, I'm going. (*He takes the bottle.*) Thanks, Pop. (*He picks up his rackets and bag.*) Good-bye, Willy, and don't worry about it. You know, "If at first you don't succeed . . ."

WILLY: Yes, I believe in that.

BERNARD: But sometimes, Willy, it's better for a man just to walk away.

WILLY: Walk away?

BERNARD: That's right.

WILLY: But if you can't walk away?

BERNARD (*after a slight pause*): I guess that's when it's tough. (*Extending his hand*) Good-bye, Willy.

WILLY (*shaking* BERNARD'*s hand*): Good-bye, boy.

CHARLEY (*an arm on* BERNARD'*s shoulder*): How do you like this kid? Gonna argue a case in front of the Supreme Court.

BERNARD (*protesting*): Pop!

WILLY (*genuinely shocked, pained, and happy*): No! The Supreme Court!

BERNARD: I gotta run. 'Bye, Dad!

CHARLEY: Knock 'em dead, Bernard!

(BERNARD *goes off.*)

WILLY (*as* CHARLEY *takes out his wallet*): The Supreme Court! And he didn't even mention it!

CHARLEY (*counting out money on the desk*): He don't have to—he's gonna do it.

WILLY: And you never told him what to do, did you? You never took any interest in him.

CHARLEY: My salvation is that I never took any interest in anything. There's some money—fifty dollars. I got an accountant inside.

WILLY: Charley, look . . . (*With difficulty*) I got my insurance to pay. If you can manage it—I need a hundred and ten dollars.

(CHARLEY *doesn't reply for a moment; merely stops moving.*)

WILLY: I'd draw it from my bank but Linda would know, and I . . .

CHARLEY: Sit down, Willy.

WILLY (*moving toward the chair*): I'm keeping an account of everything, remember. I'll pay every penny back. (*He sits.*)

CHARLEY: Now listen to me, Willy.

WILLY: I want you to know I appreciate . . .

CHARLEY (*sitting down on the table*): Willy, what're you doin'? What the hell is goin' on in your head?

WILLY: Why? I'm simply . . .

CHARLEY: I offered you a job. You can make fifty dollars a week. And I won't send you on the road.

WILLY: I've got a job.

CHARLEY: Without pay? What kind of a job is a job without pay? (*He rises.*) Now, look, kid, enough is enough. I'm no genius but I know when I'm being insulted.

WILLY: Insulted!

CHARLEY: Why don't you want to work for me?

WILLY: What's the matter with you? I've got a job.

CHARLEY: Then what're you walkin' in here every week for?

WILLY (*getting up*): Well, if you don't want me to walk in here—

CHARLEY: I am offering you a job.

WILLY: I don't want your goddam job!

CHARLEY: When the hell are you going to grow up?

WILLY (*furiously*): You big ignoramus, if you say that to me again I'll rap you one! I don't care how big you are! (*He's ready to fight.*)

(*Pause.*)

CHARLEY (*kindly, going to him*): How much do you need, Willy?

WILLY: Charley, I'm strapped. I'm strapped. I don't know what to do. I was just fired.

CHARLEY: Howard fired you?

WILLY: That snotnose. Imagine that? I named him. I named him Howard.

CHARLEY: Willy, when're you gonna realize that them things don't mean anything? You named him Howard, but you can't sell that. The only thing you got in this world is what you can sell. And the funny thing is that you're a salesman, and you don't know that.

WILLY: I've always tried to think otherwise, I guess. I always felt that if a man was impressive, and well liked, that nothing—

CHARLEY: Why must everybody like you? Who liked J. P. Morgan? Was he impressive? In a Turkish bath he'd look like a butcher. But with his pockets on he was very well liked. Now listen, Willy, I know you don't like me, and nobody can say I'm in love with you, but I'll give you a job because—just for the hell of it, put it that way. Now what do you say?

WILLY: I—I just can't work for you, Charley.

CHARLEY: What're you, jealous of me?

WILLY: I can't work for you, that's all, don't ask me why.

CHARLEY (*angered, takes out more bills*): You been jealous of me all your life, you damned fool! Here, pay your insurance. (*He puts the money in* WILLY'*s hand.*)

WILLY: I'm keeping strict accounts.

CHARLEY: I've got some work to do. Take care of yourself. And pay your insurance.

WILLY (*moving to the right*): Funny, y'know? After all the highways, and the trains, and the appointments, and the years, you end up worth more dead than alive.

CHARLEY: Willy, nobody's worth nothin' dead. (*After a slight pause.*) Did you hear what I said?

(WILLY *stands still, dreaming.*)

CHARLEY: Willy!

WILLY: Apologize to Bernard for me when you see him. I didn't mean to argue with him. He's a fine boy. They're all fine boys, and they'll end up big—all of them. Someday they'll all play tennis together. Wish me luck, Charley. He saw Bill Oliver today.

CHARLEY: Good luck.

WILLY (*on the verge of tears*): Charley, you're the only friend I got. Isn't that a remarkable thing? (*He goes out.*)

CHARLEY: Jesus!

(CHARLEY *stares after him a moment and follows. All light blacks out. Suddenly raucous music is heard, and a red glow rises behind the screen at right.* STANLEY, *a young waiter, appears, carrying a table, followed by* HAPPY, *who is carrying two chairs.*)

STANLEY (*putting the table down*): That's all right, Mr. Loman, I can handle it myself. (*He turns and takes the chairs from* HAPPY *and places them at the table.*)

HAPPY (*glancing around*): Oh, this is better.

STANLEY: Sure, in the front there you're in the middle of all kinds a noise. Whenever you got a party, Mr. Loman, you just tell me and I'll put you back here. Y'know, there's a lotta people they don't like it private, because when they go out they like to see a lotta action around them because they're sick and tired to stay in the house by theirself. But I know you, you ain't from Hackensack. You know what I mean?

HAPPY (*sitting down*): So how's it coming, Stanley?

STANLEY: Ah, it's a dog's life. I only wish during the war they'd a took me in the Army. I coulda been dead by now.

HAPPY: My brother's back, Stanley.

STANLEY: Oh, he come back, heh? From the Far West.

HAPPY: Yeah, big cattle man, my brother, so treat him right. And my father's coming too.

STANELY: Oh, your father too!

HAPPY: You got a couple of nice lobsters?

STANLEY: Hundred per cent, big.

HAPPY: I want them with the claws.

STANLEY: Don't worry, I don't give you no mice. (HAPPY *laughs.*) How about some wine? It'll put a head on the meal.

HAPPY: No. You remember, Stanley, that recipe I brought you from overseas? With the champagne in it?

STANLEY: Oh, yeah, sure. I still got it tacked up yet in the kitchen. But that'll have to cost a buck apiece anyways.

HAPPY: That's all right.

STANLEY: What'd you, hit a number or somethin'?

HAPPY: No, it's a little celebration. My brother is—I think he pulled off a big deal today. I think we're going into business together.

STANLEY: Great! That's the best for you. Because a family business, you know what I mean?—that's the best.

HAPPY: That's what I think.

STANLEY: 'Cause what's the difference? Somebody steals? It's in the family. Know what I mean? (*Sotto voce*) Like this bartender here. The boss is goin' crazy what kinda leak he's got in the cash register. You put it in but it don't come out.

HAPPY (*raising his head*): Sh!

STANLEY: What?

HAPPY: You notice I wasn't lookin' right or left, was I?

STANLEY: No.

HAPPY: And my eyes are closed.

STANLEY: So what's the—?

HAPPY: Strudel's comin'.

STANLEY (*catching on, looks around*): Ah, no, there's no—

(*He breaks off as a furred, lavishly dressed* GIRL *enters and sits at the next table. Both follow her with their eyes.*)

STANLEY: Geez, how'd ya know?

HAPPY: I got radar or something. (*Staring directly at her profile*) Ooooooooo . . . Stanley.

STANLEY: I think that's for you, Mr. Loman.

HAPPY: Look at that mouth. Oh, God. And the binoculars.

STANLEY: Geez, you got a life, Mr. Loman.

HAPPY: Wait on her.

STANLEY (*going to* THE GIRL's *table*) Would you like a menu, ma'am?

GIRL: I'm expecting someone, but I'd like a—

HAPPY: Why don't you bring her—excuse me, miss, do you mind? I sell champagne, and I'd like you to try my brand. Bring her a champagne, Stanley.

GIRL: That's awfully nice of you.

HAPPY: Don't mention it. It's all company money. (*He laughs.*)

GIRL: That's a charming product to be selling, isn't it?

HAPPY: Oh, gets to be like everything else. Selling is selling, y'know.

GIRL: I suppose.

HAPPY: You don't happen to sell, do you?

GIRL: No, I don't sell.

HAPPY: Would you object to a compliment from a stranger? You ought to be on a magazine cover.

GIRL (*looking at him a little archly*): I have been.

(STANLEY *comes in with a glass of champagne.*)

HAPPY: What'd I say before, Stanley? You see? She's a cover girl.

STANLEY: Oh, I could see, I could see.

HAPPY (*to* THE GIRL): What magazine?

GIRL: Oh, a lot of them. (*She takes the drink.*) Thank you.

HAPPY: You know what they say in France, don't you? "Champagne is the drink of the complexion"—Hya, Biff!

(BIFF *has entered and sits with* HAPPY.)

BIFF: Hello, kid. Sorry I'm late.

HAPPY: I just got here. Uh, Miss—?

GIRL: Forsythe.

HAPPY: Miss Forsythe, this is my brother.

BIFF: Is Dad here?

HAPPY: His name is Biff. You might've heard of him. Great football player.

GIRL: Really? What team?

HAPPY: Are you familiar with football?

GIRL: No, I'm afraid I'm not.

HAPPY: Biff is quarterback with the New York Giants.

GIRL: Well, that is nice, isn't it? (*She drinks.*)

HAPPY: Good health.

GIRL: I'm happy to meet you.

HAPPY: That's my name. Hap. It's really Harold, but at West Point they called me Happy.

GIRL (*now really impressed*): Oh, I see. How do you do? (*She turns her profile.*)

BIFF: Isn't Dad coming?

HAPPY: You want her?

BIFF: Oh, I could never make that.

HAPPY: I remember the time that idea would never come into your head. Where's the old confidence, Biff?

BIFF: I just saw Oliver—

HAPPY: Wait a minute. I've got to see that old confidence again. Do you want her? She's on call.

BIFF: Oh, no. (*He turns to look at* THE GIRL.)

HAPPY: I'm telling you. Watch this. (*Turning to* THE GIRL) Honey? (*She turns to him.*) Are you busy?

GIRL: Well, I am . . . but I could make a phone call.

HAPPY: Do that, will you, honey? And see if you can get a friend. We'll be here for a while. Biff is one of the greatest football players in the country.

GIRL (*standing up*): Well, I'm certainly happy to meet you.

HAPPY: Come back soon.

GIRL: I'll try.

HAPPY: Don't try, honey, try hard.

(THE GIRL *exits.* STANLEY *follows, shaking his head in bewildered admiration.*)

HAPPY: Isn't that a shame now? A beautiful girl like that? That's why I can't get married. There's not a good woman in a thousand. New York is loaded with them, kid!

BIFF: Hap, look—

HAPPY: I told you she was on call!

BIFF (*strangely unnerved*): Cut it out, will ya? I want to say something to you.

HAPPY: Did you see Oliver?

BIFF: I saw him all right. Now look, I want to tell Dad a couple of things and I want you to help me.

HAPPY: What? Is he going to back you?

BIFF: Are you crazy? You're out of your goddam head, you know that?

HAPPY: Why? What happened?

BIFF (*breathlessly*): I did a terrible thing today, Hap. It's the strangest day I ever went through. I'm all numb, I swear.

HAPPY: You mean he wouldn't see you?

BIFF: Well, I waited six hours for him, see? All day. Kept sending my name in. Even tried to date his secretary so she'd get me to him, but no soap.

HAPPY: Because you're not showin' the old confidence, Biff. He remembered you, didn't he?

BIFF (*stopping* HAPPY *with a gesture*): Finally, about five o'clock, he comes out. Didn't remember who I was or anything. I felt like such an idiot, Hap.

HAPPY: Did you tell him my Florida idea?

BIFF: He walked away. I saw him for one minute. I got so mad I could've torn the walls down! How the hell did I ever get the idea I was a salesman there? I even believed myself that I'd been a salesman for him! And then he gave me one look and—I realized what a ridiculous lie my whole life has been! We've been talking in a dream for fifteen years. I was a shipping clerk.

HAPPY: What'd you do?

BIFF (*with great tension and wonder*): Well, he left, see. And the secretary went out. I was all alone in the waiting room. I don't know what came over me, Hap. The next thing I know I'm in his office—paneled walls, everything. I can't explain it. I—Hap, I took his fountain pen.

HAPPY: Geez, did he catch you?

BIFF: I ran out. I ran down all eleven flights. I ran and ran and ran.

HAPPY: That was an awful dumb—what'd you do that for?

BIFF (*agonized*): I don't know, I just—wanted to take something, I don't know. You gotta help me, Hap, I'm gonna tell Pop.

HAPPY: You crazy? What for?

BIFF: Hap, he's got to understand that I'm not the man somebody lends that kind of money to. He thinks I've been spiting him all these years and it's eating him up.

HAPPY: That's just it. You tell him something nice.

BIFF: I can't.

HAPPY: Say you got a lunch date with Oliver tomorrow.

BIFF: So what do I do tomorrow?

HAPPY: You leave the house tomorrow and come back at night and say Oliver is thinking it over. And he thinks it over for a couple of weeks, and gradually it fades away and nobody's the worse.

BIFF: But it'll go on forever!

HAPPY: Dad is never so happy as when he's looking forward to something!

(WILLY *enters.*)

HAPPY: Hello, scout!

WILLY: Gee, I haven't been here in years!

(STANLEY *has followed* WILLY *in and sets a chair for him.* STANLEY *starts off but* HAPPY *stops him.*)

HAPPY: Stanley!

(STANLEY *stands by, waiting for an order.*)

BIFF (*going to* WILLY *with guilt, as to an invalid*): Sit down, Pop. You want a drink?

WILLY: Sure, I don't mind.

BIFF: Let's get a load on.

WILLY: You look worried.

BIFF: N-no. (*To* STANLEY) Scotch all around. Make it doubles.

STANLEY: Doubles, right. (*He goes.*)

WILLY: You had a couple already, didn't you?

BIFF: Just a couple, yeah.

WILLY: Well, what happened, boy? (*Nodding affirmatively, with a smile.*) Everything go all right?

BIFF (*takes a breath, then reaches out and grasps* WILLY's *hand*): Pal . . . (*He is smiling bravely, and* WILLY *is smiling too.*) I had an experience today.

HAPPY: Terrific, Pop.

WILLY: That so? What happened?

BIFF (*high, slightly alcoholic, above the earth*): I'm going to tell you everything from first to last. It's been a strange day. (*Silence. He looks around, composes himself as best he can, but his breath keeps breaking the rhythm of his voice.*) I had to wait quite a while for him, and—

WILLY: Oliver?

BIFF: Yeah, Oliver. All day, as a matter of cold fact. And a lot of—instances—facts, Pop, facts about my life came back to me. Who was it, Pop? Who ever said I was a salesman with Oliver?

WILLY: Well, you were.

BIFF: No, Dad, I was a shipping clerk.

WILLY: But you were practically—

BIFF (*with determination*): Dad, I don't know who said it first, but I was never a salesman for Bill Oliver.

WILLY: What're you talking about?

BIFF: Let's hold on to the facts tonight, Pop. We're not going to get anywhere bullin' around. I was a shipping clerk.

WILLY (*angrily*): All right, now listen to me—

BIFF: Why don't you let me finish?

WILLY: I'm not interested in stories about the past or any crap of that kind because the woods are burning, boys, you understand? There's a big blaze going on all around. I was fired today.

BIFF (*shocked*): How could you be?

WILLY: I was fired, and I'm looking for a little good news to tell your mother, because the woman has waited and the woman has suffered. The gist of it is that I haven't got a story left in my head, Biff. So don't give me a lecture about facts and aspects. I am not interested. Now what've you got to say to me?

(STANLEY *enters with three drinks. They wait until he leaves.*)

WILLY: Did you see Oliver?

BIFF: Jesus, Dad!

WILLY: You mean you didn't go up there?

HAPPY: Sure he went up there.

BIFF: I did. I—saw him. How could they fire you?

WILLY (*on the edge of his chair*): What kind of a welcome did he give you?

BIFF: He won't even let you work on commission?

WILLY: I'm out! (*Driving*) So tell me, he gave you a warm welcome?

HAPPY: Sure, Pop, sure!

BIFF (*driven*): Well, it was kind of—

WILLY: I was wondering if he'd remember you. (*To* HAPPY) Imagine, man doesn't see him for ten, twelve years and gives him that kind of a welcome!

HAPPY: Damn right!

BIFF (*trying to return to the offensive*): Pop, look—

WILLY: You know why he remembered you, don't you? Because you impressed him in those days.

BIFF: Let's talk quietly and get this down to the facts, huh?

WILLY (*as though* BIFF *had been interrupting*): Well, what happened? It's great news, Biff. Did he take you into his office or'd you talk in the waiting room?

BIFF: Well, he came in, see, and—

WILLY (*with a big smile*): What'd he say? Betcha he threw his arm around you.

BIFF: Well, he kinda—

WILLY: He's a fine man. (*To* HAPPY) Very hard man to see, y'know.

HAPPY (*agreeing*): Oh, I know.

WILLY (*to* BIFF): Is that where you had the drinks?

BIFF: Yeah, he gave me a couple of—no, no!

HAPPY (*cutting in*): He told him my Florida idea.

WILLY: Don't interrupt. (*To* BIFF) How'd he react to the Florida idea?

BIFF: Dad, will you give me a minute to explain?

WILLY: I've been waiting for you to explain since I sat down here! What happened? He took you into his office and what?

BIFF: Well—I talked. And—and he listened, see.

WILLY: Famous for the way he listens, y'know. What was his answer?

BIFF: His answer was—(*He breaks off, suddenly angry*) Dad, you're not letting me tell you what I want to tell you!

WILLY (*accusing, angered*): You didn't see him, did you?

BIFF: I did see him!

WILLY: What'd you insult him or something? You insulted him, didn't you?

BIFF: Listen, will you let me out of it, will you just let me out of it!

HAPPY: What the hell!

WILLY: Tell me what happened!

BIFF (*to* HAPPY): I can't talk to him!

(*A single trumpet note jars the ear. The light of green leaves stains the house, which holds the air of night and a dream.* YOUNG BERNARD *enters and knocks on the door of the house.*)

YOUNG BERNARD (*frantically*): Mrs. Loman, Mrs. Loman!

HAPPY: Tell him what happened!

BIFF (*to* HAPPY): Shut up and leave me alone!

WILLY: No, no! You had to go and flunk math!

BIFF: What math? What're you talking about?

YOUNG BERNARD: Mrs. Loman, Mrs. Loman!

(LINDA *appears in the house, as of old.*)

WILLY (*wildly*): Math, math, math!

BIFF: Take it easy, Pop!

YOUNG BERNARD: Mrs. Loman!

WILLY (*furiously*): If you hadn't flunked you'd've been set by now!

BIFF: Now, look, I'm gonna tell you what happened, and you're going to listen to me.

YOUNG BERNARD: Mrs. Loman!

BIFF: I waited six hours—

HAPPY: What the hell are you saying?

BIFF: I kept sending in my name but he wouldn't see me. So finally he . . . (*He continues unheard as light fades low on the restaurant.*)

YOUNG BERNARD: Biff flunked math!

LINDA: No!

YOUNG BERNARD: Birnbaum flunked him! They won't graduate him!

LINDA: But they have to. He's gotta go to the university. Where is he? Biff! Biff!

YOUNG BERNARD: No, he left. He went to Grand Central.

LINDA: Grand—You mean he went to Boston!

YOUNG BERNARD: Is Uncle Willy in Boston?

LINDA: Oh, maybe Willy can talk to the teacher. Oh, the poor, poor boy!

(*Light on house area snaps out.*)

BIFF (*at the table, now audible, holding up a gold fountain pen*): . . . so I'm washed up with Oliver, you understand? Are you listening to me?

WILLY (*at a loss*): Yeah, sure. If you hadn't flunked

BIFF: Flunked what? What're you talking about?

WILLY: Don't blame everything on me! I didn't flunk math—you did! What pen?

HAPPY: That was awful dumb, Biff, a pen like that is worth—

WILLY (*seeing the pen for the first time*): You took Oliver's pen?

BIFF (*weakening*): Dad, I just explained it to you.

WILLY: You stole Bill Oliver's fountain pen!

BIFF: I didn't exactly steal it! That's just what I've been explaining to you!

HAPPY: He had it in his hand and just then Oliver walked in, so he got nervous and stuck it in his pocket!

WILLY: My God, Biff!

BIFF: I never intended to do it, Dad!

OPERATOR'S VOICE: Standish Arms, good evening!

WILLY (*shouting*): I'm not in my room!

BIFF (*frightened*): Dad, what's the matter? (*He and* HAPPY *stand up.*)

OPERATOR: Ringing Mr. Loman for you!

WILLY: I'm not there, stop it!

BIFF (*horrified, gets down on one knee before* WILLY): Dad, I'll make good, I'll make good. (WILLY *tries to get to his feet.* BIFF *holds him down.*) Sit down now.

WILLY: No, you're no good, you're no good for anything.

BIFF: I am, Dad, I'll find something else, you understand? Now don't worry about anything. (*He holds up* WILLY's *face.*) Talk to me, Dad.

OPERATOR: Mr. Loman does not answer. Shall I page him?

WILLY (*attempting to stand, as though to rush and silence the* OPERATOR): No, no, no!

HAPPY: He'll strike something, Pop.

WILLY: No, no . . .

BIFF (*desperately, standing over* WILLY): Pop, listen! Listen to me! I'm telling you something good. Oliver talked to his partner about the Florida idea. You listening? He—he talked to his partner, and he came to me . . . I'm going to be all right, you hear? Dad, listen to me, he said it was just a question of the amount!

WILLY: Then you . . . got it?

HAPPY: He's gonna be terrific, Pop!

WILLY (*trying to stand*): Then you got it, haven't you? You got it! You got it!

BIFF (*agonized, holds* WILLY *down*): No, no. Look, Pop. I'm supposed to have lunch with them tomorrow. I'm just telling you this so you'll know that I can still make an impression, Pop. And I'll make good somewhere, but I can't go tomorrow, see?

WILLY: Why not? You simply—

BIFF: But the pen, Pop!

WILLY: You give it to him and tell him it was an oversight!

HAPPY: Sure, have lunch tomorrow!

BIFF: I can't say that—

WILLY: You were doing a crossword puzzle and accidentally used his pen!

BIFF: Listen, kid, I took those balls years ago, now I walk in with his fountain pen? That clinches it, don't you see? I can't face him like that! I'll try elsewhere.

PAGE's VOICE: Paging Mr. Loman!

WILLY: Don't you want to be anything?

BIFF: Pop, how can I go back?

WILLY: You don't want to be anything, is that what's behind it?

BIFF: (*now angry at* WILLY *for not crediting his sympathy*): Don't take it that way! You think it was easy walking into that office after what I'd done to him? A team of horses couldn't have dragged me back to Bill Oliver!

WILLY: Then why'd you go?

BIFF: Why did I go? Why did I go! Look at you! Look at what's become of you!

(*Off left,* THE WOMAN *laughs.*)

WILLY: Biff, you're going to go to that lunch tomorrow, or—

BIFF: I can't go. I've got no appointment!

HAPPY: Biff, for . . . !

WILLY: Are you spiting me?

BIFF: Don't take it that way! Goddammit!

WILLY (*strikes* BIFF *and falters away from the table*): You rotten little louse! Are you spiting me?

THE WOMAN: Someone's at the door, Willy!

BIFF: I'm no good, can't you see what I am?

HAPPY (*separating them*): Hey, you're in a restaurant! Now cut it out, both of you! (THE GIRLS *enter.*) Hello, girls, sit down.

(THE WOMAN *laughs, off left.*)

MISS FORSYTHE: I guess we might as well. This is Letta.

THE WOMAN: Willy, are you going to wake up?

BIFF (*ignoring* WILLY): How'r ya, miss, sit down. What do you drink?

MISS FORSYTHE: Letta might not be able to stay long.

LETTA: I gotta get up very early tomorrow. I got jury duty. I'm so excited! Were you fellows ever on a jury?

BIFF: No, but I been in front of them! (THE GIRLS *laugh.*) This is my father.

LETTA: Isn't he cute? Sit down with us, Pop.

HAPPY: Sit him down, Biff!

BIFF (*going to him*): Come on, slugger, drink us under the table. To hell with it! Come on, sit down, pal.

(*On* BIFF's *insistence,* WILLY *is about to sit.*)

THE WOMAN (*now urgently*): Willy, are you going to answer the door!

(THE WOMAN's *call pulls* WILLY *back. He starts right, befuddled.*)

BIFF: Hey, where are you going?

WILLY: Open the door.

BIFF: The door?

WILLY: The washroom . . . the door . . . where's the door?

BIFF (*leading* WILLY *to the left*): Just go straight down.

(WILLY *moves left.*)

THE WOMAN: Willy, Willy, are you going to get up, get up, get up, get up?

(WILLY *exits left.*)

LETTA: I think it's sweet you bring your daddy along.

MISS FORSYTHE: Oh, he isn't really your father!

BIFF (*at left, turning to her resentfully*): Miss Forsythe, you've just seen a prince walk by. A fine, troubled prince. A hard-working, unappreciated prince. A pal, you understand? A good companion. Always for his boys.

LETTA: That's so sweet.

HAPPY: Well, girls, what's the program? We're wasting time. Come on, Biff. Gather round. Where would you like to go?

BIFF: Why don't you do something for him?

HAPPY: Me!

BIFF: Don't you give a damn for him, Hap?

HAPPY: What're you talking about? I'm the one who—

BIFF: I sense it, you don't give a good goddam about him. (*He takes the rolled-up hose from his pocket and puts it on the table in front of* HAPPY.) Look what I found in the cellar, for Christ's sake. How can you bear to let it go on?

HAPPY: Me? Who goes away? Who runs off and—

BIFF: Yeah, but he doesn't mean anything to you. You could help him—I can't! Don't you understand what I'm talking about? He's going to kill himself, don't you know that?

HAPPY: Don't I know it! Me!

BIFF: Hap, help him! Jesus . . . help him . . . Help me, help me, I can't bear to look at his face! (*Ready to weep, he hurries out, up right.*)

HAPPY (*starting after him*): Where are you going?

MISS FORSYTHE: What's he so mad about?

HAPPY: Come on, girls, we'll catch up with him.

MISS FORSYTHE (as HAPPY pushes her out): Say, I don't like that temper of his!

HAPPY: He's just a little overstrung, he'll be all right!

WILLY (off left, as THE WOMAN laughs): Don't answer! Don't answer!

LETTA: Don't you want to tell your father—

HAPPY: No, that's not my father. He's just a guy. Come on, we'll catch Biff, and, honey, we're going to paint this town! Stanley, where's the check! Hey, Stanley!

(They exit. STANLEY looks toward left.)

STANLEY (calling to HAPPY indignantly): Mr. Loman! Mr. Loman!

(STANLEY picks up a chair and follows them off. Knocking is heard off left. THE WOMAN enters, laughing. WILLY follows her. She is in a black slip; he is buttoning his shirt. Raw, sensuous music accompanies their speech.)

WILLY: Will you stop laughing? Will you stop?

THE WOMAN: Aren't you going to answer the door? He'll wake the whole hotel.

WILLY: I'm not expecting anybody.

THE WOMAN: Whyn't you have another drink, honey, and stop being so damn self-centered?

WILLY: I'm so lonely.

THE WOMAN: You know you ruined me, Willy? From now on, whenever you come to the office, I'll see that you go right through to the buyers. No waiting at my desk any more, Willy. You ruined me.

WILLY: That's nice of you to say that.

THE WOMAN: Gee, you are self-centered! Why so sad? You are the saddest self-centeredest soul I ever did see-saw. (She laughs. He kisses her.) Come on inside, drummer boy. It's silly to be dressing in the middle of the night. (As knocking is heard.) Aren't you going to answer the door?

WILLY: They're knocking on the wrong door.

THE WOMAN: But I felt the knocking. And he heard us talking in here. Maybe the hotel's on fire!

WILLY (his terror rising): It's a mistake.

THE WOMAN: Then tell him to go away!

WILLY: There's nobody there.

THE WOMAN: It's getting on my nerves, Willy. There's somebody standing out there and it's getting on my nerves!

WILLY (pushing her away from him): All right, stay in the bathroom here, and don't come out. I think there's a law in Massachusetts about it, so don't come out. It may be that new room clerk. He looked very mean. So don't come out. It's a mistake, there's no fire.

(The knocking is heard again. He takes a few steps away from her, and she vanishes into the wing. The light follows him, and now he is facing YOUNG BIFF, who carries a suitcase. BIFF steps toward him. The music is gone.)

BIFF: Why didn't you answer?

WILLY: Biff! What are you doing in Boston?

BIFF: Why didn't you answer? I've been knocking for five minutes, I called you on the phone—

WILLY: I just heard you. I was in the bathroom and had the door shut. Did anything happen home?

BIFF: Dad—I let you down.

WILLY: What do you mean?

BIFF: Dad . . .

WILLY: Biffo, what's this about? (Putting his arm around BIFF) Come on, let's go downstairs and get you a malted.

BIFF: Dad, I flunked math.

WILLY: Not for the term?

BIFF: The term. I haven't got enough credits to graduate.

WILLY: You mean to say Bernard wouldn't give you the answers?

BIFF: He did, he tried, but I only got a sixty-one.

WILLY: And they wouldn't give you four points?

BIFF: Birnbaum refused absolutely. I begged him, Pop, to give me those points. You gotta talk to him before they close the school. Because if he saw the kind of man you are, and you just talked to him in your way, I'm sure he'd come through for me. The class came right before practice, see, and I didn't go enough. Would you talk to him? He'd like you, Pop. You know the way you could talk.

WILLY: You're on. We'll drive right back.

BIFF: Oh, Dad, good work! I'm sure he'll change it for you!

WILLY: Go downstairs and tell the clerk I'm checkin' out. Go right down.

BIFF: Yes, sir! See, the reason he hates me, Pop—one day he was late for class so I got up at the blackboard and imitated him. I crossed my eyes and talked with a lithp.

WILLY (laughing): You did? The kids like it?

BIFF: They nearly died laughing!

WILLY: Yeah? What'd you do?

BIFF: The thquare root of thixthy twee is . . . (WILLY bursts out laughing; BIFF joins him.) And in the middle of it he walked in!

(WILLY *laughs and* THE WOMAN *joins in offstage.*)

WILLY (*without hesitation*): Hurry downstairs and—
BIFF: Somebody in there?
WILLY: No, that was next door.

(THE WOMAN *laughs offstage.*)

BIFF: Somebody got in your bathroom!
WILLY: No, it's the next room, there's a party—
THE WOMAN (*enters, laughing. She lisps this*): Can I come in? There's something in the bathtub, Willy, and it's moving!

(WILLY *looks at* BIFF, *who is staring open-mouthed and horrified at* THE WOMAN.)

WILLY: Ah—you better go back to your room. They must be finished painting by now. They're painting her room so I let her take a shower here. Go back, go back . . . (*he pushes her.*)
THE WOMAN (*resisting*): But I've got to get dressed, Willy, I can't—
WILLY: Get out of here! Go back, go back . . . (*Suddenly striving for the ordinary*) This is Miss Francis, Biff, she's a buyer. They're painting her room. Go back, Miss Francis, go back . . .
THE WOMAN: But my clothes, I can't go out naked in the hall!
WILLY (*pushing her offstage*): Get outa here! Go back, go back!

(BIFF *slowly sits down on his suitcase as the argument continues offstage.*)

THE WOMAN: Where's my stockings? You promised me stockings, Willy!
WILLY: I have no stockings here!
THE WOMAN: You had two boxes of size nine sheers for me, and I want them!
WILLY: Here, for God's sake, will you get outa here!
THE WOMAN (*enters holding a box of stockings*): I just hope there's nobody in the hall. That's all I hope. (*To* BIFF): Are you football or baseball?
BIFF: Football.
THE WOMAN (*angry, humiliated*): That's me too. G'night. (*She snatches her clothes from* WILLY, *and walks out.*)
WILLY (*after a pause*): Well, better get going. I want to get to the school first thing in the morning. Get my suits out of the closet. I'll get my valise. (BIFF *doesn't move.*) What's the matter? (BIFF *remains motionless, tears falling.*) She's a buyer. Buys for J. H. Simmons. She lives down the

hall—they're painting. You don't imagine—(*He breaks off. After a pause.*) Now listen, pal, she's just a buyer. She sees merchandise in her room and they have to keep it looking just so . . . (*Pause. Assuming command*) All right, get my suits. (BIFF *doesn't move.*) Now stop crying and do as I say. I gave you an order. Biff, I gave you an order! Is that what you do when I give you an order? How dare you cry! (*Putting his arm around* BIFF) Now look, Biff, when you grow up you'll understand about these things. You mustn't—you mustn't over-emphasize a thing like this. I'll see Birnbaum first thing in the morning.
BIFF: Never mind.
WILLY (*getting down beside* BIFF): Never mind! He's going to give you those points. I'll see to it.
BIFF: He wouldn't listen to you.
WILLY: He certainly will listen to me. You need those points for the U. of Virginia.
BIFF: I'm not going there.
WILLY: Heh? If I can't get him to change that mark you'll make it up in summer school. You've got all summer to—
BIFF (*his weeping breaking from him*): Dad . . .
WILLY (*infected by it*): Oh, my boy . . .
BIFF: Dad . . .
WILLY: She's nothing to me, Biff. I was lonely, I was terribly lonely.
BIFF: You—you gave her Mama's stockings! (*His tears break through and he rises to go.*)
WILLY (*grabbing for* BIFF): I gave you an order!
BIFF: Don't touch me, you—liar!
WILLY: Apologize for that!
BIFF: You fake! You phony little fake! You fake! (*Overcome, he turns quickly and weeping fully goes out with his suitcase.* WILLY *is left on the floor on his knees.*)
WILLY: I gave you an order! Biff, come back here or I'll beat you! Come back here! I'll whip you!

(STANLEY *comes quickly in from the right and stands in front of* WILLY.)

WILLY (*shouts at* STANLEY): I gave you an order . . .
STANLEY: Hey, let's pick it up, pick it up, Mr. Loman. (*He helps* WILLY *to his feet.*) Your boys left with the chippies. They said they'll see you home.

(A *second waiter watches some distance away.*)

WILLY: But we were supposed to have dinner together.

(*Music is heard,* WILLY'S *theme.*)

STANLEY: Can you make it?

WILLY: I'll—sure, I can make it. (*Suddenly concerned about his clothes.*) Do I—I look all right?

STANLEY: Sure, you look all right. (*He flicks a speck off* WILLY's *lapel.*)

WILLY: Here—here's a dollar.

STANLEY: Oh, your son paid me. It's all right.

WILLY (*putting it in* STANLEY's *hand*): No, take it. You're a good boy.

STANLEY: Oh, no, you don't have to . . .

WILLY: Here—here's some more, I don't need it any more. (*After a slight pause.*) Tell me—is there a seed store in the neighborhood?

STANLEY: Seeds? You mean like to plant?

(*As* WILLY *turns,* STANLEY *slips the money back into his jacket pocket.*)

WILLY: Yes. Carrots, peas . . .

STANLEY: Well, there's hardware stores on Sixth Avenue, but it may be too late now.

WILLY (*anxiously*): Oh, I'd better hurry. I've got to get some seeds. (*He starts off to the right.*) I've got to get some seeds, right away. Nothing's planted. I don't have a thing in the ground.

(WILLY *hurries out as the light goes down.* STANLEY *moves over to the right after him, watches him off. The other waiter has been staring at* WILLY.)

STANLEY (*to the waiter*): Well, whatta you looking at?

(*The waiter picks up the chairs and moves off right.* STANLEY *takes the table and follows him. The light fades on this area. There is a long pause, the sound of the flute coming over. The light gradually rises on the kitchen, which is empty.* HAPPY *appears at the door of the house, followed by* BIFF. HAPPY *is carrying a large bunch of long-stemmed roses. He enters the kitchen, looks around for* LINDA. *Not seeing her, he turns to* BIFF, *who is just outside the house door, and makes a gesture with his hands, indicating "Not here, I guess." He looks into the living room and freezes. Inside,* LINDA, *unseen, is seated,* WILLY's *coat on her lap. She rises ominously and quietly and moves toward* HAPPY, *who backs up into the kitchen, afraid.*)

HAPPY: Hey, what're you doing up? (LINDA *says nothing but moves toward him implacably.*) Where's Pop? (*He keeps backing to the right, and now* LINDA *is in full view in the doorway to the living room.*) Is he sleeping?

LINDA: Where were you?

HAPPY (*trying to laugh it off*): We met two girls, Mom, very fine types. Here, we brought you some flowers. (*Offering them to her*) Put them in your room, Ma.

(*She knocks them to the floor at* BIFF's *feet. He has now come inside and closed the door behind him. She stares at* BIFF, *silent.*)

HAPPY: Now what'd you do that for? Mom, I want you to have some flowers—

LINDA (*cutting* HAPPY *off, violently to* BIFF): Don't you care whether he lives or dies?

HAPPY (*going to the stairs*): Come upstairs, Biff.

BIFF (*with a flare of disgust, to* HAPPY): Go away from me! (*To* LINDA) What do you mean, lives or dies? Nobody's dying around here, pal.

LINDA: Get out of my sight! Get out of here!

BIFF: I wanna see the boss.

LINDA: You're not going near him!

BIFF: Where is he? (*He moves into the living room and* LINDA *follows.*)

LINDA (*shouting after* BIFF): You invite him for dinner. He looks forward to it all day—(BIFF *appears in his parents' bedroom, looks around, and exits*)—and then you desert him there. There's no stranger you'd do that to!

HAPPY: Why? He had a swell time with us. Listen, when I—(LINDA *comes back into the kitchen*)—desert him I hope I don't outlive the day!

LINDA: Get out of here!

HAPPY: Now look, Mom . . .

LINDA: Did you have to go to women tonight? You and your lousy rotten whores!

(BIFF *re-enters the kitchen.*)

HAPPY: Mom, all we did was follow Biff around trying to cheer him up! (*To* BIFF) Boy, what a night you gave me!

LINDA: Get out of here, both of you, and don't come back! I don't want you tormenting him any more. Go on now, get your things together! (*To* BIFF) You can sleep in his apartment. (*She starts to pick up the flowers and stops herself.*) Pick up this stuff, I'm not your maid any more. Pick it up, you bum, you!

(HAPPY *turns his back to her in refusal.* BIFF *slowly moves over and gets down on his knees, picking up the flowers.*)

LINDA: You're a pair of animals! Not one, not another living soul would have had the cruelty to walk out on that man in a restaurant!

BIFF (*not looking at her*): Is that what he said?

LINDA: He didn't have to say anything. He was so humiliated he nearly limped when he came in.

HAPPY: But, Mom, he had a great time with us—

BIFF (*cutting him off violently*): Shut up!

(*Without another word,* HAPPY *goes upstairs.*)

LINDA: You! You didn't even go in to see if he was all right!

BIFF (*still on the floor in front of* LINDA, *the flowers in his hand; with self-loathing*): No. Didn't. Didn't do a damned thing. How do you like that, heh? Left him babbling in a toilet.

LINDA: You louse. You . . .

BIFF: Now you hit it on the nose! (*He gets up, throws the flowers in the wastebasket.*) The scum of the earth, and you're looking at him!

LINDA: Get out of here!

BIFF: I gotta talk to the boss, Mom. Where his he?

LINDA: You're not going near him. Get out of this house!

BIFF (*with absolute assurance, determination*): No. We're gonna have an abrupt conversation, him and me.

LINDA: You're not talking to him!

(*Hammering is heard from outside the house, off right.* BIFF *turns toward the noise.*)

LINDA (*suddenly pleading*): Will you please leave him alone?

BIFF: What's he doing out there?

LINDA: He's planting the garden!

BIFF (*quietly*): Now? Oh, my God!

(BIFF *moves outside,* LINDA *following. The light dies down on them and comes up on the center of the apron as* WILLY *walks into it. He is carrying a flashlight, a hoe, and a handful of seed packets. He raps the top of the hoe sharply to fix it firmly, and then moves to the left, measuring off the distance with his foot. He holds the flashlight to look at the seed packets, reading off the instructions. He is in the blue of night.*)

WILLY: Carrots . . . quarter-inch apart. Rows . . . one-foot rows. (*He measures it off.*) One foot. (*He puts down a package and measures off.*) Beets. (*He puts down another package and measures again.*) Lettuce. (*He reads the package, puts it down.*) One foot—(*He breaks off as* BEN *appears at the right and moves slowly down to him.*) What a proposition, ts, ts. Terrific, terrific. 'Cause she's suffered, Ben, the woman has suffered. You understand me? A man can't go out the way he came in, Ben, a man has got to add up to something. You can't, you can't—(*Ben moves toward him as though to interrupt.*) You gotta consider, now. Don't answer so quick. Remember, it's a guaranteed twenty-thousand-dollar proposition. Now look, Ben, I want you to go through the ins and outs of this thing with me. I've got nobody to talk to, Ben, and the woman has suffered, you hear me?

BEN (*standing still, considering*): What's the proposition?

WILLY: It's twenty thousand dollars on the barrelhead. Guaranteed, gilt-edged, you understand?

BEN: You don't want to make a fool of yourself. They might not honor the policy.

WILLY: How can they dare refuse? Didn't I work like a coolie to meet every premium on the nose? And now they don't pay off? Impossible!

BEN: It's called a cowardly thing, William.

WILLY: Why? Does it take more guts to stand here the rest of my life ringing up a zero?

BEN (*yielding*): That's a point, William. (*He moves, thinking, turns.*) And twenty thousand—that *is* something one can feel with the hand, it is there.

WILLY (*now assured, with rising power*): Oh, Ben, that's the whole beauty of it! I see it like a diamond, shining in the dark, hard and rough, that I can pick up and touch in my hand. Not like—like an appointment! This would not be another damned-fool appointment, Ben, and it changes all the aspects. Because he thinks I'm nothing, see, and so he spites me. But the funeral—(*Straightening up*) Ben, that funeral will be massive! They'll come from Maine, Massachusetts, Vermont, New Hampshire! All the old-timers with the strange license plates—that boy will be thunder-struck, Ben, because he never realized—I am known! Rhode Island, New York, New Jersey—I am known, Ben, and he'll see it with his eyes once and for all. He'll see what I am, Ben! He's in for a shock, that boy!

BEN (*coming down to the edge of the garden*): He'll call you a coward.

WILLY (*suddenly fearful*): No, that would be terrible.

BEN: Yes. And a damned fool.

WILLY: No, no, he mustn't, I won't have that! (*He is broken and desperate.*)

BEN: He'll hate you, William.

(*The gay music of the boys is heard.*)

WILLY: Oh, Ben, how do we get back to all the great times? Used to be so full of light, and comradeship, the sleigh-riding in winter, and the ruddiness on his cheeks. And always some kind of good news coming up, always something nice coming up ahead. And never even let me carry the valises in the house, and simonizing, simonizing that little red car! Why, why can't I give him something and not have him hate me?

BEN: Let me think about it. (*He glances at his watch.*) I still have a little time. Remarkable proposition, but you've got to be sure you're not making a fool of yourself.

(BEN *drifts off upstage and goes out of sight.* BIFF *comes down from the left.*)

WILLY (*suddenly conscious of* BIFF, *turns and looks up at him, then begins picking up the packages of seeds in confusion*): Where the hell is that seed? (*Indignantly*) You can't see nothing out here! They boxed in the whole goddam neighborhood!

BIFF: There are people all around here. Don't you realize that?

WILLY: I'm busy. Don't bother me.

BIFF (*taking the hoe from* WILLY): I'm saying good-bye to you, Pop. (WILLY *looks at him, silent, unable to move.*) I'm not coming back any more.

WILLY: You're not going to see Oliver tomorrow?

BIFF: I've got no appointment, Dad.

WILLY: He put his arm around you, and you've got no appointment?

BIFF: Pop, get this now, will you? Every time I've left it's been a fight that sent me out of here. Today I realized something about myself and I tried to explain it to you and I—I think I'm just not smart enough to make any sense out of it for you. To hell with whose fault it is or anything like that. (*He takes* WILLY's *arm.*) Let's just wrap it up, heh? Come on in, we'll tell Mom. (*He gently tries to pull* WILLY *to left.*)

WILLY (*frozen, immobile, with guilt in his voice*): No, I don't want to see her.

BIFF: Come on! (*He pulls again, and* WILLY *tries to pull away.*)

WILLY (*highly nervous*): No, no, I don't want to see her.

BIFF (*tries to look into* WILLY's *face, as if to find the answer there*): Why don't you want to see her?

WILLY (*more harshly now*): Don't bother me, will you?

BIFF: What do you mean, you don't want to see her? You don't want them calling you yellow, do you? This isn't your fault; it's me, I'm a bum. Now come inside! (WILLY *strains to get away.*) Did you hear what I said to you?

(WILLY *pulls away and quickly goes by himself into the house.* BIFF *follows.*)

LINDA (*to* WILLY): Did you plant, dear?

BIFF (*at the door, to* LINDA): All right, we had it out. I'm going and I'm not writing any more.

LINDA (*going to* WILLY *in the kitchen*): I think that's the best way, dear. 'Cause there's no use drawing it out, you'll just never get along.

(WILLY *doesn't respond.*)

BIFF: People ask where I am and what I'm doing, you don't know, and you don't care. That way it'll be off your mind and you can start brightening up again. All right? That clears it, doesn't it? (WILLY *is silent, and* BIFF *goes to him.*) You gonna wish me luck, scout? (*He extends his hand*) What do you say?

LINDA: Shake his hand, Willy.

WILLY (*turning to her, seething with hurt*): There's no necessity to mention the pen at all, y'know.

BIFF (*gently*): I've got no appointment, Dad.

WILLY (*erupting fiercely*): He put his arm around . . . ?

BIFF: Dad, you're never going to see what I am, so what's the use of arguing? If I strike oil I'll send you a check. Meantime forget I'm alive.

WILLY (*to* LINDA): Spite, see?

BIFF: Shake hands, Dad.

WILLY: Not my hand.

BIFF: I was hoping not to go this way.

WILLY: Well, this is the way you're going. Good-bye.

(BIFF *looks at him a moment, then turns sharply and goes to the stairs.*)

WILLY (*stops him with*): May you rot in hell if you leave this house!

BIFF (*turning*): Exactly what is it that you want from me?

WILLY: I want you to know, on the train, in the mountains, in the valleys, wherever you go, that you cut down your life for spite!

BIFF: No, no.

WILLY: Spite, spite, is the word of your undoing! And when you're down and out, remember what did it. When you're rotting somewhere beside the railroad tracks, remember, and don't you dare blame it on me!

BIFF: I'm not blaming it on you!

WILLY: I won't take the rap for this, you hear?

(HAPPY *comes down the stairs and stands on the bottom step, watching.*)

BIFF: That's just what I'm telling you!

WILLY (*sinking into a chair at the table, with full accusation*): You're trying to put a knife in me— don't think I don't know what you're doing!

BIFF: All right, phony! Then let's lay it on the line. (*He whips the rubber tube out of his pocket and puts it on the table.*)

HAPPY: You crazy—

LINDA: Biff! (*She moves to grab the hose, but* BIFF *holds it down with his hand.*)

BIFF: Leave it there! Don't move it!

WILLY (*not looking at it*): What is that?

BIFF: You know goddam well what that is.

WILLY (*caged, wanting to escape*): I never saw that.

BIFF: You saw it. The mice didn't bring it into the cellar! What is this supposed to do, make a hero out of you? This supposed to make me sorry for you?

WILLY: Never heard of it.

BIFF: There'll be no pity for you, you hear it? No pity!

WILLY (*to* LINDA): You hear the spite!

BIFF: No, you're going to hear the truth—what you are and what I am!

LINDA: Stop it!

WILLY: Spite!

HAPPY (*coming down toward* BIFF): You cut it now!

BIFF (*to* HAPPY): The man don't know who we are! The man is gonna know! (*to* WILLY) We never told the truth for ten minutes in this house!

HAPPY: We always told the truth!

BIFF (*turning on him*): You big blow, are you the assistant buyer? You're one of the two assistants to the assistant, aren't you?

HAPPY: Well, I'm practically—

BIFF: You're practically full of it! We all are! And I'm through with it. (*To* WILLY.) Now hear this, Willy, this is me.

WILLY: I know you!

BIFF: You know why I had no address for three months? I stole a suit in Kansas City and I was in jail. (*To* LINDA, *who is sobbing*) Stop crying. I'm through with it.

(LINDA *turns away from them, her hands covering her face.*)

WILLY: I suppose that's my fault!

BIFF: I stole myself out of every good job since high school!

WILLY: And whose fault is that?

BIFF: And I never got anywhere because you blew me so full of hot air I could never stand taking orders from anybody! That's whose fault it is!

WILLY: I hear that!

LINDA: Don't, Biff!

BIFF: It's goddam time you heard that! I had to be boss big shot in two weeks, and I'm through with it!

WILLY: Then hang yourself! For spite, hang yourself!

BIFF: No! Nobody's hanging himself, Willy! I ran down eleven flights with a pen in my hand today. And suddenly I stopped, you hear me? And in the middle of that office building, do you hear this? I stopped in the middle of that building and I saw—the sky. I saw the things that I love in this world. The work and the food and time to sit and smoke. And I looked at the pen and said to myself, what the hell am I grabbing this for? Why am I trying to become what I don't want to be? What am I doing in an office, making a contemptuous, begging fool of myself, when all I want is out there, waiting for me the minute I say I know who I am! Why can't I say that, Willy? (*He tries to make* WILLY *face him, but* WILLY *pulls away and moves to the left.*)

WILLY (*with hatred, threateningly*): The door of your life is wide open!

BIFF: Pop! I'm a dime a dozen, and so are you!

WILLY (*turning on him now in an uncontrolled outburst*): I am not a dime a dozen! I am Willy Loman, and you are Biff Loman!

(BIFF *starts for* WILLY, *but is blocked by* HAPPY. *In his fury,* BIFF *seems on the verge of attacking his father.*)

BIFF: I am not a leader of men, Willy, and neither are you. You were never anything but a hard-working drummer who landed in the ash can like all the rest of them! I'm one dollar an hour, Willy! I tried seven states and couldn't raise it. A buck an hour! Do you gather my meaning? I'm not bringing home any prizes any more, and you're going to stop waiting for me to bring them home!

WILLY (*directly to* BIFF): You vengeful, spiteful mutt!

(BIFF *breaks from* HAPPY. WILLY, *in fright, starts up the stairs.* BIFF *grabs him.*)

BIFF (*at the peak of his fury*): Pop, I'm nothing! I'm nothing, Pop. Can't you understand that? There's no spite in it any more. I'm just what I am, that's all.

(BIFF's *fury has spent itself, and he breaks down, sobbing, holding on to* WILLY, *who dumbly fumbles for* BIFF's *face.*)

WILLY (*astonished*): What're you doing? What're you doing? (*To* LINDA) Why is he crying?

BIFF (*crying, broken*): Will you let me go, for Christ's sake? Will you take that phony dream and burn it before something happens? (*Struggling to contain himself, he pulls away and moves to the stairs.*) I'll go in the morning. Put him—put him to bed. (*Exhausted,* BIFF *moves up the stairs to his room.*)

WILLY (*after a long pause, astonished, elevated*): Isn't that—isn't that remarkable? Biff—he likes me!

LINDA: He loves you, Willy!

HAPPY (*deeply moved*): Always did, Pop.

WILLY: Oh, Biff! (*Staring wildly*) He cried! Cried to me. (*He is choking with his love, and now cries out his promise.*) That boy—that boy is going to be magnificent!

(BEN *appears in the light just outside the kitchen.*)

BEN: Yes, outstanding, with twenty thousand behind him.

LINDA (*sensing the racing of his mind, fearfully, carefully*): Now come to bed, Willy. It's all settled now.

WILLY (*finding it difficult not to rush out of the house*): Yes, we'll sleep. Come on. Go to sleep, Hap.

BEN: And it does take a great kind of a man to crack the jungle.

(*In accents of dread,* BEN's *idyllic music starts up.*)

HAPPY (*his arm around* LINDA): I'm getting married, Pop, don't forget it. I'm changing everything. I'm gonna run that department before the year is up. You'll see, Mom. (*He kisses her.*)

BEN: The jungle is dark but full of diamonds, Willy.

(WILLY *turns, moves, listening to* BEN.)

LINDA: Be good. You're both good boys, just act that way, that's all.

HAPPY: 'Night, Pop. (*He goes upstairs.*)

LINDA (*to* WILLY): Come, dear.

BEN (*with greater force*): One must go in to fetch a diamond out.

WILLY (*to* LINDA, *as he moves slowly along the edge of the kitchen, toward the door*): I just want to get settled down, Linda. Let me sit alone for a little.

LINDA (*almost uttering her fear*): I want you upstairs.

WILLY (*taking her in his arms*): In a few minutes, Linda. I couldn't sleep right now. Go on, you look awful tired. (*He kisses her.*)

BEN: Not like an appointment at all. A diamond is rough and hard to the touch.

WILLY: Go on now. I'll be right up.

LINDA: I think this is the only way, Willy.

WILLY: Sure, it's the best thing.

BEN: Best thing!

WILLY: The only way. Everything is gonna be— go on, kid, get to bed. You look so tired.

LINDA: Come right up.

WILLY: Two minutes.

(LINDA *goes into the living room, then reappears in her bedroom.* WILLY *moves just outside the kitchen door.*)

WILLY: Loves me. (*Wonderingly*) Always loved me. Isn't that a remarkable thing? Ben, he'll worship me for it!

BEN (*with promise*): It's dark there, but full of diamonds.

WILLY: Can you imagine that magnificence with twenty thousand dollars in his pocket?

LINDA (*calling from her room*): Willy! Come up!

WILLY (*calling into the kitchen*): Yes! Yes. Coming! It's very smart, you realize that, don't you, sweetheart? Even Ben sees it. I gotta go, baby. 'Bye! 'Bye! (*Going over to* BEN, *almost dancing*) Imagine? When the mail comes he'll be ahead of Bernard again!

BEN: A perfect proposition all around.

WILLY: Did you see how he cried to me? Oh, if I could kiss him, Ben!

BEN: Time, William, time!

WILLY: Oh, Ben, I always knew one way or another we were gonna make it, Biff and I!

BEN (*looking at his watch*): The boat. We'll be late. (*He moves slowly off into the darkness.*)

WILLY (*elegiacally, turning to the house*): Now when you kick off, boy, I want a seventy-yard boot, and get right down the field under the ball, and when you hit, hit low and hit hard, because it's important, boy. (*He swings around and faces the audience.*) There's all kinds of important people in the stands, and the first thing you know . . . (*Suddenly realizing he is alone.*) Ben! Ben, where do I . . . ? (*He makes a sudden movement of search.*) Ben, how do I . . . ?

LINDA (*calling*): Willy, you coming up?

WILLY (*uttering a gasp of fear, whirling about as if to quiet her*): Sh! (*He turns around as if to find his way; sounds, faces, voices, seem to be swarming in upon him and he flicks at them, crying*) Sh! Sh! (*Suddenly music, faint and high, stops him. It rises in intensity, almost to an unbearable scream. He goes up and down on his toes, and rushes off around the house.*) Shhh!

LINDA: Willy?

(*There is no answer. LINDA waits. BIFF gets up off his bed. He is still in his clothes. HAPPY sits up. BIFF stands listening.*)

LINDA (*with real fear*): Willy, answer me! Willy!

(*There is the sound of a car starting and moving away at full speed.*)

LINDA: No!

BIFF (*rushing down the stairs*): Pop!

(*As the car speeds off, the music crashes down in a frenzy of sound, which becomes the soft pulsation of a single cello string. BIFF slowly returns to his bedroom. He and HAPPY gravely don their jackets. LINDA slowly walks out of her room. The music has developed into a dead march. The leaves of day are appearing over everything. CHARLEY and BERNARD, somberly dressed, appear and knock on the kitchen door. BIFF and HAPPY slowly descend the stairs to the kitchen as CHARLEY and BERNARD enter. All stop a moment when LINDA, in clothes of mourning, bearing a little bunch of roses, comes through the draped doorway into the kitchen. She goes to CHARLEY and takes his arm. Now all move toward the audience, through the wall-line of the kitchen. At the limit of the apron, LINDA lays down the flowers, kneels, and sits back on her heels. All stare down at the grave.*)

REQUIEM

CHARLEY: It's getting dark, Linda.

(*LINDA doesn't react. She stares at the grave.*)

BIFF: How about it, Mom? Better get some rest, heh? They'll be closing the gate soon.

(*LINDA makes no move. Pause.*)

HAPPY (*deeply angered*): He had no right to do that. There was no necessity for it. We would've helped him.

CHARLEY (*grunting*): Hmmm.

BIFF: Come along, Mom.

LINDA: Why didn't anybody come?

CHARLEY: It was a very nice funeral.

LINDA: But where are all the people he knew? Maybe they blame him.

CHARLEY: Naw. It's a rough world, Linda. They wouldn't blame him.

LINDA: I can't understand it. At this time especially. First time in thirty-five years we were just about free and clear. He only needed a little salary. He was even finished with the dentist.

CHARLEY: No man only needs a little salary.

LINDA: I can't understand it.

BIFF: There were a lot of nice days. When he'd come home from a trip; or on Sundays, making the stoop; finishing the cellar; putting on the new porch; when he built the extra bathroom; and put up the garage. You know something, Charley, there's more of him in that front stoop than in all the sales he ever made.

CHARLEY: Yeah. He was a happy man with a batch of cement.

LINDA: He was so wonderful with his hands.

BIFF: He had the wrong dreams. All, all, wrong.

HAPPY (*almost ready to fight BIFF*): Don't say that!

BIFF: He never knew who he was.

CHARLEY (*stopping HAPPY's movement and reply. To BIFF*): Nobody dast blame this man. You don't understand: Willy was a salesman. And for a salesman, there is no rock bottom to the life. He don't put a bolt to a nut, he don't tell you the law or give you medicine. He's a man way out there in the blue, riding on a smile and a shoeshine. And when they start not smiling back—that's an earthquake. And then you get yourself a couple of spots on your hat, and you're finished. Nobody dast blame this man. A salesman is got to dream, boy. It comes with the territory.

BIFF: Charley, the man didn't know who he was.

HAPPY: (*infuriated*): Don't say that!

BIFF: Why don't you come with me, Happy?

HAPPY: I'm not licked that easily. I'm staying right in this city, and I'm gonna beat this racket! (*He looks at BIFF, his chin set.*) The Loman Brothers!

BIFF: I know who I am, kid.

HAPPY: All right, boy. I'm gonna show you and everybody else that Willy Loman did not die in vain. He had a good dream. It's the only dream you can have—to come out number-one man. He fought it out here, and this is where I'm gonna win it for him.

BIFF (*with a hopeless glance at* HAPPY, *bends toward his mother*): Let's go, Mom.

LINDA: I'll be with you in a minute. Go on, Charley. (*He hesitates.*) I want to, just for a minute. I never had a chance to say good-bye.

(CHARLEY *moves away, followed by* HAPPY. BIFF *remains a slight distance up and left of* LINDA. *She sits there, summoning herself. The flute begins, not far away, playing behind her speech.*)

LINDA: Forgive me, dear. I can't cry. I don't know what it is, but I can't cry. I don't understand it. Why did you ever do that? Help me, Willy, I can't cry. It seems to me that you're just on another trip. I keep expecting you. Willy, dear, I can't cry. Why did you do it? I search and search and I search, and I can't understand it, Willy. I made the last payment on the house today. Today, dear. And there'll be nobody home. (*A sob rises in her throat.*) We're free and clear. (*Sobbing more fully, released.*) We're free. (BIFF *comes slowly toward her.*) We're free . . . We're free . . .

(BIFF *lifts her to her feet and moves out up right with her in his arms.* LINDA *sobs quietly.* BERNARD *and* CHARLEY *come together and follow them, followed by* HAPPY. *Only the music of the flute is left on the darkening stage as over the house the hard towers of the apartment buildings rise into sharp focus, and—*)

THE CURTAIN FALLS

COMMENTARY

For the ancient Greeks, at least for Aristotle, *pathos* was the destructive or painful act common in tragedy; but in English "pathos" refers to an element in art or life that evokes tenderness or sympathetic pity. Modern English critical usage distinguishes between tragic figures and pathetic figures by recognizing some element either of strength or of regeneration in the former that is not in the latter. The tragic protagonists perhaps act so that they bring their destruction upon themselves, or if their destruction comes from outside, they resist it, and in either case they come to at least a partial understanding of the causes of their suffering. Pathetic figures, however, are largely passive, unknowing, and unresisting innocents. In such a view, Macbeth is tragic, Duncan pathetic; Lear is tragic, Cordelia pathetic; Othello is tragic, Desdemona pathetic; Hamlet is tragic (the situation is not of his making, but he does what he can to alter it), Ophelia pathetic. (Note, by the way, that of the four pathetic figures named, the first is old and the remaining three are women. Pathos is more likely to be evoked by persons assumed to be relatively defenseless than by those who are able-bodied.)

That the spectators were not themselves heroic figures seems to have been assumed by the Greeks and by the Elizabethans; the lesser choral figures or nameless citizens interpret the action and call attention to the fact that even highly placed great heroes are not exempt from pain. Indeed, high place and strenuous activity invite pain: the lofty pine tree, or the mariner who ventures far from the coast, is more likely to meet destruction than the lowly shrub or the fair-weather sailor. For Greeks of the fifth century B.C., and for Elizabethans, high place was not a mere matter of rank, but of worth. In both ages, it was of course known that a king may be unkingly, but it was assumed that kingship required a special nature—though that nature was not always forthcoming. Put it this way: tragedy deals with kings not because they are men with a certain title (though of course the title does give them special power), but because they are men with a certain nature. This nature is an extraordinary capacity for action and for feeling; when they make an error its consequences are enormous, and they themselves feel it as lesser people would not. When Oedipus is polluted, all of Thebes feels it. Arthur Miller is somewhat misleading when he argues (p. 744) that because Oedipus has given his name to a complex that the common man may have, the common man is therefore "as apt a subject for tragedy." It is not Oedipus's "complex" but his unique importance that is the issue in the play. Moreover, even if one argues that a person of no public importance may suffer as much as one of public importance (and surely nobody doubts this), one may be faced with the fact that unimportant people by their ordinariness are not particularly good material for drama, and we are here concerned with drama rather than with life. In *Death of a Salesman* Willy Loman's wife says, rightly, "A small man can be just as exhausted as a great man." Yes, but is his exhaustion itself interesting, and do his activities (and this includes the words he utters) before his exhaustion have interesting dramatic possibilities? Isn't there a colorlessness that may weaken the play, an impoverishment of what John Milton called "gorgeous tragedy"?

Inevitably the rise of the bourgeoisie brought about the rise of bourgeois drama, and in the eighteenth century we get a fair number of tragedies with prologues that insist that characters like ourselves deserve our *pity*:

> No fustian hero rages here tonight,
> No armies fall, to fix a tyrant's right.
> From lower life we draw our scene's distress:
> —Let not your equals move your pity less.
> George Lillo, *Fatal Curiosity* (1733)

Note the deflation of older tragedy, the implication that its heroes were "fustian" (bombastic, pretentious) rather than genuinely heroic persons of deep feelings and high aspirations. Or, to put it differently, older tragedy in the bourgeois view dealt with persons of high rank, but rank (in this view) is not significant; therefore one may as well show persons of middle rank with whom the middle-class audience may readily identify. At the same time, the dismissal of heroic activities ("no fusion hero *rages*," "no armies *fall*") and the substitution of "distress" indicates that we are well on the road to the Hero as Victim.

And we have kept on that road. As early as the sixteenth century Copernicus had shown that humanity and its planet were not the center of the universe, but the thought did not distress most people until much later. In 1859 Darwin published *The Origin of Species*, arguing that human beings are not a special creation but creatures that have evolved because "accidental variations" have aided them in the struggle for survival. At about the same time, Marx (who wished to dedicate *Capital* to Darwin) argued that economic forces guide our lives. Early in the twentieth century Freud seemed to argue that we are conditioned by infantile experiences and are enslaved by the dark forces of the id. All in all, by the time of the Depression of the 1930s, it was difficult to have much confidence in our ability to shape our destiny. The human condition was a sorry one; we were insignificant lust-ridden, soulless creatures in a terrifying materialistic universe. A human being was no Oedipus whose moral pollution infected a great city, no Brutus whose deed might bring civil war to Rome. A human being was really not much of anything, except perhaps to a few immediate dependents.

Arthur Miller accurately noted (*Theatre Arts*, October 1953) that American drama "has been a steady year by year documentation of the frustration of man," and it is evident that Miller has set out to restore a sense of importance if not greatness to the individual. In "Tragedy and the Common Man" (see p. 744), published in the same year that *Death of a Salesman* was produced and evidently a defense of the play, he argues on behalf of the common man as a tragic figure and he insists that tragedy and pathos are very different: "Pathos truly is the mode of the pessimist. . . . The plays we revere, century after century, are the tragedies. In them, and in them alone, lies the belief—optimistic, if you will— in the perfectibility of man."

Curiously, however, many spectators and readers find that by Miller's own terms Willy Loman fails to be a tragic figure; he seems to them pathetic rather than tragic, a victim rather than a man who acts and who wins our esteem. True, he is partly the victim of his own actions (although he could have chosen to be a carpenter, he chose to live by the bourgeois code that values a white collar), but he seems in larger part to be a victim of the system itself, a system of ruthless competition that has no place for the man who can no longer produce. (Here is an echo of the social-realist drama of the thirties.) Willy had believed in this system; and although his son Biff comes to the realization that Willy "had the wrong dreams," Willy himself seems not to achieve this insight. Of course he knows that he is out of a job, that the system does not value him any longer, but he still seems not to question the values he had subscribed to. Even in the last minutes of the play, when he is planning his suicide in order to provide money for his family—really for Biff—he says such things as "Can you imagine his magnificence with twenty thousand dollars in his pocket?" and "When the mail comes he'll be ahead of Bernard again." In the preface to his *Collected Plays*, Miller comments on the "exultation" with which Willy faces the end, but it is questionable whether an audience shares it. Many people find that despite the gulf in rank, they can share King Lear's feelings more easily than Willy's.

Perhaps, however, tradition has been too arbitrary in its use of the word *tragedy*. Perhaps we should be as liberal as the ancient Greeks were, who did not withhold it from any play that was serious and dignified.

TOPICS FOR DISCUSSION

1. Miller says that tragedy shows man's struggle to secure "his sense of personal dignity" and that "his destruction in the attempt posits a wrong or an evil in his environment" (page 745). Do you think this makes sense when applied to some earlier tragedy (such as *Oedipus the King* or *Hamlet*), and does it apply convincingly to *Death of a*

Salesman? Is this the tragedy of an individual's own making? Or is society at fault for corrupting and exploiting Willy? Or both?

2. Do you find Willy pathetic rather than tragic? If pathetic, does this imply that the play is less worthy than if he is tragic?

3. Do you feel that Miller is straining too hard to turn a play about a little man into a big, impressive play? For example, do the musical themes, the unrealistic setting, the appearances of Ben, and the speech at the grave seem out of keeping in a play about the death of a salesman?

4. We don't know what Willy sells, and we don't know whether or not the insurance will be paid after his death. Do you consider these uncertainties to be faults in the play?

5. Is Howard a villain?

6. Characterize Linda.

7. The critic Kenneth Tynan has written, in *Tynan Right and Left:* "*Death of a Salesman* . . . is not a tragedy. Its catastrophe depends entirely on the fact that the company Willy Loman works for has no pension scheme for its employees. What ultimately destroys Willy is economic injustice, which is curable, as the ills that plague Oedipus do not." What do you think of Tynan's view?

HAPPY DAYS

Samuel Beckett

Samuel Beckett (b. 1906) was born in Dublin of middle-class Protestant parents. He was educated at Trinity College, Dublin, where he took his degree in modern languages, graduating in 1927. He went to Paris the next year where he met James Joyce, a fellow Irishman, and translated parts of *Finnegan's Wake* into French. He stayed in France until 1930, when he returned to Dublin to take up a lectureship in French at Trinity College. He soon decided against teaching and began a number of years of wandering, living in London, traveling about Germany and France, and then settling in Paris in 1937. During World War II, after narrowly escaping capture by the Gestapo for his work in the French Resistance, he fled to Roussillon in southwestern France, where he remained until the end of the war, when he returned to Paris. In 1961, the year he was writing *Happy Days*, he married a French woman, Suzanne Deschevaux-Dumesnil. In 1969 he was awarded the Nobel Prize for literature but refused to go to Stockholm for the ceremonies. Always a reclusive figure, he still lives in Paris with his wife. His best-known works include the novels *Molloy* (1951), *Malone Dies* (1951), and *The Unnamable* (1953); short stories collected as *More Pricks Than Kicks* (1934); and the plays *Waiting for Godot* (first published in French as *En attendant Godot* in 1952 but translated by Beckett into English and published in 1954), *Endgame* (1957), and *Happy Days* (1961). Numerous shorter works, including scripts for radio and television and even for a movie entitled *Film*, starring Buster Keaton, complete what John Updike called "a single holy book."

CHARACTERS

WINNIE, *a woman about fifty*
WILLIE, *a man about sixty*

Peggy Ashcroft in the National Theatre Production of *Happy Days*, directed by Sir Peter Hall, 1975. (Photograph: Zoë Dominic F.R.P.S.)

ACT I

Expanse of scorched grass rising centre to low mound. Gentle slopes down to front and either side of stage. Back an abrupter fall to stage level. Maximum of simplicity and symmetry.

Blazing light.

Very pompier trompe-l'oeil[1] backcloth to represent unbroken plain and sky receding to meet in far distance.

Imbedded up to above her waist in exact centre of mound, WINNIE. *About fifty, well preserved, blond for preference, plump, arms and shoulders bare, low bodice, big bosom, pearl necklet. She is discovered sleeping, her arms on the ground before her, her head on her arms. Beside her on ground to her left a capacious black bag, shopping variety, and to her right a collapsible collapsed parasol, beak of handle emerging from sheath.*

To her right and rear, lying asleep on ground, hidden by mound, WILLIE.

Long pause. A bell rings piercingly, say ten seconds, stops. She does not move. Pause. Bell more piercingly, say five seconds. She wakes. Bell stops. She raises her head, gazes front. Long pause. She straightens up, lays her hands flat on ground, throws back her head and gazes at zenith. Long pause.

WINNIE (*gazing at zenith*): Another heavenly day. (*Pause. Head back level, eyes front, pause. She clasps hands to breast, closes eyes. Lips move in inaudible prayer, say ten seconds. Lips still. Hands remain clasped. Low*) For Jesus Christ sake Amen. (*Eyes open, hands unclasp, return to mound. Pause. She clasps hands to breast again, closes eyes, lips move again in inaudible addendum, say five seconds. Low*) World without end Amen. (*Eyes open, hands unclasp, return to mound. Pause.*) Begin, Winnie. (*Pause.*) Begin your day, Winnie. (*Pause. She turns to bag, rummages in it without moving it from its place, brings out toothbrush, rummages again, brings out flat tube of toothpaste, turns back front, unscrews cap of tube, lays cap on ground, squeezes with difficulty small blob of paste on brush, holds tube in one hand and brushes teeth with other. She turns modestly aside and back to her right to spit out behind mound. In this position her eyes rest on* WILLIE. *She spits out.*

[1] Ordinary illusionistic.

She cranes a lttle further back and down. Loud) Hoo-oo! (*Pause. Louder*) Hoo-oo! (*Pause. Tender smile as she turns back front, lays down brush.*) Poor Willie—(*examines tube, smile off*)—running out—(*looks for cap*)—ah well—(*finds cap*)—can't be helped—(*screws on cap*)—just one of those old things—(*lays down tube*)—another of those old things—(*turns towards bag*)—just can't be cured—(*brings out small mirror, turns back front*)—ah yes—(*inspects teeth in mirror*)—poor dear Willie—(*testing upper front teeth with thumb, indistinctly*)—good Lord!—(*pulling back upper lip to inspect gums, do*)—good God!—(*pulling back corner of mouth, mouth open, do*)—ah well—(*other corner, do*)—no worse—(*abandons inspection, normal speech*)—no better, no worse—(*lays down mirror*)—no change—(*wipes fingers on grass*)—no pain—(*looks for toothbrush*)—hardly any—(*takes up toothbrush*)—great thing that—(*examines handle of brush*)—nothing like it—(*examines handle, reads*)—pure . . . what?—(*pause*)—what?—(*lays down brush*)—ah yes—(*turns towards bag*)—poor Willie—(*rummages in bag*)—no zest—(*rummages*)—for anything—(*brings out spectacles in case*)—no interest—(*turns back front*)—in life—(*takes spectacles from case*)—poor dear Willie—(*lays down case*)—sleep for ever—(*opens spectacles*)—marvellous gift—(*puts on spectacles*)—nothing to touch it—(*looks for toothbrush*)—in my opinion—(*takes up toothbrush*)—always said so—(*examines handle of brush*)—I wish I had it—(*examines handle, reads*)—genuine . . . pure . . . what?—(*lays down brush*)—blind next—(*takes off spectacles*)—ah well—(*lays down spectacles*)—seen enough—(*feels in bodice for handkerchief*)—I suppose—(*takes out folded handkerchief*)—by now—(*shakes out handkerchief*)—what are those wonderful lines—(*wipes one eye*)—woe woe is me—(*wipes the other*)—to see what I see—(*looks for spectacles*)—ah yes—(*takes up spectacles*)—wouldn't miss it—(*starts polishing spectacles, breathing on lenses*)—or would I?—(*polishes*)—holy light—(*polishes*)—bob up out of dark—(*polishes*)—blaze of hellish light. (*Stops polishing, raises face to sky, pause, head back level, resumes polishing, stops polishing, cranes back to her right and down.*) Hoo-oo! (*Pause. Tender smile as she turns back front and resumes polishing. Smile off.*) Marvellous gift—(*stops polishing, lays down spectacles*)—wish I had it—(*folds handkerchief*)—ah well—(*puts handkerchief back in bodice*)—can't complain—(*looks for spectacles*)—no no—(*takes* up spectacles)—mustn't complain—(holds up spectacles, looks through lens)—so much to be thankful for—(looks through other lens)—no pain—(puts on spectacles)—hardly any—(looks for toothbrush)—wonderful thing that—(takes up toothbrush)—nothing like it—(examines handle of brush)—slight headache sometimes—(examines handle, reads)—guaranteed . . . genuine . . . pure . . . what?—(looks closer)—genuine pure . . .—(takes handkerchief from bodice)—ah yes—(shakes out handkerchief)—occasional mild migraine—(starts wiping handle of brush)—it comes—(wipes)—then goes—(wiping mechanically)—ah yes—(wiping)—many mercies—(wiping)—great mercies—(stops wiping, fixed lost gaze, brokenly)—prayers perhaps not for naught—(pause, do)—first thing—(pause, do)—last thing—(head down, resumes wiping, stops wiping, head up, calmed, wipes eyes, folds handkerchief, puts it back in bodice, examines handle of brush, reads)—fully guaranteed . . . genuine pure . . .—(looks closer)—genuine pure . . . (Takes off spectacles, lays them and brush down, gazes before her.) Old things. (Pause.) Old eyes. (Long pause.) On, Winnie. (She casts about her, sees parasol, considers it at length, takes it up and develops from sheath a handle of surprising length. Holding butt of parasol in right hand she cranes back and down to her right to hang over WILLIE.) Hoo-oo! (Pause.) Willie! (Pause.) Wonderful gift. (She strikes down at him with beak of parasol.) Wish I had it. (She strikes again. The parasol slips from her grasp and falls behind mound. It is immediately restored to her by WILLIE's invisible hand.) Thank you, dear. (She transfers parasol to left hand, turns back front and examines right palm.) Damp. (Returns parasol to right hand, examines left palm.) Ah well, no worse. (Head up, cheerfully) No better, no worse, no change. (Pause. Do) No pain. (Cranes back to look down at WILLIE, holding parasol by butt as before.) Don't go off on me again now dear will you please, I may need you. (Pause.) No hurry, no hurry, just don't curl up on me again. (Turns back front, lays down parasol, examines palms together, wipes them on grass.) Perhaps a shade off colour just the same. (Turns to bag, rummages in it, brings out revolver, holds it up, kisses it rapidly, puts it back, rummages, brings out almost empty bottle of red medicine, turns back front, looks for spectacles, puts them on, reads label.) Loss of spirits . . . lack of keenness . . . want of appetite . . . infants . . . children . . . adults . . . six level . . . tablespoonfuls daily—(head up, smile)—the old style!—(smile off, head down, reads)—daily . . . before and after . . . meals . . . instantaneous . . .

(looks closer) . . . improvement. (Takes off spectacles, lays them down, holds up bottle at arm's length to see level, unscrews cap, swigs it off head well back, tosses cap and bottle away in WILLIE's direction. Sound of breaking glass.) Ah that's better! (Turns to bag, rummages in it, brings out lipstick, turns back front, examines lipstick.) Running out. (Looks for spectacles.) Ah well. (Puts on spectacles, looks for mirror.) Mustn't complain. (Takes up mirror, starts doing lips.) What is that wonderful line? (Lips.) Oh fleeting joys—(lips)—oh something lasting woe. (Lips. She is interrupted by disturbance from WILLIE. He is sitting up. She lowers lipstick and mirror and cranes back and down to look at him. Pause. Top back of WILLIE's bald head, trickling blood, rises to view above slope, comes to rest. WINNIE pushes up her spectacles. Pause. His hand appears with handkerchief, spreads it on skull, disappears. Pause. The hand appears with boater, club ribbon, settles it on head, rakish angle, disappears. Pause. WINNIE cranes a little further back and down.) Slip on your drawers, dear, before you get singed. (Pause.) No? (Pause.) Oh I see, you still have some of that stuff left. (Pause.) Work it well in, dear. (Pause.) Now the other. (Pause. She turns back front, gazes before her. Happy expression.) Oh this is going to be another happy day! (Pause. Happy expression off. She pulls down spectacles and resumes lips. WILLIE opens newspaper, hands invisible. Tops of yellow sheets appear on either side of his head. WINNIE finishes lips, inspects them in mirror held a little further away.) Ensign crimson. (WILLIE turns page. WINNIE lays down lipstick and mirror, turns towards bag.) Pale flag.

(WILLIE turns page. WINNIE rummages in bag, brings out small ornate brimless hat with crumpled feather, turns back front, straightens hat, smooths feather, raises it towards head, arrests gesture as WILLIE reads.)

WILLIE: His Grace and Most Reverend Father in God Dr. Carolus Hunter dead in tub.

(Pause.)

WINNIE (gazing front, hat in hand, tone of fervent reminiscence): Charlie Hunter! (Pause.) I close my eyes—(she takes off spectacles and does so, hat in one hand, spectacles in other, WILLIE turns page)—and am sitting on his knees again, in the back garden at Borough Green, under the horse-beech. (Pause. She opens eyes, puts on spectacles, fiddles with hat.) Oh the happy memories!

(*Pause. She raises hat towards head, arrests gesture as* WILLIE *reads.*)

WILLIE: Opening for smart youth.

(*Pause. She raises hat towards head, arrests gesture, takes off spectacles, gazes front, hat in one hand, spectacles in other.*)

WINNIE: My first ball! (*Long pause.*) My second ball! (*Long pause. Closes eyes.*) My first kiss! (*Pause.* WILLIE *turns page.* WINNIE *opens eyes.*) A Mr. Johnson, or Johnston, or perhaps I should say Johnstone. Very bushy moustache, very tawny. (*Reverently*) Almost ginger! (*Pause.*) Within a toolshed, though whose I cannot conceive. We had no toolshed and he most certainly had no toolshed. (*Closes eyes.*) I see the piles of pots. (*Pause.*) The tangles of bast. (*Pause.*) The shadows deepening among the rafters.

(*Pause. She opens eyes, puts on spectacles, raises hat towards head, arrests gesture as* WILLIE *reads.*)

WILLIE: Wanted bright boy.

(*Pause.* WINNIE *puts on hat hurriedly, looks for mirror.* WILLIE *turns page.* WINNIE *takes up mirror, inspects hat, lays down mirror, turns toward bag. Paper disappears.* WINNIE *rummages in bag, brings out magnifying-glass, turns back front, looks for toothbrush. Paper reappears, folded, and begins to fan* WILLIE'*s face, hand invisible.* WINNIE *takes up toothbrush and examines handle through glass.*)

WINNIE: Fully guaranteed . . . (WILLIE *stops fanning*) . . . genuine pure . . . (*Pause.* WILLIE *resumes fanning.* WINNIE *looks closer, reads.*) Fully guaranteed . . . (WILLIE *stops fanning*) . . . genuine pure . . . (*Pause.* WILLIE *resumes fanning.* WINNIE *lays down glass and brush, takes handkerchief from bodice, takes off and polishes spectacles, puts on spectacles, looks for glass, takes up and polishes glass, lays down glass, looks for brush, takes up brush and wipes handle, lays down brush, puts handkerchief back in bodice, looks for glass, takes up glass, looks for brush, takes up brush and examines handle through glass.*) Fully guaranteed . . . (WILLIE *stops fanning*) . . . genuine pure . . . (*pause,* WILLIE *resumes fanning*) . . . hog's (WILLIE *stops fanning, pause*) . . . setae. (*Pause.* WINNIE *lays down glass and brush, paper disappears,* WINNIE *takes off spectacles, lays them down, gazes front.*) Hog's setae. (*Pause.*) That is what I find so wonderful, that not a day goes by—(*smile*)—to speak in the old style—(*smile off*)—hardly a day,

without some addition to one's knowledge however trifling, the addition I mean, provided one takes the pains. (WILLIE'*s hand reappears with a postcard which he examines close to eyes.*) And if for some strange reason no further pains are possible, why then just close the eyes—(*she does so*)—and wait for the day to come—(*opens eyes*)—the happy day to come when flesh melts at so many degrees and the night of the moon has so many hundred hours. (*Pause.*) That is what I find so comforting when I lose heart and envy the brute beast. (*Turning towards* WILLIE) I hope you are taking in— (*She sees postcard, bends lower.*) What is that you have there, Willie, may I see? (*She reaches down with hand and* WILLIE *hands her card. The hairy forearm appears above slope, raised in gesture of giving, the hand open to take back, and remains in this position till card is returned.* WINNIE *turns back front and examines card.*) Heavens what are they up to! (*She looks for spectacles, puts them on and examines card.*) No but this is just genuine pure filth! (*Examines card.*) Make any nice-minded person want to vomit! (*Impatience of* WILLIE'*s fingers. She looks for glass, takes it up and examines card through glass. Long pause.*) What does that creature in the background think he's doing? (*Looks closer.*) Oh no really! (*Impatience of fingers. Last long look. She lays down glass, takes edge of card between right forefinger and thumb, averts head, takes nose between left forefinger and thumb.*) Pah! (*Drops card.*) Take it away! (WILLIE'*s arm disappears. His hand reappears immediately, holding card.* WINNIE *takes off spectacles, lays them down, gazes before her. During what follows* WILLIE *continues to relish card, varying angles and distance from his eyes.*) Hog's setae. (*Puzzled expression.*) What exactly is a hog? (*Pause. Do.*) A sow of course I know, but a hog . . . (*Puzzled expression off.*) Oh well what does it matter, that is what I always say, it will come back, that is what I find so wonderful, all comes back. (*Pause.*) All? (*Pause.*) No, not all. (*Smile.*) No no. (*Smile off.*) Not quite. (*Pause.*) A part. (*Pause.*) Floats up, one fine day, out of the blue. (*Pause.*) That is what I find so wonderful. (*Pause. She turns towards bag. Hand and card disappear. She makes to rummage in bag, arrests gesture.*) No. (*She turns back front. Smile.*) No no. (*Smile off.*) Gently Winnie. (*She gazes front.* WILLIE'*s hand reappears, takes off hat, disappears with hat.*) What then? (*Hand reappears, takes handkerchief from skull, disappears with handkerchief. Sharply, as to one not paying attention.*) Winnie! (WILLIE *bows head out of sight.*) What *is* the alternative? (*Pause.*) What *is* the al—(WILLIE *blows nose loud and long, head and hands invisible. She turns to look at him. Pause. Head reappears. Pause. Hand reappears with handkerchief, spreads it on skull, disappears. Pause. Hand reappears with boater, settles it on head, rakish angle, disappears. Pause.*) Would I had let you sleep on. (*She turns back front. Intermittent plucking at grass, head up and down, to animate following.*) Ah yes, if only I could bear to be alone, I mean prattle away with not a soul to hear. (*Pause.*) Not that I flatter myself you hear much, no Willie, God forbid. (*Pause.*) Days perhaps when you hear nothing. (*Pause.*) But days too when you answer. (*Pause.*) So that I may say at all times, even when you do not answer and perhaps hear nothing, something of this is being heard, I am not merely talking to myself, that is in the wilderness, a thing I could never bear to do—for any length of time. (*Pause.*) That is what enables me to go on, go on talking that is. (*Pause.*) Whereas if you were to die—(*smile*)—to speak in the old style—(*smile off*)—or go away and leave me, then what would I do, what *could* I do, all day long, I mean between the bell for waking and the bell for sleep? (*Pause.*) Simply gaze before me with compressed lips. (*Long pause while she does so. No more plucking.*) Not another word as long as I drew breath, nothing to break the silence of this place. (*Pause.*) Save possibly, now and then, every now and then, a sigh into my looking-glass. (*Pause.*) Or a brief . . . gale of laughter, should I happen to see the old joke again. (*Pause. Smile appears, broadens and seems about to culminate in laugh when suddenly replaced by expression of anxiety.*) My hair! (*Pause.*) Did I brush and comb my hair? (*Pause.*) I may have done. (*Pause.*) Normally I do. (*Pause.*) There is so little one *can* do. (*Pause.*) One does it all. (*Pause.*) All one can. (*Pause.*) Tis only human. (*Pause.*) Human nature. (*She begins to inspect mound, looks up.*) Human weakness. (*She resumes inspection of mound, looks up.*) Natural weakness. (*She resumes inspection of mound.*) I see no comb. (*Inspects.*) Nor any hairbrush. (*Looks up. Puzzled expression. She turns to bag, rummages in it.*) The comb is here. (*Back front. Puzzled expression. Back to bag. Rummages.*) The brush is here. (*Back front. Puzzled expression.*) Perhaps I put them back, after use. (*Pause. Do.*) But normally I do not put things back, after use, no, I leave them lying about and put them back all together, at the end of the day. (*Smile.*) To speak in the old style. (*Pause.*) The sweet old style. (*Smile off.*) And yet . . . I seem . . . to remember . . . (*Suddenly careless*) Oh well, what does it matter,

that is what I always say, I shall simply brush and comb them later on, purely and simply, I have the whole—(*Pause. Puzzled*) Them? (*Pause.*) Or it? (*Pause.*) Brush and comb it? (*Pause.*) Sounds improper somehow. (*Pause. Turning a little towards* WILLIE) What would you say, Willie? (*Pause. Turning a little further*) What would you say, Willie, speaking of your hair, them or it? (*Pause.*) The hair on your head, I mean. (*Pause. Turning a little further.*) The hair on your head, Willie, what would you say speaking of the hair on your head, them or it?

(*Long pause.*)

WILLIE: It.

WINNIE (*turning back front, joyful*): Oh you are going to talk to me today, this is going to be a happy day! (*Pause. Joy off.*) Another happy day. (*Pause.*) Ah well, where was I, my hair, yes, later on, I shall be thankful for it later on. (*Pause.*) I have my—(*raises hands to hat*)—yes, on, my hat on—(*lowers hands*)—I cannot take it off now. (*Pause.*) To think there are times one cannot take off one's hat, not if one's life were at stake. Times one cannot put it on, times one cannot take it off. (*Pause.*) How often I have said, Put on your hat now, Winnie, there is nothing else for it, take off your hat now, Winnie, like a good girl, it will do you good, and did not. (*Pause.*) Could not. (*Pause. She raises hand, frees a strand of hair from under hat, draws it towards eye, squints at it, lets it go, hand down.*) Golden you called it, that day, when the last guest was gone—(*hand up in gesture of raising a glass*)—to your golden . . . may it never (*voice breaks*) . . . may it never . . . (*Hand down. Head down. Pause. Low*) That day. (*Pause. Do.*) What day? (*Pause. Head up. Normal voice*) What now? (*Pause.*) Words fail, there are times when even they fail. (*Turning a little towards* WILLIE) Is that not so, Willie? (*Pause. Turning a little further*) Is not that so, Willie, that even words fail, at times? (*Pause. Back front.*) What is one to do then, until they come again? Brush and comb the hair, if it has not been done, or if there is some doubt, trim the nails if they are in need of trimming, these things tide one over. (*Pause.*) That is what I mean. (*Pause.*) That is all I mean. (*Pause.*) That is what I find so wonderful, that not a day goes by—(*smile*)—to speak in the old style—(*smile off*)—without some blessing—(WILLIE *collapses behind slope, his head disappears,* WINNIE *turns towards event*)—in disguise. (*She cranes back and down.*) Go back into your hole now, Willie, you've exposed yourself enough. (*Pause.*) Do as I say,

Willie, don't lie sprawling there in this hellish sun, go back into your hole. (*Pause*.) Go on now, Willie. (WILLIE *invisible starts crawling left towards hole*.) That's the man. (*She follows his progress with her eyes*.) Not head first, stupid, how are you going to turn? (*Pause*.) That's it . . . right round . . . now . . . back in. (*Pause*.) Oh I know it is not easy, dear, crawling backwards, but it is rewarding in the end. (*Pause*.) You have left your vaseline behind. (*She watches as he crawls back for vaseline*.) The lid! (*She watches as he crawls back towards hole. Irritated*) Not head first, I tell you! (*Pause*.) More to the right. (*Pause*.) The *right*, I said. (*Pause. Irritated*) Keep your tail down, can't you! (*Pause*.) Now. (*Pause*.) There! (*All these directions loud. Now in her normal voice, still turned towards him*) Can you hear me? (*Pause*.) I beseech you, Willie, just yes or no, can you hear me, just yes or nothing.

(*Pause*.)

WILLIE: Yes.
WINNIE (*turning front, same voice*): And now?
WILLIE (*irritated*): Yes.
WINNIE (*less loud*): And now?
WILLIE (*more irritated*): Yes.
WINNIE (*still less loud*): And now? (*A little louder*) And now?
WILLIE (*violently*): Yes!
WINNIE (*same voice*): Fear no more the heat o' the sun. (*Pause*.) Did you hear that?
WILLIE (*irritated*): Yes.
WINNIE (*same voice*): What? (*Pause*.) What?
WILLIE (*more irritated*): Fear no more.

(*Pause*.)

WINNIE (*same voice*): No more what? (*Pause*.) Fear no more what?
WILLIE (*violently*): Fear no more!
WINNIE (*normal voice, gabbled*): Bless you Willie I do appreciate your goodness I know what an effort it costs you, now you may relax I shall not trouble you again unless I am obliged to, by that I mean unless I come to the end of my own resources which is most unlikely, just to know that in theory you can hear me even though in fact you don't is all I need, just to feel you there within earshot and conceivably on the qui vive is all I ask, not to say anything I would not wish you to hear or liable to cause you pain, not to be babbling away on trust as it is were not knowing and something gnawing at me. (*Pause for breath*.) Doubt. (*Places index and second finger on heart area, moves them about, brings them to rest*.) Here. (*Moves them

slightly*.) Abouts. (*Hand away*.) Oh no doubt the time will come when before I can utter a word I must make sure you heard the one that went before and then no doubt another come another time when I must learn to talk to myself a thing I could never bear to do such wilderness. (*Pause*.) Or gaze before me with compressed lips. (*She does so*.) All day long. (*Gaze and lips again*.) No. (*Smile*.) No no. (*Smile off*.) There is of course the bag. (*Turns towards it*.) There will always be the bag. (*Back front*.) Yes, I suppose so. (*Pause*.) Even when you are gone, Willie. (*She turns a little towards him*.) You *are* going, Willie, aren't you? (*Pause. Louder*) You *will* be going soon, Willie, won't you? (*Pause. Louder*) Willie! (*Pause. She cranes back and down to look at him*.) So you have taken off your straw, that is wise. (*Pause*.) You do look snug, I must say, with your chin on your hands and the old blue eyes like saucers in the shadows. (*Pause*.) Can you see me from there I wonder, I still wonder. (*Pause*.) No? (*Back front*.) Oh I know it does not follow when two are gathered together—(*faltering*)—in this way—(*normal*)—that because one sees the other the other sees the one, life has taught me that . . . too. (*Pause*.) Yes, life I suppose, there is no other word. (*She turns a little towards him*.) Could you see me, Willie, do you think, from where you are, if you were to raise your eyes in my direction? (*Turns a little further*.) Lift up your eyes to me, Willie, and tell me can you see me, do that for me, I'll lean back as far as I can. (*Does so. Pause*.) No? (*Pause*.) Well never mind. (*Turns back painfully front*.) The earth is very tight today, can it be I have put on flesh, I trust not. (*Pause. Absently, eyes lowered*) The great heat possibly. (*Starts to pat and stroke ground*.) All things expanding, some more than others. (*Pause. Patting and stroking*) Some less. (*Pause. Do*.) Oh I can well imagine what is passing through your mind, it is not enough to have to listen to the woman, now I must look at her as well. (*Pause. Do*.) Well it is very understandable. (*Pause. Do*.) Well it is very understandable. (*Pause. Do*.) Most understandable. (*Pause. Do*.) One does not appear to be asking a great deal, indeed at times it would seem hardly possible—(*voice breaks, falls to a murmur*)—to ask less—of a fellow-creature—to put it mildly—whereas actually—when you think about it—look into your heart—see the other—what he needs—peace—to be left in peace—then perhaps the moon—all this time—asking for the moon. (*Pause. Stroking hand suddenly still. Lively*) Oh I say, what have we here? (*Bending head to ground, incredulous*) Looks like life of some kind! (*Looks for spectacles, puts them on, bends closer. Pause*.) An emmet! (*Recoils. Shrill*) Willie, an emmet, a live emmet! (*Seizes magnifying-glass, bends to ground again, inspects through glass.*) Where's it gone? (*Inspects.*) Ah! (*Follows its progress through grass.*) Has like a little white ball in its arms. (*Follows progress. Hand still. Pause.*) It's gone in. (*Continues a moment to gaze at spot through glass, then slowly straightens up, lays down glass, takes off spectacles and gazes before her, spectacles in hand. Finally*) Like a little white ball.

(*Long pause. Gesture to lay down spectacles.*)

WILLIE: Eggs.
WINNIE (*arresting gesture*): What?

(*Pause.*)

WILLIE: Eggs. (*Pause. Gesture to lay down glasses.*) Formication.
WINNIE (*arresting gesture*): What?

(*Pause.*)

WILLIE: Formication.

(*Pause. She lays down spectacles, gazes before her. Finally.*)

WINNIE (*murmur*): God. (*Pause.* WILLIE *laughs quietly. After a moment she joins in. They laugh quietly together.* WILLIE *stops. She laughs on a moment alone.* WILLIE *joins in. They laugh together. She stops.* WILLIE *laughs on a moment alone. He stops. Pause. Normal voice.*) Ah well what a joy in any case to hear you laugh again, Willie, I was convinced I never would, you never would. (*Pause.*) I suppose some people might think us a trifle irreverent, but I doubt it. (*Pause.*) How can one better magnify the Almighty than by sniggering with him at his little jokes, particularly the poorer ones? (*Pause.*) I think you would back me up there, Willie. (*Pause.*) Or were we perhaps diverted by two quite different things? (*Pause.*) Oh well, what does it matter, that is what I always say, so long as one . . . you know . . . what is that wonderful line . . . laughing wild . . .something something laughing wild amid severest woe. (*Pause.*) And now? (*Long pause.*) Was I lovable once, Willie? (*Pause.*) Was I ever lovable? (*Pause.*) Do not misunderstand my question, I am not asking you if you loved me, we know all about that, I am asking you if you found me lovable—at one stage. (*Pause.*) No? (*Pause.*) You can't? (*Pause.*) Well I admit it is a teaser. And you have done more than your bit already, for the time being, just lie back now and relax, I shall not

trouble you again unless I am
know you are there within hea
bly on the semi-alert is . . . er . . .
(*Pause.*) The day is now well advanc
To speak in the old style. (*Smile off.*) An
perhaps a little soon for my song. (*Pause.*) To
too soon is a great mistake, I find. (*Turnin*
towards bag) There is of course the bag. (*Looking at bag*) The bag. (*Back front.*) Could I enumerate its contents? (*Pause.*) No. (*Pause.*) Could I, if some kind person were to come along and ask, What all have you got in that big black bag, Winnie? give an exhaustive answer? (*Pause.*) No. (*Pause.*) The depths in particular, who knows what treasures. (*Pause.*) What comforts. (*Turns to look at bag.*) Yes, there is the bag. (*Back front.*) But something tells me, Do not overdo the bag, Winnie, make use of it of course, let it help you . . . along, when stuck, by all means, but cast your mind forward, something tells me, cast your mind forward, Winnie, to the time when words must fail—(*she closes eyes, pause, opens eyes*)—and do not overdo the bag. (*Pause. She turns to look at bag.*) Perhaps just one quick dip. (*She turns back front, closes eyes, throws out left arm, plunges hand in bag and brings out revolver. Disgusted.*) You again! (*She opens eyes, brings revolver front and contemplates it. She weighs it in her palm.*) You'd think the weight of this thing would bring it down among the . . . last rounds. But no. It doesn't. Ever uppermost, like Browning. (*Pause.*) Brownie . . . (*Turning a little towards* WILLIE) Remember Brownie, Willie? (*Pause.*) Remember how you used to keep on at me to take it away from you? Take it away, Winnie, take it away, before I put myself out of my misery. (*Back front. Derisive*) *Your* misery! (*To revolver*) Oh I suppose it's a comfort to know you're there, but I'm tired of you. (*Pause.*) I'll leave you out, that's what I'll do. (*She lays revolver on ground to her right.*) There, that's your home from this day out. (*Smile.*) The old style! (*Smile off.*) And now? (*Long pause.*) Is gravity what it was, Willie, I fancy not. (*Pause.*) Yes, the feeling more and more that if I were not held—(*gesture*)—in this way, I would simply float up into the blue. (*Pause.*) And that perhaps some day the earth will yield and let me go, the pull is so great, yes, crack all round me and let me out. (*Pause.*) Don't you ever have that feeling, Willie, of being sucked up? (*Pause.*) Don't you have to cling on sometimes, Willie? (*Pause. She turns a little towards him.*) Willie.

(*Pause.*)

WILLIE: *Sucked* up?

WINNIE: Yes, love, up into the blue, like gossamer. (*Pause.*) No? (*Pause.*) You don't? (*Pause.*) Ah well, natural laws, natural laws, I suppose it's like everything else, it all depends on the creature you happen to be. All I can say is for my part is that for me they are not what they were when I was young and . . . foolish and . . . (*faltering, head down*) . . . beautiful . . . possibly . . . lovely . . . in a way . . . to look at. (*Pause. Head up.*) Forgive me, Willie, sorrow keeps breaking in. (*Normal voice*) Ah well what a joy in any case to know you are there, as usual, and perhaps awake, and perhaps taking all this in, some of all this, what a happy day for me . . . it will have been. (*Pause.*) So far. (*Pause.*) What a blessing nothing grows, imagine if all this stuff were to start growing. (*Pause.*) Imagine. (*Pause.*) Ah yes, great mercies. (*Long pause.*) I can say no more. (*Pause.*) For the moment. (*Pause. Turns to look at bag. Back front. Smile.*) No no. (*Smile off. Looks at parasol.*) I suppose I might—(*takes up parasol*)—yes, I suppose I might . . . hoist this thing now. (*Begins to unfurl it. Following punctuated by mechanical difficulties overcome.*) One keeps putting off—putting up—for fear of putting up—too soon—and the day goes by—quite by—without one's having put up—at all. (*Parasol now fully open. Turned to her right she twirls it idly this way and that.*) Ah yes, so little to say, so little to do, and the fear so great, certain days, of finding oneself . . . left, with hours still to run, before the bell for sleep, and nothing more to say, nothing more to do, that the days go by, certain days go by, quite by, the bell goes, and little or nothing said, little or nothing done. (*Raising parasol*) That is the danger. (*Turning front*) To be guarded against. (*She gazes front, holding up parasol with right hand. Maximum pause.*) I used to perspire freely. (*Pause.*) Now hardly at all. (*Pause.*) The heat is much greater. (*Pause.*) The perspiration much less. (*Pause.*) That is what I find so wonderful. (*Pause.*) The way man adapts himself. (*Pause.*) To changing conditions. (*She transfers parasol to left hand. Long pause.*) Holding up wearies the arm. (*Pause.*) Not if one is going along. (*Pause.*) Only if one is at rest. (*Pause.*) That is a curious observation. (*Pause.*) I hope you heard that, Willie, I should be grieved to think you had not heard that. (*She takes parasol in both hands. Long pause.*) I am weary, holding it up, and I cannot put it down. (*Pause.*) I am worse off with it up than with it down, and I cannot put it down. (*Pause.*) Reason says, Put it down, Winnie, it is not helping you, put the thing down and get on with something

else. (*Pause.*) I cannot. (*Pause.*) I cannot move. (*Pause.*) No, something must happen, in the world, take place, some change, I cannot, if I am to move again. (*Pause.*) Willie. (*Mildly*) Help. (*Pause.*) No? (*Pause.*) Bid me put this thing down, Willie, I would obey you instantly, as I have always done, honoured and obeyed. (*Pause.*) Please, Willie. (*Mildly*) For pity's sake. (*Pause.*) No? (*Pause.*) You can't? (*Pause.*) Well I don't blame you, no, it would ill become me, who cannot move, to blame my Willie because he cannot speak. (*Pause.*) Fortunately I am in tongue again. (*Pause.*) That is what I find so wonderful, my two lamps, when one goes out the other burns brighter. (*Pause.*) Oh yes, great mercies. (*Maximum pause. The parasol goes on fire. Smoke, flames if feasible. She sniffs, looks up, throws parasol to her right behind mound, cranes back to watch it burning. Pause.*) Ah earth you old extinguisher. (*Back front.*) I presume this has occurred before, though I cannot recall it. (*Pause.*) Can you, Willie? (*Turns a little towards him.*) Can' you recall this having occurred before? (*Pause. Cranes back to look at him.*) Do you know what has occurred, Willie? (*Pause.*) Have you gone off on me again? (*Pause.*) I do not ask if you are alive to all that is going on, I merely ask if you have not gone off on me again. (*Pause.*) Your eyes appear to be closed, but that has no particular significance we know. (*Pause.*) Raise a finger, dear, will you please, if you are not quite senseless. (*Pause.*) Do that for me, Willie please, just the little finger, if you are still conscious. (*Pause. Joyful*) Oh all five, you are a darling today, now I may continue with an easy mind. (*Back front.*) Yes, what ever occurred that did not occur before and yet . . . I wonder, yes, I confess I wonder. (*Pause.*). With the sun blazing so much fiercer down, and hourly fiercer, is it not natural things should go on fire never known to do so, in this way I mean, spontaneous like. (*Pause.*) Shall I myself not melt perhaps in the end, or burn, oh I do not mean necessarily burst into flames, no, just little by little be charred to a black cinder, all this—(*ample gesture of arms*)—visible flesh. (*Pause.*) On the other hand, did I ever know a temperate time? (*Pause.*) No. (*Pause.*) I speak of temperate times and torrid times, they are empty words. (*Pause.*) I speak of when I was not yet caught—in this way—and had my legs and had the use of my legs, and could seek out a shady place, like you, when I was tired of the sun, or a sunny place when I was tired of the shade, like you, and they are all empty words. (*Pause.*) It is no hotter today than yesterday, it will be no hotter tomorrow than today, how could it, and so on back into the far past, forward into the far future. (*Pause.*) And should one day the earth cover my breasts, then I shall never have seen my breasts, no one ever seen my breasts. (*Pause.*) I hope you caught something of that, Willie, I should be sorry to think you had caught nothing of all that, it is not every day I rise to such heights. (*Pause.*) Yes, something seems to have occurred, something has seemed to occur, and nothing has occurred, nothing at all, you are quite right, Willie. (*Pause.*) The sunshade will be there again tomorrow, beside me on this mound, to help me through the day. (*Pause. She takes up mirror.*) I take up this little glass, I shiver it on a stone—(*does so*)—I throw it away—(*does so far behind her*)—it will be in the bag again tomorrow, without a scratch, to help me through the day. (*Pause.*) No, one can do nothing. (*Pause.*) That is what I find so wonderful, the way things . . . (*voice breaks, head down*) . . . things . . . so wonderful. (*Long pause, head down. Finally turns, still bowed, to bag, brings out unidentifiable odds and ends, stuffs them back, fumbles deeper, brings out finally musical-box, winds it up, turns it on, listens for a moment holding it in both hands, huddled over it, turns back front, straightens up and listens to tune, holding box to breast with both hands. It plays the Waltz Duet "I Love You So" from* The Merry Widow. *Gradually happy expression. She sways to the rhythm. Music stops. Pause. Brief burst of hoarse song without words—musical-box tune—from* WILLIE. *Increase of happy expression. She lays down box.*) Oh this will have been a happy day! (*She claps hands.*) Again, Willie, again! (*Claps.*) Encore, Willie, please! (*Pause. Happy expression off.*) No? You won't do that for me? (*Pause.*) Well it is very understandable, very understandable. One cannot sing just to please someone, however much one loves them, no, song must come from the heart, that is what I always say, pour out from the inmost, like a thrush. (*Pause.*) How often I have said, in evil hours, Sing now, Winnie, sing your song, there is nothing else for it, and did not. (*Pause.*) Could not. (*Pause.*) No, like the thrush, or the bird of dawning, with no thought of benefit, to oneself or anyone else. (*Pause.*) And now? (*Long pause. Low*) Strange feeling. (*Pause. Do.*) Strange feeling that someone is looking at me. I am clear, then dim, then gone, then dim again, then clear again, and so on, back and forth, in and out of someone's eye. (*Pause. Do.*) Strange? (*Pause. Do.*) No, here all is strange. (*Pause. Normal voice*) Something says, Stop talk-

ing now, Winnie, for a minute, don't squander all your words for the day, stop talking and do something for a change, will you? (*She raises hands and holds them open before her eyes. Apostrophic*) Do something! (*She closes hands.*) What claws! (*She turns to bag, rummages in it, brings out finally a nailfile, turns back front and begins to file nails. Files for a time in silence, then the following punctuated by filing.*) There floats up—into my thoughts—a Mr. Shower—a Mr. and perhaps a Mrs. Shower—no—they are holding hands—his fiancée then more likely—or just some—loved one. (*Looks closer at nails.*) Very brittle today. (*Resumes filing.*) Shower—Shower—does the name mean anything—to you, Willie—evoke any reality, I mean—for you, Willie—don't answer if you don't—feel up to it—you have done more—than your bit—already—Shower— Shower. (*Inspects filed nails.*) Bit more like it. (*Raises head, gazes front.*) Keep yourself nice, Winnie, that's what I always say, come what may, keep yourself nice. (*Pause. Resumes filing.*) Yes— Shower—Shower—(*stops filing, raises head, gazes front, pause*)—or Cooker, perhaps I should say Cooker. (*Turning a little towards* WILLIE.) Cooker, Willie, does Cooker strike a chord? (*Pause. Turns a little further. Louder*) Cooker, Willie, does Cooker ring a bell, the name Cooker? (*Pause. She cranes back to look at him. Pause.*) Oh really! (*Pause.*) Have you no handkerchief, darling? (*Pause.*) Have you no delicacy? (*Pause.*) Oh, Willie, you're not eating it! Spit it out, dear, spit it out! (*Pause. Back front.*) Ah well, I suppose it's only natural. (*Break in voice.*) Human. (*Pause. Do.*) What *is* one to do? (*Head down. Do.*) All day long. (*Pause. Do.*) Day after day. (*Pause. Head up. Smile. Calm*) The old style! (*Smile off. Resumes nails.*) No, done him. (*Passes on to next.*) Should have put on my glasses. (*Pause.*) Too late now. (*Finishes left hand, inspects it.*) Bit more human. (*Starts right hand. Following punctuated as before.*) Well anyway—this man Shower—or Cooker—no matter—and the woman—hand in hand—in the other hands bags—kind of big brown grips—standing there gaping at me—and at last this man Shower—or Cooker—ends in er anyway—stake my life on that—What's she doing? he says—What's the idea? he says—stuck up to her diddies in the bleeding ground—coarse fellow—What does it mean? he says—What's it meant to mean?—and so on—lot more stuff like that—usual drivel—Do you hear me? he says—I do, she says, God help me—What do you mean, he says, God help you? (*Stops filing, raises head, gazes front.*) And you, she says, what's the idea of you, she says, what are you meant to mean? It is because you're still on your two flat feet, with your old ditty full of tinned muck and changes of underwear, dragging me up and down this fornicating wilderness, coarse creature, fit mate—(*with sudden violence*)—let go of my hand and drop for God's sake, she says, drop! (*Pause. Resumes filing.*) Why doesn't he dig her out? he says—referring to you, my dear—What good is she to him like that?—What good is he to her like that?—and so on—usual tosh—Good! she says, have a heart for God's sake—Dig her out, he says, dig her out, no sense in her like that—Dig her out with what? she says—I'd dig her out with my bare hands, he says—must have been man and—wife. (*Files in silence.*) Next thing they're away—hand in hand—and the bags—dim—then gone—last human kind—to stray this way. (*Finishes right hand, inspects it, lays down file, gazes front.*) Strange thing, time like this, drift up into the mind. (*Pause.*) Strange? (*Pause.*) No, here all is strange. (*Pause.*) Thankful for it in any case. (*Voice breaks.*) Most thankful. (*Head down. Pause. Head up. Calm*) Bow and raise the head, bow and raise, always that. (*Pause.*) And now? (*Long pause. Starts putting things back in bag, toothbrush last. This operation, interrupted by pauses as indicated, punctuates following.*) It is perhaps a little soon— to make ready—for the night—(*stops tidying, head up, smile*)—the old style!—(*smile off, resumes tidying*)—and yet I do—make ready for the night—feeling it at hand—the bell for sleep— saying to myself—Winnie—it will not be long now, Winnie—until the bell for sleep. (*Stops tidying, head up.*) Sometimes I am wrong. (*Smile.*) But not often. (*Smile off.*) Sometimes all is over, for the day, all done, all said, all ready for the night, and the day not over, far from over, the night not ready, far, far from ready. (*Smile.*) But not often. (*Smile off.*) Yes, the bell for sleep, when I feel it at hand, and so make ready for the night— (*gesture*)—in this way, sometimes I am wrong (*smile*)—but not often. (*Smile off. Resumes tidying.*) I used to think—I say I used to think—that all these things—put back into the bag—if too soon—put back too soon—could be taken out again—if necessary—if needed—and so on—indefinitely—back into the bag—back out of the bag—until the bell—went. (*Stops tidying, head up, smile.*) But no. (*Smile broader.*) No no. (*Smile off. Resumes tidying.*) I suppose this—might seem strange—this—what shall I say—this what I have said—yes—(*she takes up revolver*)—strange—(*she turns to put revolver in bag*)—were it not—(*about to put revolver in bag she arrests gesture and turns back front*)—were it not—(*she lays down revolver to her right, stops tidying, head up*)—that all seems strange. (*Pause.*) Most strange. (*Pause.*) Never any change. (*Pause.*) And more and more strange. (*Pause. She bends to mound again, takes up last object, i.e., toothbrush, and turns to put it in bag when her attention is drawn to disturbance from* WILLIE. *She cranes back and to her right to see. Pause.*) Weary of your hole, dear? (*Pause.*) Well I can understand that. (*Pause.*) Don't forget your straw. (*Pause.*) Not the crawler you were, poor darling. (*Pause.*) No, not the crawler I gave my heart to. (*Pause.*) The hands and knees, love, try the hands and knees. (*Pause.*) The knees! The knees! (*Pause.*) What a curse, mobility! (*She follows with eyes his progress towards her behind mound, i.e., towards place he occupied at beginning of act.*) Another foot, Willie, and you're home. (*Pause as she observes last foot.*) Ah! (*Turns back front laboriously, rubs neck.*) Crick in my neck admiring you. (*Rubs neck.*) But it's worth it, well worth it. (*Turning slightly towards him*) Do you know what I dream sometimes? (*Pause.*) What I dream sometimes, Willie. (*Pause.*) That you'll come round and live this side where I could see you. (*Pause. Back front.*) I'd be a different woman. (*Pause.*) Unrecognizable. (*Turning slightly towards him*) Or just now and then, come round this side just every now and then and let me feast on you. (*Back front.*) But you can't, I know. (*Head down.*) I know. (*Pause. Head up.*) Well anyway— (*looks at toothbrush in her hand*)—can't be long now—(*looks at brush*)—until the bell. (*Top back of* WILLIE's *head appears above slope.* WINNIE *looks closer at brush.*) Fully guaranteed . . . (*head up*) . . . what's this it was? (WILLIE's *hand appears with handkerchief, spreads it on skull, disappears.*) Genuine pure . . . fully guaranteed . . . (WILLIE's *hand appears with boater, settles it on head, rakish angle, disappears*) . . . genuine pure . . . ah! hog's setae. (*Pause.*) What is a hog exactly? (*Pause. Turns slightly towards* WILLIE) What exactly is a hog, Willie, do you know, I can't remember. (*Pause. Turning a little further, pleading*) What is a hog, Willie, please!

(*Pause.*)

WILLIE: Castrated male swine. (*Happy expression appears on* WINNIE's *face.*) Reared for slaughter.

(*Happy expression increases.* WILLIE *opens newspaper, hands invisible. Tops of yellow sheets appear on either side of his head.* WINNIE *gazes before her with happy expression.*)

WINNIE: Oh this *is* a happy day! (*Pause.*) After all. (*Pause.*) So far.

(*Pause. Happy expression off.* WILLIE *turns page. Pause. He turns another page. Pause.*)

WILLIE: Opening for smart youth.

(*Pause.* WINNIE *takes off hat, turns to put it in bag, arrests gesture, turns back front. Smile.*)

WINNIE: No. (*Smile broader.*) No no. (*Smile off. Puts on hat again, gazes front, pause.*) And now? (*Pause.*) Sing. (*Pause.*) Sing your song, Winnie. (*Pause.*) No? (*Pause.*) Then pray. (*Pause.*) Pray your prayer, Winnie.

(*Pause.* WILLIE *turns page. Pause.*)

WILLIE: Wanted bright boy.

(*Pause.* WINNIE *gazes before her.* WILLIE *turns page. Pause. Newspaper disappears. Long pause.*)

WINNIE: Pray your old prayer, Winnie.

(*Long pause.*)

CURTAIN

ACT II

SCENE *as before.*

WINNIE *imbedded up to neck, hat on head, eyes closed. Her head, which she can no longer turn, nor bow, nor raise, faces front motionless throughout act. Movements of eyes as indicated.*
   Bag and parasol as before. Revolver conspicuous to her right on mound.
   Long pause.
   Bell rings loudly. She opens eyes at once. Bell stops. She gazes front. Long pause.

WINNIE: Hail, holy light. (*Long pause. She closes her eyes. Bell rings loudly. She opens eyes at once. Bell stops. She gazes front. Long smile. Smile off. Long pause.*) Someone is looking at me still. (*Pause.*) Caring for me still. (*Pause.*) That is what I find so wonderful. (*Pause.*) Eyes on my eyes. (*Pause.*) What is that unforgettable line? (*Pause. Eyes right.*) Willie. (*Pause. Louder*) Willie. (*Pause. Eyes front.*) May one still speak of time? (*Pause.*) Say it is a long time now, Willie, since I saw you. (*Pause.*) Since I heard you. (*Pause.*) May

one? (*Pause.*) One does. (*Smile.*) The old style! (*Smile off.*) There is so little one can speak of. (*Pause.*) One speaks of it all. (*Pause.*) All one can. (*Pause.*) I used to think . . . (*pause*) . . . I say I used to think that I would learn to talk alone. (*Pause.*) By that I mean to myself, the wilderness. (*Smile.*) But no. (*Smile broader.*) No no. (*Smile off.*) Ergo you are there. (*Pause.*) Oh no doubt you are dead, like the others, no doubt you have died, or gone away and left me, like the others, it doesn't matter, you are there. (*Pause. Eyes left.*) The bag too is there, the same as ever, I can see it. (*Pause. Eyes right. Louder*) The bag is there, Willie, as good as ever, the one you gave me that day . . . to go to market. (*Pause. Eyes front.*) That day. (*Pause.*) What day? (*Pause.*) I used to pray. (*Pause.*) I say I used to pray. (*Pause.*) Yes, I must confess I did. (*Smile.*) Not now. (*Smile broader.*) No no. (*Smile off. Pause.*) Then . . . now . . . what difficulties here, for the mind. (*Pause.*) To have been always what I am—and so changed from what I was. (*Pause.*) I am the one, I say the one, then the other. (*Pause.*) Now the one, then the other (*Pause.*) There is so little one can say, one says it all. (*Pause.*) All one can. (*Pause.*) And no truth in it anywhere. (*Pause.*) My arms. (*Pause.*) My breasts. (*Pause.*) What arms? (*Pause.*) What breasts? (*Pause.*) Willie. (*Pause.*) What Willie? (*Sudden vehement affirmation*) My Willie! (*Eyes right, calling*) Willie! (*Pause. Louder*) Willie! (*Pause. Eyes front.*) Ah well, not to know, not to know for sure, great mercy, all I ask. (*Pause.*) Ah yes . . . then . . . now . . . beechen green . . . this . . . Charlie . . . kisses . . . this . . . all that . . . deep trouble for the mind. (*Pause.*) But it does not trouble mine. (*Smile.*) Not now. (*Smile broader.*) No no. (*Smile off. Long pause. She closes eyes. Bell rings loudly. She opens eyes. Pause.*) Eyes float up that seem to close in peace . . . to see . . . in peace. (*Pause.*) Not mine. (*Smile.*) Not now. (*Smile broader.*) No no. (*Smile off. Long pause.*) Willie. (*Pause.*) Do you think the earth has lost its atmosphere, Willie? (*Pause.*) Do you, Willie? (*Pause.*) You have no opinion? (*Pause.*) Well that is like you, you never had any opinion about anything. (*Pause.*) It's understandable. (*Pause.*) Most. (*Pause.*) The earthball. (*Pause.*) I sometimes wonder. (*Pause.*) Perhaps not quite all. (*Pause.*) There always remains something. (*Pause.*) Of everything. (*Pause.*) Some remains. (*Pause.*) If the mind were to go. (*Pause.*) It won't of course. (*Pause.*) Not quite. (*Pause.*) Not mine. (*Smile.*) Not now. (*Smile braoder.*) No no. (*Smile off. Long pause.*) It might be the eternal cold. (*Pause.*)

Everlasting perishing cold. (*Pause.*) Just chance, I take it, happy chance. (*Pause.*) Oh yes, great mercies, great mercies. (*Pause.*) And now? (*Long pause.*) The face. (*Pause.*) The nose. (*She squints down.*) I can see it . . . (*squinting down*) . . . the tip . . . the nostrils . . . breath of life . . . that curve you so admired . . . (*pouts*) . . . a hint of lip . . . (*pouts again*) . . . if I pout them out . . . (*sticks out tongue*) . . . the tongue of course . . . you so admired . . . if I stick it out . . . (*sticks it out again*) . . . the tip . . . (*eyes up*) . . . suspicion of brow . . . eyebrow . . . imagination possibly . . . (*eyes left*) . . . cheek . . . no . . .(*eyes right*) . . . no . . . (*distends cheeks*) . . .even if I puff them out . . . (*eyes left, distends cheeks again*) . . . no . . . no damask. (*Eyes front.*) That is all. (*Pause.*) The bag of course . . . (*eyes left*) . . . a little blurred perhaps . . . but the bag. (*Eyes front. Offhand*) The earth of course and sky. (*Eyes right.*) The sunshade you gave me . . . that day . . . (*pause*) . . . that day . . . the lake . . . the reeds. (*Eyes front. Pause.*) What day? (*Pause.*) What reeds? (*Long pause. Eyes close. Bell rings loudly. Eyes open. Pause. Eyes right.*) Brownie of course. (*Pause.*) You remember Brownie, Willie, I can see him. (*Pause.*) Brownie is there, Willie, beside me. (*Pause. Loud*) Brownie is there, Willie. (*Pause. Eyes front.*) That is all. (*Pause.*) What would I do without them? (*Pause.*) What would I do without them, when words fail? (*Pause.*) Gaze before me, with compressed lips. (*Long pause while she does so.*) I cannot. (*Pause.*) Ah yes, great mercies, great mercies. (*Long pause. Low*) Sometimes I hear sounds. (*Listening expression. Normal voice*) But not often. (*Pause.*) They are a boon, sounds are a boon, they help me . . . through the day. (*Smile.*) The old style! (*Smile off.*) Yes, those are happy days, when there are sounds. (*Pause.*) When I hear sounds. (*Pause.*) I used to think . . . (*pause*) . . . I say I used to think they were in my head. (*Smile.*) But no. (*Smile broader.*) No no. (*Smile off.*) That was just logic. (*Pause.*) Reason. (*Pause.*) I have not lost my reason. (*Pause.*) Not yet. (*Pause.*) Not all. (*Pause.*) Some remains. (*Pause.*) Sounds. (*Pause.*) Like little . . . sunderings, little falls . . . apart. (*Pause. Low*) It's things, Willie. (*Pause. Normal voice*) In the bag, outside the bag. (*Pause.*) Ah yes, things have their life, that is what I always say, *things* have a life. (*Pause.*) Take my looking-glass, it doesn't need me. (*Pause.*) The bell. (*Pause.*) It hurts like a knife. (*Pause.*) A gouge. (*Pause.*) One cannot ignore it. (*Pause.*) How often . . . (*pause*) . . . I say how often I have said, Ignore it, Winnie, ignore the bell, pay no heed, just sleep and wake, sleep and wake, as

you please, open and close the eyes, as you please, or in the way you find most helpful. (*Pause.*) Open and close the eyes, Winnie, open and close, always that. (*Pause.*) But no. (*Smile.*) Not now. (*Smile broader.*) No no. (*Smile off. Pause.*) What now? (*Pause.*) What now, Willie? (*Long pause.*) There is my story of course, when all else fails. (*Pause.*) A life. (*Smile.*) A long life. (*Smile off.*) Beginning in the womb, where life used to begin, Mildred has memories, she will have memories, of the womb, before she dies, the mother's womb. (*Pause.*) She is now four or five already and has recently been given a big waxen dolly. (*Pause.*) Fully clothed, complete outfit. (*Pause.*) Shoes, socks, undies, complete set, frilly frock, gloves. (*Pause.*) White mesh. (*Pause.*) A little white straw hat with a chin elastic. (*Pause.*) Pearly necklet. (*Pause.*) A little picture-book with legends in real print to go under her arm when she takes her walk. (*Pause.*) China blue eyes that open and shut. (*Pause. Narrative*) The sun was not well up when Milly rose, descended the steep . . . (*pause*) . . . slipped on her nightgown, descended all alone the steep wooden stairs, backwards on all fours, though she had been forbidden to do so, entered the . . . (*pause*) . . . tiptoed down the silent passage, entered the nursery and began to undress Dolly. (*Pause.*) Crept under the table and began to undress Dolly. (*Pause.*) Scolding her . . . the while. (*Pause.*) Suddenly a mouse—(*Long pause.*) Gently, Winnie. (*Long pause. Calling*) Willie! (*Pause. Louder*) Willie! (*Pause. Mild reproach*) I sometimes find your attitude a little strange, Willie, all this time, it is not like you to be wantonly cruel. (*Pause.*) Strange? (*Pause.*) No. (*Smile.*) Not here. (*Smile broader.*) Not now. (*Smile off.*) And yet . . . (*Suddenly anxious*) I do hope nothing is amiss. (*Eyes right, loud*) Is all well, dear? (*Pause. Eyes front. To herself*) God grant he did not go in head foremost! (*Eyes right, loud*) You're not stuck, Willie? (*Pause. Do.*) You're not jammed, Willie? (*Eyes front, distressed*) Perhaps he is crying out for help all this time and I do not hear him! (*Pause.*) I do of course hear cries. (*Pause.*) But they are in my head surely. (*Pause.*) Is it possible that . . . (*Pause. With finality*) No no, my head was always full of cries. (*Pause.*) Faint confused cries. (*Pause.*) They come. (*Pause.*) Then go. (*Pause.*) As on a wind. (*Pause.*) That is what I find so wonderful. (*Pause.*) They cease. (*Pause.*) Ah yes, great mercies, great mercies. (*Pause.*) The day is now well advanced. (*Smile. Smile off.*) And yet it is perhaps a little soon for my song. (*Pause.*) To sing too soon is fatal, I always find.

(*Pause.*) On the other hand it is possible to leave it too late. (*Pause.*) The bell goes for sleep and one has not sung. (*Pause.*) The whole day has flown— (*smile, smile off*)—flown by, quite by, and no song of any class, kind or description. (*Pause.*) There is a problem here. (*Pause.*) One cannot sing . . . just like that, no. (*Pause.*) It bubbles up, for some unknown reason, the time is ill chosen, one chokes it back. (*Pause.*) One says, Now is the time, it is now or never, and one cannot. (*Pause.*) Simply cannot sing. (*Pause.*) Not a note. (*Pause.*) Another thing, Willie, while we are on this subject. (*Pause.*) The sadness after song. (*Pause.*) Have you run across that, Willie? (*Pause.*) In the course of your experience. (*Pause.*) No? (*Pause.*) Sadness after intimate sexual intercourse one is familiar with of course. (*Pause.*) You would concur with Aristotle there, Willie, I fancy. (*Pause.*) Yes, that one knows and is prepared to face. (*Pause.*) But after song . . . (*Pause.*) It does not last of course. (*Pause.*) That is what I find so wonderful. (*Pause.*) It wears away. (*Pause.*) What are those exquisite lines? (*Pause.*) Go forget me why should something o'er that something shadow fling . . . go forget me . . . why should sorrow . . . brightly smile . . . go forget me . . . never hear me . . . sweetly smile . . . brightly sing . . . (*Pause. With a sigh*) One loses one's classics. (*Pause.*) Oh not all. (*Pause.*) A part. (*Pause.*) A part remains. (*Pause.*) That is what I find so wonderful, a part remains, of one's classics, to help one through the day. (*Pause.*) Oh yes, many mercies, many mercies. (*Pause.*) And now? (*Pause.*) And now, Willie? (*Long pause.*) I call to the eye of the mind . . . Mr. Shower—or Cooker. (*She closes her eyes. Bell rings loudly. She opens her eyes. Pause.*) Hand in hand, in the other hands bags. (*Pause.*) Getting on . . . in life. (*Pause.*) No longer young, not yet old. (*Pause.*) Standing there gaping at me. (*Pause.*) Can't have been a bad bosom, he says, in its day. (*Pause.*) Seen worse shoulders, he says, in my time. (*Pause.*) Does she feel her legs? he says. (*Pause.*) Is there any life in her legs? he says. (*Pause.*) Has she anything on underneath? he says. (*Pause.*) Ask her, he says, I'm shy. (*Pause.*) Ask her what? she says. (*Pause.*) Is there any life in her legs. (*Pause.*) Has she anything on underneath. (*Pause.*) Ask her yourself, she says. (*Pause. With sudden violence*) Let go of me for Christ sake and drop! (*Pause. Do.*) Drop dead! (*Smile.*) But no. (*Smile broader.*) No no. (*Smile off.*) I watch them recede. (*Pause.*) Hand in hand—and the bags. (*Pause.*) Dim. (*Pause.*) Then gone. (*Pause.*) Last human kind—to stray this way. (*Pause.*) Up to

date. (*Pause.*) And now? (*Pause. Low*) Help. (*Pause. Do.*) Help, Willie. (*Pause. Do.*) No? (*Long pause. Narrative*) Suddenly a mouse . . . (*Pause.*) Suddenly a mouse ran up her little thigh and Mildred, dropping Dolly in her fright, began to scream—(WINNIE *gives a sudden piercing scream*)—and screamed and screamed—(WINNIE *screams twice*)—screamed and screamed and screamed and screamed till all came running, in their night attire, papa, mamma, Bibby and . . . old Annie, to see what was the matter . . . (*pause*) . . . what on earth could possibly be the matter. (*Pause.*) Too late. (*Pause.*) Too late. (*Long pause. Just audible*) Willie. (*Pause. Normal voice*) Ah well, not long now, Winnie, can't be long now, until the bell for sleep. (*Pause.*) Then you may close your eyes, then you *must* close your eyes— and keep them closed. (*Pause.*) Why say that again? (*Pause.*) I used to think . . . (*pause*) . . . I say I used to think there was no difference between one fraction of a second and the next. (*Pause.*) I used to say . . . (*pause*) . . . I say I used to say, Winnie, you are changeless, there is never any difference between one fraction of a second and the next. (*Pause.*) Why bring that up again? (*Pause.*) There is so little one can bring up, one brings up all. (*Pause.*) All one can. (*Pause.*) My neck is hurting me. (*Pause. With sudden violence*) My neck is hurting me! (*Pause.*) Ah that's better. (*With mild irritation*) Everything within reason. (*Long pause.*) I can do no more. (*Pause.*) Say no more. (*Pause.*) But I must say more. (*Pause.*) Problem here. (*Pause.*) No, something must move, in the world, I can't any more. (*Pause.*) A zephyr. (*Pause.*) A breath. (*Pause.*) What are those immortal lines? (*Pause.*) It might be the eternal dark. (*Pause.*) Black night without end. (*Pause.*) Just chance, I take it, happy chance. (*Pause.*) Oh yes, abounding mercies. (*Long pause.*) And now? (*Pause.*) And now, Willie? (*Long pause.*) That day. (*Pause.*) The pink fizz. (*Pause.*) The flute glasses. (*Pause.*) The last guest gone. (*Pause.*) The last bumper with the bodies nearly touching. (*Pause.*) The look. (*Long pause.*) What day? (*Long pause.*) What look? (*Long pause.*) I hear cries. (*Pause.*) Sing. (*Pause.*) Sing your old song, Winnie.

(*Long pause. Suddenly alert expression. Eyes switch right.* WILLIE's *head appears to her right round corner of mound. He is on all fours, dressed to kill—top hat, morning coat, striped trousers, etc., white gloves in hand. Very long bushy white Battle of Britain moustache. He halts, gazes front, smoothes moustache. He emerges completely from behind mound, turns to his left, halts, looks up at* WINNIE. *He advances on all fours towards centre, halts, turns head front, gazes front, strokes moustache, straightens tie, adjusts hat, advances a little further, halts, takes off hat and looks up at* WINNIE. *He is now not far from centre and within her field of vision. Unable to sustain effort of looking up he sinks head to ground.*)

WINNIE (*mondaine*): Well this is an unexpected pleasure! (*Pause.*) Reminds me of the day you came whining for my hand. (*Pause.*) I worship you, Winnie, be mine. (*He looks up.*) Life a mockery without Win. (*She goes off into a giggle.*) What a get up, you do look a sight! (*Giggles.*) Where are the flowers? (*Pause.*) That smile today. (WILLIE *sinks head.*) What's that on your neck, an anthrax? (*Pause.*) Want to watch that, Willie, before it gets a hold on you. (*Pause.*) Where were you all this time? (*Pause.*) What were you doing all this time? (*Pause.*) Changing? (*Pause.*) Did you not hear me screaming for you? (*Pause.*) Did you get stuck in your hole? (*Pause. He looks up.*) That's right, Willie, look at me. (*Pause.*) Feast your old eyes, Willie. (*Pause.*) Does anything remain? (*Pause.*) Any remains? (*Pause.*) No? (*Pause.*) I haven't been able to look after it, you know. (*He sinks his head.*) You are still recognizable, in a way. (*Pause.*) Are you thinking of coming to live this side now . . . for a bit maybe? (*Pause.*) No? (*Pause.*) Just a brief call? (*Pause.*) Have you gone deaf, Willie? (*Pause.*) Dumb? (*Pause.*) Oh I know you were never one to talk, I worship you Winnie be mine and then nothing from that day forth only tidbits from Reynolds' News. (*Eyes front. Pause.*) Ah well, what matter, that's what I always say, it will have been a happy day, after all, another happy day. (*Pause.*) Not long now, Winnie. (*Pause.*) I hear cries. (*Pause.*) Do you ever hear cries, Willie? (*Pause.*) No? (*Eyes back on* WILLIE.) Willie. (*Pause.*) Look at me again, Willie. (*Pause.*) Once more, Willie. (*He looks up. Happily*) Ah! (*Pause. Shocked*) What ails you, Willie, I never saw such an expression! (*Pause.*) Put on your hat, dear, it's the sun, don't stand on ceremony, I won't mind. (*He drops hat and gloves and starts to crawl up mound towards her. Gleeful*) Oh I say, this is terrific! (*He halts, clinging to mound with one*

hand, reaching up with the other.) Come on, dear, put a bit of jizz into it, I'll cheer you on. (*Pause.*) Is it me you're after, Willie . . . or is it something else? (*Pause.*) Do you want to touch my face . . . again? (*Pause.*) Is it a kiss you're after, Willie . . . or is it something else? (*Pause.*) There was a time when I could have given you a hand. (*Pause.*) And then a time before that again when I did give you a hand. (*Pause.*) You were always in dire need of a hand, Willie. (*He slithers back to foot of mound and lies with face to ground.*) Brrum! (*Pause. He rises to hands and knees, raises his face towards her.*) Have another go, Willie, I'll cheer you on. (*Pause.*) Don't look at me like that! (*Pause. Vehement*) Don't look at me like that! (*Pause. Low*) Have you gone off your head, Willie? (*Pause. Do.*) Out of your poor old wits, Willie?

(*Pause.*)

WILLIE (*just audible*): Win.

(*Pause.* WINNIE's *eyes front. Happy expression appears, grows.*)

WINNIE: Win! (*Pause.*) Oh this *is* a happy day, this will have been another happy day! (*Pause.*) After all. (*Pause.*) So far.

(*Pause. She hums tentatively beginning of song, then sings softly, musical-box tune.*)

> Though I say not
> What I may not
> Let you hear,
> Yet the swaying
> Dance is saying,
> Love me dear!
> Every touch of fingers
> Tells me what I know,
> Says for you,
> It's true, it's true,
> You love me so!

(*Pause. Happy expression off. She closes her eyes. Bell rings loudly. She opens her eyes. She smiles, gazing front. She turns her eyes, smiling, to* WILLIE, *still on his hands and knees looking up at her. Smile off. They look at each other. Long pause.*)

CURTAIN

COMMENTARY

Aside from the background information on the development of modern tragicomedy given in "The Nature of Drama" at the beginning of this book, especially on pages 75–79, we need perhaps only mention that Beckett wrote *Happy Days* in English, in 1960–61. (He sometimes writes his plays and novels in French, but in *Happy Days*, beyond describing the backdrop as *pompier trompe-l'oeil* ("ordinary illusionistic"), French is implied only in Winnie's uncertainty whether hair is "them" or "it," for in French "hair" is plural, *les cheveux*.)

TOPICS FOR DISCUSSION

SETTING AND PROPERTIES

1. In another of Beckett's plays, *Endgame*, two characters are in garbage cans. What do you think would be gained or lost if Winnie were in a garbage can instead of in a mound?
2. Is there some dramatic significance or advantage to burying Winnie in a mound, rather than at ground level?
3. Why is Winnie's bag black, rather than, say, brightly colored or patterned?
4. What do you imagine is the audience's reaction when the parasol goes on fire? How does this reaction compare to Winnie's and Willie's reaction?

GESTURES AND MOVEMENTS

1. In the second act, when Winnie is buried up to the chin, gestures of course are fewer than in the first act. But what gestures or movements are there in Act II?
2. When at the end Willie crawls up the mound and Winnie exclaims, "Don't look at me like that! Have you gone out of your head, Willie?" do you think Willie is expressing renewed love, or is he thinking of shooting her with the revolver? Is it relevant that Willie is said to be "dressed to kill"?

SOUND EFFECTS

1. The bell that wakes Winnie rings "piercingly." Why not, instead, a cheery cuckoo clock, or a musical sound? Winnie several times mentions "the bell for sleep," but we never hear it, even though it might easily have sounded at the end of Act I. *Should* we have heard it?
2. In the first act the bell rings twice, at the beginning. In the second act it rings several times, interrupting Winnie's monologues. Is there any meaning to this? Does it perhaps mean that time is moving faster—and what does *that* mean?
3. Why the waltz duet, "I Love You So" from *The Merry Widow*, rather than some other song?

DIALOGUE

1. How does Beckett keep Winnie's talk from being dull jabbering? By what means does the dialogue hold our attention?

2. Take the first few lines, and imagine how each is spoken:

> "Another heavenly day."
> "Fer Jesus Christ sake Amen. . . . World without end Amen."
> "Begin, Winnie. . . . Begin your day, Winnie."

CHARACTER

1. The first director of *Happy Days*, Alan Schneider, said that Beckett originally conceived of Winnie's part as a male part but changed his mind because pockets wouldn't work as well as a handbag. Does the meaning of the present play depend to any degree on the fact that one character is male, the other female?
2. One critic (A. Alvarez, in *Samuel Beckett*) says the play offers "a sour view of a cozy marriage. . . . [Beckett] finds [Winnie] and her manic defenses ludicrous at best." How profitable do you find this line of thinking?

STRUCTURE

1. It has been said of Beckett's most widely known play, *Waiting for Godot*, that in it nothing happens, twice. How appropriate is this as a summary of *Happy Days*?

MEANING

1. On page 545 Winnie tells how a man and a woman came by, and she reproduces their conversation:

> What's she doing? he says—What's the idea? he says—stuck up to her diddies in the bleeding ground—coarse fellow—What does it mean? he says— What's it meant to mean?—and so on—lot more stuff like that—usual drivel—Do you hear me? he says—I do, she says, God help me—What do you mean, he says, God help you? . . . And you, she says, what's the idea of you, she says, what are you meant to mean?

Do you think Beckett here is telling us that the play has no meaning?

2. The director Peter Brook has said of *Happy Days*, "The optimism of the lady buried in the ground is not a virtue, it is the element that blinds her to the truth of her situation." Evaluate.

EQUUS

Peter Shaffer

Peter Shaffer (b. 1926) is an Englishman who, after studying at Cambridge University, worked for three years in the United States. He returned to England, where he wrote his first play, *Five Finger Exercise* (produced in New York in 1959). Among his other plays are *The Royal Hunt of the Sun* (1964), *Black Comedy* (1965), and of course *Equus*, (1973), which when produced in New York won the Tony Award for the best play of the year.

CHARACTERS

MARTIN DYSART, *a psychiatrist* DORA STRANG, *his mother*   HARRY DALTON, *a stable owner*
ALAN STRANG   HESTHER SALOMON, *a magistrate* A YOUNG HORSEMAN
FRANK STRANG, *his father*   JILL MASON   A NURSE

SIX ACTORS—*including the* YOUNG HORSEMAN, *who also plays* NUGGET—*appear as* HORSES.

THE HORSES: The actors wear track-suits of chestnut velvet. On their feet are light strutted hooves, about four inches high, set on metal horse-shoes. On their hands are gloves of the same colour. On their heads are tough masks made of alternating bands of silver wire and leather: their eyes are outlined by leather blinkers. The actors' own heads are seen beneath them: no attempt should be made to conceal them.

Any literalism which could suggest the cosy familiarity of a domestic animal—or worse, a pantomime horse— should be avoided. The actors should never crouch on all fours, or even bend forward. They must always—except on the one occasion where NUGGET is ridden—stand upright, as if the body of the horse extended invisibly behind them. Animal effect must be created entirely mimetically, through the use of legs, knees, neck, face, and the turn of the head which can move the mask above it through all the gestures of equine wariness and pride. Great care must also be taken that the masks are put on before the audience with very precise timing—the actors watching each other, so that the masking has an exact and ceremonial effect.

Peter Firth as Alan in the New York production of *Equus*, directed by John Dexter, 1974. (Photograph: Van Williams.)

THE CHORUS: References are made in the text to the Equus Noise. I have in mind a choric effect, made by all the actors sitting round upstage, and composed of humming, thumping, and stamping—though never of neighing or whinnying. This Noise heralds or illustrates the presence of Equus the God.

A *Note on the Play*—One weekend over two years ago, I was driving with a friend through bleak countryside. We passed a stable. Suddenly he was reminded by it of an alarming crime which he had heard about recently at a dinner party in London. He knew only one horrible detail, and his complete mention of it could barely have lasted a minute—but it was enough to arouse in me an intense fascination.

The act had been committed several years before by a highly disturbed young man. It had deeply shocked a local bench of magistrates. It lacked, finally, any coherent explanation.

A few months later my friend died. I could not verify what he had said, or ask him to expand it. He had given me no name, no place, and no time. I don't think he knew them. All I possessed was his report of a dreadful event, and the feeling it engendered in me. I knew very strongly that I wanted to interpret it in some entirely personal way. I had to create a mental world in which the deed could be made comprehensible.

Every person and incident in *Equus* is of my own invention, save the crime itself: and even that I modified to accord with what I feel to be acceptable theatrical proportion. I am grateful now that I have never received confirmed details of the real story, since my concern has been more and more with a different kind of exploration.

I have been lucky, in doing final work on the play, to have enjoyed the advice and expert comment of a distinguished child psychiatrist. Through him I have tried to keep things real in a more naturalistic sense. I have also come to perceive that psychiatrists are an immensely varied breed professing immensely varied methods and techniques. MARTIN DYSART is simply one doctor in one hospital. I must take responsibility for him, as I do for his patient.

The Set—A square of wood set on a circle of wood.

The square resembles a railed boxing ring. The rail, also of wood, encloses three sides. It is perforated on each side by an opening. Under the rail are a few vertical slats, as if in a fence. On the downstage side there is no rail. The whole square is set on ball bearings, so that by slight pressure from actors standing round it on the circle, it can be made to turn round smoothly by hand.

On the square are set three little plain benches, also of wood. They are placed parallel with the rail, against the slats, but can be moved out by the actors to stand at right angles to them.

Set into the floor of the square, and flush with it, is a thin metal pole, about a yard high. This can be raised out of the floor, to stand upright. It acts as a support for the actor playing NUGGET, when he is ridden.

In the area outside the circle stand benches. Two downstage left and right, are curved to accord with the circle. The left one is used by DYSART as a listening and observing post when he is out of the square, and also by ALAN as his hospital bed. The right one is used by ALAN's parents, who sit side by side on it. (Viewpoint is from the main body of the audience.)

Further benches stand upstage and accommodate the other actors. All the cast of *Equus* sits on stage the entire evening. They get up to perform their scenes, and return when they are done to their places around the set. They are witnesses, assistants—and especially a CHORUS.

Upstage, forming a backdrop to the whole, are tiers of seats in the fashion of a dissecting theatre, formed into two railed-off blocks, pierced by a central tunnel. In these blocks sit members of the audience. During the play, DYSART addresses them directly from time to time, as he addresses the main body of the theatre. No other actor ever refers to them.

To left and right, downstage, stand two ladders on which are suspended horse masks.

The colour of all benches is olive green.

Above the stage hangs a battery of lights, set in a huge metal ring. Light cues, in this version, will be only of the most general description.

The main action of the play takes place in Rokeby Psychiatric Hospital in Southern England.

The time is the present.

The play is divided into numbered scenes, indicating a change of time or locale or mood. The action, however, is continuous.

ACT I

SCENE 1

Darkness.

Silence.

Dim light up on the square. In a spotlight stands ALAN STRANG, *a lean boy of seventeen, in sweater and jeans. In front of him, the horse* NUGGET. ALAN's *pose represents a contour of great tenderness: his head is pressed against the shoulder of the horse, his hands stretching up to fondle its head. The horse in turn nuzzles his neck.*

The flame of a cigarette lighter jumps in the dark. Lights come up slowly on the circle. On the left bench, downstage, MARTIN DYSART, *smoking. A man in his mid-forties.*

DYSART: With one particular horse, called Nugget, he embraces. The animal digs its sweaty brow into his cheek, and they stand in the dark for an hour—like a necking couple. And of all nonsensical things—I keep thinking about the *horse*! Not the boy: the horse, and what it may be trying to do. I keep seeing that huge head kissing him with its chained mouth. Nudging through the metal some desire absolutely irrelevant to filling its belly or propagating its own kind. What desire could that be? Not to stay a horse any longer? Not to remain reined up for ever in those particular genetic strings? Is it possible, at certain moments we cannot imagine, a horse can add its sufferings together—the non-stop jerks and jabs that are its daily life—and turn them into grief? What use is grief to a horse?

(ALAN *leads* NUGGET *out of the square and they disappear together up the tunnel, the horse's hooves scraping delicately on the wood.*

DYSART *rises, and addresses both the large audience in the theatre and the smaller one on stage.*)

You see, I'm lost. What use, I should be asking, are questions like these to an overworked psychiatrist in a provincial hospital? They're worse than useless: they are, in fact, subversive.

(*He enters the square. The light grows brighter.*)

The thing is, I'm desperate. You see, I'm wearing that horse's head myself. That's the feeling. All reined up in old language and old assumptions, straining to jump clean-hoofed on to a whole new track of being I only suspect is there. I can't see it, because my educated, average head is being held at the wrong angle. I can't jump because the bit forbids it, and my own basic force—my horse-power, if you like—is too little. The only thing I know for sure is this: a horse's head is finally unknowable to me. Yet I handle children's heads—which I must presume to be more complicated, at least in the area of my chief concern. . . . In a way, it has nothing to do with this boy. The doubts have been there for years, piling up steadily in this dreary place. It's only the extremity of this case that's made them active. I know that. The *extremity* is the point! All the same, whatever the reason, they are now, these doubts, not just vaguely worrying—but intolerable . . . I'm sorry. I'm not making much sense. Let me start properly: in order. It began one Monday last month, with Hesther's visit.

SCENE 2

The light gets warmer.
He sits. NURSE *enters the square.*

NURSE: Mrs. Salomon to see you, Doctor.
DYSART: Show her in, please.

(NURSE *leaves and crosses to where* HESTHER *sits.*)

Some days I blame Hesther. She brought him to see me. But of course that's nonsense. What is he but a last straw? a last symbol? If it hadn't been him, it would have been the next patient, or the next. At least, I suppose so.

(HESTHER *enters the square: a woman in her mid-forties.*)

HESTHER: Hallo, Martin.

(DYSART *rises and kisses her on the cheek.*)

DYSART: Madam Chairman! Welcome to the torture chamber!
HESTHER: It's good of you to see me right away.
DYSART: You're a welcome relief. Take a couch.
HESTHER: It's been a day?
DYSART: No—just a fifteen-year-old schizophrenic, and a girl of eight thrashed into catatonia by her father. Normal, really . . . You're in a state.
HESTHER: Martin, this is the most shocking case I ever tried.
DYSART: So you said on the phone.

HESTHER: I mean it. My bench wanted to send the boy to prison. For life, if they could manage it. It took me two hours solid arguing to get him sent to you instead.
DYSART: Me?
HESTHER: I mean, to hospital.
DYSART: Now look, Hesther. Before you say anything else, I can take no more patients at the moment. I can't even cope with the ones I have.
HESTHER: You must.
DYSART: Why?
HESTHER: Because most people are going to be disgusted by the whole thing. Including doctors.
DYSART: May I remind you I share this room with two highly competent psychiatrists?
HESTHER: Bennett and Thoroughgood. They'll be as shocked as the public.
DYSART: That's an absolutely unwarrantable statement.
HESTHER: Oh, they'll be cool and exact. And underneath they'll be revolted, and immovably English. Just like my bench.
DYSART: Well, what am I? Polynesian?
HESTHER: You know exactly what I mean! . . . (*Pause.*) Please, Martin. It's vital. You're this boy's only chance.
DYSART: Why? What's he done? Dosed some little girl's Pepsi with Spanish Fly? What could possibly throw your bench into two-hour convulsions?
HESTHER: He blinded six horses with a metal spike.

(A *long pause.*)

DYSART: Blinded?
HESTHER: Yes.
DYSART: All at once, or over a period?
HESTHER: All on the same night.
DYSART: Where?
HESTHER: In a riding stable near Winchester. He worked there at weekends.
DYSART: How old?
HESTHER: Seventeen.
DYSART: What did he say in Court?
HESTHER: Nothing. He just sang.
DYSART: Sang?
HESTHER: Any time anyone asked him anything.

(*Pause.*)

Please take him, Martin. It's the last favour I'll ever ask you.
DYSART: No, it's not.
HESTHER: No, it's not—and he's probably abominable. All I know is, he needs you badly. Because there really is nobody within a hundred

miles of your desk who can handle him. And
perhaps understand what this is about. Also . . .

DYSART: What?

HESTHER: There's something very special about
him.

DYSART: In what way?

HESTHER: Vibrations.

DYSART: You and your vibrations.

HESTHER: They're quite startling. You'll see.

DYSART: When does he get here?

HESTHER: Tomorrow morning. Luckily there
was a bed in Neville Ward. I know this is an awful
imposition, Martin. Frankly I didn't know what
else to do.

(*Pause.*)

DYSART: Can you come in and see me on
Friday?

HESTHER: Bless you!

DYSART: If you come after work I can give you a
drink. Will 6:30 be all right?

HESTHER: You're a dear. You really are.

DYSART: Famous for it.

HESTHER: Good-bye.

DYSART: By the way, what's his name?

HESTHER: Alan Strang.

(*She leaves and returns to her seat.*)

DYSART (*to audience*): What did I expect of him?
Very little, I promise you. One more dented little
face. One more adolescent freak. The usual unusual. One great thing about being in the adjustment business: you're never short of customers.

(NURSE *comes down the tunnel, followed by*
ALAN. *She enters the square.*)

NURSE: Alan Strang, Doctor.

(*The boy comes in.*)

DYSART: Hallo. My name's Martin Dysart. I'm
pleased to meet you.

(*He puts out his hand.* ALAN *does not respond in
any way.*)

That'll be all, Nurse, thank you.

SCENE 3

NURSE *goes out and back to her place.*
DYSART *sits, opening a file.*

So: did you have a good journey? I hope they gave
you lunch at least. Not that there's much to choose
between a British Rail meal and one here.

(ALAN *stands staring at him.*)

DYSART: Won't you sit down?

(*Pause. He does not.* DYSART *consults his file.*)

Is this your full name? Alan Strang?

(*Silence.*)

And you're seventeen. Is that right? Seventeen? . . .
Well?

ALAN (*singing low*):
    Double your pleasure,
    Double your fun
    With Doublemint, Doublemint
    Doublemint gum.

DYSART (*unperturbed*): Now, let's see. You work
in an electrical shop during the week. You live
with your parents, and your father's a printer.
What sort of things does he print?

ALAN (*singing louder*):
    Double your pleasure
    Double your fun
    With Doublemint, Doublemint
    Doublemint gum.

DYSART: I mean does he do leaflets and calen-
dars? Things like that?

(*The boy approaches him, hostile.*)

ALAN (*singing*):
    Try the taste of Martini
    The most beautiful drink in the world.
    It's the right one—
    The bright one—
    That's Martini!

DYSART: I wish you'd sit down, if you're going to
sing. Don't you think you'd be more comfortable?

(*Pause.*)

ALAN (*singing*):
    There's only one T in Typhoo!
    In packets and in teabags too.
    Any way you make it, you'll find it's true:
    There's only one T in Typhoo!

DYSART (*appreciatively*): Now that's a good
song. I like it better than the other two. Can I hear
that one again?

(ALAN *starts away from him, and sits on the
upstage bench.*)

ALAN (*singing*):
    Double your pleasure
    Double your fun
    With Doublemint, Doublemint
    Doublemint gum.

DYSART (*smiling*): You know I was wrong. I

really do think that one's better. It's got such a catchy tune. Please do that one again.

(*Silence. The boy glares at him.*)

I'm going to put you in a private bedroom for a little while. There are one or two available, and they're rather more pleasant than being in a ward. Will you please come and see me tomorrow? . . . (*He rises.*) By the way, which parent is it who won't allow you to watch television? Mother or father? Or is it both? (*Calling out of the door*) Nurse!

(ALAN *stares at him.* NURSE *comes in.*)

NURSE: Yes, Doctor?
DYSART: Take Strang here to Number Three, will you? He's moving in there for a while.
NURSE: Very good, Doctor.
DYSART (*to* ALAN): You'll like that room. It's nice.

(*The boy sits staring at* DYSART. DYSART *returns the stare.*)

NURSE: Come along, young man. This way. . . . I said this way, please.

(*Reluctantly* ALAN *rises and goes to* NURSE, *passing dangerously close to* DYSART, *and out through the left door.* DYSART *looks after him, fascinated.*)

Scene 4

NURSE *and patient move on to the circle, and walk downstage to the bench where the doctor first sat, which is to serve also as* ALAN's *bed.*

NURSE: Well now: isn't this nice? You're lucky to be in here, you know, rather than the ward. That ward's a noisy old place.
ALAN (*singing*):
    Let's go where you wanna go—Texaco!
NURSE (*contemplating him*): I hope you're not going to make a nuisance of yourself. You'll have a much better time of it here, you know, if you behave yourself.
ALAN: Fuck off.
NURSE (*tight*): That's the bell there. The lav's down the corridor.

(*She leaves him, and goes back to her place.* ALAN *lies down.*)

Scene 5

DYSART *stands in the middle of the square and addresses the audience. He is agitated.*

DYSART: That night, I had this very explicit dream. In it I'm a chief priest in Homeric Greece. I'm wearing a wide gold mask, all noble and bearded, like the so-called Mask of Agamemnon found at Mycenae. I'm standing by a thick round stone and holding a sharp knife. In fact, I'm officiating at some immensely important ritual sacrifice, on which depends the fate of the crops or of a military expedition. The sacrifice is a herd of children: about five hundred boys and girls. I can see them stretching away in a long queue, right across the plain of Argos. I know it's Argos because of the red soil. On either side of me stand two assistant priests, wearing masks as well: lumpy, pop-eyed masks, such as also were found at Mycenae. They are enormously strong, these other priests, and absolutely tireless. As each child steps forward, they grab it from behind and throw it over the stone. Then with a surgical skill which amazes even me, I fit in the knife and slice elegantly down to the navel, just like a seamstress following a pattern. I part the flaps, sever the inner tubes, yank them out and throw them hot and steaming on to the floor. The other two then study the pattern they make, as if they were reading hieroglyphics. It's obvious to me that I'm tops as chief priest. It's this unique talent for carving that has got me where I am. The only thing is, unknown to them, I've started to feel distinctly nauseous. And with each victim, it's getting worse. My face is going green behind the mask. Of course, I redouble my efforts to look professional—cutting and snipping for all I'm worth: mainly because I know that if ever those two assistants so much as glimpse my distress—and the implied doubt that this repetitive and smelly work is doing any social good at all—I will be the next across the stone. And then, of course—the damn mask begins to slip. The priests both turn and look at it—it slips some more—they see the green sweat running down my face—their gold pop-eyes suddenly fill up with blood—they tear the knife out of my hand . . . and I wake up.

Scene 6

HESTHER *enters the square. Light grows warmer.*

HESTHER: That's the most indulgent thing I ever heard.
DYSART: You think?
HESTHER: Please don't be ridiculous. You've done the most superb work with children. You must know that.
DYSART: Yes, but do the children?
HESTHER: Really!

DYSART: I'm sorry.

HESTHER: So you should be.

DYSART: I don't know why you listen. It's just professional menopause. Everyone gets it sooner or later. Except you.

HESTHER: Oh, of course. I feel totally fit to be a magistrate all the time.

DYSART: No, you don't—but then that's you feeling unworthy to fill a job. I feel the job is unworthy to fill me.

HESTHER: Do you seriously?

DYSART: More and more. I'd like to spend the next ten years wandering very slowly around the *real* Greece. . . . Anyway, all the dream nonsense is your fault.

HESTHER: Mine?

DYSART: It's that lad of yours who started it off. Do you know it's his face I saw on every victim across the stone?

HESTHER: Strang?

DYSART: He has the strangest stare I ever met.

HESTHER: Yes.

DYSART: It's exactly like being accused. Violently accused. But what of? . . . Treating him is going to be unsettling. Especially in my present state. His singing was direct enough. His speech is more so.

HESTHER (*surprised*): He's talking to you, then?

DYSART: Oh yes. It took him two more days of commercials, and then he snapped. Just like that—I suspect it has something to do with his nightmares.

(NURSE *walks briskly round the circle, a blanket over her arm, a clipboard of notes in her hand.*)

HESTHER: He has nightmares?

DYSART: Bad ones.

NURSE: We had to give him a sedative or two, Doctor. Last night it was exactly the same.

DYSART (*to* NURSE): What does he do? Call out?

NURSE (*to* DESK): A lot of screaming, Doctor.

DYSART (*to* NURSE): Screaming?

URSE: One word in particular.

DYSART (*to* NURSE): You mean a special word?

NURSE: Over and over again. (*Consulting clipboard*) It sounds like "Ek."

HESTHER: Ek?

NURSE: Yes, Doctor. Ek. . . . "Ek!" he goes. "Ek!"

HESTHER: How weird.

NURSE: When I woke him up he clung to me like he was going to break my arm.

(*She stops at* ALAN's *bed. He is sitting up. She*

puts the blanket over him, and returns to her place.)

DYSART: And then he burst in—just like that—without knocking or anything. Fortunately, I didn't have a patient with me.

ALAN (*jumping up*): Dad!

HESTHER: What?

DYSART: The answer to a question I'd asked him two days before. Spat out with the same anger as he sang the commercials.

HESTHER: Dad what?

ALAN: Who hates telly.

(*He lies downstage on the circle, as if watching television.*)

HESTHER: You mean his dad forbids him to watch?

DYSART: Yes.

ALAN: It's a dangerous drug.

HESTHER: Oh, really!

(FRANK *stands up and enters the scene downstage. A man in his fifties.*)

FRANK (*to* ALAN): It may not look like that, but that's what it is. Absolutely fatal mentally, if you receive my meaning.

(DORA *follows him on. She is also middle-aged.*)

DORA: That's a little extreme, dear, isn't it?

FRANK: You sit in front of that thing long enough, you'll become stupid for life—like most of the population. (*To* ALAN) The thing is, it's a *swiz*. It seems to be offering you something, but actually it's taking something away. Your intelligence and your concentration, every minute you watch it. That's a true swiz, do you see?

(*Seated on the floor,* ALAN *shrugs.*)

I don't want to sound like a spoilsport, old chum—but there really is no substitute for reading. What's the matter: don't you like it?

ALAN: It's all right.

FRANK: I know you think it's none of my beeswax, but it really is you know . . . Actually, it's a disgrace when you come to think of it. You the son of a printer, and never opening a book! If all the world was like you, I'd be out of a job, if you receive my meaning!

DORA: All the same, times change, Frank.

FRANK (*reasonably*): They change if you let them change, Dora. Please return that set in the morning.

ALAN (*crying out*): No!

DORA: Frank! No!

FRANK: I'm sorry, Dora, but I'm not having that thing in the house a moment longer. I told you I didn't want it to begin with.

DORA: But, dear, everyone watches television these days!

FRANK: Yes, and what do they watch? Mindless violence! Mindless jokes! Every five minutes some laughing idiot selling you something you don't want, just to bolster up the economic system. (*To* ALAN) I'm sorry, old chum.

(*He leaves the scene and sits again in his place.*)

HESTHER: He's a Communist, then?

DYSART: Old-type Socialist, I'd say. Relentlessly self-improving.

HESTHER: They're *both* older than you'd expect.

DYSART: So I gather.

DORA (*looking after* FRANK): Really, dear, you are very extreme!

(*She leaves the scene, too, and again sits beside her husband.*)

HESTHER: She's an ex-school teacher, isn't she?

DYSART: Yes. The boy's proud of that. We got on to it this afternoon.

ALAN (*belligerently, standing up*): She knows more than you.

(HESTHER *crosses and sits by* DYSART. *During the following, the boy walks round the circle, speaking to* DYSART *but not looking at him.* DYSART *replies in the same manner.*)

DYSART (*to* ALAN): Does she?

ALAN: I bet I do too. I bet I know more history than you.

DYSART (*to* ALAN): Well, I bet you don't.

ALAN: All right: who was the Hammer of the Scots?

DYSART (*to* ALAN): I don't know: who?

ALAN: King Edward the First. Who never smiled again?

DYSART (*to* ALAN): I don't know: who?

ALAN: You don't know anything, do you? It was Henry the First. I know all the Kings.

DYSART (*to* ALAN): And who's your favourite?

ALAN: John.

DYSART (*to* ALAN): Why?

ALAN: Because he put out the eyes of that smarty little—

(*Pause.*)

(*Sensing he has said something wrong*) Well, he didn't really. He was prevented, because the gaoler was merciful!

HESTHER: Oh dear.

ALAN: *He was prevented!*

DYSART: Something odder was to follow.

ALAN: Who said "Religion is the opium of the people"?

HESTHER: Good Lord!

(ALAN *giggles.*)

DYSART: The odd thing was, he said it with a sort of guilty snigger. The sentence is obviously associated with some kind of tension.

HESTHER: What did you say?

DYSART: I gave him the right answer. (*To* ALAN) Karl Marx.

ALAN: No.

DYSART (*to* ALAN): Then who?

ALAN: Mind your own beeswax.

DYSART: It's probably his dad. He may say it to provoke his wife.

HESTHER: And you mean she's religious?

DYSART: She could be. I tried to discover—none too successfully.

ALAN: Mind your own beeswax!

(ALAN *goes back to bed and lies down in the dark.*)

DYSART: However, I shall find out on Sunday.

HESTHER: What do you mean?

DYSART (*getting up*): I want to have a look at his home, so I invited myself over.

HESTHER: Did you?

DYSART: If there's any tension over religion, it should be evident on a Sabbath evening! I'll let you know.

(*He kisses her cheek and they part, both leaving the square.* HESTHER *sits in her place again;* DYSART *walks round the circle, and greets* DORA *who stands waiting for him downstage.*)

SCENE 7

DYSART (*shaking hands*): Mrs. Strang.

DORA: Mr. Strang's still at the Press, I'm afraid. He should be home in a minute.

DYSART: He works Sundays as well?

DORA: Oh, yes, He doesn't set much store by Sundays.

DYSART: Perhaps you and I could have a little talk before he comes in.

DORA: Certainly. Won't you come into the living room?

(*She leads the way into the square. She is very nervous.*)

Please. . . .

(She motions him to sit, then holds her hands tightly together.)

DYSART: Mrs. Strang, have you any idea how this thing could have occurred?

DORA: I can't imagine, Doctor. It's all so unbelievable! . . . Alan's always been such a gentle boy. He loves animals! Especially horses.

DYSART: Especially?

DORA: Yes. He even has a photograph of one up in his bedroom. A beautiful white one, looking over a gate. His father gave it to him a few years ago, off a claendar he'd printed—and he's never taken it down . . . And when he was seven or eight, I used to have to read him the same book over and over, all *about* a horse.

DYSART: Really?

DORA: Yes: it was called Prince, and no one could ride him.

(ALAN calls from his bed, not looking at his mother.)

ALAN *(excited, younger voice)*: Why not? . . . Why not? . . . Say it! In his voice!

DORA: He loved the idea of animals talking.

DYSART: Did he?

ALAN: *Say it! Say it! . . . Use his voice!*

DORA *("proud" voice)*: "Because I am faithful!"

(ALAN giggles.)

"My name is Prince, and I'm a Prince among horses! Only my young Master can ride me! Anyone else—I'll *throw off!*"

(ALAN giggles louder.)

And then I remember I used to tell him a funny thing about falling off horses. Did you know that when Christian cavalry first appeared in the New World, the pagans thought horse and rider was one person?

DYSART: Really?

ALAN *(sitting up, amazed)*: One person?

DORA: Actually they thought it must be a god.

ALAN: A *god!*

DORA: It was only when one rider fell off, they realized the truth.

DYSART: That's fascinating. I never heard that before. . . . Can you remember anything else like that you may have told him about horses?

DORA: Well, not really. They're in the Bible, of course. "He saith among the trumpets, Ha, ha."

DYSART: Ha, ha?

DORA: The Book of Job. Such a noble passage.

You know—*(Quoting)* "Hast thou given the horse strength?"

ALAN *(responding)*: "Hast thou clothed his neck with thunder?"

DORA *(to ALAN)*: "The glory of his nostrils is terrible!"

ALAN: "He swallows the ground with fierceness and rage!"

DORA: "He saith among the trumpets—"

ALAN *(trumpeting)*: "Ha! Ha!"

DORA *(to DYSART)*: Isn't that splendid?

DYSART: It certainly is.

ALAN *(trumpeting)*: Ha! Ha!

DORA: And then, of course, we saw an awful lot of Westerns on the television. He couldn't have enough of those.

DYSART: But surely you don't have a set, do you? I understand Mr. Strang doesn't approve.

DORA *(conspiratorially)*: He doesn't . . . I used to let him slip off in the afternoons to a friend next door.

DYSART *(smiling)*: You mean without his father's knowledge?

DORA: What the eye does not see, the heart does not grieve over, does it? Anyway, Westerns are harmless enough, surely?

(FRANK stands up and enters the square. ALAN lies back under the blanket.)

(To FRANK) Oh, hallo dear. This is Dr. Dysart.

FRANK *(shaking hands)*: How d'you do?

DYSART: How d'you do?

DORA: I was just telling the Doctor, Alan's always adored horses.

FRANK *(tight)*: We assumed he did.

DORA: You know he did, dear. Look how he liked that photograph you gave him.

FRANK *(startled)*: What about it?

DORA: Nothing dear. Just that he pestered you to have it as soon as he saw it. Do you remember? *(To DYSART)* We've always been a horsey family. At least my side of it has. My grandfather used to ride every morning on the downs behind Brighton, all dressed up in bowler hat and jodhpurs! He used to look splendid. Indulging in equitation, he called it.

(FRANK moves away from them and sits wearily.)

ALAN *(trying the word)*: Equitation. . . .

DORA: I remember I told him how that came from *equus*, the Latin word for horse. Alan was fascinated by that word, I know. I suppose because he'd never come across one with two U's together before.

ALAN *(savouring it)*: Equus!

DORA: I always wanted the boy to ride himself. He'd have so enjoyed it.

DYSART: But surely he did?

DORA: No.

DYSART: Never?

DORA: He didn't care for it. He was most definite about not wanting to.

DYSART: But he must have had to at the stables? I mean, it would be part of the job.

DORA: You'd have thought so, but no. He absolutely wouldn't, would he, dear?

FRANK (*dryly*): It seems he was perfectly happy raking out manure.

DYSART: Did he ever give a reason for this?

DORA: No. I must say we both thought it most peculiar, but he wouldn't discuss it. I mean, you'd have thought he'd be longing to get out in the air after being cooped up all week in that dreadful shop. Electrical and kitchenware! Isn't *that* an environment for a sensitive boy, Doctor? . . .

FRANK: Dear, have you offered the doctor a cup of tea?

DORA: Oh dear, no, I haven't . . . And you must be dying for one.

DYSART: That would be nice.

DORA: Of course it would. . . . Excuse me . . .

(*She goes out—but lingers on the circle, eavesdropping near the right door.* ALAN *stretches out under his blanket and sleeps.* FRANK *gets up.*)

FRANK: My wife has romantic ideas, if you receive my meaning.

DYSART: About her family?

FRANK: She thinks she married beneath her. I daresay she did. I don't understand these things myself.

DYSART: Mr. Strang, I'm fascinated by the fact that Alan wouldn't ride.

FRANK: Yes, well that's him. He's always been a weird lad, I have to be honest. Can you imagine spending your weekends like that—just cleaning out stalls—with all the things that he could have been doing in the way of Further Education?

DYSART: Except he's hardly a scholar.

FRANK: How do we know? He's never really tried. His mother indulged him. She doesn't care if he can hardly write his own name, and she a school teacher that was. Just as long as he's happy, she says . . .

(DORA *wrings her hands in anguish.*
FRANK *sits again.*)

DYSART: Would you say she was closer to him than you are?

FRANK: They've always been thick as thieves. I can't say I entirely approve—especially when I hear her whispering that Bible to him hour after hour, up there in his room.

DYSART: Your wife is religious?

FRANK: Some might say excessively so. Mind you that's her business. But when it comes to dosing it down the boy's throat—well, frankly, he's my son as well as hers. She doesn't see that. Of course, that's the funny thing about religious people. They always think their susceptibilities are more important than nonreligious.

DYSART: And you're nonreligious, I take it?

FRANK: I'm an atheist, and I don't mind admitting it. If you want my opinion, it's the Bible that's responsible for all this.

DYSART: Why?

FRANK: Well, look at it yourself. A boy spends night after night having this stuff read into him: an innocent man tortured to death—thorns driven into his head—nails into his hands—a spear jammed through his ribs. It can mark anyone for life, that kind of thing. I'm not joking. The boy was absolutely fascinated by all that. He was always mooning over religious pictures. I mean real kinky ones, if you receive my meaning. I had to put a stop to it once or twice! . . . (*Pause.*) Bloody religion—it's our only real problem in this house, but it's insuperable: I don't mind admitting it.

(*Unable to stand any more,* DORA *comes in again.*)

DORA (*pleasantly*): You must excuse my husband, Doctor. This one subject is something of an obsession with him, isn't it, dear? You must admit.

FRANK: Call it what you like. All that stuff to me is just bad sex.

DORA: And what has that got to do with Alan?

FRANK: Everything! . . . (*Seriously.*) Everything, Dora!

DORA: I don't understand. What are you saying?

(*He turns away from her.*)

DYSART (*calmingly*): Mr. Strang, exactly how informed do you judge your son to *be* about sex?

FRANK (*tight*): I don't know.

DYSART: You didn't actually instruct him yourself?

FRANK: Not in so many words, no.

DYSART: Did *you*, Mrs. Strang?

DORA: Well, I spoke a little, yes. I had to. I've been a teacher, Doctor, and I know what happens if you don't. They find out through magazines and dirty books.

DYSART: What sort of thing did you tell him? I'm sorry if this is embarrassing.

DORA: I told him the biological facts. But I also told him what I believed. That sex is not *just* a biological matter, but spiritual as well. That if God willed, he would fall in love one day. That his task was to prepare himself for the most important happening of his life. And after that, if he was lucky, he might come to know a higher love still . . . I simply . . . don't understand. . . . *Alan!* . . .

(*She breaks down in sobs. Her husband gets up and goes to her.*)

FRANK (*embarrassed*): There now. There now, Dora. Come on!

DORA (*with sudden desperation*): All right— laugh! Laugh, as usual!

FRANK (*kindly*): No one's laughing, Dora.

(*She glares at him. He puts his arms round her shoulders.*)

No one's laughing, are they, Doctor?

(*Tenderly, he leads his wife out of the square, and they resume their places on the bench.*
Lights grow much dimmer.)

SCENE 8

A *strange noise begins.* ALAN *begins to murmur from his bed. He is having a bad nightmare, moving his hands and body as if frantically straining to tug something back.* DYSART *leaves the square as the boy's cries increase.*

ALAN: Ek! . . . Ek! . . . Ek! . . .

(*Cries of* Ek! *on tape fill the theatre, from all around.*
   DYSART *reaches the foot of* ALAN's *bed as the boy gives a terrible cry—*)

EK!

(—*and wakes up. The sounds snap off.* ALAN *and the* DOCTOR *stare at each other. Then abruptly* DYSART *leaves the area and re-enters the square.*)

SCENE 9

Lights grow brighter.
   DYSART *sits on his bench, left, and opens his file.* ALAN *gets out of bed, leaves his blanket, and comes in. He looks truculent.*

DYSART: Hallo. How are you this morning?

(ALAN *stares at him.*)

Come on: sit down.

(ALAN *crosses the stage and sits on the bench, opposite.*)

Sorry if I gave you a start last night. I was collecting some papers from my office, and I thought I'd look in on you. Do you dream often?

ALAN: Do *you?*

DYSART: It's my job to ask the questions. Yours to answer them.

ALAN: Says who?

DYSART: Says me. Do you dream often?

ALAN: Do you?

DYSART: Look—Alan.

ALAN: I'll answer if you answer. In turns.

(*Pause.*)

DYSART: Very well. Only we have to speak the truth.

ALAN (*mocking*): Very well.

DYSART: So. Do you dream often?

ALAN: Yes. Do you?

DYSART: Yes. Do you have a special dream?

ALAN: No. Do you?

DYSART: Yes. What was your dream about last night?

ALAN: Can't remember. What's yours about?

DYSART: I said the truth.

ALAN: That is the truth. What's yours about? The special one.

DYSART: Carving up children.

(ALAN *smiles.*)

My turn!

ALAN: What?

DYSART: What is your first memory of a horse?

ALAN: What d'you mean?

DYSART: The first time one entered your life, in any way.

ALAN: Can't remember.

DYSART: Are you sure?

ALAN: Yes.

DYSART: You have no recollection of the first time you noticed a horse?

ALAN: I told you. Now it's my turn. Are you married?

DYSART (*controlling himself*): I am.

ALAN: Is she a doctor, too?

DYSART: It's my turn.

ALAN: Yes, well what?

DYSART: What is Ek?

(*Pause.*)

You shouted it out last night in your sleep. I thought you might like to talk about it.

ALAN (*singing*):
    Double your pleasure,
    Double your fun!

DYSART: Come on, now. You can do better than that.

ALAN (*singing louder*):
    With Doublemint, Doublemint
    Doublemint gum!

DYSART: All right. Good morning.

ALAN: What d'you mean?

DYSART: We're finished for today.

ALAN: But I've only had ten minutes.

DYSART: Too bad.

(*He picks up a file and studies it.* ALAN *lingers.*)

Didn't you hear me? I said, Good morning.

ALAN: That's not fair!

DYSART: No?

ALAN (*savagely*): The Government pays you twenty quid an hour to see me. I know. I heard downstairs.

DYSART: Well, go back there and hear some more.

ALAN: *That's not fair!*

(*He springs up, clenching his fists in a sudden violent rage.*)

You're a—you're a—You're a swiz! . . . Bloody swiz! . . . Fucking swiz!

DYSART: Do I have to call Nurse?

ALAN: She puts a finger on me, I'll bash her!

DYSART: She'll bash you much harder, I can assure you. Now go away.

(*He reads his file.* ALAN *stays where he is, emptily clenching his hands. He turns away.*
    A pause.
    A faint hum starts from the CHORUS.)

ALAN (*suddenly*): On a beach. . . .

SCENE 10

He steps out of the square, upstage, and begins to walk round the circle. Warm light glows on it.

DYSART: What?

ALAN: Where I saw a horse, Swizzy.

(*Lazily he kicks at the sand, and throws stones at the sea.*)

DYSART: How old were you?

ALAN: How should I know? . . . Six.

DYSART: Well, go on. What were you doing there?

ALAN: Digging.

(*He throws himself on the ground, downstage centre of the circle, and starts scuffing with his hands.*)

DYSART: A sandcastle?

ALAN: Well, what else?

DYSART (*warningly*): And?

ALAN: Suddenly I heard this noise. Coming up behind me.

(*A young* HORSEMAN *issues in slow motion out of the tunnel. He carries a riding crop with which he is urging on his invisible horse, down the right side of the circle. The hum increases.*)

DYSART: What noise?

ALAN: Hooves. Splashing.

DYSART: Splashing?

ALAN: The tide was out and he was galloping.

DYSART: Who was?

ALAN: This fellow. Like a college chap. He was on a big horse—urging him on. I thought he hadn't seen me. I called out: Hey!

(*The* HORSEMAN *goes into* natural time, *charging fast round the downstage corner of the square straight at* ALAN.)

and they just swerved in time!

HORSEMAN (*reining back*): Whoa! . . . Whoa there! *Whoa!* . . . Sorry! I didn't see you! . . . Did I scare you?

ALAN: No!

HORSEMAN (*looking down on him*): That's a terrific castle!

ALAN: What's his name?

HORSEMAN: Trojan. You can stroke him, if you like. He won't mind.

(*Shyly* ALAN *stretches up on tip-toe, and pats an invisible shoulder.*)

(*Amused*) You can hardly reach down there. Would you like to come up?

(ALAN *nods, eyes wide.*)

All right. Come round this side. You always mount a horse from the left. I'll give you a lift. O.K.?

(ALAN *goes round on the other side.*)

Here we go, now. Just do nothing. Upsadaisy!

(ALAN *sets his foot on the* HORSEMAN's *thigh, and is lifted by him up on to his shoulders.*

The hum from the CHORUS *becomes exultant. Then stops.)*

All right?

(ALAN nods.)

Good. Now all you do is hold onto his mane.

(He holds up the crop, and ALAN grips on to it.)

Tight now. And grip with your knees. All right? All set? . . . Come on, then, Trojan. Let's go!

(The HORSEMAN walks slowly upstage round the circle, with ALAN's legs tight round his neck.)

DYSART: How was it? Was it wonderful?

(ALAN rides in silence.)

Can't you remember?
HORSEMAN: Do you want to go faster?
ALAN: Yes!
HORSEMAN: O.K. All you have to do is say "Come on, Trojan—bear me away!" . . . Say it, then!
ALAN: Bear me away!

(The HORSEMAN starts to run with ALAN round the circle.)

DYSART: You went fast?
ALAN: Yes!
DYSART: Weren't you frightened?
ALAN: No!
HORSEMAN: Come on now. Trojan! Bear us away! Hold on! Come on now! . . .

(He runs faster. ALAN begins to laugh. Then suddenly, as they reach again the right downstage corner, FRANK and DORA stand up in alarm.)

DORA: Alan!
FRANK: Alan!
DORA: Alan, stop!

(FRANK runs round after them. DORA follows behind.)

FRANK: Hey, you! You! . . .
HORSEMAN: Whoa, boy! . . . Whoa! . . .

(He reins the horse round, and wheels to face the parents. This all goes fast.)

FRANK: What do you imagine you are doing?
HORSEMAN (*ironic*): "Imagine"?
FRANK: What is my son doing up there?
HORSEMAN: Water-skiing!

(DORA joins them, breathless.)

DORA: Is he all right, Frank? . . . He's not hurt?
FRANK: Don't you think you should ask permission before doing a stupid thing like that?
HORSEMAN: What's stupid?
ALAN: It's lovely, dad!
DORA: Alan, come down here!
HORSEMAN: The boy's perfectly safe. Please don't be hysterical.
FRANK: Don't you be la-di-da with me, young man! Come down here, Alan. You heard what your mother said.
ALAN: No.
FRANK: Come down at once. Right this moment.
ALAN: No . . . NO!
FRANK (*in a fury*): I said—this moment!

(He pulls ALAN from the HORSEMAN's shoulders. The boy shrieks, and falls to the ground.)

HORSEMAN: Watch it!
DORA: Frank!

(She runs to her son, and kneels. The HORSEMAN skitters.)

HORSEMAN: Are you mad? D'you want to terrify the horse?
DORA: He's grazed his knee. Frank—the boy's hurt!
ALAN: I'm not! I'm *not*!
FRANK: What's your name?
HORSEMAN: Jesse James.
DORA: Frank, he's bleeding!
FRANK: I intend to report you to the police for endangering the lives of children.
HORSEMAN: Go right ahead!
DORA: Can you stand, dear?
ALAN: Oh, *stop* it! . . .
FRANK: You're a public menace, d'you know that? How dare you pick up children and put them on dangerous animals.
HORSEMAN: Dangerous?
FRANK: Of course dangerous. Look at his eyes. They're rolling.
HORSEMAN: So are yours!
FRANK: In my opinion that is a dangerous animal. In my considered opinion you are both dangers to the safety of this beach.
HORSEMAN: And in my opinion, you're a stupid fart!
DORA: Frank, leave it!
FRANK: What did you say?
DORA: It's not important, Frank—really!
FRANK: *What did you say?*
HORSEMAN: Oh bugger off! Sorry, chum! Come on, Trojan!

(*He urges his horse straight at them, then wheels it and gallops off round the right side of the circle and away up the tunnel, out of sight. The parents cry out, as they are covered with sand and water. Frank runs after him, and round the left side of the circle, with his wife following after.*)

ALAN: Splash, splash, splash! All three of us got covered with water! Dad got absolutely soaked!

FRANK (*shouting after the* HORSEMAN): Hooligan! Filthy hooligan!

ALAN: I wanted to laugh!

FRANK: Upper class riff-raff! That's all they are, people who go riding! That's what they *want*—trample on ordinary people!

DORA: Don't be absurd, Frank.

FRANK: It's why they do it. It's why they bloody do it!

DORA (*amused*): Look at you. You're covered!

FRANK: Not as much as you. There's sand all over your hair!

(*She starts to laugh.*)

(*Shouting*) Hooligan! Bloody hooligan!

(*She starts to laugh more. He tries to brush the sand out of her hair.*)

What are you laughing at? It's not funny. It's not funny at all, Dora!

(*She goes off, right, still laughing.* ALAN *edges into the square, still on the ground.*)

It's just not funny! . . .

(FRANK *returns to his place on the beach, sulky. Abrupt silence.*)

ALAN: And that's all I remember.

DYSART: And a lot, too. Thank you. . . . You know, I've never been on a horse in my life.

ALAN (*not looking at him*): Nor me.

DYSART: You mean, after that?

ALAN: Yes.

DYSART: But you must have done at the stables?

ALAN: No.

DYSART: Never?

ALAN: No.

DYSART: How come?

ALAN: I didn't care to.

DYSART: Did it have anything to do with falling off like that, all those years ago?

ALAN (*tight*): I just didn't care to, that's all.

DYSART: Do you think of that scene often?

ALAN: I suppose.

DYSART: Why, do you think?

ALAN: 'Cos it's funny.

DYSART: Is that all?

ALAN: What else? My turn. . . . I told you a secret: now you tell me one.

DYSART: All right. I have patients who've got things to tell me, only they're ashamed to say them to my face. What do you think I do about that?

ALAN: What?

DYSART: I give them this little tape recorder.

(*He takes a small tape recorder and microphone from his pocket.*)

They go off to another room, and send me the tape through Nurse. They don't have to listen to it with me.

ALAN: That's stupid.

DYSART: All you do is press this button, and speak into this. It's very simple. Anyway, your time's up for today. I'll see you tomorrow.

ALAN (*getting up*): Maybe.

DYSART: Maybe?

ALAN: If I feel like it.

(*He is about to go out. Then suddenly he returns to* DYSART *and takes the machine from him.*)

It's stupid.

(*He leaves the square and goes back to his bed.*)

SCENE 11

DORA (*calling out*): Doctor!

(DORA *re-enters and comes straight on to the square from the right. She wears an overcoat, and is nervously carrying a shopping bag.*)

DYSART: That same evening, his mother appeared.

DORA: Hallo, Doctor.

DYSART: Mrs. Strang!

DORA: I've been shopping in the neighbourhood. I thought I might just look in.

DYSART: Did you want to see Alan?

DORA (*uncomfortably*): No, no . . . Not just at the moment. Actually, it's more you I wanted to see.

DYSART: Yes?

DORA: You see, there's something Mr. Strang and I thought you ought to know. We discussed it, and it might just be important.

DYSART: Well, come and sit down.

DORA: I can't stay more than a moment. I'm late as it is. Mr. Strang will be wanting his dinner.

DYSART: Ah. (*Encouragingly*) So, what was it you wanted to tell me?

(*She sits on the upstage bench.*)

DORA: Well, do you remember that photograph I mentioned to you. The one Mr. Strang gave Alan to decorate his bedroom a few years ago?

DYSART: Yes. A horse looking over a gate, wasn't it?

DORA: That's right. Well, actually, it took the place of another kind of picture altogether.

DYSART: What kind?

DORA: It was a reproduction of Our Lord on his way to Calvary. Alan found it in Reeds Art Shop, and fell absolutely in love with it. He insisted on buying it with his pocket money, and hanging it at the foot of his bed where he could see it last thing at night. My husband was very displeased.

DYSART: Because it was religious?

DORA: In all fairness I must admit it was a little extreme. The Christ was loaded down with chains, and the centurions were really laying on the stripes. It certainly would not have been my choice, but I don't believe in interfering too much with children, so I said nothing.

DYSART: But Mr. Strang did?

DORA: He stood it for a while, but one day we had one of our tiffs about religion, and he went straight upstairs, tore it off the boy's wall and threw it in the dustbin. Alan went quite hysterical. He cried for days without stopping—and he was not a crier, you know.

DYSART: But he recovered when he was given the photograph of the horse in its place?

DORA: He certainly seemed to. At least, he hung it in exactly the same position, and we had no more of that awful weeping.

DYSART: Thank you, Mrs. Strang. That *is* interesting . . . Exactly how long ago was that? Can you remember?

DORA: It must be five years ago, Doctor. Alan would have been about twelve. How is he, by the way?

DYSART: Bearing up.

(*She rises.*)

DORA: Please give him my love.

DYSART: You can see him any time you want, you know.

DORA: Perhaps if I could come one afternoon without Mr. Strang. He and Alan don't exactly get on at the moment, as you can imagine.

DYSART: Whatever you decide, Mrs. Strang . . . Oh, one thing.

DORA: Yes?

DYSART: Could you describe that photograph of the horse in a little more detail for me? I presume it's still in his bedroom?

DORA: Oh, yes. It's a most remarkable picture, really. You very rarely see a horse taken from that angle—absolutely head on. That's what makes it so interesting.

DYSART: Why? What does it look like?

DORA: Well, it's most extraordinary. It comes out all eyes.

DYSART: Staring straight at you?

DORA: Yes, that's right . . .

(*An uncomfortable pause.*)

I'll come and see him one day very soon, Doctor. Good-bye.

(*She leaves, and resumes her place by her husband.*)

DYSART (*to audience*): It was then—that moment—I felt real alarm. What was it? The shadow of a giant head across my desk? . . . At any rate, the feeling got worse with the stable-owner's visit.

SCENE 12

DALTON *comes in to the square: heavy-set: mid-fifties.*

DALTON: Dr. Dysart?

DYSART: Mr. Dalton. It's very good of you to come.

DALTON: It is, actually. In my opinion the boy should be in prison. Not in a hospital at the taxpayers' expense.

DYSART: Please sit down.

(DALTON *sits.*)

This must have been a terrible experience for you.

DALTON: Terrible? I don't think I'll ever get over it. Jill's had a nervous breakdown.

DYSART: Jill?

DALTON: The girl who worked for me. Of course, she feels responsible in a way. Being the one who introduced him in the first place.

DYSART: He was introduced to the stable by a girl?

DALTON: Jill Mason, He met her somewhere, and asked for a job. She told him to come and see me. I wish to Christ she never had.

DYSART: But when he first appeared he didn't seem in any way peculiar?

DALTON: No, he was bloody good. He'd spend hours with the horses cleaning and grooming them, way over the call of duty. I thought he was a real find.

DYSART: Apparently, during the whole time he worked for you, he never actually rode.

DALTON: That's true.

DYSART: Wasn't that peculiar?

DALTON: Very . . . *If* he didn't.

DYSART: What do you mean?

(DALTON *rises.*)

DALTON: Because on and off, that whole year, I had the feeling the horses were being taken out at night.

DYSART: At night?

DALTON: There were just odd things I noticed. I mean too often one or other of them would be sweaty first thing in the morning, when it wasn't sick. Very sweaty, too. And its stall wouldn't be near as mucky as it should be if it had been in all night. I never paid it much mind at the time. It was only when I realised I'd been hiring a loony, I came to wonder if he hadn't been riding all the time, behind our backs.

DYSART: But wouldn't you have noticed if things had been disturbed?

DALTON: Nothing ever was. Still, he's a neat worker. That wouldn't prove anything.

DYSART: Aren't the stables locked at night?

DALTON: Yes.

DYSART: And someone sleeps on the premises?

DALTON: Me and my son.

DYSART: Two people?

DALTON: I'm sorry Doctor. It's obviously just my fancy. I tell you, this thing has shaken me so bad, I'm liable to believe anything. If there's nothing else, I'll be going.

DYSART: Look: even if you were right, why should anyone do that? Why would any boy prefer to ride by himself at night, when he could go off with others during the day.

DALTON: Are you asking me? He's a loony, isn't he?

(DALTON *leaves the square and sits again in his place.* DYSART *watches him go.*)

ALAN: It was *sexy.*

DYSART: His tape arrived that evening.

SCENE 13

ALAN *is sitting on his bed holding the tape-recorder.* NURSE *approaches briskly, takes the machine from him—gives it to* DYSART *in the*

square—*and leaves again, resuming her seat.* DYSART *switches on the tape.*

ALAN: That's what you want to know, isn't it? All right: it was. I'm talking about the beach. That time when I was a kid. What I told you about. . . .

(*Pause. He is in great emotional difficulty.*
DYSART *sits on the left bench listening, file in hand.* ALAN *rises and stands directly behind him, but on the circle, as if recording the ensuing speech. He never, of course, looks directly at the* DOCTOR.)

I was pushed forward on the horse. There was sweat on my legs from his neck. The fellow held me tight, and let me turn the horse which way I wanted. All that power going any way you wanted . . . His sides were all warm, and the smell . . . Then suddenly I was on the ground, where Dad pulled me. I could have bashed him . . .

(*Pause.*)

Something else. When the horse first appeared, I looked up into his mouth. It was huge. There was this chain in it. The fellow pulled it, and cream dripped out. I said, "Does it hurt?" And he said— the horse said—said—

(*He stops, in anguish.* DYSART *makes a note in his file.*)

(*Desperately*) It was always the same, after that. Every time I heard one clop by, I had to run and see. Up a country lane or anywhere. They sort of pulled me. I couldn't take my eyes off them. Just to watch their skins. The way their necks twist, and sweat shines in the folds . . . (*Pause.*) I can't remember when it started. Mum reading to me about Prince who no one could ride, except one boy. Or the white horse in Revelations. "He that sat upon him was called Faithful and True. His eyes were as flames of fire, and he had a name written that no man knew but himself" . . . Words like reins. Stirrup. Flanks . . . "Dashing his spurs against his charger's flanks!" . . . Even the words made me feel— . . . Years, I never told anyone. Mum wouldn't understand. She likes "Equitation." Bowler hats and jodhpurs! "My grandfather dressed for the horse," she says. What does that mean? The horse isn't dressed. It's the most naked thing you ever saw! More than a dog or a cat or anything. Even the most broken down old nag has got its *life!* To put a bowler on it is *filthy!* . . . Putting them through their paces! Bloody gymkhanas! . . . No one understands! . . . Except cowboys. They do. I wish I was a cowboy. They're free. They just swing up and then it's miles of grass . . . I bet all cowboys are *orphans!* . . . I bet they are!

NURSE: Mr. Strang to see you, Doctor.

DYSART (*in surprise*): Mr. Strang? Show him up, please.

ALAN: No one ever says to cowboys "Receive my meaning"! They wouldn't dare. Or "God" all the time. (*Mimicking his mother*) "God sees you, Alan. God's got eyes everywhere—"

(*He stops abruptly.*)

I'm not doing any more! . . . I hate this! . . . You can whistle for anymore. I've had it!

(*He returns angrily to his bed, throwing the blanket over him.*
DYSART *switches off the tape.*)

SCENE 14

FRANK STRANG *comes into the square, his hat in his hand. He is nervous and embarrassed.*

DYSART (*welcoming*): Hallo, Mr. Strang.

FRANK: I was passing. I hope it's not too late.

DYSART: Of course not. I'm delighted to see you.

FRANK: My wife doesn't know I'm here. I'd be grateful to you if you didn't enlighten her, if you receive my meaning.

DYSART: Everything that happens in this room is confidential, Mr. Strang.

FRANK: I hope so . . . I hope so . . .

DYSART (*gently*): Do you have something to tell me?

FRANK: As a matter of fact I have. Yes.

DYSART: Your wife told me about the photograph.

FRANK: I know, it's not that! It's *about* that, but it's—worse. . . . I wanted to tell you the other night, but I couldn't in front of Dora. Maybe I should have. It might show her where all that stuff leads to, she drills into the boy behind my back.

DYSART: What kind of thing is it?

FRANK: Something I witnessed.

DYSART: Where?

FRANK: At home. About eighteen months ago.

DYSART: Go on.

FRANK: It was late. I'd gone upstairs to fetch something. The boy had been in bed hours, or so I thought.

DYSART: Go on.

FRANK: As I came along the passage I saw the door of his bedroom was ajar. I'm sure he didn't know it was. From inside I heard the sound of this chanting.

DYSART: Chanting?

FRANK: Like the Bible. One of those lists his mother's always reading to him.

DYSART: What kind of list?

FRANK: Those Begats. So-and-so begat, you know. Genealogy.

DYSART: Can you remember what Alan's list sounded like?

FRANK: Well, the *sort* of thing. I stood there absolutely astonished. The first word I heard was . . .

ALAN (*rising and chanting*): Prince!

DYSART: Prince?

FRANK: Prince begat Prance. That sort of nonsense.

(ALAN *moves slowly to the center of the circle, downstage.*)

ALAN: And Prance begat Prankus! And Prankus begat Flankus!

FRANK: I looked through the door, and he was standing in the moonlight in his pyjamas, right in front of that big photograph.

DYSART: The horse with the huge eyes?

FRANK: Right.

ALAN: Flankus begat Spankus. And Spankus begat Spunkus the Great, who lived three score years!

FRANK: It was all like that. I can't remember the exact names, of course. Then suddenly he knelt down.

DYSART: In front of the photograph?

FRANK: Yes. Right there at the foot of his bed.

ALAN (*kneeling*): And Legwus begat Neckwus. And Neckwus begat Fleckwus, the King of Spit. And Fleckwus spoke out of his chinkle-chankle!

(*He bows himself to the ground.*)

DYSART: What?

FRANK: I'm sure that was the word. I've never forgotten it. Chinkle-chankle.

(ALAN *raises his head and extends his hands up in glory.*)

ALAN: And he said "Behold—I give you Equus, my only begotten son!"

DYSART: Equus?

FRANK: Yes. No doubt of that. He repeated that word several times. "Equus my only begotten son."

ALAN (*reverently*): Ek . . . wus!

DYSART (*suddenly understanding: almost "aside"*): Ek . . . Ek . . .

FRANK (*embarrassed*): And then . . .

DYSART: Yes: what?

FRANK: He took a piece of string out of his pocket. Made up into a noose. And put it in his mouth.

(ALAN *bridles himself with invisible string, and pulls it back.*)

And then with his other hand he picked up a coat hanger. A wooden coat hanger, and—and—

DYSART: Began to beat himself?

(ALAN, *in mime, begins to thrash himself, increasing the strokes in speed and viciousness. Pause.*)

FRANK: You see why I couldn't tell his mother. . . . Religion. Religion's at the bottom of all this!

DYSART: What did you do?

FRANK: Nothing. I coughed—and went back downstairs.

(*The boy starts guiltily—tears the string from his mouth—and scrambles back to bed.*)

DYSART: Did you ever speak to him about it later? Even obliquely?

FRANK (*unhappily*): I can't speak of things like that, Doctor. It's not in my nature.

DYSART (*kindly*): No. I see that.

FRANK: But I thought you ought to know. So I came.

DYSART (*warmly*): Yes. I'm very grateful to you. Thank you.

(*Pause.*)

FRANK: Well, that's it. . . .

DYSART: Is there anything else?

FRANK (*even more embarrassed*): There is actually. One thing.

DYSART: What's that?

FRANK: On the night that he did it—that awful thing in the stable—

DYSART: Yes?

FRANK: That very night, he was out with a girl.

DYSART: How d'you know that?

FRANK: I just know.

DYSART (*puzzled*): Did he tell you?

FRANK: I can't say any more.

DYSART: I don't quite understand.

FRANK: Everything said in here is confidential, you said.

DYSART: Absolutely.

FRANK: Then ask him. Ask him about taking a girl out, that very night he did it. . . . (*Abruptly*) Good-bye, Doctor.

(*He goes.* DYSART *looks after him.* FRANK *resumes his seat.*)

SCENE 15

ALAN *gets up and enters the square.*

DYSART: Alan! Come in. Sit down. (*Pleasantly*) What did you do last night?

ALAN: Watched telly.

DYSART: Any good?

ALAN: All right.

DYSART: Thanks for the tape. It was excellent.

ALAN: I'm not making any more.

DYSART: One thing I didn't quite understand. You began to say something about the horse on the beach talking to you.

ALAN: That's stupid. Horses don't talk.

DYSART: So I believe.

ALAN: I don't know what you mean.

DYSART: Never mind. Tell me something else. Who introduced you to the stable to begin with?

(*Pause.*)

ALAN: Someone I met.

DYSART: Where?

ALAN: Bryson's.

DYSART: The shop where you worked?

ALAN: Yes.

DYSART: That's a funny place for you to be. Whose idea was that?

ALAN: Dad.

DYSART: I'd have thought he'd have wanted you to work with him.

ALAN: I haven't the aptitude. And printing's a failing trade. If you receive my meaning.

DYSART (*amused*): I see . . . What did your mother think?

ALAN: Shops are common.

DYSART: And you?

ALAN: I loved it.

DYSART: Really?

ALAN (*sarcastic*): Why not? You get to spend every minute with electrical things. It's fun.

(NURSE, DALTON, *and the actors playing horses call out to him as* CUSTOMERS, *seated where they are. Their voices are aggressive and demanding. There is a constant background mumbling, made up of trade names, out of which can clearly be distinguished the italicized words, which are shouted out.*)

CUSTOMER: *Philco!*

ALAN (*to* DYSART): Of course it might just drive you off your chump.

CUSTOMER: I want to buy a hot-plate. I'm told the *Philco* is a good make!

ALAN: I think it is, madam.

CUSTOMER: Remington ladies' shavers?

ALAN: I'm not sure, madam.

CUSTOMER: *Robex* tableware?

CUSTOMER: *Croydex?*

CUSTOMER: *Volex?*

CUSTOMER: *Pifco* automatic toothbrushes?

ALAN: I'll find out, sir.

CUSTOMER: Beautiflor!

CUSTOMER: Windowlene!

CUSTOMER: I want a *Philco* transistor radio!

CUSTOMER: This isn't a *Remington!* I wanted a *Remington!*

ALAN: Sorry.

CUSTOMER: I wanted the heat retaining *Pifco!*

ALAN: *Sorry!*

(JILL *comes into the square; a girl in her early twenties, pretty and middle class. She wears a sweater and jeans. The mumbling stops.*)

JILL: Hallo.

ALAN: Hallo.

JILL: Have you any blades for a clipping machine?

ALAN: Clipping?

JILL: To clip horses.

(*Pause. He stares at her, open-mouthed.*)

What's the matter?

ALAN: You work at Dalton's stables. I've seen you.

(*During the following, he mimes putting away a pile of boxes on a shelf in the shop.*)

JILL: I've seen you too, haven't I? You're the boy who's always staring into the yard around lunch-time.

ALAN: Me?

JILL: You're there most days.

ALAN: Not me.

JILL (*amused*): Of course it's you. Mr. Dalton was only saying the other day: "Who's that boy keeps staring in at the door?" Are you looking for a job or something?

ALAN (*eagerly*): Is there one?

JILL: I don't know.

ALAN: I can only do weekends.

JILL: That's when most people ride. We can always use extra hands. It'd mainly be mucking out.

ALAN: I don't mind.

JILL: Can you ride?

ALAN: No . . . No . . . I don't want to.

(*She looks at him curiously.*)

Please.

JILL: Come up on Saturday. I'll introduce you to Mr. Dalton.

(*She leaves the square.*)

DYSART: When was this? About a year ago?

ALAN: I suppose.

DYSART: And she did?

ALAN: Yes.

(*Briskly he moves the three benches to form three stalls in the stable.*)

SCENE 16

Rich light falls on the square.

An exultant humming from the CHORUS.

Tramping is heard. Three actors playing horses rise from their places. Together they unhook three horse masks from the ladders to left and right, put them on with rigid timing, and walk with swaying horse-motion into the square. Their metal hooves stamp on the wood. Their masks turn and toss high above their heads—as they will do sporadically throughout all horse scenes—making the steel gleam in the light.

For a moment they seem to converge on the boy as he stands in the middle of the stable, but then they swiftly turn and take up positions as if tethered by the head, with their invisible rumps towards him, one by each bench. ALAN *is sunk in this glowing world of horses. Lost in wonder, he starts almost involuntarily to kneel on the floor in reverence—but is sharply interrupted by the cheery voice of* DALTON, *coming into the stable, followed by* JILL. *The boy straightens up guiltily.*

DALTON: First thing to learn is drill. Learn it and keep to it. I want this place neat, dry and clean at all times. After you've mucked out, Jill will show you some grooming. What we call strapping a horse.

JILL: I think Trooper's got a stone.

DALTON: Yes? Let's see.

(*He crosses to the horse by the left bench, who is balancing one hoof on its tip. He picks up the hoof.*)

You're right. (*To* ALAN) See this? This V here. It's what's called a frog. Sort of shock-absorber. Once you pierce that, it takes ages to heal—so you want to watch for it. You clean it out with this. What we call a hoof-pick.

(*He takes from his pocket an invisible pick.*)

Mind how you go with it. It's very sharp. Use it like this.

(*He quickly takes the stone out.*)

See?

(ALAN *nods, fascinated.*)

You'll soon get the hang of it. Jill will look after you. What she doesn't know about stables, isn't worth knowing.

JILL (*pleased*): Oh yes, I'm sure!
DALTON (*handing* ALAN *the pick*): Careful how you go with that. The main rule is: anything you don't know—ask. Never pretend you know something when you don't. (*Smiling*) Actually, the main rule is: enjoy yourself. All right?
ALAN: Yes, sir.
DALTON: Good lad. See you later.

(*He nods to them cheerfully, and leaves the square.* ALAN *clearly puts the invisible hoof-pick on the rail, downstage left.*)

JILL: All right, let's start on some grooming. Why don't we begin with him? He looks as if he needs it.

(*They approach* NUGGET, *who is standing to the right. She pats him.* ALAN *sits and watches her.*)

This is Nugget. He's my favorite. He's as gentle as a baby, aren't you? But terribly fast if you want him to be.

(*During the following, she mimes both the actions and the objects, which she picks up from the right bench.*)

Now this is the dandy, and we start with that. Then you move on to the body brush. This is the most important, and you use it with this curry-comb. Now you always groom the same way: from the ears downward. Don't be afraid to do it hard. The harder you do it, the more the horse loves it. Push it right through the coat: like this.

(*The boy watches in fascination as she brushes the invisible body of* NUGGET, *scraping the dirt and hair off on to the invisible curry-comb. Now and then the horse mask moves very slighly in pleasure.*)

Down towards the tail and right through the coat. See how he loves it? I'm giving you a lovely massage, boy, aren't I? . . . You try.

(*She hands him the brush. Gingerly he rises and approaches* NUGGET. *Embarrassed and excited, he copies her movements, inexpertly.*)

Keep it nice and easy. Never rush. Down towards the tail and right through the coat. That's it. Again. Down towards the tail and right through the coat. . . . Very good. Now you keep that up for fifteen minutes and then do old Trooper. Will you?

(ALAN *nods.*)

You've got a feel for it. I can tell. It's going to be nice teaching you. See you later.

(*She leaves the square and resumes her place.* ALAN *is left alone with the horses.*
They all stamp. He approaches NUGGET *again, and touches the horse's shoulder. The mask turns sharply in his direction. The boy pauses, then moves his hand gently over the outline of the neck and back. The mask is reassured. It stares ahead unmoving. Then* ALAN *lifts his palm to his face and smells it deeply, closing his eyes.*
DYSART *rises from his bench, and begins to walk slowly upstage round the circle.*)

DYSART: Was that good? Touching them.

(ALAN *gives a faint groan.*)

ALAN: Mmm.
DYSART: It must have been marvelous, being near them at last . . . Stroking them . . . Making them fresh and glossy . . . Tell me . . .

(*Silence.* ALAN *begins to brush* NUGGET.)

How about the girl? Did you like her?
ALAN (*tight*): All right.
DYSART: Just all right?

(ALAN *changes his position, moving round* NUGGET's *rump so that his back is to the audience. He brushes harder.* DYSART *comes downstage around the circle, and finally back to his bench.*)

Was she friendly?
ALAN: Yes.
DYSART: Or stand-offish?
ALAN: Yes.
DYSART: Well which?
ALAN: What?

DYSART: Which was she?

(ALAN *brushes harder*.)

Did you take her out? Come on now: tell me. Did you have a date with her?

ALAN: What?

DYSART (*sitting*): Tell me if you did.

(*The boy suddenly explodes in one of his rages*.)

ALAN (*yelling*): TELL ME!

(*All the masks toss at the noise*.)

DYSART: What?

ALAN: *Tell me, tell me, tell me, tell me!*

(ALAN *storms out of the square, and downstage to where* DYSART *sits. He is raging. During the ensuing, the horses leave by all three openings*.)

On and on, sitting there! Nosey Parker! That's all you are! Bloody Nosey Parker! Just like Dad. On and on and bloody on! Tell me, tell me, tell me . . . Answer this. Answer that. Never stop!—

(*He marches round the circle and back into the square*. DYSART *rises and enters it from the other side*.)

SCENE 17

Lights brighten.

DYSART: I'm sorry.

(*Alan slams about what is now the office again, replacing the benches to their usual position*.)

ALAN: All right, it's my turn now. You tell me! Answer me!

DYSART: We're not playing that game now.

ALAN: We're playing what I say.

DYSART: All right. What do you want to know?

(*He sits*.)

ALAN: Do *you* have dates?

DYSART: I told you. I'm married.

(ALAN *approaches him, very hostile*.)

ALAN: I know. Her name's Margaret. She's a dentist! You see, I found out! What made you go with her? Did you use to bite her hands when she did you in the chair?

(*The boy sits next to him, close*.)

DYSART: That's not very funny.

ALAN: Do you have girls behind her back?

DYSART: No.

ALAN: Then what? Do you fuck her?

DYSART: That's enough now.

(*He rises and moves away*.)

ALAN: Come on, tell me! Tell me, tell me!

DYSART: I said that's enough now.

(ALAN *rises too and walks around him*.)

I bet you don't. I bet you never touch her. Come on, tell me. You've got no kids, have you? Is that because you don't fuck?

DYSART (*sharp*): Go to your room. Go on: quick march.

(*Pause*. ALAN *moves away from him, insolently takes up a packet of* DYSART's *cigarettes from the bench, and extracts one*.)

Give me those cigarettes.

(*The boy puts one in his mouth*.)

(*Exploding*.) Alan, *give them to me!*

(*Reluctantly* ALAN *shoves the cigarette back in the packet, turns and hands it to him*.)

Now go!

(ALAN *bolts out of the square, and back to his bed*. DYSART, *unnerved, addresses the audience*.)

Brilliant! Absolutely brilliant! The boy's on the run, so he gets defensive. What am I, then? . . . Wicked little bastard—he knows exactly what questions to try. He'd actually marched himself round hospital, making enquiries about my wife. Wicked and—of course, perceptive. Ever since I made that crack about carving up children, he's been aware of me in an absolutely specific way. Of course, there's nothing novel in that. Advanced neurotics can be dazzling at that game. They aim unswervingly at your area of maximum vulnerability . . . Which I suppose is as good a way as any of describing Margaret.

(*He sits*. HESTHER *enters the square. Light grows warmer*.)

SCENE 18

HESTHER: Now stop it.

DYSART: Do I embarrass you?

HESTHER: I suspect you're about to.

(*Pause*.)

DYSART: My wife doesn't understand me, Your Honour.

HESTHER: Do you understand her?

DYSART: No. Obviously I never did.

HESTHER: I'm sorry. I've never liked to ask but I've always imagined you weren't exactly compatible.

(*She moves to sit opposite.*)

DYSART: We were. It actually worked for a bit. I mean for both of us. We worked for each other, she actually for me through a kind of briskness. A clear, red-headed, inaccessible briskness which kept me keyed up for months. Mind you, if you're kinky for Northern Hygienic, as I am, you can't find anything much more compelling than a Scottish Lady Dentist.

HESTHER: It's *you* who are wicked, you know!

DYSART: Not at all: She got exactly the same from me. Antiseptic proficiency. I was like that in those days. We suited each other admirably. I see us in our wedding photo: Doctor and Doctor Mac Brisk. We were brisk in our wooing, brisk in our wedding, brisk in our disappointment. We turned from each other briskly into our separate surgeries: and now there's damn all.

HESTHER: You have no children, have you?

DYSART: No, we didn't go in for them. Instead, she sits beside our salmon-pink, glazed brick fireplace, and knits things for orphans in a home she helps with. And I sit opposite, turning the pages of art books on Ancient Greece. Occasionally, I still trail a faint scent of my enthusiasm across her path. I pass her a picture of the sacred acrobats of Crete leaping through the horns of running bulls—and she'll say: "Och, Martin, what an *absurrd* thing to be doing! The Highland Games, now there's *norrmal sport!*" Or she'll observe, just after I've told her a story from the Iliad: "You know, when you come to think of it, Agamemnon and that lot were nothing but a bunch of ruffians from the Gorbals, only with fancy names!" (*He rises.*) You get the picture. She's turned into a Shrink. The familiar domestic monster. Margaret Dysart: The Shrink's Shrink.

HESTHER: That's cruel, Martin.

DYSART: Yes. Do you know what it's like for two people to live in the same house as if they were in different parts of the world? Mentally, she's always in some drizzly kirk of her own inheriting: and I'm in some Doric temple—clouds tearing through pillars—eagles bearing prophecies out of the sky. She finds all that repulsive. All my wife has ever taken from the Mediterranean—from that whole vast intuitive culture—are four bottles of Chianti to make into lamps, and two china condiment donkeys labelled Sally and Peppy.

(*Pause.*)

(*More intimately*) I wish there was one person in my life I could show. One instinctive, absolutely unbrisk person I could take to Greece, and stand in front of certain shrines and sacred streams and say "Look! Life is only comprehensible through a thousand local Gods." And not just the old dead ones with names like Zeus—no, but living Geniuses of Place and Person! And not just Greece but modern England! Spirits of certain trees, certain curves of brick wall, certain chip shops, if you like, and slate roofs—just as of certain frowns in people and slouches . . . I'd say to them—"Worship as many as you can see—and more will appear!" . . . If I had a son, I bet you he'd come out exactly like his mother. Utterly worshipless. Would you like a drink?

HESTHER: No, thanks. Actually, I've got to be going. As usual . . .

DYSART: Really?

HESTHER: Really. I've got an Everest of papers to get through before bed.

DYSART: You never stop, do you?

HESTHER: Do you?

DYSART: This boy, with his stare. He's trying to save himself through me.

HESTHER: I'd say so.

DYSART: What am I trying to do to him?

HESTHER: Restore him, surely?

DYSART: To what?

HESTHER: A normal life.

DYSART: Normal?

HESTHER: It still means something.

DYSART: Does it?

HESTHER: Of course.

DYSART: You mean a normal boy has one head: a normal head has two ears?

HESTHER: You know I don't.

DYSART: Then what else?

HESTHER (*lightly*): Oh, stop it.

DYSART: No, what? You tell me.

HESTHER (*rising: smiling*): I won't be put on the stand like this, Martin. You're really disgraceful! . . . (*Pause.*) You know what I mean by a normal smile in a child's eyes, and one that isn't—even if I can't exactly define it. Don't you?

DYSART: Yes.

HESTHER: Then we have a duty to that, surely? Both of us.

DYSART: Touché. . . . I'll talk to you.

HESTHER: Dismissed?

DYSART: You said you had to go.

HESTHER: I do. . . . (*She kisses his cheek.*) Thank

you for what you're doing. . . . You're going through a rotten patch at the moment. I'm sorry . . . I suppose one of the few things one can do is simply hold on to priorities.

DYSART: Like what?

HESTHER: Oh—children before grown-ups. Things like that.

(*He contemplates her.*)

DYSART: You're really quite splendid.

HESTHER: Famous for it. Goodnight.

(*She leaves him.*)

DYSART (*to himself—or to the audience*): Normal! . . . Normal!

SCENE 19

ALAN *rises and enters the square. He is subdued.*

DYSART: Good afternoon.

ALAN: Afternoon.

DYSART: I'm sorry about our row yesterday.

ALAN: It was stupid.

DYSART: It was.

ALAN: What I said, I mean.

DYSART: How are you sleeping?

(ALAN *shrugs.*)

You're not feeling well, are you?

ALAN: All right.

DYSART: Would you like to play a game? It could make you feel better.

ALAN: What kind?

DYSART: It's called *Blink*. You have to fix your eyes on something: say, that little stain over there on the wall—and I tap this pen on the desk. The first time I tap it, you close your eyes. The next time you open them. And so on. Close, open, close, open, till I say Stop.

ALAN: How can that make you feel better?

DYSART: It relaxes you. You'll feel as though you're talking to me in your sleep.

ALAN: It's stupid.

DYSART: You don't have to do it, if you don't want to.

ALAN: I didn't say I didn't want to.

DYSART: Well?

ALAN: I don't mind.

DYSART: Good. Sit down and start watching that stain. Put your hands by your sides, and open the fingers wide.

(*He opens the left bench and* ALAN *sits on the end of it.*)

The thing is to feel comfortable, and relax absolutely. . . . Are you looking at the stain?

ALAN: Yes.

DYSART: Right. Now try and keep your mind as blank as possible.

ALAN: That's not difficult.

DYSART: Ssh. Stop talking . . . On the first tap, close. On the second, open. Are you ready?

(ALAN *nods.* DYSART *taps his pen on the wooden rail.* ALAN *shuts his eyes.* DYSART *taps again.* ALAN *opens them. The taps are evenly spaced. After four of them the sound cuts out, and is replaced by a louder, metallic sound, on tape.* DYSART *talks through this, to the audience—the light changes to cold—while the boy sits in front of him, staring at the wall, opening and shutting his eyes.*)

The Normal is the good smile in a child's eyes— all right. It is also the dead stare in a million adults. It both sustains and kills—like a God. It is the Ordinary made beautiful: it is also the Average made lethal. The Normal is the indispensable, murderous God of Health, and I am his Priest. My tools are very delicate. My compassion is honest. I have honestly assisted children in this room. I have talked away terrors and relieved many agonies. But also—beyond question—I have cut from them parts of individuality repugnant to this God, in both his aspects. Parts sacred to rarer and more wonderful Gods. And at what length . . . Sacrifices to Zeus took at the most surely, sixty seconds each. Sacrifices to the Normal can take as long as sixty months.

(*The natural sound of the pencil resumes. Light changes back.*)

(*To* ALAN) Now your eyes are feeling heavy. You want to sleep, don't you? You want a long, deep sleep. Have it. Your head is heavy. Very heavy. Your shoulders are heavy. Sleep.

(*The pencil stops.* ALAN's *eyes remain shut and his head has sunk on his chest.*)

Can you hear me?

ALAN: Mmm.

DYSART: You can speak normally. Say Yes, if you can.

ALAN: Yes.

DYSART: Good boy. Now raise your head, and open your eyes.

(*He does so.*)

Now, Alan, you're going to answer questions I'm going to ask you. Do you understand?

ALAN: Yes.

DYSART: And when you wake up, you are going to remember everything you tell me. All right?

ALAN: Yes.

DYSART: Good. Now I want you to think back in time. You are on that beach you told me about. The tide has gone out, and you're making sandcastles. Above you, staring down at you, is that great horse's head, and the cream dropping from it. Can you see that?

ALAN: Yes.

DYSART: You ask him a question. "Does the chain hurt?"

ALAN: Yes.

DYSART: Do you ask him aloud?

ALAN: No.

DYSART: And what does the horse say back?

ALAN: "Yes."

DYSART: Then what do you say?

ALAN: "I'll take it out for you."

DYSART: And he says?

ALAN: "It never comes out. They have me in chains."

DYSART: Like Jesus?

ALAN: Yes!

DYSART: Only his name isn't Jesus, is it?

ALAN: No.

DYSART: What is it?

ALAN: No one knows but him and me.

DYSART: You can tell me, Alan. Name him.

ALAN: Equus.

DYSART: Thank you. Does he live in all horses or just some?

ALAN: All.

DYSART: Good boy. Now: you leave the beach. You're in your bedroom at home. You're twelve years old. You're in front of the picture. You're looking at Equus from the foot of your bed. Would you like to kneel down?

ALAN: Yes.

DYSART (encouragingly): Go on, then.

(ALAN kneels.)

Now tell me. Why is Equus in chains?

ALAN: For the sins of the world.

DYSART: What does he say to you?

ALAN: "I see you." "I will save you."

DYSART: How?

ALAN: "Bear you away. Two shall be one."

DYSART: Horse and rider shall be one beast?

ALAN: One person!

DYSART: Go on.

ALAN: "And my chinkle-chankle shall be in thy hand."

DYSART: Chinkle-chankle? That's his mouth chain?

ALAN: Yes.

DYSART: Good. You can get up . . . Come on.

(ALAN rises.)

Now: think of the stable. What is the stable? His Temple? His Holy of Holies?

ALAN: Yes.

DYSART: Where you wash him? Where you tend him, and brush him with many brushes?

ALAN: Yes.

DYSART: And there he spoke to you, didn't he? He looked at you with his gentle eyes, and spake unto you?

ALAN: Yes.

DYSART: What did he say? "Ride me? Mount me, and ride me forth at night?"

ALAN: Yes.

DYSART: And you obeyed?

ALAN: Yes.

DYSART: How did you learn? By watching others?

ALAN: Yes.

DYSART: It must have been difficult. You bounced about?

ALAN: Yes.

DYSART: But he showed you, didn't he? Equus showed you the way.

ALAN: No!

DYSART: He didn't?

ALAN: He showed me nothing! He's a mean bugger! Ride—or fall! That's Straw Law.

DYSART: Straw Law?

ALAN: He was born in the straw, and this is his law.

DYSART: But you managed? You mastered him?

ALAN: Had to!

DYSART: And then you rode in secret?

ALAN: Yes.

DYSART: How often?

ALAN: Every three weeks. More, people would notice.

DYSART: On a particular horse?

ALAN: No.

DYSART: How did you get into the stable?

ALAN: Stole a key. Had it copied at Bryson's.

DYSART: Clever boy.

(ALAN smiles.)

Then you'd slip out of the house?

ALAN: Midnight! On the stroke!

DYSART: How far's the stable?
ALAN: Two miles.

(*Pause.*)

DYSART: Let's do it! Let's go riding! . . . Now!

(*He stands up, and pushes in his bench.*)

You are there now, in front of the stable door.

(ALAN *turns upstage.*)

That key's in your hand. Go and open it.

SCENE 20

ALAN *moves upstage, and mimes opening the
door.*
    Soft light on the circle.
    Humming from the CHORUS: *the Equus noise.
The horse-actors enter, raise high their masks,
and put them on all together. They stand around
the circle—*NUGGET *in the mouth of the tunnel.*

DYSART: Quietly as possible. Dalton may still be
awake. Sssh . . . Quietly . . . Good. Now go in.

(ALAN *steps secretly out of the square through the
central opening on to the circle, now glowing
with a warm light. He looks about him. The
horses stamp uneasily: their masks turn towards
him.*)

You are on the inside now. All the horses are
staring at you. Can you see them?
ALAN (*excited*): Yes!
DYSART: Which one are you going to take?
ALAN: Nugget.

(ALAN *reaches up and mimes leading* NUGGET
*carefully round the circle downstage with a rope,
past all the horses on the right.*)

DYSART: What colour is Nugget?
ALAN: Chestnut.

(*The horse picks his way with care.* ALAN *halts
him at the corner of the square.*)

DYSART: What do you do, first thing?
ALAN: Put on his sandals.
DYSART: Sandals?

(*He kneels, downstage centre.*)

ALAN: Sandals of majesty! . . . Made of sack.

(*He picks up the invisible sandals, and kisses
them devoutly.*)

Tie them round his hooves.

(*He taps* NUGGET's *right leg: the horse raises it
and the boy mimes tying the sack round it.*)

DYSART: All four hooves?
ALAN: Yes.
DYSART: Then?
ALAN: Chinkle-chankle.

(*He mimes picking up the bridle and bit.*)

He doesn't like it so late, but he takes it for my
sake. He bends for me. He stretches forth his neck
to it.

(NUGGET *bends his head down.* ALAN *first ritually puts the bit into his own mouth, then
crosses, and transfers it into* NUGGET's. *He
reaches up and buckles on the bridle. Then he
leads him by the invisible reins, across the front
of the stage and up round the left side of the
circle.* NUGGET *follows obediently.*)

ALAN: Buckle and lead out.
DYSART: No saddle?
ALAN: Never.
DYSART: Go on.
ALAN: Walk down the path behind. He's quiet.
Always is, this bit. Meek and mild legs. At least till
the field. Then there's trouble.

(*The horse jerks back. The mask tosses.*)

DYSART: What kind?
ALAN: Won't go in.
DYSART: Why not?
ALAN: It's his place of Ha Ha.
DYSART: What?
ALAN: Ha Ha.
DYSART: Make him go into it.
ALAN (*whispering fiercely*): Come on! . . . Come
on! . . .

(*He drags the horse into the square as* DYSART
steps out of it.)

SCENE 21

NUGGET *comes to a halt staring diagonally
down what is now the field. The Equus noise dies
away. The boy looks about him.*

DYSART (*from the circle*): Is it a big field?
ALAN: Huge!
DYSART: What's it like?
ALAN: Full of mist. Nettles on your feet.

(*He mimes taking off his shoes—and the sting.*)

Ah!

DYSART (*going back to his bench*): You take your shoes off?

ALAN: Everything.

DYSART: All your clothes?

ALAN: Yes.

(*He mimes undressing completely in front of the horse. When he is finished and obviously quite naked, he throws out his arms and shows himself fully to his God, bowing his head before* NUGGET.)

DYSART: Where do you leave them?

ALAN: Tree hole near the gate. No one could find them.

(*He walks upstage and crouches by the bench, stuffing the invisible clothes beneath it.* DYSART *sits again on the left bench, downstage beyond the circle.*)

DYSART: How does it feel now?

ALAN (*holds himself*): Burns.

DYSART: Burns?

ALAN: The mist!

DYSART: Go on. Now what?

ALAN: The Manbit.

(*He reaches again under the bench and draws out an invisible stick.*)

DYSART: Manbit?

ALAN: The stick for my mouth.

DYSART: Your mouth?

ALAN: To bite on.

DYSART: Why? What for?

ALAN: So's it won't happen too quick.

DYSART: Is it always the same stick?

ALAN: Course. Sacred stick. Keep it in the hole. The Ark of the Manbit.

DYSART: And now what? . . . What do you do now?

(*Pause. He rises and approaches* NUGGET.)

ALAN: Touch him!

DYSART: Where?

ALAN (*in wonder*): All over. Everywhere. Belly. Ribs. His ribs are of ivory. Of great value! . . . His flank is cool. His nostrils open for me. His eyes shine. They can see in the dark . . . *Eyes!*—

(*Suddenly he dashes in distress to the farthest corner of the square.*)

DYSART: Go on! . . . Then?

(*Pause.*)

ALAN: Give sugar.

DYSART: A lump of sugar?

(ALAN *returns to* NUGGET.)

ALAN: His Last Supper.

DYSART: Last before what?

ALAN: Ha Ha.

(*He kneels before the horse, palms upward and joined together.*)

DYSART: Do you say anything when you give it to him?

ALAN (*offering it*): Take my sins. Eat them for my sake . . . He always does.

(NUGGET *bows the mask into* ALAN's *palm, then takes a step back to eat.*)

And then he's ready.

DYSART: You can get up on him now?

ALAN: Yes!

DYSART: Do it, then. Mount him.

(ALAN, *lying before* NUGGET, *stretches out on the square. He grasps the top of the thin metal pole embedded in the wood. He whispers his God's name ceremonially.*)

ALAN: Equus! . . . Equus! . . . Equus!

(*He pulls the pole upright. The actor playing* NUGGET *leans forward and grabs it. At the same instant all the other horses lean forward around the circle, each placing a gloved hand on the rail.* ALAN *rises and walks right back to the upstage corner, left.*)

Take me!

(*He runs and jumps high on to* NUGGET's *back.*)

(*crying out*) Ah!

DYSART: What is it?

ALAN: Hurts!

DYSART: Hurts?

ALAN: Knives in his skin! Little knives—all inside my legs.

(NUGGET *mimes restiveness.*)

ALAN: Stay, Equus. No one said Go! . . . That's it. He's good. Equus the Godslave, Faithful and True. Into my hands he commends himself— naked in his chinkle-chankle. (*He punches.*) Stop it! . . . He wants to go so badly.

DYSART: Go, then. Leave me behind. Ride away now, Alan. Now! . . . Now you are alone with Equus.

(ALAN *stiffens his body.*)

ALAN (*ritually*): Equus—son of Fleckwus—son of Neckwus—*Walk.*

(*A hum from the* CHORUS.

   Very slowly the horses standing on the circle begin to turn the square by gently pushing the wooden rail. ALAN *and his mount start to revolve. The effect, immediately is of a statue being slowly turned round on a plinth. During the ride however the speed increases, and the light decreases until it is only a fierce spotlight on horse and rider, with the overspill glinting on the other masks leaning in towards them.*)

Here we go. The King rides out on Equus, mightiest of horses. Only I can ride him. He lets me turn him this way and that. His neck comes out of my body. It lifts in the dark. Equus, my Godslave! . . . Now the King commands you. Tonight, we ride against them all.

DYSART: Who's all?

ALAN: My foes and His.

DYSART: Who are your foes?

ALAN: The Hosts of Hoover. The Hosts of Philco. The Hosts of Pifco. The House of Remington and all its tribe!

DYSART: Who are His foes?

ALAN: The Hosts of Jodhpur. The Hosts of Bowler and Gymkhana. All those who show him off for their vanity. Tie rosettes on his head for their vanity! Come on, Equus. Let's get them! . . . *Trot!*

(*The speed of the turning square increases.*)

Stead-y! Stead-y! Stead-y! Stead-y! Cowboys are watching! Take off their stetsons. They know who we are. They're admiring us! Bowing low unto us! Come on now—show them! *Canter!* . . . CANTER!

(*He whips* NUGGET.)

   And Equus the Mighty rose against All!
   His enemies scatter, his enemies fall!
   TURN!
   Trample them, trample them,
   Trample them, trample them,
   TURN!
   TURN!!
   TURN!!!

(*The Equus noise increases in volume.*)

(*Shouting.*) WEE! . . . WAA! . . . WONDER-FUL! . . .
I'm stiff! Stiff in the wind!
My mane, stiff in the wind!

My flanks! *My* hooves!
Mane on my legs, on my flanks, like whips!
Raw!
Raw!
I'm raw! Raw!
Feel me on you! *On* you! *On* you! *On* you!
I want to be *in* you!
I want to BE you forever and ever!—
Equus, I love you!
Now!—
Bear me away!
Make us One Person!

(*He rides Equus frantically.*)

One Person! One Person! One Person! One Person!

(*He rises up on the horse's back, and calls like a trumpet.*)

Ha-HA! . . . Ha-HA! . . . Ha HA!

(*The trumpet turns to great cries.*)

HA-HA! HA-HA! HA-HA! HA-HA! HA! . . . HA! . . . HAAAAA!

(*He twists like a flame.
   Silence.
   The turning square comes to a stop in the same position it occupied at the opening of the Act.
   Slowly the boy drops off the horse's back on to the ground.
   He lowers his head and kisses* NUGGET's *hoof.
   Finally he flings back his head and cries up to him:*)

AMEN!

(NUGGET *snorts, once.*)

                  BLACKOUT

ACT 2

SCENE 22

Darkness.
   Lights come slowly up on ALAN *kneeling in the night at the hooves of* NUGGET. *Slowly he gets up, climbing lovingly up the body of the horse until he can stand and kiss it.*
   DYSART *sits on the downstage bench where he began Act 1.*

DYSART: With one particular horse, called Nugget, he embraces. He showed me how he stands with it afterwards in the night, one hand on its chest, one on its neck, like a frozen tango dancer,

inhaling its cold sweet breath. "Have you noticed," he said, "about horses: how they'll stand
one hoof on its end, like those girls in the ballet?"

(ALAN *leads* NUGGET *out of the square.* DYSART
*rises. The horse walks away up the tunnel and
disappears. The boy comes downstage and sits on
the bench* DYSART *has vacated.* DYSART *crosses
downstage and moves slowly up round the circle,
until he reaches the central entrance to the
square.*)

Now he's gone off to rest, leaving me alone with
Equus. I can hear the creature's voice. It's calling
me out of the black cave of the Psyche. I shove in
my dim little torch, and there he stands—waiting
for me. He raises his matted head. He opens his
great square teeth, and says—(*Mocking*) "Why? . . .
Why Me? . . . Why—ultimately—Me? . . . Do
you really imagine you can account for Me?
Totally, infallibly, inevitably account for Me? . . .
Poor Doctor Dysart!"

(*He enters the square.*)

Of course I've stared at such images before. Or
been stared at by them, whichever way you look at
it. And weirdly often now with me the feeling is
that *they* are staring at *us*—That in some quite
palpable way they precede us. Meaningless, but
unsettling . . . In either case, this one is the most
alarming yet. It asks questions I've avoided all my
professional life. (*Pause.*) A child is born into a
world of phenomena all equal in their power to
enslave. It sniffs—it sucks—it strokes its eyes over
the whole uncountable range. Suddenly one
strikes. Why? Moments snap together like mag-
nets, forging a chain of shackles. Why? I can trace
them. I can even, with time, pull them apart
again. But why at the start they were ever magne-
tized at all—just those particular moments of
experience and no others—I don't know. *And nor
does anyone else.* Yet *if* I don't know—if I can
never know that—then what am I doing here? I
don't mean clinically doing or socially doing—I
mean *fundamentally!* These questions, these
Whys, are fundamental—yet they have no place
in a consulting room. So then, do I? . . . This is
the feeling more and more with me—No Place.
Displacement. . . . "Account for me," says staring
Equus. "First account for Me! . . ." I fancy this is
more than menopause.

(NURSE *rushes in.*)

NURSE: Doctor! . . . Doctor! There's a terrible

scene with the Strang boy. His mother came to
visit him, and I gave her the tray to take in. He
threw it at her. She's saying the most dreadful
things.

(ALAN *springs up, down left.* DORA *springs up,
down right. They face each other across the
bottom end of the stage. It is observable that at
the start of this Act* FRANK *is not sitting beside
his wife on their bench. It is hopefully not
observable that he is placed among the audience
upstage, in the gloom, by the central tunnel.*)

DORA: Don't you dare! *Don't you dare!*
DYSART: Is she still there?
NURSE: Yes!

(*He quickly leaves the square, followed by the*
NURSE. DORA *moves towards her son.*)

DORA: Don't you look at me like that! I'm not a
doctor, you know, who'll take anything. Don't you
dare give me that stare, young man!

(*She slaps his face.* DYSART *joins them.*)

DYSART: Mrs. Strang!
DORA: I know your stares. They don't work on
me!
DYSART (*to her*): Leave this room.
DORA: What did you say?
DYSART: I tell you to leave here at once.

(DORA *hesitates. Then:*)

DORA: Good-bye, Alan.

(*She walks past her son, and round into the
square.* DYSART *follows her. Both are very upset.*
ALAN *returns to his bench and* NURSE *to her
place.*)

SCENE 23

Lights up on the square.

DYSART: I must ask you never to come here
again.
DORA: Do you think I want to? Do you think I
want to?
DYSART: Mrs. Strang, what on earth has got into
you? Can't you see the boy is highly distressed?
DORA (*ironic*): Really?
DYSART: Of course! He's at a most delicate stage
of treatment. He's totally exposed. Ashamed. Ev-
erything you can imagine!
DORA (*exploding*): *And me? What about me? . . .
What do you think I am? . . .* I'm a parent, of

course—so it doesn't count. That's a dirty word in here, isn't it, "parent"?

DYSART: You know that's not true.

DORA: Oh, I know. I know, all right! I've heard it all my life. It's *our* fault. Whatever happens, *we* did it. Alan's just a little victim. He's really done nothing at all! (*Savagely*) What do you have to do in this world to get any sympathy—blind animals?

DYSART: Sit down, Mrs. Strang.

DORA (*ignoring him: more and more urgently*): Look, Doctor: you don't have to live with this. Alan is one patient to you: one out of many. He's my son. I lie awake every night thinking about it. Frank lies there beside me. I can hear him. Neither of us sleeps all nght. You come to us and say Who forbids television? who does what behind whose back?—as if we're criminals. Let me tell you something. We're not criminals. We've done nothing wrong. We loved Alan. We gave him the best love we could. All right, we quarrel some-times—all parents quarrel—we always make it up. My husband is a good man. He's an upright man, religion or no religion. He cares for his home, for the world, and for his boy. Alan had love and care and treats, and as much fun as any boy in the world. I know about loveless homes: I was a teacher. Our home wasn't loveless. I know about privacy too—not invading a child's privacy. All right, Frank may be at fault there—he digs into him too much—but nothing in excess. He's not a bully. . . . (*Gravely*) No, doctor. Whatever's happened has happened *because of Alan*. Alan is himself. Every soul is itself. If you added up everything we ever did to him, from his first day on earth to this, you wouldn't find why he did this terrible thing—because that's *him*: not just all of our things added up. Do you understand what I'm saying? I want you to understand, because I lie awake and awake thinking it out, and I want you to know that I deny it absolutely what he's doing now, staring at me, attacking me for what *he's* done, for what *he* is! (*Pause; calmer*) You've got your words, and I've got mine. You call it a complex, I suppose. But if you knew God, Doctor, you would know about the Devil. You'd know the Devil isn't made by what mummy says and daddy says. The Devil's *there*. It's an old-fashioned word, but a true thing . . . I'll go. What I did in there was inexcusable. I only know he was my little Alan, and then the Devil came.

(*She leaves the square, and resumes her place.* DYSART *watches her go, then leaves himself by the opposite entrance, and approaches* ALAN.)

SCENE 24

Seated on his bench, the boy glares at him.

DYSART: I thought you liked your mother.

(*Silence.*)

She doesn't know anything, you know. I haven't told her what you told me. You do know that, don't you?

ALAN: It was lies anyway.

DYSART: What?

ALAN: You and your pencil. Just a con trick, that's all.

DYSART: What do you mean?

ALAN: Made me say a lot of lies.

DYSART: Did it? . . . Like what?

ALAN: All of it. Everything I said. Lot of lies.

(*Pause.*)

DYSART: I see.

ALAN: You ought to be locked up. Your bloody tricks.

DYSART: I thought you liked tricks.

ALAN: It'll be the drug next. I know.

(DYSART *turns, sharply.*)

DYSART: What drug?

ALAN: I've heard. I'm not ignorant. I know what you get up to in here. Shove needles in people, pump them full of truth drug, so they can't help saying things. That's next, isn't it?

(*Pause.*)

DYSART: Alan, do you know why you're here?

ALAN: So you can give me truth drugs.

(*He glares at him.*
DYSART *leaves abruptly, and returns to the square.*)

SCENE 25

HESTHER *comes in simultaneously from the other side.*

DYSART (*agitated*): He actually thinks they exist! And of course he wants one.

HESTHER: It doesn't sound like that to me.

DYSART: Of course he does. Why mention them otherwise? He wants a way to speak. To finally tell me what happened in that stable. Tape's too isolated, and hypnosis is a trick. At least that's the pretense.

HESTHER: Does he still say that today?

DYSART: I haven't seen him. I cancelled his appointment this morning, and let him stew in his own anxiety. Now I am almost tempted to play a real trick on him.

HESTHER (*sitting*): Like what?

DYSART: The old placebo.

HESTHER: You mean a harmless pill?

DYSART: Full of *alleged* Truth Drug. Probably an aspirin.

HESTHER: But he'd deny it afterwards. Same thing all over.

DYSART: No. Because he's ready to abreact.

HESTHER: Abreact?

DYSART: Live it all again. He won't be able to deny it after that, because he'll have shown me. Not just told me—but acted it out in front of me.

HESTHER: Can you get him to do that?

DYSART: I think so. He's nearly done it already. Under all that glowering, he trusts me. Do you realise that?

HESTHER (*warmly*): I'm sure he does.

DYSART: Poor bloody fool.

HESTHER: Don't start that again.

(*Pause.*)

DYSART (*quietly*): Can you think of anything worse one can do to anybody than take away their worship?

HESTHER: Worship?

DYSART: Yes, that word again!

HESTHER: Aren't you being a little extreme?

DYSART: Extremity's the point.

HESTHER: Worship isn't destructive, Martin. I know that.

DYSART: I don't. I only know it's the core of his life. What else has he got? Think about him. He can hardly read. He knows no physics or engineering to make the world real for him. No paintings to show him how others have enjoyed it. No music except television jingles. No history except tales from a desperate mother. No friends. Not one kid to give him a joke, or make him know himself more moderately. He's a modern citizen for whom society doesn't exist. He lives *one hour* every three weeks—howling in a mist. And after the service kneels to a slave who stands over him obviously and unthrowably his master. With my body I thee worship! . . . Many men have less vital with their wives.

(*Pause.*)

HESTHER: All the same, they don't usually blind their wives, do they?

DYSART: Oh, come on!

HESTHER: Well, do they?

DYSART (*sarcastically*): You mean he's dangerous? A violent, dangerous madman who's going to run round the country doing it again and again?

HESTHER: I mean he's in pain, Martin. He's been in pain for most of his life. That much, at least, you *know*.

DYSART: Possibly.

HESTHER: *Possibly?* ! . . . That cut-off little figure you just described must have been in pain for years.

DYSART (*doggedly*): Possibly.

HESTHER: And you can take it away.

DYSART: Still—possibly.

HESTHER: Then that's enough. That simply has to be enough for you, surely?

DYSART: No!

HESTHER: Why not?

DYSART: Because it's his.

HESTHER: I don't understand.

DYSART: His pain. His own. He made it.

(*Pause.*)

(*Earnestly*) Look . . . to go through life and call it yours—*your life*—you first have to get your own pain. Pain that's unique to you. You can't just dip into the common bin and say "That's enough!" . . . He's done that. All right, he's sick. He's full of misery and fear. He was dangerous, and could be again, though I doubt it. But that boy has known a passion more ferocious than I have felt in any second of my life. And let me tell you something: I envy it.

HESTHER: You can't.

DYSART (*vehemently*): Don't you see? That's the Accusation! That's what his stare has been saying to me all the time. "*At least I galloped! When did you?*" . . . (*Simply*) I'm jealous, Hesther. Jealous of Alan Strang.

HESTHER: That's absurd.

DYSART: Is it? . . . I go on about my wife. That smug woman by the fire. Have you thought of the fellow on the other side of it? The finicky, critical husband looking through his art books on mythical Greece. What worship has *he* ever known? Real worship! Without worship you shrink, it's as brutal as that . . . I shrank my *own* life. No one can do it for you. I settled for being pallid and provincial, out of my own eternal timidity. The old story of bluster, and do bugger-all . . . I imply that we can't have children: but actually, it's only me. I had myself tested behind her back. The lowest sperm count you could find. And I never told her. That's all I need—her sympathy mixed with resentment

. . . I tell everyone Margaret's the puritan, I'm the pagan. Some pagan! Such wild returns I make to the womb of civilization. Three weeks a year in the Peleponnese, every bed booked in advance, every meal paid for by vouchers, cautious jaunts in hired Fiats, suitcase crammed with Kao-Pectate! Such a fantastic surrender to the primitive. And I use that word endlessly: "primitive." "Oh, the primitive world," I say. "What instinctual truths were lost with it!" And while I sit there, baiting a poor unimaginative woman with the word, that freaky boy tries to conjure the reality! I sit looking at pages of centaurs trampling the soil of Argos—and outside my window he is trying to *become one*, in a Hampshire field! . . . I watch that woman knitting, night after night—a woman I haven't *kissed* in six years—and he stands in the dark for an hour, sucking the sweat off his God's hairy cheek! (*Pause.*) Then in the morning, I put away my books on the cultural shelf, close up the koda-chrome snaps of Mount Olympus, touch my re-production statue of Dionysus for luck—and go off to hospital to treat him for insanity. Do you see?

HESTHER: The boy's in pain, Martin. That's all I see. In the end . . . I'm sorry.

(*He looks at her.* ALAN *gets up from his bench and stealthily places an envelope in the left-hand entrance of the square, then goes back and sits with his back to the audience, as if watching television.*
HESTHER *rises.*)

HESTHER: That stare of his. Have you thought it might not be accusing you at all?
DYSART: What then?
HESTHER: Claiming you.
DYSART: For what?
HESTHER (*mischievously*): A new God.

(*Pause.*)

DYSART: Too conventional, for him. Finding a religion in Psychiatry is really for very ordinary patients.

(*She laughs.*)

HESTHER: Maybe he just wants a new Dad. Or is that too conventional, too? . . . Since you're questioning your profession anyway, perhaps you ought to try it and see.
DYSART (*amused*): I'll talk to you.
HESTHER: Good-bye.

(*She smiles, and leaves him.*)

SCENE 26

DYSART *becomes aware of the letter lying on the floor. He picks it up, opens and reads it.*

ALAN (*speaking stiffly, as* DYSART *reads*): "It is all true, what I said after you tapped the pencil. I'm sorry if I said different. Post Scriptum: I know why I'm in here."

(*Pause.*)

DYSART (*calling, joyfully*): Nurse!

(NURSE *comes in.*)

NURSE: Yes, Doctor?
DYSART (*trying to conceal his pleasure*): Good evening!
NURSE: You're in late tonight.
DYSART: Yes! . . . Tell me, is the Strang boy in bed yet?
NURSE: Oh no, Doctor. He's bound to be up-stairs looking at television. He always watches to the last possible moment. He doesn't like going to his room at all.
DYSART: You mean he's still having nightmares?
NURSE: He had a bad one last night.
DYSART: Would you ask him to come down here, please?
NURSE (*faint surprise*): Now?
DYSART: I'd like a word with him.
NURSE (*puzzled*): Very good, Doctor.
DYSART: If he's not back in his room by lights out, tell Night Nurse not to worry. I'll see he gets back to bed all right. And would you phone my home and tell my wife I may be in late?
NURSE: Yes, Doctor.
DYSART: Ask him to come straight away, please.

(NURSE *goes to the bench, taps* ALAN *on the shoulder, whispers her message in his ear, and returns to her place.* ALAN *stands up and pauses for a second—then steps into the square.*)

SCENE 27

He stands in the doorway, depressed.

DYSART: Hallo.
ALAN: Hallo.
DYSART: I got your letter. Thank you. (*Pause.*) Also the Post Scriptum.
ALAN (*defensively*): That's the right word. My mum told me. It's Latin for "After-writing."
DYSART: How are you feeling?
ALAN: All right.
DYSART: I'm sorry I didn't see you today.

ALAN: You were fed up with me.
DYSART: Yes. (*Pause.*) Can I make it up to you now?
ALAN: What d'you mean?
DYSART: I thought we'd have a session.
ALAN (*startled*): Now?
DYSART: Yes! At dead of night! . . . Better than going to sleep, isn't it?

(*The boy flinches.*)

Alan—look. Everything I say has a trick or a catch. Everything I do is a trick or a catch. That's all I know to do. But they work—and you know that. Trust me.

(*Pause.*)

ALAN: You got another trick, then?
DYSART: Yes.
ALAN: A truth drug?
DYSART: If you like.
ALAN: What's it do?
DYSART: Make it easier for you to talk.
ALAN: Like you can't help yourself?
DYSART: That's right. Like you have to speak the truth at all costs. And all of it.

(*Pause.*)

ALAN (*slyly*): Comes in a needle, doesn't it?
DYSART: No.
ALAN: Where is it?
DYSART (*indicating his pocket*): In here.
ALAN: Let's see.

(DYSART *solemnly takes a bottle of pills out of his pocket.*)

DYSART: There.
ALAN (*suspicious*): That really it?
DYSART: It is . . . Do you want to try it?
ALAN: No.
DYSART: I think you do.
ALAN: I don't. Not at all.
DYSART: Afterwards you'd sleep. You'd have no bad dreams all night. Probably many nights, from then on . . .

(*Pause.*)

ALAN: How long's it take to work?
DYSART: It's instant. Like coffee.
ALAN (*half believing*): It isn't!
DYSART: I promise you . . . Well?
ALAN: Can I have a fag?
DYSART: Pill first. Do you want some water?
ALAN: No.

(DYSART *shakes one out on to his palm.* ALAN *hesitates for a second—then takes it and swallows it.*)

DYSART: Then you can chase it down with this. Sit down.

(*He offers him a cigarette, and lights it for him.*)

ALAN (*nervous*): What happens now?
DYSART: We wait for it to work.
ALAN: What'll I feel first?
DYSART: Nothing much. After a minute, about a hundred green snakes should come out of that cupboard singing the Hallelujah Chorus.
ALAN (*annoyed*): I'm serious!
DYSART (*earnestly*): You'll feel nothing. Nothing's going to happen now but what you want to happen. You're not going to say anything to me but what you want to say. Just relax. Lie back and finish your fag.

(ALAN *stares at him. Then accepts the situation, and lies back.*)

DYSART: Good boy.
ALAN: I bet this room's heard some funny things.
DYSART: It certainly has.
ALAN: I like it.
DYSART: This room?
ALAN: Don't you?
DYSART: Well, there's not much to like, is there?
ALAN: How long am I going to be in here?
DYSART: It's hard to say. I quite see you want to leave.
ALAN: No.
DYSART: You don't?
ALAN: Where would I go?
DYSART: Home. . . .

(*The boy looks at him.* DYSART *crosses and sits on the rail upstage, his feet on the bench. A pause.*)

Actually, I'd like to leave this room and never see it again in my life.
ALAN (*surprise*): Why?
DYSART: I've been in it too long.
ALAN: Where would you go?
DYSART: Somewhere.
ALAN: Secret?
DYSART: Yes. There's a sea—a great sea—I love . . . It's where the Gods used to go to bathe.
ALAN: What Gods?
DYSART: The old ones. Before they died.
ALAN: Gods don't die.
DYSART: Yes, they do.

(Pause.)

There's a village I spent one night in, where I'd like to live. It's all white.

ALAN: How would you Nosey Parker, though? You wouldn't have a room for it any more.

DYSART: I wouldn't mind. I don't actually enjoy being a Nosey Parker, you know.

ALAN: Then why do it?

DYSART: Because you're unhappy.

ALAN: So are you.

(DYSART looks at him sharply. ALAN sits up in alarm.)

Oooh, I didn't mean that!

DYSART: Didn't you?

ALAN: Here—is that how it works? Things just slip out, not feeling anything?

DYSART: That's right.

ALAN: But it's so quick!

DYSART: I told you: it's instant.

ALAN *(delighted)*: It's wicked, isn't it? I mean, you can say anything under it.

DYSART: Yes.

ALAN: Ask me a question.

DYSART: Tell me about Jill.

(Pause. The boy turns away.)

ALAN: There's nothing to tell.

DYSART: Nothing?

ALAN: No.

DYSART: Well, for example—is she pretty? You've never described her.

ALAN: She's all right.

DYSART: What colour hair?

ALAN: Dunno.

DYSART: Is it long or short?

ALAN: Dunno.

DYSART *(lightly)*: You must know that.

ALAN: I don't remember. *I don't!*

(DYSART rises and comes down to him. He takes the cigarette out of his hand.)

DYSART *(firmly)*: Lie back . . . Now listen. You have to do this. And now. You are going to tell me everything that happened with this girl. And not just *tell* me—*show* me. Act it out, if you like—even more than you did when I tapped the pencil. I want you to feel free to do absolutely anything in this room. The pill will help you. I will help you. . . . Now, where does she live?

(A long pause.)

ALAN *(tight)*: Near the stables. About a mile.

(DYSART steps down out of the square as JILL enters it. He sits again on the downstage bench.)

SCENE 28

The light grows warmer.

JILL: It's called The China Pantry.

(She comes down and sits casually on the rail. Her manner is open and lightly provocative. During these scenes ALAN acts directly with her, and never looks over at DYSART when he replies to him.)

When Daddy disappeared, she was left without a bean. She had to earn her own living. I must say she did jolly well, considering she was never trained in business.

DYSART: What do you mean, "disappeared"?

ALAN *(to DYSART)*: He ran off. No one ever saw him again.

JILL: Just left a note on her dressing table saying "Sorry. I've had it." Just like that. She never got over it. It turned her right off men. All my dates have to be sort of secret. I mean, she knows about them, but I can't ever bring anyone back home. She's so rude to them.

ALAN *(to DYSART)*: She was always looking.

DYSART: At you?

ALAN *(to DYSART)*: Saying stupid things.

(She jumps off the bench.)

JILL: You've got super eyes.

ALAN *(to DYSART)*: Anyway, *she* was the one who had them.

(She sits next to him. Embarrassed, the boy tries to move away as far as he can.)

JILL: There was an article in the paper last week saying what points about boys fascinate girls. They said Number One is bottoms. I think it's eyes every time. . . . They fascinate you too, don't they?

ALAN: Me?

JILL *(sly)*: Or is it only horses' eyes?

ALAN *(startled)*: What d'you mean?

JILL: I saw you staring into Nugget's eyes yesterday for ages. I spied on you through the door!

ALAN *(hotly)*: There must have been something in it!

JILL: You're a real Man of Mystery, aren't you?

ALAN *(to DYSART)*: Sometimes, it was like she knew.

DYSART: Did you ever hint?

ALAN *(to DYSART)*: Course not!

JILL: I love horses' eyes. The way you can see yourself in them. D'you find them sexy?

ALAN (*outraged*): What? !

JILL: Horses.

ALAN: Don't be daft!

(*He springs up, and away from her.*)

JILL: Girls do. I mean, they go through a period when they pat them and kiss them a lot. I know *I* did. I suppose it's just a substitute, really.

ALAN (*to* DYSART): That kind of thing, all the time. Until one night . . .

DYSART: Yes? What?

ALAN (*to* DYSART: *defensively*): She did it! Not me. It was her idea, the whole thing! . . . She got me into it!

DYSART: What are you saying? "One night": go on from there.

(*A pause.*)

ALAN (*to* DYSART): Saturday night. We were just closing up.

JILL: How would you like to take me out?

ALAN: What?

JILL (*coolly*): How would you like to take me out tonight?

ALAN: I've got to go home.

JILL: What for?

(*He tries to escape upstage.*)

ALAN: They expect me.

JILL: Ring up and say you're going out.

ALAN: I can't.

JILL: Why?

ALAN: They expect me.

JILL: Look. Either we go out together and have some fun, or you go back to your boring home, *as usual*, and I go back to mine. That's the situation, isn't it?

ALAN: Well . . . where would we go?

JILL: The pictures! There's a skinflick over in Winchester! I've never seen one, have you?

ALAN: No.

JILL: Wouldn't you like to? *I* would. All those heavy Swedes, panting at each other! . . . What d'you say?

ALAN (*grinning*): Yeh! . . .

JILL: Good! . . .

(*He turns away.*)

DYSART: Go on, please.

(*He steps off the square.*)

ALAN (*to* DYSART): I'm tired now!

DYSART: Come on now. You can't stop there.

(*He storms round the circle to* DYSART, *and faces him directly.*)

ALAN: I'm *tired!* I want to go to bed!

DYSART (*sharply*): Well, you can't. I want to hear about the film.

ALAN (*hostile*): Hear what? . . . *What?* . . . It was bloody awful!

(*The actors playing horses come swiftly on to the square, dressed in sports coats or raincoats. They move the benches to be parallel with the audience, and sit on them—staring out front.*)

DYSART: Why?

ALAN: Nosey Parker!

DYSART: *Why?*

ALAN: *Because!* . . . Well—we went into the Cinema!

SCENE 29

A burst of Rock music, instantly fading down. Lights darken.

ALAN *re-enters the square.* JILL *rises and together they grope their way to the downstage bench, as if in a dark auditorium.*

ALAN (*to* DYSART): The whole place was full of men. Jill was the only girl.

(*They push by a patron seated at the end, and sit side by side, staring up at the invisible screen, located above the heads of the main audience. A spotlight hits the boy's face.*)

We sat down and the film came on. It was daft. Nothing happened for ages. There was this girl Brita, who was sixteen. She went to stay in this house, where there was an older boy. He kept giving her looks, but she ignored him completely. In the end she took a shower. She went into the bathroom and took off all her clothes. The lot. Very slowly. . . . What she didn't know was the boy was looking through the door all the time. . . . (*He starts to become excited.*) It was fantastic! The water fell on her breasts, bouncing down her . . .

(FRANK *steps into the square furtively from the back, hat in hand, and stands looking about for a place.*)

DYSART: Was that the first time you'd seen a girl naked?

ALAN (*to* DYSART): Yes! You couldn't see everything, though. . . . (*Looking about him*) All round me they were all looking. All the men—staring up like they were in church. Like they were a sort of congregation. And then—(*He sees his father.*) Ah!

(*At the same instant* FRANK *sees him.*)

FRANK: Alan!
ALAN: God!
JILL: What is it?
ALAN: *Dad!*
JILL: *Where?*
ALAN: At the back! *He saw me!*
JILL: You sure?
ALAN: Yes!
FRANK (*calling*): Alan!
ALAN: Oh God!

(*He tries to hide his face in the girl's shoulder. His father comes down the aisle towards him.*)

FRANK: Alan! You can hear me! Don't pretend!
PATRONS: *Ssssh!*
FRANK (*approaching the row of seats*): Do I have to come and fetch you out? . . . Do I? . . .

(*Cries of "Sssh!" and "Shut up!"*)

Do I, Alan?
ALAN (*through gritted teeth*): Oh, fuck!

(*He gets up as the noise increases.* JILL *gets up too and follows him.*)

DYSART: You went?
ALAN (*to* DYSART): What else could I do? He kept shouting. Everyone was saying Shut up!

(*They go out, right, through the group of* PA-TRONS—*who rise protesting as they pass, quickly replace the benches and leave the square.*
DYSART *enters it.*)

SCENE 30

Light brightens from the cinema, but remains cold: streets at night.
  The three walk round the circle downstage in a line: FRANK *leading, wearing his hat. He halts in the middle of the left rail, and stands staring straight ahead of him, rigid with embarrassment.*
  ALAN *is very agitated.*

ALAN (*to* DYSART): We went into the street, all three of us. It was weird. We just stood there by the bus stop—like we were three people in a queue, and we didn't know each other. Dad was all white and sweaty. He didn't look at us at all. It must have

gone on for about five minutes. I tried to speak. I said—(*To his father*) I—I—I've never been there before. Honest . . . Never . . . (*To* DYSART) He didn't seem to hear. Jill tried.
JILL: It's true. Mr. Strang. It wasn't Alan's idea to go there. It was mine.
ALAN (*to* DYSART): He just went on staring, straight ahead. It was awful.
JILL: I'm not shocked by films like that. I think they're just silly.
ALAN (*to* DYSART): The bus wouldn't come. We just stood and stood. . . . Then suddenly he spoke.

(FRANK *takes off his hat.*)

FRANK (*stiffly*): I'd like you to know something. Both of you. I came here tonight to see the Manager. He asked me to call on him for business purposes. I happen to be a printer, Miss. A picture house needs posters. That's entirely why I'm here. To discuss posters. While I was waiting I happened to glance in, that's all. I can only say I'm going to complain to the council. I had no idea they showed films like this. I'm certainly going to refuse my services.
JILL (*kindly*): Yes, of course.
FRANK: So long as that's understood.
ALAN (*to* DYSART) Then the bus came along.
FRANK: Come along now, Alan.

(*He moves away downstage.*)

ALAN: No.
FRANK (*turning*): No fuss, please. Say Good-night to the young lady.
ALAN (*timid but firm*): No. I'm stopping here . . . I've got to see her home . . . It's proper.

(*Pause.*)

FRANK (*as dignified as possible*): Very well. I'll see you when you choose to return. Very well then . . . Yes . . .

(*He walks back to his original seat, next to his wife. He stares across the square at his son—who stares back at him. Then, slowly, he sits.*)

ALAN (*to* DYSART): And he got in, and we didn't. He sat down and looked at me through the glass. And I saw . . .
DYSART (*soft*): What?
ALAN (*to* DYSART): His face. It was scared.
DYSART: Of you?
ALAN (*to* DYSART): It was terrible. We had to walk home. Four miles. I got the shakes.
DYSART: You were scared, too?

ALAN (*to* DYSART): It was like a hole had been drilled in my tummy. A hole—right here. And the air was getting in!

(*He starts to walk upstage, round the circle.*)

SCENE 31

The girl stays still.

JILL (*aware of other people looking*): Alan . . .
ALAN (*to* DYSART): People kept turning round in the street to look.
JILL: Alan!
ALAN (*to* DYSART): I kept seeing him, just as he drove off. Scared of me. . . . And me scared of *him.* . . . I kept thinking—all those airs he put on! . . . "Receive my meaning. Improve your mind!" . . . All those nights he said he'd be in late. "Keep my supper hot, Dora!" "Your poor father: he works so hard!" . . . Bugger! Old bugger! . . . Filthy old bugger!

(*He stops, clenching his fists.*)

JILL: Hey! Wait for me!

(*She runs after him. He waits.*)

What are you thinking about?
ALAN: Nothing.
JILL: Mind my own beeswax?

(*She laughs.*)

ALAN (*to* DYSART): And suddenly she began to laugh.
JILL: I'm sorry. But it's pretty funny, when you think of it.
ALAN (*bewildered*): What?
JILL: Catching him like that! I mean, it's terrible—but it's very funny.
ALAN: Yeh!

(*He turns from her.*)

JILL: No, wait! . . . I'm sorry. I know you're upset. But it's not the end of the world, is it? I mean, what was he doing? Only what we were. Watching a silly film. It's a case of like father like son, I'd say! . . . I mean, when that girl was taking a shower, you were pretty interested, weren't you?

(*He turns round and looks at her.*)

We keep saying old people are square. Then when they suddenly aren't—we don't like it!
DYSART: What did you think about that?
ALAN (*to* DYSART): I don't know. I kept looking

at all the people in the street. They were mostly men coming out of pubs. I suddenly thought— *they all do it! All of them!* . . . They're not just Dads—they're people with pricks! . . . And Dad— he's just not Dad either. He's a man with a prick, too. You know, I'd never thought about it.

(*Pause.*)

We went into the country.

(*He walks again.* JILL *follows. They turn the corner and come downstage, right.*)

We kept walking. I just thought about Dad, and how he was nothing special—just a poor old sod on his own.

(*He stops.*)

(*To* JILL: *realising it*) Poor old sod!

JILL: That's right!
ALAN (*grappling with it*): I mean, what else has he got? . . . He's got mum, of course, but well— she—she—she—
JILL: She doesn't give him anything?
ALAN: That's right. I bet you . . . She doesn't give him anything. That's right . . . That's really right! . . . She likes Ladies and Gentlemen. Do you understand what I mean?
JILL (*mischievously*): Ladies and gentlemen aren't naked?
ALAN: That's right! Never! . . . *Never!* That would be disgusting! She'd have to put bowler hats on them! . . . Jodhpurs!

(JILL *laughs.*)

DYSART: Was that the first time you ever thought anything like that about your mother? . . . I mean, that she was unfair to your dad?
ALAN (*to* DYSART): Absolutely!
DYSART: How did you feel?
ALAN (*to* DYSART): Sorry. I mean for him. Poor old sod, that's what I felt—he's just like me! He hates ladies and gents just like me! Posh things— and la-di-da. He goes off by himself at night, and does his own secret thing which no one'll know about, just like me! There's no difference—he's just the same as me—just the same!—

(*He stops in distress, then bolts back a little upstage.*)

Christ!

DYSART (*sternly*): Go on.
ALAN (*to* DYSART): I can't.

DYSART: Of course you can. You're doing wonderfully.

ALAN (*to* DYSART): No, please. *Don't make me!*

DYSART (*firm*): Don't think: just answer. You were happy at that second, weren't you? When you realised about your dad. How lots of people have secrets, not just you?

ALAN (*to* DYSART): Yes.

DYSART: You felt sort of free, didn't you? I mean, free to do anything?

ALAN (*to* DYSART, *looking at* JILL): Yes!

DYSART: What was she doing?

ALAN (*to* DYSART): Holding my hand.

DYSART: And that was good?

ALAN (*to* DYSART): Oh, yes!

DYSART: Remember what you thought. *As if it's happening to you now. This very moment* . . . What's in your head?

ALAN (*to* DYSART): Her eyes. *She's* the one with eyes! . . . I keep looking at them, because I really want—

DYSART: To look at her breasts?

ALAN (*to* DYSART): Yes.

DYSART: Like in the film.

ALAN (*to* DYSART): Yes . . . Then she starts to scratch my hand.

JILL: You're really very nice, you know that?

ALAN (*to* DYSART): Moving her nails on the back. Her face so warm. Her eyes.

DYSART: You want her very much?

ALAN (*to* DYSART): Yes . . .

JILL: I love your eyes.

(*She kisses him.*)

(*Whispering*) Let's go!

ALAN: Where?

JILL: I know a place. It's right near here.

ALAN: Where?

JILL: Surprise! . . . Come on!

(*She darts away round the circle, across the stage and up the left side.*)

Come *on!*

ALAN (*to* DYSART): She runs ahead. I follow. And then—and then—!

(*He halts.*)

DYSART: What?

ALAN (*to* DYSART): I see what she means.

DYSART: What? . . . Where are you? . . . Where has she taken you?

ALAN (*to* JILL): *The Stables?*

JILL: Of course!

CHORUS *makes a warning hum.*

The horse-actors enter, and ceremonially put on their masks—first raising them high above their heads. NUGGET *stands in the central tunnel.*

ALAN (*recoiling*): No!

JILL: Where else? They're perfect!

ALAN: No!

(*He turns his head from her.*)

JILL: Or do you want to go home now and face your dad?

ALAN: No!

JILL: Then come on!

(*He edges nervously past the horse standing at the left, which turns its neck and even moves a challenging step after him.*)

ALAN: Why not your place?

JILL: I can't. Mother doesn't like me bringing back boys. I told you. . . . Anyway, the Barn's better.

ALAN: No!

JILL: All that straw. It's cosy.

ALAN: No.

JILL: *Why not?*

ALAN: Them!

JILL: Dalton will be in bed . . . What's the matter? . . . Don't you want to?

ALAN (*aching to*): Yes!

JILL: So?

ALAN (*desperate*): Them! . . . Them! . . .

JILL: *Who?*

ALAN (*low*): Horses.

JILL: *Horses?* . . . You're really dotty, aren't you? . . . What do you mean?

(*He starts shaking.*)

Oh, you're freezing . . . Let's get under the straw. You'll be warm there.

ALAN (*pulling away*): No!

JILL: What on earth's the matter with you? . . .

(*Silence. He won't look at her.*)

Look, if the sight of horses offends you, my lord, we can just shut the door. You won't have to see them. All right?

DYSART: What door is that? In the barn?

ALAN (*to* DYSART): Yes.

DYSART: So what do you do? You go in?

ALAN (*to* DYSART): Yes.

SCENE 33

A rich light falls.

Furtively ALAN *enters the square from the top end, and* JILL *follows. The horses on the circle retire out of sight on either side.* NUGGET *retreats up the tunnel and stands where he can just be glimpsed in the dimness.*

DYSART: Into the Temple? The Holy of Holies?

ALAN (*to* DYSART: *desperate*): What else can I do? . . . I can't say! I can't tell her. . . . (*To* JILL) Shut it tight.

JILL: All right . . . You're crazy!

ALAN: Lock it.

JILL: Lock?

ALAN: Yes.

JILL: It's just an old door. What's the matter with you? They're in their boxes. They can't get out . . . Are you all right?

ALAN: Why?

JILL: You look weird.

ALAN: *Lock it!*

JILL: Ssssh! D'you want to wake up Dalton? . . . Stay there, idiot.

(*She mimes locking a heavy door, upstage.*)

DYSART: Describe the barn, please.

ALAN (*walking round it: to* DYSART): Large room. Straw everywhere. Some tools . . . (*as if picking it up off the rail where he left it in Act 1*) A hoof-pick! . . .

(*He "drops" it hastily, and dashes away from the spot.*)

DYSART: Go on.

ALAN (*to* DYSART): At the end this big door. Behind it—

DYSART: Horses.

ALAN (*to* DYSART): Yes.

DYSART: How many?

ALAN (*to* DYSART): Six.

DYSART: Jill closes the door so you can't see them?

ALAN (*to* DYSART): Yes.

DYSART: And then? . . . What happens now? . . . Come on, Alan. Show me.

JILL: See, it's all shut. There's just us . . . Let's sit down. Come on.

(*They sit together on the same bench, left.*)

Hallo.

ALAN (*quickly*): Hallo.

(*She kisses him lightly. He responds. Suddenly a* faint trampling of hooves, off-stage, makes him jump up.*)

JILL: What is it?

(*He turns his head upstage, listening.*)

Relax, there's no one there. Come here.

(*She touches his hand. He turns to her again.*)

You're very gentle. I love that . . .

ALAN: So are you . . . I mean . . .

(*He kisses her spontaneously. The hooves trample again, harder. He breaks away from her abruptly towards the upstage corner.*)

JILL (*rising*): What is it?

ALAN: Nothing!

(*She moves towards him. He turns and moves past her. He is clearly distressed. She contemplates him for a moment.*)

JILL (*gently*): Take your sweater off.

ALAN: What?

JILL: I will, if you will.

(*He stares at her. A pause.*

She lifts her sweater over head: he watches— then unzips his. They each remove their shoes, their socks, and their jeans. Then they look at each other diagonally across the square, in which the light is gently increasing.)

ALAN: You're . . . You're very . . .

JILL: So are you. . . . (*Pause.*) Come here.

(*He goes to her. She comes to him. They meet in the middle, and hold each other, and embrace.*)

ALAN (*to* DYSART): She put her mouth in mine. It was lovely! *Oh, it was lovely!*

(*They burst into giggles. He lays her gently on the floor in the centre of the square, and bends over her eagerly. Suddenly the noise of Equus fills the place. Hooves smash on wood. Alan straightens up, rigid. He stares straight ahead of him over the prone body of the girl.*)

DYSART: Yes, what happened then, Alan?

ALAN (*to* DYSART: *brutally*): I put it in her!

DYSART: Yes?

ALAN (*to* DYSART): I put it in her.

DYSART: You did?

ALAN (*to* DYSART): Yes!

DYSART: Was it easy?

ALAN (*to* DYSART): Yes.

DYSART: Describe it.

ALAN (*to* DYSART): I told you.

DYSART: More exactly.

ALAN (*to* DYSART): I put it in her!

DYSART: Did you?

ALAN (*to* DYSART): All the way!

DYSART: Did you, Alan?

ALAN (*to* DYSART): All the way. I shoved it. I put it in her all the way.

DYSART: Did you?

ALAN (*to* DYSART): Yes!

DYSART: Did you?

ALAN (*to* DYSART): Yes! . . . Yes!

DYSART: Give me the TRUTH! . . . Did you? . . . *Honestly?*

ALAN (*to* DYSART): Fuck off!

(*He collapses, lying upstage on his face.* JILL *lies on her back motionless, her head downstage, her arms extended behind her. A pause.*)

DYSART (*gently*): What was it? You couldn't? Though you wanted to very much?

ALAN (*to* DYSART): I couldn't . . . see her.

DYSART: What do you mean?

ALAN (*to* DYSART): Only Him. Every time I kissed her—*He* was in the way.

DYSART: Who?

(ALAN *turns on his back.*)

ALAN (*to* DYSART): You *know* who! . . . When I touched her, I felt *Him*. Under me . . . His side, waiting for my hand . . . His flanks . . . I refused him. I looked. I looked right at her . . . and I couldn't do it. When I shut my eyes, I saw him at once. The streaks on his belly . . . (*With more desperation*) I couldn't feel *her* flesh at all! I wanted the foam off his neck. His sweaty hide. Not flesh. Hide! Horse-hide! . . . Then I couldn't even kiss her.

(JILL *sits up.*)

JILL: What is it?

ALAN (*dodging her hand*): No!

(*He scrambles up and crouches in the corner against the rails, like a little beast in a cage.*)

JILL: Alan!

ALAN: Stop it!

(JILL *gets up.*)

JILL: It's all right . . . It's all right . . . Don't worry about it. It often happens—honest. . . . There's nothing wrong. I don't mind, you know . . . I don't at all.

(*He dashes past her downstage.*)

Alan, look at me . . . Alan? . . . Alan!

(*He collapses again by the rail.*)

ALAN: Get out!

JILL: What?

ALAN (*soft*): Out!

JILL: There's nothing wrong: believe me! It's very common.

ALAN: *Get out!*

(*He snatches up the invisible pick.*)

GET OUT!

JILL: Put that down!

ALAN: Leave me alone!

JILL: Put that down, Alan. It's very dangerous. Go on, please—drop it.

(*He "drops" it, and turns from her.*)

ALAN: You ever tell anyone. Just you tell . . .

JILL: Who do you think I am? . . . I'm your friend—Alan . . .

(*She goes towards him.*)

Listen: you don't have to do anything. Try to realize that. Nothing at all. Why don't we just lie here together in the straw. And talk.

ALAN (*low*): Please . . .

JILL: Just talk.

ALAN: *Please!*

JILL: All right, I'm going . . . Let me put my clothes on first.

(*She dresses, hastily.*)

ALAN: You tell anyone! . . . Just tell and see. . . .

JILL: *Oh, stop it!* . . . I wish you could believe me. It's not in the least important.

(*Pause.*)

Anyway, I won't say anything. You know that. You know I won't. . . .

(*Pause. He stands with his back to her.*)

Goodnight, then, Alan. . . . I wish—I really wish—

(*He turns on her, hissing. His face is distorted— possessed. In horrified alarm she turns—fumbles the door open—leaves the barn—shuts the door hard behind her, and dashes up the tunnel out of sight, past the barely visible figure of* NUGGET.)

Scene 34

ALAN *stands alone, and naked.*

A faint humming and drumming. The boy looks about him in growing terror.

DYSART: What?

ALAN (*to* DYSART): He was there. Through the door. The door was shut, but he was there! . . . He'd seen everything. I could hear him. He was laughing.

DYSART: Laughing?

ALAN (*to* DYSART): Mocking! . . . *Mocking!* . . .

(*Standing downstage he stares up towards the tunnel. A great silence weighs on the square.*)

(*To the silence: terrified.*) Friend . . . Equus the Kind . . . The Merciful! . . . *Forgive me!* . . .

(*Silence.*)

It wasn't me. Not really me. Me! . . . Forgive me! . . . Take me back again! Please! . . . PLEASE!

(*He kneels on the downstage lip of the square, still facing the door, huddling in fear.*)

I'll never do it again. I swear . . . I swear! . . .

(*Silence.*)

(*In a moan*) Please! ! ! . . .

DYSART: And He? What does He say?

ALAN (*to* DYSART: *whispering*): "Mine! . . . You're mine! . . . I am yours and you are mine!" . . . Then I see his eyes. They are rolling!

(NUGGET *begins to advance slowly, with relentless hooves, down the central tunnel.*)

"I see you. I see you. Always! Everywhere! Forever!"

DYSART: Kiss anyone and I will see?

ALAN (*to* DYSART): Yes!

DYSART: And you will fail! Forever and ever you will *fail!* You will see ME—and you will FAIL!

(*The boy turns round, hugging himself in pain. From the sides two more horses converge with* NUGGET *on the rails. Their hooves stamp angrily. The Equus noise is heard more terribly.*)

The Lord thy God is a Jealous God. He sees you. He sees you forever and ever, Alan. He sees you! . . . *He sees you!*

ALAN (*in terror*): Eyes! . . . White eyes—never closed! Eyes like flames—coming—coming! . . . God seest! God seest! . . . NO! . . .

(*Pause. He steadies himself. The stage begins to blacken.*)

(*Quieter*) No more. No more, Equus.

(*He gets up. He goes to the bench. He takes up the invisible pick. He moves slowly upstage towards* NUGGET, *concealing the weapon behind his naked back, in the growing darkness. He stretches out his hand and fondles* NUGGET'*s mask.*)

(*Gently*) Equus . . . Noble Equus . . . Faithful and True . . . Godslave . . . Thou—God—Seest— NOTHING!

(*He stabs out* NUGGET'*s eyes. The horse stamps in agony. A great screaming begins to fill the theatre, growing ever louder.* ALAN *dashes at the other two horses and blinds them too, stabbing over the rails. Their metal hooves join in the stamping.*

Relentlessly, as this happens, three more horses appear in cones of light: not naturalistic animals like the first three, but dreadful creatures out of nightmare. Their eyes flare—their nostrils flare—their mouths flare. They are archetypal images—judging, punishing, pitiless. They do not halt at the rail, but invade the square. As they trample at him, the boy leaps desperately at them, jumping high and naked in the dark, slashing at their heads with arms upraised.

The screams increase. The other horses follow into the square. The whole place is filled with cannoning, blinded horses—and the boy dodging among them, avoiding their slashing hooves as best he can. Finally they plunge off into darkness and away out of sight. The noise dies abruptly, and all we hear is ALAN *yelling in hysteria as he collapses on the ground—stabbing at his own eyes with the invisible pick.*)

ALAN: Find me! . . . Find me! . . . Find me! . . . KILL ME! . . . KILL ME! . . .

Scene 35

The light changes quickly back to brightness. DYSART *enters swiftly, hurls a blanket on the left bench, and rushes over to* ALAN. *The boy is having convulsions on the floor.* DYSART *grabs his hands, forces them from his eyes, scoops him up in his arms and carries him over to the bench.* ALAN *hurls his arms round* DYSART *and clings to him, gasping and kicking his legs in dreadful frenzy.*

DYSART *lays him down and presses his head back on the bench. He keeps talking—urgently talking—soothing the agony as he can.*

DYSART: Here . . . Here . . . Sssssh . . . Sssssh . . . Calm now . . . Lie back. *Just lie back!* Now breathe in deep. Very deep. In . . . Out . . . In . . . Out . . . That's it. . . . In. . . . *Out* . . . *In* . . . *Out* . . .

(The boy's breath is drawn into his body with a harsh rasping sound, which slowly grows less. DYSART *puts the blanket over him.)*

Keep it going . . . That's a good boy . . . Very good boy . . . It's all over now, Alan. It's all over. He'll go away now. You'll never see him again, I promise. You'll have no more bad dreams. No more awful nights. Think of that! . . . You are going to be well. I'm going to make you well, I promise you. . . . You'll be here for a while, but I'll be here too, so it won't be so bad. Just trust me . . .

(He stands upright. The boy lies still.)

Sleep now. Have a good long sleep. You've earned it. . . . Sleep. Just sleep. . . . I'm going to make you well.

(He steps backwards into the centre of the square. The light brightens some more. A pause.)

DYSART: I'm lying to you, Alan. He won't really go that easily. Just clop away from you like a nice old nag. Oh, no! When Equus leaves—if he leaves at all—it will be with your intestines in his teeth. And I don't stock replacements. . . . If you knew anything, you'd get up this minute and run from me fast as you could.

(HESTHER speaks from her place.)

HESTHER: The boy's in pain, Martin.
DYSART: Yes.
HESTHER: And you can take it away.
DYSART: Yes.
HESTHER: Then that has to be enough for you, surely? . . . In the end!
DYSART *(crying out)*: All right! *I'll take it away!* He'll be delivered from madness. *What then?* He'll feel himself acceptable! *What then?* Do you think feelings like his can be simply reattached, like plasters? Stuck on to other objects we select? *Look at him!* . . . My desire might be to make this boy an ardent husband—a caring citizen—a wor-

shipper of abstract and unifying God. My achievement, however, is more likely to make a ghost! . . . Let me tell you exactly what I'm going to do to him!

(He steps out of the square and walks round the upstage end of it, storming at the audience.)

I'll heal the rash on his body. I'll erase the welts cut into his mind by flying manes. When that's done, I'll set him on a nice mini-scooter and send him puttering off into the Normal world where animals are treated *properly:* made extinct, or put into servitude, or tethered all their lives in dim light, just to feed it! I'll give him the good Normal world where we're tethered beside them—blinking our nights away in a nonstop drench of cathode-ray over our shrivelling heads! I'll take away his Field of Ha Ha, and give him Normal places for his ecstasy—multi-lane highways driven through the guts of cities, extinguishing Place altogether, *even the idea of Place!* He'll trot on his metal pony tamely through the concrete evening—and one thing I promise you: he will never touch hide again! With any luck his private parts will come to feel as plastic to him as the products of the factory to which he will almost certainly be sent. Who knows? He may even come to find sex funny. Smirky funny. Bit of grunt funny. Trampled and furtive and entirely in control. Hopefully, he'll feel nothing at his fork but Approved Flesh. *I doubt, however, with much passion! . . .* Passion, you see can be destroyed by a doctor. It cannot be created.

(He addresses ALAN *directly, in farewell.)*

You won't gallop any more, Alan. Horses will be quite safe. You'll save your pennies every week, till you can change that scooter in for a car, and put the odd fifty P on the gee-gees, quite forgetting that they were ever anything more to you than bearers of little profits and little losses. You will, however, be without pain. More or less completely without pain.

(Pause.
He speaks directly to the theatre, standing by the motionless body of ALAN STRANG, *under the blanket.)*

And now for me it never stops: that voice of Equus out of the cave—"Why Me? . . . Why Me? . . . Account for Me!" . . . All right—I surrender! I say it . . . In an ultimate sense I cannot know what I do in this place—yet I do ultimate things. Essentially I cannot know what I do—yet I do essential things. Irreversible, terminal things. I stand in the dark with a pick in my hand, striking at heads!

(*He moves away from* ALAN, *back to the down-stage bench, and finally sits.*)

I need—more desperately than my children need me—a way of seeing in the dark. What way is this? . . . *What dark is this?* . . . I cannot call it ordained of God: I can't get that far. I will however pay it so much homage. There is now, in my mouth, this sharp chain. And it never comes out.

(*A long pause.* DYSART *sits staring.*)

BLACKOUT

COMMENTARY

The first tragedy in this book is Sophocles's *Oedipus the King* (about 430 B.C.). It is a commonplace of dramatic criticism that *Oedipus* is a sort of detective story in which the detective, Oedipus, searches for the criminal and discovers that he himself is the object of his search. Part of the greatness of the play surely resides in the fact that Oedipus, in his relentless search for the truth, strips away all comforting illusions, pursuing his quest even when it becomes evident that he himself may be the culprit. Oedipus' triumph, and, in part, ours as we watch him, is that he is determined to know the truth at whatever cost.

In some ways, Peter Shaffer's *Equus*, too, is a sort of detective story. We are told at the start of the play that Alan Strang has blinded six horses. As the play progresses, we learn, through the psychiatrist's careful analytic or detective work, why Alan blinded the horses. The analyst uses the devices of a detective: for example, he invites himself to the boy's home to see what he can learn, and he does so on a Sunday: "If there's any tension over religion, it should be evident on a Sabbath evening." And bit by bit the full story of the crime is revealed. In Scene 6 we are told that Alan screams something that sounds like "Ek," but not until Scene 14 is this puzzle explained, when Alan's father mentions that he heard the boy say, "Equus my only begotten son." Similarly, we first hear about Jill, very casually, in Scene 12, but not until much later do we understand the part she played in Alan's life.

Alan at first seems to be a fairly ordinary boy; but of course he is not. Although it is risky enough even for experts to try to psychoanalyze real people, and it is usually foolish to try to psychoanalyze characters in a play, it seems fairly clear that Alan is schizoid. That is, he has markedly withdrawn from reality. As the play progresses, we come to see that Alan, like the classic schizophrenic—at least as understood by R. D. Laing in *The Politics of Experience* (1967)—allows his outer self to live in the normal world (Alan lives a humdrum life at home and in the electrical supply store) but preserves an inner self that is radically contemptuous of the normal world and that sometimes suddenly shows itself in some violent, unsocial action. The inner life of such a person is more "real" than the outer, daily bodily life, and so Alan can insist to his god Equus, after the abortive sexual episode with Jill, "It wasn't me. Not really me." This is not mere weaseling; for the schizophrenic, there is a sharp separation between the real, inner "me" and the body that goes through a daily hateful routine.

It is interesting to note that in the early drafts of the play both parents were religiously obsessed, but Shaffer reduced the mother's obsession and eliminated the father's, lest the audience find the boy too obvious or neat a case. As we shall see, the boy is not supposed to be understood as the sick manifestation of sick parents. The play seeks to be much more than a dramatization of schizoid behavior, and that is why it concerns us. It claims, finally, not to present one strange case but to offer a vision of life. (Similarly, if Sophocles's *Oedipus the King* were merely a dramatization of a man who killed his father and married his mother—if it were simply a dramatization of a curious episode rooted in the Oedipus complex—rather than a dramatization of what can be taken as a story of a hero, it would scarcely be of interest to more than a few psychiatrists.)

Any comments on what a play is "about" must, of course, be imprecise, for a play consists of thousands of details that inevitably make any summary and brief interpretation a distortion. Still, we can say that the play dramatizes not a curious case history but the tragic conflict between the world of passion and mystery and the world of numbness and sociability. We have seen glimpses of some such conflict in other tragedies: Oedipus's passionate desire to find out the truth about his origins versus Iocasta's sensible suggestion that it is best to let sleeping dogs lie; or King Lear's madness on the heath ("I abjure all roofs") versus his wicked daughters' seemingly reasonable view that old men should not try to hang on to the power they cannot effectively wield. The paradox in this play is that Dysart, the apparently rational psychiatrist who is charged with restoring Alan to the normal world, envies Alan's irrationality. It is Dysart's fate to be married to a dentist, a thoroughly sensible Scottish woman who cannot share his interest in the world of ancient art and ritual:

> I pass her a picture of the sacred acrobats of Crete leaping through the horns of running bulls—and she'll say "Och, Martin, what an *absurred* thing to be doing! The Highland Games, now there's a *norrmal sport!*" Or, she'll observe, just after I've told her a story from the Iliad: "You know, when you come to think of it, Agamemnon and that lot were nothing but a bunch of ruffians from the Gorbals, only with fancy names!" You get the picture. She's turned into a Shrink.

But what of Dysart himself? Is he an Alan who has somehow bridged the gulf and managed to live a socially useful life? First of all, as he knows, he has none of Alan's passion. His trips to Greece are not "wild returns . . . to the womb of civilization":

> Three weeks a year in the Peloponnese, every bed booked in advance, every meal paid for by vouchers, cautious jaunts in hired Fiats, suitcase crammed with Kao-Pectate! Such a fantastic surrender to the primitive. And I use that word endlessly: "primitive." "Oh, the primitive world," I say. "What instinctual truths were lost with it!" . . . I sit looking at pages of centaurs trampling the soil of Argos—and outside my window he is trying to *become one*, in a Hampshire field!

Dysart's awareness of his own lack of deep feeling and of separation from mystery makes him envy Alan, particularly Alan's pain. "His pain. His own. He made it." It is a curious fact that as we look at the sufferings of tragic characters—Oedipus insisting on an agonizing search for the truth that culminates when he blinds himself, Lear rejecting the shelter of a daughter's roof in preference to a stormy heath—we feel that these sufferings are, in a way, their most precious possession. Lesser people are numbed by sufferings, but by taking on sufferings tragic heroes somehow fulfill themselves. They choose their way of life, and all that it entails. With Melville's Ahab they say, "Oh, now I feel my topmost greatness lies in my topmost grief." Some such awareness causes Dysart to say, "That boy has known a passion more ferocious than I have felt in any second of my life. And let me tell you something: I envy it." He has been critical of his way, and he goes on to dissect his own failure:

> The finicky, critical husband looking through his art books on mythical Greece. What worship has *he* ever known? Real worship! Without worship you shrink, it's as brutal as that . . . I shrank my own life.

If Alan's tragedy is that he has chosen a life radically different from the normal world's, and so he must suffer for it, Dysart's is that he chose the normal world, and thus he suffers—though less intensely—from the knowledge that he has made the wrong choice.

TOPICS FOR DISCUSSION

1. Shaffer describes the set for *Equus* as "tiers of seats in the fashion of a dissecting theatre." The tiers surround a square that "resembles a railed boxing ring." What does this set contribute to the play?
2. On the first night after he meets Alan, Dysart dreams that he sacrifices children to the "normal." In this play, how is the normal world presented?
3. The film version of *Equus* used real horses rather than actors wearing stylized masks. Do you think that this was a good idea or a poor idea? Would the element of reality add to or detract from the play?
4. The nudity in scene 33 aroused much comment when the play was first produced. Do you think it is theatrically meaningful, or merely sensational? Or what?

THE DUMB WAITER

Harold Pinter

Harold Pinter (b. 1930) was born in London, the son of a tailor. He attended the Royal Academy of Dramatic Art, and from 1949 until 1957 he acted in a touring repertory company throughout the British Isles. In 1957 he wrote his first play; later in the same year he wrote *The Dumb Waiter*—though it was not produced until 1960. Another play, *The Birthday Party*, was produced in 1958. He won critical acclaim finally with *The Caretaker* in 1960. Besides *The Homecoming* (1965), he has written radio and television scripts, and several films, most notably *The Servant* and *The Go-Between*. His as yet unproduced film adaptation of Marcel Proust's *Remembrance of Things Past* was published in 1977.

CHARACTERS

BEN
GUS

A scene from *The Dumb Waiter*. (Photograph: Joseph Abeles Studio.)

Scene: A basement room. Two beds, flat against the back wall. A serving hatch, closed, between the beds. A door to the kitchen and lavatory, left. A door to a passage, right.

BEN *is lying on a bed, left, reading a paper.* GUS *is sitting on a bed, right, tying his shoe laces, with difficulty. Both are dressed in shirts, trousers and braces.*

Silence.

GUS *ties his laces, rises, yawns and begins to walk slowly to the door, left. He stops, looks down, and shakes his foot.*

BEN *lowers his paper and watches him.* GUS *kneels and unties his shoe-lace and slowly takes off the shoe. He looks inside it and brings out a flattened matchbox. He shakes it and examines it. Their eyes meet.* BEN *rattles his paper and reads.* GUS *puts the matchbox in his pocket and bends down to put on his shoe. He ties his lace, with difficulty.* BEN *lowers his paper and watches him.* GUS *walks to the door, left, stops, and shakes the other foot. He kneels, unties his shoe-lace, and slowly takes off the shoe. He looks inside it and brings out a flattened cigarette packet. He shakes it and examines it. Their eyes meet.* BEN *rattles his paper and reads.* GUS *puts the packet in his pocket, bends down, puts on his shoe and ties the lace.*

He wanders off, left.

BEN *slams the paper down on the bed and glares after him. He picks up the paper and lies on his back, reading.*

Silence.

A lavatory chain is pulled twice off, but the lavatory does not flush.

Silence.

GUS *re-enters, left, and halts at the door, scratching his head.* BEN *slams down the paper.*

BEN: Kaw!

(*He picks up the paper.*)

What about this? Listen to this!

(*He refers to the paper.*)

A man of eighty-seven wanted to cross the road. But there was a lot of traffic, see? He couldn't see how he was going to squeeze through. So he crawled under a lorry.

GUS: He what?

BEN: He crawled under a lorry. A stationary lorry.

GUS: No?

BEN: The lorry started and ran over him.

GUS: Go on!

BEN: That's what it says here.

GUS: Get away.

BEN: It's enough to make you want to puke, isn't it?

GUS: Who advised him to do a thing like that?

BEN: A man of eighty-seven crawling under a lorry!

GUS: It's unbelievable.

BEN: It's down here in black and white.

GUS: Incredible.

(*Silence.*

GUS *shakes his head and exits.* BEN *lies back and reads.*

The lavatory chain is pulled once off left, but the lavatory does not flush.

BEN *whistles at an item in the paper.*

GUS *re-enters.*)

I want to ask you something.

BEN: What are you doing out there?

GUS: Well, I was just—

BEN: What about the tea?

GUS: I'm just going to make it.

BEN: Well, go on, make it.

GUS: Yes, I will. (*He sits in a chair. Ruminatively*) He's laid on some very nice crockery this time, I'll say that. It's sort of striped. There's a white stripe.

(BEN *reads.*)

It's very nice. I'll say that.

(BEN *turns the page.*)

You know, sort of round the cup. Round the rim. All the rest of it's black, you see. Then the saucer's black, except for right in the middle, where the cup goes, where it's white.

(BEN *reads.*)

Then the plates are the same, you see. Only they've got a black stripe—the plates—right across the middle. Yes, I'm quite taken with the crockery.

BEN (*still reading*): What do you want plates for? You're not going to eat.

GUS: I've brought a few biscuits.

BEN: Well, you'd better eat them quick.

GUS: I always bring a few biscuits. Or a pie. You know I can't drink tea without anything to eat.

BEN: Well, make the tea then, will you? Time's getting on.

(GUS *brings out the flattened cigarette packet and examines it.*)

GUS: You got any cigarettes? I think I've run out.

(*He throws the packet high up and leans forward to catch it.*)

I hope it won't be a long job, this one.

(*Aiming carefully, he flips the packet under his bed.*)

Oh, I wanted to ask you something.
  BEN (*slamming his paper down*): Kaw!
  GUS: What's that?
  BEN: A child of eight killed a cat!
  GUS: Get away.
  BEN: It's a fact. What about that, eh? A child of eight killing a cat!
  GUS: How did he do it?
  BEN: It was a girl.
  GUS: How did she do it?
  BEN: She—

(*He picks up the paper and studies it.*)

It doesn't say.
  GUS: Why not?
  BEN: Wait a minute. It just says—Her brother, aged eleven, viewed the incident from the toolshed.
  GUS: Go on!
  BEN: That's bloody ridiculous.

(*Pause.*)

  GUS: I bet he did it.
  BEN: Who?
  GUS: The brother.
  BEN: I think you're right.

(*Pause.*)

(*Slamming down the paper*) What about that, eh? A kid of eleven killing a cat and blaming it on his little sister of eight! It's enough to—

(*He breaks off in disgust and seizes the paper. GUS rises.*)

GUS: What time is he getting in touch?

(BEN *reads.*)

What time is he getting in touch?
  BEN: What's the matter with you? It could be any time. Any time.
  GUS (*moves to the foot of BEN's bed*): Well, I was going to ask you something.

  BEN: What?
  GUS: Have you noticed the time that tank takes to fill?
  BEN: What tank?
  GUS: In the lavatory.
  BEN: No. Does it?
  GUS: Terrible.
  BEN: Well, what about it?
  GUS: What do you think's the matter with it?
  BEN: Nothing.
  GUS: Nothing?
  BEN: It's got a deficient ballcock, that's all.
  GUS: A deficient what?
  BEN: Ballcock.
  GUS: No? Really?
  BEN: That's what I should say.
  GUS: Go on! That didn't occur to me.

(GUS *wanders to his bed and presses the mattress.*)

I didn't have a very restful sleep today, did you? It's not much of a bed. I could have done with another blanket, too. (*He catches sight of a picture on the wall.*) Hello, what's this? (*Peering at it*) "The First Eleven." Cricketers. You seen this, Ben?
  BEN (*reading*): What?
  GUS: The first eleven.
  BEN: What?
  GUS: There's a photo here of the first eleven.
  BEN: What first eleven?
  GUS (*studying the photo*): It doesn't say.
  BEN: What about that tea?
  GUS: They all look a bit old to me.

(GUS *wanders downstage, looks out front, then all about the room.*)

I wouldn't like to live in this dump. I wouldn't mind if you had a window, you could see what it looked like outside.
  BEN: What do you want a window for?
  GUS: Well, I like to have a bit of a view, Ben. It whiles away the time.

(*He walks around the room.*)

I mean, you come into a place when it's still dark, you come into a room you've never seen before, you sleep all day, you do your job, and then you go away in the night again.

(*Pause.*)

I like to get a look at the scenery. You never get the chance in this job.
  BEN: You get your holidays, don't you?
  GUS: Only a fortnight.
  BEN (*lowering the paper*): You kill me. Anyone

would think you're working every day. How often do we do a job? Once a week? What are you complaining about?

GUS: Yes, but we've got to be on tap though, haven't we? You can't move out of the house in case a call comes.

BEN: You know what your trouble is?

GUS: What?

BEN: You haven't got any interests.

GUS: I've got interests.

BEN: What? Tell me one of your interests.

(*Pause.*)

GUS: I've got interests.

BEN: Look at me. What have I got?

GUS: I don't know. What?

BEN: I've got my woodwork. I've got my model boats. Have you ever seen me idle? I'm never idle. I know how to occupy my time, to its best advantage. Then when a call comes, I'm ready.

GUS: Don't you ever get a bit fed up?

BEN: Fed up? What with?

(*Silence.*

BEN *reads.* GUS *feels in the pocket of his jacket, which hangs on the bed.*)

GUS: You got any cigarettes? I've run out.

(*The lavatory flushes off left.*)

There she goes.

(GUS *sits on his bed.*)

No, I mean, I say the crockery's good. It is. It's very nice. But that's about all I can say for this place. It's worse than the last one. Remember that last place we were in? Last time, where was it? At least there was a wireless there. No, honest. He doesn't seem to bother much about our comfort these days.

BEN: When are you going to stop jabbering?

GUS: You'd get rheumatism in a place like this, if you stay long.

BEN: We're not staying long. Make the tea, will you? We'll be on the job in a minute.

(GUS *picks up a small bag by his bed and brings out a packet of tea. He examines it and looks up.*)

GUS: Eh, I've been meaning to ask you.

BEN: What the hell is it now?

GUS: Why did you stop the car this morning, in the middle of that road?

BEN (*lowering the paper*): I thought you were asleep.

GUS: I was, but I woke up when you stopped. You did stop, didn't you?

(*Pause.*)

In the middle of that road. It was still dark, don't you remember? I looked out. It was all misty. I thought perhaps you wanted to kip, but you were sitting up dead straight, like you were waiting for something.

BEN: I wasn't waiting for anything.

GUS: I must have fallen asleep again. What was all that about then? Why did you stop?

BEN (*picking up the paper*): We were too early.

GUS: Early? (*He rises.*) What do you mean? We got the call, didn't we, saying we were to start right away. We did. We shoved out on the dot. So how could we be too early?

BEN (*quietly*): Who took the call, me or you?

GUS: You.

BEN: We were too early.

GUS: Too early for what?

(*Pause.*)

You mean someone had to get out before we got in?

(*He examines the bedclothes.*)

I thought these sheets didn't look too bright. I thought they ponged a bit. I was too tired to notice when I got in this morning. Eh, that's taking a bit of a liberty, isn't it? I don't want to share my bed-sheets. I told you things were going down the drain. I mean, we've always had clean sheets laid on up till now. I've noticed it.

BEN: How do you know those sheets weren't clean?

GUS: What do you mean?

BEN: How do you know they weren't clean? You've spent the whole day in them, haven't you?

GUS: What, you mean it might be my pong? (*He sniffs sheets.*) Yes. (*He sits slowly on bed.*) It could be my pong, I suppose. It's difficult to tell. I don't really know what I pong like, that's the trouble.

BEN (*referring to the paper*): Kaw!

GUS: Eh, Ben.

BEN: Kaw!

GUS: Ben.

BEN: What?

GUS: What town are we in? I've forgotten.

BEN: I've told you. Birmingham.

GUS: Go on!

(*He looks with interest about the room.*)

That's in the Midlands. The second biggest city in Great Britain. I'd never have guessed.

(*He snaps his fingers.*)

Eh, it's Friday today, isn't it? It'll be Saturday tomorrow.

BEN: What about it?

GUS (*excited*): We could go and watch the Villa.

BEN: They're playing away.

GUS: No, are they? Caarr! What a pity.

BEN: Anyway, there's no time. We've got to get straight back.

GUS: Well, we have done in the past, haven't we? Stayed over and watched a game, haven't we? For a bit of relaxation.

BEN: Things have tightened up, mate. They've tightened up.

(GUS *chuckles to himself.*)

GUS: I saw the Villa get beat in a cup tie once. Who was it against now? White shirts. It was one-all at half-time. I'll never forget it. Their opponents won by a penalty. Talk about drama. Yes, it was a disputed penalty. Disputed. They got beat two-one, anyway, because of it. You were there yourself.

BEN: Not me.

GUS: Yes, you were there. Don't you remember that disputed penalty?

BEN: No.

GUS: He went down just inside the area. Then they said he was just acting. I didn't think the other bloke touched him myself. But the referee had the ball on the spot.

BEN: Didn't touch him! What are you talking about? He laid him out flat!

GUS: Not the Villa. The Villa don't play that sort of game.

BEN: Get out of it.

(*Pause.*)

GUS: Eh, that must have been here, in Birmingham.

BEN: What must?

GUS: The Villa. That must have been here.

BEN: They were playing away.

GUS: Because you know who the other team was? It was the Spurs. It was Tottenham Hotspur.

BEN: Well, what about it?

GUS: We've never done a job in Tottenham.

BEN: How do you know?

GUS: I'd remember Tottenham.

(BEN *turns on his bed to look at him.*)

BEN: Don't make me laugh, will you?

(BEN *turns back and reads.* GUS *yawns and speaks through his yawn.*)

GUS: When's he going to get in touch!

(*Pause.*)

Yes, I'd like to see another football match. I've always been an ardent football fan. Here, what about coming to see the Spurs tomorrow?

BEN (*tonelessly*): They're playing away.

GUS: Who are?

BEN: The Spurs.

GUS: Then they might be playing here.

BEN: Don't be silly.

GUS: If they're playing away they might be playing here. They might be playing the Villa.

BEN (*tonelessly*): But the Villa are playing away.

(*Pause. An envelope slides under the door, right,* GUS *sees it. He stands, looking at it.*)

GUS: Ben.

BEN: Away. They're all playing away.

GUS: Ben, look here.

BEN: What?

GUS: Look.

(BEN *turns his head and sees the envelope. He stands.*)

BEN: What's that?

GUS: I don't know.

BEN: Where did it come from?

GUS: Under the door.

BEN: Well, what is it?

GUS: I don't know.

(*They stare at it.*)

BEN: Pick it up.

GUS: What do you mean?

BEN: Pick it up!

(GUS *slowly moves towards it, bends and picks it up.*)

What is it?

GUS: An envelope.

BEN: Is there anything on it?

GUS: No.

BEN: Is it sealed?

GUS: Yes.

BEN: Open it.

GUS: What?

BEN: Open it!

(GUS *opens it and looks inside.*)

What's in it?

(GUS *empties twelve matches into his hand.*)

GUS: Matches.
BEN: Matches?
GUS: Yes.
BEN: Show it to me.

(GUS *passes the envelope.* BEN *examines it.*)

Nothing on it. Not a word.

GUS: That's funny, isn't it?
BEN: It came under the door?
GUS: Must have done.
BEN: Well, go on.
GUS: Go on where?
BEN: Open the door and see if you can catch anyone outside.
GUS: Who, me?
BEN: Go on!

(GUS *stares at him, puts the matches in his pocket, goes to his bed and brings a revolver from under the pillow. He goes to the door, opens it, looks out and shuts it.*)

GUS: No one.

(*He replaces the revolver.*)

BEN: What did you see?
GUS: Nothing.
BEN: They must have been pretty quick.

(GUS *takes the matches from pocket and looks at them.*)

GUS: Well, they'll come in handy.
BEN: Yes.
GUS: Won't they?
BEN: Yes, you're always running out, aren't you?
GUS: All the time.
BEN: Well, they'll come in handy then.
GUS: Yes.
BEN: Won't they?
GUS: Yes, I could do with them. I could do with them, too.
BEN: You could, eh?
GUS: Yes.
BEN: Why?
GUS: We haven't got any.
BEN: Well, you've got some now, haven't you?
GUS: I can light the kettle now.
BEN: Yes, you're always cadging matches. How many have you got there?
GUS: About a dozen.
BEN: Well, don't lose them. Red, too. You don't even need a box.

(GUS *probes his ear with a match.*)

(*Slapping his hand*). Don't waste them! Go on, go and light it.

GUS: Eh?
BEN: Go and light it.
GUS: Light what?
BEN: The kettle.
GUS: You mean the gas.
BEN: Who does?
GUS: You do.
BEN (*his eyes narrowing*): What do you mean, I mean the gas?
GUS: Well, that's what you mean, don't you? The gas.
BEN (*powerfully*): If I say go and light the kettle I mean go and light the kettle.
GUS: How can you light a kettle?
BEN: It's a figure of speech! Light the kettle. It's a figure of speech!
GUS: I've never heard it.
BEN: Light the kettle! It's common usage!
GUS: I think you've got it wrong.
BEN (*menacing*): What do you mean?
GUS: They say put on the kettle.
BEN (*taut*): Who says?

(*They stare at each other, breathing hard.*)

(*Deliberately*) I have never in all my life heard anyone say put on the kettle.

GUS: I bet my mother used to say it.
BEN: Your mother? When did you last see your mother?
GUS: I don't know, about—
BEN: Well, what are you talking about your mother for?

(*They stare.*)

Gus, I'm not trying to be unreasonable. I'm just trying to point out something to you.

GUS: Yes, but—
BEN: Who's the senior partner here, me or you?
GUS: You.
BEN: I'm only looking after your interests, Gus. You've got to learn, mate.
GUS: Yes, but I've never heard—
BEN (*vehemently*): Nobody says light the gas! What does the gas light?
GUS: What does the gas—?
BEN (*grabbing him with two hands by the throat, at arm's length*): THE KETTLE, YOU FOOL!

(GUS *takes the hands from his throat.*)

GUS: All right, all right.

(Pause.)

BEN: Well, what are you waiting for?
GUS: I want to see if they light.
BEN: What?
GUS: The matches.

(He takes out the flattened box and tries to strike.)

No.

(He throws the box under the bed. BEN stares at him. GUS raises his foot.)

Shall I try it on here?

(BEN stares. GUS strikes a match on his shoe. It lights.)

Here we are.
BEN *(wearily)*: Put on the bloody kettle, for Christ's sake.

(BEN goes to his bed, but, realising what he has said, stops and half turns. They look at each other. GUS slowly exits, left. BEN slams his paper down on the bed and sits on it, head in hands.)

GUS *(entering)*: It's going.
BEN: What?
GUS: The stove.

(GUS goes to his bed and sits.)

I wonder who it'll be tonight.

(Silence.)

Eh, I've been wanting to ask you something.
BEN *(putting his legs on the bed)*: Oh, for Christ's sake.
GUS: No. I was going to ask you something.

(He rises and sits on BEN's bed.)

BEN: What are you sitting on my bed for?

(GUS sits.)

What's the matter with you? You're always asking me questions. What's the matter with you?
GUS: Nothing.
BEN: You never used to ask me so many damn questions. What's come over you?
GUS: No, I was just wondering.
BEN: Stop wondering. You've got a job to do. Why don't you just do it and shut up?
GUS: That's what I was wondering about.
BEN: What?
GUS: The job.
BEN: What job?

GUS *(tentatively)*: I thought perhaps you might know something.

(BEN looks at him.)

I thought perhaps you—I mean—have you got any idea—who it's going to be tonight?
BEN: Who what's going to be?

(They look at each other.)

GUS *(at length)*: Who it's going to be.

(Silence.)

BEN: Are you feeling all right?
GUS: Sure.
BEN: Go and make the tea.
GUS: Yes, sure.

(GUS exits, left, BEN looks after him. He then takes his revolver from under the pillow and checks it for ammunition. GUS re-enters.)

The gas has gone out.
BEN: Well, what about it?
GUS: There's a meter.
BEN: I haven't got any money.
GUS: Nor have I.
BEN: You'll have to wait.
GUS: What for?
BEN: For Wilson.
GUS: He might not come. He might just send a message. He doesn't always come.
BEN: Well, you'll have to do without it, won't you?
GUS: Blimey.
BEN: You'll have a cup of tea afterwards. What's the matter with you?
GUS: I like to have one before.

(BEN holds the revolver up to the light and polishes it.)

BEN: You'd better get ready anyway.
GUS: Well, I don't know, that's a bit much, you know, for my money.

(He picks up a packet of tea from the bed and throws it into the bag.)

I hope he's got a shilling, anyway, if he comes. He's entitled to have. After all, it's his place, he could have seen there was enough gas for a cup of tea.
BEN: What do you mean, it's his place?
GUS: Well, isn't it?
BEN: He's probably only rented it. It doesn't have to be his place.

GUS: I know it's his place. I bet the whole house is. He's not even laying on any gas now either.

(GUS *sits on his bed.*)

It's his place all right. Look at all the other places. You go to this address, there's a key there, there's a teapot, there's never a soul in sight—(*He pauses.*) Eh, nobody ever hears a thing, have you ever thought of that? We never get any complaints, do we, too much noise or anything like that? You never see a soul, do you?—except the bloke who comes. You ever noticed that? I wonder if the walls are sound-proof. (*He touches the wall above his head.*) Can't tell. All you do is wait, eh? Half the time he doesn't even bother to put in an appearance, Wilson.

BEN: Why should he? He's a busy man.

GUS (*thoughtfully*): I find him hard to talk to, Wilson. Do you know that, Ben?

BEN: Scrub round it, will you?

(*Pause.*)

GUS: There are a number of things I want to ask him. But I can never get round to it, when I see him.

(*Pause.*)

I've been thinking about the last one.

BEN: What last one?

GUS: That girl.

(BEN *grabs the paper, which he reads.*)

(*Rising, looking down at* BEN) How many times have you read that paper?

(BEN *slams the paper down and rises.*)

BEN (*angrily*): What do you mean?

GUS: I was just wondering how many times you'd—

BEN: What are you doing, criticising me?

GUS: No, I was just—

BEN: You'll get a swipe round your earhole if you don't watch your step.

GUS: Now look here, Ben—

BEN: I'm not looking anywhere! (*He addresses the room.*) How many times have I—! A bloody liberty!

GUS: I didn't mean that.

BEN: You just get on with it, mate. Get on with, that's all.

(BEN *gets back on the bed.*)

GUS: I was just thinking about that girl, that's all.

(GUS *sits on his bed.*)

She wasn't much to look at, I know, but still. It was a mess though, wasn't it? What a mess. Honest, I can't remember a mess like that one. They don't seem to hold together like men, women. A looser texture, like. Didn't she spread, eh? She didn't half spread. Kaw! But I've been meaning to ask you.

(BEN *sits up and clenches his eyes.*)

Who clears up after we've gone? I'm curious about that. Who does the clearing up? Maybe they don't clear up. Maybe they just leave them there, eh? What do you think? How many jobs have we done? Blimey, I can't count them. What if they never clear anything up after we've gone.

BEN (*pityingly*): You mutt. Do you think we're the only branch of this organisation? Have a bit of common. They got departments for everything.

GUS: What cleaners and all?

BEN: You birk!

GUS: No, it was that girl made me start to think—

(*There is a loud clatter and racket in the bulge of wall between the beds, of something descending. They grab their revolvers, jump up and face the wall. The noise comes to a stop. Silence. They look at each other.* BEN *gestures sharply towards the wall.* GUS *approaches the wall slowly. He bangs it with his revolver. It is hollow.* BEN *moves to the head of his bed, his revolver cocked.* GUS *puts his revolver on his bed and pats along the bottom of the centre panel. He finds a rim. He lifts the panel. Disclosed is a serving-hatch, a "dumb waiter." A wide box is held by pulleys.* GUS *peers into the box. He brings out a piece of paper.*)

BEN: What is it?

GUS: You have a look at it.

BEN: Read it.

GUS (*reading*): Two braised steak and chips. Two sago puddings. Two teas without sugar.

BEN: Let me see that. (*He takes the paper.*)

GUS (*to himself*): Two teas without sugar.

BEN: Mmmnn.

GUS: What do you think of that?

BEN: Well—

(*The box goes up.* BEN *levels his revolver.*)

GUS: Give us a chance! They're in a hurry, aren't they?

(BEN *re-reads the note.* GUS *looks over his shoulder.*)

That's a bit—that's a bit funny, isn't it?

BEN (*quickly*): No. It's not funny. It probably used to be a café here, that's all. Upstairs. These places change hands very quickly.

GUS: A café?

BEN: Yes.

GUS: What, you mean this was the kitchen, down here?

BEN: Yes, they change hands overnight, these places. Go into liquidation. The people who run it, you know, they don't find it a going concern, they move out.

GUS: You mean the people who ran this place didn't find it a going concern and moved out?

BEN: Sure.

GUS: WELL, WHO'S GOT IT NOW?

(*Silence.*)

BEN: What do you mean, who's got it now?

GUS: Who's got it now? If they moved out, who moved in?

BEN: Well, that all depends—

(*The box descends with a clatter and bang.* BEN *levels his revolver.* GUS *goes to the box and brings out a piece of paper.*)

GUS (*reading*): Soup of the day. Liver and onions. Jam tart.

(*A pause.* GUS *looks at* BEN. BEN *takes the note and reads it. He walks slowly to the hatch.* GUS *follows.* BEN *looks into the hatch but not up it.* GUS *puts his hand on* BEN's *shoulder.* BEN *throws it off.* GUS *puts his finger to his mouth. He leans on the hatch and swiftly looks up it.* BEN *flings him away in alarm.* BEN *looks at the note. He throws his revolver on the bed and speaks with decision.*)

BEN: We'd better send something up.

GUS: Eh?

BEN: We'd better send something up.

GUS: Oh! Yes. Yes. Maybe you're right.

(*They are both relieved at the decision.*)

BEN (*purposefully*): Quick! What have you got in that bag?

GUS: Not much.

(GUS *goes to the hatch and shouts up it.*)

Wait a minute!

BEN: Don't do that!

(GUS *examines the contents of the bag and brings them out, one by one.*)

GUS: Biscuits. A bar of chocolate. Half a pint of milk.

BEN: That all?

GUS: Packet of tea.

BEN: Good.

GUS: We can't send the tea. That's all the tea we've got.

BEN: Well, there's no gas. You can't do anything with it, can you?

GUS: Maybe they can send us down a bob.

BEN: What else is there?

GUS (*reaching into bag*): One Eccles cake.

BEN: One Eccles cake?

GUS: Yes.

BEN: You never told me you had an Eccles cake.

GUS: Didn't I?

BEN: Why only one? Didn't you bring one for me?

GUS: I didn't think you'd be keen.

BEN: Well, you can't send up one Eccles cake, anyway.

GUS: Why not?

BEN: Fetch one of those plates.

GUS: All right.

(GUS *goes towards the door, left, and stops.*)

Do you mean I can keep the Eccles cake then?

BEN: Keep it?

GUS: Well, they don't know we've got it, do they?

BEN: That's not the point.

GUS: Can't I keep it?

BEN: No, you can't. Get the plate.

(GUS *exits, left.* BEN *looks in the bag. He brings out a packet of crisps. Enter* GUS *with a plate.*)

(*Accusingly, holding up the crisps*) Where did these come from?

GUS: What?

BEN: Where did these crisps come from?

GUS: Where did you find them?

BEN (*hitting him on the shoulder*): You're playing a dirty game, my lad!

GUS: I only eat those with beer!

BEN: Well, where were you going to get the beer?

GUS: I was saving them till I did.

BEN: I'll remember this. Put everything on the plate.

(*They pile everything on to the plate. The box goes up without the plate.*)

Wait a minute!

(*They stand.*)

GUS: It's gone up.
BEN: It's all your stupid fault, playing about!
GUS: What do we do now?
BEN: We'll have to wait till it comes down.

(BEN *puts the plate on the bed, puts on his shoulder holster, and starts to put on his tie.*)

You'd better get ready.

(GUS *goes to his bed, puts on his tie, and starts to fix his holster.*)

GUS: Hey, Ben.
BEN: What?
GUS: What's going on here?

(*Pause.*)

BEN: What do you mean?
GUS: How can this be a café?
BEN: It used to be a café.
GUS: Have you seen the gas stove?
BEN: What about it?
GUS: It's only got three rings.
BEN: So what?
GUS: Well, you couldn't cook much on three rings, not for a busy place like this.
BEN (*irritably*): That's why the service is slow!

(BEN *puts on his waistcoat.*)

GUS: Yes, but what happens when we're not here? What do they do then? All these menus coming down and nothing going up. It might have been going on like this for years.

(BEN *brushes his jacket.*)

What happens when we go?

(BEN *puts on his jacket.*)

They can't do much business.

(*The box descends. They turn about.* GUS *goes to the hatch and brings out a note.*)

GUS (*reading*): Macaroni Pastitsio. Ormitha Macarounada.
BEN: What was that?
GUS: Macaroni Pastitsio. Ormitha Macarounada.
BEN: Greek dishes.
GUS: No.
BEN: That's right.
GUS: That's pretty high class.
BEN: Quick before it goes up.

(GUS *puts the plate in the box.*)

GUS (*calling up the hatch*): Three McVitie and Price! One Lyons Red Label! One Smith's Crisps! One Eccles cake! One Fruit and Nut!
BEN: Cadbury's.
GUS (*up the hatch*): Cadbury's!
BEN (*handing the milk*): One bottle of milk.
GUS (*up the hatch*): One bottle of milk! Half a pint! (*He looks at the label.*) Express Dairy! (*He puts the bottle in the box.*)

(*The box goes up.*)

Just did it.
BEN: You shouldn't shout like that.
GUS: Why not?
BEN: It isn't done.

(BEN *goes to his bed.*)

Well, that should be all right, anyway, for the time being.
GUS: You think so, eh?
BEN: Get dressed, will you? It'll be any minute now.

(GUS *puts on his waistcoat.* BEN *lies down and looks up at the ceiling.*)

GUS: This is some place. No tea and no biscuits.
BEN: Eating makes you lazy, mate. You're getting lazy, you know that? You don't want to get slack on your job.
GUS: Who me?
BEN: Slack, mate, slack.
GUS: Who me? Slack?
BEN: Have you checked your gun? You haven't even checked your gun. It looks disgraceful, anyway. Why don't you ever polish it?

(GUS *rubs his revolver on the sheet.* BEN *takes out a pocket mirror and straightens his tie.*)

GUS: I wonder where the cook is. They must have had a few, to cope with that. Maybe they had a few more gas stoves. Eh! Maybe there's another kitchen along the passage.
BEN: Of course there is! Do you know what it takes to make an Ormitha Macarounada?
GUS: No, what?
BEN: An Ormitha—! Buck your ideas up, will you?
GUS: Takes a few cooks, eh?

(GUS *puts his revolver in his holster.*)

The sooner we're out of this place the better.

(*He puts on his jacket.*)

Why doesn't he get in touch? I feel like I've been here years. (*He takes his revolver out of its holster to check the ammunition.*) We've never let him down though, have we? We've never let him down. I was thinking only the other day, Ben. We're reliable, aren't we?

(*He puts his revolver back in its holster.*)

Still, I'll be glad when it's over tonight.

(*He brushes his jacket.*)

I hope the bloke's not going to get excited tonight, or anything. I'm feeling a bit off. I've got a splitting headache.

(*Silence. The box descends. BEN jumps up. GUS collects the note.*)

(*Reading.*) One Bamboo Shoots, Water Chestnuts and Chicken. One Char Siu and Beansprouts.
BEN: Beansprouts?
GUS: Yes.
BEN: Blimey.
GUS: I wouldn't know where to begin.

(*He looks back at the box. The packet of tea is inside it. He picks it up.*)

They've sent back the tea.
BEN (*anxious*): What'd they do that for?
GUS: Maybe it isn't tea-time.

(*The box goes up. Silence.*)

BEN (*throwing the tea on the bed, and speaking urgently*): Look here. We'd better tell them.
GUS: Tell them what?
BEN: That we can't do it, we haven't got it.
GUS: All right then.
BEN: Lend us your pencil. We'll write a note.

(*GUS, turning for a pencil, suddenly discovers the speaking-tube, which hangs on the right wall of the hatch facing his bed.*)

GUS: What's this?
BEN: What?
GUS: This.
BEN (*examining it*): This? It's a speaking-tube.
GUS: How long has that been there?
BEN: Just the job. We should have used it before, instead of shouting up there.
GUS: Funny I never noticed it before.
BEN: Well, come on.
GUS: What do you do?
BEN: See that? That's a whistle.
GUS: What, this?
BEN: Yes, take it out. Pull it out.

(*GUS does so.*)

That's it.
GUS: What do we do now?
BEN: Blow into it.
GUS: Blow?
BEN: It whistles up there if you blow. Then they know you want to speak. Blow.

(*GUS blows. Silence.*)

GUS (*tube at mouth*): I can't hear a thing.
BEN: Now you speak! Speak into it!

(*GUS looks at BEN, then speaks into the tube.*)

GUS: The larder's bare!
BEN: Give me that!

(*He grabs the tube and puts it to his mouth.*)

(*Speaking with great deference*): Good evening. I'm sorry to—bother you, but we just thought we'd better let you know that we haven't got anything left. We sent up all we had. There's no more food down here.

(*He brings the tube slowly to his ear.*)

What?

(*To mouth.*)

What?

(*To ear. He listens. To mouth.*)

No, all we had we sent up.

(*To ear. He listens. To mouth.*)

Oh, I'm very sorry to hear that.

(*To ear. He listens. To GUS.*)

The Eccles cake was stale.

(*He listens. To GUS.*)

The chocolate was melted.

(*He listens. To GUS.*)

The milk was sour.
GUS: What about the crisps?
BEN (*listening*): The biscuits were mouldy.

(*He glares at GUS. Tube to mouth.*)

Well, we're very sorry about that.

(*Tube to ear.*)

What?

(*To mouth.*)

What?

(*To ear.*)

Yes. Yes.

(*To mouth.*)

Yes certainly. Certainly. Right away.

(*To ear. The voice has ceased. He hangs up the tube.*)

(*Excitedly.*) Did you hear that?
GUS: What?
BEN: You know what he said? Light the kettle! Not put on the kettle! Not light the gas! But light the kettle!
GUS: How can we light the kettle?
BEN: There's no gas.
BEN (*clapping hand to head*): Now what do we do?
GUS: What did he want us to light the kettle for?
BEN: For tea. He wanted a cup of tea.
GUS: *He* wanted a cup of tea! What about me? I've been wanting a cup of tea all night!
BEN (*despairingly*): What do we do now?
GUS: What are we supposed to drink?

(BEN *sits on his bed, staring.*)

What about us?

(BEN *sits.*)

I'm thirsty, too. I'm starving. And he wants a cup of tea. That beats the band, that does.

(BEN *lets his head sink on to his chest.*)

I could do with a bit of sustenance myself. What about you? You look as if you could do with something too.

(GUS *sits on his bed.*)

We send him up all we've got and he's not satisfied. No, honest, it's enough to make the cat laugh. Why did you send him up all that stuff? (*Thoughtfully*) Why did I send it up?

(*Pause.*)

Who knows what he's got upstairs? He's probably got a salad bowl. They must have something up there. They won't get much from down here. You notice they didn't ask for any salads? They've probably got a salad bowl up there. Cold meat, radishes, cucumbers. Watercress. Roll mops.

(*Pause.*)

Hardboiled eggs.

(*Pause.*)

The lot. They've probably got a crate of beer too. Probably eating my crisps with a pint of beer now. Didn't have anything to say about those crisps, did he? They do all right, don't worry about that. You don't think they're just going to sit there and wait for stuff to come up from down here, do you? That'll get them nowhere.

(*Pause.*)

They do all right.

(*Pause.*)

And he wants a cup of tea.

(*Pause.*)

That's past a joke, in my opinion.

(*He looks over at* BEN, *rises, and goes to him.*)

What's the matter with you? You don't look too bright. I feel like an Alka-Seltzer myself.

(BEN *sits up.*)

BEN (*in a low voice*): Time's getting on.
GUS: I know. I don't like doing a job on an empty stomach.
BEN (*wearily*): Be quiet a minute. Let me give you your instructions.
GUS: What for? We always do it the same way, don't we?
BEN: Let me give you your instructions.

(GUS *sighs and sits next to* BEN *on the bed. The instructions are stated and repeated automatically.*)

When we get the call, you go over and stand behind the door.
GUS: Stand behind the door.
BEN: If there's a knock on the door you don't answer it.
GUS: If there's a knock on the door I don't answer it.
BEN: But there won't be a knock on the door.
GUS: So I won't answer it.
BEN: When the bloke comes in—
GUS: When the bloke comes in—
BEN: Shut the door behind him.
GUS: Shut the door behind him.
BEN: Without divulging your presence.
GUS: Without divulging my presence.
BEN: He'll see me and come towards me.
GUS: He'll see you and come towards you.
BEN: He won't see you.

GUS (*absently*): Eh?

BEN: He won't see you.

GUS: He won't see me.

BEN: But he'll see me.

GUS: He'll see you.

BEN: He won't know you're there.

GUS: He won't know you're there.

BEN: He won't know *you're* there.

GUS: He won't know I'm there.

BEN: I take out my gun.

GUS: You take out your gun.

BEN: He stops in his tracks.

GUS: He stops in his tracks.

BEN: If he turns round—

GUS: If he turns round—

BEN: You're there.

GUS: I'm here.

(BEN *frowns and presses his forehead.*)

You've missed something out.

BEN: I know. What?

GUS: I haven't taken my gun out, according to you.

BEN: You take your gun out—

GUS: After I've closed the door.

BEN: After you've closed the door.

GUS: You've never missed that out before, you know that?

BEN: When he sees you behind him—

GUS: Me behind him—

BEN: And me in front of him—

GUS: And you in front of him—

BEN: He'll feel uncertain—

GUS: Uneasy.

BEN: He won't know what to do.

GUS: So what will he do?

BEN: He'll look at me and he'll look at you.

GUS: We won't say a word.

BEN: We'll look at him.

GUS: He won't say a word.

BEN: He'll look at us.

GUS: And we'll look at him.

BEN: Nobody says a word.

(*Pause.*)

GUS: What do we do if it's a girl?

BEN: We do the same.

GUS: Exactly the same?

BEN: Exactly.

(*Pause.*)

GUS: We don't do anything different?

BEN: We do exactly the same.

GUS: Oh.

(GUS *rises, and shivers.*)

Excuse me.

(*He exits through the door on the left.* BEN *remains sitting on the bed, still.*
    The lavatory chain is pulled once off left, but the lavatory does not flush.
    Silence.
    GUS *re-enters and stops inside the door, deep in thought. He looks at* BEN, *then walks slowly across to his own bed. He is troubled. He stands, thinking. He turns and looks at* BEN. *He moves a few paces towards him.*)

(*Slowly in a low, tense voice*) Why did he send us matches if he knew there was no gas?

(*Silence.*
    BEN *stares in front of him.* GUS *crosses to the left side of* BEN, *to the foot of his bed, to get to his other ear.*)

BEN: Why did he send us matches if he knew there was no gas?

(BEN *looks up.*)

Why did he do that?

BEN: Who?

GUS: Who sent us those matches?

BEN: What are you talking about?

(GUS *stares down at him.*)

GUS (*thickly*): Who is it upstairs?

BEN (*nervously*): What's one thing to do with another?

GUS: Who is it, though?

BEN: What's one thing to do with another?

(BEN *fumbles for his paper on the bed.*)

GUS: I asked you a question.

BEN: Enough!

GUS (*with growing agitation*): I asked you before. Who moved in? I asked you. You said the people who had it before moved out. Well, who moved in?

BEN (*hunched*): Shut up.

GUS: I told you, didn't I?

BEN (*standing*): Shut up!

GUS (*feverishly*): I told you before who owned this place, didn't I? I told you.

(BEN *hits him viciously on the shoulder.*)

I told you who ran this place, didn't I?

(BEN *hits him viciously on the shoulder.*)

(*Violently*) Well, what's he playing all these games for? That's what I want to know. What's he doing it for?

BEN: What games?

GUS (*passionately, advancing*): What's he doing it for? We've been through our tests, haven't we? We got right through our tests, years ago, didn't we? We took them together, don't you remember, didn't we? We've proved ourselves before now, haven't we? We've always done our job. What's he doing all this for? What's the idea? What's he playing these games for?

(*The box in the shaft comes down behind them. The noise is this time accompanied by a shrill whistle, as it falls.* GUS *rushes to the hatch and seizes the note.*)

(*Reading.*) Scampi!

(*He crumples the note, picks up the tube, takes out the whistle, blows and speaks.*)

WE'VE GOT NOTHING LEFT! NOTHING! DO YOU UNDERSTAND?

(BEN *seizes the tube and flings* GUS *away. He follows* GUS *and slaps him hard, back-handed, across the chest.*)

BEN: Stop it! You maniac!

GUS: But you heard!

BEN (*savagely*): That's enough! I'm warning you!

(*Silence.*
BEN *hangs the tube. He goes to his bed and lies down. He picks up his paper and reads.*
Silence.
The box goes up.
They turn quickly, their eyes meet. BEN *turns to his paper.*
Slowly GUS *goes back to his bed, and sits.*
Silence.
The hatch falls back into place.
They turn quickly, their eyes meet. BEN *turns back to his paper.*
Silence.
BEN *throws his paper down.*)

BEN: Kaw!

(*He picks up the paper and looks at it.*)

Listen to this!

(*Pause.*)

What about that, eh?

(*Pause.*)

Kaw!

(*Pause.*)

Have you ever heard such a thing?

GUS (*dully*): Go on!

BEN: It's true.

GUS: Get away.

BEN: It's down here in black and white.

GUS (*very low*): Is that a fact?

BEN: You can imagine it.

GUS: It's unbelievable.

BEN: It's enough to make you want to puke, isn't it?

GUS (*almost inaudible*): Incredible.

(BEN *shakes his head. He puts the paper down and rises. He fixes the revolver in his holster.*
GUS *stands up. He goes towards the door on the left.*)

BEN: Where are you going?

GUS: I'm going to have a glass of water.

(*He exits.* BEN *brushes dust off his clothes and shoes. The whistle in the speaking-tube blows. He goes to it, takes the whistle out and puts the tube to his ear. He listens. He puts it to his mouth.*)

BEN: Yes.

(*To ear. He listens. To mouth.*)

Straight away. Right.

(*To ear. He listens. To mouth.*)

Sure we're ready.

(*To ear. He listens. To mouth.*)

Understood. Repeat. He has arrived and will be coming in straight away. The normal method to be employed. Understood.

(*To ear. He listens. To mouth.*)

Sure we're ready.

(*To ear. He listens. To mouth.*)

Right.

(*He hangs the tube up.*)

Gus!

(*He takes out a comb and combs his hair, adjusts his jacket to diminish the bulge of the revolver. The lavatory flushes off left.* BEN *goes quickly to the door, left.*)

Gus!

(The door right opens sharply. BEN *turns, his revolver levelled at the door.*
GUS *stumbles in.*
He is stripped of his jacket, waistcoat, tie, holster and revolver.
He stops, body stooping, his arms at his sides.

He raises his head and looks at BEN.
A long silence.
They stare at each other.)

CURTAIN

COMMENTARY

I've never started a play from any kind of abstract idea or theory and never envisaged my own characters as messengers of death, doom, heaven or the milky way or, in other words, as allegorical representations of any particular force, whatever that may mean. When a character cannot be comfortably defined or understood in terms of the familiar, the tendency is to perch him on a symbolic shelf, out of harm's way. Once there, he can be talked about but not lived with.*

Probably most or even all of the dramatists represented in this book could say the same thing: it is impossible to believe that (for example) Shakespeare began *King Lear* with "any kind of abstract idea"—in fact, he must have begun it with reading or seeing the old play *King Leir*, and felt that he could do it much better, make the characters breathe and make the story move us. And probably every dramatist in this book would be distressed if, because we could not find a character familiar, we turned the character into a tidy symbol and talked about it but did not live with it in all its unfamiliarity.

Still, when we read or see a good play we inevitably feel that it has some meaning, that it adds up to something. That's what makes any work of art different from, say, a story in a newspaper. If we read on page 1 of *The Daily Record* that a gunman killed another, we don't bother to think of the meaning; the story is in the paper simply because it happened, not because the happening has any significance. But a work of art has not only the concrete immediacy of experience—the sort of thing that newspapers and history books are full of; it has something of the distillation or significance of experience that we find (usually in a highly abstract form) in philosophy.

The meaning of a good play, however, is not usually to be found in a philosophical or preachy speech; rather, it is diffused throughout the play, from the first line to the last, or, rather, from our first view of the stage to the last. In "The Language of Drama" (pages 3–9) we call attention to the meaning of Ibsen's set in *A Doll's House*, and to the meanings of the costumes and gestures, as well as of the dialogue and even of the sound of the door slamming at the end of the play. If we were similarly analyzing *The Dumb Waiter* we would, for example, call attention to the fact that near the end of the play, when he is probably about to be murdered by his partner Ben, Gus "is stripped of his jacket,

*Harold Pinter, "Writing for the Theatre," in *The New British Drama*, ed. Henry Popkin (New York: Grove, 1964), pp. 575–576.

waistcoat, tie, holster, and revolver." Here, as when Nora in A *Doll's House* takes off her fancy costume, or when the mad King Lear tears off his clothing, we see the stripping away of those accoutrements that conceal humanity's essential vulnerability.

We might consider, too, the characterization in the play (What sort of people are Gus and Ben? Why is it that we learn almost nothing of their background, nothing about why they do what they do?), or we might consider the setting (What is implied by "a basement room"?), but instead we shall briefly glance at the structure of the play. The germ of the play—two hit-men wait to do a job—probably owes something to Ernest Hemingway's short story "The Killers," in which two hired assassins engage in flat small talk while waiting for their victim; but it owes something also to gangster films and suspense films. The gangster film, however, usually has a plot, with what Aristotle calls a beginning, a middle, and an end: it begins with a situation that is fairly stable, fairly understandable (for instance, a young hood joins an organization of gangsters); the film proceeds to a middle—the consequences of the beginning and the causes of the end (the middle of the gangster film may show the youngster pushing his way to the top of the mob); and it concludes with the end, which is caused by the middle and which does not seem to lead to anything further (having rubbed out the apparent opposition, the new boss is now himself rubbed out by a younger contender or by the police, or—as in *The Godfather, Part II*— the central figure finds that his success has brought him nothing, for he cannot share it with his family). A suspense film, too, usually has an easily perceptible structure, for example, the scary hunt for the criminals, the forces of evil waiting behind closed doors for the good guy who pursues them, mysterious messages, and finally a resolution in which (usually) virtue is rewarded.

In *The Dumb Waiter* we get suspense and mystery (the sudden clatter of the previously unnoticed dumb waiter, the envelope with matches that is slipped under the door, the erratic flushing of the toilet, the whistling of the speaking-tube, and, of course, the mysterious orders from above), but we are not given the satisfaction of witnessing a story unfold episode by episode. Gus and Ben are waiting for their victim, and near the end of the play, when Gus goes to the toilet, Ben learns that the victim will be "coming in straight away." He levels his revolver at the door—and Gus walks in. The two stare at each other, there is "a long silence," and the play ends. Anton Chekhov, talking about the importance of foreshadowing and of inevitability in drama, said that if there is a gun on the wall in the first act, it must go off in the last act—but here no gun goes off.

Has Pinter, then, merely written an hour's worth of small talk with no shape to it? Not quite. First, although at the start of the drama we see two men waiting, we do not clearly understand until about the middle that they are hired murderers waiting for their victim. And it is not until the end of the play that we learn (as the two men themselves learn) who the victim is. Ben does not kill Gus in the play, but it seems almost certain that he will kill Gus, for Ben has been consistently presented (in contrast to Gus) as a mindless hood who unthinkingly follows the orders given to him. Or, to put it a little differently, we come to understand that Gus, by the very doubts he has expressed throughout the play, is doomed to be eradicated (the toilet flushes, just before the end) by a system that brooks no questions. The play is not mere chitchat; it progresses, in the sense that *we* come to an understanding.

Second, and more obvious as a structural pattern, at the start of the play we hear Ben recount two newspaper stories of death—one of an eighty-seven-year-old man who was killed while crawling under a lorry (i.e., a truck), and the other of an eight-year-old girl who killed a cat. The first story, then, introduces the motif of the unpredictability of death (at the end of the play, Gus, who thinks he is the killer, finds that he is the victim); the second news story, too, introduces a note of surprise, but now the surprise is tinged with the mystery of the suspense story, for Gus doubts the accuracy of the newspaper report and he conjectures that in fact the girl's eleven-year-old brother was the real killer of the cat. Whether or not Gus is right, then, the seemingly trivial dialogue at the beginning of the play is preparation for the dialogue and the action at the end of the play. Or, rather, for the silence and the inaction. We are left wondering, just as at the start we wonder which child did in fact kill the cat.

At the end of the play, then, Pinter leaves us with an ambiguity, but the play has been ambiguous from the start. If we are annoyed by the uncertainty of the resolution of the plot, we may be even more annoyed by the uncertainty of the meaning, but this is perhaps because we mistakenly expect playwrights to be philosophers who answer our largest questions. Perhaps we should recall that in *King Lear* we get no answer to Lear's agonized question, asked over the body of his beloved daughter Cordelia, "Why should a dog, a horse, a rat, have life, / And thou no breath at all?" The question is unforgettable; the answer is not forthcoming. In *A Midsummer Night's Dream*, Lear's question is asked comically, when Pyramus laments the seeming death, at the jaws of a lion, of his beloved Thisby: "O wherefore, Nature, didst thou lions frame?" Not answers, but an experience of life, is what the best playwrights offer.

TOPICS FOR DISCUSSION

1. Ben and Gus, though gangsters, often express moral indignation. How do you explain this? Is Pinter saying something about the hypocrisy of society?
2. What speeches, actions, or situations in the play might be called comic? Are some or all of these tinged with the urgency or desperation that one also finds in tragedy?
3. The commentary offers brief characterizations of Ben and Gus. Amplify these by citing concrete details, or, if you see the two characters differently, set forth your own generalizations and support them with details.
4. Would the play be better or worse if at the end we saw Ben kill Gus?

DUTCHMAN

LeRoi Jones (Imamu Amiri Baraka)

LeRoi Jones (born in 1934), who has taken the name Imamu Amiri Baraka, was born in Newark, N.J., attended Rutgers and graduated from Howard University. After his graduation he served for three years in the United States Air Force and then did graduate work at the New School for Social Research and at Columbia, where he took an M.A. in German literature. Although early in his career Jones was associated with such Beat writers as Allen Ginsburg, in the 1960s he came to adopt an explicitly black revolutionary position, announcing that "the Black Artist's role in America is to aid in the destruction of America as he knows it." Among his writing are plays, poetry, stories, essays, and a book on black music. Also as part of his program he founded the Black Arts Repertory Theater/School, an institution that excluded white audiences.

He wrote his first play in 1958, but his reputation as a playwright was not established until he wrote *Dutchman*, produced Off Broadway in 1966 and made into a film in 1967. He continues to write while serving as a professor at the State University of New York at Stony Brook.

CHARACTERS

CLAY, *twenty-year-old Negro*
LULA, *thirty-year-old white woman*
RIDERS OF COACH, *white and black*
YOUNG NEGRO
CONDUCTOR

In the flying underbelly of the city. Steaming hot, and summer on top, outside. Underground. The subway heaped in modern myth.

Opening scene is a man sitting in a subway seat, holding a magazine but looking vacantly just above its wilting pages. Occasionally he looks blankly toward the window on his right. Dim lights and darkness whistling by against the glass. (Or paste the lights, as admitted props, right on the subway windows. Have them move, even dim and flicker. But give the sense of speed. Also stations, whether the train is stopped or the glitter and activity of these stations merely flashes by the windows.)

The man is sitting alone. That is, only his seat is visible, though the rest of the car is outfitted as a complete subway car. But only his seat is shown. There might be, for a time, as the play begins, a loud scream of the actual train. And it can recur throughout the play, or continue on a lower key once the dialogue starts.

Calvin Lockhart as Clay and Tony Robbins as Lula in the Hampstead Theatre Club production directed by Charles Jarrott, London, 1967. (Photograph: © 1972 John Haynes.)

The train slows after a time, pulling to a brief stop at one of the stations. The man looks idly up, until he sees a woman's face staring at him through the window; when it realizes that the man has noticed the face, it begins very premeditatedly to smile. The man smiles, too, for a moment, without a trace of self-consciousness. Almost an instinctive though undesirable response. Then a kind of awkwardness or embarrassment sets in, and the man makes to look away, is further embarrassed, so he brings back his eyes to where the face was, but by now the train is moving again, and the face would seem to be left behind by the way the man turns his head to look back through the other windows at the slowly fading platform. He smiles then; more comfortably confident, hoping perhaps that his memory of this brief encounter will be pleasant. And then he is idle again.

SCENE I

Train roars. Lights flash outside the windows.

LULA *enters from the rear of the car in bright, skimpy summer clothes and sandals. She carries a net bag full of paper books, fruit, and other anonymous articles. She is wearing sunglasses, which she pushes up on her forehead from time to time.* LULA *is a tall, slender, beautiful woman with long red hair hanging straight down her back, wearing only loud lipstick in somebody's good taste. She is eating an apple, very daintily. Coming down the car toward* CLAY.

She stops beside CLAY's *seat and hangs languidly from the strap, still managing to eat the apple. It is apparent that she is going to sit in the seat next to* CLAY, *and that she is only waiting for him to notice her before she sits.*

CLAY *sits as before, looking just beyond his magazine, now and again pulling the magazine slowly back and forth in front of his face in a hopeless effort to fan himself. Then he sees the woman hanging there beside him and he looks up into her face, smiling quizzically.*

LULA: Hello.
CLAY: Uh, hi're you?
LULA: I'm going to sit down. . . . O.K.?
CLAY: Sure.
LULA (*swings down onto the seat, pushing her legs straight out as if she is very weary*): Oooof! Too much weight.
CLAY: Ha, doesn't look like much to me. (*Leaning back against the window, a little surprised and maybe stiff.*)

LULA: It's so anyway.

(*And she moves her toes in the sandals, then pulls her right leg up on the left knee, better to inspect the bottoms of the sandals and the back of her heel. She appears for a second not to notice that* CLAY *is sitting next to her or that she has spoken to him just a second before.* CLAY *looks at the magazine, then out the black window. As he does this, she turns very quickly toward him.*)

Weren't you staring at me through the window?
CLAY (*wheeling around and very much stiffened*): What?
LULA: Weren't you staring at me through the window? At the last stop?
CLAY: Staring at you? What do you mean?
LULA: Don't you know what staring means?
CLAY: I saw you through the window . . . if that's what it means. I don't know if I was staring. Seems to me you were staring through the window at me.
LULA: I was. But only after I'd turned around and saw you staring through that window down in the vicinity of my ass and legs.
CLAY: Really?
LULA: Really. I guess you were just taking those idle potshots. Nothing else to do. Run your mind over people's flesh.
CLAY: Oh boy. Wow, now I admit I was looking in your direction. But the rest of that weight is yours.
LULA: I suppose.
CLAY: Staring through train windows is weird business. Much weirder than staring very sedately at abstract asses.
LULA: What's why I came looking through the

window . . . so you'd have more than that to go on. I even smiled at you.

CLAY: That's right.

LULA: I even got into this train, going some other way than mine. Walked down the aisle . . . searching you out.

CLAY: Really? That's pretty funny.

LULA: That's pretty funny. . . . God, you're dull.

CLAY: Well, I'm sorry, lady, but I really wasn't prepared for party talk.

LULA: No, you're not. What are you prepared for? (*Wrapping the apple core in a Kleenex and dropping it on the floor.*)

CLAY (*takes her conversation as pure sex talk. He turns to confront her squarely with this idea*): I'm prepared for anything. How about you?

LULA (*laughing loudly and cutting it off abruptly*): What do you think you're doing?

CLAY: What?

LULA: You think I want to pick you up, get you to take me somewhere and screw me, huh?

CLAY: Is that the way I look?

LULA: You look like you been trying to grow a beard. That's exactly what you look like. You look like you live in New Jersey with your parents and are trying to grow a beard. That's what. You look like you've been reading Chinese poetry and drinking lukewarm sugarless tea. (*Laughs, uncrossing and recrossing her legs.*) You look like death eating a soda cracker.

CLAY (*cocking his head from one side to the other, embarrassed and trying to make some comeback, but also intrigued by what the woman is saying . . . even the sharp city coarseness of her voice, which is still a kind of gentle sidewalk throb*): Really? I look like all that?

LULA: Not all of it. (*She feints a seriousness to cover an actual somber tone.*) I lie a lot. (*Smiling*) It helps me control the world.

CLAY (*relieved and laughing louder than the humor*): Yeah, I bet.

LULA: But it's true, most of it, right? Jersey? Your bumpy neck?

CLAY: How'd you know all that? Huh? Really, I mean about Jersey . . . and even the beard. I met you before? You know Warren Enright?

LULA: You tried to make it with your sister when you were ten.

(CLAY *leans back hard against the back of the seat, his eyes opening now, still trying to look amused.*)

But I succeeded a few weeks ago. (*She starts to laugh again.*)

CLAY: What're you talking about? Warren tell you that? You're a friend of Georgia's?

LULA: I told you I lie. I don't know your sister. I don't know Warren Enright.

CLAY: You mean you're just picking these things out of the air?

LULA: Is Warren Enright a tall skinny black boy with a phony English accent?

CLAY: I figured you knew him.

LULA: But I don't. I just figured you would know somebody like that. (*Laughs.*)

CLAY: Yeah, yeah.

LULA: You're probably on your way to his house now.

CLAY: That's right.

LULA (*putting her hand on* CLAY'*s closest knee, drawing it from the knee up to the thigh's hinge, then removing it, watching his face very closely, and continuing to laugh, perhaps more gently than before*): Dull, dull, dull. I bet you think I'm exciting.

CLAY: You're O.K.

LULA: Am I exciting you now?

CLAY: Right. That's not what's supposed to happen?

LULA: How do I know? (*She returns her hand, without moving it, then takes it away and plunges it in her bag to draw out an apple.*) You want this?

CLAY: Sure.

LULA (*she gets one out of the bag for herself*): Eating apples together is always the first step. Or walking up uninhabited Seventh Avenue in the twenties on weekends. (*Bites and giggles, glancing at* CLAY *and speaking in loose sing-song*) Can get you involved . . . boy! Get us involved. Um-huh. (*Mock seriousness*) Would you like to get involved with me, Mister Man?

CLAY (*trying to be as flippant as* LULA, *whacking happily at the apple*): Sure. Why not? A beautiful woman like you. Huh, I'd be a fool not to.

LULA: And I bet you're sure you know what you're talking about. (*Taking him a little roughly by the wrist, so he cannot eat the apple, then shaking the wrist*) I bet you're sure of almost everything anybody ever asked you about . . . right? (*Shakes his wrist harder.*) Right?

CLAY: Yeah, right. . . . Wow, you're pretty strong, you know? Whatta you, a lady wrestler or something?

LULA: What's wrong with lady wrestlers? And don't answer because you never knew any. Huh. (*Cynically*) That's for sure. They don't have any lady wrestlers in that part of Jersey. That's for sure.

CLAY: Hey, you still haven't told me how you know so much about me.

LULA: I told you I didn't know anything about *you* . . . you're a well-known type.

CLAY: Really?

LULA: Or at least I know the type very well. And your skinny English friend, too.

CLAY: Anonymously?

LULA (*settles back in seat, single-mindedly finishing her apple and humming snatches of rhythm and blues song*): What?

CLAY: Without knowing us specifically?

LULA: Oh boy. (*Looking quickly at* CLAY) What a face. You know, you could be a handsome man.

CLAY: I can't argue with you.

LULA (*vague, off-center response*): What?

CLAY (*raising his voice, thinking the train noise has drowned part of his sentence*): I can't argue with you.

LULA: My hair is turning gray. A gray hair for each year and type I've come through.

CLAY: Why do you want to sound so old?

LULA: But it's always gentle when it starts. (*Attention drifting*) Hugged against tenements, day or night.

CLAY: What?

LULA: (*refocusing*): Hey, why don't you take me to that party you're going to?

CLAY: You must be a friend of Warren's to know about the party.

LULA: Wouldn't you like to take me to the party? (*Imitates clinging vine*) Oh, come on, ask me to your party.

CLAY: Of course I'll ask you to come with me to the party. And I'll bet you're a friend of Warren's.

LULA: Why not be a friend of Warren's? Why not? (*Taking his arm*) Have you asked me yet?

CLAY: How can I ask you when I don't know your name?

LULA: Are you talking to my name?

CLAY: What is it, a secret?

LULA: I'm Lena the Hyena.

CLAY: The famous woman poet?

LULA: Poetess! The same!

CLAY: Well, you know so much about me . . . what's my name?

LULA: Morris the Hyena.

CLAY: The famous woman poet?

LULA: The same. (*Laughing and going into her bag*) You want another apple?

CLAY: Can't make it, lady. I only have to keep one doctor away a day.

LULA: I bet your name is . . . something like . . . uh, Gerald or Walter. Huh?

CLAY: God, no.

LULA: Lloyd, Norman? One of those hopeless colored names creeping out of New Jersey. Leonard? Gag. . . .

CLAY: Like Warren?

LULA: Definitely. Just exactly like Warren. Or Everett.

CLAY: Gag. . . .

LULA: Well, for sure, it's not Willie.

CLAY: It's Clay.

LULA: Clay? Really? Clay what?

CLAY: Take your pick. Jackson, Johnson, or Williams.

LULA: Oh, really? Good for you. But it's got to be Williams. You're too pretentious to be a Jackson or Johnson.

CLAY: Thass right.

LULA: But Clay's O.K.

CLAY: So's Lena.

LULA: It's Lula.

CLAY: Oh?

LULA: Lula the Hyena.

CLAY: Very good.

LULA (*starts laughing again*): Now you say to me, "Lula, Lula, why don't you go to this party with me tonight?" It's your turn, and let those be your lines.

CLAY: Lula, why don't you go to this party with me tonight, huh?

LULA: Say my name twice before you ask, and no huh's.

CLAY: Lula, Lula, why don't you go to this party with me tonight?

LULA: I'd like to go, Clay, but how can you ask me to go when you barely know me?

CLAY: That is strange, isn't it?

LULA: What kind of reaction is that? You're supposed to say, "Aw, come on, we'll get to know each other better at the party."

CLAY: That's pretty corny.

LULA: What are you into anyway? (*Looking at him half sullenly but still amused*) What thing are you playing at, Mister? Mister Clay Williams? (*Grabs his thigh, up near the crotch.*) What are *you* thinking about?

CLAY: Watch it now, you're gonna excite me for real.

LULA (*taking her hand away and throwing her apple core through the window*): I bet. (*She slumps in the seat and is heavily silent.*)

CLAY: I thought you knew everything about me? What happened?

(LULA *looks at him, then looks slowly away, then over where the other aisle would be. Noise of the train. She reaches in her bag and pulls out one of the paper books. She puts it on her leg and thumbs the pages listlessly.* CLAY *cocks his head to see the title of the book. Noise of the train.* LULA *flips pages and her eyes drift. Both remain silent.*)

Are you going to the party with me, Lula?

LULA (*bored and not even looking*): I don't even know you.

CLAY: You said you know my type.

LULA (*strangely irritated*): Don't get smart with me, Buster. I know you like the palm of my hand.

CLAY: The one you eat the apples with?

LULA: Yeh. And the one I open doors late Saturday evening with. That's my door. Up at the top of the stairs. Five flights. Above a lot of Italians and lying Americans. And scrape carrots with. Also . . . (*looks at him*) the same hand I unbutton my dress with, or let my skirt fall down. Same hand. Lover.

CLAY: Are you angry about something? Did I say something wrong?

LULA: Everything you say is wrong. (*Mock smile.*) That's what makes you so attractive. Ha. In that funnybook jacket with all the buttons. (*More animate, taking hold of his jacket*) What've you got that jacket and tie on in all this heat for? And why're you wearing a jacket and tie like that? Did your people ever burn witches or start revolutions over the price of tea? Boy, those narrow-shoulder clothes come from a tradition you ought to feel oppressed by. A three-button suit. What right do you have to be wearing a three-button suit and striped tie? Your grandfather was a slave, he didn't go to Harvard.

CLAY: My grandfather was a night watchman.

LULA: And you went to a colored college where everybody thought they were Averell Harriman.

CLAY: All except me.

LULA: And who did you think you were? Who do you think you are now?

CLAY (*laughs as if to make light of the whole trend of the conversation*): Well, in college I thought I was Baudelaire. But I've slowed down since.

LULA: I bet you never once thought you were a black nigger.

(*Mock serious, then she howls with laughter.* CLAY *is stunned but after initial reaction, he quickly tries to appreciate the humor.* LULA *almost shrieks.*)

A black Baudelaire.

CLAY: That's right.

LULA: Boy, are you corny. I take back what I said

before. Everything you say is not wrong. It's perfect. You should be on television.

CLAY: You act like you're on television already.

LULA: That's because I'm an actress.

CLAY: I thought so.

LULA: Well, you're wrong. I'm no actress. I told you I always lie. I'm nothing, honey, and don't you ever forget it. (*Lighter*) Although my mother was a Communist. The only person in my family ever to amount to anything.

CLAY: My mother was a Republican.

LULA: And your father voted for the man rather than the party.

CLAY: Right!

LULA: Yea for him. Yea, yea for him.

CLAY: Yea!

LULA: And yea for America where he is free to vote for the mediocrity of his choice! Yea!

CLAY: Yea!

LULA: And yea for both your parents who even though they differ about so crucial a matter as the body politic still forged a union of love and sacrifice that was destined to flower at the birth of the noble Clay . . . what's your middle name?

CLAY: Clay.

LULA: A union of love and sacrifice that was destined to flower at the birth of the noble Clay Clay Williams. Yea! And most of all yea yea for you, Clay Clay. The Black Beaudelaire! Yes! (*And with knifelike cynicism*) My Christ. My Christ.

CLAY: Thank you, ma'am.

LULA: May the people accept you as a ghost of the future. And love you, that you might not kill them when you can.

CLAY: What?

LULA: You're a murderer, Clay, and you know it. (*Her voice darkening with significance*) You know goddamn well what I mean.

CLAY: I do?

LULA: So we'll pretend the air is light and full of perfume.

CLAY (*sniffing at her blouse*): It is.

LULA: And we'll pretend the people cannot see you. That is, the citizens. And that you are free of your own history. And I am free of my history. We'll pretend that we are both anonymous beauties smashing along through the city's entrails. (*She yells as loud as she can.*) GROOVE!

BLACK

SCENE II

Scene is the same as before, though now there are other seats visible in the car. And throughout the scene other people get on the subway. There are maybe one or two seated in the car as the scene opens, though neither CLAY *nor* LULA *notices them.* CLAY'S *tie is open.* LULA *is hugging his arm.*

CLAY: The party!

LULA: I know it'll be something good. You can come in with me, looking casual and significant. I'll be strange, haughty, and silent, and walk with long slow strides.

CLAY: Right.

LULA: When you get drunk, pat me once, very lovingly on the flanks, and I'll look at you cryptically, locking my lips.

CLAY: It sounds like something we can do.

LULA: You'll go around talking to young men about your mind, and to old men about your plans. If you meet a very close friend who is also with someone like me, we can stand together, sipping our drinks and exchanging codes of lust. The atmosphere will be slithering in love and half-love and very open moral decision.

CLAY: Great. Great.

LULA: And everyone will pretend they don't know your name, and then . . . (*she pauses heavily*) later, when they have to, they'll claim a friendship that denies your sterling character.

CLAY (*kissing her neck and fingers*): And then what?

LULA: Then? Well, then we'll go down the street, late night, eating apples and winding very deliberately toward my house.

CLAY: Deliberately?

LULA: I mean, we'll look in all the shopwindows, and make fun of the queers. Maybe we'll meet a Jewish Buddhist and flatten his conceits over some very pretentious coffee.

CLAY: In honor of whose God?

LULA: Mine.

CLAY: Who is . . . ?

LULA: Me . . . and you?

CLAY: A corporate Godhead.

LULA: Exactly. Exactly. (*Notices one of the other people entering.*)

CLAY: Go on with the chronicle. Then what happens to us?

LULA (*a mild depression, but she still makes her description triumphant and increasingly direct*): To my house, of course.

CLAY: Of course.

LULA: And up the narrow steps of the tenement.

CLAY: You live in a tenement?

LULA: Wouldn't live anywhere else. Reminds me specifically of my novel form of insanity.

CLAY: Up the tenement stairs.

LULA: And with my apple-eating hand I push open the door and lead you, my tender big-eyed prey, into my . . . God, what can I call it . . . into my hovel.

CLAY: Then what happens?

LULA: After the dancing and games, after the long drinks and long walks, the real fun begins.

CLAY: Ah, the real fun. (*Embarrassed, in spite of himself.*) Which is . . . ?

LULA (*laughs at him*): Real fun in the dark house. Hah! Real fun in the dark house, high up above the street and the ignorant cowboys. I lead you in, holding your wet hand gently in my hand . . .

CLAY: Which is not wet?

LULA: Which is dry as ashes.

CLAY: And cold?

LULA: Don't think you'll get out of your responsibility that way. It's not cold at all. You Fascist! Into my dark living room. Where we'll sit and talk endlessly, endlessly.

CLAY: About what?

LULA: About what? About your manhood, what do you think? What do you think we've been talking about all this time?

CLAY: Well, I didn't know it was that. That's for sure. Every other thing in the world but that. (*Notices another person entering, looks quickly, almost involuntarily up and down the car, seeing the other people in the car.*) Hey, I didn't even notice when those people got on.

LULA: Yeah, I know.

CLAY: Man, this subway is slow.

LULA: Yeah, I know.

CLAY: Well, go on. We were talking about my manhood.

LULA: We still are. All the time.

CLAY: We were in your living room.

LULA: My dark living room. Talking endlessly.

CLAY: About my manhood.

LULA: I'll make you a map of it. Just as soon as we get to my house.

CLAY: Well, that's great.

LULA: One of the things we do while we talk. And screw.

CLAY (*trying to make his smile broader and less shaky*): We finally got there.

LULA: And you'll call my rooms black as a grave. You'll say, "This place is like Juliet's tomb."

CLAY (*laughs*): I might.

LULA: I know. You've probably said it before.

CLAY: And is that all? The whole grand tour?

LULA: Not all. You'll say to me very close to my

face, many, many times, you'll say, even whisper, that you love me.

CLAY: Maybe I will.

LULA: And you'll be lying.

CLAY: I wouldn't lie about something like that.

LULA: Hah. It's the only kind of thing you will lie about. Especially if you think it'll keep me alive.

CLAY: Keep you alive? I don't understand.

LULA (*bursting out laughing, but too shrilly*): Don't understand? Well, don't look at me. It's the path I take, that's all. Where both feet take me when I set them down. One in front of the other.

CLAY: Morbid. Morbid. You sure you're not an actress? All that self-aggrandizement.

LULA: Well, I told you I wasn't an actress . . . but I also told you I lie all the time. Draw your own conclusions.

CLAY: Morbid. Morbid. You sure you're not an actress? All scribed? There's no more?

LULA: I've told you all I know. Or almost all.

CLAY: There's no funny parts?

LULA: I thought it was all funny.

CLAY: But you mean peculiar, not ha-ha.

LULA: You don't know what I mean.

CLAY: Well, tell me the almost part then. You said almost all. What else? I want the whole story.

LULA (*searching aimlessly through her bag. She begins to talk breathlessly, with a light and silly tone*): All stories are whole stories. All of 'em. Our whole story . . . nothing but change. How could things go on like that forever? Huh? (*Slaps him on the shoulder, begins finding things in her bag, taking them out and throwing them over her shoulder into the aisle.*) Except I do go on as I do. Apples and long walks with deathless intelligent lovers. But you mix it up. Look out the window, all the time. Turning pages. Change change change. Till, shit, I don't know you. Wouldn't, for that matter. You're too serious. I bet you're even too serious to be psychoanalyzed. Like all those Jewish poets from Yonkers, who leave their mothers looking for other mothers, or others' mothers, on whose baggy tits they lay their fumbling heads. Their poems are always funny, and all about sex.

CLAY: They sound great. Like movies.

LULA: But you change. (*Blankly*) And things work on you till you hate them.

(*More people come into the train. They come closer to the couple, some of them not sitting, but swinging drearily on the straps, staring at the two with uncertain interest.*)

CLAY: Wow. All these people, so suddenly. They must all come from the same place.

LULA: Right. That they do.

CLAY: Oh? You know about them too?

LULA: Oh yeah. About them more than I know about you. Do they frighten you?

CLAY: Frighten me? Why should they frighten me?

LULA: 'Cause you're an escaped nigger.

CLAY: Yeah?

LULA: 'Cause you crawled through the wire and made tracks to my side.

CLAY: Wire?

LULA: Don't they have wire around plantations?

CLAY: You must be Jewish. All you can think about is wire. Plantations didn't have any wire. Plantations were big open white-washed places like heaven, and everybody on 'em was grooved to be there. Just strummin' and hummin' all day.

LULA: Yes, yes.

CLAY: And that's how the blues was born.

LULA: Yes, yes. And that's how the blues was born. (*Begins to make up a song that becomes quickly hysterical. As she sings she rises from her seat, still throwing things out of her bag into the aisle, beginning a rhythmical shudder and twistlike wiggle, which she continues up and down the aisle, bumping into many of the standing people and tripping over the feet of those sitting. Each time she runs into a person she lets out a very vicious piece of profanity, wiggling and stepping all the time.*) And that's how the blues was born. Yes. Yes. Son of a bitch, get out of the way. Yes. Quack. Yes. Yes. And that's how the blues was born. Ten little niggers sitting on a limb, but none of them ever looked like him. (*Points to* CLAY, *returns toward the seat, with her hands extended for him to rise and dance with her.*) And that's how the blues was born. Yes. Come on, Clay. Let's do the nasty. Rub bellies. Rub bellies.

CLAY (*waves his hands to refuse. He is embarrassed, but determined to get a kick out of the proceedings*): Hey, what was in those apples? Mirror, mirror on the wall, who's the fairest one of all? Snow White, baby, and don't you forget it.

LULA (*grabbing for his hands, which he draws away*): Come on, Clay. Let's rub bellies on the train. The nasty. The nasty. Do the gritty grind, like your ol' rag-head mammy. Grind till you lose your mind. Shake it, shake it, shake it, shake it! OOOOweeee! Come on, Clay. Let's do the choochoo train shuffle, the navel scratcher.

CLAY: Hey, you coming on like the lady who smoked up her grass skirt.

LULA (*becoming annoyed that he will not dance, and becoming more animate as if to embarrass him still further*): Come on, Clay . . . let's do the thing. Uhh! Uhh! Clay! Clay! You middle-class black bastard. Forget your social-working mother for a few seconds and let's knock stomachs. Clay, you liver-lipped white man. You would-be Christian. You ain't no nigger, you're just a dirty white man. Get up, Clay. Dance with me, Clay.

CLAY: Lula! Sit down, now. Be cool.

LULA (*mocking him, in wild dance*): Be cool. Be cool. That's all you know . . . shaking that wildroot cream-oil on your knotty head, jackets buttoning up to your chin, so full of white man's words. Christ. God. Get up and scream at these people. Like scream meaningless shit in these hopeless faces. (*She screams at people in train, still dancing.*) Red trains cough Jewish underwear for keeps! Expanding smells of silence. Gravy snot whistling like sea birds. Clay. Clay, you got to break out. Don't sit there dying the way they want you to die. Get up.

CLAY: Oh, sit the fuck down. (*He moves to restrain her.*) Sit down, goddamn it.

LULA (*twisting out of his reach*): Screw yourself, Uncle Tom. Thomas Woolly-Head. (*Begins to dance a kind of jig, mocking CLAY with loud forced humor.*) There is Uncle Tom . . . I mean, Uncle Thomas Woolly-Head. With old white matted mane. He hobbles on his wooden cane. Old Tom. Old Tom. Let the white man hump his ol' mama, and he jes' shuffle off in the woods and hide his gentle gray head. Ol' Thomas Woolly-Head.

(*Some of the other riders are laughing now. A drunk gets up and joins LULA in her dance, singing, as best he can, her "song." CLAY gets up out of his seat and visibly scans the faces of the other riders.*)

CLAY: Lula! Lula!

(*She is dancing and turning, still shouting as loud as she can. The drunk, too, is shouting, and waving his hands wildly.*)

Lula . . . you dumb bitch. Why don't you stop it? (*He rushes half stumbling from his seat, and grabs one of her flailing arms.*)

LULA: Let me go! You black son of a bitch. (*She struggles against him.*) Let me go! Help!

(*CLAY is dragging her toward her seat, and the drunk seeks to interfere. He grabs CLAY around the shoulders and begins wrestling with him. CLAY clubs the drunk to the floor without releas-*

ing LULA, *who is still screaming.* CLAY *finally gets her to the seat and throws her into it.*)

CLAY: Now you shut the hell up. (*Grabbing her shoulders*) Just shut up. You don't know what you're talking about. You don't know anything. So just keep your stupid mouth closed.

LULA: You're afraid of white people. And your father was. Uncle Tom Big Lip!

CLAY (*slaps her as hard as he can, across the mouth.* LULA's *head bangs against the back of the seat. When she raises it again,* CLAY *slaps her again*): Now shut up and let me talk.

(*He turns toward the other riders, some of whom are sitting on the edge of their seats. The drunk is on one knee, rubbing his head, and singing softly the same song. He shuts up too when he sees* CLAY *watching him. The others go back to newspapers or stare out the windows.*)

Shit, you don't have any sense, Lula, nor feelings either. I could murder you now. Such a tiny ugly throat. I could squeeze it flat, and watch you turn blue, on a humble. For dull kicks. And all these weak-faced ofays squatting around here, staring over their papers at me. Murder them too. Even if they expected it. That man there . . . (*Points to well-dressed man.*) I could rip that *Times* right out of his hand, as skinny and middle-classed as I am, I could rip that paper out of his hand and just as easily rip out his throat. It takes no great effort. For what? To kill you soft idiots? You don't understand anything but luxury.

LULA: You fool!

CLAY (*pushing her against the seat*): I'm not telling you again, Tallulah Bankhead! Luxury. In your face and your fingers. You telling me what I ought to do. (*Sudden scream frightening the whole coach.*) Well, don't! Don't you tell me anything! If I'm a middle-class fake white man . . . let me be. And let me be in the way I want. (*Through his teeth*) I'll rip your lousy breasts off! Let me be who I feel like being. Uncle Tom. Thomas. Whoever. It's none of your business. You don't know anything except what's there for you to see. An act. Lies. Device. Not the pure heart, the pumping black heart. You don't ever know that. And I sit here, in this buttoned-up suit, to keep myself from cutting all your throats. I mean wantonly. You great liberated whore! You fuck some black man, and right away you're an expert on black people. What a lotta shit that is. The only thing you know is that you come if he bangs you hard enough. And that's all. The belly rub? You wanted to do the belly rub? Shit, you don't even know how. You don't know how. That ol' dipty-dip shit you do, rolling your ass like an elephant. That's not my kind of belly rub. Belly rub is not Queens. Belly rub is dark places, with big hats and overcoats held up with one arm. Belly rub hates you. Old bald-headed four-eyed ofays popping their fingers . . . and don't know yet what they're doing. They say, "I love Bessie Smith." And don't even understand that Bessie Smith is saying, "Kiss my ass, kiss my black unruly ass." Before love, suffering, desire, anything you can explain, she's saying, and very plainly, "Kiss my black ass." And if you don't know that, it's you that's doing the kissing.

Charlie Parker? Charlie Parker. All the hip white boys scream for Bird. And Bird saying, "Up your ass, feeble-minded ofay! Up your ass." And they sit there talking about the tortured genius of Charlie Parker. Bird would've played not a note of music if he just walked up to East Sixty-seventh Street and killed the first ten white people he saw. Not a note! And I'm the great would-be poet. Yes. That's right! Poet. Some kind of bastard literature . . . all it needs is a simple knife thrust. Just let me bleed you, you loud whore, and one poem vanished. A whole people of neurotics, struggling to keep from being sane. And the only thing that would cure the neurosis would be your murder. Simple as that. I mean if I murdered you, then other white people would begin to understand me. You understand? No. I guess not. If Bessie Smith had killed some white people she wouldn't have needed that music. She could have talked very straight and plain about the world. No metaphors. No grunts. No wiggles in the dark of her soul. Just straight two and two are four. Money. Power. Luxury. Like that. All of them. Crazy niggers turning their backs on sanity. When all it needs is that simple act. Murder. Just murder! Would make us all sane.

(*Suddenly weary.*) Ahhh. Shit. But who needs it? I'd rather be a fool. Insane. Safe with my words, and no deaths, and clean, hard thoughts, urging me to new conquests. My people's madness. Hah! That's a laugh. My people. They don't need me to claim them. They got legs and arms of their own. Personal insanities. Mirrors. They don't need all those words. They don't need any defense. But listen, though, one more thing. And you tell this to your father, who's probably the kind of man who needs to know at once. So he can plan ahead. Tell him not to preach so much rationalism and cold logic to these niggers. Let them alone. Let them sing curses at you in code and see your filth as simple lack of style. Don't make the mistake, through some irresponsible surge of Christian charity, of talking too much about the advantages of Western rationalism, or the great intellectual legacy of the white man, or maybe they'll begin to listen. And then, maybe one day, you'll find they actually do understand exactly what you are talking about, all these fantasy people. All these blues people. And on that day, as sure as shit, when you really believe you can "accept" them into your fold, as half-white trusties late of the subject peoples. With no more blues, except the very old ones, and not a watermelon in sight, the great missionary heart will have triumphed, and all of those ex-coons will be stand-up Western men, with eyes for clean hard useful lives, sober, pious and sane, and they'll murder you. They'll murder you, and have very rational explanations. Very much like your own. They'll cut your throats, and drag you out to the edge of your cities so the flesh can fall away from your bones, in sanitary isolation.

LULA (*her voice takes on a different, more businesslike quality*): I've heard enough.

CLAY (*reaching for his books*): I bet you have. I guess I better collect my stuff and get off this train. Looks like we won't be acting out that little pageant you outlined before.

LULA: No. We won't. You're right about that, at least. (*She turns to look quickly around the rest of the car.*) All right!

(*The others respond.*)

CLAY (*bending across the girl to retrieve his belongings*): Sorry, baby, I don't think we could make it.

(*As he is bending over her, the girl brings up a small knife and plunges it into* CLAY's *chest. Twice. He slumps across her knees, his mouth working stupidly.*)

LULA: Sorry is right. (*Turning to the others in the car who have already gotten up from their seats*) Sorry is the rightest thing you've said. Get this man off me! Hurry, now!

(*The others come and drag* CLAY's *body down the aisle.*)

Open the door and throw his body out.

(*They throw him off.*)

And all of you get off at the next stop.

(LULA *busies herself straightening her things. Getting everything in order. She takes out a* notebook and makes a quick scribbling note. Drops it in her bag. The train apparently stops and all the others get off, leaving her alone in the coach.

Very soon a young Negro of about twenty comes into the coach, with a couple of books under his arm. He sits a few seats in back of LULA. When he is seated she turns and gives him a long slow look. He looks up from his book and drops the book on his lap. Then an old Negro conductor comes into the car, doing a sort of restrained soft shoe, and half mumbling the words of some song. He looks at the young man, briefly, with a quick greeting.)

CONDUCTOR: Hey, brother!
YOUNG MAN: Hey.

(The conductor continues down the aisle with his little dance and the mumbled song. LULA turns to stare at him and follows his movements down the aisle. The conductor tips his hat when he reaches her seat, and continues out the car.)

CURTAIN

COMMENTARY

In a very limited sense, black theater in the United States has a long history. At least as early as 1821 a semiprofessional black company performed in New York; and in the middle of the nineteenth century the black actor Ira Aldridge achieved international fame. But both of these facts are misleading: the early nineteenth-century black company chiefly performed plays by Shakespeare, and Aldridge—not welcome in the white companies of the United States—had to go to Europe to achieve his fame. At the end of the nineteenth century, and in the first decades of the twentieth, things were not much different, though a few black playwrights were emerging, and some black companies performed original plays, chiefly musicals. Still, it was not until the 1920s that black companies did much in the way of performing serious plays written by blacks, about blacks, and even then black actors chiefly found employment as performers in plays about black life written by white playwrights. But in 1926 William E. DuBois, a black leader, organized a black theater in Harlem and enunciated his vision of a new black drama:

> The plays of a real Negro theatre must be: 1. About us. That is, they must have plots that reveal Negro life as it is. 2. By us; they must be written by Negro authors who understand from birth and continued association just what it means to be a Negro today. 3. For us; that is, the Negro theatre must cater primarily to Negro audiences and be supported by their entertainment and approval. 4. Near us. The theatre must be in a neighborhood near the mass of Negro people.

But when it came to putting ink on paper, not every black writer was quite sure about how to proceed. In 1928, in an article titled "The Dilemma of the Negro Artist," James Weldon Johnson wrote:

> The moment a Negro writer picks up his pen and sits down to his typewriter he is immediately called upon to solve, consciously or unconsciously, this problem of the double audience. To whom shall he address himself, to his own black group or to white America?

Johnson in fact went on to assert that the black writer's audience "is always both white America and black America," but as we shall see in a moment, in the

1960s—the period of *Dutchman* and the period when "black" displaced "Negro"—not all black writers agreed.

The plays written by blacks from, say, 1920 to the early 1960s fit rather comfortably into the mainstream of American drama. Two plays by and about blacks, Langston Hughes's *Mulatto* (1938) and Lorraine Hansberry's *A Raisin in the Sun* (1959), enjoyed long runs on Broadway, which is to say that much of their support came from whites. These plays are not fundamentally different from, say, Philip Yordan's *Anna Lucasta*, which is by a white playwright and originally dealt with a working-class Polish family in Philadelphia but was altered for a black cast and then became a Broadway hit. With the growth of the civil rights movement in the 1960s, however, black theater changed decisively, helping to form the black power movement. Central to any study of black drama in the 1960s is LeRoi Jones (now known by his Muslim name Imamu Amiri Baraka), who was already established as a poet. In the early 1960s he visited Cuba, where he became deeply impressed by the revolution's ideals. Convinced that a revolution, not a grdual transformation, was needed in the United States, Jones founded the Black Arts Repertory Theater in Harlem, from which he excluded white audiences. *Dutchman* (1964) had already been staged to considerable acclaim at the Cherry Lane Theater, a predominantly white theater in New York, but when it was done at the Black Arts Repertory Theater—that is, when it was done for an all-black audience—it seemed to take on a new, revolutionary meaning, more dangerous in the white view, more liberating in the black.

In several essays in a volume called *Home* Jones argues that blacks, by virtue of their status as outsiders in American society, are especially equipped to see what the white Establishment cannot see. Not surprisingly, Jones has been harassed by public officials (they withdrew support from his Black Arts Repertory Theater), who claim that his revolutionary vision is a threat to public morality.

Jones admits the charge. Several quotations from "The Revolutionary Theatre" (included in *Home*) will give the gist of his position:

> The Revolutionary Theatre should force change; it should be change. . . .
> The Revolutionary Theatre must EXPOSE! Show up the insides of these humans, look into black skulls. White men will cower before this theatre because it hates them. Because they themselves have been trained to hate.

> The Revolutionary Theatre must take dreams and give them a reality. . . . It must be food for all those who need food, and daring propaganda for the beauty of the Human Mind. It is a political theatre, a weapon to help in the slaughter of these dim-witted fatbellied white guys who somehow believe that the rest of the world is here for them to slobber on.

> Our theatre will show victims so that their brothers in the audience will be better able to understand that they are the brothers of victims, and that they themselves are victims if they are blood brothers.[1]

---

[1] The four extracts on this page and the one on page 630 are reprinted from LeRoi Jones's *Home*, pages 210—11, 211–12, 213, 251, and 188, by permission of The Sterling Lord Agency, Inc. Copyright © 1961, 1962, 1963, 1964, 1965, 1966 by LeRoi Jones.

Finally, here is a passage from the short essay that concludes *Home*:

> The Black Artist's role in America is to aid in the destruction of America as he
> knows it. His role is to report and reflect so precisely the nature of the society,
> that other men will be moved by the exactness of his rendering and, if they are
> black men, grow strong through this moving, having seen their own strength,
> and weakness; and if they are white men, tremble, curse, and go mad,
> because they will be drenched with the filth of their evil.

Jones thus assumes that art is enormously potent, and in so doing he takes his
place in a tradition that can be traced back to Chekhov (who said that he wrote
his plays in order to make people see that their lives were dreary and to make
them create a better life for themselves), back to Shakespeare (whose Hamlet had
heard that "guilty creatures sitting at a play" may see their own image on the
stage and may be moved to "proclaim" their malefactions), and finally back to
Plato, who in the fourth century B.C. argued that the tragic dramatists should be
barred from the ideal commonwealth precisely because they have the power to
stir up pity and terror and thus to obscure a human being's rational faculty.
Much black writing of the 1960s assumes, with Jones, that theater should be
revolutionary. Indeed, it usually asserts that all theater is political; traditional
white drama expresses the values of an exploitive capitalism, and so the new
black drama is new not in expressing political values but in at last daring to
express the values of an exploited group. (Interested readers should consult the
summer 1968 issues of *The Drama Review*, which was devoted to essays by
blacks on black drama.)

In *Dutchman* Jones shows us an intolerable society. He does this not by
abstract preaching (though his essays are full of such preaching) but by vividly
setting forth on the stage characters engaged in a human relationship. Jones has
denied that Clay and Lula are symbols: they are, he says, real people in a real
world. At the same time, however, he admits that these characters are not only
individuals but are recognizable human types:

> Lula, for all her alleged insanity, just barely reflects the insanity of this
> hideous place. And Clay is a young boy trying desperately to become a man.
> *Dutchman* is about the difficulty of becoming a man in America. It is very
> difficult, to be sure, if you are black, but I think it is now much harder to
> become one if you're white. In fact, you will find very few white American
> males with the slightest knowledge of what manhood involves. They are too
> busy running the world, or running from it.

Let us begin with Lula. Jones presents her in such a way that we see her, we
know her, and he does this as a dramatist must, by endowing the character with
gestures and with language that ring true. Early in the play we see her as a vivid
rendition of a fairly common type, someone whose precise kind of vulgarity is
especially revealed in pretentiousness. She says that Clay was staring "in the
vicinity of my ass" (not "at my ass"), and before she tosses her apple core onto the
floor of the subway car she wraps it in a Kleenex. Through such bits of dialogue
and such gestures a very real human being is rendered visible to us—but our

perception of her reality is partly indebted to our recognition of her as a type. Moreover, she is not just one of millions of people whose special sort of coarseness reveals itself in ludicrous attempts at being genteel: she is also a *femme fatale*, a woman who seeks out victims, an Eve tempting Adam with her apple—specifically, the white woman who, surrounded by a myth of purity, lures black men to their destruction. Early in her conversation with Clay, Lula admits that she sought him out, and that she often lies because "it helps me to control the world." We can say that Lula—while never ceasing to be a specific woman who encounters a specific man on the subway—at least in part stands for, or, perhaps better, embodies the white society that Jones sees as enslaving all blacks.

And what of Clay, the black man? Jones said that "Clay is a young boy trying desperately to become a man." Just because Jones said so in an essay does not make it true in the play, but when we return to the play we can see ample evidence. Lula immediately sees Clay's effort to mature: "You look like you live in New Jersey with your parents and are trying to grow a beard." Again the specific details embody a type. She knows him well because he is, as she says, "a well-known type," and she later calls to Clay's attention that they have all the while been talking (however indirectly) about his manhood. The kind of man Clay wants to be is clear to Lula and to us, from his clothing:

> Boy, those narrow-shoulder clothes come from a tradition you ought to feel oppressed by. A three-button suit. What right do you have to be wearing a three-button suit and striped tie? Your grandfather was a slave, he didn't go to Harvard.

Clay is, Lula says, a "middle-class black bastard. . . . You ain't no nigger, you're just a dirty white man." Clay half knows that he is trying to surrender his black identity, and he also knows that he embodies the slave's murderous impulses toward his white oppressor. But Clay's bourgeois aspirations enslave him, and rather than achieve manhood by murdering his oppressor (so Jones seems to see it) Clay makes the mistake of thinking that murder can be avoided. "I sit here, in this buttoned-up suit, to keep myself from cutting your throats." Clay, self-imprisoned in the white man's clothes, thinks he is achieving manhood but he is ensuring his own destruction. The white oppressor, having none of Clay's illusions, knows that in white America the whites must murder the blacks (deprive them of "manhood") or the whites will be murdered by the blacks.

There is no Dutchman in the play; in fact the word is never used within the play. But, in conjunction with the description of the locale—"the *flying* underbelly of the city . . . the subway heaped in modern *myth*"—is it fanciful to see the endlessly shuttling subway as a modern version of the ship of the mythical flying Dutchman, who was condemned to sail the stormy seas until redeemed by the love of a pure woman? Both Lula and Clay are condemned to restlessness; Clay thinks he can find peace in the white man's world but he finds only the loss of identity; Lula's fate is that she is condemned to go on riding the subway, murdering one black after another.

TOPICS FOR DISCUSSION

1. Jones has written: "My ideas revolve around the rotting and destruction of America, so I can't really expect anyone who is part of that to accept my ideas." What assumptions does Jones here make about the spectator at a play? Do you think they are valid?
2. Characterize Clay. Do you think that Jones regards Clay as a hero or, on the contrary, as the sort of black who must be disposed of before blacks can have freedom?
3. Why does Lula kill Clay? Fear? Hatred? Frustration? Or what?
4. Do you think that Clay and Lula are believable characters, or are they only allegorical types? A comment by Jones may be useful in formulating your answer:

> [Lula] does not represent any thing—she is one. And perhaps that thing is America, or at least its spirit. You remember America, don't you, where they have unsolved murders happening before your eyes on television? How crazy, extreme, neurotic does that sound? Lula, for all her alleged insanity, just barely reflects the insanity of this hideous place. And Clay is a young boy trying desperately to be a man. *Dutchman* is about the difficulty of becoming a man in America.

5. Imagine a day when racial conflict is no more. Will the play be dated?

OUT OF OUR FATHERS' HOUSE

Eve Merriam, Paula Wagner, and Jack Hofsiss

When the actress Paula Wagner expressed dissatisfaction with some of the roles she had played, Eve Merriam suggested that Wagner do a one-woman show drawing on Merriam's anthology of journals and letters, *Growing Up Female* (1971). Merriam and Wagner together made the selections for the performance, and then, in collaboration with the director Jack Hofsiss, decided to convert the work, now titled *Out of Our Fathers' House*, into a play for three actresses and several musicians. It was first produced in 1975.

Eve Merriam has written plays, poetry, fiction, and nonfiction. Among her awards is an Obie for *The Club*. Paula Wagner, now a film agent in Hollywood, has played major roles in classical and modern dramas. Jack Hofsiss, director of many productions, won a Tony award for his direction of *The Elephant Man*.

CHARACTERS

ELIZA SOUTHGATE (1783–1809), *schoolgirl*
ELIZABETH CADY STANTON (1815–1902), *founder of the Women's Suffrage Movement*
MARIA MITCHELL (1818–1889), *astronomer*
"MOTHER" MARY JONES (1830–1930), *labor organizer*
DR. ANNA HOWARD SHAW (1847–1919), *minister and doctor*
ELIZABETH GERTRUDE STERN (1890–1954), *in the Jewish ghetto*

Three actresses play all six women and the minor characters. Musicians perform the songs (number of singers and instruments used are at the discretion of the director). ACTRESS #1 plays ELIZA SOUTHGATE and GERTRUDE STERN; ACTRESS #2 plays MARIA MITCHELL and ANNA HOWARD SHAW; ACTRESS #3 plays ELIZABETH CADY STANTON and MOTHER MARY JONES. *Out of Our Fathers' House* may also be performed by six actresses.

Out of Our Fathers' House, while taken from the actual writings of the characters portrayed, takes the theatrical form of a hypothetical conversation among the different woman characters. This is historically impossible, since these women could never have had such a conversation, but it is valid for the purposes of the piece. This is a timeless interaction in which these women act out for both themselves and each other the stories of their lives—in particular the accounts of their emergence "out of their fathers' house." It is essential that the piece be personal and conversational. The characters are not retelling but rather reliving their experiences. Both together and alone they make the journey into a world of self-sufficiency and the "solitude of self."

The stage is an abandoned summerhouse; there is a carousel horse, battered and broken, upstage right; a wicker table upstage center, or possibly an old coatrack, and another coatrack upstage left. Down center are three chairs placed in a semicircle in which musicians sit playing as the audience enters. The mood should be warm and comfortable. This is the secret place where one would run off to think and be alone.

Scene from Minor Latham's production. (Photo by Lowell Handler.)

As the lights dim, the musicians begin to sing.

Song: "Built My Lady a Fine Brick House"
I built my lady a fine brick house,
I built it in a garden.
I put her in, but she jumped out,
Oh, fare thee well, my darling.

I built my lady a high stone wall,
I built it in a garden.
I put her in, but she jumped out,
Oh, fare thee well, my darling.

I built my lady a gate with a lock,
I built it in a garden.
I put her in, but she jumped out,
So fare thee well, my darling.

(ACTRESS #1 *has entered during the last part of the song and states the first of the rules of etiquette for young ladies of the late eighteenth century in America. Others follow and take lines in sequence. The actresses carry with them lanterns and large wicker baskets which contain any props and costumes they might need for the show. It has the effect of running away from home. Rules of etiquette:*)

ACTRESS #1: Bite not thy bread, but break it.
ACTRESS #2: Look not earnestly at any other that is eating.
ACTRESS #3: Never sit down at the table until asked, and after the blessing.
ACTRESS #1: When moderately satisfied, leave the table.
ACTRESS #2: Sing not, hum not, wriggle not.
ACTRESS #3: When any speak to thee, stand up.
ACTRESS #2: Say not "I have heard it before."
ACTRESS #1: Never endeavor to help him out if he tell it not right.
ACTRESS #3: Snigger not. Never question the truth of it.
ACTRESS #2: Do not remove the gloves.
ACTRESS #3: Do not make a call of ceremony on a wet day . . . Always have an umbrella beside you and overshoes.
ACTRESS #1: Getting wet seldom fails to produce a cold.
ACTRESS #2: To lose your dinner is not half so dangerous.
ACTRESS #3: Wet feet and wet clothes have sent thousands to eternity before their time.
ACTRESS #1: Avoid unnecessary exposure to the evening air.
ACTRESS #2: Do not touch the piano unless asked.

ACTRESS #3: Do not call upon a gentleman unless he is a confirmed invalid.

(*The musicians are offstage by now*)

Song: "Little Bird"
(Theme for Gertrude Stern)
I'm as free a little bird as I can be
I'm as free a little bird as I can be
I will build my nest in the sour apple tree
Where those bad boys will never bother me.

VOICE: Elizabeth Gertrude Stern, born in 1890 in a Jewish ghetto of a large Midwestern city, growing up to obey her father's commandments.
Oh, who will shoe your little foot?
And who will glove your little hand?
(*Pause.*)

GERTRUDE (*Sings*):
Oh, it's papa will shoe my little foot
And it's mama will glove my little hand
(*Spoken*)
I remember looking down at the face of my father, beautiful and still in death, and for a brief moment, feeling my heart rise up . . . Surely it was in a strange suffocating relief . . . Now I am free!
(*Sings*)
And it's you who'll kiss my red-rosy cheek
When you come from that far-distant land.

Song: "Molly Hare" (Theme for Mother Jones)
Old Molly Hare, what are you doing there?
Running through a cotton patch as fast as I can tear.
Riding of a goat, leading of a sheep,
I won't be back till the middle of the week.

VOICE: Mary Harris Jones, born in 1830, lived to be one hundred years old and became known to children and adults alike as "Mother Jones."

MARY: I asked a man in prison once how he happened to be there, and he said that he had stolen a pair of shoes. I told him if he had stolen a railroad he would be a United States Senator.

Song: "My Horses Ain't Hungry"
(Theme for Anna Shaw)
My horses ain't hungry, they won't eat your hay,
So I'll get on my pony, I'm going away.
With all our belongings we'll ride till we come
To a lonely little cabin, we'll call it our home.

VOICE: Anna Howard Shaw, at age twelve, moved from a manufacturing town in Massachusetts to the wild woods of Michigan in 1859.

ANNA: Once when I was fourteen, I had been in the woods all day, buried in my books, and when I returned home at night, still in the dream world these books had opened to me, Father was awaiting my coming, dark with disapproval . . . *I was an idler who wasted time.* He ended a long arraignment by predicting that with such tendencies I would make nothing of my life.

> Song: "What'll We Do with the Baby?"
> (Theme for Elizabeth)
> What'll we do with the baby?
> What'll we do with the baby?
> What'll we do with the baby-o?
> We'll wrap it up in calico!
> Wrap it up in calico and send it to its pappy-o.

VOICE: Elizabeth Cady Stanton, born in New York State in 1815 . . . The same year her father was elected to Congress.

ELIZABETH: The custom of calling women Mrs. John This and Mrs. Tom That, and colored men Sambo and Zip-coon, is founded on the principle that white men are the lords of all. I cannot acknowledge this principle, and therefore I cannot bear the name of another. If the nineteenth century is to be governed by the opinions of the eighteenth, and the twentieth by the nineteenth, then the world will always be governed by dead men. I would rather make a few slanders from a superabundance of life than to have all the proprieties of a well-embalmed mummy.

> Song: "Rose, Rose and Up She Rises"
> (Theme for Maria Mitchell)
> Rose, rose and up she rises,
> Rose, rose and up she rises,
> Rose, rose and up she rises
> So early in the morning.
> I wonder where Maria's gone?
> I wonder where Maria's gone?
> I wonder where Maria's gone
> So early in the morning?

VOICE: Maria Mitchell, born on Nantucket Island in 1818. Her father was devoted to astronomy, and all the children were drafted into the service of counting seconds by the chronometer during his observations.

MARIA: Once a lady asked me if I told fortunes, and when I replied in the negative, she asked me if I weren't an astronomer. I admitted that I made efforts in that direction. She then asked me what could I tell if not fortunes. I told her that I could

tell when the moon would rise, and when the sun would set. She said, "Oh," in a tone which plainly implied "Is that all?"

> Song: "Young Maid"
> (Theme for Eliza Southgate)
> When I was a young maid, young maid,
> When I was a young maid, then oh then
> It was ha, ha, this-a-way, ha, ha, that-a-way
> This-a-way, that-a-way, then.

VOICE: Eliza Southgate, born in 1783 in Scarborough, Maine . . . sent by her parents to finishing school near Boston when she was fourteen.

ELIZA: You may justly say, my best of fathers, that every letter of mine is one which is asking for something more; never contented . . . I only ask. If you refuse me, I know you do what you think best, and I am sure I ought not to complain, for you have never yet refused me anything that I have asked, my best of parents, how shall I repay you?

> Song: "Listen to the Voices"
> Listen to the voices
> Out of darkness into daybreak
> Making their lives.

(*At this point, the actresses sit in the chairs that are placed center, and begin to knit, and write, and comb their hair. A musician sings. The song is "Monday Morning."*)

MUSICIAN:
> How old are you, my fair young maid?
> I'm going to be sixteen next Monday morning.

ELIZA: Such a frolic! Such a chain of adventures I never before met with. For two days it had been storming so much that the snow drifts were very large; however, as it was the last assembly, I could not resist the temptation of going, as I knew all the world would be there. About seven I went downstairs and immediately slipt on my socks and coat, and met Mr. Motley in the entry. The snow was deep, but Mr. Motley took me up in his arms, and sat me in the carriage without difficulty. I found a full assembly, many married ladies, and every one disposed to end the winter in good spirits. At one we left dancing. It stormed dreadfully, we could not get a coach until three o'clock. There were now twenty in waiting, the gentlemen scolding and fretting, the ladies murmuring and complaining as they all flocked to engage a seat. Luckily I was one of the first. Mr. Motley took me up in his arms and carried me till my weight pressed him so far into the snow that he had no power to move his feet. I rolled out of his arms and wallowed till I reached the gate; then rising to shake off the snow, I turned and beheld my beau fixed and immovable; he could not get his feet out to take another step! At length, making a great exertion to spring his whole length forward, he made out to reach the poor horse, who lay in a worse condition than his master. By this time all the family had gathered to the window. Indeed they saw the whole frolic. I was perfectly convulsed with laughter.

MARIA: I was up before six, made the fire in the kitchen and made coffee. Then I set the table in the dining room, and made the fire there. Toasted the bread and trimmed the lamps. Rang the breakfast bell at seven. After breakfast, made my bed, and "put up" the room. Then I came down to the library and looked over my comet computations till noon. I am just beginning to notice the different colors of the stars. I wonder that I have been so long insensible to this charm in the skies. The tints of different stars are so delicate in their variety . . . Before dinner I did some tatting, and made seven button-holes for K. I dressed and then dined.

ELIZABETH: The first event engraved on my memory was the birth of a sister when I was four years old. I heard so many friends remark, "What a pity it is she is a girl!" that I felt a kind of compassion for the little baby. True, our family consisted of five girls and only one boy, but I did not understand at the time that girls were considered an inferior order of beings.

ELIZA: Mother dear: You mentioned in yours of the sixteenth that it was a long time since you had received a letter from me; but it was owing to my studies. Now, Mama, what do you think I am going to ask you for? A wig. Eleanor Coffin has got a new one just like my hair, and it's only five dollars. I must either cut my hair or have one—I cannot dress it at all stylish. How much time it will save. In one year's time we could save it in pins and paper, besides the trouble. At the assembly I was quite ashamed of my head, for nobody has long hair. If you will consent to my having one, do send me a five-dollar bill by the post immediately after you receive this, for I am in hopes to have it for the next assembly.

MARIA: Came back again to the library at one-thirty . . . and looked over another set of computations, which took me until four o'clock. I was pretty tired by that time, and rested by reading "Cosmos." Lizzie E. came in, and I gossiped for half an hour. I went home to tea, and that over, I made a loaf of bread. Then I went up to my room and read through—partly writing—two exercises in German, which took me thirty-five minutes. It was stormy, and I had no observing to do, so I sat down to my tatting. Lizzie E. came in and I took a new lesson in tatting, so as to make the pearl-edge. I made about half a yard during the evening. What a pity that we cannot take dye stuff from the stars, so as to create a new brilliancy in fashion . . . At a little after nine I went home with Lizzie, and carried to the post office. I had kept steadily at work for sixteen hours when I went to bed.

(*At this point, the actresses begin to act out what they are saying. They can move around the stage, showing us and themselves just what they have gone through. They also play parts in each other's stories, gently aiding each other in their growth.*)

ELIZABETH: A student in my father's office told me one day, after conning my features carefully, that I had one defect that he could remedy. "Your eyebrows should be darker and heavier," he said, "and if you will let me shave them once or twice, you will be much improved." I consented, and slight as my eyebrows were, they seemed to have a handsome expression, for the loss of them had a most singular effect on my appearance. Everybody, including the shaver, laughed at my odd-looking face, and I was in the depths of humiliation while my eyebrows were growing out again. Needless to say, I never permitted the young man to repeat the experiment, although strongly urged to do so.

MARIA: I swept the sky two hours last night. Not a fringe of a cloud, all clear, all beautiful. I really enjoy that kind of work, but my back soon becomes tired, long before the cold chills me. I saw two nebulae in Leo with which I was not familiar, and that repaid me for the time . . . There will come with the greater love of science greater love to one another. We cannot see how impartially Nature gives of her riches to all without loving all, and helping all.

ELIZABETH: When I was eleven years old, my only brother, who had just graduated from Union College, came home to die. A young man of great talent and promise, he was the pride of my father's heart. I recall going into the large darkened parlor and finding the casket, mirrors and pictures all draped in white, and my father seated, pale and immovable as he took no notice of me. After standing a long while, I climbed upon his knee, when he mechanically put his arm about me, and with my head resting against his beating heart, we both sat in silence, he thinking of the wreck of all his hopes in the loss of a dear son—and I wondering what could be said or done to fill the void in his breast. At length he heaved a deep sigh and said, "Oh, my daughter, I wish you were a boy!" Throwing my arms about his neck, I replied, "I will try to be all my brother was." All that day, and far into the night I pondered the problems of boyhood. I thought that the chief thing to be done in order to equal boys was to be learned and courageous. So I decided to study Greek and learn to manage a horse. I learned to leap a fence on horseback. I began to study Latin, Greek and mathematics with a class of boys in the Academy, many of whom were much older than I. For three years one boy kept his place at the head of the class, and I always stood next. Two prizes were offered in Greek. I strove for one and took the second. One thought alone filled my mind. "Now," said I, "my father will be satisfied with me." I rushed into his office, laid the new Greek testament, which was my prize, on his table, and exclaimed: "I got it!" He took up the book, asked me some questions about the class, and evidently pleased, handed it back to me. Then he kissed me on the forehead and exclaimed with a sigh, "You should have been a boy!"

ELIZA: I thank heaven I was born a woman. I have now only patiently to wait till some clever fellow shall take a fancy to me and place me in a situation, I am determined to make the best of it, let it be what it will. We ladies, you know, possess that "sweet pliability of temper." But remember, I desire to be thankful I am not a man—I should not be content with mediocrity in any thing, but as a woman I am equal to the generality of my sex, and I do not feel that great desire of fame I think I should if I was a man. Were I a man, the law would be my choice. When I might hope to arrive at an eminence which would be gratifying to my feelings, I should then hope to be a public character, respected and admired. To be an eloquent speaker would be the delight of my heart.

ELIZABETH: As my father's office joined the house, I spent much of my time there, when out of school, talking with the students, and reading the laws in regard to women. One Christmas morning I went into the office to show them, among others of my presents, a new coral necklace and bracelets. They all admired the jewelry and then began to tease me with hypothetical cases of future ownership. "Now," said one, "If in due time you should be my wife, those ornaments would be mine. I could take them and lock them up, and you could never wear them except with my permission. I could even exchange them for a box of cigars, and you could watch them evaporate in smoke." When my attention was called to these odious laws, I would mark them in my father's books with a pencil, and I resolved to seize the first opportunity, when alone in the office, to cut every one of them out of the books; supposing my father and his library were the beginning and end of the law . . . However, this mutilation of his volumes was never accomplished. He explained to me one evening how laws were made, and that if his library should burn up it would make no difference in woman's condition. "When you are grown up, and able to prepare a speech," said he, "you must go down to Albany and talk to the legislators; tell them all you have seen in this office: the sufferings of women, robbed of their inheritance and left dependent on their unworthy sons, and if you can persuade them to pass new laws, the old ones will be a dead letter." Thus was the future object of my life foreshadowed and my duty plainly outlined by him who was most opposed to my public career when, in due time, I entered upon it.

MARIA: It seems to me that the needle is the chain of woman and has fettered her more than the laws of the country.

ELIZABETH: Sewing as an amusement is contemptible. It should be the study of every woman to do as little of it as possible.

MARIA: Once you emancipate her from the stitch-stitch-stitch, she would have time for studies which engross as never the needle can. I have a hunger of the mind which longs for knowledge of all around. Astronomy seems to me particularly fitted to women. A girl's eye is trained from early childhood to be keen, trained to the nicety of color. The eye that directs a needle in the delicate meshes of embroidery will equally bisect a star with the spider web of the micrometer.

ELIZABETH: When a woman pulls a cotton washrag from her pocket and begins to knit with a bowed head, fixing her eyes and concentrating her thoughts on a rag one foot square, it is impossible for conversation to rise above the washrag level. Think of the optic nerves being concentrated on a cotton rag. One can buy a whole dozen of these useful appliances with red borders and fringed for twenty-five cents. I beseech you, knit no more!

VOICE: Anna Howard Shaw, at age twelve, moved from a manufacturing town in Massachusetts to the wild woods of Michigan in 1859.

ANNA: Like most men, my dear father should

have never married. In practical matters he remained a child. To him, an acorn was not an acorn, but a forest of young oaks; thus when he took up his claim of three hundred and sixty acres of land in the wilderness of northern Michigan, and sent my mother and five young children to live there alone until he could join us, he gave no thought to the matter in which we were to make the struggle and survive the hardships before us. From his viewpoint, he was doing a man's duty. He had furnished us with land and the four walls of a log cabin. Some day, he reasoned, the place would be a fine estate which his sons would inherit, and in the course of time pass on to their sons. But to the present, we were one hundred miles from a railroad, forty miles from the nearest post office, and half a dozen miles from any neighbors, save Indians, wolves and wildcats; we were wholly unlearned in the ways of the woods, yet we faced our situation with clear and unalarmed eyes the morning after our arrival. We held a family council after breakfast and in this, though I was only twelve, I took an eager and determined part. I loved work—it has always been my favorite form of recreation—and my spirit rose to the opportunities of it which smiled on us from every side. You see, I knew I was doing my share for the family, and already too, I had begun to feel the call of my career. For some reason I wanted to preach . . . to talk to people, to tell them things. Just why, just what, I did not yet know, but I had begun to preach in the silent woods—to stand upon tree stumps and address the unresponsive trees—to feel the stir of aspiration within me. Some day I am going to college. And before I die I shall be worth ten thousand dollars.

GERTRUDE: The first clear impression of my childhood is a summer day.

VOICE: Elizabeth Gertrude Stern, born in 1890 in a Jewish ghetto of a large Midwestern city, growing up to obey her father's commandments.

GERTRUDE: My mother, in her puffed sleeves and tight-fitting dress, walked near my father, in his long coat and high hat: for he was assistant to the rabbi in our city. We children trudged behind. We came at last to the river's edge. Our father stood, waited a moment, and then prayed that his sins should be washed away by the river. I looked into the muddy waters below us, and at my father. All my life I had believed that, even when I resisted him, he was right. But today it seemed to me childish and perhaps even silly to be standing there, chanting that beautiful old tongue, the Hebrew, that I too had been taught, and asking

that our sins be washed away. Most of the people who lived near us were Catholics. They believed that if you told the priest what you had done, you would not be punished for your misdeeds. When I told my father one day of the Catholics, he looked down at me from his tall height, and said, "You can see how foolish and childish ignorant people are. A priest tells them that if they go to him, and confess, he can forgive them. Can a sin be undone by confession?" And yet here was my father, grave and pleading, sending our own sins down the waters of the Ohio. I looked at him, opened my mouth, but did not speak. I knew he would be angry. From that day, however, I did not accept anything he told me about our faith until I analyzed it myself.

MARIA: How can we dispute authority which has come down to us all established for ages? We cannot accept anything as granted beyond the first mathematical formula. Question everything else.

MARY: My husband was an iron moulder and a staunch member of the Iron Moulders' Union. We were living in Memphis when a yellow fever epidemic swept the city. Its victims were mainly among the poor and the workers. The rich and the well-to-do fled the city. Schools and churches were closed. People were not permitted to enter the house of a yellow fever victim without permits. The poor could not afford nurses. Across the street from me, ten persons lay dead from the plague. The dead surrounded us. They were buried at night, quickly and without ceremony. All about my house I could hear weeping and the cries of delirium. One by one, my four little children sickened and died. I washed their little bodies and got them ready for burial.

My husband caught the fever and died. I sat alone through nights of grief. No one came to me. No one could. Other homes were as stricken as mine. All day long, all night long, I heard the grating of the wheels of the death cart.

After the union had buried my husband I got a permit to nurse the sufferers. This I did until the plague was stamped out. I returned to Chicago and went again into the dress-making business. I became more and more engrossed with the labor struggle and I decided to take an active part in the efforts of the working people to better the conditions under which they worked and lived. I became a member of the Knights of Labor. From that time on, I became wholly engrossed in the labor movement.

GERTRUDE: My father did not approve of my continuing high school. It was time for me to think of marrying a pious man. He and Mother disagreed about it—their one quarrel. It was perhaps due to my going to high school, Mother said, gently and dubiously, that I wanted something new. I wanted to dance, to play, to have fun. I didn't mean to go to work at fourteen or fifteen, marry at sixteen, be a mother at eighteen, and an old woman at thirty. My mother drew her fine dark brows together. She took my face in her little hands, round and soft, in spite of her constant work. "You shall learn to dance, my daughter." And dance I did. I learned to dance in what, I suppose, was a dreadful public dance hall, for I paid a quarter a lesson there once every Wednesday night, and I danced with the lady instructor whenever she thought of me. But I faithfully put my foot out . . . one-two-three and turn . . . as the long line of men and women learned the steps of the waltz. I learned to two-step, and to Schottische, and even—wild days those—to do the barn dance. I wanted a new thing: happiness.

ELIZABETH: "What to do with a baby!" Though motherhood is the most important of all the professions, requiring more knowledge than any other department in human affairs, there was no attention given to preparation for this office. When my baby was four days old, we discovered that his collarbone was bent. The physician, wishing to get a pressure on the shoulder, braced the bandage round the wrist.

FIRST DOCTOR: Leave that ten days, and then it will be all right.

ELIZABETH: Soon after he left, I noticed that the baby's hand was blue, showing that the circulation had been impeded. This will never do. Nurse, take it off.

NURSE: No, indeed. I shall never interfere with the doctor.

ELIZABETH: So I took it on myself to send for another doctor. He expressed great surprise that the first should have put on so severe a bandage.

SECOND DOCTOR: That would do for a grown man, but ten days of it on a child would make him a cripple.

ELIZABETH: However, he did nearly the same thing, only fastening it round the hand, instead of the wrist. I soon saw that the ends of the fingers were all purple. So I took it off. What we want is a little pressure on that bone; that is what both those men have aimed at. How can we get it without involving the arm is the question.

NURSE: I'm sure I don't know.

ELIZABETH: Well, bring me three strips of linen rolled double. I then folded one, wet in arnica and water, and laid it on the collarbone. I put two other bands, like a pair of suspenders, over the shoulders, crossing them both in front and behind, pinning the ends to the diaper, which gave the needed pressure without impeding the circulation anywhere. Several times night and day, we wet the compress and readjusted the bands, until the inflammation had subsided. At the end of ten days, the doctors appeared and made their examination. All was right. Whereupon I told them how badly their bandages worked, and what I had done myself. They smiled at each other and said:

FIRST DOCTOR: Well . . .

SECOND DOCTOR: Well . . .

FIRST DOCTOR: Well . . .

SECOND DOCTOR: Well . . .

FIRST DOCTOR: After all, a mother's instinct . . .

SECOND DOCTOR: . . . is better than a man's reason.

ELIZABETH: Thank you, gentlemen, there was no instinct about it. I did some hard thinking before I saw how I could get pressure on the shoulder without impeding the circulation, as you did. . . . I trusted neither men nor books completely after this, either in regard to the heavens above or the earth below, but continued to use my "mother's instinct," if "reason" is too dignified a term to apply to a woman's thoughts.

MARIA: People have to learn sometimes not only how much the heart, but how much the head can bear.

ANNA: As an aid to public speaking I was taught to "elocute," and I remember in every mournful detail the occasion on which I gave my first recitation. We were having our monthly "public exhibition night," and the audience included not only my classmates, but their parents and friends as well. The selection I intended to recite was a poem entitled "No Sects in Heaven." But, when I faced my audience, I was so appalled by its size and by the sudden realization of my own temerity, that I fainted during the delivery of the first verse. Sympathetic classmates carried me into an anteroom and revived me, after which they naturally assumed that the entertainment I furnished was over for the evening. I, however, felt that if I let that failure stand against me I could never afterward speak in public; and within ten minutes, notwithstanding the protests of my friends, I was back in the hall and beginning my recitation a second time. The audience gave me its eager attention. Possibly it hoped to see me topple off the platform again, but nothing of the sort occurred. I went through the recitation with self-possession and even received some friendly applause at the end.

MARY: I organized an army of women house-keepers. On a given day they were to bring their mops and brooms and "the Army" would charge the scabs up at the mines. The general manager, the sheriff, and the corporation hirelings heard of our plans and were on hand. The day came and the women came with the mops and brooms and pails of water. I decided not to go up to the drip mouth myself, for I knew they would arrest me and that might rout the Army. I selected as leader an Irish woman who had a most picturesque appearance. She had slept late and her husband had told her to hurry up and get into the Army. She had grabbed a red petticoat and slipped it over a thick cotton nightgown. She wore a black stocking and a white one. She had tied a little red fringed shawl over her wild red hair. Her face was red and her eyes were mad. I looked at her and felt that she could raise a rumpus. I said, "You lead the Army up to the drip mouth, take that tin dishpan you have with you and your hammer, and when the scabs and the mules come up, begin to hammer and howl. Then all of you hammer and howl and be ready to chase the scabs with your mops and brooms. Don't be afraid of anyone!" Up the mountainside, yelling and hollering, she led the women, and when the mules came up with the scabs and the coal, she began beating on the dishpan and hollering, and all the Army joined in with her. The sheriff tapped her on the shoulder. "My dear lady," said he, "remember the mules. Don't frighten them." She took the old tin pan and she hit him with it and she hollered, "To hell with you and the mules!" He fell over and dropped into the creek. Then the mules began to rebel against scabbing. They bucked and kicked the scab drivers and started off for the barn. The scabs started running down the hill, followed by the army of women with their mops and pails and brooms. A poll parrot in a nearby shack screamed at the superintendent, "Ya got hell, did you? Ya got hell?" There was a great big doctor in the crowd, a company lap dog. He had a little satchel in his hand, and he said to me, "Mrs. Jones, I have a warrant for your arrest." "All right," said I, "keep it in your pill bag until I call for it. I am going to hold a meeting now." From that day on the women kept continual watch of the mines to see that the company did not bring in scabs. Every day women with brooms or mops in one hand and babies in the other arm, wrapped in little blankets, went to the mines and watched that no one went in. And all night long they kept watch.

There had been no bloodshed. There had been no riots. And the victory was due to the army of women with their mops and brooms.

GERTRUDE: I had known for months that I loved Dr. Morton. That was why I could speak to him of those things I felt most deeply, and why I felt the peace of my work. We were young, and we were well. We were mysterious and beautiful to one another. I had, all my life, thought of the woman-hood in me as something to be deprecated. I knew that a man of my faith must absent himself from his wife, as from defilement at certain holy times of his life. And always she must humbly beg God to pardon her that she is a woman. Had I not read in the prayer book the words my brothers and my father spoke daily . . . thanking God they were not women?

But my husband was modern. He said I must do anything I wanted to do, just as he did what he chose. Only, he must earn our living. Whatever I did I could do without thinking whether it was successful or not, only whether it made me happy. I took his hands in mine. I kissed him. But as I did, I know I wished he had said that my work was as practical a need to me as his. He thought I might do social work as a volunteer, without pay. I was, however, determined not to be an amateur. I wanted to work just as he did. I would not be happy otherwise. "So you want a career," he smiled, "and a husband tacked on?" "Haven't you one with me tacked on?" He kissed me then and laughed very tenderly indeed. "I like to work," I then said quietly, "I enjoy being important." He laughed then, relieved. He was delighted that I spoke like a child about my work. He kissed me and held me close.

MARIA: I put some wires into my telescope this morning. I dreaded it so much when I found yesterday that it must be done, that it disturbed my sleep. It was much easier than I expected. I took out the little collimating screws first, then I drew out the tube, and in that I found a brass plate which contained the lines . . . I was at first a little puzzled to know which screws held this in its place, and as I was very anxious not to unscrew the wrong ones, I took time to consider and found I need turn only two. Then out slipped the little plate with its three wires where five should have been, two having been broken. I took the hairs from my own head, taking care to pick out white ones because I have no dark ones to spare. I put in the two, by sticking them with sealing wax dissolved in alcohol into the little grooved lines which I had found. When I had, with great labor, adjusted these, as I thought, firmly, I perceived that some of the wax was still on the hairs and would make them yet coarser, and they were already too coarse: so I washed them with clear alcohol. Almost at once I washed out another wire and soon another. I went to work patiently and put in the five perpendicular ones besides the horizontal one, which like the others, had frizzled up and appeared to melt away. With another hour's labor I got in the five, when a rude motion raised them all again and I began over.

ELIZABETH: When I married Mr. Stanton, he announced to me that his business would occupy all his time, and that I must take charge of the housekeeping.

It is a proud moment in a woman's life to reign supreme within four walls. I studied up everything pertaining to housekeeping. Even washing day had its charms for me. The clean clothes on the lines and on the grass looked so white and smelled so sweet. I inspired my laundress with an ambition to get the clothes out earlier than our neighbors, and to have them ironed and put away sooner. I also felt the same ambition to excel in all departments of the culinary arts that I did at school in the different branches of learning. My love of order and cleanliness was carried throughout, from parlor to kitchen, from front door to back. I even gave the man an extra shilling to pile the logs of firewood with their smooth ends outward.

MARIA: There is an article on the study of medicine by women that states it would be better for the husband always to be superior to the wife. Why? And if so, doesn't this condemn the ablest of women to a single life? It is sad to see a woman sacrificing the ties of affection, even to do good.

GERTRUDE: During the influenza epidemic of 1917 my husband came down with the sickness. We already had two children. I knew that I must get work. Not, now, work to fill the time, or to express myself, but to earn the living of my family. What could I do?

One day it came to me. A big store needed a personnel director. The store manager spoke to me, smiled to hear I was a college woman, was interested but not antagonistic when he heard I was married. "Now, if you prove to be what we're looking for, there is a big job ahead of you, but first, you must know the work. First you must be a saleswoman." I was sent to the linen department,

then to the dress department. From there I was promoted to hats, and then to jewelry and books.

I had a problem not different from those many others were facing. I learned how to adjust things a bit. I prepared breakfast the night before. I taught my young daughter how to feed her little brother. I arranged for lunches for my children with a woman who lived near the school. Sometimes, I would run out to my home at noon, missing my own lunch, but having the peace of seeing that everything went well with my husband. He was tired and lonely, but he said nothing. He would sit, waiting till the children came home. After months I was promoted to the position of personnel director. I was a woman with a career for certain now. I was shown to my office. A pretty little thing with a real desk, a telephone, and a tray . . . for what? . . . for business letters. It looked just like the wire tray in which I drained dishes.

MARIA: Just at one o'clock I had got them all back in again. I attempted to put the plate back into its place. The sealing wax was not dry, and with a sudden motion I sent the wires all agog . . .

ELIZABETH: My second son was born, and a *third*. We moved from Boston to Seneca Falls, where our residence was on the outskirts of town . . . roads often muddy and no sidewalks most of the way. Mr. Stanton was frequently away from home. I had poor servants, and a fourth son was born. I have so much care with all these boys on my hands. How much I long to be free from housekeeping and children so as to have some time to read and think and write.

MARIA: Endow the already established institution with money. Endow the woman who shows genius with time.

> Song: "Housewife's Lament"
> With grease and with grime from corner to corner,
> Forever at war and forever alert,
> No rest for a day lest the enemy enter,
> I spend my whole life in a struggle with dirt.
> Oh, life is a toil and love is a trouble,
> Beauty will fade and riches will flee,
> Pleasures they dwindle and prices they double,
> And nothing is as I would wish it to be.

This time they did not come out of the little grooved lines into which they were put, and I hastened to set them in parallel lines. I gave up then for the day, but, as they looked well and were certainly in firmly, I did not consider that I had made an entire failure.

I thought it nice ladylike work to manage such slight threads and turn such delicate screws; but fine as are the hairs on one's head, I shall seek something finer, for I can see how clumsy they will appear when I get on with the eyepiece and magnify their imperfections. They look parallel to the eye, but with a little magnifying power a very little crook will seem a billowy wave, and a faint star will hide itself in one of the yawning abysses.

I remembered at once that I had seen some cocoons in the library which I had carefully refrained from disturbing. I found them perfect, and unrolled them. I made the perpendicular wires of the spider's web, breaking them and doing the work over again a great many times.

GERTRUDE: My husband got well. Well enough to go to work again. I believed in my equal rights as a woman, but I was happy that day because he was head of our life and of our home. That was something I yielded to him. As I gave my love to him. I left the store. I was thirty-eight years old. More than half of my life had been lived. I was doing nothing: I went to my desk, and there, like an old friend, stood a typewriter. I could write . . . Sometimes it seemed to me my fingers burned with the need to write. I realized that all that I had been living through all these years—the years of my work, of my past, were a mine on which I could draw. I went to see a magazine editor. I received a first assignment, and then another. At the end of the first year, I had earned almost three thousand dollars. I earned it so easily it seemed criminal to be so successful, for I was so happy in this work.

MARIA: I at length got all the wires in—crossing the five perpendicular ones with a horizontal one . . . After twenty-four hours' exposure to the weather, I looked at them. The spider webs had not changed. They were plainly used to a chill and made to endure changes of temperature.

ELIZA: Among the many gentlemen I have become acquainted with and who have been attentive, one I believe is serious. I know not how to introduce this subject, yet, as I fear you may hear it from others and feel anxious for my welfare, I consider it a duty to tell you all. I felt cautious of encouraging his attentions tho' I did not wish to *discourage* them . . . He is a man of business, uniform in his conduct and *very much respected.* He is a man in whom I could place the most unbounded confidence. Nothing rash or impetuous in his disposition, but weighs maturely every

circumstance: He appeared as solicitous that I should act with strict propriety as one of my most disinterested friends. He advises me like a friend and would not discourage his addresses till he had an opportunity of making known to my parents his character and wishes—this I promised, but the decision must rest with my parents, their wishes were my law. He insisted upon coming on immediately: that I refused to consent to. He is coming in October. And now, my dearest mother, I submit myself wholly to the wishes of my father and you, convinced that my happiness is your warmest wish, and to promote it has ever been your study. That I feel deeply interested in Mr. Bowne I candidly acknowledge. He is a firm, steady, serious man, there is nothing light or trifling in his character.

Song: "Monday Morning"
And now I am determined to have my own way and I'm
Going to be married next Monday morning.

Here we are at Mrs. Carter's boarding house, and though we have endeavored to keep ourselves as much out of the way as possible, a great many people have called to pay their respects to Mr. and Mrs. Bowne. When I hear an old acquaintance call me Mrs. Bowne, it really makes me stare at first, it sounds so very odd. I am enraptured with New York. You cannot imagine anything half so beautiful as Broadway. Mr. Bowne brings me a pocket full of fruit every day he comes home. I eat as many as I want, and I'm thinking how much I would give to get them to you. But this early fruit won't keep at all. As to news, New York is not so gay as last winter, few balls, but a great many tea parties. The city air has not stolen my country bloom yet, for everyone says, "I need not ask how you do, Mrs. Bowne, you look in such fine health."

ELIZABETH: My fifth child is a girl. The particulars I must give you. On Wednesday morning at six I awoke with a little pain which I well understood. Thereupon I jumped up, bathed and dressed myself, hurried the breakfast, eating none myself, of course, and got the house and all things in order, working bravely between the pains. I neither sat down nor lay down until half past nine, when I gave up all my vocations and avocations, secular and domestic, and devoted myself wholly to the one matter then brought before my mind. At ten o'clock the whole work was completed—the nurse and Amelia our housekeeper alone officiating. I had no doctor, and Mr. Stanton was away on business. When the baby was twenty-four hours old, I got up, bathed, making a sponge and sitz bath, put on my wet bandage, dressed, ate my breakfast, walked on the piazza, and the day being beautiful, I took a ride of three miles on the old plank road. Then I came home, rested an hour or so, read the newspaper and wrote a long letter to Mama . . . My joy in being the mother of a precious little girl is more than I can tell you. The baby is very large and plump, and her head is covered with black curly hair. Oh, how I do rejoice in her!

ELIZA: Walter Bowne, *Junior*. He is so hearty and well, he has not had a day's sickness. I am just starting to leave off his caps, I want his hair to grow before his grandmama sees him. He won't look so pretty without his caps. He creeps so much I find it hard to keep him so nice as I used to.

ANNA: The first notice of me ever printed in the newspaper. This was instigated by my brother-in-law, and was brief, but pointed. It read, "A young girl named Anna Shaw preached her first sermon at Ashton yesterday. Her real friends deprecate the course she is pursuing."

The members of my family, meeting in solemn conclave, sent for me. They had a proposition to make. If I gave up my preaching, they would send me to college and pay for the entire course. We had a long evening together, and it was a very unhappy one. At the end of it, I was given twenty-four hours in which to decide whether I would choose my people and college, or my pulpit and the Arctic loneliness of a life that held no family circle. It did not take me twenty-four hours of reflection to convince me that I must go my solitary way.

ELIZA: You are anxious, my dear mother, to hear from my own hand how I am. My cough is extremely obstinate, I have occasionally a little fever, tho' quite irregular and sometimes a week without any. I have a new physician to attend me: he keeps me on a milk diet, but allows me to eat eggs and oysters. I am much better already, my cough seems to be my only disorder, he thinks he can cure that. Indeed he speaks with perfect confidence and says he has no doubt that as soon as I leave this severe New York winter and get to warmer weather in South Carolina, my cough will soon leave me. You will hear from me often, my dear mother. At present my mind seems so occupied: leaving my children, preparing to go, making arrangements to shut up my house. 'Tis quite a trial to leave my little ones . . . My little Mary has a

wet nurse, she is a fine lively child . . . Adieu, my dear mother, I did not think I could have written half so much. Love to all my friends.

MARY: I went to Kensington, Pennsylvania, where seventy-five thousand textile workers were on strike. Of this number, more than ten thousand were little children. They were all stooped little things, round shouldered and skinny, some with their fingers off at the knuckles. Many of them were not yet ten years of age. I asked the newspapermen why they hadn't published the facts about child labor in Pennsylvania. They said that they couldn't because all ten mill owners had stock in the papers. "Well, I've got stock in these little children, and I'll arrange a little publicity." I decided that the children and I would go on a tour. I asked some of the parents if they'd let me have their little boys and girls for a week or ten days. I promised to bring them back safe and sound. They consented. The children carried knapsacks on their backs. They each had a knife and fork, a tin cup and plate. One little girl had a fife, and her brother had a drum. That was our band. The children were very happy, having plenty to eat, taking baths in the streams and rivers every day. I thought, When this strike is over and they go back to the mills, they will never have another holiday like this one. We marched to Jersey City, Hoboken, Princeton and into New York. Our march was doing its work. We were bringing to the attention of the nation the crime of child labor. In Coney Island, after the wild animal show, I put my little children into the empty iron cages and they clung to the bars while I talked. "You see those monkeys in those cages over there? The professors are trying to teach them to talk. The monkeys are too smart, for they fear that the manufacturers would buy them for slaves in their factories. And you see those little boys in those cages? Well, we are told that every American boy has the chance of being President. I tell you that those little boys would sell their chances any day for good square meals and a chance to play."

MARIA: A few evenings ago a meteor flashed upon me suddenly, very bright, very short-lived. It seemed to me that it was sent just for me especially, for it greeted me almost the first instant I looked up and was gone in a second, fleeting and beautiful. I am but a woman. For women there are, undoubtedly, great difficulties in the path, but so much the more to overcome. First, no woman should say, "I am but a woman." *But a woman—* what more can you ask to be?

ELIZA: I send a little pair of shoes for Mary, a

little cuckoo toy for Walter, and a tumbler of orange marmalade. I have had only one letter from New York since I have been here . . . not one line from my husband. I can tell you nothing flattering of my health. I am very miserable at present. How are my dear little ones? I hope not too troublesome. I hardly trust myself to think of them, precious children—how they bind me to life. Adieu. I have a bad headache and am low-spirited today.

Song: "When the Train Comes Along"
When the train comes along, when the train comes along,
I'm going to meet you at the station when the train comes along.

If my mother asks for me, tell her death doth summon me,
I'm going to meet her at the station when the train comes along.

If my father asks for me, tell him death doth summon me,
I'm going to meet him at the station when the train comes along.

VOICE UNDER MUSIC: Inscription on the monument in Archdale Churchyard, Charleston, South Carolina . . . "Sacred to the memory of Eliza Southgate Bowne, wife of Walter Bowne of New York, daughter of Robert Southgate Esquire of Scarborough, District of Maine, who departed this life on the nineteenth day of February, aged twenty-five years."

ANNA: The stagecoach took me within twenty-two miles of my destination. To my dismay, however, when I arrived Saturday evening, I found that the rest of the journey lay through a dense woods, and that I could reach my pulpit in time the next morning only by having someone drive me through the woods that night. It was not a pleasant prospect, for I had heard appalling tales of the stockades in this region and of the women who were kept prisoners there. But to miss the engagement was not to be thought of, and when, after I had made several vain efforts to find a driver, a man appeared in a two-seated wagon and offered to take me to my destination, I felt that I had to go with him, though I did not like his appearance. He was a huge, muscular person, with a protruding jaw and singularly evasive eye; but I reflected that his forbidding expression might be due, in part at least, to the prospect of the long night drive through the woods, to which possibly he objected as much as I did. It was already growing dark when

we started, and within a few moments we were out of the little settlement and entering the woods. With me I had a revolver I had long since learned to use, but which I very rarely carried. I had hesitated to bring it now—had even left home without it; and then, impelled by some impulse I never afterward ceased to bless, had returned for it and dropped it into my handbag. I sat on the back seat of the wagon, directly behind the driver, and for a time, as we entered the darkening woods, his great shoulders blotted out all perspective as he drove on in stolid silence. Soon the darkness folded around us like a garment. I could see neither the driver nor his horses. I could hear only the sibilant whisper of the trees and the creak of our slow wheels in the rough forest road. Suddenly the driver began to talk, and at first I was glad to hear the reassuring human tones, for the experience had begun to seem like a bad dream. I replied readily, and at once regretted that I had done so, for the man's choice of topics was most unpleasant. He began to tell me stories of the stockades— grim stories with horrible details, repeated so fully and with such gusto that I soon realized he was deliberately affronting my ears. I told him I could not listen to such talk. He replied with a series of oaths and shocking vulgarities, stopping his horses that he might turn and fling the words into my face. He ended by snarling that I must think him a fool to imagine he did not know the kind of woman I was. What was I doing in that rough country, and why was I alone with him in those dark woods at night? I tried to answer him calmly. "You know perfectly well who I am, and you understand that I am making this journey tonight because I am to preach tomorrow morning and there is no other way to keep my appointment." He uttered a laugh which was a most unpleasant sound. "Well," he said, coolly, "I'm damned if I'll take you. I've got you here, and I'm going to keep you here!" I slipped my hand into the satchel in my lap, and it touched my revolver. No touch of human fingers ever brought such comfort. With a deep breath of thanksgiving I drew it out and cocked it. "Here! What have you got there?" "I have a revolver," I replied, as steadily as I could. "And it is cocked and aimed straight at your back. Now, drive on. If you stop again, or speak, I'll shoot you." For an instant or two he blustered. "By God," he cried, "you wouldn't dare." "Wouldn't I?" I asked. "Try me by speaking just once more." Even as I spoke I felt my hair rise on my scalp with the horror of the moment, which seemed worse than any nightmare a woman could experience.

But the man was conquered by the knowledge of the waiting, willing weapon just behind him. He laid his whip savagely on the backs of his horses, and they responded with a leap that almost knocked me out of the wagon. He did not speak again, nor stop, but I dared not relax my caution for an instant. Hour after hour crawled toward day, and still I sat in the unpierced darkness, the revolver ready. I knew he was inwardly raging, and that at any instant he might make a sudden jump and try to get the revolver away from me. I decided that at his slightest movement I must shoot. But dawn came at last, and just as its bluish light touched the dark tips of the pines we drove up to the log hotel in the settlement that was our destination. Here my driver spoke. "Get down," he said gruffly. "This is the place." I sat still. Even yet I dared not trust him. Moreover, I was so stiff after my vigil that I was not sure I could move. "You get down, and wake up the landlord. Bring him out here." He sullenly obeyed and aroused the hotel owner, and when the latter appeared I climbed out of the wagon with some effort but without explanation. That morning I preached in my friend's pulpit as I had promised to do, and the rough building was packed with lumber men who had come in from the neighboring camp. Their appearance caused a great stir. There were forty or fifty of them, and when we took up our collection it was the largest that had ever been taken in the history of the settlement, but I soon learned that it wasn't spiritual comfort that I offered which appealed to the men. My driver of the night before, who was one of their number, had told his pals of his experience, and the whole camp had poured into town to see the woman minister who carried a revolver. "Her sermon?" I overheard one of them say. "I dunno what she preached. But, sure don't make no mistake about one thing, the little lady preacher has sure got grit!"

(*All the characters alternate the lines of "Solitude of Self."*)

ALL (*alternating*): We must make the voyage of life alone.

It matters not whether the solitary voyager be a man or a woman.

We come into the world alone, unlike all who have gone before us: we leave it alone under circumstances peculiar to ourselves.

No mortal ever has been, no mortal ever will be like the soul just launched on the sea of life.

Nature never repeats herself, and the possibilities of one human soul will never be found in another.

The same individual is not the same at all times. Each individual has a middle self, which is not the one of today, nor of yesterday, nor of tomorrow, but among these different selves.

In youth our most bitter disappointments, our brightest hopes and ambitions are known only to ourselves. Even our friendship and love we never fully share with another.

The solitude of individual life: its pains, its penalties, its responsibilities.

The solitude of self. It is the height of cruelty to rob the individual of a single natural right.

Our inner being, which we call our self, no eye nor touch has ever pierced.

Such is individual life. Who can take/ . . . dare take/ . . . on himself/herself/the rights,/the responsibilities, the duties/of another human soul?

(*During the course of the preceding section, the actresses have moved their chairs into a close-knit semicircle downstage center: They place their lanterns on the floor in front of them. When they are done speaking, they stare out at the audience for the first time, seemingly to ask the audience to make its own choice. They stay looking at the audience as the lights dim slowly to darkness.*)

COMMENTARY

Although in England in the late seventeenth century a woman, Aphra Behn, was one of the most popular playwrights, and although in America in the mid-nineteenth century another woman, Anna Cora Mowatt, wrote *Fashion*, the best-known social comedy of the period, it is nevertheless true that very few women wrote for the theater until about 1915. And even when women did achieve some prominence as playwrights in the earlier twentieth century (for instance, Anne Nichols, author of the immensely popular *Abie's Irish Rose* [1922], and Lillian Hellman and Clare Boothe Luce in the 1930s), their plays usually did not reveal a distinctly feminist point of view. Nor were they (especially Hellman) noticeably sympathetic in their characterizations of women. In short, despite some important exceptions, women have not played a large role as writers for the theater, even though, of course, many women have made great contributions to the theater as actresses.

Honor Moore, in *The New Women's Theatre*, suggests an explanation: theater (unlike writing fiction or poetry) is a communal activity, and men have not welcomed women into this community. "Male exclusion of women," she says, "perhaps more than any other single factor, has been responsible for the lack of a female tradition in playwriting similar to that which exists in both fiction and poetry." Then, too, writing for the theater requires larger chunks of time—for instance, whole days at early rehearsals—than most women in the past, tied to households, were able to spare.

In any case, not until the late 1960s, as part of the women's movement, did a substantial number of women begin to set forth on the stage a drama of feminine sensibility—writing, for example, about the difficult business of surviving as a woman in a man's world. As Eve Merriam said in 1976, surveying playwrighting since 1960, "First you had to write an Arthur Miller play, then you had to write an absurd play. Now there is a new freedom—you can write empathetic women characters."

But, as Ms. Merriam demonstrates in *Out of Our Fathers' House*, a woman playwright may want to do more than depict empathetic women. She may want to write a new kind of play, a play fundamentally different from the kind of play that men (and a very few women) have been writing for almost 2,500 years. Let us approach this matter a bit indirectly. Earlier in this book we quoted a passage by William Butler Yeats on the tragic hero's passionate assertion of his identity. The passage is worth quoting again, for it conveys the dominant view of what a tragic play is about:

> Know that when all words are said
> And a man is fighting mad,
> Something drops from eyes long blind,
> He completes his partial mind,
> For an instant stands at ease,
> Laughs aloud, his heart at peace.
> Even the wisest man grows tense
> With some sort of violence
> Before he can accomplish fate,
> Know his work or choose his mate.

This is all very male; possibly "man" is used generically, standing for humanity (that mght be offensive enough), but more likely Yeats meant "man" when he said "man"; only a male, he probably felt, can achieve this sort of tragic status.

Women have, of course, often played significant roles in early drama, even in tragedies, usually as secondary characters (King Lear's daughters are obvious examples) but sometimes even as the major character (Antigone is an example). Usually, however, when a woman is at the center of a play she is either like a male (and therefore is regarded as unwomanly and unnatural), or acts so passionately that she is regarded as neurotic (and as all too female). What Merriam, Wagner, and Hofsiss give us in *Out of Our Fathers' House* is a drama about six women—a sort of communal play that joins women from the late eighteenth century through the mid-twentieth century. There is no central hero; instead, we get a group of women who share the problem of living in male-dominated societies. The very idea of the nature of a play, then, is reconceived; instead of seeing one character pitted against another or perhaps against a group of characters, we see a sort of consciousness-raising group. There is plenty of conflict in the play, explicit in many speeches, but the conflict is not embodied in opposing characters and therefore the play "says" something that traditional plays do not usually say.

TOPICS FOR DISCUSSION

1. Take one character and trace, through her speeches, the forces that impede her development as an individual.
2. Take another character and summarize her personality.
3. What do you think Eliza Southgate contributes to the play? What would be lost if she were omitted?
4. What sort of structure does the play have? To what extent are speeches related to previous speeches? Does the play have any significant organization? Explain.
5. Discuss the use of music in the play. Are some—or all—of the songs relevant? What, if anything, would be lost if they were omitted?
6. Three actresses play the six women, and the authors specify which two roles each actress is to perform. Are the pairings significant? If so, how? If you were producing *Out of Our Fathers' House*, would you use three actresses or (also acceptable, the authors say) six actresses? Why?
7. Exactly what is the attitude toward work revealed by Gertrude's husband? What is Gertrude's attitude toward work?
8. The longest speech in the play is Anna's, about her ride in a two-seated wagon, which comes just before the alternating lines spoken by all of the women at the end of the play. What is the point of her speech? Why do you suppose it comes so late in the play?
9. The play is certainly serious, but it also includes some comic passages, for instance the responses of the doctors to Elizabeth Cady Stanton when she corrects them. Do you find other amusing passages in this serious play? If so, specify a few.

"MASTER HAROLD" . . . AND THE BOYS

Athol Fugard

Athol Fugard (his full name is Athol Harold Lannigan Fugard) was born in 1932 in Cape Province, South Africa. In 1958 he organized a multiracial theater, for which he wrote plays (A *Lesson of Aloes* won the New York Drama Critics' Circle Award as the best play of 1980) and also served as a director and an actor. In addition to writing plays, he has written a novel and an autobiographical volume entitled *Notebooks 1960–1977.* "*MASTER HAROLD*" . . . *and the boys* was first produced in 1982 at the Yale Repertory Theatre.

The St. George's Park Tea Room on a wet and windy Port Elizabeth afternoon.

Tables and chairs have been cleared and are stacked on one side except for one which stands apart with a single chair. On this table a knife, fork, spoon and side plate in anticipation of a simple meal, together with a pile of comic books.

Other elements: a serving counter with a few stale cakes under glass and a not very impressive display of sweets, cigarettes and cool drinks, etc.; a few cardboard advertising handouts—Cadbury's Chocolate, Coca-Cola—and a blackboard on which an untrained hand has chalked up the prices of Tea, Coffee, Scones, Milkshakes—all flavors—and Cool Drinks; a few sad ferns in pots; a telephone; an old-style jukebox.

There is an entrance on one side and an exit into a kitchen on the other.

Leaning on the solitary table, his head cupped in one hand as he pages through one of the comic books, is SAM. A black man in his midforties. He wears the white coat of a waiter. Behind him on his knees, mopping down the floor with a bucket of water and a rag, is WILLIE. Also black and about the same age as Sam. He has his sleeves and trousers rolled up.

The year: 1950.

Ramolao Makhene as Willie, Duart Sylwain as Hally, and John Kani as Sam in a 1983 Market Theatre Company production at Cottesloe. (Photo by Donald Cooper © Photostage.)

WILLIE (*singing as he works*):
> "She was scandalizin' my name,
> She took my money
> She called me honey
> But she was scandalizin' my name.
> Called it love but was playin' a game . . ."

(*He gets up and moves the bucket. Stands thinking for a moment, then, raising his arms to hold an imaginary partner, he launches into an intricate ballroom dance step. Although a mildly comic figure, he reveals a reasonable degree of accomplishment.*)

Hey, Sam.

(SAM, *absorbed in the comic book, does not respond.*)

Hey, Boet[1] Sam!

(SAM *looks up.*)

I'm getting it. The quickstep. Look now and tell me. (*He repeats the step.*) Well?
SAM (*encouragingly*): Show me again.
WILLIE: Okay, count for me.
SAM: Ready?
WILLIE: Ready.
SAM: Five, six, seven, eight. . . . (WILLIE *starts to dance.*) A-n-d one two three four . . . and one two three four. . . . (*Ad libbing as* WILLIE *dances*) Your shoulders, Willie . . . your shoulders! Don't look down! Look happy, Willie! Relax, Willie!
WILLIE (*desperate but still dancing*): I am relax.
SAM: No, you're not.
WILLIE (*he falters*): Ag no man, Sam! Mustn't talk. You make me make mistakes.
SAM: But you're stiff.
WILLIE: Yesterday I'm not straight . . . today I'm too stiff!
SAM: Well, you are. You asked me and I'm telling you.
WILLIE: Where?
SAM: Everywhere. Try to glide through it.
WILLIE: Glide?
SAM: Ja, make it smooth. And give it more style. It must look like you're enjoying yourself.
WILLIE (*emphatically*): I wasn't.
SAM: Exactly.
WILLIE: How can I enjoy myself? Not straight, too stiff and now it's also glide, give it more style,

make it smooth. . . . Haai! Is hard to remember all those things, Boet Sam.
SAM: That's your trouble. You're trying too hard.
WILLIE: I try hard because it *is* hard.
SAM: But don't let me see it. The secret is to make it look easy. Ballroom must look happy, Willie, not like hard work. It must . . . Ja! . . . it must look like romance.
WILLIE: Now another one! What's romance?
SAM: Love story with happy ending. A handsome man in tails, and in his arms, smiling at him, a beautiful lady in evening dress!
WILLIE: Fred Astaire, Ginger Rogers.
SAM: You got it. Tapdance or ballroom, it's the same. Romance. In two weeks' time when the judges look at you and Hilda, they must see a man and a woman who are dancing their way to a happy ending. What I saw was you holding her like you were frightened she was going to run away.
WILLIE: Ja! Because that is what she wants to do! I got no romance left for Hilda anymore, Boet Sam.
SAM: Then pretend. When you put your arms around Hilda, imagine she is Ginger Rogers.
WILLIE: With no teeth? You try.
SAM: Well, just remember, there's only two weeks left.
WILLIE: I know, I know! (*To the jukebox.*) I do it better with music. You got sixpence for Sarah Vaughan?
SAM: That's a slow foxtrot. You're practicing the quickstep.
WILLIE: I'll practice slow foxtrot.
SAM (*shaking his head*): It's your turn to put money in the jukebox.
WILLIE: I only got bus fare to go home. (*He returns disconsolately to his work.*) Love story and happy ending! She's doing it all right, Boet Sam, but is not me she's giving happy endings. Fuckin' whore! Three nights now she doesn't come practice. I wind up gramophone, I get record ready and I sit and wait. What happens? Nothing. Ten o'clock I start dancing with my pillow. You try and practice romance by yourself, Boet Sam. Struesgod, she doesn't come tonight I take back my dress and ballroom shoes and I find me new partner. Size twenty-six. Shoes size seven. And now she's also making trouble for me with the baby again. Reports me to Child Wellfed, that I'm not giving her money. She lies! Every week I am giving her money for milk. And how do I know is my baby? Only his hair looks like me. She's fucking around

   [1] **Boet**: Brother

all the time I turn my back. Hilda Samuels is a bitch! (*Pause.*) Hey, Sam!

SAM: Ja.

WILLIE: You listening?

SAM: Ja.

WILLIE: So what you say?

SAM: About Hilda?

WILLIE: Ja.

SAM: When did you last give her a hiding?

WILLIE (*reluctantly*): Sunday night.

SAM: And today is Thursday.

WILLIE (*he knows what's coming*): Okay.

SAM: Hiding on Sunday night, then Monday, Tuesday and Wednesday she doesn't come to practice . . . and you are asking me why?

WILLIE: I said okay, Boet Sam!

SAM: You hit her too much. One day she's going to leave you for good.

WILLIE: So? She makes me the hell-in too much.

SAM (*emphasizing his point*): *Too* much and *too* hard. You had the same trouble with Eunice.

WILLIE: Because she also make the hell-in, Boet Sam. She never got the steps right. Even the waltz.

SAM: Beating her up every time she makes a mistake in the waltz? (*Shaking his head*) No, Willie! That takes the pleasure out of ballroom dancing.

WILLIE: Hilda is not too bad with the waltz, Boet Sam. Is the quickstep where the trouble starts.

SAM (*testing him gently*): How's your pillow with the quickstep?

WILLIE (*ignoring the tease*): Good! And why? Because it got no legs. That's her trouble. She can't move them quick enough, Boet Sam. I start the record and before halfway Count Basie is already winning. Only time we catch up with him is when gramophone runs down. (SAM *laughs.*) Haaikona, Boet Sam, is not funny.

SAM (*snapping his fingers*): I got it! Give her a handicap.

WILLIE: What's that?

SAM: Give her a ten-second start and then let Count Basie go. Then I put my money on her. Hot favorite in the Ballroom Stakes: Hilda Samuels ridden by Willie Malopo.

WILLIE (*turning away*): I'm not talking to you no more.

SAM (*relenting*): Sorry, Willie. . . .

WILLIE: It's finish between us.

SAM: Okay, okay . . . I'll stop.

WILLIE: You can also fuck off.

SAM: Willie, listen! I want to help you!

WILLIE: No more jokes?

SAM: I promise.

WILLIE: Okay. Help me.

SAM (*his turn to hold an imaginary partner*): Look and learn. Feet together. Back straight. Body relaxed. Right hand placed gently in the small of her back and wait for the music. Don't start worrying about making mistakes or the judges or the other competitors. It's just you, Hilda and the music, and you're going to have a good time. What Count Basie do you play?

WILLIE: "You the cream in my coffee, you the salt in my stew."

SAM: Right. Give it to me in strict tempo.

WILLIE: Ready?

SAM: Ready.

WILLIE: A-n-d . . . (*Singing*)
"You the cream in my coffee.
You the salt in my stew.
You will always be
my necessity.
I'd be lost without you. . . ." (*etc.*)

(SAM *launches into the quickstep. He is obviously a much more accomplished dancer than* WILLIE. HALLY *enters. A seventeen-year-old white boy. Wet raincoat and school case. He stops and watches* SAM. *The demonstration comes to an end with a flourish. Applause from* HALLY *and* WILLIE.)

HALLY: Bravo! No question about it. First place goes to Mr. Sam Semela.

WILLIE (*in total agreement*): You was gliding with style, Boet Sam.

HALLY (*cheerfully*): How's it, chaps?

SAM: Okay, Hally.

WILLIE (*springing to attention like a soldier and saluting*): At your service, Master Harold!

HALLY: Not long to the big event, hey!

SAM: Two weeks.

HALLY: You nervous?

SAM: No.

HALLY: Think you stand a chance?

SAM: Let's just say I'm ready to go out there and dance.

HALLY: It looked like it. What about you, Willie?

(WILLIE *groans.*)

What's the matter?

SAM: He's got leg trouble.

HALLY (*innocently*): Oh, sorry to hear that, Willie.

WILLIE: Boet Sam! You promised. (WILLIE *returns to his work.*)

(HALLY *deposits his school case and takes off his raincoat. His clothes are a little neglected and untidy: black blazer with school badge, gray flannel trousers in need of an ironing, khaki shirt and tie, black shoes. SAM has fetched a towel for* HALLY *to dry his hair.*)

HALLY: God, what a lousy bloody day. It's coming down cats and dogs out there. Bad for business, chaps . . . (*conspiratorial whisper*) . . . but it also means we're in for a nice quiet afternoon.

SAM: You can speak loud. Your Mom's not here.

HALLY: Out shopping?

SAM: No. The hospital.

HALLY: But it's Thursday. There's no visiting on Thursday afternoons. Is my Dad okay?

SAM: Sounds like it. In fact, I think he's going home.

HALLY (*stopped short by* SAM's *remark*): What do you mean?

SAM: The hospital phoned.

HALLY: To say what?

SAM: I don't know. I just heard your Mom talking.

HALLY: So what makes you say he's going home?

SAM: It sounded as if they were telling her to come and fetch him.

(HALLY *thinks about what* SAM *has said for a few seconds.*)

HALLY: When did she leave?

SAM: About an hour ago. She said she would phone you. Want to eat?

(HALLY *doesn't respond.*)

Hally, want your lunch?

HALLY: I suppose so. (*His mood has changed.*) What's on the menu? . . . as if I don't know.

SAM: Soup, followed by meat pie and gravy.

HALLY: Today's?

SAM: No.

HALLY: And the soup?

SAM: Nourishing pea soup.

HALLY: Just the soup. (*The pile of comic books on the table.*) And these?

SAM: For your Dad. Mr. Kempston brought them.

HALLY: You haven't been reading them, have you?

SAM: Just looking.

HALLY (*examining the comics*): *Jungle Jim* . . . *Batman and Robin* . . . *Tarzan* . . . God, what rubbish! Mental pollution. Take them away.

(SAM *exits waltzing into the kitchen.* HALLY *turns to* WILLIE.)

HALLY: Did you hear my Mom talking on the telephone, Willie?

WILLIE: No, Master Hally. I was at the back.

HALLY: And she didn't say anything to you before she left?

WILLIE: She said I must clean the floors.

HALLY: I mean about my Dad.

WILLIE: She didn't say nothing to me about him, Master Hally.

HALLY (*with conviction*): No! It can't be. They said he needed at least another three weeks of treatment. Sam's definitely made a mistake. (*Rummages through his school case, finds a book and settles down at the table to read.*) So, Willie!

WILLIE: Yes, Master Hally! Schooling okay today?

HALLY: Yes, okay. . . . (*He thinks aobut it.*). . . . No, not really. Ag, what's the difference? I don't care. And Sam says you've got problems.

WILLIE: Big problems.

HALLY: Which leg is sore?

(WILLIE *groans.*)

Both legs.

WILLIE: There is nothing wrong with my legs. Sam is just making jokes.

HALLY: So then you *will* be in the competition.

WILLIE: Only if I can find a partner.

HALLY: But what about Hilda?

SAM (*returning with a bowl of soup*): She's the one who's got trouble with her legs.

HALLY: What sort of trouble, Willie?

SAM: From the way he describes it, I think the lady has gone a bit lame.

HALLY: Good God! Have you taken her to see a doctor?

SAM: I think a vet would be better.

HALLY: What do you mean?

SAM: What do you call it again when a racehorse goes very fast?

HALLY: Gallop?

SAM: That's it!

WILLIE: Boet Sam!

HALLY: "A gallop down the homestretch to the winning post." But what's that got to do with Hilda?

SAM: Count Basie always gets there first.

(WILLIE *lets fly with his slop rag. It misses* SAM *and hits* HALLY.)

HALLY (*furious*): For Christ's sake, Willie! What the hell do you think you're doing!

WILLIE: Sorry, Master Hally, but it's him. . . .

HALLY: Act your bloody age! (*Hurls the rag back at* WILLIE.) Cut out the nonsense now and get on with your work. And you too, Sam. Stop fooling around.

(SAM *moves away.*)

No. Hang on. I haven't finished! Tell me exactly what my Mom said.

SAM: I have. "When Hally comes, tell him I've gone to the hospital and I'll phone him."

HALLY: She didn't say anything about taking my Dad home?

SAM: No. It's just that when she was talking on the phone. . . .

HALLY (*interrupting him*): No, Sam. They can't be discharging him. She would have said so if they were. In any case, we saw him last night and he wasn't in good shape at all. Staff nurse even said there was talk about taking more X-rays. And now suddenly today he's better? If anything, it sounds more like a bad turn to me . . . which I sincerely hope it isn't. Hang on . . . how long ago did you say she left?

SAM: Just before two . . . (*his wrist watch*) . . . hour and a half.

HALLY: I know how to settle it. (*Behind the counter to the telephone. Talking as he dials*) Let's give her ten minutes to get to the hospital, ten minutes to load him up, another ten, at the most, to get home and another ten to get him inside. Forty minutes. They should have been home for at least half an hour already. (*Pause—he waits with the receiver to his ear.*) No reply, chaps. And you know why? Because she's at his bedside in hospital helping him pull through a bad turn. You definitely heard wrong.

SAM: Okay.

(*As far as* HALLY *is concerned, the matter is settled. He returns to his table, sits down and divides his attention between the book and his soup.* SAM *is at his school case and picks up a textbook.*)

Modern Graded Mathematics for Standards Nine and Ten. (*Opens it at random and laughs at something he sees.*) Who is this supposed to be?

HALLY: Old fart-face Prentice.

SAM: Teacher?

ALLY: Thinks he is. And believe me, that is not a bad likeness.

SAM: Has he seen it?

HALLY: Yes.

SAM: What did he say?

HALLY: Tried to be clever, as usual. Said I was no Leonardo da Vinci and that bad art had to be punished. So, six of the best, and his are bloody good.

SAM: On your bum?

HALLY: Where else? The days when I got them on my hands are gone forever, Sam.

SAM: With your trousers down!

HALLY: No. He's not quite that barbaric.

SAM: That's the way they do it in jail.

HALLY (*flicker of morbid interest*): Really?

SAM: Ja. When the magistrate sentences you to "strokes with a light cane."

HALLY: Go on.

SAM: They make you lie down on a bench. One policeman pulls down your trousers and holds your ankles, another one pulls your shirt over your head and holds your arms. . . .

HALLY: Thank you! That's enough.

SAM: . . . and the one that gives you the strokes talks to you gently and for a long time between each one. (*He laughs.*)

HALLY: I've heard enough, Sam! Jesus! It's a bloody awful world when you come to think of it. People can be real bastards.

SAM: That's the way it is, Hally.

HALLY: It doesn't *have* to be that way. There is something called progress, you know. We don't exactly burn people at the stake anymore.

SAM: Like Joan of Arc.

HALLY: Correct. If she was captured today, she'd be given a fair trial.

SAM: And then the death sentence.

HALLY (*a world-weary sigh*): I know, I know! I oscillate between hope and despair for this world as well, Sam. But things will change, you wait and see. One day somebody is going to get up and give history a kick up the backside and get it going again.

SAM: Like who?

HALLY (*after thought*): They're called social reformers. Every age, Sam, has got its social reformer. My history book is full of them.

SAM: So where's ours?

HALLY: Good question. And I hate to say it, but the answer is: I don't know. Maybe he hasn't even been born yet. Or is still only a babe in arms at his mother's breast. God, what a thought.

SAM: So we just go on waiting.

HALLY: Ja, looks like it. (*Back to his soup and the book*.)

SAM (*reading from the textbook*): "Introduction: In some mathematical problems only the magnitude . . ." (*He mispronounces the word "magnitude."*)

HALLY (*correcting him without looking up*): Magnitude.

SAM: What's it mean?

HALLY: How big it is. The size of the thing.

SAM: (*reading*): ". . . magnitude of the quantities is of no importance. In other problems we need to know whether these quantities are negative or positive. For example, whether there is a debit or credit bank balance . . ."

HALLY: Whether you're broke nor not.

SAM: ". . .whether the temperature is above or below Zero. . . ."

HALLY: Naught degrees. Cheerful state of affairs! No cash and you're freezing to death. Mathematics won't get you out of that one.

SAM: "All these quantities are called . . ." (*spelling the word*) . . . s-c-a-l . . .

HALLY: Scalars.

SAM: Scalars! (*Shaking his head with a laugh*) You understand all that?

HALLY (*turning a page*): No. And I don't intend to try.

SAM: So what happens when the exams come?

HALLY: Failing a maths exam isn't the end of the world, Sam. How many times have I told you that examination results don't measure intelligence?

SAM: I would say about as many times as you've failed one of them.

HALLY (*mirthlessly*): Ha, ha, ha.

SAM (*simultaneously*): Ha, ha, ha.

HALLY: Just remember Winston Churchill didn't do particularly well at school.

SAM: You've also told me that one many times.

HALLY: Well, it just so happens to be the truth.

SAM (*enjoying the word*): Magnitude! Magnitude! Show me how to use it.

HALLY (*after thought*): An intrepid social reformer will not be daunted by the magnitude of the task he has undertaken.

SAM (*impressed*): Couple of jaw-breakers in there!

HALLY: I gave you three for the price of one. Intrepid, daunted and magnitude. I did that once in an exam. Put five of the words I had to explain in one sentence. It was half a page long.

SAM: Well, I'll put my money on you in the English exam.

HALLY: Piece of cake. Eighty percent without even trying.

SAM (*another textbook from* HALLY's *case*): And history?

HALLY: So-so. I'll scrape through. In the fifties if I'm lucky.

SAM: You didn't do too badly last year.

HALLY: Because we had World War One. That at least has some action. You try to find that in the South African Parliamentary system.

SAM (*reading from the history textbook*): "Napoleon and the principle of equality." Hey! This sounds interesting. "After concluding peace with Britain in 1802, Napoleon used a brief period of calm to in-sti-tute . . ."

HALLY: Introduce.

SAM: ". . . many reforms. Napoleon regarded all people as equal before the law and wanted them to have equal opportunities for advancement. All ves-ti-ges of the feu-dal system with its oppression of the poor were abolished." Vestiges, feudal system and abolished. I'm all right on oppression.

HALLY: I'm thinking. He swept away . . . abolished . . . the last remains . . . vestiges . . . of the bad old days . . . feudal system.

SAM: Ha! There's the social reformer we're waiting for. He sounds like a man of some magnitude.

HALLY: I'm not so sure about that. It's a damn good title for a book, though. A man of magnitude!

SAM: He sounds pretty big to me, Hally.

HALLY: Don't confuse historical significance with greatness. But maybe I'm being a bit prejudiced. Have a look in there and you'll see he's two chapters long. And hell! . . . has he only got dates, Sam, all of which you've got to remember! This campaign and that campaign, and then, because of all the fighting, the next thing is we get Peace Treaties all over the place. And what's the end of the story? Battle of Waterloo, which he loses. Wasn't worth it. No, I don't know about him as a man of magnitude.

SAM: Then who would you say was?

HALLY: To answer that, we need a definition of greatness, and I suppose that would be somebody who . . . somebody who benefited all mankind.

SAM: Right. But like who?

HALLY (*his speaks with total conviction*): Charles Darwin. Remember him? That big book from the library. *The Origin of the Species.*

SAM: Him?

HALLY: Yes. For his Theory of Evolution.

SAM: You didn't finish it.

HALLY: I ran out of time. I didn't finish it

because my two weeks was up. But I'm going to take it out again after I've digested what I read. It's safe. I've hidden it away in the Theology section. Nobody ever goes in there. And anyway who are you to talk? You hardly even looked at it.

SAM: I tried. I looked at the chapters in the beginning and I saw one called "The Struggle for an Existence." Ah ha, I thought. At last! But what did I get? Something called the mistiltoe which needs the apple tree and there's too many seeds and all are going to die except one . . . ! No, Hally.

HALLY (*intellectually outraged*): What do you mean, No! The poor man had to start somewhere. For God's sake, Sam, he revolutionized science. Now we know.

SAM: What?

HALLY: Where we come from and what it all means.

SAM: And that's a benefit to mankind? Anyway, I still don't believe it.

HALLY: God, you're impossible. I showed it to you in black and white.

SAM: Doesn't mean I got to believe it.

HALLY: It's the likes of you that kept the Inquisition in business. It's called bigotry. Anyway, that's my man of magnitude. Charles Darwin! Who's yours?

SAM (*without hesitation*): Abraham Lincoln.

HALLY: I might have guessed as much. Don't get sentimental, Sam. You've never been a slave, you know. And anyway we freed your ancestors here in South Africa long before the Americans. But if you want to thank somebody on their behalf, do it to Mr. William Wilberforce. Come on. Try again. I want a real genius.

(*Now enjoying himself, and so is* SAM. HALLY *goes behind the counter and helps himself to a chocolate.*)

SAM: William Shakespeare.

HALLY (*no enthusiasm*): Oh. So you're also one of them, are you? You're basing that opinion on only one play, you know. You've only read my *Julius Caesar* and even I don't understand half of what they're talking about. They should do what they did with the old Bible: bring the language up to date.

SAM: That's all you've got. It's also the only one *you've* read.

HALLY: I know. I admit it. That's why I suggest we reserve our judgment until we've checked upon on a few others. I've got a feeling, though, that by the end of this year one is going to be enough for

me, and I can give you the names of twenty-nine other chaps in the Standard Nine class of the Port Elizabeth Technical College who feel the same. But if you want him, you can have him. My turn now. (*Pacing*) This is a damned good exercise, you know! It started off looking like a simple question and here it's got us really probing into the intellectual heritage of our civilization.

SAM: So who is it going to be?

HALLY: My next man . . . and he gets the title on two scores: social reform and literary genius . . . is Leo Nikolaevich Tolstoy.

SAM: That Russian.

HALLY: Correct. Remember the picture of him I showed you?

SAM: With the long beard.

HALLY (*trying to look like Tolstoy*): And those burning, visionary eyes. My God, the face of a social prophet if ever I saw one! And remember my words when I showed it to you? Here's a *man*, Sam!

SAM: Those were words, Hally.

HALLY: Not many intellectuals are prepared to shovel manure with the peasants and then go home and write a "little book" called *War and Peace*. Incidentally, Sam, he was somebody else who, to quote, ". . . did not distinguish himself scholastically."

SAM: Meaning?

HALLY: He was not good at school.

SAM: Like you and Winston Churchill.

HALLY (*mirthlessly*): Ha, ha, ha.

SAM (*simultaneously*): Ha, ha, ha.

HALLY: Don't get clever, Sam. That man freed his serfs of his own free will.

SAM: No argument. He was somebody, all right. I accept him.

HALLY: I'm sure Count Tolstoy will be very pleased to hear that. Your turn. Shoot. (*Another chocolate from behind the counter.*) I'm waiting, Sam.

SAM: I've got him.

HALLY: Good. Submit your candidate for examination.

SAM: Jesus.

HALLY (*stopped dead in his tracks*): Who?

SAM: Jesus Christ.

HALLY: Oh, come on, Sam!

SAM: The Messiah.

HALLY: Ja, but still . . . No, Sam. Don't let's get started on religion. We'll just spend the whole afternoon arguing again. Suppose I turn around and say Mohammed?

SAM: All right.

HALLY: You can't have them both on the same list!

SAM: Why not? You like Mohammed, I like Jesus.

HALLY: I *don't* like Mohammed. I never have. I was merely being hypothetical. As far as I'm concerned, the Koran is as bad as the Bible. No. Religion is out! I'm not going to waste my time again arguing with you about the existence of God. You know perfectly well I'm an atheist . . . and I've got homework to do.

SAM: Okay, I take him back.

HALLY: You've got time for one more name.

SAM (*after thought*): I've got one I know we'll agree on. A simple straightforward great Man of Magnitude . . . and no arguments. And *he* really *did* benefit all mankind.

HALLY: I wonder. After your last contribution I'm beginning to doubt whether anything in the way of an intellectual agreement is possible between the two of us. Who is he?

SAM: Guess.

HALLY: Socrates? Alexandre Dumas? Karl Marx, Dostoevsky? Nietzsche?

(SAM *shakes his head after each name.*)

Give me a clue.

SAM: The letter P is important. . . .

HALLY: Plato!

SAM: . . . and his name begins with an F.

HALLY: I've got it. Freud and Psychology.

SAM: No. I didn't understand him.

HALLY: That makes two of us.

SAM: Think of mouldy apricot jam.

HALLY (*after a delighted laugh*): Penicillin and Sir Alexander Fleming! And the title of the book: *The Microbe Hunters.* (*Delighted*) Splendid, Sam! Splendid. For once we are in total agreement. The major breakthrough in medical science in the Twentieth Century. If it wasn't for him, we might have lost the Second World War. It's deeply gratifying, Sam, to know that I haven't been wasting my time in talking to you. (*Strutting around proudly*) Tolstoy may have educated his peasants, but I've educated you.

SAM: Standard Four to Standard Nine.

HALLY: Have we been at it as long as that?

SAM: Yep. And my first lesson was geography.

HALLY (*intrigued*): Really? I don't remember.

SAM: My room there at the back of the old Jubilee Boarding House. I had just started working for your Mom. Little boy in short trousers walks in one afternoon and asks me seriously: "Sam, do you

want to see South Africa?" Hey man! Sure I wanted to see South Africa!

HALLY: Was that me?

SAM: . . . So the next thing I'm looking at a map you had just done for homework. It was your first one and you were very proud of yourself.

HALLY: Go on.

SAM: Then came my first lesson. "Repeat after me, Sam: Gold in the Transvaal, mealies in the Free State, sugar in Natal and grapes in the Cape." I still know it!

HALLY: Well, I'll be buggered. So that's how it all started.

SAM: And your next map was one with all the rivers and the mountains they came from. The Orange, the Vaal, the Limpopo, the Zambezi. . . .

HALLY: You've got a phenomenal memory!

SAM: You should be grateful. That is why you started passing your exams. You tried to be better than me.

(*They laugh together.* WILLIE *is attracted by the laughter and joins them.*)

HALLY: The old Jubilee Boarding House. Sixteen rooms with board and lodging, rent in advance and one week's notice. I haven't thought about it for donkey's years . . . and I don't think that's an accident. God, was I glad when we sold it and moved out. Those years are not remembered as the happiest ones of an unhappy childhood.

WILLIE (*knocking on the table and trying to imitate a woman's voice*): "Hally, are you there?"

HALLY: Who's that supposed to be?

WILLIE: "What you doing in there, Hally? Come out at once!"

HALLY (*to* SAM): What's he talking about?

SAM: Don't you remember?

WILLIE: "Sam, Willie . . . is he in there with you boys?"

SAM: Hiding away in our room when your mother was looking for you.

HALLY (*another good laugh*): Of course! I used to crawl and hide under your bed! But finish the story, Willie. Then what used to happen? You chaps would give the game away by telling her I was in there with you. So much for friendship.

SAM: We couldn't lie to her. She knew.

HALLY: Which meant I got another rowing for hanging around the "servants' quarters." I think I spent more time in there with you chaps than anywhere else in that dump. And do you blame me? Nothing but bloody misery wherever you went. Somebody was always complaining about the food, or my mother was having a fight with

Micky Nash because she'd caught her with a petty officer in her room. Maud Meiring was another one. Remember those two? They were prostitutes, you know. Soldiers and sailors from the troopships. Bottom fell out of the business when the war ended. God, the flotsam and jetsam that life washed up on our shores! No joking, if it wasn't for your room, I would have been the first certified ten-year-old in medical history. Ja, the memories are coming back now. Walking home from school and thinking: "What can I do this afternoon?" Try out a few ideas, but sooner or later I'd end up in there with you fellows. I bet you I could still find my way to your room with my eyes closed. (*He does exactly that.*) Down the corridor . . . telephone on the right, which my Mom keeps locked because somebody is using it on the sly and not paying . . . past the kitchen and unappetizing cooking smells . . . around the corner into the backyard, hold my breath again because there are more smells coming when I pass your lavatory, then into that little passageway, first door on the right and into your room. How's that?

SAM: Good. But, as usual, you forgot to knock.

HALLY: Like that time I barged in and caught you and Cynthia . . . at it. Remember? God, was I embarrassed! I didn't know what was going on at first.

SAM: Ja, that taught you a lesson.

HALLY: And about a lot more than knocking on doors, I'll have you know, and I don't mean geography either. Hell, Sam, couldn't you have waited until it was dark?

SAM: No.

HALLY: Was it that urgent?

SAM: Yes, and if you don't believe me, wait until your time comes.

HALLY: No, thank you. I am not interested in girls. (*Back to his memories. . . . Using a few chairs he re-creates the room as he lists the items.*) A gray little room with a cold cement floor. Your bed against that wall . . . and I now know why the mattress sags so much! . . . Willie's bed . . . it's propped up on bricks because one leg is broken . . .that wobbly little table with the washbasin and jug of water . . . Yes! . . . stuck to the wall above it are some pin-up pictures from magazines. Joe Louis . . .

WILLIE: Brown Bomber. World Title. (*Boxing pose.*) Three rounds and knockout.

HALLY: Against who?

SAM: Max Schmeling.

HALLY: Correct. I can also remember Fred Astaire and Ginger Rogers, and Rita Hayworth in a bathing costume which always made me hot and bothered when I looked at it. Under Willie's bed is an old suitcase with all his clothes in a mess, which is why I never hide there. Your things are neat and tidy in a trunk next to your bed, and on it there is a picture of you and Cynthia in your ballroom clothes, your first silver cup for third place in a competition and an old radio which doesn't work anymore. Have I left out anything?

SAM: No.

HALLY: Right, so much for the stage directions. Now the characters. (SAM *and* WILLIE *move to their appropriate positions in the bedroom.*) Willie is in bed, under his blankets with his clothes on, complaining nonstop about something, but we can't make out a word of what he's saying because he's got his head under the blankets as well. You're on your bed trimming your toenails with a knife—not a very edifying sight—and as for me . . . What am I doing?

SAM: You're sitting on the floor giving Willie a lecture about being a good loser while you get the checker board and pieces ready for a game. Then you go to Willie's bed, pull off the blankets and make him play with you first because you know you're going to win, and that gives you the second game with me.

HALLY: And you certainly were a bad loser, Willie!

WILLIE: Haai!

HALLY: Wasn't he, Sam? And so slow! A game with you almost took the whole afternoon. Thank God I gave up trying to teach you how to play chess.

WILLIE: You and Sam cheated.

HALLY: I never saw Sam cheat, and mine were mostly the mistakes of youth.

WILLIE: Then how is it you two was always winning?

HALLY: Have you ever considered the possibility, Willie, that it was because we were better than you?

WILLIE: Every time better?

HALLY: Not every time. There were occasions when we deliberately let you win a game so that you would stop sulking and go on playing with us. Sam used to wink at me when you weren't looking to show me it was time to let you win.

WILLIE: So then you two didn't play fair.

HALLY: It was for your benefit, Mr. Malopo, which is more than being fair. It was an act of self-sacrifice. (*To* SAM) But you know what my best memory is, don't you?

SAM: No.

HALLY: Come on, guess. If your memory is so good, you must remember it as well.

SAM: We got up to a lot of tricks in there, Hally.

HALLY: This one was special, Sam.

SAM: I'm listening.

HALLY: It started off looking like another of those useless nothing-to-do afternoons. I'd already been down to Main Street looking for adventure, but nothing had happened. I didn't feel like climbing trees in the Donkin Park or pretending I was a private eye and following a stranger . . . so as usual: See what's cooking in Sam's room. This time it was you on the floor. You had two thin pieces of wood and you were smoothing them down with a knife. It didn't look particularly interesting, but when I asked you what you were doing, you just said, "Wait and see, Hally. Wait . . . and see" . . . in that secret sort of way of yours, so I knew there was a surprise coming. You teased me, you bugger, by being deliberately slow and not answering my questions!

(SAM *laughs*.)

And whistling while you worked away! God, it was infuriating! I could have brained you! It was only when you tied them together in a cross and put that down on the brown paper that I realized what you were doing. "Sam is making a kite?" And when I asked you and you said "Yes" . . . ! (*Shaking his head with disbelief.*) The sheer audacity of it took my breath away! I mean, seriously, what the hell does a black man know about flying a kite? I'll be honest with you, Sam, I had no hopes for it. If you think I was excited and happy, you got another guess coming. In fact, I was shit-scared that we were going to make fools of ourselves. When we left the boarding house to go up onto the hill, I was praying quietly that there wouldn't be any other kids around to laugh at us.

SAM (*enjoying the memory as much as* HALLY): Ja, I could see that.

HALLY: I made it obvious, did I?

SAM: Ja. You refused to carry it.

HALLY: Do you blame me? Can you remember what the poor thing looked like? Tomato-box wood and brown paper! Flour and water for glue! Two of my mother's old stockings for a tail, and then all those bits and pieces of string you made me tie together so that we could fly it! Hell, no, that was now only asking for a miracle to happen.

SAM: Then the big argument when I told you to hold the string and run with it when I let go.

HALLY: I was prepared to run, all right, but straight back to the boarding house.

SAM (*knowing what's coming*): So what happened?

HALLY: Come on, Sam, you remember as well as I do.

SAM: I want to hear it from you.

(HALLY *pauses. He wants to be as accurate as possible.*)

HALLY: You went a little distance from me down the hill, you held it up ready to let it go. . . . "This is it," I thought. "Like everything else in my life, here comes another fiasco." Then you shouted, "Go, Hally!" and I started to run. (*Another pause.*) I don't know how to describe it, Sam. Ja! The miracle happened! I was running, waiting for it to crash to the ground, but instead suddenly there was something alive behind me at the end of the string, tugging at it as if it wanted to be free. I looked back . . . (*Shakes his head.*) . . . I still can't believe my eyes. It was flying! Looping around and trying to climb even higher into the sky. You shouted to me to let it have more string. I did, until there was none left and I was just holding that piece of wood we had tied it to. You came up and joined me. You were laughing.

SAM: So were you. And shouting, "It works, Sam! We've done it!"

HALLY: And we had! I was so proud of us! It was the most splendid thing I had ever seen. I wished there were hundreds of kids around to watch us. The part that scared me, though, was when you showed me how to make it dive down to the ground and then just when it was on the point of crashing, swoop up again!

SAM: You didn't want to try yourself.

HALLY: Of course not! I would have been suicidal if anything had happened to it. Watching you do it made me nervous enough. I was quite happy just to see it up there with its tail fluttering behind it. You left me after that, didn't you? You explained how to get it down, we tied it to the bench so that I could sit and watch it, and you went away. I wanted you to stay, you know. I was a little scared of having to look after it by myself.

SAM (*quietly*): I had work to do, Hally.

HALLY: It was sort of sad bringing it down, Sam. And it looked sad again when it was lying there on the ground. Like something that had lost its soul. Just tomato-box wood, brown paper and two of my mothers' old stockings! But, hell, I'll never forget that first moment when I saw it up there. I had a stiff neck the next day from looking up so much.

(SAM *laughs.* HALLY *turns to him with a question he never thought of asking before.*)

Why did you make that kite, Sam?

SAM (*evenly*): I can't remember.

HALLY: Truly?

SAM: Too long ago, Hally.

HALLY: Ja, I suppose it was. It's time for another one, you know.

SAM: Why do you say that?

HALLY: Because it feels like that. Wouldn't be a good day to fly it, though.

SAM: No. You can't fly kites on rainy days.

HALLY (*he studies* SAM. *Their memories have made him conscious of the man's presence in his life*): How old are you, Sam?

SAM: Two score and five.

HALLY: Strange, isn't it?

SAM: What?

HALLY: Me and you.

SAM: What's strange about it?

HALLY: Little white boy in short trousers and a black man old enough to be his father flying a kite. It's not every day you see that.

SAM: But why strange? Because the one is white and the other black?

HALLY: I don't know. Would have been just as strange, I suppose, if it had been me and my Dad . . . cripple man and a little boy! Nope! There's no chance of me flying a kite without it being strange. (*Simple statement of fact—no self-pity.*) There's a nice little short story there. "The Kite-Flyers." But we'd have to find a twist in the ending.

SAM: Twist?

HALLY: Yes. Something unexpected. The way it ended with us was too straightforward . . . me on the bench and you going back to work. There's no drama in that.

WILLIE: And me?

HALLY: You?

WILLIE: Yes me.

HALLY: You want to get into the story as well, do you? I got it! Change the title: "Afternoons in Sam's Room" . . . expand it and tell all the stories. It's on its way to being a novel. Our days in the old Jubilee. Sad in a way that they're over. I almost wish we were still in that little room.

SAM: We're still together.

HALLY: That's true. It's just that life felt the right size in there . . . not too big and not too small. Wasn't so hard to work up a bit of courage. It's got so bloody complicated since then.

(*The telephone rings.* SAM *answers it.*)

SAM: St. George's Park Tea Room . . . Hello, Madam . . . Yes, Madam, he's here. . . . Hally, it's your mother.

HALLY: Where is she phoning from?

SAM: Sounds like the hospital. It's a public telephone.

HALLY (*relieved*): You see! I told you. (*The telephone.*) Hello, Mom . . . Yes . . . Yes no fine. Everything's under control here. How's things with poor old Dad? . . . Has he had a bad turn? . . . What? . . . Oh, God! . . . Yes, Sam told me, but I was sure he'd made a mistake. But what's this all about, Mom? He didn't look at all good last night. How can he get better so quickly? . . . Then very obviously you must say no. Be firm with him. You're the boss. . . . You know what it's going to be like if he comes home. . . . Well then, don't blame me when I fail my exams at the end of the year. . . . Yes! How am I expected to be fresh for school when I spend half the night massaging his gammy leg? . . . So am I! . . . So tell him a white lie. Say Dr. Colley wants more X-rays of his stump. Or bribe him. We'll sneak in double tots of brandy in future. . . . What? . . . Order him to get back into bed at once! If he's going to behave like a child, treat him like one. . . . All right, Mom! I was just trying to . . . I'm sorry. . . . I said I'm sorry. . . . Quick, give me your number. I'll phone you back. (*He hangs up and waits a few seconds.*) Here we go again! (*He dials.*) I'm sorry, Mom. . . . Okay. . . . But now listen to me carefully. All it needs is for you to put your foot down. Don't take no for an answer. . . . Did you hear me? And whatever you do, don't discuss it with him. . . . Because I'm frightened you'll give in to him. . . . Yes, Sam gave me lunch. . . . I ate all of it! . . . No, Mom not a soul. It's still raining here. . . . Right, I'll tell them. I'll just do some homework and then lock up. . . . But remember now, Mom. Don't listen to anything he says. And phone me back and let me know what happens. . . . Okay. Bye, Mom. (*He hangs up. The men are staring at him.*) My Mom says that when you're finished with the floors you must do the windows. (*Pause.*) Don't misunderstand me, chaps. All I want is for him to get better. And if he was, I'd be the first person to say: "Bring him home." But he's not, and we can't give him the medical care and attention he needs at home. That's what hospitals are there for. (*Brusquely*) So don't just stand there! Get on with it!

(SAM *clears* HALLY's *table.*)

You heard right. My Dad wants to go home.

SAM: Is he better?

HALLY (*sharply*): No! How the hell can he be

better when last night he was groaning with pain? This is not an age of miracles!

SAM: Then he should stay in hospital.

HALLY (*seething with irritation and frustration*): Tell me something I don't know, Sam. What the hell do you think I was saying to my Mom? All I can say is fuck-it-all.

SAM: I'm sure he'll listen to your Mom.

HALLY: You don't know what she's up against. He's already packed his shaving kit and pajamas and is sitting on his bed with his crutches, dressed and ready to go. I know him when he gets in that mood. If she tries to reason with him, we've had it. She's no match for him when it comes to a battle of words. He'll tie her up in knots. (*Trying to hide his true feelings.*)

SAM: I suppose it gets lonely for him in there.

HALLY: With all the patients and nurses around? Regular visits from the Salvation Army? Balls! It's ten times worse for him at home. I'm at school and my mother is here in the business all day.

SAM: He's at least got you at night.

HALLY (*before he can stop himself*): And we've got him! Please! I don't want to talk about it anymore. (*Unpacks his school case, slamming down books on the table.*) Life is just a plain bloody mess, that's all. And people are fools.

SAM: Come on, Hally.

HALLY: Yes, they are! They bloody well deserve what they get.

SAM: Then don't complain.

HALLY: Don't try to be clever, Sam. It doesn't suit you. Anybody who thinks there's nothing wrong with this world needs to have his head examined. Just when things are gong along all right, without fail someone or something will come along and spoil everything. Somebody should write that down as a fundamental law of the Universe. The principle of perpetual disappointment. If there is a God who created this world, he should scrap it and try again.

SAM: All right, Hally, all right. What you got for homework?

HALLY: Bullshit, as usual. (*Opens an exercise book and reads*) "Write five hundred words describing an annual event of cultural or historical significance."

SAM: That should be easy enough for you.

HALLY: And also plain bloody boring. You know what he wants, don't you? One of their useless old ceremonies. The commemoration of the landing of the 1820 Settlers, or if it's going to be culture, Carols by Candlelight every Christmas.

SAM: It's an impressive sight. Make a good description, Hally. All those candles glowing in the dark and the people singing hymns.

HALLY: And it's called religious hysteria. (*Intense irritation*) Please, Sam! Just leave me alone and let me get on with it. I'm not in the mood for games this afternoon. And remember my Mom's orders . . . you're to help Willie with the windows. Come on now, I don't want any more nonsense in here.

SAM: Okay, Hally, okay.

(HALLY *settles down to his homework; determined preparations . . . pen, ruler, exercise book, dictionary, another cake . . . all of which will lead to nothing.*)

(SAM *waltzes over to* WILLIE *and starts to replace tables and chairs. He practices a ballroom step while doing so.* WILLIE *watches. When* SAM *is finished,* WILLIE *tries.*)

Good! But just a little bit quicker on the turn and only move in to her after she's crossed over. What about this one?

(*Another step. When* SAM *is finished,* WILLIE *again has a go.*)

Much better. See what happens when you just relax and enjoy yourself? Remember that in two weeks' time you'll be all right.

WILLIE: But I haven't got partner, Boet Sam.

SAM: Maybe Hilda will turn up tonight.

WILLIE: No, Boet Sam. (*Reluctantly*) I gave her a good hiding.

SAM: You mean a bad one.

WILLIE: Good bad one.

SAM: Then you mustn't complain either. Now you pay the price for losing your temper.

WILLIE: I also pay two pounds ten shilling entrance fee.

SAM: They'll refund you if you withdraw now.

WILLIE (*appalled*): You mean, don't dance?

SAM: Yes.

WILLIE: No! I wait too long and I practice too hard. If I find me new partner, you think I can be ready in two weeks? I ask Madam for my leave now and we practice every day.

SAM: Quickstep nonstop for two weeks. World record, Willie, but you'll be mad at the end.

WILLIE: No jokes, Boet Sam.

SAM: I'm not joking.

WILLIE: So then what?

SAM: Find Hilda. Say you're sorry and promise you won't beat her again.

WILLIE: No.

SAM: Then withdraw. Try again next year.

WILLIE: No.

SAM: Then I give up.

WILLIE: Haaikona, Boet Sam, you can't.

SAM: What do you mean, I can't? I'm telling you: I give up.

WILLIE (*adamant*): No! (*Accusingly*) It was you who start me ballroom dancing.

SAM: So?

WILLIE: Before that I use to be happy. And is you and Miriam who bring me to Hilda and say here's partner for you.

SAM: What are you saying, Willie?

WILLIE: You!

SAM: But me what? To blame?

WILLIE: Yes.

SAM: Willie . . . ? (*Bursts into laughter.*)

WILLIE: And now all you do is make jokes at me. You wait. When Miriam leaves you is my turn to laugh. Ha! Ha! Ha!

SAM (*he can't take* WILLIE *seriously any longer*): She can leave me tonight! I know what to do. (*Bowing before an imaginary partner.*) May I have the pleasure? (*He dances and sings*)
> "Just a fellow with his pillow . . .
> Dancin' like a willow . . .
> In an autumn breeze . . ."

WILLIE: There you go again!

(SAM *goes on dancing and singing.*)

Boet Sam!

SAM: There's the answer to your problem! Judges' announcement in two weeks' time: "Ladies and gentlemen, the winner in the open section . . . Mr. Willie Malopo and his pillow!"

(*This is too much for a now really angry* WILLIE. *He goes for* SAM, *but the latter is too quick for him and puts* HALLY's *table between the two of them.*)

HALLY (*exploding*): For Christ's sake, you two!

WILLIE (*still trying to get at* SAM): I donner you, Sam! Struesgod!

SAM (*still laughing*): Sorry, Willie . . . Sorry. . . .

HALLY: Sam! Willie! (*Grabs his ruler and gives* WILLIE *a vicious whack on the bum.*) How the hell am I supposed to concentrate with the two of you behaving like bloody children!

WILLIE: Hit him, too!

HALLY: Shut up, Willie.

WILLIE: He started jokes again.

HALLY: Get back to your work. you too, Sam. (*His ruler.*) Do you want another one, Willie?

(SAM *and* WILLIE *return to their work.* HALLY *uses the opportunity to escape from his unsuccessful attempt at homework. He struts around like a little despot, ruler in hand, giving vent to his anger and frustration.*)

Suppose a customer had walked in then? Or the Park Superintendent. And seen the two of you behaving like a pair of hooligans. That would have been the end of my mother's license, you know. And your jobs? Well, this is the end of it. From now on there will be no more of your ballroom nonsense in here. This is a business establishment, not a bloody New Brighton dancing school. I've been far too lenient with the two of you. (*Behind the counter for a green cool drink and a dollop of ice cream. He keeps up his tirade as he prepares it.*) But what really makes me bitter is that I allow you chaps a little freedom in here when business is bad and what do you do with it? The foxtrot! Specially you, Sam. There's more to life than trotting around a dance floor and I thought at least you knew it.

SAM: It's a harmless pleasure, Hally. It doesn't hurt anybody.

HALLY: It's also a rather simple one, you know.

SAM: You reckon so? Have you ever tried?

HALLY: Of course not.

SAM: Why don't you? Now.

HALLY: What do you mean? Me dance?

SAM: Yes. I'll show you a simple step—the waltz—then you try it.

HALLY: What will that prove?

SAM: That it might not be as easy as you think.

HALLY: I didn't say it was easy. I said it was simple—like in simple-minded, meaning mentally retarded. You can't exactly say it challenges the intellect.

SAM: It does other things.

HALLY: Such as?

SAM: Make people happy.

HALLY (*the glass in his hand*): So do American cream sodas with ice cream. For God's sake, Sam, you're not asking me to take ballroom dancing serious, are you?

SAM: Yes.

HALLY (*sigh of defeat*): Oh, well, so much for trying to give you a decent education. I've obviously achieved nothing.

SAM: You still haven't told me what's wrong with admiring something that's beautiful and then trying to do it yourself.

HALLY: Nothing. But we happen to be talking about a foxtrot, not a thing of beauty.

SAM: But that is just what I'm saying. If you were to see two champions doing, two masters of the art . . . !

HALLY: Oh God, I give up. So now it's also art!

SAM: Ja.

HALLY: There's a limit, Sam. Don't confuse art and entertainment.

SAM: So then what is art?

HALLY: You want a definition?

SAM: Ja.

HALLY (*He realizes he has got to be careful. He gives the matter a lot of thought before answering*): Philosophers have been trying to do that for centuries. What is Art? What is Life? But basically I suppose it's . . . the giving of meaning to matter.

SAM: Nothing to do with beautiful?

HALLY: It goes beyond that. It's the giving of form to the formless.

SAM: Ja, well, maybe it's not art, then. But I still say it's beautiful.

HALLY: I'm sure the word you mean to use is entertaining.

SAM (*adamant*): No. Beautiful. And if you want proof come along to the Centenary Hall in New Brighton in two weeks' time.

(*The mention of the Centenary Hall draws* WILLIE *over to them.*)

HALLY: What for? I've seen the two of you prancing around in here often enough.

SAM (*he laughs*): This isn't the real thing, Hally. We're just playing around in here.

HALLY: So? I can use my imagination.

SAM: And what do you get?

HALLY: A lot of people dancing around and having a so-called good time.

SAM: That all?

HALLY: Well, basically it is that, surely.

SAM: No, it isn't. Your imagination hasn't helped you at all. There's a lot more to it than that. We're getting ready for the championships, Hally, not just another dance. There's going to be a lot of people, all right, and they're going to have a good time, but they'll only be spectators, sitting around and watching. It's just the competitors out there on the dance floor. Party decorations and fancy lights all around the walls! The ladies in beautiful evening dresses!

HALLY: My mother's got one of those, Sam, and, quite frankly, it's an embarrassment every time she wears it.

SAM (*undeterred*): Your imagination left out the excitement.

(HALLY *scoffs.*)

Oh, yes. The finalists are not going to be out there just to have a good time. One of those couples will be the 1950 Eastern Province Champions. And your imagination left out the music.

WILLIE: Mr. Elijah Gladman Guzana and his Orchestral Jazzonions.

SAM: The sound of the big band, Hally. Trombone, trumpet, tenor and alto sax. And then, finally, your imagination also left out the climax of the evening when the dancing is finished, the judges have stopped whispering among themselves and the Master of Ceremonies collects their scorecards and goes up onto the stage to announce the winners.

HALLY: All right. So you make it sound like a bit of a do. It's an occasion. Satisfied?

SAM (*victory*): So you admit that!

HALLY: Emotionally yes, intellectually no.

SAM: Well, I don't know what you mean by that, all I'm telling you is that it is going to be *the* event of the year in New Brighton. It's been sold out for two weeks already. There's only standing room left. We've got competitors coming from Kingwilliamstown, East London, Port Alfred.

(HALLY *starts pacing thoughfully.*)

HALLY: Tell me a bit more.

SAM: I thought you weren't interested . . . intellectually.

HALLY (*mysteriously*): I've got my reasons.

SAM: What do you want to know?

HALLY: It takes place every year?

SAM: Yes. But only every third year in New Brighton. It's East London's turn to have the championships next year.

HALLY: Which, I suppose, makes it an even more significant event.

SAM: Ah ha! We're getting somewhere. Our "occasion" is now a "significant event."

HALLY: I wonder.

SAM: What?

HALLY: I wonder if I would get away with it.

SAM: But what?

HALLY (*to the table and his exercise book*): "Write five hundred words describing an annual event of cultural or historical significance." Would I be stretching poetic license a little too far if I called your ballroom championships a cultural event?

SAM: You mean . . . ?

HALLY: You think we could get five hundred words out of it, Sam?

SAM: Victor Sylvester has written a whole book on ballroom dancing.

WILLIE: You going to write about it, Master Hally?

HALLY: Yes, gentlemen, that is precisely what I am considering doing. Old Doc Bromely—he's my English teacher—is going to argue with me, of course. He doesn't like natives. But I'll point out to him that in strict anthropological terms the culture of a primitive black society includes its dancing and singing. To put my thesis into a nutshell: The war-dance has been replaced by the waltz. But it still amounts to the same thing: the release of primitive emotions through movement. Shall we give it a go?

SAM: I'm ready.

WILLIE: Me also.

HALLY: Ha! This will teach the old bugger a lesson. (*Decision taken.*) Right. Let's get ourselves organized (*This means another cake on the table. He sits.*) I think you've given me enough general atmosphere, Sam, but to build the tension and suspense I need facts. (*Pencil poised.*)

WILLIE: Give him facts, Boet Sam.

HALLY: What you called the climax . . . how many finalists?

SAM: Six couples.

HALLY (*making notes*): Go on. Give me the picture.

SAM: Spectators seated right around the hall. (WILLIE *becomes a spectator.*)

HALLY: . . . and it's a full house.

SAM: At one end, on the stage, Gladman and his Orchestral Jazzonions. At the other end is a long table with the three judges. The six finalists go onto the dance floor and take up their positions. When they are ready and the spectators have settled down, the Master of Ceremonies goes to the microphone. To start with, he makes some jokes to get people laughing. . . .

HALLY: Good touch (*as he writes*) ". . . creating a relaxed atmosphere which will change to one of tension and drama as the climax is approached."

SAM (*onto a chair to act out the M.C.*): "Ladies and gentlemen, we come now to the great moment you have all been waiting for this evening. . . . The finals of the 1950 Eastern Province Open Ballroom Dancing Championships. But first let me introduce the finalists! Mr. and Mrs. Welcome Tchabalala from Kingwilliamstown . . ."

WILLIE (*he applauds after every name*): Is when the people clap their hands and whistle and make a lot of noise, Master Hally.

SAM: "Mr. Mulligan Njikelane and Miss Nomhle Nkonyeni of Grahamstown; Mr. and Mrs. Norman Nchinga from Port Alfred; Mr. Fats Bokolane and Miss Dina Plaatjies from East London; Mr. Sipho Dugu and Mrs. Mable Magada from Peddie; and from New Brighton our very own Mr. Willie Malopo and Miss Hilda Samuels."

(WILLIE *can't believe his ears. He abandons his role as spectator and scrambles into position as a finalist.*)

WILLIE: Relaxed and ready to romance!

SAM: The applause dies down. When everybody is silent, Gladman lifts up his sax, nods at the Orchestral Jazzonions. . . .

WILLIE: Play the jukebox please, Boet Sam!

SAM: I also only got bus fare, Willie.

HALLY: Hold it, everybody. (*Heads for the cash register behind the counter.*) How much is in the till, Sam?

SAM: Three shillings. Hally . . . Your Mom counted it before she left.

(HALLY *hesitates.*)

HALLY: Sorry, Willie. You know how she carried on the last time I did it. We'll just have to pool our combined imaginations and hope for the best. (*Returns to the table.*) Back to work. How are the points scored, Sam?

SAM: Maximum of ten points each for individual style, deportment, rhythm and general appearance.

WILLIE: Must I start?

HALLY: Hold it for a second, Willie. And penalties?

SAM: For what?

HALLY: For doing something wrong. Say you stumble or bump into somebody . . . do they take off any points?

SAM (*aghast*): Hally . . . !

HALLY: When you're dancing. If you and your partner collide into another couple.

(HALLY *can get no further.* SAM *has collapsed with laughter. He explains to* WILLIE.)

SAM: If me and Miriam bump into you and Hilda. . . .

(WILLIE *joins him in another good laugh.*)

Hally, Hally . . .!

HALLY (*perplexed*): Why? What did I say?

SAM: There's no collisions out there, Hally. Nobody trips or stumbles or bumps into anybody else. That's what that moment is all about. To be one of those finalists on that dance floor is like . . . like being in a dream about a world in which accidents don't happen.

HALLY (*genuinely moved by* SAM'*s image*): Jesus, Sam! That's beautiful!

WILLIE (*can endure waiting no longer*): I'm starting!

(WILLIE *dances while* SAM *talks.*)

SAM: Of course it is. That's what I've been trying to say to you all afternoon. And it's beautiful because that is what we want life to be like. But instead, like you said, Hally, we're bumping into each other all the time. Look at the three of us this afternoon: I've bumped into Willie, the two of us have bumped into you, you've bumped into your mother, she bumping into your Dad. . . . None of us knows the steps and there's no music playing. And it doesn't stop with us. The whole world is doing it all the time. Open a newspaper and what do you read? America has bumped into Russia, England is bumping into India, rich man bumps into poor man. Those are big collisions, Hally. They make for a lot of bruises. People get hurt in all that bumping, and we're sick and tired of it now. It's been going on for too long. Are we never going to get it right? . . . Learn to dance life like champions instead of always being just a bunch of beginners at it?

HALLY (*deep and sincere admiration of the man*): You've got a vision, Sam!

SAM: Not just me. What I'm saying to you is that everybody's got it. That's why there's only standing room left for the Centenary Hall in two week's time. For as long as the music lasts, we are going to see six couples get it right, the way we want life to be.

HALLY: But is that the best we can do, Sam . . . watch six finalists dreaming about the way it should be?

SAM: I don't know. But it starts with that. Without the dream we won't know what we're going for. And anyway I reckon there are a few people who have got past just dreaming about it and are trying for something real. Remember that thing we read once in the paper about the Mahatma Gandhi? Going without food to stop those riots in India?

HALLY: You're right. He certainly was trying to teach people to get the steps right.

SAM: And the Pope.

HALLY: Yes, he's another one. Our old General Smuts as well, you know. He's also out there dancing. You know, Sam, when you come to think of it, that's what the United Nations boils down to . . . a dancing school for politicians!

SAM: And let's hope they learn.

HALLY: (*a little surge of hope*): You're right. We mustn't despair. Maybe there's some hope for mankind after all. Keep it up, Willie. (*Back to his table with determination.*) This is a lot bigger than I thought. So what have we got? Yes, our title: "A World Without Collisions."

SAM: That sounds good! "A World Without Collisions."

HALLY: Subtitle: "Global Politics on the Dance Floor." No. A bit too heavy, hey? What about "Ballroom Dancing as Political Vision"?

(*The telephone rings.* SAM *answers it.*)

SAM: St. George's Park Tea Room . . . Yes, Madam . . . Hally, it's your Mom.

HALLY (*back to reality*): Oh, God, yes! I'd forgotten all about that. Shit! remember my words, Sam? Just when you're enjoying yourself, someone or something will come along and wreck everything.

SAM: You haven't heard what she's got to say yet.

HALLY: Public telephone?

SAM: No.

HALLY: Does she sound happy or unhappy?

SAM: I couldn't tell. (*Pause.*) She's waiting, Hally.

HALLY (*to the telephone*): Hello, Mom . . . No, everything is okay here. Just doing my homework. . . . What's your news? . . . You've what? . . . (*Pause. He takes the receiver away from his ear for a few seconds. In the course of* HALLY'*s telephone conversation,* SAM *and* WILLIE *discreetly position the stacked tables and chairs.* HALLY *places the receiver back to his ear.*) Yes, I'm still here. Oh, well, I give up now. Why did you do it, Mom? . . . Well, I just hope you know what you've let us in for. . . . (*Loudly*) I said I hope you know what you've let us in for! It's the end of the peace and quiet we've been having. (*Softly*) Where is he? (*Normal voice*) He can't hear us from in there. But for God's sake, Mom, what happened? I told you to be firm with him. . . . Then you and the nurses should have held him down, taken his crutches away. . . . I know only too well he's my father! . . . I'm not being disrespectful, but I'm sick and tired of emptying stinking chamber pots full of phlegm and piss. . . . Yes, I do! When you're not there, he asks *me* to do it. . . . If you really want to know the truth, that's why I've got no appetite for my food.

. . . Yes! For your information, I still haven't got that science textbook I need. And you know why? He borrowed the money you gave me for it. . . . Because I didn't want to start another fight between you two. . . . He says that every time. . . . All right, Mom! (*Viciously*) Then just remember to start hiding your bag away again, because he'll be at your purse before long for money for booze. And when he's well enough to come down here, you better keep an eye on the till as well, because that is also going to develop a leak. . . . Then don't complain to me when he starts his old tricks. . . . Yes, you do. I get it from you on one side and from him on the other, and it makes life hell for me. I'm not going to be the peacemaker anymore. I'm warning you now: when the two of you start fighting again, I'm leaving home. . . . Mom, if you start crying, I'm going to put down the receiver. . . . Okay. . . . (*Lowering his voice to a vicious whisper*) Okay, Mom. I heard you. (*Desperate*) No. . . . Because I don't want to. I'll see him when I get home! Mom! . . . (*Pause. When he speaks again, his tone changes completely. It is not simply pretense. We sense a genuine emotional conflict.*) Welcome home, chum! . . . What's that? . . . Don't be silly, Dad. You being home is just about the best news in the world. . . . I bet you are. Bloody depressing there with everybody going on about their ailments, hey! . . . How you feeling? . . . Good. . . . Here as well, pal. Coming down cats and dogs. . . . That's right. Just the day for a kip and a toss in your old Uncle Ned. . . . Everything's just hunky-dory on my side, Dad. . . . Well, to start with, there's a nice pile of comics for you on the counter. . . . Yes, old Kemple brought them in. *Batman and Robin, Supermariner* . . . just your cup of tea . . . I will. . . . Yes, we'll spin a few yarns tonight. . . . Okay, chum, see you in a little while. . . . No, I promise. I'll come straight home. . . . (*Pause—his mother comes back on the phone.*) Mom? Okay. I'll lock up now. . . . What? . . . Oh, the brandy . . . Yes, I'll remember! . . . I'll put it in my suitcase now, for God's sake. I know well enough what will happen if he doesn't get it. . . . (*Places a bottle of brandy on the counter.*) I was kind to him, Mom. I didn't say anything nasty! . . . All right. Bye. (*End of telephone conversation. A desolate* HALLY *doesn't move. A strained silence.*)

SAM (*quietly*): That sounded like a bad bump, Hally.

HALLY (*having a hard time controlling his emotions. He speaks carefully*): Mind your own business, Sam.

SAM: Sorry. I wasn't trying to interfere. Shall we

carry on? Hally? (*He indicates the exercise book. No response from* HALLY.)

WILLIE (*also trying*): Tell him about when they give out the cups, Boet Sam.

SAM: Ja! That's another big moment. The presentation of the cups after the winners have been announced. You've got to put that in.

(*Still no response from* HALLY.)

WILLIE: A big silver one, Master Hally, called floating trophy for the champions.

SAM: We always invite some big-shot personality to hand them over. Guest of honor this year is going to be His Holiness Bishop Jabulani of the All African Free Zionist Church.

(HALLY *gets up abruptly, goes to his table and tears up the page he was writing on.*)

HALLY: So much for a bloody world without collisions.

SAM: Too bad. It was on its way to being a good composition.

HALLY: Let's stop bullshitting ourselves, Sam.

SAM: Have we been doing that?

HALLY: Yes! That's what all our talk about a decent world has been . . . just so much bullshit.

SAM: We did say it was still only a dream.

HALLY: And a bloody useless one at that. Life's a fuckup and it's never going to change.

SAM: Ja, maybe that's true.

HALLY: There's no maybe about it. It's a blunt and brutal fact. All we've done this afternoon is waste our time.

SAM: Not if we'd got your homework done.

HALLY: I don't give a shit about my homework, so for Christ's sake, just shut up about it. (*Slamming books viciously into his school case.*) Hurry up now and finish your work. I want to lock up and get out of here. (*Pause.*) And then go where? Home-sweet-fucking-home. Jesus, I hate that word.

(HALLY *goes to the counter to put the brandy bottle and comics in his school case. After a moment's hesitation, he smashes the bottle of brandy. He abandons all further attempts to hide his feelings.* SAM *and* WILLIE *work away as unobtrusively as possible.*)

Do you want to know what is really wrong with your lovely little dream, Sam? It's not just that we are all bad dancers. That does happen to be perfectly true, but there's more to it than just that. You left out the cripples.

SAM: Hally!

HALLY (*now totally reckless*): Ja! Can't leave them out, Sam. That's why we always end up on our backsides on the dance floor. They're also out there dancing . . . like a bunch of broken spiders trying to do the quickstep! (*An ugly attempt at laughter.*) When you come to think of it, it's a bloody comical sight. I mean, it's bad enough on two legs . . . but one and a pair of crutches! Hell, no, Sam. That's guaranteed to turn that dance floor into a shambles. Why you shaking your head? Picture it, man. For once this afternoon let's use our imaginations sensibly.

SAM: Be careful, Hally.

HALLY: Of what? The truth? I seem to be the only one around here who is prepared to face it. We've had the pretty dream, it's time now to wake up and have a good long look at the way things really are. Nobody knows the steps, there's no music, the cripples are also out there tripping up everybody and trying to get into the act, and it's all called the All-Comers-How-to-Make-a-Fuckup-of-Life Championships. (*Another ugly laugh.*) Hang on, Sam! The best bit is still coming. Do you know what the winner's trophy is? A beautiful big chamber pot with roses on the side, and it's full to the brim with piss. And guess who I think is going to be this year's winner.

SAM (*almost shouting*): Stop now!

HALLY (*suddenly appalled by how far he has gone*): Why?

SAM: Hally? It's your father you're talking about.

HALLY: So?

SAM: Do you know what you've been saying?

(HALLY *can't answer. He is rigid with shame.* SAM *speaks to him sternly.*)

No, Hally, you mustn't do it. Take back those words and ask for forgiveness! It's a terrible sin for a son to mock his father with jokes like that. You'll be punished if you carry on. Your father is your father, even if he is a . . . cripple man.

WILLIE: Yes, Master Hally. Is true what Sam say.

SAM: I understand how you are feeling, Hally, but even so. . . .

HALLY: No, you don't!

SAM: I think I do.

HALLY: And I'm telling you you don't. Nobody does. (*Speaking carefully as his shame turns to rage at* SAM) It's your turn to be careful, Sam. Very careful! You're treading on dangerous ground. Leave me and my father alone.

SAM: I'm not the one who's been saying things about him.

HALLY: What goes on between me and my Dad is none of your business!

SAM: Then don't tell me about it. If that's all you've got to say about him, I don't want to hear.

(*For a moment* HALLY *is at loss for a response.*)

HALLY: Just get on with your bloody work and shut up.

SAM: Swearing at me won't help you.

HALLY: Yes, it does! Mind your own fucking business and shut up!

SAM: Okay. If that's the way you want it. I'll stop trying.

(*He turns away. This infuriates* HALLY *even more.*)

HALLY: Good. Because what you've been trying to do is meddle in something you know nothing about. All that concerns you in here, Sam, is to try and do what you get paid for—keep the place clean and serve the customers. In plain words, just get on with your job. My mother is right. She's always warning me about allowing you to get too familiar. Well, this time you've gone too far. It's going to stop right now.

(*No response from* SAM.)

You're only a servant in here, and don't forget it.

(*Still no response.* HALLY *is trying hard to get one.*)

And as far as my father is concerned, all you need to remember is that he is your boss.

SAM (*needled at last*): No, he isn't. I get paid by your mother.

HALLY: Don't argue with me, Sam!

SAM: Then don't say he's my boss.

HALLY: He's a white man and that's good enough for you.

SAM: I'll try to forget you said that.

HALLY: Don't! Because you won't be doing me a favor if you do. I'm telling you to remember it.

(*A pause.* SAM *pulls himself together and makes one last effort.*)

SAM: Hally, Hally . . . ! Come on now. Let's stop before it's too late. You're right. We *are* on dangerous ground. If we're not careful, somebody is going to get hurt.

HALLY: It won't be me.

SAM: Don't be so sure.

HALLY: I don't know what you're talking about, Sam.

SAM: Yes, you do.

HALLY (*furious*): Jesus, I wish you would stop trying to tell me what I do and what I don't know.

(SAM *gives up. He turns to* WILLIE.)

SAM: Let's finish up.

HALLY: Don't turn your back on me! I haven't finished talking.

(*He grabs* SAM *by the arm and tries to make him turn around.* SAM *reacts with a flash of anger.*)

SAM: Don't do that, Hally! (*Facing the boy*) All right, I'm listening. Well? What do you want to say to me?

HALLY (*pause as* HALLY *looks for something to say*): To begin with, why don't you also start calling me Master Harold, like Willie.

SAM: Do you mean it?

HALLY: Why the hell do you think I said it?

SAM: And if I don't?

HALLY: You might just lose your job.

SAM (*quietly and very carefully*): If you make me say it once, I'll never call you anything else again.

HALLY: So? (*The boy confronts the man.*) Is that meant to be a threat?

SAM: Just telling you what will happen if you make me do that. You must decide what it means to you.

HALLY: Well, I have. It's good news. Because that is exactly what Master Harold wants from now on. Think of it as a little lesson in respect, Sam, that's long overdue, and I hope you remember it as well as you do your geography. I can tell you now that somebody who will be glad to hear I've finally given it to you will be my Dad. Yes! He agrees with my Mom. He's always going on about it as well. "You must teach the boys to show you more respect, my son."

SAM: So now you can stop complaining about going home. Everybody is going to be happy tonight.

HALLY: That's perfectly correct. You see, you mustn't get the wrong idea about me and my Dad, Sam. We also have our good times together. Some bloody good laughs. He's got a marvelous sense of humor. Want to know what our favorite joke is? He gives out a big groan, you see, and says: "It's not fair, is it, Hally?" Then I have to ask: "What, chum?" And then he says: "A nigger's arse" . . . and we both have a good laugh.

(*The men stare at him with disbelief.*)

What's the matter, Willie? Don't you catch the joke? You always were a bit slow on the uptake. It's what is called a pun. You, see, fair means both

light in color and to be just and decent. (*He turns to* SAM.) I thought *you* would catch it, Sam.

SAM: Oh ja, I catch it all right.

HALLY: But it doesn't appeal to your sense of humor.

SAM: Do you really laugh?

HALLY: Of course.

SAM: To please him? Make him feel good?

HALLY: No, for heavens sake! I laugh because I think it's a bloody good joke.

SAM: You're really trying hard to be ugly, aren't you? And why drag poor old Willie into it? He's done nothing to you except show you the respect you want so badly. That's also not being fair, you know . . . and *I* mean just or decent.

WILLIE: It's all right, Sam. Leave it now.

SAM: It's me you're after. You should just have said "Sam's arse" . . . because that's the one you're trying to kick. Anyway, how do you know it's not fair? You've never seen it. Do you want to? (*He drops his trousers and underpants and presents his backside for* HALLY's *inspection.*) Have a good look. A real Basuto arse . . . which is about as nigger as they can come. Satisfied? (*Trousers up.*) Now you can make your Dad even happier when you go home tonight. Tell him I showed you my arse and he is quite right. It's not fair. And if it will give him an even better laugh next time, I'll also let *him* have a look. Come, Willie, let's finish up and go.

(SAM *and* WILLIE *start to tidy up the tea room.* HALLY *doesn't move. He waits for a moment when* SAM *passes him.*)

HALLY (*quietly*): Sam . . .

(SAM *stops and looks expectantly at the boy.* HALLY *spits in his face. A long and heartfelt groan from* WILLIE. *For a few seconds* SAM *doesn't move.*)

SAM (*taking out a handkerchief and wiping his face.*): It's all right, Willie.

(*To* HALLY)

Ja, well, you've done it . . . Master Harold. Yes, I'll start calling you that from now on. It won't be difficult anymore. You've hurt yourself, Master Harold. I saw it coming. I warned you, but you wouldn't listen. You've just hurt yourself *bad.* And you're a coward, Master Harold. The face you should be spitting in is your father's . . . but you used mine, because you think you're safe inside your fair skin . . . and this time I don't mean just or decent. (*Pause, then moving violently towards* HALLY) Should I hit him, Willie?

WILLIE (*stopping* SAM): No, Boet Sam.

SAM (*violently*): Why not?

WILLIE: It won't help, Boet Sam.

SAM: I don't want to help! I want to hurt him.

WILLIE: You also hurt yourself.

SAM: And if he had done it to you, Willie?

WILLIE: Me? Spit at me like I was a dog? (*A thought that had not occurred to him before. He looks at* HALLY.) Ja. Then I want to hit him. I want to hit him hard!

(*A dangerous few seconds as the men stand staring at the boy.* WILLIE *turns away, shaking his head.*)

But maybe all I do is go cry at the back. He's little boy, Boet Sam. Little *white* boy. Long trousers now, but he's still little boy.

SAM (*his violence ebbing away into defeat as quickly as it flooded*): You're right. So go on, then: groan again, Willie. You do it better than me. (*To* HALLY) You don't know all of what you've just done . . . Master Harold. It's not just that you've made me feel dirtier than I've ever been in my life . . . I mean, how do I wash off yours and your father's filth? . . . I've also failed. A long time ago I promised myself I was going to try and do something, but you've just shown me . . . Master Harold . . . that I've failed. (*Pause.*) I've also got a memory of a little white boy when he was still wearing short trousers and a black man, and they're not flying a kite. It was the old Jubilee days, after dinner one night. I was in my room. You came in and just stood against the wall, looking down at the ground, and only after I'd asked you what you wanted, what was wrong, I don't know how many times, did you speak and even then so softly I almost didn't hear you. "Sam, please help me to go and fetch my Dad." Remember? He was dead drunk on the floor of the Central Hotel Bar. They'd phoned for your Mom, but you were the only one at home. And do you remember how we did it? You went in first by yourself to ask permission for me to go into the bar. Then I loaded him onto my back like a baby and carried him back to the boarding house with you following behind carrying his crutches. (*Shaking his head as he remembers*) A crowded Main Street with all the people watching a little white boy following his drunk father on a nigger's back! I felt for that little boy . . . Master Harold. I felt for him. After that we still had to clean him up, remember? He'd messed in his trousers, so we had to clean him up and get him into bed.

HALLY (*great pain*): I love him, Sam.

SAM: I know you do. That's why I tried to stop you from saying these things about him. It would have been so simple if you could have just despised him for being a weak man. But he's your father. You love him and you're ashamed of him. You're ashamed of so much! . . . And now that's going to include yourself. That was the promise I made to myself: to try and stop that happening. (*Pause.*) After we got him to bed you came back with me to my room and sat in a corner and carried on just looking down at the ground. And for days after that! You hadn't done anything wrong, but you went around as if you owed the world an apology for being alive. I didn't like seeing that! That's not the way a boy grows up to be a man! . . . But the one person who should have been teaching you what that means was the cause of your shame. If you really want to know, that's why I made you that kite. I wanted you to look up, be proud of something, of yourself . . . (*bitter smile at the memory*) . . . and you certainly were that when I left you with it up there on the hill. Oh, ja . . . something else! . . . If you ever do write it as a short story, there *was* a twist in our ending. I couldn't sit down there and stay with you. It was a "Whites Only" bench. You were too young, too excited to notice then. But not anymore. If you're not careful . . . Master Harold . . . you're going to be sitting up there by yourself for a long time to come, and there won't be a kite in the sky. (SAM *has got nothing more to say. He exits into the kitchen, taking off his waiter's jacket.*)

WILLIE: Is bad. Is all bad in here now.

HALLY (*books into his school case, raincoat on*): Willie . . . (*It is difficult to speak.*) Will you lock up for me and look after the keys?

WILLIE: Okay.

(SAM *returns.* HALLY *goes behind the counter and collects the few coins in the cash register. As he starts to leave . . .*)

SAM: Don't forget the comic books.

(HALLY *returns to the counter and puts them in his case. He starts to leave again.*)

SAM (*to the retreating back of the boy*): Stop . . . Hally. . . .

(HALLY *stops, but doesn't turn to face him.*)

Hally . . . I've got no right to tell you what being a man means if I don't behave like one myself, and I'm not doing so well at that this afternoon. Should we try again, Hally?

HALLY: Try what?

SAM: Fly another kite, I suppose. It worked once, and this time I need it as much as you do.

HALLY: It's still raining, Sam. You can't fly kites on rainy days, remember.

SAM: So what do we do? Hope for better weather tomorrow?

HALLY (*helpless gesture*): I don't know. I don't know anything anymore.

SAM: You sure of that, Hally? Because it would be pretty hopeless if that was true. It would mean nothing has been learnt in here this afternoon, and there was a hell of a lot of teaching going on . . . one way or the other. But anyway, I don't believe you. I reckon there's one thing you know. You don't *have* to sit up there by yourself. You know what that bench means now, and you can leave it any time you choose. All you've got to do is stand up and walk away from it.

(HALLY *leaves*. WILLIE *goes up quietly to* SAM.)

WILLIE: Is okay, Boet Sam. You see. Is . . . (*He can't find any better words.*) . . . is going to be okay tomorrow. (*Changing his tone*) Hey, Boet Sam! (*He is trying hard.*) You right. I think about it and you right. Tonight I find Hilda and say sorry. And make promise I won't beat her no more. You hear me, Boet Sam?

SAM: I hear you, Willie.

WILLIE: And when we practice I relax and romance with her from beginning to end. Non-stop! You watch! Two weeks' time: "First prize for promising newcomers: Mr. Willie Malopo and Miss Hilda Samuels." (*Sudden impulse.*) To hell with it! I walk home. (*He goes to the jukebox, puts in a coin and selects a record. The machine comes to life in the gray twilight, blushing its way through a spectrum of soft, romantic colors.*) How did you say it, Boet Sam? Let's dream. (WILLIE *sways with the music and gestures for* SAM *to dance.*)

(*Sarah Vaughan sings*)

> "Little man you're crying,
> I know why you're blue,
> Someone took your kiddy car away;
> Better go to sleep now,
> Little man you've had a busy day."
>   (*etc., etc.*)

You lead. I'll follow.

(*The men dance together.*)

> "Johnny won your marbles,
> Tell you what we'll do;
> Dad will get you new ones
>   right away;
> Better go to sleep now,
> Little man you've had a busy day."

TOPICS FOR DISCUSSION

1. Exactly what do you think is implied in the title? Why is "*MASTER HAROLD*" in capital letters and in quotation marks, while *and the boys* (separated by three dots from Harold) is in lowercase letters? Why "Harold" rather than Hally, since he is called Hally in the play? Why "boys" for grown men?

2. Compare Sam and Willie, making specific references to the text in order to support your characterizations.

3. Characterize Hally, taking account of his relationships to his parents as well as to Sam and Willie. In his autobiographical volume, *Notebooks*, Fugard tells how as an adolescent he spat at Sam "out of a spasm of acute loneliness." In your characterization of Hally you may want to discuss the degree (if any) to which loneliness helps to explain the boy's behavior.

4. The play is set in Fugard's native country, South Africa, in the 1950s. How closely does that world resemble the United States of the 1950s?

5. Can it be argued that the relationship dramatized in this play is not limited to South Africa in the 1950s but is essentially rooted in the situation, that is, in the relationship of employees to the child of the employer?

6. Early in the play (page 655), when Sam describes policemen whipping a prisoner, Hally says "People can be real bastards," and Sam replies, "That's the way it is,

Hally." Does the play as a whole suggest that hostility and cruelty are "the way it is," despite Hally's belief that "there is something called progress, you know"? Later (page 662), speaking of his father's plan to leave the hospital, Hally says "This is not an age of miracles!" Is it legitimate to connect these passages, and to relate them to the theme of the play?

7. Why does Fugard introduce (pages 660–661) the episode of the kite?

8. On page 668 Sam cautions Hally, "Be careful." Exactly what is he cautioning Hally against? And what is Hally cautioning Sam against when he says (page 668) "Very careful! You're treading on dangerous ground"?

9. "Reversal" (Aristotle's *peripeteia*) and "recognition" (Aristotle's *anagnorisis*) are discussed above, in the Nature of Drama (page 68), and below, in the Glossary, and in Aristotle's essay (page 741). Consider the relevance of these terms to this play.

10. In Mary McCarthy's novel *A Charmed Life*, one of the characters says that tragedies depict "growing pains." How apt a characterization is this of other tragedies that you have read, and of this play?

11. In your opinion, why does Fugard end the play not with Hally's final exit but with three speeches and a song?

'NIGHT, MOTHER

Marsha Norman

Marsha Norman was born in Louisville, Kentucky, in 1947. After receiving a bachelor's degree from Agnes Scott College and a master of arts in teaching from the University of Louisville, she taught gifted children and disturbed children. Her reputation as a playwright was established with a two-act play, *Getting Out*, which was produced in Louisville (1977) and subsequently in New York (1978). *'night, Mother*, which had its world premiere in Cambridge, Massachusetts, in 1983, won the Pulitzer Prize for drama in that year.

CHARACTERS

JESSIE CATES, *in her late thirties or early forties, is pale and vaguely unsteady physically. It is only in the last year that Jessie has gained control of her mind and body, and tonight she is determined to hold on to that control. She wears pants and a long black sweater with deep pockets, which contain scraps of paper, and there may be a pencil behind her ear or a pen clipped to one of the pockets of the sweater.*

As a rule, Jessie doesn't feel much like talking. Other people have rarely found her quirky sense of humor amusing. She has a peaceful energy on this night, a sense of purpose, but is clearly aware of the time passing moment by moment. Oddly enough, Jessie has never been as communicative or as enjoyable as she is on this evening, but we must know she has not always been this way. There is a familiarity between these two women that comes from having lived together for a long time. There is a shorthand to the talk and a sense of routine comfort in the way they relate to each other physically. Naturally, there are also routine aggravations.

THELMA CATES, "MAMA," *is Jessie's mother, in her late fifties or early sixties. She has begun to feel her age and so takes it easy when she can, or when it serves her purpose to let someone help her. But she speaks quickly and enjoys talking. She believes that things are what she says they are. Her sturdiness is more a mental quality than a physical one, finally. She is chatty and nosy, and this is her house.*

Kathy Bates as Jessie and Anne Pitoniak as Mama in a scene from the American Repertory Theatre production of *'night Mother*. (Photograph: Richard Feldman, courtesy of the American Repertory Theatre Company Inc., Cambridge, MA.)

The play takes place in a relatively new house built way out on a country road, with a living room and connecting kitchen, and a center hall that leads off to the bedrooms. A pull cord in the hall ceiling releases a ladder which leads to the attic. One of these bedrooms opens directly onto the hall, and its entry should be visible to everyone in the audience. It should be, in fact, the focal point of the entire set, and the lighting should make it disappear completely at times and draw the entire set into it at others. It is a point of both threat and promise. It is an ordinary door that opens onto absolute nothingness. That door is the point of all the action, and the utmost care should be given to its design and construction.

The living room is cluttered with magazines and needlework catalogues, ashtrays and candy dishes. Examples of Mama's needlework are everywhere—pillows, afghans, and quilts, doilies and rugs, and they are quite nice examples. The house is more comfortable than messy, but there is quite a lot to keep in place here. It is more personal than charming. It is not quaint. Under no circumstances should the set and its dressing make a judgment about the intelligence or taste of Jessie and Mama. It should simply indicate that they are very specific real people who happen to live in a particular part of the country. Heavy accents, which would further distance the audience from Jessie and Mama, are also wrong.

The time is the present, with the action beginning about 8:15. Clocks onstage in the kitchen and on a table in the living room should run throughout the performance and be visible to the audience.

There will be no intermission.

MAMA *stretches to reach the cupcakes in a cabinet in the kitchen. She can't see them, but she can feel around for them, and she's eager to have one, so she's working pretty hard at it. This may be the most serious exercise* MAMA *ever gets. She finds a cupcake, the coconut-covered, raspberry-and-marshmallow-filled kind known as a snowball, but sees that there's one missing from the package. She calls to* JESSIE, *who is apparently somewhere else in the house.*

MAMA (*unwrapping the cupcake*): Jessie, it's the last snowball, sugar. Put it on the list, O.K.? And we're out of Hershey bars, and where's that peanut brittle? I think maybe Dawson's been in it again. I

ought to put a big mirror on the refrigerator door. That'll keep him out of my treats, won't it? You hear me, honey? (*Then more to herself*) I hate it when the coconut falls off. Why does the coconut fall off?

(JESSIE *enters from her bedroom, carrying a stack of newspapers.*)

JESSIE: We got any old towels?
MAMA: There you are!
JESSIE (*holding a towel that was on the stack of newspapers*): Towels you don't want anymore. (*Picking up* MAMA's *snowball wrapper*) How about this swimming towel Loretta gave us? Beach towel, that's the name of it. You want it? (MAMA *shakes her head no.*)

MAMA: What have you been doing in there?

JESSIE: And a big piece of plastic like a rubber sheet or something. Garbage bags would do if there's enough.

MAMA: Don't go making a big mess, Jessie. It's eight o'clock already.

JESSIE: Maybe an old blanket or towels we got in a soap box sometime?

MAMA: I said don't make a mess. Your hair is black enough, hon.

JESSIE (*continuing to search the kitchen cabinets, finding two or three more towels to add to her stack*): It's not for my hair, Mama. What about some old pillows anywhere, or a foam cushion out of a yard chair would be real good.

MAMA: You haven't forgot what night it is, have you? (*Holding up her fingernails*) They're all chipped, see? I've been waiting all week, Jess. It's Saturday night, sugar.

JESSIE: I know. I got it on the schedule.

MAMA (*crossing to the living room*): You want me to wash 'em now or are you making your mess first? (*Looking at the snowball*) We're out of these. Did I say that already?

JESSIE: There's more coming tomorrow. I ordered you a whole case.

MAMA (*checking the* TV Guide): A whole case will go stale, Jessie.

JESSIE: They can go in the freezer till you're ready for them. Where's Daddy's gun?

MAMA: In the attic.

JESSIE: Where in the attic? I looked your whole nap and couldn't find it anywhere.

MAMA: One of his shoeboxes, I think.

JESSIE: Full of shoes. I looked already.

MAMA: Well, you didn't look good enough, then. There's that box from the ones he wore to the hospital. When he died, they told me I could have them back, but I never did like those shoes.

JESSIE (*pulling them out of her pocket*): I found the bullets. They were in an old milk can.

MAMA (*as* JESSIE *starts for the hall*): Dawson took the shotgun, didn't he? Hand me that basket, hon.

JESSIE (*getting the basket for her*): Dawson better not've taken that pistol.

MAMA (*stopping her again*): Now my glasses, please. (JESSIE *returns to get the glasses.*) I told him to take those rubber boots, too, but he said they were for fishing. I told him to take up fishing.

(JESSIE *reaches for the cleaning spray, and cleans* MAMA's *glasses for her.*)

JESSIE: He's just too lazy to climb up there, Mama. Or maybe he's just being smart. That floor's not very steady.

MAMA (*getting out a piece of knitting*): It's not a floor at all, hon, it's a board now and then. Measure this for me. I need six inches.

JESSIE (*as she measures*): Dawson could probably use some of those clothes up there. Somebody should have them. You ought to call the Salvation Army before the whole thing falls in on you. Six inches exactly.

MAMA: It's plenty safe! As long as you don't go up there.

JESSIE (*turning to go again*): I'm careful.

MAMA: What do you want the gun for, Jess?

JESSIE (*not returning this time. Opening the ladder in the hall*): Protection. (*She steadies the ladder as* MAMA *talks.*)

MAMA: You take the TV way too serious, hon. I've never seen a criminal in my life. This is way too far to come for what's out here to steal. Never seen a one.

JESSIE (*taking her first step up*): Except for Ricky.

MAMA: Ricky is mixed up. That's not a crime.

JESSIE: Get your hands washed. I'll be right back. And get 'em real dry. You dry your hands till I get back or it's no go, all right?

MAMA: I thought Dawson told you not to go up those stairs.

JESSIE (*going up*): He did.

MAMA: I don't like the idea of a gun, Jess.

JESSIE (*calling down from the attic*): Which shoebox, do you remember?

MAMA: Black.

JESSIE: The box was black?

MAMA: The shoes were black.

JESSIE: That doesn't help much, Mother.

MAMA: I'm not trying to help, sugar. (*No answer.*) We don't have anything anybody'd want, Jessie. I mean, I don't even want what we got, Jessie.

JESSIE: Neither do I. Wash your hands. (MAMA *gets up and crosses to stand under the ladder.*)

MAMA: You come down from there before you have a fit. I can't come up and get you, you know.

JESSIE: I know.

MAMA: We'll just hand it over to them when they come, how's that? Whatever they want, the criminals.

JESSIE: That's a good idea, Mama.

MAMA: Ricky will grow out of this and be a real fine boy, Jess. But I have to tell you, I wouldn't want Ricky to know we had a gun in the house.

JESSIE: Here it is. I found it.

MAMA: It's just something Ricky's going through. Maybe he's in with some bad people. He just needs some time, sugar. He'll get back in school or get a job or one day you'll get a call and he'll say he's sorry for all the trouble he's caused and invite you out for supper someplace dress-up.

JESSIE (coming back down the steps): Don't worry. It's not for him, it's for me.

MAMA: I didn't think you would shoot your own boy, Jessie. I know you've felt like it, well, we've all felt like shooting somebody, but we don't do it. I just don't think we need . . .

JESSIE (interrupting): Your hands aren't washed. Do you want a manicure or not?

MAMA: Yes, I do, but . . .

JESSIE (crossing to the chair): Then wash your hands and don't talk to me any more about Ricky. Those two rings he took were the last valuable things I had, so now he's started in on other people, door to door. I hope they put him away sometime. I'd turn him in myself if I knew where he was.

MAMA: You don't mean that.

JESSIE: Every word. Wash your hands and that's the last time I'm telling you.

(JESSIE sits down with the gun and starts cleaning it, pushing the cylinder out, checking to see that the chambers and barrel are empty, then putting some oil on a small patch of cloth and pushing it through the barrel with the push rod that was in the box. MAMA goes to the kitchen and washes her hands, as instructed, trying not to show her concern about the gun.)

MAMA: I shoulda got you to bring down that milk can. Agnes Fletcher sold hers to somebody with a flea market for forty dollars apiece.

JESSIE: I'll go back and get it in a minute. There's a wagon wheel up there, too. There's even a churn. I'll get it all if you want.

MAMA (coming over, now, taking over now): What are you doing?

JESSIE: The barrel has to be clean, Mama. Old powder dust gets in it. . . .

MAMA: What for?

JESSIE: I told you.

MAMA (reaching for the gun): And I told you, we don't get criminals out here.

JESSIE (quickly pulling it to her): And I told you . . . (Then trying to be calm) The gun is for me.

MAMA: Well, you can have it if you want. When I die, you'll get it all, anyway.

JESSIE: I'm going to kill myself, Mama.

MAMA (returning to the sofa): Very funny. Very funny.

JESSIE: I am.

MAMA: You are not! Don't even say such a thing, Jessie.

JESSIE: How would you know if I didn't say it? You want it to be a surprise? You're lying there in your bed or maybe you're just brushing your teeth and you hear this . . . noise down the hall?

MAMA: Kill yourself.

JESSIE: Shoot myself. In a couple of hours.

MAMA: It must be time for your medicine.

JESSIE: Took it already.

MAMA: What's the matter with you?

JESSIE: Not a thing. Feel fine.

MAMA: You feel fine. You're just going to kill yourself.

JESSIE: Waited until I felt good enough, in fact.

MAMA: Don't make jokes, Jessie. I'm too old for jokes.

JESSIE: It's not a joke, Mama.

(MAMA watches for a moment in silence.)

MAMA: That gun's no good, you know. He broke it right before he died. He dropped it in the mud one day.

JESSIE: Seems O.K. (She spins the chamber, cocks the pistol, and pulls the trigger. The gun is not yet loaded, so all we hear is the click, but it will definitely work. It's also obvious that JESSIE knows her way around a gun. MAMA cannot speak.) I had Cecil's all ready in there, just in case I couldn't find this one, but I'd rather use Daddy's.

MAMA: Those bullets are at least fifteen years old.

JESSIE (pulling out another box): These are from last week.

MAMA: Where did you get those?

JESSIE: Feed store Dawson told me about.

MAMA: Dawson!

JESSIE: I told him I was worried about prowlers. He said he thought it was a good idea. He told me what kind to ask for.

MAMA: If he had any idea . . .

JESSIE: He took it as a compliment. He thought I might be taking an interest in things. He got through telling me all about the bullets and then he said we ought to talk like this more often.

MAMA: And where was I while this was going on?

JESSIE: On the phone with Agnes. About the milk can, I guess. Anyway, I asked Dawson if he thought they'd send me some bullets and he said he'd just call for me, because he knew they'd send them if he told them to. And he was absolutely right. Here they are.

MAMA: How could he do that?

JESSIE: Just trying to help, Mama.

MAMA: And then I told you where the gun was.

JESSIE (*smiling, enjoying this joke*): See? Everybody's doing what they can.

MAMA: You told me it was for protection!

JESSIE: It *is*! I'm still doing your nails, though. Want to try that new Chinaberry color?

MAMA: Well, I'm calling Dawson right now. We'll just see what he had to say about this little stunt.

JESSIE: Dawson doesn't have any more to do with this.

MAMA: He's your brother.

JESSIE: And that's all.

MAMA (*stands up, moves toward the phone*): Dawson will put a stop to this. Yes he will. He'll take the gun away.

JESSIE: If you call him, I'll just have to do it before he gets here. Soon as you hang up the phone, I'll just walk in the bedroom and lock the door. Dawson will get here just in time to help you clean up. Go ahead, call him. Then call the police. Then call the funeral home. Then call Loretta and see if *she'll* do your nails.

MAMA: You will not! This is crazy talk, Jessie!

(MAMA *goes directly to the telephone and starts to dial, but* JESSIE *is fast, coming up behind her and taking the receiver out of her hand, putting it back down.*)

JESSIE (*firm and quiet*): I said no. This is private. Dawson is not invited.

MAMA: Just me.

JESSIE: I don't want anybody else over here. Just you and me. If Dawson comes over, it'll make me feel stupid for not doing it ten years ago.

MAMA: I think we better call the doctor. Or how about the ambulance. You like that one driver, I know. What's his name, Timmy? Get you somebody to talk to.

JESSIE (*going back to her chair*): I'm through talking, Mama. You're it. No more.

MAMA: We're just going to sit around like every other night in the world and then you're going to kill yourself? (JESSIE *doesn't answer.*) You'll miss. (*Again there is no response.*) You'll just wind up a vegetable. How would you like that? Shoot your ear off? You know what the doctor said about getting excited. You'll cock the pistol and have a fit.

JESSIE: I think I can kill myself, Mama.

MAMA: You're not going to kill yourself, Jessie. You're not even upset! (JESSIE *smiles, or laughs quietly, and* MAMA *tries a different approach.*) People don't really kill themselves, Jessie. No, mam, doesn't make sense, unless you're retarded or deranged, and you're as normal as they come, Jessie, for the most part. We're all *afraid* to die.

JESSIE: I'm not, Mama. I'm cold all the time, anyway.

MAMA: That's ridiculous.

JESSIE: It's exactly what I want. It's dark and quiet.

MAMA: So is the back yard, Jessie! Close your eyes. Stuff cotton in your ears. Take a nap! It's quiet in your room. I'll leave the TV off all night.

JESSIE: So quiet I don't know it's quiet. So nobody can get me.

MAMA: You don't know what dead is like. It might not be quiet at all. What if it's like an alarm clock and you can't wake up so you can't shut it off. Ever.

JESSIE: Dead is everybody and everything I ever knew, gone. Dead is dead quiet.

MAMA: It's a sin. You'll go to hell.

JESSIE: Uh-huh.

MAMA: You will!

JESSIE: Jesus was a suicide, if you ask me.

MAMA: You'll go to hell just for saying that. Jessie!

JESSIE (*with genuine surprise*): I didn't know I thought that.

MAMA: Jessie!

(JESSIE *doesn't answer. She puts the now-loaded gun back in the box and crosses to the kitchen. But* MAMA *is afraid she's headed for the bedroom.*)

MAMA (*in a panic*): You can't use my towels! They're my towels. I've had them for a long time. I like my towels.

JESSIE: I asked you if you wanted that swimming towel and you said you didn't.

MAMA: And you can't use your father's gun, either. It's mine now, too. And you can't do it in my house.

JESSIE: Oh, come on.

MAMA: No. You can't do it. I won't let you. The house is in my name.

JESSIE: I have to go in the bedroom and lock the door behind me so they won't arrest you for killing me. They'll probably test your hands for gunpowder, anyway, but you'll pass.

MAMA: Not in my house!

JESSIE: If I'd known you were going to act like this, I wouldn't have told you.

MAMA: How am I supposed to act? Tell you to go ahead? O.K. by me, sugar? Might try it myself. What took you so long?

JESSIE: There's just no point in fighting me over it, that's all. Want some coffee?

MAMA: Your birthday's coming up, Jessie. Don't you want to know what we got you?

JESSIE: You got me dusting powder, Loretta got me a new housecoat, pink probably, and Dawson got me new slippers, too small, but they go with the robe, he'll say. (MAMA *cannot speak. Apparently* JESSIE *is right.*) Be back in a minute.

(JESSIE *takes the gun box, puts it on top of the stack of towels and garbage bags, and takes them into her bedroom.* MAMA, *alone for a moment, goes to the phone, picks up the receiver, looks toward the bedroom, starts to dial, and then replaces the receiver in its cradle as* JESSIE *walks back into the room.* JESSIE *wonders, silently. They have lived together for so long there is very rarely any reason for one to ask what the other was about to do.*)

MAMA: I started to, but I didn't. I didn't call him.

JESSIE: Good. Thank you.

MAMA (*starting over, a new approach*): What's this all about, Jessie?

JESSIE: About?

(JESSIE *now begins the next task she had "on the schedule" which is refilling all the candy jars, taking the empty papers out of the boxes of chocolates, etc.* MAMA *generally snitches when* JESSIE *does this. Not tonight, though. Nevertheless,* JESSIE *offers.*)

MAMA: What did I do?

JESSIE: Nothing. Want a caramel?

MAMA (*ignoring the candy*): You're mad at me.

JESSIE: Not a bit. I am worried about you, but I'm going to do what I can before I go. We're not just going to sit around tonight. I made a list of things.

MAMA: What things?

JESSIE: How the washer works. Things like that.

MAMA: I know how the washer works. You put the clothes in. You put the soap in. You turn it on. You wait.

JESSIE: You do something else. You don't just wait.

MAMA: Whatever else you find to do, you're still mainly waiting. The waiting's the worst part of it.

The waiting's what you pay somebody else to do, if you can.

JESSIE (*nodding*): O.K. Where do we keep the soap?

MAMA: I could find it.

JESSIE: See?

MAMA: If you're mad about doing the wash, we can get Loretta to do it.

JESSIE: Oh now, that might be worth staying to see.

MAMA: She'd never in her life, would she?

JESSIE: Nope.

MAMA: What's the matter with her?

JESSIE: She thinks she's better than we are. She's not.

MAMA: Maybe if she didn't wear that yellow all the time.

JESSIE: The washer repair number is on a little card taped to the side of the machine.

MAMA: Loretta doesn't ever have to come over here again. Dawson can just leave her at home when he comes. And we don't ever have to see Dawson either if he bothers you. Does he bother you?

JESSIE: Sure he does. Be sure you clean out the lint tray every time you use the dryer. But don't you ever put your house shoes in, it'll melt the shoes.

MAMA: What does Dawson do, that bothers you?

JESSIE: He just calls me Jess like he knows who he's talking to. He's always wondering what I do all day. I mean, I wonder that myself, but it's my day, so it's mine to wonder about, not his.

MAMA: Family is just accident, Jessie. It's nothing personal, hon. They don't mean to get on your nerves. They don't even mean to be your family, they just are.

JESSIE: They know too much.

MAMA: About what?

JESSIE: They know things about you, and they learned it before you had a chance to say whether you wanted them to know it or not. They were there when it happened and it don't belong to them, it belongs to you, only they got it. Like my mail-order bra got delivered to their house.

MAMA: By accident!

JESSIE: All the same . . . they opened it. They saw the little rosebuds on it. (*Offering her another candy*) Chewy mint?

MAMA (*shaking her head no*): What do they know about you? I'll tell them never to talk about it again. Is it Ricky or Cecil or your fits or your hair is falling out or you drink too much coffee or you never go out of the house or what?

JESSIE: I just don't like their talk. The account at the grocery is in Dawson's name when you call. The number's on a whole list of numbers on the back cover of the phone book.

MAMA: Well! Now we're getting somewhere. They're none of them ever setting foot in this house again.

JESSIE: It's not them, Mother. I wouldn't kill myself just to get away from them.

MAMA: You leave the room when they come over, anyway.

JESSIE: I stay as long as I can. Besides, it's you they come to see.

MAMA: That's because I stay in the room when they come.

JESSIE: It's not them.

MAMA: Then what is it?

JESSIE (*checking the list on her note pad*): The grocery won't deliver on Saturday anymore. And if you want your order the same day, you have to call before ten. And they won't deliver less than fifteen dollars' worth. What I do is tell them what we need and tell them to add on cigarettes until it gets to fifteen dollars.

MAMA: It's Ricky. You're trying to get through to him.

JESSIE: If I thought I could do that, I would stay.

MAMA: Make him sorry he hurt you, then. That's it, isn't it?

JESSIE: He's hurt me, I've hurt him. We're about even.

MAMA: You'll be telling him killing is O.K. with you, you know. Want him to start killing next? Nothing wrong with it. Mom did it.

JESSIE: Only a matter of time, anyway, Mama. When the call comes, you let Dawson handle it.

MAMA: Honey, nothing says those calls are always going to be some new trouble he's into. You could get one that he's got a job, that he's getting married, or how about he's joined the army, wouldn't that be nice?

JESSIE: If you call the Sweet Tooth before you call the grocery, that Susie will take your fudge next door to the grocery and it'll all come out together. Be sure you talk to Susie, though. She won't let them put it in the bottom of a sack like that one time, remember?

MAMA: Ricky could come over, you know. What if he calls us?

JESSIE: It's not Ricky, Mama.

MAMA: Or anybody could call us, Jessie.

JESSIE: Not on Saturday night, Mama.

MAMA: Then what is it? Are you sick? If your gums are swelling again, we can get you to the dentist in the morning.

JESSIE: No. Can you order your medicine or do you want Dawson to? I've got a note to him. I'll add that to it if you want.

MAMA: Your eyes don't look right. I thought so yesterday.

JESSIE: That was just the ragweed. I'm not sick.

MAMA: Epilepsy is sick, Jessie.

JESSIE: It won't kill me. (*A pause.*) If it would, I wouldn't have to.

MAMA: You don't *have* to.

JESSIE: No, I don't. That's what I like about it.

MAMA: Well, I won't let you!

JESSIE: It's not up to you.

MAMA: Jessie!

JESSIE: I want to hang a big sign around my neck, like Daddy's on the barn. GONE FISHING.

MAMA: You don't like it here.

JESSIE (*smiling*): Exactly.

MAMA: I meant here in my house.

JESSIE: I know you did.

MAMA: You never should have moved back in here with me. If you'd kept your little house or found another place when Cecil left you, you'd have made some new friends at least. Had a life to lead. Had your own things around you. Give Ricky a place to come see you. You never should've come here.

JESSIE: Maybe.

MAMA: But I didn't force you, did I?

JESSIE: If it was a mistake, we made it together. You took me in. I appreciate that.

MAMA: You didn't have any business being by yourself right then, but I can see how you might want a place of your own. A grown woman should . . .

JESSIE: Mama . . . I'm just not having a very good time and I don't have any reason to think it'll get anything but worse. I'm tired. I'm hurt. I'm sad. I feel used.

MAMA: Tired of what?

JESSIE: It all.

MAMA: What does that mean?

JESSIE: I can't say it any better.

MAMA: Well, you'll have to say it better because I'm not letting you alone till you do. What were those other things? Hurt . . . (*Before* JESSIE *can answer*) You had this all ready to say to me, didn't you? Did you write this down? How long have you been thinking about this?

JESSIE: Off and on, ten years. On all the time, since Christmas.

MAMA: What happened at Christmas?

JESSIE: Nothing.

MAMA: So why Christmas?

JESSIE: That's it. On the nose.

(*A pause.* MAMA *knows exactly what* JESSIE *means. She was there, too, after all.*)

JESSIE (*putting the candy sacks away*): See where all this is? Red hots up front, sour balls and horehound mixed together in this one sack. New packages of toffee and licorice right in back there.

MAMA: Go back to your list. You're hurt by what?

JESSIE: (MAMA *knows perfectly well*): Mama . . .

MAMA: O.K. Sad about what? There's nothing real sad going on right now. If it was after your divorce or something, that would make sense.

JESSIE (*looking at her list, then opening the drawer*): Now, this drawer has everything in it that there's no better place for. Extension cords, batteries for the radio, extra lighters, sandpaper, masking tape, Elmer's glue, thumbtacks, that kind of stuff. The mousetraps are under the sink, but you call Dawson if you've got one and let him do it.

MAMA: Sad about what?

JESSIE: The way things are.

MAMA: Not good enough. What things?

JESSIE: Oh, everything from you and me to Red China.

MAMA: I think we can leave the Chinese out of this.

JESSIE (*crosses back into the living room*): There's extra light bulbs in a box in the hall closet. And we've got a couple of packages of fuses in the fuse box. There's candles and matches in the top of the broom closet, but if the lights go out, just call Dawson and sit tight. But don't open the refrigerator door. Things will stay cool in there as long as you keep the door shut.

MAMA: I asked you a question.

JESSIE: I read the paper. I don't like how things are. And they're not any better out there than they are in here.

MAMA: If you're doing this because of the newspapers, I can sure fix that!

JESSIE: There's just more of it on TV.

MAMA (*kicking the television set*): Take it out, then!

JESSIE: You wouldn't do that.

MAMA: Watch me.

JESSIE: What would you do all day?

MAMA (*desperately*): Sing. (JESSIE *laughs.*) I would, too. You want to watch? I'll sing till morning to keep you alive, Jessie, please!

JESSIE: No. (*Then affectionately*) It's a funny idea, though. What do you sing?

MAMA (*has no idea how to answer this*): We've got a good life here!

JESSIE (*going back into the kitchen*): I called this morning and canceled the papers, except for Sunday, for your puzzles; you'll still get that one.

MAMA: Let's get another dog, Jessie! You liked a big dog, now, didn't you? That King dog, didn't you?

JESSIE (*washing her hands*): I did like that King dog, yes.

MAMA: I'm so dumb. He's the one run under the tractor.

JESSIE: That makes him dumb, not you.

MAMA: For bringing it up.

JESSIE: It's O.K. Handi-Wipes and sponges under the sink.

MAMA: We could get a new dog and keep him in the house. Dogs are cheap!

JESSIE (*getting big pill jars out of the cabinet*): No.

MAMA: Something for you to take care of.

JESSIE: I've had you, Mama.

MAMA (*frantically starting to fill pill bottles*): You do too much for me. I can fill pill bottles all day, Jessie, and change the shelf paper and wash the floor when I get through. You just watch me. You don't have to do another thing in this house if you don't want to. You don't have to take care of me, Jessie.

JESSIE: I know that. You've just been letting me do it so I'll have something to do, haven't you?

MAMA (*realizing this was a mistake*): I don't do it as well as you. I just meant if it tires you out or makes you feel used . . .

JESSIE: Mama, I know you used to ride the bus. Riding the bus and it's hot and bumpy and crowded and too noisy and more than anything in the world you want to get off and the only reason in the world you don't get off is it's still fifty blocks from where you're going? Well, I can get off right now if I want to, because even if I ride fifty more years and get off then, it's the same place when I step down to it. Whenever I feel like it, I can get off. As soon as I've had enough, it's my stop. I've had enough.

MAMA: You're feeling sorry for yourself!

JESSIE: The plumber's helper is under the sink, too.

MAMA: You're not having a good time! Whoever promised you a good time? Do you think I've had a good time?

JESSIE: I think you're pretty happy, yeah. You have things you like to do.

MAMA: Like what?

JESSIE: Like crochet.

MAMA: I'll teach you to crochet.

JESSIE: I can't do any of that nice work, Mama.

MAMA: Good time don't come looking for you, Jessie. You could work some puzzles or put in a garden or go to the store. Let's call a taxi and go to the A&P!

JESSIE: I shopped you up for about two weeks already. You're not going to need toilet paper till Thanksgiving.

MAMA (interrupting): You're acting like some little brat, Jessie. You're mad and everybody's boring and you don't have anything to do and you don't like me and you don't like going out and you don't like staying in and you never talk on the phone and you don't watch TV and you're miserable and it's your own sweet fault.

JESSIE: And it's time I did something about it.

MAMA: Not something like killing yourself. Something like . . . buying us all new dishes! I'd like that. Or maybe the doctor would let you get a driver's license now, or I know what let's do right this minute, let's rearrange the furniture.

JESSIE: I'll do that. If you want. I always thought if the TV was somewhere else, you wouldn't get such a glare on it during the day. I'll do whatever you want before I go.

MAMA (badly frightened by those words): You could get a job!

JESSIE: I took that telephone sales job and I didn't even make enough money to pay the phone bill, and I tried to work at the gift shop at the hospital and they said I made people real uncomfortable smiling the way I did.

MAMA: You could keep books. You kept your dad's books.

JESSIE: But nobody ever checked them.

MAMA: When he died, they checked them.

JESSIE: And that's when they took the books away from me.

MAMA: That's because without him there wasn't any business, Jessie!

JESSIE (putting the pill bottles away): You know I couldn't work. I can't do anything. I've never been around people my whole life except when I went to the hospital. I could have a seizure any time. What good would a job do? The kind of job I could get would make me feel worse.

MAMA: Jessie!

JESSIE: It's true!

MAMA: It's what you think is true!

JESSIE (struck by the clarity of that): That's right. It's what I think is true.

MAMA (hysterically): But I can't do anything about that!

JESSIE (quietly): No. You can't. (MAMA slumps, if not physically, at least emotionally.) And I can't do anything either, about my life, to change it, make it better, make me feel better about it. Like it better, make it work. But I can stop it. Shut it down, turn it off like the radio when there's nothing on I want to listen to. It's all I really have that belongs to me and I'm going to say what happens to it. And it's going to stop. And I'm going to stop it. So. Let's just have a good time.

MAMA: Have a good time.

JESSIE: We can't go on fussing all night. I mean, I could ask you things I always wanted to know and you could make me some hot chocolate. The old way.

MAMA (in despair): It takes cocoa, Jessie.

JESSIE (gets it out of the cabinet): I bought cocoa, Mama. And I'd like to have a caramel apple and do your nails.

MAMA: You didn't eat a bit of supper.

JESSIE: Does that mean I can't have a caramel apple?

MAMA: Of course not. I mean. . . . (Smiling a little) Of course you can have a caramel apple.

JESSIE: I thought I could.

MAMA: I make the best caramel apples in the world.

JESSIE: I know you do.

MAMA: Or used to. And you don't get cocoa like mine anywhere anymore.

JESSIE: It takes time, I know, but . . .

MAMA: The salt is the trick.

JESSIE: Trouble and everything.

MAMA (backing away toward the stove): It's no trouble. What trouble? You put it in the pan and stir it up. All right. Fine. Caramel apples. Cocoa. O.K.

(JESSIE walks to the counter to retrieve her cigarettes as MAMA looks for the right pan. There are brief near-smiles, and maybe MAMA clears her throat. We have a truce, for the moment. A genuine but nevertheless uneasy one. JESSIE, who has been in constant motion since the beginning, now seems content to sit.

MAMA starts looking for a pan to make the cocoa, getting out all the pans in the cabinets in the process. It looks like she's making a mess on purpose so JESSIE will have to put them all away again. MAMA is buying time, or trying to, and entertaining.)

JESSIE: You talk to Agnes today?

MAMA: She's calling me from a pay phone this week. God only knows why. She has a perfectly good Trimline at home.

JESSIE (*laughing*): Well, how is she?

MAMA: How is she every day, Jessie? Nuts.

JESSIE: Is she really crazy or just silly?

MAMA: No, she's really crazy. She was probably using the pay phone because she had another little fire problem at home.

JESSIE: Mother . . .

MAMA: I'm serious! Agnes Fletcher's burned down every house she ever lived in. Eight fires, and she's due for a new one any day now.

JESSIE (*laughing*): No!

MAMA: Wouldn't surprise me a bit.

JESSIE (*laughing*): Why didn't you tell me this before? Why isn't she locked up somewhere?

MAMA: 'Cause nobody ever got hurt, I guess. Agnes woke everybody up to watch the fires as soon as she set 'em. One time she set out porch chairs and served lemonade.

JESSIE (*shaking her head*): Real lemonade?

MAMA: The houses they lived in, you knew they were going to fall down anyway, so why wait for it, is all I could ever make out about it. Agnes likes a feeling of accomplishment.

JESSIE: Good for her.

MAMA (*finding the pan she wants*): Why are you asking about Agnes? One cup or two?

JESSIE: One. She's your friend. No marshmallows.

MAMA (*getting the milk, etc.*): You have to have marshmallows. That's the old way, Jess. Two or three? Three is better.

JESSIE: Three, then. Her whole house burns up? Her clothes and pillows and everything? I'm not sure I believe this.

MAMA: When she was a girl, Jess, not now. Long time ago. But she's still got it in her, I'm sure of it.

JESSIE: She wouldn't burn her house down now. Where would she go? She can't get Buster to build her a new one, he's dead. How could she burn it up?

MAMA: Be exciting, though, if she did. You never know.

JESSIE: You do too know, Mama. She wouldn't do it.

MAMA (*forced to admit, but reluctant*): I guess not.

JESSIE: What else? Why does she wear all those whistles around her neck?

MAMA: Why does she have a house full of birds?

JESSIE: I didn't know she had a house full of birds!

MAMA: Well, she does. And she says they just follow her home. Well, I know for a fact she's still paying on the last parrot she bought. You gotta keep your life filled up, she says. She says a lot of stupid things. (JESSIE *laughs*, MAMA *continues, convinced she's getting somewhere*.) It's all that okra she eats. You can't just willy-nilly eat okra two meals a day and expect to get away with it. Made her crazy.

JESSIE: She really eats okra twice a day? Where does she get it in the winter?

MAMA: Well, she eats it a lot. Maybe not two meals, but . . .

JESSIE: More than the average person.

MAMA (*beginning to get irritated*): I don't know how much okra the average person eats.

JESSIE: Do you know how much okra Agnes eats?

MAMA: No.

JESSIE: How many birds does she have?

MAMA: Two.

JESSIE: Then what are the whistles for?

MAMA: They're not real whistles. Just little plastic ones on a necklace she won playing Bingo, and I only told you about it because I thought I might get a laugh out of you for once even if it wasn't the truth, Jessie. Things don't have to be true to talk about 'em, you know.

JESSIE: Why won't she come over here?

(MAMA *is suddenly quiet, but the cocoa and milk are in the pan now, so she lights the stove and starts stirring.*)

MAMA: Well now, what a good idea. We should've had more cocoa. Cocoa is perfect.

JESSIE: Except you don't like milk.

MAMA (*another attempt, but not as energetic*): I hate milk. Coats your throat as bad as okra. Something just downright disgusting about it.

JESSIE: It's because of me, isn't it?

MAMA: No, Jess.

JESSIE: Yes, Mama.

MAMA: O.K. Yes, then, but she's crazy. She's as crazy as they come. She's a lunatic.

JESSIE: What is it exactly? Did I say something, sometime? Or did she see me have a fit and's afraid I might have another one if she came over, or what?

MAMA: I guess.

JESSIE: You guess what? What's she ever said? She must've given you some reason.

MAMA: Your hands are cold.

JESSIE: What difference does that make?

MAMA: "Like a corpse," she says, "and I'm gonna be one soon enough as it is."

JESSIE: That's crazy.

MAMA: That's Agnes. "Jessie's shook the hand of death and I can't take the chance it's catching, Thelma, so I ain't comin' over, and you can understand or not, but I ain't comin'. I'll come up the driveway, but that's as far as I go."

JESSIE (*laughing, relieved*): I thought she didn't like me! She's scared of me! How about that! Scared of me.

MAMA: I could make her come over here, Jessie. I could call her up right now and she could bring the birds and come visit. I didn't know you ever thought about her at all. I'll tell her she just has to come and she'll come, all right. She owes me one.

JESSIE: No, that's all right. I just wondered about it. When I'm in the hospital, does she come over here?

MAMA: Her kitchen is just a tiny thing. When she comes over here, she feels like . . . (*Toning it down a little*) Well, we all like a change of scene, don't we?

JESSIE (*playing along*): Sure we do. Plus there's no birds diving around.

MAMA: I hate those birds. She says I don't understand them. What's there to understand about birds?

JESSIE: Why Agnes likes them, for one thing. Why they stay with her when they could be outside with the other birds. What their singing means. How they fly. What they think Agnes is.

MAMA: Why do you have to know so much about things, Jessie? There's just not that much *to* things that I could ever see.

JESSIE: That you could ever *tell*, you mean. You didn't have to lie to me about Agnes.

MAMA: I didn't lie. You never asked before!

JESSIE: You lied about setting fire to all those houses and about how many birds she has and how much okra she eats and why she won't come over here. If I have to keep dragging the truth out of you, this is going to take all night.

MAMA: That's fine with me. I'm not a bit sleepy.

JESSIE: Mama . . .

MAMA: All right. Ask me whatever you want. Here.

(*They come to an awkward stop, as the cocoa is ready and* MAMA *pours it into the cups* JESSIE *has set on the table.*)

JESSIE (*as* MAMA *takes her first sip*): Did you love Daddy?

MAMA: No.

JESSIE (*pleased that* MAMA *understands the rules better now*): I didn't think so. Were you really fifteen when you married him?

MAMA: The way he told it? I'm sitting in the mud, he comes along, drags me in the kitchen, "She's been there ever since"?

JESSIE: Yes.

MAMA: No. It was a big fat lie, the whole thing. He just thought it was funnier that way. God, this milk in here.

JESSIE: The cocoa helps.

MAMA (*pleased that they agree on this, at least*): Not enough, though, does it? You can still taste it, can't you?

JESSIE: Yeah, it's pretty bad. I thought it was my memory that was bad, but it's not. It's the milk, all right.

MAMA: It's a real waste of chocolate. You don't have to finish it.

JESSIE (*putting her cup down*): Thanks, though.

MAMA: I should've known not to make it. I knew you wouldn't like it. You never did like it.

JESSIE: You didn't ever love him, or he did something and you stopped loving him, or what?

MAMA: He felt sorry for me. He wanted a plain country woman and that's what he married, and then he held it against me the rest of my life like I was supposed to change and surprise him somehow. Like I remember this one day he was standing on the porch and I told him to get a shirt on and he went in and got one and then he said, real peaceful, but to the point, "You're right, Thelma. If God had meant for people to go around without any clothes on, they'd have been born that way."

JESSIE (*sees* MAMA*'s hurt*): He didn't mean anything by that, Mama.

MAMA: He never said a word he didn't have to, Jessie. That was probably all he'd said to me all day, Jessie. So if he said it, there was something to it, but I never did figure that one out. What did that mean?

JESSIE: I don't know. I liked him better than you did, but I didn't know him any better.

MAMA: How could I love him, Jessie. I didn't have a thing he wanted. (JESSIE *doesn't answer.*) He got his share, though. You loved him enough for both of us. You followed him around like some . . . Jessie, all the man ever did was farm and sit . . . and try to think of somebody to sell the farm to.

JESSIE: Or make me a boyfriend out of pipe cleaners and sit back and smile like the stick man was about to dance and wasn't I going to get a kick out of that. Or sit up with a sick cow all night and leave me a chain of sleepy stick elephants on my bed in the morning.

MAMA: Or just sit.

JESSIE: I liked him sitting. Big old faded blue man in the chair. Quiet.

MAMA: Agnes gets more talk out of her birds than I got from the two of you. He could've had that GONE FISHING sign around his neck in that chair. I saw him stare off at the water. I saw him look at the weather rolling in. I got where I could practically see the boat myself. But you, you knew what he was thinking about and you're going to tell me.

JESSIE: I don't know, Mama! His life, I guess. His corn. His boots. Us. Things. You know.

MAMA: No, I don't know, Jessie! You had those quiet little conversations after supper every night. What were you whispering about?

JESSIE: We weren't whispering, you were just across the room.

MAMA: What did you talk about?

JESSIE: We talked about why black socks are warmer than blue socks. Is that something to go tell Mother? You were just jealous because I'd rather talk to him than wash the dishes with you.

MAMA: I was jealous because you'd rather talk to him than anything! (JESSIE *reaches across the table for the small clock and starts to wind it.*) If I had died instead of him, he wouldn't have taken you in like I did.

JESSIE: I wouldn't have expected him to.

MAMA: Then what would you have done?

JESSIE: Come visit.

MAMA: Oh, I see. He died and left you stuck with me and you're mad about it.

JESSIE (*getting up from the table*): Not anymore. He didn't mean to. I didn't have to come here. We've been through this.

MAMA: He felt sorry for you, too, Jessie, don't kid yourself about that. He said you were a runt and he said it from the day you were born and he said you didn't have a chance.

JESSIE (*getting the canister of sugar and starting to refill the sugar bowl*): I know he loved me.

MAMA: What if he did? It didn't change anything.

JESSIE: It didn't have to. I miss him.

MAMA: He never really went fishing, you know. Never once. His tackle box was full of chewing tobacco and all he ever did was drive out to the lake and sit in his car. Dawson told me. And Bennie at the bait shop, he told Dawson. They all laughed about it. And he'd come back from fishing and all he'd have to show for it was . . . a whole pipe-cleaner *family*—chickens, pigs, a dog with a bad leg—it was creepy strange. It made me sick to look at them and I hid his pipe cleaners a couple of times but he always had more somewhere.

JESSIE: I thought it might be better for you after he died. You'd get interested in things. Breathe better. Change somehow.

MAMA: Into what? The Queen? A clerk in a shoe store? Why should I? Because he said to? Because you said to? (JESSIE *shakes her head.*) Well I wasn't here for his entertainment and I'm not here for yours either, Jessie. I don't know what I'm here for, but then I don't think about it. (*Realizing what all this means*) But I bet you wouldn't be killing yourself if he were still alive. That's a fine thing to figure out, isn't it?

JESSIE (*filling the honey jar now*): That's not true.

MAMA: Oh no? Then what were you asking about him for? Why did you want to know if I loved him?

JESSIE: I didn't think you did, that's all.

MAMA: Fine then. You were right. Do you feel better now?

JESSIE (*cleaning the honey jar carefully*): It feels good to be right about it.

MAMA: It didn't matter whether I loved him. It didn't matter to me and it didn't matter to him. And it didn't mean we didn't get along. It wasn't important. We didn't talk about it. (*Sweeping the pots off the cabinet*) Take all these pots out to the porch!

JESSIE: What for?

MAMA: Just leave me this one pan. (*She jerks the silverware drawer open.*) Get me one knife, one fork, one big spoon, and the can opener, and put them out where I can get them. (*Starts throwing knives and forks in one of the pans.*)

JESSIE: Don't do that! I just straightened that drawer!

MAMA (*throwing the pan in the sink*): And throw out all the plates and cups. I'll use paper. Loretta can have what she wants and Dawson can sell the rest.

JESSIE (*calmly*): What are you doing?

MAMA: I'm not going to cook. I never liked it, anyway. I like candy. Wrapped in plastic or coming in sacks. And tuna. I like tuna. I'll eat tuna, thank you.

JESSIE (*taking the pan out of the sink*): What if you want to make apple butter? You can't make apple butter in that little pan. What if you leave carrots on cooking and burn up that pan?

MAMA: I don't like carrots.

JESSIE: What if the strawberries are good this year and you want to go picking with Agnes.

MAMA: I'll tell her to bring a pan. You said you would do whatever I wanted! I don't want a bunch of pans cluttering up my cabinets I can't get down to, anyway. Throw them out. Every last one.

JESSIE (*gathering up the pots*): I'm putting them all back in. I'm not taking them to the porch. If you want them, they'll be here. You'll bend down and get them, like you got the one for the cocoa. And if somebody else comes over here to cook, they'll have something to cook in, and that's the end of it!

MAMA: Who's going to come cook here?

JESSIE: Agnes.

MAMA: In my pots? Not on your life.

JESSIE: There's no reason why the two of you couldn't just live here together. Be cheaper for both of you and somebody to talk to. And if the birds bothered you, well, one day when Agnes is out getting her hair done, you could take them all for a walk!

MAMA (*as* JESSIE *straightens the silverware*): So that's why you're pestering me about Agnes. You think you can rest easy if you get me a new babysitter? Well, I don't want to live with Agnes. I barely want to talk with Agnes. She's just around. We go back, that's all. I'm not letting Agnes near this place. You don't get off as easy as that, child.

JESSIE: O.K., then. It's just something to think about.

MAMA: I don't like things to think about. I like things to go on.

JESSIE (*closing the silverware drawer*): I want to know what Daddy said to you the night he died. You came storming out of his room and said I could wait it out with him if I wanted to, but you were going to watch *Gunsmoke*. What did he say to you?

MAMA: He didn't have *anything* to say to me, Jessie. That's why I left. He didn't say a thing. It was his last chance not to talk to me and he took full advantage of it.

JESSIE (*after a moment*): I'm sorry you didn't love him. Sorry for you, I mean. He seemed like a nice man.

MAMA (*as* JESSIE *walks to the refrigerator*): Ready for your apple now?

JESSIE: Soon as I'm through here, Mama.

MAMA: You won't like the apple, either. It'll be just like the cocoa. You never liked eating it all, did you? Any of it! What have you been living on all these years, toothpaste?

JESSIE (*as she starts to clean out the refrigerator*): Now, you know the milkman comes on Wednesdays and Saturdays, and he leaves the order blank in an egg box, and you give the bills to Dawson once a month.

MAMA: Do they still make that orangeade?

JESSIE: It's not orangeade, it's just orange.

MAMA: I'm going to get some. I thought they stopped making it. You just stopped ordering it.

JESSIE: You should drink milk.

MAMA: Not anymore, I'm not. That hot chocolate was the last. Hooray.

JESSIE (*getting the garbage can from under the sink*): I told them to keep delivering a quart a week no matter what you said. I told them you'd run out of Cokes and you'd have to drink it. I told them I knew you wouldn't pour it on the ground . . .

MAMA (*finishing her sentence*): And you told them you weren't going to be ordering anymore?

JESSIE: I told them I was taking a little holiday and to look after you.

MAMA: And they didn't think something was funny about that? You who doesn't go to the front steps? You, who only sees the driveway looking down from a stretcher passed out cold?

JESSIE (*enjoying this, but not laughing*): They said it was about time, but why didn't I take you with me? And I said I didn't think you'd want to go, and they said, "Yeah, everybody's got their own idea of vacation."

MAMA: I guess you think that's funny.

JESSIE (*pulling jars out of the refrigerator*): You know there never was any reason to call the ambulance for me. All they ever did for me in the emergency room was let me wake up. I could've done that here. Now, I'll just call them out and you say yes or no. I know you like pickles. Ketchup?

MAMA: Keep it.

JESSIE: We've had this since last Fourth of July.

MAMA: Keep the ketchup. Keep it all.

JESSIE: Are you going to drink ketchup from the bottle or what? How can you want your food and not want your pots to cook it in? This stuff will all spoil in here, Mother.

MAMA: Nothing I ever did was good enough for you and I want to know why.

JESSIE: That's not true.

MAMA: And I want to know why you've lived here this long feeling the way you do.

JESSIE: You have no earthly idea how I feel.

MAMA: Well, how could I? You're real far back there, Jessie.

JESSIE: Back where?

MAMA: What's it like over there, where you are? Do people always say the right thing or get whatever they want, or what?

JESSIE: What are you talking about?

MAMA: Why do you read the newspaper? Why don't you wear that sweater I made for you? Do you remember how I used to look, or am I just any old woman now? When you have a fit, do you see stars or what? How did you fall off the horse, really? Why did Cecil leave you? Where did you put my old glasses?

JESSIE (*stunned by* MAMA's *intensity*): They're in the bottom drawer of your dresser in an old Milk of Magnesia box. Cecil left me because he made me choose between him and smoking.

MAMA: Jessie, I know he wasn't that dumb.

JESSIE: I never understood why he hated it so much when it's so good. Smoking is the only thing I know that's always just what you think it's going to be. Just like it was the last time, right there when you want it and real quiet.

MAMA: Your fits made him sick and you know it.

JESSIE: Say seizures, not fits. Seizures.

MAMA: It's the same thing. A seizure in the hospital is a fit at home.

JESSIE: They didn't bother him at all. Except he did feel responsible for it. It *was* his idea to go horseback riding that day. It was his idea I could do *anything* if I just made up my mind to. I fell off the horse because I didn't know how to hold on. Cecil left me for pretty much the same reason.

MAMA: He had a girl, Jessie. I walked right in on them in the toolshed.

JESSIE (*after a moment*): O.K. That's fair. (*Lighting another cigarette*) Was she very pretty?

MAMA: She was Agnes's girl, Carlene. Judge for yourself.

JESSIE (*as she walks to the living room*): I guess you and Agnes had a good talk about that, huh?

MAMA: I never thought he was good enough for you. They moved here from Tennessee, you know.

JESSIE: What are you talking about? You liked him better than I did. You flirted him out here to build your porch or I'd never even met him at all. You thought maybe he'd help you out around the place, come in and get some coffee and talk to you. God knows what you thought. All that curly hair.

MAMA: He's the best carpenter I ever saw. That little house of yours will still be standing at the end of the world, Jessie.

JESSIE: You didn't need a porch, Mama.

MAMA: All right! I wanted you to have a husband.

JESSIE: And I couldn't get one on my own, of course.

MAMA: How were you going to get a husband never opening your mouth to a living soul?

JESSIE: So I was quiet about it, so what?

MAMA: So I should have let you just sit here? Sit like your daddy? Sit here?

JESSIE: Maybe.

MAMA: Well, I didn't think so.

JESSIE: Well, what did you know?

MAMA: I never said I knew much. How was I supposed to learn anything living out here? I didn't know enough to do half the things I did in my life. Things happen. You do what you can about them and you see what happens next. I married you off to the wrong man, I admit that. So I took you in when he left. I'm sorry.

JESSIE: He wasn't the wrong man.

MAMA: He didn't love you, Jessie, or he wouldn't have left.

JESSIE: He wasn't the wrong man, Mama. I loved Cecil so much. And I tried to get more exercise and I tried to stay awake. I tried to learn to ride a horse. And I tried to stay outside with him, but he always knew I was trying, so it didn't work.

MAMA: He was a selfish man. He told me once he hated to see people move into his houses after he built them. He knew they'd mess them up.

JESSIE: I loved that bridge he built over the creek in back of the house. It didn't have to be anything special, a couple of boards would have been just fine, but he used that yellow pine and rubbed it so smooth . . .

MAMA: He had responsibilities here. He had a wife and son here and he failed you.

JESSIE: Or that baby bed he built for Ricky. I told him he didn't have to spend so much time on it, but he said it had to last, and the thing ended up weighing two hundred pounds and I couldn't move it. I said, "How long does a baby bed have to last, anyway?" But maybe he thought if it was strong enough, it might keep Ricky a baby.

MAMA: Ricky is too much like Cecil.

JESSIE: He is not. Ricky is as much like me as it's possible for any human to be. We even wear the same size pants. These are his, I think.

MAMA: That's just the same size. That's not you're the same person.

JESSIE: I see it on his face. I hear it when he talks. We look out at the world and we see the same thing: Not Fair. And the only difference between us is Ricky's out there trying to get even. And he knows not to trust anybody and he got it straight from me. And he knows not to try to get work, and guess where he got that. He walks around like there's loose boards in the floor, and you know who laid that floor, I did.

MAMA: Ricky isn't through yet. You don't know how he'll turn out!

JESSIE (*going back to the kitchen*): Yes I do and so did Cecil. Ricky is the two of us together for all time in too small a space. And we're tearing each other apart, like always, inside that boy, and if you don't see it, then you're just blind.

MAMA: Give him time, Jess.

JESSIE: Oh, he'll have plenty of that. Five years for forgery, ten years for armed assault. . . .

MAMA (*furious*): Stop that! (*Then pleading*) Jessie, Cecil might be ready to try it again, honey, that happens sometimes. Go downtown. Find him. Talk to him. He didn't know what he had in you. Maybe he sees things different now, but you're not going to know that till you go see him. Or call him up! Right now! He might be home.

JESSIE: And say what? Nothing's changed, Cecil, I'd just like to look at you, if you don't mind? No. He loved me, Mama. He just didn't know how things fall down around me like they do. I think he did the right thing. He gave himself another chance, that's all. But I did beg him to take me with him. I did tell him I would leave Ricky and you and everything I loved out here if only he would take me with him, but he couldn't and I understood that. (*Pause.*) I wrote that note I showed you. I wrote it. Not Cecil. I said, "I'm sorry, Jessie, I can't fix it all for you." I said I'd always love me, not Cecil. But that's how he felt.

MAMA: Then he should've taken you with him!

JESSIE (*picking up the garbage bag she has filled*): Mama, you don't pack your garbage when you move.

MAMA: You will not call yourself garbage, Jessie.

JESSIE (*taking the bag to the big garbage can near the back door*): Just a way of saying it, Mama. Thinking about my list, that's all. (*Opening the can, putting the garbage in, then securing the lid*) Well, a little more than that. I was trying to say it's all right that Cecil left. It was . . . a relief in a way. I never was what he wanted to see, so it was better when he wasn't looking at me all the time.

MAMA: I'll make your apple now.

JESSIE: No thanks. You get the manicure stuff and I'll be right there.

(JESSIE *ties up the big garbage bag in the can and replaces the small garbage bag under the sink, all the time trying desperately to regain her calm.* MAMA *watches, from a distance, her hand reaching unconsciously for the phone. Then she has a better idea. Or rather she thinks of the only other thing left and is willing to try it. Maybe she is even convinced it will work.*)

MAMA: Jessie, I think your daddy had little . . .

JESSIE (*interrupting her*): Garbage night is Tuesday. Put it out as late as you can. The Davis's dogs get in it if you don't. (*Replacing the garbage bag in the can under the sink*) And keep ordering the heavy black bags. It doesn't pay to buy the cheap ones. And I've got all the ties here with the hammers and all. Take them out of the box as soon as you open a new one and put them in this drawer. They'll get lost if you don't, and rubber bands or something else won't work.

MAMA: I think your daddy had fits, too. I think he sat in his chair and had little fits. I read this a long time ago in a magazine, how little fits go, just little blackouts where maybe their eyes don't even close and people just call them "thinking spells."

JESSIE (*getting the slipcover out of the laundry basket*): I don't think you want this manicure we've been looking forward to. I washed this cover for the sofa, but it'll take both of us to get it back on.

MAMA: I watched his eyes. I know that's what it was. The magazine said some people don't even know they've had one.

JESSIE: Daddy would've known if he'd had fits, Mama.

MAMA: The lady in this story had kept track of hers and she'd had eighty thousand of them in the last seven years.

JESSIE: Next time you wash this cover, it'll dry better if you put it on wet.

MAMA: Jessie, listen to what I'm telling you. This lady had anywhere between five and five hundred fits a day and they lasted maybe fifteen seconds apiece, so that out of her life, she'd only lost about two weeks altogether, and she had a full-time secretary job and an IQ of 120.

JESSIE (*amused by* MAMA'*s approach*): You want to talk about fits, is that it?

MAMA: Yes. I do. I want to say. . . .

JESSIE (*interrupting*): Most of the time I wouldn't even know I'd had one, except I wake up with different clothes on, feeling like I've been run over. Sometimes I feel my head start to turn around or hear myself scream. And sometimes there *is* this dizzy stupid feeling a little before it, but if the TV's on, well, it's easy to miss.

(As JESSIE *and* MAMA *replace the slipcover on the sofa and the afghan on the chair, the physical struggle somehow mirrors the emotional one in the conversation.*)

MAMA: I can tell when you're about to have one. Your eyes get this big! But, Jessie, you haven't . . .

JESSIE (*taking charge of this*): What do they look like? The seizures?

MAMA (*reluctant*): Different each time, Jess.

JESSIE: O.K. Pick one, then. A good one. I think I want to know now.

MAMA: There's not much to tell. You just . . . crumple, in a heap, like a puppet and somebody cut the strings all at once, or like the firing squad in some Mexican movie, you just slide down the wall, you know. You don't know what happens? How can you not know what happens?

JESSIE: I'm busy.

MAMA: That's not funny.

JESSIE: I'm not laughing. My head turns around and I fall down and then what?

MAMA: Well, your chest squeezes in and out, and you sound like you're gagging, sucking air in and out like you can't breathe.

JESSIE: Do it for me. Make the sound for me.

MAMA: I will not. It's awful-sounding.

JESSIE: Yeah. It felt like it might be. What's next?

MAMA: Your mouth bites down and I have to get your tongue out of the way fast, so you don't bite yourself.

JESSIE: Or you. I bite you, too, don't I?

MAMA: You got me once real good. I had to get a tetanus! But I know what to watch for now. And then you turn blue and the jerks start up. Like I'm standing there poking you with a cattle prod or you're sticking your finger in a light socket as fast as you can. . . .

JESSIE: Foaming like a mad dog the whole time.

MAMA: It's bubbling, Jess, not foam like the washer overflowed, for God's sake; it's bubbling like a baby spitting up. I go get a wet washcloth, that's all. And then the jerks slow down and you wet yourself and it's over. Two minutes tops.

JESSIE: How do I get to the bed?

MAMA: How do you think?

JESSIE: I'm too heavy for you now. How do you do it?

MAMA: I call Dawson. But I get you cleaned up before he gets here and I make him leave before you wake up.

JESSIE: You could just leave me on the floor.

MAMA: I want you to wake up someplace nice, O.K.? (*Then making a real effort*) But, Jessie, and this is the reason I even brought this up! You haven't had a seizure for a solid year. A whole year, do you realize that?

JESSIE: Yeah, the phenobarb's about right now, I guess.

MAMA: You bet it is. You might never have another one, ever! You might be through with it for all time!

JESSIE: Could be.

MAMA: You are. I know you are!

JESSIE: I sure am feeling good. I really am. The double vision's gone and my gums aren't swelling. No rashes or anything. I'm feeling as good as I ever felt in my life. I'm even feeling like worrying or getting mad and I'm not afraid it will start a fit if I do, I just go ahead.

MAMA: Of course you do! You can even scream at me, if you want to. I can take it. You don't have to act like you're visiting here, Jessie. This is your house, too.

JESSIE: The best part is, my memory's back.

MAMA: Your memory's always been good. When couldn't you remember things? You're always reminding me what . . .

JESSIE: Because I've made lists for everything. But now I remember what things mean on my lists. I see "dish towels," and I used to wonder whether I was supposed to wash them, buy them, or look for them because I wouldn't remember where I put them after I washed them, and now I know it means wrap them up, they're a present for Loretta's birthday.

MAMA (*finished with the sofa now*): You used to go looking for your lists, too. I've noticed that. You always know where they are now! (*Then suddenly worried*) Loretta's birthday isn't coming up, is it?

JESSIE: I made a list of all the birthdays for you. I even put yours on it. (*A small smile.*) So you can call Loretta and remind her.

MAMA: Let's take Loretta to Howard Johnson's and have those fried clams. I *know* you love that clam roll.

JESSIE (*slight pause*): I won't be here, Mama.

MAMA: What have we just been talking about? You'll be here. You're well, Jessie. You're starting all over. You said it yourself. You're remembering things and . . .

JESSIE: I won't be here. If I'd ever had a year like this, to think straight and all, before now, I'd be gone already.

MAMA (*not pleading, commanding*): No, Jessie.

JESSIE (*folding the rest of the laundry*): Yes, Mama. Once I started remembering, I could see what it all added up to.

MAMA: The fits are over!

JESSIE: It's not the fits, Mama.

MAMA: Then it's me for giving them to you, but I didn't do it!

JESSIE: It's not the fits! You said it yourself, the medicine takes care of the fits.

MAMA (*interrupting*): Your daddy gave you those fits, Jessie. He passed it down to you like your green eyes, and your straight hair. It's not my fault!

JESSIE: So what if he had little fits? It's not inherited. I fell off the horse. It was an accident.

MAMA: The horse wasn't the first time, Jessie. You had a fit when you were five years old.

JESSIE: I did not.

MAMA: You did! You were eating a popsicle and down you went. He gave it to you. It's *his* fault, not mine.

JESSIE: Well, you took your time telling me.

MAMA: How do you tell that to a five-year-old?

JESSIE: What did the doctor say?

MAMA: He said kids have them all the time. He said there wasn't anything to do but wait for another one.

JESSIE: But I didn't have another one.

(*Now there is a real silence.*)

JESSIE: You mean to tell me I had fits all the time as a kid and you just told me I fell down or something and it wasn't till I had the fit when Cecil was looking that anybody bothered to find out what was the matter with me?

MAMA: It wasn't *all the time*, Jessie. And they changed when you started to school. More like your daddy's. Oh, that was some swell time, sitting here with the two of you turning off and on like light bulbs some nights.

JESSIE: How many fits did I have?

MAMA: You never hurt yourself. I never let you out of my sight. I caught you every time.

JESSIE: But you didn't tell anybody.

MAMA: It was none of their business.

JESSIE: You were ashamed.

MAMA: I didn't want anybody to know. Least of all you.

JESSIE: Least of all me. Oh, right. That was mine to know, Mama, not yours. Did Daddy know?

MAMA: He thought you were . . . you fell down a lot. That's what he thought. You were careless. Or maybe he thought I beat you. I don't know what he thought. He didn't think about it.

JESSIE: Because you didn't tell him!

MAMA: If I told him about you, I'd have to tell him about him!

JESSIE: I don't like this. I don't like this one bit.

MAMA: I didn't think you'd like it. That's why I didn't tell you.

JESSIE: If I'd known I was epileptic, Mama, I wouldn't have ridden any horses.

MAMA: Make you feel like a freak, is that what I should have done?

JESSIE: Just get the manicure tray and sit down!

MAMA (*throwing it to the floor*): I don't want a manicure!

JESSIE: Doesn't look like you do, no.

MAMA: Maybe I did drop you, you don't know.

JESSIE: If you say you didn't, you didn't.

MAMA (*beginning to break down*): Maybe I fed you the wrong thing. Maybe you had a fever sometime and I didn't know it soon enough. Maybe it's a punishment.

JESSIE: For what?

MAMA: I don't know. Because of how I felt about your father. Because I didn't want any more children. Because I smoked too much or didn't eat right when I was carrying you. It has to be something I did.

JESSIE: It does not. It's just a sickness, not a curse. Epilepsy doesn't mean anything. It just is.

MAMA: I'm not talking about the fits here, Jessie! I'm talking about this killing yourself. It has to be me that's the matter here. You wouldn't be doing this if it wasn't. I didn't tell you things or I married you off to the wrong man or I took you in and let your life get away from you or all of it put together. I don't know what I did, but I did it, I know. This is all my fault, Jessie, but I don't know what to do about it now!

JESSIE (*exasperated at having to say this again*): It doesn't have anything to do with you!

MAMA: Everything you do has to do with me, Jessie. You can't do *anything*, wash your face or cut your finger, without doing it to me. That's right! You might as well kill me as you, Jessie, it's the same thing. This has to do with me, Jessie.

JESSIE: Then what if it does! What if it has everything to do with you! What if you are all I have and you're not enough? What if I could take all the rest of it if only I didn't have you here? What if the only way I can get away from you for good is to kill myself? What if it is? I can *still* do it!

MAMA (*in desperate tears*): Don't leave me, Jessie! (JESSIE *stands for a moment, then turns for the bedroom.*) No! (*She grabs* JESSIE's *arm.*)

JESSIE (*carefully taking her arm away*): I have a box of things I want people to have. I'm just going to go get it for you. You . . . just rest a minute.

(JESSIE *is gone.* MAMA *heads for the telephone, but she can't even pick up the receiver this time and, instead, stoops to clean up the bottles that have spilled out of the manicure tray.*

JESSIE *returns, carrying a box that groceries were delivered in. It probably says Hershey Kisses or Starkist Tuna.* MAMA *is still down on the floor cleaning up, hoping that maybe if she just makes it look nice enough,* JESSIE *will stay.*)

MAMA: Jessie, how can I live here without you? I need you! You're supposed to tell me to stand up straight and say how nice I look in my pink dress, and drink my milk. You're supposed to go around and lock up so I know we're safe for the night, and when I wake up, you're supposed to be out there making the coffee and watching me get older every day, and you're supposed to help me die when the time comes. I can't do that by myself, Jessie. I'm not like you, Jessie. I hate the quiet and I don't want to die and I don't want you to go, Jessie. How can I . . . (*Has to stop a moment.*) How can I get up every day knowing you had to kill yourself to make it stop hurting and I was here all the time and I never even saw it. And then you gave me this chance to make it better, convince you to stay alive, and I couldn't do it. How can I live with myself after this, Jessie?

JESSIE: I only told you so I could explain it, so you wouldn't blame yourself, so you wouldn't feel bad. There wasn't anything you could say to change my mind. I didn't want you to save me. I just wanted you to know.

MAMA: Stay with me just a little longer. Just a few more years. I don't have that many more to go, Jessie. And as soon as I'm dead, you can do whatever you want. Maybe with me gone, you'll have all the quiet you want, right here in the house. And maybe one day you'll put in some begonias up the walk and get just the right rain for them all summer. And Ricky will be married by then and he'll bring your grandbabies over and you can sneak them a piece of candy when their daddy's not looking and then be real glad when they've gone home and left you to your quiet again.

JESSIE: Don't you see, Mama, everything I do winds up like this. How could I think you would understand? How could I think you would want a manicure? We could hold hands for an hour and then I could go shoot myself? I'm sorry about tonight, Mama, but it's exactly why I'm doing it.

MAMA: If you've got the guts to kill yourself, Jessie, you've got the guts to stay alive.

JESSIE: I know that. So it's really just a matter of where I'd rather be.

MAMA: Look, maybe I can't think of what you should do, but that doesn't mean there isn't something that would help. *You* find it. *You* think of it. You can keep trying. You can get brave and try some more. You don't have to give up!

JESSIE: I'm *not* giving up! This *is* the other thing I'm trying. And I'm sure there are some other things that might work, but *might* work isn't good enough anymore. I need something that *will* work. *This* will work. That's why I picked it.

MAMA: But something might happen. Something that could change everything. Who knows what it might be, but it might be worth waiting for! (JESSIE *doesn't respond.*) Try it for two more weeks. We could have more talks like tonight.

JESSIE: No, Mama.

MAMA: I'll pay more attention to you. Tell the truth when you ask me. Let you have your say.

JESSIE: No, Mama! We wouldn't have more talks like tonight, because it's this next part that's made this last part so good, Mama. No, Mama. *This* is how I have my say. This is how I say what I thought about it *all* and I say no. To Dawson and Loretta and the Red Chinese and epilepsy and Ricky and Cecil and you. And me. And hope. I say no! (*Then going to* MAMA *on the sofa*) Just let me go easy, Mama.

MAMA: How can I let you go?

JESSIE: You can because you have to. It's what you've always done.

MAMA: You are my child!

JESSIE: I am what became of your child. (MAMA *cannot answer.*) I found an old baby picture of me. And it was somebody else, not me. It was somebody pink and fat who never heard of sick or lonely, somebody who cried and got fed, and reached up and got held and kicked but didn't hurt anybody, and slept whenever she wanted to, just by closing her eyes. Somebody who mainly just laid there and laughed at the colors waving around over her head and chewed on a polka-dot whale and woke up knowing some new trick nearly every day, and rolled over and drooled on the sheet and felt your hand pulling my quilt back up over me. That's who I started out and this is who is left. (*There is no self-pity here.*) That's what this is about. Its somebody I lost, all right, it's my own self. Who I never was. Or who I tried to be and never got there. Somebody I waited for who never came. And never will. So, see, it doesn't much matter what else happens in the world or in this house, even. I'm what was worth waiting for and I didn't make it. Me . . . who might have made a difference to me . . . I'm not going to show up, so there's no reason to stay, except to keep you company, and that's . . . not reason enough because I'm not . . . very good company. (*Pause.*) Am I.

MAMA (*knowing she must tell the truth*): No. And neither am I.

JESSIE: I had this strange little thought, well, maybe it's not so strange. Anyway, after Christmas, after I decided to do this, I would wonder, sometimes, what might keep me here, what might be worth staying for, and you know what it was? It was maybe if there was something I really liked, like maybe if I really liked rice pudding or cornflakes for breakfast or something, that might be enough.

MAMA: Rice pudding is good.

JESSIE: Not for me.

MAMA: And you're not afraid?

JESSIE: Afraid of what?

MAMA: I'm afraid of it, for me, I mean. When my time comes. I know it's coming, but . . .

JESSIE: You don't know when. Like in a scary movie.

MAMA: Yeah, sneaking up on me like some killer on the loose, hiding out in the back yard just waiting for me to have my hands full someday and how am I supposed to protect myself anyhow when I don't know what he looks like and I don't know how he sounds coming up behind me like that or if it will hurt or take very long or what I don't get done before it happens.

JESSIE: You've got plenty of time left.

MAMA: I forget what for, right now.

JESSIE: For whatever happens, I don't know. For the rest of your life. For Agnes burning down one more house or Dawson losing his hair or . . .

MAMA (*quickly*): Jessie. I can't just sit here and say O.K., kill yourself if you want to.

JESSIE: Sure you can. You just did. Say it again.

MAMA: (*really startled*): Jessie! (*Quiet horror*) How dare you! (*Furious*) How dare you! You think you can just leave whenever you want, like you're watching television here? No, you can't, Jessie. You make me feel like a fool for being alive, child, and you are so wrong! I like it here, and I will stay here until they make me go, until they drag me screaming and I mean screeching into my grave, and you're real smart to get away before then because, I mean, honey, you've never heard noise like that in your life. (JESSIE *turns away.*) Who am I talking to? You're gone already, aren't you? I'm looking right through you! I can't stop you because

you're already gone! I guess you think they'll all have to talk about you now! I guess you think this will really confuse them. Oh, yes, ever since Christmas you've been laughing to yourself and thinking, "Boy, are they all in for a surprise." Well, nobody's going to be a bit surprised, sweetheart. This is just like you. Do it the hard way, that's my girl, all right. (JESSIE *gets up and goes into the kitchen, but* MAMA *follows her.*) You know who they're going to feel sorry for? Me! How about that! Not you, me! They're going to be *ashamed* of you. Yes. *Ashamed!* If somebody asks Dawson about it, he'll change the subject as fast as he can. He'll talk about how much he has to pay to park his car these days.

JESSIE: Leave me alone.

MAMA: It's the truth!

JESSIE: I should've just left you a note!

MAMA (*screaming*): Yes! (*Then suddenly understanding what she has said, nearly paralyzed by the thought of it, she turns slowly to face* JESSIE, *nearly whispering.*) No. No. I . . . might not have thought of all the things you've said.

JESSIE: It's O.K., Mama.

(MAMA *is nearly unconscious from the emotional devastation of these last few moments. She sits down at the kitchen table, hurt and angry and desperately afraid. But she looks almost numb. She is so far beyond what is known as pain that she is virtually unreachable and* JESSIE *knows this, and talks quietly, watching for signs of recovery.*)

JESSIE (*washes her hands in the sink*): I remember you liked that preacher who did Daddy's, so if you want to ask him to do the service, that's O.K. with me.

MAMA (*not an answer, just a word*): What.

JESSIE (*putting on hand lotion as she talks*): And pick some songs you like or let Agnes pick, she'll know exactly which ones. Oh, and I had your dress cleaned that you wore to Daddy's. You looked real good in that.

MAMA: I don't remember, hon.

JESSIE: And it won't be so bad once your friends start coming to the funeral home. You'll probably see people you haven't seen for years, but I thought about what you should say to get you over that nervous part when they first come in.

MAMA (*simply repeating*): Come in.

JESSIE: Take them up to see their flowers, they'd like that. And when they say, "I'm so sorry, Thelma," you just say, "I appreciate your coming, Connie." And then ask how their garden was this summer or what they're doing for Thanksgiving or how their children . . .

MAMA: I don't think I should ask about their children. I'll talk about what they have on, that's always good. And I'll have some crochet work with me.

JESSIE: And Agnes will be there, so you might not have to talk at all.

MAMA: Maybe if Connie Richards does come, I can get her to tell me where she gets that Irish yarn, she calls it. I know it doesn't come from Ireland. I think it just comes with a green wrapper.

JESSIE: And be sure to invite enough people home afterward so you get enough food to feed them all and have some left for you. But don't let anybody take anything home, especially Loretta.

MAMA: Loretta will get all the food set up, honey. It's only fair to let her have some macaroni or something.

JESSIE: No, Mama. You have to be more selfish from now on. (*Sitting at the table with* MAMA.) Now, somebody's bound to ask you why I did it and you just say you don't know. That you loved me and you know I loved you and we just sat around tonight like every other night of our lives, and then I came over and kissed you and said, "'Night, Mother," and you heard me close my bedroom door and the next thing you heard was the shot. And whatever reasons I had, well, you guess I just took them with me.

MAMA (*quietly*): It was something personal.

JESSIE: Good. That's good, Mama.

MAMA: That's what I'll say, then.

JESSIE: Personal. Yeah.

MAMA: Is that what I tell Dawson and Loretta, too? We sat around, you kissed me, "'Night, Mother"? They'll want to know more, Jessie. They won't believe it.

JESSIE: Well, then, tell them what we did. I filled up the candy jars. I cleaned out the refrigerator. We made some hot chocolate and put the cover back on the sofa. You had no idea. All right? I really think it's better that way. If they know we talked about it, they really won't understand how you let me go.

MAMA: I guess not.

JESSIE: It's private. Tonight is private, yours and mine, and I don't want anybody else to have any of it.

MAMA: O.K., then.

JESSIE (*standing behind* MAMA *now, holding her shoulders*): Now, when you hear the shot, I don't want you to come in. First of all, you won't be able to get in by yourself, but I don't want you trying.

Call Dawson, then call the police, and then call Agnes. And then you'll need something to do till somebody gets here, so wash the hot-chocolate pan. You wash that pan till you hear the doorbell ring and I don't care if it's an hour, you keep washing that pan.

MAMA: I'll make my calls and then I'll just sit. I won't need something to do. What will the police say?

JESSIE: They'll do that gunpowder test, I guess, and ask you what happened, and by that time, the ambulance will be here and they'll come in and get me and you know how that goes. You stay out here with Dawson and Loretta. You keep Dawson out here. I want the police in the room first, not Dawson, O.K.?

MAMA: What if Dawson and Loretta want me to go home with them?

JESSIE (*returning to the living room*): That's up to you.

MAMA: I think I'll stay here. All they've got is Sanka.

JESSIE: Maybe Agnes could come stay with you for a few days.

MAMA (*standing up, looking into the living room*): I'd rather be by myself, I think. (*Walking toward the box* JESSIE *brought in earlier*) You want me to give people those things?

JESSIE (*they sit down on the sofa,* JESSIE *holding the box on her lap*): I want Loretta to have my little calculator. Dawson bought it for himself, you know, but then he saw one he liked better and he couldn't bring both of them home with Loretta counting every penny the way she does, so he gave the first one to me. Be funny for her to have it now, don't you think? And all my house slippers are in a sack for her in my closet. Tell her I know they'll fit and I've never worn any of them, and make sure Dawson hears you tell her that. I'm glad he loves Loretta so much, but I wish he knew not everybody has her size feet.

MAMA (*taking the calculator*): O.K.

JESSIE (*reaching into the box again*): This letter is for Dawson, but it's mostly about you, so read it if you want. There's a list of presents for you for at least twenty more Christmases and birthdays, so if you want anything special you better add it to this list before you give it to him. Or if you want to be surprised, just don't read that page. This Christmas, you're getting mostly stuff for the house, like a new rug in your bathroom and needlework, but next Christmas, you're really going to cost him next Christmas. I think you'll like it a lot and you'd never think of it.

MAMA: And you think he'll go for it?

JESSIE: I think he'll feel like a real jerk if he doesn't. Me telling him to, like this and all. Now, this number's where you call Cecil. I called it last week and he answered, so I know he still lives there.

MAMA: What do you want me to tell him?

JESSIE: Tell him we talked about him and I only had good things to say about him, but mainly tell him to find Ricky and tell him what I did, and tell Ricky you have something for him, out here, from me, and to come get it. (*Pulls a sack out of the box.*)

MAMA (*the sack feels empty*): What is it?

JESSIE (*taking it off*): My watch. (*Putting it in the sack and taking a ribbon out of the sack to tie around the top of it.*)

MAMA: He'll sell it!

JESSIE: That's the idea. I appreciate him not stealing it already. I'd like to buy him a good meal.

MAMA: He'll buy dope with it!

JESSIE: Well, then, I hope he gets some good dope with it, Mama. And the rest of this is for you. (*Handing* MAMA *the box now.* MAMA *picks up the things and looks at them.*)

MAMA (*surprised and pleased*): When did you do all this? During my naps, I guess.

JESSIE: I guess. I tried to be quiet about it. (*As* MAMA *is puzzled by the presents.*) Those are just little presents. For whenever you need one. They're not bought presents, just things I thought you might like to look at, pictures or things you think you've lost. Things you didn't know you had, even. You'll see.

MAMA: I'm not sure I want them. They'll make me think of you.

JESSIE: No they won't. They're just things, like a free tube of toothpaste I found hanging on the door one day.

MAMA: Oh. All right, then.

JESSIE: Well, maybe there's one nice present in there somewhere. It's Granny's ring she gave me and I thought you might like to have it, but I didn't think you'd wear it if I gave it to you right now.

MAMA (*taking the box to a table nearby*): No. Probably not. (*Turning back to face her*) I'm ready for my manicure, I guess. Want me to wash my hands again?

JESSIE (*standing up*): It's time for me to go, Mama.

MAMA (*starting for her*): No, Jessie, you've got all night!

JESSIE (*as* MAMA *grabs her*): No, Mama.

MAMA: It's not even ten o'clock.

JESSIE (*very calm*): Let me go, Mama.

MAMA: I can't. You can't go. You can't do this. You didn't say it would be so soon, Jessie. I'm scared. I love you.

JESSIE (*takes her hands away*): Let go of me, Mama. I've said everything I had to say.

MAMA (*standing still a minute*): You said you wanted to do my nails.

JESSIE (*taking a small step backward*): I can't. It's too late.

MAMA: It's not too late!

JESSIE: I don't want you to wake Dawson and Loretta when you call. I want them to still be up and dressed so they can get right over.

MAMA (*as* JESSIE *backs up,* MAMA *moves in on her, but carefully*): They wake up fast, Jessie, if they have to. They don't matter here, Jessie. You do. I do. We're not through yet. We've got a lot of things to take care of here. I don't know where my prescriptions are and you didn't tell me what to tell Dr. Davis when he calls or how much you want me to tell Ricky or who I call to rake the leaves or . . .

JESSIE: Don't try to stop me, Mama, you can't do it.

MAMA (*grabbing her again, this time hard*): I can too! I'll stand in front of this hall and you can't get past me. (*They struggle.*) You'll have to knock me down to get away from me, Jessie. I'm not about to let you . . .

(MAMA *struggles with* JESSIE *at the door and in the struggle* JESSIE *gets away from her and—*

JESSIE (*almost a whisper*): 'Night, Mother. (*She vanishes into her bedroom and we hear the door lock just as* MAMA *gets to it.*)

MAMA (*screams*): Jessie! (*Pounding on the door*) Jessie, you let me in there. Don't you do this, Jessie. I'm not going to stop screaming until you open this door, Jessie. Jessie! Jessie! What if I don't do any of the things you told me to do! I'll tell Cecil what a miserable man he was to make you feel the way he did and I'll give Ricky's watch to Dawson if I feel like it and the only way you can make sure I do what you want is you come out here and make me. Jessie! (*Pounding again*) Jessie! Stop this! I didn't know! I was here with you all the time. How could I know you were so alone?

(And MAMA *stops for a moment, breathless and frantic, putting her ear to the door, and when she doesn't hear anything, she stands up straight again and screams once more.*)

Jessie! Please!

(*And we hear the shot, and it sounds like an answer, it sounds like No.*

MAMA *collapses against the door, tears streaming down her face, but not screaming anymore. In shock now*):

Jessie, Jessie, child . . . Forgive me. (*Pause.*) I thought you were mine.

(*And she leaves the door and makes her way through the living room, around the furniture, as* though she didn't know where it was, not knowing what to do. Finally, she goes to the stove in the kitchen and picks up the hot-chocolate pan and carries it with her to the telephone, and holds on to it while she dials the number. She looks down at the pan, holding it tight like her life depended on it. She hears Loretta answer.)

MAMA: Loretta, let me talk to Dawson, honey.

COMMENTARY

In our commentary following *Death of a Salesman* (p. 532), where we sketch the rise of the middle class, we mention that the ideas of Copernicus, Darwin, and Freud have contributed to the view that human beings are "lust-ridden, soulless creatures in a terrifying materialistic universe."

In contrast to this somewhat despairing view, Marsha Norman gives us a figure whom she sees as very strong. In an interview published in *Interviews with Contemporary Women Playwrights* (eds. Kathleen Betsko and Rachel Koenig), Norman said that Jessie achieves a "nearly total triumph. Jessie is able to get what she feels she needs. It may look despairing from the outside, but it has cost her everything she has. If Jessie says it is worth it, it is."

In this quotation Norman is pretty much saying that Jessie is a traditional tragic hero, someone who ventures boldly and, in a way, turns apparent material defeat into some sort of spiritual triumph. Interestingly, the very success of Norman's play brought fairly widespread criticism from persons interested in the development of women's theater. The two chief objections are somewhat contradictory: (1) *'night, Mother* suggests that women are self-destructive neurotics; (2) *'night, Mother* is just another drama in the male tradition—that is, it emphasizes the heroism of the isolated individual and it ignores the strength born out of communal action, a kind of action that many women today regard as necessary if they are to escape from the assigned roles of housewife and sexual object. (Many feminist theater groups reject the usual hierarchical structure—a director dominating actors, designers, and technicians—in favor of a leaderless group.) If feminist theater interests you, you may want to read another play in this book, *Out of Our Fathers' House* (page 635), and our commentary.

TOPICS FOR DISCUSSION

1. Early in the play, on page 677, Jessie says she wants the gun for "protection." In the context of the entire play, what does this mean?
2. On page 678 Jessie says she would rather use her father's gun than her husband's. Why?

3. The playwright specifies that "The time is the present, with the action beginning about 8:15. Clocks on stage in the kitchen and on a table in the living room should run throughout the performance and be visible to the audience." Why?

4. Jessie insists (page 688) that Ricky is like her and not like his father Cecil. Exactly what do you think she is getting at?

5. On page 679 Mama says, "People don't really kill themselves. Jessie. No, mam, doesn't make sense, unless you're retarded or deranged." Specify the various reasons that Mama assumes are the motives for Jessie's suicide.

6. Most theories of suicide can be classified into one of two groups, psychoanalytical and sociological. Psychoanalytical theories (usually rooted in Freud) assume that human beings have dual impulses, *eros* (life instinct) and *thanatos* (death instinct). When the death instinct, expressed as hostility and aggression, is turned against others, it takes the form of homicide; but when it is turned against the self, it takes the form of suicide. Most sociological theories assume that suicide occurs among three types of people: egoistic suicides, people who are excessively individualistic (i.e., who are not integrated into society); altruistic suicides, people who have an excessive sense of duty to society and who die willingly to serve society; and anomic suicides, people who find their usual lifestyles disrupted by sudden social changes such as the loss of a job during an economic depression. Do any of these theories strike you as helpful in explaining Jessie's suicide? Exactly why *does* Jessie kill herself? (You may want to do some research on suicide, for instance by consulting Freud's *Civilization and Its Discontents*, or Andrew F. Henry and James F. Short, *Homicide and Suicide*, or Edwin S. Scheidman, ed., *Essays in Self-Destruction*, or A. Alvarez, *The Savage God*.)

7. The greatest tragedies somehow suggest that the tragic figures are not only particular individuals—Oedipus, Lear, and so forth—but also are universal figures who somehow embody our own hopes and fears. Another way of putting it is to say that the greatest plays are not case histories but are visions of a central aspect of life. To what extent do you think *'night, Mother* meets this criterion?

FENCES

August Wilson

for Lloyd Richards,
who adds to whatever he touches

When the sins of our fathers visit us
We do not have to play host.
We can banish them with forgiveness
As God, in His Largeness and Laws.
                    —August Wilson

August Wilson was born in Pittsburgh in 1945, the son of a black woman and a white man. After dropping out of school at the age of fifteen, Wilson took various odd jobs, such as stock clerk and short-order cook, in his spare time educating himself in the public library, chiefly by reading works by such black writers as Richard Wright, Ralph Ellison, Langston Hughes, and Amiri Baraka (LeRoi Jones). In 1978 the director of a black theater in St. Paul, Minnesota, who had known Wilson in Pittsburgh, invited him to write a play for the theater. Six months later Wilson moved permanently to St. Paul.

The winner of the Pulitzer Prize for drama in 1987, Wilson's *Fences* was first presented as a staged reading in 1983 and was later performed in Chicago, Seattle, Rochester (New York), and New Haven (Connecticut) before reaching New York City in 1987. An earlier play, *Ma Rainey's Black Bottom*, was voted Best Play of the Year 1984–85 by the New York Drama Critics' Circle. In 1981 when *Ma Rainey* was first read at the O'Neill Center in Waterford, Connecticut, Wilson met Lloyd Richards, a black director with whom he has continued to work closely.

CHARACTERS

TROY MAXSON
JIM BONO, *Troy's friend*
ROSE, *Troy's wife*
LYONS, *Troy's oldest son by previous marriage*
GABRIEL, *Troy's brother*
CORY, *Troy and Rose's son*
RAYNELL, *Troy's daughter*

Seattle Repertory Theatre production with (left to right) Francis Foster as Rose Maxon, Keith Amos, as Cory Maxon, William Jay as Gabriel, and Gilbert Lewis as Troy Maxon. (Photo © Chris Bennion.)

Setting

The setting is the yard which fronts the only entrance to the MAXSON household, an ancient two-story brick house set back off a small alley in a big-city neighborhood. The entrance to the house is gained by two or three steps leading to a wooden porch badly in need of paint.

A relatively recent addition to the house and running its full width, the porch lacks congruence. It is a sturdy porch with a flat roof. One or two chairs of dubious value sit at one end where the kitchen window opens onto the porch. An old-fashioned icebox stands silent guard at the opposite end.

The yard is a small dirt yard, partially fenced, except for the last scene, with a wooden sawhorse, a pile of lumber, and other fence-building equipment set off to the side. Opposite is a tree from which hangs a ball made of rags. A baseball bat leans against the tree. Two oil drums serve as garbage receptacles and sit near the house at right to complete the setting.

The Play

Near the turn of the century, the destitute of Europe sprang on the city with tenacious claws and an honest and solid dream. The city devoured them. They swelled its belly until it burst into a thousand furnaces and sewing machines, a thousand butcher shops and bakers' ovens, a thousand churches and hospitals and funeral parlors and moneylenders. The city grew. It nourished itself and offered each man a partnership limited only by his talent, his guile, and his willingness and capacity for hard work. For the immigrants of Europe, a dream dared and won true.

The descendants of African slaves were offered no such welcome or participation. They came from places called the Carolinas and the Virginias, Georgia, Alabama, Mississippi, and Tennessee. They came strong, eager, searching. The city rejected them and they fled and settled along the riverbanks and under bridges in shallow, ramshackle houses made of sticks and tar-paper. They collected rags and wood. They sold the use of their muscles and their bodies. They cleaned houses and washed clothes, they shined shoes, and in quiet desperation and vengeful pride, they stole, and lived in pursuit of their own dream. That they could breathe free, finally, and stand to meet life with the force of dignity and whatever eloquence the heart could call upon.

By 1957, the hard-won victories of the European immigrants had solidifed the industrial might of America. War had been confronted and won with new energies that used loyalty and patriotism as its fuel. Life was rich, full, and flourishing. The Milwaukee Braves won the World Series, and the hot winds of change that would make the sixties a turbulent, racing, dangerous, and provocative decade had not yet begun to blow full.

ACT I

SCENE I

It is 1957. TROY *and* BONO *enter the yard, engaged in conversation.* TROY *is fifty-three years old, a large man with thick, heavy hands; it is this largeness that he strives to fill out and make an accommodation with. Together with his blackness, his largeness informs his sensibilities and the choices he has made in his life.*

Of the two men, BONO *is obviously the follower. His commitment to their friendship of thirty-odd years is rooted in his admiration of* TROY's *honesty, capacity for hard work, and his strength, which* BONO *seeks to emulate.*

It is Friday night, payday, and the one night of the week the two men engage in a ritual of talk and drink. TROY *is usually the most talkative and at times he can be crude and almost vulgar, though he is capable of rising to profound heights of expression. The men carry lunch buckets and wear or carry burlap aprons and are dressed in clothes suitable to their jobs as garbage collectors.*

BONO: Troy, you ought to stop that lying!

TROY: I ain't lying! The nigger had a watermelon this big. (*He indicates with his hands.*) Talking about . . . "What watermelon, Mr. Rand?" I liked to fell out! "What watermelon, Mr. Rand?" . . . And it sitting there big as life.

BONO: What did Mr. Rand say?

TROY: Ain't said nothing. Figure if the nigger too dumb to know he carrying a watermelon, he wasn't gonna get much sense out of him. Trying to hide that great big old watermelon under his coat. Afraid to let the white man see him carry it home.

BONO: I'm like you . . . I ain't got no time for them kind of people.

TROY: Now what he look like getting mad cause he see the man from the union talking to Mr. Rand?

BONO: He come to me talking about . . . "Maxson gonna get us fired." I told him to get away from me with that. He walked away from me calling you a troublemaker. What Mr. Rand say?

TROY: Ain't said nothing. He told me to go down the Commissioner's office next Friday. They called me down there to see them.

BONO: Well, as long as you got your complaint filed, they can't fire you. That's what one of them white fellows tell me.

TROY: I ain't worried about them firing me.

They gonna fire me cause I asked a question? That's all I did. I went to Mr. Rand and asked him, "Why?" Why you got the white mens driving and the colored lifting?" Told him, "what's the matter, don't I count? You think only white fellows got sense enough to drive a truck. That ain't no paper job! Hell, anybody can drive a truck. How come you got all whites driving and the colored lifting?" He told me "take it to the union." Well, hell, that's what I done! Now they wanna come up with this pack of lies.

BONO: I told Brownie if the man come and ask him any questions . . . just tell the truth! It ain't nothing but something they done trumped up on you cause you filed a complaint on them.

TROY: Brownie don't understand nothing. All I want them to do is change the job description. Give everybody a chance to drive the truck. Brownie can't see that. He ain't got that much sense.

BONO: How you figure he be making out with that gal be up at Taylors' all the time . . . that Alberta gal?

TROY: Same as you and me. Getting just as much as we is. Which is to say nothing.

BONO: It is, huh? I figure you doing a little better than me . . . and I ain't saying what I'm doing.

TROY: Aw, nigger, look here . . . I know you. If you had got anywhere near that gal, twenty minutes later you be looking to tell somebody. And the first one you gonna tell . . . that you gonna want to brag to . . . is gonna be me.

BONO: I ain't saying that. I see where you be eyeing her.

TROY: I eye all the women. I don't miss nothing. Don't never let nobody tell you Troy Maxson don't eye the women.

BONO: You been doing more than eyeing her. You done bought her a drink or two.

TROY: Hell yeah, I bought her a drink! What that mean? I bought you one, too. What that mean cause I buy her a drink? I'm just being polite.

BONO: It's all right to buy her one drink. That's what you call being polite. But when you wanna be buying two or three . . . that's what you call eyeing her.

TROY: Look here, as long as you known me . . . you ever known me to chase after women?

BONO: Hell yeah! Long as I done known you. You forgetting I knew you when.

TROY: Naw, I'm talking about since I been married to Rose?

BONO: Oh, not since you been married to Rose. Now, that's the truth, there. I can say that.

TROY: All right then! Case closed.

BONO: I see you be walking up around Alberta's house. You supposed to be at Taylors' and you be walking up around there.

TROY: What you watching where I'm walking for? I ain't watching after you.

BONO: I seen you walking around there more than once.

TROY: Hell, you liable to see me walking anywhere! That don't mean nothing cause you see me walking around there.

BONO: Where she come from anyway? She just kinda showed up one day.

TROY: Tallahassee. You can look at her and tell she one of them Florida gals. They got some big healthy women down there. Grow them right up out the ground. Got a little bit of Indian in her. Most of them niggers down in Florida got some Indian in them.

BONO: I don't know about that Indian part. But she damn sure big and healthy. Woman wear some big stockings. Got them great big old legs and hips as wide as the Mississippi River.

TROY: Legs don't mean nothing. You don't do nothing but push them out of the way. But them hips cushion the ride!

BONO: Troy, you ain't got no sense.

TROY: It's the truth! Like you riding on Goodyears!

(ROSE *enters from the house. She is ten years younger than* TROY, *her devotion to him stems from her recognition of the possibilities of her life without him: a succession of abusive men and their babies, a life of partying and running the streets, the Church, or aloneness with its attendant pain and frustration. She recognizes* TROY's *spirit as a fine and illuminating one and she either ignores or forgives his faults, only some of which she recognizes. Though she doesn't drink, her presence is an integral part of the Friday night rituals. She alternates between the porch and the kitchen, where supper preparations are under way.*)

ROSE: What you all out here getting into?

TROY: What you worried about what we getting into for? This is men talk, woman.

ROSE: What I care what you all talking about? Bono, you gonna stay for supper?

BONO: No, I thank you, Rose. But Lucille say she cooking up a pot of pigfeet.

TROY: Pigfeet! Hell, I'm going home with you! Might even stay the night if you got some pigfeet. You got something in there to top them pigfeet, Rose?

ROSE: I'm cooking up some chicken. I got some chicken and collard greens.

TROY: Well, go on back in the house and let me and Bono finish what we was talking about. This is men talk. I got some talk for you later. You know what kind of talk I mean. You go on and powder it up.

ROSE: Troy Maxson, don't you start that now!

TROY (*puts his arm around her*): Aw, woman . . . come here. Look here, Bono . . . when I met this woman . . . I got out that place, say, "Hitch up my pony, saddle up my mare . . . there's a woman out there for me somewhere. I looked here. Looked there. Saw Rose and latched on to her." I latched on to her and told her—I'm gonna tell you the truth—I told her, "Baby, I don't wanna marry, I just wanna be your man." Rose told me . . . tell him what you told me, Rose.

ROSE: I told him if he wasn't the marrying kind, then move out the way so the marrying kind could find me.

TROY: That's what she told me. "Nigger, you in my way. You blocking the view! Move out the way so I can find me a husband." I thought it over two or three days. Come back—

ROSE: Ain't no two or three days nothing. You was back the same night.

TROY: Come back, told her . . . "Okay, baby . . . but I'm gonna buy me a banty rooster and put him out there in the backyard . . . and when he sees a stranger come, he'll flap his wings and crow . . ." Look here, Bono, I could watch the front door by myself . . . it was that back door I was worried about.

ROSE: Troy, you ought not talk like that. Troy ain't doing nothing but telling a lie.

TROY: Only thing is . . . when we first got married . . . forget the rooster . . . we ain't had no yard!

BONO: I hear you tell it. Me and Lucille was staying down there on Logan Street. Had two rooms with the outhouse in the back. I ain't mind the outhouse none. But when that goddamn wind blow through there in the winter . . . that's what I'm talking about! To this day I wonder why in the hell I ever stayed down there for six long years. But see, I didn't know I could do no better. I thought only white folks had inside toilets and things.

ROSE: There's a lot of people don't know they can do no better than they doing now. That's just something you got to learn. A lot of folks still shop at Bella's.

TROY: Ain't nothing wrong with shopping at Bella's. She got fresh food.

ROSE: I ain't said nothing about if she got fresh food. I'm talking about what she charge. She charge ten cents more than the A&P.

TROY: The A&P ain't never done nothing for me. I spends my money where I'm treated right. I go down to Bella, say, "I need a loaf of bread, I'll pay you Friday." She give it to me. What sense that make when I got money to go and spend it somewhere else and ignore the person who done right by me? That ain't in the Bible.

ROSE: We ain't talking about what's in the Bible. What sense it make to shop there when she overcharge?

TROY: You shop where you want to. I'll do my shopping where the people been good to me.

ROSE: Well, I don't think it's right for her to overcharge. That's all I was saying.

BONO: Look here . . . I got to get on. Lucille going be raising all kind of hell.

TROY: Where you going, nigger? We ain't finished this pint. Come here, finish this pint.

BONO: Well, hell, I am . . . if you ever turn the bottle loose.

TROY (hands him the bottle): The only thing I say about the A&P is I'm glad Cory got that job down there. Help him take care of his school clothes and things. Gabe done moved out and things getting tight around here. He got that job. . . . He can start to look out for himself.

ROSE: Cory done went and got recruited by a college football team.

TROY: I told that boy about that football stuff. The white man ain't gonna let him get nowhere with that football. I told him when he first come to me with it. Now you come telling me he done went and got more tied up in it. He ought to go and get recruited in how to fix cars or something where he can make a living.

ROSE: He ain't talking about making no living playing football. It's just something the boys in school do. They gonna send a recruiter by to talk to you. He'll tell you he ain't talking about making no living playing football. It's a honor to be recruited.

TROY: It ain't gonna get him nowhere. Bono'll tell you that.

BONO: If he be like you in the sports . . . he's gonna be all right. Ain't but two men ever played baseball as good as you. That's Babe Ruth and Josh Gibson. Them's the only two men ever hit more home runs than you.

TROY: What it ever get me? Ain't got a pot to piss in or a window to throw it out of.

ROSE: Times have changed since you was playing baseball, Troy. That was before the war. Times have changed a lot since then.

TROY: How in hell they done changed?

ROSE: They got lots of colored boys playing ball now. Baseball and football.

BONO: You right about that, Rose. Times have changed, Troy. You just come along too early.

TROY: There ought not never have been no time called too early! Now you take that fellow . . . what's that fellow they had playing right field for the Yankees back then? You know who I'm talking about, Bono. Used to play right field for the Yankees.

ROSE: Selkirk?

TROY: Selkirk! That's it! Man batting .269, understand? .269. What kind of sense that make? I was hitting .432 with thirty-seven home runs! Man batting .269 and playing right field for the Yankees! I saw Josh Gibson's daughter yesterday. She walking around with raggedy shoes on her feet. Now I bet you Selkirk's daughter ain't walking around with raggedy shoes on her feet! I bet you that!

ROSE: They got a lot of colored baseball players now. Jackie Robinson was the first. Folks had to wait for Jackie Robinson.

TROY: I done seen a hundred niggers play baseball better than Jackie Robinson. Hell, I know some teams Jackie Robinson couldn't even make! What you talking about Jackie Robinson. Jackie Robinson wasn't nobody. I'm talking about if you could play ball then they ought to have let you play. Don't care what color you were. Come telling me I come along too early. If you could play . . . then they ought to have let you play.

(TROY takes a long drink from the bottle.)

ROSE: You gonna drink yourself to death. You don't need to be drinking like that.

TROY: Death ain't nothing. I done seen him. Done wrassled with him. You can't tell me nothing about death. Death ain't nothing but a fastball on the outside corner. And you know what I'll do to that! Lookee here, Bono . . . am I lying? You get one of them fastballs, about waist high, over the outside corner of the plate where you can get the meat of the bat on it . . . and good god! You can kiss it goodbye. Now, am I lying?

BONO: Naw, you telling the truth there. I seen you do it.

TROY: If I'm lying . . . that 450 feet worth of lying! (*Pause.*) That's all death is to me. A fastball on the outside corner.

ROSE: I don't know why you want to get on talking about death.

TROY: Ain't nothing wrong with talking about death. That's part of life. Everybody gonna die. You gonna die, I'm gonna die. Bono's gonna die. Hell, we all gonna die.

ROSE: But you ain't got to talk about it. I don't like to talk about it.

TROY: You the one brought it up. Me and Bono was talking about baseball . . . you tell me I'm gonna drink myself to death. Ain't that right, Bono? You know I don't drink this but one night out of the week. That's Friday night. I'm gonna drink just enough to where I can handle it. Then I cuts it loose. I leave it alone. So don't you worry about me drinking myself to death. 'Cause I ain't worried about Death. I done seen him. I done wrestled with him.

Look here, Bono . . . I looked up one day and Death was marching straight at me. Like Soldiers on Parade! The Army of Death was marching straight at me. The middle of July, 1941. It got real cold just like it be winter. It seem like Death himself reached out and touched me on the shoulder. He touch me just like I touch you. I got cold as ice and Death standing there grinning at me.

ROSE: Troy, why don't you hush that talk.

TROY: I say . . . What you want, Mr. Death? You be wanting me? You done brought your army to be getting me? I looked him dead in the eye. I wasn't fearing nothing. I was ready to tangle. Just like I'm ready to tangle now. The Bible say be ever vigilant. That's why I don't get but so drunk. I got to keep watch.

ROSE: Troy was right down there in Mercy Hospital. You remember he had pneumonia? Laying there with a fever talking plumb out of his head.

TROY: Death standing there staring at me . . . carrying that sickle in his hand. Finally he say, "You want bound over for another year?" See, just like that . . . "You want bound over for another year?" I told him, "Bound over hell! Let's settle this now!"

It seem like he kinda fell back when I said that, and all the cold went out of me. I reached down and grabbed that sickle and threw it just as far as I could throw it . . . and me and him commenced to wrestling.

We wrestled for three days and three nights. I can't say where I found the strength from. Every time it seemed like he was gonna get the best of me, I'd reach way down deep inside myself and find the strength to do him one better.

ROSE: Every time Troy tell that story he find different ways to tell it. Different things to make up about it.

TROY: I ain't making up nothing. I'm telling you the facts of what happened. I wrestled with Death for three days and three nights and I'm standing here to tell you about it. (*Pause.*) All right. At the end of the third night we done weakened each other to where we can't hardly move. Death stood up, throwed on his robe . . . had him a white robe with a hood on it. He throwed on that robe and went off to look for his sickle. Say, "I'll be back." Just like that. "I'll be back." I told him, say, "Yeah, but . . . you gonna have to find me!" I wasn't no fool. I wasn't going looking for him. Death ain't nothing to play with. And I know he's gonna get me. I know I got to join his army . . . his camp followers. But as long as I keep my strength and see him coming . . . as long as I keep up my vigilance . . . he's gonna have to fight to get me. I ain't going easy.

BONO: Well, look here, since you got to keep up your vigilance . . . let me have the bottle.

TROY: Aw hell, I shouldn't have told you that part. I should have left out that part.

ROSE: Troy be talking that stuff and half the time don't even know what he be talking about.

TROY: Bono know me better than that.

BONO: That's right. I know you. I know you got some Uncle Remus in your blood. You got more stories than the devil got sinners.

TROY: Aw hell, I done seen him too! Done talked with the devil.

ROSE: Troy, don't nobody wanna be hearing all that stuff.

(LYONS *enters the yard from the street. Thirty-four years old,* TROY's *son by a previous marriage, he sports a neatly trimmed goatee, sport coat, white shirt, tieless and buttoned at the collar. Though he fancies himself a musician, he is more caught up in the rituals and "idea" of being a musician than in the actual practice of the music. He has come to borrow money from* TROY, *and while he knows he will be successful, he is uncertain as to what extent his lifestyle will be held up to scrutiny and ridicule.*)

LYONS: Hey, Pop.

TROY: What you come "Hey, Popping" me for?

LYONS: How you doing, Rose? (*He kisses her.*) Mr. Bono. How you doing?

BONO: Hey, Lyons . . . how you been?

TROY: He must have been doing all right. I ain't seen him around here last week.

ROSE: Troy, leave your boy alone. He come by to see you and you wanna start all that nonsense.

TROY: I ain't bothering Lyons. (*Offers him the bottle.*) Here . . . get you a drink. We got an understanding. I know why he come by to see me and he know I know.

LYONS: Come on, Pop . . . I just stopped by to say hi . . . see how you was doing.

TROY: You ain't stopped by yesterday.

ROSE: You gonna stay for supper, Lyons? I got some chicken cooking in the oven.

LYONS: No, Rose . . . thanks. I was just in the neighborhood and thought I'd stop by for a minute.

TROY: You was in the neighborhood alright, nigger. You telling the truth there. You was in the neighborhood cause it's my payday.

LYONS: Well, hell, since you mentioned it . . . let me have ten dollars.

TROY: I'll be damned! I'll die and go to hell and play blackjack with the devil before I give you ten dollars.

BONO: That's what I wanna know about . . . that devil you done seen.

LYONS: What . . . Pop done seen the devil? You too much, Pops.

TROY: Yeah, I done seen him. Talked to him too!

ROSE: You ain't seen no devil. I done told you that man ain't had nothing to do with the devil. Anything you can't understand, you want to call it the devil.

TROY: Look here, Bono . . . I went down to see Hertzberger about some furniture. Got three rooms for two-ninety-eight. That what it say on the radio. "Three rooms . . . two-ninety-eight." Even made up a little song about it. Go down there . . . man tell me I can't get no credit. I'm working every day and can't get no credit. What to do? I got an empty house with some raggedy furniture in it. Cory ain't got no bed. He's sleeping on a pile of rags on the floor. Working every day and can't get no credit. Come back here—Rose'll tell you—madder than hell. Sit down . . . try to figure what I'm gonna do. Come a knock on the door. Ain't been living here but three days. Who know I'm here? Open the door . . . devil standing there bigger than life. White fellow . . . got on good clothes and everything. Standing there with a clipboard in his hand. I ain't had to say nothing. First words come out of his mouth was . . . "I understand you need some furniture and can't get no credit." I liked to fell over. He say, "I'll give you all the credit you want, but you got to pay the interest on it." I told him, "Give me three rooms worth and charge whatever you want." Next day a truck pulled up here and two men unloaded them three rooms. Man what drove the truck give me a book. Say send ten dollars, first of every month to the address in the book and everything will be alright. Say if I miss a payment the devil was coming back and it'll be hell to pay. That was fifteen years ago. To this day . . . the first of the month I send my ten dollars, Rose'll tell you.

ROSE: Troy lying.

TROY: I ain't never seen that man since. Now you tell me who else that could have been but the devil? I ain't sold my soul or nothing like that, you understand. Naw, I wouldn't have truck with the devil about nothing like that. I got my furniture and pays my ten dollars the first of the month just like clockwork.

BONO: How long you say you been paying this ten dollars a month?

TROY: Fifteen years!

BONO: Hell, ain't you finished paying for it yet? How much the man done charged you.

TROY: Aw hell, I done paid for it. I done paid for it ten times over! The fact is I'm scared to stop paying it.

ROSE: Troy lying. We got that furniture from Mr. Glickman. He ain't paying no ten dollars a month to nobody.

TROY: Aw hell, woman. Bono know I ain't that big a fool.

LYONS: I was just getting ready to say . . . I know where there's a bridge for sale.

TROY: Look here, I'll tell you this . . . it don't matter to me if he was the devil. It don't matter if the devil give credit. Somebody has got to give it.

ROSE: It ought to matter. You going around talking about having truck with the devil . . . God's the one you gonna have to answer to. He's the one gonna be at the Judgment.

LYONS: Yeah, well, look here, Pop . . . let me have that ten dollars. I'll give it back to you. Bonnie got a job working at the hospital.

TROY: What I tell you, Bono? The only time I see this nigger is when he wants something. That's the only time I see him.

LYONS: Come on, Pop, Mr. Bono don't want to hear all that. Let me have the ten dollars. I told you Bonnie working.

TROY: What that mean to me? "Bonnie working." I don't care if she working. Go ask her for the ten dollars if she working. Talking about "Bonnie working." Why ain't you working?

LYONS: Aw, Pop, you know I can't find no decent job. Where am I gonna get a job at? You know I can't get no job.

TROY: I told you I know some people down there. I can get you on the rubbish if you want to work. I told you that the last time you came by here asking me for something.

LYONS: Naw, Pop . . . thanks. That ain't for me. I don't wanna be carrying nobody's rubbish. I don't wanna be punching nobody's time clock.

TROY: What's the matter, you too good to carry people's rubbish? Where you think that ten dollars you talking about come from? I'm just supposed to haul people's rubbish and give my money to you cause you too lazy to work. You too lazy to work and wanna know why you ain't got what I got.

ROSE: What hospital Bonnie working at? Mercy?

LYONS: She's down at Passavant working in the laundry.

TROY: I ain't got nothing as it is. I give you that ten dollars and I got to eat beans the rest of the week. Naw . . . you ain't getting no ten dollars here.

LYONS: You ain't got to be eating no beans. I don't know why you wanna say that.

TROY: I ain't got no extra money. Gabe done moved over to Miss Pearl's paying her the rent and things done got tight around here. I can't afford to be giving you every payday.

LYONS: I ain't asked you to give me nothing. I asked you to loan me ten dollars. I know you got ten dollars.

TROY: Yeah, I got it. You know why I got it? Cause I don't throw my money away out there in the streets. You living the fast life . . . wanna be a musician . . . running around in them clubs and things . . . then, you learn to take care of yourself. You ain't gonna find me going and asking nobody for nothing. I done spent too many years without.

LYONS: You and me is two different people, Pop.

TROY: I done learned my mistake and learned to do what's right by it. You still trying to get something for nothing. Life don't owe you nothing. You owe it to yourself. Ask Bono. He'll tell you I'm right.

LYONS: You got your way of dealing with the world . . . I got mine. The only thing that matters to me is the music.

TROY: Yeah, I can see that! It don't matter how you gonna eat . . . where your next dollar is coming from. You telling the truth there.

LYONS: I know I got to eat. But I got to live too. I need something that gonna help me to get out of the bed in the morning. Make me feel like I belong in the world. I don't bother nobody. Just stay with my music cause that's the only way I can find to live in the world. Otherwise there ain't no telling what I might do. Now I don't come criticizing you and how you live. I just come by to ask you for ten dollars. I don't wanna hear all that about how I live.

TROY: Boy, your mama did a hell of a job raising you.

LYONS: You can't change me, Pop. I'm thirty-four years old. If you wanted to change me, you should have been there when I was growing up. I come by to see you . . . ask for ten dollars and you want to talk about how I was raised. You don't know nothing about how I was raised.

ROSE: Let the boy have ten dollars, Troy.

TROY (To LYONS): What the hell you looking at me for? I ain't got no ten dollars. You know what I do with my money. (To ROSE) Give him ten dollars if you want him to have it.

ROSE: I will. Just as soon as you turn it loose.

TROY (handing ROSE the money): There it is. Seventy-six dollars and forty-two cents. You see this, Bono? Now, I ain't gonna get but six of that back.

ROSE: You ought to stop telling that lie. Here, Lyons. (She hands him the money.)

LYONS: Thanks, Rose. Look . . . I got to run . . . I'll see you later.

TROY: Wait a minute. You gonna say, "thanks, Rose" and ain't gonna look to see where she got that ten dollars from? See how they do me, Bono?

LYONS: I know she got it from you, Pop. Thanks. I'll give it back to you.

TROY: There he go telling another lie. Time I see that ten dollars . . . he'll be owing me thirty more.

LYONS: See you, Mr. Bono.

BONO: Take care, Lyons!

LYONS: Thanks, Pop. I'll see you again.

(LYONS exits the yard.)

TROY: I don't know why he don't go and get him a decent job and take care of that woman he got.

BONO: He'll be alright, Troy. The boy is still young.

TROY: The boy is thirty-four years old.

BONO: Let's not get off into all that.

BONO: Look here . . . I got to be going. I got to be getting on. Lucille gonna be waiting.

TROY (*puts his arm around* ROSE): See this woman, Bono? I love this woman. I love this woman so much it hurts. I love her so much . . . I done run out of ways of loving her. So I got to go back to basics. Don't you come by my house Monday morning talking about time to go to work . . . 'cause I'm still gonna be stroking!

ROSE: Troy! Stop it now!

BONO: I ain't paying him no mind, Rose. That ain't nothing but gin-talk. Go on, Troy. I'll see you Monday.

TROY: Don't you come by my house, nigger! I done told you what I'm gonna be doing.

(*The lights go down to black.*)

SCENE II

The lights come up on ROSE *hanging up clothes. She hums and sings softly to herself. It is the following morning.*

ROSE (*Sings*):
> Jesus, be a fence all around me every day
> Jesus, I want you to protect me as I travel
>   on my way
> Jesus, be a fence all around me every day.

(TROY *enters from the house.*)

ROSE (*continues*):
> Jesus, I want you to protect me
> As I travel on my way.

(*To* TROY) 'Morning. You ready for breakfast? I can fix it soon as I finish hanging up these clothes?

TROY: I got the coffee on. That'll be all right. I'll just drink some of that this morning.

ROSE: That 651 hit yesterday. That's the second time this month. Miss Pearl hit for a dollar . . . seem like those that need the least always get lucky. Poor folks can't get nothing.

TROY: Them numbers don't know nobody. I don't know why you fool with them. You and Lyons both.

ROSE: It's something to do.

TROY: You ain't doing nothing but throwing your money away.

ROSE: Troy, you know I don't play foolishly. I just play a nickel here and a nickel there.

TROY: That's two nickels you done thrown away.

ROSE: Now I hit sometimes . . . that makes up for it. It always comes in handy when I do hit. I don't hear you complaining then.

TROY: I ain't complaining now. I just say it's foolish. Trying to guess out of six hundred ways which way the number gonna come. If I had all the money niggers, these Negroes, throw away on numbers for one week—just one week—I'd be a rich man.

ROSE: Well, you wishing and calling it foolish ain't gonna stop folks from playing numbers. That's one thing for sure. Besides . . . some good things come from playing numbers. Look where Pope done bought him that restaurant off of numbers.

TROY: I can't stand niggers like that. Man ain't had two dimes to rub together. He walking around with his shoes all run over bumming money for cigarettes. All right. Got lucky there and hit the numbers . . .

ROSE: Troy, I know all about it.

TROY: Had good sense, I'll say that for him. He ain't throwed his money away. I seen niggers hit the numbers and go through two thousand dollars in four days. Man bought him that restaurant down there . . . fixed it up real nice . . . and then didn't want nobody to come in it! A Negro go in there and can't get no kind of service. I seen a white fellow come in there and order a bowl of stew. Pope picked all the meat out the pot for him. Man ain't had nothing but a bowl of meat! Negro come behind him and ain't got nothing but the potatoes and carrots. Talking about what numbers do for people, you picked a wrong example. Ain't done nothing but make a worser fool out of him than he was before.

ROSE: Troy, you ought to stop worrying about what happened at work yesterday.

TROY: I ain't worried. Just told me to be down there at the Commissioner's office on Friday. Everybody think they gonna fire me. I ain't worried about them firing me. You ain't got to worry about that. (*Pause.*) Where's Cory? Cory in the house? (*Calls*) Cory?

ROSE: He gone out.

TROY: Out, huh? He gone out 'cause he know I want him to help me with this fence. I know how he is. That boy scared of work.

(GABRIEL *enters. He comes halfway down the alley and, hearing* TROY's *voice, stops.*)

TROY (*continues*): He ain't done a lick of work in his life.

ROSE: He had to go to football practice. Coach wanted them to get in a little extra practice before the season start.

TROY: I got his practice . . . running out of here before he get his chores done.

ROSE: Troy, what is wrong with you this morning? Don't nothing set right with you. Go on back in there and go to bed . . . get up on the other side.

TROY: Why something got to be wrong with me? I ain't said nothing wrong with me.

ROSE: You got something to say about everything. First it's the numbers . . . then it's the way the man runs his restaurant . . . then you done got on Cory. What's it gonna be next? Take a look up there and see if the weather suits you . . . or is it gonna be how you gonna put up the fence with the clothes hanging in the yard.

TROY: You hit the nail on the head then.

ROSE: I know you like I know the back of my hand. Go on in there and get you some coffee . . . see if that straighten you up. 'Cause you ain't right this morning.

(TROY *starts into the house and sees* GABRIEL. GABRIEL *starts singing.* TROY's *brother, he is seven years younger than* TROY. *Injured in World War II, he has a metal plate in his head. He carries an old trumpet tied around his waist and believes with every fiber of his being that he is the Archangel Gabriel. He carries a chipped basket with an assortment of discarded fruits and vegetables he has picked up in the strip district and which he attempts to sell.*)

GABRIEL (*singing*):
Yes, ma'am, I got plums
You ask me how I sell them
Oh ten cents apiece
Three for a quarter
Come and buy now
'Cause I'm here today
And tomorrow I'll be gone

(GABRIEL *enters.*)

Hey, Rose!

ROSE: How you doing, Gabe?

GABRIEL: There's Troy . . . Hey, Troy!

TROY: Hey, Gabe. (*Exits into kitchen.*)

ROSE (*to* GABRIEL): What you got there?

GABRIEL: You know what I got, Rose. I got fruits and vegetables.

ROSE (*looking in basket*): Where's all these plums you talking about?

GABRIEL: I ain't got no plums today, Rose. I was just singing that. Have some tomorrow. Put me in a big order for plums. Have enough plums tomorrow for St. Peter and everybody.

(TROY *re-enters from kitchen, crosses to steps.*)

(*To* ROSE) Troy's mad at me.

TROY: I ain't mad at you. What I got to be mad at you about? You ain't done nothing to me.

GABRIEL: I just moved over to Miss Pearl's to keep out from in your way. I ain't mean no harm by it.

TROY: Who said anything about that? I ain't said anything about that.

GABRIEL: You ain't mad at me, is you?

TROY: Naw . . . I ain't mad at you, Gabe. If I was mad at you I'd tell you about it.

GABRIEL: Got me two rooms. In the basement. Got my own door, too. Wanna see my key? (*He holds up a key.*) That's my own key! Ain't nobody else got a key like that. That's my key! My two rooms!

TROY: Well, that's good, Gabe. You got your own key . . . that's good.

ROSE: You hungry, Gabe? I was just fixing to cook Troy his breakfast.

GABRIEL: I'll take some biscuits. You got some biscuits? Did you know when I was in heaven . . . every morning me and St. Peter would sit down by the gate and eat some big fat biscuits? Oh, yeah! We had us a good time. We'd sit there and eat us them biscuits and then St. Peter would go off to sleep and tell me to wake him up when it's time to open the gates for the judgment.

ROSE: Well, come on . . . I'll make up a batch of biscuits.

(ROSE *exits into the house.*)

GABRIEL: Troy . . . St. Peter got your name in the book. I seen it. It say . . . Troy Maxson. I say . . . I know him! He got the same name like what I got. That's my brother!

TROY: How many times you gonna tell me that, Gabe?

GABRIEL: Ain't got my name in the book. Don't have to have my name. I done died and went to heaven. He got your name though. One morning St. Peter was looking at his book . . . marking it up for the judgment . . . and he let me see your name. Got it in there under M. Got Rose's name . . . I ain't seen it like I seen yours . . . but I know it's in there. He got a great big book. Got everybody's name what was ever been born. That's what he told me. But I seen your name. Seen it with my own eyes.

TROY: Go on in the house there. Rose going to fix you something to eat.

GABRIEL: Oh, I ain't hungry. I done had breakfast with Aunt Jemimah. She come by and cooked me up a whole mess of flapjacks. Remember how we used to eat them flapjacks?

TROY: Go on in the house and get you something to eat now.

GABRIEL: I got to go sell my plums. I done sold some tomatoes. Got me two quarters. Wanna see? (*He shows* TROY *his quarters.*) I'm gonna save them and buy me a new horn so St. Peter can hear me when it's time to open the gates. (GABRIEL *stops suddenly. Listens.*) Hear that? That's the hellhounds. I got to chase them out of here. Go on get out of here! Get out! (GABRIEL *exits singing.*)

Better get ready for the judgment
Better get ready for the judgment
My Lord is coming down

(ROSE *enters from the house.*)

TROY: He gone off somewhere.

GABRIEL (*offstage*):
Better get ready for the judgment
Better get ready for the judgment morning
Better get ready for the judgment
My God is coming down

ROSE: He ain't eating right. Miss Pearl say she can't get him to eat nothing.

TROY: What you want me to do about it, Rose? I done did everything I can for the man. I can't make him get well. Man got half his head blown away . . . what you expect?

ROSE: Seem like something ought to be done to help him.

TROY: Man don't bother nobody. He just mixed up from that metal plate he got in his head. Ain't no sense for him to go back into the hospital.

ROSE: Least he be eating right. They can help him take care of himself.

TROY: Don't nobody wanna be locked up, Rose. What you wanna lock him up for? Man go over there and fight the war . . . messin' around with them Japs, get half his head blown off . . . and they give him a lousy three thousand dollars. And I had to swoop down on that.

ROSE: Is you fixing to go into that again?

TROY: That's the only way I got a roof over my head . . . cause of that metal plate.

ROSE: Ain't no sense you blaming yourself for nothing. Gabe wasn't in no condition to manage that money. You done what was right by him. Can't nobody say you ain't done what was right by him. Look how long you took care of him . . . till he wanted to have his own place and moved over there with Miss Pearl.

TROY: That ain't what I'm saying, woman! I'm just stating the facts. If my brother didn't have that metal plate in his head . . . I wouldn't have a pot to piss in or a window to throw it out of. And I'm fifty-three years old. Now see if you can understand that!

(TROY *gets up from the porch and starts to exit the yard.*)

ROSE: Where you going off to? You been running out of here every Saturday for weeks. I thought you was gonna work on this fence?

TROY: I'm gonna walk down to Taylors'. Listen to the ball game. I'll be back in a bit. I'll work on it when I get back.

(*He exits the yard. The lights go to black.*)

SCENE III

The lights come up on the yard. It is four hours later. ROSE *is taking down the clothes from the line.* CORY *enters carrying his football equipment.*

ROSE: Your daddy like to had a fit with you running out of here without doing your chores.

CORY: I told you I had to go to practice.

ROSE: He say you were supposed to help him with this fence.

CORY: He been saying that the last four or five Saturdays, and then he don't never do nothing, but go down to Taylors'. Did you tell him about the recruiter?

ROSE: Yeah, I told him.

CORY: What he say?

ROSE: He ain't said nothing too much. You get in there and get started on your chores before he gets back. Go on and scrub down them steps before he gets back here hollering and carrying on.

CORY: I'm hungry. What you got to eat, Mama?

ROSE: Go on and get started on your chores. I got some meat loaf in there. Go on and make you a sandwich . . . and don't you leave no mess in there. (CORY *exits into the house.* ROSE *continues to take down the clothes.* TROY *enters the yard and sneaks up and grabs her from behind.*) Troy! Go on, now. You liked to scared me to death. What was the score of the game? Lucille had me on the phone and I couldn't keep up with it.

TROY: What I care about the game? Come here, woman. (*He tries to kiss her.*)

ROSE: I thought you went down Taylors' to listen to the game. Go on, Troy! You supposed to be putting up this fence.

TROY (*attempting to kiss her again*): I'll put it up when I finish with what is at hand.

ROSE: Go on, Troy. I ain't studying you.

TROY (*chasing after her*): I'm studying you . . . fixing to do my homework!

ROSE: Troy, you better leave me alone.

TROY: Where's Cory? That boy brought his butt home yet?

ROSE: He's in the house doing his chores.

TROY (*calling*): Cory! Get your butt out here, boy!

(ROSE *exits into the house with the laundry.* TROY *goes over to the pile of wood, picks up a board, and starts sawing.* CORY *enters from the house.*)

TROY: You just now coming in here from leaving this morning?

CORY: Yeah, I had to go to football practice.

TROY: Yeah, what?

CORY: Yessir.

TROY: I ain't but two seconds off you noway. The garbage sitting in there overflowing . . . you ain't done none of your chores . . . and you come in here talking about "Yeah."

CORY: I was just getting ready to do my chores now, Pop . . .

TROY: Your first chore is to help me with this fence on Saturday. Everything else come after that. Now get that saw and cut them boards.

(CORY *takes the saw and begins cutting the boards.* TROY *continues working. There is a long pause.*)

CORY: Hey, Pop . . . why don't you buy a TV?

TROY: What I want with a TV? What I want one of them for?

CORY: Everybody got one. Earl, Ba Bra . . . Jesse!

TROY: I ain't asked you who had one. I say what I want with one?

CORY: So you can watch it. They got lots of things on TV. Baseball games and everything. We could watch the World Series.

TROY: Yeah . . . and how much this TV cost?

CORY: I don't know. They got them on sale for around two hundred dollars.

TROY: Two hundred dollars, huh?

CORY: That ain't that much, Pop.

TROY: Naw, it's just two hundred dollars. See that roof you got over your head at night? Let me tell you something about that roof. It's been over ten years since that roof was last tarred. See now . . . the snow come this winter and sit up there on

that roof like it is . . . and it's gonna seep inside. It's just gonna be a little bit . . . ain't gonna hardly notice it. Then the next thing you know, it's gonna be leaking all over the house. Then the wood rot from all that water and you gonna need a whole new roof. Now, how much you think it cost to get that roof tarred?

CORY: I don't know.

TROY: Two hundred and sixty-four dollars . . . cash money. While you thinking about a TV, I got to be thinking about the roof . . . and whatever else go wrong around here. Now if you had two hundred dollars, what would you do . . . fix the roof or buy a TV?

CORY: I'd buy a TV. Then when the roof started to leak . . . when it needed fixing . . . I'd fix it.

TROY: Where you gonna get the money from? You done spent it for a TV. You gonna sit up and watch the water run all over your brand new TV.

CORY: Aw, Pop. You got money. I know you do.

TROY: Where I got it at, huh?

CORY: You got it in the bank.

TROY: You wanna see my bankbook? You wanna see that seventy-three dollars and twenty-two cents I got sitting up in there?

CORY: You ain't got to pay for it all at one time. You can put a down payment on it and carry it on home with you.

TROY: Not me. I ain't gonna owe nobody nothing if I can help it. Miss a payment and they come and snatch it right out your house. Then what you got? Now, soon as I get two hundred dollars clear, then I'll buy a TV. Right now, as soon as I get two hundred and sixty-four dollars, I'm gonna have this roof tarred.

CORY: Aw . . . Pop!

TROY: You go on and get you two hundred dollars and buy one if ya want it. I got better things to do with my money.

CORY: I can't get no two hundred dollars. I ain't never seen two hundred dollars.

TROY: I'll tell you what . . . you get you a hundred dollars and I'll put the other hundred with it.

CORY: All right, I'm gonna show you.

TROY: You gonna show me how you can cut them boards right now.

(CORY *begins to cut the boards. There is a long pause.*)

CORY: The Pirates won today. That make five in a row.

TROY: I ain't thinking about the Pirates. Got an all-white team. Got that boy . . . that Puerto Rican boy . . . Clemente. Don't even half-play him. That boy could be something if they give him a chance. Play him one day and sit him on the bench the next.

CORY: He gets a lot of chances to play.

TROY: I'm talking about playing regular. Playing every day so you can get your timing. That's what I'm talking about.

CORY: They got some white guys on the team that don't play every day. You can't play everybody at the same time.

TROY: If they got a white fellow sitting on the bench . . . you can bet your last dollar he can't play! The colored guy got to be twice as good before he get on the team. That's why I don't want you to get all tied up in them sports. Man on the team and what it get him? They got colored on the team and don't use them. Same as not having them. All them teams the same.

CORY: The Braves got Hank Aaron and Wes Covington. Hank Aaron hit two home runs today. That makes forty-three.

TROY: Hank Aaron ain't nobody. That's what you supposed to do. That's how you supposed to play the game. Ain't nothing to it. It's just a matter of timing . . . getting the right follow-through. Hell, I can hit forty-three home runs right now!

CORY: Not off no major-league pitching, you couldn't.

TROY: We had better pitching in the Negro leagues. I hit seven home runs off of Satchel Paige. You can't get no better than that!

CORY: Sandy Koufax. He's leading the league in strikeouts.

TROY: I ain't thinking of no Sandy Koufax.

CORY: You got Warren Spahn and Lew Burdette. I bet you couldn't hit no home runs off of Warren Spahn.

TROY: I'm through with it now. You go on and cut them boards. (*Pause.*) Your mama tell me you done got recruited by a college football team? Is that right?

CORY: Yeah. Coach Zellman say the recruiter gonna be coming by to talk to you. Get you to sign the permission papers.

TROY: I thought you supposed to be working down there at the A&P. Ain't you suppose to be working down there after school?

CORY: Mr. Stawicki say he gonna hold my job for me until after the football season. Say starting next week I can work weekends.

TROY: I thought we had an understanding about this football stuff? You suppose to keep up with your chores and hold that job down at the A&P.

Ain't been around here all day on a Saturday. Ain't none of your chores done . . . and now you telling me you done quit your job.

CORY: I'm gonna be working weekends.

TROY: You damn right you are! And ain't no need for nobody coming around here to talk to me about signing nothing.

CORY: Hey, Pop . . . you can't do that. He's coming all the way from North Carolina.

TROY: I don't care where he coming from. The white man ain't gonna let you get nowhere with that football noway. You go on and get your book-learning so you can work yourself up in that A&P or learn how to fix cars or build houses or something, get you a trade. That way you have something can't nobody take away from you. You go on and learn how to put your hands to some good use. Besides hauling people's garbage.

CORY: I get good grades, Pop. That's why the recruiter wants to talk with you. You got to keep up your grades to get recruited. This way I'll be going to college. I'll get a chance . . .

TROY: First you gonna get your butt down there to the A&P and get your job back.

CORY: Mr. Stawicki done already hired somebody else 'cause I told him I was playing football.

TROY: You a bigger fool than I thought . . . to let somebody take away your job so you can play some football. Where you gonna get your money to take out your girlfriend and whatnot? What kind of foolishness is that to let somebody take away your job?

CORY: I'm still gonna be working weekends.

TROY: Naw . . . naw. You getting your butt out of here and finding you another job.

CORY: Come on, Pop! I got to practice. I can't work after school and play football, too. The team needs me. That's what Coach Zellman say . . .

TROY: I don't care what nobody else say. I'm the boss . . . you understand? I'm the boss around here. I do the only saying what counts.

CORY: Come on, Pop!

TROY: I asked you . . . did you understand?

CORY: Yeah . . .

TROY: What?!

CORY: Yessir.

TROY: You go on down there to that A&P and see if you can get your job back. If you can't do both . . . then you quit the football team. You've got to take the crookeds with the straights.

CORY Yessir. (*Pause.*) Can I ask you a question?

TROY: What the hell you wanna ask me? Mr. Stawicki the one you got the questions for.

CORY: How come you ain't never liked me?

TROY: Liked you? Who the hell say I got to like you? What law is there say I got to like you? Wanna stand up in my face and ask a damn fool-ass question like that. Talking about liking somebody. Come here, boy, when I talk to you.

(CORY *comes over to where* TROY *is working. He stands slouched over and* TROY *shoves him on his shoulder.*)

Straighten up, goddammit! I asked you a question . . . what law is there say I got to like you?

CORY: None.

TROY: Well, all right then! Don't you eat every day? (*Pause.*) Answer me when I talk to you! Don't you eat every day?

CORY: Yeah.

TROY: Nigger, as long as you in my house, you put that sir on the end of it when you talk to me!

CORY: Yes . . . sir.

TROY: You eat every day.

CORY: Yessir!

TROY: Got a roof over your head.

CORY: Yessir!

TROY: Got clothes on your back.

CORY: Yessir.

TROY: Why you think that is?

CORY: Cause of you.

TROY: Aw, hell I know it's 'cause of me . . . but why do you think that is?

CORY (*hesitant*): Cause you like me.

TROY: Like you? I go out of here every morning . . . bust my butt . . . putting up with them crackers every day. . . cause I like you? You about the biggest fool I ever saw. (*Pause.*) It's my job. It's my responsibility! You understand that? A man got to take care of his family. You live in my house . . . sleep you behind on my bedclothes . . . fill you belly up with my food . . . cause you my son. You my flesh and blood. Not 'cause I like you! Cause it's my duty to take care of you. I owe a responsibility to you!

Let's get this straight right here . . . before it go along any further . . . I ain't got to like you. Mr. Rand don't give me my money come payday cause he likes me. He gives me cause he owe me. I done give you everything I had to give you. I gave you your life! Me and your mama worked that out between us. And liking your black ass wasn't part of the bargain. Don't you try and go through life worrying about if somebody like you or not. You best be making sure they doing right by you. You understand what I'm saying, boy?

CORY: Yessir.

TROY: Then get the hell out of my face, and get on down to that A&P.

(ROSE *has been standing behind the screen door for much of the scene. She enters as* CORY *exits.*)

ROSE: Why don't you let the boy go ahead and play football, Troy? Ain't no harm in that. He's just trying to be like you with the sports.

TROY: I don't want him to be like me! I want him to move as far away from my life as he can get. You the only decent thing that ever happened to me. I wish him that. But I don't wish him a thing else from my life. I decided seventeen years ago that boy wasn't getting involved in no sports. Not after what they did to me in the sports.

ROSE: Troy, why don't you admit you was too old to play in the major leagues? For once . . . why don't you admit that?

TROY: What do you mean too old? Don't come telling me I was too old. I just wasn't the right color. Hell, I'm fifty-three years old and can do better than Selkirk's .269 right now!

ROSE: How's was you gonna play ball when you were over forty? Sometimes I can't get no sense out of you.

TROY: I got good sense, woman. I got sense enough not to let my boy get hurt over playing no sports. You been mothering that boy too much. Worried about if people like him.

ROSE: Everything that boy do . . . he do for you. He wants you to say "Good job, son." That's all.

TROY: Rose, I ain't got time for that. He's alive. He's healthy. He's got to make his own way. I made mine. Ain't nobody gonna hold his hand when he get out there in that world.

ROSE: Times have changed from when you was young, Troy. People change. The world's changing around you and you can't even see it.

TROY (*slow, methodical*): Woman . . . I do the best I can do. I come in here every Friday. I carry a sack of potatoes and a bucket of lard. You all line up at the door with your hands out. I give you the lint from my pockets. I give you my sweat and my blood. I ain't got no tears. I done spent them. We go upstairs in that room at night . . . and I fall down on you and try to blast a hole into forever. I get up Monday morning . . . find my lunch on the table. I go out. Make my way. Find my strength to carry me through to the next Friday. (*Pause.*) That's all I got, Rose. That's all I got to give. I can't give nothing else.

(TROY *exits into the house. The lights go down to black.*)

SCENE IV

It is Friday. Two weeks later. CORY *starts out of the house with his football equipment. The phone rings.*

CORY (*calling*): I got it!

(*He answers the phone and stands in the screen door talking.*)

Hello? Hey, Jesse. Naw . . . I was just getting ready to leave now.

ROSE (*calling*): Cory!

CORY: I told you, man, them spikes is all tore up. You can use them if you want, but they ain't no good. Earl got some spikes.

ROSE (*calling*): Cory!

CORY (*calling to* ROSE): Mam? I'm talking to Jesse. (*Into phone*) When she say that? (*Pause.*) Aw, you lying, man. I'm gonna tell her you said that.

ROSE (*calling*): Cory, don't you go nowhere!

CORY: I got to go to the game, Ma! (*Into the phone*) Yeah, hey, look, I'll talk to you later. Yeah, I'll meet you over Earl's house. Later. Bye, Ma.

(CORY *exits the house and starts out the yard.*)

ROSE: Cory, where you going off to? You got that stuff all pulled out and thrown all over your room.

CORY (*in the yard*): I was looking for my spikes. Jesse wanted to borrow my spikes.

ROSE: Get up there and get that cleaned up before your daddy get back in here.

CORY: I got to go to the game! I'll clean it up *when I get back.*

(CORY *exits.*)

ROSE: That's all he need to do is see that room all messed up.

(ROSE *exits into the house.* TROY *and* BONO *enter the yard.* TROY *is dressed in clothes other than his work clothes.*)

BONO: He told him the same thing he told you. Take it to the union.

TROY: Brownie ain't got that much sense. Man wasn't thinking about nothing. He wait until I confront them on it . . . then he wanna come crying seniority. (*Calls*) Hey Rose!

BONO: I wish I could have seen Mr. Rand's face when he told you.

TROY: He couldn't get it out of his mouth! Liked to bit his tongue! When they called me down there

to the Commissioner's office . . . he thought they was gonna fire me. Like everybody else.

BONO: I didn't think they was gonna fire you. I thought they was gonna put you on the warning paper.

TROY: Hey, Rose! (*To* BONO): Yeah, Mr. Rand like to bit his tongue.

(TROY *breaks the seal on the bottle, takes a drink, and hands it to* BONO.)

BONO: I see you run right down to Taylors' and told that Alberta gal.

TROY (*calling*): Hey Rose! (*To* BONO) I told everybody. Hey, Rose! I went down there to cash my check.

ROSE (*entering from the house*): Hush all that hollering, man! I know you out here. What they say down there at the Commissioner's office?

TROY: You supposed to come when I call you, woman. Bono'll tell you that. (*To* BONO): Don't Lucille come when you call her?

ROSE: Man, hush your mouth. I ain't no dog . . . talk about "come when you call me."

TROY (*puts his arm around* ROSE): You hear this, Bono? I had me an old dog used to get uppity like that. You say, "C'mere, Blue!" . . . and he just lay there and look at you. End up getting a stick and chasing him away trying to make him come.

ROSE: I ain't studying you and your dog. I remember you used to sing that old song.

TROY (*he sings*):
Hear it ring! Hear it ring!
I had a dog and his name was Blue.

ROSE: Don't nobody wanna hear you sing that old song.

TROY (*sings*):
You know Blue was mighty true.

ROSE: Used to have Cory running around here singing that song.

BONO: Hell, I remember that song myself.

TROY (*sings*):
You know Blue was a good old dog
Blue treed a possum in a hollow log.
That was my daddy's song. My daddy made up that song.

ROSE: I don't care who made it up. Don't nobody wanna hear you sing it.

TROY (*makes a song like calling a dog*): Come here, woman.

ROSE: You come in here carrying on, I reckon they ain't fired you. What they say down there at the Commissioner's office?

TROY: Look here, Rose . . . Mr. Rand called me

into his office today when I got back from talking to them people down there . . . it come from up top . . . he called me in and told me they was making me a driver.

ROSE: Troy, you kidding!

TROY: No I ain't. Ask Bono.

ROSE: Well, that's great, Troy. Now you don't have to hassle them people no more.

(LYONS *enters from the street.*)

TROY: Aw hell, I wasn't looking to see you today. I thought you was in jail. Got it all over the front page of the *Courier* about them raiding Sefus' place . . . where you be hanging out with all them thugs.

LYONS: Hey, Pop . . . that ain't got nothing to do with me. I don't go down there gambling. I go down there to sit in with the band. I ain't got nothing to do with the gambling part. They got some good music down there.

TROY: They got some rogues . . . is what they got.

LYONS: How you been, Mr. Bono? Hi, Rose.

BONO: I see where you playing down at the Crawford Grill tonight.

ROSE: How come you ain't brought Bonnie like I told you. You should have brought Bonnie with you, she ain't been over in a month of Sundays.

LYONS: I was just in the neighborhood . . . thought I'd stop by.

TROY: Here he come . . .

BONO: Your daddy got a promotion on the rubbish. He's gonna be the first colored driver. Ain't got to do nothing but sit up there and read the paper like them white fellows.

LYONS: Hey, Pop . . . if you knew how to read you'd be all right.

BONO: Naw . . . naw . . . you mean if the nigger knew how to *drive* he'd be all right. Been fighting with them people about driving and ain't even got a license. Mr. Rand know you ain't got no driver's license?

TROY: Driving ain't nothing. All you do is point the truck where you want it to go. Driving ain't nothing.

BONO: Do Mr. Rand know you ain't got no driver's license? That's what I'm talking about. I ain't asked if driving was easy. I asked if Mr. Rand know you ain't got no driver's license.

TROY: He ain't got to know. The man ain't got to know my business. Time he find out, I have two or three driver's licenses.

LYONS (*going into his pocket*): Say, look here, Pop . . .

TROY: I knew it was coming. Didn't I tell you, Bono? I know what kind of "Look here, Pop" that was. The nigger fixing to ask me for some money. It's Friday night. It's my payday. All them rogues down there on the avenue . . . the ones that ain't in jail . . . and Lyons is hopping in his shoes to get down there with them.

LYONS: See, Pop . . . if you give somebody else a chance to talk sometime, you'd see that I was fixing to pay you back your ten dollars like I told you. Here . . . I told you I'd pay you when Bonnie got paid.

TROY: Naw . . . you go ahead and keep that ten dollars. Put it in the bank. The next time you feel like you wanna come by here and ask me for something . . . you go on down there and get that.

LYONS: Here's your ten dollars, Pop. I told you I don't want you to give me nothing. I just wanted to borrow ten dollars.

TROY: Naw . . . you go on and keep that for the next time you want to ask me.

LYONS: Come on, Pop . . . here go your ten dollars.

ROSE: Why don't you go on and let the boy pay you back, Troy?

LYONS: Here you go, Rose. If you don't take it I'm gonna have to hear about it for the next six months. (*He hands her the money.*)

ROSE: You can hand yours over here too, Troy.

TROY: You see this, Bono. You see how they do me.

BONO: Yeah, Lucille do me the same way.

(GABRIEL *is heard singing offstage. He enters.*)

GABRIEL: Better get ready for the Judgment! Better get ready for . . . Hey! . . . Hey! . . . There's Troy's boy!

LYONS: How you doing, Uncle Gabe?

GABRIEL: Lyons . . . The King of the Jungle! Rose . . . hey, Rose. Got a flower for you. (*He takes a rose from his pocket.*) Picked it myself. That's the same rose like you is!

ROSE: That's right nice of you, Gabe.

LYONS: What you been doing, Uncle Gabe?

GABRIEL: Oh, I been chasing hellhounds and waiting on the time to tell St. Peter to open the gates.

LYONS: You been chasing helhounds, huh? Well . . . you doing the right thing, Uncle Gabe. Somebody got to chase them.

GABRIEL: Oh, yeah . . . I know it. The devil's

strong. The devil ain't no pushover. Hellhounds snipping at everybody's heels. But I got my trumpet waiting on the judgment time.

LYONS: Waiting on the Battle of Armageddon, huh?

GABRIEL: Ain't gonna be too much of a battle when God get to waving that Judgment sword. But the people's gonna have a hell of a time trying to get into heaven if them gates ain't open.

LYONS (*putting his arm around* GABRIEL): You hear this, Pop. Uncle Gabe, you all right!

GABRIEL (*laughing with* LYONS): Lyons! King of the Jungle.

ROSE: You gonna stay for supper, Gabe. Want me to fix you a plate?

GABRIEL: I'll take a sandwich, Rose. Don't want no plate. Just wanna eat with my hands. I'll take a sandwich.

ROSE: How about you, Lyons? You staying? Got some short ribs cooking.

LYONS: Naw, I won't eat nothing till after we finished playing. (*Pause.*) You ought to come down and listen to me play, Pop.

TROY: I don't like that Chinese music. All that noise.

ROSE: Go on in the house and wash up, Gabe . . . I'll fix you a sandwich.

GABRIEL (*to* LYONS, *as he exits*): Troy's mad at me.

LYONS: What you mad at Uncle Gabe for, Pop?

ROSE: He thinks Troy's mad at him cause he moved over to Miss Pearl's.

TROY: I ain't mad at the man. He can live where he want to live at.

LYONS: What he move over there for? Miss Pearl don't like nobody.

ROSE: She don't mind him none. She treats him real nice. She just don't allow all that singing.

TROY: She don't mind that rent he be paying . . . that's what she don't mind.

ROSE: Troy, I ain't going through that with you no more. He's over there cause he want to have his own place. He can come and go as he please.

TROY: Hell, he could come and go as he please here. I wasn't stopping him. I ain't put no rules on him.

ROSE: It ain't the same thing, Troy. And you know it. (GABRIEL *comes to the door*). Now, that's the last I wanna hear about that. I don't wanna hear nothing else about Gabe and Miss Pearl. And next week . . .

GABRIEL: I'm ready for my sandwich, Rose.

ROSE: And next week . . . when that recruiter come from that school . . . I want you to sign that paper and go on and let Cory play football. Then that'll be the last I have to hear about that.

TROY (*to* ROSE *as she exits into the house*): I ain't thinking about Cory nothing.

LYONS: What . . . Cory got recruited? What school he going to?

TROY: That boy walking around here smelling his piss . . . thinking he's grown. Thinking he's gonna do what he want, irrespective of what I say. Look here, Bono . . . I left the Commissioner's office and went down to the A&P . . . that boy ain't working down there. He lying to me. Telling me he got his job back . . . telling me he working weekends . . . telling me he working after school . . . Mr. Stawicki tell me he ain't working down there at all!

LYONS: Cory just growing up. He's just busting at the seams trying to fill out your shoes.

TROY: I don't care what he's doing. When he get to the point where he wanna disobey me . . . then it's time for him to move on. Bono'll tell you that. I bet he ain't never disobeyed his daddy without paying the consequences.

BONO: I ain't never had a chance. My daddy came on through . . . but I ain't never knew him to see him . . . or what he had on his mind or where he went. Just moving on through. Searching out the New Land. That's what the old folks used to call it. See a fellow moving around from place to place . . . woman to woman . . . called it searching out the New Land. I can't say if he ever found it. I come along, didn't want no kids. Didn't know if I was gonna be in one place long enough to fix on them right as their daddy. I figured I was going searching, too. As it turned out I been hooked up with Lucille near about as long as your daddy been with Rose. Going on sixteen years.

TROY: Sometimes I wish I hadn't known my daddy. He ain't cared nothing about no kids. A kid to him wasn't nothing. All he wanted was for you to learn how to walk so he could start you to working. When it come time for eating . . . he ate first. If there was anything left over, that's what you got. Man would sit down and eat two chickens and give you the wing.

LYONS: You ought to stop that, Pop. Everybody feed their kids. No matter how hard times is . . . everybody care about their kids. Make sure they have something to eat.

TROY: The only thing my daddy cared about was getting them bales of cotton in to Mr. Lubin. That's the only thing that mattered to him. Sometimes I used to wonder why he was living. Wonder why the devil hadn't come and got him. "Get them bales of cotton in to Mr. Lubin" and find out he owe him money . . .

LYONS: He should have just went on and left when he saw he couldn't get nowhere. That's what I would have done.

TROY: How he gonna leave with eleven kids? And where he gonna go? He ain't knew how to do nothing but farm. No, he was trapped and I think he knew it. But I'll say this for him . . . he felt a responsibility toward us. Maybe he ain't treated us the way I felt he should have . . . but without that responsibility he could have walked off and left us . . . made his own way.

BONO: A lot of them did. Back in those days what you talking about . . . they walk out their front door and just take on down one road or another and keep on walking.

LYONS: There you go! That's what I'm talking about.

BONO: Just keep on walking till you come to something else. Ain't you never heard of nobody having the walking blues? Well, that's what you call it when you just take off like that.

TROY: My daddy ain't had them walking blues! What you talking about? He stayed right there with his family. But he was just as evil as he could be. My mama couldn't stand him. Couldn't stand that evilness. She run off when I was about eight. She sneaked off one night after he had gone to sleep. Told me she was coming back for me. I ain't never seen her no more. All his women run off and left him. He wasn't good for nobody.

When my turn come to head out, I was fourteen and got to sniffing around Joe Canewell's daughter. Had us an old mule we called Greyboy. My daddy sent me out to do some plowing and I tied up Greyboy and went to fooling around with Joe Canewell's daughter. We done found us a nice little spot, got real cozy with each other. She about thirteen and we done figured we was grown anyway . . . so we down there enjoying ourselves . . . ain't thinking about nothing. We didn't know Greyboy had got loose and wandered back to the house and my daddy was looking for me. We down there by the creek enjoying ourselves when my daddy come up on us. Surprised us. He had them leather straps off the mule and commenced to whupping me like there was no tomorrow. I jumped up, mad and embarrassed. I was scared of my daddy. When he commenced to whupping on me . . . quite naturally I run to get out of the way. (Pause.)

Now I thought he was mad cause I ain't done my work. But I see where he was chasing me off so he could have the gal for himself. When I see what the matter of it was, I lost all fear of my daddy. Right there is where I become a man . . . at fourteen years of age. (Pause.)

Now it was my turn to run him off. I picked up them same reins that he had used on me. I picked up them reins and commenced to whupping on him. The gal jumped up and run off . . . and when my daddy turned to face me, I could see why the devil had never come to get him . . . cause he was the devil himself. I don't know what happened. When I woke up, I was laying right there by the creek, and Blue . . . this old dog we had . . . was licking my face. I thought I was blind. I couldn't see nothing. Both my eyes were swollen shut. I layed there and cried. I didn't know what I was gonna do. The only thing I knew was the time had come for me to leave my daddy's house. And right there the world suddenly got big. And it was a long time before I could cut it down to where I could handle it.

Part of that cutting down was when I got to the place where I could feel him kicking in my blood and knew that the only thing that separated us was the matter of a few years.

(GABRIEL *enters from the house with a sandwich.*)

LYONS: What you got there, Uncle Gabe?

GABRIEL: Got me a ham sandwich. Rose gave me a ham sandwich.

TROY: I don't know what happened to him. I done lost touch with everybody except Gabriel. But I hope he's dead. I hope he found some peace.

LYONS: That's a heavy story, Pop. I didn't know you left home when you was fourteen.

TROY: And didn't know nothing. The only part of the world I knew was the forty-two acres of Mr. Lubin's land. That's all I knew about life.

LYONS: Fourteen's kinda young to be out on your own. (*Phone rings.*) I don't even think I was ready to be out on my own at fourteen. I don't know what I would have done.

TROY: I got up from the creek and walked on down to Mobile. I was through with farming. Figured I could do better in the city. So I walked the two hundred miles to Mobile.

LYONS: Wait a minute . . . you ain't walked no two hundred miles, Pop. Ain't nobody gonna walk no two hundred miles. You talking about some walking there.

BONO: That's the only way you got anywhere back in them days.

LYONS: Shhh. Damn if I wouldn't have hitched a ride with somebody!

TROY: Who you gonna hitch it with? They ain't had no cars and things like they got now. We talking about 1918.

ROSE (*entering*): What you all out here getting into?

TROY (*to* ROSE): I'm telling Lyons how good he got it. He don't know nothing about this I'm talking.

ROSE: Lyons, that was Bonnie on the phone. She say you supposed to pick her up.

LYONS: Yeah, okay, Rose.

TROY: I walked on down to Mobile and hitched up with some of them fellows that was heading this way. Got up here and found out . . . not only couldn't you get a job . . . you couldn't find no place to live. I thought I was in freedom. Shhh. Colored folks living down there on the riverbanks in whatever kind of shelter they could find for themselves. Right down there under the Brady Street Bridge. Living in shacks made of sticks and tarpaper. Messed around there and went from bad to worse. Started stealing. First it was food. Then I figure, hell, if I steal money I can buy me some food. Buy me some shoes, too! One thing led to another. Met your mama. I was young and anxious to be a man. Met your mama and had you. What I do that for? Now I got to worry about feeding you and her. Got to steal three times as much. Went out one day looking for somebody to rob . . . that's what I was, a robber. I'll tell you the truth. I'm ashamed of it today. But it's the truth. Went to rob this fellow . . . pulled out my knife . . . and he pulled out a gun. Shot me in the chest. It felt just like somebody had taken a hot branding iron and laid it on me. When he shot me I jumped at him with my knife. They told me I killed him and they put me in the penitentiary and locked me up for fifteen years. That's where I met Bono. That's where I learned how to play baseball. Got out that place and your mama had taken you and went on to make life without me. Fifteen years was a long time for her to wait. But that fifteen years cured me of that robbing stuff. Rose'll tell you. She asked me when I met her if I had gotten all that foolishness out of my system. And I told her, "Baby, it's you and baseball all what count with me." You hear me, Bono? I meant it, too. She say, "Which one comes first?" I told her, "Baby, ain't no doubt it's baseball . . . but you stick and get old with me and we'll both outlive this baseball." Am I right, Rose? And it's true.

ROSE: Man, hush your mouth. You ain't said no such thing. Talking about "Baby, you know you'll always be number one with me." That's what you was talking.

TROY: You hear that, Bono. That's why I love her.

BONO: Rose'll keep you straight. You get off the track, she'll straighten you up.

ROSE: Lyons, you better get on up and get Bonnie. She waiting on you.

LYONS: (*gets up to go*): Hey, Pop, why don't you come on down to the Grill and hear me play?

TROY: I ain't going down there. I'm too old to be sitting around in them clubs.

BONO: You got to be good to play down at the Grill.

LYONS: Come on, Pop . . .

TROY: I got to get up in the morning.

LYONS: You ain't got to stay long.

TROY: Naw, I'm gonna get my supper and go on to bed.

LYONS: Well, I got to go. I'll see you again.

TROY: Don't you come around my house on my payday.

ROSE: Pick up the phone and let somebody know you coming. And bring Bonnie with you. You know I'm always glad to see her.

LYONS: Yeah, I'll do that, Rose. You take care now. See you, Pop. See you, Mr. Bono. See you, Uncle Gabe.

GABRIEL: Lyons! King of the Jungle!

(LYONS *exits.*)

TROY: Is supper ready, woman? Me and you got some business to take care of. I'm gonna tear it up, too.

ROSE: Troy, I done told you now!

TROY (*puts his arm around* BONO): Aw hell, woman . . . this is Bono. Bono like family. I done known this nigger since . . . how long I done know you?

BONO: It's been a long time.

TROY: I done known this nigger since Skippy was a pup. Me and him done been through some times.

BONO: You sure right about that.

TROY: Hell, I done know him longer than I known you. And we still standing shoulder to shoulder. Hey, look here, Bono . . . a man can't ask for no more than that. (*Drinks to him.*) I love you, nigger.

BONO: Hell, I love you too . . . but I got to get home see my woman. You got yours in hand. I got to go get mine.

(BONO *starts to exit as* CORY *enters the yard, dressed in his football uniform. He gives* TROY *a hard, uncompromising look.*)

CORY: What you do that for, Pop? (*He throws his helmet down in the direction of* TROY.)

ROSE: What's the matter? Cory . . . what's the matter?

CORY: Papa done went up to the school and told Coach Zellman I can't play football no more. Wouldn't even let me play the game. Told him to tell the recruiter not to come.

ROSE: Troy . . .

TROY: What you Troying me for. Yeah, I did it. And the boy know why I did it.

CORY: Why you wanna do that to me? That was the one chance I had.

ROSE: Ain't nothing wrong with Cory playing football, Troy.

TROY: The boy lied to me. I told the nigger if he wanna play football . . . to keep up his chores and hold down that job at the A&P. That was the conditions. Stopped down there to see Mr. Stawicki . . .

CORY: I can't work after school during the football season, Pop! I tried to tell you that Mr. Stawicki's holding my job for me. You don't never want to listen to nobody. And then you wanna go and do this to me!

TROY: I ain't done nothing to you. You done it to yourself.

CORY: Just cause you didn't have a chance! You just scared I'm gonna be better than you, that's all.

TROY: Come here.

ROSE: Troy . . .

(CORY *reluctantly crosses over to* TROY.)

TROY: All right! See. You done made a mistake.

CORY: I didn't even do nothing!

TROY: I'm gonna tell you what your mistake was. See . . . you swung at the ball and didn't hit it. That's strike one. See, you in the batter's box now. You swung and you missed. That's strike one. Don't you strike out!

(*Lights fade to black.*)

ACT II

Scene I

The following morning. CORY *is at the tree hitting the ball with the bat. He tries to mimic* TROY, *but his swing is awkward, less sure.* ROSE *enters from the house.*

ROSE: Cory, I want you to help me with this cupboard.

CORY: I ain't quitting the team. I don't care what Poppa say.

ROSE: I'll talk to him when he gets back. He had to go see about your Uncle Gabe. The police done arrested him. Say he was disturbing the peace. He'll be back directly. Come on in here and help me clean out the top of this cupboard.

(CORY *exits into the house.* ROSE *sees* TROY *and* BONO *coming down the alley.*)

Troy . . . what they say down there?

TROY: Ain't said nothing. I give them fifty dollars and they let him go. I'll talk to you about it. Where's Cory?

ROSE: He's in there helping me clean out these cupboards.

TROY: Tell him to get his butt out here.

(TROY *and* BONO *go over to the pile of wood.* BONO *picks up the saw and begins sawing.*)

TROY (*to* BONO): All they want is the money. That makes six or seven times I done went down there and got him. See me coming they stick out their *hands.*

BONO: Yeah. I know what you mean. That's all they care about . . . that money. They don't care about what's right. (*Pause.*) Nigger, why you got to go and get some hard wood? You ain't doing nothing but building a little old fence. Get you some soft pine wood. That's all you need.

TROY: I know what I'm doing. This is outside wood. You put pine wood inside the house. Pine wood is inside wood. This here is outside wood. Now you tell me where the fence is gonna be?

BONO: You don't need this wood. You can put it up with pine wood and it'll stand as long as you gonna be here looking at it.

TROY: How you know how long I'm gonna be here, nigger? Hell, I might just live forever. Live longer than old man Horsely.

BONO: That's what Magee used to say.

TROY: Magee's a damn fool. Now you tell me who you ever heard of gonna pull their own teeth with a pair of rusty pliers.

BONO: The old folks . . . my granddaddy used to pull his teeth with pliers. They ain't had no dentists for the colored folks back then.

TROY: Get clean pliers! You understand? Clean pliers! Sterilize them! Besides we ain't living back then. All Magee had to do was walk over to Doc Goldblums.

BONO: I see where you and that Tallahassee gal

. . . that Alberta . . . I see where you all done got tight.

TROY: What do you mean "got tight?"

BONO: I see where you be laughing and joking with her all the time.

TROY: I laughs and jokes with all of them, Bono. You know me.

BONO: That ain't the kind of laughing and joking I'm talking about.

(CORY *enters from the house.*)

CORY: How you doing, Mr. Bono?

TROY: Cory? Get that saw from Bono and cut some wood. He talking about the wood's too hard to cut. Stand back there, Jim, and let that young boy show you how it's done.

BONO: He's sure welcome to it.

(CORY *takes the saw and begins to cut the wood.*)

Whew-e-e! Look at that. Big old strong boy. Look like Joe Louis. Hell, must be getting old the way I'm watching that boy whip through that wood.

CORY: I don't see why Mama want a fence around the yard noways.

TROY: Damn if I know either. What the hell she keeping out with it? She ain't got nothing nobody want.

BONO: Some people build fences to keep people out . . . and other people build fences to keep people in. Rose wants to hold on to you all. She loves you.

TROY: Hell, nigger, I don't need nobody to tell me my wife loves me. Cory . . . go on in the house and see if you can find that other saw.

CORY: Where's it at?

TROY: I said find it! Look for it till you find it!

(CORY *exits into the house.*)

What's that supposed to mean? Wanna keep us in?

BONO: Troy . . . I done known you seem like damn near my whole life. You and Rose both. I done know both of you all for a long time. I remember when you met Rose. When you was hitting them baseball out the park. A lot of them old gals was after you then. You had the pick of the litter. When you picked Rose, I was happy for you. That was the first time I knew you had any sense. I said . . . My man Troy knows what he's doing . . . I'm gonna follow this nigger . . . he might take me somewhere. I been following you, too. I done learned a whole heap of things about life watching you. I done learned how to tell where the shit lies. How to tell it from the alfalfa. You done learned me a lot of things. You showed me how to not

make the same mistakes . . . to take life as it comes along and keep putting one foot in front of the other. (*Pause.*) Rose a good woman, Troy.

TROY: Hell, nigger, I know she a good woman. I been married to her for eighteen years. What you got on your mind, Bono?

BONO: I just say she a good woman. Just like I say anything. I ain't got to have nothing on my mind.

TROY: You just gonna say she a good woman and leave it hanging out there like that? Why you telling me she a good woman?

BONO: She loves you, Troy. Rose loves you.

TROY: You saying I don't measure up. That's what you trying to say. I don't measure up cause I'm seeing this other gal. I know what you trying to say.

BONO: I know what Rose means to you, Troy. I'm just trying to say I don't want to see you mess up.

TROY: Yeah, I appreciate that, Bono. If you was messing around on Lucille I'd be telling you the same thing.

BONO: Well that's all I got to say. I just say that because I love you both.

TROY: Hell, you know me . . . I wasn't out there looking for nothing. You can't find a better woman than Rose. I know that. But seems like this woman just stuck onto me where I can't shake her loose. I done wrestled with it, tried to throw her off me . . . but she just stuck on tighter. Now she's stuck on for good.

BONO: You's in control . . . that's what you tell me all the time. You responsible for what you do.

TROY: I ain't ducking the responsibility of it. As long as it sets right in my heart . . . then I'm okay. Cause that's all I listen to. It'll tell me right from wrong every time. And I ain't talking about doing Rose no bad turn. I love Rose. She done carried me a long ways and I love and respect her for that.

BONO: I know you do. That's why I don't want to see you hurt her. But what you gonna do when she find out? What you got then? If you try to juggle both of them . . . sooner or later you gonna drop one of them. That's common sense.

TROY: Yeah, I hear what you saying, Bono. I been trying to figure a way to work it out.

BONO: Work it out right, Troy. I don't want to be getting all up between you and Rose's business . . . but work it so it come out right.

TROY: Aw hell, I get all up between you and Lucille's business. When you gonna get that woman that refrigerator she been wanting? Don't tell me you ain't got no money now. I know who your banker is. Mellon don't need that money bad as Lucille want that refrigerator. I'll tell you that.

BONO: Tell you what I'll do . . . when you finish building this fence for Rose . . . I'll buy Lucille that refrigerator.

TROY: You done stuck your foot in your mouth now! (TROY *grabs up a board and begins to saw.* BONO *starts to walk out the yard.*) Hey, nigger . . . where you going?

BONO: I'm going home. I know you don't expect me to help you now. I'm protecting my money. I wanna see you put that fence up by yourself. That's what I want to see. You'll be here another six months without me.

TROY: Nigger, you ain't right.

BONO: When it comes to my money . . . I'm right as fireworks on the Fourth of July.

TROY: All right, we gonna see now. You better get out your bankbook.

(BONO *exits, and* TROY *continues to work.* ROSE *enters from the house.*)

ROSE: What they say down there? What's happening with Gabe?

TROY: I went down there and got him out. Cost me fifty dollars. Say he was disturbing the peace. Judge set up a hearing for him in three weeks. Say to show cause why he shouldn't be recommitted.

ROSE: What was he doing that cause them to arrest him?

TROY: Some kids was teasing him and he run them off home. Say he was howling and carrying on. Some folks seen him and called the police. That's all it was.

ROSE: Well, what's you say? What'd you tell the judge?

TROY: Told him I'd look after him. It didn't make no sense to recommit the man. He stuck out his big greasy palm and told me to give him fifty dollars and take him on home.

ROSE: Where's he at now? Where'd he go off to?

TROY: He's gone on about his business. He don't need nobody to hold his hand.

ROSE: Well, I don't know. Seem like that would be the best place for him if they did put him into the hospital. I know what you're gonna say. But that's what I think would be best.

TROY: The man done had his life ruined fighting for what? And they wanna take and lock him up. Let him be free. He don't bother nobody.

ROSE: Well, everybody got their own way of looking at it I guess. Come on and get your lunch. I got a bowl of lima beans and some cornbread in the oven. Come on get something to eat. Ain't no sense you fretting over Gabe.

(ROSE *turns to go into the house.*)

TROY: Rose . . . got something to tell you.

ROSE: Well, come on . . . wait till I get this food on the table.

TROY: Rose! (*She stops and turns around.*) I don't know how to say this. (*Pause.*) I can't explain it none. It just sort of grows on you till it gets out of hand. It starts out like a little bush . . . and the next thing you know it's a whole forest.

ROSE: Troy . . . what is you talking about?

TROY: I'm talking, woman, let me talk. I'm trying to find a way to tell you . . . I'm gonna be a daddy. I'm gonna be somebody's daddy.

ROSE: Troy . . . you're not telling me this? You're gonna be . . . what?

TROY: Rose . . . now . . . see . . .

ROSE: You telling me you gonna be somebody's daddy? You telling your *wife* this?

(GABRIEL *enters from the street. He carries a rose in his hand.*)

GABRIEL: Hey, Troy! Hey, Rose!

ROSE: I have to wait eighteen years to hear something like this.

GABRIEL: Hey, Rose . . . I got a flower for you. (*He hands it to her.*) That's a rose. Same rose like you is.

ROSE: Thanks, Gabe.

GABRIEL: Troy, you ain't mad at me is you? Them bad mens come and put me away. You ain't mad at me is you?

TROY: Naw, Gabe, I ain't mad at you.

ROSE: Eighteen years and you wanna come with this.

GABRIEL (*takes a quarter out of his pocket*): See what I got? Got a brand new quarter.

TROY: Rose . . . it's just . . .

ROSE: Ain't nothing you can say, Troy. Ain't no way of explaining that.

GABRIEL: Fellow that give me this quarter had a whole mess of them. I'm gonna keep this quarter till it stop shining.

ROSE: Gabe, go on in the house there. I got some watermelon in the frigidaire. Go on and get you a piece.

GABRIEL: Say, Rose . . . you know I was chasing hellhounds and them bad mens come and get me and take me away. Troy helped me. He come down there and told them they better let me go before he beat them up. Yeah, he did!

ROSE: You go on and get you a piece of watermelon, Gabe. Them bad mens is gone now.

GABRIEL: Okay, Rose . . . gonna get me some watermelon. The kind with the stripes on it.

(GABRIEL *exits into the house.*)

ROSE: Why, Troy? Why? After all these years to come dragging this in to me now. It don't make no sense at your age. I could have expected this ten or fifteen years ago, but not now.

TROY: Age ain't got nothing to do with it, Rose.

ROSE: I done tried to be everything a wife should be. Everything a wife could be. Been married eighteen years and I got to live to see the day you tell me you been seeing another woman and done fathered a child by her. And you know I ain't never wanted no half nothing in my family. My whole family is half. Everybody got different fathers and mothers . . . my two sisters and my brother. Can't hardly tell who's who. Can't never sit down and talk about Papa and Mama. It's your papa and your mama and my papa and my mama . . .

TROY: Rose . . . stop it now.

ROSE: I ain't never wanted that for none of my children. And now you wanna drag your behind in here and tell me something like this.

TROY: You ought to know. It's time for you to know.

ROSE: Well, I don't want to know, goddamn it!

TROY: I can't just make it go away. It's done now. I can't wish the circumstance of the thing away.

ROSE: And you don't want to either. Maybe you want to wish me and my boy away. Maybe that's what you want? Well, you can't wish us away. I've got eighteen years of my life invested in you. You ought to have stayed upstairs in my bed where you belong.

TROY: Rose . . . now listen to me . . . we can get a handle on this thing. We can talk this out . . . come to an understanding.

ROSE: All of a sudden it's "we." Where was "we" at when you was down there rolling around with some god-forsaken woman? "We" should have come to an understanding before you started making a damn fool of yourself. You're a day late and a dollar short when it comes to an understanding with me.

TROY: It's just . . . She gives me a different idea . . . a different understanding about myself. I can step out of this house and get away from the pressures and problems . . . be a different man. I ain't got to wonder how I'm gonna pay the bills or get the roof fixed. I can just be a part of myself that I ain't never been.

ROSE: What I want to know . . . is do you plan to continue seeing her. That's all you can say to me.

TROY: I can sit up in her house and laugh. Do you understand what I'm saying. I can laugh out loud . . . and it feels good. It reaches all the way down to the bottom of my shoes. (*Pause.*) Rose, I can't give that up.

ROSE: Maybe you ought to go on and stay down there with her . . . if she a better woman than me.

TROY: It ain't about nobody being a better woman or nothing. Rose, you ain't the blame. A man couldn't ask for no woman to be a better wife than you've been. I'm responsible for it. I done locked myself into a pattern trying to take care of you all that I forgot about myself.

ROSE: What the hell was I there for? That was my job, not somebody else's.

TROY: Rose, I done tried all my life to live decent . . . to live a clean . . . hard . . . useful life. I tried to be a good husband to you. In every way I knew how. Maybe I come into the world backwards, I don't know. But . . . you born with two strikes on you before you come to the plate. You got to guard it closely . . . always looking for the curve-ball on the inside corner. You can't afford to let none get past you. You can't afford a call strike. If you going down . . . you going down swinging. Everything lined up against you. What you gonna do. I fooled them, Rose. I bunted. When I found you and Cory and a halfway decent job . . . I was safe. Couldn't nothing touch me. I wasn't gonna strike out no more. I wasn't going back to the penitentiary. I wasn't gonna lay in the streets with a bottle of wine. I was safe. I had me a family. A job. I wasn't gonna get that last strike. I was on first looking for one of them boys to knock me in. To get me home.

ROSE: You should have stayed in my bed, Troy.

TROY: Then when I saw that gal . . . she firmed up my backbone. And I got to thinking that if I tried . . . I just might be able to steal second. Do you understand after eighteen years I wanted to steal second.

ROSE: You should have held me tight. You should have grabbed me and held on.

TROY: I stood on first base for eighteen years and I thought . . . well, goddamn it . . . go on for it!

ROSE: We're not talking about baseball! We're talking about you going off to lay in bed with another woman . . . and then bring it home to me. That's what we're talking about. We ain't talking about no baseball.

TROY: Rose, you're not listening to me. I'm trying the best I can to explain it to you. It's not easy for me to admit that I been standing in the same place for eighteen years.

ROSE: I been standing with you! I been right here with you, Troy. I got a life too. I gave eighteen years of my life to stand in the same spot with you. Don't you think I ever wanted other things? Don't you think I had dreams and hopes? What about my life? What about me. Don't you think it ever crossed my mind to want to know other men? That I wanted to lay up somewhere and forget about my responsibilities? That I wanted someone to make me laugh so I could feel good? You not the only one who's got wants and needs. But I held on to you, Troy. I took all my feelings, my wants and needs, my dreams . . . and I buried them inside you. I planted a seed and watched and prayed over it. I planted myself inside you and waited to bloom. And it didn't take me no eighteen years to find out the soil was hard and rocky and it wasn't never gonna bloom.

But I held on to you, Troy. I held on tighter. You was my husband. I owed you everything I had. Every part of me I could find to give you. And upstairs in that room . . . with the darkness falling in on me . . . I gave everything I had to try and erase the doubt that you wasn't the finest man in the world. And wherever you was going . . . I wanted to be there with you. Cause you was my husband. Cause that's the only way I was gonna survive as your wife. You always talking about what you give . . . and what you don't have to give. But you take, too. You take . . . and don't even know nobody's giving!

(ROSE *turns to exit into the house;* TROY *grabs her arm.*)

TROY: You say I take and don't give!
ROSE: Troy! You're hurting me!
TROY: You say I take and don't give.
ROSE: Troy . . . you're hurting my arm! Let go!
TROY: I done give you everything I got. Don't you tell that lie on me.
ROSE: Troy!
TROY: Don't you tell that lie on me!

(CORY *enters from the house.*)

CORY: Mama!
ROSE: Troy. You're hurting me.
TROY: Don't you tell me about no taking and giving.

(CORY *comes up behind* TROY *and grabs him.* TROY, *surprised, is thrown off balance just as* CORY *throws a glancing blow that catches him on the chest and knocks him down.* TROY *is stunned, as is* CORY.)

ROSE: Troy. Troy. No!

(TROY *gets to his feet and starts at* CORY.)

Troy . . . no. Please! Troy!

(ROSE *pulls on* TROY *to hold him back.* TROY *stops himself.*)

TROY (*to* CORY): All right. That's strike two. You stay away from around me, boy. Don't you strike out. You living with a full count. Don't you strike out.

(TROY *exits out the yard as the lights go down.*)

SCENE II

It is six months later, early afternoon. TROY *enters from the house and starts to exit the yard.* ROSE *enters from the house.*

ROSE: Troy, I want to talk to you.
TROY: All of a sudden, after all this time, you want to talk to me, huh? You ain't wanted to talk to me for months. You ain't wanted to talk to me last night. You ain't wanted no part of me then. What you wanna talk to me about now?
ROSE: Tomorrow's Friday.
TROY: I know what day tomorrow is. You think I don't know tomorrow's Friday? My whole life I ain't done nothing but look to see Friday coming and you got to tell me it's Friday.
ROSE: I want to know if you're coming home.
TROY: I always come home, Rose. You know that. There ain't never been a night I ain't come home.
ROSE: That ain't what I mean . . . and you know it. I want to know if you're coming straight home after work.
TROY: I figure I'd cash my check . . . hang out at Taylors' with the boys . . . maybe play a game of checkers . . .
ROSE: Troy, I can't live like this. I won't live like this. You livin' on borrowed time with me. It's been going on six months now you ain't been coming home.
TROY: I be here every night. Every night of the year. That's 365 days.
ROSE: I want you to come home tomorrow after work.
TROY: Rose . . . I don't mess up my pay. You know that now. I take my pay and I give it to you. I don't have no money but what you give me back. I just want to have a little time to myself . . . a little time to enjoy life.
ROSE: What about me? When's my time to enjoy life?
TROY: I don't know what to tell you, Rose. I'm doing the best I can.

ROSE: You ain't been home from work but time enough to change your clothes and run out . . . and you wanna call that the best you can do?

TROY: I'm going over to the hospital to see Alberta. She went into the hospital this afternoon. Look like she might have the baby early. I won't be gone long.

ROSE: Well, you ought to know. They went over to Miss Pearl's and got Gabe today. She said you told them to go ahead and lock him up.

TROY: I ain't said no such thing. Whoever told you that is telling a lie. Pearl ain't doing nothing but telling a big fat lie.

ROSE: She ain't had to tell me. I read it on the papers.

TROY: I ain't told them nothing of the kind.

ROSE: I saw it right there on the papers.

TROY: What it say, huh?

ROSE: It said you told them to take him.

TROY: Then they screwed that up, just the way they screw up everything. I ain't worried about what they got on the paper.

ROSE: Say the government send part of his check to the hospital and the other part to you.

TROY: I ain't got nothing to do with that if that's the way it works. I ain't made up the rules about how it work.

ROSE: You did Gabe just like you did Cory. You wouldn't sign the paper for Cory . . . but you signed for Gabe. You signed that paper.

(*The telephone is heard ringing inside the house.*)

TROY: I told you I ain't signed nothing, woman! The only thing I signed was the release form. Hell, I can't read, I don't know what they had on that paper! I ain't signed nothing about sending Gabe away.

ROSE: I said send him to the hospital . . . you said let him be free . . . now you done went down there and signed him to the hospital for half his money. You went back on yourself, Troy. You gonna have to answer for that.

TROY: See now . . . you been over there talking to Miss Pearl. She done got mad cause she ain't getting Gabe's rent money. That's all it is. She's liable to say anything.

ROSE: Troy, I seen where you signed the paper.

TROY: You ain't seen nothing I signed. What she doing got papers on my brother anyway? Miss Pearl telling a big fat lie. And I'm gonna tell her about it too! You ain't seen nothing I signed. Say . . . you ain't seen nothing I signed.

(ROSE *exits into the house to answer the telephone. Presently she returns.*)

ROSE: Troy . . . that was the hospital. Alberta had the baby.

TROY: What she have? What is it?

ROSE: It's a girl.

TROY: I better get on down to the hospital to see her.

ROSE: Troy . . .

TROY: Rose . . . I got to go see her now. That's only right . . . what's the matter . . . the baby's all right, ain't it?

ROSE: Alberta died having the baby.

TROY: Died . . . you say she's dead? Alberta's dead?

ROSE: They said they done all they could. They couldn't do nothing for her.

TROY: The baby? How's the baby?

ROSE: They say it's healthy. I wonder who's gonna bury her.

TROY: She had family, Rose. She wasn't living in the world by herself.

ROSE: I know she wasn't living in the world by herself.

TROY: Next thing you gonna want to know if she had any insurance.

ROSE: Troy, you ain't got to talk like that.

TROY: That's the first thing that jumped out your mouth. "Who's gonna bury her?" Like I'm fixing to take on that task for myself.

ROSE: I am your wife. Don't push me away.

TROY: I ain't pushing nobody away. Just give me some space. That's all. Just give me some room to breathe.

(ROSE *exits into the house.* TROY *walks about the yard.*)

TROY (*with a quiet rage that threatens to consume him*): All right . . . Mr. Death. See now . . . I'm gonna tell you what I'm gonna do. I'm gonna take and build me a fence around this yard. See? I'm gonna build me a fence around what belongs to me. And then I want you to stay on the other side. See? You stay over there until you're ready for me. Then you come on. Bring your army. Bring your sickle. Bring your wrestling clothes. I ain't gonna fall down on my vigilance this time. You ain't gonna sneak up on me no more. When you ready for me . . . when the top of your list say Troy Maxson . . . that's when you come around here. You come up and knock on the front door. Ain't nobody else got nothing to do with this. This is between you and me. Man to man. You stay on the other side of that fence until you ready for me. Then you come up and knock on the front door. Anytime you want. I'll be ready for you.

(*The lights go down to black.*)

SCENE III

The lights come up on the porch. It is late evening three days later. ROSE *sits listening to the ball game waiting for* TROY. *The final out of the game is made and* ROSE *switches off the radio.* TROY *enters the yard carrying an infant wrapped in blankets. He stands back from the house and calls.*

    ROSE *enters and stands on the porch. There is a long, awkward silence, the weight of which grows heavier with each passing second.*

TROY: Rose . . . I'm standing here with my daughter in my arms. She ain't but a wee bittie little old thing. She don't know nothing about grownups' business. She innocent . . . and she ain't got no mama.

ROSE: What you telling me for, Troy?

(She turns and exits into the house.)

TROY: Well . . . I guess we'll just sit out here on the porch.

(He sits down on the porch. There is an awkward indelicateness about the way he handles the baby. His largeness engulfs and seems to swallow it. He speaks loud enough for ROSE *to hear.)*

A man's got to do what's right for him. I ain't sorry for nothing I done. It felt right in my heart. (*To the baby*) What you smiling at? Your daddy's a big man. Got these great big old hands. But sometimes he's scared. And right now your daddy's scared cause we sitting out here and ain't got no home. Oh, I been homeless before. I ain't had no little baby with me. But I been homeless. You just be out on the road by your lonesome and you see one of them trains coming and you just kinda go like this . . . (*He sings as a lullaby*)

    Please, Mr. Engineer let a man ride the
      line
    Please, Mr. Engineer let a man ride the
      line
    I ain't got no ticket please let me ride the
      blinds

*(*ROSE *enters from the house.* TROY *hearing her steps behind him, stands and faces her.)*

She's my daughter, Rose. My own flesh and blood. I can't deny her no more than I can deny them boys. (*Pause.*) You and them boys is my family. You and them and this child is all I got in the world. So I guess what I'm saying is . . . I'd appreciate it if you'd help me take care of her.

ROSE: Okay, Troy . . . you're right. I'll take care of your baby for you . . . cause . . . like you say . . . she's innocent . . . and you can't visit the sins of the father upon the child. A motherless child has got a hard time. (*She takes the baby from him.*) From right now . . . this child got a mother. But you a womanless man.

*(*ROSE *turns and exits into the house with the baby. Lights go down to black.)*

SCENE IV

It is two months later. LYONS *enters from the street. He knocks on the door and calls.*

LYONS: Hey, Rose! (*Pause.*) Rose!

ROSE (*from inside the house*): Stop that yelling. You gonna wake up Raynell. I just got her to sleep.

LYONS: I just stopped by to pay Papa this twenty dollars I owe him. Where's Papa at?

ROSE: He should be here in a minute. I'm getting ready to go down to the church. Sit down and wait on him.

LYONS: I got to go pick up Bonnie over her mother's house.

ROSE: Well, sit it down there on the table. He'll get it.

LYONS (*enters the house and sets the money on the table*): Tell Papa I said thanks. I'll see you again.

ROSE: All right, Lyons. We'll see you.

*(*LYONS *starts to exit as* CORY *enters.)*

CORY: Hey, Lyons.

LYONS: What's happening, Cory. Say man, I'm sorry I missed your graduation. You know I had a gig and couldn't get away. Otherwise, I would have been there, man. So what you doing?

CORY: I'm trying to find a job.

LYONS: Yeah I know how that go, man. It's rough out here. Jobs are scarce.

CORY: Yeah, I know.

LYONS: Look here, I got to run. Talk to Papa . . . he know some people. He'll be able to help get you a job. Talk to him . . . see what he say.

CORY: Yeah . . . all right, Lyons.

LYONS: You take care. I'll talk to you soon. We'll find some time to talk.

*(*LYONS *exits the yard.* CORY *wanders over to the tree, picks up the bat and assumes a batting stance. He studies an imaginary pitcher and swings. Dissatisfied with the result, he tries again.* TROY *enters. They eye each other for a beat.* CORY *puts the bat down and exits the yard.*

TROY *starts into the house as* ROSE *exits with* RAYNELL. *She is carrying a cake.*)

TROY: I'm coming in and everybody's going out.

ROSE: I'm taking this cake down to the church for the bake sale. Lyons was by to see you. He stopped by to pay you your twenty dollars. It's laying in there on the table.

TROY (*going into his pocket*): Well . . . here go this money.

ROSE: Put it in there on the table, Troy. I'll get it.

TROY: What time you coming back?

ROSE: Ain't no use you studying me. It don't matter what time I come back.

TROY: I just asked you a question, woman. What's the matter . . . can't I ask you a question?

ROSE: Troy, I don't want to go into it. Your dinner's in there on the stove. All you got to do is heat it up. And don't you be eating the rest of them cakes in there. I'm coming back for them. We having a bake sale at the church tomorrow.

(ROSE *exits the yard.* TROY *sits down on the steps, takes a pint bottle from his pocket, opens it and drinks. He begins to sing.*)

TROY:

> Hear it ring! Hear it ring!
> Had an old dog his name was Blue
> You know Blue was mighty true
> You know Blue as a good old dog
> Blue trees a possum in a hollow log
> You know from that he was a good old dog

(BONO *enters the yard.*)

BONO: Hey, Troy.

TROY: Hey, what's happening, Bono?

BONO: I just thought I'd stop by to see you.

TROY: What you stop by and see me for? You ain't stopped by in a month of Sundays. Hell, I must owe you money or something.

BONO: Since you got your promotion I can't keep up with you. Used to see you every day. Now I don't even know what route you working.

TROY: They keep switching me around. Got me out in Greentree now . . . hauling white folks' garbage.

BONO: Greentree, huh? You lucky, at least you ain't got to be lifting them barrels. Damn if they ain't getting heavier. I'm gonna put in my two years and call it quits.

TROY: I'm thinking about retiring myself.

BONO: You got it easy. You can *drive* for another five years.

TROY: It ain't the same, Bono. It ain't like working the back of the truck. Ain't got nobody to talk to . . . feel like you working by yourself. Naw, I'm thinking about retiring. How's Lucille?

BONO: She all right. Her arthritis get to acting up on her sometime. Saw Rose on my way in. She going down to the church, huh?

TROY: Yeah, she took up going down there. All them preachers looking for somebody to fatten their pockets. (*Pause.*) Got some gin here.

BONO: Naw, thanks. I just stopped by to say hello.

TROY: Hell, nigger . . . you can take a drink. I ain't never known you to say no to a drink. You ain't got to work tomorrow.

BONO: I just stopped by. I'm fixing to go over to Skinner's. We got us a domino game going over his house every Friday.

TROY: Nigger, you can't play no dominoes. I used to whup you four games out of five.

BONO: Well, that learned me. I'm getting better.

TROY: Yeah? Well, that's all right.

BONO: Look here . . . I got to be getting on. Stop by sometime, huh?

TROY: Yeah, I'll do that, Bono. Lucille told Rose you bought her a new refrigerator.

BONO: Yeah, Rose told Lucille you had finally built your fence . . . so I figured we'd call it even.

TROY: I knew you would.

BONO: Yeah . . . okay. I'll be talking to you.

TROY: Yeah, take care, Bono. Good to see you. I'm gonna stop over.

BONO: Yeah. Okay, Troy.

(BONO *exits.* TROY *drinks from the bottle.*)

TROY:

> Old Blue died and I dig his grave
> Let him down with a golden chain
> Every night when I hear old Blue bark
> I know Blue treed a possum in Noah's Ark.
> Hear it ring! Hear it ring!

(CORY *enters the yard. They eye each other for a beat.* TROY *is sitting in the middle of the steps.* CORY *walks over.*)

CORY: I got to get by.

TROY: Say what? What's you say?

CORY: You in my way. I got to get by.

TROY: You got to get by where? This is my house. Bought and paid for. In full. Took me fifteen years. And if you wanna go in my house and I'm sitting on the steps . . . you say excuse me. Like your mama taught you.

CORY: Come on, Pop . . . I got to get by.

(CORY *starts to maneuver his way past* TROY. TROY *grabs his leg and shoves him back.*)

TROY: You just gonna walk over top of me?

CORY: I live here, too!

TROY (*advancing toward him*): You just gonna walk over top of me in my own house?

CORY: I ain't scared of you.

TROY: I ain't asked if you was scared of me. I asked you if you was fixing to walk over top of me in my own house? That's the question. You ain't gonna say excuse me? You just gonna walk over top of me?

CORY: If you wanna put it like that.

TROY: How else am I gonna put it?

CORY: I was walking by you to go into the house cause you sitting on the steps drunk, singing to yourself. You can put it like that.

TROY: Without saying excuse me???

(CORY *doesn't respond.*)

I asked you a question. Without saying excuse me???

CORY: I ain't got to say excuse me to you. You don't count around here no more.

TROY: Oh, I see . . . I don't count around here no more. You ain't got to say excuse me to your daddy. All of a sudden you done got so grown that your daddy don't count around here no more . . . Around here in his own house and yard that he done paid for with the sweat of his brow. You done got so grown to where you gonna take over. You gonna take over my house. Is that right? You gonna wear my pants. You gonna go in there and stretch out on my bed. You ain't got to say excuse me cause I don't count around here no more. Is that right?

CORY: That's right. You always talking this dumb stuff. Now, why don't you just get out my way.

TROY: I guess you got someplace to sleep and something to put in your belly. You got that, huh? You got that? That's what you need. You got that, huh?

CORY: You don't know what I got. You ain't got to worry about what I got.

TROY: You right! You one hundred percent right! I done spent the last seventeen years worrying about what you got. Now it's your turn, see? I'll tell you what to do. You grown . . . we done established that. You a man. Now, let's see you act like one. Turn your behind around and walk out this yard. And when you get out there in the alley . . . you can forget about this house. See? 'Cause this is my house. You go on and be a man and get your own house. You can forget about this. 'Cause this is mine. You go on and get yours 'cause I'm through with doing for you.

CORY: You talking about what you did for me . . . what'd you ever give me?

TROY: Them feet and bones! That pumping heart, nigger! I give you more than anybody else is ever gonna give you.

CORY: You ain't never gave me nothing! You ain't never done nothing but hold me back. Afraid I was gonna be better than you. All you ever did was try and make me scared of you. I used to tremble every time you called my name. Every time I heard your footsteps in the house. Wondering all the time . . . what's Papa gonna say if I do this? . . . What's he gonna say if I do that? . . . What's Papa gonna say if I turn on the radio? And Mama, too . . . she tries . . . but she's scared of you.

TROY: You leave your mama out of this. She ain't got nothing to do with this.

CORY: I don't know how she stands you . . . after what you did to her.

TROY: I told you to leave your mama out of this!

(*He advances toward* CORY.)

CORY: What you gonna do . . . give me a whupping? You can't whup me no more. You're too old. You just an old man.

TROY (*shoves him on his shoulder*): Nigger! That's what you are. You just another nigger on the street to me!

CORY: You crazy! You know that?

TROY: Go on now! You got the devil in you. Get on away from me!

CORY: You just a crazy old man . . . talking about I got the devil in me.

TROY: Yeah, I'm crazy! If you don't get on the other side of that yard . . . I'm gonna show you how crazy I am! Go on . . . get the hell out of my yard.

CORY: It ain't your yard. You took Uncle Gabe's money he got from the army to buy this house and then you put him out.

TROY (*advances on* CORY): Get your black ass out of my yard!

(TROY's *advance backs* CORY *up against the tree.* CORY *grabs up the bat.*)

CORY: I ain't going nowhere! Come on . . . put me out! I ain't scared of you.

TROY: That's my bat!

CORY: Come on!

TROY: Put my bat down!
CORY: Come on, put me out.

(CORY *swings at* TROY, *who backs across the yard.*)

What's the matter? You so bad . . . put me out!

(TROY *advances toward* CORY.)

CORY (*backing up*): Come on! Come on!
TROY: You're gonna have to use it! You wanna draw that bat back on me . . . you're gonna have to use it.
CORY: Come on! . . . Come on!

(CORY *swings the bat at* TROY *a second time. He misses.* TROY *continues to advance toward him.*)

TROY: You're gonna have to kill me! You wanna draw that bat back on me. You're gonna have to kill me.

(CORY, *backed up against the tree, can go no farther.* TROY *taunts him. He sticks out his head and offers him a target.*)

Come on! Come on!

(CORY *is unable to swing the bat.* TROY *grabs it.*)

TROY: Then I'll show you.

(CORY *and* TROY *struggle over the bat. The struggle is fierce and fully engaged.* TROY *ultimately is the stronger, and takes the bat from* CORY *and stands over him ready to swing. He stops himself.*)

Go on and get away from around my house.

(CORY, *stung by his defeat, picks himself up, walks slowly out of the yard and up the alley.*)

CORY: Tell Mama I'll be back for my things.
TROY: They'll be on the other side of that fence.

(CORY *exits.*)

TROY: I can't taste nothing. Helluljah! I can't taste nothing no more. (TROY *assumes a batting posture and begins to taunt Death, the fastball in the outside corner.*) Come on! It's between you and me now! Come on! Anytime you want! Come on! I be ready for you . . . but I ain't gonna be easy.

(*The lights go down on the scene.*)

SCENE V

The time is 1965. The lights come up in the yard. It is the morning of TROY's *funeral. A funeral plaque with a light hangs beside the door. There is a small garden plot off to the side. There is noise and activity in the house as* ROSE, LYONS, *and* BONO *have gathered. The door opens and* RAYNELL, *seven years old, enters dressed in a flannel nightgown. She crosses to the garden and pokes around with a stick.* ROSE *calls from the house.*

ROSE: Raynell!
RAYNELL: Mam?
ROSE: What you doing out there?
RAYNELL: Nothing.

(ROSE *comes to the door.*)

ROSE: Girl, get in here and get dressed. What you doing?
RAYNELL: Seeing if my garden growed.
ROSE: I told you it ain't gonna grow overnight. You got to wait.
RAYNELL: It don't look like it never gonna grow. Dag!
ROSE: I told you a watched pot never boils. Get in here and get dressed.
RAYNELL: This ain't even no pot, Mama.
ROSE: You just have to give it a chance. It'll grow. Now you come on and do what I told you. We got to be getting ready. This ain't no morning to be playing around. You hear me?
RAYNELL: Yes, mam.

(ROSE *exits into the house.* RAYNELL *continues to poke at her garden with a stick.* CORY *enters. He is dressed in a Marine corporal's uniform, and carries a duffel bag. His posture is that of a military man, and his speech has a clipped sternness.*)

CORY (*to* RAYNELL): Hi. (*Pause.*) I bet your name is Raynell.
RAYNELL: Uh huh.
CORY: Is your mama home?

(RAYNELL *runs up on the porch and calls through the screendoor.*)

RAYNELL: Mama . . . there's some man out here. Mama?

(ROSE *comes to the door.*)

ROSE: Cory? Lord have mercy! Look here, you all!

(ROSE *and* CORY *embrace in a tearful reunion as* BONO *and* LYONS *enter from the house dressed in funeral clothes.*)

BONO: Aw, looka here . . .

ROSE: Done got all grown up!

CORY: Don't cry, Mama. What you crying about?

ROSE: I'm just so glad you made it.

CORY: Hey Lyons. How you doing, Mr. Bono.

(LYONS *goes to embrace* CORY.)

LYONS: Look at you, man. Look at you. Don't he look good, Rose? Got them Corporal stripes.

ROSE: What took you so long?

CORY: You know how the Marines are, Mama. They got to get all their paperwork straight before they let you do anything.

ROSE: Well, I'm sure glad you made it. They let Lyons come. Your Uncle Gabe's still in the hospital. They don't know if they gonna let him out or not. I just talked to them a little while ago.

LYONS: A Corporal in the United States Marines.

BONO: Your daddy knew you had it in you. He used to tell me all the time.

LYONS: Don't he look good, Mr. Bono?

BONO: Yeah, he remind me of Troy when I first met him. (*Pause.*) Say, Rose, Lucille's down at the church with the choir. I'm gonna go down and get the pallbearers lined up. I'll be back to get you all.

ROSE: Thanks, Jim.

CORY: See you, Mr. Bono.

LYONS (*with his arm around* RAYNELL): Cory . . . look at Raynell. Ain't she precious? She gonna break a whole lot of hearts.

ROSE: Raynell, come and say hello to your brother. This is your brother, Cory. You remember Cory.

RAYNELL: No, Mam.

CORY: She don't remember me, Mama.

ROSE: Well, we talk about you. She heard us talk about you. (*To* RAYNELL) This is your brother, Cory. Come on and say hello.

RAYNELL: Hi.

CORY: Hi. So you're Raynell. Mama told me a lot about you.

ROSE: You all come on into the house and let me fix you some breakfast. Keep up your strength.

CORY: I ain't hungry, Mama.

LYONS: You can fix me something, Rose. I'll be in there in a minute.

ROSE: Cory, you sure you don't want nothing? I know they ain't feeding you right.

CORY: No, Mama . . . thanks. I don't feel like eating. I'll get something later.

ROSE: Raynell . . . get on upstairs and get that dress on like I told you.

(ROSE *and* RAYNELL *exit into the house.*)

LYONS: So . . . I hear you thinking about getting married.

CORY: Yeah, I done found the right one, Lyons. It's about time.

LYONS: Me and Bonnie been split up about four years now. About the time Papa retired. I guess she just got tired of all them changes I was putting her through. (*Pause.*) I always knew you was gonna make something out yourself. Your head was always in the right direction. So . . . you gonna stay in . . . make it a career . . . put in your twenty years?

CORY: I don't know. I got six already, I think that's enough.

LYONS: Stick with Uncle Sam and retire early. Ain't nothing out here. I guess Rose told you what happened with me. They got me down the workhouse. I thought I was being slick cashing other people's checks.

CORY: How much time you doing?

LYONS: They give me three years. I got that beat now. I ain't got but nine more months. It ain't so bad. You learn to deal with it like anything else. You got to take the crookeds with the straights. That's what Papa used to say. He used to say that when he struck out. I seen him strike out three times in a row . . . and the next time up he hit the ball over the grandstand. Right out there in Homestead Field. He wasn't satisfied hitting in the seats . . . he want to hit it over everything! After the game he had two hundred people standing around waiting to shake his hand. You got to take the crookeds with the straights. Yeah, Papa was something else.

CORY: You still playing?

LYONS: Cory . . . you know I'm gonna do that. There's some fellows down there we got us a band . . . we gonna try and stay together when we get out . . . but yeah, I'm still playing. It still helps me to get out of bed in the morning. As long as it do that I'm gonna be right there playing and trying to make some sense out of it.

ROSE (*calling*): Lyons, I got these eggs in the pan.

LYONS: Let me go on and get these eggs, man. Get ready to go bury Papa. (*Pause.*) How you doing? You doing all right?

(CORY *nods.* LYONS *touches him on the shoulder and they share a moment of silent grief.* LYONS *exits into the house.* CORY *wanders about the yard.* RAYNELL *enters.*)

RAYNELL: Hi.

CORY: Hi.

RAYNELL: Did you used to sleep in my room?

CORY: Yeah . . . that used to be my room.

RAYNELL: That's what Papa call it. "Cory's room." It got your football in the closet.

(ROSE *comes to the door.*)

ROSE: Raynell, get in there and get them good shoes on.

RAYNELL: Mama, can't I wear these? Them other one hurt my feet.

ROSE: Well, they just gonna have to hurt your feet for a while. You ain't said they hurt your feet when you went down to the store and got them.

RAYNELL: They didn't hurt then. My feet done got bigger.

ROSE: Don't you give me no backtalk now. You get in there and get them shoes on. (RAYNELL *exits into the house.*) Ain't too much changed. He still got that piece of rag tied to that tree. He was out here swinging that bat. I was just ready to go back in the house. He swung that bat and then he just fell over. Seem like he swung it and stood there with this grin on his face . . . and then he just fell over. They carried him on down to the hospital, but I knew there wasn't no need . . . why don't you come on in the house?

CORY: Mama . . . I got something to tell you. I don't know how to tell you this . . . but I've got to tell you . . . I'm not going to Papa's funeral.

ROSE: Boy, hush your mouth. That's your daddy you talking about. I don't want hear that kind of talk this morning. I done raised you to come to this? You standing there all healthy and grown talking about you ain't going to your daddy's funeral?

CORY: Mama . . . listen . . .

ROSE: I don't want to hear it, Cory. You just get that thought out of your head.

CORY: I can't drag Papa with me everywhere I go. I've got to say no to him. One time in my life I've got to say no.

ROSE: Don't nobody have to listen to nothing like that. I know you and your daddy ain't seen eye to eye, but I ain't got to listen that that kind of talk this morning. Whatever was between you and your daddy . . . the time has come to put it aside. Just take it and set it over there on the shelf and forget about it. Disrespecting your daddy ain't gonna make you a man, Cory. You got to find a way to come to that on your own. Not going to your daddy's funeral ain't gonna make you a man.

CORY: The whole time I was growing up . . . living in his house . . . Papa was like a shadow that followed you everywhere. It weighed on you and sunk into your flesh. It would wrap around you and lay there until you couldn't tell which one was you anymore. That shadow digging in your flesh. Trying to crawl in. Trying to live through you. Everywhere I looked, Troy Maxson was staring back at me . . . hiding under the bed . . . in the closet. I'm just saying I've got to find a way to get rid of that shadow, Mama.

ROSE: You just like him. You got him in you good.

CORY: Don't tell me that, Mama.

ROSE: You Troy Maxson all over again.

CORY: I don't want to be Troy Maxson. I want to be me.

ROSE: You can't be nobody but who you are, Cory. That shadow wasn't nothing but you growing into yourself. You either got to grow into it or cut it down to fit you. But that's all you got to make life with. That's all you got to measure yourself against that world out there. Your daddy wanted you to be everything he wasn't . . . and at the same time he tried to make you into everything he was. I don't know if he was right or wrong . . . but I do know he meant to do more good than he meant to do harm. He wasn't always right. Sometimes when he touched he bruised. And sometimes when he took me in his arms he cut.

When I first met your daddy I thought . . . Here is a man I can lay down with and make a baby. That's the first thing I thought when I seen him. I was thirty years old and had done seen my share of men. But when he walked up to me and said, "I can dance a waltz that'll make you dizzy," I thought, Rose Lee, here is a man that you can open yourself up to and be filled to bursting. Here is a man that can fill all them empty spaces you been tipping around the edges of. One of them empty spaces was being somebody's mother.

I married your daddy and settled down to cooking his supper and keeping clean sheets on the bed. When your daddy walked through the house he was so big he filled it up. That was my first mistake. Not to make him leave some room for me. For my part in the matter. But at that time I wanted that. I wanted a house that I could sing in. And that's what your daddy gave me. I didn't know to keep up his strength I had to give up little pieces of mine. I did that. I took on his life as mine and mixed up the pieces so that you couldn't hardly tell which was which anymore. It was my choice. It was my life and I didn't have to live it like that. But that's what life offered me in the way of being a woman and I took it. I grabbed hold of it with both hands.

By the time Raynell came into the house, me and your daddy had done lost touch with one another. I didn't want to make my blessing off of nobody's misfortune . . . but I took on to Raynell like she was all them babies I had wanted and never had. (*The phone rings.*) Like I'd been blessed to relive a part of my life. And if the Lord see fit to keep up my strength . . . I'm gonna do her just like your daddy did you . . . I'm gonna give her the best of what's in me.

RAYNELL (*entering, still with her old shoes*): Mama . . . Reverend Tollivier on the phone.

(ROSE *exits into the house.*)

RAYNELL: Hi.
CORY: Hi.
RAYNELL: You in the Army or the Marines?
CORY: Marines.
RAYNELL: Papa said it was the Army. Did you know Blue?
CORY: Blue? Who's Blue?
RAYNELL: Papa's dog what he sing about all the time.

CORY (*singing*):
Hear it ring! Hear it ring!
I had a dog his name was Blue
You know Blue was mighty true
You know Blue was a good old dog
Blue treed a possum in a hollow log
You know from that he was a good old dog.
Hear it ring! Hear it ring!

(RAYNELL *joins in singing*)

CORY *and* RAYNELL:
Blue treed a possum out on a limb
Blue looked at me and I looked at him
Grabbed that possum and put him in a sack
Blue stayed there till I came back
Old Blue's feets was big and round
Never allowed a possum to touch the ground.

Old Blue died and I dug his grave
I dug his grave with a silver spade
Let him down with a golden chain
And every night I call his name
Go on Blue, you good dog you
Go on Blue, you good dog you.

RAYNELL:
Blue laid down and died like a man
Blue laid down and died . . .

BOTH:
Blue laid down and died like a man

Now he's treeing possums in the Promised Land
I'm gonna tell you this to let you know
Blue's gone where the good dogs go
When I hear old Blue bark
When I hear old Blue bark
Blue treed a possum in Noah's Ark
Blue treed a possum in Noah's Ark.

(ROSE *comes to the screendoor.*)

ROSE: Cory, we gonna be ready to go in a minute.
CORY (*to* RAYNELL): You go on in the house and change them shoes like Mama told you so we can go to Papa's funeral.
RAYNELL: Okay, I'll be back.

(RAYNELL *exits into the house.* CORY *gets up and crosses over to the tree.* ROSE *stands in the screendoor watching him.* GABRIEL *enters from the alley.*)

GABRIEL (*calling*): Hey, Rose!
ROSE: Gabe?
GABRIEL: I'm here, Rose. Hey Rose, I'm here!

(ROSE *enters from the house.*)

ROSE: Lord . . . Look here, Lyons!
LYONS: See, I told you, Rose . . . I told you they'd let him come.
CORY: How you doing, Uncle Gabe?
LYONS: How you doing, Uncle Gabe?
GABRIEL: Hey, Rose. It's time. It's time to tell St. Peter to open the gates. Troy, you ready? You ready, Troy. I'm gonna tell St. Peter to open the gates. You get ready now.

(GABRIEL, *with great fanfare, braces himself to blow. The trumpet is without a mouthpiece. He puts the end of it into his mouth and blows with great force, like a man who has been waiting some twenty-odd years for this single moment. No sound comes out of the trumpet. He braces himself and blows again with the same result. A third time he blows. There is a weight of impossible description that falls away and leaves him bare and exposed to a frightful realization. It is a trauma that a sane and normal mind would be unable to withstand. He begins to dance. A slow, strange dance, eerie and life-giving. A dance of atavistic signature and ritual.* LYONS *attempts to embrace him.* GABRIEL *pushes* LYONS *away. He begins to howl in what is an attempt at song, or perhaps a song turning back*

into itself in an attempt at speech. He finishes his   That's the way that go!
dance and the gates of heaven stand open as wide
as God's closet.)   BLACKOUT

COMMENTARY

Something about the history of blacks in the American theater has already been said in our commentary on *Dutchman* (page 628), but it is worth repeating here that in the 1940s and 1950s black playwrights faced the difficult problem of deciding what audience they were writing for—an audience of blacks or of whites? The difficulty was compounded by the fact that although there were a number of black theater groups—for example, the American Negro Theatre (founded by blacks in 1940)—there was not a large enough black theater-going public to make such groups commercially successful. In fact, although the original ideal of the American Negro Theatre was "to portray Negro life . . . honestly," within a few years it was doing plays by white writers, such as Thornton Wilder's *Our Town* (not only by a white but about whites) and Philip Yordan's *Anna Lucasta* (by a white, and originally about a Polish working-class family, but transformed into a play about a black family). Further, the aim of such groups usually was in large measure to employ black actors and theater technicians; some of the most talented of these, including Harry Belafonte, Sidney Poitier, and Ruby Dee, then went on to enter the mainstream of white theater, on Broadway or—a short step—in Hollywood. Meanwhile, such writers as James Baldwin and Lorraine Hansberry, though writing about black life, wrote plays that were directed at least as much at whites as at blacks. That is, their plays were in large measure attempts to force whites to look at what they had done to blacks.

In the mid-1960s, however, the most talented black dramatists, including LeRoi Jones (Imamu Amiri Baraka) and Ed Bullins, largely turned their backs on white audiences and in effect wrote plays aimed at showing blacks that *they*— not their white oppressors—must change, must cease to accept the myths that whites had created. Today, however, strongly revolutionary plays by and about blacks have difficulty getting a hearing. Instead, the newest black writers seem to be concerned less with raising the consciousness of blacks than with depicting black life and with letting both blacks and whites respond aesthetically rather than politically. Baraka has attributed the change to a desire by many blacks to become assimilated in today's society, and surely there is much to his view. One might also say, however, that black dramatists may for other reasons have come to assume that the business of drama is not to preach but to show, and that a profound, honest depiction—in a traditional, realistic dramatic form—of things as they are, or in Wilson's play, things as they were in the 1950s—will touch audiences whatever their color. "Part of the reason I wrote *Fences*," Wilson has said, "was to illuminate that generation, which shielded its children from all of the indignities they went through."

This is not to say, of course, that *Fences* is a play about people who just happen to be black. The Polish family of *Anna Lucasta* could easily be converted to a black family (though perhaps blacks may feel that there is something unconvincing about this family), but Troy Maxson's family cannot be whitewashed. The play is very much about persons who are what they are because they are blacks living in an unjust society run by whites. We are not allowed to forget this. Troy is a baseball player who was too old to join a white team when the major leagues began to hire blacks. For Troy's friend, Bono, "Troy just came along too early"; but Troy pungently replies, "There ought not never have been no time called too early." Blacks of Troy's day were expected to subscribe to American ideals—for instance, to serve in the army in time of war—but they were also expected to sit in the back of the bus and to accept the fact that they were barred from decent jobs. Wilson shows us the scars that such treatment left. Troy is no paragon. Although he has a deep sense of responsibility to his family, his behavior toward them is deeply flawed: he oppresses his son Cory, he is unfaithful to his wife, Rose, and he exploits his brother Gabriel.

Wilson, as we have seen, calls attention to racism in baseball, and he indicates that Troy turned to crime because he could not earn money. But Wilson does not allow *Fences* to become a prolonged protest against white oppression—though one can never quite forget that Troy insists on a high personal ideal in a world that has cheated him. The interest in the play is in Troy as a human being, or, rather, in all of the characters as human beings rather than as representatives of white victimization. As Troy sees it, by preventing Cory from engaging in athletics—the career that frustrated Troy—he is helping rather than oppressing Cory: "I don't want him to be like me. I want him to move as far from me as he can." But Wilson also makes it clear that Troy has other (very human) motives, of which Troy perhaps is unaware.

A Note on the Word *Black*: The play is set in 1957 and (the last scene) 1965, before *black* was the word commonly applied to persons of African descent. The blacks in the play speak of "coloreds" and of "niggers." *Black* did not become the preferred word until the late 1960s. For instance, the question was still open in November 1967, when *Ebony* magazine asked its (black, chiefly middle-class) readers whether the word *Negro* should be replaced by *black* or *Afro-American*. The results of polls at that time chiefly suggested that *Afro-American* was the preferred choice.

TOPICS FOR DISCUSSION

1. What do you think Bono means when he says, early in Act II (page 719), "Some people build fences to keep people out . . . and some people build fences to keep people in"? Why is the play called *Fences*? What has fenced Troy in? What is Troy

fencing in? (Take account of Troy's last speech in Act II, Scene ii, but do not limit your discussion to this speech.)

2. What do you think Troy's reasons are—conscious and unconscious—for not wanting Cory to play football at college?

3. Compare and contrast Cory and Lyons. Consider, too, in what ways they resemble Troy, and in what ways they differ from him.

4. In what ways is Troy like his father, and in what ways unlike?

5. What do you make out of the prominence given to the song about Blue?

6. There is a good deal of anger in the play, but there is also humor. Which passages do you find humorous, and why?

7. Characterize Rose Maxson.

8. Some scenes begin by specifying that "the lights come up." Others do not, presumably beginning with an illuminated stage. All scenes except the last one end with the lights going down to blackness. Explain Wilson's use of lighting.

ESSAYS

The Poetics

Aristotle

Translated by L. J. Potts

It is no exaggeration to say that the history of tragic criticism is a series of footnotes to Aristotle. In a fragmentary treatise usually called the *Poetics*, Aristotle (384–322 B.C.) raises almost all the points that have subsequently been argued, such as the nature of the hero, the emotional effect on the spectator, the coherence of the plot. Whether or not he gave the right answers, it has seemed for more than two thousand years that he asked the right questions.

[ART IS IMITATION]

Let us talk of the art of poetry as a whole, and its different species with the particular force of each of them; how the fables must be put together if the poetry is to be well formed; also what are its elements and their different qualities; and all other matters pertaining to the subject.

To begin in the proper order, at the beginning. The making of epics and of tragedies, and also comedy, and the art of the dithyramb, and most flute and lyre art, all have this in common, that they are imitations. But they differ from one another in three respects: the different kinds of medium in which they imitate, the different objects they imitate, and the different manner in which they imitate (when it does differ). . . . When the imitators imitate the doings of people, the people in the imitation must be either high or low; the characters almost always follow this line exclusively, for all men differ in character according to their degree of goodness or badness. They must therefore be either above our

Reprinted from *Aristotle on the Art of Fiction* by L. J. Potts by permission of Cambridge University Press. © 1953 by Cambridge University Press.

norm, or below it, or normal; as, in painting, Polygnōtus depicted superior, Pauson inferior, and Dionysius normal, types. It is clear that each variant of imitation that I have mentioned will have these differences, and as the object imitated varies in this way so the works will differ. Even in the ballet, and in flute and lyre music, these dissimilarities can occur; and in the art that uses prose, or verse without music. . . . This is the difference that marks tragedy out from comedy; comedy is inclined to imitate persons below the level of our world, tragedy persons above it.

[ORIGINS OF POETRY]

There seem to be two causes that gave rise to poetry in general, and they are natural. The impulse to imitate is inherent in man from his childhood; he is distinguished among the animals by being the most imitative of them, and he takes the first steps of his education by imitating. Everyone's enjoyment of imitation is also inborn. What happens with works of art demonstrates this: though a thing itself is disagreeable to look at, we enjoy contemplating the most accurate representations of it—for instance, figures of the most despicable animals, or of human corpses. The reason for this lies in another fact: learning is a great pleasure, not only to philosophers but likewise to everyone else, however limited his gift for it may be. He enjoys looking at these representations, because in the act of studying them he is learning—identifying the object by an inference (for instance, recognizing who is the original of a portrait); since, if he happens not to have already seen the object depicted, it will not be the imitation as such that is giving him pleasure, but the finish of the workmanship, or the colouring, or some such other cause.

And just as imitation is natural to us, so also are music and rhythm (metres, clearly, are constituent parts of rhythms). Thus, from spontaneous beginnings, mankind developed poetry by a series of mostly minute changes out of these improvisations.

[THE ELEMENTS OF TRAGEDY]

Let us now discuss tragedy, having first picked up from what has been said the definition of its essence that has so far emerged. Tragedy, then, is an imitation of an action of high importance, complete and of some amplitude; in language enhanced by distinct and varying beauties; acted not narrated; by means of pity and fear effecting its purgation of these emotions. By the beauties enhancing the language I mean rhythm and melody; by "distinct and varying" I mean that some are produced by metre alone, and others at another time by melody.

Now since the imitating is done by actors, it would follow of necessity that one element in a tragedy must be the *Mise en scène*. Others are Melody and Language, for these are the media in which the imitating is done. By Language, I mean the component parts of the verse, whereas Melody has an entirely sensuous effect. Again, since the object imitated is an action, and doings are done by persons, whose individuality will be determined by

their Character and their Thought (for these are the factors we have in mind when we define the quality of their doings), it follows that there are two natural causes of these doings, Thought and Character; and these causes determine the good or ill fortune of everyone. But the Fable is the imitation of the action; and by the Fable I mean the whole structure of the incidents. By Character I mean the factor that enables us to define the particular quality of the people involved in the doings; and Thought is shown in everything they say when they are demonstrating a fact or disclosing an opinion. There are therefore necessarily six elements in every tragedy, which give it its quality; and they are the Fable, Character, Language, Thought, the *Mise en scène*, and Melody. Two of these are the media in which the imitating is done, one is the manner of imitation, and three are its objects; there is no other element besides these. Numerous poets have turned these essential components to account; all of them are always present—the *Mise en scène*, Character, the Fable, Language, Melody, and Thought.

The chief of these is the plotting of the incidents; for tragedy is an imitation not of men but of doings, life, happiness; unhappiness is located in doings, and our end is a certain kind of doing, not a personal quality; it is their characters that give men their quality, but their doings that make them happy or the opposite. So it is not the purpose of the actors to imitate character, but they include character as a factor in the doings. Thus it is the incidents (that is to say the Fable) that are the end for which tragedy exists; and the end is more important than anything else. Also, without an action there could not be a tragedy, but without Character there could. (In fact, the tragedies of most of the moderns are non-moral, and there are many non-moral poets of all periods; this also applies to the paintings of Zeuxis, if he is compared with Polygnōtus, for whereas Polygnōtus is a good portrayer of character the painting of Zeuxis leaves it out.) Again, if any one strings together moral speeches with the language and thought well worked out, he will be doing what is the business of tragedy; but it will be done much better by a tragedy that handles these elements more weakly, but has a fable with the incidents connected by a plot. Further, the chief means by which tragedy moves us, Irony of events and Disclosure, are elements in the Fable. A pointer in the same direction is that beginners in the art of poetry are able to get the language and characterization right before they can plot their incidents, and so were almost all the earliest poets.

So the source and as it were soul of tragedy is the Fable; and Character comes next. For, to instance a parallel from the art of painting, the most beautiful colours splashed on anyhow would not be as pleasing as a recognizable picture in black and white. Tragedy is an imitation of an action, and it is chiefly for this reason that it imitates the persons involved.

Third comes Thought: that is, the ability to say what circumstances allow and what is appropriate to them. It is the part played by social morality and rhetoric in making the dialogue: the old poets made their characters talk like men of the world, whereas our contemporaries make them talk like public speakers. Character is what shows a man's disposition—the kind of things he chooses or rejects when his choice is not obvious. Accordingly those speeches where the speaker shows no preferences or aversions whatever are non-moral. Thought, on the other hand, is shown in demonstrating a matter of fact or disclosing a significant opinion.

Fourth comes the Language. By Language I mean, as has already been said, words used semantically. It has the same force in verse as in prose.

Of the remaining elements, Melody is the chief of the enhancing beauties. The *Mise en scène* can excite emotion, but it is the crudest element and least akin to the art of poetry; for the force of tragedy exists even without stage and actors; besides, the fitting out of a *Mise en scène* belongs more to the wardrobe-master's art than to the poet's.

[THE TRAGIC FABLE]

So much for analysis. Now let us discuss in what sort of way the incidents should be plotted, since that is the first and chief consideration in tragedy. Our data are that tragedy is an imitation of a whole and complete action of some amplitude (a thing can be whole and yet quite lacking in amplitude). Now a whole is that which has a beginning, a middle, and an end. A beginning is that which does not itself necessarily follow anything else, but which leads naturally to another event or development; an end is the opposite, that which itself naturally (either of necessity or most commonly) follows something else, but nothing else comes after it; and a middle is that which itself follows something else and is followed by another thing. So, well-plotted fables must not begin or end casually, but must follow the pattern here described.

But, besides this, a picture, or any other composite object, if it is to be beautiful, must not only have its parts properly arranged, but be of an appropriate size; for beauty depends on size and structure. Accordingly, a minute picture cannot be beautiful (for when our vision has almost lost its sense of time it becomes confused); nor can an immense one (for we cannot take it all in together, and so our vision loses its unity and wholeness)— imagine a picture a thousand miles long! So, just as there is a proper size for bodies and pictures (a size that can be well surveyed), there is also a proper amplitude for fables (what can be kept well in one's mind). The length of the performance on the stage has nothing to do with art; if a hundred tragedies had to be produced, the length of the production would be settled by the clock, as the story goes that another kind of performance once was. But as to amplitude, the invariable rule dictated by the nature of the action is the fuller the more beautiful so long as the outline remains clear; and for a simple rule of size, the number of happenings that will make a chain of probability (or necessity) to change a given situation from misfortune to good fortune or from good fortune to misfortune is the minimum.

[UNITY]

Unity in a fable does not mean, as some think, that it has one man for its subject. To any one man many things happen—an infinite number—and some of them do not make any sort of unity; and in the same way one man has many doings which cannot be made into a unit of action. . . . Accordingly, just as in the other imitative arts the object of each imitation is a unit, so, since the fable is an imitation of an action, that action must be a complete unit, and the events of which it is made up must be so plotted that if any of these elements is moved or removed the whole is altered and upset. For when a thing can be included or not included without making any noticeable difference, that thing is no part of the whole.

[PROBABILITY]

From what has been said it is also clear that it is not the poet's business to tell what has happened, but the kind of things that would happen—what is possible according to probability or necessity. The difference between the historian and the poet is not the difference between writing in verse or prose; the work of Herodotus could be put into verse, and it would be just as much a history in verse as it is in prose. The difference is that the one tells what has happened, and the other the kind of things that would happen. It follows therefore that poetry is more philosophical and of higher value than history; for poetry unifies more, whereas history aggregates. To unify is to make a man of a certain description say or do the things that suit him, probably or necessarily, in the circumstances (this is the point of the descriptive proper names in poetry); what Alcibiades did or what happened to him is an aggregation. In comedy this has now become clear. They first plot the fable on a base of probabilities, and then find imaginary names for the people—unlike the lampooners, whose work was an aggregation of personalities. But in tragedy they keep to the names of real people. This is because possibility depends on conviction; if a thing has not happened we are not yet convinced that it is possible, but if it has happened it is clearly possible, for it would not have happened if it were impossible. Even tragedies, however, sometimes have all their persons fictitious except for one or two known names; and sometimes they have not a single known name, as in the *Anthos* of Agathon, in which both the events and the names are equally fictitious, without in the least reducing the delight it gives. It is not, therefore, requisite at all costs to keep to the traditional fables from which our tragedies draw their subject-matter. It would be absurd to insist on that, since even the known legends are known only to a few, and yet the delight is shared by every one. . . .

[SIMPLE AND COMPLEX FABLES]

The action imitated must contain incidents that evoke fear and pity, besides being a complete action; but this effect is accentuated when these incidents occur logically as well as unexpectedly, which will be more sensational than if they happen arbitrarily, by chance. Even when events are accidental the sensation is greater if they appear to have a purpose, as when the statue of Mitys at Argos killed the man who had caused his death, by falling on him at a public entertainment. Such things appear not to have happened blindly. Inevitably, therefore, plots of this sort are finer.

Some fables are simple, others complex: for the obvious reason that the original actions imitated by the fables are the one or the other. By a simple action I mean one that leads to the catastrophe in the way we have laid down, directly and singly, without Irony of events or Disclosure.

An action is complex when the catastrophe involves Disclosure, or Irony, or both. But these complications should develop out of the very structure of the fable, so that they fit what has gone before, either necessarily or probably. To happen after something is by no means the same as to happen because of it.

[IRONY]

Irony is a reversal in the course of events, of the kind specified, and, as I say, in accordance with probability or necessity. Thus in the *Oedipus* the arrival of the messenger, which was expected to cheer Oedipus up by releasing him from his fear about his mother, did the opposite by showing him who he was; and in the *Lynceus* [Abas], who was awaiting sentence of death, was acquitted, whereas his prosecutor Dānaüs was killed, and all this arose out of what had happened previously.

A Disclosure, as the term indicates, is a change from ignorance to knowledge; if the people are marked out for good fortune it leads to affection, if for misfortune, to enmity. Disclosure produces its finest effect when it is connected with Irony, as the disclosure in the *Oedipus* is. There are indeed other sorts of Disclosure: the process I have described can even apply to inanimate objects of no significance, and mistakes about what a man has done or not done can be cleared up. But the sort I have specified is more a part of the fable and of the action than any other sort; for this coupling of Irony and Disclosure will carry with it pity or fear, which we have assumed to be the nature of the doings tragedy imitates; and further, such doings will constitute good or ill fortune. Assuming then that it is a disclosure of the identity of persons, it may be of one person only, to the other, when the former knows who the latter is; or sometimes both have to be disclosed—for instance, the sending of the letter led Orestes to the discovery of Iphigeneia, and there had to be another disclosure to make him known to her.

This then is the subject-matter of two elements in the Fable, Irony and Disclosure. A third element is the Crisis of feeling. Irony and Disclosure have been defined; the Crisis of feeling is a harmful or painful experience, such as deaths in public, violent pain, physical injuries, and everything of that sort.

[THE TRAGIC PATTERN]

Following the proper order, the next subject to discuss after this would be: What one should aim at and beware of in plotting fables; that is to say, What will produce the tragic effect. Since, then, tragedy, to be at its finest, requires a complex, not a simple, structure, and its structure should also imitate fearful and pitiful events (for that is the peculiarity of this sort of imitation), it is clear: first, that decent people must not be shown passing from good fortune to misfortune (for that is not fearful or pitiful but disgusting); again, vicious people must not be shown passing from misfortune to good fortune (for that is the most untragic situation possible—it has none of the requisites, it is neither humane, nor pitiful, nor fearful); nor again should an utterly evil man fall from good fortune into misfortune (for though a plot of that kind would be humane, it would not induce pity or fear—pity is induced by undeserved misfortune, and fear by the misfortunes of normal people, so that this situation will be neither pitiful nor fearful). So we are left with the man between these extremes: that is to say, the kind of man who neither is distinguished for excellence and virtue, nor comes to grief on account of baseness and vice, but on account of some error; a man of great reputation and prosperity, like Oedipus and Thyestes and conspicuous people of such families as theirs. So, to be well informed, a fable must be single rather than (as some say) double—there must be no change from misfortune to good fortune, but only the opposite, from good fortune to misfortune; the cause must not be vice, but a great error; and the man must be either of the type specified or better, rather than worse. This is borne out by the practice of poets; at first they picked a fable at random and made an inventory of its contents, but now the finest tragedies are plotted, and concern a few families—for example, the tragedies about Alcmeon, Oedipus, Orestes, Mĕlĕăger, Thyestes, Tĕlĕphus, and any others whose lives were attended by terrible experiences or doings.

This is the plot that will produce the technically finest tragedy. Those critics are therefore wrong who censure Euripides on this very ground—because he does this in his tragedies, and many of them end in misfortune; for it is, as I have said, the right thing to do. This is clearly demonstrated on the stage in the competitions, where such plays, if they succeed, are the most tragic, and Euripides, even if he is inefficient in every other respect, still shows himself the most tragic of our poets. The next best plot, which is said by some people to be the best, is the tragedy with a double plot, like the *Odyssey*, ending in one way for the better people and in the opposite way for the worse. But it is the weakness of theatrical performances that gives priority to this kind; when poets write what the audience would like to happen, they are in leading strings. This is not the pleasure proper to

tragedy, but rather to comedy, where the greatest enemies in the fable, say Orestes and Aegisthus, make friends and go off at the end, and nobody is killed by anybody.

[THE TRAGIC EMOTIONS]

The pity and fear can be brought about by the *Mise en scène*; but they can also come from the mere plotting of the incidents, which is preferable, and better poetry. For, without seeing anything, the fable ought to have been so plotted that if one heard the bare facts, the chain of circumstances would make one shudder and pity. That would happen to anyone who heard the fable of the *Oedipus*. To produce this effect by the *Mise en scène* is less artistic and puts one at the mercy of the technician; and those who use it not to frighten but merely to startle have lost touch with tragedy altogether. We should not try to get all sorts of pleasure from tragedy, but the particular tragic pleasure. And clearly, since this pleasure coming from pity and fear has to be produced by imitation, it is by his handling of the incidents that the poet must create it.

Let us, then, take next the kind of circumstances that seem terrible or lamentable. Now, doings of that kind must be between friends, or enemies, or neither. If an enemy injures an enemy, there is no pity either beforehand or at the time, except on account of the bare fact; nor is there if they are neutral; but when sufferings are engendered among the affections—for example, if murder is done or planned, or some similar outrage is committed, by brother on brother, or son on father, or mother on son, or son on mother— that is the thing to aim at.

Though it is not permissible to ruin the traditional fables—I mean, such as the killing of Clytemnestra by Orestes, or Erīphўle by Alcmeon—the poet should use his own invention to refine on what has been handed down to him. Let me explain more clearly what I mean by "refine." The action may take place, as the old poets used to make it, with the knowledge and understanding of the participants; this was how Euripides made Medea kill her children. Or they may do it, but in ignorance of the horror of the deed, and then afterwards discover the tie of affection, like the Oedipus of Sophocles; his act was outside the play, but there are examples where it is inside the tragedy itself—Alcmeon in the play by Astydămas, or Tēlĕgōnus in *The Wounded Odysseus*. Besides these, there is a third possibility: when a man is about to do some fatal act in ignorance, but is enlightened before he does it. These are the only possible alternatives. One must either act or not act, and either know or not know. Of these alternatives, to know, and to be about to act, and then not to act, is thoroughly bad—it is disgusting without being tragic, for there is no emotional crisis; accordingly poets only rarely create such situations, as in the *Antigone*, when Haemon fails to kill Creon. Next in order is to act; and if the deed is done in ignorance and its nature is disclosed afterwards, so much the better—there is no bad taste in it, and the revelation is overpowering. But the last is best; I mean, like Mĕrŏpe in the *Cresphontes*, intending to kill her son, but recognizing him and not killing him; and the brother and sister in the *Iphigeneia*; and in the *Helle*, the son recognizing his mother just as he was going to betray her.—This is the reason for what was mentioned earlier: that the subject-matter of our tragedies is drawn from a few families. In their search for matter they discovered this recipe in the fables, not by cunning but by luck. So they are driven to have recourse to those families where such emotional crises have occurred. . . .

[CHARACTER]

And in the characterization, as in the plotting of the incidents, the aim should always be either necessity or probability: so that they say or do such things as it is necessary or probable that they would, being what they are; and that for this to follow that is either necessary or probable. . . . As for extravagant incidents, there should be none in the story, or if there are they should be kept outside the tragedy, as is the one in the *Oedipus* of Sophocles.

Since tragedy is an imitation of people above the normal, we must be like good portrait-painters, who follow the original model closely, but refine on it; in the same way the poet, in imitating people whose character is choleric or phlegmatic, and so forth, must keep them as they are and at the same time make them attractive. So Homer made Achilles noble, as well as a pattern of obstinacy. . . .

[CHORUS]

Treat the chorus as though it were one of the actors; it should be an organic part of the play and reinforce it, not as it is in Euripedes, but as in Sophocles. In their successors the songs belong no more to the fable than to that of any other tragedy. This has led to the insertion of borrowed lyrics, an innovation for which Agathon was responsible.

Tragedy and the Common Man

Arthur Miller

Arthur Miller's "Tragedy and the Common Man" was written while his *Death of a Salesman* was running on Broadway. Implicitly a defense of his play, the essay's assertions about the nature of the tragic hero have implications for other plays about middle-class figures and even for earlier tragedies with heroes of high rank.

In this age few tragedies are written. It has often been held that the lack is due to a paucity of heroes among us, or else that modern man has had the blood drawn out of his organs of belief by the skepticism of science, and the heroic attack on life cannot feed on an attitude of reserve and circumspection. For one reason or another, we are often held to be below tragedy—or tragedy above us. The inevitable conclusion is, of course, that the tragic mode is archaic, fit only for the very highly placed, the kings or the kingly, and where this admission is not made in so many words it is most often implied.

I believe that the common man is as apt a subject for tragedy in its highest sense as kings were. On the face of it this ought to be obvious in the light of modern psychiatry, which bases its analysis upon classific formulations, such as the Oedipus and Orestes complexes, for instance, which were enacted by royal beings, but which apply to everyone in similar emotional situations.

More simply, when the question of tragedy in art is not at issue, we never hesitate to attribute to the well-placed and the exalted the very same mental processes as the lowly.

And finally, if the exaltation of tragic action were truly a property of the high-bred character alone, it is inconceivable that the mass of mankind should cherish tragedy above all other forms, let alone be capable of understanding it.

As a general rule, to which there may be exceptions unknown to me, I think the tragic feeling is evoked in us when we are in the presence of a character who is ready to lay down his life, if need be, to secure one thing—his sense of personal dignity. From Orestes to Hamlet, Medea to Macbeth, the underlying struggle is that of the individual attempting to gain his "rightful" position in his society.

Sometimes he is one who has been displaced from it, sometimes one who seeks to attain it for the first time, but the fateful wound from which the inevitable events spiral is the wound of indignity, and its dominant force is indignation. Tragedy, then, is the consequence of a man's total compulsion to evaluate himself justly.

In the sense of having been initiated by the hero himself, the tale always reveals what has been called his "tragic flaw," a failing that is not peculiar to grand or elevated characters. Nor is it necessarily a weakness. The flaw, or crack in the character, is really nothing—and need be nothing—but his inherent unwillingness to remain passive in the face of what he conceives to be a challenge to his dignity, his image of his rightful status. Only the passive, only those who accept their lot without active retaliation, are "flawless." Most of us are in that category.

But there are among us today, as there always have been, those who act against the scheme of things that degrades them, and in the process of action, everything we have accepted out of fear or insensitivity or ignorance is shaken before us and examined, and from this total onslaught by an individual against the seemingly stable cosmos surrounding us—from this total examination of the "unchangeable" environment—comes the terror and the fear that is classically associated with tragedy.

More important, from this total questioning of what has been previously unquestioned, we learn. And such a process is not beyond the common man. In revolutions around the world, these past thirty years, he has demonstrated again and again this inner dynamic of all tragedy.

Insistence upon the rank of the tragic hero, or the so-called nobility of his character, is really but a clinging to the outward forms of tragedy. If rank or nobility of character were indispensable, then it would follow that the problems of those with rank were the particular problems of tragedy. But surely the right of one monarch to capture the domain from another no longer raises our passions, nor are our concepts of justice what they were to the mind of an Elizabethan king.

The quality in such plays that does shake us, however, derives from the underlying fear of being displaced, the disaster inherent in being torn away from our chosen image of what and who we are in this world. Among us today this fear is as strong, and perhaps stronger, than it ever was. In fact, it is the common man who knows this fear best.

Now, if it is true that tragedy is the consequence of a man's total compulsion to evaluate himself justly, his destruction in the attempt posits a wrong or an evil in his environment. And this is precisely the morality of tragedy and its lesson. The discovery of the moral law, which is what the enlightenment of tragedy consists of, is not the discovery of some abstract or metaphysical quantity.

The tragic right is a condition of life, a condition in which the human personality is able to flower and realize itself. The wrong is the condition which suppresses man, perverts the flowing out of his love and creative instinct. Tragedy enlightens—and it must, in that it points the heroic finger at the enemy of man's freedom. The thrust for freedom is the quality in tragedy which exalts. The revolutionary questioning of the stable environment is what terrifies. In no way is the common man debarred from such thoughts or such actions.

Seen in this light, our lack of tragedy may be partially accounted for by the turn which modern literature has taken toward the purely psychiatric view of life, or the purely sociological. If all our miseries, our indignities, are born and bred within our minds, then all action, let alone the heroic action, is obviously impossible.

And if society alone is responsible for the cramping of our lives, then the protagonist must needs be so pure and faultless as to force us to deny his validity as a character. From neither of these views can tragedy derive, simply because neither represents a balanced concept of life. Above all else, tragedy requires the finest appreciation by the writer of cause and effect.

No tragedy can therefore come about when its author fears to question absolutely everything, when he regards any institution, habit or custom as being either everlasting, immutable or inevitable. In the tragic view the need of man to wholly realize himself is the only fixed star, and whatever it is that hedges his nature and lowers it is ripe for attack and examination. Which is not to say that tragedy must preach revolution.

The Greeks could probe the very heavenly origin of their ways and return to confirm the rightness of laws. And Job could face God in anger, demanding his right, and end in submission. But for a moment everything is in suspension, nothing is accepted, and in this stretching and tearing apart of the cosmos, in the very action of so doing, the character gains "size," the tragic stature which is spuriously attached to the royal or the high born in our minds. The commonest of men may take on that stature to the extent of his willingness to throw all he has into the contest, the battle to secure his rightful place in his world.

There is a misconception of tragedy with which I have been struck in review after review, and in many conversations with writers and readers alike. It is the idea that tragedy is of necessity allied to pessimism. Even the dictionary says nothing more about the word than that it means a story with a sad or unhappy ending. This impression is so firmly fixed that I almost hesitate to claim that in truth tragedy implies more optimism in its author than does comedy, and that its final result ought to be the reinforcement of the onlooker's brightest opinions of the human animal.

For, if it is true to say that in essence the tragic hero is intent upon claiming his whole due as a personality, and if this struggle must be total and without reservation, then it automatically demonstrates the indestructible will of man to achieve his humanity.

The possibility of victory must be there in tragedy. Where pathos rules, where pathos is finally derived, a character has fought a battle he could not possibly have won. The pathetic is achieved when the protagonist is, by virtue of his witlessness, his insensitivity, or the very air he gives off, incapable of grappling with a much superior force.

Pathos truly is the mode for the pessimist. But tragedy requires a nicer balance between what is possible and what is impossible. And it is curious, although edifying, that the plays we revere, century after century, are the tragedies. In them, and in them alone, lies the belief—optimistic, if you will—in the perfectibility of man.

It is time, I think, that we who are without kings, took up this bright thread of our history and followed it to the only place it can possibly lead in our time—the heart and spirit of the average man.

The Comic Rhythm

Susanne K. Langer

In Boswell's *Life of Doctor Johnson* we hear of a man who intended to be a philosopher but who failed because "cheerfulness was always breaking in." Susanne K. Langer is a philosopher, but she does not see cheerfulness as an enemy. She sees in comedy a dramatization of the basic biological patterns of persistence and growth, "human vitality holding its own in the world amid the surprises of unplanned coincidence."

The pure sense of life is the underlying feeling of comedy, developed in countless different ways. To give a general phenomenon one name is not to make all its manifestations one thing, but only to bring them conceptually under one head. Art does not generalize and classify; art sets forth the individuality of forms which discourse, being essentially general, has to suppress. The sense of life is always new, infinitely complex, therefore infinitely variable in its possible expressions. This sense, or "enjoyment" as Alexander would call it,[1] is the realization in direct feeling of what sets organic nature apart from inorganic: self-preservation, self-restoration, functional tendency, purpose. Life is teleological, the rest of nature is, apparently, mechanical; to maintain the pattern of vitality in a non-living universe is the most elementary instinctual purpose. An organism tends to keep its equilibrium amid the bombardment of aimless forces that beset it, to regain

[1] S. Alexander, *Space, Times and Deity*. See Vol. I, p. 12.

equilibrium when it has been disturbed, and to pursue a sequence of actions dictated by the need of keeping all its interdependent parts constantly renewed, their structure intact. Only organisms have needs; lifeless objects whirl or slide or tumble about, are shattered and scattered, stuck together, piled up, without showing any impulse to return to some pre-eminent condition and function. But living things strive to persist in a particular chemical balance, to maintain a particular temperature, to repeat particular functions, and to develop along particular lines, achieving a growth that seems to be preformed in their earliest, rudimentary, protoplasmic structure.

That is the basic biological pattern which all living things share: the round of conditioned and conditioning organic processes that produces the life rhythm. When this rhythm is disturbed, all activities in the total complex are modified by the break; the organism as a whole is out of balance. But, within a wide range of conditions, it struggles to retrieve its original dynamic form by overcoming and removing the obstacle, or if this proves impossible, it develops a slight variation of its typical form and activity and carries on life with a new balance of functions—in other words, it adapts itself to the situation. A tree, for instance, that is bereft of the sunshine it needs by the encroachment of other trees, tends to grow tall and thin until it can spread its own branches in the light. A fish that has most of its tail bitten off partly overcomes the disturbance of its locomotion patterns by growing new tissue, replacing some of the tail, and partly adapts to its new condition by modifying the normal uses of its fins, swimming effectively without trying to correct the list of its whole body in the water, as it did at first.

But the impulse to survive is not spent only in defense and accommodation; it appears also in the varying power of organisms to seize on opportunities. Consider how chimney swifts, which used to nest in crevasses among rocks, have exploited the products of human architecture, and how unfailingly mice find the warmth and other delights of our kitchens. All creatures live by opportunities, in a world fraught with disasters. That is the biological pattern in most general terms. . . .

Mankind has its rhythm of animal existence, too—the strain of maintaining a vital balance amid the alien and impartial chances of the world, complicated and heightened by passional desires. The pure sense of life springs from that basic rhythm, and varies from the composed well-being of sleep to the intensity of spasm, rage, or ecstasy. But the process of living is incomparably more complex for human beings than for even the highest animals; man's world is, above all, intricate and puzzling. The powers of language and imagination have set it utterly apart from that of other creatures. In human society an individual is not, like a member of a herd or a hive, exposed only to others that visibly or tangibly surround him, but is consciously bound to people who are absent, perhaps far away, at the moment. Even the dead may still play into his life. His awareness of events is far greater than the scope of his physical perceptions. Symbolic construction has made this vastly involved and extended world: and mental adroitness is his chief asset for exploiting it. The pattern of his vital feeling, therefore, reflects his deep emotional relation to those symbolic structures that are his realities, and his instinctual life modified in almost every way by thought—a brainy opportunism in face of an essentially dreadful universe.

This human life-feeling is the essence of comedy. It is at once religious and ribald, knowing and defiant, social and freakishly individual. The illusion of life which the comic poet creates is the oncoming future fraught with dangers and opportunities, that is, with physical or social events occurring by chance and building up the coincidences with which individuals cope according to their lights. This ineluctable future—ineluctable because its countless factors are beyond human knowledge and control—is Fortune. Destiny in the guise of Fortune is the fabric of comedy; it is developed by comic action, which is the upset and recovery of the protagonist's equilibrium, his contest with the world and his triumph by wit, luck, personal power, or even humorous, or ironical, or philosophical acceptance of mischance. Whatever the theme—serious and lyrical as in *The Tempest*, coarse slapstick as in the *Schwänke* of Hans Sachs, or clever and polite social satire—the immediate sense of life is the underlying feeling of comedy, and dictates its rhythmically structured unity, that is to say its organic form.

Comedy is an art form that arises naturally wherever people are gathered to celebrate life, in spring festivals, triumphs, birthdays, weddings, or initiations. For it expresses the elementary strains and resolutions of animate nature, the animal drives that persist even in human nature, the delight man takes in his special mental gifts that make him the lord of creation; it is an image of human vitality

holding its own in the world amid the surprises of unplanned coincidence. The most
obvious occasions for the performance of
comedies are thanks or challenges to fortune.
What justifies the term "Comedy" is not that
the ancient ritual procession, the Comus,
honoring the god of that name, was the
source of this great art form—for comedy has
arisen in many parts of the world, where the
Greek god with his particular worship was
unknown—but that the Comus was a fertility
rite, and the god it celebrated a fertility god, a
symbol of perpetual rebirth, eternal life. . . .

Because comedy abstracts, and reincarnates
for our perception, the motion and rhythm of
living, it enhances our vital feeling, much as
the presentation of space in painting enhances our awareness of visual space. The
virtual life on the stage is not diffuse and only
half felt, as actual life usually is: virtual life,
always moving visibly into the future, is in-
tensified, speeded up, exaggerated; the exhibition of vitality rises to a breaking point, to
mirth and laughter. We laugh in the theater
at small incidents and drolleries which would
hardly rate a chuckle offstage. It is not for
such psychological reasons that we go there to
be amused, nor are we bound by rules of
politeness to hide our hilarity, but these trifles
at which we laugh are really funnier *where
they occur* than they would be elsewhere; they
are employed in the play, not merely brought
in casually. They occur where the tension of
dialogue or other action reaches a high point.
As thought breaks into speech—as the wave
breaks into form—vitality breaks into humor.

Humor is the brilliance of drama, a sudden
heightening of the vital rhythm. A good comedy, therefore, builds up to every laugh; a
performance that has been filled up with jokes
at the indiscretion of the comedian or of his
writer may draw a long series of laughs, yet
leave the spectator without any clear impression of a very funny play. The laughs, moreover, are likely to be of a peculiar sameness,
almost perfunctory, the formal recognition of
a timely "gag."

The amoral character of the comic protagonist goes through the whole range of what
may be called the comedy of laughter. Even
the most civilized products of this art—
plays that George Meredith would honor
with the name of "comedy," because they
provoke "thoughtful laughter"—do not present moral distinctions and issues, but only
the ways of wisdom and of folly. Aristophanes, Menander, Molière—practically the
only authors this most exacting of critics
admitted as truly comic poets—are not mor-
alists, yet they do not flout or deprecate
morality; they have, literally, "no use" for
moral principles—that is, they do not use
them. Meredith, like practically all his contemporaries, labored under the belief that
poetry must teach society lessons, and that
comedy was valuable for what it revealed
concerning the social order.[2] He tried hard to
hold its exposé of foibles and vindications of
common sense to an ethical standard, yet in
his very efforts to justify its amoral personages
he only admitted their amoral nature, and
their simple relish for life, as when he said:
"The heroines of comedy are like women of
the world, not necessarily heartless from being clear-sighted. . . . Comedy is an exhibi-

---

[2] His well-known little work is called *An Essay on
Comedy, and the Uses of the Comic Spirit.* These uses
are entirely non-artistic. Praising the virtues of "good
sense" (which is whatever has survival value in the eyes
of society), he says: "The French have a school of stately
comedy to which they can fly for renovation whenever
they have fallen away from it; and their having such a
school is the main reason why, as John Stuart Mill
pointed out, they know men and women more accurately than we do." And a few pages later: "The *Femmes
Savantes* is a capital instance of the uses of comedy in
teaching the world to understand what ails it. The
French had felt the burden of this new nonsense [the fad
of academic learning, new after the fad of excessive
nicety and precision in speech, that had marked the
Précieuses]; but they had to see the comedy several times
before they were consoled in their suffering by seeing the
cause of it exposed."

tion of their battle with men, and that of men with them. . . ."

There it is, in a nutshell: the contest of men and women—the most universal contest, humanized, in fact civilized, yet still the primitive joyful challenge, the self-preservation and self-assertion whose progress is the comic rhythm. . . .

The same impulse that drove people, even in prehistoric times, to enact fertility rites and celebrate all phases of their biological existence sustains their eternal interest in comedy. It is in the nature of comedy to be erotic, risqué, and sensuous if not sensual, impious, and even wicked. This assures it a spontaneous emotional interest, yet a dangerous one: for it is easy and tempting to command an audience by direct stimulation of feeling and fantasy, not by artistic power. But where the formulation of feeling is really achieved, it probably reflects the whole development of mankind and man's world, for feeling is the intaglio image of reality. The sense of precariousness that is the typical tension of light comedy was undoubtedly developed in the eternal struggle with chance that every farmer knows only too well—with weather, blights, beasts, birds and beetles. The embarrassments, perplexities and mounting panic which characterize that favorite genre, comedy of manners, may still reflect the toils of ritual and taboo that complicated the cave-man's existence. Even the element of aggressiveness in comic action serves to develop a fundamental trait of the comic rhythm—the deep cruelty of it, as all life feeds on life. There is no biological truth that feeling does not reflect, and that good comedy, therefore, will not be prone to reveal.

But the fact that the rhythm of comedy is the basic rhythm of life does not mean that biological existence is the "deeper meaning" of all its themes, and that to understand the play is to interpret all the characters as symbols and the story as a parable, a disguised rite of spring or fertility magic, performed four hundred and fifty times on Broadway. The stock characters are probably symbolic both in origin and in appeal. There are such independently symbolic factors, or residues of them, in all the arts,[3] but their value for art lies in the degree to which their significance can be "swallowed" by the single symbol, the art work. Not the derivation of personages and situations, but of the rhythm of "felt life" that the poet puts upon them, seems to me to be of artistic importance: the essential comic feeling, which is the sentient aspect of organic unity, growth, and self-preservation.

---

[3] E.g., the symbolization of the zodiac in some sacred architecture, of our bodily orientation in the picture plane, or of walking measure, a primitive measure of actual time, in music. But a study of such non-artistic symbolic functions would require a monograph.

The Deadly Theatre

Peter Brook

A director devoted to exploring new forms of drama, Peter Brook has been a major force in the theater since 1945. English by birth but since 1970 resident chiefly in France, his productions of classics and of new plays have been staged throughout the world. "The Deadly Theatre" comes from his first book, *The Empty Space*, in which, apart from the Deadly Theatre, he distinguishes three kinds of theater: (1) the Holy Theatre ("The notion that the stage is a place where the invisible can appear"); (2) the Rough Theatre (a "popular" theater that is "close to the people," for instance a puppet theater); and (3) the Immediate Theatre (the theater of our time, in which Brook works).

I can take any empty space and call it a bare stage. A man walks across this empty space whilst someone else is watching him, and this is all that is needed for an act of theatre to be engaged. Yet when we talk about theatre this is not quite what we mean. Red curtains, spotlights, blank verse, laughter, darkness, these are all confusedly superimposed in a messy image covered by one all-purpose word. We talk of the cinema killing the theatre, and in that phrase we refer to the theatre as it was when the cinema was born, a theatre of box office, foyer, tie-up seats, footlights, scene changes, intervals, music, as though the theatre was by very definition these and little more.

I will try to split the word four ways and distinguish four different meanings—and so will talk about a Deadly Theatre, a Holy Theatre, a Rough Theatre and an Immediate Theatre. Sometimes these four theatres really exist, standing side by side, in the West End of London, or in New York off Times Square. Sometimes they are hundreds of miles apart,

the Holy in Warsaw and the Rough in Prague, and sometimes they are metaphoric: two of them mixing together within one evening, within one act. Sometimes within one single moment, the four of them, Holy, Rough, Immediate and Deadly intertwine.

The Deadly Theatre can at first sight be taken for granted, because it means bad theatre. As this is the form of theatre we see most often, and as it is most closely linked to the despised, much-attacked commercial theatre, it might seem a waste of time to criticize it further. But it is only if we see that deadliness is deceptive and can appear anywhere that we will become aware of the size of the problem.

The condition of the Deadly Theatre at least is fairly obvious. All through the world theatre audiences are dwindling. There are occasional new movements, good new writers and so on, but as a whole, the theatre not only fails to elevate or instruct, it hardly even entertains. The theatre has often been called a whore, meaning its art is impure, but today this is true in another sense—whores take the money and then go short on the pleasure. The Broadway crisis, the Paris crisis, the West End crisis are the same: we do not need the ticket agents to tell us that the theatre has become a deadly business and the public is smelling it out. In fact, were the public ever really to demand the true entertainment it talks about so often, we would almost all be hard put to know where to begin. A true theatre of joy is non-existent and it is not just the trivial comedy and the bad musical that fail to give us our money's worth—the Deadly Theatre finds its deadly way into grand opera and tragedy, into the plays of Molière and the plays of Brecht. Of course nowhere does the Deadly Theatre install itself so securely, so comfortably and so slyly as in the works of William Shakespeare. The Deadly Theatre takes easily to Shakespeare. We see his plays done by good actors in what seems like the proper way—they look lively and colourful, there is music and everyone is all dressed up, just as they are supposed to be in the best of classical theatres. Yet secretly we find it excruciatingly boring—and in our hearts we either blame Shakespeare, or theatre as such, or even ourselves. To make matters worse there is always a deadly spectator, who for special reasons enjoys a lack of intensity and even a lack of entertainment, such as the scholar who emerges from routine performances of the classics smiling because nothing has distracted him from trying over and confirming his pet theories to himself, whilst reciting his favourite lines under his breath. In his heart he sincerely wants a theatre that is nobler-than-life and he confuses a sort of intellectual satisfaction with the true experience for which he craves. Unfortunately, he lends the weight of his authority to dullness and so the Deadly Theatre goes on its way.

Anyone who watches the real successes as they appear each year will see a very curious phenomenon. We expect the so-called hit to be livelier, faster, brighter than the flop—but this is not always the case. Almost every season in most theatre-loving towns, there is one great success that defies these rules; one play that succeeds not despite but because of dullness. After all, one associates culture with

a certain sense of duty, historical costumes and long speeches with the sensation of being bored: so, conversely, just the right degree of boringness is a reassuring guarantee of a worthwhile event. Of course, the dosage is so subtle that it is impossible to establish the exact formula—too much and the audience is driven out of their seats, too little and it may find the theme too disagreeably intense. However, mediocre authors seem to feel their way unerringly to the perfect mixture—and they perpetuate the Deadly Theatre with dull successes, universally praised. Audiences crave for something in the theatre that they can term "better" than life and for this reason are open to confuse culture, or the trappings of culture, with something they do not know, but sense obscurely could exist—so, tragically, in elevating something bad into a success they are only cheating themselves.

If we talk of deadly, let us note that the difference between life and death, so crystal clear in man, is somewhat veiled in other fields. A doctor can tell at once between the trace of life and the useless bag of bones that life has left; but we are less practised in observing how an idea, an attitude or a form can pass from the lively to the moribund. It is difficult to define but a child can smell it out. Let me give an example. In France there are two deadly ways of playing classical tragedy. One is traditional, and this involves using a special voice, a special manner, a noble look and an elevated musical delivery. The other way is no more than a half-hearted version of the same thing. Imperial gestures and royal values are fast disappearing from everyday life, so each new generation finds the grand manner more and more hollow, more and more meaningless. This leads the young actor to an angry and impatient search for what he calls truth. He wants to play his verse more realistically, to get it to sound like honest-to-God real speech, but he finds that the formality of the writing is so rigid that it resists this treatment. He is forced to an uneasy compromise that is neither refreshing, like ordinary talk, nor defiantly histrionic, like what we call ham. So his acting is weak and because ham is strong, it is remembered with a certain nostalgia. Inevitably, someone calls for tragedy to be played once again "the way it is written." This is fair enough, but unfortunately all the printed word can tell us is what was written on paper, not how it was once brought to life. There are no records, no tapes—only experts, but not one of them, of course, has first-hand knowledge. The real antiques have all gone—only some imitations have survived, in the shape of traditional actors, who continue to play in a traditional way, drawing their inspiration not from real sources, but from imaginary ones, such as the memory of the sound an older actor once made—a sound that in turn was a memory of a predecessor's way.

I once saw a rehearsal at the Comedie Française—a very young actor stood in front of a very old one and spoke and mimed the role with him like a reflection in a glass. This must not be confused with the great tradition, say, of the Noh actors passing knowledge orally from father to son. There it is meaning that is communicated—and meaning never belongs to the past. It can be checked in each man's own present experience. But to imitate the externals of acting only perpetuates manner—a manner hard to relate to anything at all.

Again with Shakespeare we hear or read the same advice—"Play what is written." But what is written? Certain ciphers on paper. Shakespeare's words are records of the words that he wanted to be spoken, words issuing as sounds from people's mouths, with pitch, pause, rhythm and gesture as part of their meaning. A word does not start as a word—it is an end product which begins as an impulse, stimulated by attitude and behaviour which dictate the need for expression. This process occurs inside the dramatist; it is repeated inside the actor. Both may only be conscious of the words, but both for the author and then for the actor the word is a small visible portion of a gigantic unseen formation. Some writers attempt to nail down their meaning and intentions in stage directions and explanations, yet we cannot help being struck by the fact that the best dramatists explain themselves the least. They recognize that further indications will most probably be useless. They recognize that the only way to find the true path to the speaking of a word is through a process that parallels the original creative one. This can neither be by-passed nor simplified. Unfortunately, the moment a lover speaks, or a king utters, we rush to give them a label: the lover is "romantic," the king is "noble"—and before we know it we are speaking of romantic love and kingly nobility or princeliness as though they are things we can hold in our hand and expect the actors to observe. But these are not substances and they do not exist. If we search for them, the best we can do is to make guesswork reconstructions from books and paintings. If you ask an actor to play in a "romantic style" he will valiantly have a go, thinking he knows what you mean. What actually can he draw on? Hunch, imagination and a scrapbook of theatrical memories, all of which will give him a vague "romanticness" that he will mix up with a disguised imitation of whatever older actor he happens to admire. If he digs into his own experiences the result may not marry with the text; if he just plays what he thinks is the text, it will be imitative and conventional. Either way the result is a compromise: at most times unconvincing.

It is vain to pretend that the words we apply to classical plays like "musical," "poetic," "larger than life," "noble," "heroic," "romantic," have any absolute meaning. They are the reflections of a critical attitude of a particular period, and to attempt to build a performance today to conform to these canons is the most certain road to deadly theatre—deadly theatre of a respectability that makes it pass as living truth.

Once, when giving a lecture on this theme, I was able to put it to a practical test. By luck, there was a woman in the audience who had neither read nor seen *King Lear*. I gave her Goneril's first speech and asked her to recite it as best she could for whatever values she found in it. She read it very simply—and the speech itself emerged full of eloquence and charm. I then explained that it was supposed to be the speech of a wicked woman and suggested her reading every word for hypocrisy. She tried to do so, and the audience saw what a hard unnatural wrestling with the simple music of the words was involved when she sought to act to a definition:

> Sir, I love you more than words can
>   wield the matter;
> Dearer than eyesight, space, and
>   liberty;
> Beyond that can be valued, rich or
>   rare;
> No less than life, with grace, health,
>   beauty, honour;
> As much as child e'er loved, or
>   father found;
> A love that makes breath poor, and
>   speech unable;
> Beyond all manner of so much I
>   love you.

Anyone can try this for himself. Taste it on the tongue. The words are those of a lady of style and breeding accustomed to expressing herself in public, someone with ease and social aplomb. As for clues to her character, only the facade is presented and this, we see, is elegant and attractive. Yet if one thinks of the performances where Goneril speaks these first lines as a macabre villainess, and looks at the speech again, one is at a loss to know what suggests this—other than preconceptions of Shakespeare's moral attitudes. In fact, if Goneril in her first appearance does not play a "monster," but merely what her given words suggest, then all the balance of the play changes—and in the subsequent scenes her villainy and Lear's martyrdom are neither as crude nor as simplified as they might appear. Of course, by the end of the play we learn that Goneril's actions make her what we call a monster—but a real monster, both complex and compelling.

In a living theatre, we would each day approach the rehearsal putting yesterday's discoveries to the test, ready to believe that the true play has once again escaped us. But the Deadly Theatre approaches the classics from the viewpoint that somewhere, someone has found out and defined how the play should be done.

Staging

Kenneth M. Cameron and Patti P. Gillespie

Reading a play in a book such as this one inevitably focuses attention on the written lines. But plays are written to be performed, and it is the reader's job to see the play in the mind's eye—to see, that is, the characters acting and reacting on the stage. In the following essay Kenneth M. Cameron and Patti P. Gillespie help a reader to acquire the skill of envisioning the text as performed, rather than as merely spoken.

"Blocking," "staging," or "traffic direction," as some people wryly call it, is one of the director's inescapable responsibilities. No matter how much the actors and even the director are devoted to inner truth and to characterization, the time must come when the director must shape the actors' moves and timing, must give careful attention to *picturization* and *composition* and to *movement*. It is in the very nature of modern theater that the visual details of the stage have significance, and the director must make that significance jibe with his interpretation.

For significance is the crux of the matter. We live in a world where movement and visual arrangement signify: they give signals. In the realistic theater, the same things signify that do in life; in the nonrealistic theater, these things can be kept from signifying or can be made to signify differently only with careful control and effort.

Before the appearance of the director, audiences seemingly found less significance in stage movement, gesture, and picture—or, more accurately, they found a *theatrical* significance in them: the star took center stage, facing front, with other actors flanking and

balancing him; a hero's movement pattern and posture was heroic; the heroine moved so as to show herself off and to divide or punctuate her speeches. We cannot say with certainty what the audiences made of what they saw, but we can say with certainty what they did not see: modern staging, with its meticulous attention to visual symbolism (picturization), beauty (composition), and movement.

Much of what is taught about directing today is devoted to these matters. By and large, what is taught has been established by tradition and extended by popular theory, little of it having been tested objectively. Much of the theory of picturization—especially the supposed "meanings" of various stage areas—derives from traditional use of the proscenium stage and probably has less relevance for thrust and arena staging. Indeed, as realistic plays exert less influence on the theater and as new theories of theater evolve, many of these traditional theories of directing will probably fade.

MOVEMENT

As actors are aware of and exploit "body language," so the director is aware of and uses "movement language." Stage movement is more abundant than real-life movement; in a real situation, people often sit for a very long time to talk, for example, while on a stage characters in the same situation will be seen to stand, walk, change chairs, and move a good deal. Partly this abundance of movement results from the physical distance of the audience—small movements of eyes and facial muscles do not carry the length of a theater; and partly it results from the director's need for variety, for punctuation of action and lines, for the symbolic values of movement itself, and for the changing symbolic values of picturization.

Stage movement is based partly on the received wisdom of statements like "Face up to it," "She turned her back on it," "He rose to the occasion." Too, it serves to get characters into positions with which we have similar associations—"at the center of things," "way off in the blue," "out in left field."

The director is concerned with *speed*, *amount*, and *direction* of movement. Direction includes both motivation and human interaction; speed shows strength of desire or strength of involvement (impassioned haste, for example, and ambling indifference); amount shows much less than the other two and is perhaps most useful for contrast (a character making a very long movement after several short ones or in contrast with the small moves of several other characters).

Movement also *punctuates* the lines. It introduces speech: the character moves, catches our attention, stops and speaks; it breaks up speech: the character speaks, moves, speaks again, or moves while speaking and breaks the lines with turns or about-faces. (Pacing is frequently used for this reason. In life, we associate pacing with thought, and so a pacing character may seem thoughtful, but his turns are carefully timed by the director to mark changes in the speech itself.)

Movement *patterns* have a symbolic value much like that of individual movements and can be derived from the same figures of speech: "twisting him around her finger,"

"winding her in," "going in circles," "following like sheep," "on patrol," and many others suggest patterns for characters or groups. They are used, of course, to underscore a pattern already perceived in the play or the scene.

PICTORIALISM

Pictorialism—the exploitation of the stage's potential for displaying pictures—is not entirely limited to the proscenium theater but does have its greatest use there. From the late nineteenth century through the middle of the twentieth, the proscenium was seen literally as a picture frame, and the audience sat in locations that allowed it to look through the frame at its contents. With the advent of thrust and round stages, however, this "framing" became impossible, and audiences were located on three or all four sides of the stage, so that each segment of the audience saw quite a different picture. Thus only certain aspects of pictorialism have universal application, and of these the most important by far is picturization.

Of considerably less importance, except on the proscenium stage, is the symbolic value of *stage areas* (see drawing). These areas (on the proscenium stage) are Down Center, Right, and Left (*Down* meaning toward the audience, *Right* meaning to the actor's right and thus the audience's left) and Up Center, Right, and Left. Down Center is unquestionably the most important (or "strongest") area, followed by Down Right and Down Left. (Traditional wisdom has it that Down Right is more important than Down Left and that it has a "warmth" that Down Left lacks. The point is questionable.) The Upper areas are weaker and Up Left is the "coldest," hence appropriate for scenes of menace and the supernatural and inappropriate for love scenes, or so traditional wisdom has it. The real value of identifying the stage areas is in

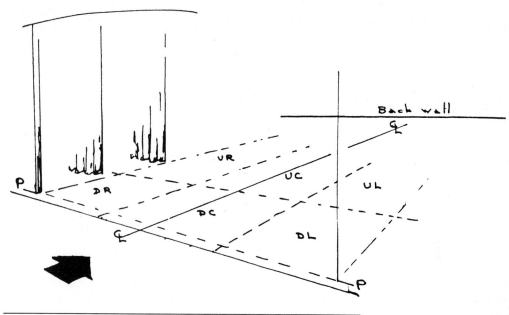

Stage areas as seen from the audience (arrow).

creating *variety* and *identification*, variety because it is tedious if the audience has to watch scene after scene played in the same area, and identification because the association of an area with a character or a feeling is an important tool for conveying emotional meaning to the audience. And, unquestionably, the matter of "strength" does have some importance, if only because common sense tells us that the downstage areas are stronger because we can see the actors more clearly there—and, as a result, we want to play our most important (but not all) scenes there.

PICTURIZATION

Puns and traditional sayings give us a clue to how picturization works—and also suggest to us how the mind of the director works as it creates visual images of the sort that communicate to us in dreams. "Caught in the middle," "one up on him," and "odd man out" all suggest strong pictorial arrangements of actors. When a director combines them with area identification, for example, they become richer and more complex. The additional use of symbolic properties or set pieces—a fireplace, associated with the idea of home ("hearth and family"), for example—gives still greater force to the picture. Thus a character who "moves in" on the hearth of a setting while also moving physically between a husband and wife ("coming between them") and sitting in the husband's armchair ("taking his place") has told the audience a complicated story without saying a word.

Sometimes as in Shakespeare's *Richard II* (Act II, Scene iii), the playwright's own symbolism creates a rich texture of both picture and movement.

("KING RICHARD *appeareth on the walls,*" (First Quarto), "*Enter on the walls,*" (First Folio).)

NORTH:
My lord, in the base court he doth attend
To speak with you; may it please you to come
    down?

RICHARD:
Down, down I come, like glist'ring Phaeton . . .,
Wanting the manage of unruly jades.
Is this the base court? Base court, where kings grow
   base . . .

[*Richard comes down to stage level; the usurper Bolingbroke kneels to him, as is evident from omitted material*]

BOLINGBROKE:
Stand all apart,
And show fair duty to his Majesty. ("*He kneels downe.*" First Quarto.)
My gracious lord.
   RICHARD:
Fair cousin, you debase your princely knee
To make the base earth proud with kissing it. . . .
Up, cousin, up; your heart is up, I know,
Thus high at least, although your knee be low.

The scene begins with Richard "on high" while his enemies are in the "base court" at stage level. (A base court was a part of a castle, but *base* means "common" or "unworthy," as well as "low" in both the physical and the social sense.) Richard says he will come "down, like glist'ring Phaeton," that is, like the young man who drove the chariot of the sun too near the earth because he could not control the horses that pulled it ("wanting the manage of unruly jades"). But the audience already knows (from earlier reference) that the sun is Richard's emblem, and the director has probably made sure that it is visible on Richard's costume and may even be suggested by the shape of his crown, so the sun is being *debased*, brought down, even as Richard physically moves down to stage level. There, the usurper tells everyone else to "stand apart," that is, to give them room, but the word *stand* may be ironic and the director may use it to make an ironic picture, because they should kneel to the king. Bolingbroke himself does kneel (stage direction, First Quarto), but the gesture is a mockery, as Richard notes, "You debase your princely knee/To make the base earth proud. . . ./Up, cousin, up . . . ," reminding the audience that Richard himself was, only moments ago,

"up" on the higher level. And Richard goes on: touching his crown (a traditional bit of business), he says, "Up, cousin, up . . ./Thus high at least . . ." That is, he will raise himself high enough in the presence of his king (though he should be kneeling) to seize the crown.

Thus, in a quick sequence of moves and gestures, the symbolic flow of the scene is given to the audience. With a scene of this richness and detail, the director need only follow its lead; few modern scenes are this explicitly symbolic, however, and the director usually has to create his own picturization to match his interpretation.

FOCUS

A stage is a visually busy place, with many things to look at; therefore, the audience's eyes must be directed to the important point at each moment. There are a number of principal devices for achieving *focus: framing* (in a doorway, between other actors, and so on); *isolating* (one character against a crowd, one character on a higher or lower level); *elevating* (standing while others sit, or the reverse, or getting on a higher level); *enlarging* (with costume, properties, or the mass of a piece of furniture); *illuminating* (in a pool of light or with a brighter costume); and *indicating* (putting the focal character at the intersection of "pointers"—pointing arms, swords, eyes, and so on).

Focus is largely a mechanical matter, but it is an important one that affects both movement and picturization.

COMPOSITION AND BALANCE

Most stage pictures that are picturized and focused are also rather well *composed*, or good to look at, but directors are often careful to study the production with an eye to improving the aesthetic quality of the scenes. What is *not* wanted is easier to say than what is: straight lines, lines parallel to the stage front, evenly spaced figures like ducks in a shooting gallery, and so on. *Balance* is also sought so that the stage does not seem heavy with characters on one side, light on the other. Composition is, finally, an irrational matter and a highly subjective one; directors who concern themselves with it in depth learn much from the other visual arts, especially traditional painting.

MOOD

Mood is established most readily with lighting and sound and with the behavior of characters. However, certain visual effects of character arrangement contribute, as well: horizontals, perhaps, for a quiet, resigned scene from Chekhov; looming verticals and skewed lines for a suspense melodrama. Mood values are as subjective and irrational as those of composition, however, and as hard to describe. In reality, what the director remains watchful for are clashes of mood, where movement and picturization conflict with other mood establishers.

The Script and the Stage

Peter Arnott

Peter Arnott was born and educated in Great Britain, where he received degrees from the University of Wales and Oxford University. Currently professor of drama at Tufts University, he has written numerous books on the theater and on ancient civilizations. Arnott is also an actor, director, and the creator of the Marionette Theater of Peter Arnott, which specializes in performing Greek drama for audiences throughout the continent.

The dramatic author writing his play is engaged in the same one-to-one relationship as the artist with his canvas or the sculptor with his block of stone. He shapes his material as his particular genius dictates, and is responsive only to those imperatives that he decides to set himself. The production of a play, however, is a much more complex process, involving a variety of factors, and a number of professional skills, each of which may influence the way in which the work is finally presented to the public. Theater is community, and the author must resign himself to being merely one, and not necessarily the most important member, of the group.

Of whom does this group consist? In the modern theater, the production of a play normally involves, besides the author, the director and his assistants; the actors; the set and costume designer (who may not be the same person); the lighting designer; and a stage staff responsible for the mechanical execution of the project. Although these elements have always been present, in some degree, in the theater, their relative importance has changed over the centuries, and it is

necessary to consider which held first place when the play was originally conceived.

THE AUTHOR

For those accustomed to think of a play primarily as a work of literature, it comes as a shock to learn that, at some of the most productive periods of the theater, the author was by no means the most important figure. In Elizabethan London, for example, the playwright was often no more than a hack, turning out material on demand as the company's needs and the public taste dictated. As well as writing his own material, he was expected to collaborate with others, to be able to work up a scenario suggested by someone else, or to write new scenes to freshen an old play. Once his work had been sold to the company, he had no further financial interest in it, and no artistic control. Several plays which enjoyed a long life in the Elizabethan public playhouse have come down to us as patchwork pieces, continually revised or added to by different hands over the years. For a long time plays, however distinguished, were not considered as literature. It was not until Ben Jonson had the effrontery to publish his dramatic with his nondramatic works that the playwright's status began to show a change. French playwrights of the seventeenth century were the first who found themselves able to charge substantial sums for their works, and the first, tentative beginnings of the modern system of author's royalties appeared at the same time.

THE ACTORS

In the modern commercial theater, actors are normally cast for each new production on an *ad hoc* basis. When the play closes they go their separate ways, and though their paths may sometimes recross, it may well be that they never meet on the stage again. There are, of course, important exceptions to this. The national theaters of various countries—the United States still does not have one—try to retain at least the nucleus of a permanent company for a period of years. In France, once an actor has been admitted to full membership of the Comédie Française, he may remain, if he wishes, for life. Theaters with a particular aim or identity, such as the Stratford, Ontario, Shakespeare Festival, recruit a large company for a number of plays and then stage the works in repertory. What is the exception now, however, was common practice until the present century. For most of the history of the theater, actors formed themselves into companies that worked together for years, so that the members grew to know one another's work intimately. This gave dramatists of earlier periods an advantage that they rarely enjoy today. They were writing for a known group, and could tailor the roles to particular abilities and talents. Shakespeare wrote *Hamlet* and *Othello* with Richard Burbage in mind. Molière's comedies made the best of his company's physical characteristics. Congreve and Sheridan, similarly, knew who was going to play each part before they wrote them. In this kind of company, actors tended

to fall into what were called "lines of business": that is, they would specialize in playing the same kind of character, whatever the play. Certain members of the King's Men would always play the fools and clowns. Sheridan had a gallery of comic types around which to build a new work. Dickens, in *Nicholas Nickleby*, gives a delightful description of a nineteenth-century touring company in which the members are identified, not by their names, but by the roles they customarily play on stage: the swaggering hero, the angry old father, the ingenue, and so forth. You will often find, therefore, that this kind of company organization induces certain sorts of dramatic formulae in playwrights. As early as Sophocles, dramatists were returning to the same types of character, and similar kinds of dramatic situation, because they could rely on actors who were able to exploit them powerfully. The modern author usually lacks this resource. He creates his characters out of the blue. It is up to the producing agency, and the casting director, to find actors capable of bringing them to life.

THE DIRECTOR

The director is the most recent member of the producing group, and still one of the most controversial. Throughout the history of the theater, obviously, someone always had to be in charge. In the Greek theater it was usually the playwright. Aeschylus played his own leading parts and supervised his assistant actors; as well as providing the script, he was his own composer, choreographer, and designer. The medieval theater provided a *maître de jeu*, who had general responsibility for seeing that his actors knew their lines, rehearsed their moves, and stood more or less in the right places. Shakespeare's playhouse had its "bookholder," who combined the functions of prompter and stage manager. In the eighteenth and nineteenth centuries we see the emergence of the actor-manager, a paternalistic figure who played the leading roles himself and imposed some cohesion on the company—sometimes a difficult task, for many actors were individualists, intent on drawing attention to their own performance at the expense of the ensemble effect. In the late nineteenth century the growing complexity of the theater's technical resources, and dissatisfaction with certain haphazard methods of the past, combined to create the need for a master mind who would stand apart from the production, see it as a whole, and harness its various resources to a common end. This figure emerges, in the twentieth century, as the American director, the British producer, or the European *régisseur*, and there are still widely different views as to what his function should be. Some directors have established themselves as autocrats, allowing nothing to happen on the stage that has not evolved from their minds or, at least, won their considered approval. In many cases, it has been possible to identify a given directorial style as easily as a writing style. A production by Tyrone Guthrie, or by Roger Planchon, was unmistakably his, and could be no one else's. Other directors have considered their function to be to allow the actor's initiative to predominate; they merely shape and control his creative imagination, offering suggestions, not directives. As the theater is constantly in a state of flux, so the director's role is still changing. Twenty years ago, the director expected to walk into his first rehearsal with every move of the play blocked out on paper, or at least in his mind. Now, he hopes to come to the same result after long working sessions with his actors, in the course of which a number of different approaches may be tried and discarded. Particular directors and actors may achieve a long and mutually fruitful working relationship over a number of productions, each helping and inspiring the other. The same may happen between directors and playwrights. Elia Kazan has had a long partnership with Tennessee Williams, contributing materially to the final shaping of the plays. Alan Schneider has done the same for Edward Albee.

THE DESIGNERS

Designers, too, represent a fairly recent innovation in theater practice. For most eras of the past, design as we now know it did not exist. The theater provided a conventional background for its actors. Sometimes, as in the Greek and Elizabethan theaters, this was simply the permanent architectural structure of the stage building, with the audience left to imagine the settings suggested by the language of the author. Even when the theater began to develop painted, illusionistic scenery the same stock settings were used for play after play; each playhouse owned a basic collection which could be used, with minimal adaptation, for the entire repertoire. Costumes, similarly, were drawn from stock, with the actors most of the time wearing the same sorts of clothes that they, and the audience, wore for everyday usage. The role of the designer begins to emerge in the early nineteenth century, out of the same dissatisfactions that eventually created the director. There was a growing desire for greater consistency, and greater appropriateness, in the stage picture, coupled with an increased concern for historical accuracy. The first "designed" production is usually said, with some justice, to be Shakespeare's *King John* as presented on the London stage in 1823, with every character dressed in the historical period indicated by the play, and the settings inspired by authentic medieval records. Since then, of course, the designer has developed into far more than a historical researcher, though that kind of study may still represent the basis of his design. He is expected, first, to lay out the playing space in a way that will be usable by actors, and at the same time say something about the play's intent; in other words, he must provide a visual metaphor of the play's action. In the same way, the costumes must be related to the dramatic intent, as seen by the director either alone or in combination with the author. Each costume must make a statement about the character who wears it, and be related to the others as part of a unified concept. The stage lighting, usually in different hands, must also contribute to the total effect, illuminating selectively and significantly the crucial moments of the action and suggesting mood and contrast.

All these things have to be kept in mind when taking a play from the printed page and translating it into stage action. As we have stated, many of the above are functions of the modern theater only. Selective stage lighting was impossible before the appearance of gas; seventeenth-century audiences would have been astonished at the suggestion that they should sit in the dark, while only the stage was lit. But even when considering the plays of the past, it is essential to consider what practical facilities were available to the playwright, and how these influenced the form in which he wrote. Plays are rarely written in a vacuum. When they are, they tend not to be good plays. Normally, an author writes with a particular kind of theater in mind, a particular acting style, a particular audience with reasonably predictable responses. The final shape of his play will be determined by all these things.

THE PLAYHOUSE

Particularly important is the shape of the playhouse at any given period, for this largely determines not what the author says, but how he says it. Was it large or small? Spectacular or intimate? Designed to provide elaborate scenic illusion, or working largely through the active complicity of the audience's im-

agination? Greek plays, for instance, were written for open-air theaters which were enormous by today's standards (see photo on page 80). They held upwards of 15,000 spectators, and the actor was dwarfed by his environment. In such a theater there was little place for subtle visual effect, or for the intricate physical business that a modern dramatist now writes into his stage directions. As a compensating factor, the acoustics of these theaters, by reason of their bowl-shaped structure, were superb. Audiences could hear every word, even at so great a remove from the action. Thus, by necessity, the dramatist worked largely in terms of language. In Greek plays, characters tell you everything: who and what they are, what they are doing and going to do, what they feel about it all. In the smaller, more intimate modern theater, Greek plays often seem unnecessarily wordy because the actors now have other resources. A modern actor may show in a look what his ancient counterpart had to express in a sentence. Directors who revive Greek plays have to keep these problems of transposition in mind.

In the Elizabethan theater, as most scholars now assume, actors worked on a deep thrust stage which could carry them into the center of their audience (see illustrations on pages 764–765). Thus, a characteristic feature of the theater building encouraged the use of the stage soliloquy. Also, Elizabethan theaters seem to have relied very little on illusionistic, representational scenery. They offered, instead, a neutral space defined largely by the words of the actors. Shakespeare's characters tell you where they are, if it matters; if they do not, then the precise location is unimportant. In these circumstances the theater could develop a fast-moving pattern of action in which one scene followed rapidly on the heels of another with no necessity to drop the curtain for a change of setting. Victorian actor-managers, mounting Shakespeare on their own

Johannes de Witt, a Continental vistor to London, made a drawing of the Swan
Theatre in about the year 1596. The original drawing is lost; this is Arend van
Buchel's copy of it. For additional details about the Elizabethan theater, see the
Glossary, p. 816.

C. Walter Hodges's drawing (1965) of an Elizabethan playhouse.

heavily pictorial stages, found this to be a major problem, for their productions stretched out to an inordinate length as one elaborately painted set was replaced by another. Once again, the factors governing the original production have to be taken into account, even if one intends to depart from them.

INTERPRETING A PLAY FOR THE STAGE

Let us now trace the progress of a production through its various stages. First, it is the task of the director to consider his interpretation of the play, and how this may be realized in practical terms. He must determine what he thinks the play means, for on this everything else will hang. If the author is living and accessible, the director will almost certainly consult him. This may be a mixed blessing, for the author will usually have his private vision of the play, shaped by his own proximity to it. The director, standing apart from the work, is able to be more objective. Authors are, notoriously, fallible directors of their own work, though a number have refused to recognize this and tried to impose their will on actors and director alike. George Bernard Shaw is a case in point; his plays contain inordinately lengthy stage directions, dictating the appearance of the stage setting, the properties, costumes and movements in such explicit detail that, if followed to the letter, they would leave the director nothing to do.

In the case of a dead, particularly a long-dead, author the director has different problems. He must arrive at the best interpretation that he can, aided only by the second-hand resources of scholarship. This is not to denigrate the scholar. Any intelligent director will read all the editions and commentaries that he can. But it is in the matter of bringing the play to the stage that the practitioner and the scholar conspicuously part company. Scholarship has space and leisure to be expansive. It can discuss alternative explanations, point to ambiguities, and illuminate textual problems with footnotes suggesting various ways in which they may be resolved. A good scholar is more inclined to discuss a range of interpretations than to commit himself to one. The theater, on the other hand, has to be decisive. It offers no footnotes. It cannot ask the spectator to go back and reconsider. In performance, if something is not clear at first hearing, it is not clear at all. Therefore the director, for better or worse, has to commit himself to one interpretation, to one vision of the play; and inevitably, there will be those who disagree with him. Laurence Olivier prefaced his film of *Hamlet* with the statement that this is a play about a man who could not make up his mind. An immediate response rang out from a segment of the audience: "Wrong!" It is ever thus. The theater, unfortunately, cannot offer a variety of interpretations and ask the audience to choose. It has to settle for one; and what this is will vary with the director and his times. Part of the measure of greatness of a play is the number of different interpretations it can bear without forfeiting its dramatic viability.

The initial decision, once arrived at, carries others in its train. A directorial interpretation involves matters of setting and costume, and these are usually worked out well in advance with the appropriate people. Let us take, as an example, the case of *King Lear*. The same play may assume a number of stage shapes, depending on what the director assumes its meaning and purpose to be. Does he see it, for instance, on the most rudimentary level, as a chronicle play about certain events in remote British history? (Unlikely, perhaps; but it has been done.) The name of Lear, after all, appears in early British records, and a rough date may be assigned to him. In this case we will have a *Lear* dressed in furs and skins, and set again a background of rocks and monoliths. Alternatively, does the director see the play, as some scholars have suggested, as closely related to political events of Shakespeare's own time? Does Lear's division of his kingdom give stage form to the fears of those who looked uneasily into the future of an England whose queen would die unmarried and childless? This gives another line for sets and costumes to take. Does the director envisage the work as having a particular meaning for now, for the present generation? He may therefore decide to stage it in modern dress, against settings evoking the audience's present. As noted above, "modern-dress" Shakespeare was the regular practice before the nineteenth century; it became modish again in the 1920s and 30s, and still occasionally reappears with value today, though perhaps *Lear* is not the ideal play for such treatment. Is it a cosmic drama, located in no particular time and place, but expressive only of man's constant inhumanity to man, and his subservience to forces beyond his control? Sets and costumes may display this too, by choosing forms linked to no specific style or period but creating their own theatrical logic. Thus the stage has shown us all manner of Lears. One has been Ancient British, another Elizabethan. Olivier's production suggested an almost prehistoric world without actually depicting it, a world of towering crags and swirling mists. Gielgud chose a timeless *Lear*, dressed in costumes of stylized shape and set among abstract sculptural forms. Yet another production looked to the future and set the play in a blackened, smouldering landscape, the neo-primitive world that had survived the atomic war.

The director's basic interpretation must also decide the placement and movement of his characters. It is his task to illuminate what he considers to be the underlying pattern of the play through significant action. To this end he will create a subtext, working with his actors to build up a mental background and justification for the lines they speak. In *Lear* again, the play begins with the King's announcement that he proposes to divide his kingdom, and his challenge to his daughters to proclaim their love for him. Why does he do this? Is it simply the datum, the formal beginning to the play, which neither asks nor needs explanation? In this case, the director may stage the opening scenes almost as a prologue, quite simply and formally, a bare proclamation. Or is there a more complex human explanation? Olivier saw Lear in this scene as a man on the verge of senility, making his momentous decision almost as a whim; and he worked up to this from his first appearance on stage, having Lear stop as if to address a remark to a soldier, then changing his mind and going on. Why does Cordelia refuse to answer? Is she simply revolted by her sisters' protestations, or is there some other reason? Nahum Tate, the Restoration playwright, was so obsessed by this problem that he postulated a love affair between Cordelia and Edgar dividing her loyalty so that she was unable to answer her father as he wished; and he carried this idea to such lengths that he rewrote the play. So far may interpretation go.

A further example. What relationship exists between Lear and the Fool? Is the latter intended to be the King's conscience? His *alter ego*? A daughter-substitute? Or an objective commentator on his master's folly? Once again, whatever interpretation is decided upon can be emphasized by the relative placing of the characters and their contact, or lack of it. Gloucester is blinded. Is the director concerned with the physical violence of the act, or its symbolic performance? If the former, the deed can be portrayed most graphically on the stage. If the latter, it can be merely suggested, not shown. All these are things which must be worked out by the director with his actors, and they must ultimately agree on the meaning of what is being

Engraving of Benjamin Wilson's painting of David Garrick (1717–1770) as King Lear, Act III. (Photograph: Raymond Mander and Joe Mitchenson Theatre Collection.)

John Gielgud as Lear in the Royal Shakespeare Theatre production, Stratford-upon-Avon, England, 1955. (Photograph: Royal Shakespeare Theatre.)

done. Discrepancies of interpretation show up with painful clarity in performance. An actor may sometimes disagree totally with his director's interpretation. He will usually follow it, none the less. In the long rehearsal process, the interpretation may change. Alec Guinness has recorded that he went through several interpretations of Shakespeare's *Richard II* before he found a view of the character that satisfied him as being logical and self-consistent.

Amid all these interpretations, then, where is the play? The answer must be that it is in none of them, and all of them. The play's values change as the theaters, the actors, and the audiences change. The *Lear* we see is not the *Lear* that Burbage performed, and the Elizabethan playgoers saw, though the text is the same. The Lear of Garrick (1717–1779) was totally different from that of Edmund Kean (1787–1833). In the same way, Lincoln Center bears small resemblance to the Globe Playhouse, Drury Lane, or the Lyceum. Each generation finds a new meaning in the script, illuminating it with contemporary concerns and preoccupations. It is the theater's continual task to bring about a rapprochement between the play and its successive audiences, finding a new frame of reference in which it will be meaningful. The actor, who works in the ephemeral, who sculpts, as has been said, in snow, accepts this as a condition of his art. The text remains, but its illumination changes.

THE MECHANICS OF PRODUCTION

However ornate the director's conception, the commercial theater imposes strict limitations on time and cost. A Broadway production may expect a minimum of three weeks' rehearsal; the cost, regulated by strict union standards for actors and stage crew, may be upwards of $1,000,000 for a nonmusical play, vastly more for a musical. In university theaters, which have tended to become more and more the home of the classics, conditions are somewhat happier. Campus productions usually work with five or six weeks of rehearsal time, uninhibited by union hours, and the budget is far smaller when salaries do not have to be paid: perhaps as little as $2,500 for a *King Lear*. Given these differences, rehearsals in both situations tend to follow the same pattern. They will begin with a general reading of the play, during which the director explains his conception; the cast may also see preliminary designs of sets and costumes, so that they know the environment in which they will be working. Early rehearsals are conducted book-in-hand, with normally only the barest indication of a set. The principal acting areas, steps and levels are marked out on the floor with tape. Any furniture that is to hand may be used; a chair may stand in for a throne, a bench for a bed. During this period cuts and changes may still be made, imposed sometimes by such commercial considerations as the length and expense of the performance, sometimes by changes in the director's conception as he absorbs what his actors bring to their parts. Gradually, the actors memorize. It is the director's hope that parts will be learnt as rapidly as possible, as only then can serious work begin. Once they have discarded their scripts, actors can relate to one another and to their surroundings.

During the course of rehearsals the other production elements are added. Actors start to work with the actual props, instead of rehearsal equivalents. In a university theater, the setting begins to grow around the actors as they rehearse. Actual steps replace the lines on the floor and walls appear where there was only empty space. In the commercial theater, again because of expense, the company may never know the actual set until the last stages of rehearsal; they do most of their work in an empty hall lit by a single bulb. In either case,

The University of Minnesota production of *King Lear* in Minneapolis, 1956.
(Photograph: The University of Minnesota Theatre.)

Paul Scofield as Lear in Peter Brook's production by the Royal Shakespeare
Company in London, 1962. (Photograph: Angus McBean. Harvard Theatre
Collection.)

the last days are spent in integrating the total production. The full set appears, and actors have to adjust to its intricacies. The full lighting plot is put into action. Sound effects and music are added. The actors are introduced to their costumes, and have to master, very rapidly, the difficulties of wearing them. There is usually one technical rehearsal, during which the actors are subordinated to the other demands of the performance; they usually move from one lighting or scene cue to the next, so that the technical staff may become accustomed to the changes. Finally, full dress rehearsals, run like a full performance, with the director no longer intervening, but confining himself to notes at the end.

In the commercial theater, even this may not be the end of the process. Most Broadway productions go through a series of tryouts out-of-town, before paying public audiences. Depending on the reaction, important changes may be made in the production, or even in the script itself. It is not unknown for actors to be handed new material every day. Thus the production is established; it opens; and even then, over a long commercial run, it may change, as new actors replace the original cast or as those who were with the play from the beginning make new discoveries about it and about each other. A script, once it has been published, achieves a certain permanency. A production is always changing, and no two audiences ever see exactly the same dramatic event.

WRITING ABOUT DRAMA

People write about plays in order to clarify and to account for their WHY WRITE? responses to works that interest or excite or frustrate them. In order to put words on paper we have to take a second and a third look at what is in front of us and at what is within us. And so writing is a way of learning. The last word is never said about complex thoughts and feelings, but when we write we hope to make at least a little progress in the difficult but rewarding job of talking about our responses. We learn, and then we hope to interest our reader because we are communicating our responses to something that for one reason or another is worth talking about.

This communication is, in effect, teaching. You may think that you are writing for the teacher, but such a belief is a misconception; when you write, *you* are the teacher. An essay on a play is an attempt to help someone to see the play as you see it. If this chapter had to be boiled down to a single sentence of advice, that sentence would be: Because you are teaching, your essay should embody those qualities that you value in teachers—probably intelligence, open-mindedness, and effort; certainly a desire to offer what help you can.

Analysis is, literally, a separation into parts in order to understand. An ANALYSIS analysis commonly considers one part and the relation of this part to the whole. For example, it may consider only the functions of the setting in *The Sandbox*, of the Fool in *King Lear*, or of the music in *Happy Days*.

Analysis, of course, is not a process used only in talking about literature. It is commonly applied in thinking about almost any complex matter. Boris Becker plays a deadly game of tennis; what makes it so good? How does his backhand contribute to his game? What does his serve do to the opponent? Because a play is usually long and complicated, in a paper written for a college course you probably do not have enough space to analyze all aspects of the play, and so you will probably choose one aspect and relate it to the whole. Of course all of the parts are related; a study of one character, for example, will have to take some account of other characters and of plot and perhaps even of setting; but, still, an analysis may legitimately devote most of its space to one part, taking account of other parts only insofar as they are relevant to the topic.

If a work is fairly long and complex, and you are writing only a few pages, FINDING A TOPIC almost surely you will write an analysis of some part. Unless you have an enormous amount of time for reflection and revision, you cannot write a meaningful essay of five hundred or even a thousand words on *Oedipus* or *The Cherry Orchard*. You cannot even write on "Character in *Oedipus*" or "Symbolism in *The Cherry Orchard*." And probably you won't really want to write on such topics anyway. Probably *one* character or *one* symbol has caught your interest. Trust your feelings; you are probably on to something interesting, and it will be best to think about this smaller topic for the relatively few hours that you have. A "smaller" topic need not be dull or trivial; treated properly, it may illuminate the entire work, or, to change the metaphor, it may serve as a mine shaft that gives entry to the work. "The Dramatic Function of the Gloucester

Subplot in *King Lear*," carefully thought about, will in five hundred or a thousand words tell a reader more (and will have taught its author more) than will "*King Lear* as a Tragedy." Similarly, "Imagery of Blindness in *King Lear*" is a better topic than "Imagery in *King Lear*," and "The Meanings of 'Nature' in *King Lear*" is a better topic than "The Meaning of *King Lear*."

Every play affords its own topics for analysis, and every essayist must set forth his or her own thesis, but a few useful generalizations may be made. You can often find a thesis by asking one of two questions:

1. *What is this doing?* That is, why is this scene in the play? Why is the Fool in *King Lear*? Why the music in *Happy Days*? Why are these lines verse and those lines prose? Why is a certain action reported to us rather than represented on the stage? What is the significance of the parts of the work? (Titles are often highly significant parts of the work: Ibsen's *A Doll's House* and Chekhov's *The Cherry Orchard* would be slightly different if they had other titles.)

2. *Why do I have this response?* Why do I find this scene clever, or moving, or puzzling? How did the author make this character funny or dignified or pathetic? How did he or she communicate the idea that this character is a bore without boring me?

The first of these questions, "What is this doing?" requires that you identify yourself with the dramatist, wondering, for example, whether this opening scene is the best possible for this story. The second question, "Why do I have this response?" requires that you trust your feelings. If you are amused or bored or puzzled or annoyed, assume that these responses are appropriate and follow them up, at least until a rereading of the play provides other responses.

FROM TOPIC TO THESIS

How do you find a topic and how do you turn it into a thesis, that is, a point you want to make? An idea may hit you suddenly; as you are reading you find yourself jotting it in the margin, "Contrast with Nora's earlier response," or "Note the change of costume," or "too heavy irony," or "ugh." Or an idea may come slowly on rereading. Perhaps you gradually become aware that in *Antigone* the chorus may not be a static character but changes its views as the play progresses. At this point, then, you have a thesis—an angle—as well as a topic.

Think of it this way: a topic is a subject, and a thesis is a subject with a predicate: "Imagery in *King Lear*" is a topic, but it can be turned into a thesis thus: "Imagery helps to distinguish the characters in *King Lear*." Once you can formulate a thesis, you are well on the way to writing a good paper. But note that the more precise the formulation of the thesis, the better the paper will probably be. After all, "Imagery in *King Lear* is interesting" is a thesis, but such a vague formulation gives you little to go on. Not until you can turn it into something like "Imagery in *King Lear* serves three important purposes" are you anywhere near to being able to draft your essay.

Following is a short essay written by a student. The student told us privately that when she began work on the paper she was hoping to write on the irrationality of the fairies in *A Midsummer Night's Dream* as a sort of mirror of the irrationality of the young lovers, but when she searched the play for supporting detail she found, to her surprise, that she had to revise her thesis.

Her earliest jottings—a sort of preliminary outline and guide to rereading the play—looked like this:

> faries -- like lovers, irrational?
>
> Puck
> mischievous
>
> Titania and Oberon
> equally quarrelsome ?
> quarrel disturbs human world
> Titania wants Indian boy
> isn't she right ?
> if so, she's **not** irrational
>
> Oberon
> jealous
> cruel to Titania ?
> unfaithful?
>
> Other faries
> do they **do** anything?
> T's different from O's ?

In rereading the play, and in jotting down notes, she came to see that the supernatural characters were not as malicious and irrational as she had thought, and so she changed the focus of her thesis.

A SAMPLE ANALYSIS

Fairy Mischief and Morality
and A Midsummer Night's Dream

Title is informative.

If we read <u>A Midsummer Night's Dream</u> casually, or come away from a delightful performance, we may have the vague impression that the fairies are wild, mischievous, willful creatures who perhaps represent the irrational qualities of mankind. But in fact the text lends only a little support to this view. The irrationality of mankind is really represented chiefly by the human beings in the play—we are told in the first scene, for example, that Demetrius used to love Helena, but now loves Hermia—and the fairies are really largely responsible for the happy ending finally achieved.

Opening paragraph leads us into the subject.

It is, of course, easy to see why we may think of the fairies as wild and mischievous. Titania and Oberon have quarreled over a little Indian boy, and their quarrel had led to fogs, floods, and other disorders in nature. Moreover, Titania accuses Oberon of infidelity, and Oberon returns the charge:

Short quotation provides evidence.

> How canst thou thus for shame, Titania,
> Glance at my credit with Hippolyta,
> Knowing I know thy love to Theseus?
> (2.1.74-76)[1]

Titania rejects this countercharge, saying "These are the forgeries of jealousy" (2.1.81), but we are not convinced of her innocence. It would be easy to give additional examples of speeches in which the king and queen of fairyland present unflattering pictures of each other, but probably one of the strongest pieces of evidence of their alleged irrationality is the fact that Oberon causes Titania to fall in love with the asinine Bottom. We should not forget, however, that later Oberon will take pity on her: "Her dotage now I do begin to pity" (4.1.51).

Citation in parentheses to reduce the number of footnotes.

In fact, it is largely through Oberon's sense of pity—this time for the quarreling young lovers in the forest—that the lovers finally are successfully paired off. And we should remember, too, before we claim that the fairies are consistently quarrelsome and mischievous, that at the very end of the play Oberon and Titania join in a song and dance blessing the newlyweds and promising healthy offspring. The fairies, though quarrelsome, are fundamentally benevolent spirits.

The main point having been set forth, essayist now turns to an apparent exception.

But what of Robin Goodfellow, the Puck of this play? Is he not mischievous? One of the fairies says Robin is a "shrewd and

Footnote gives source, and explains that other footnotes will not be necessary.

---

[1]All quotations from this play are from the text reprinted in Sylvan Barnet, Morton Berman, and William Burto, <u>Types of Drama</u>, 5th ed. (Boston: Scott, Foresman/Little, Brown, 1989). Further references to the play will be given parenthetically, within the text of the essay.

knavish sprite" (2.1.33) who frightens maids and plays tricks on

housewives; Robin admits the charge, saying "Thou speakest

aright" (2.1.42), and two lines later he says "I jest to Oberon, and

make him smile," and then he goes on to describe some of his

practical jokes, including his fondness for neighing to tease a

horse, and pulling a stool from under an old lady. But this is not

quite the whole story. The fact is, despite this speech, that we do

not see Robin engage in any mischievous pranks. After all, he

does not deliberately anoint the eyes of the wrong Athenian lover.

Oberon tells Robin that he will recognize the young man by his

Athenian clothing, and when Puck encounters a young man in

Athenian clothing he anoints the youth's eyes. The fault is really

Oberon's, though of course Oberon meant well when he instructed

Robin:

> A sweet Athenian lady is in love
> With a disdainful youth. Anoint his eyes;
> But do it when the next thing he espies
> May be the lady.
>   (2.1.260-263)

So Robin's error is innocent. He is speaking honestly when he

says, "Believe me, king of shadows, I mistook" (3.2.347). Of

course he does enjoy the confusion he mistakenly causes, but we

can hardly blame him severely for that. After all, we enjoy it, too.

The fairies, by their very nature, of course suggest a myste-

rious, irrational world, but—even though, as we have just seen,

Oberon is called the "king of shadows"—they are not to be con-

fused with "ghosts, wand'ring here and there," "damnèd spirits"

who "willfully themselves exile from light/ And must for aye con-

sort with black-browed night" (3.2.381-387). Oberon explicitly

says, after this speech, "But we are spirits of another sort," and

his speech is filled with references not to darkness but to light:

"morning," "eastern gate," "blessèd beams." The closer we observe

Essayist concedes a point, but then goes on in the rest of the paragraph to argue that the main point nevertheless still holds.

Concluding paragraph summarizes, but it does not merely repeat what has come before; it offers a few brief new quotations. The paragraph ends by setting the conclusion (fairies are decent) in a fresh context (it's the mortals who are irrational).

them in the play, then, the closer their behavior is to that of nor-

mal, decent human beings. There is plenty of irrationality in the

play, but it is found for the most part in the mortals.

Notice that this first-rate essay

1. has a thesis, and
2. develops the thesis effectively.

Notice also that

3. the title gives the reader some idea of what is coming, and
4. the first paragraph pretty clearly sets forth the thesis.
5. The essay next takes up the evidence that might seem to contradict the thesis—Oberon and Titania, and Robin Goodfellow—and it shows that this evidence is not decisive.
6. All the while, then, the essay is moving forward, substantiating the thesis,
7. especially by using well-chosen quotations.
8. The last paragraph slightly restates the thesis, in light of what the essay has demonstrated.

WRITING A
REVIEW

Your instructor may ask you to write a review of a local production. A review requires analytic skill but it is not identical with an analysis. First of all, a reviewer normally assumes that the reader is unfamiliar with the production being reviewed, and unfamiliar with the play if the play is not a classic. Thus, the first paragraph usually provides a helpful introduction, along these lines:

> Marsha Norman's new play, 'night, Mother, a tragedy with only two actors and one set, shows us a woman's preparation for suicide. Jessie has concluded that she no longer wishes to live, and so she tries to put her affairs into order, which chiefly means preparing her rather uncomprehending mother to get along without her.

Inevitably some retelling of the plot is necessary if the play is new, and a summary of a sentence or two is acceptable even for a familiar play, but the review will chiefly be concerned with

1. describing,
2. analyzing, and, especially,
3. evaluating.

(By the way, don't confuse description with analysis. Description tells what something—for instance, the set or the costumes—looks like; analysis tells us how they work, what they add up to, what they contribute to the total effect.) If the play is new, much of the evaluation may center on the play itself, but if the play is a classic, the evaluation probably will be devoted chiefly to the acting, the set, and the direction.

Other points:

1. Save the playbill; it will give you the names of the actors, and perhaps a brief biography of the author, a synopsis of the plot, and a photograph of the set, all of which may be helpful.

2. Draft your review as soon as possible, while the performance is still fresh in your mind. If you can't draft it immediately after seeing the play, at least jot down some notes about the setting and the staging, the acting, and the audience's response.

3. If possible, read the play—ideally, before the performance and again after it.

4. In your first draft, don't worry about limitations of space; write as long a review as you can, putting down everything that comes to mind. Later you can cut it to the required length, retaining only the chief points and the necessary supporting details. But in your first draft try to produce a fairly full record of the performance and your response to it, so that a day or two later, when you revise, you won't have to trust a fading memory for details.

If you read reviews of plays in *Time*, *Newsweek*, or a newspaper, you will soon develop a sense of what reviews normally do. The following example, an undergraduate's review of a college production of *Macbeth*, is typical except in one respect: reviews of new plays customarily include a few sentences summarizing the plot and classifying the play (a tragedy, a farce, a rock musical, or whatever), perhaps briefly putting it into the context of the author's other works, but because *Macbeth* is so widely known the reviewer has chosen not to insult his readers by telling them that *Macbeth* is a tragedy by Shakespeare.

A SAMPLE REVIEW

An Effective <u>Macbeth</u>

<u>Macbeth</u> at the University Theater is a thoughtful and occa-
sionally exciting production, partly because the director, Mark
Urice, has trusted Shakespeare and has not imposed a gimmick
on the play. The characters do not wear cowboy costumes as they
did in last year's production of <u>A Midsummer Night's Dream</u>.

Probably the chief problem confronting a director of
<u>Macbeth</u> is how to present the witches so that they are powerful

Title implies thesis.

Opening paragraph is informative, letting the reader know the reviewer's overall attitude.

Reviewer promptly turns to a major issue.

supernatural forces and not silly things that look as though they came from a Halloween party. Urice gives us ugly but not absurdly grotesque witches, and he introduces them most effectively. The stage seems to be a bombed-out battlefield littered with rocks and great chunks of earth, but some of these begin to stir—the earth seems to come alive—and the clods move, unfold, and become the witches, dressed in brown and dark gray rags. The suggestion is that the witches are a part of nature, elemental forces that can hardly be escaped. This effect is increased by the moans and creaking noises that they make, all of which could be comic but which in this production are impressive.

First sentence of this paragraph provides an effective transition.

The witches' power over Macbeth is further emphasized by their actions. When the witches first meet Macbeth, they encircle him, touch him, caress him, even embrace him, and he seems helpless, almost their plaything. Moreover, in the scene in which he imagines that he sees a dagger, the director has arranged for one of the witches to appear, stand near Macbeth, and guide his hand toward the invisible dagger. This is, of course, not in the text, but the interpretation is reasonable rather than intrusive. Finally, near the end of the play, just before Macduff kills Macbeth, a witch appears and laughs at Macbeth as Macduff explains that he was not "born of woman." There is no doubt that throughout the tragedy Macbeth has been a puppet of the witches.

Paragraph begins with a broad assertion and then offers supporting details.

Macbeth (Stephen Beers) and Lady Macbeth (Tina Peters) are excellent. Beers is sufficiently brawny to be convincing as a battlefield hero, but he also speaks the lines sensitively, so the audience feels that in addition to being a hero, he is a man of gentleness. One can believe Lady Macbeth when she says that she fears he is "too full o' the milk of human kindness" to murder

Duncan. Lady Macbeth is especially effective in the scene in
which she asks the spirits to "unsex her." During this speech she
is reclining on a bed and as she delivers the lines she becomes
increasingly sexual in her bodily motions, deriving excitement
from her own stimulating words. Her attachment to Macbeth is
strongly sexual, and so is his attraction to her. The scene when
she persuades him to kill Duncan ends with them passionately
embracing. The strong attraction of each for the other, so evident
in the early part of the play, disappears after the murder, when
Macbeth keeps his distance from Lady Macbeth and does not allow her to touch him. The acting of the other performers is
effective, except for Duncan (John Berens), who recites the lines
mechanically and seems not to take much account of their
meaning.

Reference to a particular scene.

   The set consists of a barren plot at the rear of which stands
a spidery framework of piping of the sort used by construction
companies, supporting a catwalk. This framework fits with the
costumes (lots of armor, leather, heavy boots), suggesting a sort
of elemental, primitive, and somewhat sadistic world. The catwalk,
though effectively used when Macbeth goes off to murder Duncan
(whose room is presumably upstairs and offstage) is not much
used in later scenes. For the most part it is an interesting piece
of scenery but it is not otherwise helpful. For instance, there is
no reason why the scene with Macduff's wife and children is
staged on it. The costumes are not in any way Scottish—no
plaids—but in several scenes the sound of a bagpipe is heard, adding another weird or primitive tone to the production.

Description, but also analysis.

Concrete details to support evaluation.

   This Macbeth appeals to the eye, the ear, and the mind. The
director has given us a unified production that makes sense and
that is faithful to the spirit of Shakespeare's play.

Summary.

Much of what we want to say about this review we have already said in our marginal notes, but three additional points should be made:

1. The reviewer's feelings and evaluations are clearly expressed, not in such tedious and egotistical-sounding expressions as "furthermore I feel," and "it is also my opinion," but in such expressions as "a thoughtful and occasionally exciting production," "excellent," and "appeals to the eye, the ear, and the mind."

2. The evaluations are supported by details. For instance, the evaluation that the witches are effectively presented is supported by a brief description of their appearance.

3. The reviewer is courteous, even when (as in the discussion of the catwalk, in the next-to-last paragraph) she is talking about aspects of the production she doesn't care for.

WRITING A
COMPARISON

Something should be said about an essay organized around a comparison or a contrast between, say, two characters—in one play or even in two plays. Probably the student's first thought, after making some jottings, is to discuss half of the comparison and then go on to the second half. Instructors and textbooks usually condemn such an organization, arguing that the essay breaks into two parts and that the second part involves a good deal of repetition of categories set up in the first part. Usually they recommend that the student organize his or her thoughts differently, somewhat along the lines:

1. First similarity
   a. first work (or character, or characteristic)
   b. second work
2. Secondary similarity
   a. first work
   b. second work
3. First difference
   a. first work
   b. second work
4. Second difference
   a. first work
   b. second work

and so on, for as many additional differences as seen relevant. For example, if one wishes to compare King Lear with King Oedipus, one may organize the material thus:

1. First similarity: Each figure is a person of great authority
   a. Lear
   b. Oedipus
2. Second similarity: Each figure is ignorant
   a. Lear's ignorance of his daughters
   b. Oedipus's ignorance of his birth

3. First difference: Stage at which the character attains self-knowledge
   a. Lear's early recognition
   b. Oedipus's continuing ignorance until late in the play

Here is another way of organizing a comparison and contrast:

1. First point: Lack of self-knowledge
   a. similarities between Lear and Oedipus
   b. differences between Lear and Oedipus
2. Second point: The corrupt world
   a. similarities between the worlds in *King Lear* and *Oedipus*
   b. differences between the worlds in *King Lear* and *Oedipus*
3. Third point: Degree of attainment of self-knowledge
   a. similarities between Lear and Oedipus
   b. differences between Lear and Oedipus

But a comparison need not employ either of these structures. There is even the danger that an essay employing either of them may not come into focus until the essayist stands back from the seven-layer cake and announces, in the concluding paragraph, that the odd layers taste better. In one's preparatory thinking, one may want to make comparisons in pairs (Faults: Lear and Oedipus; Children: Lear's daughters, Oedipus's sons; Comments by others: the Fool on Lear, the Chorus on Oedipus . . .), but one must come to some conclusions about what these add up to before writing the final version. This final version should not duplicate one's thought processes; rather, it should be organized so as to make the point clearly and effectively. After reflection, one may believe that although there are superficial similarities between Lear and Oedipus, there are essential differences; then in the finished essay one probably will not wish to obscure the main point by jumping back and forth from play to play, working through a series of similarities and differences. It may be better to discuss King Lear and then point out that, although Oedipus resembles him in A, B, and C, Oedipus in D, E, and F does *not* resemble Lear. Some repetition in the second half of the essay (for example, "Oedipus comes very late to the deep self-knowledge that we see Lear achieve by the middle of the play") will serve to bind the two halves into a meaningful whole, making clear the degree of similarity or difference.

A SIMPLE, EFFECTIVE ORGANI-ZATION FOR A COMPO-SITION

The point of the essay presumably is not to list pairs of similarities or differences but to illuminate a work, or works, by making thoughtful comparison. Although in a long essay one cannot postpone until page 30 a discussion of the second half of the comparison, in an essay of, say, fewer than ten pages nothing is wrong with setting forth first one half of the comparison and then, in light of it, the second half. The essay will break into two unrelated parts if the second half makes no use of the first, or if it fails to modify the first half, but not if the second half looks back to the first half and calls attention to differences that the new material reveals. Students ought to learn how to write an essay with interwoven comparisons, but they ought also to know that there is another, simpler and clearer way to write a comparison.

COMMUNI-
CATING
JUDGMENTS
Because a critical essay on a play is a judicious attempt to help a reader see what is going on in a work or in a part of a work, the voice of the critic sounds, on first hearing, impartial; but good criticism includes—at least implicitly— evaluation. You can say not only that the setting changes (a neutral expression) but also that "the playwright aptly shifts the setting" or "unconvincingly introduces a new character," or "effectively juxtaposes . . ." These evaluations you support with evidence. You have feelings about the work under discussion, and you reveal them, as we have already pointed out in our discussion of the review of *Macbeth*, not by continually saying "I feel" and "this moves me," but by calling attention to the degree of success or failure you perceive. Nothing is wrong with occasionally using "I," and noticeable avoidances of it—passives, "this writer," "we," and the like—suggest an offensive sham modesty; but too much talk of "I" makes a writer sound like an egomaniac.

ASKING
QUESTIONS
TO GET
ANSWERS
We have already suggested that you can often find a thesis by asking two questions: *What is this doing?* and *Why do I have this response?* In a moment we will suggest many additional questions, but first we want to mention that the editorial apparatus throughout this book is intended to help you to read, enjoy, and discuss drama as fully as possible. When you are sitting down to write about a play, you may want to reread some parts of this apparatus for guidance on your topic, perhaps paying special attention to the Glossary entries on **character, convention, dialogue, diction, foil, irony, motivation, plot, suspense,** and **unity.** You may also want to reread some of the earlier material in the book, especially "The Language of Drama."

Now for additional questions that may help you to find topics and to sharpen them into theses.

Plot. Are certain developments (for example, Lear's madness) prepared for by foreshadowing?

Are certain happenings or situations recurrent? If so, what significance do you attach to them?

If there is a subplot, as in *King Lear,* how is it related?

What is the function of a particular scene? Why do certain scenes occur when and where they do?

Why are certain episodes reported rather than presented on the stage?

Are there irrelevant scenes?

Does the plot depend on chance?

Is the resolution satisfactory?

Character. What sort of person is So-and-so? (Of course a dramatic character is not likely to be thoroughly realistic in the sense of being a copy of someone we might know, but is the character coherent, perhaps representative of some human type?)

How is the character defined?

How trustworthy are the characters when they characterize themselves?

Others? (Consider what the character says and does, what others say about him or her and do to him or her and also consider other characters who more or less resemble the character in question, because the similarities—and the differences—may be significant.)

If a character is tragic, does the tragedy proceed from a flaw, from an intellectual error, from the malice of others, from sheer chance, or from some combination of these? If comic, do we laugh with, or at, the character?

Are the characters adequately motivated?

Do the characters change as the play goes on, or do we simply know them better at the end?

Is the character so meditative that we feel he or she is engaged less in a dialogue with others than in a dialogue with his or her own mind? If so, do we feel that this character is in large degree a spokesperson for the author, commenting not only on the world of the play but on the outside world too?

In a typical course paper you need not and probably should not take on all aspects of a character. With a play of great complexity—for example, one of Shakespeare's major plays—a short essay may do well to take an even smaller topic, such as Lear's use of prose (Why does he sometimes speak in prose, sometimes in verse, and what does it tell us about him?) or Lear's denunciation of sex (Why is the king obsessed with the idea of lechery?). Even here you will not be able merely to hunt through the play looking at Lear's prose or his remarks about sex; you will have to pay some attention to other uses of prose in *King Lear*, or to references to sex in the play, if you are to see the exact nature of the problem you have chosen to isolate.

Nonverbal Language. Words are not, it has been suggested in our discussion of drama (see especially pages 3–7), the only language of drama, and a student will sometimes want to explore matters of staging. What is especially difficult for most of us confronted with only a printed page is to catch the full dramatic quality of a play—to read the words and also to have a sense of how they will sound in the context of gestures and a setting. We tend to read drama as literature rather than as dramatic literature, or theater. (When the author is Shakespeare or Shaw, we can sometimes justly examine his works as literature, although even here we may find that things that seem flat on the page come alive in the theater.) Consider the setting, for example. Is it symbolic? Drama of the nineteenth and early twentieth centuries (for example, plays of Ibsen and Chekhov) is often thought to be "realistic," but of course even a realistic playwright or stage designer selects his or her material. A realistic setting can say a great deal, can serve as a symbol. Here is Ibsen on nonverbal devices:

> I can do quite a lot by manipulating the prosaic details of my plays so that they become theatrical metaphors and come to mean more than what they are; I have used costume in this way, lighting, scenery, landscape, weather; I have used trivial everyday things like inky fingers and candles; and I have used living figures as symbols of spiritual forces that act upon the hero. Perhaps

these things could be brought into the context of a modern realistic play to help me to portray the modern hero and the tragic conflict which I now understand so well.[1]

Over and over again in Ibsen we find the realistic setting of a nineteenth-century drawing room, with its heavy draperies and its bulky furniture, helping to convey his vision of a bourgeois world that oppresses the individual who struggles to affirm other values.

Contemporary dramatists are often explicit about the symbolic qualities of the setting. For example, in *The Glass Menagerie* Tennessee Williams says that the Wingfield apartment is

> one of those vast hive-like conglomerations of cellular living-units that flower as warty growths in overcrowded urban centers of lower middle-class popula-tion and are symptomatic of the impulse of this largest and fundamentally enslaved section of American society to avoid fluidity and differentiation. . . . The apartment faces an alley and is entered by a fire-escape, a structure whose name is a touch of accidental poetic truth, for all of these huge buildings are always burning with the slow and implacable fires of human desperation.

Gestures, too, can be symbolic. If you set out to write an essay on gestures in *King Lear*, you may come to see how rich the play is in such a symbolic gesture as kneeling or stripping off clothing, and it is similarly rich in sound effects—chiefly, of course, the storm, but also sounds of music and of fighting.

Similarly, costume (as we point out on pp. 5–6) often reveals rather than conceals. Again, even a realistic playwright such as Ibsen uses costume symbolically, as a close reading of *A Doll's House* will show.

Staging and Production. How would you stage the first scene of a given play? What kinds of costumes should the characters wear (assuming that these are not specified by the playwright)?

If you were producing the play, what scenes or speeches might you cut, and why?

Prepare a television script for the first scene of a play, indicating what the viewer would see at first (for example, a group of characters talking to each other) and then, bit by bit, what the camera would focus on. (Because the television screen is small, it cannot accommodate a view of the whole stage for more than a few moments; it must focus on a few figures in proximity, or even on the face of a single speaker or on the face of a character listening to a speaker.)

ORGANIZING AN ESSAY

Like a play, an essay on a play should be organized, and one can hardly go wrong in saying (as Aristotle said of plays) that an essay should have a beginning, a middle, and an end.

In the *beginning*, probably in the first paragraph, it's usually a good idea to state your thesis. You don't have to state it in the first sentence (you may, for

---

[1] Quoted by John Northam, "Ibsen's Search for the Hero," in *Ibsen*, ed. Rolf Fjelde (Englewood Cliffs, N.J.: Prentice-Hall, 1965), p. 99.

example, want to open with a quotation from the play), but state it early and clearly. In the *middle*, support your thesis with evidence, probably including some brief quotations from the play.

The middle, like the essay as a whole, should be organized. For example, if you are discussing the development of a character, you will probably want to move through the play act by act; if you are discussing symbolism—maybe blindness in *King Lear*—you may first want to discuss literal blindness (Gloucester's eyes are put out), and then figurative blindness (Lear doesn't "see" what he is doing). Probably you'll move from the obvious to the less obvious, or from the less important to the more important, in order to avoid a sense of anticlimax.

In the *end*, or conclusion, you will briefly recapitulate, but try also (lest your conclusion strike the reader as nothing more than an unnecessary restatement of what you said a moment ago) to set your findings in a larger context, the context of the entire play.

All writers must work out their own procedures and rituals (John C. Calhoun liked to plough his farm before writing), but the following suggestions may provide some help.

SUMMARY: HOW TO WRITE AN EFFECTIVE ESSAY[2]

1. **Read the play carefully.**

2. **Choose a worthwhile and manageable subject,** something that interests you and is not so big that your handling of it must be superficial. As you work, shape your topic into a thesis, moving, for example, from "The Character of King Lear" to "Change in King Lear."

3. **Reread the play, jotting down notes** of all relevant matters. As you read, reflect on your reading and record your reflections. If you have a feeling or an idea, jot it down; don't assume that you will remember it when you get around to writing your essay. The margins of this book are a good place for initial jottings, but many people find that in the long run it is easier to transfer these notes to 3 × 5 cards, writing on one side only.

4. **Sort out your cards** into some kind of reasonable divisions, and reject cards irrelevant to your topic. If you have adequately formulated your thesis (let's say, "Tom, not Laura, is the central character in *The Glass Menagerie*") you ought to be able to work out a tentative organization. As you work you may discover a better way to group your notes. If so, start reorganizing. Speaking generally, it is a good idea to organize your essay from the lesser material to the greater (to avoid anticlimax) or from the simple to the complex (to ensure intelligibility). If, for example, you are discussing the roles of three characters, it may be best to build up to the one of the three that you think the most important. If you are comparing two characters, it may be best to move from the most obvious contrasts to the least obvious. (In your opening paragraph, which will probably be almost the last thing you will write, you should of course give the reader an idea of the scope of the paper, but at this stage you are organizing the

---

[2] This section is adapted from Sylvan Barnet, *A Short Guide to Writing about Literature*, 5th ed. (Boston: Little, Brown, 1985), pp.41–44.

material chiefly for yourself and so you need not yet worry about an introductory paragraph.) When you have arranged your notes into a meaningful sequence of packets, you have approximately divided your material into paragraphs.

5. **Get it down on paper.** Most essayists find it useful to jot down some sort of outline, indicating the main idea of each paragraph and, under each main idea, supporting details that give it substance. An outline—not necessarily anything highly formal with capital and lowercase letters and roman and arabic numerals but merely key phrases in some sort of order—will help you to overcome the paralysis called "writer's block" that commonly afflicts professionals as well as students. A page of paper with ideas in some sort of sequence, however rough, ought to encourage you that you do have something to say. And so, despite the temptation to sharpen another pencil or to put a new ribbon into the typewriter, the best thing to do at this point is to sit down and start writing.

If you don't feel that you can work from note cards and a rough outline, try another method: get something down on paper, writing freely, sloppily, automatically, or whatever, but allow your ideas about what the work means to you and how it conveys its meaning—rough as they may be—to begin to take visible form. If you are like most people, you can't do much precise thinking until you have committed to paper at least a rough sketch of your initial ideas. Later you can push and polish your ideas into shape, perhaps even deleting all of them and starting over, but it's a lot easier to improve your ideas once you see them in front of you than it is to do the job in your head. On paper (or on a computer screen) one word leads to another; in your head one word often blocks another.

Just keep going; you may realize, as you near the end of a sentence, that you no longer believe it. O.K.; be glad that your first idea led you to a better one, and pick up your better one and keep going with it. What you are doing is, in a sense, by trial and error pushing your way not only toward clear expression but toward sharper ideas and richer responses.

6. If there is time, **reread the play,** looking for additional material that strengthens or weakens your main point; take account of it in your outline or draft.

7. **With your outline or draft in front of you, write a more lucid version,** checking your notes for fuller details, such as supporting quotations. If, as you work, you find that some of the points in your earlier jottings are no longer relevant, eliminate them; but make sure that the argument flows from one point to the next. As you write, your ideas will doubtless become clearer; some may prove to be poor ideas. (We rarely know exactly what our ideas are until we have them set down on paper. As the little girl said, replying to the suggestion that she should think before she spoke, "How do I know what I think until I say it?") Not until you have written a draft do you really have a strong sense of how good your essay may be.

8. After a suitable interval, preferably a few days, **read the draft with a view toward revising it,** not with a view toward congratulating yourself. A revision, after all, is a re-vision, a second (and presumably sharper) view. When you revise, you will be in the company of Picasso, who said that in painting a

picture he advanced by a series of destructions. A revision—say, the addition of an example, or the reorganization of the sequence of examples, or even the substitution of a precise word for an imprecise one—is not a matter of prettifying but of thinking. As you read, correct things that disturb you (for example, awkward repetitions that bore, inflated utterances that grate), add supporting detail where the argument is undeveloped (a paragraph of only one or two sentences is usually an undeveloped paragraph), and ruthlessly delete irrelevancies however well written they may be. But remember that a deletion probably requires some adjustment in the preceding and subsequent material. Make sure that the opening paragraph gives the readers some sense of where they will be going, and that between the opening and the closing paragraphs the argument, aided by transitions (such as "furthermore," "on the other hand," "in the next scene"), runs smoothly. The details should be relevant, the organization reasonable, the argument clear. Check all quotations for accuracy. Quotations are evidence, usually intended to support your assertions, and it is not nice to alter the evidence, even unintentionally. If there is time (there almost never is), put the revision aside, reread it in a day or two, and revise it again, especially with a view toward shortening it.

9. **Type or write a clean copy,** following the principles concerning margins, pagination, footnotes, and so on set forth in the next section of this discussion. If you have borrowed any ideas, be sure to give credit, usually in footnotes, to your sources. Remember that plagiarism is not limited to the unacknowledged borrowing of words; a borrowed idea, even when put into your own words, requires acknowledgment.

10. **Proofread and make corrections.**

Much of what follows regarding basic manuscript form is nothing more than common sense.

BASIC MANUSCRIPT FORM

1. Use 8½ × 11 paper of good weight. Keep as lightweight a carbon copy as you wish, or make a photocopy, but hand in a sturdy original.

2. If you typewrite or use a word processor, be sure to use a reasonably fresh ribbon, double-space, and type on one side of the page only. If you submit a handwritten copy, use lined paper and write on one side of the page only, in ink, on every other line. Most instructors do *not* want papers to be enclosed in any sort of binder; and most instructors want papers to be stapled in the upper left corner; do not crimp or crease corners and expect them to hold together.

3. Leave an adequate margin—an inch or an inch and a half—at top, bottom, and sides.

4. Number the pages consecutively, using arabic numerals in the upper right-hand corner.

5. Put your name and class or course number in the upper left-hand corner of the first page. It is a good idea to put your name in the upper right corner of each page so that your essay can be easily reassembled if a page gets separated.

6. Create your own title—one that reflects your topic or thesis. For example, a paper on *The Glass Menagerie* should *not* be called *"The Glass Menagerie"* but might be called "Tom's Romanticization of Laura: A View of *The Glass Menagerie."*

7. Center the title of your essay below the top margin of the first page. Begin the first word of the title with a capital, and capitalize each subsequent word except articles, conjunctions, and prepositions, thus: The Truth of Dreams in A *Midsummer Night's Dream.*

8. Begin the essay an inch or two below the title.

9. Your extensive revisions should have been made in your drafts, but minor last-minute revisions may be made—neatly—on the finished copy. Proofreading may catch some typographical errors, and you may notice some small weaknesses. Additions should be made *above* the line, with a caret (∧) *below* the line to indicate placement of the correction. Mark deletions by drawing a horizontal line through the word or words you wish to delete. Delete a single letter by drawing a vertical line through it. Use a vertical line, too, to separate words that should not have been run together.

QUOTATION
AND
QUOTATION
MARKS

Excerpts from the plays you are writing about are indispensable. Such quotations not only let the reader know what you are talking about, they present the material you are responding to, thus letting the reader share your responses. Here are some mechanical matters:

1. Identify the speaker or writer of the quotation, so that the reader is not left with a sense of uncertainty. Usually this identification precedes the quoted material (for example, "Smith says . . .") in accordance with the principle of letting readers know where they are going, but occasionally it may follow the quotation, especially if it will provide something of a pleasant surprise. For instance, in a discussion of Williams's *The Glass Menagerie*, you might quote a comment that seems to belittle the play and then reveal that Williams himself was the speaker.

2. The quotation must fit grammatically into your sentence. Suppose you want to use Lear's line, addressed to the Fool, "In boy; go first." Do *not* say:

In 3.4, in response to Lear's command, the Fool "go first."

You'll have to say something like this:

In 3.4, in response to Lear's command to "go first," the Fool enters the

hovel.

Or, of course, you can say,

In 3.4, Lear says to the Fool, "In boy; go first," and the Fool obeys.

3. The quotation must be exact. Any material that you add—even one or two words—must be in square brackets, thus:

When Lear says, "In boy; go [into the hovel] first," he shows a touch of

humility.

If you wish to omit material from within a quotation, indicate the ellipsis by three spaced periods. If a sentence ends in an omission, add a closed-up period and then three spaced periods to indicate the omission. The following example is based on a quotation from the sentences immediately above this one:

> The chapter says that "if you . . . omit material from within a quotation, [you must] indicate the ellipsis. . . . If a sentence ends in an omission, add a closed-up period and then three spaced periods. . . ."

Notice that although material preceded "If you," periods are not needed to indicate the omission because "If you" began a sentence in the original. Customarily, initial and terminal omissions are indicated only when they are part of the sentence you are quoting. Even such omissions need not be indicated when the quoted material is obviously incomplete—when, for instance, it is a word or phrase. Notice, too, that although quotations must be given word for word, the initial capitalization can be adapted, as here where "If" is reduced to "if."

When a line or more of verse is omitted from a passage that is set off, the three spaced periods are printed on a separate line:

> If we shadows have offended,
> Think but this, and all is mended;
> .   .   .
> Give me your hands, if we be friends,
> And Robin shall restore amends.

4. Distinguish between short and long quotations, and treat each appropriately. Short quotations (usually defined as fewer than three lines of verse or five lines of prose) are enclosed within quotation marks and run into the text (rather than set off, without quotation marks). Examples:

Near the end of Oedipus Rex the Chorus reminds the audience that

Oedipus "solved the famous riddle," but it does not tell us what the riddle

was.

King Lear's first long speech begins authoritatively: "Meantime we shall

express our darker purpose. / Give me the map there. Know that we have

divided / In three our kingdom."

Notice in the first passage that although four words only are being quoted, quotation marks are used, indicating that these are Sophocles's words, not the essayist's. Notice that in the second example a slash (diagonal line, virgule) is used to indicate the end of a line of verse other than the last line quoted. The slash is, of course, not used for prose, and it is not used if poetry is set off, indented, and printed as verse, thus:

King Lear's first long speech begins authoritatively:

> Meantime we shall express our darker purpose.
> Give me the map there. Know that we have divided
> In three our kingdom; and 'tis our fast intent
> To shake all cares and business from our age,
> Conferring them on younger strengths, while we
> Unburthened crawl toward death.

Material that is set off (usually three or more lines of verse, five or more lines of prose) is *not* enclosed within quotation marks. To set it off, triple-space before and after the quotation and single-space the quotation. Poetry should be centered; prose quotations should be flush with both right and left margins. (Note: Some manuals of style call for double-spacing, some for indenting prose quotations; but whichever procedure you adopt, be consistent. Be sparing in your use of long quotations.) Use quotations as evidence, not as padding. Do not bore the reader with material that can be effectively reduced either by paraphrase or by cutting. If you cut, indicate ellipses as explained above under 3.

5. Commas and periods go inside the quotation marks. (Exception: if the quotation is immediately followed by material in parentheses or in square brackets, close the quotation, then give the parenthetic or bracketed material, and then—after the closing parenthesis or bracket, put the comma or period.)

Marks of punctuation other than periods and commas (that is, semicolons, colons, and dashes) go outside quotation marks. Question marks and exclamation points go inside if they are part of the quotation, outside if they are your own. In the following example, the first two question marks are Shakespeare's, so they go *inside* of the quotation marks. The third question mark, however, is the essayist's, so it goes *outside* of the quotation marks.

> Lear asks the beggar, "Dids't thou give all to thy daughters?" The beg-
> gar's reply is, "Who gives anything to Poor Tom?" Are we surprised
> when he goes on to say, "Do Poor Tom some charity, whom the foul fiend
> vexes"?

6. Use *single* quotation marks for material contained within a quotation that itself is within quotation marks, thus:

> The editors of <u>Types of Drama</u> say, "With Puck we look at the antics in
>
> the forest, smile tolerantly, and say with a godlike perspective, 'Lord,
>
> what fools these mortals be!'"

7. Use quotation marks around titles of short works, that is, for titles of chapters in books and for essays that might not be published by themselves. Unpublished works, even book-length dissertations, are also enclosed in quota-

tion marks. Use italics (indicated by underlining) for books, that is, for plays, periodicals, and collections of essays.

You may wish to use a footnote, telling the reader that the passage you are quoting is found in this book on such-and-such a page. Let us assume that you have already mentioned the author and the title of the play and have just quoted a passage. At the end of the sentence that includes the quotation, or at the end of the quotation if you are offering it as an independent sentence, following the period type or write the number 1, elevating it slightly above the line. Do not put a period after the digit. Near the bottom of the paper, indent five spaces and type or write the number 1, elevated and without a period. Then write (giving the appropriate page number): A NOTE ON FOOTNOTES

> [1] Reprinted in Sylvan Barnet, Morton Berman, and William Burto, <u>Types of Drama</u>, 5th ed. (Boston: Scott, Foresman / Little, Brown, 1989), p. 236.

Notice that the abbreviation for *page* is p., not pg.; the abbreviation for *pages* is pp., thus: pp. 236–237. For verse plays, whose lines are numbered, the usual procedure is not to cite a page but to cite act, scene, and line numbers in parentheses after the quotation. The preferred method now is to give the act, scene, and line (if numbered in the text) in arabic numerals, with periods but no extra spaces (5.1.7–11) between the act and the scene. Or you may use the older method, and give the act in capital roman numerals, the scene in small roman numerals, and the line in arabic numerals, with periods following the act and scene: CITING ACT, SCENE, AND LINE

> The lunatic, the lover and the poet
> Are of imagination all compact.
> One sees more devils than vast hell can hold,
> That is the madman. The lover, all as frantic,
> Sees Helen's beauty in a brow of Egypt.
>
> (V.i.7–11)[1]

The footnote will then read:

> [1] All quotations from <u>A Midsummer Night's Dream</u> are from the text reprinted in Sylvan Barnet, Morton Berman, and William Burto, <u>Types of Drama</u>, 5th ed. (Boston: Scott, Foresman / Little, Brown, 1989).

If you have not mentioned the author or title of the work quoted, you need to give that information in the note, thus:

> [1] William Shakespeare, <u>A Midsummer Night's Dream</u>, reprinted in Sylvan Barnet, Morton Berman, and William Burto, <u>Types of Drama</u>, 5th ed. (Boston: Scott, Foresman / Little Brown, 1989).

If you have mentioned the author, but not the work, the note will go thus:

> [1] <u>A Midsummer Night's Dream</u>, reprinted in Sylvan Barnet, Morton Berman, and William Burto, <u>Types of Drama</u>, 5th ed. (Boston: Scott, Foresman / Little, Brown, 1989).

In short, you need not give information in the note that is already given in the main body of the essay.

In order to eliminate writing many footnotes, each one merely citing the page of a quotation, you can say, in the first footnote, after giving the bibliographical information as above, something like this:

> All further references to this work will be given parenthetically, within the text of the essay.

Thus, when you quote the next passage from the play, at the end of the sentence—just before the period—you need only insert a pair of parentheses enclosing the page number or the act, scene, and line number. Here is an example:

> At this point Lear goes out, saying, "O Fool, I shall go mad!" (p. 172).

or

> At this point Lear goes out, saying, "O Fool, I shall go mad!" (II.iv.287).

Notice that in the sample analysis on pp. 777–780 the author used only one footnote and then cited all of the other quotations parenthetically.

A NOTE ON INTERNAL CITATIONS
 If you use secondary sources, your instructor may want you to cite your source—usually an authority you are quoting or summarizing—parenthetically, within the body of your paper. Here is an example, citing page 29 of a book:

> In Comic Woman, Tragic Men, Linda Bamber says that in Shakespeare's
>
> plays, "The natural order, the status quo, is for men to rule women"
>
> (29).

Or:

> In Shakespeare's plays "the natural order," Bamber says, "is for men to
>
> rule women" (29), but she goes on to modify this statement.

At the end of your paper, on a separate page, give a list headed "Works Cited," listing all of your sources, alphabetically by author, with last name first, then the title (underlined, to indicate italics), then the place of publication, the publisher, and the date. After the date, type a period.

> Bamber, Linda. Comic Women, Tragic Men. Stanford. Stanford UP, 1982.

For details on how to cite journals, books published in more than one volume, translations, and dozens of other troublesome works, see Joseph Gibaldi and Walter S. Achtert, *MLA Handbook for Writers of Research Papers*, 2nd ed. (New York: MLA, 1984). (By the way, MLA stands for Modern Language Association.)

WRITING DRAMA

Your instructor may ask you to write some dialogue, such as might constitute one scene in a play; or you may be asked to turn some classic short story into a one-act play, or even to write an original one-act play.

WRITING A SCENE

If you are asked to write a scene that might be part of a longer work, once you have settled on the situation, on what is happening (we will give some examples in a moment), try to get your characters fairly clearly in mind even before you begin writing—though of course once you start writing you will doubtless revise your view of them. For instance, if in your scene a college student tells her parents that she is dropping out of college, think hard about who these people are. What is their ethnic background, what do they wear, what sort of furnishings surround them, and what kinds of food do they eat? How old are they? How much money do they have? What attitudes toward education do they have? Why? Is the student immature, mature, troubled, timid, adventurous, or what? What gestures do the characters use? How do they stand or sit? How do they speak (thoughtfully, hesitantly, vigorously)? With what sort of vocabulary? With what sort of rhythm? What sorts of people are the parents? Is the father intolerant but the mother sympathetic, or the father baffled and the mother hostile, or what? Further, if (for instance) you conceive of the mother as intolerant of the daughter's goals, *why* is she intolerant? Because she is afraid that her daughter will excel her? Or because, on the contrary, she strongly feels her own limitations and is so eager for her daughter to transcend them that she cannot understand the daughter's choice of what seems to the mother to be a very limited goal?

In short, what is said (and done) in any given situation will largely depend on the particular people who are talking and acting. Only if you have a strong sense of what kinds of people your characters are—so strong a sense of them that you can imagine what their homes look like, what they wear, and how they would behave not only in this situation but in almost any situation—will you be able to write convincing, interesting dialogue. The point: as they speak and act, the characters reveal more of themselves than they are aware of.

Following is a list of encounters you might want to try to set forth in a scene of two or three pages. But first we want to add three points.

1. We leave to you the difficult job of creating the particular personalities who are in these situations. In your introductory stage directions you can describe and briefly characterize the speakers and the setting, but remember that an audience will not be aware of these comments. The audience will understand the characters only through the language, gestures (stage business), and setting.

2. Your characters should be believable individuals, not mere stereotypes. Nevertheless, since each will be a coherent personality, in some degree each will stand for something. That is, each will be a concrete embodiment (but not a flat or abstract version) of a type of person and a point of view.

3. Among the most interesting confrontations in drama are those of one right with another, not of right against wrong.

Now for the sample encounters:

1. A female college student tells her drama instructor (a male) that she wants to stage Eve Merriam's *Out of Our Fathers' House*. (How does he respond, and why?)

2. A person responding to an ad offering to sell a car comes to talk to the owner. (Your dialogue should give the reader a strong sense of what sort of person each one is.)

3. A young woman, seeking a job as a driver, is interviewed by the male owner of a taxi cab company.

4. A Chicano or Asian American is telling a friend (of similar ethnic background) about a job interview that he or she has just had with an Anglo employer.

5. A young white man tells his parents that he intends to marry a young black woman.

6. A black woman tells some black friends that she plans to marry a white man.

7. A middle-aged married woman, assuming that her older unmarried sister must be unhappy, tells her that marriage isn't so great.

8. A character wants something (perhaps money, a job, or approval) that another character does not want to give.

9. A member of some minority group is talking with a friend who makes what is supposed to be an amusing ethnic slur.

10. If you have read Clare Boothe Luce's update (*Slam the Door Softly*) of Ibsen's *A Doll's House* and feel that you want the characters to say something quite different, write your own version. Or take two characters from some other play—perhaps from Molière's *The Misanthrope* or from Wilson's *Fences*—and let them continue the issue, in today's terms.

Two additional points:

1. Before you set to work, please read the rest of this discussion; it concerns the importance of giving a shape or pattern to a scene.

2. After you have drafted and revised your scene, ask some friends to take the roles and to read the dialogue aloud. Listen as impartially as possible, and then revise your work where necessary, making the dialogue more convincing and the dramatic conflict more effective.

Your instructor may want not just a scene but a play, perhaps your dramatized version of a short story, say by Hawthorne or Poe or Updike or Flannery O'Connor. If so, your plot and characters (and some of your lines) are already established for you, but you will still have to invent much of the dialogue and the gestures. Almost surely you will have to arrange the dialogue to include exposition that a storyteller may simply tell the reader directly, and probably you will have to omit some episodes and combine some others into one episode. The author of the original story will doubtless have given it a significant structure, but you may have to reshape it at least slightly, since you are converting a story into a play.

At this point we may digress for a moment, and talk about construction in drama. A playwright (not "playwrite") is a *wright*, that is, a maker—a maker of plays, just as a shipwright is a maker of ships. And a play is made with characters engaged in a plot. The word *plot* itself suggests the importance of "making" or "building" or "constructing," since the original meaning of the word was a parcel of land (as in "a plot of ground"); the plot originally was the area staked out, on which one might then build. When one looks closely at a good play, one always sees that it has been designed carefully and built well. Consider, for instance, the basic pattern or groundplan of A *Midsummer Night's Dream*. The play begins (1.1) and ends (5.1) in Athens. Just after the first scene, and then again just before the last scene, Shakespeare gives us scenes of the comic workmen (1.2 and 4.2). And in between these scenes we are in the forest (2.1–4.1). A close analysis will reveal numerous contrasts and similarities between scenes. Few if any viewers are conscious of the pattern—of the architecture, we might say— but the pattern probably makes its effect nevertheless. In the words of the dramatist Friedrich Hebbel,

CONSTRUC-
TION IN
DRAMA

> A genuine drama is comparable to one of those big buildings which have almost as many rooms and corridors below ground as above ground. People in general are aware only of the latter; the master builder is aware of the former as well.

Or take the structure not of an entire play but of a single scene, the first in *King Lear*, where Lear makes the enormous mistake of giving his kingdom to two of his daughters and of banishing the third. If (so to speak) we stand back from the scene, we notice that it falls into three parts, which we can characterize as a prologue (lines 1–35, in prose), a central portion (Lear's decisions), and an epilogue (lines 270–312, the latter part of it in prose). The prologue is rather intimate; Gloucester and Kent begin the play by chatting about public affairs, and then their conversation turns to talk about Gloucester's sons. The epilogue, too (which is about the same length as the prologue), is relatively intimate or private; it begins with the banished sister taking her farewell of her two wicked sisters, and it ends with the two wicked sisters, speaking prose, plotting against Lear. Between these two passages, beginning with Lear's entrance at line 36 and ending with Lear's exit at line 268, is, of course, the highly ceremonial scene of Lear inviting his three daughters to speak, their speeches, and his responses. Further, within this central part of the scene the speeches of the three daughters fall into patterns, but here we need not go into that.

Your instructor may ask you to write a one-act play of your own invention. A distinction is often made between the one-act play and the full-length play,

THE ONE-
ACT PLAY

but the terms are a bit misleading. A one-act play, like a three-act play or a five-act play, is "full-length" in the sense that it treats its material as fully as is appropriate. Usually, of course, the material of the one-act play is more limited than that of a longer play. For instance, it usually covers less time and deals with fewer characters. Thus, if the piece really is a one-act play and not just a short play with two or more scenes, the time covered by the play usually corresponds closely to real time; that is, the play covers something like from twenty to perhaps forty minutes. And, again, the action probably involves only a few characters; indeed, some one-act plays are monologues, although most use two or three characters.

Generally only a single incident is dramatized: two strangers exchange words on a park bench, and one ends up dead (Albee, *The Zoo Story*); an angry man goes to a woman to collect an overdue payment and ends up courting her (Chekhov, *The Boor*); sailors on a ship during war suspect a fellow sailor or being a spy, break into his locker, and find not incriminating documents but a letter concerning a failed love affair (O'Neill, *In the Zone*). None of these plays has the scope of, say, *King Lear*, which covers several months and which is rich in parallels and contrasts. For instance, in *Lear* the stories of Cordelia, Kent, and Edgar all involve persons whose love is so deep that they can forgive actions that others might think intolerable.

A one-act play cannot have the complexity of a three- or five-act play; still, we will see something of the subtlety that even a one-act play can convey if we think about Susan Glaspell's *Trifles* (page 399). To take perhaps the two most obvious examples: (1) the men form a contrast to the women (though the two women are by no means interchangeable), and (2) the broken hinge of the bird cage, the broken neck of the bird, the broken neck of the man, and the broken spirit of the wife are all part of a pattern.

James Joyce spoke unkindly of one-act plays as "dwarf drama," implying that the one-act play is a miniature three-act play. But most writers of one-act plays do not pack a three-act play into one act; rather, as we have already said, they severely limit the time covered and the number of characters, usually concentrating on one or two figures involved in a single episode. Although Joyce scorned the form, major playwrights (we have already mentioned Albee, Chekhov, and O'Neill, and many others could be named) have found the one-act play a worthy vehicle.

What sort of structure does a one-act play have? In the late nineteenth century, and in the first half of the twentieth, it was commonplace to say that a play, whether in three acts or in one, has a pyramidal structure; that is, it rises to a climax, and it then descends or unknots. A variation was to say that the structure of a play is like an arch, with the turning point in the plot resembling the keystone. Or, to go back more than two thousand years, in Aristotle's terms a play has a beginning, a middle, and an end. Although some plays since the 1950s have seemed to use a different structure (a wit has said that in Beckett's *Waiting for Godot*—a play in two acts—nothing happens, twice), the old pattern is still often used effectively, and indeed it may be found even in many works that, at first glance, seem not to use it.

There are other ways of expressing the idea: one ancient formula (speaking of the three-act play, but applicable also to the structure of a one-act play) goes thus: In the first act, get your people up a tree, in the second act throw stones at them, and in the third act get them down. In romantic comedy this formula often takes the shape of "Boy meets girl, boy loses girl, boy gets girl." With a little thought it is evident that such formulas are versions of Aristotle's beginning, middle, and end—or, as Peter De Vries cleverly put it, "beginning, muddle, and end." That is, a stable situation (the beginning) is disrupted (the middle) and then resolved (the end).

Almost every scene or act in a long play has something of this structure, at least to the extent that a scene or act develops. Line by line it may seem to be simply adding a unit to a unit, but in retrospect the whole has a unity, a definite shape. Even a scene that consists of a single speech is likely to move from (in effect), "What am I to do?" to "I'll do X," to "Now I feel better (or worse)"; that is, the scene builds to a climax in complexity or tension and then settles toward a resolution or relaxation.

Almost surely your first few drafts of a scene or an act will *not* have an effective pattern—but then comes the job of rewriting the material so that it becomes not mere dialogue but drama. You can test your scene by rewriting it in a few sentences as a scenario, that is, without any dialogue. Does the summary of the encounter have a shape—a beginning, a middle, and an end?

And this gets us to our final point. An effective scene, or an effective one-act play, of course gives us characters in whom we are interested—characters whose ideas or passions hold our attention—but it also gives a shape to the presentation of those ideas or passions. Aristotle said that the arts arise from two impulses, the impulse to imitate, and the impulse toward harmony. The first of these (except in certain forms, such as farce) requires realistic dialogue and convincing characterization; we listen to the characters speak and we say, "Yes, that is how people sound, that's the way they behave." But obviously works of art do not simply offer language that imitates the language we can hear on the campus or in a bus. Works of art—songs are the most obvious example—put language into a harmonious shape. They impose a pattern (songs use meter, melody, and rhyme), and here we get to Aristotle's second point, that works of art arise partly from the human instinct for harmony. The impulse toward harmony requires a shapely "plot," a territory staked out, and then a blueprint or plan that is converted into a well-ordered construction.

LAST WORDS

A GLOSSARY
OF DRAMATIC TERMS

Absurd, Theater of the. Drama of such writers as Eugène Ionesco and Samuel Beckett in France and Harold Pinter in England that imitates the absurdity of our existence. "Everything, as I see it, is an aberration," Ionesco has said. Among the basic themes are: loneliness in a world without God; inability to communicate; dehumanization at the hands of mass media; and impotence in the face of society and of death. Though the plays are serious, they may contain extravagantly comic scenes in depicting a reality that is absurd, illogical, senseless, a world of futility and meaningless clichés. In Ionesco's *The Chairs* (1951) an elderly couple rush about, filling a room with chairs for nonexistent visitors. Old age is a fact, but an absurdity, too, and old people are incomprehensible. At the end of *The Chairs*, an orator who is to deliver a solemn talk about the truths of life turns out to be deaf and dumb and merely makes unintelligible noises and gestures to the invisible crowd. Ionesco summarizes the theme of *The Chairs* (*The New York Times*, June 1, 1958): "I have tried to deal . . . with emptiness, with frustration, with this world, at once fleeting and crushing. The characters I have used are not fully conscious of their spiritual rootlessness, but they feel it instinctively and emotionally." One basis of the inability to communicate, and one that the "Absurd" dramatists seize upon, is the corruption of language. The absurdity of trying to communicate by means of a debased language is dramatized by Ionesco in *The Bald Soprano* (1948), where the characters speak in clichés. Because the characters are incomprehensible and the happenings illogical and baffling, the spectators cannot simply sit back in ease but are continually challenged to grasp the play's meaning. The theater of the absurd (pp. 146–147) can be said to be a descendent of expressionism (see p. 817). Consult M. Esslin, *The Theatre of the Absurd*.

act. A main division in drama or opera. Act divisions probably arose in Roman theory and derive ultimately from the Greek practice of separating episodes in a play by choral interludes, but Greek (and probably Roman) plays were performed without interruption, for the choral interludes were part of the plays themselves. The division of Elizabethan plays into five acts is often the work of editors rather than authors. No play of Shakespeare's was published in his lifetime with divisions into five acts. Today an act division is commonly indicated by lowering the curtain and turning up the houselights. A **scene** is a smaller unit, either (1) a division with no change of locale or abrupt shift of time, or (2) a division consisting of an actor or a group of actors on the stage. According to the second definition, the departure or entrance of an actor changes the composition of the group and thus produces a new scene. In an entirely different sense, the scene is the locale where a work is set. The first speech in *Romeo and Juliet* informs the audience of the play's locale: "In fair Verona, where we lay our scene." Often the décor lets the spectator know where the play is set, but during the last hundred years playwrights have tended, for the convenience of readers, to write long stage directions describing the scene. Here is the beginning of the first stage direction in Shaw's *Candida*: "A fine morning in October 1894 in the north east quarter of London, a vast district miles away from the London of Mayfair and St. James's, and much less narrow, squalid, fetid and airless in its slums."

action. (1) The physical movement of an actor, whether he is leaping into Ophelia's grave or speaking softly to himself. That talk is action is easily seen in the Bastard's remark (*King John*, 2.1.466): "Zounds! I was never so bethumped with words / Since I first called my brother's father dad." (2) An incident in the plot, an episode. Aristotle's statement that a drama is an "imitation of an action" (*praxis*) has provoked considerable controversy; recently there has been a tendency to regard this action as the motive underlying the outward deeds of the plot. Francis Fergusson says (in *The Human Image in Dramatic Literature,* p. 116), for example, that the action of *Oedipus the King* "is the quest for Laius's slayer, . . . which persists through the changing circumstances of the play."

acto. A short dramatic sketch, written in a mixture of Spanish and English, often with stereotyped characters satirizing the anglo establishment. The form, developed by Luis Valdez in 1965 during a strike by farm workers in California, aims at stimulating Chicanos to value their culture and to unite against exploitation. Consult *The Drama Review* 11:4 (1967).

aesthetic distance, or **psychical distance.** The detachment between the receptor and the work of art. The concept is chiefly associated with Edward Bullough (see the essay in his *Aesthetics,* reprinted in Melvin Rader, *A Modern Book of Aesthetics*). Bullough explains that there must be some sort of psychical "distance" (gap) between our practical self (our personal needs) and the work of art. Thus, an old man who has been treated harshly by his children may be unable to divorce his personal feelings from *King Lear.* He may be too involved with the piece as life to see it as art. But "distance" does not mean that the receptor is totally detached or objective. Rather, he is detached from his usual personal involvements, and because of this detachment he can look with a new vigorous interest—he can look with a new sort of passion born of his new personality—at the work of art as art. Persons who do not understand the need for distance between themselves and a work, Bullough explains,

commonly say that they do not wish to see a tragedy because there is enough suffering in real life. But the more sophisticated spectator at a tragedy realizes that as a picture is distanced by the frame, a play is distanced from the audience (the characters may speak verse, they perform behind footlights, and their deeds cohere to make a unified harmonious pattern); the feelings it evokes are not the feelings evoked by a roughly similar event in real life. In the theater we feel "rapturous awe" at what in life would be depressing. See also *dramatic illusion, empathy, epic drama.*

agon (Greek: *contest*). A debate in a Greek comedy. See p. 199. In the last few decades the term has been used (e.g., by Francis Fergusson, *The Idea of a Theater*) to designate a scene of conflict in tragedy, such as the agonizing struggle between Oedipus and Teiresias.

agroikos. See *character.*

alazon. See *character.*

alienation effect. See *epic drama.*

allegory. Often a narrative wherein abstractions (e.g., virtue, fear) are made concrete (Mr. Virtue, Giant Fear), for the purpose of effectively communicating a moral. But in essence an allegory is merely a system of equivalents. Though allegory need not personify abstractions, allegoric drama almost always does. *Everyman* (c. 1500), an allegoric morality play, includes among its dramatis personae Death, Good Deeds, Beauty, and of course, Everyman. But morality plays may also include allegoric castles (standing for strength or chastity), roses (standing for love or virtue), and so on. Consult Bernard Spivack, *Shakespeare and the Allegory of Evil.* (See also *symbolism.*)

anagnorisis, or **disclosure, discovery, recognition.** For Aristotle the "recognition" or "disclosure" seemed to be merely a recognition of who is who, by such tokens as birthmarks, clothes, and so on, but the term has been extended to include the tragic hero's recognition of himself and/or the essence of life. Thus Othello, having murdered his faithful wife, learns he was beguiled into thinking her dishonest and finally recognizes himself as "one not easily jealous, but being wrought / Perplexed in the extreme"; and he exacts justice from himself by suicide. For examples from *King Lear, Hamlet,* and *Macbeth,* see pp. 68–69.

antagonist. See *plot, protagonist.*

antecedent action. See *plot.*

anticlimax. A descent, the lines or happenings being markedly less important or less impressive than their predecessors. In melodrama, a decrease in tension may cause disappointment and loss of interest; in comedy, a sharp descent (the beautiful princess opens her mouth and sounds like a burlesque queen) may get a desirable laugh. On the desirability of a gradual decrease in tension in tragedy (i.e., a "quiet ending"), consult Max Beerbohm, "Last Acts," in *Around Theatres.*

antimasque. See *masque.*

arena stage. (1) In British usage, a stage with a back wall and with an audience on three sides. (2) In American usage, a playing space surrounded by spectators, **theater-in-the-round.** Proponents of arena staging (in the American sense) stress the intimacy afforded by having actors in the midst of the audience, but opponents suggest that at least for some plays the intimacy ought not to be very great. (See *aesthetic distance.*) It has

been noted, too, that even in arena staging the audience normally feels set apart from the actors, for the audience is in the dark while the actors are in an illuminated playing area. Critics of arena staging cite the following difficulties: soliloquies, asides, and direct addresses are hard to deliver in such a theater; directors, aware that the back of an actor's head is not very expressive, tend to have the actors gyrate disturbingly and meaninglessly; entrances and exits are cumbersome; little use can be made of elevation and of groupings of actors.

Apollonian. See *Dionysus.*

arras. See *Elizabethan playhouse.*

aside. See *convention, soliloquy.*

atmosphere. The mood created by setting, language, and happenings.

blocking. The director's organization of the movement on the stage, including the chief stage business (e.g., head scratching) and exits and entrances.

bombast. Rant, speech that is too inflated for the occasion; from a word meaning "cotton stuffing." In Marlowe's *Tamburlaine* (c. 1587), Tamburlaine brags thus:

Our quivering lances, shaking in the air,
And bullets, like Jove's dreadful thunderbolts,
Enrolled in flames and fiery smoldering mists,
Shall threat the gods more than Cyclopian wars:
And with our sun-bright armor as we march,
Will chase the stars from Heaven and dim their
 eyes
That stand and muse at our admirèd arms.

bomolochos. See *character.*

bourgeois drama. A serious play with middle-class dramatis personae. There are a few Elizabethan tragedies of middle-class life, but bourgeois drama, with its emphasis on pathos, is more or less an eighteenth-century invention. Bourgeois dramas were written in the eighteenth and nineteenth centuries, apparently in response to the middle class's desire to see itself on the stage; the bourgeoisie by the eighteenth century regarded themselves as a suitable replacement for the noblemen of earlier tragedy. Speaking generally, the characteristics of these plays are middle-class dramatis personae, virtue in distress, sentimentality, and an unreasonably high moral tone. Eighteenth-century critics, not sure what to do with pathetic plays on middle-class life, used the terms **drame, drame bourgeois, comédie larmoyante** (tearful comedy), **tragédie bourgeoise,** and **bürgerliches Trauerspiel** (bourgeois tragedy) interchangeably. (Note that a *comédie larmoyante* need not end happily, nor a *tragédie bourgeoise* end sadly.) In England, George Lillo's *The London Merchant* (1731), "a tale of private woe. A London 'prentice ruined," depicted an apprentice who murdered his benefactor. Bourgeois drama in the nineteenth century became melodrama in many hands and tragedy in Ibsen's hands. Consult Fred O. Nolte, *Early Middle Class Drama*; and Eric Auerback, *Mimesis*, Ch. 17. On Ibsen as a bourgeois dramatist, consult Eric Bentley, *The Playwright as Thinker*. See *domestic tragedy, sentimental,* and pp. 76–78, 532–534.

box set. See *realism.*

burla. See *commedia dell'arte.*

burlesque. Any imitation that, by distortion, aims to amuse. Its subject matter is sometimes said to be faults rather than vices, and its tone is neither shrill nor savage. Thus, in distinction from satire it can be defined as a comic imitation of a mannerism or a minor fault (either in style or subject matter), con-

trived to arouse amusement rather than indignation. In the theater, a burlesque may be a play that amusingly criticizes another play by grotesquely imitating aspects of it, as Gay's *The Beggar's Opera* (1728) mimicked serious operas. In England, a burlesque may be a musical extravaganza in which fantasy has almost entirely ousted criticism. In America, burlesque (especially popular in the late nineteenth and first half of the twentieth century) is usually a sort of vaudeville or variety show stressing bawdy humor and sex. The sexual theme is most fully revealed in the striptease, introduced about 1920. See *comedy, satire.*

catastrophe. See *plot.*

catharsis. Aristotle and countless followers said that tragedy evokes pity and fear and that it produces in the spectator a catharsis (purgation, or, some scholars hold, purification) of these emotions: it drains or perhaps refines or modifies these emotions, and thus tragedy is socially useful. (Aristotle's *Poetics* is the subject of much controversy; one cannot with security assert that Aristotle said anything without a counter-argument being offered. For various views of catharsis, consult F. L. Lucas, *Tragedy*, and Gerald F. Else's monumental *Aristotle's Poetics*.)

character. (1) One of the dramatis personae, e.g., King Lear. (2) The personality of such a figure. Characters are sometimes divided into **flat** and **round characters.** The former have only one "side," representing a single trait (e.g., the faithful wife, the genial drunkard); the latter have many traits and are seen, as it were, from all sides, in the round. The behavior of flat characters is thoroughly predictable; that of round characters is sometimes unexpected though credible. A **stock character** is a type that recurs in many works. For example, from Greek comedy to the present there have been numerous braggart soldiers, stubborn fathers, jealous husbands. Northrop Frye finds four chief types of comic figures: (1) the **alazon,** the imposter, boaster, hypocrite; (2) the **eiron** (see irony), the man who deprecates himself and exposes the boaster; (3) the **bomolochos,** the buffoon, or more generally, the man who entertains by his mannerisms and talk; and (4) the **agroikos,** the straightman who is the unwitting butt of humor. Each of these types appears in many dresses; the *alazon*, for example, is most commonly the braggart soldier (*miles gloriosus*), but he is also the pedant, the crank, or anyone who is full of ideas that have no relation to reality. (See *commedia dell'arte*; consult Northrop Frye, *Anatomy of Criticism*, pp. 171–176, and R. L. Hunter, *The New Comedy of Greece and Rome.*) Stock characters are not limited to comedy: the proud tragic hero is a stock character, as are, for example, the cruel stepmother and the son who wishes to avenge his father. See also *motivation, plot*. Consult J. L. Styan, *The Elements of Drama*, Ch. 8.

chorus. In Greek drama, a group of singers and dancers (*khoros* in Greek means "dancer") who play a role, e.g., Old Men of Corinth. (The chorus leader is the **koryphaios.**) In Aeschylus's *The Suppliants* (c. 490 B.C.), perhaps the earliest extant play, the chorus consists of the heroines, but in most Greek plays the chorus consists of subsidiary figures who comment rather helplessly on what is happening to the important people. Aeschylus reduced the chorus of fifty to twelve; Sophocles increased it to fifteen, where it remained. The Greek chorus, it is often said, is a sort of middleman between the unusual main figures and the humdrum spectators. Elizabethan dramas occasionally had a chorus of one actor who, not a participant in the story, commented on it. The Chorus (or

prologue) in Shakespeare's *Henry* V urges the audience to

> Think when we talk of horses that you see them
> Printing their proud hoofs i' the receiving earth;
> For 'tis your thoughts that now must deck our
>   kings.
> Carry them here and there, jumping o'er times,
> Turning the accomplishment of many years
> Into an hour-glass: for the which supply,
> Admit me Chorus to this history:
> Who prologue-like your humble patience pray,
> Gently to hear, kindly to judge, our play.

A **chorus character,** or *raisonneur,* however, such as Enobarbus in *Antony and Cleopatra*, is a character who participates in the story yet seems to be the author's mouthpiece, intelligently commenting (often with irony) on the actions of the other characters. But Alfred Harbage, in *As They Liked It*, skeptically and aptly calls such a figure "The Unreliable Spokesman." The use of the chorus, in one form or another, continues into our times, for example in T. S. Eliot's *Murder in the Cathedral*, whose "Chorus of Women of Canterbury," like a Greek chorus and like the audience, "are forced to bear witness"; and in Tennessee Williams's *The Glass Menagerie*, whose Tom Wingfield tells the audience he is "the narrator of the play, and also a character in it." See also *plot*.

climax. See *plot*.

closet drama. A play suited only for reading, not for acting. Most nineteenth-century English poetic dramas (e.g., Coleridge's, Shelley's, Tennyson's) fit into this category, although Byron's plays have recently been moving out of the closet. Consult Moody Prior, *The Language of Tragedy*.

comedy. Most broadly, anything amusing, whether a literary work or a situation. More specifically, comedy is (in Dr. Johnson's words) "such a dramatic representation of human life, as may excite mirth." Dramatic comedies generally depict a movement from unhappiness to happiness, from (for example) young lovers frustrated by their parents to young lovers happily married. The unhappy situation is so presented that it entertains rather than distresses the spectator; it is ridiculous or diverting rather than painful.

Comic drama seems related to fertility rituals; it celebrates generation, renewal, variety (laughing away any narrow-minded persons who seek to limit life's abundance), and it celebrates human triumphs over the chances of life. Irate parents and shipwrecks cannot prevent journeys from ending with lovers meeting. For the kinds of Greek comedy (Old, Middle, and New) see pp. 198–202. For the stock characters in Greek comedy, see *character*. Consult C. Hoy, *The Hyacinth Room; Theories of Comedy*, ed. P. Lauter; L. J. Potts, *Comedy*.

comedy of humors. A term sometimes applied to plays—notably those of Ben Jonson—wherein the characters, though somewhat individualized, obviously represent types or moods (the jealous husband, the witless pedant). A humor was a bodily liquid (blood [Latin: *sanguis*], phlegm, yellow bile, black bile) thought to control one's behavior. Allegedly, a proper mixture produced a well-adjusted person, but a preponderance of any one humor produced a distorted personality. The old sense of the word survives in the phrase, "He is in a bad humor"; *sanguine, phlegmatic,* and *bilious* are also modern survivals of the old psychology of humors. **Humor characters** are common in **situational comedy**; they are engineered by a clever plot into a situation that displays their absurdity: the man who craves silence is confronted with a talkative woman; the coward is confronted by the braggart.

comedy of manners, comedy of wit. See *high comedy*.

comic relief. Humorous episodes in tragedy, alleged to alleviate or lighten the tragic effect. Some comic scenes in tragedy, however, not only provide "relief" but enlarge the canvas of tragedy, showing us a fuller picture of life. The clown who brings Cleopatra the poisonous asp sets her tragedy against the daily world. Critics have increasingly noted that the comic scenes (such as the macabre comments of the gravediggers in *Hamlet*) often deepen rather than alleviate the tragic effect. See *tragicomedy*. Consult A. P. Rossiter, *Angel with Horns*, Ch. 14.

commedia dell'arte. Italian drama, more or less improvised, performed by professionals in Italy and abroad, mostly in the sixteenth century but still alive in the early eighteenth century. In contrast to the classically inspired written drama (**commedia erudita**) performed by actors who memorized their lines, *commedia dell'arte* (perhaps best translated as "professional drama") employed sketches of plots (**scenario;** plural: **scenarii**) specifying entrances and exits and the gist of the dialogue; in performance these *scenarii* were fleshed out with stock bits of comic stage business (**lazzi**) or larger pieces of business (**burle**) such as practical jokes. (The singulars are **lazzo** and **burla**.) Thus a *scenario* may call for the *lazzo* of anger, or the *burla* of chasing a fly, and leave it to the actor to work out the swats and the smile when at last he munches the fly. Though these plays are said to have been improvised, the stock characters, stock situations, and stock stage business make them something more—or less—than improvised. The chief characters—most of whom wore masks—are Pantolone, an elderly Venetian merchant wearing a little cap, a red jacket, loose trousers (hence our word "pants"), and slippers; his age, amours, and avarice make him ridiculous; Dottore, a Bolognese doctor wearing a black academic gown: his age and his pedantry make him ridiculous; Capitano, a soldier, ridiculous because a braggart and a coward; several servants called *zanne* (singular: *zanni*, from *Gianni*, "Johnny"), including Arlecchino (later Harlequin), who in the sixteenth century wore patches that in the next century were represented by triangles or diamonds; Brighella, a rather cruel and crafty rogue; Pulcinella, noted for his resourcefulness and his disguises; Pedrolino, a naive valet who becomes the melancholy Pagliacci and Pierrot; Colombina, who later becomes Columbine and loves Harlequin. Further, there are usually four lovers, children of the two Old Men. Consult Allardyce Nicoll, *Masks, Mimes and Miracles*, and *The World of Harliquin*; and K. M. Lea, *Italian Popular Comedy*.

complication. See *plot*.

confidant (feminine: **confidante**); A character in whom a principal character confides, revealing his state of mind and often furthering the exposition. Horatio is Hamlet's confidant; Oenone is Phèdre's. Although Horatio and Oenone are memorable, the confidant is sometimes absurdly vapid; though the French defended the device as more plausible than the soliloquy, the confidant may be more trouble than he is worth. In *The Critic* (1779), Sheridan ridiculed it thus: "Enter Tilburina stark mad in white satin, and her confidante stark mad in white linen."

conflict. See *plot*.

convention. An unrealistic device that the public agrees to tolerate. Thus, a character in a drama may express her thoughts aloud and not be heard by other characters (the **aside**), or she may speak her thoughts aloud on the empty stage (the **soliloquy**). Italian characters (e.g., Desdemona and Iago) speak English, yet are understood to be speaking Italian. In motion pictures, one image fades out, another fades in, and through this convention

the audience knows that there is a shift in time or place. More generally any character-type, any theme or motif (e.g., the suspected butler), widely used in literature or drama is a convention. Similarly, **realism,** though apparently opposed to conventions, has its own conventions. For instance, a realistic set showing a room is, when one thinks about it, highly conventional since the room lacks a fourth wall. Consult Harry Levin, *Refractions*; M. C. Bradbrook, *Themes and Conventions of Elizabethan Tragedy*.

cosmic irony. See *irony*.

cothurnus. See *sock and buskin*.

coup de théatre. A surprise, especially a striking turn of events in the plot. Consult Alan R. Thompson, *The Anatomy of Drama*.

crisis. See *plot*.

Cruelty, theater of. Antonin Artaud (1896–1948) used the term in 1933 to refer to a drama that, working rather like a plague, would shock people out of the bonds of their "logical" or "civilized" conceptions and would release the suppressed primitive or prelogical powers within them, such as criminal instincts and erotic obsessions, revealing the "cruelty" or terrible mystery of existence. This drama, relying more on gestures, shapes, music, and light than on words (Artaud was immensely impressed by Balinese drama although he did not understand Indonesian), would bypass mere realism (i.e., psychology) and would make manifest the truly real supernatural, creating in the spectator a "kind of terror" or a purifying delirium. Artaud, a poet, actor, and director, published relatively little, but his metaphysics and his emphasis on an antirealistic theater in various ways have influenced Sartre, Camus, Beckett, Ionesco, Genet (consult the preface to

The Maids) and others: language sometimes becomes gibberish, and madness and violence are presented in order to jolt spectators out of their comfortable false view of humankind and of the universe—or, in less metaphysical plays, in order to reflect on the stage the cruelty of the modern world. Consult Artaud's *The Theater and Its Double*; several articles in *Tulane Drama Review*, 8 (Winter 1963); and the "Conclusion" in Jacques Guicharnaud and June Beckelman, *Modern French Theatre*.

denouement. See *plot*.

deus ex machina. Literally, a god out of a machine. (1) In Greek drama a god who descends by a cranelike arrangement and solves a problem in the story, thus allowing the play to end. It was much used by Euripides; Sophocles in his old age borrowed the idea and introduced Heracles at the end of *Philoctetes* to induce the title character to go to Troy. (2) Any unexpected and improbable device (e.g., an unexpected inheritance from a long-lost uncle in Australia) used to unknot a problem and thus conclude the work.

deuteragonist. See *protagonist*.

dialogue. The speech exchanged between characters or, loosely, even the speech of a single character. Dialogue is sometimes contrasted to action, but Elizabeth Bowen aptly says that dialogue is what the characters *do* to each other, and Shaw aptly says that his plays are all talk just as Beethoven's symphonies are all music. **Stichomythia** is a special form of dialogue, wherein two speakers in a verbal duel thrust and parry in alternating lines. Example:

QUEEN:
Hamlet, thou hast thy father much offended.
HAMLET:
Mother, you have my father much offended.

QUEEN:
Come, come, you answer with an idle tongue.
HAMLET:
Go, go, you question with a wicked tongue.

See *action, soliloquy*. Consult J. L. Styan, *The Elements of Drama*, Chs. 1–2, and Eric Bentley, *The Life of the Drama*.

diction. (1) Choice of words, wording. Dr. Johnson objected to the "knife" ("an instrument used by butchers and cooks," he said) that Lady Macbeth says she will use to murder the King. "Words too familiar, or too remote," Johnson said, "defeat the purpose of a poet." Consult Moody Prior, *The Language of Tragedy*. (2) A performer's manner or style of speaking, including pronunciation and phrasing.

Dionysus. Greek god of wine, the phallus, the surge of growth, and (to join all these) irrational impulse. It is commonly held that Greek tragedy grew from choral celebrations in his honor; in any case, from the sixth century B.C. tragedies were performed in Athens at the **Great** (or **Greater,** or **City**) **Dionysia,** a festival in Dionysus's honor. (For a survey of theories of the origin of tragedy, see A. W. Pickard-Cambridge, *Dithyramb, Tragedy and Comedy*, 2nd ed., revised by T. B. L. Webster. For a brief rejection of the theory that drama originated in Dionysian festivals, see H. D. F. Kitto, in *Theatre Survey*, 1 [1960], 3–17.) Friedrich Nietzsche suggested in *The Birth of Tragedy* (1872) that Greek tragedy, usually considered calm and poised, was not the product of quiet minds. If tragedy, Nietzsche said, showed light and beauty (over which the god Apollo presided), it was nevertheless also indebted to Dionysus, who represented the frenzied, buried self-assertions of the mind. That is, Greek tragedy was the product of **Dionysian** ecstatic and violent self-assertion tamed by (or fused with) the **Apollonian** sense of reason, of moderation, and of external order. "Apollonian" is often associated with classicism, and "Dionysian" with romanticism.

direct address. See *soliloquy*.

disclosure, discovery. See *anagnorisis*.

disguising. See *masque*.

domestic tragedy. A serious play showing the misfortunes (especially within the family) of a private citizen rather than of a person of high rank who is involved in events that shake a realm. See *bourgeois drama*. Consult Henry H. Adams, *English Domestic or Homiletic Tragedy 1575 to 1642*.

double plot. See *plot*.

downstage. The front half of the stage, or any part of the stage considered in relation to someone or something further from the audience.

drama (from Greek *dran*: to do). (1) A play, a work that tells a story by means of impersonators. (2) The whole body of work written for the theater. (3) A serious but untragic play (see *drame*). (4) Events containing conflict, tension, surprise ("life is full of drama"; "the first act lacks drama"). See *closet drama, comedy, melodrama, tragedy*. A play is written by a **dramatist;** the art of writing plays is **dramaturgy.** A person who writes plays is also a **playwright.** (Note that the last syllable is not "-write" but "-wright," denoting a maker, as a shipwright is a maker of ships.) Consult Kenneth T. Rowe, *Write That Play*; Walter Kerr, *How Not to Write a Play*; Bernard Grebanier, *Playwriting*.

drama of ideas. See *pièce à thèse*.

dramatic illusion. The state between delusion (the spectators think the world on the stage is real) and full awareness (the spectators never forget they are looking at scenery and actors). In *A Midsummer Night's Dream*, Bottom fears that delusion will occur unless the audience is carefully warned: "Write me a prologue, and let the prologue seem to say we will do no harm with our swords, and that Pyramus is not killed indeed. And, for the more better assurance, tell them that I Pyramus am not Pyramus, but Bottom the Weaver. This will put them out of fear." See *aesthetic distance*.

George Henry Lewes (1817–1878) introduced into English dramatic criticism the term ***optique du théâtre,*** taken from the French actor Francois René Molé (1734–1802). Spectators must have this "theater view," this understanding of "scenic illusion," if they are to enjoy the theater; if they lack it, they will complain that Hamlet ought to be speaking Danish (see *convention*). *Optique du théâtre* requires that we be given not reality but a symbolic representation of it. A stage miser should finger his gold differently from a real miser; a stage character must be heard, even though in real life the character might speak inaudibly.

Staging that aims at delusion or a high degree of illusion is **representational** staging. Here the stage characters eat real food on stage, speak with their backs to the audience, and so on. (See *naturalism, realism*.) When David Belasco staged *The Governor's Lady* in 1912, he was representational, placing on the stage an exact duplicate of a particular (Child's) restaurant. On the other hand, **presentational** staging is antirealistic; in Thornton Wilder's *Our Town* (1938), a drugstore counter, for example, consisted of a board across the backs of two chairs. The staging in musical comedies, ballets, and puppet shows is, of course, presentational. Presentational staging is sometimes called **theatrical** staging. **Theatricalism,** by its unreality, continually reminds us that we are in the theater, not in the street. On theatricalism, see *style*. A derogatory way of saying a work is theatrical is to say it is "**stagy**."

dramatic irony. See *irony*.

dramatist. See *drama*.

dramaturgy. See *drama*.

drame. A solemn but untragic play, especially an eighteenth-century play that, quietly glorifying the bourgeois virtues, preaches and appeals to the audience's emotions. See *bourgeois drama*. Consult Alan R. Thompson, *The Anatomy of Drama*, which classifies most naturalistic and realistic plays (e.g., Ibsen's and Chekhov's) as *drames*.

eiron. See *character*.

Elizabethan playhouse. The first permanent structure built in England for plays was The Theatre, built outside the city limits of London in 1576 by James Burbage. It soon had several competitors, but little is known about any of these playhouses. The contract for one, The Fortune (built in 1600), survives; it tells us that the three-storied building was square, 80 feet on the outside, 55 feet on the inside. The stage was 43 feet broad and 27½ feet deep. It has been calculated that about 800 people (the **groundlings**) could stand around the three sides of the stage on the ground that was called the *yard*, and another 1500 could be seated in the three galleries. The other chief pieces of evidence concerning the physical nature of the theater are (1) the "De Witt drawing," which is really a copy of a sketch made by a visitor (c. 1596) to The Swan (see illustration, p. 764), and (2) bits of evidence that can be gleaned from the plays themselves, such as "Enter a Fairy at one door, and Robin Goodfellow at another." Conclusions vary and scholarly tempers run

high; the following statements are not indisputable. Most theaters were polygonal or round structures (Shakespeare calls the theater a "wooden O") with three galleries; the yard was open to the sky. From one side a raised stage (or open *platform*) jutted into the middle. A sort of wooden canopy (the *heavens*, or the *shadow*) projected over the stage and in some theaters rested on two pillars; these pillars could conveniently serve as a hiding place for an actor supposed to be unseen by the other characters. At the rear of the stage there sometimes was a curtained alcove or booth, which when uncurtained might represent a room or a cave. The curtain is often called an *arras*, and it was probably behind this curtain that Polonius hid, only to be stabbed. At the rear of the stage (flanking the curtained space?) there were perhaps also two or three doors, through which entrances and exits were made. Probably the *tiring house* ("attiring house," i.e., dressing room) was behind the stage. Above the alcove or booth was an area that could be used for an *upper stage* (for example, in scenes of people standing on a city's walls); flanking the upper stage were windows, one of which may have served Juliet for her misnamed balcony scene. Some scholars argue that in a yet higher place were musicians, and at the very top—called the *top*—was an opening from which an actor could look; in *Henry VI, Part I*, Joan of Arc appears "on the top, thrusting out a torch burning." Most of the acting was done on the main stage (the platform), but the "inner stage," "upper stage," "windows," and "top" must have been useful occasionally (if they existed). The *cellar* (beneath the stage) was used, for example, for the voice of the ghost in *Hamlet* and for Ophelia's grave. Though some scenery was used, the absence of a front curtain precluded many elaborate scenic effects (much, however, could be done by carrying banners) and encouraged continuous action. The stage that was a battlefield could in an instant, by the introduction of a throne, become a room in a palace. Two readable books are A. M. Nagler, *Shakespeare's Stage*, and C. Walter Hodges, *The Globe Restored*. Nagler (Ch. 12) also gives information about a second kind of Elizabethan theater—basically a platform at one end of a hall—that catered to a courtly group. Interesting specialized items on playhouses can be found in *Shakespeare Survey*, 1 and 12, ed. Allardyce Nicoll.

empathy. The projection of one's feelings into a perceived object. The Germans call it *Einfühling*—"a feeling into." Vernon Lee, one of the formulators of the idea, claimed that when we say "the mountain rises" we do so not because the mountain rises (it doesn't) but because we have often raised our eyes, head, and total muscular structure to look at mountains or other tall objects. In perceiving a mountain, we merge (unawares) its image with the previously accumulated idea of rising. We are said to empathize with a character if we flinch at a blow directed at him, or if we feel bowed with his grief—if, in short, we *experience* as well as *see* his behavior. Empathy is often distinguished from **sympathy:** we empathize if we feel *with* the character; we sympathize if we feel *for* the character. See *aesthetic distance*. Consult Vernon Lee's essay in *A Modern Book of Aesthetics*, ed. Melvin Rader; and Herbert S. Langfield, *The Aesthetic Attitude*.

epic drama. Bertolt Brecht (1898–1956) labeled "Aristotelian" most drama before his own. He held that it aimed at enthralling the spectators by building up to a climax, thus arousing and then purging their emotions. In contrast, Brecht said, epic drama (he borrowed the phrase from Erwin Piscator) aims at arousing the audience's detached thought; it teaches, keeping the spectators alert by preventing any emotional involvement. The epic

drama (probably so-called because it resembles the epic in its abundance of loosely connected scenes and its tendency to deal with a society rather than merely with a few individuals) achieves this estrangement, or **alienation effect** (German: *Verfremdungseffekt*), by many means: the epic play (e.g., Brecht's *The Good Woman of Setzuan*, or his *Mother Courage*) commonly consists of a series of loosely connected scenes rather than a tightly organized plot with a climax; the settings are not realistic but merely suggest the locale, and they are often changed in full view of the audience, preventing any entrancing illusion (a night scene may be done on an illuminated stage, again to prevent the audience from emotionally entering into the play); the actor may address the audience directly, sometimes in song, and he aims not at becoming the character but at presenting him, or, to put it differently, at making a comment on him, as we might do when we put aside a cigarette and say, "He said to me, '. . .'"; loudspeakers, films, and placards may be used; and the whole is something of a lecture-demonstration, aimed not at arousing and then quieting the audience's emotions but at making things somewhat strange to the audience so that the audience will look sharply and will think. Consult Bertolt Brecht, "A Short Organum," in *Playwrights on Playwriting*, ed. Toby Cole; *Brecht on Theatre*, trans. John Willett; R. Gray, "Brecht," *The Tulane Drama Review*, 6 (Sept. 1961).

epilogue. (1) An appendix (usually a concluding address) to a play; (2) the actor who recites such an appendix (e.g., Puck, at the close of Shakespeare's *A Midsummer Night's Dream*).

exposition. See *plot*.

expressionism. An antinaturalistic movement chiefly associated with Germany just after World War I. It was foreshadowed by Strindberg, notably in his trilogy *To Damascus* (1898–1904) and in his *A Dream Play* (1902). Expressionism does not seek to "hold the mirror up to nature" (Hamlet's words) or to present reality dispassionately; rather, it seeks to show the world as we feel (rather than literally see) it. Thus, when Mr. Zero shakes his employer (in Elmer Rice's *The Adding Machine* [1923]), the office spins; when he is on trial, the walls of the courtroom veer crazily. Speaking broadly, expressionist plays (in addition to being unrealistic) usually (1) depict types or classes (Rice's Mr. Zero; the Man, the Woman, the Nameless One in Ernst Toller's *Man and Masses* [1921]), (2) employ dream sequences and (3) assume that society is responsible for our troubles. Though Arthur Miller's *Death of a Salesman* (1949) is in many ways "realistic," it also is indebted to expressionism, especially in the scenes involving Willy's memories. (Miller originally planned to call the play *The Inside of His Head.*) Note, too, the name of Miller's hero—Loman, i.e., low man. O'Neill's *The Emperor Jones* (see page 409) and Tennessee Williams's *The Glass Menagerie* (see p. 453) similarly reveal a modified—one might say Americanized—expressionism. Consult John Willett, *Expressionism*.

falling action. See *plot*.

farce. A sort of comedy based not on clever language or subtleties of character but on broadly humorous situations (a man mistakenly enters the ladies' locker room). Farce is lucidly defended by Eric Bentley in his introduction to *"Let's Get a Divorce" and Other Plays*, where he suggests that farce, like dreams, shows "the disguised fulfillment of repressed wishes." Farce is usually filled with surprise, with swift physical action, and with assault. The characters are physically and intellectually insensitive, and characteriza-

tion is subordinated to plot. See also Bentley's *The Life of the Drama*. **Slapstick,** named for an implement made of two slats that resound when slapped against a posterior, is farce that relies on physical assault. Farce and slapstick are **low comedy,** as is comedy that depends on obscenity.

foil. A character who sets off another, as Laertes and Fortinbras—young men who, like Hamlet, have lost a father—help to set off Hamlet, or as a braggart soldier helps to set off a courageous one.

foreshadowing. See *suspense*.

Great Dionysia. See *Dionysus*.

Greek theater. The great age of the Greek drama was the fifth century B.C. The audience sat on wooden benches in tiers on a hillside (see photo, p. 80), looking down at a flat circular dancing place (the **orchestra**), about eight-five feet in diameter, in the middle of which was an altar to Dionysus; behind the dancing place was a playing area, which logic (but no concrete evidence) suggests may have been slightly elevated. Visible behind the playing area was the **skene,** a wooden "scene-building" introduced about 458 B.C. that served as a background, as a place for actors to make entrances from and exits to, and as a dressing room. To speak of these elements in a little more detail: the seating area, which held as many as 16,000 people, was the *theatron* ("seeing-place"); fan-shaped or horseshoe-shaped, it swept around the orchestra in a segment a little greater than a semicircle. The chorus of singers and dancers, entering by an aisle (***parodos***) at each side of the *theatron*, danced in the orchestra. The front (i.e., the façade) of the *skene* (or perhaps a temporary screen) and sometimes the playing area in front of it seem to have been called the *proskenion*. Though the *skene*'s façade perhaps suggested the front of a temple or a palace, there were further efforts at indicating locale: Sophocles is said to have invented scene painting (a painted cloth or screen in front of the *skene?*), and there are allusions to *periaktoi*, upright prisms bearing a different decoration on each side. Apparently when a new locality in the same town was to be indicated, the *periaktos* at the right was turned; when an entirely new locality was to be indicated, both *periaktoi* were turned. Other machines were the *eccyclema*, a platform that was rolled out of the *skene* to indicate a scene indoors, and the *mechane*, a crane from which a god could escend or by means of which a character could soar through the air. (See *deus ex machina.*)

Speaking a bit broadly, we can say that the Greek theater, open to the heavens, with its orchestra representing a city square and the skene representing a temple or palace, is itself a symbol of the ancient Athenian world view of a society that operates under divine and human law. Plays were put on chiefly during two holidays, the **Lenaea** (Feast of the Wine Press) in January, and the **Great** (or **City**) **Dionysia** in March or April. The Lenaea was chiefly associated with comedy, the Great Dionysia with tragedy. At the latter, on each of three mornings a tragic dramatist presented three tragedies and one **satyr-play**. The expense was born by a *choregos*, a rich citizen ordered by the state to assume the financial burden. See *comedy, tragedy*. Consult Margarete Bieber, *The History of the Greek and Roman Theater*; T. B. L. Webster, *Greek Theatre Production*, 2nd ed.; and Peter Arnott, *The Ancient Greek and Roman Theatre.*

groundlings. See *Elizabethan playhouse.*

guerilla theater. Dramatic performances, especially in the 1960s, seeking to help the populace to throw off what was said to be an oppressive bourgeois government. Theater was viewed not as a means of producing beauty or of exploring ideas but as a weapon in a class war. Performances were given in such places as streets, fields, and gymnasiums rather than in conventional theaters. Thus, the traditional separation of players from audience was broken down; moreover, the audience itself might be in some degree assaulted, for instance by obscenities or by the spectacle of nudity, offered in an effort to shock the spectators into an awareness of new ideals. Further, "performance" and "drama" were loosely interpreted. For example, Luis Valdez, founder of El Teatro Campesino (1965) in *Actos* wrote, "A demonstration with a thousand Chicanos, all carrying flags and picket signs, shouting 'Chicago Power!' is . . . theater." Consult Henry Lesnik, ed., *Guerilla Street Threatre*, and (especially for El Teatro Campesino) C. W. E. Bigsby, *A Critical Introduction to Twentieth-Century American Drama*, vol. 3.

hamartia. A Greek word variously translated as "tragic flaw" or "error" or "shortcoming" or "weakness." In many plays it *is* a flaw or even a vice such as *hybris* (also *hubris*)—a word that in classical Greek meant bullying, or even assault and battery, but that in discussions of tragedy means overweening pride, arrogance, excessive confidence. But in other plays it is merely a misstep, such as a choice that turns out badly. Indeed, the tragic hero may be undone by his virtue—his courage, for example, when others are not merely prudent but cowardly. See pp. 67–68. On *hamartia* and *hybris* see Richmond Lattimore, *Story Patterns in Greek Tragedy.*

Hellenistic theater. Theaters of, say, the third and second centuries B.C. erected in towns to which Greek culture had been spread by Alexander's conquests seem to have been much like the Greek theater, though the *proskenion* was apparently more highly decorated, having pillars a few feet in front of it and being fitted with painted panels called *pinakes*. And the *skene*, now of stone rather than of wood, may have had projections at the sides (*paraskenia*) and an upper story (*episkenion*). The playing area on this supper level is the *logeion*. Consult Margarete Bieber, *The History of the Greek and Roman Theater*.

high comedy. Intellectual rather than physical, a type of comedy that required the close attention of a sophisticated audience, flourishing (says George Meredith in his *Essay on Comedy* [1877]) in a "society of cultivated men and women . . . wherein ideas are current, and the perceptions quick." Etherege, Wycherley, Congreve, and other playwrights of the decades following the Restoration of Charles II to the throne of England (1660) wrote **Restoration comedy,** high comedy of a particular sort, often called **comedy of manners** or **comedy of wit.** Their plays abound in witty **repartee** (what Dr. Johnson called "gay remarks and unexpected answers") and often strike modern audiences as cynical. Restoration comedy has no precise terminal date, but can be said to have ended about 1700, with the development of sentimental comedy, plays of venerable parents and middle-class dutiful sons who love pure young things. Example: Richard Steele's *The Conscious Lovers* (1722). Consult Thomas H. Fujimura, *The Restoration Comedy of Wit*; Louis Kronenberger, *The Thread of Laughter*; Norman N. Holland, *The First Modern Comedies*.

humor character. See *comedy of humors*.

hubris (*hybris*). See *hamartia*.

imitation (Greek: *mimesis*). Not a pejorative term in much criticism, for it often implies a "making" or "re-creating" or "representing" of a form in a substance not natural to it. Thus Michelangelo reproduced or imitated the form of Moses, in stone. For Aristotle, tragedy was the imitation (i.e., representation, re-creation) by means of words, gesture, music, and scenery, of an important action.

irony. Irony is of several sorts. **Socratic irony,** named for Socrates, who commonly feigned more ignorance than he possessed, denotes understatement. The *eiron* (see character) is the cunning fellow who plays the underdog. **Dramatic irony,** or **Sophoclean irony,** or **tragic irony** refers to a condition of affairs that is the tragic reverse of what the participants think. Thus, it is ironic that Macbeth kills Duncan, thinking he will achieve happiness; he later finds he loses all that makes life worth living. Oedipus accuses the blind prophet of corruption, but by the end of the play Oedipus learns (as the audience knew at the outset) that he himself is corrupt, that he has been mentally blind (ignorant) and that the prophet has had vision (knowledge). Oedipus meant what he said, but his words have proved to be ironic. (Aristotle's word for reversal is *peripeteia*.) We have dramatic irony, it can be said, when a speech or action is more fully understood by the spectators than by the characters. This sort of irony, based on misunderstanding, or partial knowledge, is common in tragedy, but comedy too has its misunderstandings; comic speeches or actions are ironic if they bring about the opposite of what is intended. More generally, the contrast implied in irony need be neither tragic nor comic; it is ironic that the strong man is overthrown by the weak man and that the liar unknowingly tells the truth. **Irony of fate** (a phrase that H. W. Fowler's *Modern English Usage* aptly says is hackneyed), or **cosmic irony,** denotes the view that God, or fate, or some sort of supernatural figure, is amused to manipulate human beings as a puppeteer manipulates his puppets. Thus, by an irony of fate the messenger delivers the prisoner's pardon an instant too late. Consult Garnett G. Sedgewick, *Of Irony*, and Alan R. Thompson, *The Dry Mock*.

koryphaios. See *chorus*.

kothurnus. See *sock and buskin*.

lazzo. See *commedia dell'arte*.

Lenaea. See *Greek theater*.

liturgical drama. A play that is part of the church service or liturgy. In the tenth century the churchmen put on a playlet of a few lines as part of the Easter liturgy. The text was based on Mark 16:1–7: clerics dressed as the Three Marys approached the "tomb" of Christ (the altar) and were asked by a cleric, disguised as an angel, whom they sought. When they replied that they sought Christ, he told them that Christ had risen and showed them the empty "tomb." The performers were all male, and the dialogue (in Latin) was chanted or sung; probably the gestures were stylized.

low comedy. See *farce*.

masque, mask, disguising. An entertainment (apparently derived from an ancient ritual) in the Renaissance court, wherein noblemen performed a dignified playlet, usually allegorical and mythological. The masque was lavishly produced, but its basic structure was generally simple: the masquers (costumed and masked noble performers) entered, supposedly having come from afar, they danced with the ladies of the court, and then they departed. Because the masquers were of the same rank as the ladies, and because performers and audience joined in a dance, the masque was very close to the masked ball. Ben Jonson (1572–1637) popularized what he called the **antimasque** (a grotesque dance of monsters or clowns), performed by professionals representing chaos, who were dispelled by the courtly performers. (*Anti*, from *antic*, meaning "a grotesque caper" or "a fool," is sometimes written *ante* because the antimasque precedes the masque.) Consult Enid Welsford, *The Court Masque*, and E. K. Chambers, *The Mediaeval Stage* and *The Elizabethan Stage*.

melodrama. Originally, in Renaissance Italy, an opera; later, a drama with occasional songs, or with music (*melos* is Greek for "song") expressing a character's thoughts, much as in films today. In the early nineteenth century plays with musical accompaniment became so stereotyped that the word acquired a second (and now dominant) meaning: a play wherein characters clearly virtuous or vicious are pitted against each other in sensational situations filled with suspense, until justice triumphs. The situations, not the characters, are exciting. The exotic horror (castles and dungeons) dominant in early nineteenth-century melodramas was often replaced later in the century by local horror (the cruel landlord), but whether exotic or local, melodrama is improbable, and virtue—unsullied by any touch of guilt—triumphs over unlikely circumstances. Melodrama is sometimes said to be tragedy with character left out (i.e., it contains serious happenings), but by virtue of its happy ending and its one-sided characters it can better be described as comedy with good-humor left out. Some critics use *melodrama* without any pejorative connotation to describe such serious, often sensational, plays as Emlyn Williams's *Night Must Fall* (1935), Robert Ardrey's *Thunder Rock* (1939), and Arthur Miller's *All My Sons*. Consult Robert B. Heilman, *Tragedy and Melodrama*.

miracle play. A medieval play on a biblical episode or a saint's life. Consult Arnold Williams, *The Drama of Medieval England*.

monologue. See *soliloquy*.

morality play. A late medieval development, popular well into the sixteenth century, allegorically dramatizing some aspect of the moral life, including such characters as Everyman, Good Deeds, and Avarice. It usually showed the conflict between good and evil, or the way in which the Christian faces death. Consult Arnold Williams, *The Drama of Medieval England*; Bernard Spivack, *Shakespeare and the Allegory of Evil*; and R. Potter, *The English Morality Play*.

motivation. Grounds in character and situation that make behavior plausible. Such grounds are not always present, even in great drama: when Othello asks why Iago "hath thus ensnared my soul," Iago replies, "Demand me nothing: what you know, you know." See *character*. Consult J. I. M. Stewart, *Character and Motive in Shakespeare*.

naturalism. Sometimes defined, like realism, as the portrayal of "a scientifically accurate, detached picture of life, including everything and selecting nothing." The spectators looking through the peephole of the proscenium, as a scientist looks through the eyepiece of a microscope, are to feel they are witnessing life rather than a symbolic representation of life. More commonly, however, *naturalism* alludes neither to a panoramic view nor to the detailed presentation of a narrow **slice of life** (French: *tranche de vie*) but to a particular attitude held by some writers since the middle of the nineteenth century. Though claiming to be dispassionate observers, they were influenced by evolutionary thought and regarded humans not as possessed of a soul and of free will but as creatures determined by their heredity and environment. The movement in drama can be said to have begun with the Goncourt Brothers' unsuccessful *Henriette Maréchal* (1865), but it is usual to say that the opening gun in the battle for naturalism was fired in Emile Zola's dramatization (1873) of his novel *Thérèse Raquin*. Thérèse and her lover drown her husband but are then so guilt-ridden that they poison themselves. In his preface Zola urged that the theater be brought "into closer relation with the great movement toward truth and experimental science which has since the last century been on the increase. . . . I have chosen characters who were completely dominated by their nerves and blood." In Paris, André Antoine opened his Théâtre Libre in 1887, devoting it mostly to plays showing the power of instincts and the influence of heredity and environment. These plays were staged as untheatrically as possible; for example, the actors turned their backs to the audience. In Germany, Otto Brahm opened the Freie Bühne in 1889, and in England J. T. Grein opened the Independent Theatre in 1891, both with Ibsen's *Ghosts* (1881), a play showing the destruction of a young man by inherited syphilis. Ibsen's greatness does not allow him to be pinned down by the label "naturalist," but he can be said to be naturalistic (among other things) by virtue of his serious interests in the effects of heredity and environment. Other dramatists who wrote naturalistic plays include August Strindberg (e.g., his *Miss Julie* [1888]) and Gerhart Hauptmann (early in his career, say, through *The Weavers* [1892]), and Eugene O'Neill (again, the early plays such as *The Rope* [1918] and *Diff'rent* [1920]). Note, however, that the major naturalistic writers usually are more than naturalistic; Strindberg's *Miss Julie*, for example, has a preface that talks about the influence of heredity and environment, and it deals with sordid aspects of reality, but it also has symbolic overtones, notably in Julie's and Jean's dreams. Consult Mordecai Gorelik, *New Theatres for Old*; *TDR: The Drama Review*, 13 (Winter 1968); and (for Strindberg, O'Neill, and the sources of their ideas) Oscar Cargill, *Intellectual America*.

nuntius. See *Senecan* tragedy.

obligatory scene. See *scène à faire.*

optique du théâtre. See dramatic illusion.

orchestra. See *Greek theater.*

pathos. The quality that evokes pity. The pathetic is often distinguished from the tragic; in the former, the suffering is experienced by the passive and the innocent (especially women and children), while in the latter it is experienced by persons who act, struggle, and are in some measure responsible for their sufferings. Discussing Aeschylus's *The Suppliants,* H. D. F. Kitto says in *Greek Tragedy* (2nd ed.): "The Suppliants are not only pathetic, as the victims of outrage, but also tragic, as the victims of their own misconceptions." See *bourgeois drama.*

performance theater. A movement in the 1960s and early 1970s especially associated with Julian Beck, a co-founder of the Living Theatre. Influenced by Antonin Artaud's **theater of cruelty**, performance theater rejected the gap between performers and spectators (performers moving on stage, spectators impassively sitting in the dark); it therefore necessarily minimized the role of the playwright and gave the actors freedom to improvise. Verbal and visual assaults (for instance nudity) on the audience, as well as physical contact with it, supposedly gave actor and spectator freedom to celebrate bodily and spiritual unity and liberation. Consult Julian Beck, *The Life of the Theatre,* and for a critical and historical survey, see part 2 of the third volume of C. W. E. Bigsby, *A Critical Introduction to Twentieth-Century American Drama.*

peripeteia (anglicized to **peripety,** meaning **reversal**). The reversal occurs when an action produces the opposite of what was intended or expected, and it is therefore a kind of irony. In *Julius Caesar,* Brutus kills Caesar in order to free Rome from tyranny, but the deed introduces tyranny into Rome. See *irony, plot.*

picture-frame stage. See *proscenium stage.*

pièce à thèse. A play with a thesis, a play in which the dramatist argues a point. Commonly the thesis is not about, say, the benevolence of God, but about the merits or defects of some social institution; a play dealing with a social institution may also be called a **problem play** or a **drama of ideas.** Some critics distinguish between the terms, saying that a problem play merely poses a social problem, as Galsworthy does in *Strife* (1909), while a thesis play propounds a solution. Shaw says that "the material of the dramatist is always some conflict of human feeling with circumstances"; when the circumstances are "human institutions" (e.g., divorce laws, penal codes) rather than unchanging facts of life (e.g., death) and the audience is forced to meditate on the value of the institutions, we have a problem play. Shaw's essay, "The Play of Ideas," is in *Shaw on Theatre,* ed. E. J. West. Consult also Walter Kerr, *How Not to Write a Play,* Ch. 5.

pièce bien faite, or **well-made play.** A play, with much suspense and with little depth of characterization, that relies on a cleverly constructed plot, first developing a situation, then building the crisis to a climax, and then resolving the business. The type, which perhaps can be described as melodrama with the fisticuffs left out, is chiefly associated with Victorien Sardou (1831–1908), but Sardou was indebted to Eugène Scribe (1791–1861). Shaw called their plays clockwork mice, and Sardoodledom, but the influence of Sardou on Shaw's hero, Ibsen, is undeniable. See *plot,* and consult Walter Kerr, *How Not to*

Write a Play, Ch. 10; Eric Bentley, "Homage to Scribe," *What Is Theatre?*; C. E. Montague, *Dramatic Values*, pp. 63–74; *Camille and Other Plays*, ed. Stephen S. Stanton.

plot and **character.** The plot is sometimes the "story," the "narrative," but usually it is the happenings *as the author arranges them*. In *Hamlet*, for example, the story involves the poisoning of Hamlet's father, but Shakespeare omits this scene from his plot. Aristotle, in Chapter 6 of the *Poetics*, calls plot "the whole structure of the incidents," and he speaks of plot as the "soul of tragedy," thus making it more important than character. By *character* he means the personalities of the figures in the story. Menander (a Greek comic dramatist) is said to have told a friend that he had finished a comedy, though he had not yet written a line of dialogue; the anecdote implies that Menander had completed his idea of *what happens* (action) and in *what order* (plot), and he would find it easy then to write the lines of the characters necessary to his plot. The separation, however, between plot and character is misleading, for the two usually interplay. Although it is true that there may be much plot and little character (as in a thriller), in most great plays there is such a fusion between what is done and the personality of the doer that we feel the truth of Henry James's questions: "What is character but the determination of incident? What is incident but the illustration of character?" (See also *character*).

Most plots entail a **conflict,** wherein the protagonist is somehow opposed. If he is opposed chiefly by another person rather than by a force such as Fate or God or by an aspect of himself, the opposing figure is the **antagonist.** The German critic Gustav Freytag, in *Technique of the Drama* (1863), held that a play dramatizes "the rushing forth of will power from the depths of man's soul toward the external world" and "the coming into being of a deed and its consequences on the human soul." The five-act play, he said, commonly arranged such an action into a **pyramidal structure,** consisting of a **rising action,** a **climax,** and **falling action.** (In Peter de Vries's witty formulation, a plot has a beginning, a muddle, and an end.) The rising action begins with the **exposition,** in which is given essential information, especially about the **antecedent action** (what has occurred before this piece of action begins). The two gossiping servants who tell each other that after a year away in Paris the young master is coming home today with his new wife are giving the audience the exposition. The action rises through a **complication** (the protagonist is opposed) to a high point or **crisis** or **climax** (a moment at which tension is high, and which is a decisive turning point). The falling action goes through a **reversal** (if a tragedy, the protagonist loses power), and then into a **catastrophe,** also called a **denouement** (unknotting) or resolution. (Aristotle's word for the reversal is *peripeteia,* anglicized to **peripety,** and, translated as "irony of events," would in a comedy be a change from bad fortune to good, and the catastrophe would thus be happy.) The denouement frequently involves what Aristotle called an *anagnorisis* (**recognition, disclosure, discovery**). This recognition may be as simple as the identification of a long-lost brother by a birth mark, or it may involve a character's recognition of his own true condition. Shakespeare sometimes used a pyramidal structure, placing his climax neatly in the middle of what seems to us to be the third of five acts. In *Julius Caesar*, Brutus rises in the first half of the play, reaching his height in 3.1, with the death of Caesar; but later in this scene he gives Marc Antony permission to speak at Caesar's funeral and thus sets in motion his own fall, which occupies the second half of the play. In *Macbeth*, the protagonist attains his height in 3.1 ("Thou hast it now: King"), but he soon perceives that he is going downhill:

I am in blood
Stepped in so far that, should I wade no more,
Returning were as tedious as go o'er.

Some works have a **double plot,** that is, two plots, usually with some sort of relation. For example, the **subplot** or **underplot** (the secondary narrative) might be a grotesque version of the serious main plot. In Shakespeare's *The Tempest*, the main plot and subplot both deal with usurpation. In *King Lear*, the main plot concerns Lear's relation to his daughters, while the parallel subplot concerns Gloucester's relation to his sons. For another aspect of the subplot, see *comic relief*. Consult William Empson, *Some Versions of Pastoral*, Ch. 2. On plotting see *pièce bien faite* and *scène à faire*.

poetic justice. A term coined by Thomas Rymer in 1678, denoting the reward of the virtuous and the punishment of the vicious. Aristotle had said or implied that the tragic hero is undone partly by some sort of personal flaw—i.e., he is at least partly responsible for the suffering he later encounters. (See *hamartia* and p. 67). Poetic justice, with its idea that all characters reap the harvest of their just deserts, is a hardening of Aristotle's suggestion. Consult M. A. Quinlan, *Poetic Justice in the Drama*.

presentational theater. A type of theater in which there is little or no illusionism in the acting and staging (as opposed to realistic or naturalistic or representational theater). Communication is achieved by means of evident conventions. For instance, a voyage in a boat may be indicated by pantomiming the motion of rowing. Virtually all drama before the middle of the nineteenth century was highly presentational, if only because of the inability to produce illusionistic lighting effects. But a largely presentational theater, such as Shakespeare's (where, on the open-air stage, a night scene might be indicated in daylight by the presence of characters holding torches), also might aim at realism. For instance, in Shakespeare's *The Tempest* a stage direction specifies that the sailors are "wet." On the other hand, even highly illusionistic sets of the later nineteenth century also employ conventions; for instance, the audience agrees to pretend that there is a fourth wall for the living room it sees exposed on the stage. On one form of twentieth-century presentational theater, see *expressionism*.

problem play. See *pièce à thèse*.

prologue. (1) A preface or introduction. For the Greeks the *prologos* was the first scene, which gave the exposition. Elizabethan prologues commonly summarize the plot, as the Chorus does in the prologue to *Romeo and Juliet*, but in the English theater of the late seventeenth century, the prologue was almost an independent verse essay spoken before the play began. (2) The actor who speaks a piece of the sort described above.

properties, props. Objects used on the stage, other than scenery and costumes. Examples: umbrellas, books, food.

proscenium stage, or **picture-frame stage.** A playing-area framed in the front, and thus separated from the audience. This frame is the *proscenium arch* or the *proscenium;* the empty space it contains, sometimes filled with a curtain, is the *proscenium opening*. Basically a **proscenium theater** has two rooms, one for the audience and another (with a hole in the mutual wall) for the performers. Such a theater is at least as old as the early seventeenth century, when the Farnese Theater was built in Parma. Consult Allardyce Nicoll, *The Development of the Theatre*.

protagonist. The chief figure in a play. In Greek the word means literally the "first contender," i.e., the chief actor (*protos:* first). The second role was given to the **deuteragonist,** the third to the **tritagonist.** The protagonist is commonly opposed by the **antagonist,** played by the deuteragonist. For the relationship between the protagonist and the antagonist, see *plot*.

psychical distance. See *aesthetic distance*.

pyramidal structure. See *plot*.

raisonneur. See *chorus*.

realism. The reproduction of life, especially as it appears to the eye and ear; the illusion of nature. Usually it deals with ordinary people in ordinary situations, moving in scenery that closely imitates reality. In England, T. W. Robertson (1829–1871) insisted, for example, that doorknobs not be painted on the doors but be three-dimensional. Wings and a backcloth (i.e., projecting flats at the sides and a painted cloth at the rear) were increasingly replaced by the **box set** (a room with the front wall missing, containing real furniture) for interior scenes. Gas lighting, introduced to the stage about 1820, soon became capable of producing effects of sunlight, moonlight, and so on. The dialogue, as well as the sets, came closer to what the senses perceive. Realistic plays (in prose, of course) avoid soliloquies, asides, and declamation. (On the other hand, realism makes use of its own conventions. See pp. 3–5 and the entry on *convention*.) The great playwrights of the movement are Ibsen and Chekhov. As Mary McCarthy says of American realistic drama (*On the Contrary*), "realism is a depreciation

of the real," for in "its resolve to tell the whole truth" it tends to deflate, to reveal human littleness. (It doesn't believe in exceptional, heroic people; when it treats the upper classes, it usually tends toward satire.) The oppressive box set of realistic plays, Miss McCarthy points out, "is the box or 'coffin' of average middle-class life opened at one end to reveal the corpse within." That realism shades into naturalism is clear; that in Ibsen it shades into symbolism is less obvious but is well demonstrated by John Northam, *Ibsen's Dramatic Method*. A simple example of Ibsen's symbolism: In *Hedda Gabler*, Hedda's hair is "not particularly ample," but Thea's is "unusually rich and wavy," suggesting Hedda's barrenness and Thea's fertility. Consult Mordecai Gorelik, *New Theatres for Old*; A. Nicholas Vardac, *Stage to Screen*, Chs. 4, 9; and Ernest B. Watson, *Sheridan to Robertson*. In **selective realism,** some of the scenery (e.g., a window and a door) closely reproduce reality, but some (e.g., a framework *suggesting* a roof) does not.

recognition. See *anagnorisis*.

repartee. See *high comedy*.

Restoration comedy. See *high comedy*.

revenge play. See *Senecan tragedy*.

reversal. See *peripeteia*.

rising action. See *plot*.

Roman theater. A permanent theater was not built at Rome until the first century B.C. The plays of Plautus (254?–184 B.C.) and Terence (190?–159? B.C.) were performed on temporary stages erected in the Circus Maximus and the Forum during holidays. In the permanent Roman theater, the enormous audience (40,000 or more) sat in a semicircle around a level space that was a vestige of what had been called the *orchestra* ("dancing place") of the Greek theater. Behind this vestige was the stage, running through what would have been the diameter of the circle. The long, slightly elevated stage was backed by a façade (painted to resemble two or three houses) with several doors through which actors made some of their exits and entrances, the others being made at the ends of the stage. Behind the façade was the dressing-room. The Roman theater, unlike the Greek and Hellenistic theaters, was a self-enclosed structure, built on level ground, not against a hillside. Consult Margarete Bieber, *The History of the Greek and Roman Theater*.

satire. A work ridiculing aspects of human behavior and seeking to arouse in the audience contempt for its object. Satirists almost always justify their attacks by claiming that satire is therapeutic. Shaw says, in the preface to his *Complete Plays*, "If I make you laugh at yourself, remember that my business as a classic writer of comedies is to 'chasten morals with ridicule'; and if I sometimes make you feel like a food, remember that I have by the same action cured your folly." Satire, however, is sometimes distinguished from comedy on the grounds that satire aims to correct by ridiculing, while comedy aims simply to evoke amusement. Among notable satires are the plays of Aristophanes; Gay's *The Beggar's Opera* (1728); Brecht's *The Threepenny Opera* (1928); and Kaufman, Ryskind, and Gershwin's *Of Thee I sing* (1931)—though Kaufman himself has defined satire as "that which closes on Saturday night." See *burlesque, comedy*. Consult Northrop Frye, *Anatomy of Criticism*.

satyr-play. A piece in which there is a chorus of lewd satyrs (creatures half-man, the other half either horse or goat). The Greek tragic playwrights of the fifth century B.C.

presented three tragedies and a satyr-play for the dramatic festival. Apparently the satyr-play often burlesqued a hero, showing him in a ludicrous situation. Only one complete satyr-play (Euripides' *The Cyclops*) is extant; it travesties the legend of Odysseus's encounter with Polyphemus. Consult Philip W. Harsh, A *Handbook of Classical Drama*.

scenario. See *commedia dell'arte*.

scene. *See* act.

scène à faire, or (in William Archer's translation of Francisque Sarcey's term) **obligatory scene.** "An obligatory scene [Archer says] is one which the audience (more or less clearly and consciously) foresees and desires, and the absence of which it may with reason resent." For example, a familiar legend may make a scene obligatory, or a dramatist may cause the audience to expect a certain scene. In *Hamlet* the play-within-the-play (3.2) has been called such a scene: Hamlet has doubted the ghost, and we must see the ghost's words verified. But most often an obligatory scene is an expected critical confrontation in which information previously hidden from a character or from the audience is revealed. Consult William Archer, *Play-making*.

scenery. The carpentry and painted cloths (and projected images) used on a stage. Scenery may be used to conceal parts of the stage, to decorate, to imitate or suggest locales, to establish time, or to evoke mood. For comments on early scenery, see *Greek theater* and *Elizabethan playhouse*. The Elizabethan public theater did not use much scenery. In *Twelfth Night*, when Viola asks, "What country, friends, is this?" she is told, "This is Illyria, lady," and the audience knows all that carpenters and painters can tell them. But even before Shakespeare's birth, Renaissance Italians had placed buildings, probably of lath and cloth, at the right and left of the stage. Behind the buildings, which were three-dimensional and were embellished with moldings, projected flat pieces cut and painted to look like other buildings at a distance, and behind these flat pieces were yet other flats, still smaller. On the symbolic use of scenery, see pp. 3–5.

selective realism. See *realism*.

Senecan tragedy. Any of the serious plays by the Roman author Seneca (4 B.C.–65 A.D.), or imitations of them. Of the ten extant Roman tragedies, nine are attributed to Seneca, and these were probably written not for the stage but for private readings. The heroes seem to us to be almost madmen, but perhaps they are to be regarded sympathetically as people overwhelmed by passion. Seneca's influence on the Elizabethan dramatists was considerable; the **revenge play,** with its ghosts and its deranged hero who seeks vengeance, doubtless would have been different had Seneca not existed. Among the signs of Seneca's influence are ghosts, revenge, deeds of horror (e.g., children stewed and served to their parents), occasional stoical speeches but a predominance of passionate speeches, use of stichomythia (see *dialogue*), and a *nuntius* (messenger) who recites in a heightened style an off-stage happening (e.g., the wounded soldier in *Macbeth*, 1.1). But, of course, not every use of any of these characteristics is necessarily attributable to Seneca's influence. And there are differences; for example, the horrors in Seneca are narrated, but in *King Lear* Gloucester is blinded on the stage. Consult F. L. Lucas, *Seneca and Elizabethan Tragedy*; Madeleine Doran, *Endeavors of Art*; and Willard Farnham, *The Medieval Heritage of Elizabethan Tragedy*. Howard Baker, *Induction to Tragedy*, minimizes Seneca's influence.

sensibility. See *sentimental*.

sentimental. Generally a pejorative word in criticism, indicating a superabundance of tender emotion, a disproportionate amount of sentiment (feeling). It is sentimental to be intensely distressed because one has stepped on a flower. A character, say Hamlet, may display deep emotions, but they are sentimental only if they are in excess of what the situation warrants. More specifically, "sentimental" writing refers to writing wherein evil is facilely conquered, denied, overlooked, or bathed in a glow of forgiving tenderness. In the eighteenth century the ability to respond emotionally (usually tearfully) to acts of benevolence or malevolence was called **sensibility.** In its **sentimental drama** there is at the expense of reason an emphasis on tearful situations; people's benevolent emotions are overestimated, for they are assumed to be innately good, and villains reform, usually in bursts of repenting tears. There is little wit, the characters are usually of the middle class, and they demonstrate their virtue by weeping at the sight of distress. In his "Comparison between Sentimental and Laughing Comedy" (1772), Oliver Goldsmith attacked sentimental comedy, saying that in it

> the virtues of private life are exhibited, rather than the vices exposed; and the distresses rather than the faults of mankind make our interest in the piece. . . . Almost all the characters are good, . . . and though they want humor, have abundance of sentiment and feeling. If they happen to have faults or foibles, the spectator is taught, not only to pardon, but to applaud them, in consideration of the goodness of their hearts; so that folly, instead of being ridiculed, is commended, and the comedy aims at touching our passions, without the power of being truly pathetic.

See *bourgeois drama*. Consult Ernest Bernbaum, *The Drama of Sensibility*, and Arthur Sherbo, *English Sentimental Drama*.

situational comedy. See *comedy of humors*.

slapstick. See *farce*.

slice of life. See *naturalism*.

sock and **buskin.** Performers of Latin comedy wore a light slipper or sandal called the *soccus*. The sock is either this piece of footwear or comedy itself. The high boot worn by Greek tragic actors was the *cothurnus* or *kothurnus.* In Hellenistic times it acquired a very thick sole, giving the performer the height appropriate to a great man. In English this footgear (or tragic drama in general) is called the buskin, apparently from Old French *broissequin*, from Middle Dutch *brosekin*, a small leather boot. Consult Margarete Bieber, *The History of the Greek and Roman Theater*.

Socratic irony. See *irony*.

soliloquy. A speech wherein a character utters his or her thoughts aloud while alone. An **aside** is a speech wherein a character expresses his or her thoughts in words audible to the spectators but supposedly unheard by the other stage characters present. Both were important conventions in Elizabethan drama and, later, in melodrama, but the late nineteenth century sought so vigorously to present on the stage the illusion of real life that both techniques were banished. They have, however, been revived in the twentieth century, as in Eugene O'Neill's *Strange Interlude*, where the asides represent the characters' thoughts and unspoken desires. In **direct address,** a character turns from the world on the stage and speaks directly to the audience, telling it, for instance, to watch closely. Consult Una Ellis-Fermor, *The Frontiers of Drama*, Ch. 6; George E. Duckworth, *The Nature of Roman Comedy*; and Max Beerbohm, "Soliloquies in Drama," *Around Theatres*. The soliloquy, the aside, and direct address are all monologues, but more often a **monologue** is either a long speech delivered by one character, which may be heard but not interrupted by others in his presence, or a performance by a single actor.

Sophoclean irony. See *irony*.

sound effect. An imitative noise, usually produced by simple machinery. Though a sound effect may be a mere imitation of nature, it may also be a richly symbolic suggestion. Chekhov's *The Cherry Orchard* (1904) concludes: "There is a far-off sound as if out of the sky, the sound of a snapped string, dying away, sad. A stillness falls, and there is only the thud of an ax on a tree, far away in the orchard." Consult Frank Napier, *Noises Off*.

spectacle. The last of Aristotle's six elements of drama, spectacle denotes what appeals to the eye, such as costume and scenery. Greek drama was splendidly costumed and made some use of scenery. Aeschylus especially seems to have contrived moments that caught the eye, such as Agamemnon's entrance in a chariot. The Elizabethan stage, though sparse in scenery, apparently was architecturally impressive, and doubtless military scenes were embellished with waving banners. In the Restoration, spectacle sometimes got the upper hand. Alexander Pope complained:

> The play stands still; damn action and discourse,
> Back fly the scenes, and enter foot and horse;
> Pageants on pageants, in long order drawn,
> Peers, heralds, bishops, ermine, gold, and lawn.

In the nineteenth century the development of gas light and then electric light made possible elaborate sunrises and twilights, and at the end of the century (especially in Russia) there was an emphasis on ensemble acting that gave a tableau effect. Pictorial effects in late-nineteenth-century productions of Shakespeare were often achieved at the cost of Shakespeare's lines. At the very end of the century William Poel rejected spectacle and helped establish a trend to stage Shakespeare in what was thought to be an Elizabethan manner: an uncluttered stage, allowing the action to proceed rapidly. Consult James Laver, *Drama*, and A. Nicholas Vardac, *Stage to Screen*, Chs. 3–4.

stage business. Minor physical action— including posture and facial expression— by a performer. Business ranges from head scratching to an addition Henry Irving made to *The Merchant of Venice*, 2.4: in Shakespeare's scene, Jessica and Lorenzo elope and the scene ends quietly; Irving added business in which Shylock entered and knocked on the door of his empty house while the curtain fell. Irving's successors amplified his business: Shylock entered the house, cried out, reappeared, and so on. Consult Arthur C. Sprague, *Shakespeare and the Actors*.

stichomythia. See *dialogue*.

stock character. See *character*.

structure. The arrangement of episodes.

style. The mode of expression. Newman, talking of the writer's style, called it "a thinking out into language." This idea of "a thinking out" (but not into language) is applicable also to the style of the scene designer, the costume designer, and so on. Kenneth Tynan in *Curtains* defines good style as "a happy consonance of manner with matter, of means with end, of tools with job." To *stylize* a play commonly means to present it with a noticeable artful manner rather than to present it realistically, though in fact realism itself is a style. A **stylized production** usually is presentational or anti-illusionistic rather than repre-

sentational (see *dramatic illusion*). Consult George R. Kernodle, "Style, Stylization, and Styles of Acting," *Educational Theatre Journal*, 12 (1960), 251–261.

subplot. See *plot*.

surprise. See *suspense*.

surrealism. A literary movement, especially vigorous in France in the 1920s and 1930s, that insisted that reality is grasped by the unconscious, the irrational, rather than by the conscious. The best art, it is held, is the dream. Among the forerunners were Alfred Jarry, whose *Ubu Roi* (1896) combined grotesque farce with antibourgeois satire; August Strindberg, whose *To Damascus* (three parts, 1898–1904) and *The Dream Play* (1902) had presented dreamlike worlds; and Guillaume Apollinaire, whose *Breasts of Tiresias* (1917) was called a *"drame surréaliste"* (the first use of the word) by the author. Perhaps the chief surrealist dramatist is Jean Cocteau, notably in his *Orpheus* (1926), in which a glazier is an angel and a horse dictates prophetic words. Consult Georges E. Lamaître, *From Cubism to Surrealism in French Literature*.

suspense. Uncertainty, often characterized by anxiety. Suspense is usually a curious mixture of pain and pleasure, as Gwendolen, in Oscar Wilde's *The Importance of Being Earnest*, implies: "This suspense is terrible. I hope it will last." Most great art relies more heavily on suspense than on **surprise** (the unexpected). One can rarely sit twice through a play depending on surprise; the surprise gone, the interest is gone. Suspense is usually achieved in part by **foreshadowing**—hints of what is to come. Dumas *fils* put it this way: "The art of the theater is the art of preparations." Coleridge, who held that Shakespeare gives us not surprise but expectation and then the satisfaction of perfect knowledge, once wrote: "As the feeling with which we startle at a shooting star, compared with that of watching the sunrise at the pre-establish moment, such and so low is surprise compared with expectation." Thus, in *Hamlet*, the ghost does not pop up surprisingly, but satisfies the eager expectations that have been aroused by references to "this thing," "this dreaded sight," and "this apparition." Often, in fact, Shakespeare—like the Greek dramatists—used traditional stories; the audience presumably was not surprised by the deaths of Caesar and Brutus, and it enjoyed the suspense of anticipating them. Suspense is thus related to tragic irony. The tragic character moves closer and closer to his doom, and though he may be surprised by it, we are not; we are held by suspense. On surprise, consult David L. Grossvogel, *The Self-Conscious Stage in Modern French Drama* (reprinted in paperback as *Twentieth-Century French Drama*).

symbolism. Derived from Greek *symballein*, "to throw together," which thus suggests the essential quality of symbolism, the drawing together of two worlds; it presents the concrete material world of roses, toads, caves, stars, and so on and through them reveals an otherwise invisible world. As a noun, the original Greek word denoted half of something broken in two, and thus the word suggests not something that stands for something else but something that is part of a larger unit.

Symbolism is often distinguished from **allegory.** Where the allegorist commonly invents a world (the author of *Everyman* [c. 1500] invents a figure called Everyman, who seeks aid from figures called Goods, Kindred, etc.) in order to talk about the real world, the symbolist commonly presents the phenomena of what we usually call the real world in order to reveal a "higher," eternal world of which the symbol is a part. The allegorist is free to invent any number of imaginary worlds to talk about the real world, but the symbolist feels that there is only one way by which he or she can present the "higher" real world he or she envisions. The everyday world is often considered by symbolists as a concrete but transient version of a more important realm, and the symbolist who presents, say, a rose, is (he might hold) speaking about a rose and also about the eternal beauty of womanhood in the only possible way.

In the second half of the nineteenth century there arose in France the so-called **Symbolist Movement,** but it must be emphasized that symbolism of a sort is probably as old as literature. An author's insistence on some object may cause us to regard it as more than its apparent nature. For example, the forest or greenwood in *As You Like It* suggests a benevolent nature that restores humans to their best part. But on the whole Shakespeare's plays do not leave the world of sensible reality. The plays of the Symbolists do. The Symbolic writer presents a world that seems to be a dream world, a world that is not the usual world enriched, but a new world. In his preface to *The Dream Play* (1902), Strindberg says he "has tried to imitate the disconnected but seemingly logical form of the dream. Anything may happen. . . . The characters split, double, multiply, vanish, solidify, blur, clarify." A play is the expression of a "soul-state" (Stéphane Mallarmé's term) rather than an imitation of an external action. See *surrealism.*

The best naturalists (Ibsen, Chekhov, Strindberg, and Hauptmann) at times wrote symbolic works, but the chief Symbolic dramatists are the French (if we include the Belgian Maurice Maeterlinck) and William Butler Yeats. In Maeterlinck's *The Intruder* (1890) a blind old man sees with his soul the approach of Death. In *The Blind* (1890) a group of blind men are lost in a forest; their leader was a priest, but he has died. Maeterlinck occasionally said some of his plays were for marionettes, and though his statement is sometimes held to be a mildly self-deprecating joke, in fact there is much in the plays that belongs to the realm of impassive, other-worldly dolls, not surprising in the work of a writer who said he wished to study "man . . . in the presence of eternity and mystery." Paul Claudel's *Tidings Brought to Mary* (written in 1892, revised in 1899 and 1912) was acted in 1912. Claudel, who said he had gained from Arthur Rimbaud (one of the leading Symbolists) "an almost physical impression of the supernatural," in this play envelops his medieval characters in a divine world, and dramatizes salvation. In Ireland, Yeats, who compared an artistic work to a magic talisman ("it entangles . . . a part of the Divine essence") wrote verse plays of Irish supernatural creatures and heroes. In *On Baile's Strand* (1903), for instance, Cuchulain, the protagonist, is said to have been sired by a hawk. The bird imagery is insisted on; Cuchalain's associates are chicks and nestlings, and the Fool (who represents Cuchulain on another level) is delighted with feathers. Near the conclusion of the play, Cuchulain rushes out to fight the waves, literally doing what Hamlet spoke metaphorically of doing.

In Russia, Meyerhold in 1906 staged Ibsen's *Hedda Gabler* (1890) as symbolically as possible, turning what had been a naturalistic play into a vision suggestive of another world, something (in the words of a hostile critic) "halfway between metaphysics and ballet." (Consult Nikolai Gorchakov, *The Theater in Soviet Russia*.) For symbolism in the sense of richly suggestive images, consult Alan S. Downer, "The Life of Our Design: the Function of Imagery in the Poetic Drama," *The Hudson Review*, 2 (Summer 1949), 242–260. On the Symbolist Movement, consult William Butler Yeats, *Essays and Introductions*; Arthur Symons, *The Symbolist Move-*

ment in Literature; *Yale French Studies*, No. 9; Eric Bentley, *The Playwright as Thinker*; and John Gassner, *Form and Idea in the Modern Theatre*.

sympathy. See *empathy*.

theater-in-the-round. See *arena stage*.

theater of the absurd. See Absurd, Theater of the.

theatrical. Literally, characteristic of the theater, but often (unfortunately) used pejoratively, to suggest artificially contrived, melodramatic, implausible.

theme. The underlying idea, such as the triumph of love or the failure of idealism. A *theme* can thus be distinguished from a *thesis*, which is a message, such as "Love ought to triumph" or "Idealism is short-sighted."

Three Unities. See *unity*.

total theater. The idea that the theater should not try to imitate realistically an aspect of life but should embody a synthesis of all of the expressive arts—music, movement, speech, lighting, and so on. The expression *total theater* is probably derived from Richard Wagner's *Gesamtkunstwerk*, "united" or "total artwork." Consult *Total Theatre*, ed. E. T. Kirby.

tragedy. For Aristotle, tragedy was a dramatic imitation (representation) of an "action of high importance." A Greek tragedy was serious, but it did not necessarily end unhappily. Aeschylus's *Eumenides*, for example, ends on a note of solemn joy. For us a tragedy is generally a play that faces evil, depicts suffering, and ends with death or (especially in the naturalistic tragedies since the latter part of the nineteenth century) ends with the hero alive but spiritually crushed. Tragedy's essence, Alfred North Whitehead says (*Science and the Modern World*, Ch. 1) resides not in unhappiness but "in the solemnity of the remorseless working of things." H. D. F. Kitto says (*The Greeks*, Ch. 4) that Greek tragedy—and perhaps one might add the great tragedy of other countries—was in part the product of intellectualism and humanism. Intellectualism let the Greeks see that human life must be lived within a great framework of what might be called the will of the gods, or Necessity: "Actions must have their consequences; ill-judged actions must have uncomfortable results." Humanism denied the Greeks an easy view of a heavenly life and gave them an "almost fierce joy in life, the exultation in human achievement and in human personality." The tragic note, Kitto suggests, is produced by a tension between this unalterable framework and this passionate delight in life. Consult R. Sewall, *The Vision of Tragedy*; T. R. Henn, *The Harvest of Tragedy*; and H. J. Muller, *The Spirit of Tragedy*.

tragic irony. See *irony*.

tragicomedy. Renaissance critical theorists, embroidering on Aristotle's *Poetics*, assumed that tragedy dealt with noble (important) figures and ended with a death; comedy dealt with trivial (laughable) figures and ended with a celebration. A tragicomedy was some sort of mixture: high characters in a play ending happily, or a mingling of deaths and feasts, or, most often (as in many American films) threats of death that are happily—and unconvincingly—evaded. John Fletcher (1579–1625), who with his collaborator Francis Beaumont wrote graceful dramas relying heavily on passionate outbursts and surprising turns of plot, defined a tragicomedy as a play that lacks deaths (and thus is no tragedy) but "brings some near it, which is enough to make it no comedy." One of the speakers in John Dryden's *Essay of Dramatick Poesie* (1668) says: "There is no theater in the world has anything so absurd as the English tragicomedy; . . . here a course of mirth, there another of sadness and passion, and a third of honor and a duel: thus, in two hours and a half, we run through all the fits of Bedlam." Consult Eugene Waith, *The Pattern of Tragi-Comedy*. On what can roughly be called the bitter or ironic comedy of the nineteenth and twentieth centuries, consult K. S. Guthke, *Modern Tragicomedy*; C. Hoy, *The Hyacinth Room*; and Eric Bentley, *The Life of the Drama*.

trilogy. A unit of three works. Though Greek tragic dramatists submitted three tragedies at a time, the plays are only a trilogy if they have an internal unity. Aeschylus's *Oresteia* (458 B.C.) is the only extant complete Greek trilogy; Sophocles's three plays on the Oedipus legend—*Antigone* (c. 422 B.C.), *Oedipus the King* (c. 425), and *Oedipus at Colonus* (c. 406) are not properly a trilogy because they were written at widely separated times and do not cohere into a consistent, unified whole. A modern trilogy: O'Neill's *Mourning Becomes Electra* (1931).

tritagonist. See *protagonist*.

underplot. See *plot*.

unity. Generally means something like "coherence," "congruence"; in a unified piece the parts work together and jointly contribute to the whole. The subplot of a play may parallel the main plot, or one character may be a foil to another. In any case, unity suggests "completeness" or "pattern" resulting from a controlling intelligence. In the

Poetics, Aristotle said that a tragedy should have a unified action, and he mentioned that most tragedies cover a period of twenty-four hours. Italian critics, making his comments rigid, in the late sixteenth century established the **Three Unities** of Time, Place, and Action: a play (1) must not cover more than twenty-four hours, (2) must be set in one locale only or, at worst, in various parts of a single city, and (3) must be either entirely tragic or entirely comic, rather than a mixture of (as Sir Philip Sidney said) "hornpipes and funerals." (Consult H. B. Charlton, *Castelvetro's Theory of Poetry*.) Actually, the time covered by Greek tragedies is vague; characters come from distant places in the space of relatively few lines. For example, in *Oedipus the King*, a shepherd who lives in the "farthest" fields from Corinth is sent for in line 863 and arrives in line 1108. Nor is unity of place invariable in Greek tragedy; there are violations of it in, for example, Aeschylus's *The Eumenides* and Sophocles's *Ajax*.

upstage. The back half of the acting area, or any part of the stage considered in relation to someone or something nearer the audience.

well-made play. See *pièce bien faite*.

As educational publishers we realize it is our responsiblity to try constantly to improve the textbooks we publish. In order to make TYPES OF DRAMA, 5th EDITION, a better book next time, we need to know what you, our ultimate consumer, think of what we've already done. Please help us by filling out this questionnaire and returning it to Scott, Foresman College English Developmental Group, 1900 East Lake Avenue, Glenview, IL 60025.

School _____ City and State _____

Instructor's Name _____

Please give us your reaction to the selections:

	Keep	Drop	Didn't Read	Read in High School
A DOLL'S HOUSE	___	___	___	___
SLAM THE DOOR SOFTLY	___	___	___	___
OEDIPUS THE KING	___	___	___	___
THE IMPORTANCE OF BEING EARNEST	___	___	___	___
THE SANDBOX	___	___	___	___
ANTIGONE	___	___	___	___
LYSISTRATA	___	___	___	___
A MIDSUMMER NIGHT'S DREAM	___	___	___	___
THE TRAGEDY OF KING LEAR	___	___	___	___
THE MISANTHROPE	___	___	___	___
ARMS AND THE MAN	___	___	___	___
THE CHERRY ORCHARD	___	___	___	___
TRIFLES	___	___	___	___
THE EMPEROR JONES	___	___	___	___
THE HOUSE OF BERNARDA ALBA	___	___	___	___
THE GLASS MENAGERIE	___	___	___	___
DEATH OF A SALESMAN	___	___	___	___
HAPPY DAYS	___	___	___	___
EQUUS	___	___	___	___
THE DUMB WAITER	___	___	___	___
DUTCHMAN	___	___	___	___
OUT OF OUR FATHERS' HOUSE	___	___	___	___
"MASTER HAROLD" . . . AND THE BOYS	___	___	___	___
'NIGHT, MOTHER	___	___	___	___
FENCES	___	___	___	___

1. Are there any plays or playwrights not included that you would like to see included next time? _____

_____

2. Did you find the general introduction helpful? _____ How might it have been improved? _____

3. Were the commentaries for each play useful? _____ Did they tell you too much? _____ Too little? _____

4. Did you read the "Theory" section? _____ Did you find it interesting? _____
How might it be improved? _____

5. Did you read the "Practice" section? _____ Did you find it interesting? _____
How might it be improved? _____

6. Was the section "Writing About Drama" helpful? _____
How might it be improved? _____

7. Was the section "Writing Drama" helpful? _____
How might it be improved? _____

8. Did you use the glossary of dramatic terms? _____
How might it be improved? _____

9. Do you like the book's appearance (cover, illustrations, layout)? _____

_____

10. Do you feel you instructor should continue to assign this book? _____
Why, or why not? _____

11. Will you keep this book? _____

12. Please add any further comments or suggestions on how we might improve this book.

_____

_____

Optional: Your name _____ Date _____

Address _____

May we quote you, either in promotion for this book or in future publishing ventures?

Yes _____ No _____

THANK YOU!